FedEx®

SECOND EDITION

Organizational Behavior

Foundations, Realities, and Challenges

ANNOTATED INSTRUCTOR'S EDITION

SECOND EDITION

Organizational Behavior

Foundations, Realities, and Challenges

ANNOTATED INSTRUCTOR'S EDITION

Debra L. Nelson
OKLAHOMA STATE UNIVERSITY

James Campbell Quick
UNIVERSITY OF TEXAS AT ARLINGTON

WEST PUBLISHING COMPANY
ITP AN INTERNATIONAL THOMPSON COMPANY
MINNEAPOLIS/ST. PAUL NEW YORK LOS ANGELES SAN FRANCISCO

COPYEDITOR Sheryl Rose
COVER DESIGN K. M. Weber
TEXT DESIGN K. M. Weber
PAGE LAYOUT By Design/Wendy LaChance
PHOTO RESEARCH Kathy Ringrose
ARTWORK Randy Miyake
COMPOSITION Parkwood Composition Services, Inc.
INDEX Theresa Casey
PHOTO CREDITS FOLLOW THE INDEX.

WEST'S COMMITMENT TO THE ENVIRONMENT

In 1906, West Publishing Company began recycling materials left over from the production of books. This began a tradition of efficient and responsible use of resources. Today, 100% of our legal bound volumes are printed on acid-free, recycled paper consisting of 50% new fibers. West recycles nearly 27,700,000 pounds of scrap paper annually—the equivalent of 229,300 trees. Since the 1960s, West has devised ways to capture and recycle waste inks, solvents, oils, and vapors created in the printing process. We also recycle plastics of all kinds, wood, glass, corrugated cardboard, and batteries, and have eliminated the use of polystyrene book packaging. We at West are proud of the longevity and the scope of our commitment to the environment.

West pocket parts and advance sheets are printed on recyclable paper and can be collected and recycled with newspapers. Staples do not have to be removed. Bound volumes can be recycled after removing the cover.

Production, Prepress, Printing and Binding by West Publishing Company.

British Library Cataloguing-in-Publication Data. A catalogue record for this book is available from the British Library.

610 Opperman Drive
P.O. Box 64526
St. Paul, MN 55164-0526

Printed in the United States of America

04 03 02 01 00 99 98 97 8 7 6 5 4 3 2 1 0 (Hardcover Student Edition)
04 03 02 01 00 99 98 97 8 7 6 5 4 3 2 1 0 (Softcover Student Edition)
04 03 02 01 00 99 98 97 8 7 6 5 4 3 2 1 0 (Loose-Leaf Student Edition)
04 03 02 01 00 99 98 97 8 7 6 5 4 3 2 1 0 (Annotated Instructor's Edition)
04 03 02 01 00 99 98 97 8 7 6 5 4 3 2 1 0 (Loose-Leaf Annotated Instructor's Edition)

Library of Congress Cataloging-in-Publication Data

Nelson, Debra L., 1956–
Organizational behavior : foundations, realities, and challenges / Debra L. Nelson, James Campbell Quick.— 2nd ed.
p. cm.
Includes index.
ISBN 0-314-09626-4 (hardcover : alk. paper). — ISBN 0-314-20567-5 (pbk. : alk. paper) —ISBN 0-314-20566-7 (looseleaf : alk. paper)—ISBN 0-314-20558-6 (annotated instructor's edition : alk. paper).—ISBN 0-314-21353-8 (annotated instructor's edition, looseleaf : alk. paper)
1. Organizational Behavior. I. Quick, James C. II. Title.
HD58.7.N44 1997
658.3—dc20

96-35205
CIP

To our students, who challenge us to be better than we are, who keep us in touch with reality, and who are the foundation of our careers.

Contents in Brief

Contents

Chapter 2 Organizations 2001 and Managerial Challenges 31

Part II Individual Processes and Behavior 69

Chapter 3 Personality, Perception, and Attribution 71

Chapter 4 Attitudes, Values, and Ethics 101

Chapter 5 Motivation in Organizations 131

Part III Interpersonal Processes and Behavior 219

Chapter 8 Communication 221

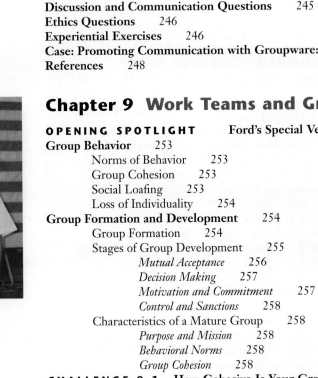

Chapter 9 Work Teams and Groups 251

Chapter 10 Decision Making By Individuals and Groups 281

Chapter 11 Power and Political Behavior 315

Chapter 12 Leadership and Followership 345

Chapter 13 Conflict at Work 377

Part IV Organizational Processes and Structure 413

Chapter 14 Jobs and the Design of Work 415

Chapter 15 Organizational Design and Structure 445

Chapter 16 ORGANIZATIONAL CULTURE 475

Chapter 17 Career Management 505

Chapter 18 Managing Change 539

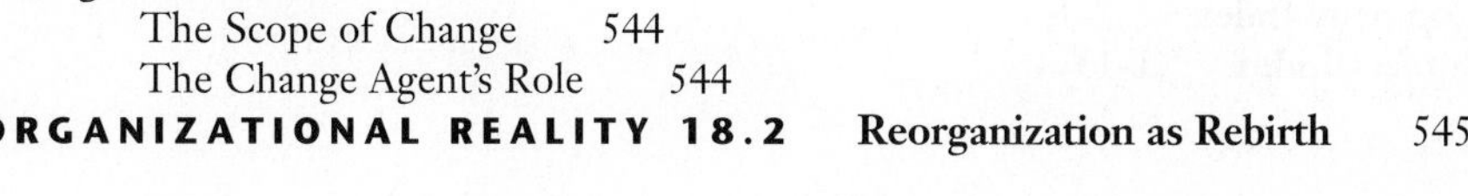

Preface

Organizational Behavior addresses ageless topics concerning how we live, work, and thrive in organizations. Motivation, teamwork, and leadership questions, for example, have fascinated us for decades. What are my most important needs and values? Why does my group, team, or family have difficulty functioning at times? How can I most effectively exercise power and influence with other people? What is the ethical thing to do in a complex, conflicted situation? Many books on organizational behavior address these and other important questions in the field.

Organizational Behavior's distinctiveness is reflected in its subtitle: *Foundations, Realities, and Challenges. Foundations* refers to the scientific and scholarly underpinnings of organizational behavior as a discipline. Extensive and intensive research and theory building have characterized a century of scholarly work on organizational behavior. *Realities* refers to the contemporary practice of organizational behavior in a variety of settings: large corporations, medium-sided manufacturers, and small businesses; private, public sector, and military organizations; product-oriented and service-oriented firms. The realities in contemporary organizations include both applications, and misapplications, of our knowledge about behavior. *Challenges* refer to the opportunities we have to better understand ourselves and the organizational worlds in which we live.

Organizational behavior is the study of individual and group behavior in organizational settings. This study is made more complex by the changes that have been unfolding for over a decade. Changes in the American economy were seen in a wide range of merger, acquisition, and downsizing activities during the 1980s and early 1990s. These changes affected large numbers of people. Some left their places of employment, while others stayed. All were changed by the experience. Changes in the global economy have also occurred. The 1990s are characterized by efforts to create free enterprise organizations in Russia, Eastern Europe, and the People's Republic of China, the creation of a unified European market system; and significant efforts at privatization throughout Central and South America. This is an era of dramatic change with significant consequences for American business and for you.

The overarching theme in the book is *change*, consistent with all the changes occurring domestically and globally. Change is the overarching theme that has been embedded throughout the text and pedagogical features. Total quality management is still an important issue and driving force in the 1990s. David Kearns, former chairman and CEO of Xerox, says leadership-through-quality is what earned Xerox a Malcolm Baldrige National Quality Award.

Four supporting subthemes continue to be woven into the second edition of text: globalization, cultural diversity, technology, and ethics. These themes are the challenges that managers face. Each places demands on people to grow and adjust. People must come to grips with them to maintain the health and well-being of themselves and their organizations. Our organizational behavior book can equip individuals, managers, and groups with the knowledge and skills needed to achieve this goal.

A second distinguishing feature of *Organizational Behavior* continues to be its pedagogical assumption that learning involves both acquiring objective knowledge and developing skills. Theory and research in an applied discipline such as organizational behavior must be translated into application. Hence, the text is based on the belief that organizational behavior includes *knowing* concepts, ideas, and theories as well as *practicing* skills, abilities, and behaviors to enhance the management of human behavior at work.

The book now concludes with two Appendices. Appendix A is titled "A Brief History of Organizational Behavior" and focuses on a century of research and scholarship in the discipline. Appendix B is titled "How Do We Know What We Know about Organizational Behavior?", which discusses the various ways of conducting research in organizational behavior.

Special Features

■ Several special features of the book extend the subtitle *Foundations, Realities, and Challenges* to specific applications. These features are designed to enhance the application of theory and research in practice, to stimulate student interest and discussion, and to facilitate cognitive as well as skill-based learning.

Foundations

SCIENTIFIC FOUNDATION Each chapter includes one inset summarizing an important research study related to the content of the chapter. This feature enables the student to appreciate the details and contributions of specific studies to organizational behavior.

EXTENSIVE TEXT REFERENCES The authors have read and reviewed an extensive body of literature on each topic. Each chapter includes dozens of references to which the student may refer for an in-depth treatment of the subject.

Realities

OPENING AND CLOSING SPOTLIGHTS The new and revised Opening Spotlights for each chapter focus on one of six key organizations, briefly developing an issue or raising a question based on an actual organizational situation related to the chapter topic. The companies—Chaparral Steel, Ford, Motorola, Federal Express, Citicorp, and Southwest Airlines—represent both manufacturing and service industries. This approach familiarizes the student with organizations, without claiming they are "ideal." The Closing Spotlight answers the question raised in the Opening Spotlight or analyzes the spotlight to underscore its relevance to the chapter material.

ORGANIZATIONAL REALITIES Each chapter includes two new Organizational Reality boxes, which consist of examples from organizations outside our group of six spotlighted companies. The boxes focus on what is happening in contemporary organizations, specifically on how organizations are managing the challenges of globalization, diversity, technology, and ethics.

Challenges

CHALLENGE EXERCISES Two Challenges are included in the body of each chapter. They are self-assessment exercises that provide the student with feedback on one aspect of the topic. Examples are the Self-Reliance questionnaire in Chapter 7 and the Ethical Culture questionnaire in Chapter 16. The latter asks the student to analyze whether an organization's culture supports ethical behavior. Each Challenge is designed to enhance self-knowledge or to promote skill development in the subject matter. The student is able to use the results of the Challenge for self-discovery or behavioral change.

EXPERIENTIAL EXERCISES Two group-oriented experiential exercises are included at the end of each chapter. They are designed for students to work in teams to learn more about an important aspect of the chapter's topic. The exercises give students opportunities to develop interpersonal skills and to process their thinking within a teamwork setting. The Chapter 2 exercise "Is This Behavior Ethical?" asks student teams to examine one of the twelve top ethical challenges identified in a *Wall Street Journal* study and to devise a workable solution to the dilemma.

CASES A case is included at the end of each chapter. It is based on real-world situations that have been modified slightly for learning purposes. Students have an opportunity to discuss and reflect on the content of the case, drawing on and then applying the content material of the chapter within the framework of the case. Illustrative videos supplement several of these cases.

VIDEO COHESION CASE This section includes four cases dealing with various organizational behavior issues facing PriceCostco, a company resulting from the merger of Price company and Costco Wholesale. The cases are interrelated, but each can stand alone. Each case is supplemented with videos that present the challenges faced by a corporation formed from two diverse companies seeking to create a single company with a unified philosophy and culture. These cases immediately follow Chapter 18 on page 573.

ETHICS QUESTIONS A set of ethics questions and dilemmas at the end of each chapter provokes students to think about what is right and wrong as well as about the best ways to resolve ethical conflicts in organizations. Many of the ethical questions and dilemmas do not have a single answer; rather, they raise key issues for the students to think through.

COMMUNICATION QUESTIONS All students need help in developing their oral and written communication skills. The second edition includes communication questions at the end of each chapter to give students practice in applying chapter material using some form of communication. The questions challenge students to write memos and brief reports, prepare oral presentations for class, interview experts in the field and conduct research to gather information on important management topics for discussion in class.

Some Distinctive Features Students Will Like

■ *Organizational Behavior* offers a number of distinctive, time tested and interesting features for students as well as new and innovative features. Each chapter begins with a clear statement of learning objectives to provide students with expectations about what is to come. The chapter summaries are designed to bring closure to these learning objectives. Graphics and tables enhance students' ease in grasping the topical material and involve students actively in the learning process. Photos throughout each chapter include clear captions that reinforce, and in many cases supplement, the text.

Interesting and relevant end-of-chapter features such as the list of key terms, review questions, discussion questions, and/or videocases reflect practical and applied aspects of organizational behavior. This second edition has added new internet exercises and communication questions to enhance student learning and interest.

Examples from diverse organizations (multinational, regional, nonprofit, public) and industries (manufacturing, service, defense) are included. These examples are integrated throughout the text. A unique feature of the book is its focus on the six organizations mentioned earlier—three of them manufacturing companies and three of them service organizations. Each is featured in three Opening and Closing Spotlights. The purpose of this approach is to provide a sense of continuity and depth not achieved in single examples. Also appearing throughout the text are many illustrations from a wide range of organizations.

Some Distinctive Features Instructors Will Like

■ Professors have demanding jobs. They should expect textbook authors and publishers to provide them with the support they need to do an excellent job for students. Among their expectations should be a well-integrated, complete ancillary package and an annotated instructor's edition. *Organizational Behavior* has these features.

Ancillary Package

A comprehensive set of ancillaries supports the basic text. Eleven ancillaries are available to the instructor; the annotated instructor's edition of the text, advanced instructional modules, transparency masters and acetates, an instructor's resource manual, a test bank, WESTEST™ (computerized testing software), West's Classroom Management Software, PowerPoint Presentation Files, West's CD-ROM Product Manager, Organizational Behavior Online, and a video program and video guide. The videos include a variety of short vignettes from some of the six featured companies and other organizations. They enhance the text presentation and reinforce its themes, adding continuity and integration to the overall understanding of organizational behavior.

ANNOTATED INSTRUCTOR'S EDITION J. Lee Whittington of Texas Wesleyan University has prepared an outstanding set of annotations to enhance lectures. The annotations include the following:

- Discussion considerations, which suggest additional topics for discussion.
- Alternative examples of current topics related to the text discussion.
- Points to emphasize in discussing text concepts.

ADVANCED INSTRUCTIONAL MODULES The advanced instructional modules are four self-contained units on current hot topics in organizational behavior, each of which is related to one of the themes in the book. The objective of each module is to provide additional lecture material to enhance and expand what is discussed in the book. Along with the lectures, each module contains student learning objectives, outlines of the lectures, transparency masters to support the lectures, and test questions covering the module's content. The modules average more than fifty pages each and are available free to instructors. The subjects and authors of the modules are as follows:

- *New* "Organizational Change" by Coy A. Jones of the University of Memphis.
- "Total Quality Management" by Professor Roger McGrath, Jr., of the University of South Florida.

- "International Organizational Behavior" by Professor Sunil Babbar of Kansas State University.
- "Diversity" by Professor Barbara J. Parker of Seattle University.
- "Business Ethics" by Professor Susan J. Harrington of Kent State University.

NEW **POWERPOINT® PRESENTATION FILES** Zulema C. C. Seguel has developed over 500 PowerPoint® slides for this text. These slides feature figures from the text, lecture outlines, and innovative adaptations to enhance classroom presentation. These files are available on disk in PowerPoint® 4.0 for Windows.

TRANSPARENCY ACETATES More than 100 full-color acetates are provided with *Organizational Behavior.* These transparency acetates include important figures and tables from the text and additional transparencies from the PowerPoint® files.

TRANSPARENCY MASTERS Over 200 transparency masters are printed from the PowerPoint® Presentation Files, and include figures from the text and innovative adaptations to enhance classroom presentation.

INSTRUCTOR'S MANUAL The instructor's manual for *Organizational Behavior* was prepared by Linda Parrack Livingstone of Baylor University. It is available in printed and in disk form. Each chapter contains the following information:

- Chapter scan—a brief overview of the chapter.
- Suggested learning objectives—expanded versions of the objectives presented in the textbook.
- Key terms—a list of key terms from the chapter.
- The chapter summarized—an extended outline with narratives under each major point to flesh out the discussion and offer alternative examples and issues to bring forward. The extended outlines are several pages long and incorporate many teaching suggestions.
- Answer guidelines for end-of-chapter materials—detailed responses to the review questions, discussion questions, and ethics questions, with suggestions for keeping discussion on track in the classroom.
- Experiential exercises—a brief description of each exercise as well as a detailed summary of anticipated results. Discussion questions provided with selected experiential exercises are put in perspective so instructors can conduct classroom discussion in an efficient manner.
- Cases—suggested answers for discussion questions are provided in a detailed form.
- Challenges—suggested answers for the Challenges where appropriate.
- Alternate experiential exercises—one additional exercise per chapter. Suggested answers are incorporated where appropriate.
- Integration of Myers-Briggs Type indicator material (optional)—including full descriptions and exercises in communication, leadership, motivation, decision making, conflict resolution, power, stress and time management, and managing change. For instructors unfamiliar with the Myers-Briggs test, a general introduction to this instrument is provided at the end of Chapter 3 of the instructor's manual. The introduction includes several good references for additional information about testing.
- Extra Experiential Exercises—references to additional exercises appropriate for the chapter material.

TEST BANK The *Test Bank*, prepared by Jon G. Kalinowski of Mankato State University, has been thoroughly revised and expanded for this edition. The test bank contains over 1,200 multiple choice, true/false, matching, and essay questions. Each question has been coded according to Bloom's Taxonomy, a widely-known testing and measurement device used to classify questions according to level (easy, medium, or hard) and type (application, recall, or comprehension).

WESTEST™ COMPUTERIZED TESTING SOFTWARE WESTEST™ allows instructors to create, edit, store, and print exams. The system is menu-driven with a desktop format to make the program quick and easy to use. WESTEST is available in Macintosh, IBM and IBM-compatible Windows® and MS-DOS® versions.

NEW **WEST'S CLASSROOM MANAGEMENT SOFTWARE** West's Classroom Management Software enables instructors to keep track of student performance using a spreadsheet format. This program allows for each entry of student information (name, ID number, social security number, etc.) and assignment data. The instructor can customize grading parameters by changing grading criteria or determining assignment weighting.

NEW **WEST'S CD-ROM PRODUCT MANAGER** West's CD-ROM Product Manager provides a simple way to install WESTEST™ microcomputer testing software with the complete test bank, West's Classroom Management Software and the PowerPoint® Presentation Files for this text. Using this CD-ROM and its installer, you can immediately access and use all of these valuable resources.

NEW **ORGANIZATIONAL BEHAVIOR ONLINE** Organizational Behavior Online puts the most current information in instructor's hands as soon as it is available. Adopters can log onto Organizational Behavior Online through West's home page on the Internet (http://www.westpub.com/Educate). New information includes updated pedagogy, information on the Internet Exercises, information on the companies profiled in the book, and other materials that professors might find newsworthy for teaching organizational behavior.

VIDEO PROGRAM An extensive updated video program has been developed especially for use with *Organizational Behavior*. Video segments have been selected by Professor Michael K. McCuddy of Valparaiso University to support the themes of the book, video cases, video cohesion case, and featured companies in the text. Sources for the videos include West's Business Video Profiles, Association for Manufacturing Excellence and the Blue Chip Enterprise Initiative.

VIDEO GUIDE The video guide was developed by Professor Michael K. McCuddy of Texas Wesleyan University. It provides running times, video descriptions, discussion considerations, and alternate places for the use of each tape in the series.

For the Student:

NEW INSIGHTS: READINGS IN ORGANIZATIONAL BEHAVIOR

This new reader for students includes multiple selections from academic and popular sources such as the American Management Association, Academy of Management Executive, Organizational Dynamics, Journal of Business Ethics, and Fortune.

NEW Student Note-Taking Guide

The Student Note-Taking Guide, prepared by Zulema C. C. Sequel, addresses the frustration of professors who find that students spend most of their time during lectures frantically copying material from the overheads. The Student Note-Taking Guide contains reduced images of the PowerPoint® Presentation Files with space for lecture notes on each page.

ORGANIZATIONAL BEHAVIOR: EXPERIENCES AND CASES Written by Dorothy Marcic, *Organizational Behavior: Experiences and Cases* contains experiential exercises and cases that emphasize management skill development and practical application of theory integral to the study of organizational behavior.

Management Skills: Practice and Experience

For instructors who emphasize skill development in the classroom. Professor Patricia M. Fandt of the University of Washington-Tacoma has created the integrated book *Management Skills: Practice and Experience.* It consists of nine modules: interpersonal skills, leadership, written communication, oral communication, perception, organizing and planning, decision making, decisiveness, and flexibility, designed to provide theory, exercises, and assessments to assist students in developing these important skills. Each module can be custom-bound for flexibility, and each has its own professionally developed role model video.

Our Reviewers Are Appreciated

■ We would like to thank our professional peers and colleagues who reviewed each draft of the manuscript to evaluate scholarly accuracy, writing style, and pedagogy. The many changes we made are based on their suggestions. We gratefully acknowledge the help of the following individuals:

Nathan Bennett
Louisiana State University

Meg G. Birdseye
Augusta College

Gerald Blakely
West Virginia University

Gary Blau
Temple University

Charles Burney
San Jacinto College South

Cliff Cheng
Loyola Marymount University

Sharon Clinebell
University of Northern Colorado

Lori Coakley
Bryant College

Carol Danehower
Memphis State University

Cathy L. Z. Dubois
Kent State University

Kenneth Dunegan
Cleveland State University

Joseph Foerst
Georgia State University

Cynthia Fukami
University of Denver

Robert Giacalone
University of Richmond

Roy Gordon
Hofstra University

Richard Grover
University of Southern Maine

Susan Halfhill
California State University at Fresno

Stanley Harris
Auburn University

Nell T. Hartley
Robert Morris College

Sandra J. Hartmun
University of New Orleans

Jacqueline Hood
University of New Mexico

Eugene Hunt
Virginia Commonwealth University

Natalie Hunter
Portland State University

George W. Jacobs
Middle Tennessee State University

Richard Jette
Northeastern University

Ahmad Karim
Indiana University—Purdue University at Fort Wayne

John Kimmel
Grande Visar Consulting

Donald C. King
Purdue University

Ron Klocke
Mankato State University

Stephen Knouse
University of Southwestern Louisiana

Rodney Lim
Tulane University

Bonnie Lindemann
University of Iowa

Rebecca Long
Louisiana Tech University

Thomas Martin
University of Nebraska at Omaha

Regan McLaurin
Western Carolina University

Ed Miles
Georgia State University

Paula C. Morrow
Iowa State University

Brian Niehoff
Kansas State University

Robert Nixon
University of South Florida

Mark Peterson
Texas Tech University

Marcia Pulich
University of Wisconsin at Whitewater

Elizabeth Ravlin
University of South Carolina

Tina Robbins
Clemson University

Joseph G. Rosse
University of Colorado at Boulder

Elizabeth Ryland
California State University of San Bernadino

David Savino
Ohio Northern University

Jane Siebler
Oregon State University

P. C. Smith
University of Tulsa

Steve Sommer
University of Nebraska at Lincoln

Gregory Stephens
Texas Christian University

Dana L. Stover
University of Idaho

Paul Sweeney
Marquette University

Jay Tombaugh
University of Houston at Clear Lake

Harold White
Arizona State University

J. Lee Whittington
Texas Wesleyan University

Joseph P. Yaney
Northern Illinois University

We would also like to thank those individuals who helped us with Opening and Closing Spotlights as well as other aspects of the Focus Companies features in various important ways. These individuals are Dennis Beach (Chaparral Steel), Jim Bright (Ford Motor Company), Margo Brown (Motorola), George Grimsrud (Motorola), Tom Martin (Federal Express), Paul McElligatt (Ford Motor Company), John M. Morris (Citibank), Tom Rhoades (Special Vehicle Team, Ford Motor Company), Jeff Roesler (Chaparral Steel), James D. Sawyer (Special Vehicle Team, Ford Motor Company) and Susan Yancey (Southwest Airlines).

Acknowledgments

■ *Organizational Behavior* was completed because of the hard work of many people at West Publishing Company. Our editor, Rick Leyh, showed the depth of his experience on the project. He provided several wonderful suggestions and worked closely with us to help us make the important decisions that kept this book on track for the second edition. We greatly appreciate his help and value him as a collaborator in the development process.

The efforts of Brent Gordon, developmental editor, and Paul O'Neill, production editor, resulted in a book that is again reader-friendly and an example of state-of-the-art publishing. We appreciate their professionalism and expertise.

Preparation of the instructional materials to enhance classroom efforts required an army of people. Ken Eastman of Oklahoma State University was great in creating the Internet Exercises, as was Michael McCuddy of Valparaiso University in developing the Video Cases and Video Cohesion Case. Linda Livingstone of Baylor University has been an invaluable partner through both editions of the book, and created an outstanding instructor's manual. Jon Kalinowski of Mankato State University developed the test bank. Hyler Bracey and Aubrey Sanford of the Atlanta Consulting Group shared their knowledge of experiential managerial learning. John Kimmel was an important source of information on team leader and teamwork training, an area in which he is an expert. Uma Sekaran created a superb research appendix. Coy A. Jones of the University of Memphis developed the new Organizational Change advanced instructional module. Margaret A. White of Oklahoma State University provided the innovative approach to Chapter 15, and we are indebted to her for her contribution to that chapter. Linda Trevino of Pennsylvania State University contributed her expertise on ethics. Many thanks also go to Zulelma C. C. Seguel for developing the PowerPoint Presentation Files, Transparency Masters, and the Student Note-Taking Guide.

We are extremely grateful to the following colleagues who made helpful contributions and supported our development through both editions of the book: Mike Hitt of Texas A & M University; Kenneth G. Wheeler, Jerry C. Wofford, Abdul Rasheed, and Richard Priem, all of the University of Texas at Arlington; Wayne Meinhart and Raja Basu of Oklahoma State University; and Lisa Kennedy of Baylor College of Medicine.

Many individuals assisted us with the preparation of the manuscript. We especially appreciate the efforts of Bev Dunham of Oklahoma State University, and Nancy A. Foster, Beverly Antilley, Beverly Gilbert, all of the University of Texas at Arlington. Vickie Turner Vogel conducted valuable library research for the book. J. Lee Whittington and Paula Daly made additional specific contributions.

We would like to thank Dianne Nelson and Sheri Shember Quick for their many important contributions and support in the development of this book. We benefited immensely from their suggestions, and students will as well.

In healthy human development, the roles of professor and student often become blurred. A professor must also be a good learner and student; a student must become a good teacher. Although we began to work together as student and professor fourteen years ago, the student has become a professor and the professor a student. Or, more accurately, we have become colleagues, each learning from the other in an ongoing, reciprocal process of education, growth, and development. We hope you will engage in open and reciprocal learning relationships.

Debra L. Nelson

James Campbell Quick

P A R T

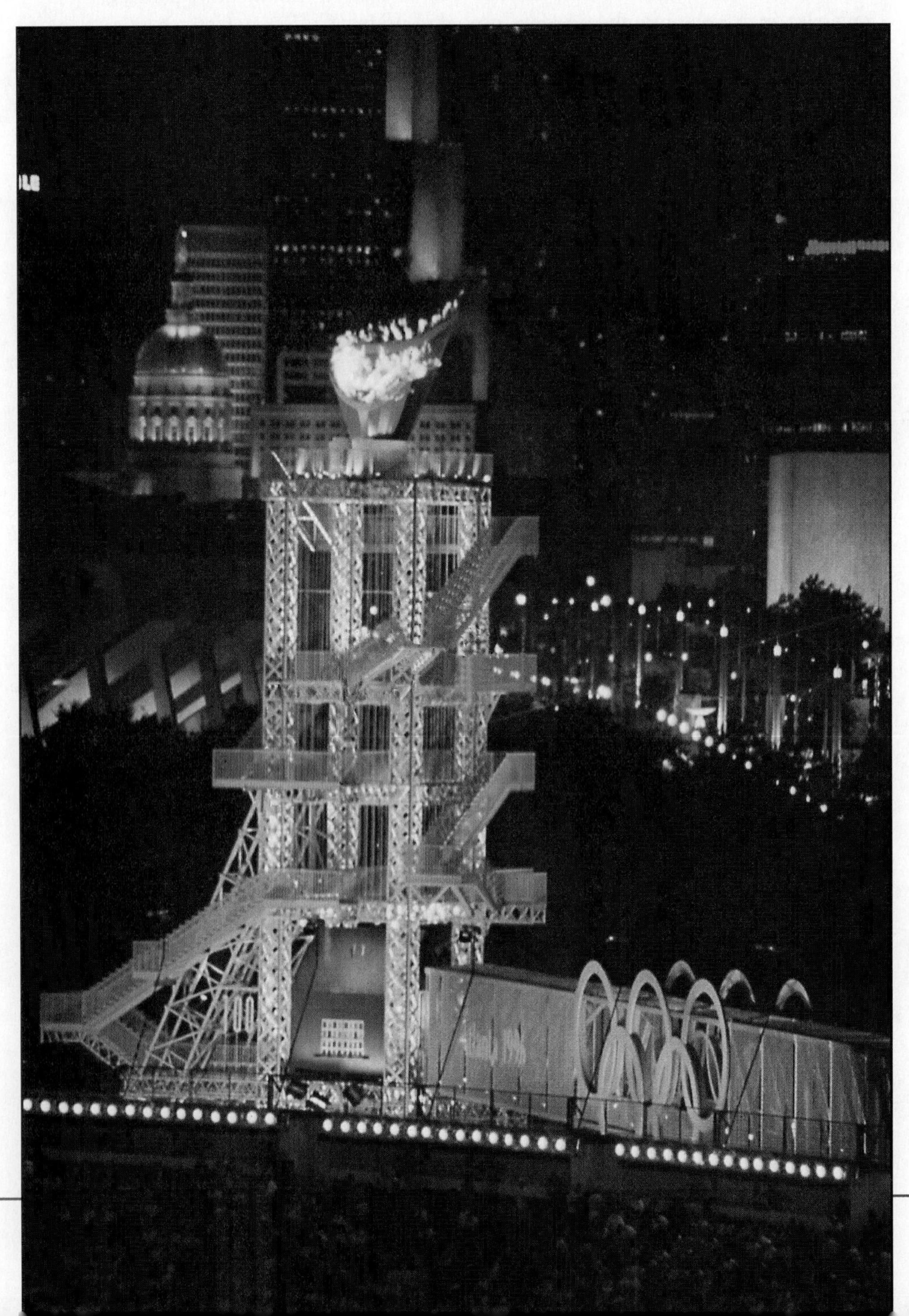

Introduction

CHAPTER

1

Organizational Behavior in the 1990s

LEARNING OBJECTIVES

After reading this chapter, you should be able to do the following:

- Define *organizational behavior.*
- Identify six interdisciplinary contributions to the study of organizational behavior.
- Identify the important system components of an organization.
- Describe the formal and informal elements of an organization.
- Understand the difference between manufacturing and service organizations in the economy, as exemplified by the six focus companies in this book.
- Recognize the importance of change and challenge for organizational behavior in the 1990s.
- Demonstrate the importance of objective knowledge and skill development in the study of organizational behavior.

OPENING SPOTLIGHT

Change and Challenge at Motorola

The competition in the automotive industry during the 1990s is not the first time the industry has been challenged. The automotive industry experienced a painful downturn in the early 1980s. In contrast, several sectors of the high technology industry in which Motorola did business were doing well during the same period. Further, Motorola was a very successful company in 1983, with an enlightened and progressive senior management team. In spite of the absence of immediate internal or external pressure for change, Chairman and CEO Bob Galvin saw a need for Motorola to change and reposition itself in response to a changing external environment.[1]

http://www.mot.com/

As a change strategist, Bob Galvin attempted to challenge and stimulate his senior managers to create their own vision for the Motorola of the future. He did not have a carefully crafted vision of the future for Motorola nor did he want to impose a vision of the future on a successful company. However, he did sense that the rapid expansion that Motorola had experienced had left some structural and managerial problems, which would eventually cause the company difficulty unless they were addressed.

"Managing Change" was the theme of Motorola's biennial meeting of its top 153 officers on April 23–24, 1983. Rather than providing his usual clear, concise summary at the conclusion of the two-day meeting, Bob Galvin stood and issued a spontaneous challenge, both in tone and mood, to his senior officers to take a fresh look at their organizations. How would Motorola's officers respond to this challenge by 1995? The Closing Spotlight continues Motorola's story of managing change. ■

Human Behavior in Organizations

organizational behavior

The study of individual behavior and group dynamics in organizational settings.

■ **Organizational behavior** is individual behavior and group dynamics in organizations. The study of organizational behavior is primarily concerned with the psychosocial, interpersonal, and behavioral dynamics in organizations. However, organizational variables that affect human behavior at work are also relevant to the study of organizational behavior. These organizational variables include jobs, the design of work, communication, performance appraisal, organizational design, and organizational structure. Therefore, although individual behavior and group dynamics are the primary concerns in the study of organizational behavior, organizational variables are important as the context in which human behavior occurs.

change

The transformation or modification of an organization and/or its stakeholders.

challenge

The call to competition, contest, or battle.

This chapter presents an introduction to organizational behavior. The first section provides an overview of human behavior in organizations and its interdisciplinary origins. The second section presents an organizational context within which behavior occurs and briefly introduces the six focus companies used in the book. The third section highlights the importance of **change** and **challenge** for organizational behavior in the 1990s. The accompanying Organizational Reality feature shows that change is on managers' minds today. The fourth section addresses the ways people learn about organizational behavior and explains how the text's pedagogical features relate to the various ways of learning. The final section of the chapter presents the plan for the book.

Human behavior in organizations is complex and often difficult to understand. Organizations have been described as clockworks in which human behavior is logical and rational, but they often seem like snake pits to those who work in them.[2] The clockwork metaphor reflects an orderly, idealized view of organizational behavior devoid of conflict or dilemma because all the working parts (the people) mesh smoothly together. The snake pit metaphor conveys the daily conflict, distress, and struggle in organizations. Each metaphor reflects reality from a different point of view—the organization's versus the individual's point of view.

This section briefly contrasts two perspectives for understanding human behavior, the external and the internal perspectives. It then discusses the six scientific disciplines from which the study of organizational behavior has emerged. Each discipline has made a unique contribution to organizational behavior.

Understanding Human Behavior

The vast majority of theories and models of human behavior fall into one of two basic categories. One category has an internal perspective, and the other has an external perspective. The internal perspective considers factors inside the person to understand behavior. This view is psychodynamically oriented. People who subscribe to this view understand human behavior in terms of the thoughts,

ORGANIZATIONAL REALITY

The Challenge of Change: The Heat Is On!

Change is the biggest challenge on American managers' minds! Changing realities in the workplace are challenging managers, employees, and executives alike to learn new skills and to adapt themselves to new work environments. Change becomes its own challenge and it is driven by global markets, diminishing product life cycles, more intense competition, evolving customer needs, and breakthrough technological developments. Organization around "customer requirements" and "flexibility" in meeting market conditions have moved ahead of "quality" and "service leadership" as the top two capabilities according to one survey of managers. This has occasioned a shift for managers and executives from an internal focus on their organizations to an external focus on their customers, competitors, and others in their external environments.

Where change is especially rapid, organizations must be responsive and flexible. For example, Welch's has invested heavily in its employees to create a new high-performance design to quickly meet changing demands for customerization of their products.

One of the biggest forces for change comes from the competition. The retail sector of the economy is one in which the sheer intensity of competition really turns the heat on managers, employees and executives. This intensity, especially for small retailers, is driven in part through the overpowering advertising and operating efficiencies of large organizations such as Wal-Mart, Kmart, Toys Я Us and Home Depot.

SOURCE: E. Davis, "What's on American Managers' Minds," *Management Review*, April 1995, 14–20.

Change from many directions is turning the heat on for American managers, challenging and stressing them to face difficult decisions which they may not want to face. Complacency is shattered. Managing in the 1990s is difficult for managers, who must think carefully and exhibit patience at the same time they work with a sense of urgency.

feelings, past experiences and needs of the individual. The internal perspective explains people's actions and behavior in terms of their history and personal value systems. The internal processes of thinking, feeling, perceiving, and judging lead people to act in specific ways. The internal perspective has given rise to a wide range of motivational and leadership theories. This perspective implies that people are best understood from the inside and that people's behavior is best interpreted after understanding their thoughts and feelings.

The other category of theories and models of human behavior takes an external perspective. This perspective focuses on factors outside the person to under-

Alternate Example
An individual's view of human nature may also influence their approach to understanding behavior. Some view humans as relatively simple, while others view humans as highly complex. These underlying assumptions may guide the approach used by researchers attempting to explain behavior.

stand behavior. People who subscribe to this view understand human behavior in terms of external events, consequences of behavior, and the environmental forces to which a person is subject. From the external perspective, a person's history, feelings, thoughts, and personal value systems are not very important in interpreting actions and behavior. This perspective has given rise to an alternative set of motivational and leadership theories. The external perspective implies that a person's behavior is best understood by examining the surrounding external events and environmental forces.

The internal and external perspectives offer alternative explanations for human behavior. For example, the internal perspective might say Mary is an outstanding employee because she has a high need for achievement, whereas the external perspective might say Mary is an outstanding employee because she is paid extremely well for her work. Kurt Lewin captured both perspectives in saying that behavior is a function of both the person and the environment.[3]

Points to Emphasize
Social psychologists make a distinction between critical multiplism and perspectivism. Critical multiplism seeks to explain a given phenomena from as many different theoretical perspectives as possible. Perspectivism uses only one perspective to explain human behavior. Given the interdisciplinary nature of organizational behavior, critical multiplism approach seems most appropriate.

Interdisciplinary Influences

Organizational behavior is a blended discipline that has grown out of contributions from numerous earlier fields of study, only one of which is the psychological discipline from which Kurt Lewin came. These interdisciplinary influences are the roots for what is increasingly recognized as the independent discipline of organizational behavior. The sciences of psychology, sociology, engineering, anthropology, management, and medicine are the primary fields of study out of which organizational behavior has grown. Each of these sciences has had its own important and unique influence on the discipline of organizational behavior.

psychology
The science of human behavior.

Psychology is the science of human behavior and dates back to the closing decades of the nineteenth century. Psychology traces its own origins to philosophy and the science of physiology. One of the most prominent early psychologists, William James, actually held a degree in medicine (M.D.). Since its origin, psychology has itself become differentiated into a number of specialized fields, such as clinical, experimental, military, organizational, and social psychology. The topics in organizational psychology, which include work teams, work motivation, training and development, power and leadership, human resource planning, and workplace wellness, are very similar to the topics covered by organizational behavior.[4] Robert Yerkes was an early leader in the field of psychology whose research efforts for the American military during World War I had later implications for sophisticated personnel selection methods used by corporations such as Johnson and Johnson, Valero Energy, and Chaparral Steel.[5]

sociology
The science of society.

Sociology, the science of society, has made important contributions to knowledge about group and intergroup dynamics in the study of organizational behavior. Because sociology takes the society rather than the individual as its point of departure, the sociologist is concerned with the variety of roles within a society or culture, the norms and standards of behavior that emerge within societies and groups, and the examination of the consequences of compliant and deviant behavior within social groups. For example, the concept of *role set* was a key contribution to role theory by Robert Merton.[6] The role set consisted of a person in a social role and all others who had expectations of the person. A team of Harvard educators used the concept to study the school superintendent role in Massachusetts.[7] These sociological contributions were the basis for subsequent studies of role conflict and ambiguity in companies such as Tenneco, Purex, and The Western Company of North America.

engineering
The applied science of energy and matter.

Engineering is the applied science of energy and matter. Engineering has made important contributions to our understanding of the design of work. By taking basic engineering ideas and applying them to human behavior in work organizations, Frederick Taylor had a profound influence on the early years of the study of organizational behavior.[8] Taylor's engineering background led him to place special emphasis on human productivity and efficiency in work behavior. His notions of performance standards and differential piece-rate systems contributed to a congressional investigation into scientific management at the behest of organized labor.[9] Taylor was ahead of his times in many ways, and his ideas were often controversial during his lifetime. However, the application of his original ideas is embedded in organizational goal-setting programs, such as at Black and Decker, IBM, and Weyerhauser. Even the notions of *stress* and *strain* have their origins in the lexicon of engineering.

Anthropology is the science of human learned behavior and is especially important to understanding organizational culture. Cultural anthropology focuses on the origins of culture and the patterns of behavior as culture is communicated symbolically. Current research in this tradition has examined the effects of efficient cultures on organization performance[10] and how pathological personalities may lead to dysfunctional organizational cultures.[11] Schwartz uses a psychodynamic, anthropological mode of inquiry in exploring the corporate decay in General Motors and NASA during the 1980s.[12]

anthropology
The science of the learned behavior of human beings.

Management, originally called administrative science, is a discipline concerned with the study of overseeing activities and supervising people in organizations. It emphasizes the design, implementation, and management of various administrative and organizational systems. March and Simon take the human organization as their point of departure and concern themselves with the administrative practices that will enhance the effectiveness of the system.[13] Management is the first discipline to take the modern corporation as the unit of analysis, and this viewpoint distinguishes the discipline's contribution to the study of organizational behavior.

management
The study of overseeing activities and supervising people in organizations.

Medicine is the applied science of healing or treatment of diseases to enhance an individual's health and well being. Medicine embraces concern for both physical and psychological health, with the concern for industrial mental health dating back at least sixty years.[14] More recently, as the war against acute diseases is being won, medical attention has shifted from the acute diseases, such as influenza, to the more chronic, such as hypertension.[15] Individual behavior and lifestyle patterns play a more important role in treating chronic diseases than in treating acute diseases.[16] These trends have contributed to the growth of wellness programs in the context of corporate medicine, such as Johnson and Johnson's "Live for Life Program" and Control Data Corporation's STAY-WELL program. These programs have led to the increasing attention to medicine in organizational behavior. The surge in health care costs through the past two decades has increased organizational concern with medicine and health care in the workplace.[17]

medicine
The applied science of healing or treatment of diseases to enhance an individual's health and well-being.

The Organizational Context

■ A complete understanding of organizational behavior requires both an understanding of human behavior and an understanding of the organizational context within which human behavior is acted out. The organizational context is the specific setting within which organizational behavior is enacted. This section discusses several aspects of this organizational context and includes specific organizational examples. First, organizations are presented as systems. Second, the formal and informal organization is discussed. Finally, six focus companies are presented as contemporary examples, which are drawn on throughout the text.

Organizations as Systems

Just as two different perspectives offer complementary explanations for human behavior, two other perspectives offer complementary explanations of organizations. Organizations are systems of interacting components, which are people, tasks, technology, and structure. These internal components also interact with components in the organization's task environment. Organizations as open systems have people, technology, structure, and purpose, which interact with elements in the organization's environment.

What, exactly, is an organization? The corporation is the dominant organizational form for much of the twentieth-century Western world, but other organizational forms have dominated other times and societies. Some societies have been dominated by religious organizations, such as the temple corporations of ancient Mesopotamia and the churches in colonial America.[18] Other societies have been dominated by military organizations, such as the clans of the Scottish Highlands and the regional armies of the People's Republic of China.[19, 20] All these societies are woven together by family organizations, which themselves may vary from nuclear and extended families to small, collective communities.[21, 22] The purpose and structure of the religious, military, and family organizational forms may vary, but people's behavior in these organizations may be very similar. In fact, early discoveries about power and leadership in work organizations were remarkably similar to findings about power and leadership within families.[22]

Organizations may manufacture products, such as aircraft components or steel, or deliver services, such as managing money or providing insurance protection. To understand how organizations do these things requires an understanding of the open system components of the organization and the components of its task environment.

Leavitt sets out a basic framework for understanding organizations, a framework that emphasizes four major internal components.[24] The four internal components of organizational systems are task, people, technology, and structure. These four components, along with the organization's inputs, outputs, and key elements in the task environment, are depicted in Figure 1.1. The **task** of the organization is its mission, purpose, or goal for existing. The **people** are the human resources of the organization. The technology is the wide range of tools, knowledge, and/or techniques used to transform the inputs into outputs. The **structure** is how work is designed at the micro level, as well as how departments, divisions, and the overall organization are designed at the macro level.

task

An organization's mission, purpose, or goal for existing.

people

The human resources of the organization.

structure

The manner in which an organization's work is designed at the micro level, as well as how departments, divisions, and the overall organization are designed at the macro level.

In addition, to these major internal components of the organization as a system, there is the organization's external task environment. The task environment is composed of different constituents, such as suppliers, customers, and federal regulators. Thompson describes the task environment as that element of the environment related to the organization's degree of goal attainment; that is, the task environment is composed of those elements of the environment related to the organization's basic task.[25] For example, when steel was a major component in the production of cars, U.S. Steel was a major supplier for General Motors and Ford Motor Company—U.S. Steel was a major component of their task environments. As less steel and more aluminum was used to make cars, U.S. Steel became a less important supplier for General Motors and Ford—it was no longer a major component in their task environments.

Discussion Consideration

Organizations are systems of interrelated components. What happens when managers attempt to change one of the components without considering the others?

Discussion Consideration

Are students inputs to the university, outputs (products) of the university, or customers of the university? What are the implications of the various answers to this question?

Discussion Consideration

What are the implications of the United States' economy shifting from a manufacturing economy to a service economy?

The organization system works by taking inputs, converting them into throughputs, and delivering outputs to its task environment. Inputs consist of the human, informational, material, and financial resources used by the organization. Throughputs are the materials and resources as they are transformed by the organization's technology component. Once the transformation is complete, they become outputs for customers, consumers, and clients. The actions of suppliers, customers, regulators, and other elements of the task environment affect the organization and the behavior of people at work. For example, Onsite Engineering and Management of Norcross, Georgia, experienced a threat to its survival in the mid-1980s by being totally dependent on one large utility for its outputs. By broadening its client base and improving the quality of its services (that is, its outputs) over the next several years, Onsite became a healthier, more suc-

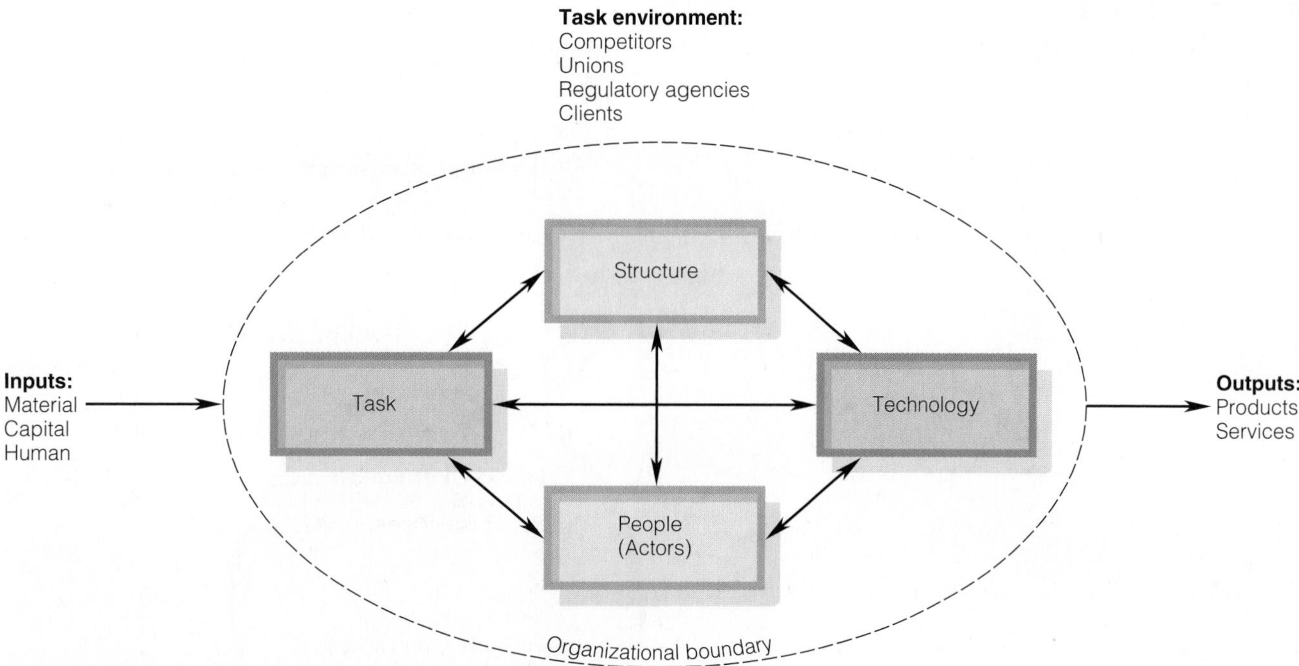

■ **FIGURE 1.1**

A Systems View of Organization

SOURCE: A Framework for Viewing Organizational Health. Based on Harold Levitt, "Applied Organizational Change in Industry: Structural, Technological, and Humanistic Approaches," in J. G. March (ed.), *Handbook of Organizations,* Rand McNally, Chicago, 1965, p. 1145.

cessful small company. Transforming inputs into high-quality outputs is critical to an organization's success.

Alternate Example

Kinko's Copies views itself as a "just in time" manufacturing organization. Like many service organizations they create their products in close conjunction with their customers, in many cases while the customer waits.

The Formal and Informal Organization

The systems view of organization may lead one to view the design of an organization as a clockwork with a neat, precise, interrelated functioning. The **formal organization** is the part of the system that has legitimacy and official recognition. The snake pit organizational metaphor mentioned earlier has its roots in the study and examination of the **informal organization,** which is the unofficial part of the system. The informal organization was first fully appreciated as a result of the **Hawthorne Studies** (discussed in detail in Appendix A), conducted during the 1920s and 1930s. It was during the interview study, the third of the four Hawthorne studies, that the researchers began to develop a fuller appreciation for the informal elements of the Hawthorne Works as an organization.[26] The formal and informal elements of the organization are depicted in Figure 1.2.[27]

formal organization

The part of the organization that has legitimacy and official recognition.

informal organization

The unofficial part of the organization.

Hawthorne Studies

Studies conducted during the 1920s and 1930s that discovered the existence of the informal organization.

Potential conflict between the formal and informal elements of the organization makes an understanding of both important. Conflicts between these two elements erupted in many organizations during the early years of this century and were embodied in the union-management strife of that era. The conflicts escalated into violence in a number of cases. For example, every supervisor in the Homestead Works of U.S. Steel was issued a pistol and a box of ammunition during the 1920s "just in case" it was necessary to shoot an unruly, dangerous steelworker. Not all organizations are characterized by such potential formal-informal, management-labor conflict. During the same era, Eastman Kodak was very progressive. The company helped with financial backing for employees' neighborhood communities, such as Meadowbrook in Rochester, New York.

Points to Emphasize

The distinction between formal and informal organizations parallels the image of an iceberg. The formal organization can be seen like the tip of an iceberg. The informal organization lies below the surface and is much more difficult to analyze. Despite this difficulty, the informal organization provides the energy for the organization, and may be critical to the organization's effectiveness.

FIGURE 1.2
Formal and Informal Elements of Organizations

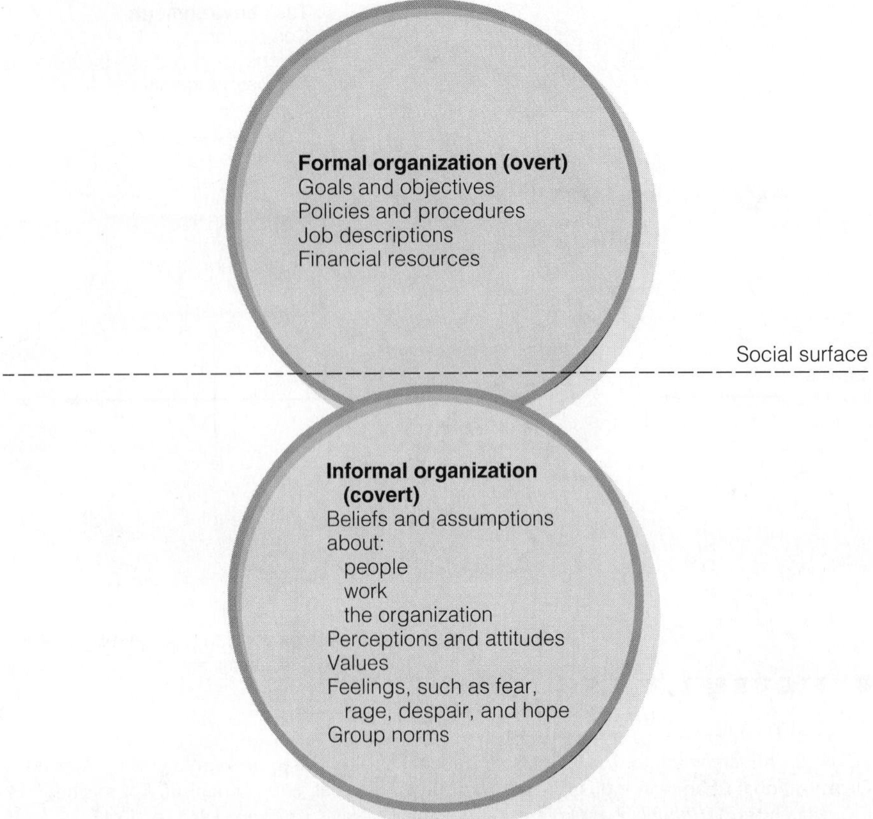

Alternate Example
Eastman Kodak pays attention to its organizational culture to assist its employees. During the 1980s the company devoted a room to be a tension release room. The "humor room" was filled with cartoons, rubber bats, and other paraphernalia to help employees release tension at work.

Kodak's concern for employees and attention to informal issues made unions unnecessary within the company.

The informal organization is a frequent point of diagnostic and intervention activities in organization development.[28] The informal organization is important because people's feelings, thoughts, and attitudes about their work do make a difference in their behavior and performance. Individual behavior plays out in the context of the formal and informal elements of the system, becoming organizational behavior. The existence of the informal organization was one of the major discoveries of the Hawthorne Studies.

Six Focus Companies

Organizational behavior always occurs in the context of a specific organizational setting. Most attempts at explaining or predicting organizational behavior rely heavily on factors within the organization and give less weight to external environmental considerations.[29] We think it is important for students to be sensitive to the industrial context of organizations and to develop an appreciation for each organization as a whole. In this vein, we draw on the experiences of six companies, each being used in the Opening and Closing Spotlights in three chapters. Motorola is the company illustrated in this chapter.

The U.S. economy is the largest economy in the world, with a gross domestic product of more than $7 trillion in 1995. Figure 1.3 shows the major sectors of the economy. The largest sectors of the economy are service (39 percent) and product manufacture for nondurable goods (20 percent) and durable goods (9 percent). Taken together, the production of products and the delivery of services account for 69 percent of the U.S. economy. Government and fixed investments

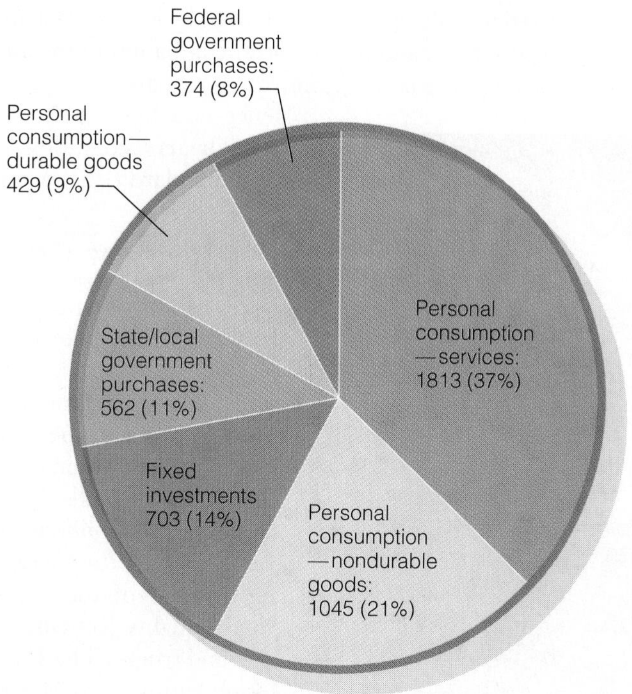

■ **FIGURE 1.3**

U.S. Gross Domestic Product
(Total is $7,113,200,000,000.)

account for the remaining 31 percent. Large and small organizations operate in each sector of the economy. Figure 1.3 shows the context in which each organization and company fits.

Our primary, but not exclusive, focus is on the private sectors of the economy. The manufacturing sector of the economy includes the production of basic materials, such as steel, and the production of finished products, such as automobiles and electronic equipment. The service sector of the economy includes transportation, financial services, insurance, and retail sales. We have chosen three manufacturing and three service organizations to highlight throughout the text. The three manufacturing organizations are Chaparral Steel Company, Ford Motor Company, and Motorola. The three service organizations are Federal Express, Citicorp, and Southwest Airlines.

Each of these six organizations makes an important and unique contribution to the manufacturing and service sectors of the national economy. However, these companies are not alone. Hundreds of other small, medium, and large organizations are making valuable and significant contributions to the economic health of the United States. We use brief examples from many organizations throughout the book. We hope that by your better understanding these organizations, you have a greater appreciation for your own organization and others within the diverse world of private business enterprises.

Chaparral Steel Company

Chaparral Steel Company is a producer of bar and medium-sized structural steel products from scrap steel. Much of its scrap steel comes from used cars. Chaparral can shred a car in eighteen seconds and begin steel production with the results. The company owns and operates a technologically advanced steel mill located in Midlothian, Texas.

Chaparral Steel is a small- to medium-sized manufacturing company with fewer than 1,000 employees. The officers of the company describe themselves as refugees from the large, bureaucratic steel companies they found inhibiting. Gordon Forward, the president and chief executive officer, is an internationally recognized metallurgist and steel industry leader.[30] Chaparral Steel outperforms all other domestic and foreign steel companies in the amount of steel produced per person each year. The company is recognized around the world for its excellence and high-quality steel products, as indicated by its recognition with the Japanese Industrial Standard (JIS) certification.

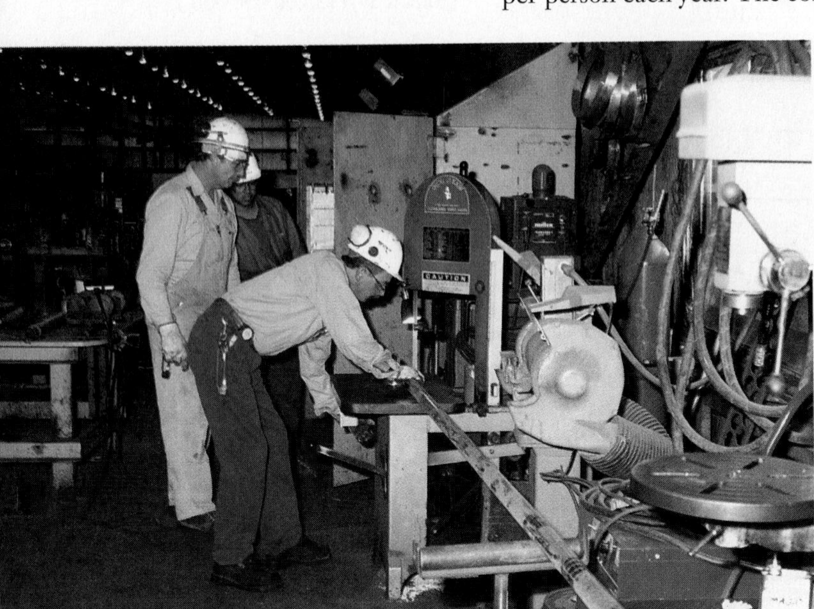

Rocky Turner, a skilled senior operator at Chaparral Steel, demonstrates his skills at cutting pipe on a ban saw in the set-up shop of the company's section mill while former employee Leon Gee looks on. A wide range of intellectual, physical, and interpersonal skills are essential to the success of any organization.

Ford Motor Company

Ford Motor Company is the world's second largest industrial corporation, serving the automobile, agricultural, financial, and communications industries through three operating groups. Ford is probably best known for the cars and trucks that its Automotive Group manufactures, assembles, and sells. Ford has tens of thousands of employees, billions of dollars in sales each year, and operating locations all over the world. At the end of the 1970s, Ford committed to "make quality Job One" in the production of its cars and trucks. The 1980s saw an internal revolution within Ford Motor Company resulting in a dramatic improvement in its financial health and the quality of its cars and trucks.[31] With continuing quality pressure from the Japanese and domestic pressure for safer and more fuel-efficient cars, Ford faces challenges through the 1990s and the early twenty-first century.

Motorola

Motorola provides electronics equipment, system components, and services for markets throughout the world. Motorola is a large manufacturing organization that has been recognized for excellence with the Malcolm Baldrige National Quality Award. The company is headquartered near Chicago and has operating locations throughout the United States and the world.

Motorola has a long history of, and takes great pride in, the ability to create world-class products.[32] Therefore, the company invests heavily in research and development activities. Less than 10 percent of its revenues and profits come from service activities, and the chairman of the board does not expect that to change. Like Chaparral Steel and Ford, Motorola has worldwide recognition and reach.

Federal Express

Federal Express is an internationally recognized service company specializing in the transportation and distribution of priority goods and documents throughout the world. Like Motorola, Federal Express has been honored with a Malcolm Baldrige National Quality Award for service. The company uses a systematic goal-setting program to achieve high levels of performance throughout the organization. Federal Express is a medium- to large-sized organization headquartered in Memphis.

In 1989, Federal Express acquired Tiger International and positioned itself for international service. It currently serves 119 countries through 167 airports. Federal Express has created a "people first" work environment that emphasizes a nonhierarchical structure and, in some cases, an inverted hierarchical structure.[33]

Citicorp

Citicorp is the leading bank in the United States, one of the largest financial companies in the world, and the parent of Citibank.[34] Citicorp has its origin in the First Bank of the United States, founded in 1791. Because of a weak domestic economy and unprofitable business loans, Citicorp had a challenging time in the early 1990s, finishing 1991 with its first loss since 1813. However, Chairman John Reed has Citicorp on a strong road to growth, finishing 1994 with $26 billion in total capital.

Widely known for its Citibank global card products, worldwide consumer business is one of three franchises that distinguish Citicorp. The other two are its local and regional banking businesses in the emerging world economies and its role as a provider of global products and services aimed at major corporations and institutions.

Southwest Airlines

Southwest Airlines is an air transportation service company providing single-class, high-frequency service to thirty-seven cities in the midwestern, southwestern, and western United States. Southwest is a medium-sized service organization based on number of employees, yet it is the seventh largest airline based on number of passengers carried in 1992. The company is headquartered in Dallas. It has been recognized with numerous Triple Crown Awards.

Southwest has an informal organizational culture.[35] In 1996, the company celebrated its twenty-fifth anniversary of incorporation. Southwest emphasizes high aircraft utilization and high employee productivity. It has created a unique niche in the air transportation industry because it competes against ground and rail transportation, not against the major airlines.

Change and Challenge in the 1990s

■ Change and challenge are two new realities at work in the 1990s. Competition is a leading force driving change at work. Competition in the United States and world economies has increased significantly during the past couple of decades, especially in industries such as banking, finance, and air transportation. Corporate competition creates performance and cost pressures, which have a ripple effect on people and their behavior at work. Competition will continue to create pressure through the 1990s. In some cases, this leads to downsizing and layoffs. Although these can be challenging experiences for organizations and individuals alike, negative outcomes are not inevitable, as the accompanying Scientific Foundation feature reports. Further, small companies are not necessarily the losers in this competitive environment. Scientech, a small power and energy company headquartered in Idaho Falls, Idaho, found it had to enhance its managerial talent and service quality to meet the challenges of growth and big-company competitors. Product and service quality is one tool that can help companies become winners in a competitive environment. Problem-solving skills are another tool used by IBM, CDC, Northwest Airlines, and Northwestern National Life to help achieve high-quality products and services.

Too much change leads to chaos; too little change leads to stagnation. Terrence Murray is chairman of Fleet Financial Group, the New England financial organization that has grown dramatically in ten years. As Mr. Murray says, "When there is change, morale is never going to be perfect." What are your perceptions of change? Complete Challenge 1.1 and see how positive your perceptions of change are.

Discussion Consideration
Some have characterized organizational change as an episodic event that occurs only occasionally. Others have suggested that working in today's organizations is like a raft trip through "permanent white water". Which characterization of the change process best describes the students' experience?

Alternate Example
"The location of opportunities is shifting. Succeeding at work today demands strategies and career paths that are often different from mid-20th century norms. Increasingly, the new rule is: beware of the conventional and traditional. In a time of rapid change, the unconventional often wins." Source: John Kotter, *The New Rules: How to Succeed in Today's Post-Corporate World.* New York: The Free Press, 1995.

SCIENTIFIC FOUNDATION

Job Loss and a Soft Landing

Job loss through organizational downsizing can be a difficult and painful experience, as many employees and managers found during the early 1990s. Even though job loss may be an inevitable consequence of changing organizational realities for some people at work, it may not be inevitable that employees and managers who lose their jobs end up bitter or angry; there may be a soft landing depending on how the company handles the process.

J. Brockner and his colleagues examined the attitudes and feelings of more than 200 unemployed people (i.e., layoff victims), 150 survivors in the financial services industry who had lost many coworkers to layoffs, and about 150 lame ducks (i.e., people scheduled to lose their manufacturing jobs). The research team found that companies who downsize may significantly reduce adverse, negative employee reactions by focusing on *how* they conduct the layoffs and whether they provide an attractive severance package.

The findings suggest that when companies use a process seen as fair and equitable to conduct the layoffs and provide an attractive severance package, employees have a much more positive attitude toward the company. In addition, they are more prone to trust the organization and be supportive in their responses. Providing a soft landing for employees can be good for the company in survivor productivity and the absence of retaliation, as well as good for the manager or employee in helping them move on in their work life with a positive attitude.

SOURCE: J. Brockner, M. Konovsky, R. Cooper-Schneider, R. Folger, C. Martin, and R. J. Bies, "Interactive Effects of Procedural Justice and Outcome Negativity on Victims and Survivors of Job Loss," *Academy of Management Journal* 37 (1994): 397–409.

The changes in the workplace are nowhere more prevalent than in information technology, which is on the leading edge of change in communication and how business is conducted globally. IBM technicians and employees test out new information and communication technology in a usability laboratory.

CHALLENGE

1.1

Analyze Your Perceptions of a Change

Everyone perceives change differently. Think of a change situation you are currently experiencing. It can be any business, school-related, or personal experience that requires a significant change in your attitude or behavior. Rate your feelings about this change using the following scales. For instance, if you feel the change is more of a threat than an opportunity, you would circle 0, 2, or 4 on the first scale.

1. Threat	0	2	4	6	8	10	Opportunity
2. Holding on to the past	0	2	4	6	8	10	Reaching for the future
3. Immobilized	0	2	4	6	8	10	Activated
4. Rigid	0	2	4	6	8	10	Versatile
5. A loss	0	2	4	6	8	10	A gain
6. Victim of change	0	2	4	6	8	10	Agent of change
7. Reactive	0	2	4	6	8	10	Proactive
8. Focused on the past	0	2	4	6	8	10	Focused on the future
9. Separate from change	0	2	4	6	8	10	Involved with change
10. Confused	0	2	4	6	8	10	Clear

How positive are your perceptions of this change?

SOURCE: Aftershock: Helping People through Corporate Change by H. Woodward and S. Bucholz. Copyright © 1987 John Wiley & Sons, Inc. Reprinted by permission of John Wiley & Sons, Inc.

International Competition in Business

Organizations in the United States are changing radically in response to increased international competition. According to noted economist Lester Thurow, the next several decades in business will be characterized by intense competition between the United States, Japan, and Europe in core industries.[36] Economic competition will place pressure on all categories of employees to be productive and to add value to the firm. The uncertainty of unemployment resulting from corporate warfare and competition is an ongoing feature of organizational life for people in companies or industries that pursue cost-cutting strategies to achieve economic success. The international competition in the automotive industry between the Japanese, U.S., and European car companies embodies the intensity that can be expected in other industries in the future. We will see how Motorola has fared against the competition in the Closing Spotlight.

Some people feel that the future must be the focus in coming to grips with this international competition, whereas others believe we can only deal with the future by studying the past.[37, 38] Global, economic, and organizational changes will have dramatic effects on the study and management of organizational behavior. How positive were your perceptions of the change you analyzed in Challenge 1.1?

Success in international competition requires organizations to be more responsive to ethnic, religious, and gender diversity in the workforce, in addition to responding positively to the dramatic changes occurring in the international marketplace. Workforce demographic change will be a critical challenge in itself for the study and management of organizational behavior.[39, 40] The theories of motivation, leadership, and group behavior based on research in a workforce of one composition may not be applicable in a workforce of a very different composition. This may be especially problematic if ethnic, gender, and/or religious differences lead to conflict between leaders and followers in organizations. For example, the former Soviet Union's military establishment found ethnic and religious conflicts between the officers and enlisted corps a real impediment to unit cohesion and performance during the 1980s.

Customer-Focused for High Quality

Organizations are becoming more customer-focused with changing product and service demands as well as customers' expectations of high quality. Quality has the potential for giving organizations in viable industries a competitive edge in meeting international competition. Some of the consequences of this increased customer focus are discussed in the accompanying Organizational Reality feature.

total quality management
The total dedication to continuous improvement and to customers so that the customers' needs are met and their expectations exceeded.

Quality has become a rubric for products and services that are of high status. Total quality has been defined in many ways.[41] We define **total quality management** as the total dedication to continuous improvement and to customers so that the customers' needs are met and their expectations exceeded. Quality is a customer-oriented philosophy of management with important implications for virtually all aspects of organizational behavior. Quality cannot be optimized, because customer needs and expectations are always changing. Quality is a cultural value embedded in highly successful organizations. Ford Motor Company's dramatic metamorphosis during the 1980s is attributable to the decision to "make quality Job One" in all aspects of the design and manufacture of cars.

Discussion Consideration
Using the definition of TQM as a guide, what aspects of the students' university experience could benefit from a quality improvement program?

The pursuit of total quality improves the probability of organizational success in increasingly competitive industries. Quality is more than a fad; it is an enduring feature of an organization's culture and of the economic competition we face in the 1990s. Quality is not an end in itself. It leads to competitive advantage through customer responsiveness, results acceleration, and resource effectiveness.[42] The three key questions in evaluating quality-improvement ideas for people at work are these: (1) Does the idea improve customer response? (2) Does the idea accelerate results? (3) Does the idea raise the effectiveness of resources? A yes answer means the idea should be implemented to improve total quality. Total quality is also dependent upon how people behave at work.

Behavior and Quality at Work

Whereas total quality may draw upon reliability engineering or just-in-time management, total quality improvement can only be successful when employees have the skills and authority to respond to customer needs.[43] Total quality has direct and important effects on the behavior of employees at all levels in the organization, not just on employees working directly with customers. Chief executives can advance total quality by engaging in participative management, being willing to change everything, focusing quality efforts on customer service (not cost cutting), including quality as a criterion in reward systems, improving the flow information regarding quality improvement successes or failures, and being actively and personally involved in quality efforts. George Fisher, chairman of Eastman Kodak, considers behavioral attributes such as leadership, cooperation, communication, and participation important elements in a total quality system.

http://www.Kodak.com

Quality has become so important to our future competitiveness that the U.S. Department of Commerce now sponsors an annual award in the name of Malcolm Baldrige, former secretary of commerce in the Reagan administration, to recognize companies excelling in total quality management. The Malcolm

ORGANIZATIONAL REALITY

The Customer as Boss

In January 1996, AT&T announced that it would reduce the size of its workforce by 40,000 employees, 65 percent of whom would be managers and 85 percent of whom were in the United States, over a three-year period. Another large-scale layoff? More downsizing? More people out of work? What is going on? Who's the boss?

What is happening in the telecommunications and other industries is a fundamental change in how companies organize and do business. Dramatic technological advances, such as in information technology, are leading to breathtaking productivity improvements in how products are manufactured, sold, and delivered. Hence, more is produced with fewer people and that trend will continue in manufacturing just as it did in agriculture throughout the United States.

These changes are driven by a focus on the customer. Customers can no longer be taken for granted. In this customer revolution the customer is now the boss, not the company nor the employee. As a result of this intense customer focus, there is less employment security because companies need to be flexible and have low fixed costs so as to be able to respond to the changing demands of their customers.

Increasingly, executives link customers and employees, in a sense serving as representatives of customers. As customers become more demanding, employees are increasingly put in a position to accede to these demands. This is a fundamental change at work.

SOURCE: M. Hammer, "Manager's Journal: Who's to Blame for All the Layoffs?" *Wall Street Journal*, 22 January 1996, A14.

How satisfied are you as a customer? Taco Bell, Dunkin Donuts and other fast food organizations are locating outlets on college and university campuses as one way of being more responsive to this sector of their constituency.

Baldrige National Quality Award examination evaluates an organization in seven categories: leadership, information and analysis, strategic quality planning, human resource utilization, quality assurance of products and services, quality results, and customer satisfaction. Challenge 1.2 gives you an opportunity to evaluate an organization of which you are a customer in eight categories of customer satisfaction. You are the boss; how satisfied are you?

According to former president George Bush, "Quality management is not just a strategy. It must be a new style of working, even a new style of thinking. A dedication to quality and excellence is more than good business. It is a way of life, giving something back to society, offering your best to others."

CHALLENGE

■ 1.2

Are You Highly Satisfied as a Customer

Think of an organization or business with whom you have frequent contact and interaction. How satisfied are you with the products or services provided to you by this organization or business? Would the organization or business be competitive in the Customer Satisfaction category for a Malcolm Baldrige National Quality Award?

Complete the following eight questions to rate the quality of the organization's or business's customer satisfaction. Use a scale of 1 (definitely not), 2 (probably not), 3 (unsure), 4 (probably yes), and 5 (definitely yes).

_____ **1.** Do you believe the organization knows what you expect as a customer?
_____ **2.** Has the organization improved the quality of its customer relationships over a period of time?
_____ **3.** Do you receive the same standard of service from different people in this organization?
_____ **4.** Do you believe that each and every employee is committed to serving your needs and satisfying you as a customer?
_____ **5.** Whenever you have had even the smallest complaint about the organization, has that complaint been resolved satisfactorily?
_____ **6.** Have you ever completed any sort of customer satisfaction survey, card, or feedback form for the organization?
_____ **7.** Have you heard that people were more satisfied with the organization's products and services in the past than today?
_____ **8.** Compared with similar organizations, do you consider this organization to be superior in serving customers?

☐ Total points

Scoring
35–40: This organization provides world-class customer service and deserves quality recognition in this area.
28–34: This organization provides high-quality service to its customers.
20–27: This organization is mediocre in its service to customers.
8–19: This organization needs to improve its service to customers.

Quality is one watchword for competitive success during the 1990s and beyond. Organizations that do not respond to customer needs find their customers choosing alternative product and service suppliers who are willing to exceed customer expectations. With this said, you should not conclude that total quality is a panacea for all organizations or that total quality guarantees unqualified success.

Discussion Consideration
Of the challenges listed, which do you feel will be most difficult for managers to deal with in the 21st century?

Points to Emphasize
The globalization of markets and competition is increasing at an increasing rate. Success in this environment requires individuals and organizations to be constantly aware of these changes. Often opportunities present themselves quickly. Only those who are alert will be able to take advantage of these "strategic windows."

Managing Organizational Behavior in the 1990s

Over and above the challenge of enhancing quality to meet international competition, managing organizational behavior during the 1990s is challenging for at least four reasons: (1) the increasing globalization of organizations' operating territory, (2) the increasing diversity of organizational workforces, (3) continuing technological innovation with its companion need for skill enhancement, and (4) the continuing demand for higher levels of moral and ethical behavior at work. These are the issues managers need to address in managing people at work.

Each of these four issues is explored in detail in Chapter 2 and highlighted throughout the text because they are intertwined in the contemporary practice of organizational behavior. For example, the issue of women in the workplace concerns workforce diversity while at the same time overlapping the globalization issue. Gender roles are often defined differently in various cultures and societies. In addition, sexual harassment is a frequent ethical problem for organizations as more women enter the workforce. The student of organizational behavior must appreciate and understand the importance of these issues.

Learning about Organizational Behavior

■ Organizational behavior is neither a purely scientific area of inquiry nor a strictly intellectual endeavor. It involves the study of abstract ideas, such as valence and expectancy in motivation, as well as the study of concrete matters, such as observable behaviors and physiological symptoms of distress at work. Therefore, learning about organizational behavior is a multidimensional activity, as shown in Figure 1.4. First, it requires the mastery of a certain body of **objective knowledge.** Objective knowledge results from research and scholarly activities. Second, the study of organizational behavior requires **skill development** and the mastery of abilities essential to successful functioning in organizations. Third, it requires the integration of objective knowledge and skill development in order to apply both appropriately in specific organizational settings.

objective knowledge
Knowledge that results from research and scholarly activities.

skill development
The mastery of abilities essential to successful functioning in organizations.

Objective Knowledge

Objective knowledge, in any field of study, is developed through basic and applied research. Research in organizational behavior has continued since Frederick Taylor's early research on scientific management. Acquiring objective knowledge requires the cognitive mastery of theories, conceptual models, and research findings. The Scientific Foundation feature in each chapter of this book reflects how objective knowledge is acquired. The feature draws from a wide body of published literature on organizational behavior developed during the past few years. This feature is designed to enable the student to see how organizational behavior research is conducted and how this research adds to the body of objective knowledge in the field. In addition to the Scientific Foundation feature, the objective knowledge in each chapter is reflected in the notes used to support the text material. Mastering the concepts and ideas that come from these notes enables you to intelligently discuss topics such as motivation and performance,[44] leadership,[45] and executive stress.[46]

We encourage instructors and students of organizational behavior to think critically about the objective knowledge in organizational behavior and about the Scientific Foundation feature in each chapter. Only by engaging in critical thinking can one question or challenge the results of specific research and responsibly consider how to apply research results in a particular work setting. Rote memorization does not enable the student to appreciate the complexity of specific theories or the interrelationships among concepts, ideas, and topics. Good critical thinking, in contrast, enables the student to identify inconsistencies and limitations in the current body of objective knowledge.

Critical thinking, based on knowledge and understanding of basic ideas, leads to inquisitive exploration. A questioning, probing attitude is as the core of critical thinking. The student of organizational behavior should evolve into a critical consumer of knowledge related to organizational behavior—one who is able

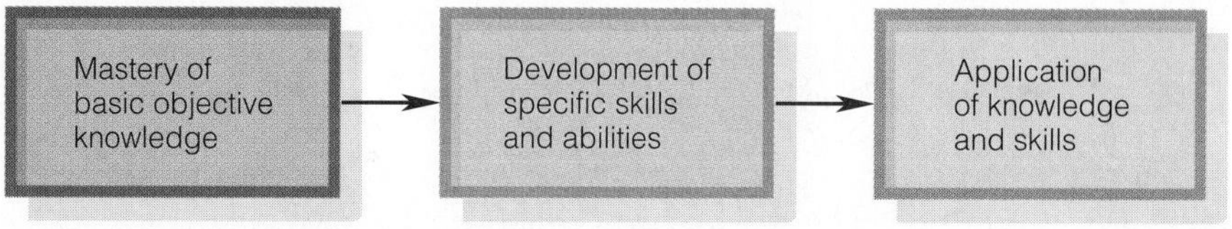

Mastery of basic objective knowledge → Development of specific skills and abilities → Application of knowledge and skills

■ **FIGURE 1.4**
Learning about Organizational Behavior

to intelligently question the latest research results and distinguish plausible, sound new approaches from fads that lack substance or adequate foundation. Ideally, the student of organizational behavior develops into a scientific professional manager who is knowledgeable in the art and science of organizational behavior.

Skill Development

Learning about organizational behavior requires doing as well as knowing. The development of skills and abilities requires that students be challenged, by the instructor or by themselves. Skill development is a very active component of the learning process.

The U.S. Department of Labor is concerned that people achieve the necessary skills to be successful in the workplace.[47] The essential skills identified by the Department of Labor are: (1) resource management skills, such as time management; (2) information management skills, such as data interpretation; (3) personal interaction skills, such as teamwork; (4) systems behavior and performance skills, such as cause-effect relationships; and (5) technology utilization skills, such as troubleshooting. Many of these skills, such as decision making and information management, are directly related to the study of organizational behavior.

Point to Emphasize
Although they are technically competent, graduates of business schools have been criticized for a lack of interpersonal skills. The skill-building experiences and self-assessment exercises in this book will assist students in developing their interpersonal skills.

Developing skills is different from acquiring objective knowledge in that it requires structured practice and feedback. A key function of experiential learning is to engage the student in individual or group activities that are systematically reviewed, leading to new skills and understandings. Objective knowledge acquisition and skill development are interrelated. The process for learning from structured or experiential activities is depicted in Figure 1.5. The student engages in an individual or group structured activity and systematically reviews that activity, which leads to new or modified knowledge and skills.

If skill development and structured learning occur in this way, there should be an inherently self-correcting element to learning because of the modification of the student's knowledge and skills over time.[48] To ensure that skill development does occur and that the learning is self-correcting as it occurs, three basic assumptions that underlie the previous model must be followed.

FIGURE 1.5
Learning from Structured Activity

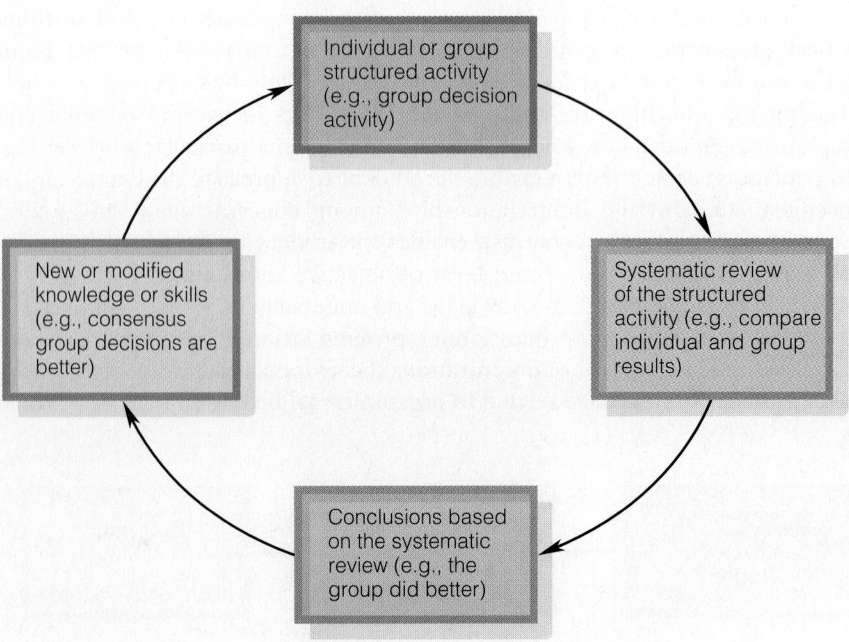

First, each student must accept responsibility for his or her own behavior, actions, and learning. A group cannot learn for its members. Each member must accept responsibility for what he or she does and learns. Denial of responsibility helps no one, least of all the learner.

Second, each student must actively participate in the individual or group structured learning activity. Structured learning is not passive; it is active. In group activities, everyone suffers if just one person adopts a passive attitude. Hence, all must actively participate.

Third, each student must be open to new information, new skills, new ideas, and experimentation. This does not mean that students should be indiscriminately open. It does mean that students should have a nondefensive, open attitude so that change is possible through the learning process.

Application of Knowledge and Skills

One of the advantages of structured, experiential learning is that a person can explore new behaviors and skills in a comparatively safe environment. Losing your temper in a classroom activity and learning about the potential adverse impact on other people will probably have dramatically different consequences from losing your temper with an important customer in a tense work situation. The ultimate objective of skill development and experiential learning is that one transfers the process employed in learning from structured activities in the classroom to learning from unstructured opportunities in the workplace.

Although organizational behavior is an applied discipline, a student is not "trained" in organizational behavior. Rather, one is "educated" in organizational behavior. The distinction between these two modes of learning is found in the degree of direct and immediate applicability of either knowledge or skills. As an activity, training more nearly ties direct objective knowledge or skill development to specific applications. By contrast, education enhances a person's residual pool of objective knowledge and skills that may then be selectively applied later—sometimes significantly later—when the opportunity presents itself.

Plan for the Book

■ Change and challenge are the watchwords in organizations during the 1990s. Managers and employees alike are challenged to meet change in the workplace; change in how work gets done, change in psychological and legal contracts between individuals and organizations, change in who is working in the organization, and change in the basis for organization. The four major challenges facing managers in the 1990s are the global environment, workplace diversity, technological innovation, and ethical issues at work. These four challenges are discussed in detail in Chapter 2 and they are the challenges shaping the changes occurring in organizations throughout the world. For example, the increasing globalization of business has led to intense international competition in core industries and the changing demographics of the workplace have led to gender, age, racial, and ethnic diversity among working populations.

The first two chapters compose Part I of the book, the introduction. It is against the backdrop of the challenges discussed here that the specific content subjects in organizational behavior must be understood. In addition to the introduction, the text has three major parts. Part II addresses individual processes and behavior. Part III addresses interpersonal processes and behavior. Part IV addresses organizational processes and behavior.

The five chapters in Part II are designed to help the reader understand specific aspects of human behavior. Chapter 3 discusses personality, perception, and attribution, better preparing one to understand how specific individuals might respond to change. Chapter 4 examines attitudes, values, and ethics. You already looked at your attitude toward change in Challenge 1.1. Once the basics of attitudes and values are understood, consideration may be given to attitude or value change. Chapters 5 and 6 address the broad range of motivational theories, learning, and performance management in organizations. These basic theories present alternative tools for changing and influencing behavior in organizations. Finally, Chapter 7 considers stress and well-being at work. The natural sequence of change in organizations often leads individuals to feel threatened rather than feeling they are on the verge of a new opportunity. Therefore, recognizing the signs and signals of stress and strain are a basis for preventive stress management.

Part III is composed of six chapters designed to help the reader better understand interpersonal and group dynamics in organizations. Chapter 8 examines interpersonal and electronic communication at work, with attention given to overcoming barriers to communication and defensiveness at work, both consequences of changing or chaotic work environments. Chapter 9 focuses on an increasingly prominent feature of the workplace, teamwork and groups. Chapter 10 examines how individuals and groups make decisions, which is a vital skill in adjusting to new organizational realities. Chapter 11 is about power and politics, the bases of which shift as the organization shifts. Chapter 12 addresses the companion topics of leadership and followership, posing the consideration of new paradigms for a changing workplace. Finally, Chapter 13 examines conflict at work, one natural outcome of changing interpersonal dynamics at work.

Part IV's five chapters are designed to help the reader better understand organizational processes and the organizational context of behavior at work. Chapter 14 examines traditional and contemporary approaches to job design. This is the foundation of job-based organization, for which competency-based organization is an alternative.[49] Chapter 15 develops the topics of organizational design and structure, giving special attention to contemporary forces reshaping organizations and to emerging forms of organization, such as the modular corporation. Chapter 16 addresses the culture of the organization, which is shaped by the dynamics of globalization, technological innovations, and changing workplace demographics. Chapter 17 is about careers and career management, vital topics in a world of work that is reshaping itself each year. Finally, Chapter 18 brings closure to the text and the main theme of change by addressing the topic of managing change. Managing change is the proactive individual and organizational alternative to letting change manage you.

Managerial Implications: Foundations for the Future

■ Managers must consider personal and environmental factors to fully understand how people behave in organizations. Human behavior is complex and at times confusing. Characteristics of the organizational system and formal-informal dynamics at work are important environmental factors that influence people's behavior. Managers should look for similarities and differences in manufacturing, service-oriented, nonprofit, and governmental organizations.

Change is a primary concern for managers in the 1990s. Changing customer demands for high-quality outputs challenge companies to meet the international competition. Organizations making a commitment to total quality are more likely to succeed in the face of the competition. Another aspect of meeting the competition is learning. Managers must continually upgrade their knowledge about all aspects of their businesses. They also must hone their technical and interpersonal skills.

CLOSING SPOTLIGHT

. . . and Still Repositioning!

Motorola's officers responded positively to the challenge issued them in 1983 and twelve years later in 1995, Motorola continued to be a global leader in the manufacture and sale of consumer and communication products.[50] Motorola continues as a successful, profitable American corporation, reporting a 21 percent increase in sales for the third quarter in 1995. The company's success is in part attributable to growth in the wireless communications and semiconductors markets it serves.

From 1983 to 1995, Motorola continued to reposition itself and became much more global. In 1985, 75 percent of its business was American and 25 percent was global. A decade later in 1995, these percentages were well on the way to reversing themselves; 60 percent of Motorola's business was global and 40 percent was American.

Where it was doing business was not the only big change for Motorola. In 1995, the company continued to be an innovative leader with new technologies and new products. For example, during its 1995 biannual Horizons media conference, Motorola debuted "Virtual Display," a new display technology designed to bring high-quality graphics to hand-held portable devices and other graphic-intensive applications.

Motorola is working with the Chinese government related to the manufacturing of pagers, cellular phones, and two-way radios. China is seeing explosive growth in these technologies. For example, only 500,000 pagers were estimated to be in use in China during 1990. The estimate in 1995 was 17 million, a 3400 percent increase. ■

Chapter Summary

- Organizational behavior is individual behavior and group dynamics in organizations.
- The disciplines of psychology, sociology, engineering, anthropology, management, and medicine have contributed to the development of the discipline of organizational behavior.
- Organizations are systems composed of people, structure, and technology committed to a task.
- Organizations have formal and informal elements within them.
- Manufacturing organizations (such as Chaparral Steel, Ford, and Motorola) and service organizations (such as Citicorp, Federal Express, and Southwest Airlines) constitute 67 percent of the U.S. economy based on gross domestic purchases.
- The changes and challenges facing managers in the 1990s are driven by international competition and customer demands.
- Learning about organizational behavior requires a mastery of objective knowledge and specific skill development.

Key Terms

organizational behavior (p. 6)
change (p. 6)
challenge (p. 6)
psychology (p. 8)
sociology (p. 8)
engineering (p. 8)
anthropology (p. 9)
management (p. 9)
medicine (p. 9)
task (p. 10)
people (p. 10)
structure (p. 10)
formal organization (p. 11)
informal organization (p. 11)
Hawthorne Studies (p. 11)
total quality management (p. 18)
objective knowledge (p. 21)
skill development (p. 21)

Review Questions

1. Define *organizational behavior.*
2. Identify how six disciplines have contributed to the development of organizational behavior.
3. What are the four components of all organizational systems? Give examples of each.
4. Briefly describe the elements of the formal and the informal organization. Give examples of each.
5. Classify the six focus companies in sectors of the economy.
6. Describe how change, challenge, competition, and total quality are affecting the study of organizational behavior.

Discussion and Communication Questions

1. How do the formal aspects of your work environment affect you? What informal aspects of your work environment are important?
2. What is the biggest competitive challenge or change facing the businesses in your industry today? Will that change in the next five years?
3. What will the next chief executive of your company be like?
4. How would you describe a scientific manager?
5. Discuss two ways people learn about organizational behavior.
6. Which of the focus companies is your own company most like? Do you work for one of these focus companies? Which company would you most like to work for?
7. *(communication question)* Prepare a memo about an organizational change occurring where you work or in your college or university. Write a 100-word description of the change and, using Figure 1.1, identify how it is affecting the people, structure, task, and technology of the organization.
8. *(communication question)* Develop an oral presentation about the changes and challenges facing your college or university based on an interview with a faculty member or administrator. Be prepared to describe the changes and challenges, as well as whether they are good or bad.
9. *(communication question)* Prepare a brief description of a service or manufacturing company of your choice. Go to the library and read about the company from several sources, then use these multiple sources to write your description.

Ethics Questions

1. Suppose two people at work have a personal, informal relationship unrelated to the formal organization and further assume their relationship could affect people in the formal organization. As an aware employee, should you tell the people who are unaware of it and may be affected by the relationship?
2. Which disciplines are important in understanding moral and ethical issues for organizations and management?
3. Suppose you would be able to beat the competition if you presented a prospective customer with negative information about the competition's quality program. Should you provide the information? Further assume that the information relates to safety. Would that make a difference in whether you told the customer?
4. What are the most sensitive ethical issues in your business today?

Experiential Exercises

1.1 What's Changing at Work?

This exercise provides an opportunity to discuss changes occurring in your workplace and university. These changes may be for the better or the worse. However, rather than evaluating whether they are good or bad changes, begin by simply identifying the changes that are occurring. Later you can evalutate whether they are good or bad.

Step 1. The class forms into groups of approximately six members each. Each group elects a spokesperson and answers the following questions. The group should spend at least five minutes on each question. Make sure that each member of the group makes a contribution to each question. The spokesperson for each group should be ready to share the group's collective responses to these questions.

a. *What are the changes occurring in your workplace and university?* Members should focus both on internal changes, such as reorganizations, as well as external changes, such as new customers or competitors. Develop a list of the changes discussed in your group.
b. *What are the forces that are driving the changes?* To answer this question, look for the causes of the changes members of the group are observing. For example, a reorganization may be caused by new business opportunities, by new technologies, or by a combination of factors.
c. *What signs of resistance to change do you see occurring?* Change is not always easy for people or organizations. Do you see signs of resistance, such as frustration, anger, increased absences, or other forms of discomfort with the changes you observe?

Step 2. Once you have answered the three questions in Step 1, your group needs to spend some time evaluating whether these changes are good or bad. For each change on the list developed in Step 1a, identify whether this is a good or bad change. In addition, answer the question "Why?" That is, why is this change good? Why is that change bad?

Step 3. Each group shares the results of its answers to the questions in Step 1 and its evaluation of the changes completed in Step 2. Cross-team questions and discussion follows.

Step 4. Your instructor may allow a few minutes at the end of the class period to comment on his or her perceptions of changes occurring within the university, or businesses with which he or she is familiar.

1.2 My Absolute Worst Job

Purpose: To become acquainted with fellow classmates.
Group size: Any number of groups of two.
Exercise schedule:

1. Write answers to the following questions:
   a. What was the worst job you ever had? Describe the following:
      (1) The type of work you did.
      (2) Your boss.
      (3) Your co-workers.
      (4) The organization and its policies.
      (5) What made the job so bad?
   b. What is your dream job?
2. Find someone you do not know, and share your responses.
3. Get together with another dyad, preferably new people. Partner a of one dyad introduces partner b to the other dyad, then b introduces a. The same process is followed by the other dyad. The introduction should follow this format: "This is Mary Cullen. Her very worst job was putting appliqués on bibs at a clothing factory, and the reason she disliked it was because of the following. What she would rather do is be a financial analyst for a big corporation."
4. Each group of four meets with another quartet and is introduced, as before.
5. Your instructor asks for a show of hands on the number of people whose worst jobs fit into the following categories:
   a. Factory
   b. Restaurant
   c. Manual labor.
   d. Driving or delivery.
   e. Professional.
   f. Health care.
   g. Phone sales or communication.
   h. Other.
6. Your instructor gathers data from each group on worst jobs and asks the groups to answer these questions:
   a. What are the common characteristics of the worst jobs in your group?
   b. How did your co-workers feel about their jobs?
   c. What happens to morale and productivity when a worker hates the job?
   d. What was the difference between your own morale and productivity in your worst job and in a job you really enjoyed?
   e. Why do organizations continue to allow unpleasant working conditions to exist?
7. Your instructor leads a group discussion on Questions a through e.

SOURCE: D. Marcic, "My Absolute Worst Job: An Icebreaker," *Organizational Behavior: Experiences and Cases* (St. Paul, Minn.: West, 1989), 5–6.

VIDEO CASE

Lanier's Customer Vision[1]

Lanier Worldwide, Inc. sells and services copying systems, facsimile products, digital dictating systems, presentation systems products, and electronic optical systems for storage and retrieval. "We are a distribution company, which means that everything we sell, we source from some place else," says Lanier's David Marini. Lanier contracts other companies to manufacture products to Lanier's high standards—most of which is done overseas, and primarily in Japan. These products are then distributed throughout the United States and the rest of the world. Lanier's international operations consists of five regions: Latin America, three European regions (North, Central, and South), and a catchall region including Canada, Australia, Asia, and Africa.

Lanier faces formidable competition in its different product areas. For example, Xerox, Cannon, Sharp, and Mita are among its primary competitors in the copying systems and facsimile products areas. Dictaphones and Sony compete with Lanier on dictation and voice systems products. IBM is a competitor on imaging products or optical disk storage and retrieval systems.

Lanier does not compete with any of these firms on the basis of price or technology. Rather, it competes on the basis of how they treat the customer. Known as customer vision, this is the defining element of the Lanier's corporate culture. According to Lanier executive Lance Herrin, customer vision enables the company ". . . to see our business through the customers' eyes and to respond as a team . . . to their concerns and needs at (and preferably above) their expectations." Customer vision "has really been ingrained into the processes of the company," says Brian Bergin, another Lanier executive.

At Lanier, customer vision involves four key components. First, a customer performance promise guarantees that Lanier will provide equipment or systems that meet customer needs and expectations. If the customer isn't satisfied, Lanier will exchange the product to make sure the customer is happy—no questions asked. The customer makes the decision, not Lanier employees. Second, Lanier guarantees that purchased or leased products will be up and running 98 percent of the time. Plus, if the equipment is unusable for eight hours, a loaner is provided at no cost to the customer. Third, Lanier maintains a round-the-clock, 365 day a year toll free help line to assist in solving any customer problems with its products. Fourth, the company guarantees the availability of service and parts on any of its products for a minimum of five years after installation.

Lanier has an obsessive focus on customer satisfaction and it fully embraces total quality management (TQM) concepts. Similar to Ford's *Quality is Job One* and Motorola's *Six Sigma Quality*, Lanier's approach to total quality management is called *LTMP—Lanier Team Management Process.* The basic pillars of LTMP include employee involvement, customer focus, and teamwork at all levels of the organization.

Lanier's employees are critical in fulfilling the customer vision and helping the company become successful. Says Terry Geraghty, Director of Organizational Development, "We feel that we can only achieve business results by capturing the hearts and minds of all our employees—which is, I guess, one of our fundamental tenets associated with quality."

DISCUSSION QUESTIONS

1. What marketplace advantages and disadvantages might Lanier realize as a result of their customer vision competitive strategy?
2. What implications do the four key components of Lanier's customer vision have for the job behavior of their employees?
3. What skills and knowledge do you think are crucial to the success of Lanier's employees? Explain your answer.
4. Would you like to work for a company like Lanier? Why or why not?

SOURCE: This case was written by Michael K. McCuddy, the Louis S. and Mary L. Morgal Professor of Christian Business Ethics, College of Business Administration, Valparaiso University.

[1]This case is based on transcripts of interviews that representatives of West Educational Publishing conducted with various Lanier executives during 1994.

References

1. R. M. Kanter, B. A. Stein, and T. D. Jick, *The Challenge of Organizational Change* (New York: Free Press, 1992).
2. H. Schwartz, "The Clockwork or the Snakepit: An Essay on the Meaning of Teaching Organizational Behavior," *Organizational Behavior Teaching Review* 11, No. 2 (1987): 19–26.
3. K. Lewin, "Field Theory in Social Science," selected theoretical papers (edited by Dorin Cartwright) (NY: Harper, 1951).
4. L. R. Offermann and M. K. Gowing, guest eds., "Special Issue: Organizational Psychology," *American Psychologist* 45 (1990): 95–283.
5. R. M. Yerkes, "The Relation of Psychology to Military Activities," *Mental Hygiene* 1 (1917): 371–376.
6. R. K. Merton, "The Role Set," *British Journal of Sociology* 8 *(1957): 106–120.*
7. N. Gross, W. Mason, and A. McEachen, *Explorations in Role Analysis: Studies of the School Superintendency Role* (New York: Wiley, 1958)
8. F. W. Taylor, *The Principles of Scientific Management* (New York: Norton, 1911).
9. Hearings before Special Committee of the House of Representatives to Investigate the Taylor and Other Systems of Shop Management under Authority of House Resolution 90; Vol. 3: 1377–1508 contains Dr. Taylor's testimony before the committee from Thursday, January 25, through Tuesday, January 30, 1912.
10. A. L. Wilkins and W. G. Ouchi, "Efficient Cultures: Exploring the Relationship between Culture and Organizational Performance," *Administrative Science Quarterly* 28 (1983): 468–481.
11. M. F. R. Kets de Vries and D. Miller, "Personality, Culture, and Organization," *Academy of Management Review* 11 (1986): 266–279.
12. H. Schwartz, *Narcissistic Process and Corporate Decay: The Theory of the Organizational Ideal* (New York: NYU Press, 1990).
13. J. G. March and H. A. Simon, *Organizations* (New York: Wiley, 1958).
14. H. B. Elkind, *Preventive Management: Mental Hygiene in Industry* (New York: B. C. Forbes, 1931).
15. L. Foss and K. Rothenberg, *The Second Medical Revolution: From Biomedical to Infomedical* (Boston: New Science Library, 1987).
16. K. R. Pelletier, *Mind as Healer, Mind as Slayer: A Holistic Approach to Preventing Stress Disorders* (New York: Delacorte, 1977).
17. D. R. Ilgen, "Health Issues at Work," *American Psychologist* 45 (1990): 273–283.
18. R. L. A. Sterba, "The Organization and Management of the Temple Corporations in Ancient Mesopotamia," *Academy of Management Review* 1 (1976): 16–26; S. P. Dorsey, *Early English Churches in America* (New York: Oxford University Press, 1952).
19. Sir I. Moncreiffe of That Ilk, *The Highland Clans: The Dynastic Origins, Chiefs, and Background of the Clans and of Some Other Families Connected to Highland History*, rev. ed. (New York: C. N. Potter, 1982).
20. D. Shambaugh, "The Soldier and the State in China: The Political Work System in the People's Liberation Army," *Chinese Quarterly* 127 (1991): 527–568.
21. L. L'Abate, ed., *Handbook of Developmental Family Psychology and Psychopathology* (New York: Wiley, 1993).
22. J. A. Hostetler, *Communitarian Societies* (New York: Holt, Rinehart & Winston, 1974).
23. J. M. Lewis, "The Family System and Physical Illness" in *No Single Thread: Psychological Health in Family Systems* (New York: Brunner/Mazel, 1976).
24. H. J. Leavitt, "Applied Organizational Change in Industry: Structural, Technological, and Humanistic Approaches," in J. G. March, ed., *Handbook of Organizations* (Chicago: Rand McNally, 1965), 1144–1170.
25. J. D. Thompson, *Organizations in Action* (New York: McGraw-Hill, 1967).
26. F. J. Roethlisberger and W. J. Dickson, *Management and the Worker* (Cambridge, Mass.: Harvard University Press, 1939).
27. R. J. Selfridge and S. L. Sokolik, "A Comprehensive View of Organizational Development, *MSU Business Topics*, Winter 1975, 47.
28. W. L. French and C. H. Bell, *Organization Development*, 4th ed. (Englewood Cliffs, N. J.: Prentice-Hall, 1990).
29. J. P. Kotter, "Managing External Dependence," *Academy of Management Review* 4 (1979): 87–92.
30. G. J. McManus, "Beaming with Pride: Steelmaker of the Year," *Iron Age*, August 1992, 14–21.
31. R. L. Shook, *Turn Around: The New Ford Motor Company* (New York: Prentice-Hall, 1990).
32. H. M. Petrakis, *The Founder's Touch: The Life of Paul Galvin of Motorola* (New York: McGraw-Hill, 1965).
33. American Management Association, *Blueprints for Service Quality: The Federal Express Approach* (New York: American Management Association, 1991).
34. L. Mirabile (ed.), *International Directory of Company Histories: Volume II* (Chicago: St. James Press, 1990): 253–255 and P. Kepos (ed.), *International Directory of Company Histories: Volume 9* (London: St. James Press, 1994): 123–126.
35. J. C. Quick, "Crafting an Organizational Culture: Herb's Hand at Southwest Airlines," *Organizational Dynamics* 21 (1992): 45–56.
36. L. E. Thurow, *Head to Head: The Coming Economic Battle among Japan, Europe, and America* (New York: William Morrow, 1992).
37. J. E. Patterson, *Acquiring the Future: America's Survival and Success in the Global Economy* (Homewood, Ill.: Dow Jones–Irwin, 1990).
38. H. B. Stewart, *Recollecting the Future: A View of Business, Technology, and Innovation in the Next 30 Years* (Homewood, Ill.: Dow Jones–Irwin, 1989).
39. L. R. Offermann and M. K. Gowing, "Organizations of the Future," *American Psychologist* 45 (1990): 95–108.
40. R. S. Fosler, W. Alonso, J. A. Meyer, and R. Kern, *Demographic Change and the American Future* (Pittsburgh, Pa.: University of Pittsburgh Press, 1990).
41. D. Ciampa, *Total Quality* (Reading, Mass.: Addison-Wesley, 1992).
42. P. R. Thomas, L. J. Gallace, and K. R. Martin, *Quality Alone is Not Enough* (New York: American Management Association, 1992).
43. J. A. Edosomwan, "Six Commandments to Empower Employees for Quality Improvement," *Industrial Engineering* 24 (1992): 14–15.
44. R. M. Steers and L. W. Porter, *Motivation and Work Behavior*, 5th ed. (New York: McGraw-Hill, 1991).
45. B. M. Bass, *Stogdill's Handbook of Leadership* (New York: Free Press, 1982).
46. H. Levinson, *Executive Stress* (New York: New American Library, 1975).
47. D. L. Whetzel, "The Department of Labor Identifies Workplace Skills," *Industrial/Organizational Psychologist* 29 (1991): 89–90.
48. C. Argyris and D. A. Schon, *Organizational Learning: A Theory of Action Perspective* (Reading, Mass.: Addison-Wesley, 1978).
49. E. E. Lawler III, "From Job-Based to Competency-Based Organizations," *Journal of Organizational Behavior* 15 (1994): 3–15.
50. J. DeTar, "Motorola in 'Dramatic' Global Shift," *Electronic News* (2 October 1995): 4–6; "Motorola Sales Climb 21% as Wireless, Semi Prosper," *Electronic News* (16 October 1995): 12.

CHAPTER 2

Organizations 2001 and Managerial Challenges

LEARNING OBJECTIVES

After reading this chapter, your should be able to do the following:

- Describe the dimensions of cultural differences in societies that affect work-related attitudes.
- Explain the social and demographic changes that are producing diversity in organizations.
- Describe actions managers can take to help their employees value diversity.
- Understand the technological changes that will affect organizations most dramatically by the year 2000.
- Explain the ways managers can help employees adjust to technological change.
- Discuss the assumptions of consequential, rule-based, and cultural ethical theories.
- Explain eight issues that pose ethical dilemmas for managers.

OPENING SPOTLIGHT

Meeting the Challenges at Federal Express

Global competition, workforce diversity, technological change, and ethical behavior are challenges that Federal Express manages well. Federal Express faces tremendous competition in the overnight delivery business. Domestic rivals like the U.S. postal system and United Parcel Service (UPS) keep up the competition on the domestic side. FedEx also faces stiff competition in the

http://fedex.com/

global market, particularly in Europe and Asia. Its chief competitors overseas are DHL Express International of Belgium and Australia's TNT Express. The goals of the three cargo carriers are the same: total domination of Europe and Asia. FedEx's niche is transcontinental delivery, as opposed to intracountry delivery. How does Federal Express manage the global competitive challenge? One key is the company's emphasis on *service quality*.

Federal Express was the first service company to win the coveted Malcolm Baldridge National Quality Award. Service quality can only be measured by customer satisfaction. FedEx developed a list of service quality indicators, which are potential problems weighted according to their seriousness as determined by customer satisfaction surveys. A late delivery by a few hours rates a 1, and a missed pickup or a damaged shipment rates a 10. By quantifying part of service quality, FedEx workers can focus on the things that customers find most dissatisfying and view them as key problems to avoid. FedEx also uses teams that work on improving service quality to its advantage. One quality team developed a simpler way to memorize the company's 700 three-letter city codes, and its method cut training time from six months to five weeks.

Managing workforce diversity is another challenge that Federal Express has tackled head-on. Its Leadership Institute offers a 4½-day workshop, "Diversity: The Leadership Challenge," that helps managers explore issues of race, gender, and disability as sources of diversity. The goal of the workshop is to help managers lead people of all types and value the differences they bring to the workplace.

In the Closing Spotlight, we'll examine FedEx's innovative ways of managing technological change and ethical behavior.[1, 2] ■

Competition: The Challenges Managers Face

Alternate Example
Not all approaches to meeting competition are "high tech" and automated. For example, in the 1970s, Phillips 66 in Bartlesville, Oklahoma, utilized ham radio hobbyists to monitor the global environment. Knowing that a large community of ham radio operators stayed up all night to listen to the wires across the world, the company had one of its security guards pick up their "listenings" early each morning. The guard delivered the information and had it transcribed and placed on the marketing manager's desk before 8:00 A.M. each morning. This gave Phillips 66 a competitive advantage that cost the company nothing while it developed community support.

■ Federal Express is not alone in its attempt to meet the competitive challenges of today's environment. Recent surveys indicate that the vast majority of U.S. executives believe U.S. firms are encountering unprecedented global competition.[3] Research data also support this belief. The United States has not performed as well as Canada, Germany, Japan, or the United Kingdom in terms of increases in living standards, productivity, and investment in recent years.[4] With competition increasing both at home and abroad, managers must find creative ways to deal with the competitive challenges they face.

What are the major challenges? Chief executive officers of U.S. corporations of all sizes responded to a survey that asked them to identify the greatest challenges they face in the 1990s and beyond.[5] The top three responses were global competition and globalizing the firm's operations, making sure the human side of the enterprise works at all levels, and keeping up with technology and implementing it in the workplace. Complementing these challenges is the challenge of managing ethical behavior. Some believe that management abuses of trust are the most serious threat to organizations today.[6]

This chapter introduces these four specific challenges for managers and describes how some organizations are tackling the challenges. First, the *challenge of globalization* is discussed. Rapid political and social changes have broken down national barriers, and the push for global expansion has become a reality in many organizations.

Discussion Consideration
What technological changes have occurred in the students' lifetime? How have these changes impacted their approach to learning? How have these changes impacted organizations?

Second, the *challenge of workforce diversity* is presented. The human side of the enterprise is more diverse than ever before. When managers try to bring together employees of different backgrounds, they face the challenge of varied communication styles, insensitivity, and ignorance of others' motivations and cultures.[7]

Third, the *challenge of technological change* is explored. Organizations must take advantage of technology as a key to strategic competitiveness. Technological change is complex, because it often necessitates changes in individual and group behavior, information flows, work design, social interactions, and organizational structure.

Finally, the *challenge of managing ethical behavior* is discussed. With recent insider trading scandals, junk bond proliferation, savings and loan crises, contract frauds, check-kiting practices, and influence peddling, ethical behavior has come to the forefront of public consciousness. These four challenges are the engines that drive organizations in their pursuit of competitiveness.

Managing in a Global Environment

■ Only a few years ago, business conducted across national borders was referred to as "international"activity. The word *international* carries with it a connotation that the individual's or the organization's nationality is held strongly in consciousness.[8] *Globalization*, in contrast, implies that the world is free from national boundaries and that it is really a borderless world.[9] U.S. workers are now competing with workers in other countries. Organizations from other countries are locating subsidiaries in the United States, such as the U.S. manufacturing locations of Honda and Mazda.

Similarly, what were once referred to as multinational organizations (organizations that did business in several countries) are now referred to as transnational companies. In **transnational organizations,** the global viewpoint supersedes national issues.[10] Transnational organizations operate over large global distances and are multicultural in terms of the people they employ. 3M, Dow Chemical, Coca-Cola, and other transnational organizations operate worldwide with diverse populations of employees.

transnational organization

An organization in which the global viewpoint supersedes national issues.

Point to Emphasize

U.S. firms will be able to use a base in one country to develop a network for selling their products throughout the EC, resulting in lower transportation and capital costs. Even more interesting is that European countries cooperating with the EC will have the same cultural difficulties in negotiations that the United States has traditionally had from country to country. SOURCE: T. Bennett and C. S. Hakkio, "Europe 1992: Implications for U.S. Firms," *Economic Review,* April 1989.

Changes in the Global Marketplace

Social and political upheavals have led organizations to change the way they conduct business and to encourage their members to think globally. The collapse of Eastern Europe was followed quickly by the demise of the Berlin Wall. East and West Germany were united into a single country. In the Soviet Union, perestroika led to the liberation of the satellite countries and the breaking away of the Soviet Union's member nations. Perestroika also brought about many opportunities for U.S. businesses, as witnessed by the press releases showing extremely long waiting lines at Moscow's first McDonald's restaurant.

Business ventures in China have become increasingly attractive to U.S. businesses. One challenge U.S. managers have tackled is attempting to understand the Chinese way of doing business. Chinese managers' business practices have been shaped by the Communist party, socialism, feudalistic values, and ***guanxi*** (building networks for social exchange). For example, it is common in China to use *guanxi*, or personal connections, to conduct business or to obtain jobs.[11] The term *guanxi* is sometimes a sensitive word, because Communist party policies oppose the use of such practices to gain influence. In China, the family is regarded as being responsible for a worker's productivity, and in turn, the company is responsible for the worker's family. Because of socialism, Chinese managers have very little experience with rewards and punishments, and are reluctant to use them in the workplace. To work with Chinese managers, Americans can learn to build their own *guanxi;* understand the Chinese chain of command; and negotiate slow, general agreements in order to interact effectively. Using the foreign government as the local franchisee may be effective in China. For example, Kentucky Fried Chicken's operation in China is a joint venture between KFC (60 percent) and two Chinese government bodies (40 percent).[12]

guanxi

The Chinese practice of building networks for social exchange.

In 1993, the European Union integrated fifteen nations into a single market by removing trade barriers. The member nations of the European Union are

Belgium, Denmark, France, Germany, Greece, Ireland, Italy, Luxembourg, the Netherlands, Portugal, Spain, Austria, Finland, Sweden, and the United Kingdom. The integration of Europe provides many opportunities for U.S. organizations, including 350 million potential customers. Companies like Ford Motor Company and IBM, which entered the market early with wholly owned subsidiaries, will have a head start on these opportunities.[13] However, competition within the European Union will increase, as will competition from Japan and the former Soviet nations.

The United States, Canada, and Mexico have dramatically reduced trade barriers in accordance with the North American Free Trade Agreement (NAFTA), which took effect in 1994. Organizations have found promising new markets for their products, and many companies have located plants in Mexico to take advantage of low labor costs. Chrysler, for example, has a massive assembly plant in Saltillo. Prior to NAFTA, Mexico placed heavy tariffs on U.S. exports. The agreement immediately eliminated many of these tariffs, and provided that the remaining tariffs be phased out over time.

All of these changes have brought about the need to think globally. Given the domestic economic problems in the United States, a global focus provides a way to maintain profitability. To benefit from global thinking, managers will also need to take a long-term view. Entry into global markets is a long-term proposition, and it requires long-term strategies.

Understanding Cultural Differences

One of the keys for any company competing in the global marketplace is to understand the diverse cultures of the individuals involved. Whether managing culturally diverse individuals within a single location or managing individuals at remote locations around the globe, an appreciation of the differences among cultures is crucial. Knowing cultural differences in symbols may even be important. Computer icons may not translate well in other cultures. The thumbs up sign, for example, means approval in the U.S. In Australia, however, it is an obscene gesture. And manila file folders, like the icons used in Windows applications, aren't used in many European countries and therefore aren't recognized.[14]

Do cultural differences translate into differences in work-related attitudes? The pioneering work of Dutch researcher Geert Hofstede has focused on this question.[15] He and his colleagues surveyed 160,000 managers and employees of IBM who were represented in sixty countries.[16] In this way, the researchers were able to study individuals from the same company in the same jobs, but working in different countries. Hofstede's work is important, because his studies showed that national culture explains more differences in work-related attitudes than does age, gender, profession, or position within the organization. Thus, cultural differences do affect individuals' work-related attitudes. Hofstede found five dimensions of cultural differences that formed the basis for work-related attitudes. These dimensions are shown in Figure 2.1.

individualism

A cultural orientation in which people belong to loose social frameworks, and their primary concern is for themselves and their families.

collectivism

A cultural orientation in which individuals belong to tightly knit social frameworks, and they depend strongly on large extended families or clans.

INDIVIDUALISM VERSUS COLLECTIVISM In cultures where **individualism** predominates, people belong to loose social frameworks, but their primary concern is for themselves and their families. People are responsible for taking care of their own interests. They believe that individuals should make decisions. Cultures characterized by **collectivism** are tightly knit social frameworks in which individual members depend strongly on extended families or clans. Group decisions are valued and accepted.

The North American culture is individualistic in orientation. It is a "can-do" culture that values individual freedom and responsibility. In contrast, collectivist cultures emphasize group welfare and harmony. Israeli kibbutzim and the Japanese culture are examples of societies in which group loyalty and unity are para-

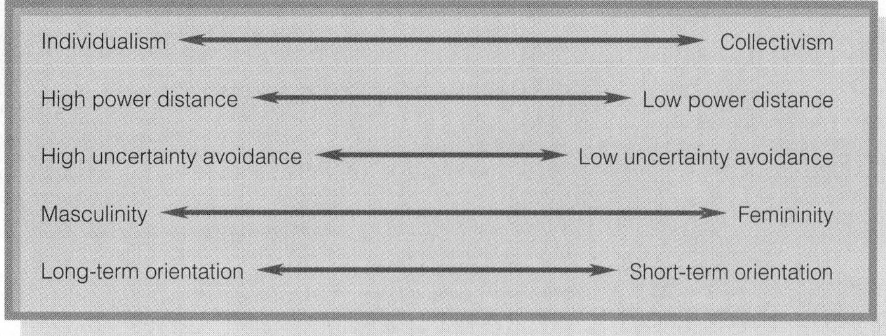

■ **FIGURE 2.1**

Hofstede's Dimensions of Cultural Differences

SOURCE: G. Hofstede, "Cultural Constraints in Management Theories," *Academy of Management Executive* 7 (1993): 81–94. Reprinted with permission.

mount. Organization charts show these orientations. In Canada and the United States, which are individualistic cultures, organization charts show individual positions. In Malaysia, which is a collectivist culture, organization charts show only sections or departments.[17]

This dimension of cultural differences has other workplace implications. Individualistic managers, as found in Great Britain and the Netherlands, emphasize and encourage individual achievement. In contrast, collectivistic managers, such as in Japan and Colombia, seek to fit harmoniously within the group. They also encourage these behaviors among their employees.

Alternate Example

Hofstede's framework may also be a useful framework for understanding the cultures of organizations and the differences between individuals.

Discussion Consideration

Ask students how they would feel if their grade for this course was based solely on what their project team did rather than each student's individual performance. What advantages and disadvantages do they see in this approach?

POWER DISTANCE The second dimension of cultural differences examines the acceptance of unequal distribution of power. In countries with a high **power distance,** bosses are afforded more power simply because they are the bosses. Titles are used, formality is the rule, and bypassing authority is seldom seen. Power holders are entitled to their privileges, and managers and employees see one another as fundamentally different kinds of people. India is a country with a high power distance, as are Venezuela and Mexico.

power distance

The degree to which a culture accepts unequal distribution of power.

In countries with a low power distance, people believe that inequality in society should be minimized. People at various power levels are less threatened by, and more willing to trust, one another. Managers and employees see one another as similar. Managers are given power only if they have expertise. Employees frequently bypass the boss in order to get work done in countries with a low power distance, such as Denmark and Australia.

UNCERTAINTY AVOIDANCE Some cultures are quite comfortable with ambiguity and uncertainty, whereas others do not tolerate these conditions as well. Cultures with high **uncertainty avoidance** are concerned with security and tend to avoid conflict. People have a need for consensus. The inherent uncertainty in life is a threat against which people in such cultures constantly struggle.

uncertainty avoidance

The degree to which a culture tolerates ambiguity and uncertainty.

Cultures with low uncertainty avoidance are more tolerant of ambiguity. People are more willing to take risks and more tolerant of individual differences. Conflict is seen as constructive, and people accept dissenting viewpoints. Norway and Australia are characterized by low uncertainty avoidance, and this trait is seen in the value placed on job mobility. Japan and Italy are characterized by high uncertainty avoidance, so career stability is emphasized.

MASCULINITY VERSUS FEMININITY In cultures that are characterized by **masculinity,** assertiveness and materialism are valued. Men should be assertive, and women should be nurturing. Money and possessions are important, and performance is what counts. Achievement is admired. Cultures that are characterized by **femininity** emphasize relationships and concern for others. Men and women are expected to assume both assertive and nurturing roles. Quality of life is important, and people and the environment are emphasized.

masculinity

The cultural orientation in which assertiveness and materialism are valued.

femininity

The cultural orientation in which relationships and concern for others are valued.

Academy Award winning actress Susan Sarandon has said she would rather be "best mom" than best actress. In addition to balancing career and family, she is known for her political activism and her efforts to aid victims of poverty and injustice.

Masculine societies, such as in Austria and Venezuela, define gender roles strictly. Feminine societies, in contrast, tend to have gender roles that are blurred. Women may be the providers, and men may stay home with the children. The Scandinavian countries of Norway, Sweden, and Denmark exemplify the feminine orientation.

time orientation

Whether a culture's values are oriented toward the future (long-term orientation) or toward the past and present (short-term orientation).

TIME ORIENTATION Cultures also differ in **time orientation;** that is, whether the culture's values are oriented toward the future (long-term orientation) or toward the past and present (short-term orientation).[18] In China, a culture with a long-term orientation, values such as thrift and persistence, which focus on the future, are emphasized. In Russia, the orientation is short-term. Values such as respect for tradition (past) and meeting social obligations (present) are emphasized.

Point to Emphasize

Although corporate America is embracing teamwork, a number of obstacles still must be overcome to move from individual teamwork to group teamwork, as stressed in quality management teams. The United States has always rewarded individual effort, from competing in school to annual performance appraisals at work based on individual contributions. Today, the emphasis has shifted to group achievement. SOURCE: "Out of the Crisis," W. Edwards Deming, Massachusetts Institute of Technology, 1986.

U.S. CULTURE The position of the United States on these five dimensions is interesting. Hofstede found the United States to be the most individualistic country of any studied. On the power distance dimension, the United States ranked among the countries with weak power distance. Its rank on uncertainty avoidance indicated a tolerance of uncertainty. The United States also ranked as a masculine culture with a short-term orientation. These values have shaped U.S. management theory, and Hofstede's work casts doubt on the universal applicability of U.S. management theories. Because cultures differ so widely on these dimensions, management practices should be adjusted to account for cultural differences. Managers in transnational organizations must learn as much as they can about other cultures in order to lead their culturally diverse organizations effectively.

expatriate manager

A manager who works in a country other than his or her home country.

Careers in management have taken on a global dimension. Working in transnational organizations will likely give managers the opportunity to work in other countries. **Expatriate managers,** those who work in a country other than their home country, should know as much as possible about cultural differences. Because many future managers will have global work experience, it is never too early to begin planning for this aspect of your career. Challenge 2.1 asks you to

CHALLENGE

■ **2.1**

Planning for a Global Career

Think of a country you would like to work in, do business in, or visit. Find out about its culture, using Hofstede's dimensions as guidelines. You can use a variety of sources to accomplish this, particularly your school library, government offices, faculty members, or others who have global experience. You will want to answer the following questions:

1. Is the culture individualistic or collectivist?
2. Is the power distance high or low?
3. Is uncertainty avoidance high or low?
4. Is the country masculine or feminine in its orientation?
5. Is the time orientation short-term or long-term?
6. How did you arrive at your answers to the first four questions?
7. How will these characteristics affect business practices in the country you chose to investigate?

begin gathering information about a country in which you would like to work, including information on its culture.

Understanding cultural differences becomes especially important for companies that are considering opening foreign offices, because workplace customs can vary widely from one country to another. Carefully searching out this information in advance can help companies successfully manage foreign operations. Consulate offices and companies operating within the foreign country are excellent sources of information about national customs and legal requirements. Table 2.1 presents a series of differences among five countries to highlight what a company might encounter in opening a foreign office in any one of them.

Another reality that can affect global business practices is the cost of layoffs in other countries. The practice of downsizing is not unique to the United States. Dismissing a forty-five-year-old middle manager with twenty years of service and a $50,000 annual salary can vary in cost from a low of $13,000 in Ireland to a high of $130,000 in Italy.[19] The cost of laying off this manager in the United States would be approximately $19,000. The wide variability in costs stems from the various legal protections that certain countries give workers. In Italy, laid-off employees must receive a "notice period" payment (one year's pay if they have nine years or more of service) plus a severance payment (based on pay and years of service). U.S. companies operating overseas often adopt the European tradition of spending more time training and retraining workers to avoid overstaffing and potential layoffs. An appreciation of the customs and rules for doing business in another country is essential if a company wants to go global.

Developing Cross-Cultural Sensitivity

As organizations compete in the global marketplace, employees must learn to deal with individuals from diverse cultural backgrounds. Stereotypes may pervade employees' perceptions of other cultures. In addition, employees may be unaware of others' perceptions of the employees' national culture. A potentially valuable exercise is to ask members from various cultures to describe one another's cultures. This provides a lesson on the misinterpretation of culture.

Cultural sensitivity training is a popular method for helping employees recognize and appreciate cultural differences. Northern Telecom, for example, conducts a sixteen-hour training program to help employees modify negative attitudes toward individuals from different cultures.[20]

■ **TABLE 2.1**

Opening a Foreign Office: A Five-Country Comparison

Some of the knottiest problems a company faces when it opens a foreign office are right inside that office. Few U.S. companies are prepared for how different the workplace "rules" abroad can be from U.S. norms—and how these norms differ from one country to another. Knowing some of these customs in advance can make a huge difference in the ability to manage a foreign operation successfully, as well as in the profitability of the operation. Few prerequisites and compensation levels are mandated. The benefits offered by companies are typically a blend of what is legally required and what is voluntary. The following are work force highlights from five countries, gathered from consulate offices and owners of U.S. companies.
BELGIUM **Perks:** As elsewhere in Europe, a car and a cellular phone for managers and salespeople. Discretionary use of an expense account. **Benefits:** Health care and social security are required by law; these amount to 33% of gross salary. Even a secretary signs a contract when hired, and cannot be fired just like that. Severance provisions are much higher than in the United States. After 10 years, a middle manager could expect severance pay of one to two years' salary. **Compensation:** Almost every employee participates in a bonus plan. Employees also get a separate bonus, equal to three weeks' salary, when they take their vacation. Cost of a good electronic engineer: $35,000. **Vacation:** Four weeks, by law. **Holidays:** Twelve days. **Language:** English is all that's necessary. **U.S. Workers:** Relatively easy to bring in. **Other:** Dated attitudes toward women employees and minorities prevail here and throughout Europe, but upcoming legislation should force attitudes to change.
GREAT BRITAIN **Perks:** Managers and salespeople expect company cars, often with cellular phones. High tax rates have made objects, rather than cash, preferred by employees. **Benefits:** Private medical insurance to complement national health care. Pension plans are not as common as in the United States. **Compensation:** It's difficult to find people to work for straight commission. A Christmas bonus is expected by all. Cost of a good electronic engineer: $25,000. **Vacation:** Three to five weeks typically, but not mandated by law. **Holidays:** Eight legal holidays; most companies offer twelve. **Language:** English. **U.S. workers:** It's not easy, but the Brits are cooperative if you want to bring in U.S. citizens to seed a company. **Other:** The buying cycle is much longer. What takes two visits to sell here, might take five there.
HUNGARY **Perks:** Company car for managers and salespeople. Pay in hard currency. Travel abroad is prized. **Benefits:** Health-care coverage is legally required and costs plenty—some 40% of wages. But wage rates are low. Many companies also make home-construction loans and provide lunch, commuting, and day-care allowances. There's a heavy penalty for trying to reduce benefits to employees. **Compensation:** High tax rate makes bonuses not very rewarding, so they aren't expected. Cost of a good electronic engineer: $10,000. **Vacation:** Fifteen days required by law. Companies typically add one to nine days for every three years of service. **Holidays:** Eight days. **Language:** Most Hungarians speak German or Russian as a second language. **U.S. workers:** Laws recently became more restrictive, but there's little problem for managers or technical employees. **Other:** Buying a Hungarian property is complicated because of the privatization process, but overhead is easily lowered. Office space is scarce and expensive. Never toast a contract with beer mugs—it recalls the conquest of Hungary. Use slivovitz instead.
JAPAN **Perks:** Company car for executives. Add a chauffeur for the president, vice-presidents, and perhaps managing director of a U.S. company's office. **Benefits:** National health-care and social-security costs are split 50-50 by employer and employee. Companies also pay for workers' compensation insurance, unemployment insurance, and pension costs. Transportation allowance (four-hour daily train commutes aren't unusual), lunch allowance. Expense budgets can run very high; a middle manager might entertain clients five nights a week. **Compensation:** Bonuses for individual performance are unpopular. Employees prefer straight salary. All receive New Year's bonus based on company's performance: 1.2 times a month's salary in a good year, half a month's salary in a bad year. Cost of a good electronic engineer: $30,000. **Vacation:** Two weeks, by law, usually taken a day or two at a time. **Holidays:** Twenty legally mandated days, including New Year's and August holidays, during which the whole country shuts down. **Language:** English fluency is very rare. Many Japanese understand English, but they are taught to write, rather than speak it. Outside the cities, no English. **U.S. workers:** Not difficult; U.S. limitations pose more difficulty than Japanese rules do. **Other:** There's a tremendous shortage of people for management positions, and head-hunting is not accepted. Communication problems can be awesome. There is no effective, acceptable way to say no in Japanese, so you often don't know where you stand.
SOUTH KOREA **Perks:** Pick-up by a car pool, graduating to a company car and driver. For a vice-president, a golf-club membership and lessons, for any salesperson, a generous lump-sum expense account, which employee may keep if he or she does not spend it all. **Benefits:** Law requires companies with more than 10 employees to pay for one medical examination each year and set aside one month's salary per year, per employee, as severance. Many companies offer low- or no-interest car and housing loans; some build their own apartment buildings and offer cheap leases to key employees. **Compensation:** Employees respond well to commission only. Spring, fall, and New Year's bonuses are expected; size of bonus reflects company performance. Cost of a good engineer: $19,000. **Vacation:** Law requires three vacation days. **Holidays:** Nineteen days. **U.S. workers:** Company must prove no Korean could do the job, but criteria for this are not rigorous. **Language:** It's easy to find people who speak English, though not as easy among production people. **Other:** South Koreans hold the United States in high esteem.

SOURCE: Reprinted with permission, *Inc, Magazine* (April, 1992). Copyright 1992 by Goldhirsh Group, Inc., 38 Commercial Wharf, Boston, MA 02110.

Another way of developing sensitivity is to use cross-cultural task forces or teams. The Milwaukee-based GE Medical Systems Group (GEMS) has 7,000 of its 15,000 employees working outside the United States. GEMS has developed a vehicle for bringing managers from each of its three regions (the Americas, Europe, and Asia) together to work on a variety of business projects. The plan is called the Global Leadership Program, and several work groups made up of managers from various regions of the world are formed in the program. The teams work on important projects, such as worldwide employee integration to increase the employees' sense of belonging throughout the GEMS international organization.[21]

The globalization of business affects all parts of the organization, and human resource management is affected in particular. Companies have employees around the world, and human resource managers face the daunting task of effectively supporting a culturally diverse work force. Human resource managers must adopt a global view of all functions, including human resource planning, recruitment and selection, compensation, and training and development. They must have a working knowledge of the legal systems in various countries, as well as of global economics, culture, and customs. Human resource managers must not only prepare U.S. workers to become expatriates but also help foreign employees interact with U.S. culture. Global human resource management is a complex endeavor, but it is critical to the success of organizations in the global marketplace.

Globalization is one challenge managers must face in order to remain competitive in the changing world. Related to globalization is the challenge of managing an increasingly diverse workforce. Cultural differences contribute a great deal to the diversity of the workforce, but there are other forms of diversity as well.

Managing Workforce Diversity

■ Workforce diversity has always been an important issue for organizations. The United States, as a melting pot nation, has always had a mix of individuals in its workforce. We once sought to be all alike, as in the melting pot. However, we now recognize and try to appreciate individual differences. **Diversity** encompasses all forms of differences among individuals, including culture, gender, age, ability, religious affiliation, personality, economic class, social status, military attachment, and sexual orientation.

diversity

All forms of individual differences, including culture, gender, age, ability, personality, religious affiliation, economic class, social status, military attachment, and sexual orientation.

Attention to diversity has increased in recent years, particularly because of the changing demographics of the working population. Managers feel that dealing with diversity successfully is an issue of paramount concern. Two reasons are given for this emphasis. First, managers may lack the knowledge of how to motivate diverse work groups. Second, managers are unsure of how to communicate effectively with employees who have different values and language skills.[22]

Several demographic trends, in particular, will be forced upon organizations in the coming years. By the year 2000, the workforce is predicted to be more culturally diverse, more female, and older than ever.[23] In addition, new legislation and new technologies will bring more disabled workers into the workforce.

Alternate Example

Although most international companies do not want to advertise the issue, corporate terrorism in an increasing concern for employers. Large multinational corporations are particularly vulnerable because terrorists operate widely and boldly overseas. To help executives be more aware of their surroundings, many companies provide seminars and guidelines for increasing personal security. SOURCE: W. J. Heisler, W. D. Jones, and P. O. Benham, Jr., *Managing Human Resources Issues* (San Francisco: Jossey-Bass, 1988).

Cultural Diversity

Cultural diversity in the workplace is growing because of the globalization of business, as we discussed earlier. People of diverse national origins—Koreans, Bolivians, Pakistanis, Vietnamese, Swedes, Australians, and others—will find themselves cooperating in teams to perform the work of the organization. In addition, changing demographics within the United States will significantly affect the cultural diversity in organizations. Over the next ten years, only 58 percent of the new entrants to the labor force will be white Americans ("majority"workers).[24] The participation rates of African-Americans and Hispanic-Americans in the labor force have increased dramatically in recent years. African-American women are predicted to make up the largest share of the increase in the minority labor force, and they are expected to outnumber the African-American men in the workforce by the year 2000.

Alternate Example
Many members of minority groups have come to resent the implications that have been connected with Equal Employment Opportunity Commission (EEOC) and affirmative action programs that are directed at them. For example, some find that the programs make them appear as if they were not qualified, resulting in unwarranted skepticism about their abilities. Instead of fighting the stigma of always having to be above reproach and better than average, some minorities are banning together in a selective segregation to avoid these additional pressures. Some students have gone out of their way to ensure that this bias is not directed at them. SOURCE: Sonia L. Nazario, "Many Minorities Feel Torn by Experience of Affirmative Action," *Wall Street Journal,* 27 June 1989; and *Sixty Minutes,* 25 April 1993.

These trends have important implications for organizations. African-Americans and Hispanic-Americans are overrepresented in declining occupations, thus limiting their opportunities. Further, African-Americans and Hispanic-Americans tend to live in a small number of large cities that are facing severe economic difficulties and high crime rates. Because of these factors, minority workers are likely to be at a disadvantage within organizations.

The jobs available in the future will require more skill than has been the case in the past. Often, minority workers have not had opportunities to develop their skills. Minority skills deficits are large, and the proportions of African-Americans and Hispanic-Americans who are qualified for higher-level jobs are often much lower than the proportions of qualified whites and Asian-Americans.[25] Minority workers are less likely to be prepared because they are less likely to have had satisfactory schooling and on-the-job training. Educational systems within the workplace are needed to supply minority workers with the skills necessary for success. Companies such as Motorola are already recognizing and meeting this need by focusing on basic skills training.

The globalization of business and changing demographic trends will present organizations with a tremendously culturally diverse workforce. This represents both a challenge and a risk. The challenge is to harness the wealth of differences that cultural diversity provides. The risk is that prejudices and stereotypes will prevent managers and employees from developing a synergy that can benefit the organization.

Gender Diversity

The feminization of the workforce has increased substantially. The number of women in the labor force increased from 31.5 million in 1970 to 60 million in 1994. This increase accounts for almost 60 percent of the overall expansion of the entire labor force in the United States for this time period. In 1994, women made up almost 46 percent of the labor force, and by the year 2000, the labor force is predicted to be balanced with respect to gender. Women are also better prepared to contribute in organizations than ever before. Women earned 35 percent of the master of business administration (MBA) degrees, 43 percent of the law degrees, 15 percent of the engineering degrees, and 54 percent of all undergraduate degrees awarded in 1992. Thus, women are better educated, and more are electing to work: in 1994, 70 percent of U.S. women were employed.[26]

Women's participation in the workforce is increasing, but their share of the rewards of participation is not increasing commensurately. Women hold only 5 percent of senior management positions in organizations (vice president level and above).[27] Salaries for women persist at a level of 70 percent of their male counterparts' earnings.[28] Furthermore, because benefits are tied to compensation, women also receive lower levels of benefits.

glass ceiling
A transparent barrier that keeps women from rising above a certain level in organizations.

In addition to lower earnings, women face other obstacles at work. The **glass ceiling** is a transparent barrier that keeps women from rising above a certain level in organizations. In the United States, it is rare to find women in positions above middle management in corporations.[29] The glass ceiling is not a barrier that is based on women's lack of ability to handle upper-level management positions. Instead, the barrier keeps women from advancing higher in an organization because they are women. The glass ceiling is not a phenomenon unique to the United States. In Nigeria, for example, males hold more negative attitudes toward women as managers than do U.S. males. American managers who work in Nigeria thus have a double burden. Cultural differences and attitudes toward women managers make the integration of expatriate and indigenous work groups a real challenge.[30]

Removing the glass ceiling and other obstacles to women's success represents a major challenge to organizations. Policies that promote equity in pay and benefits, encourage benefit programs of special interest to women, and provide equal starting salaries for jobs of equal value are needed in organizations.

Although women in our society have adopted the provider role, men have not been as quick to share domestic responsibilities. Managing the home and arranging for child care are still seen as the woman's domain. In addition, working women often find themselves in the position of caretaker for their elderly parents. Because of their multiple roles, women are more likely than men to experience conflicts between work and home. Organizations can offer incentives such as flexible work schedules, child care, elder care, and work site health promotion programs to assist working women in managing the stress of their lives.[31]

More women in the workforce means that organizations must help them achieve their potential. To do less would be to underutilize the talents of half of the U.S. workforce.

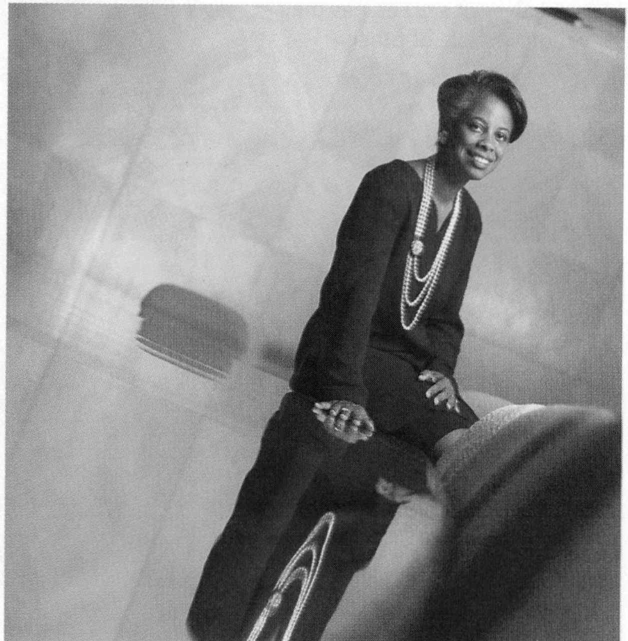

After eight years with Kraft General Foods, Ann Fudge was promoted to president of Maxwell House Coffee Company. An advocate of teamwork, she gives the team a charge and turns them loose. She has also won numerous awards for fostering diversity.

Age Diversity

The graying of the U.S. workforce is another source of diversity in organizations. Aging baby boomers (those individuals born from 1946 through 1964) will contribute to the rise of the median age in the United States to thirty-six by the year 2000—six years older than at any earlier time in history. This means also that the number of middle-aged Americans will rise dramatically. In the workforce, the number of younger workers will decline, as will the number of older workers (over age sixty-five). The net result will be a gain in workers aged thirty-five to fifty-four.[32]

This change in worker profile has profound implications for organizations. The job crunch among middle-aged workers will become more intense as companies seek flatter organizations and the elimination of middle-management jobs. Older workers are often higher paid, and companies that employ large numbers of aging baby boomers may find these pay scales a handicap to competitiveness.[33] However, a more experienced, stable, reliable, and healthy workforce can pay dividends to companies. The baby boomers are well trained and educated, and their knowledge can be a definite asset to organizations.

Another effect of the aging workforce is greater intergenerational contact in the workplace.[34] As organizations grow flatter, workers who were traditionally segregated by old corporate hierarchies (with older workers at the top and younger workers at the bottom) will be working together. Four generations will be cooperating: the swing generation (those born from 1910 through 1929), who lived through the Great Depression and World War II and are now in their sixties to eighties; the silent generation (people born from 1930 through 1945), a small group that includes most organizations' top managers; the baby boomers, whose substantial numbers give them a strong influence; and the baby bust generation (those born from 1965 through 1976).[35] Although there is certainly diversity within each generation, each generation differs in general ways from other generations.

Discussion Consideration

Deborah Tannen, in her book *You Just Don't Understand,* suggested that men talking to women is cross-cultural communication. Ask students to identify the differences in the communication styles of men and women.

Discussion Consideration

Should men in organizations be granted the same leave opportunities for child care that women have?

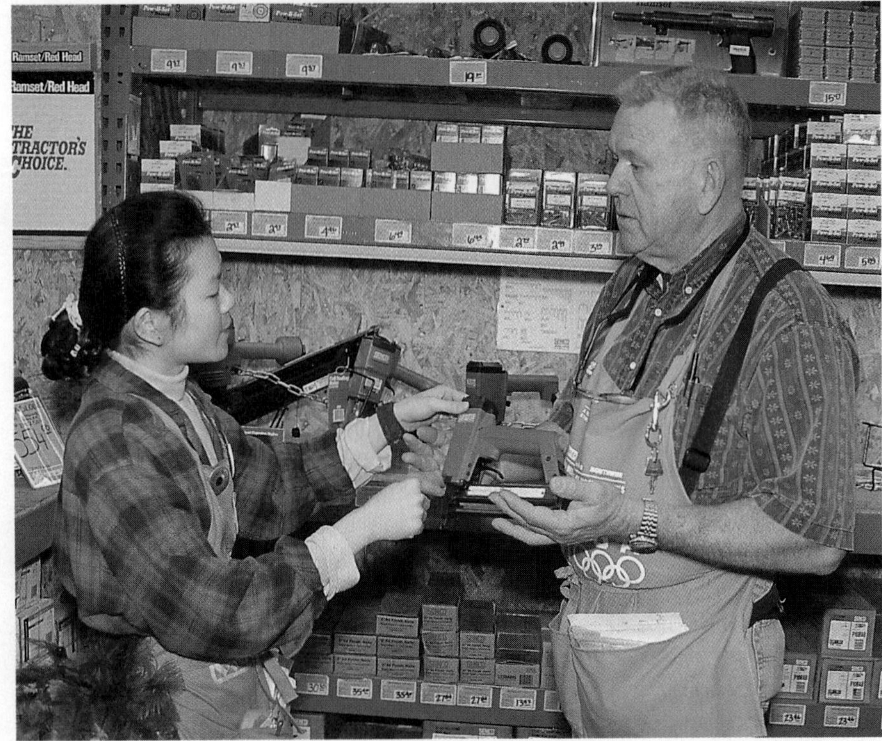

At Home Depot, younger and older workers team up to provide the quality service that customers count on. When younger and older workers have such experiences, they tend to rid themselves of stereotypes they hold about people of other generations.

The differences in attitudes and values among these four generations can be substantial, and managers face the challenge of integrating these individuals into a cohesive group. Currently, as already noted, most positions of leadership are held by members of the silent generation. Baby boomers regard the silent generation as complacent and as having done little to reduce social inequities. Baby boomers strive for moral rights in the workplace and take a more activist position regarding employee rights. The baby busters, new to the workplace, are impatient, want short-term gratification, and believe that family should come before work. They scorn the achievement orientation and materialism of the baby boomers. Managing such diverse perspectives is a challenge that must be addressed.

http://www.patagonia.com/

One company that is succeeding in accommodating the baby busters is Patagonia, a manufacturer of products for outdoor enthusiasts. Although the company does not actively recruit 20-year-olds, approximately 20 percent of Patagonia's workers are in this age group because they are attracted to its products. To retain baby busters, the company offers several options, one of which is flextime. Employees can arrive at work as early as 6 A.M., and work as late as 6 P.M., as long as they work the core hours between 9 A.M. and 3 P.M. Workers also have the option of working at the office for five hours a day and at home for three hours.

Personal leaves of absence are also offered, generally unpaid, for as much as four months per year. This allows employees to take an extended summer break and prevents job burnout. Patagonia has taken into consideration the baby busters' desires for more time for personal concerns and has incorporated these desires into the company.[36]

Younger workers may have false impressions of older workers, viewing them as resistant to change, unable to learn new work methods, less physically capable, and less creative than younger employees. Research indicates, however, that older employees are more satisfied with their jobs, are more committed to the organization, and possess more internal work motivation than their younger cohorts.[37] Recent research indicates that direct experience with older workers reduces younger workers' negative beliefs.[38] Motivating the aging workforce and helping them maintain high levels of contribution to the organization will be a key task for managers.

Ability Diversity

The workforce is full of individuals with different abilities, which presents another form of diversity. Individuals with disabilities are an underutilized human resource. An estimated 43 million disabled individuals live in the United States, and their unemployment rate is estimated to exceed 60 percent.[39] The representation of disabled individuals in the workforce is expected to increase dramatically because of the Americans with Disabilities Act, which went into effect in the summer of 1992. Under this law, employers are required to make reasonable accommodations to permit workers with disabilities to perform jobs. The act defines a disabled person as "anyone possessing a physical or mental impairment that substantially limits one or more major life activities."[40] It protects individuals with temporary, as well as permanent, disabilities. A broad range of illnesses that produce disabilities are included in the act's protection. Among these are acquired immune deficiency syndrome (AIDS), cancer, hypertension, anxiety disorders, dyslexia, blindness, and cerebral palsy, to name only a few.

Alternate Example
Passage of the Americans with Disabilities Act (ADA) has sensitized American organizations to an additional aspect of diversity: People with disabilities and handicaps.

Some companies recognized the value of employing disabled workers long before the legislation. Pizza Hut employs 3,000 disabled workers and plans to hire more. The turnover rates for disabled Pizza Hut workers is only one-fifth of the normal turnover rate.[41]

McDonald's created McJobs, a program that has trained and hired more than 9,000 mentally and physically challenged individuals since 1981.[42] McJobs is a corporate plan to recruit, train, and retain disabled individuals. Its participants include workers with visual, hearing, or orthopedic impairments; learning disabilities; and mental retardation. Through classroom and on-site training, the McJobs program prepares disabled individuals for the work environment. Before McJobs workers go on-site, sensitivity training sessions are held with store managers and crew members. These sessions help nondisabled workers understand what it means to be a worker with a disabling condition. Most McJobs workers start part-time and advance according to their own abilities and the opportunities available. Some visually impaired McJobs workers prefer to work on the back line, whereas others who are wheelchair users can work the drive-through window.

http://www.mcdonalds.com/

Companies like Pizza Hut and McDonald's have led the way in hiring disabled individuals. One key to the success of these firms is helping able-bodied employees understand how disabled workers can contribute to the organization. In this way, ability diversity becomes an asset and helps organizations meet the challenge of unleashing the talents of disabled workers.

Differences Are Assets

Diversity involves much more than culture, gender, age, ability, or personality. It also encompasses religious affiliation, economic class, social status, military attachment, and sexual orientation. The scope of diversity is broad and inclusive. All these types of diversity lend heterogeneity to the workforce.

The issue of sexual orientation as a form of diversity has received increasing attention by organizations. In a 1992 U.S. Census Bureau survey, 1.5 million households were identified as homosexual domestic partnerships.[43] Sexual orientation is an emotionally charged issue. Often, heterosexual resisitance to accepting gay, lesbian, or bisexual workers is caused by moral beliefs. Although organizations must respect these beliefs, they must also send a message that all people are valued. People who work in organizations full of fear, distrust, stigmatization, and harassment are not likely to be able to perform well. A tolerant atmosphere can improve the productivity of heterosexual and homosexual workers alike. Training must explain how homophobia hinders everyone's productivity. Education and training can be supplemented by everyday practices like using inclusive language—for example, using the term "partner" instead of "spouse" in verbal and written communication. Some companies offer benefits to same-sex partners. Coors Brewing Company, the Walt Disney Company, and Lotus Development Corporation were among the first to extend these benefits.

Part of the challenge in managing diversity lies in attempting to combat prejudices and discrimination. Whereas prejudice is an attitude, discrimination is behavior. Both are detrimental to organizations that depend on productivity from every single worker. Often, in studies of ratings of promotion potential, minorities are rated lower than whites, and females are rated lower than males.[44] The disparity between the pay of women and minority group members relative to white men increases with age.[45] It is to organizations' benefit to make sure that good workers are promoted and compensated fairly, but as the workforce becomes increasingly diverse, the potential for unfair treatment also increases.

Diversity is advantageous to the organization in a multitude of ways. Some organizations have recognized the potential benefits of aggressively working to increase the diversity of their workforces. Pepsico's Kentucky Fried Chicken (KFC) has a goal of attracting and retaining female and minority-group executives. Kyle Craig, president of KFC's U.S. operations, recently said, "We want to bring in the best people. If there are two equally qualified people, we'd clearly like to have diversity."[46]

http://www.pepsico.com/

Digital Equipment Corporation (DEC) faced a challenge in managing diversity in its Springfield, Massachusetts, plant, which employed predominantly African-American workers. The task was to overcome the perception that the plant was separate from, different from, and not as good as DEC's predominantly white plants. DEC's Springfield employees succeeded in tackling the issue by stressing empowerment (sharing power throughout the organization) and pushing for high-technology products that would give it a solid identity. The model used by the plant, called Valuing Differences, was based on two key ideas. First, people work best when they are valued and when diversity is taken into account. Second, when people feel valued, they build relationships and work together as a team.[47]

http://www.digital.com/

Managing diversity is one way a company can become more competitive, as shown in the Scientific Foundation feature. It is more than simply being a good corporate citizen or complying with affirmative action.[48] It is also more than assimilating women and minorities into a dominant male culture. Managing diversity includes a painful examination of hidden assumptions that employees hold. Biases and prejudices about people's differences must be uncovered and dealt with so that differences can be celebrated and exploited to their full advantage.

Diversity is a performance issue. Pillsbury is one company that lays out the performance case for managing and valuing differences. Pillsbury's managers argue that the same business rationale for cross-functional teams is relevant to all kinds of diversity. Managing differences includes race and gender, but also marketing expertise brought into a team. To open up a very profitable baked-goods market in a tough-to-crack niche, Pillsbury hired some Spanish-speaking Hispanics. The company lacked the language expertise and cultural access to the Hispanic community. Pillsbury's vice president of human resources conducted his own study of the food industry, asking an independent group to rate the diversity performance of ten companies and correlating it with financial performance over a ten-year period. Along with many other studies, the Pillsbury research suggests that diversity is a strong contributor to financial performance.[49]

Managing diversity also involves helping employees understand their own cultures.[50] Whites of European heritage do not think of themselves as having a

SCIENTIFIC FOUNDATION

Managing Diversity Makes Economic Sense

If competitive advantage is based on effective use of resources, then managing diversity is one way to effectively utilize human resources. In an innovative study, Wright, Ferris, Hiller, and Kroll examined whether companies' records in managing diversity affected the companies' stock price valuations. Using data from 1986 to 1992, the authors used an event study method to conduct their research. In the event study approach, researchers determine whether there is a significant change in the price of a firm's stock on days immediately surrounding the announcement of a particular event.

In this study, the authors used high-quality affirmative action programs as a proxy for effective management of diversity. The U.S. Department of Labor provides awards for exemplary affirmative action programs, and the announcements of these awards were used as the event of interest. Similarly, discrimination lawsuits were used as a proxy for poor management of diversity. The announcements of damage awards from discrimination lawsuits were the other events of interest.

The results supported the authors' hypotheses. Announcement of firms' receiving the award for high-quality voluntary affirmative action programs were associated with positive stock price changes for those firms. Announcements that conveyed that firms were guilty of discriminatory practices were associated with negative stock returns for those firms.

It appears from this study that efforts toward managing diversity are valued in the marketplace. Investors bid up the price of stocks for firms who receive DOL awards for their efforts. It may be that investors realize that firms who manage diversity well attract more talented human resources and may have lower costs and better reputations with customers.

SOURCE: P. Wright, S. P. Ferris, J. S. Hiller, and M. Kroll, "Competitiveness Through Management of Diversity: Effects on Stock Price Valuation," *Academy of Management Journal* 38 (1995): 272–288.

culture—they often believe culture is something that only minorities have. Whereas the struggle for equal employment opportunity is a battle against racism and prejudice, managing diversity is a battle to value the differences that individuals bring to the workplace. Organizations that manage diversity effectively can reap the rewards of increased productivity and improved organizational health.[51]

Managing Technological Innovation

Another challenge that managers face is effectively managing technological innovation. **Technology** consists of the intellectual and mechanical processes used by an organization to transform inputs into products or services that meet organizational goals. Managers face the challenge of rapidly changing technology and of putting the technology to optimum use in organizations. The inability of managers to incorporate new technologies successfully into their organizations is a major factor that has limited economic growth in the United States.[52] Although the United States still leads the way in developing new technologies, it lags behind in making productive use of these new technologies in workplace settings.[53]

technology
The intellectual and mechanical processes used by an organization to transform inputs into products or services that meet organizational goals.

The information superhighway has radically changed the way organizations communicate and perform work. By integrating computer, cable, and telecommunications technologies, businesses have learned new ways to compete. In networked organizations, time, distance, and space become irrelevant. A networked organization can do business anytime and anywhere, which is essential in the global marketplace. And networking is essential for companies who want to provide quality service to customers. Del Monte Corporation gets daily inventory reports electronically from grocers. When inventory falls to a certain level, the Del Monte network processes a restocking order. This allows retailers to drastically cut their investments in inventories. The World Wide Web has created a

Point to Emphasize
More managers are opting for flexible work schedules. Flextime is an attempt to break the stranglehold of the five-day workweek. In many cases, this flexibility actually helps careers prosper. It turns out that professionals who have such arrangements are fiercely loyal to their employers. SOURCE: "Pioneers of the New Balance," *Fortune,* 20 May 1991.

http://www.delmonte.com/

virtual commercial district. Customers can book air travel, buy compact discs, and "surf the Net" to conduct business around the globe.[54]

Any change that affects the way work is performed is a technological change. One such change is **telecommuting,** transmitting work from a home computer to the office using a modem. IBM, for example, was one of the first companies to experiment with the notion of installing computer terminals at employees' homes and having employees work at home. By telecommuting, employees gain flexibility, save the commute to work, and enjoy the comforts of being at home. There are disadvantages of telecommuting as well. Distractions, lack of opportunities to socialize with other workers, lack of interaction with supervisors, and decreased identification with the organization are a few of these disadvantages. Telecommuting is but one of the many technological changes that organizations must face.

telecommuting

Transmitting work from a home computer to the office using a modem.

http://www.ibm.com/

Another technological change is **expert systems,** computer-based applications that use a representation of human expertise in a specialized field of knowledge to solve problems. Expert systems can be used in many ways, including providing advice to nonexperts, providing assistance to experts, replacing experts, and serving as a training and development tool in organizations.[55] MYCIN, a medically-oriented expert system, diagnoses diseases and recommends treatment.[56] One organization currently using an expert system is Anheuser Busch.[57] The company uses an expert system to assist managers in ensuring that personnel decisions comply with antidiscrimination laws.

expert system

A computer-based application that uses a representation of human expertise in a specialized field of knowledge to solve problems.

http://www.budweiser.com/

Robots, another technological innovation, were invented in the United States, and advanced research on **robotics** is still conducted here. However, Japan leads the world in the use of robotics in organizations. The United States has fewer total robots in organizations than were added in 1989 alone in Japan.[58] Robots in Japan are treated like part of the family. They are even named after favorite celebrities, singers, and movie stars. Whereas Japanese workers are happy to let robots take over repetitive or dangerous work, Americans are more suspicious of the labor-saving robots because employers often use them to cut jobs.[59] The main reason for the reluctance of U.S. organizations to use robots is their slow payout. Robotics represents a big investment that does not pay off in the short term. Japanese managers are more willing to use a long-term horizon to evaluate the effectiveness of robotics technology. Labor unions may also resist robotics because of the fear that robots will replace employees.

robotics

The use of robots in organizations.

Some U.S. companies that experimented with robotics had bad experiences. John Deere and Company originally used robots to paint its tractors, but the company scrapped them because the robots took too long to program for the multitude of types of paint used. Now Deere uses robots to torque cap screws on tractors, a repetitive job that once had a high degree of human error.

http://www.deere.com/

Technologies of the Future

The technological innovations already described may seem like dramatic examples, but they are realities in many organizations. The challenge that managers face is putting advanced technologies into productive use by employees. What can be expected in terms of technological changes managers will face between now and the year 2000?

New technologies, as well as exploitations of older technologies, continue to reshape jobs and organizations. Five technologies in particular are predicted to have the greatest impact from now until the year 2000. These technologies are information storage and processing, communications, advanced materials, biotechnologies, and superconductivity.[60]

INFORMATION STORAGE AND PROCESSING Continuing improvements in information storage and processing will ensure that by the year 2000, desktop computing capability will be measured by gigabytes (billion words) and terabytes (trillion words) instead of the megabytes (million words) that are used today. Improvements in the price/performance ratios of equipment will mean that it will be very inexpensive to apply machine intelligence to jobs currently performed by humans.

COMMUNICATIONS By the year 2000, the United States will have a digital telecommunications network made possible by fiber optics technology. This innovation will mean that most homes will use a computer terminal as much or more than they use the telephone to access systems for home shopping, banking, and entertainment. Print media such as newspapers and magazines will fade in use in favor of electronic media.

Alternate Example
Technology has an impact on student cultures. Many experts believe that in the future resumé data bases will be the major method for recruiting. Many companies are now using the Internet to post job opportunities. Many universities recruiting potential faculty members prefer to receive resume information via E-mail.

ADVANCED MATERIALS Improvements in the traditional materials used in industry will mean declines in jobs that produce raw materials by the year 2000. Coatings such as ceramics and reinforced plastics will extend the life of manufactured products. Because of this increase in durability, fewer raw materials will be used.

BIOTECHNOLOGIES By the year 2000, agriculture and health care will be dramatically affected by advances in biotechnology, especially by the increased ability to manipulate life forms at the cellular and subcellular levels. New plant varieties that can withstand extreme environmental conditions will be introduced. Pork with less cholesterol is being produced, as are cows that produce better milk. These innovations will produce an abundance of farm produce.

The impacts of biotechnologies on health care will be delayed by extensive testing and licensing requirements. Although AIDS may not be cured by the year 2000, the knowledge gained about the immune system will lead to vastly improved treatments for a host of diseases. Mapping the human genetic system will make it possible to predict and treat birth defects and other diseases.

SUPERCONDUCTIVITY The development of superconductive materials (those that carry electric current without energy loss) is predicted to be the technology that has the most rapid impact on industry. The efficiency of electric motors of all kinds will be improved. Electric cars could become commonplace.

These five areas of technological change are only a few that affect organizations. There are other innovative uses of technology. In the accompanying Organizational Reality feature, you will see how a three-generation family business grew 100 percent because of the creative use of new technology.

Workers face changes in the way their work is performed on a daily basis, and these changes range from being relatively minor to having a major effect on the worker and the job. In addition, technological changes bring with them a host of changes in the way managerial work is performed.

The Changing Nature of Managerial Work

Technological innovation affects the very nature of the management job. Managers who once had to coax workers back to their desks from coffee breaks now find that they need to encourage workers mesmerized by new technology to take more frequent breaks.[61] Working with a computer can be stressful, both physically and psychologically. Eye strain, neck and back strain, and headaches can result from sitting at a computer terminal too long. In addition, workers can become accustomed to the fast response time of the computer and expect the same from their coworkers. When coworkers do not respond with the speed and accuracy of the computer, they may receive a harsh retort.[62]

ORGANIZATIONAL REALITY

Bissett Nursery Uses Imaging Technology to Gain a Competitive Edge

Bissett Nursery, a rewholesaler of nursery materials, was hit hard by the recession. Its customers, who are landscape contractors, were hit hard too. Landscape contractors had to deal with Long Island customers who were becoming more demanding, and who were having trouble envisioning what their homes would look like with plants and shrubs drawn on blueprints. The owners of Bissett Nursery came up with an idea. Why not use an imaging system to depict the landscape plans for the contractors? They hired a former landscape contractor to design the system. At first, Jim Vazanna, the designer, purchased a database of photographs. He became disenchanted with the resolution and detail of the images, and hit the road with his own 35-millimeter camera, taking pictures of trees, shrubs, waterfalls, all the parts of landscaping. Then he built his own database.

Contractors were skeptical at first, because imaging was unknown in the nursery business. Vazanna took his camera to new homes, scanned the photos into the computer, and produced a rendering of the house fully landscaped. He gave the photos to the landscape contractors and told them to pay him if they got the job. In 95 percent of the cases, the contractors did. Bissett's investment in imaging technology has generated about $7.5 million in sales for its customers and $3 million in new business for Bissett in just two years. More importantly, it provided Bissett's customers with a powerful marketing tool and tied them to Bissett more strongly than ever. ■

SOURCE: Adapted with permission. *Inc.* Magazine, February 1994. Copyright © by Goldhirsch Group, Inc., 38 Commercial Wharf, Boston, MA 02110.

Computerized monitoring provides managers with a wealth of information about employee performance, but it also holds great potential for misuse. The telecommunications, airline, and mail-order merchandise industries make wide use of systems that secretly monitor employees' interactions with customers. Employers praise such systems, saying that they improve customer service. Workers, however, are not so positive; they react with higher levels of depression, anxiety, and exhaustion from working under such secret scrutiny. At Bell Canada, operators were evaluated on a system that tabulated average working time with customers. Operators found the practice highly stressful, and they sabotaged the system by giving callers wrong directory assistance numbers rather than taking the time to look up the correct ones. As a result, Bell Canada now uses average working time scores for entire offices rather than for individuals.[63]

New technologies and rapid innovation place a premium on a manager's technical skills. Early management theories rated technical skills as less important than human and conceptual skills, but this has become wisdom of the past. Managers today must develop technical competence in order to gain workers' respect, which does not come automatically. Computer-integrated manufacturing systems, for example, have been shown to require managers to use participative management styles, open communication, and greater technical expertise in order to be effective.[64]

In a world of rapid technological innovation, managers must focus more carefully on helping workers manage the stress of their work. They must also take advantage of the wealth of information at their disposal to motivate, coach, and counsel workers rather than try to control them more stringently or police them. In addition, managers will need to develop their technical competence in order to gain workers' respect.

Technological change occurs so rapidly that turbulence characterizes most organizations. Workers must constantly learn and adapt to changing technology so that organizations can remain competitive. Managers must grapple with the challenge of helping workers adapt and make effective use of new technologies.

Helping Employees Adjust to Technological Change

Most workers are well aware of the benefits of modern technologies. The availability of skilled jobs and improved working conditions has been the by-product of innovation in many organizations. Technology is also bringing disadvantaged individuals into the workforce. Microchips have dramatically increased opportunities for visually impaired workers. Information can be decoded into speech using a speech synthesizer, into braille using a hard-copy printer, or into enlarged print visible on a computer monitor. Visually impaired workers are no longer dependent on sighted persons to translate printed information for them, and this has opened new doors of opportunity.[65] Engineers at Carnegie-Mellon University have developed PizzaBot, a robot that disabled individuals can operate using a voice-recognition system. Despite knowledge of these and other benefits of new technology in the workplace, however, employees may still resist change.

Technological innovations bring about changes in employees' work environments, and change has been described as the ultimate stressor. Many workers react negatively to change that they perceive will threaten their work situation. Many of their fears center around loss—of freedom, of control, of the things they like about their jobs.[66] Employees may fear that their quality of work life will deteriorate and that pressure at work will increase. Further, employees may fear being replaced by technology or being displaced into jobs of lower skill levels.

Managers can take several actions to help employees adjust to changing technology. The workers' participation in early phases of the decision-making process regarding technological changes is important.[67] Individuals who participate in planning for the implementation of new technology gain important information about the potential changes in their jobs; therefore, they are less resistant to the change. Workers are the users of the new technology. Their input in early stages can lead to a smoother transition into the new ways of performing work.

Another action managers can take is to keep in mind the effects that new technology will have on the skill requirements of workers. Many employees support changes that increase the skill requirements of their jobs.[68] Increased skill requirements often lead to increases in job autonomy, responsibility, and potential pay increases, all of which are received positively by employees. Whenever possible, managers should select technology that increases workers' skill requirements.

Providing effective training about ways to use the new technology also is essential. Training helps employees increase their perceptions that they control the technology rather than being controlled by it. The training should be designed to match workers' needs, and it should increase the workers' sense of mastery of the new technology.

Support groups within the organization are another way of helping employees adjust to technological change. Technological change is stressful, and support groups are important emotional outlets for workers.[69] Support groups can also function as information exchanges so that workers can share advice on using the technology. The sense of communion provided helps workers feel less alone with the problem through the knowledge that other workers share their frustration.

A related challenge is to encourage workers to invent new uses for technology already in place. **Reinvention** is the term for creatively applying new technology.[70] Innovators should be rewarded for their efforts. Individuals who explore the boundaries of a new technology can personalize the technology and adapt it to their own job needs, as well as share this information with others in the work group. In one large public utility, service representatives (without their supervisor's knowledge) developed a personal note-passing system that later became the basis of a formal communication system that improved the efficiency of their work group.

reinvention
The creative application of new technology.

Managers face a substantial challenge in leading organizations to adopt new technologies more humanely and effectively. Technological changes are essential for earnings growth and for expanded employment opportunities. The adoption of new technologies is a critcal determinant of U.S. competitiveness in the global marketplace.[71]

Managing Ethical Issues at Work

■ In addition to the challenges of globalization, workforce diversity, and technology, managers must confront the ethical challenges that are encountered in organizations. Some organizations manage ethical issues well. Johnson & Johnson employees operate under an organizational credo, which we will present later in this section. Another organization that manages ethical issues well is Merck and Company. Merck's emphasis on ethical behavior has earned the pharmaceutical company its recognition as one of America's most admired companies in *Fortune's* polls of CEOs.

http://www.jnj.com/

Points to Emphasize
So far, codes of ethics do not matter much in outcomes of behavior unless they have been emphasized by top management as important. The mere existence of a code of ethics in a company does not have the desired effect of changing behavior. Formal training and rigorous enforcement of the code do make a difference in how seriously employees think the company is with its ethical principles. SOURCE: Sara A. Morris, "Do Corporate Codes of Ethics Matter? An Empirical Test," *Southern Management Association Proceedings,* October, 1992.

Despite the positive way some organizations handle ethical issues, however, there is plenty of evidence that unethical conduct does occur in other organizations. In April 1992 alone, billionaire financier and Olivetti chief executive Carlo DeBenedetti was convicted in a Milan court as an accessory in the 1982 collapse of Banco Ambrosiano and was sentenced to six years and four months in prison; self-crowned hotel queen Leona Helmsley began her four-year sentence for tax evasion; and Charles Keating, former chief executive officer of American Continental Corporation, began a ten-year stretch for defrauding the thrift institution's customers.[72]

In examining the corporate misbehavior at Manville Corporation, Continental Illinois Bank, and E.F. Hutton, Saul Gellerman examined why "good" managers sometimes make bad ethical choices.[73] How can people in organizations rationally think through ethical decisions so that they make the "right" choices? Ethical theories give us a basis for understanding, evaluating, and classifying moral arguments, and then defending conclusions about what is right and wrong. Ethical theories can be classified as consequential, rule-based, or cultural.

consequential theory
An ethical theory that emphasizes the consequences or results of behavior.

Consequential theories of ethics emphasize the consequences or results of behavior. John Stuart Mill's utilitarianism, a well-known consequential theory, suggests that right and wrong is determined by the consequences of the action.[74] "Good" is the ultimate moral value, and we should maximize the most good for the greatest number of people. But do good ethics make for good business?[75] Right actions do not always produce good consequences, and good consequences do not always follow from right actions. And how do we determine the greatest good—in short-term or long-term consequences? Using the "greatest number"criterion can imply that minorities (less than 50 percent) might be excluded in evaluating the morality of actions. An issue that may be important for a minority but unimportant for the majority might be ignored. These are but a few of the dilemmas raised by utilitarianism.

rule-based theory
An ethical theory that emphasizes the character of the act itself rather than its effects.

In contrast, **rule-based theories** of ethics emphasize the character of the act itself, not its effects, in arriving at universal moral rights and wrongs.[76] Moral rights, the basis for legal rights, are associated with such theories. In a theological context, the Bible, the Talmud, and the Koran are rule-based guides to ethical behavior. Immanuel Kant worked toward the ultimate moral principle in formulating his categorical imperative, a universal standard of behavior.[77] Kant argued that individuals should be treated with respect and dignity, and that they should not be used as a means to an end. He argued that we should put ourselves in the other person's position and ask if we would make the same decision if we were in the other person's situation.

Corporations and business enterprises are more prone to subscribe to consequential ethics than rule-based ethics, in part due to the persuasive arguments of the Scottish political economist and moral philosopher Adam Smith.[78] He believed that the self-interest of human beings is God's providence, not the government's. Smith set forth a doctrine of natural liberty, presenting the classical argument for open market competition and free trade. Within this framework, people should be allowed to pursue what is in their economic self-interest, and the natural efficiency of the marketplace would serve the well-being of society.

Cultural theories are a third type of ethical theory.[79] Cultural relativism contends that there are no universal ethical principles and that people should not impose their own ethical standards on others. Local standards should be the guides for ethical behavior. Cultural theories encourage individuals to operate under the old adage "When in Rome, do as the Romans do." Strict adherence to cultural relativism can lead individuals to deny their accountability for their own decisions and to avoid difficult ethical dilemmas.

cultural theory
An ethical theory that emphasizes respect for different cultural values.

People need ethical theories to help them think through confusing, complex, difficult moral choices and ethical decisions. In contemporary organizations, people face ethical and moral dilemmas in many diverse areas. The key areas we will address are white-collar crime, computer use, employee rights, sexual harassment, romantic involvements, organizational justice, whistle-blowing, and social responsibility. We conclude with a discussion of professionalism and codes of ethics.

White-Collar Crime

Corporate criminal behaviors have resulted in tough new sentencing guidelines for corporate crimes and in corporate America's teaching employees about ethics.[80] In addition, corporations have set up ethics committees or appointed ethics officers. However, such practices do not always work. For example, Dow Corning had an ethics program for eighteen years before its breast-implant scandal, in which the implants were found to leak and cause several health problems. No questions of safety or testing of the implants were ever given to the ethics committee.[81] Since the savings and loan scandals of the late 1980s, the U.S. Justice Department has been keener on catching and punishing white-collar criminals such as Charles Keating. In April 1992, prosecutors ended some of the biggest 1980s financial scandals, as previously discussed.

White-collar crime may occur in more subtle forms as well. Using work hours for conducting personal business, sending out personal mail using the company postage meter, and padding an expense account are all examples of practices some individuals would consider unethical. Whether the impact is large or small, white-collar crimes are important issues in organizations.

Computer Use

Computers are one of the core technologies of our times and give rise to various ethical dilemmas for computer professionals and users.[82] People in organizations face a wide range of ethical questions and dilemmas with regard to the use and abuse of computerized information. What constitutes a computer crime? Software theft? Invasion of privacy?

As organizations computerize the workplace, what are the responsibilities of the corporation for the stress and health risks posed by computers? To what extent should the organization be allowed to secure itself against hackers and computer viruses? What are the moral, ethical, and legal obligations of designers and producers of unreliable computers? Who has moral, ethical, and legal liability for expert systems that go wrong?[83]

Discussion Consideration
Does your college or university have a code of ethics for student behavior? What effect does the code have? Should students be required to report the ethical violations by other students?

Employee Rights

Managing the rights of employees at work creates many ethical dilemmas in organizations. Some of these dilemmas are privacy issues related to technology. Computerized monitoring, as we discussed earlier in the chapter, constitutes an invasion of privacy in the minds of some individuals. The use of employee data from computerized information systems presents many ethical concerns. Safeguarding the employee's right to privacy and at the same time preserving access to the data for those who need it requires that the manager balance competing interests.

Drug testing, free speech, downsizing and layoffs, and due process are but a few of the employee rights concerns with which managers must deal. Perhaps no other issue generates as much need for managers to balance the interests of employees and the interests of the organization as the reality of AIDS in the workplace. New drugs have shown the promise of extended lives for people with human immunodeficiency virus (HIV), and this means that HIV-infected individuals can remain in the workforce and stay productive. Managers will be caught in the middle of a conflict between the rights of HIV-infected workers and the rights of their co-workers who feel threatened.

Employers are not required to make concessions to coworkers, but employers do have obligations to educate, reassure, and provide emotional support to coworkers. Confidentiality may also be a difficult issue. Some employees with HIV or AIDS will not wish to waive confidentiality and will not want to reveal their condition to their coworkers because of fears of stigmatization or even reprisals. In any case, management should discuss with the affected employee the ramifications of trying to maintain confidentiality, and should assure the employee that every effort will be made to see that there are no negative ramifications for him or her in the workplace.[84]

Laws exist that protect HIV-infected workers. As stated earlier, the Americans with Disabilities Act requires employees to treat HIV-infected workers as disabled individuals and to make reasonable accommodations for them. However, the ethical dilemmas involved with this situation go far beyond the legal issues. How does a manager protect the dignity of the person with AIDS and preserve the morale and productivity of the work group when so much prejudice and ignorance surround this disease? Many organizations, such as Wells Fargo, believe the answer is education.[85] Wells Fargo has a written AIDS policy because of the special issues associated with the disease—such as confidentiality, employee socialization, co-worker education, and counseling—that must be addressed. The Body Shop's employee education program consists of factual seminars combined with interactive theater workshops. The workshops depict a scenario in which an HIV-positive worker has decisions to make, and the audience decides what she should do. This helps participants explore the emotional and social issues surrounding HIV.[86] Many of us do not know as much about AIDS as we should, and many of our fears arise because of a lack of knowledge. Assessment tools like the one in Challenge 2.2 are used by employers to help employees surface their concerns about AIDS and pinpoint specific content needed in education programs.

http://www.wellsfargo.com/

http://www.bodyshop.com/

Points to Emphasize
Now that sexual harassment issues are more widely understood, debate has extended to sexual harassment by third parties in the workplace. For example, what are the ramifications of sexual intimidation when the harasser is a client, customer, or supplier? Sexual harassment of workers by third parties can lead into a maze of legal and moral issues. An employer has the responsibility to provide an environment that does not permit sexual harassment. A salesman was terminated by his employer because one of his customers had complained that he had continually harassed a female employee.

Sexual Harassment

Anita Hill's sexual harassment charges against Associate Supreme Court Justice Clarence Thomas during his 1991 Senate hearings generated a tremendous national controversy. According to the Equal Employment Opportunity Commission, sexual harassment is unwelcome sexual attention, whether verbal or physical, that affects an employee's job conditions or created a hostile working environment.[87] Recent court rulings, too, have broadened the definition of sexual harassment beyond job-related abuse to include acts that create a hostile

CHALLENGE

■ 2.2

How Much Do You Know About AIDS?

Rate the following terms on a scale of 1 to 5 to indicate the extent to which you agree or disagree with each statement (1 = strongly disagree, 5 = strongly agree).

____ **1.** It may be dangerous for me to work around someone with AIDS.
____ **2.** Working with employees who have AIDS places co-workers in a life-threatening situation.
____ **3.** There is a reason to fear employees who have AIDS.
____ **4.** Employees who have AIDS pose a threat to their co-workers.
____ **5.** There is a reason to single out employees who have AIDS.

Please indicate whether you believe each statement below is true (T) or false (F).

____ **6.** AIDS is a highly contagious disease.
____ **7.** Most people who contract AIDS die from the disease.
____ **8.** AIDS can be contracted when an employee with AIDS sneezes or coughs on others.
____ **9.** AIDS can be contracted through nonsexual touching, such as shaking hands.
____**10.** Persons who share tools or equipment with employees who have AIDS are likely to contract the disease.
____**11.** AIDS cannot be contracted through face-to-face conversation with an AIDS-infected co-worker.
____**12.** AIDS can be transmitted when people eat or drink after one another.
____**13.** AIDS can be transmitted through blood.
____**14.** There is a vaccine to prevent AIDS.
____**15.** AIDS can be contracted from toilet seats.

Now, for items 1 through 5, add your score. Your total reflects your fear of AIDS. Scores range from 5 (low fear) to 25 (high fear). Score greater than 15 indicate a high-level, work-related fear of AIDS.

Finally, look at items 6 through 15. All of these items are false except 7 and 11. Give yourself 1 point for each correct answer. This scale reflects knowledge of AIDS. Scores can range from 0 (poorly informed about AIDS) to 10 (well informed about AIDS). If your score was less than 5, you need to learn more about AIDS.

SOURCE: Adapted from J. M. Vest, F. P. O'Brien, and M. J. Vest, "AIDS Training in the Workplace," *Training and Development Journal* 45 (1991): 59–64.

work environment. Sexual harassment costs the typical Fortune 500 company $6.7 million per year in absenteeism, turnover, and loss of productivity. By 1997, it is estimated that companies will have spent $1 billion to settle and pay damages for sexual harassment cases. Plaintiffs may now sue not only for back pay, but also for compensatory and punitive damages. And these costs do not take into account the negative publicity that firms may encounter from sexual harassment cases, which may cost untold millions.[88] Some of the best training programs use role-playing, videotapes, and group discussions of real cases to help supervisors recognize unlawful sexual harassment and investigate complaints properly.

Romantic Involvements

Hugging, sexual innuendos, and repeated requests for dates may constitute sexual harassment for some, but they are a prelude to romance for others. This situation carries with it a different set of ethical dilemmas for organizations.

Paula Coughlin, a Navy lieutenant, blew the whistle on sexual harassment at the Tailhook convention and was the first of 83 women to come forward. Women now are able to serve on warships and fly in combat squads due in part to Coughlin's persistence.

Discussion Consideration
Universities have been passing bans against faculty-student dating. This step addresses the faculty's professional conduct and implications of sexual harassment. But, on the other hand, are blanket prohibitions constitutional? SOURCE: "Hands Off, Mr. Chips!" *Newsweek,* 3 May 1993; and "Colleges Puzzle over Banning Faculty-Student Dating," *USA Today,* 30 April 1993.

Discussion Consideration
Some organizations have bans against husband-wife relationships among employees. Should companies ban romantic involvements among employees?

http://www.wal-mart.com/

Discussion Consideration
Ask students which of the concepts of justice is most important to them in the classroom: distributive justice or procedural justice?

distributive justice
The fairness of the outcomes that individuals receive in an organization.

procedural justice
The fairness of the process by which outcomes are allocated in an organization.

The office romance between William Agee, at the time chairman of Bendix Corporation, and Mary Cunningham, a corporate vice president at Bendix, was one of the first cases to bring the ethical dilemmas of office romance to the fore. Their much-publicized liaison exemplified the conflicts that occur within an organization when romantic involvements at work become disruptive. Both Agee and Cunningham ultimately left Bendix and went on to a long-term marital and family relationship. Unfortunately, many office romances do not lead to such positive outcomes.

A recent fax poll indicated that three-fourths of the respondents felt it was okay to date a coworker, while three-fourths disapproved of dating a superior or subordinate. In *Meritor vs. Vinson,* the Supreme Court ruled that the agency principle applies to supervisor-subordinate relationships. Employers are liable for acts of their agents (supervisors) and can thus be held liable for sexual harassment. Other employees might claim that the subordinate who is romantically involved with the supervisor gets preferential treatment. Dating between coworkers poses less liability for the company because the agency principle doesn't apply. However, policing coworker dating can backfire: WalMart lost a lawsuit when it tried to forbid coworkers from dating.

Romatic involvements at work can create a conflict of interest. A comprehensive dating policy should require anyone who might be experiencing a conflict of interest to report it to his or her supervisor. The policy should also include an explanation of how unwelcome romantic advances can turn into sexual harassment.[89]

Organizational Justice

Another area in which moral and ethical dilemmas may arise for people at work concerns organizational justice, both distributive and procedural. **Distributive justice** concerns the fairness of outcomes individuals receive. For example, the salaries and bonuses for U.S. corporate executives became a central issue with Japanese executives during President George Bush's 1992 visit to Japan with accompanying American CEOs in key industries. The Japanese CEOs questioned the distributive justice in the American CEOs' salaries at a time when so many companies were in difficulty and laying off workers.

Procedural justice concerns the fairness of the process by which outcomes are allocated.[90] The ethical questions here do not concern the just or unjust distribution of organizational resources. Rather, the ethical questions in procedural justice concern the process. Has the organization used the correct procedures in allocating resources? Have the right considerations, such as competence and skill, been brought to bear in the decision process? And have the wrong considerations, such as race and gender, been excluded from the decision process?

Whistle-blowing

Whistle-blowers are employees who inform authorities of wrongdoings of their companies or coworkers. Whistle-blowers can be perceived as either heroes or "vile wretches" depending on the circumstances of the situation. For a whistle-blower to be considered a public hero, the gravity of the situation that the whistle-blower reports to authorities must be of such magnitude and quality as to be perceived as abhorrent by others.[91] In contrast, the whistle-blower is considered a vile wretch if the act of whistle-blowing is seen by others as more offensive than the situation the whistle-blower reports to authorities.

whistle-blower

An employee who informs authorities of the wrongdoings of his or her company or coworkers.

Whistle-blowing is important in the United States because committed organizational members sometimes engage in unethical behavior in an intense desire to succeed. Many examples of whistle-blowing can be found in corporate America. For example, in 1984, a laboratory technician employed at a General Electric Company nuclear fuels production facility complained to management that fellow workers were failing to clean up radioactive spills. Although the spills were later cleaned up, the complaining employee was later laid off.[92] Laws are now in place to provide a remedy for workers who suffer employment discrimination in retaliation for whistle-blowing.

http://www.ge.com/

Organizations can manage whistle-blowing by communicating the conditions that are appropriate for the disclosure of wrongdoing.[93] Clearly delineating wrongful behavior and the appropriate ways to respond are important organizational actions.

Social Responsibility

Corporate **social responsibility** is the obligation of an organization to behave in ethical ways in the social environment in which it operates. Ethical conduct at the individual level can translate into social responsibility at the organizational level. Johnson & Johnson, for example, acted in a socially responsible fashion in 1984 and 1985 when it was discovered that some bottles of Tylenol had been tampered with and poisoned. Managers moved quickly to remove Tylenol from the retailers and held press conferences to warn the public about the situation. The company had encouraged ethical behavior among employees for years, and thus employees knew how to respond to the crisis.

social responsibility

The obligation of an organization to behave in ethical ways.

Alternate Example

Employers who avoid setting AIDS corporate policies in the workplace do so because they hope they will never be confronted with the issue. Many initially view the HIV-positive case as a single, unusual occurrence. However, statistics illustrate that this is a naive assumption. Additionally, the neglect of a policy renders an organization liable regarding health benefits, and may be viewed as insensitive to employee concerns. The sad fact is that lost labor and lost production are beginning to be apparent in the urban professional ranks because of the spread of AIDS. SOURCE: "The Hidden Cost of AIDS," *U.S. News and World Report*, 27 July 1992.

Socially responsible actions are expected of organizations. Current concerns include protecting the environment, promoting worker safety, supporting social issues, and investing in the community, among others. Some organizations, like IBM, loan executives to inner-city schools to teach science and math. Other organizations like Patagonia demonstrate social responsibility through environmentalism, as seen in the Organizational Reality feature. Managers must encourage both individual ethical behavior and organizational social responsibility.

Codes of Ethics

One of the characteristics of mature professions is the existence of a code of ethics to which the practitioners adhere in their actions and behavior. Such is the case with the Hippocratic oath in medicine. Although some of the individual differences we will address in Chapter 4 produce ethical or unethical orientations in specific people, a profession's code of ethics becomes a standard against which members can measure themselves in the absence of internalized standards.

No universal code of ethics or oath exists for business as it does for medicine. However, Paul Harris and four business colleagues, who founded Rotary International in 1904, made an effort to address ethical and moral behavior right from the beginning. They developed the Four-Way Test, shown in Figure 2.2, which is now used in over 180 nations throughout the world by the nearly 2 million

ORGANIZATIONAL REALITY

Patagonia's Dirt Bag Environmental Agenda

As founder and CEO of Patagonia Outdoor Clothing, Yvon Chouinard prefers to be called a Dirt Bag. He has worn several hats in his life—blacksmith, professional surfer, climber, kayaker—and prefers to sleep on the ground with no tent (hence the name Dirt Bag). He describes working in an office as "an unnatural situation." All Patagonia employees are given an official Dirt Bag camping mug, with the words "Live, Take Risks, Die, Compost" describing their existence as a linked circle.

The head Dirt Bag's love of the environment has resulted in Patagonia's putting its money where its mouth is. Chouinard developed an environmental grants program and the company donates 1 percent of its annual revenue to groups ranging from the Sierra Club to Planned Parenthood to Earth First! Chouinard is committed to Deep Ecology, an analysis that examines the farm-to-landfill impact of every company action. This triggered an internal assessment that revealed the environmental damage that Patagonia's own products were causing. Patagonia then declared that its popular polyester fleece jackets would be produced from recycled soda bottles, and that the cotton for its T-shirts would come only from organic farmers. The company hopes to prove that business can earn reasonable profits without destroying the environment. Such environmental concern has earned Patagonia quite a following, not only for its functional products for wilderness adventure, but also for its corporate social responsibility. ■

SOURCE: P. Carlin, "Will Rapid Growth Stunt Corporate Do-Gooders?" *Business & Society Review* (Spring 1995): 36–43.

■ **FIGURE 2.2**
The Four-Way Test

The Four-Way Test
OF WHAT WE THINK, SAY, OR DO

1. Is it the TRUTH?
2. Is it FAIR to all concerned?
3. Will it build GOODWILL and better friendships?
4. Will it be BENEFICIAL to all concerned?

Rotarians in 25,000 Rotary clubs. Figure 2.2 focuses the questioner on key ethical and moral questions.

Beyond the individual and profession level, corporate culture is another excellent starting point for addressing ethics and morality. In Chapter 16 we will examine how corporate culture and leader behavior trickles down the company, setting a standard for all below. In some cases, the corporate ethics may be captured in a regulation. For example, the Joint Ethics Regulation (DOD 5500.7-R, August 1993) specifies the ethical standards to which all U.S. military personnel are to adhere. In other cases, the corporate ethics may be in the form of a credo. Johnson & Johnson's credo, shown in Figure 2.3, helped hundreds of employees ethically address the criminal tampering with Tylenol products already mentioned. In its 1986 centennial annual report, J & J attributed its success in this crisis, as well as its long-term business growth (a compound sales rate of 11.6 percent for 100 years), to "our unique form of decentralized management, our adherence to the ethical principles embodied in our credo, and our emphasis on managing the business for the long term."

Individual codes of ethics, professional oaths, and organizational credos all must be anchored in a moral, ethical framework. They are always open to ques-

We believe our first responsibility is to the doctors, nurses and patients,
to mothers and all others who use our products and services.
In meeting their needs everything we do must be of high quality.
We must constantly strive to reduce our costs
in order to maintain reasonable prices.
Customers' orders must be serviced promptly and accurately.
Our suppliers and distributors must have an opportunity
to make a fair profit.

We are responsible to our employees,
the men and women who work with us throughout the world.
Everyone must be considered as an individual.
We must respect their dignity and recognize their merit.
They must have a sense of security in their jobs.
Compensation must be fair and adequate,
and working conditions clean, orderly and safe.
Employees must feel free to make suggestions and complaints.
There must be equal opportunity for employment, development
and advancement for those qualified.
We must provide competent management,
and their actions must be just and ethical.

We are responsible to the communities in which we live and work
and to the world community as well.
We must be good citizens—support good works and charities
and bear our fair share of taxes.
We must encourage civic improvements and better health and education.
We must maintain in good order
the property we are privileged to use,
protecting the environment and natural resources.

Our final responsibility is to our stockholders.
Business must make a sound profit.
We must experiment with new ideas.
Research must be carried on, innovative programs developed
and mistakes paid for.
New equipment must be purchased, new facilities provided
and new products launched.
Reserves must be created to provide for adverse times.
When we operate according to these principles,
the stockholders should realize a fair return.

FIGURE 2.3

The Johnson & Johnson Credo

tion and continuous improvement using ethical theories as a toll for reexamining the soundness of the current standard. Although a universal right and wrong may exist, it would be hard to argue that there is only one code of ethics to which all individuals, professions, and organizations can subscribe.

Managerial Implications: Facing the Challenges

Globalization, workforce diversity, emerging technologies, and ethical dilemmas are challenges that managers in all organizations will face during the next decade. If organizations are to gain competitive advantage, they must meet these challenges head-on, as well as in a proactive manner. You will find these challenges addressed in each chapter as you continue through this textbook.

Managers will face ethical and diversity challenges when they make employee selection decisions and complete performance evaluations. They will face technology challenges when they learn new methods and take advantage of new tools for performing their jobs, as well as when they help implement technological innovation throughout their organizations. Managers will face global competition issues when the industries they work in are challenged by foreign competition. They will encounter diversity challenges when they work side by side with people who are ethnically, sexually, or in any other way different from them. The success of organizations during the next decade will be dependent upon managers' success in addressing these four challenges.

CLOSING SPOTLIGHT

Federal Express Uses Technology to Gain Competitive Advantage and Corporate Philosophy to Encourage Ethical Behavior

In managing the challenge of technology, Federal Express has passed technology's advantages along to its customers. The company has installed more than 70,000 POWERSHIP computer terminals at its customers' offices and plans to install 100,000 more by the year 2000. Using a POWERSHIP terminal, a FedEx customer can electronically track its shipments from initial shipping point to final destination, as if the goods were moving within the customer's own warehousing system. This gives the customer sophisticated information and a sense of comfort in knowing where its shipment is at any point in the process. It also creates a seamless interface between customers, suppliers, and FedEx.

Managing ethical behavior is a challenge that Federal Express addresses in its *Manager's Guide*, a 200-page statement of the company's expectations of managerial behavior. Ethical behavior is also encouraged by the corporate culture and is embedded in the corporate philosophy: "People/Service/Profit." The idea is that FedEx puts its employees first, who are then motivated to provide the 100 percent quality service that ensures a profit. Putting people first is an ethical issue with Federal Express. Seminars on topics like leadership ethics are also offered to help managers explore their own values and ethics.

Federal Express faces tremendous competition both at home and abroad, and it has managed the competitive challenge successfully. Part of this success can be credited to the proactive manner in which FedEx tackles the challenges of globalization, workforce diversity, technology, and ethical behavior.[94] ■

Chapter Summary

- To ensure that their organizations meet the competition, managers must tackle four important challenges: globalization, workforce diversity, technological change, and ethical behavior at work.
- The five cultural differences that affect work-related attitudes are individualism versus collectivism, power distance, uncertainty avoidance, masculinity versus femininity, and time orientation.
- Diversity encompasses gender, culture, personality, sexual orientation, religion, military affiliation, ability, economic class, social status, and a host of other differences.
- Managers must take a proactive approach to managing diversity so that differences are valued and capitalized upon.
- Technological changes will have dramatic effects on organizations by the year 2000.
- Through supportive relationships and training, managers can help employees adjust to technological change.
- Three types of ethical theories include consequential theories, rule-based theories, and cultural theories.
- Ethical dilemmas emerge for people at work in the areas of white-collar crime, computer use, employee rights, sexual harassment, romantic involvements, organizational justice, whistle-blowing, and social responsibility.

Key Terms

transnational organization (p. 33)
***guanxi* (p. 33)**
individualism (p. 34)
collectivism (p. 34)
power distance (p. 35)
uncertainty avoidance (p. 35)
masculinity (p. 35)
femininity (p. 35)
time orientation (p. 36)
expatriate manager (p. 36)
diversity (p. 39)
glass ceiling (p. 40)
technology (p. 45)
telecommuting (p. 46)
expert system (p. 46)
robotics (p. 46)
reinvention (p. 49)
consequential theory (p. 50)
rule-based theory (p. 50)
cultural theory (p. 51)
distributive justice (p. 54)
procedural justice (p. 54)
whistle-blower (p. 55)
social responsibility (p. 55)

Review Questions

1. What are Hofstede's five dimensions of cultural differences that affect work attitudes? Using these dimensions, describe the United States.
2. What are the primary sources of diversity in the U.S. workforce?
3. What specific actions can managers take to manage a diverse workforce?
4. Discuss five areas of rapid technological advancement that will affect organizations by the year 2000.
5. Explain four ways managers can help employees adjust to technology.
6. Describe three types of ethical theories and their assumptions.
7. Discuss the ethical dilemmas people face at work concerning crime, computer use, employee rights, sexual harassment, romantic involvements, organizational justice, whistle-blowing, and social responsibility.

Discussion and Communication Questions

1. How can managers be encouraged to develop global thinking? How can managers dispel stereotypes about other cultures?
2. Some people have argued that in designing expert systems, human judgment is made obsolete. What do you think?
3. What areas of managerial work could be improved with new technologies?
4. What effects will the globalization of business have on a company's culture? How can an organization with a strong "made in America" identity compete in the global marketplace?
5. Why is diversity such an important issue? Is the workforce more diverse today than in the past?
6. How does a manager strike a balance between encouraging employees to celebrate their own cultures and forming a single unified culture within the organization?
7. Do you agree with Hofstede's findings about U.S. culture? On what do you base your agreement or disagreement?
8. *(communication question)* Select one of the four challenges (globalization, diversity, technology, ethics) and write a brief position paper arguing for its importance to managers.
9. *(communication question)* Find someone whose home country is not your own. This might be a classmate or an international student at your university. Interview them about their culture, using Hof-stede's dimensions. Ask them also to tell you anything you might need to know about doing business in their country (e.g., customs, etiquette). Be prepared to share this information in class.

Ethics Questions

1. Suppose your company has the opportunity to install a marvelous new technology, but it will mean that 20 percent of the jobs in the company will be lost. As a manager, would you adopt the new technology? How would you make the decision?
2. What is the most difficult ethical dilemma you have ever faced at work or school? Why? How was it resolved?
3. Some companies have a policy that employees should not become romantically involved with each other. Is this ethical?
4. What are some of the concerns that a person with AIDS would have about his or her job? What are some of the fears that co-workers would have? How can a manager balance these two sets of concerns?
5. Suppose you are visiting Taiwan and attempting to do business there. You are given a gift by your Taiwanese host, who is your prospective client. Your interpreter explains that it is customary to exchange gifts before transacting business. You have no gift to offer. How would you handle the situation?

Experiential Exercises

2.1: International Orientations

1 Preparation (pre-class)

Read the background on the scale, the case study "Office Supplies International," complete the ratings and questions, and fill out the self-assessment inventory.

2 Group Discussions

Groups of four to six people discuss their answers to the case study questions and their own responses to the self-assessment.

3 Class Discussion

Instructor leads a discussion on the International Orientation Scale and the difficulties and challenges of adjusting to a new culture. Why do some people adjust more easily than others? What can you do to adjust to a new culture? What can you regularly do that will help you adjust in the future to almost any new culture?

Office Supplies International—marketing associate*

Jonathan Fraser is a marketing associate for a large multinational corporation, Office Supplies International (OSI), in Buffalo, New York. He is being considered for a transfer to the International division of OSI. This position will require that he spend between one and three years living abroad in any one of the OSI's three foreign subsidiaries: OSI-France, OSI-Japan or OSI-Australia. This transfer is considered a fast track career move at OSI, and Jonathan feels honored to be in the running for the position.

Jonathan has been working at OSI since he graduated with his bachelor's degree in marketing ten years ago. He is married and has lived and worked in Buffalo all his life. Jonathan's parents are first-generation German-Americans. His grandparents, although deceased, spoke only German at home and upheld many of their traditional ethnic traditions. His parents, although quite "Americanized," have retained some of their German traditions. In order to communicate better with his grandparents, Jonathan took German in high school, but never used it because his grandparents had passed away.

In college, Jonathan joined the German club and was a club officer for two years. His other collegiate extra-curricular activity was playing for the varsity baseball team. Jonathan still enjoys playing in a summer softball league with his college friends. Given his athletic interests, he volunteered to be the athletic programming coordinator at OSI, where he organizes the company's softball and volleyball teams. Jonathan has been making steady progress at OSI. Last year, he was named marketing associate of the year.

His wife, Sue, is also a Buffalo native. She teaches English literature at the high school in one of the middle-class suburbs of Buffalo. Sue took five years off from teaching after she had a baby, but returned to teaching this year when Janine, their 5-year-old daughter, started kindergarten. She is happy to be resuming her career. One or two nights a week, Sue volunteers her time at the city mission where she works as a career counselor and a basic skills trainer. For fun, she takes both pottery and ethnic cooking classes.

Both Sue and Jonathan are excited about the potential transfer and accompanying pay raise. They are, however, also feeling apprehensive and cautious. Neither Sue nor Jonathan has ever lived away from their families in Buffalo, and Sue is concerned about giving up her newly reestablished career. Their daughter Janine has just started school, and Jonathan and Sue are uncertain whether living abroad is the best thing for her at her age.

Using the three-point scale below, try to rate Jonathan and Sue as potential expatriates. Write a sentence or two on why you gave the ratings you did.

Rating scale

1. Based on this dimension, this person would adjust well to living abroad.
2. Based on this dimension, this person may or may not adjust well to living abroad.
3. Based on this dimension, this person would not adjust well to living abroad.

Jonathan's International Orientation

rating dimension	rating and reason for rating
International attitudes	
Foreign Experiences	
Comfort with Differences	
Participation in Cultural Events	

Sue's International Orientation

rating dimension	rating and reason for rating
International attitudes	
Foreign Experiences	
Comfort with Differences	
Participation in Cultural Events	

Discussion Questions: Office Supplies International

1. Imagine that you are the international human resource manager for OSI. Your job is to interview both Jonathan and Sue to determine whether they should be sent abroad. What are some of the questions you would ask? What critical information do you feel is missing? It might be helpful to role play the three parts and evaluate your classmates' responses as Jonathan and Sue.
2. Suppose France is the country where they would be sent. To what extent woud your ratings change? What else would you change about the way you are assessing the couple?
3. Now answer the same questions, except this time they are being sent to Japan. Repeat the exercise for Australia.
4. For those dimensions that you rated Sue and Jonathan either 2 or 3, (indicating that they might have a potential adjustment problem), what would you suggest for training and development? What might be included in a training program?
5. Reflect on your own life for a moment and give yourself a rating on each of the following dimensions. Try to justify why you rated yourself as you did. Do you feel that you would adjust well to living abroad? What might be difficult for you?

rating dimension	rating and reason for rating France, Spain, Australia (or other)
International Attitudes	
Foreign Experiences	
Comfort with Differences	
Participation in Cultural Events	

6. Generally, what are some of the potential problems a dual career couple might face? What are some of the solutions to those problems?

7. How would the various ages of children affect the expatriate's assignment? At what age should the children's international orientations be assessed along with their parents?

International Orientation Scale

The following sample items are taken from the International Orientation Scale. Answer each question and give yourself a score for each dimension. The highest possible score for any dimension is 20 points.

Dimension 1: International attitudes

Use the following scale to answer question Q1 through Q4.

1 *Strongly agree*
2 *Agree somewhat*
3 *Maybe or unsure*
4 *Disagree somewhat*
5 *Strongly disagree*

Q1. Foreign language skills should be taught (as early as) elementary school. _____

Q2. Traveling the world is a priority in my life. _____

Q3. A year-long overseas assignment (from my company) would be a fantastic opportunity for my family and me. _____

Q4. Other countries fascinate me. _____

Total Dimension 1 _____

Dimension 2: Foreign experiences

Q1. I have studied a foreign language.

1 Never
2 For less than a year
3 For a year
4 For a few years
5 For several years

Q2. I am fluent in another language.

1 I don't know another language.
2 I am limited to very short and simple phrases.
3 I know basic grammatical structure and speak with a limited vocabulary.
4 I understand conversation on most topics.
5 I am very fluent in another language.

Q3. I have spent time overseas (traveling, studying abroad, etc.).

1 Never
2 About a week
3 A few weeks
4 A few months
5 Several months or years

Q4. I was overseas before the age of 18.

1 Never
2 About a week
3 A few weeks
4 A few months
5 Several months or years

Total dimension 2 _____

Dimension 3: Comfort with differences

Use the following scale for questions Q1 through Q4.

1 *Quite similar*
2 *Mostly similar*
3 *Somewhat different*
4 *Quite different*
5 *Extremely different*

Q1. My friends' career goals, interests and education are . . . _____

Q2. My friends' ethnic backgrounds are . . . _____

Q3. My friends' religious affiliations are . . . _____

Q4. My friends' first languages are . . . _____

Total Dimension 3 _____

Dimension 4: Participation in cultural events

Use the following scale to answer questions Q1 through Q4.

1 *Never*
2 *Seldom*
3 *Sometimes*
4 *Frequently*
5 *As often as possible*

Q1. I eat at a variety of ethnic restaurants (e.g., Greek, Polynesian, Thai, German). _____

Q2. I watch the major networks' world news programs. _____

Q3. I attend ethnic festivals. _____

Q4. I visit art galleries and museums. _____

Total Dimension 4 _____

Self-assessment discussion questions:

Do any of these scores suprise you?
Would you like to improve your international orientation?
If so, what could you do to change various aspects of your life?

*By Paula M. Caligiuri, Dept. of Psychology, Pennsylvania State University. Used with permission.

Dorothy Marcic and Sheila Puffer, *Management International*, West Publishing, 1994.

2.2 Ethical Dilemmas

Divide the class into five groups. Each group should choose one of the following scenarios and agree on a course of action.

1. Sam works for you. He is technically capable and a good worker, but he does not get along well with others in the work group. When Sam has an opportunity to transfer, you encourage him to take it. What would you say to Sam's potential supervisor when he asks about Sam?

2. Your boss has told you that you must reduce your work group by 30 percent. Which of the following criteria would you use to lay off workers?

a. Lay off older, higher-paid employees.
b. Lay off younger, lower-paid employees.
c. Lay off workers based on seniority only.
d. Lay off workers based on performance only.

3. You are an engineer, but you are not working on your company's Department of Transportation (DOT) project. One day you overhear a conversation in the cafeteria between the program manager and the project engineer that makes you reasonably sure a large contract will soon be given to the ABC Company to develop and manufacture a key DOT subsystem. ABC is a small firm, and its stock is traded over the counter. You feel sure that the stock will rise from its present $2.25 per share as soon as news of the DOT contract gets out. Would you go out and buy ABC's stock?

4. You are the project engineer working on the development of a small liquid rocket engine. You know that if you could achieve a throttling ratio greater than 8 to 1, your system would be considered a success and continue to receive funding support. To date, the best you have achieved is a 4 to 1 ratio. You have an unproven idea that you feel has a 50 percent chance of being successful. Your project is currently being reviewed to determine if it should be continued. You would like to continue it. How optimistically should you present test results?

5. Imagine that you are the president of a company in a highly competitive industry. You learn that a competitor has made an important scientific discovery that is not patentable and that will give him an advantage that will substantially reduce the profits of your company for about a year. There is some hope of hiring one of the competitor's employees who knows the details of the discovery. Would you try to hire this person?

Each group should present its scenario and chosen course of action to the class. The class should then evaluate the ethics of the course of action, using the following questions to guide discussion:

1. Are you following rules that are understood and accepted?
2. Are you comfortable discussing and defending your action?
3. Would you want someone to do this to you?
4. What if everyone acted this way?
5. Are there alternatives that rest on firmer ethical ground?

Scenarios adapted from R.A. DiBattista, "Providing a Rationale for Ethical Conduct from Alternatives Taken in Ethical Dilemmas," *Journal of General Psychology* 116 (1989): 207–214; discussion questions reprinted with the permission of the Free Press, a Division of Macmillan, Inc. from *The Manager as Negotiator: Bargaining for Cooperation and Competitive Gain* by David A. Lax and James K. Sebenius.

CASE

Developing Global Management Talent at Gillette[1]

Gillette, a company strongly oriented toward international growth, has more than 57 manufacturing facilities located in 28 different countries, and distributes its products in more than 200 countries and territories. With product lines focusing on personal grooming, stationery, and small electrical appliances, about 70 percent of Gillette's sales and operating profits come from international markets. Approximately 75 percent of its employees work outside the United States.

Michael Duerr, a member of the Conference Board, has observed that having the right people in the right place at the right time is the key to a company's global growth. Gillette takes a proactive approach to developing the management talent that it needs to successfully implement its business strategy of global growth.

Since the mid-1980s, Gillette has recruited top business students from international universities to participate in its international-trainee program. These trainees usually work for six months at Gillette subsidiaries in their home countries. In addition, highly qualified employees who have more than two year's experience at Gillette are selected for participation in the international-trainee program.

After their on-the-job experience in their home country, trainees are then transferred to Boston, London, or Singapore—the locations of Gillette's three international headquarters—for an eighteen-month training stint. Trainees usually are assigned to the headquarters that serves the region in which their home country is located. Headquarters training focuses on getting the trainees to learn (a) everything they can about the functional area[1] to which they are assigned, and (b) "how to work effectively in the Gillette organization." After their headquarters stint, the graduates take appropriate entry-level management positions in their home countries. With continued success, the graduates receive assignments in other countries to further expand their global visions and capabilities. Eventually, the graduates return to "their home countries as general managers or senior operating managers." Many graduates have risen to mid- to senior-level management positions within five to six years after completing the international-trainee program.

Another approach that Gillette uses to develop its global management talent is to recruit foreign nationals who are studying for their MBAs at U.S. universities. Upon graduation with their MBAs, these new hires are usually assigned to Boston headquarters for a year. They then return to their home countries to work in Gillette subsidiaries for about four years. Then they move to other countries and other assignments. As they ". . . build their international experience, they also teach and develop other potential managers within the organization."

DISCUSSION QUESTIONS

1. How can Hofstede's dimensions of cultural differences help Gillette employees in understanding the global challenges that result from manufacturing products in 28 different countries and distributing them in over 200 countries and territories?
2. What advantages and disadvantages do you see in the methods that Gillette uses to develop global managerial talent?
3. How can Gillette's approach to developing global management talent help the company in capitalizing on workforce diversity?

SOURCE: This case was written by Michael K. McCuddy, the Louis S. and Mary L. Morgal Professor of Christian Business Ethics, College of Business Administration, Valparaiso University.

1. These functional areas parallel Gillette's five major business areas: finance, marketing, manufacturing, human resources, and market research and sales. Adapted from: M. G. Duerr, "International Business Management: Its Four Tasks," *Conference Board Record* (October 1986): 43; J. J. Laabs, "Building a Global Management Team," *Personnel Journal* (August 1993): 75; J. J. Laabs, "How Gillette Grooms Global Talent," *Personnel Journal* (August 1993): 65–68+.

References

1. A. Salomon, "Air Cargo Carriers Fight for Global Dominance," *Advertising Age's Marketing* 8 (1995): 10.
2. F. Rose, "Now Quality Means Service Too," *Fortune,* 22 April 1991, 100–108.
3. M. A. Hitt, R. E. Hoskisson, and J. S. Harrison, "Strategic Competitiveness in the 1990s: Challenges and Opportunities for U.S. Executives," *Academy of Management Executive* 5 (1991): 7–22.
4. "Competitiveness Survey: *HBR* Readers Respond," *Harvard Business Review* 65 (1987): 8–11.
5. S. C. Harper, "The Challenges Facing CEOs: Past, Present, and Future," *Academy of Management Executive* 6 (1992): 7–25.
6. T. R. Mitchell and W. G. Scott, "America's Problems and Needed Reforms: Confronting the Ethic of Personal Advantage," *Academy of Management Executive* 4 (1990): 23–25.
7. D. Jamieson and J. O'Mara, *Managing Workforce 2000* (San Francisco: Jossey-Bass, 1991).
8. K. Sera, "Corporate Globalization: A New Trend," *Academy of Management Executive* 6 (1992): 89–96.
9. K. Ohmae, *Borderless World: Power and Strategies in the Interlinked Economy* (New York: Harper & Row,1990).
10. C. A. Bartlett and S. Ghoshal, *Managing across Borders: The Transnational Solution* (Boston: Harvard Business School Press,1989).
11. Y. Bian, "*Guanxi* and the Allocation of Urban Jobs in China," *The China Quarterly* (December 1994): 971–999.
12. P. S. Chan, "Franchise Management in East Asia," *Academy of Management Executive* 4 (1990): 75–85.
13. H. Weihrich, "Europe 1992: What the Future May Hold," *Academy of Management Executive* 4 (1990): 7–18.
14. R. Sharpe, "Hi-Tech Taboos," *Wall Street Journal*, October 31, 1995, A1.
15. G. Hofstede, *Culture's Consequences: International Differences in Work-Related Values* (Beverly Hills, Calif.: Sage Publications, 1980).
16. G. Hofstede, "Motivation, Leadership, and Organization: Do American Theories Apply Abroad?" *Organizational Dynamics* (Summer 1980): 42–63.
17. S. G. Redding and T. A. Martyn-Johns, "Paradigm Differences and Their Relation to Management with Reference to Southeast Asia," in G. W. England, A. R. Negandhi, and B. Wilpert, eds., *Organizational Functioning in a Cross-Cultural Perspective* (Kent, Ohio: Kent State University Press, 1979).
18. G. Hofstede, "Cultural Constraints in Management Theories," *Academy of Management Executive* 7 (1993): 81–94.
19. A. J. Michel, "Goodbyes Can Cost Plenty in Europe," *Fortune*, 6 April 1992,16.
20. T. Cox, "The Multicultural Organization," *Academy of Management Executive* 5 (1991): 34–47.
21. E. Brandt, "Global HR," *Personnel Journal* 70 (1991): 38–44.
22. Towers Perrin and Hudson Institute, *Workforce 2000: Competing in a Seller's Market* (Valhalla, N.Y.: Towers Perrin, 1990).
23. W. B. Johnston and E. A. Packer, *Workforce 2000: Work and Workers for the 21st Century* (Indianapolis: Hudson Institute, 1987).
24. Johnston and Packer, *Workforce 2000*.
25. L. S. Gottfredson, "Dilemmas in Developing Diversity Programs," in S. E. Jackson, ed., *Diversity in the Workplace: Human Resources Initiatives* (New York: Guilford Press, 1992), 279–305.
26. U.S. Bureau of the Census, *Statistical Abstract of the United States: 1995* (Washington, D.C.: Government Printing Office, 1995).
27. Glass Ceilings and Concrete Walls Do Not Shatter Easily," *HR Focus* (June 1995): 17.
28. J. Bound and G. Johnson, "What Are the Causes of Rising Wage Inequality in the United States?" *Economic Policy Review* 1(1995): 9–16.
29. A. M. Morrison, R. P. White, E. Van Velsor, and the Center for Creative Leadership, *Breaking the Glass Ceiling: Can Women Reach the Top of America's Largest Corporations?* (Reading, Mass.: Addison-Wesley, 1987).
30. J. Tomkiewicz and T. Adeyemi-Bello, "A Cross-Sectional Analysis of Attitudes of Nigerians and Americans Toward Women as Managers," *Journal of Social Behavior and Personality*, 10 (1995): 189–198.
31. D. L. Nelson and M. A. Hitt, "Employed Women and Stress: Implications for Enhancing Women's Mental Health in the Workplace," in J. C. Quick, L. R. Murphy, and J. J. Hurrell, Jr., eds., *Stress and Well-Being at Work* (Washington, D.C.: American Psychological Association, 1992), 164–177.
32. Johnston and Packer, *Workforce 2000*.
33. W. B. Johnston, "Global Workforce 2000: The New World Labor Market," *Harvard Business Review* 69 (1991): 115–127.
34. S. E. Jackson and E. B. Alvarez, "Working through Diversity as a Strategic Imperative," in S. E. Jackson, ed., *Diversity in the Workplace: Human Resources Initiatives* (New York: Guilford Press, 1992), 13–36.
35. "Managing Generational Diversity," *HR Magazine* 36 (1991): 91–92.
36. C. M. Solomon, "Managing the Baby Busters," *Personnel Journal* (March 1992): 52–59.
37. S. R. Rhodes, "Age-related Differences in Work Attitudes and Behavior: A Review and Conceptual Analysis," *Psychological Bulletin* 93 (1983): 338–367.
38. B. L. Hassell and P. L. Perrewe, "An Examination of Beliefs about Older Workers: Do Stereotypes Still Exist?" *Journal of Organizational Behavior* 16 (1995): 457–468.
39. J. J. Laabs, "The Golden Arches Provide Golden Opportunities," *Personnel Journal* (July 1991): 52–57.
40. W. J. Rothwell, "HRD and the Americans with Disabilities Act," *Training and Development Journal* (August 1991): 45–47.
41. J. Waldrop, "The Cost of Hiring the Disabled," *American Demographics* (March 1991): 12.
42. Laabs, "The Golden Arches," 52–57.
43. L. Winfield and S. Spielman, "Making Sexual Orientation Part of Diversity," *Training and Development* (April 1995): 50–51.
44. J. Landau, "The Relationship of Race and Gender to Managers' Ratings of Promotion Potential," *Journal of Organizational Behavior* 16 (1995): 391–400.
45. P. Barnum, "Double Jeopardy for Women and Minorities: Pay Differences with Age," *Academy of Management Journal* 38 (1995): 863–880.
46. J. E. Rigdon, "PepsiCo's KFC Scouts for Blacks and Women for Its Top Echelons," *Wall Street Journal,* 13 November 1991, A1.

47. P. A. Galagan, "Tapping the Power of a Diverse Workforce," *Training and Development Journal* 26 (1991): 38–44.

48. R. Thomas, "From Affirmative Action to Affirming Diversity," *Harvard Business Review* 68 (1990): 107–117.

49. J. Gordon, "Different From What?" *Training* (May 1995): 25–33.

50. L. Copeland, "Learning to Manage a Multicultural Workforce," *Training* 25 (1988): 48–56.

51. Jackson and Alvarez, "Working through Diversity," 13–36.

52. Task Force on Management of Innovation, *Technology and Employment: Innovation and Growth in the U.S. Economy* (Washington, D.C.: U.S. Government Research Council, 1987).

53. C. H. Ferguson, "Computers and the Coming of the U.S. Keiretsu," *Harvard Business Review* 68 (1990): 55–70.

54. C. Arnst, "The Networked Corporation," *Business Week*, June 26, 1995, 86–89.

55. J. A. Senn, *Information Systems in Management*, 4th ed. (Belmont, Calif.: Wadsworth, 1990).

56. R. Forsyth, "The Anatomy of Expert Systems," in M. Yazdani and A. Narayanan, eds., *Artificial Intelligence: Human Effects* (Chichester, England: Ellis Horwood, 1984), 186–199.

57. M. T. Damore, "A Presentation and Examination of the Integration of Unlawful Discrimination Practices in the Private Business Sector with Artificial Intelligence" (Thesis, Oklahoma State University, 1992).

58. A. Tanzer and R. Simon, "Why Japan Loves Robots and We Don't," *Forbes*, 16 April 1990, 148–153.

59. E. Fingleton, "Jobs for Life: Why Japan Won't Give Them Up," *Fortune*, March 20, 1995, 119–125.

60. Johnston and Packer, *Workforce 2000*.

61. D. L. Nelson, "Individual Adjustment to Information-driven Technologies: A Critical Review," *MIS Quarterly* 14 (1990): 79–98.

62. C. Brod, *Technostress* (Reading, Mass.: Addison-Wesley, 1984).

63. M. Allen, "Legislation Could Restrict Bosses from Snooping on Their Workers," *Wall Street Journal*, 24 September 1991, B1–B8.

64. K. D. Hill and S. Kerr, "The Impact of Computer-integrated Manufacturing Systems on the First Line Supervisor," *Journal of Organizational Behavior Management* 6 (1984): 81–87.

65. J. Anderson, "How Technology Brings Blind People into the Workplace," *Harvard Business Review* 67 (1989): 36–39.

66. D. L. Nelson and M. G. Kletke, "Individual Adjustment during Technological Innovation: A Research Framework," *Behaviour and Information Technology* 9 (1990): 257–271.

67. A. Majchrzak, *The Human Side of Factory Automation* (San Francisco: Jossey-Bass, 1988).

68. B. Bemmels and Y. Reshef, "Manufacturing Employees and Technological Change," *Journal of Labor Research* 12 (1991): 231–246.

69. Y. V. H. Morieux and E. Sutherland, "The Interaction between the Use of Information Technology and Organizational Culture," *Behaviour and Information Technology* 7 (1988): 205–213.

70. D. Mankin, T. Bikson, B. Gutek, and C. Stasz, "Managing Technological Change: The Process Is the Key," *Datamation* 34 (1988), 69–80.

71. R. M. Cyert and D. C. Mowery, "Technology, Employment, and U.S. Competitiveness," *Scientific American* May (1989): 54–62.

72. L. Kretchmar, "Another CEO Told: Go to Jail," *Fortune*, 18 May 1992,113.

73. S. W. Gellerman, "Why 'Good' Managers Make Bad Ethical Choices," *Harvard Business Review* 64 (1986): 85–90.

74. J. S. Mill, *Utilitarianism, Liberty, and Representative Government* (London: Dent, 1910).

75. K. H. Blanchard and N.V. Peale, *The Power of Ethical Management* (New York: Morrow, 1988).

76. C. Fried, *Right and Wrong* (Cambridge, Mass.: Harvard University Press, 1978).

77. I. Kant, *Groundwork of the Metaphysics of Morals*, trans. H. J. Paton (New York: Harper & Row, 1964).

78. A. Smith, *An Inquiry into the Nature and Causes of the Wealth of Nations*, vol. 10 of *The Harvard Classics*, ed. C. J. Bullock (New York: P. F. Collier & Son, 1909).

79. H. W. Lane and J. J. DiStefano, *International Management Behavior*, 2d ed. (Boston: PWS-Kent, 1992).

80. S. J. Harrington, "What Corporate America Is Teaching about Ethics," *Academy of Management Executive* 5 (1991): 21–30.

81. K. Labich, "The New Crisis in Business Ethics," *Fortune*, 20 April 1992, 167–176.

82. T. Forester and P. Morrison, *Computer Ethics: Cautionary Tales and Ethical Dilemmas in Computing* (Cambridge, Mass.: MIT Press, 1990).

83. P. Mykytyn, K. Mykytyn, and C. Slinkman, "Expert Systems: A Question of Liability?" *MIS Quarterly* 14 (1990): 27–42.

84. D. Kemp, "Employers and AIDS: Dealing with the Psychological and Emotional Issues of AIDS in the Workplace," *American Review of Public Administration* 25 (1995): 263–278.

85. J. J. Koch, "Wells Fargo's and IBM's HIV Policies Help Protect Employees' Rights," *Personnel Journal*, April 1990, 40–48.

86. A. Arkin, "Positive HIV and AIDS Policies at Work," *Personnel Management* (December 1994): 34–37.

87. S. J. Adler, "Lawyers Advise Concerns to Provide Precise Written Policy to Employees," *Wall Street Journal*, 9 October 1991,B1.

88. D. Gross, "The High Price of Harassment," *CFO*, (February 1994): 57–58.

89. M. H. Peak, "Cupid in a Three-Piece Suit," *Management Review* (April 1995): 5.

90. J. Greenberg and R. Folger, "Procedural Justice, Participation, and the Fair Process Effect in Groups and Organizations," in P. B. Paulus, ed., *Basic Group Processes* (New York: Springer-Verlag, 1983), 235–256.

91. H. L. Laframboise, "Vile Wretches and Public Heroes: The Ethics of Whistleblowing in Government," *Canadian Public Administration* (Spring 1991): 73–78.

92. C. Hukill, "Whistleblowers," *Monthly Labor Review* (October 1990): 41.

93. M. P. Miceli and J. P. Near, "Who Blows the Whistle and Why," *Industrial and Labor Relations Review* 45 (1991): 113–130.

94. "Aligning the Process with the People," *Chief Executive* (March 1995): 8–13.

INTERNET EXERCISE

Part of understanding organizational behavior issues as a manager is to be aware of the resources available to you. Progressive managers do not rely solely on common sense or "gut-hunches." Rather, they stay informed and are knowledgeable about new ideas and research. The Internet is becoming a more popular forum for many ideas including organizational behavior. This assignment will allow you to begin to investigate the resources available on the Internet.

Listserv

The globalization of organizations is a growing trend. Managers will not only have to understand the behavior of their domestic employees, but also those in the various countries in which they do business. To find out more about international business, via e-mail, subscribe to:
listserve@dekker.mtsu.edu

In the message portion of your e-mail type: **subscribe IMD-L "YOUR NAME"**

Gopher

While the World Wide Web is growing in popularity, many organizations still maintain extensive gopher sites. Use gopher to find the "Management Working Paper Archive."

What topics are covered here? How do they relate to the topics covered in this section?

World Wide Web

The Academy of Management is the leading professional organization for management and organizational behavior. Use your Web browser to go to the Academy of Management's home page.

What information is provided here? How could a manager make use of this information?

E-Mail

E-mail your professor two titles from the "Management Working Paper Archive" mentioned earlier. Discuss how these papers relate to a topic you have covered in class.

VIDEO COHESION CASE

This section includes four cases dealing with various organizational behavior issues facing PriceCostco, a company resulting from the merger of Price Company and Costco Wholesale. The cases are interrelated, but each can stand alone. Each case is supplemented with videos that present the challenges faced by a corporation formed from two diverse companies seeking to create a single company with a unified philosophy and culture. These cases immediately follow Chapter 18 on page 573.

PART II

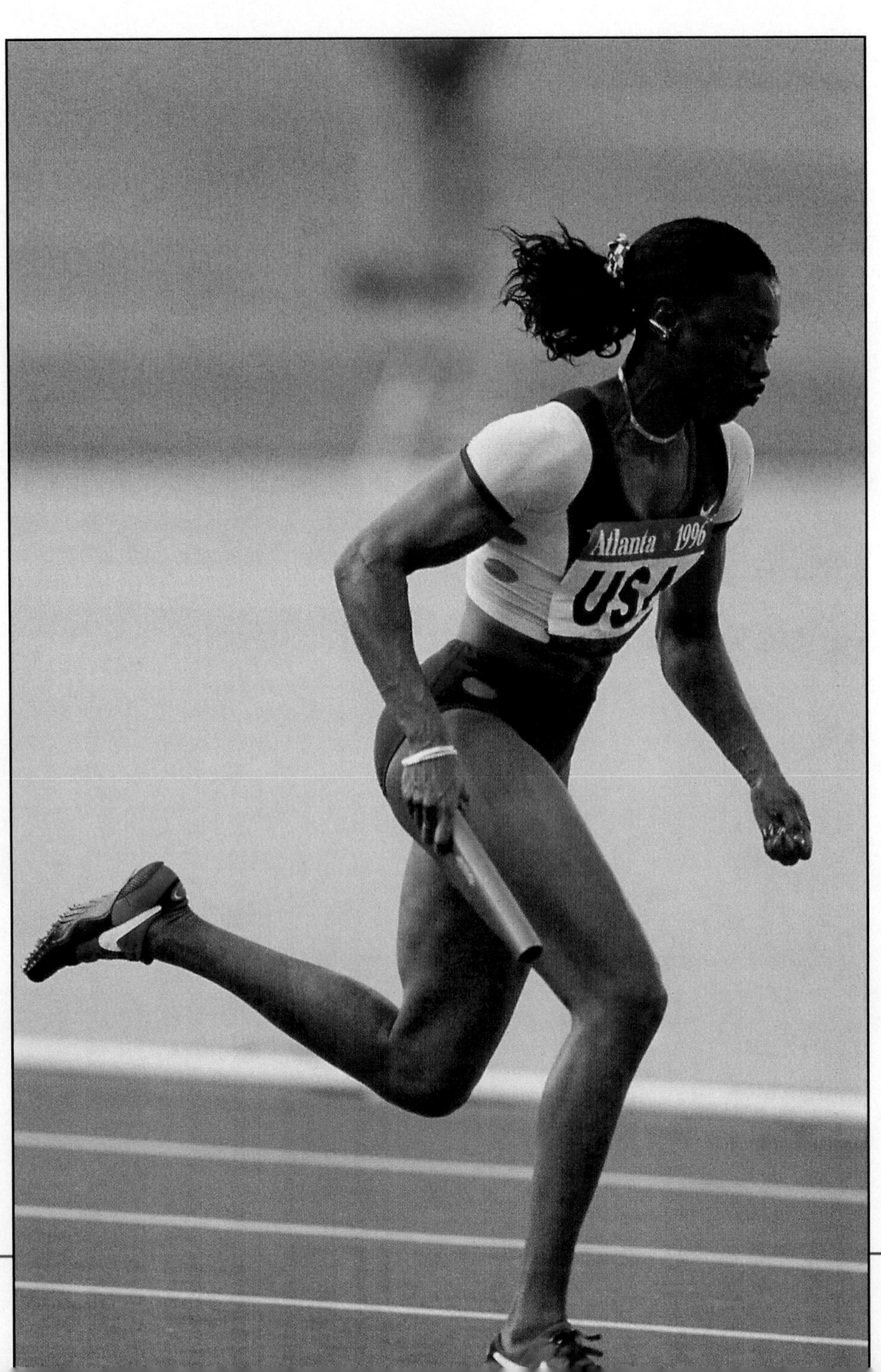

Individual Processes and Behavior

CHAPTER

3

Personality, Perception, and Attribution

LEARNING OBJECTIVES

After reading this chapter, you should be able to do the following:

- Describe individual differences and their importance in understanding behavior.
- Define *personality.*
- Explain four theories of personality.
- Identify several personality characteristics and their influences on behavior in organizations.
- Explain how personality is measured.
- Discuss Carl Jung's contribution to our understanding of individual differences, and explain how his theory is used in the Myers-Briggs Type Indicator.
- Define *social perception* and explain how characteristics of the perceiver, the target, and the situation affect it.
- Identify five common barriers to social perception.
- Explain the attribution process and how attributions affect managerial behavior.

OPENING SPOTLIGHT

Celebrating Individual Differences at Southwest Airlines

BRIAN SHOWS AN EARLY APTITUDE FOR WORKING AT SOUTHWEST AIRLINES.
SOUTHWEST AIRLINES

Southwest Airlines presented the accompanying recruiting advertisement in its inflight magazine, *Spirit.* Coloring outside the lines is encouraged at Southwest; in fact, the airline specifically seeks to hire creative people. Although the staff at Southwest has grown 97 percent in four years, the informal hiring process remains the same. In addition to creative people, Southwest looks for self-starters who will pitch in on any task, even blowing up balloons for celebrations.[1] Southwest stresses a spirit of teamwork but places a premium on individuality. On Southwest flights, chances are that you may hear the traditional instructions to passengers to prepare for landing sung to the tune of the theme http://www.iflyswa.com/

song from *The Beverly Hillbillies.* An in-flight contest may be held in which the winner is the passenger who displays the most holes in his or her socks. Humor is a crucial ingredient in Southwest's organizational culture. In the Closing Spotlight, we'll explore how Southwest's emphasis on encouraging individuals to be themselves is translated into "Positively Outrageous Service." ■

Individual Differences and Organizational Behavior

individual differences

The way in which factors such as skills, abilities, personalities, perceptions, attitudes, values, and ethics differ from one individual to another.

■ In this chapter and continuing in Chapter 4, we explore the concept of **individual differences.** Individuals are unique in terms of their skills, abilities, personalities, perceptions, attitudes, values, and ethics. These are just a few of the ways individuals may be similar to or different from one another. Individual differences represent the essence of the challenge of management, because no two individuals are completely alike. Managers face the challenge of working with people who possess a multitude of individual characteristics, so the more managers understand individual differences, the better they can work with others. Figure 3.1 illustrates how individual differences affect human behavior.

The basis for understanding individual differences stems from Lewin's early contention that behavior is a function of the person and the environment.[2] Lewin expressed this idea in an equation: $B=f(P, E)$, where B=behavior, P=person, and E=environment. This idea has been developed by the **interactional psychology** approach.[3] Basically, this approach says that in order to understand human behavior, we must know something about the person and something about the situation. There are four basic propositions of interactional psychology:

interactional psychology

The psychological approach that emphasizes that in order to understand human behavior, we must know something about the person and about the situation.

1. Behavior is a function of a continuous, multidirectional interaction between the person and the situation.
2. The person is active in this process and both is changed by situations and changes situations.
3. People vary in many characteristics, including cognitive, affective, motivational, and ability factors.
4. Two interpretations of situations are important: the objective situation and the person's subjective view of the situation.[4]

Alternate Example

Developmental psychologists suggest that 80-90% of an individual's personality is determined by the time they are six years old.

■ **FIGURE 3.1**

Variables Influencing Individual Behavior

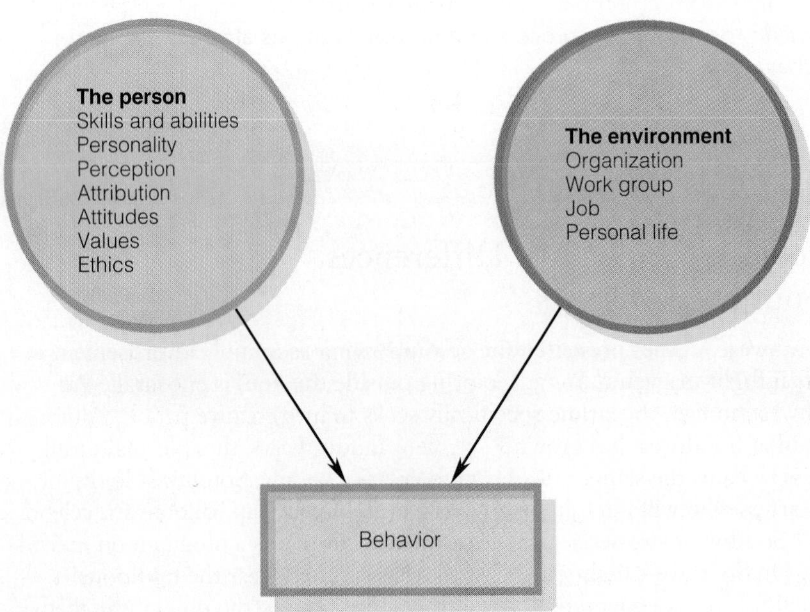

The interactional psychology approach points out the need to study both persons and situations. We will focus on personal and situational factors throughout the text. The person consists of individual differences such as those we emphasize in this chapter and Chapter 4: personality, perception, attribution, attitudes, values, and ethics. The situation consists of the environment the person operates in, and it can include things like the organization, work group, personal life situation, job characteristics, and many other environmental influences. One important and fascinating individual difference is personality.

Personality

■ What makes an individual behave in consistent ways in a variety of situations? Personality is an individual difference that lends consistency to a person's behavior. **Personality** is defined as a relatively stable set of characteristics that influence an individual's behavior. Although there is debate about the determinants of personality, we conclude that there are several origins. One determinant is heredity, and some interesting studies have supported this position. Identical twins who are separated at birth and raised apart in very different situations have been found to share personality traits and job preferences. For example, about half of the variation in traits like extraversion, impulsiveness, and flexibility was found to be genetically determined; that is, identical twins who grew up in different environments shared these traits.[5] In addition, the twins held similar jobs.[6] Thus, there does appear to be a genetic influence on personality.

personality

A relatively stable set of characteristics that influences an individual's behavior.

Another determinant of personality is the environment a person is exposed to. Family influences, cultural influences, educational influences, and other environmental forces shape personality. Personality is therefore shaped by both heredity and environment.

Personality Theories

Four major theories of personality are the trait theory, psychodynamic theory, humanistic theory, and the integrative approach. Each theory has influenced the study of personality in organizations.

Points to Emphasize

Personality traits have been found to be accurate in predicting behavior only in those situations where the trait is in extreme tail of the normal distribution.

TRAIT THEORY Some early personality researchers believed that to understand individuals, we must break down behavior patterns into a series of observable traits. According to **trait theory,** combining these traits into a group forms an individual's personality. Gordon Allport, a leading trait theorist, saw traits as broad, general guides that lend consistency to behavior.[7] Thousands of traits have been identified over the years. Raymond Cattell, another prominent trait theorist, identified sixteen traits that formed the basis for differences in individual behavior. He described traits in bipolar adjective combinations such as self-assured/apprehensive, reserved/outgoing, and submissive/dominant.[8]

trait theory

The personality theory that states that in order to understand individuals, we must break down behavior patterns into a series of observable traits.

More recently, researchers have argued that all traits can be reduced to five basic factors. The "big five" traits include extraversion, agreeableness, conscientiousness, emotional stability, and openness to experience.[9] Although there is evidence to support the existence of the big five traits, research is needed to see whether these five traits actually predict behavior. Preliminary results indicate that one of the big five, conscientiousness, is related to job performance. Across five different occupations, people who were responsible, dependable, persistent, and achievement-oriented performed better than people who lacked conscientiousness.

The trait approach has been the subject of considerable criticism. Some theorists argue that simply identifying traits is not enough; instead, personality is dynamic and not completely stable. Further, trait theorists tended to ignore the influence of situations. [10]

psychodynamic theory
The personality theory that emphasizes the unconscious determinants of behavior.

PSYCHODYNAMIC THEORY Based on the work of Sigmund Freud, **psychodynamic theory** emphasizes the unconscious determinants of behavior.[11] Freud saw personality as the interaction between three elements of personality: the id, ego, and superego. The id is the most primitive element, the source of drives and impulses that operates in an uncensored manner. The superego, similar to what we know as conscience, contains values and the "shoulds and should nots" of the personality. There is an ongoing conflict between the id and the superego. The ego serves to manage the conflict between the id and the superego. In this role, the ego compromises, and the result is the individual's use of defense mechanisms such as denial of reality. The contribution of psychodynamic theory to our understanding of personality is its focus on unconscious influences on behavior.

humanistic theory
The personality theory that emphasizes individual growth and improvement.

HUMANISTIC THEORY Carl Rogers believed that all people have a basic drive toward self-actualization, which is the quest to be all you can be.[12] The **humanistic theory** focuses on individual growth and improvement. It is distinctly people centered and also emphasizes the individual's view of the world. The humanistic approach contributes an understanding of the self to personality theory and contends that the self-concept is the most important part of an individual's personality.

integrative approach
The broad theory that describes personality as a composite of an individual's psychological processes.

INTEGRATIVE APPROACH Recently, researchers have taken a broader, more **integrative approach** to the study of personality.[13] To capture its influence on behavior, personality is described as a composite of the individual's psychological processes. Personality dispositions include emotions, cognitions, attitudes, expectancies, and fantasies.[14] *Dispositions,* in this approach, simply means the tendencies of individuals to respond to situations in consistent ways. Influenced by both genetics and experiences, dispositions can be modified. The integrative approach focuses on both person (dispositions) and situational variables as combined predictors of behavior.

Alternate Example
Externals may need to be encouraged to view their effort as a determinant of their own outcomes on the job and as something they can control. In some cases, internals will ascribe to supervisor the positive factors of their job, rather than take credit for their achievements. SOURCE: A. L. Johnson, F. Luthans, and H. W. Hennesey, "The Role of Locus of Control in Leader Influence Behavior," *Personnel Psychology,* 1984, 61–75.

Personality Characteristics in Organizations

Managers should learn as much as possible about personality in order to understand their employees. Hundreds of personality characteristics have been identified. We have selected five characteristics because of their particular influences on individual behavior in organizations: locus of control, self-esteem, self-efficacy, self-monitoring, and positive/negative affect.

locus of control
An individual's generalized belief about internal control (self-control) versus external control (control by the situation or by others).

LOCUS OF CONTROL An individual's generalized belief about internal (self) versus external (situation or others) control is called **locus of control.** People who believe they control what happens to them are said to have an internal locus of control, whereas people who believe that circumstances or other people control their fate have an external locus of control.[15] Research on locus of control has strong implications for organizations. Internals (those with an internal locus of control) have been found to have higher job satisfaction, to be more likely to assume managerial positions, and to prefer participative management styles.[16] In addition, internals have been shown to display higher work motivation, hold stronger beliefs that effort leads to performance, receive higher salaries, and display less anxiety than externals (those with an external locus of control).[17]

Knowing about locus of control can prove valuable to managers. Because internals believe they control what happens to them, they will want to exercise control in their work environment. Allowing internals considerable voice in how work is performed is important. Internals will not react well to being closely supervised. Externals, in contrast, may prefer a more structured work setting, and they may be more reluctant to participate in decision making.

SELF-ESTEEM **Self-esteem** is an individual's general feeling of self-worth. Individuals with high self-esteem have positive feelings about themselves, perceive themselves to have strengths as well as weaknesses, and believe their strengths are more important than their weaknesses.[18] Individuals with low self-esteem view themselves negatively. They are more strongly affected by what other people think of them, and they compliment individuals who give them positive feedback while cutting down people who give them negative feedback.[19]

self-esteem

An individual's general feeling of self-worth.

A person's self-esteem affects a host of other attitudes and has important implications for behavior in organizations. People with high self-esteem perform better and are more satisfied with their jobs.[20] When they are involved in a job search, they seek out higher-status jobs.[21] A work team made up of individuals with high self-esteem is more likely to be successful than a team with lower average self-esteem.[22]

Points to Emphasize

Stanford psychologist Albert Bandura's research indicates that past experience is the major force for establishing our self-efficacy. This counters the often easily cited expression "they need to pull themselves up by their bootstraps." In short, winning breeds the winners.

Very high self-esteem may be too much of a good thing. When people with high self-esteem find themselves in stressful situations, they may brag inappropriately.[23] This may be viewed negatively by others, who see spontaneous boasting as egotistical.

Self-esteem may be strongly affected by situations. Success tends to raise self-esteem, whereas failure tends to lower it. Given that high self-esteem is generally a positive characteristic, managers should encourage employees to raise their self-esteem by giving them appropriate challenges and opportunities for success. One company that believes in self-esteem is Fantastic Foods, as shown in the Organizational Reality feature.

SELF-EFFICACY An individual's beliefs and expectancies about his or her ability to accomplish a specific task effectively is known as **self-efficacy.**[24] Individuals with high self-efficacy believe that they have the ability to get things done, that they are capable of putting forth the effort to accomplish the task, and that they can overcome any obstacles to their success. There are four sources of self-efficacy: prior experiences, behavior models (witnessing the success of others), persuasion from other people, and assessment of current physical and emotional capabilities.[25] Believing in one's own capability to get something done is an important facilitator of success. There is strong evidence that self-efficacy leads to high performance on a wide variety of physical and mental tasks.[26] High self-efficacy has also led to success in breaking addictions, increasing pain tolerance, and recovering from illnesses.

self-efficacy

An individual's beliefs and expectancies about his or her ability to accomplish a specific task effectively.

Discussion Consideration

Much of the recent emphasis on empowerment involves building up the employee's self efficacy. What can managers do to enhance an employee's self-efficacy?

Managers can help employees develop their self-efficacy. This can be done by providing job challenges, coaching and counseling for improved performance, and rewarding employees' achievements. Empowerment, or sharing power with employees, can be accomplished by interventions that help employees increase their self-esteem and self-efficacy.[27] Given the increasing diversity of the work force, managers may want to target their efforts toward women and minorities in particular. Research has indicated that women and minorities tend to have lower than average self-efficacy.[28]

Points to Emphasize

Self-esteem and self-efficacy are easy to confuse. A good way to keep these constructs clear is to realize that self-esteem is a general construct, whereas self-efficacy is a task-specific construct. A person may have positive self-esteem, yet have a low level of self-efficacy on a particular task or activity.

SELF-MONITORING A characteristic with great potential for affecting behavior in organizations is **self-monitoring**—the extent to which people base their behavior on cues from people and situations.[29] High self-monitors pay attention to what is appropriate in particular situations and to the behavior of other people, and they behave accordingly. Low self-monitors, in contrast, are not as vigilant to situational cues and act from internal states rather than paying attention to the situation. As a result, the behavior of low self-monitors is consistent across

self-monitoring

The extent to which people base their behavior on cues from other people and situations.

ORGANIZATIONAL REALITY

Building Fantastic Self-Esteem

Jim Rosen, president of Fantastic Foods, learned everything he needed to know about management in nursery school. The Entrepreneur of the Year winner was a Montessori teacher for twenty years, and he uses the same techniques with the 90 employees of the Petaluma, California, dry soup manufacturing company. Rosen reasons that "big people are just little people who got big."

Some of the Montessori philosophy is recast by Rosen for the production floor. He believes that self-esteem is critical to employee satisfaction and productivity. "With kids," he says, "the most important thing is how they feel about themselves. With employees also, if you want them to have the right attitude, you have to help build self-esteem." How does he do this? First, by giving employees tasks that stretch them, and making sure they have the ability and tools to achieve their goals. Second, he lets employees run with their ideas and risk failure. They learn something powerful from this.

Montessori classroom materials let children gauge their own progress. At Fantastic Foods, daily production goals are posted in the factory and provide automatic feedback on performance. Each person evaluates himself or herself, which builds self-esteem. ■

SOURCE: Reprinted through the courtesy of CIO. © 1995 CIO Communications Inc.

Employees at Fantastic Foods are satisfied with their jobs and are high performers. The company's CEO, Jim Rosen, believes that helping workers build self-esteem leads to success.

Points to Emphasize

Self-monitoring is not necessarily negative. In fact, it may be useful in many situations. For instance, when someone first joins an organization, self-monitoring helps the person pick up cues from their environment about appropriate and inappropriate behavior.

Discussion Consideration

Are some jobs more suitable for self-monitoring individuals? Some jobs that come to mind are in marketing, teaching, and in organizations that are structured around work teams.

situations. High self-monitors, because their behavior varies with the situation, appear to be more unpredictable and less consistent. You can use Challenge 3.1 to assess your own self-monitoring tendencies.

Research is currently focusing on the effects of self-monitoring in organizations. In one study, the authors tracked the careers of 139 MBAs for five years to see whether high self-monitors were more likely to be promoted, change employers, or make a job-related geographic move. The results were "yes" to each question. High self-monitors get promoted because they accomplish tasks through meeting the expectations of others. However, the high self-monitor's flexibility may not be suited for every job, and the tendency to move may not fit every organization.[30]

Although research on self-monitoring in organizations is in its early stages, we can speculate that high self-monitors respond more readily to work group norms, organizational culture, and supervisory feedback than do low self-monitors, who adhere more to internal guidelines for behavior ("I am who I am"). In addition, high self-monitors may be enthusiastic participants in the trend toward work teams because of their ability to assume flexible roles.

Like chameleons who change their appearance to blend in with the environment, high self-monitors change their behavior in accordance with cues provided in the situation.

Points to Emphasize
Affect is often a contagious process in organizations. That is, positive or negative affect can spread from one person to another.

POSITIVE/NEGATIVE AFFECT Recently, researchers have explored the effects of persistent mood dispositions at work. Individuals who focus on the positive aspects of themselves, other people, and the world in general are said to have **positive affect.**[31] In contrast, those who accentuate the negative in themselves, others, and the world are said to possess **negative affect** (also referred to as negative affectivity).[32] Interviewers who exhibit positive affect evaluate job candidates more favorably than do interviewers whose affect is neutral.[33] Employees with positive affect are absent from work less often.[34] Individuals with negative affect report more work stress.[35] Individual affect also influences the work group. Negative individual affect produces negative group affect, and this leads to less cooperative behavior in the work group.[36]

positive affect
An individual's tendency to accentuate the positive aspects of himself or herself, other people, and the world in general.

negative affect
An individual's tendency to accentuate the negative aspects of himself or herself, other people, and the world in general.

Positive affect is a definite asset in work settings. Managers can do several things to promote positive affect, including allowing participative decision making and providing pleasant working conditions. We need to know more about inducing positive affect in the workplace.

The characteristics previously described are but a few of the personality characteristics that affect behavior in organizations. Can managers predict the behavior of their employees by knowing their personalities? Not completely. You may recall that the interactional psychology model (Figure 3.1) requires both person and situation variables to predict behavior. Another idea to remember in predicting behavior is the strength of situational influences. Some situations are **strong situations** in that they overwhelm the effects of individual personalities. These situations are interpreted in the same way by different individuals, evoke agreement on the appropriate behavior in the situation, and provide cues to appropriate behavior. A performance appraisal session is an example of a strong situation. Employees know to listen to their boss and to contribute when asked to do so.

strong situation
A situation that overwhelms the effects of individual personalities by providing strong cues for appropriate behavior.

CHALLENGE

■ 3.1

Are You a High or Low Self-Monitor?

For the following items, circle T (true) if the statement is characteristic of your behavior. Circle F (false) if the statement does not reflect your behavior.

1. I find it hard to imitate the behavior of other people. T F
2. At parties and social gatherings, I do not attempt to do or say things that others will like. T F
3. I can only argue for ideas that I already believe. T F
4. I can make impromptu speeches even on topics about which I have almost no information. T F
5. I guess I put on a show to impress or entertain others. T F
6. I would probably make a good actor. T F
7. In a group of people, I am rarely the center of attention. T F
8. In different situations and with different people, I often act like very different persons. T F
9. I am not particularly good at making other people like me. T F
10. I am not always the person I appear to be. T F
11. I would not change my opinions (or the way I do things) in order to please others or win their favor. T F
12. I have considered being an entertainer. T F
13. I have never been good at games like charades or at improvisational acting. T F
14. I have trouble changing my behavior to suit different people and different situations. T F
15. At a party, I let others keep the jokes and stories going. T F
16. I feel a bit awkward in company and do not show up quite as well as I should. T F
17. I can look anyone in the eye and tell a lie with a straight face (if it is for a good cause). T F
18. I may deceive people by being friendly when I really dislike them. T F

To score this questionnaire, give yourself 1 point for each of the following items that you answered T (true): 4, 5, 6, 8, 10, 12, 17, and 18. Now give yourself 1 point for each of the following items that you answered F (false): 1, 2, 3, 7, 9, 11, 13, 14, 15, and 16. Add both subtotals to find your overall score. If you scored 11 or above, you are probably a *high self-monitor*. If you scored 10 or under, you are probably a *low self-monitor*.

SOURCE: From *Public Appearances, Private Realities: The Psychology of Self-Monitoring* by M. Snyder. Copyright © 1987 by W. H. Freeman and Co. Reprinted by permission.

A weak situation, in contrast, is one that is open to many interpretations. It provides few cues to appropriate behavior and no obvious rewards for one behavior over another. Thus, individual personalities have a stronger influence in weak situations than in strong situations. An informal meeting without an agenda can be seen as a weak situation.

Organizations present combinations of strong and weak situations; therefore, personality has a stronger effect on behavior in some situations than in others.[37] Southwest Airlines, as you saw in the Opening Spotlight, chooses to let individual personalities shine through rather than creating strong cues for behavior.

Measuring Personality

Several methods can be used to assess personality. These include projective tests, behavioral measures, and self-report questionnaires.

The **projective test** is one method used to measure personality. In these tests, individuals are shown a picture, abstract image, or photo and are asked to describe what they see or to tell a story about what they see. The rationale behind projective tests is that each individual responds to the stimulus in a way that reflects his or her unique personality. The Rorschach ink blot test is a projective test commonly used to assess personality.[38] Like other projective tests, however, it has low reliability.

projective test

A personality test that elicits an individual's response to abstract stimuli.

There are **behavioral measures** of personality as well. Measuring behavior involves observing an individual's behavior in a controlled situation. We might assess a person's sociability, for example, by counting the number of times he or she approaches strangers at a party. The behavior is scored in some manner to produce an index of personality.

behavioral measures

Personality assessments that involve observing an individual's behavior in a controlled situation.

The most common method of assessing personality is the **self-report questionnaire.** Individuals respond to a series of questions, usually in an agree/disagree or true/false format. One of the more widely recognized questionnaires is the Minnesota Multiphasic Personality Inventory (MMPI). The MMPI is comprehensive and assesses a variety of traits, as well as various neurotic or psychotic disorders. Used extensively in psychological counseling to identify disorders, the MMPI is a long questionnaire. The big five traits we discussed earlier are measured by another self-report questionnaire, the NEO Personality Inventory.

self-report questionnaire

A common personality assessment that involves an individual's responses to a series of questions.

Another popular self-report questionnaire is the **Myers-Briggs Type Indicator (MBTI).** In the next section, we will introduce the Jungian theory of personality. The Myers-Briggs Type Indicator is an instrument that has been developed to measure Jung's ideas about individual differences. Many organizations use the MBTI, and we will focus on it as an example of how some organizations use personality concepts to help employees appreciate diversity.

Myers-Briggs Type Indicator (MBTI)

An instrument developed to measure Carl Jung's theory of individual differences.

Points to Emphasize

The MBTI is one of the most widely utilized personality tests in the United States. In one year alone, over 20 million people take the MBTI.

Jungian Theory and the Myers-Briggs Type Indicator

■ One approach to applying personality theory in organizations is the Jungian approach and its measurement tool, the MBTI.

Swiss psychiatrist Carl Jung built his work upon the notion that people are fundamentally different, but also fundamentally alike. His classic treatise *Psychological Types* proposed that the population was made up of two basic types—extraverted and introverted.[39] He went on to identify two types of perception (sensing and intuiting) and two types of judgment (thinking and feeling). Perception (how we gather information) and judgment (how we make decisions) represent the basic mental functions that everyone uses.

Jung suggested that human similarities and differences could be understood by combining preferences. We prefer and choose one way of doing things over another. We are not exclusively one way or another; rather, we have a preference for extraversion or introversion, just as we have a preference for right-handedness or left-handedness. We may use each hand equally well, but when a ball is thrown at us by surprise, we will reach to catch it with our preferred hand. Jung's type theory argues that no preferences are better than others. Differences are to be understood, celebrated, and appreciated.

Discussion Consideration

Personality has been defined as a set of relatively stable traits. Do students think their personality is set and fixed, or can it change? Ask them for examples of changes in their own personality they have observed.

During the 1940s, a mother-daughter team became fascinated with individual differences among people and with the work of Carl Jung. Katharine Briggs and her daughter, Isabel Briggs Myers, developed the Myers-Briggs Type Indicator to put Jung's type theory into practical use. The MBTI is used extensively in organizations as a basis for understanding individual differences. More than twenty million people completed the instrument in 1991.[40] The MBTI has been used in career counseling, team building, conflict management, and understanding management styles.[41]

The Preferences

There are four basic preferences in type theory, and two possible choices for each of the four preferences. Table 3.1 shows these preferences. The combination of these preferences makes up an individual's psychological type.

extraversion

A preference indicating that an individual is energized by interaction with other people.

introversion

A preference indicating that an individual is energized by time alone.

EXTRAVERSION/INTROVERSION The **extraversion/introversion** preference represents where you get your energy. The extravert (E) is energized by interaction with other people. The introvert (I) is energized by time alone. Extraverts typically have a wide social network, whereas introverts have a more narrow range of relationships. As articulated by Jung, this preference has nothing to do with social skills. Many introverts have excellent social skills but prefer the internal world of ideas, thoughts, and concepts. Extraverts represent approximately 70 percent of the U.S. population.[42] Our culture rewards extraversion and nurtures it. Jung contended that the extraversion/introversion preference reflects the most important distinction between individuals.

In work settings, extraverts prefer variety, and they do not mind the interruptions of the phone or visits from coworkers. They communicate freely but may say things that they regret later. Introverts prefer quiet for concentration, and they like to think things through in private. They do not mind working on a project for a long time and are careful with details. Introverts dislike telephone interruptions, and they may have trouble recalling names and faces.

TABLE 3.1

Type Theory Preferences and Descriptions

EXTRAVERSION	INTROVERSION
Outgoing	Quiet
Publicly expressive	Reserved
Interacting	Concentrating
Speaks, then thinks	Thinks, then speaks
Gregarious	Reflective
SENSING	**INTUITING**
Practical	General
Specific	Abstract
Feet on the ground	Head in the clouds
Details	Possibilities
Concrete	Theoretical
THINKING	**FEELING**
Analytical	Subjective
Clarity	Harmony
Head	Heart
Justice	Mercy
Rules	Circumstances
JUDGING	**PERCEIVING**
Structured	Flexible
Time oriented	Open ended
Decisive	Exploring
Makes lists/uses them	Makes lists/loses them
Organized	Spontaneous

SOURCE: Adapted from O. Kroeger and J. Thuesen, *Typewatching Training Workshop* (Fairfax, VA: Otto Kroeger Associates, 1981).

SENSING/INTUITING The **sensing/intuiting** preference represents perception or how we prefer to gather information. In essence this preference reflects what we pay attention to. The sensor (S) pays attention to information gathered through the five senses and to what actually exists. The intuitor (N) pays attention to a "sixth sense" and to what could be rather than to what actually exists.[43] Approximately 70 percent of people in the United States are sensors.[44]

At work, sensors prefer specific answers to questions and can become frustrated with vague instructions. They like jobs that yield tangible results, and they enjoy using established skills more than learning new ones. Intuitors like solving new problems and are impatient with routine details. They enjoy learning new skills more than actually using them. Intuitors tend to think about several things at once, and they may be seen by others as absentminded. They like figuring out how things work just for the fun of it.

sensing

Gathering information through the five senses.

intuiting

Gathering information through "sixth sense" and focusing on what could be rather than what actually exists.

THINKING/FEELING The **thinking/feeling** preference represents the way we prefer to make decisions. The thinker (T) makes decisions in a logical, objective fashion, whereas the feeler (F) makes decisions in a personal, value-oriented way. The general U.S. population is divided 50/50 on the thinking/feeling preference, but it is interesting that two-thirds of all males are thinkers, whereas two-thirds of all females are feelers. It is the one preference in type theory that has a strong gender difference. Thinkers tend to analyze decisions, whereas feelers sympathize. Thinkers try to be impersonal, whereas feelers base their decisions on how the outcome will affect the people involved.

In work settings, thinkers do not show much emotion, and they may become uncomfortable with people who do. They respond more readily to other people's thoughts. They are firm minded and like putting things into a logical framework. Feelers, in contrast, are more comfortable with emotion in the workplace. They enjoy pleasing people and need a lot of praise and encouragement.

thinking

Making decisions in a logical, objective fashion.

feeling

Making decisions in a personal, value-oriented way.

JUDGING/PERCEIVING The **judging/perceiving** preference reflects one's orientation to the outer world. The judger (J) loves closure. Judgers prefer to lead a planned, organized life and like making decisions. The perceiver (P), in contrast, prefers a more flexible and spontaneous life and wants to keep options open. Imagine a J and a P going out for dinner. The J asks the P to choose a restaurant, and the P suggests ten alternatives. The J just wants to decide and get on with it, whereas the P wants to explore all the options.

For judgers in all arenas of life, and especially at work, there is a right and a wrong way to do everything. They love getting things accomplished and delight in marking off the completed items on their calendars. Perceivers tend to adopt a wait-and-see attitude and to collect new information rather than draw conclusions. Perceivers are curious and welcome new information. They may start too many projects and not finish them.

judging

Preferring closure and completion in making decisions.

perceiving

Preferring to explore many alternatives and flexibility.

Discussion Consideration

Ask the class if students from cultures that are perceived as extraverted or introverted should adapt to the cultures they are visiting. What about class participation? Is it fair to grade students on class participation when students are from cultures that are not accustomed to talking in class? If the students think that exceptions should be made for members of introverted cultures, ask them if exceptions should be made for introverted students in general, regardless of cultural background.

The Sixteen Types

The preferences combine to form sixteen distinct types, as shown in Table 3.2. For example, let's examine ESTJ. This type is extraverted, sensing, thinking, and judging. ESTJs see the world as it is (S); make decisions objectively (T); and like structure, schedules, and order (J). Combining these qualities with their preference for interacting with others makes them natural managers. ESTJs are seen by others as dependable, practical, and able to get any job done. They are conscious of the chain of command and see work as a series of goals to be reached by following rules and regulations. They may have little tolerance for disorganization and have a high need for control. Research results from the *MBTI Atlas* show that most of the 7,463 managers studied were ESTJs.[45]

TABLE 3.2

Characteristics Frequently Associated with Each Type

ISTJ	ISFJ	INFJ	INTJ
"Doing what should be done" Organizer, compulsive, private, trustworthy, rules and regulations, practical	"A high sense of duty" Amiable, works behind the scenes, ready to sacrifice, accountable, prefers "doing"	"An inspiration to others" Reflective/introspective, quietly caring, creative, linguistically gifted, psychic	"Everything has room for improvement" Theory based, skeptical, "my way," high need for competency, sees world as a chessboard
Most responsible	Most loyal	Most contemplative	Most independent
ISTP	**ISFP**	**INFP**	**INTP**
"Ready to try anything once" Very observant, cool and aloof, hands-on practicality, unpretentious, ready for what happens.	"Sees much but shares little" Warm and sensitive, unassuming, short-range planner, good team member, in touch with self and nature	"Performing noble service to aid society" Strict personal values, seeks inner order/peace, creative, nondirective, reserved	"A love of problem solving" Challenges others to think, absentminded professor, competency needs, socially cautious
Most pragmatic	Most artistic	Most idealistic	Most conceptual
ESTP	**ESFP**	**ENFP**	**ENTP**
"The ultimate realist" Unconventional approach, fun, gregarious, lives for here and now, good at problem solving	"You only go around once in life" Sociable, spontaneous, loves surprises, cuts red tape, juggles multiple projects/events, quip master	"Giving life an extra squeeze" People oriented, creative, seeks harmony, life of party, more starts than finishes	"One exciting challenge after another" Argues both sides of a point to learn, brinksmanship, tests the limits, enthusiastic, new ideas
Most spontaneous	Most generous	Most optimistic	Most inventive
ESTJ	**ESFJ**	**ENFJ**	**ENTJ**
"Life's administrators" Order and structure, sociable, opinionated, results driven, producer, traditional	"Hosts and hostesses of the world" Gracious, good interpersonal skills, thoughtful, appropriate, eager to please	"Smooth-talking persuaders" Charismatic, compassionate, possibilities for people, ignores the unpleasant, idealistic	"Life's natural leaders" Visionary, gregarious, argumentative, systems planner, takes charge, low tolerance for incompetence
Most hard charging	Most harmonizing	Most persuasive	Most commanding

NOTE: I = introvert; E = extravert; S = sensor; N = intuitor; T = thinker; F = feeler; J = judger; and P = perceiver.

SOURCE: Reproduced by special permission of the publisher, Consulting Psychologists Press, Inc., Palo Alto, CA 94303, from *Report Form for the Myers-Briggs Type Indicator* by Isabel Briggs Myers.

There are no good and bad types, and each type has its own strengths and weaknesses. There is a growing volume of research on type theory. The MBTI has been found to have good reliability and validity as a measurement instrument for identifying type.[46,47] Type has been found to be related to learning style, teaching style, choice of occupation, decision-making style, and management style.

Recent studies have begun to focus on the relationship between type and specific managerial behaviors. The introvert (I) and the feeler (F), for example, have been shown to be more effective at participative management than their counterparts, the extravert and the thinker.[48] Companies like AT&T, Exxon, and Honeywell use the MBTI in their management development programs to help

ORGANIZATIONAL REALITY

"I'm Okay, You're Really Weird"

Companies like Hewlett-Packard and Armstrong World Industries often find that working in teams poses challenges for many employees. Stereotypes and perceptual barriers lead team members to point fingers and claim that others are "weird." Many companies use the Myers-Briggs Type Indicator to build a trusting, collaborative environment that emphasizes the value of different type combinations. When Hewlett-Packard's North American distribution organization created a team to implement new software, it invested time up front to do the preparatory work to head off the stereotyping. Initially team members felt it was a waste of time, and that the team was spinning its wheels. They later realized that "it wasn't like losing days—it was like gaining weeks" in terms of productivity. The MBTI helps team members learn to increase their tolerance for others' different strokes.

Armstong World Industries' information services group switched from a hierarchical structure to self-directed work teams, and they used the MBTI as a tool for the change. The team found that a majority of its members were introverts—good at working long hours with a computer, but less skilled at helping users with their problems. The Myers-Briggs raised the team's consciousness about the importance of communication skills to complement technical expertise.

For Hewlett-Packard and Armstrong, the Myers-Briggs was a turning point. It ignited the team when members realized that diversity and differences are what make teams successful in the first place. ■

SOURCE: C. Hildebrand, "I'm Okay, You're Really Weird," *CIO* (October 1, 1995): 86–96.

employees understand the different viewpoints of others in the organization. The MBTI can be used for team building, as seen in the Organizational Reality feature.

Now that you understand the theory behind the MBTI, you can use Challenge 3.2 to speculate about your own type. Before you can understand others, you must understand yourself.

Type theory is valued by managers for its simplicity and accuracy in depicting personalities. It is a useful tool for helping managers develop interpersonal skills. Type theory is also used by managers to build teams that capitalize on individuals' strengths and to help individual team members appreciate differences.

It should be recognized that there is the potential for individuals to misuse the information from the MBTI in organizational settings. Some inappropriate uses include labeling one another, providing a convenient excuse that they simply can't work with someone else, and avoiding responsibility for their own personal development with respect to working with others and becoming more flexible. One's type is not an excuse for inappropriate behavior.

We turn now to another psychological process that forms the basis for individual differences. Perception shapes the way we view the world, and it varies greatly among individuals.

Points to Emphasize

The MBTI does not make value judgements about right or wrong, correct or incorrect, or strengths and weaknesses. Rather, it measures preferences. As such, each style has its own advantages and disadvantages. There may be situations where an individual has to work against their personal preference in order to be successful. For instance, someone who prefers flexibility may have to set deadlines to force a structure on themselves in order to meet deadlines.

Social Perception

■ Perception involves the way we view the world around us. It adds meaning to information gathered via the five senses of touch, smell, hearing, vision, and taste. Perception is the primary vehicle through which we come to understand ourselves and our surroundings. **Social perception** is the process of interpreting information about another person. Virtually all management activities rely

social perception

The process of interpreting information about another person.

CHALLENGE

■ 3.2

Guess Your Myers-Briggs Type

Review the section on Jungian theory and the MBTI. You have probably begun to evaluate your own type while reading the section. Now you can formulate an idea of your type.
Circle one:

Are you	an Extravert	or	an Introvert?
	a Sensor	or	an Intuitor?
	a Feeler	or	a Thinker?
	a Judger	or	a Perceiver?

Place the letters corresponding to your guesses on the following line:

Your type is: __ __ __ __

Alternate Example
Social psychologists have identified implicit personality theories and person schemas as powerful cognitive structures that may influence our perception of others. As implicit personality theory includes assumptions we make about the relationship between two or more personality traits. For instance, if a person is humorous, we may also assume they are intelligent even though we have no evidence of their intelligence.

on perception. In appraising performance, managers use their perceptions of an employee's behavior as a basis for the evaluation.

One work situation that highlights the importance of perception is the selection interview. The consequences of a bad match between an individual and the organization are devastating for both parties, so it is essential that the data gathered be accurate. Typical first interviews are brief, and the candidate is usually one of many seen by an interviewer during a day. How long does it take for the interviewer to reach a decision about a candidate? In the first four to five minutes, the interviewer has often made an accept or reject decision based on his or her perception of the candidate.[49]

Perception is also culturally determined. Based on our cultural backgrounds, we tend to perceive things in certain ways. Read the following sentence:

> Finished files are the result of years of scientific study combined with the experience of years.

Now quickly count the number of *F*s in the sentence. Individuals for whom English is their second language see all six *F*s. Most native English speakers report that there are three *F*s. Because of cultural conditioning, *of* is not an important word and is ignored.[50] Culture affects our interpretation of the data we gather, as well as the way we add meaning to it.

Valuing diversity, including cultural diversity, has been recognized as the key to international competitiveness.[51] This challenge and others make social perception skills essential to managerial success.

Three major categories of factors influence our perception of another person: characteristics of ourselves, as perceivers; characteristics of the target person we are perceiving; and characteristics of the situation in which the interaction takes place. Figure 3.2 shows a model of social perception.

Characteristics of the Perceiver

Discussion Consideration
Ask students to identify their own biases, stereotypes, and implicit personality theories. How do these affect their perceptions of others?

Several characteristics of the perceiver can affect social perception. One such characteristic is *familiarity* with the target (the person being perceived). When we are familiar with a person, we have multiple observations upon which to base our impression of him or her. If the information we have gathered during these observations is accurate, we may have an accurate perception of the other person. Familiarity does not always mean accuracy, however. Sometimes, when we

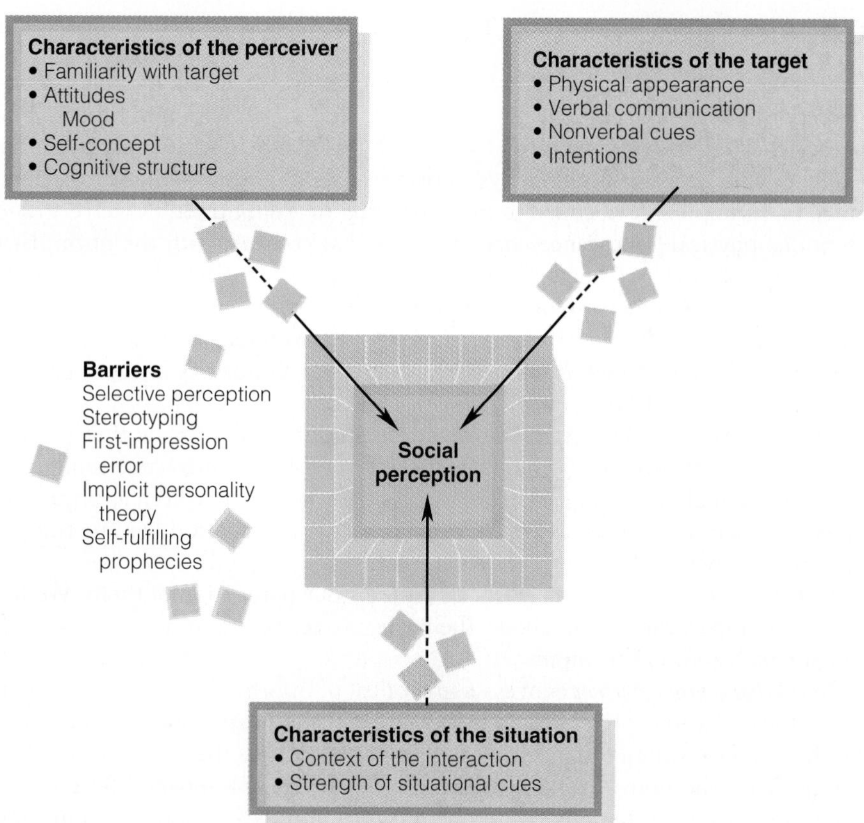

FIGURE 3.2

A Model for Social Perception

know a person well, we tend to screen out information that is inconsistent with what we believe the person is like. This is a particular danger in performance appraisals where the rater is familiar with the person being rated.

The perceiver's *attitudes* also affect social perception. Suppose you are interviewing candidates for a very important position in your organization—a position that requires negotiating contracts with suppliers, most of whom are male. You may feel that women are not capable of holding their own in tough negotiations. This attitude will doubtless affect your perceptions of the female candidates you interview.

Mood can have a strong influence on the way we perceive someone.[52] We think differently when we are happy than we do when we are depressed. In addition, we remember information that is consistent with our mood state better than information that is inconsistent with our mood state. When in a positive mood, we form more positive impressions of others. When in a negative mood, we tend to evaluate others unfavorably.

Another factor that can affect social perception is the perceiver's *self-concept.* An individual with a positive self-concept tends to notice positive attributes in another person. In contrast, a negative self-concept can lead a perceiver to pick out negative traits in another person. Greater understanding of self allows us to have more accurate perceptions of others.

Cognitive structure, an individual's pattern of thinking, also affects social perception. Some people have a tendency to perceive physical traits, such as height, weight, and appearance, more readily. Others tend to focus more on central traits, or personality dispositions. Cognitive complexity allows a person to perceive multiple characteristics of another person rather than attending to just a few traits.

Characteristics of the Target

Characteristics of the target, who is the person being perceived, influence social perception. *Physical appearance* plays a big role in our perception of others. The perceiver will notice the target's physical features like height, weight, estimated age, race, and gender. Clothing says a great deal about a person. Blue pin-striped suits, for example, are decoded to mean banking or Wall Street. Perceivers tend to notice physical appearance characteristics that contrast with the norm, that are intense, or that are new or unusual.[53] A loud person, one who dresses outlandishly, a very tall person, or a hyperactive child will be noticed because he or she provides a contrast to what is commonly encountered. In addition, people who are novel can attract attention. Newcomers or minorities in the organization are examples of novel individuals.

Discussion Consideration
Many individuals with disabilities are in the workforce now. What are some of the perceptions, stereotypes and stigmas that these individuals have to overcome in their work?

Physical attractiveness often colors our entire impression of another person. Interviewers rate attractive candidates more favorably, and attractive candidates are awarded higher starting salaries.[54,55] People who are perceived as physically attractive face stereotypes as well. We will discuss these and other stereotypes later in this chapter.

Discussion Consideration
What are some specific steps that could be taken by organizations trying to increase diversity in the workplace? For example, recruiters could consciously avoid first impressions of appearance.

Verbal communication from targets also affects our perception of them. We listen to the topics they speak about, their voice tone, and their accent and make judgments based on this input.

Nonverbal communication conveys a great deal of information about the target. Eye contact, facial expressions, body movements, and posture all are deciphered by the perceiver in an attempt to form an impression of the target. It is interesting that some nonverbal signals mean very different things in different cultures. The "okay" sign in the United States (forming a circle with the thumb and forefinger) is an insult in South America. Facial expressions, however, seem to have universal meanings. Individuals from different cultures are able to recognize and decipher expressions the same way.[56]

Alternate Example
Recently, Barry and Bateman have suggested that diversity programs may be a "social trap" for organizations. A social trap is a situation where multiple but conflicting reward structures impinge upon individual and group decision behavior in social settings. According to Barry and Bateman, diversity issues often require organization members to make behavioral choices that place self-interest and the interest of others in conflict. Diversity issues also challenge managers to manage inconsistencies between short-term and long-term consequences of the choices they make and compel choice making without the benefit of explicit knowledge of the conflicts of interest and the consequences of their choices. Finally, diversity issues typically involve social issues that have substantial societal implications. SOURCE: B. Barry and T. S. Bateman, "A Social Trap Analysis of the Management of Diversity," *Academy of Management Review*, 1996, Vol. 21, No. 3, 757-790.

The *intentions* of the target are inferred by the perceiver, who observes the target's behavior. We may see our boss appear in our office doorway and think, "Oh no! She's going to give me more work to do." Or we may perceive that her intention is to congratulate us on a recent success. In any case, the perceiver's interpretation of the target's intentions affects the way the perceiver views the target.

Characteristics of the Situation

The situation in which the interaction between the perceiver and the target takes place has an influence on the perceiver's impression of the target. The *social context* of the interaction is a major influence. Meeting a professor in his or her office affects your impression in a certain way that may contrast with the impression you would form had you met the professor in a local restaurant. In Japan, social context is very important. Business conversations after working hours or at lunch are taboo. If you try to talk business during these times, you may be perceived as rude.[57]

The *strength of situational cues* also affects social perception. As we discussed earlier in the chapter, some situations provide strong cues as to appropriate behavior. In these situations, we assume that the individual's behavior can be accounted for by the situation, and that it may not reflect the individual's disposition. This is the **discounting principle** in social perception.[58] For example, you may encounter an automobile salesperson who has a warm and personable manner, asks about your work and hobbies, and seems genuinely interested in your taste in cars. Can you assume that this behavior reflects the salesperson's personality? You probably cannot, because of the influence of the situation. This person is trying to sell you a car, and in this particular situation he or she probably treats all customers in this manner.

discounting principle
The assumption that an individual's behavior is accounted for by the situation.

You can see that characteristics of the perceiver, the target, and the situation all affect social perception. It would be wonderful if all of us had accurate social perception skills. Unfortunately, barriers often prevent us from perceiving another person accurately.

Barriers to Social Perception

Several factors lead us to form inaccurate impressions of others. Five of these barriers to social perception are selective perception, stereotyping, first-impression error, implicit personality theories, and self-fulfilling prophecies.

We receive a vast amount of information. **Selective perception** is our tendency to choose information that supports our viewpoints. Individuals often ignore information that makes them feel uncomfortable or threatens their viewpoints. Suppose, for example, that a sales manager is evaluating the performance of his employees. One employee does not get along well with colleagues and rarely completes sales reports on time. This employee, however, generates the most new sales contracts in the office. The sales manager may ignore the negative information, choosing to evaluate the salesperson only on contracts generated. The manager is exercising selective perception.

selective perception

The process of selecting information that supports our individual viewpoints while discounting information that threatens our viewpoints.

A **stereotype** is a generalization about a group of people. Stereotypes reduce information about other people to a workable level, and they are efficient for compiling and using information. Stereotypes can be accurate, and when they are accurate, they can be useful perceptual guidelines. Most of the time, however, stereotypes are inaccurate. They harm individuals when inaccurate impressions of them are inferred and are never tested or changed.[59] Thus, stereotypes may not be effective if they are too rigid or based on false information.

stereotype

A generalization about a group of people.

Alternate Example

Part of the reason there was such shock value connected to the Branch Davidian episode in Texas was because it defied the traditional situational cues for what is assumed to exist in Christian-run groups. SOURCE: "Children of the Cult," *Newsweek,* 17 May 1993, 48.

Suppose that a white male manager passes the coffee area and notices two African-American men talking there. He becomes irritated at them for wasting time. Later in the day, he sees two women talking in the coffee area. He thinks they should do their gossiping on their own time. The next morning, the same manager sees two white men talking in the coffee area. He thinks nothing of it; he is sure they are discussing business. The manager may hold a stereotype that women and minorities do not work hard unless closely supervised.

In multicultural work teams, members often stereotype foreign coworkers rather than getting to know them before forming an impression. Team members from less developed countries are often assumed to have less knowledge simply because their homeland is economically or technologically less developed.[60] Stereotypes like these can deflate the productivity of the work team, as well as create low morale.

Alternate Example

A common problem in social perception is the false consensus bias This refers to our belief that others share our attitudes and behaviors.

Attractiveness is a powerful stereotype. We assume that attractive individuals are also warm, kind, sensitive, poised, sociable, outgoing, independent, and strong. Are attractive people really like this? Certainly all of them are not. A recent study of romantic relationships showed that most attractive individuals do not fit the stereotype, except for possessing good social skills and being popular.[61]

Some individuals may seem to us to fit the stereotype of attractiveness because our behavior elicits behavior that confirms the stereotype from them. Consider, for example, a situation in which you meet an attractive fellow student. Chances are that you respond positively to this person, because you assume he or she is warm, sociable, and so on. Even though the person may not possess these traits, your positive response may bring out these behaviors in the person. The interaction between the two of you may be channeled such that the stereotype confirms itself.[62]

First impressions are lasting impressions, so the saying goes. Individuals place a good deal of importance on first impressions, and for good reason. We tend to remember what we perceive first about a person, and sometimes we are quite reluctant to change our initial impressions.[63] **First-impression error** means

first-impression error

The tendency to form lasting opinions about an individual based on initial perceptions.

that we observe a very brief bit of a person's behavior in our first encounter and infer that this behavior reflects what the person is really like. Primacy effects can be particularly dangerous in interviews, given that we form first impressions quickly and that these impressions may be the basis for long-term employment relationships.

implicit personality theory

Opinions formed about other people that are based on our own mini-theories about how people behave.

Implicit personality theories can also lead to inaccurate perceptions.[64] We tend to have our own mini-theories about how people look and behave. These theories help us organize our perceptions and take shortcuts instead of integrating new information all the time. We are *cognitive misers*. Because the world is complex and ambiguous and we have a limited mental capacity, we try to expend the least amount of effort possible in attempting to make sense of the world.[65] We group traits and appearances into clusters that seem to go together. For example, you may believe that introverted people are also worriers and intellectuals, or that fashionable dressers are also up on current events and like modern music. These implicit personality theories are barriers, because they limit our ability to take in new information when it is available.

self-fulfilling prophecy

The situation in which our expectations about people affect our interaction with them in such a way that our expectations are fulfilled.

Discussion Consideration

How could a manager use the pygmalion effect to improve the effectiveness of an organizational team?

Self-fulfilling prophecies are also barriers to social perception. Sometimes our expectations affect the way we interact with others such that we get what we wish for. Self-fulfilling prophecy is also known as the Pygmalion effect, named for the sculptor in Greek mythology who carved a statue of a woman that came to life when he prayed for this wish and it was granted.

Early studies of self-fulfilling prophecy were conducted in elementary school classrooms. Teachers were given bogus information that some of their pupils had high intellectual potential. These pupils were chosen randomly; there were really no differences among the students. Eight months later, the "gifted" pupils scored significantly higher on an IQ test. The teachers' expectations had elicited growth from these students, and teachers had given them tougher assignments and more feedback on their performance.[66] Self-fulfilling prophecy has been studied in many settings, including at sea. The Scientific Foundation feature explains how the Israeli Defense Forces used it to combat seasickness.

The Pygmalion effect has been observed in work organizations as well. A manager's expectations of an individual affect both the manager's behavior toward the individual and the individual's response.[67] For example, suppose you have an initial impression of an employee as having the potential to move up within the organization. Chances are you will spend a great deal of time coaching and counseling the employee, providing challenging assignments, and grooming the individual for success.

Managers can harness the power of the Pygmalion effect to improve productivity in the organization. It appears that high expectations of individuals come true. Can a manager extend these high expectations to an entire group and have similar positive results? The answer is yes. When a manager expects positive things from a group, the group delivers.[68]

Impression Management

impression management

The process by which individuals try to control the impression others have of them.

Most people want to make favorable impressions on others. This is particularly true in organizations, where individuals compete for jobs, favorable performance evaluations, and salary increases. The process by which individuals try to control the impressions others have of them is called **impression management.** Individuals use several techniques to control others' impressions of them.[69]

Some impression management techniques are self-enhancing. These techniques focus on enhancing others' impressions of the person using the technique. Name-dropping, which involves mentioning an association with important people in the hopes of improving one's image, is often used. Managing one's appearance is another technique for impression management. Individuals dress carefully for interviews because they want to "look the part" in order to get the

SCIENTIFIC FOUNDATION

Seasickness as Self-Fulfilling Prophecy

Virtually no one is immune to seasickness, especially those in the Navy who must perform their jobs on rough seas. While there are drugs for the problem, some of the side effects are the very symptoms that the drugs are intended to prevent: drowsiness, blurred vision, and dryness of the mouth. Naval and aviation medicine continue to try to solve the challenge of motion sickness.

The authors of one study devised an experiment to see whether self-fulfilling prophecy could help. They assigned twenty-five naval cadets in the Israeli Defense Forces to experimental and control conditions. Before their first cruise, the cadets in the experimental group were told that they were unlikely to experience seasickness and that, if they did, it was unlikely to affect their performance at sea. Cadets in the control group were told about research on seasickness and its prevention. At the end of the five-day cruise, cadets in the experimental group reported less seasickness and were rated as better performers by their training officers. These cadets also had higher self-efficacy; that is, they believed they could perform well at sea despite seasickness.

The pills and patches that physicians often prescribe for seasickness are unpleasant to the point of deterring their use, are of short-term effectiveness, and have undesirable side effects. Self-fulfilling prophecy has none of these problems, and it appears to work in combating seasickness.

SOURCE: D. Eden and Y. Zuk, "Seasickness as a Self-Fulfilling Prophecy: Raising Self-Efficacy to Boost Performance at Sea," *Journal of Applied Psychology* 80 (1995): 628–635.

job. Self-descriptions, or statements about one's characteristics, are used to manage impressions as well.

Another group of impression management techniques are other-enhancing. The aim of these techniques is to focus on the individual whose impression is to be managed. Flattery is a common other-enhancing technique whereby compliments are given to an individual in order to win his or her approval. Favors are also used to gain the approval of others. Agreement with someone's opinion is a technique often used to gain a positive impression.

In situations like job interviews, good social perceptions skills are essential. Candidates often try to control the interviewer's impression of them using impression management techniques—and many are successful in doing so.

Some employees may engage in impression management to intentionally look bad at work. Methods for creating a poor impression include decreasing performance, not working to one's potential, skipping work, displaying a bad attitude, or broadcasting one's limitations. Why would someone try to look bad to others? Sometimes employees want to avoid additional work or a particular task. They may try to look bad in hopes of being laid off. Or they may create poor impressions in order to get attention.[70]

Are impression management techniques effective? Most of the research has focused on employment interviews, and the results indicate that candidates who engage in impression management by self-promoting performed better in interviews, were more likely to obtain site visits with potential employers, and were more likely to get hired.[71,72] In addition, employees who engage in impression management are rated more favorably in performance appraisals than those who do not.[73]

Impression management seems to have an impact on others' impressions. As long as the impressions conveyed are accurate, this process can be a beneficial one in organizations. If the impressions are found to be false, however, a strongly negative overall impression may result. Furthermore, excessive impression management can lead to the perception that the user is manipulative or insincere.[74]

We have discussed the influences on social perception, the potential barriers to perceiving another person, and impression management. Another psychological process that managers should understand is attribution.

Attribution in Organizations

attribution theory

A theory that explains how individuals pinpoint the causes of the behavior of themselves and others.

As human beings, we are innately curious. We are not content merely to observe the behavior of others; rather, we want to know *why* they behave the way they do. We also seek to understand and explain our own behavior. **Attribution theory** explains how we pinpoint the causes of our own behavior and that of other people.

The attributions, or inferred causes, we provide for behavior have important implications in organizations. In explaining the causes of employee performance, good or bad, we are asked to explain the behavior that was the basis for the performance. We explore Harold Kelley's attribution model, which is based on the pioneering work of Fritz Heider, the founder of attribution theory.[75]

Alternate Example
An interesting finding in light of attribution theory is that when writing a resume, women and minorities tend to think in terms of specific jobs held, whereas white males think in terms of tasks and successes. SOURCE: L. E. Zeff and B. Fregren, "Attribution Theory: Helping Woman and Minorities Get Promoted," *Association of Management Proceedings 10* (1992): 12-17.

Internal and External Attributions

Attributions can be made to an internal source of responsibility (something within the individual's control) or an external source (something outside the individual's control). Suppose you perform well on an exam in this course. You might say you aced the test because you are smart, or because you studied hard. If you attribute your success to ability or effort, you are citing an internal source.

Alternatively, you might cite external sources for your performance. You might say it was an easy test (you would attribute your success to degree of task difficulty) or that you had good luck. In this case, you are attributing your performance to sources beyond your control, or external attributions. You can see that internal attributions include such causes as ability and effort, whereas external attributions include causes like task difficulty or luck.

Attribution patterns differ among individuals.[76] Achievement-oriented individuals attribute their success to ability and their failures to lack of effort, both internal causes. Failure-oriented individuals attribute their failures to lack of ability, and they may develop feelings of incompetence as a result of their attributional pattern. Evidence indicates that this attributional pattern also leads to depression.[77]

Kelley's Attribution Theory

consensus

An informational cue indicating the extent to which peers in the same situation behave in a similar fashion.

distinctiveness

An informational cue indicating the degree to which an individual behaves the same way in other situations.

consistency

An informational cue indicating the frequency of behavior over time.

Attribution is a perceptual process. The way we explain success or failure—whether our own or that of another person—affects our feelings and our subsequent behavior. Harold Kelley extended attribution theory by trying to identify the antecedents of internal and external attributions. Kelley proposed that individuals make attributions based on information gathered in the form of three informational cues: consensus, distinctiveness, and consistency.[78,79] We observe an individual's behavior and then seek out information in the form of these three cues. **Consensus** is the extent to which peers in the same situation behave the same way. **Distinctiveness** is the degree to which the person behaves the same way in other situations. **Consistency** refers to the frequency of a particular behavior over time.

We form attributions based on whether these cues are low or high. Figure 3.3 shows how the combination of these cues helps us form internal or external attributions. Suppose you have received several complaints from customers regarding

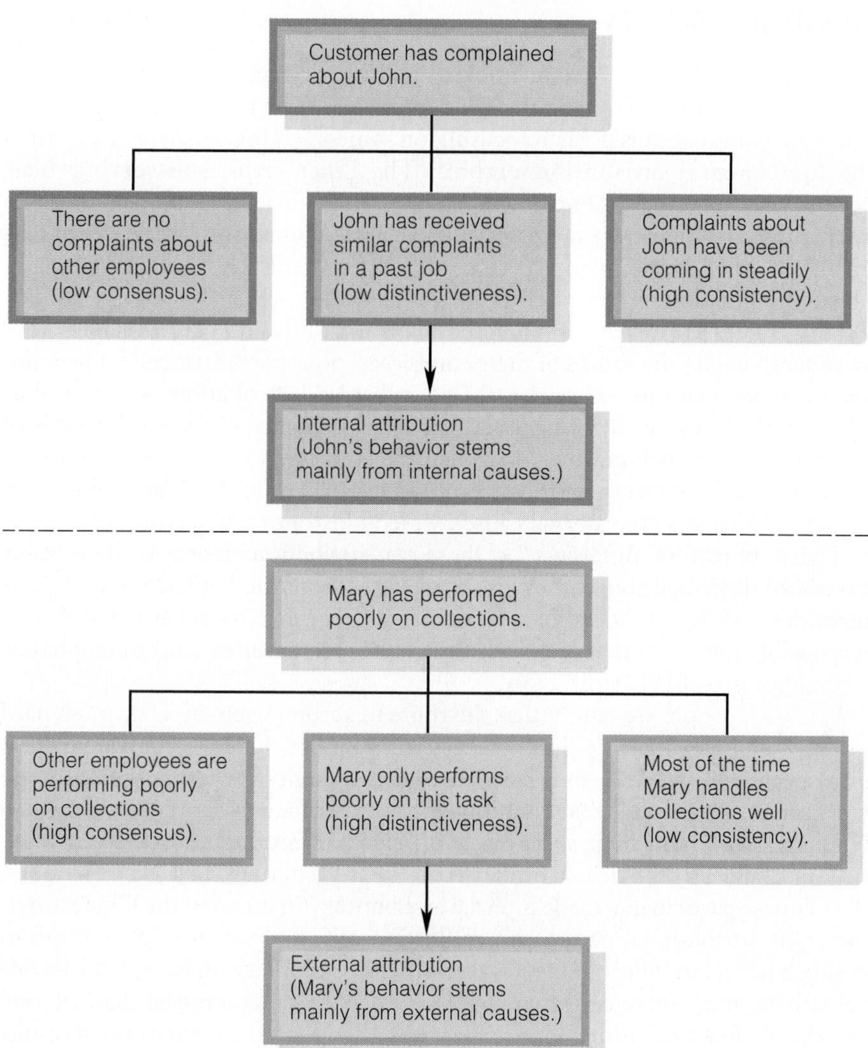

■ **FIGURE 3.3**
Informational Cues and Attributions

one of your customer service representatives, John. You have not received complaints about your other service representatives (low consensus). Upon reviewing John's records, you note that he also received customer complaints during his previous job as a sales clerk (low distinctiveness). The complaints have been coming in steadily for about three months (high consistency). In this case, you would most likely make an internal attribution and conclude that the complaints must stem from John's behavior. The combination of low consensus, low distinctiveness, and high consistency leads to internal attributions.

Other combinations of these cues, however, produce external attributions. High consensus, high distinctiveness, and low consistency, for example, produce external attributions. Suppose one of your employees, Mary, is performing poorly on collecting overdue accounts. You find that the behavior is widespread within your work team (high consensus), that Mary is only performing poorly on this aspect of the job (high distinctiveness), and that most of the time she handles this aspect of the job well (low consistency). You will probably decide that something about the work situation caused the poor performance—perhaps work overload or an unfair deadline.

Consensus, distinctiveness, and consistency are the cues used to determine whether the cause of behavior is internal or external. The process of determining the cause of a behavior may not be simple and clear-cut, however, because of some biases that occur in forming attributions.

Attributional Biases

fundamental attribution error

The tendency to make attributions to internal causes when focusing on someone else's behavior.

self-serving bias

The tendency to attribute one's own successes to internal causes and one's failures to external causes.

Discussion Consideration
How might the fundamental attribution error impact the performance appraisal process?

The attribution process may be affected by two very common errors: the fundamental attribution error and the self-serving bias. The tendency to make attributions to internal causes when focusing on someone else's behavior is known as the **fundamental attribution error.**[80] The other error, **self-serving bias,** occurs when focusing on one's own behavior. Individuals tend to make internal attributions for their own successes and external attributions for their own failures.[81] In other words, when we succeed, we take credit for it; when we fail, we blame the situation or other people.

Both of these biases were illustrated in a study of health care managers who were asked to cite the causes of their employees' poor performance.[82] The managers claimed that internal causes (their employees' lack of effort or lack of ability) were the basis for their employees' poor performance. This is an example of the fundamental attribution error. When the employees were asked to pinpoint the cause of their own performance problems, they blamed a lack of support from the managers (an external cause), which illustrates self-serving bias.

There are cultural differences in these two attribution errors. As these biases have been described above, they apply to people from the United States. In cultures that are more fatalistic, as is India, people tend to believe that fate is responsible for much that happens. People in such cultures tend to emphasize external causes of behavior.[83]

In China, people are taught that the route to accomplishment is through hard work. When faced with either a success or a failure, Chinese individuals first introspect about whether they have tried hard enough or whether their attitude was correct. In a study of attributions for performance in sports, Chinese athletes attributed both their successes and failures to internal causes. Even when the cause of poor athletic performance was clearly external, such as bad weather, the Chinese participants made internal attributions. In terms of the Chinese culture, this attributional pattern is a reflection of moral values that are used to evaluate behavior. The socialistic value of selfless morality dictates that individual striving must serve collective interests. Mao Ze-dong stressed that external causes only function through internal causes; therefore, the main cause of results lies within oneself. Chinese are taught this from childhood, and form a corresponding attributional tendency. In analyzing a cause, they first look to their own effort.[84]

The way individuals interpret the events around them has a strong influence on their behavior. People try to understand the causes of behavior in order to gain predictability and control over future behavior. Managers use attributions in all aspects of their jobs. In evaluating performance and rewarding employees, managers must determine the causes of behavior and a perceived source of responsibility. Attribution theory can explain how performance evaluation judgments can lead to differential rewards. A supervisor attributing an employee's good performance to internal causes, such as effort or ability, may give a larger raise than a supervisor attributing the good performance to external causes, such as help from others or good training. Managers are often called upon to explain their own actions as well, and in doing so they make attributions about the causes of their own behavior. We continue our discussion of attributions in Chapter 6 in terms of how attributions are used in managing performance.

Managerial Implications: Using Personality, Perception, and Attribution at Work

■ Managers need to know as much as possible about individual differences in order to understand themselves and those with whom they work. An understanding of personality characteristics can help a manager appreciate differences in employees. With the increased diversity of the workforce, tools like the MBTI can be used to help employees see someone else's point of view. These tools also can help make communication among diverse employees more effective.

Managers use social perception constantly on the job. Knowledge of the forces that affect perception and the barriers to accuracy can help the manager form more accurate impressions of others.

Determining the causes of job performance is a major task for the manager, and attribution theory can be used to explain how managers go about determining causality. In addition, knowledge of the fundamental attribution error and self-serving bias can help a manager guard against these biases in the processes of looking for causes of behavior on the job.

In this chapter, we have explored the psychological processes of personality, perception, and attribution as individual differences. In the following chapter, we will continue our discussion of individual differences in terms of attitudes, values and ethics.

CLOSING SPOTLIGHT

Positively Outrageous Service at Southwest Airlines

By encouraging employees to be themselves and to be creative, Southwest Airlines motivates employees to deliver "Positively Outrageous Service" to customers, fellow employees, and anyone affected by the company. The Winning Spirit Award is given each month to employees who demonstrate Positively Outrageous Service. Winning Spirit awardees have demonstrated Positively Outrageous Service in a variety of ways. One customer service agent lent his personal telephone calling card to a man desperately trying to locate his wife, who was stranded at another airport. A group of three customer service agents performed cardiopulmonary resuscitation (CPR) on a customer who collapsed at the ticket counter.

Positively Outrageous Service is a level of service that is unexpected, extraordinary, and delivered at random.[85] Southwest empowers its creative employees to "color outside the lines." If a passenger has an emergency and needs to use a restricted ticket that is only valid for a certain flight, agents are empowered to make exceptions. The company lets employees know that their ideas are valued, and recognizes and rewards them for creative contributions. By encouraging individuals to be themselves, Southwest Airlines continues to reinforce Positively Outrageous Service. ■

Chapter Summary

- Individual differences are factors that make individuals unique. They include personalities, perceptions, skills and abilities, attitudes, values, and ethics.
- The trait theory, psychodynamic theory, humanistic theory, and integrative approach are all personality theories.
- Managers should understand personality because of its effect on behavior. Several characteristics affect behavior in organizations, including locus of control, self-esteem, self-efficacy, self-monitoring, and positive/negative affect.
- Personality has a stronger influence in weak situations, where there are few cues to guide behavior.
- One useful framework for understanding individual differences is type theory, developed by Carl Jung and measured by the Myers-Briggs Type Indicator (MBTI).
- Social perception is the process of interpreting information about another person. It is influenced by characteristics of the perceiver, the target, and the situation.
- Barriers to social perception include selective perception, stereotyping, first-impression error, implicit personality theories, and self-fulfilling prophecies.
- Impression management techniques such as name-dropping, managing one's appearance, self-descriptions, flattery, favors, and agreement are used by individuals to control others' impressions of them.
- Attribution is the process of determining the cause of behavior. It is used extensively by managers, especially in evaluating performance.

Key Terms

individual differences (p. 72)
interactional psychology (p. 72)
personality (p. 73)
trait theory (p. 73)
psychodynamic theory (p. 74)
humanistic theory (p. 74)
integrative approach (p. 74)
locus of control (p. 74)
self-esteem (p. 75)
self-efficacy (p. 75)
self-monitoring (p. 75)
positive affect (p. 77)
negative affect (p. 77)
strong situation (p. 77)
projective test (p. 79)
behavioral measures (p. 79)
self-report questionnaire (p. 79)
Myers-Briggs Type Indicator (MBTI) (p. 79)
extraversion (p. 80)
introversion (p. 80)
sensing (p. 81)
intuiting (p. 81)
thinking (p. 81)
feeling (p. 81)
judging (p. 81)
perceiving (p. 81)
social perception (p. 83)
discounting principle (p. 86)
selective perception (p. 87)
stereotype (p. 87)
first-impression error (p. 87)
implicit personality theory (p. 88)
self-fulfilling prophecy (p. 88)
impression management (p. 88)
attribution theory (p. 90)
consensus (p. 90)
distinctiveness (p. 90)
consistency (p. 90)
fundamental attribution error (p. 92)
self-serving bias (p. 92)

Review Questions

1. What are individual differences, and why should managers understand them?
2. Define *personality*, and describe its origins.
3. Describe four theories of personality and what each contributes to our knowledge of personality.
4. Describe the eight preferences of the Myers-Briggs Type Indicator. How does this instrument measure Carl Jung's ideas?
5. What factors influence social perception? What are the barriers to social perception?
6. What are the three types of informational cues used to make attributions? Describe each one.
7. Describe the errors that affect the attribution process.

Discussion and Communication Questions

1. What contributions can high self-monitors make in organizations? Low self-monitors?
2. How can managers improve their perceptual skills?
3. Which has the strongest impact on personality: heredity or environment?
4. How can managers make more accurate attributions?
5. How can managers encourage self-efficacy in employees?
6. How can self-serving bias and the fundamental attribution error be avoided?
7. *(communication question)* You have been asked to develop a training program for interviewers. An integral part of this training program is focused on helping interviewers develop better social perception skills. Write an outline for this section of the training program. Be sure to address barriers to social perception and ways to avoid these barriers.
8. *(communication question)* Form groups of 4 to 6, then split each group in half. Debate the origins of personality, with one half taking the position that personality is inherited, and the other half taking the position that personality is formed by the environment. Each half should also discuss the implications of their position for managers.

Ethics Questions

1. What are the ethical uses of personality tests? What are the unethical uses?
2. Suppose a manager makes an incorrect attribution for an employee's poor performance (for instance, the manager cites equipment failure), and peers know the employee is at fault. Should they blow the whistle on their colleague?
3. Suppose one of your colleagues wants to eliminate all biases and stereotypes from the hiring process. He suggests that only résumés be used, with no names or other identifying data—only experience and education. What are the ethical consequences of this approach? Would any group be unfairly disadvantaged by this approach?
4. Suppose a manager makes a misattribution of an employee's poor performance. What are the ethical consequences of this?

Experiential Exercises

3.1 MBTI Types and Management Styles

Part I. This questionnaire will help you determine your preferences. For each item, circle either a or b. If you feel both a and b are true, decide which one is more like you, even if it is only slightly more true.

1. I would rather
a. Solve a new and complicated problem.
b. Work on something I have done before.

2. I like to
a. Work alone in a quiet place.
b. Be where the action is.

3. I want a boss who
a. Establishes and applies criteria in decisions.
b. Considers individual needs and makes exceptions.

4. When I work on a project, I
a. Like to finish it and get some closure.
b. Often leave it open for possible changes.

5. When making a decision, the most important considerations are
a. Rational thoughts, ideas, and data.
b. People's feelings and values.

6. On a project, I tend to
a. Think it over and over before deciding how to proceed.
b. Start working on it right away, thinking about it as I go along.

7. When working on a project, I prefer to
a. Maintain as much control as possible.
b. Explore various options.

8. In my work, I prefer to
a. Work on several projects at a time, and learn as much as possible about each one.
b. Have one project that is challenging and keeps me busy.

9. I often
a. Make lists and plans whenever I start something and may hate to seriously alter my plans.
b. Avoid plans and just let things progress as I work on them.

10. When discussing a problem with colleagues, it is easy for me to
a. See "the big picture."
b. Grasp the specifics of the situation.

11. When the phone rings in my office or at home, I usually
a. Consider it an interruption.
b. Do not mind answering it.

12. Which word describes you better?
a. Analytical.
b. Empathetic.

13. When I am working on an assignment, I tend to
a. Work steadily and consistently.
b. Work in bursts of energy with "down time" in between.

14. When I listen to someone talk on a subject, I usually try to
a. Relate it to my own experience and see if it fits.
b. Assess and analyze the message.

15. When I come up with new ideas, I generally
a. "Go for it."
b. Like to contemplate the ideas some more.

16. When working on a project, I prefer to
a. Narrow the scope so it is clearly defined.
b. Broaden the scope to include related aspects.

17. When I read something, I usually
a. Confine my thoughts to what is written there.
b. Read between the lines and relate the words to other ideas.

18. When I have to make a decision in a hurry, I often
a. Feel uncomfortable and wish I had more information.
b. Am able to do so with available data.

19. In a meeting, I tend to
a. Continue formulating my ideas as I talk about them.
b. Only speak out after I have carefully thought the issue through.

20. In work, I prefer spending a great deal of time on issues of
a. Ideas.
b. People.

21. In meetings, I am most often annoyed with people who
a. Come up with many sketchy ideas.
b. Lengthen meetings with many practical details.

22. I am a
a. Morning person.
b. Night owl.

23. What is your style in preparing for a meeting?
a. I am willing to go in and be responsive.
b. I like to be fully prepared and usually sketch an outline of the meeting.

24. In a meeting, I would prefer for people to
a. Display a fuller range of emotions.
b. Be more task oriented.

25. I would rather work for an organization where
a. My job was intellectually stimulating.
b. I was committed to its goals and mission.

26. On weekends, I tend to
a. Plan what I will do.
b. Just see what happens and decide as I go along.

27. I am more
a. Outgoing.
b. Contemplative.

28. I would rather work for a boss who is
a. Full of new ideas.
b. Practical.

In the following, choose the word in each pair that appeals to you more:

29. a. Social.
b. Theoretical.

30. a. Ingenuity.
b. Practicality.

31. a. Organized.
b. Adaptable.

32. a. Active.
b. Concentration.

SCORING KEY

Count one point for each item listed below that you have circled in the inventory.

Score for I	Score for E	Score for S	Score for N
2a	2b	1b	1a
6a	6b	10b	10a
11a	11b	13a	13b
15b	15a	16a	16b
19b	19a	17a	17b
22a	22b	21a	21b
27b	27a	28b	28a
32b	32a	30b	30a
Total			

Circle the one with more points—I or E.

Circle the one with more points—S or N.

Score for T	Score for F	Score for J	Score for P
3a	3b	4a	4b
5a	5b	7a	7b
12a	12b	8b	8a
14b	14a	9a	9b
20a	20b	18b	18a
24b	24a	23b	23a
25a	25b	26a	26b
29b	29a	31a	31b
Total			

Circle the one with more points—T or F.

Circle the one with more points—J or P.

Your score is

I or E ___

S or N ___

T or F ___

J or P ___

Part II. The purpose of this part of the exercise is to give you experience in understanding some of the individual differences that were proposed by Carl Jung and are measured by the MBTI.

Step 1. Your instructor will assign you to a group.

Step 2. Your group is a team of individuals who want to start a business. You are to develop a mission statement and a name for your business.

Step 3. After you have completed Step 2, analyze the decision process that occurred within the group. How did you decide on your company's name and mission?

Step 4. Your instructor will have each group report to the class the name and mission of the company, and then the decision process used. Your instructor will also give you some additional information about the exercise and provide some interesting insights about your management style.

SOURCE: D. Marcic and P. Nutt, "Personality Inventory," in D. Marcic, (ed.), *Organizational Behavior: Experiences and Cases*, 9–6 (St. Paul: West, 1989).

3.2 Stereotypes in Employment Interviews

Step 1. Your instructor will give you a transcript that records an applicant's interview for a job as a laborer. Your task is to memorize as much of the interview as possible.

Step 2. Write down everything you can remember about the job candidate.

Step 3. Your instructor will lead you in a discussion.

SOURCE: Adapted from D. A. Sachau and M. Hussang, "How Interviewers' Stereotypes Influence Memory: An Exercise," *Journal of Management Education*, 16 (1992): 391–396.

CASE

Jeremy Jonston's Job Reference

Upon returning to his office from a meeting, Bill Williams checked his voice mail messages. He was so stunned by one message that he replayed it twice to make sure that he heard it correctly. Kathy Meyers from the midwest office of Consulting Associates International had called, seeking a reference for Jeremy Jonston, an applicant she had interviewed for a managing director's position in their firm. Bill knew that Jeremy, his former boss, would not list him as a reference on his résumé. Williams, like numerous others in the division, had been on Jonston's "list" when Jonston was demoted from his position as division head. Although not in a management capacity, Jeremy was still on the staff— and an irritant to many of his former subordinates.

Everyone knew that Jeremy was unhappy because of his demotion and that he was looking for employment elsewhere. Almost everyone—including Bill—hoped he would find it.

Bill wondered to himself: "Should I return this call? If I do, what do I say? Do I tell lies in the hopes that he'll get the job and get out of here? Or do I tell the truth so that, at least, I have a clear conscience?"

Since Bill had met Kathy at a trade show some years earlier, he decided to return the call. Other than social pleasantries, what follows is essence of their telephone conversation.

Kathy: "Do you know why Mr. Jonston is looking to change jobs?"

Bill: (Thinking to himself, "I don't think I want to say that Jonston was demoted for questionable managerial competence. So I'll finesse this one . . .") "Mr. Jonston was hired with the mandate of obtaining a specific set of objectives for the division. He was probably the appropriate person to help the division achieve those objectives. But he isn't the appropriate person to help the division move beyond achieving those objectives. In the process of achieving those objectives, Jonston assembled a group of capable, talented, and independent individuals. But he didn't know how to manage those people."

Kathy: "What do you mean?"

Bill: "Let me use a metaphor. Managing people is like driving a team of horses. When you have a good team, you hold the reins loosely and they will enthusiastically take you where you want to go. Hold the reins tightly, and they will resist your will. Jonston held the reins tightly."

Kathy: "Mr. Jonston creates a very favorable first impression. When I met him, he seemed to be very smooth in interacting with others. What's your reaction?"

Bill: "Are you familiar with eastern religions?"

Kathy: "Well . . . not real familiar—but a little!"

Bill: "OK, so you probably know something about reincarnation?"

Kathy: "Yes!"

Bill: "I think Jonston probably was a used car salesman in a former life."

Kathy: "Is Mr. Jonston able to make decisions?"

Bill: "Hmm . . . let me tell you a story. Two or three years ago, the microwave in the employee lounge self-destructed. Several employees asked Jonston to replace it—not really expecting that it would be done anytime soon. We even had a betting pool organized on when he would actually make a decision to replace the equipment."

Kathy: "Well . . . did it ever get replaced?"

Bill: "Yes . . . a couple of weeks after his successor took over the job."

Kathy: "What about Mr. Jonston's honesty? Can you rely on him? Can you trust him?"

Bill: " . . . Let me think about how I want to respond to that question . . . I think someone else could give him a stronger recommendation on that than I could."

DISCUSSION QUESTIONS

1. What perceptions have you formed of Jeremy Jonston? Of Bill Williams? How do you think your perceptions would affect the judgments that you might make about Jonston? About Williams?
2. Using the various personality characteristics discussed in this chapter, how would you describe Jeremy Jonston's personality?
3. To what extent are barriers to social perception evident in the conversation between Bill and Kathy? Explain your answer.
4. How would you use attribution theory to explain Jonston's behavior?
5. If you were Kathy Meyers, what recommendation would you make about extending a job offer to Mr. Jonston? Explain your answer.

SOURCE: This case was written by Michael K. McCuddy, Professor of Management, College of Business Administration, Valparaiso University. The names in this case have been disguised.

References

1. W. Zellner, "Southwest," *Business Week*, (February 13, 1995): 68–69.
2. K. Lewin, "Formalization and Progress in Psychology," in D. Cartwright, ed., *Field Theory in Social Science* (New York: Harper, 1951).
3. N. S. Endler and D. Magnusson, "Toward an Interactional Psychology of Personality," *Psychological Bulletin* 83 (1976): 956–974.
4. J. R. Terborg, "Interactional Psychology and Research on Human Behavior in Organizations," *Academy of Management Review* 6 (1981): 561–576.
5. T. J. Bouchard, Jr., "Twins Reared Together and Apart: What They Tell Us about Human Diversity," in S. W. Fox, ed., *Individuality and Determinism* (New York: Plenum Press, 1984).
6. R. D. Arvey, T. J. Bouchard, Jr., N. L. Segal, and L. M. Abraham, "Job Satisfaction: Environmental and Genetic Components," *Journal of Applied Psychology* 74 (1989): 235–248.
7. G. Allport, *Pattern and Growth in Personality* (New York: Holt, 1961).
8. R. B. Cattell, *Personality and Mood by Questionnaire* (San Francisco: Jossey-Bass, 1973).
9. J. M. Digman, "Personality Structure: Emergence of a Five-Factor Model," *Annual Review of Psychology* 41 (1990): 417–440.
10. M. R. Barrick and M. K. Mount, "The Big Five Personality Dimensions and Job Performance: A Meta-Analysis," *Personnel Psychology* 44 (1991): 1–26.
11. S. Freud, *An Outline of Psychoanalysis* (New York: Norton, 1949).
12. C. Rogers, *On Becoming a Person: A Therapist's View of Psychotherapy*, 2d ed. (Boston: Houghton Mifflin, 1970).
13. D. D. Clark and R. Hoyle, "A Theoretical Solution to the Problem of Personality-Situational Interaction," *Personality and Individual Differences* 9 (1988): 133–138.
14. D. Byrne and L. J. Schulte, "Personality Dimensions as Predictors of Sexual Behavior," in J. Bancroft, ed., *Annual Review of Sexual Research*, vol. 1 (Philadelphia: Society for the Scientific Study of Sex, 1990).
15. J. B. Rotter, "Generalized Expectancies for Internal vs. External Control of Reinforcement," *Psychological Monographs* 80, whole No. 609 (1966).
16. T. R. Mitchell, C. M. Smyser, and S. E. Weed, "Locus of Control: Supervision and Work Satisfaction," *Academy of Management Journal* 18 (1975): 623–631.
17. P. Spector, "Behavior in Organizations as a Function of Locus of Control," *Psychological Bulletin* 93 (1982): 482–497.
18. B. W. Pelham and W. B. Swann, Jr., "From Self-Conceptions to Self-Worth: On the Sources and Structure of Global Self-Esteem," *Journal of Personality and Social Psychology* 57 (1989): 672–680.
19. A. H. Baumgardner, C. M. Kaufman, and P. E. Levy, "Regulating Affect Interpersonally: When Low Esteem Leads to Greater Enhancement," *Journal of Personality and Social Psychology* 56 (1989): 907–921.
20. P. Tharenou and P. Harker, "Moderating Influences of Self-Esteem on Relationships between Job Complexity, Performance, and Satisfaction," *Journal of Applied Psychology* 69 (1984): 623–632.
21. R. A. Ellis and M. S. Taylor, "Role of Self-Esteem within the Job Search Process," *Journal of Applied Psychology* 68 (1983): 632–640.
22. J. Brockner and T. Hess, "Self-Esteem and Task Performance in Quality Circles," *Academy of Management Journal* 29 (1986): 617–623.
23. B. R. Schlenker, M. F. Weingold, and J. R. Hallam, "Self-Serving Attributions in Social Context: Effects of Self-Esteem and Social Pressure," *Journal of Personality and Social Psychology* 57 (1990): 855–863.
24. A. Bandura, *Social Learning Theory* (Englewood Cliffs, N.J.: Prentice-Hall, 1977).
25. A. Bandura, "Regulation of Cognitive Processes through Perceived Self-Efficacy," *Developmental Psychology* (September 1989): 729–735.
26. H. Garland, R. Weinberg, L. Bruya, and A. Jackson, "Self-Efficacy and Endurance Performance: A Longitudinal Field Test of Cognitive Mediation Theory," *Applied Psychology: An International Review* 37 (1988): 381–394.
27. K. W. Thomas and B. A. Velthouse, "Cognitive Elements of Empowerment: An 'Interpretive' Model of Intrinsic Task Motivation," *Academy of Mangement Review* 15 (1990): 666–681.
28. V. Gecas, "The Social Psychology of Self-Efficacy," *Annual Review of Sociology* 15 (1989): 291–316.
29. M. Snyder and S. Gangestad, "On the Nature of Self-Monitoring: Matters of Assessment, Matters of Validity," *Journal of Personality and Social Psychology* 51 (1986): 123–139.
30. M. Kilduff and D. V. Day, "Do Chameleons Get Ahead? The Effects of Self-Monitoring on Managerial Careers," *Academy of Management Journal* 37 (1994): 1047–1060.
31. A. M. Isen and R. A. Baron, "Positive Affect and Organizational Behavior," in B. M. Staw and L. L. Cummings, eds., *Research in Organizational Behavior*, vol. 12 (Greenwich, Conn.: JAI Press, 1990).
32. D. Watson and L. A. Clark, "Negative Affectivity: The Disposition to Experience Aversive Emotional States," *Psychological Bulletin* 96 (1984): 465–490.
33. R. A. Baron, "Interviewer's Moods and Reactions to Job Applicants: The Influence of Affective States on Applied Social Judgments," *Journal of Applied Social Psychology* 16 (1987): 16–28.
34. J. M. George, "Mood and Absence," *Journal of Applied Psychology* 74 (1989): 287–324.
35. M. J. Burke, A. P. Brief and J. M. George, "The Role of Negative Affectivity in Understanding Relations Between Self-Reports of Stressors and Strains: A Comment on the Applied Psychology Literature," *Journal of Applied Psychology* 78 (1993): 402–412.
36. J. M. George, "Personality, Affect, and Behavior in Groups," *Journal of Applied Psychology* 75 (1990): 107–116.
37. W. Mischel, "The Interaction of Person and Situation," in D. Magnusson and N. S. Endler, eds., *Personality at the Crossroads: Current Issues in Interactional Psychology* (Hillsdale, N.J.: Erlbaum, 1977).
38. H. Rorschach, *Psychodiagnostics* (Bern: Hans Huber, 1921).
39. C. G. Jung, *Psychological Types* (New York: Harcourt & Brace, 1923).
40. Consulting Psychologists Press.
41. R. Benfari and J. Knox, *Understanding Your Management Style* (Lexington, Mass.: Lexington Books, 1991).
42. O. Kroeger and J. M. Thuesen, *Type Talk* (New York: Delacorte Press, 1988).
43. S. Hirsch and J. Kummerow, *Life Types* (New York: Warner Books, 1989).
44. I. B. Myers and M. H. McCaulley, *Manual: A Guide to the Development and Use of the Myers-Briggs Type Indicator* (Palo Alto, Calif. Consulting Psychologists Press, 1990).
45. G. P. Macdaid, M. H. McCaulley, and R. I. Kainz, *Myers-Briggs Type Indicator: Atlas of Type Tables* (Gainesville, Fla.: Center for Application of Psychological Type, 1987).
46. J. B. Murray, "Review of Research on the Myers-Briggs

Type Indicator," *Perceptual and Motor Skills* 70 (1990): 1187–1202.

47. J. G. Carlson, "Recent Assessment of the Myers-Briggs Type Indicator," *Journal of Personality Assessment* 49 (1985): 356–365.
48. C. Walck, "Training for Participative Management: Implications for Psychological Type," *Journal of Psychological Type* 21 (1991): 3–12.
49. E. C. Webster, *The Employment Interview: A Social Judgment Process* (Schomberg, Canada: SIP, 1982).
50. N. Adler, *International Dimensions of Organizational Behavior,* 2d ed. (Boston: PWS-Kent, 1991).
51. L. R. Offerman and M. K. Gowing, "Personnel Selection in the Future: The Impact of Changing Demographics and the Nature of Work," in Schmitt, Borman & Associates, eds., *Personnel Selection in Organizations* (San Francisco: Jossey-Bass, 1993).
52. A. M. Isen and R. Baron, "Positive Affect as a Factor in Organizational Behavior," in B. M. Staw and L. L. Cummins (eds.), *Research in Organizational Behavior* 13 (1991): 1–54.
53. M. W. Levine and J. M. Shefner, *Fundamentals of Sensation and Perception* (Reading, Mass.: Addison-Wesley, 1981).
54. R. L. Dipboye, H. L. Fromkin, and K. Willback, "Relative Importance of Applicant Sex, Attractiveness, and Scholastic Standing in Evaluations of Job Applicant Resumes," *Journal of Applied Psychology* 60 (1975): 39–43.
55. I. H. Frieze, J. E. Olson, and J. Russell, "Attractiveness and Income for Men and Women in Management," *Journal of Applied Social Psychology* 21 (1991): 1039–1057.
56. P. Ekman and W. Friesen, *Unmasking the Face* (Englewood Cliffs, N.J.: Prentice-Hall, 1975).
57. J. E. Rehfeld, "What Working for a Japanese Company Taught Me," *Harvard Business Review,* (November–December 1990): 167–176.
58. M.W. Morris and R. P. Larrick, "When One Cause Casts Doubt on Another: A Normative Analysis of Discounting in Causal Attribution," *Psychological Review* 102 (1995): 331–355.
59. L. Copeland, "Learning to Manage a Multicultural Workforce," *Training,* May 1988, 48–56.
60. S. Ferrari, "Human Behavior in International Groups," *Management International Review* 7 (1972): 31–35.
61. A. Feingold, "Gender Differences in Effects of Physical Attractiveness on Romantic Attraction: A Comparison across Five Research Paradigms," *Journal of Personality and Social Psychology* 59 (1990): 981–993.
62. M. Snyder, "When Belief Creates Reality," *Advances in Experimental Social Psychology* 18 (1984): 247–305.
63. E. Burnstein and Y. Schul, "The Informational Basis of Social Judgments: Operations in Forming an Impression of Another Person," *Journal of Experimental Social Psychology* 18 (1982): 217–234.
64. J. Bruner, D. Shapiro, and R. Tagiuri, "The Meaning of Traits in Isolation and in Combination," in R. Tagiuri and L. Petrullo, eds., *Person Perception and Interpersonal Behavior* (Stanford, Calif.: Stanford University Press, 1958).
65. S. T. Fiske and S. E. Taylor, *Social Cognition* (Reading, Mass.: Addison-Wesley, 1984).
66. R. Rosenthal and L. Jacobson, *Pygmalion in the Classroom: Teacher Expectations and Pupils' Intellectual Development* (New York: Holt, Rinehart & Winston, 1968).
67. D. Eden, *Pygmalion in Management: Productivity as a Self-Fulfilling Prophecy* (Lexington, Mass.: Lexington Books, 1990).
68. D. Eden, "Pygmalion Without Interpersonal Contrast Effects: Whole Groups Gain from Raising Manager Expectations," *Journal of Applied Psychology* 75 (1990): 394–398.
69. R. A. Giacolone and P. Rosenfeld, eds., *Impression Management in Organizations* (Hillsdale, N.J.: Erlbaum, 1990); J. Tedeschi and V. Melburg, "Impression Management and Influence in the Organization," in S. Bacharach and E. Lawler, eds., *Research in the Sociology of Organizations* (Greenwich, Conn.: JAI Press, 1984), 31–58.
70. T.E. Becker and S. L. Martin, "Trying to Look Bad at Work: Methods and Motives for Managing Poor Impressions in Organizations," *Academy of Management Journal* 38 (1995): 174–199.
71. D. C. Gilmore and G. R. Ferris, "The Effects of Applicant Impression Management Tactics on Interviewer Judgments," *Journal of Management* (December 1989): 557–564.
72. C.K. Stevens and A. L. Kristof, "Making the Right Impression: A Field Study of Applicant Impressions Management During Job Interviews," *Journal of Applied Psychology* 80 (1995): 587–606.
73. S. J. Wayne and R. C. Liden, "Effects of Impression Management on Performance Ratings: A Longitudinal Study," *Academy of Management Journal* 38 (1995): 232–260.
74. R. A. Baron, "Impression Management by Applicants during Employment Interviews: The 'Too Much of a Good Thing' Effect," in R. W. Eder and G. R. Ferris, eds., *The Employment Interview: Theory, Research, and Practice* (Newbury Park, Calif.: Sage Publications, 1989).
75. F. Heider, *The Psychology of Interpersonal Relations* (New York: Wiley, 1958).
76. B. Weiner, "An Attributional Theory of Achievement Motivation and Emotion," *Psychological Review* (October 1985): 548–573.
77. P. D. Sweeney, K. Anderson, and S. Bailey, "Attributional Style in Depression: A Meta-Analytic Review," *Journal of Personality and Social Psychology* 51 (1986): 974–991.
78. H. H. Kelley, *Attribution in Social Interaction* (New York: General Learning Press, 1971).
79. H. H. Kelley, "The Processes of Causal Attribution," *American Psychologist,* February 1973, 107–128.
80. L. Ross, "The Intuitive Psychologist and His Shortcomings: Distortions in the Attribution Process," in L. Berkowitz, ed., *Advances in Experimental Social Psychology* (New York: Academic Press, 1977).
81. D. T. Miller and M. Ross, "Self-Serving Biases in the Attribution of Causality: Fact or Fiction?" *Psychological Bulletin* 82 (1975): 313–325.
82. J. R. Schermerhorn, Jr., "Team Development for High-Performance Management," *Training and Development Journal* 40 (1986): 38–41.
83. J. G. Miller, "Culture and the Development of Everyday Causal Explanation," *Journal of Personality and Social Psychology* 46 (1984): 961–978.
84. G. Si, S. Rethorst, and K. Willimczik, "Causal Attribution Perception in Sports Achievement: A Cross-Cultural Study on Attributional Concepts in Germany and China," *Journal of Cross-Cultural Psychology* 26 (1995): 537–553.
85. C. Barrett, "Giving Customers P.O.S.," *Sales and Marketing Management* (November 1993): 52.

CHAPTER

4

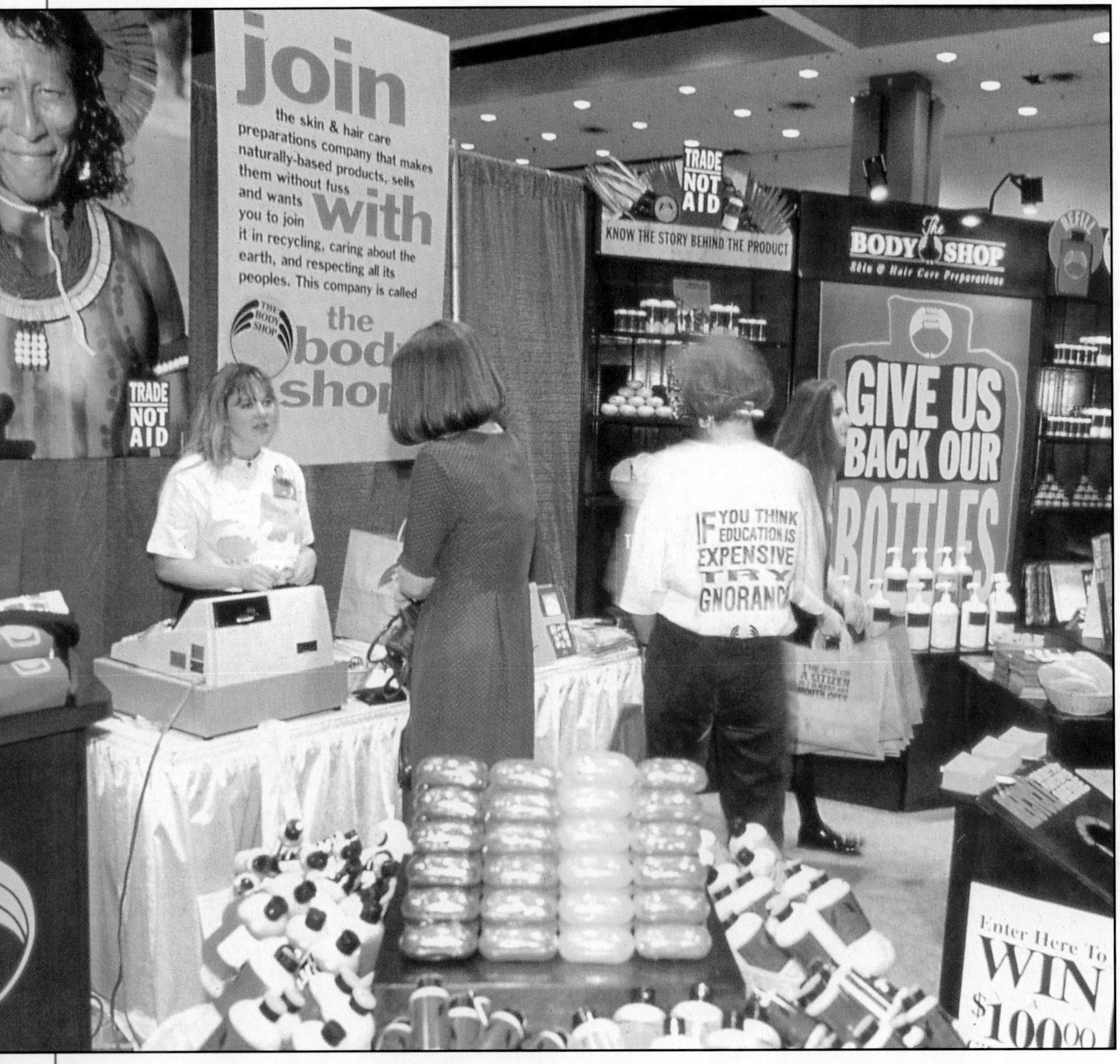

join
the skin & hair care preparations company that makes naturally-based products, sells them without fuss and wants you to join with it in recycling, caring about the earth, and respecting all its peoples. This company is called
TRADE NOT AID
TRADE NOT AID
KNOW THE STORY BEHIND THE PRODUCT
The BODY SHOP
Skin & Hair Care Preparations
GIVE US BACK OUR
YOU THINK EDUCATION IS EXPENSIVE TRY
Enter Here To WIN

Attitudes, Values, and Ethics

LEARNING OBJECTIVES

After reading this chapter, you should be able to do the following:

- Explain the ABC model of an attitude.
- Describe how attitudes are formed.
- Define *job satisfaction* and *organizational commitment* and discuss the importance of these two work attitudes.
- Identify the characteristics of the source, target, and message that affect persuasion.
- Distinguish between instrumental and terminal values.
- Explain how managers can deal with the diverse value systems that characterize the global environment.
- Describe a model of individual and organizational influences on ethical behavior.
- Discuss how value systems, locus of control, Machiavellianism, and cognitive moral development affect ethical behavior.

OPENING SPOTLIGHT

Citicorp Wins "The Ethics Game"

http://www.citicorp.com/

Citicorp has always focused on ethical behavior. It has used speeches, training sessions, and a lengthy policy manual to communicate its ethics policies to employees. Every three years, officers worldwide receive a sixty-page booklet describing the company's ethical standards. With all this exposure to ethics, you might think top management would be satisfied that they had covered all the bases. However, they wanted even more exposure for one particular ethical issue: integrity. Senior management asked the corporate communications department to come up with a program that would teach Citicorp's ethical culture and encourage ethical behavior through a continuous dialogue about ethical issues.

Corporate communications employees had a creative idea. They developed "The Ethics Game," a board and card game that presents ethical dilemmas and challenges employees to think about ethical issues beyond the obvious right and wrong.[1] The playing board is divided into four levels: entry level, supervisor, manager, and senior manager. The points a team can win or lose differ by level, because as a person advances in the organization the consequences of ethical decisions have increasingly serious implications. Each card presents ethical dilemmas like insider trading, conflicts of interest, and sexual harassment. Four solutions are offered, none of which is ideal. Players win or lose points based on their answers, end up in the penalty box, or are fired (out of the game). The game generates tremendous disagreement among players, which gets them to hash out the difficult issues. In the Closing Spotlight, you can try your hand at one of the game's dilemmas. ■

In this chapter, we continue the discussion of individual differences we began in Chapter 3 with personality, perception, and attribution. Persons and situations are joint influences on behavior, and individual differences help us to better understand the influence of the person. Our focus now is on three other individual difference factors: attitudes, values, and ethics.

Attitudes

attitudes

Individuals' general affective, cognitive, and intentional responses toward objects, other people, themselves, or social issues.

■ **Attitudes** are individuals' general affective, cognitive, and intentional responses toward objects, other people, themselves, or social issues.[2] As individuals, we respond favorably or unfavorably toward many things: animals, coworkers, our own appearance, politics. The importance of attitudes lies in their link to behavior. For example, some people prefer either cats or dogs. Individuals who prefer cats may be friendly to cats but hesitate in approaching dogs.

Attitudes are an integral part of the world of work. Managers speak of workers who have "bad attitudes" and conduct "attitude adjustment" talks with employees. Often, poor performance attributed to bad attitudes really stems from lack of motivation, minimal feedback, lack of trust in management, or other problems. These are areas that managers must explore.

You can see that it is important for managers to understand the antecedents to attitudes as well as their consequences. Managers also need to understand the different components of attitudes, how attitudes are formed, the major attitudes that affect work behavior, and how to use persuasion to change attitudes.

The ABC Model

We tend to associate attitudes with surveys; therefore, we believe that to find out how a person feels about an issue, we simply ask him or her. This method is incomplete, however. To understand the complexity of an attitude, we can break it down into three components, as depicted in Table 4.1.

affect

The emotional component of an attitude.

These components—affect, behavioral intentions, and cognition—compose what we call the ABC model of an attitude.[3] **Affect** is the emotional component of an attitude. It refers to an individual's feeling about something or someone. Statements such as "I like this" or "I prefer that" reflect the affective component of an attitude. Affect is measured by physiological indicators such as galvanic skin response (changes in electrical resistance of skin which indicate emotional arousal) and blood pressure. These indicators show changes in emotions by measuring physiological arousal. If an individual is trying to hide his or her feelings, this might be shown by a change in arousal.

The second component is the intention to behave in a certain way toward an object or person. Our attitudes toward women in management, for example, may be inferred from an observation of the way we behave toward a female

■ **TABLE 4.1**

The ABC Model of an Attitude

	COMPONENT	MEASURED BY
A	Affect	Physiological indicators Verbal statements about feelings
B	Behavioral intentions	Observed behavior Verbal statements about intentions
C	Cognition	Attitude scales Verbal statements about beliefs

SOURCE: Adapted from M. J. Rosenberg and C. I. Hovland, "Cognitive, Affective, and Behavioral Components of Attitude," in M. J. Rosenberg, C. I. Hovland, W. J. McGuire, R. P. Abelson, and J. H. Brehm, *Attitude Organization and Change* (New Haven: Yale University Press, 1960). Copyright 1960 Yale University Press. Used with permission.

supervisor. We may be supportive, passive, or hostile, depending on our attitude. The behavioral component of an attitude is measured by observing behavior or by asking a person about behavior or intentions. The statement "If I were asked to speak at commencement, I'd be willing to try to do so, even though I'd be nervous" reflects a behavioral intention.

The third component of an attitude, cognition (thought), reflects a person's perceptions or beliefs. Cognitive elements are evaluative beliefs and are measured by attitude scales or by asking about thoughts. The statement "I believe Japanese workers are industrious" reflects the cognitive component of an attitude.

The ABC model shows that to thoroughly understand an attitude, we must assess all three components. Suppose, for example, you want to evaluate your employees' attitudes toward flextime (flexible work scheduling). You would want to determine how they feel about flextime (affect), whether they would use flextime (behavioral intention), and what they think about the policy (cognition). The most common method of attitude measurement, the attitude scale, measures only the cognitive component.

As rational beings, individuals try to be consistent in everything they believe in and do. They prefer consistency (consonance) between their attitudes and behavior. Anything that disrupts this consistency causes tension (dissonance), which motivates individuals to change either their attitudes or their behavior to return to a state of consistency. The tension produced when there is a conflict between attitudes and behavior is **cognitive dissonance.**[4]

cognitive dissonance

A state of tension that is produced when an individual experiences conflict between attitudes and behavior.

Suppose, for example, a salesperson is required to sell damaged televisions for the full retail price, without revealing the damage to customers. She believes, however, that doing so constitutes unethical behavior. This creates a conflict between her attitude (concealing information from customers is unethical) and her behavior (selling defective TVs without informing customers about the damage).

The salesperson, experiencing the discomfort from dissonance, will try to resolve the conflict. She might change her behavior by refusing to sell the defective TV sets. Alternatively, she might rationalize that the defects are minor and that the customers will not be harmed by their lack of awareness of them. These are attempts by the salesperson to restore equilibrium between her attitudes and behavior, thereby eliminating the tension from cognitive dissonance.

Managers need to understand cognitive dissonance because employees often find themselves in situations in which their attitudes conflict with their behavior. They manage the tension by changing their attitudes or behavior. Employees who display sudden shifts in behavior may be attempting to reduce dissonance.

Discussion Consideration

Students have access to good examples of cognitive dissonance in trying to balance their school, work, and social obligations. Cognitive dissonance can be experienced when you purchase something you want but do not need. This impulsive move is termed buyer's remorse. Discuss how the concept of buyer's remorse is like cognitive dissonance.

Some employees find the conflicts between strongly held attitudes and required work behavior so uncomfortable that they leave the organization to escape the dissonance.

Attitude Formation

Attitudes are learned. Our responses to people and issues evolve over time. Two major influences on attitudes are direct experience and social learning.

Direct experience with an object or person is a powerful influence on attitudes. How do you know that you like biology or dislike math? You have probably formed these attitudes from experience in studying the subjects. Research has shown that attitudes that are derived from direct experience are stronger, are held more confidently, and are more resistant to change than are attitudes formed through indirect experience.[5] One reason attitudes derived from direct experience are so powerful is because of their availability. This means that the attitudes are easily accessed and are active in our cognitive processes.[6] When attitudes are available, we can call them quickly into consciousness. Attitudes that are not learned from direct experience are not as available, and therefore we do not recall them as easily.

social learning

The process of deriving attitudes from family, peer groups, religious organizations, and culture.

In **social learning,** the family, peer groups, religious organizations, and culture shape an individual's attitudes in an indirect manner.[7] Children learn to adopt certain attitudes by the reinforcement they are given by their parents when they display behaviors that reflect an appropriate attitude. This is evident when very young children express political preferences similar to their parents'. Peer pressure molds attitudes through group acceptance of individuals who express popular attitudes and through sanctions, such as exclusion from the group, placed on individuals who espouse unpopular attitudes.

Substantial social learning occurs through *modeling,* in which individuals acquire attitudes by merely observing others. The observer overhears other individuals expressing an opinion or watches them engaging in a behavior that reflects an attitude, and this attitude is adopted by the observer.

Oprah Winfrey has been the model for many talk show hosts and interviewers. Through social learning, others observe her behavior and imitate her style.

For an individual to learn from observing a model, four processes must take place:

1. The learner must focus attention on the model.
2. The learner must retain what was observed from the model. Retention is accomplished in two basic ways. One way is for the learner to "stamp in" what was observed by forming a verbal code for it. The other way is through symbolic rehearsal, by which the learner forms a mental image of himself or herself behaving like the model.
3. Behavioral reproduction must occur; that is, the learner must practice the behavior.
4. The learner must be motivated to learn from the model.

Culture also plays a definitive role in attitude development. Consider, for example, the contrast in the North American and European attitudes toward vacation and leisure. The typical vacation in the United States is two weeks, and some workers do not use all of their vacation time. In Europe, the norm is longer vacations; and in some countries, *holiday* means everyone taking a month off. The European attitude is that an investment in longer vacations is important to health and performance.

Attitudes and Behavior

If you have a favorable attitude toward participative management, will your management style be participative? As managers, if we know an employee's attitude, to what extent can we predict the person's behavior? These questions illustrate the fundamental issue of attitude-behavior correspondence; that is, the degree to which an attitude predicts behavior.

This correspondence has concerned organizational behaviorists and social psychologists for quite some time. Some studies suggested that attitudes and behavior are closely linked, while others found no relationship at all or a weak relationship at best. Attention then became focused on when attitudes predict behavior and when they do not. Attitude-behavior correspondence depends on five things: attitude specificity, attitude relevance, timing of measurement, personality factors, and social constraints.

Individuals possess both general and specific attitudes. You may favor women's right to reproductive freedom (a general attitude) and prefer pro-choice political candidates (a specific attitude). However, you may not attend pro-choice rallies or send money to Planned Parenthood. The fact that you don't perform these behaviors may make the link between your attitude and behavior on this issue seem rather weak. However, given a choice between a pro-choice and an anti-abortion political candidate you will probably vote for the pro-choice candidate. In this case, your attitude seems quite predictive of your behavior. The point is that the greater the attitude specificity, the stronger its link to behavior.[8]

Another factor that affects the attitude-behavior link is relevance.[9] Attitudes that address an issue in which we have some self-interest are more relevant for us, and our subsequent behavior is consistent with our expressed attitude. Suppose there is a proposal to raise income taxes on those who earn $150,000 or more. If you are a student, you may not find the issue of great personal relevance. Individuals in that income bracket, however, might find it highly relevant; their attitude toward the issue would be strongly predictive of whether they would vote for the tax increase.

The timing of the measurement also affects attitude-behavior correspondence. The shorter the time between the attitude measurement and the observed behavior, the stronger the relationship. For example, voter preference polls taken close to an election are more accurate than earlier polls are.

Personality factors also influence the attitude-behavior link. One personality disposition that affects the consistency between attitudes and behavior is self-monitoring. Recall from Chapter 3 that low self-monitors rely on their internal states when making decisions about behavior, while high self-monitors are more responsive to situational cues. Low self-monitors therefore display greater correspondence between their attitudes and behaviors.[10] High self-monitors display little correspondence between their attitudes and behavior because they behave according to signals from others and from the environment.

Finally, social constraints affect the relationship between attitudes and behavior.[11] The social context provides information about acceptable attitudes and behaviors.[12,13] New employees in an organization, for example, are exposed to the attitudes of their work group. Suppose a newcomer from Afghanistan holds a negative attitude toward women in management because in his country the prevailing attitude is that women should not be in positions of power. He sees, however, that his work group members respond positively to their female supervisor. His own behavior may therefore be compliant because of social constraints. This behavior is inconsistent with his attitude and cultural belief system.

Discussion Consideration
Do affect and cognition always lead to behavior? Ask students to think of situations in which they may have experienced the affective or cognitive components of an attitude, but did not express the attitude through their behavior. Have there been times when their behavior contradicted their attitude?

Points to Emphasize
The connection between attitudes and behavior may be tenuous. Social psychologists point out several problems that make it difficult to explain the relationship between attitudes and behavior. First, there may be a problem with the level of specificity at which behaviors and attitudes are measured. A general attitude may have been measured, then a specific behavior observed. Second, there is a problem of inferring attitudes from single, rather than multiple acts. Third, when situational pressures are strong, people of widely differing attitudes may behave the same way. Finally, given behavior may be related to more than one attitude. SOURCE: K. Deaux, F. C. Dane, and L. W. Wrightsman, *Social Psychology in the 90's,* Pacific Grove, CA: Brooks/Cole, 1993.

Alternate Example
The theory of planned behavior provides another explanation of the connection between behavior and attitudes. According to this theory, attitudes toward the behavior, subjective norms, and perceived behavioral control combine to determine an individual's behavioral intention, which in turn causes the behavior. SOURCE: I. Ajzen, "Attitudes, Traits, and Actions: Dispositional Prediction of Behavior in Personality and Social Psychology," in *Advances in Experimental Social Psychology,* 1987, 20, pp. 1–63.

Work Attitudes

Alternate Example
Recent trends in downsizing, reengineering and restructuring have placed emphasis on change in organizations. These tasks may be relatively easy compared to the task of changing attitudes.

Attitudes at work are important because, directly or indirectly, they affect work behavior. This was dramatically illustrated in a comparison of product quality among air conditioners manufactured in the United States versus those made in Japan.[14] In general, there is a perception that Japanese products are of higher quality. The product quality of air conditioners from nine U.S. plants and seven Japanese plants was compared, and the results were bad news for the U.S. plants. The Japanese products had significantly fewer defects than the U.S. products.

The researchers continued their study by asking managers in both countries' plants about their attitudes toward various goals. Japanese supervisors reported that their companies had strong attitudes favoring high-quality products, while U.S. supervisors reported quality goals to be less important. U.S. supervisors reported strong attitudes favoring the achievement of production scheduling goals, while Japanese supervisors indicated that schedules were less important. The researchers' conclusion was that the attitudes of U.S. managers toward quality were at least partly responsible for lower-quality products.

Discussion Consideration
Why is it so difficult to change attitude in the work place?

Although many work attitudes are important, two attitudes in particular have been emphasized. Job satisfaction and organizational commitment are key attitudes of interest to managers and researchers.

job satisfaction
A pleasurable or positive emotional state resulting from the appraisal of one's job or job experiences.

JOB SATISFACTION Most of us believe that work should be a positive experience. **Job satisfaction** is a pleasurable or positive emotional state resulting from the appraisal of one's job or job experiences.[15] It has been treated both as a general attitude and as satisfaction with five specific dimensions of the job: pay, the work itself, promotion opportunities, supervision, and coworkers.[16] You can assess your own job satisfaction by completing Challenge 4.1.

Alternate Example
In our society we often view success from the perspective of our careers. However, an alternative view of success is the "pentathlon." According to this view, success is a whole life concept that encompasses the career, personal, family, social, and spiritual arenas of an individual's life. From this viewpoint, success requires setting and achieving goals in each of these areas, not just the career arena. SOURCE: D. Sherman and W. Hendricks, *How to Balance Competing Time Demands,* Colorado Springs: NAVPRESS. 1987.

An individual may hold different attitudes toward various aspects of the job. For example, an employee may like her job responsibilities but be dissatisfied with the opportunities for promotion. Characteristics of individuals also affect job satisfaction. Those with high negative affectivity are more likely to be dissatisfied with their jobs. Challenging work, valued rewards, opportunities for advancement, competent supervision, and supportive coworkers are dimensions of the job that can lead to satisfaction.

There are several measures of job satisfaction. One of the most widely used measures comes from the Job Descriptive Index (JDI). This index measures the specific facets of satisfaction by asking employees to respond yes, no, or cannot decide to a series of statements describing their jobs. Another popular measure is the Minnesota Satisfaction Questionnaire (MSQ).[17] This survey also asks employees to respond to statements about their jobs, using a five-point scale that ranges from very dissatisfied to very satisfied. Figure 4.1 presents some sample items from each questionnaire.

Discussion Consideration
Ask students if they believe that American corporations place the proper emphasis on balancing work, leisure, and family.

Are satisfied workers more productive? Or, are more productive workers more satisfied? The link between satisfaction and performance has been widely explored. One view holds that satisfaction causes good performance. If this were true, then the manager's job would simply be to keep workers happy. Although this may be the case for certain individuals, job satisfaction for most people is one of several causes of good performance.

Another view holds that good performance causes satisfaction. If this were true, managers would need to help employees perform well, and satisfaction would follow. However, some employees who are high performers are not satisfied with their jobs.

Point to Emphasize
Satisfaction is a multifaceted construct that includes satisfaction with supervision, compensation, task design, coworkers, and the general environment of the organization.

The research shows weak support for both views, but no simple, direct relationship between satisfaction and performance has been found.[18] One reason for these results may be the difficulty of demonstrating the attitude-behavior links we described earlier in this chapter. Future studies using specific, relevant

CHALLENGE

■ **4.2**

Assess Your Job Satisfaction

Think of the job you have now, or a job you've had in the past. Indicate how satisfied you are with each aspect of your job below, using the following scale:

1 = Extremely dissatisfied
2 = Dissatisfied
3 = Slightly dissatisfied
4 = Neutral
5 = Slightly satisfied
6 = Satisfied
7 = Extremely satisfied

1. The amount of job security I have.
2. The amount of pay and fringe benefits I receive.
3. The amount of personal growth and development I get in doing my job.
4. The people I talk to and work with on my job.
5. The degree of respect and fair treatment I receive from my boss.
6. The feeling of worthwhile accomplishment I get from doing my job.
7. The chance to get to know other people while on the job.
8. The amount of support and guidance I receive from my supervisor.
9. The degree to which I am fairly paid for what I contribute to this organization.
10. The amount of independent thought and action I can exercise in my job.
11. How secure things look for me in the future in this organization.
12. The chance to help other people while at work.
13. The amount of challenge in my job.
14. The overall quality of the supervision I receive on my work.

Now, compute your scores for the facets of job satisfaction.

Pay satisfaction:

Q2 + Q9 = Divided by 2:

Security satisfaction:

Q1 + Q11 = Divided by 2:

Social satisfaction:

Q4 + Q7 + Q12 = Divided by 3:

Supervisory satisfaction:

Q5 + Q8 + Q14 = Divided by 3:

Growth satisfaction:

Q3 + Q6 + Q10 + Q13 = Divided by 4:

Scores on the facets range from 1 to 7. (Scores lower than 4 suggest there is room for change.

This questionnaire is an abbreviated version of the Job Diagnostic Survey, a widely used tool for assessing individual's attitudes about their jobs.

SOURCE: R. Hackman/G. Oldham, *Work Redesign*, © 1980 by Addison-Wesley Publishing Company, Inc. Reprinted with permission of Addison-Wesley Publishing Company, Inc.

FIGURE 4.1

Sample Items from Satisfaction Questionnaires

SOURCE: The Job Descriptive Index is copyrighted by Bowling Green State University. The complete forms, scoring key, instructions, and norms can be obtained from Dr. Patricia C. Smith, Department of Psychology, Bowling Green State University, Bowling Green, OH 43403. Minnesota Satisfaction Questionnaire from D. J. Weiss, R. V. Davis, G. W. England, and L. H. Lofquist, *Manual for the Minnesota Satisfaction Questionnaire* (University of Minnesota Industrial Relations Center, 1967).

Job Descriptive Index

Think of the work you do at present. How well does each of the following words or phrases describe your work? In the blank beside each word given below, write

__Y__ for "Yes" if it describes your work
__N__ for "No" if it does NOT describe it
__?__ if you cannot decide

WORK ON YOUR PRESENT JOB:

______ Routine
______ Satisfying
______ Good

Think of the majority of the people that you work with now or the people you meet in connection with your work. How well does each of the following words or phrases describe these people? In the blank beside each word, write

__Y__ for"Yes" if it describes the people you work with
__N__ for "No" if it does NOT describe them
__?__ if you cannot decide

CO-WORKERS (PEOPLE):

______ Boring
______ Responsible
______ Intelligent

Minnesota Satisfaction Questionnaire

1 = Very dissatisfied
2 = Dissatisfied
3 = I can't decide whether I am satisfied or not
4 = Satisfied
5 = Very satisfied

On my present job, this is how I feel about:

______ The chance to work alone on the job (Independence)
______ My chances for advancement on this job (Advancement)
______ The chance to tell people what to do (Authority)
______ The praise I get for a good job (Recognition)
______ My pay and the amount of work I do (Compensation)

SOURCE: The Job Descriptive Index is copyrighted by Bowling Green State University. The complete forms, scoring key, instructions, and norms can be obtained form Dr. Patricia C. Smith, Department of Psychology, Bowling Green State University, Bowling Green, OH 43403. Minnesota Satisfaction Questionnaire form D. J. Weiss, R. V. Davis, G. W. England, and L. H. Lofquist, *Manual for the Minnesota Satisfaction Questionnaire* (University of Minnesota Industrial Relations Center, 1967).

Alternate Example

Felice Schwartz, known for her Harvard Business Review article on the mommy track, provides a straightforward set of recommendations for women to test the work attitudes in an organization for which they are interested in working. She recommends reviewing family policies, counting the number of women at high levels, and, if possible, choosing a company whose CEO has daughters with MBAs. SOURCE: C. Pasternak, "Mommy Track Author, Catalyst for Women Retires," *HR News, Society for Human Resource Management,* May 1993, A7.

organizational citizenship behavior

Behavior that is above and beyond the call of duty.

attitudes and measuring personality variables and behavioral intentions may be able to demonstrate a link between job satisfaction and performance.

Another reason for the lack of a clear relationship between satisfaction and performance is the intervening role of rewards. Employees who receive valued rewards are more satisfied. In addition, employees who receive rewards that are contingent on performance (the higher the performance, the larger the reward) tend to perform better. Rewards thus influence both satisfaction and performance. The key to influencing both satisfaction and performance through rewards is that the rewards are valued by employees and are tied directly to performance.

Job satisfaction has been shown to be related to many other important personal and organizational outcomes. People who are dissatisfied with their jobs are absent more frequently, are more likely to quit, and report more psychological and medical problems than do satisfied employees.[19] In addition, job satisfaction may be related to **organizational citizenship behavior**—behavior that is above and beyond the call of duty.[20] Satisfied employees are more likely to help their coworkers, make positive comments about the company, and refrain from complaining when things at work do not go well. Going beyond the call of duty is especially important to organizations using teams to get work done. Employees depend on extra help from each other to get things accomplished.

Satisfied workers are more likely to want to give something back to the organization because they want to reciprocate their positive experiences.[21] Often, employees may feel that citizenship behaviors are not recognized because they occur outside the confines of normal job responsibilities. Organizational citizenship behaviors do, however, influence performance evaluations. Employees who exhibit behaviors such as helping others, making suggestions for innovations, and developing their skills receive higher performance ratings.[22]

Organizational citizenship behaviors vary from everyday individual acts to group efforts. Albany Ladder, a New York-based construction equipment sales firm, can attest to the value of such behaviors. Top managers at the company believe that they owe their company's ability to make it through the decline in the construction industry to employees who went the extra mile without being asked. For example, Albany Ladder desperately needed to put a concrete pad for equipment in the corner of their parking lot. A crew of employee volunteers, doing a job that didn't remotely resemble their regular ones, pitched in and built the pad on a Saturday, with no pay. Organizational citizenship behaviors like this can be essential to a firm's survival.

Like all attitudes, job satisfaction is influenced by culture. One study found that Japanese workers reported significantly lower job satisfaction than did U.S. workers.[23] Interestingly, the study showed that job satisfaction in both Japan and the United States could be improved by participative techniques such as quality circles and social activities sponsored by the company. Research also has shown that executives in less industrialized countries have lower levels of job satisfaction.[24]

Culture may also affect the factors that lead to job satisfaction. In a comparison of employees in the United States and India, the factors differed substantially. Leadership style, pay, and security influenced job satisfaction for the Americans. For the employees in India, however, recognition, innovation, and the absence of conflict led to job satisfaction.[25]

Because organizations face the challenge of operating in the global environment, managers must understand that job satisfaction is significantly affected by culture. Employees from different cultures may have differing expectations of their jobs; thus, there may be no single prescription for increasing the job satisfaction of a multicultural work force.

ORGANIZATIONAL COMMITMENT The strength of an individual's identification with an organization is known as **organizational commitment.** There are two kinds of organizational commitment: affective and continuance.[26] **Affective commitment** is an employee's intention to remain in an organization because of a strong desire to do so. It consists of three factors:

- A belief in the goals and values of the organization.
- A willingness to put forth effort on behalf of the organization.
- A desire to remain a member of the organization.[27]

Affective commitment encompasses loyalty, but it is also a deep concern for the organization's welfare.

Continuance commitment is an employee's tendency to remain in an organization because the person cannot afford to leave.[28] Sometimes, employees believe that if they leave, they will lose a great deal of their investments in time, effort, and benefits and that they cannot replace these investments.

Certain organizational conditions encourage commitment. Participation in decision making and job security are two such conditions. Certain job characteristics also positively affect commitment. These include autonomy, responsibility, and interesting work.[29]

organizational commitment

The strength of an individual's identification with an organization.

affective commitment

The type of organizational commitment that is based on an individual's desire to remain in an organization.

continuance commitment

The type of organizational commitment that is based on the fact that an individual cannot afford to leave.

Alternate Example
A third type of organizational commitment involves normative commitment. This type commitment may be rooted in a person's value system. According to normative commitment, a person ought to be loyal to an organization because loyalty is the right thing to do. SOURCE: J. P. Meyer, and N. J. Allen, "The Three-Component Conceptualization of Organizational Commitment," *Human Resource Management Review,* 1991, 1, 69–89.

Points to Emphasize
Students may assume there is a direct relationship between organizational commitment and career progress. However, recent studies have indicated that there is little reason to believe such a relationship exists. SOURCE: N. J. Allen and J. P. Meyer, "Organizational Commitment: Evidence of Career Stage effects?" *Journal of Business Research* 26 (1993): 49–61.

Organizational commitment is related to lower rates of absenteeism, higher quality of work, and increased productivity. Managers should be concerned about affective commitment because committed individuals expend more task-related effort and are less likely than others to leave the organization.[30]

Recent research on organizational commitment has been conducted in different countries. One study of workers in Saudi Arabia found that Asians working there were more committed to the organization than were Westerners and Arab workers.[31] Another study revealed that American workers displayed higher affective commitment than did Korean and Japanese workers.[32] The reasons for these differences need to be explored.

Job satisfaction and organizational commitment are two important work attitudes that managers can strive to improve among their employees. And these two attitudes are strongly related, so increasing job satisfaction is likely to increase commitment as well. To begin with, managers can use attitude surveys to reveal employees' satisfaction or dissatisfaction with specific facets of their jobs. Then they can take action to make the deficient aspects of the job more satisfying. Participative management has been shown to increase both satisfaction and commitment. Managers can give employees opportunities to participate in decision making to help improve these attitudes.

Persuasion and Attitude Change

To understand how attitudes can change, it is necessary to understand the process of persuasion. Through persuasion, one individual (the source) tries to change the attitude of another person (the target). Certain characteristics of the source, the target, and the message affect the persuasion process. There are also two cognitive routes to persuasion.

SOURCE CHARACTERISTICS Three major characteristics of the source affect persuasion: expertise, trustworthiness, and attractiveness.[33] A source who is perceived as an expert is particularly persuasive. Ken Cooper, founder of Cooper Aerobics Center, is a persuasive force for changing attitudes toward aerobic fitness. His expertise persuaded many sedentary people to get moving and led to the boom in aerobics classes, running, swimming, and other aerobic activities. Trustworthiness is also important. Richard Simmons, also a persuasive force in the fitness movement, has a style that certainly contrasts with that of Dr.

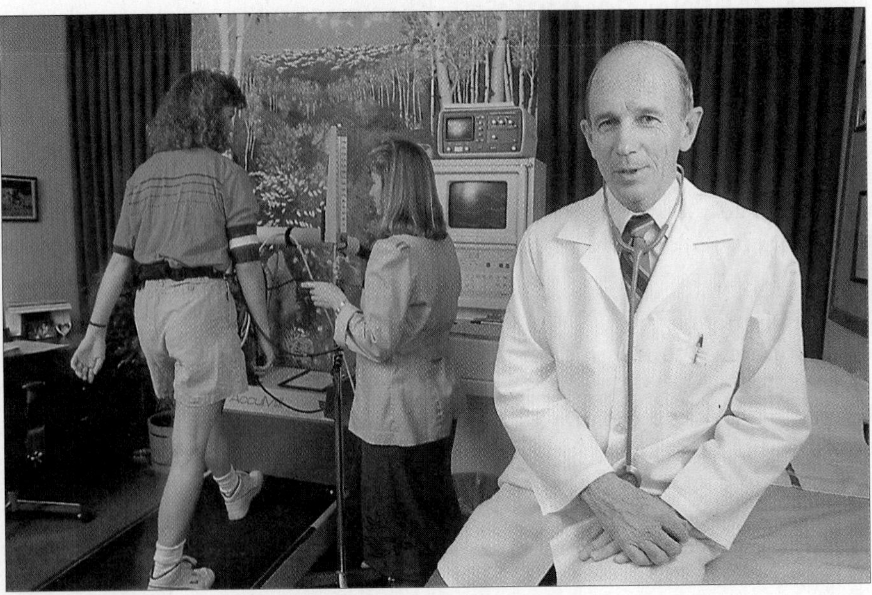

Dr. Ken Cooper's expertise has shaped Americans' attitudes toward exercise and fitness. He is regarded as one of the foremost authorities on aerobic exercise and health.

Cooper. His energetic, sometimes zany approach has motivated many overweight people to exercise. Simmons's ability to persuade comes from the trust he has earned by being forthright about his own weight problems. He combated obesity himself and won, and thus many people trust him to help them succeed in the battle to become fit. Finally, attractiveness and likability play a role in persuasion. Attractive communicators have long been used in advertising to persuade consumers to buy certain products. As a source of persuasion, managers who are perceived as being experts, who are trustworthy, or who are attractive or likable will have an edge in changing employee attitudes.

TARGET CHARACTERISTICS Some people are more easily persuaded than others. Individuals with low self-esteem are more likely to change their attitudes in response to persuasion than are individuals with high self-esteem. Individuals who hold very extreme attitudes are more resistant to persuasion, and people who are in a good mood are easier to persuade.[34] Undoubtedly, individuals differ widely in their susceptibility to persuasion. Managers must recognize these differences and realize that their attempts to change attitudes may not receive universal acceptance.

Points to Emphasize
A hotly debated issue is companies' smoke-free policies. One of the difficulties in implementing such a policy is that there are strong views and values on both sides of the question. One survey found that the reasons given for a ban on smoking are important for both smokers and nonsmokers. Many organizational members rebel against the smoke-free policy if it is viewed as "Big Brotherish." SOURCE: J. S. Harris, "Clearing the Air," *HR Magazine, Society for Human Resources Management,* February 1993, 72–79.

MESSAGE CHARACTERISTICS Suppose you must implement an unpopular policy at work. You want to persuade your employees that the policy is a positive change. Should you present one side of the issue or both sides? Given that your employees are already negatively inclined toward the policy, you will have more success in changing their attitudes if you present both sides. This shows support for one side of the issue while acknowledging that another side does exist. Moreover, refuting the other side makes it more difficult for the targets to hang on to their negative attitudes.

Messages that are obviously designed to change the target's attitude may be met with considerable negative reaction. In fact, undisguised deliberate attempts at changing attitudes may cause attitude change in the opposite direction! This is most likely to occur when the target of the persuasive communication feels her or his freedom is threatened.[35] Less threatening approaches are less likely to elicit negative reactions.

COGNITIVE ROUTES TO PERSUASION When are message characteristics more important, and when are other characteristics more important in persuasion? The elaboration likelihood model of persuasion, presented in Figure 4.2, proposes that persuasion occurs over one of two routes: the central route and the peripheral route.[36] The routes are differentiated by the amount of elaboration, or scrutiny, the target is motivated to give the message.

The *central route* to persuasion involves direct cognitive processing of the message's content. When an issue is personally relevant, the individual is motivated to think carefully about it. In the central route, the content of the message is very important. If the arguments presented are logical and convincing, attitude change will follow.

In the *peripheral route* to persuasion, the individual is not motivated to pay much attention to the message's content. The message may not be perceived as personally relevant, or the individual may be distracted. Instead, the individual is persuaded by characteristics of the persuader—for example, expertise, trustworthiness, and attractiveness. In addition, the individual may be persuaded by statistics, the number of arguments presented, or the method of presentation—all of which are nonsubstantial aspects of the message.

The elaboration likelihood model shows that the target's level of involvement with the issue is important. That involvement also determines which route to persuasion will be more effective.

We have seen that the process of persuading individuals to change their attitudes is affected by the source, the target, the message, and the route. When all

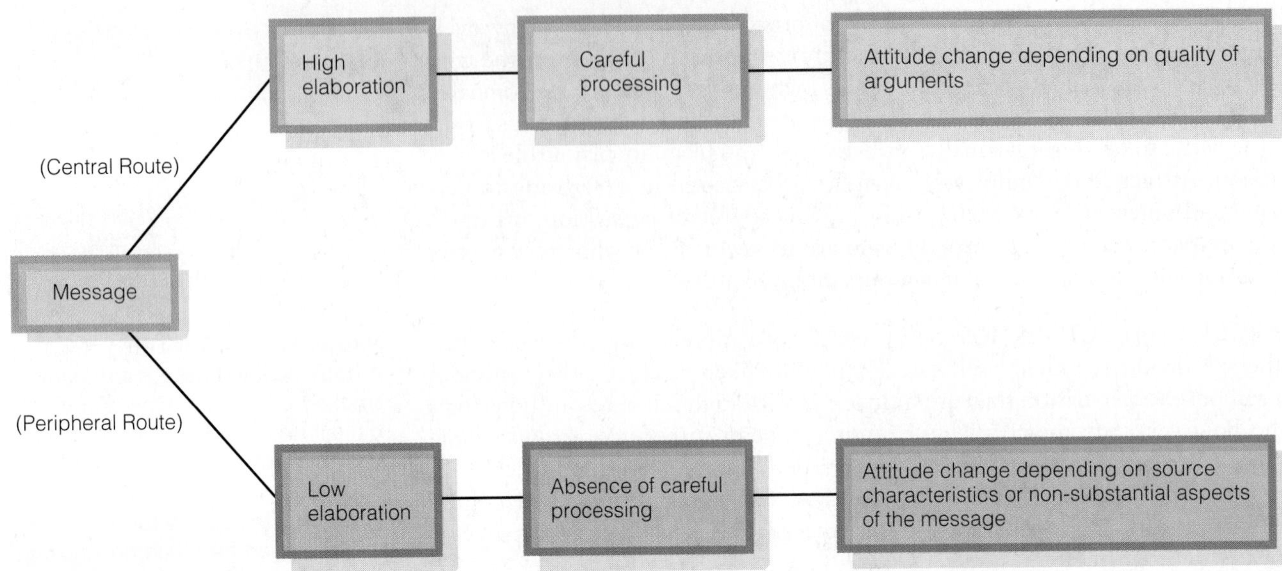

FIGURE 4.2

The Elaboration Likelihood Model of Persuasion

SOURCE: Adapted from R. E. Petty and J. T. Cacioppo, "The Elaboration Likelihood Model of Persuasion," in L. Berkowitz, ed., *Advances in Experimental Social Psychology,* vol. 19 (New York: Academic Press, 1986): 123–205.

is said and done, however, managers are merely catalysts for encouraging attitude change.

Values

Another source of individual differences is values. Values exist at a deeper level than attitudes and are more general and basic in nature. We use them to evaluate our own behavior and that of others. As such, they vary widely among individuals. **Values** are enduring beliefs that a specific mode of conduct or end state of existence is personally or socially preferable to an opposite or converse mode of conduct or end state of existence.[37] This definition was proposed by Rokeach, an early scholar of human values. Values give us a sense of right and wrong, good and bad.

values
Enduring beliefs that a specific mode of conduct or end state of existence is personally or socially preferable to an opposite or converse mode of conduct or end state of existence.

Values are learned by individuals as they grow and mature. They may change over the life span as an individual develops a sense of self. Cultures, societies, and organizations shape values. Parents and others who are respected by the individual play crucial roles in value development by providing guidance about what is right and wrong. Adolescence is a time when values come to the forefront of an individual's development, and many individuals stabilize their value systems during this life stage.

Discussion Consideration
Should an organization let an employee off work to campaign for public office?

Discussion Consideration
Ask students if they think the value systems of their parents is substantially different from their own. What are the implications for organizations if they have widely divergent sets of work values among their employees?

Businesses have shown increasing interest in values over recent years. This interest goes along with the emphasis on ethics in organizations that we described in Chapter 2. Because values are general beliefs about right and wrong, they form the basis for ethical behavior. Tandem Computers hires individuals who share the company's values of personal growth and freedom. Six-week sabbaticals every four years allow Tandem employees to pursue personal growth in areas as diverse as climbing the mountains of Nepal and studying at a world-renowned cooking school.[38] We will focus on the importance of shared values in the organization in Chapter 16. Our emphasis in this chapter is on values as sources of variation among individuals.

http://www.tandem.com/

Instrumental and Terminal Values

instrumental values
Values that represent the acceptable behaviors to be used in achieving some end state.

Rokeach distinguished between two types of values: instrumental and terminal. **Instrumental values** reflect the means to achieving goals; that is, they represent

CHALLENGE

■ 4.2

Rank Your Instrumental and Terminal Value

Look at Table 4.2. Check off the five instrumental values that you consider most important. Now enter them, in order of importance, below (most important first).

1. ____________________
2. ____________________
3. ____________________
4. ____________________
5. ____________________

Now perform the same exercise for the terminal values in Table 4.2. Check off the five terminal values that you consider most important. Now enter them, in order of importance, below (most important first).

1. ____________________
2. ____________________
3. ____________________
4. ____________________
5. ____________________

How were your rankings shaped by the generation you belong to?

As you continue reading the text, you can compare your rankings with those of national samples of Americans from earlier generations.

■ **TABLE 4.2**

Instrumental and Terminal Values

INSTRUMENTAL VALUES		
Honesty	Ambition	Responsibility
Forgiving nature	Open-mindedness	Courage
Helpfulness	Cleanliness	Competence
Self-control	Affection/love	Cheerfulness
Independence	Politeness	Intelligence
Obedience	Rationality	Imagination
TERMINAL VALUES		
World peace	Family security	Freedom
Happiness	Self-respect	Wisdom
Equality	Salvation	Prosperity
Achievement	Friendship	National security
Inner peace	Mature love	Social respect
Beauty in art and nature	Pleasure	Exciting, active life

SOURCE: Adapted with the permission of The Free Press, a Division of Macmillan, Inc. from *The Nature of Human Values,* by Milton Rokeach. Copyright © 1973 by *The Free Press.*

the acceptable behaviors to be used in achieving some end state. Instrumental values identified by Rokeach include ambition, honesty, self-sufficiency, and courageousness. **Terminal values,** in contrast, represent the goals to be achieved, or the end states of existence. Rokeach identified happiness, love, pleasure, self-respect, and freedom among the terminal values. A complete list of instrumental and terminal values is presented in Table 4.2. Instrumental and terminal values work in concert to provide individuals with goals to strive for and acceptable ways to achieve the goals.

terminal values

Values that represent the goals to be achieved, or the end states of existence.

SCIENTIFIC FOUNDATION

European Values Change with the Times

As European nations shift to a postindustrial society with an emphasis on the service sector, knowledge workers have filled organizations. A shift in values would be reflective of this broad societal change. Because older and younger workers' values were shaped by different experiences, a contrast in values would be expected. Thus, as younger workers replace older workers, the authors of one study hypothesized that (a) the workforce is now more demanding of personal involvement at work, and (b) that the workforce is more critical and demanding of employers.

To test their ideas, the authors used data from the European Values Surveys, which are massive, random national samples of many countries. This particular study focused on France, Great Britain, Germany, Denmark, the Republic of Ireland, Northern Ireland, Belgium, and the Netherlands. Respondents were asked to rank the importance of fifteen job attributes in three categories: personal development (use initiative, responsible job, achieve something, meet one's abilities, interesting job), comfort (not too much pressure, generous holidays, good hours, respected job), and material conditions (good pay and job security.) The authors used data from national samples taken in 1981 and again in 1990.

Their analysis confirmed the hypotheses. There was clear evidence of an increase in personal development as a work value in 1990 compared with 1981. The strongest emphasis on personal development was seen in Germany, the Netherlands, Great Britain, and Denmark. The authors reason that employees were indeed more demanding of employers from the finding that "good pay" showed a large net increase in importance from 1981 to 1990. Studies such as this remind managers that they must be aware of value shifts in other countries.

SOURCE: S. D. Harding and F. J. Hikspoors, "New Work Values: In Theory and Practice," *International Social Science Journal* 47 (1995): 441–455.

What are the instrumental and terminal values you consider most important? Do you think your values have been shaped by the generation you belong to? Challenge 4.2 will help you answer these questions.

Americans' rankings of instrumental and terminal values have shown remarkable stability over time.[39] Rokeach studied their rankings in four national samples from 1968, 1971, 1974, and 1981. There was considerable stability in the rankings across the studies, which spanned a thirteen-year period. Most of the values shifted only one position in the rankings over this time span. The highest-ranked instrumental values were honesty, ambition, responsibility, forgiving nature, open-mindedness, and courage. The highest-ranked terminal values were world peace, family security, freedom, happiness, self-respect, and wisdom.

Although the values of Americans as a group have been stable, individuals vary widely in their value systems. For example, social respect is one terminal value that people differ on. Some people desire respect from others and work diligently to achieve it, and other people place little importance on what others think of them. Individuals may agree that achievement is an important terminal value but may disagree on how to attain that goal.

Age also affects values. Baby boomers' values contrast with those of the baby busters, who are beginning to enter the work force. The baby busters value family life and time off from work, and prefer a balance between work and home life. This contrasts with the more driven, work-oriented value system of the boomers. The U.S. is not the only nation affected by age differences in values. Many European nations have found that values of young workers differ from those of older generations, as the Scientific Foundation feature shows.

Work Values

Work values are important because they affect how individuals behave on their jobs in terms of what is right and wrong.[40] The work values most relevant to individuals are achievement, concern for others, honesty, and fairness.[41] Achievement is a concern for the advancement of one's career. This is shown in such behaviors as working hard and seeking opportunities to develop new skills. Concern for others reflects caring, compassionate behaviors such as encouraging other employees or helping others work on difficult tasks. These behaviors constitute organizational citizenship, as we discussed earlier. Honesty is accurately providing information and refusing to mislead others for personal gain. Fairness emphasizes impartiality and recognizes different points of view. Individuals can rank-order these values in terms of their importance in their work lives.[42]

Although individuals vary in their value systems, when they share similar values at work, the results are positive. Employees who share their supervisor's values are more satisfied with their jobs and more committed to the organization.[43] Values also have profound effects on the choice of jobs. Traditionally, pay and advancement potential have been the strongest influences on job choice decisions. However, a recent study found that three other work values—achievement, concern for others, and fairness—exerted more influence on job choice decisions than did pay and promotion opportunities.[44]

This means that organizations recruiting job candidates should pay careful attention to individuals' values and to the messages that organizations send about company values. At Prudential Insurance, the key value is integrity; it is Prudential's "rock" in guiding relationships among employees, customers, and regulatory agencies.[45] At Harley-Davidson, shared values produce success, as you can see in the accompanying Organizational Reality feature.

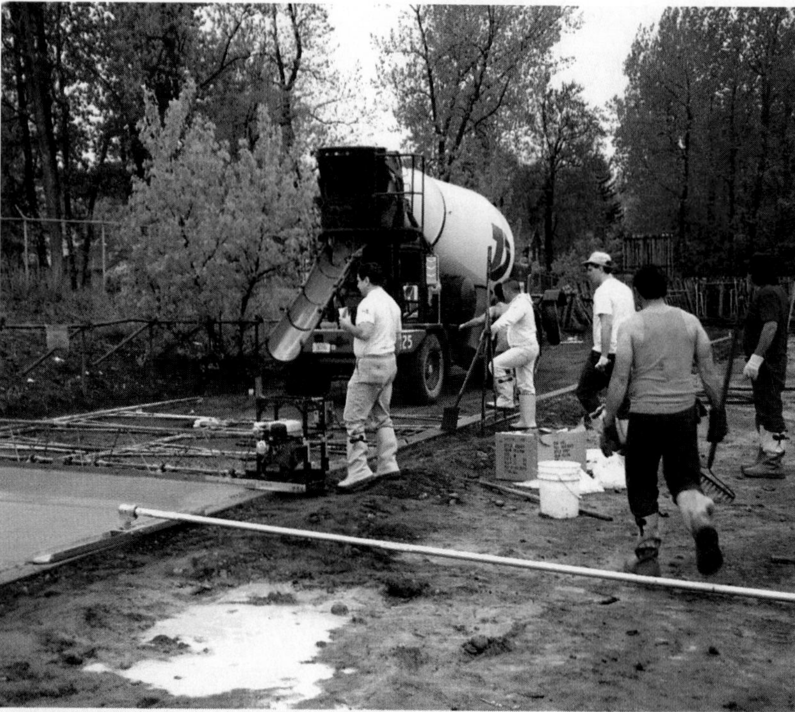

Albany Ladder needed to put a concrete equipment pad in the corner of the parking lot. To get the job done quickly, a crew of volunteers came to work on a Saturday, doing a job that was not their regular one, and with no hourly wage or overtime pay. The company is characterized by values-based management that emphasizes consensus decision making, empowerment, and shared ownership.

Cultural Differences in Values

As organizations face the challenges of an increasingly diverse work force and a global marketplace, it becomes more important than ever for them to understand the influence of culture on values. Doing business in a global marketplace often means that managers encounter a clash of values between different cultures. Take the value of loyalty, for example. Japanese workers are completely loyal to their companies; corporate loyalty is more important than even family loyalty and political loyalty.[46] In contrast, Koreans value loyalty to the person for whom one works.[47] In the United States, family and other personal loyalties are more highly valued than is loyalty to the company or one's supervisor.

Doing business in the new Russia has its challenges in terms of value differences. Cargill, a Minnesota company that is trying to establish a food-processing plant in Russia, faces many challenges. Among them is dealing with the country's nonconvertible currency. But the toughest challenge, according to Jules Carson, who heads the project, centers around value differences. "The main obstacle is getting the people to adopt a business attitude and business ethics," he said. "I don't know any short way to solve that. It will take persistence and coaching."[48]

Values also affect individuals' views of what constitutes authority. French managers value authority as a right of office and rank. Their behavior reflects this value, as they tend to use power based on their position in the organization. In contrast, managers from the Netherlands and Scandinavia value group inputs to decisions and expect their decisions to be challenged and discussed by employees.[49]

Alternate Example
Many American managers are naive in their dealings with companies in other countries. Consequently, they assume that the way they conduct business should be the norm in all situations. This is perceived as arrogance on the part of the American managers. SOURCE: A. W. Singer, "Ethics: Are Standards Lower Overseas?" *Ethicos,* March 1991.

ORGANIZATIONAL REALITY

Shared Values at Harley-Davidson Produce Bottom-Line Results

As a learning organization, Harley-Davidson Motor Company has clear objectives. Employees must understand what caused prior successes and failures. Then success can be capitalized upon and failures can be prevented. Part of Harley-Davidson's concept of the learning organization is an emphasis on shared values—ideals such as intellectual curiosity, participation, flexibility, and productivity. Key operating values include telling the truth, keeping promises, being fair, and respecting all individuals.

Harley-Davidson's past has not always been positive. In 1983, the motorcycle company was on the verge of extinction. A phenomenal turnaround was made possible by shared values centered around learning. One example is the way the company solved a problem with its assembly facility. Because their goal was to increase production, managers believed they needed to build another plant. Through big-picture, systems thinking, part of the philosophy of the learning organization, they came around to the idea of using the existing assembly plant in a different way. Shared values also create shared understandings. Because everyone learns what everyone else does, there is a shared understanding of what Harley-Davidson is all about. Employees are constantly searching for different ways of organizing, different ways of connecting everyone, different ways of improving business processes, and different ways of satisfying stakeholders. ■

SOURCES: C. Solomon, "HR Facilitates the Learning Organization Concept," *Personnel Journal*, (November 1994): 56–66, reprinted by permission of Kluwer Academic Publishers; and "Circles and Cycles," *Executive Excellence* (September 1995): 6–7. For subscription information, call 1-800-304-9782.

The sound of a Harley-Davidson Heritage Softail Classic is music to mechanic Jim Water's ears. The company is trying to patent the distinctive sound of its motorcycles.

Conducting business on a global scale often presents managers with dilemmas that call their own value systems into question. The solicitation or exchange of gifts among business people in the United States is frowned upon. In Asia and in some parts of Mexico, however, it is traditional to exchange gifts in business relationships. These gifts begin a cycle of future favors to be exchanged between the parties. What American managers may consider payoffs and bribes may be considered legitimate ways of doing business in other countries.

Value differences between cultures must be acknowledged in today's global economy. We may be prone to judging the value systems of others, but we should resist the temptation to do so. Tolerating diversity in values can help us understand other cultures. Value systems of other nations are not necessarily right or wrong—they are merely different. The following suggestions can help managers understand and work with the diverse values that characterize the global environment:[50]

1. Learn more about and recognize the values of other peoples. They view their values and customs as moral, traditional, and practical.
2. Avoid prejudging the business customs of others as immoral or corrupt. Assume they are legitimate unless proven otherwise.
3. Find legitimate ways to operate within others' ethical points of view—do not demand that they operate within your value system.
4. Avoid rationalizing "borderline" actions with excuses such as the following:
   - "This isn't really illegal or immoral."
   - "This is in the organization's best interest."
   - "No one will find out about this."
   - "The organization will back me up on this."
5. Refuse to do business when stakeholder actions violate or compromise laws or fundamental organizational values.
6. Conduct relationships as openly and as above board as possible.

Values are important because they provide guidance for behavior. They are intertwined with the concept of ethics, the next dimension of individual differences to be examined.

Ethical Behavior

■ *Ethics* is the study of moral values and moral behavior. **Ethical behavior** is acting in ways consistent with one's personal values and the commonly held values of the organization and society.[51] As we saw in Chapter 2, ethical issues are a major concern in organizations. There is evidence that paying attention to ethical issues pays off for companies. James Burke, CEO of Johnson & Johnson, put together a list of companies that devoted a great deal of attention to ethics. The group included Johnson & Johnson, Coca-Cola, Gerber, Kodak, 3M, and Pitney Bowes, among others. From 1950 to 1990, the market value of these organizations grew at an annual rate of 11.3 percent, as compared to 6.2 percent for the Dow Jones industrials as a whole.[52] Doing the right thing can positively affect an organization's performance.

ethical behavior

Acting in ways consistent with one's personal values and the commonly held values of the organization and society.

Unethical behavior by employees can affect individuals, work teams, and even the organization. Organizations thus depend on individuals to act ethically. One company recognized for its comprehensive efforts to encourage ethical behavior is General Dynamics. Several years ago, the company launched a program to integrate its ethical standards into everyday business conduct.[53] It developed a booklet of ethical standards, distributed it to all employees, and undertook a massive training effort to express to all employees the importance of ethical behavior. The company also appointed employees throughout the corporation to serve as ethics directors. The directors answer employees' questions about ethical problems and screen allegations about potential violations of General Dynamics' code of conduct. Many of the directors maintain hotlines for employees to use.

Discussion Consideration

Should ethical standards be applied universally? Or, does right and wrong change when you cross national boundaries?

Discussion Consideration

Ask students for examples of when unethical behavior has worked against a company. Can they identify situations when ethical behavior has worked against a company?

Since the hotlines were established in 1985, General Dynamics employees have contacted ethics directors more than 30,000 times. Although most employee calls are requests for information or advice, some calls have been of a more serious nature. Ethics contacts have resulted in 1,400 sanctions, the most common being warnings. Violations of time reporting, in which employees

ORGANIZATIONAL REALITY

Jack in the Box's Long Road to Recovery

The public's judgment can be harsh when it is felt that a company didn't "do the right thing." In early 1993, four children died and 300 people got sick from eating at Jack in the Box restaurants in Idaho, Nevada, and Washington. The culprit was deadly E. coli bacteria in hamburger meat. The company responded by scrapping thousands of pounds of meat, changing suppliers, installing a toll-free number for consumer complaints, and telling employees to cook the meat at a higher temperature to kill the deadly bacteria.

What angered the public, however, was the fact that it took a week for the company to admit responsibility for the food poisonings. Company officials first criticized health authorities for not telling them about new cooking regulations, and then tried to blame the problem on their meat suppliers. Even more damaging, it took two weeks after the news of the first poisoning for the parent company, Foodmaker Inc., to offer to pay for victims' hospitalization costs.

A quick response, such as Johnson & Johnson demonstrated during the Tylenol crisis, might have convinced the public of the company's concern. Since the E. coli crisis, Jack in the Box has been plagued with brand-image and financial problems. It settled with victims for more than $50 million. It also designed one of the most stringent food safety programs in the industry, which includes recalibrating grill thermostats daily. It will take the public, however, a long time to forget that the company took too long to "do the right thing." ■

SOURCES: R. Martin, "Foodmaker Revives 'Jack' to Aid Turnaround Efforts." *Nation's Restaurant News* 29 (1995): 20–21; Reprinted from *Nation's Restaurant News.*

overstate the number of hours they work, are the most frequent reasons for warnings.

Today's high-intensity business environment makes it more important to have a strong ethics program in place. In a survey of more than 4,000 employees conducted by the Washington, D.C.-based Ethics Resource Center, one-third of the employees said that they had witnessed ethical misconduct in the past year. If that many employees actually saw unethical acts, imagine how many unethical behaviors occurred behind closed doors! The most common unethical deeds witnessed were lying to supervisors (56 percent), lying on reports or falsifying records (41 percent,) stealing or theft (35 percent), sexual harassment (35 percent), drug or alcohol abuse (31 percent), and conflicts of interest (31 percent).[54]

One of the toughest challenges managers face is aligning the ideal of ethical behavior with the reality of everyday business practices. Violations of the public's trust are costly. Jack in the Box's parent company, Foodmaker, Inc., is still reeling from the effects of the burger chain's food poisoning crisis. The accompanying Organizational Reality feature presents their struggle to regain the public's confidence.

The ethical issues that individuals face at work are complex. A review of articles appearing in the *Wall Street Journal* during just one week in 1991 revealed more than sixty articles dealing with ethical issues in business.[55] As Table 4.3 shows, the themes appearing throughout the articles were distilled into twelve major ethical issues. You can see that few of these issues are clear-cut. All of them depend on the specifics of the situation, and their interpretation depends on the characteristics of the individuals examining them. For example, look at issue 2: lying. We all know that "white lies" are told in business. Is this acceptable? The answer to this question varies from person to person. Thus, the perception of what constitutes ethical versus unethical behavior in organizations varies among individuals.

■ **TABLE 4.3**

Ethical Issues from One Week in the *Wall Street Journal*

1. **Stealing:** Taking things that don't belong to you.
2. **Lying:** Saying things you know aren't true.
3. **Fraud and deceit:** Creating or perpetuating false impressions.
4. **Conflict of interest and influence buying:** Bribes, payoffs, and kickbacks.
5. **Hiding versus divulging information:** Concealing information that another party has a right to know, or failing to protect personal or proprietary information.
6. **Cheating:** Taking unfair advantage of a situation.
7. **Personal decadence:** Aiming below excellence in terms of work performance (e.g., careless or sloppy work).
8. **Interpersonal abuse:** Behaviors that are abusive of others (e.g., sexism, racism, emotional abuse).
9. **Organizational abuse:** Organizational practices that abuse members (e.g., inequitable compensation, misuses of power).
10. **Rule violations:** Breaking organizational rules.
11. **Accessory to unethical acts:** Knowing about unethical behavior and failing to report it.
12. **Ethical dilemmas:** Choosing between two equally desirable or undesirable options.

SOURCE: Adapted from J. O. Cherrington, and D. J. Cherrington, "A Menu of Moral Issues: One Week in the Life of the *Wall Street Journal*," *Journal of Business Ethics* 11 (1992): 255–265. Reprinted by permission of Kluwer Academic Publishers.

Ethical behavior is influenced by two major categories of factors: individual characteristics and organizational factors.[56] Our purpose in this section is to look at the individual influences on ethical behavior. We examine organizational influences throughout the remainder of the book—particularly in Chapter 16, where we focus on creating an organizational culture that reinforces ethical behavior.

The model that guides our discussion of individual influences on ethical behavior is presented in Figure 4.3. It shows both individual and organizational influences.

Making ethical decisions is part of each manager's job. It has been suggested that ethical decision making requires three qualities of individuals:[57]

1. The competence to identify ethical issues and evaluate the consequences of alternative courses of action.
2. The self-confidence to seek out different opinions about the issue and decide what is right in terms of a particular situation.
3. Toughmindedness—the willingness to make decisions when all that needs to be known cannot be known and when the ethical issue has no established, unambiguous solution.

Alternate Example
In their book, The Power of Ethical Management, Norman Vincent Peale and Ken Blanchard provide the following ethics check: Is it legal? Is it balanced? How will it make me feel about myself? When faced with an ethical dilemma they suggest asking yourself those three questions before proceeding. SOURCE: N. V. Peale and K. Blanchard, *The Power of Ethical Management.*

What are the individual characteristics that lead to these qualities? Our model presents four major individual differences that affect ethical behavior: value systems, locus of control, Machiavellianism, and cognitive moral development.

Value Systems

Values are systems of beliefs that affect what the individual defines as right, good, and fair. Ethics reflects the way the values are acted out. Ethical behavior, as noted earlier, is acting in ways consistent with one's personal values and the commonly held values of the organization and society.

Employees are exposed to multiple value systems: their own, their supervisor's, the company's, the customers', and others'. In most cases, the individual's greatest allegiance will be to personal values. When the value system conflicts with the behavior the person feels must be exhibited, the person experiences a value conflict. Suppose, for example, that an individual believes honesty is important in all endeavors. Yet this individual sees that those who get ahead in

■ **FIGURE 4.3**

Individual/Organizational Model of Ethical Behavior

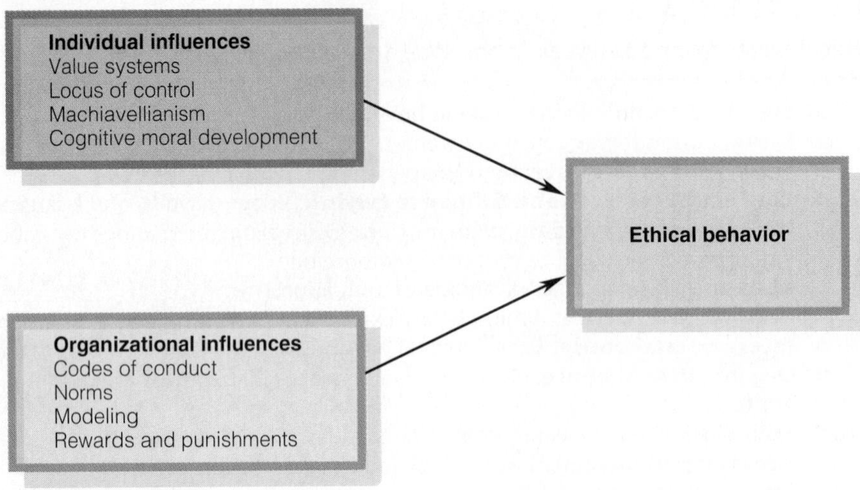

business fudge their numbers and deceive other people. Why should the individual be honest if honesty doesn't pay? It is the individual's values, a basic sense of what is right and wrong, that override the temptation to be dishonest.[58]

One person who believes that good values make good business is Kim Dawson, founder of the internationally known Kim Dawson Agency. Values have shaped her approach to the modeling and talent industries. One important value is the long-term development of people. The product that the Dawson Agency sells is the freshness of a youthful face. The modeling career ends for some at a very early age, so the agency counsels young models to pursue their education at college and plan for the future. When Dawson models work in Europe or Japan, they study by correspondence. By emphasizing honesty and long-term development, Kim Dawson demonstrates concern for her models' futures.

Locus of Control

Discussion Consideration

What are the implications of locus of control for ethical behavior? For example, are internal locus of control individuals more likely to be whistle blowers? Are externals more likely to "just go along" with an action even if they think it may not be legal or ethical?

Another individual influence on ethical behavior is locus of control. In Chapter 3, we introduced locus of control as a personality variable that affects individual behavior. Recall that individuals with an internal locus of control believe that they control events in their lives and that they are responsible for what happens to them. In contrast, individuals with an external locus of control believe that outside forces such as fate, chance, or other people control what happens to them.[59]

Internals are more likely than externals to take personal responsibility for the consequences of their ethical or unethical behavior. Externals are more apt to believe that external forces caused their ethical or unethical behavior. Research has shown that internals make more ethical decisions than do externals.[60] Internals also are more resistant to social pressure and are less willing to hurt another person, even if ordered to do so by an authority figure.[61]

Machiavellianism

Machiavellianism

A personality characteristic indicating one's willingness to do whatever it takes to get one's own way.

Another individual difference that affects ethical behavior is Machiavellianism. Niccolò Machiavelli was a sixteenth century Italian statesman. He wrote *The Prince*, a guide for acquiring and using power.[62] The primary method for achieving power that he suggested was manipulation of others. **Machiavellianism,** then, is a personality characteristic indicating one's willingness to do whatever it takes to get one's own way.

A high-Mach individual behaves in accordance with Machiavelli's ideas, which include the notion that it is better to be feared than loved. High-Machs tend to use deceit in relationships, have a cynical view of human nature, and have little concern for conventional notions of right and wrong.[63] They are skilled manipulators of other people, relying on their persuasive abilities. Low-Machs, in contrast, value loyalty and relationships. They are less willing to manipulate others for personal gain and are concerned with others' opinions.

High-Machs believe that any means justify the desired ends. They believe that manipulation of others is fine if it helps achieve a goal. Thus, high-Machs are likely to justify their manipulative behavior as ethical.[64] They are emotionally detached from other people and are oriented toward objective aspects of situations. And high-Machs are likelier than low-Machs to engage in behavior that is ethically questionable.[65] Employees can counter Machiavellian individuals by focusing on teamwork instead of on one-on-one relationships, where high-Machs have the upper hand. It is also beneficial to make interpersonal agreements public and thus less susceptible to manipulation by high-Machs.

Cognitive Moral Development

An individual's level of **cognitive moral development** also affects ethical behavior. Psychologist Lawrence Kohlberg proposed that as individuals mature, they move through a series of six stages of moral development.[66] With each successive stage, they become less dependent on other people's opinions of right and wrong and less self-centered (acting in one's own interest). At higher levels of moral development, individuals are concerned with broad principles of justice and with their self-chosen ethical principles. Kohlberg's model focuses on the decision-making process and on how individuals justify ethical decisions. His model is a cognitive developmental theory about how people think about what is right and wrong and how the decision-making process changes through interaction with peers and the environment.

cognitive moral development
The process of moving through stages of maturity in terms of making ethical decisions.

Cognitive moral development occurs at three levels, and each level consists of two stages. In Level I, called the premoral level, the person's ethical decisions are based on rewards, punishments, and self-interest. In Stage 1, the individual obeys rules to avoid punishment. In Stage 2, the individual follows the rules only if it is in his or her immediate interest to do so.

In Level II, the conventional level, the focus is on the expectations of others (parents, peers) or society. In Stage 3, individuals try to live up to the expectations of people close to them. In Stage 4, they broaden their perspective to include the laws of the larger society. They fulfill duties and obligations and want to contribute to society.

In Level III, the principled level, what is "right" is determined by universal values. The individual sees beyond laws, rules, and the expectations of other people. In Stage 5, individuals are aware that people have diverse value systems. They uphold their own values despite what others think. For a person to be classified as being in Stage 5, decisions must be based on principles of justice and rights. For example, a person who decides to picket an abortion clinic just because his religion says abortion is wrong is not a Stage 5 individual. A person who arrived at the same decision through a complex decision process based on justice and rights may be a Stage 5 individual. The key is the process rather than the decision itself. In Stage 6, the individual follows self-selected ethical principles. If there is a conflict between a law and a self-selected ethical principle, the individual acts according to the principle.

Discussion Consideration
Assume we had an accurate, easy to use measure of cognitive moral development. Should the level of an individual's cognitive moral development be a consideration in hiring decisions?

As individuals mature, their moral development passes through these stages in an irreversible sequence. Research suggests that most adults are in Stage 3 or 4. Most adults thus never reach the principled level of development (Stages 5 and 6).

Since it was proposed, more than twenty years ago, Kohlberg's model of cognitive moral development has received a great deal of research support. Individuals at higher stages of development are less likely to cheat,[67] more likely to engage in whistle-blowing,[68] and more likely to make ethical business decisions.[69,70]

Kohlberg's model has also been criticized. Gilligan, for example, has argued that the model does not take gender differences into account. Kohlberg's model was developed from a twenty-year study of eighty-four boys.[71] Gilligan contends that women's moral development follows a different pattern—one that is based not on individual rights and rules but on responsibility and relationships. Women and men face the same moral dilemmas but approach them from different perspectives—men from the perspective of equal respect and women from the perspective of compassion and care. More research is needed on gender differences in cognitive moral development.

Individual differences in values, locus of control, Machiavellianism, and cognitive moral development are important influences on ethical behavior in organizations. Given that these influences vary widely from person to person, how can organizations use this knowledge to increase ethical behavior? One action would be to hire individuals who share the organization's values. Another would be to hire only internals, low-Machs, and individuals at higher stages of cognitive moral development. This strategy obviously presents practical and legal problems.

There is evidence that cognitive moral development can be increased through training.[72] Organizations could help individuals move to higher stages of moral development by providing educational seminars. However, values, locus of control, Machiavellianism, and cognitive moral development are fairly stable in adults.

The best way to use the knowledge of individual differences may be to recognize that they help explain why ethical behavior differs among individuals and to focus managerial efforts on creating a work situation that supports ethical behavior.

Most adults are susceptible to external influences; they do not act as inde- pendent ethical agents. Instead, they look to others and to the organization for guidance. Managers can offer such guidance by providing encouragement of ethical behavior through codes of conduct, norms, modeling, and rewards and punishments, as is shown in Figure 4.3. We discuss these areas further in Chapter 16.

Managerial Implications: Attitudes, Values, and Ethics at Work

■ Managers must understand attitudes because of their effects on work behavior. By understanding how attitudes are formed and how they can be changed, managers can shape employee attitudes. Attitudes are learned through observation of other employees and by the way they are reinforced. Job satisfaction and organizational commitment are important attitudes to encourage among employees, and participative management is an excellent tool for doing so.

Values affect work behavior because they affect employees' views of what constitutes right and wrong. The diversity of the work force makes it imperative that managers understand differences in value systems. Shared values within an organization can provide the foundation for cooperative efforts toward achieving organizational goals.

Ethical behavior at work is affected by individual and organizational influences. A knowledge of individual differences in value systems, locus of control, Machiavellianism, and cognitive moral development helps managers understand why individuals have diverse views about what constitutes ethical behavior.

This chapter concludes our discussion of individual differences that affect behavior in organizations. Attitudes, values, and ethics combine with personality, perception, and attribution to make individuals unique. Individual uniqueness is a major managerial challenge, and it is one reason there is no single best way to manage people.

CLOSING SPOTLIGHT

The Ethics Game Goes Global

Ready to try a dilemma from Citicorp's Ethics Game? Suppose a vice president of your organization asks you, as corporate recruiter, to find a career opportunity for a manager in his area. You know the manager is a poor performer, although the vice president hasn't mentioned any performance issues on the manager's performance appraisal. The VP tells you he wants this manager out of his area within three months. Your rapport with the VP is critical to the success of your job. You:

a. Insist that the manager be counseled on his performance before any transfer process begins.
b. Present the manager to your fellow recruiters with the performance appraisal and say nothing about his performance.
c. Refuse to help in this transfer.
d. Present the candidate to your fellow recruiters, but are frank about the performance issues.

Teams that select *a* receive 20 points; *b*, −10; *c*, 0; *d*, 10. Employees can appeal to an appeals board if they wish. This promotes dialogue between all parties.

Since the first edition of the game, new questions have been developed for lawyers, traders, recruiters, international money managers, and a wide variety of other Citicorp employees. The game has been translated into Spanish, Portuguese, French, German, Flemish, Italian and Japanese, and has been played in sixty countries. Citicorp, which operates worldwide, uses the game as a basis for emphasizing integrity as a core value, and for shaping employees' attitudes about ethical behavior.[73] ■

Chapter Summary

- The ABC model of an attitude contends that there are three components in an attitude: affect, behavioral intentions, and cognition. Cognitive dissonance is the tension produced by a conflict between attitudes and behavior.
- Attitudes are formed through direct experience and social learning. Direct experience creates strong attitudes because the attitudes are easily accessed and active in cognitive processes.
- Attitude-behavior correspondence depends on attitude specificity, attitude relevance, timing of measurement, personality factors, and social constraints.
- Two important work attitudes are job satisfaction and organizational commitment. There are cultural differences in these attitudes, and both attitudes can be improved by providing employees with opportunities for participation in decision making.
- A manager's ability to persuade employees to change their attitudes depends on characteristics of the manager (expertise, trustworthiness, and attractiveness), the employees (self-esteem, original attitude, and mood), the message (one-sided versus two-sided), and the route (central versus peripheral).
- Values are enduring beliefs and are strongly influenced by cultures, societies, and organizations.
- Instrumental values reflect the means to achieving goals; terminal values represent the goals to be achieved.
- Ethical behavior is influenced by the individual's value system, locus of control, Machiavellianism, and cognitive moral development.

Key Terms

attitudes (p. 102)
affect (p. 102)
cognitive dissonance (p. 103)
social learning (p. 104)
job satisfaction (p. 106)
organizational citizenship behavior (p. 108)
organizational commitment (p. 109)
affective commitment (p. 109)
continuance commitment (p. 109)
values (p. 112)
instrumental values (p. 112)
terminal values (p. 113)
ethical behavior (p. 117)
Machiavellianism (p. 120)
cognitive moral development (p. 121)

Review Questions

1. Describe the ABC model of an attitude. How should each component be measured?
2. How are attitudes formed? Which source is stronger?
3. Discuss cultural differences in job satisfaction and organizational commitment.
4. What are the major influences on attitude-behavior correspondence? Why do some individuals seem to exhibit behavior that is inconsistent with their attitudes?
5. What should managers know about the persuasion process?
6. Define *values*. Distinguish between instrumental values and terminal values. Are these values generally stable, or do they change over time?
7. What is the relationship between values and ethics?
8. How does locus of control affect ethical behavior?
9. What is Machiavellianism, and how does it relate to ethical behavior?
10. Describe the stages of cognitive moral development. How does this concept affect ethical behavior in organizations?

Discussion and Communication Questions

1. What jobs do you consider to be most satisfying? Why?
2. How can managers increase their employees' job satisfaction?
3. Suppose you have an employee whose lack of commitment is affecting others in the work group. How would you go about persuading the person to change this attitude?
4. In Rokeach's studies on values, the most recent data are from 1981. Do you think values have changed since then? If so, how?
5. What are the most important influences on an individual's perceptions of ethical behavior? Can organizations change these perceptions? If so, how?
6. How can managers encourage organizational citizenship?
7. *(communication question)* Suppose you are a manager in a customer service organization. Your group includes seven supervisors who report directly to you. Each supervisor manages a team of seven customer service representatives. One of your supervisors, Linda, has complained that Joe, one of her employees, has "an attitude problem." She has requested that Joe be transferred to another team. Write a memo to Linda explaining your position on this problem and what should be done.
8. *(communication question)* Select a company that you admire for its values. Use the resources of your university library to answer two questions. First, what are the company's values? Second, how do employees enact these values? Prepare an oral presentation to present in class.
9. Think of a time when you have experienced cognitive dissonance. Analyze your experience in terms of the attitude and behavior involved. What did you do to resolve the cognitive dissonance? What other actions could you have taken? Write a brief description of your experience and your responses to the questions.

Ethics Questions

1. Is it ethical for an organization to influence an individual's ethical behavior? In other words, is ethics a personal issue that organizations should stay away from? Is it an invasion of privacy to enforce codes of conduct?
2. Suppose a coworker is engaging in behavior that you find personally unethical, but the behavior is not prohibited by the company's ethical standards. How would you handle the issue?
3. Some people have argued that the biggest deficiency of business school graduates is that they have no sense of ethics. What do you think?
4. Is it possible to operate in a completely ethical manner and be successful in business when your competitors engage in unethical tactics?
5. How do Machiavellianism and locus of control affect an individual's cognitive moral development?

Experiential Exercises

4.1 Chinese, Indian, and American Values

PURPOSE

To learn some differences between Chinese, Indian, and American value systems.

Group size

Any number of groups of five to eight people.

Time required

20+ minutes

EXERCISE SCHEDULE

1. Complete rankings (preclass)

Students rank the 15 values for either Chinese and American orientations or for Indian and American systems. If time permits, all three can be done.

	Unit time	Total time
2. Small groups (optional)	**15 min.**	**15 min.**

Groups of five to eight members try to achieve consensus on the ranking values for both Chinese and American cultures.

3. Group presentations (optional)	**15 min.**	**30 min.**

Each group presents its rankings and discusses reasons for making those decisions.

4. Discussion	**20+ min.**	**50 min.**

Instructor leads a discussion on the differences between Chinese and American value systems and presents the correct rankings.

Value rankings

Rank each of the 15 values below according to what you think they are in the Chinese, Indian (from India) and American cultures. Use "1" as the most important value for the culture and "15" as the least important value for that culture.

VALUE	AMERICAN	CHINESE	INDIAN
Achievement			
Deference			
Order			
Exhibition			
Autonomy			
Affiliation			
Intraception			
Succorance			
Dominance			
Abasement			
Nurturance			
Change			
Endurance			
Heterosexuality			
Aggression			

SOME DEFINITIONS

Succorance: Willingness to help another or to offer relief.

Abasement: To lower oneself in rank, prestige, or esteem.

Intraception: The other side of extraception, where one is governed by concrete, clearly observable physical conditions. Intraception, on the other hand, is the tendency to be governed by more subjective factors, such as feelings, fantasies, speculations and aspirations.

INTERNAL/EXTERNAL LOCUS OF CONTROL

Consider American and Chinese groups. Which one would be more internal locus of control (tend to feel in control of one's destiny, that rewards come as a result of hard work, perseverance, and responsibility)? Which one would be more external (fate, luck or other outside forces control destiny)?

MACHIAVELLIANISM

This concept was defined by Christie and Geis as the belief that one can manipulate and deceive people for personal gain. Do you think Americans or Chinese would score higher on the Machiavellian scale?

Discussion Questions

1. What are some main differences between the cultures? Did any pattern emerge?
2. Were you surprised by the results?
3. What behaviors could you expect in business dealings with Chinese (or Indians) based on their value system?
4. How do American values dictate Americans' behaviors in business situations?

1. Copyright 1993 by Dorothy Marcic. Adapted from Michael Harris Bond, ed., *The Psychology of the Chinese People, Hong Kong:* Oxford University Press, 200 Madison Ave., NY 10016, 1986. The selection used here is a portion of "Chinese Personality and Its Change," by Kuo-Shu Yang, pp. 106–170. Used with permission. Dorothy Marcic and Sheila Puffer, *Management International,* West Publishing, 1994. *All rights reserved. May not be reproduced without written permission of the publisher. For more information, contact West Publishing, Publications Dept., 610 Opperman Drive, St. Paul, MN 55164.*

4.2 Is This Behavior Ethical?

The purpose of this exercise is to explore your opinions about ethical issues faced in organizations. The class should be divided into twelve groups. Each group will randomly be assigned one of the following issues, which reflect the twelve ethical themes found in the *Wall Street Journal* study shown in Table 4.3.

1. Is it ethical to take office supplies from work for home use? Make personal long-distance calls from the office? Use company time for personal business? Or do these behaviors constitute stealing?
2. If you exaggerate your credentials in an interview, is it lying? Is lying in order to protect a coworker acceptable?
3. If you pretend to be more successful than you are in order to impress your boss, are you being deceitful?
4. How do you differentiate between a bribe and a gift?
5. If there are slight defects in a product you are selling, are you obligated to tell the buyer? If an advertised "sale" price is really the everyday price, should you divulge the information to the customer?
6. Suppose you have a friend who works at the ticket office for the convention center where Garth Brooks will be appearing. Is it cheating if you ask the friend to get you tickets so that you won't have to fight the crowd to get them? Is buying merchandise for your family at your company's cost cheating?
7. Is it immoral to do less than your best in terms of work performance? Is it immoral to accept worker's compensation when you are fully capable of working?
8. What behaviors constitute emotional abuse at work? What would you consider an abuse of one's position power?
9. Are high-stress jobs a breach of ethics? What about transfers that break up families?
10. Are all rule violations equally important? Do employees have an ethical obligation to follow company rules?
11. To what extent are you responsible for the ethical behavior of your coworkers? If you witness unethical behavior and don't report it, are you an accessory?
12. Is it ethical to help one work group at the expense of another group? For instance, suppose one group has excellent performance and you want to reward its members with an afternoon off. The other work group will have to pick up the slack and work harder if you do this. Is this ethical?

Once your group has been assigned its issue, you have two tasks:

1. First, formulate your group's answer to the ethical dilemmas.
2. After you have formulated your group's position, discuss the individual differences that may have contributed to your position. You will want to discuss the individual differences presented in this chapter as well as any others that you feel affected your position on the ethical dilemma.

Your instructor will lead the class in a discussion of how individual differences may have influenced your positions on these ethical dilemmas.

SOURCE: Issues adapted from J. O. Cherrington and D. J. Cherrington, "A Menu of Moral Issues: One Week in the Life of the *Wall Street Journal*," *Journal of Business Ethics* 11 (1992): 255–265. Reprinted by permission of Kluwer Academic Publishers.

CASE

Kidder, Peabody's Trading Scandal[1]

Kidder, Peabody & Co., once a prestigious and profitable Wall Street brokerage firm, ceased operating in December of 1994 after having a net loss for the year of almost $1 billion and selling "most of its assets to Paine Webber Group, Inc. for the fire-sale price of $670 million." Kidder, Peabody—an operating unit of General Electric Co.—self-destructed for three main reasons. First, a costly bond-trading scandal broke in April, 1994. Second, Kidder pursued a high-risk strategy of trying to dominate the market in its mortgage-backed bond business. Third, top management was unfamiliar with the ways of Wall Street and didn't properly oversee its business.

On April 17, 1994, Kidder, Peabody fired Joseph Jett for allegedly engaging in illegal trading on government bonds. Jett made both phantom trades and legitimate trades. The phantom trades were allegedly set up as forward trades to be executed within ninety days, but, in fact, were never executed. The trades were simply rolled over on a continuing basis. And the trades were allegedly handled through two bogus Federal Reserve Bank custodial accounts that Jett had set up at Kidder, Peabody.

The phantom trading produced a phony profit of $350 million, which according to some observers indicates that Jett likely made around $35 billion in illegal trades. Jett's legal trades produced a $90 million loss for Kidder, Peabody—mistakes that Jett allegedly was trying to cover with the phony profits from the phantom trades.

Jett was routinely generating $5 million to $10 million or more in profits each month for Kidder. Prior to Jett's arrival at Kidder in July, 1991, the previous record had been "some $20 million in a full year." In January and February of 1994, Jett's profits totaled $66 million—more than double his reported profits for all of 1992.

Prior to working at Kidder, Joe Jett had been with Morgan Stanley & Co. as a mortgage-backed bond trader, and then with CS First Boston Corp., working in a lesser-paying position creating packages of mortgage-backed securities. Jett's performance at Morgan Stanley was undistinguished, and he was laid off in the spring of 1989. In 1990, First Boston fired Jett for poor performance.

Jett did not have any experience in trading government securities, but was nonetheless hired in that capacity at Kidder, Peabody. Edward Cerullo, Jett's boss and the second in command at Kidder, subsequently promoted Jett because he had "a high energy level, was very executive oriented, and had the drive to succeed." However, some Kidder traders believed that Jett's hiring and subsequent promotion were due more to the firm's minority recruitment efforts than to his abilities. Some of these traders claim to have raised questions with management concerning Jett's competence and the legality of his trading activities.

In 1993, the government bond trading desk that Jett headed produced a significant portion of Kidder's $439 million operating profit. On the basis of 1993 performance, Jett was paid $9 million, promoted to managing director, and given the company's "Chairman's Award." With his promotion, Jett became the highest-ranking African-American employee at Kidder, Peabody.

Joe Jett desired to "distance himself from the experience of many blacks in American society." His classmates recall that, during his student days at Harvard Business School in the mid-1980s, he was against affirmative action and attributed the poverty of African-Americans to their laziness. At Kidder, however, "Mr. Jett set a grueling pace. On the government trading desk he was the first one in, arriving at 7:30 A.M., and the last one to leave, rarely before 7:00 P.M."

Jett's boss, Edward Cerullo, reportedly created a "produce or perish culture" but exercised lax supervision. Traders who produced were rewarded handsomely—and Cerullo is alleged to have personally benefitted as well. Indeed, Cerullo's own $20 million compensation for 1993 apparently was at least partly tied to Jett's success.

Other evidence of lax supervision at Kidder, Peabody began to emerge after Jett was fired on April 17. In late April another Kidder trader was fired for allegedly concealing an $11 million loss on bond derivatives. Then in June an options trader in London was fired for allegedly hiding $6 million in losses.

Jett attributed his firing to racism. He "denies any wrongdoing, saying he was framed by Kidder because his race makes him 'a more believable criminal' than whites at the firm." He also asserted in a counterclaim in arbitration proceedings "that his superiors at Kidder knew about and directed his trading."

General Electric chairman Jack Welch observed, "It's a pity that this ever happened." Jett "could have made $2 or $3 million honestly."

DISCUSSION QUESTIONS

1. Using the attitude model shown in Table 4.1, describe Joseph Jett's attitudes. Describe the attitudes of Jett's boss, Edward Cerullo. Describe the attitudes of other Kidder, Peabody employees.
2. How would you characterize Joseph Jett's values? How might Jett's values have influenced his behavior?
3. How would you characterize the values of other Kidder, Peabody traders? The values of Kidder, Peabody managers? What impact might their values have had on their behavior? On the behavior of others in the firm?
4. In addition to attitudes and values, what other possible explanations exist for the occurrence of unethical behavior at Kidder, Peabody?
5. What are some potential individual and organizational consequences of unethical behavior? Ethical behavior?
6. What kinds of management controls should be used to prevent a situation like the Kidder, Peabody scandal from developing?
7. Suppose that you could make considerably more money by being dishonest rather than by being honest. What would you do? Explain your answer.

SOURCE: This case was written by Michael K. McCuddy, the Louis S. and Mary L. Morgal Professor of Christian Business Ethics, College of Business Administration, Valparaiso University.

1. Adapted from W. M. Carley, M. Siconolfi, and A. K. Naj, "Major Challenge: How Will Welch Deal with Kidder Scandal? Problems Keep Coming," *The Wall Street Journal* (May 3, 1994): A1, A6; L. P. Cohen and A. M. Freedman, "A Tale of Unusual Trades," *The Wall Street Journal* (June 3, 1994): A4; L. P. Cohen, A. M. Freedman, and W. Power, "Growing Mess: Kidder's No. 2 Man Comes Under Scrutiny in Trading Scandal," *The Wall Street Journal* (May 2, 1994): A1, A10; A. M. Freedman and L. P. Cohen, "Jett's Passage: How a Kidder Trader Stumbled Before Scandal Struck," *The Wall Street Journal* (June 3, 1994): A1, A4; M. Siconolfi, "Bond Epic: How Kidder, a Tiger in April, Found Itself the Prey in December," *The Wall Street Journal* (December 29, 1994): A1, A4.

References

1. L. K. Trevino and K. A. Nelson, *Managing Business Ethics: Straight Talk About How to Do It Right* (New York: John Wiley & Sons, 1995).
2. R. E. Petty and J. T. Cacioppo, *Attitudes and Persuasion: Classic and Contemporary Approaches* (Dubuque, Iowa: Wm. C. Brown, 1981).
3. M. J. Rosenberg, C. I. Hovland, W. J. McGuire, R. P. Abelson, and J. H. Brehm, *Attitude Organization and Change* (New Haven: Yale University Press, 1960).
4. L. Festinger, *A Theory of Cognitive Dissonance* (Evanston, Ill.: Row, Peterson, 1957).
5. R. H. Fazio and M. P. Zanna, "On the Predictive Validity of Attitudes: The Roles of Direct Experience and Confidence," *Journal of Personality* 46 (1978): 228–243.
6. A. Tversky and D. Kahneman, "Judgment under Uncertainty: Heuristics and Biases," in D. Kahneman, P. Slovic, and A. Tversky, eds., *Judgment under Uncertainty* (New York: Cambridge University Press, 1982), 3–20.
7. D. Rajecki, *Attitudes*, 2d ed. (Sunderland, Mass.: Sinauer Associates, 1989).
8. I. Ajzen and M. Fishbein, "Attitude-Behavior Relations: A Theoretical Analysis and Review of Empirical Research," *Psychological Bulletin* 84 (1977): 888–918.
9. B. T. Johnson and A. H. Eagly, "Effects of Involvement on Persuasion: A Meta-Analysis," *Psychological Bulletin* 106 (1989): 290–314.
10. M. Snyder and W. B. Swann, "When Actions Reflect Attitudes: The Politics of Impression Management," *Journal of Personality and Social Psychology* 34 (1976): 1034–1042.
11. I. Ajzen and M. Fishbein, *Understanding Attitudes and Predicting Social Behavior* (Englewood Cliffs, N.J.: Prentice-Hall, 1980).
12. I. Ajzen, "From Intentions to Action: A Theory of Planned Behavior," in J. Kuhl and J. Beckmann, eds., *Action-Control: From Cognition to Behavior* (Heidelberg: Springer, 1985).
13. I. Ajzen, "The Theory of Planned Behavior," *Organizational Behavior and Human Decision Processes* 50 (1991): 1–33.
14. D. A. Garvin, "Quality Problems, Policies, and Attitudes in the United States and Japan: An Exploratory Study," *Academy of Management Journal* 29 (1986): 653–673.
15. E. A. Locke, "The Nature and Causes of Job Satisfaction," in M. Dunnette, ed., *Handbook of Industrial and Organizational Psychology* (Chicago: Rand McNally, 1976).
16. P. C. Smith, L. M. Kendall, and C. L. Hulin, *The Measurement of Satisfaction in Work and Retirement* (Skokie, Ill.: Rand McNally, 1969).
17. D. J. Weiss, R. V. Davis, G. W. England, and L. H. Lofquist, *Manual for the Minnesota Satisfaction Questionnaire* (Minneapolis: Industrial Relations Center, University of Minnesota, 1967).
18. M. T. Iaffaldano and P. M. Muchinsky, "Job Satisfaction and Job Performance: A Meta-Analysis," *Psychological Bulletin* 97 (1985): 251–273.
19. R. Griffin and T. Bateman, "Job Satisfaction and Organizational Commitment," in C. Cooper and I. Robertson, eds., *International Review of Industrial and Organizational Psychology* (New York: Wiley, 1986).
20. D. W. Organ and M. Konovsky, "Cognitive versus Affective Determinants of Organizational Citizenship Behavior," *Journal of Applied Psychology* 74 (1989): 157–164.
21. D. W. Organ, *Organizational Citizenship Behavior: The Good Soldier Syndrome* (Lexington, Mass.: Lexington Books, 1988).
22. P. M. Podsakoff, S. B. Mackenzie, and C. Hui, "Organizational Citizenship Behaviors and Managerial Evaluations of Employee Performance: A Review and Suggestions for Future Research," in *Research in Personnel and Human Resources Management*, ed. G. Ferris (Greenwich, Conn.: JAI Press, 1993), 1–40.
23. J. R. Lincoln, "Employee Work Attitudes and Management Practice in the U.S. and Japan: Evidence from a Large Comparative Survey," *California Management Review*, (Fall 1989): 89–106.
24. I. A. McCormick and C. L. Cooper, "Executive Stress: Extending the International Comparison," *Human Relations* 41 (1988): 65–72.
25. A. Krishnan and R. Krishnan, "Organizational Variables and Job Satisfaction," *Psychological Research Journal* 8 (1984): 1–11.
26. J. P. Meyer, N. J. Allen, and I. R. Gellatly, "Affective and Continuance Commitment to Organizations: Evaluation of Measures and Analysis of Concurrent and Time-Lagged Relations," *Journal of Applied Psychology* 75 (1990): 710–720.
27. R. T. Mowday, L. W. Porter, and R. M. Steers, *Employee-Organization Linkages: The Psychology of Commitment* (New York: Academic Press, 1982).
28. H. S. Becker, "Notes on the Concept of Commitment," *American Journal of Sociology* 66 (1960): 32–40.
29. J. P. Curry, D. S. Wakefield, J. L. Price, and C. W. Mueller, "On the Causal Ordering of Job Satisfaction and Organizational Commitment," *Academy of Management Journal* 29 (1986): 847–858.
30. M. J. Somers, "Organizational Commitment, Turnover, and Absenteeism: An Examination of Direct and Interaction Effects," *Journal of Organizational Behavior* 16 (1995): 49–58.
31. A. al-Meer, "Organizational Commitment: A Comparison of Westerners, Asians, and Saudis," *International Studies of Management and Organization* 19 (1989): 74–84.
32. F. Luthans, H. S. McCaul, and N. C. Dodd, "Organizational Commitment: A Comparison of American, Japanese, and Korean Employees," *Academy of Management Journal* 28 (1985): 213–219.
33. J. Cooper and R. T. Croyle, "Attitudes and Attitude Change," *Annual Review of Psychology* 35 (1984): 395–426.
34. D. M. Mackie and L. T. Worth, "Processing Deficits and the Mediation of Positive Affect in Persuasion," *Journal of Personality and Social Psychology* 57 (1989): 27–40.
35. J. W. Brehm, *Responses to Loss of Freedom: A Theory of Psychological Reactance* (New York: General Learning Press, 1972).

36. R. E. Petty and J. T. Cacioppo, *Communication and Persuasion: Central and Peripheral Routes to Attitude Change* (New York: Springer-Verlag, 1985).
37. M. Rokeach, *The Nature of Human Values* (New York: Free Press, 1973).
38. L. Bruce, "Exporting Tandem's Californiaesque Corporate Culture," *International Management* (July–August 1987): 35.
39. M. Rokeach and S. J. Ball-Rokeach, "Stability and Change in American Value Priorities, 1968–1981," *American Psychologist* 44 (1989): 775–784.
40. G. W. England, "Organizational Goals and Expected Behavior of American Managers," *Academy of Management Journal* 10 (1967): 107–117.
41. E. C. Ravlin and B. M. Meglino, "Effects of Values on Perception and Decision Making: A Study of Alternative Work Values Measures," *Journal of Applied Psychology* 72 (1987): 666–673.
42. E. C. Ravlin and B. M. Meglino, "The Transitivity of Work Values: Hierarchical Preference Ordering of Socially Desirable Stimuli," *Organizational Behavior and Human Decision Processes* 44 (1989): 494–508.
43. B. M. Meglino, E. C. Ravlin, and C. L. Adkins, "A Work Values Approach to Corporate Culture: A Field Test of the Value Congruence Process and Its Relationship to Individual Outcomes," *Journal of Applied Psychology* 74 (1989): 424–432.
44. T. A. Judge and R. D. Bretz, Jr., "Effects of Work Values on Job Choice Decisions," *Journal of Applied Psychology* 77 (1992): 261–271.
45. A. Weiss, "The Value System," *Personnel Administrator* (July 1989): 40–41.
46. R. H. Doktor, "Asian and American CEOs: A Comparative Study," *Organizational Dynamics* 18 (1990): 46–56.
47. R. L. Tung, "Handshakes across the Sea: Cross-Cultural Negotiating for Business Success," *Organizational Dynamics* (Winter 1991): 30–40.
48. S. E. Peterson, "3M Company Announces the Establishment of Wholly Owned Subsidiary in Moscow," *Minneapolis Star Tribune*, 30 January 1992, 1–2.
49. R. Neale and R. Mindel, "Rigging Up Multicultural Teamworking," *Personnel Management* (January 1992): 27–30.
50. K. Hodgson, "Adapting Ethical Decisions to a Global Marketplace," *Management Review* 81 (1992): 53–57.
51. F. Navran, "Your Role in Shaping Ethics," *Executive Excellence* 9 (1992): 11–12.
52. K. Labich, "The New Crisis in Business Ethics," *Fortune*, 20 April 1992, 167–176.
53. W. H. Wagel, "A New Focus on Business Ethics at General Dynamics," *Personnel* (August 1987): 4–8.
54. G. Flynn, "Make Employee Ethics Your Business," *Personnel Journal* (June 1995): 30–40.
55. J. O. Cherrington and D. J. Cherrington, "A Menu of Moral Issues: One Week in the Life of the *Wall Street Journal*," *Journal of Business Ethics* 11 (1992): 255–265.
56. L. K. Trevino, "Ethical Decision Making in Organizations: A Person-Situation Interactionist Model," *Academy of Management Review* 11 (1986): 601–617.
57. K. R. Andrews, "Ethics in Practice," *Harvard Business Review* (September–October 1989): 99–104.
58. A. Bhide and H. H. Stevens, "Why Be Honest if Honesty Doesn't Pay?" *Harvard Business Review* (September–October 1990): 121–129.
59. J. B. Rotter, "Generalized Expectancies for Internal versus External Control of Reinforcement," *Psychological Monographs* 80 (1966): 1–28.
60. L. K. Trevino and S. A. Youngblood, "Bad Apples in Bad Barrels: A Causal Analysis of Ethical Decision-Making Behavior," *Journal of Applied Psychology* 75 (1990): 378–385.
61. H. M. Lefcourt, *Locus of Control: Current Trends in Theory and Research*, 2d ed. (Hillsdale, N.J.: Erlbaum, 1982).
62. N. Machiavelli, *The Prince*, trans. George Bull (Middlesex, England: Penguin Books, 1961).
63. R. Christie and F. L. Geis, *Studies in Machiavellianism* (New York: Academic Press, 1970).
64. R. A. Giacalone and S. B. Knouse, "Justifying Wrongful Employee Behavior: The Role of Personality in Organizational Sabotage," *Journal of Business Ethics* 9 (1990): 55–61.
65. S. B. Knouse and R. A. Giacalone, "Ethical Decision-Making in Business: Behavioral Issues and Concerns," *Journal of Business Ethics* 11 (1992): 369–377.
66. L. Kohlberg, "Stage and Sequence: The Cognitive Developmental Approach to Socialization," in D. A. Goslin, ed., *Handbook of Socialization Theory and Research* (Chicago: Rand McNally, 1969), 347–480.
67. C. I. Malinowski and C. P. Smith, "Moral Reasoning and Moral Conduct: An Investigation Prompted by Kohlberg's Theory," *Journal of Personality and Social Psychology* 49 (1985): 1016–1027.
68. M. Brabeck, "Ethical Characteristics of Whistleblowers," *Journal of Research in Personality* 18 (1984): 41–53.
69. W. Y. Penn and B. D. Collier, "Current Research in Moral Development as a Decision Support System," *Journal of Business Ethics* 4 (1985): 131–136.
70. Trevino and Youngblood, "Bad Apples in Bad Barrels."
71. C. Gilligan, *In a Different Voice: Psychological Theory and Women's Development* (Cambridge: Harvard University Press, 1982).
72. S. A. Goldman and J. Arbuthnot, "Teaching Medical Ethics: The Cognitive-Developmental Approach," *Journal of Medical Ethics* 5 (1979): 171–181.
73. K. Ireland, "The Ethics Game," *Personnel Journal* 70 (1991): 72–75.

CHAPTER

5

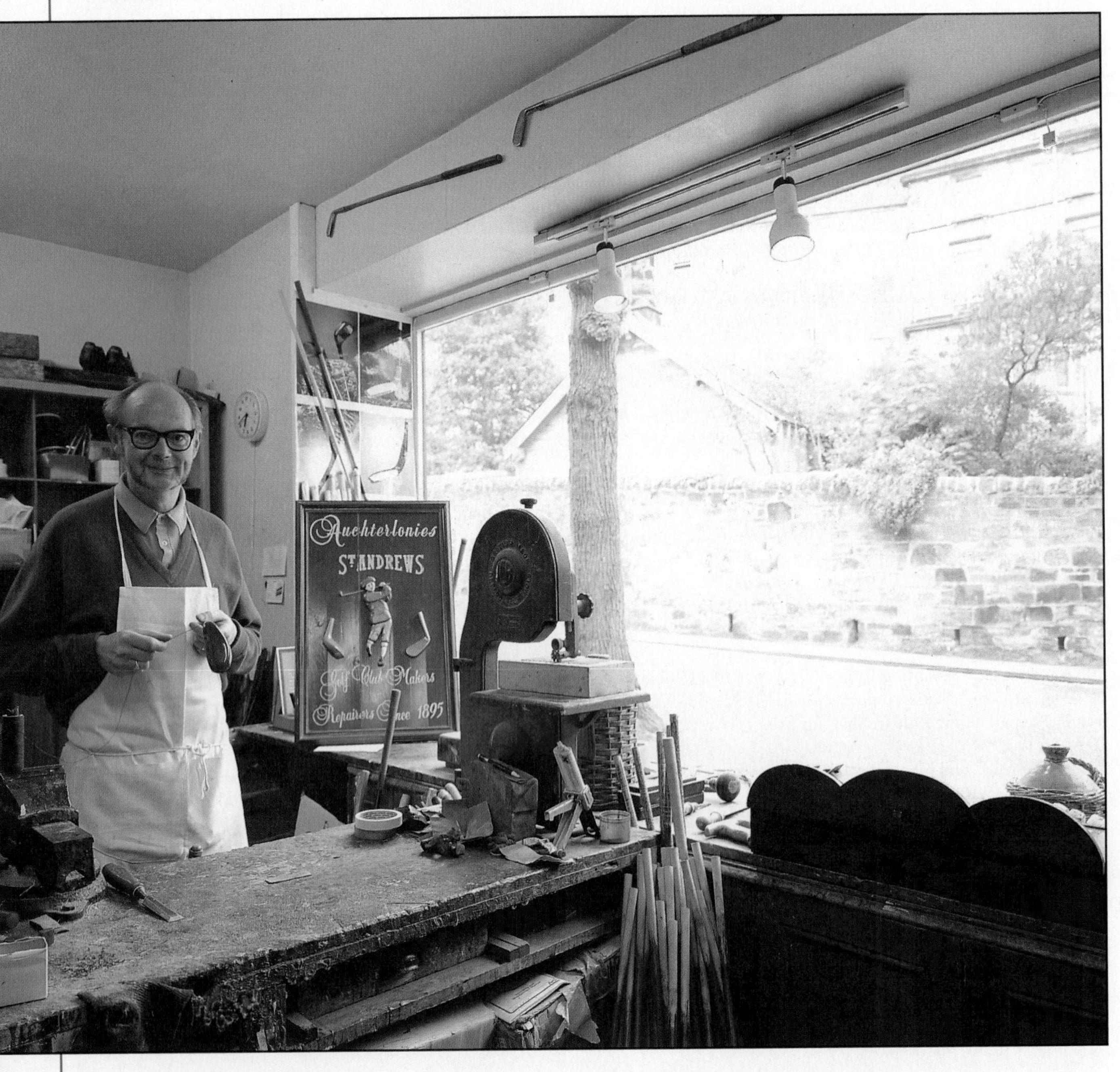
Auchterlonies
St ANDREWS
Golf Club Makers
Repairers Since 1895

Motivation in Organizations

LEARNING OBJECTIVES

After reading this chapter, you should be able to do the following:

- Define *motivation.*
- Explain how McGregor's Theory X and Theory Y relate to Maslow's Hierarchy of needs.
- Describe Herzberg's two-factor theory of motivation.
- Discuss the needs for achievement, power, and affiliation.
- Describe how inequity is determined in individual-organizational exchange relationships.
- Explain seven different strategies for resolving inequity.
- Describe the expectancy theory of motivation.
- Describe the cultural differences in motivation.

OPENING SPOTLIGHT

Motivated to Compete and Excel

http://www.ford.com/

Ford Motor Company has come a long way since its survival-motivated days in the early 1980s, once again becoming a successful, competitive American industrial leader. Although survival may not be a major issue now for Ford and its employees, being successful in a highly competitive industry that has worldwide overcapacity is a major issue. Successful in Europe for decades, Ford is now reaching out to Asia, forming a joint venture with Kia Motors Corporation in South Korea in 1995.

One of the ways in which Ford has maintained its competitive edge is through extensive training and continuing education programs to keep employees current. Ford's emphasis on employee training, development, and excellence helps increase productivity. Ford has shared its in-house training

There is no single, one best way to motivate people to work because of the variety of human needs. These two South Korean workers are welding parts to an engine on a production line in Kia Motors plant at Asan, south of Seoul.

programs with other organizations as well, such as the U.S. Air Force. Training programs can increase employee motivation and loyalty.[1]

Ford's in-house training to keep employees motivated and current draws on the latest technology, is consistent with its corporate goals and objectives, is integrated with its other established organizational systems, and draws on the best practices in the industry. Ford's instructional modules include health and safety, technology, employee relations, and product quality. Having pioneered "Quality is Job One," Ford continues to make quality a backbone of its training initiatives. If employees remain highly motivated and learn their lessons well, then what is the payoff? ■

This is the first of two chapters about motivation, behavior, and performance in work organizations. This chapter emphasizes factors within the person that explain behavior, and Chapter 6 emphasizes factors outside the person that explain behavior. In this chapter, the early sections examine needs and motives in several content theories of motivation, beginning with the early work of Abraham Maslow and Douglas McGregor. Frederick Herzberg's two-factor theory and David McClelland's need theory are then addressed in some detail. Next, the discussion turns to Adams's theory of inequity, a process theory of motivation, in the context of a contractual exchange relationship between an individual and an organization. The last section addresses expectancy theory, another process theory of motivation.

Work, Needs, Motives, and Behavior

motivation

The process of arousing and sustaining goal-directed behavior.

exogenous cause

A factor external to an individual that may help predict his or her behavior.

endogenous process

One of an individual's many internal attributes and characteristics that may help predict his or her behavior.

■ **Motivation** is the process of arousing and sustaining goal-directed behavior. Motivation is one of the more complex topics in organizational behavior. *Motivation* comes from the Latin root word *movere*, which means "to move."

Motivation theories attempt to explain and predict observable behavior. Some motivation theories emphasize factors external to the person, or **exogenous causes,** in attempting to explain and predict the person's behavior. Other theories emphasize internal attributes and characteristics of the person, or **endogenous processes,** to do the same thing.[2] Exogenous theories include reinforcement theory and goal setting, whereas endogenous theories include need theories of motivation, equity theory, and expectancy theory. This chapter focuses on the endogenous theories.

Even within these two classes of theoretical perspectives, there are substantial numbers of specific motivation theories. This is attributable to two factors. The first factor is the diversity of basic assumptions and beliefs about human nature. There are both philosophical and theological differences in perspective that have important implications for theories of motivation. Second, any single motivation theory explains only a small proportion of the variance in human behavior. Therefore, alternative theories have developed over time in an effort to account for the unexplained portions of the variance in behavior. To explain the variety of endogenous attributes and processes that influence human behavior, motivation theories have examined the depth and the breadth of internal needs and motives.

Points to Emphasize
The problem with definite explanations for motivation is typical of many problems in management, sociology, and psychology. Social sciences are often referred to as "soft sciences" because not all the variables can be controlled in studies involving human beings. The natural and physical sciences have an advantage in that they typically can control all of the variables; consequently, they are called "hard sciences."

The Depth of Internal Needs

Philosophers and scholars have theorized for centuries about internal needs and motives. Over the past century, attention has narrowed to understanding motivation in businesses and other organizations.[3] Max Weber, an early German organizational scholar, argued that the meaning of work lay not in the work itself but in its deeper potential for contributing to a person's ultimate salvation.[4] From this Calvinistic perspective, the Protestant Ethic was the fuel for human industriousness. The Protestant Ethic said a person should work hard because a person who prospered at work was more likely to find a place in heaven. Challenge 5.1 gives you an opportunity to evaluate how strongly you adhere to the Protestant Ethic.

A significantly deeper and more complex motivation theory was proposed by Sigmund Freud. He argued that a person's organizational life was founded on the compulsion to work and the power of love.[5] For Freud, much of human motivation had a sexual and unconscious basis. **Psychoanalysis** was Freud's method for delving into the unconscious mind to better understand a person's motives and needs. Freud's psychodynamic theory offers explanations for irrational and self-destructive behavior, such as the behavior manifested by the postal worker in Oklahoma who gunned down several coworkers in the late 1980s.[6] The motives underlying such traumatic work events can be understood by analyzing a person's unconscious needs and motives. Freud's theorizing is important as the basis for subsequent need theories of motivation.

psychoanalysis
Sigmund Freud's method for delving into the unconscious mind to understand better a person's motives and needs.

The Breadth of Internal Needs

Whereas Freud's research focused on the depth of human nature, later research with people in industrial settings focused on a greater breadth of internal needs and motives. Early organizational scholars made economic assumptions about human motivation and developed corresponding differential piece rate systems of pay.[7] These organizational scholars assumed that people were motivated by self-interest for economic gain. The Hawthorne Studies found social and interpersonal motives in behavior to be important while also confirming the beneficial effects of pay incentives on productivity.[8]

Each motivation theory makes assumptions about human nature and offers explanations for behavior. However, no one motivation theory or set of theories has been found universally superior. For this reason, it is important to appreciate the diversity of motivation theories. One or another may be useful in specific organizational contexts, with specific individuals or groups, or at particular times.

Discussion Consideration
Can you really motivate another individual? Football coach, Lou Holtz does not think so. Holtz said, "I'm not a great motivator, I just get rid of the guys who can't motivate themselves."

Early Theories of Motivation

■ Because motivators may change over time, we will examine two early theoretical perspectives of motivation that make fundamentally different assumptions about human nature. One perspective assumes that people act out of self-interest for the purpose of economic and material gain. Early proponents of this perspective were Adam Smith and Frederick Taylor. The other perspective assumes that people behave in ways that will gratify differing emotional needs.

Alternate Example
What may appear to be an unpleasant job to some people may have hidden motivators. For example, there is a defined advancement track for Domino's pizza delivery people. Ninety-eight percent of the owners of franchises are former delivery people. Some people delay gratification for long-term opportunities.

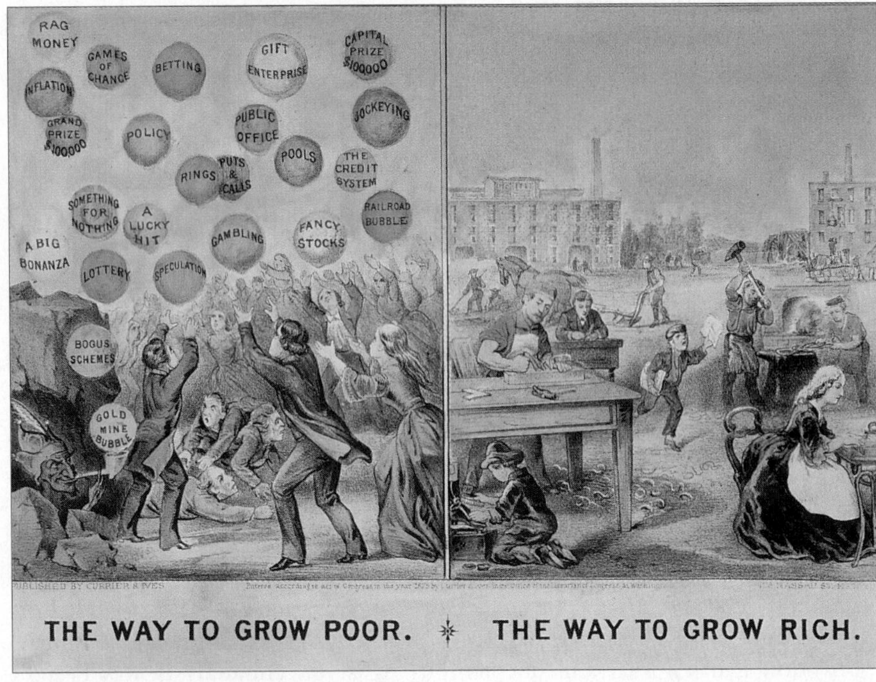

The Protestant Work Ethic is embodied in the right half of this 1875 lithograph by Currier and Ives. The way to grow rich is to be disciplined and to work hard. Weber translated this to spiritual richness as well. The left side of the lithograph suggests that frivolity is the way to poverty.

Proponents of this perspective were Sigmund Freud, Abraham Maslow, and Clayton Alderfer. Neither perspective accounted for individual diversity in needs because both perspectives assume that all people are basically the same.

Adam Smith, Economics and Frederick Taylor

self-interest

What is in the best interest and benefit to an individual.

Adam Smith was a Scottish political economist and moral philosopher who argued that a person's **self-interest** was God's providence, not the government's.[9] Gordon E. Forward, president and CEO of Chaparral Steel, believes people are motivated by "enlightened" self-interest. Self-interest is what is in the best interest and benefit to the individual; enlightened self-interest additionally recognizes the self-interest of other people. Adam Smith laid the cornerstone for the free enterprise system of economics when he formulated the "invisible hand" and the free market to explain the motivation for individual behavior. The "invisible hand" refers to the unseen forces of a free market system that shape the most efficient use of people, money, and resources for productive ends. His theory of political economy subsequently explained collective economic behavior. Smith's basic assumption was that people are motivated by self-interest for economic gain to provide the necessities and conveniences of life. This implies that financial and economic incentives to work are the most important considerations in understanding human behavior. Further, employees are most productive when motivated by self-interest.

Technology is an important concept in Smith's view, because two circumstances regulate the wealth of a nation. These are (1) the skill, dexterity, and judgment with which labor is applied and (2) the proportion of the nation's population employed in useful labor versus the proportion not so employed. It is the first of these circumstances that Smith considers more important. The more efficient and effective labor is, the greater the abundance of the nation. Technology is important because it is a factor that multiplies the productivity of labor in the creation of products or the delivery of services.

Frederick Taylor, the founder of scientific management, was a scholar also concerned with labor efficiency and effectiveness.[10] The central concern in sci-

CHALLENGE

■ 3.1

Protestant Ethic

Rate the following statements from 1 (for *disagree completely*) to 6 (for *agree completely*).

____ **1.** When the workday is finished, people should forget their jobs and enjoy themselves.
____ **2.** Hard work makes us better people.
____ **3.** The principal purpose of people's jobs is to provide them with the means for enjoying their free time.
____ **4.** Wasting time is as bad as wasting money.
____ **5.** Whenever possible, a person should relax and accept life as it is rather than always striving for unreachable goals.
____ **6.** A good indication of a person's worth is how well he or she does his or her job.
____ **7.** If all other things are equal, it is better to have a job with a lot of responsibility than one with little responsibility.
____ **8.** People who "do things the easy way" are the smart ones.

____ Total your score for the pro-Protestant Ethic items (2, 4, 6, and 7).
____ Total your score for the non-Protestant Ethic items (1, 3, 5, and 8).

A pro-Protestant Ethic score of 20 or over indicates you have a strong work ethic; 15–19 indicates a moderately strong work ethic; 9–14 indicates a moderately weak work ethic; 8 or less indicates a weak work ethic.

A non-Protestant Ethic score of 20 or over indicates you have a strong non-work ethic; 15–19 indicates a moderately strong non-work ethic; 9–14 indicates a moderately weak non-work ethic; 8 or less indicates a weak non-work ethic.

SOURCE: M. R. Blood, "Work Values and Job Satisfaction," *Journal of Applied Psychology* 53 (1969): 456–459.

entific management was with the reformation of the relationship between management and labor from one of conflict to one of cooperation.[11] Taylor saw the basis of the conflict between the two to be the division of the profits within the company. Taylor argued that instead of continuing this conflict over how to divide the profits, labor and management should form a cooperative relationship aimed at enlarging the total profits.

The basic motivational assumption within Taylor's scientific management is the same as within Adam Smith's political economic notions. Specifically, people are motivated by self-interest and economic gain. This line of reasoning stands in contrast to the more psychological theories of motivation embodied in the works of Freud, Maslow, Alderfer, and McGregor.

Abraham Maslow, Human Needs, and Clayton Alderfer

Abraham Maslow was a psychologist who proposed a theory of human motivation for understanding behavior based primarily upon a hierarchy of five need categories.[12] He recognized that there were factors other than one's needs (for example, culture) that were determinants of behavior. However, he focused his theoretical attention on specifying people's internal needs. Maslow labeled the five hierarchical categories as physiological needs, safety and security needs, love

Discussion Consideration
Do you think everyone is seeking to satisfy the entire hierarchy of needs in the workplace?

■ **FIGURE 5.1**

Human Needs, Theory X, and Theory Y

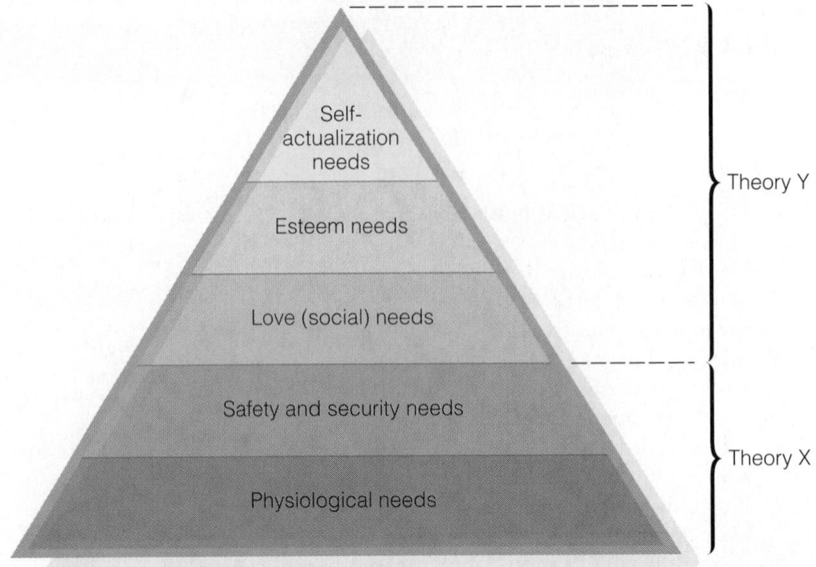

need hierarchy

The theory that behavior is determined by a progression of physical, social, and psychological needs. by higher-order needs.

Points to Emphasize

It may be useful to distinguish between primary needs and secondary needs. Primary needs are innate, or in-born. The physiological and safety needs in Maslow's hierarchy are primary needs. Secondary needs are learned through the process of socialization. The secondary needs include the social, esteem, and self-actualization needs in Maslow's hierarchy. Extending the analysis, Theory X corresponds with primary needs and Theory Y corresponds with secondary needs.

(social) needs, esteem needs, and the need for self-actualization. Maslow's **need hierarchy** is depicted in Figure 5.1, along with how the needs relate to Douglas McGregor's assumptions about people, which will be discussed next.

Maslow conceptually derived the five need categories from the early thoughts of William James[13] and John Dewey,[14] coupled with the psychodynamic thinking of Sigmund Freud and Alfred Adler.[15] Maslow's need theory was later tested in research with working populations. For example, one study reported that middle managers had different perceptions than lower-level managers of their need deficiencies and the importance of their needs.[16] More recently, Motorola has adapted motivational techniques in teamwork aimed at the social and interpersonal needs from its Penang operations in Malaysia to its 2,300-person factory in Plantation, Florida. One distinguishing feature of Maslow's need hierarchy is the following progression hypothesis. Although some research has challenged the assumption, the theory says that only ungratified needs motivate behavior.[17] Further, it is the lowest level of ungratified needs in the hierarchy that motivate behavior. As a lower level of need is met, a person progresses to the next higher level of need as a source of motivation. Hence, people progress up the hierarchy as they successively gratify each level of need. For example, an employee may satisfy security needs by obtaining two big promotions and then be motivated by developing good working relationships with coworkers. The problem with the progression hypothesis is that it leaves no way to move down the hierarchy, which could occur, for example, if a person at the esteem level lost a job and was now worried about security.

One important organizational implication of the need hierarchy concerns how to manage people at work (see Figure 5.1). Douglas McGregor understood people's motivation using Maslow's need theory. He grouped the physiological and safety needs as "lower-order" needs and the social, esteem, and self-actualization needs as "upper-order" needs. McGregor proposed two alternative sets of assumptions about people at work based upon which set of needs were the motivators.[18] He labeled these sets of assumptions **Theory X** and **Theory Y.** They are included in Table 5.1. Regardless of people's motivation to work, McGregor saw the responsibility of management as being the same. Specifically, "management is responsible for organizing the elements of productive enterprise—money, materials, equipment, people—in the interest of economic ends."[19]

Theory X

A set of assumptions of how to manage individuals who are motivated by lower-order needs.

Theory Y

A set of assumptions of how to manage individuals who are motivated by higher-order needs.

■ **TABLE 5.1**

McGregor's Assumptions about People

THEORY X	THEORY Y
■ People are by nature indolent. That is, they work as little as possible. ■ People lack ambition, dislike responsibility, and prefer to be led. ■ People are inherently self-centered and indifferent to organizational needs. ■ People are by nature resistant to change. ■ People are gullible and not very bright, the ready dupes of the charlatan and the demagogue.	■ People are not by nature passive or resistant to organizational needs. They have become so as a result of experience in organizations. ■ The motivation, the potential for development, the capacity for assuming responsibility, and the readiness to direct behavior toward organizational goals are all present in people. Management does not put them there. It is a responsibility of management to make it possible for people to recognize and develop these human characteristics for themselves. ■ The essential task of management is to arrange conditions and methods of operation so that people can achieve their own goals best by directing their own efforts toward organizational objectives.

SOURCE: D. M. McGregor, "The Human Side of Enterprise," *Management Review,* November 1957: 22–28, 88–92. Reprinted by permission of the publisher, from *Management Review,* November 1957, Copyright 1957. American Management Association, New York.

Discussion Consideration

According to Maslow, a satisfied need is not a motivator. What are the implications of this statement for managers attempting to manage highly compensated professionals?

According to McGregor, people should be treated differently according to whether they are motivated by lower-order or higher-order needs. Specifically, McGregor believed that Theory X assumptions are appropriate for employees motivated by lower-order needs. Theory Y assumptions, in contrast, are appropriate for employees motivated by higher-order needs, and Theory X assumptions are then inappropriate. In addition, McGregor believed that in the 1950s, when he was writing, the majority of American workers had satisfied their lower-order needs and were therefore motivated by higher-order needs.

Employee participation programs are one consequence of McGregor's Theory Y assumptions. Ford Motor Company's first step in revitalizing its workforce through an employee involvement (EI) program is based on Theory Y assumptions about human nature.[20] However, some companies, such as Lincoln Electric, use money as the chief source of employee motivation.

Gordon E. Forward, CEO of Chaparral Steel Company, considers the assumptions made about people central to motivation and management.[21] He views employees as resources to be developed, not labor costs to be charged off. A future-thinking, enlightened executive, Forward has fun at work and at play. Chaparral Steel has cultivated and developed a productive, loyal workforce using Maslow's need hierarchy and Theory Y assumptions about people.

Clayton Alderfer, while recognizing the value of Maslow's contribution to understanding motivation, believed that the original need hierarchy was not quite accurate in identifying and categorizing human needs.[22] As an evolutionary development of the need hierarchy, Alderfer proposed the ERG theory of motivation, which grouped human needs into only three basic categories: existence, relatedness, and growth.[23] Alderfer classified Maslow's physiological and physical safety needs in an existence need category; Maslow's interpersonal safety, love, and interpersonal esteem needs in a relatedness need category; and Maslow's self-actualization and self-esteem needs in a growth need category.

In addition to the differences in categorization of human needs, ERG theory added a regression hypothesis to go along with the progression hypothesis originally proposed by Maslow. Alderfer's regression hypothesis helped explain people's behavior when frustrated at meeting needs at the next higher level in the hierarchy. Specifically, the regression hypothesis states that people regress to the next lower category of needs and intensify their desire to gratify these needs. Hence, ERG theory explains both progressive need and gratification up the hierarchy and regression when people are faced with frustration.

Herzberg's Two-Factor Theory

■ Frederick Herzberg departed from the need hierarchy approach to motivation and examined the experiences that satisfied or dissatisfied people's needs at work. This need motivation theory became known as the two-factor theory.[24] Herzberg's original study included 200 engineers and accountants in western Pennsylvania during the 1950s. Herzberg asked these people to describe two important incidents at their jobs: one that was very satisfying and made them feel exceptionally good at work, and another that was very dissatisfying and made them feel exceptionally bad at work.

Herzberg and his colleagues believed that people had two sets of needs—one related to the animalistic avoidance of pain and one related to the humanistic desire for psychological growth. Conditions in the work environment would affect one or the other of these needs. Work conditions related to satisfaction of the need for psychological growth were labeled **motivation factors.** Work conditions related to dissatisfaction caused by discomfort or pain were labeled **hygiene factors.** Each set of factors related to one aspect of what Herzberg identified as the human being's dual nature regarding the work environment. Thus, motivation factors relate to job satisfaction, and hygiene factors relate to job dissatisfaction.[25] These two independent factors are depicted in Figure 5.2.

motivation factor
A work condition related to satisfaction of the need for psychological growth.

hygiene factor
A work condition related to dissatisfaction caused by discomfort or pain.

Motivation Factors

Job satisfaction is produced by building motivation factors into a job, according to Herzberg. This process is known as job enrichment. In the original research, the motivation factors were identified as responsibility, achievement, recognition, advancement, and the work itself. These factors relate to the content of the job and what the employee actually does on the job. When these factors are present, they lead to superior performance and effort on the part of job incumbents. These factors directly influence the way people feel about their work. Motivation factors lead to positive mental health and challenge people to grow, contribute to the work environment, and invest themselves in the organization. Recognition as an important motivation factor is used at Perpetual Financial Corporation, which hosts a companywide "Salute to Associates" to thank employees. However, programs like this one require constant supervision and do not eliminate the need for other rewards.

According to the theory and Herzberg's original results, the absence of these factors does not lead to dissatisfaction. Rather, it leads to the lack of satisfaction. The motivation factors are the more important of the two sets of factors, because they directly affect a person's motivational drive to do a good job. When they are absent, the person will be demotivated to perform well and achieve excellence. The hygiene factors are a completely distinct set of factors unrelated to the motivation to achieve and do excellent work.

Points to Emphasize
Although Herzberg has been permanently associated with research on human motivation, his larger frame of reference is questioning whether current methods of organizing work is appropriate for people's total needs and happiness. Herzberg suggested that the way tasks are designed could actually impact the level of employee motivation. Source: D. S. Pugh and D. J. Hickson, *Writers on Organizations*, 4th ed. (Newbury Park, CA: Sage Publications, 1991), 199.

Discussion Consideration
Does everyone want an enriched job? Can every job be enriched?

Hygiene Factors

Job dissatisfaction occurs when the hygiene factors are either not present or not sufficient. In the original research, the hygiene factors were company policy and administration, technical supervision, salary, interpersonal relations with one's supervisor, and working conditions, salary, and status. These factors relate to the

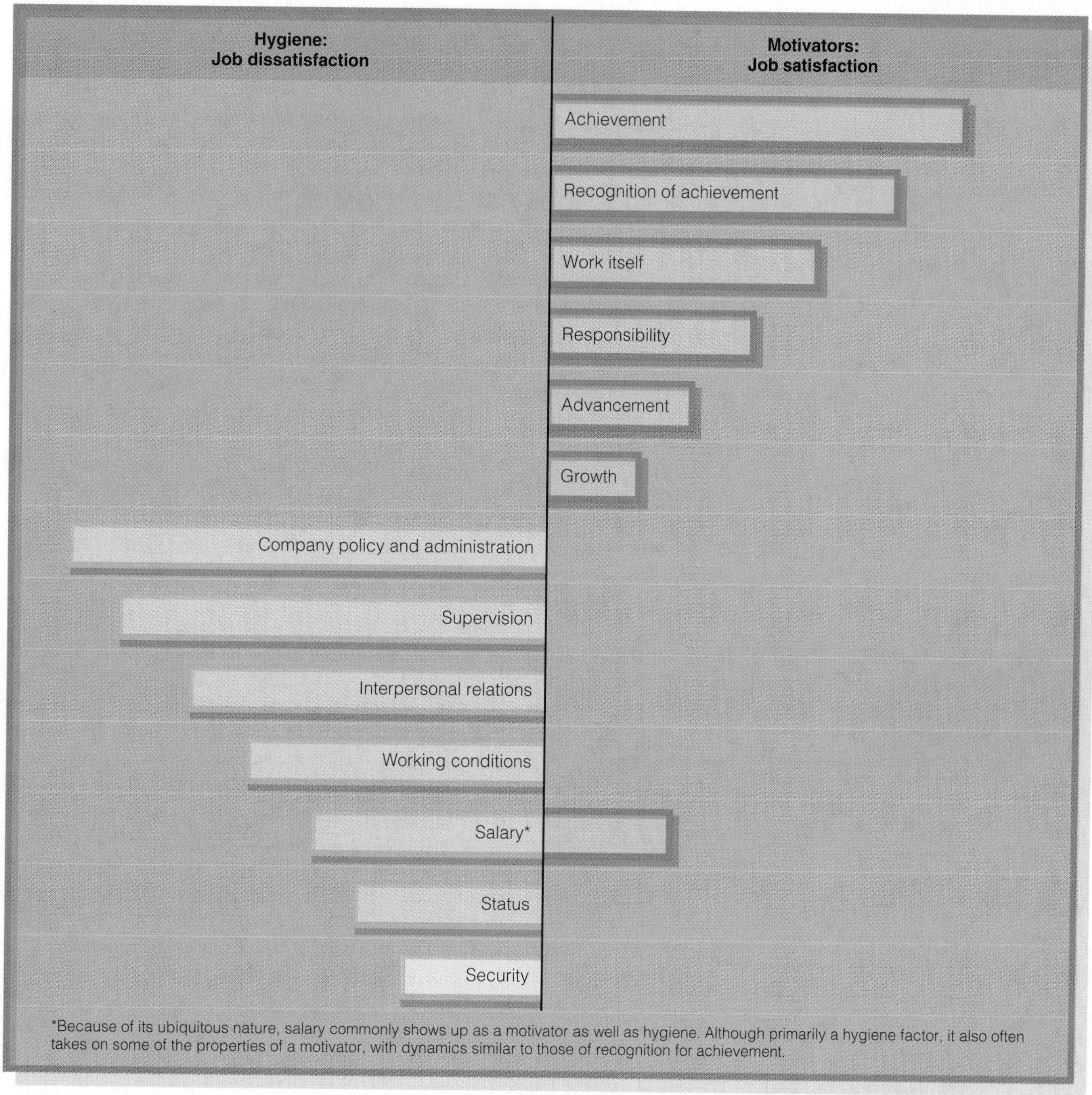

FIGURE 5.2

The Motivation-Hygiene Theory of Motivation

SOURCE: Reprinted from Frederick Herzberg, *The Managerial Choice: To Be Efficient or to Be Human* (Salt Lake City: Olympus, 1982).

context of the job and may be considered support factors. They do not directly affect a person's motivation to work but influence the extent of the person's discontent. These factors cannot stimulate psychological growth or human development. They may be thought of as maintenance factors, because they contribute to an individual's basic needs. Excellent hygiene factors result in employees' being *not dissatisfied* and contribute to the absence of complaints about these contextual considerations.

When these hygiene factors are poor or absent, the person complains about "poor supervision," "poor medical benefits," or whatever the hygiene factor is that is poor. Employees experience a deficit and are dissatisfied when the hygiene factors are not present. Employees may still be very motivated to perform their jobs well if the motivation factors are present, even in the absence of good hygiene factors. Although this may appear to be a paradox, it is not, because the motivation and hygiene factors are independent of each other.

The combination of motivation and hygiene factors can result in one of four possible job conditions. First, a job high in both motivation and hygiene factors leads to high motivation and few complaints among employees. In this job condition, employees are motivated to perform well and are contented with the conditions of their work environment. Second, a job low in both factors leads to low motivation and many complaints among employees. Under such conditions, employees are not only demotivated to perform well but are also discontented with the conditions of their work environment. Third, a job high in motivation factors and low in hygiene factors leads to high employee motivation to perform coupled with complaints about aspects of the work environment. Discontented employees may still be able to do an excellent job if they take pride in the product or service. Fourth, a job low in motivation factors and high in hygiene factors leads to low employee motivation to excel but few complaints about the work environment. These complacent employees have little motivation to do an outstanding job.

Two conclusions may be drawn at this point. First, hygiene factors are of some importance up to a threshold level, and beyond the threshold there is little value in improving the hygiene factors. Second, the presence of motivation factors is essential to enhancing employee motivation to excel at work. Challenge 5.2 asks you to rank a set of ten job rewards factors in terms of their importance to the average employee, to supervisors, and to you.

Alternate Example
A criticism of Herzberg's and Maslow's premises is that they assume that motivation focuses heavily on self-interest. Yet, history is full of examples of people who are motivated by causes, personal mission, discovery, service, beliefs, and creativity. Source: D. Osgood, "Developing a New Kind of Motivation," *Supervisory Management,* August 1992, 6.

Criticisms have been made of Herzberg's two-factor theory. One criticism concerns the classification of motivation and hygiene factors. Data have not shown a clear dichotomization of incidents into hygiene and motivator factors. For example, pay is classified by employees almost equally as a hygiene factor and a motivation factor. A second criticism is the absence of individual differences in the theory. Specifically, individual differences such as age, sex, social status, education, or occupational level may influence the classification of factors as motivation or hygiene. A third criticism is that intrinsic job factors, such as the work flow process, may be more important in determining satisfaction or dissatisfaction on the job.[26] Finally, almost all of the supporting data for the theory come from Herzberg and his students using his peculiar type of critical-incident storytelling technique. These criticisms challenge and qualify, yet do not invalidate, the theory. Herzberg's two-factor theory has important implications for job enrichment and the design of work, as discussed in Chapter 14.

McClelland's Need Theory

■ The final need theory of motivation we consider focuses on personality, as opposed to satisfaction-dissatisfaction or a hierarchy of needs. Henry Murray developed a long list of motives and manifest needs in his early studies of personality.[27] David McClelland was one psychologist inspired by Murray's early work.[28] McClelland identified three learned or acquired needs he called manifest needs. These manifest needs were the needs for achievement, for power, and for affiliation. Individuals and national cultures differ in their levels of these needs. Some individuals have a high need for achievement, whereas others have a moderate or low need for achievement. The same is true for the other two needs. Each need has quite different implications for people's behavior. The Murray Thematic Apperception Test (TAT) was used as an early measure of the achievement motive and was further developed, both qualitatively and quantitatively, by McClelland and his associates.[29] The TAT is a projective test, as was discussed in Chapter 3.

CHALLENGE

■ 5.2

What's Important to Employees?

There are many possible job rewards that employees may receive. Listed below are ten possible job reward factors. Rank these factors three times. First, rank them as you think the average employee would rank them. Second, rank them as you think the average employee's *supervisor* would rank them *for the employee*. Finally, rank them according to what *you* consider important.

Employee	*Supervisor*	*You*	
			1. job security
			2. full appreciation of work done
			3. promotion and growth in the organization
			4. good wages
			5. interesting work
			6. good working conditions
			7. tactful discipline
			8. sympathetic help with personal problems
			9. personal loyalty to employees
			10. a feeling of being in on things

Your instructor has normative data for 1,000 employees and their supervisors which will help you interpret your results and place the results in the context of Maslow's need hierarchy and Herzberg's two-factor theory of motivation.

SOURCE: "Crossed Wires on Employee Motivation," *Training and Development* 49 (1995): 59–60. American Society for Training and Development.

Need for Achievement

The **need for achievement** concerns issues of excellence, competition, challenging goals, persistence, and overcoming difficulties.[30] A person with a high need for achievement is one who seeks excellence in performance, enjoys difficult and challenging goals, and is persevering and competitive in work activities. Questions that address the need for achievement are ones like these: Do you enjoy difficult, challenging work activities? Do you strive to exceed your performance objectives? Do you seek out new ways to overcome difficulties?

McClelland found that people with a high need for achievement perform better than those with a moderate or low need for achievement, and he has noted national differences in achievement motivation. Individuals with a high need for achievement have three unique characteristics. First, they set moderately difficult goals, yet ones that are achievable, because they want both challenge and a good chance for success. Second, they like to receive feedback on their progress toward these goals. Because success is important to them, they like to know how they are doing. Third, they do not like having external events or other people interfere with their progress toward the goals. They are most comfortable working on individual tasks and activities that they control.

High achievers often hope and plan for success. They may be quite content to work alone or with other people—whichever is most appropriate to their task. High achievers like being very good at what they do, and they establish expertise and competence in their chosen endeavors. An example of a person with a high need for achievement is an information systems engineer who declines supervisory or managerial responsibility and devotes her energy to being the very best information systems engineer she can be.

need for achievement

A manifest (easily perceived) need that concerns individuals' issues of excellence, competition, challenging goals, persistence, and overcoming difficulties.

Points to Emphasize

Highly educated individuals may assume that achievement is only correlated with work. However, it is important to illustrate that some individuals may not achieve in traditional work paths, but may excel in other areas of their lives.

Discussion Consideration

High achievers like to work in circumstances where they can control the outcome. Yet, in many organizational situations, high achievers may work in teams or manage the work of others. In these situations, they do not have direct control over the outcomes. How can high achievers satisfy their need for achievement in these situations?

People with moderate and low needs for achievement will be satisfied with less challenging goals, lower levels of excellence, and less persistence in the face of difficulty. However, these same people may have high needs for power or affiliation.

Need for Power

need for power

A manifest (easily perceived) need that concerns an individual's need to make an impact on others, influence others, change people or events, and make a difference in life

Discussion Consideration

There are 2 faces of power: socialized and personalized. Have students identify historical figures they think exemplified these two faces of power.

The **need for power** is concerned with making an impact on others, the desire to influence others, the urge to change people or events, and the desire to make a difference in life.[31] The need for power is interpersonal, because it involves influence attempts directed at other people. People with a high need for power are people who like to be in control of people and events. McClelland makes an important distinction between socialized power, which is used for the social benefit of many, and personalized power, which is used for the personal gain of the individual. The former is a constructive force in organizations, whereas the latter may be a very disruptive, destructive force in organizations.

A high need for power was one distinguishing characteristic of managers rated the "best" in McClelland's research. Specifically, the best managers had a very high need for socialized power, used for the collective well-being of the group, as opposed to personalized power. These managers are concerned for others; have an interest in the organization's larger goals; and have a desire to be useful to the larger group, organization, and society.[32]

Social and hierarchical status are important considerations for people with a high need for power. The more they are able to rise to the top of their organizations, the greater is their ability to exercise power, influence, and control so as to make an impact. Successful managers have the greatest upward velocity in an organization; they rise to higher managerial levels more quickly than their contemporaries.[33] These successful managers benefit their organizations most if they have a high socialized power need. The need for power is discussed further in Chapter 11, on power and politics.

Need for Affiliation

need for affiliation

A manifest (easily perceived) need that concerns an individual's need to establish and maintain warm, close, intimate relationships with other people.

Discussion Consideration

What occupations do students think of for people with a high need for affiliation? A high need for autonomy?

The **need for affiliation** is concerned with establishing and maintaining warm, close, intimate relationships with other people.[34] People with a high need for affiliation are motivated to express their emotions and feelings to others while expecting other people to do the same in return. They find conflicts and complications in their relationships disturbing and are strongly motivated to work through any such barriers to closeness. The relationships they have with others are therefore close and personal, emphasizing friendship and companionship.

People who have moderate to low needs for affiliation are more likely to feel comfortable working alone for extended periods of time. Modest or low levels of interaction with others are likely to satisfy these people's affiliation needs, allowing them to focus their attention on other needs and activities. People with a high need for affiliation, in contrast, always hope to be included in a range of interpersonal activities, in or away from work. They may play important integrative roles in group or intergroup activities because they work to achieve harmony and closeness in all relationships.

Over and above these three needs, Murray's manifest needs theory included the need for autonomy.[35] This is the desire for independence and freedom from any constraints. People with a high need for autonomy like to work alone and to control the pace of their work. They dislike bureaucratic rules, regulations, and procedures. Figure 5.3 is a summary chart of the four need theories of motivation just discussed; it shows the parallel relationships between the needs in each of the theories. Where Maslow and Alderfer would refer to higher- and lower-

	Maslow	Alderfer		Herzberg	McClelland
Higher order needs	Self-actualization	Growth	Motivational factors	The work itself: • Responsibility • Advancement • Growth	Need for achievement
	Esteem			Achievement	
	Belongingness (social and love)	Relatedness		Recognition	Need for power
			Hygiene factors	Quality of interpersonal working relationships	Need for affiliation
				Job security	
Lower order needs	Safety and security	Existence		Working conditions	
	Physiological			Salary	

■ **FIGURE 5.3**

Four Need Theories of Motivation

order needs, Herzberg would refer to motivation and hygiene factors. The accompanying Organizational Reality feature shows how the Calvert Group has organized employees' needs in still a different way.

Individual-Organizational Exchanges

■ Each need theory we have examined focuses on the internal human needs that motivate behavior. We now turn our attention to the social processes that influence motivation and behavior. For example, Peter Blau's examination of social life suggested that power and exchange are important considerations in understanding human behavior.[36] In the same vein, Amitai Etzioni developed three categories of exchange relationships or involvements people have with organizations: committed, calculated, and alienated involvements.[37] The implications of these involvements for power are discussed in detail in Chapter 11. Etzioni characterized committed involvements as moral relationships of high positive intensity, calculated involvements as ones of low positive or low negative intensity, and alienated involvements as ones of high negative intensity. Committed involvements may characterize a person's relationship with a religious group, and alienated involvements may characterize a person's relationship with a prison system. Calculated involvements and Blau's ideas about power in social exchange are the best frameworks for understanding a person's relationship with a work organization.

Discussion Consideration
Ask students to provide an example of social exchange theory from their university setting. What would be an example in a personal relationship? Is it appropriate to apply social exchange theory in a calculated way in a relationship?

Demands and Contributions

Calculated involvements are based on the notion of social exchange in which each party in the relationship demands certain things of the other and contributes accordingly to the exchange. Business partnerships and commercial deals are excellent examples of calculated involvements. When they work well and both parties to the exchange benefit, the relationship has a positive orientation. When losses occur or conflicts arise, the relationship has a negative orientation. A model for examining these calculated exchange relationships is set out in Figure 5.4. We use this model to examine the nature of the relationship between a person and his or her employing organization.[38] The same basic

ORGANIZATIONAL REALITY

Calvert Group Fulfills Basic Needs

Calvert Group is a mutual funds company in Bethesda, Maryland. Concerned that a 30 percent turnover rate was too high, Calvert executives restructured their benefits and human resource programs to address four human needs. These are: survival, social/emotional, psychological, and spiritual.

Survival needs are addressed through a Personal Choices Benefits Plan that offers different medical, dental, long-term care, time-off benefit, and savings plans. These plans are concerned with employee health, wellness, and long-term well-being; and employees are able to make choices.

Social/emotional needs are addressed through work and family programs, such as flextime, job sharing, and parental leave, as well as through a variety of training programs in diversity, sexual harassment, and ADA awareness.

Psychological needs are addressed through job opportunities, educational assistance, on-site learning opportunities, management development, employee empowerment, and numerous reward systems.

Spiritual needs are addressed through career development, community involvement, volunteerism, and an employee giving campaign.

Calvert Group's explicit recognition of employees' basic needs and providing choices in meeting these needs is a human investment with high returns. Calvert has become an employer of choice and the turnover rate dropped to 5 percent in 1995. ■

SOURCE: D. Anfuso, "Creating a Culture of Caring Pays Off," *Personnel Journal* (August 1995): 70–77.

model can be used to examine the relationship between two individuals or two organizations.

DEMANDS Each party to the exchange makes demands upon the other. These demands express the expectations that each party has of the other in the relationship. The organization expresses its demands on the individual in the form of goal or mission statements, job expectations, performance objectives, and performance feedback. These are among the primary and formal mechanisms through which people learn about the organization's demands and expectations of them.

The organization is not alone in making demands of the relationship. The individual has needs to be satisfied as well, as we have previously discussed. These needs form the basis for the expectations or demands placed on the organization by the individual. These needs may be conceptualized from the perspective of Maslow, Alderfer, Herzberg, or McClelland. Different individuals have different needs.

Alternate Example
Annual performance appraisals are negative motivators for total quality management (TQM) programs. TQM teams are empowered to make crucial decisions, and many feel that to keep the morale and motivation intact, compensation should be determined for a group rather than for individuals.

CONTRIBUTIONS Whereas each party to the exchange makes demands upon the other, each also has contributions to make to the relationship. These contributions are the basis for satisfying the demands expressed by the other party in the relationship. The process of person-organization fit in this regard and of reciprocity are discussed in Chapter 17. Employees are able to satisfy organizational demands through a range of contributions. These contributions include their skills, abilities, knowledge, energy, professional contacts, and native talents. As people grow and develop over time, they are able to increasingly satisfy the range of demands and expectations placed upon them by the organization.

In a similar fashion, organizations have a range of contributions available to the exchange relationship to meet individual needs. These contributions include salary, benefits, advancement opportunities, security, status, and social affilia-

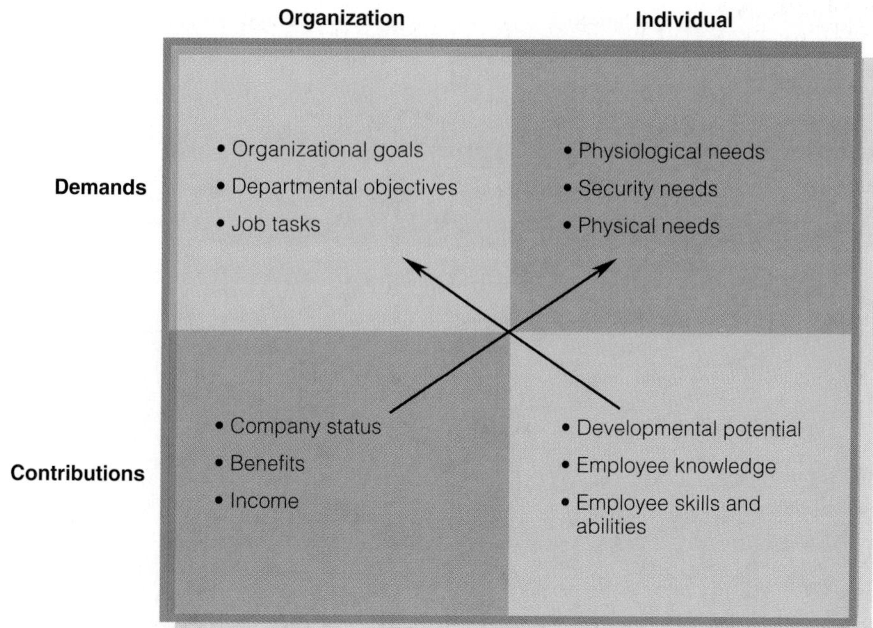

FIGURE 5.4

The Individual-Organizational Exchange Relationship

SOURCE: Reproduced with permission from McGraw-Hill, Inc.

tion. Some organizations are richer in resources and better able to meet employee needs, whereas other organizations have fewer resources available to meet employee needs. Thus, one of the concerns that individuals and organizations alike have is whether the relationship is a fair deal or an equitable arrangement for both members of the relationship.

Adams's Theory of Inequity

Blau's and Etzioni's ideas about social exchange and relationship provide a context for understanding fairness, equity, and inequity in work relationships. Stacy Adams explicitly developed the issue of **inequity** in the social exchange process.[39] Adams's theory of inequity suggests that people are motivated when they find themselves in situations of inequity or unfairness.[40] Inequity is when a person receives more, or less, than the person believes is deserved based on effort and/or contribution. Inequity leads to the experience of tension, and tension motivates a person to act in a manner to resolve the inequity.

inequity
The situation in which a person perceives he or she is receiving less than he or she is giving, or is giving less than he or she is receiving.

When does a person know that the situation is inequitable or unfair? Adams suggests that people examine the contribution portion of the exchange relationship just discussed. Specifically, people consider their inputs (their own contributions to the relationship) and their outcomes (the organization's contributions to the relationship). People then calculate an input/outcome ratio, which they compare with that of a generalized or comparison other. An inequitable situation is depicted in Figure 5.5. In the example, the comparison other is making $11,000 more per year than the person while all other input and outcome considerations are the same. This underpayment condition motivates the person to resolve the inequity, according to Adams.

Although not illustrated in the example, nontangible inputs, like emotional investment, and nontangible outcomes, like job satisfaction, may well enter into a person's equity equation. With regard to pay inequity, this has been a particularly thorny issue for women in some professions and companies. Eastman Kodak and other companies have made real progress in addressing this inequity through pay equity.[41] As organizations become increasingly international, it may be difficult to determine pay and benefit equity/inequity across national borders.

■ **FIGURE 5.5**
Inequity in the Work Environment

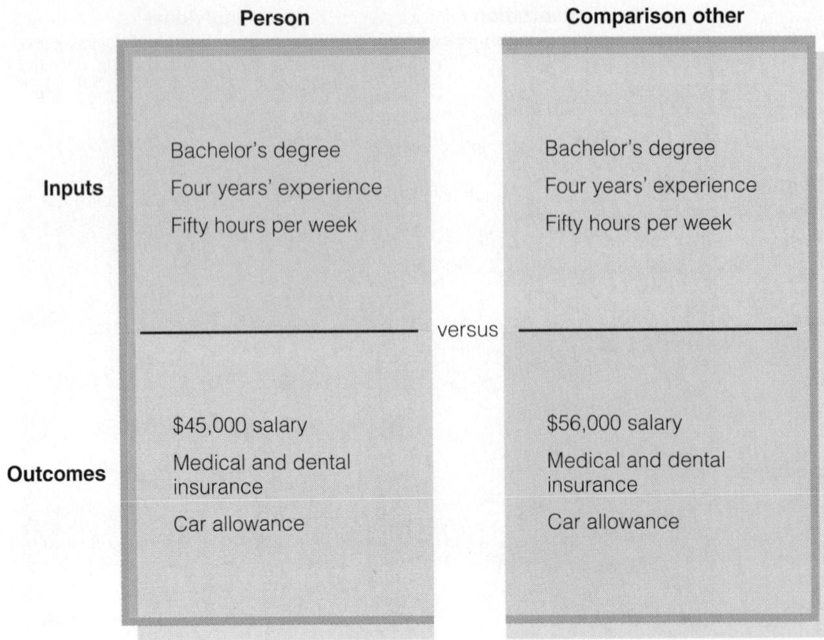

Adams would consider the inequity in Figure 5.5 to be a first level of inequity. A more severe, second level of inequity would occur if the comparison other's inputs were lower than the person's. This would occur, for example, if the comparison other worked only thirty-five hours a week or had only two years of experience. Inequalities in one (inputs or outcomes) coupled with equality in the other (inputs or outcomes) is experienced as a less severe inequity than inequalities in both inputs and outcomes. Adams's theory, however, does not provide a way of determining if some inputs (such as effort or experience) or some outcomes are more important or weighted more than others, such as a degree or certification.

The Resolution of Inequity

Once a person establishes the existence of an inequity, a number of strategies can be used to restore equity to the situation. Adams's theory provides seven basic strategies to restore equity for the person. These strategies are (1) to alter the person's outcomes, (2) to alter the person's inputs, (3) to alter the comparison other's outcomes, (4) to alter the comparison other's inputs, (5) to change who is used as a comparison other, (6) to rationalize the inequity, and (7) to leave the organizational situation. The accompanying Scientific Foundation feature examines one study of exceptionally high salaries.

Within each of the first four strategies, a wide variety of tactics can be employed. For example, if the strategy in the example shown in Figure 5.5 is to increase the person's outcomes by $11,000 per year, the tactic would be a meeting between the person and the manager concerning the issue of salary equity. The person would present relevant data on the issue. Another tactic would be for the person to work with the company's compensation specialists. A third tactic would be for the person to bring the matter before an equity committee in the company. A fourth tactic would be for the person to seek advice from the legal department.

The selection of a strategy and a set of tactics is a sensitive issue with possible long-term consequences. In this example, a strategy aimed at reducing the comparison other's outcomes may have the desired short-term effect of restoring equity while having adverse long-term consequences in terms of morale and

SCIENTIFIC FOUNDATION

Are You Worth $2 Million?

Graduate students in a business school read a salary scenario and a brief description of a senior executive who made $2 million for one year. The descriptions included job title and responsibility, a brief history of the executive, and personal and/or family information about the executive. In addition, some students were asked to assume that they were the executive.

The students rated how fair the salary was on a five-point scale: very fair to very unfair. Then students were asked to rate the extent to which the following 14 factors justified the salary: personal need, hard work, work experience and training, market forces, level of performance, company's ability to pay, unique talents and abilities, contribution to the reputation of the company, positive benefit to society, "in America, people should be able to make this much," similar executives make similar amounts, difficulty of the job, good luck, and high job responsibility.

Justifications for exceptionally high salaries varied by job and rater perspective. The results indicated that different justifications were associated with different occupations, but the justifications were consistent across genders. Hard work, talent, and performance factors were viewed as more important considerations than were external factors. The perceptions of salary fairness increased when the rater was the recipient (I'm worth $2 million!). While the sensitivity to the obvious inequity of a $2 million salary was low, tomorrow's managers are likely to base pay on performance, not social norms, the market, or gender.

SOURCE: T. R. Mitchell, J. George-Falvy, and S. R. Crandall, "Business Students' Justifications of Exceptionally High Salaries: Is It OK to Make $2 Million a Year?" *Group & Organization Management* 18 (1993): 500–522.

productivity. Similarly, the choice of legal tactics may result in equity but have the long-term consequence of damaged relationships in the workplace. Therefore, as a person formulates the strategy and tactics to restore equity, the range of consequences of alternative actions must be taken into account. Hence, not all strategies or tactics are equally preferred. The equity theory does not include a hierarchy predicting which inequity reduction strategy a person will or should choose.

Field studies on equity theory suggest that it may help explain important organizational behaviors. For example, one study found that workers who perceived compensation decisions as equitable displayed greater job satisfaction and organizational commitment.[42] In addition, equity theory may play an important role in labor-management relationships with regard to union-negotiated benefits.

New Perspectives on Equity Theory

Since the original formulation of the theory of inequity, now usually referred to as equity theory, a number of revisions have been made in light of new theories and research. One important theoretical revision proposes three types of individuals based on preferences for equity.[43] **Equity sensitives** are those people who prefer equity based on the originally formed theory. **Benevolents** are people who are comfortable with an equity ratio less than their comparison other, as exhibited in the Calvinistic heritage of the Dutch.[44] These people may be thought of as givers. **Entitleds** are people who are comfortable with an equity ratio greater than their comparison other, as exhibited by some offspring of the affluent who want and expect more.[45] These people may be thought of as takers.

Recent research found that a person's organizational position influences self-imposed performance expectations.[46] Specifically, a two-level move up in an organization with no additional pay creates a higher self-imposed performance expectation than a one-level move up with modest additional pay. Similarly, a two-level move down in an organization with no reduction in pay creates a lower self-imposed performance expectation than a one-level move down with a modest decrease in pay. This suggests that organizational position may be more

equity sensitive
An individual who prefers an equity ratio equal to that of his or her comparison other.

benevolent
An individual who is comfortable with an equity ratio less than that of his or her comparison other.

entitled
An individual who is comfortable with an equity ratio greater than that of his or her comparison other.

Discussion Consideration
Is equity sensitivity a stable trait? Or, does it vary from situation to situation? Ask the students to identify situations when they have been equity sensitive, benevolent, or felt entitled.

important than pay in determining the level of a person's performance expectations. Some limitations of equity theory are its heavy emphasis on pay as an outcome, the difficulty in controlling the choices of a comparison other, and the difficulty the theory has had in explaining the overpayment condition.

Most studies of equity theory take a short-term perspective.[47] However, equity comparisons over the long term should be considered as well. Increasing, decreasing, or constant experiences of inequity over time may have very different consequences for people.[48] For example, do increasing experiences of inequity have a debilitating effect on people? In addition, equity theory may help companies implement two-tiered wage structures, such as those at American Airlines. In a two-tiered system, one group of employees receives different pay and benefits than another group of employees. A study of 1,935 rank-and-file members in one retail chain using a two-tiered wage structure confirmed the predictions of equity theory.[49] The researchers suggest that unions and management may want to consider work location and employment status (part-time versus full-time) prior to the implementation of a two-tiered system.

http://www.americanair.com

Expectancy Theory of Motivation

■ Whereas Adams's theory of inequity focuses on a social process, Vroom's expectancy theory of motivation focuses on personal perceptions. His theory is founded on the basic notions that people desire certain outcomes of behavior, which may be thought of as rewards or consequences of behavior, and that they believe there are relationships between the effort they put forth, the performance they achieve, and the outcomes they receive. Expectancy theory is a cognitive, process theory of motivation.

valence
The value or importance one places on a particular reward.

expectancy
The belief that effort leads to performance.

instrumentality
The belief that performance is related to rewards.

The key constructs in the expectancy theory of motivation are the **valence** of an outcome, **expectancy,** and **instrumentality.**[50] Valence is the value or importance one places on a particular reward. Expectancy is the belief that effort leads to performance (for example, "If I try harder, I can do better"). Instrumentality is the belief that performance is related to the rewards (for example, "If I perform better, I will get more pay"). A model for the expectancy theory notions of effort, performance, and rewards is depicted in Figure 5.6.

Discussion Consideration
Should the three components of expectancy theory be given equal weight or is one component more important than the others?

Valence, expectancy, and instrumentality are all important to a person's motivation. Expectancy and instrumentality concern a person's beliefs about how effort, performance, and rewards are related. For example, a person may firmly believe that an increase in effort has a direct, positive effect on improved performance and that a reduced amount of effort results in a commensurate reduction in performance. Another person may have a very different set of beliefs about the effort-performance link. The person might believe that regardless of the amount of additional effort put forth, no improvement in performance is possible. Therefore, the perceived relationship between effort and performance varies from person to person and from activity to activity.

In a similar fashion, people's beliefs about the performance-reward link varies. One person may believe that an improvement in performance has a direct, positive effect on the rewards received, whereas another person may believe that an improvement in performance has no effect on the rewards received. Again, the perceived relationship between performance and rewards varies from person to person and from situation to situation. From a motivation perspective, it is the person's belief about the relationships between these constructs that is important, not the actual nature of the relationship. The accompanying Organizational Reality feature shows J. H. "Bud" Morgan's attempt to make a clear connection between performance and reward.

http://www.tenneco.com/

Expectancy theory has been used by managers and companies to design motivation programs,[51] such as Tenneco's PP&E (Performance Planning and Evaluation) system.[52] In Tenneco's case, the PP&E system was designed to enhance a

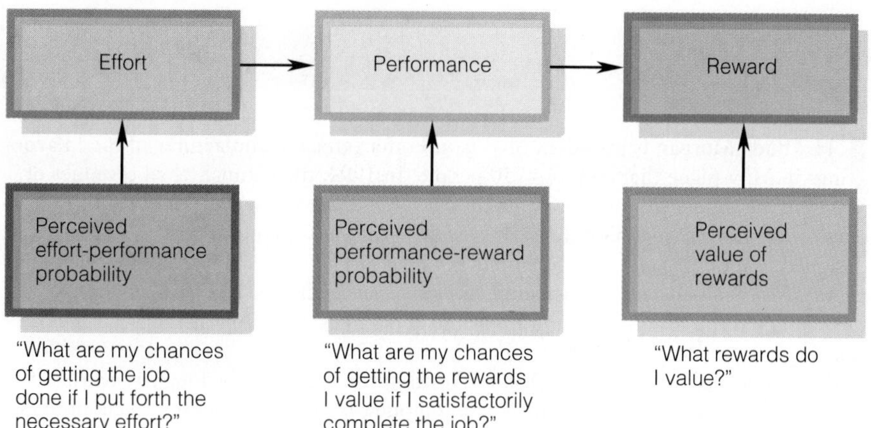
Effort
Performance
Reward
Perceived effort-performance probability
Perceived performance-reward probability
Perceived value of rewards
"What are my chances of getting the job done if I put forth the necessary effort?"
"What are my chances of getting the rewards I value if I satisfactorily complete the job?"
"What rewards do I value?"

FIGURE 5.6

An Expectancy Model for Motivation

person's belief that effort would lead to better performance and that better performance would lead to merit pay increases and other rewards. Valence and expectancy are particularly important in establishing priorities for people pursuing multiple goals.[53]

A person's motivation increases along with his or her belief that effort leads to performance and that performance leads to rewards, assuming the person wants the rewards. This is the third key idea within the expectancy theory of motivation. It is the idea that the valence, or value, that people place on various rewards varies. One person prefers salary to benefits, whereas another person prefers just the reverse. All people do not place the same value on each reward.

Points to Emphasize
Note the parallel between the perceived effort-performance probability of expectancy theory and the concept of self-efficacy developed in chapter 3. A similar parallel could be drawn to the perceived behavioral control component of Ajzen's theory of planned behavior.

Motivational Problems

Motivational problems stem from three basic causes within the expectancy theory framework. These causes are a disbelief in a relationship between effort and performance, a disbelief in a relationship between performance and rewards, and lack of desire for the rewards offered.

If the motivational problem is related to the person's belief that effort will not result in performance, the solution lies in altering this belief. The person can be shown how an increase in effort or an alteration in the kind of effort put forth can be converted into improved performance. For example, the textbook salesperson who does not believe more calls (effort) will result in greater sales (performance) might be shown how to distinguish departments with high-probability sales opportunities from those with low-probability sales opportunities. Hence, more calls (effort) can be converted into greater sales (performance).

Alternate Example
Expectancy theory may explain the behavior of survivors of layoffs. It appears they work harder when they believe that the layoff of a coworker was based on a random process rather than on the relative merits of their own and their coworker's performance. Source: J. Brockner, et al., *Academy of Management Journal* 29 (1985):373–384.

If the motivational problem is related to the person's belief that performance will not result in rewards, the solution lies in altering this belief. The person can be shown how an increase in performance or a somewhat altered form of performance will be converted into rewards. For example, the textbook salesperson who does not believe greater sales (performance) will result in overall higher commissions (rewards) might be shown computationally or graphically that a direct relationship does exist. Hence, greater sales (performance) are directly converted into higher commissions (rewards).

If the motivational problem is related to the value the person places on, or the preference the person has for certain rewards, the solution lies in influencing the value placed on the rewards or altering the rewards themselves. For example, the textbook salesperson may not particularly want higher commissions, given the small incremental gain to the salesperson at his tax level. In this case, the company might establish a mechanism for sheltering commissions from being taxed or alternative mechanisms for deferred compensation.

ORGANIZATIONAL REALITY

Wixon Fontarome at Walt Disney World

J. H. "Bud" Morgan is president of Wixon Fontarome, a manufacturer of food flavorings in Milwaukee that employs 150 people. In 1994, the company had revenues of $50 million. "Bud" Morgan used $300,000 to finance a trip for each of Wixon's 150 employees, and a companion, to Walt Disney World in Orlando, Florida. The trip was designed to motivate and reward employees for years of consistent growth in sales and profits. Morgan believed that Wixon's employees had achieved the performance, so they deserved the reward. In addition to fun and games, the trip was designed as a learning experience.

The employees went to Walt Disney World in three groups for four-day trips each. Each employee was given $300 in spending money, a park pass, and the freedom to go, play, and observe. There were two mandatory employee meetings at Walt Disney World that focused on quality and teamwork; hence, the learning component of the trip. Morgan saw Walt Disney World as a quality organization that could provide an ideal model for training in total quality and from which Wixon's employees could learn.

Who said training, learning, and total quality cannot be fun? "Bud" Morgan thinks they can be. He was also clear that the reward followed the performance, and was designed as a possible investment in future performance. ■

SOURCE: R. Maynard, "Building Teamwork for Fun and Profit," *Nations Business* (April 1995): 10. Reprinted by permission, Nation's Business, April, 1995. Copyright © 1995, U.S. Chamber of Commerce.

Joseph H. (Bud) Morgan, president of Wixon/Fontarome of Milwaukee, Wisconsin, stands to Mickey Mouse's left, along with a few of the nearly 300 employees and guests that Wixon took on a trip to Disney World. Morgan's wife Joan is in the wheelchair in front.

Research results on expectancy theory have been mixed.[54] The theory has been shown to predict job satisfaction accurately.[55] However, the theory's complexity makes it difficult to test the full model, and the measures of instrumentality, valence, and expectancy have only weak validity.[56] In addition, it is time-consuming to measure the expectancy constructs, and the values for each construct change over time for an individual. Finally, a theory assumes the individual is totally rational and acts as a minicomputer, calculating probabilities and values. In reality, the theory may be more complex than people as they typically function.

Motivation and Moral Maturity

Expectancy theory would predict that people work to maximize their personal outcomes. This is consistent with Adam Smith's ideas of working in one's own self-interest. Ultimately, Adam Smith and expectancy theories believe that people work to benefit themselves alone. Expectancy theory would not explain altruistic behavior for the benefit of others. Therefore, it may be necessary to consider an individual's **moral maturity** in order to better understand altruistic, fair, and equitable behavior. Cognitive moral development was discussed in Chapter 4. Moral maturity is the measure of a person's cognitive moral development. Morally mature people act and behave based on universal ethical principles, whereas morally immature people act and behave based on egocentric motivations.[57]

moral maturity
The measure of a person's cognitive moral development.

Cultural Differences in Motivation

Most motivation theories in use today have been developed by Americans in the United States and are about Americans.[58] Recent efforts have examined the universality of these theories and cultural differences have been found to exist, at least with regard to Maslow's, McClelland's, Herzberg's, and Vroom's theories. For example, while self-actualization may be the pinnacle need for Americans in Maslow's need hierarchy, security may be the most important need for people in cultures such as Greece and Japan who have a high need to avoid uncertainty.[59] Although achievement is an important need for Americans, other cultures do not value achievement as much as Americans do.

Herzberg's theory has been tested in other countries as well. Results in New Zealand did not replicate the results found in the United States, with supervision and interpersonal relationships being important motivators in New Zealand rather than hygienic factors as in America.[60] Finally, expectancy theory may hold up very nicely in cultures that value individualism while breaking down in more collectivist cultures that value cooperative efforts. In collectivist cultures, rewards are more closely tied to group and team efforts, thus obviating the utility of expectancy theory.

Managerial Implications: The Many Methods to Motivate People

■ Managers must realize that all motivation theories are not equally good or equally useful. The later motivation theories, such as the equity and expectancy theories, may be more scientifically sound than earlier theories, such as the two-factor theory. However, the older theories of motivation have conceptual value, show us the importance of human needs, and provide a basis for the later theories. Many motivation theories are less than perfect. Each has faults, as well as strengths, and none works all of the time for all people.

Managers cannot assume they understand employees' needs. They should recognize the variety of needs that motivate employee behavior and solicit input from employees to better understand their needs. Individual employees differ in their needs, and managers should be sensitive to ethnic, national, gender, and age differences in this regard. Employees with high needs for power must be given opportunities to exercise influence, and employees with high needs for achievement must be allowed to excel at work.

Managers can increase employee motivation by training (increased perceptions of success because of increased ability), coaching (increased confidence), and task assignments (increased perceptions of success because of more experience). Managers should ensure that rewards are contingent on good performance and that valued rewards, such as time off or flexible work schedules, are available. Managers must understand what their employees want.

Finally, managers should be aware that morally mature employees are more likely to be sensitive to inequities at work. At the same time, these employees are less likely to be selfish or self-centered and more likely to be concerned about equity issues for all employees. Morally mature employees will act ethically for the common good of all employees and the organization.

CLOSING SPOTLIGHT

The Henry Ford Technology Awards

A Henry Ford Technology Award is an important recognition reward for individual employees, teams, or non-Ford employees who have made a significant advance in automotive technology during the previous year.

Ford people who learn their lessons well may be recognized with a Henry Ford Technology Award. First presented in 1981, the Henry Ford Technology Awards are presented to individuals and teams who make significant advances in automotive technology.[61] Up to fifteen awards are presented annually in three categories: research (up to 3), product engineering (up to 6), and manufacturing (up to 6).

The September 1995 Henry Ford Technology Awards ceremonies recognized 62 individuals, including two academics from Wayne State University and five supplier personnel from MTS Corp., US Trailer Co., and Cyber, Inc., over a three-day period in Dearborn, Michigan. Spouses were included. The first day was one for introductions, photo opportunities for individuals and teams, and a keynote address from Lou Ross, chief technical officer and vice chairman of Ford. The second day featured a design center tour of future models, a ride and drive opportunity, a luncheon with an address from Ed Hagenlocker, president of Ford, and an afternoon of sessions in groups of 20 with Ford's most senior officers, such as Alexander Trotman, chairman of the board. Day two finished with a reception hosted by Ed Hagenlocker, a keynote address by Alexander Trotman, and the presentation of awards by John McTague, vice president of technical affairs.

Before leaving Dearborn on day three, the honorees had the opportunity to tour the Henry Ford museum. All in all, it was a fitting three-day recognition for individuals who were motivated to excel and be the best at what they do. ■

Chapter Summary

- Early economic theories of motivation emphasized self-interest as the basis for motivation and technology as a force with great impact.
- Early psychological theories of motivation emphasized internal needs but did not take into account individual diversity in these needs.
- Maslow's hierarchy of needs theory of motivation was the basis for McGregor's assumptions about how people should be treated at work.
- Herzberg found that the presence of motivation factors led to job satisfaction, and the presence of hygiene factors prevented job dissatisfaction.
- According to McClelland, the needs for achievement, power, and affiliation are learned needs that differ among cultures.
- Social exchange theory holds that people form calculated working relationships and expect fair, equitable, ethical treatment.
- Expectancy theory says that effort is the basis for motivation and that people want their effort to lead to performance and rewards.
- Theories of motivation are culturally bound and differences occur between nations.

Key Terms

motivation (p. 132)
exogenous cause (p. 132)
endogenous process (p. 132)
psychoanalysis (p. 133)
self-interest (p. 134)
need hierarchy (p. 136)
Theory X (p. 136)
Theory Y (p. 136)
motivation factor (p. 138)
hygiene factor (p. 138)
need for achievement (p. 141)
need for power (p. 142)
need for affiliation (p. 142)
inequity (p. 145)
equity sensitive (p. 147)
benevolent (p. 147)
entitled (p. 147)
valence (p. 148)
expectancy (p. 148)
instrumentality (p. 148)
moral maturity (p. 151)

Review Questions

1. Define the terms *motivation*, *needs*, and *equity*.
2. What is the role of self-interest in motivation? What is the role of the deeper psychological needs and drives?
3. What are the five categories of motivational needs described by Maslow? Give an example of how each can be satisfied.
4. What are the Theory X and Theory Y assumptions about human nature proposed by McGregor? How do they relate to Maslow's needs?
5. What three manifest needs does McClelland identify?
6. How is inequity determined by a person in an organization? How can inequity be resolved if it exists?
7. What are the key concepts in the expectancy theory of motivation?

Discussion and Communication Questions

1. What do you think are the most important motivational needs for the majority of people? Do you think your needs differ from those of most people?
2. At what level in Maslow's hierarchy of needs are you living? Are you basically satisfied at this level?
3. Assume you are leaving your current job to look for employment elsewhere. What will you look for that you do not have now? Or, if you do not have a job, assume you will be looking for one soon. What will be the most important factors for you to seek?
4. If you were being inequitably paid in your job, which strategy do you think would be the most helpful to you in resolving the inequity? What tactics would you consider using?
5. Do you believe you can do a better job of working or do a better job of studying than you are currently doing? Do you think you would get more pay and benefits or better grades if you did a better job? Do you care about the rewards (or grades) in your organization (or university)?
6. What important experiences have contributed to your moral and ethical development? Are you working to further your own moral maturity at this time?
7. *(communication question)* Prepare a memo describing the two employees you work with who most closely operate according to McGregor's Theory X and Theory Y assumptions about human nature. Be as specific and detailed in your description as you can, using quotes and/or observational examples.
8. *(communication question)* Develop an oral presentation about the most current management practices in employee motivation. Go to the library and read about what at least four different companies are doing in this area. Be prepared to compare these practices with the theory and research in the chapter.
9. *(communication question)* Interview a manager and prepare a memo summarizing the relative importance that manager places on the needs for achievement, power, and affiliation. Include (1) whether these needs have changed over time and (2) what job aspects satisfy these needs.

Ethics Questions

1. Is it ethical for you to pursue your self-interest at work? Is your self-interest in conflict with what is fair and equitable for others at work? Do you consider the thoughts and feelings of other people at work?
2. Suppose your company knew what employees wanted at work and was unwilling to spend the money to meet their needs. Do you think this would be unethical?
3. Assume you know an employee who is being underpaid because the company believes it will save money and the employee will not complain. Is this unethical? Should you tell the employee about the underpayment condition?
4. Suppose your company has an employee who has been with the company for a long time and now has health problems that will prevent him or her from being fully productive for at least a year. Should the company attempt to carry this person for that period of time, even though the person will not be able to perform? Should the person's pay and benefits be reduced according to performance?

Experiential Exercises

5.1 What Do You Need from Work?

This exercise provides an opportunity to discuss your basic needs and those of other students in your class. Refer back to Challenge 5.2: What's Important to Employees? on page 000 and look over your ranking of the ten possible job reward factors. Think about what basic needs you may have that are possibly work-related and yet would not be satisfied by one or another of these ten job reward factors.

Step 1. The class will form into groups of approximately six members each. Each group elects a spokesperson and answers the following questions. The group should spend at least five minutes on the first question and make sure each member of the group makes a contribution. The second question will probably take longer for your group to answer, up to 15 minutes. The spokesperson should be ready to share the group's answers.

a. *What important basic needs do you have that are not addressed by one or another of these ten job reward factors?* Members should focus on the whole range of needs discussed in the different need theories of motivation covered in Chapter 5. Develop a list of the basic needs overlooked by these ten factors.

b. *What is important to members of your group?* Rank order all job reward factors (the original ten and any new ones your group came up with in Step 1) in terms of their importance for your group. If there are disagreements among group members in the rankings, take time to discuss the differences among group members. Work for consensus and also note points of disagreement.

Step 2. Each group will share the results of its answers to the questions in Step 1. Cross-team questions and discussion follow.

Step 3. If your instructor has not already shared the normative data for 1,000 employees and their supervisors mentioned in Challenge 5.2, the instructor may do that at this time.

Step 4 (Optional). Your instructor may ask you to discuss the similarities and differences in your group's rankings with the employee and supervisory normative rankings. If he or she does, spend some time addressing two questions.

a. *What are the underlying reasons that you think may account for the differences that exist?*

b. *How have the needs of employees and supervisors changed over the past twenty years? Are they likely to change in the future?*

5.2 Work versus Play

Gordon Forward believes that work and play are not mutually exclusive activities. He believes that work can be a fun and playful activity. This also seems to be the view of J. H. "Bud" Morgan, as discussed in the Organizational Reality feature near the end of the chapter. What do you and your classmates believe?

Step 1. Working in groups of six, develop two lists of activities, one classified as work and the other as play. What are the similarities and differences between these two lists of activities?

Step 2. Examine the lists again. What motivates the members of your group to work? What motivates them to play?

Step 3. Attempt to develop (1) a set of characteristics that will distinguish work activities from play activities and (2) a list of characteristics common to both work and play.

Step 4. Share the results of your group discussions with the class in a cross-team exchange.

CASE

Delighting Cast Members Through Disney World's "Pixie Dust"[1]

Walt Disney World Resort in Lake Buena Vista, Florida, contains theme parks, golf courses, restaurants, hotels, stores, condominiums, and conference centers spread over 30,000 acres. Perhaps most famous are the theme parks—Disney World's Magic Kingdom and EPCOT Center.

Nearly 60 percent of the resort's 35,000 employees have direct contact with customers. At Disney, employees are called *cast members* and customers are *guests.* Everyone in the Disney family is a cast member, not just the performers in shows. Every cast member is expected to delight the guests and to exceed the guest's expectations.

Disney's management believes that in order for cast members to delight the guests, Disney as an employer must delight its cast members. This is accomplished by creating a "pixie dust" culture to emotionally involve cast members in their jobs.

Exposure to Disney's "pixie dust" culture begins even before cast members are hired. The spacious casting center (known as the human resources department in most organizations) is decorated with statues of Disney characters, amusing wall murals, and the original model of Snow White's castle. The fun atmosphere is intended to create an immediate emotional bond.

Less than 20 percent of the people who apply are hired as cast members. Duncan Dickson, director of casting, says that Disney is "looking for personality. We can train for skills. We want people who are enthusiastic, who have pride in their work, who can take charge of a situation without supervision." Additionally, Disney seeks to promote a clean-cut, conservative image. In fact, a 36-page guidebook covers numerous aspects of cast members' personal appearance.

Once cast members are hired they undergo a two-day orientation at Disney University. Called *Traditions*, the orientation program provides cast members with a solid understanding of Disney's culture and values. *Traditions* also provides instruction in the people skills and work attitudes that are essential to being a successful cast member. Additionally, the orientation program is designed to strengthen the cast members' self-image and to promote a team spirit among them.

After the two-day *Traditions* program, cast members begin up to fourteen days of training. Part of the training consists of classes at Disney University and on-site practice sessions. Part of the training also involves pairing the trainee with experienced and highly respected cast members for several days of on-the-job training. Only after completion of the paired training are the new cast members allowed to perform their jobs on a solo basis.

Even after the cast members learn their roles, training, reinforcement, and recognition continue. As in the *Traditions* orientation and the initial training period, the emphasis is on reinforcing Disney's commitment to delight its guests through its "pixie dust" culture.

DISCUSSION QUESTIONS

1. Given Disney's approach to hiring, orienting, and training cast members, what insights have you gained about Disney's approach to employee motivation? Explain your answer.
2. What needs does Disney appeal to through its emphasis on emotionally connecting cast members to their jobs, and on delighting guests by delighting cast members?
3. Using the model of the individual-organizational exchange relationship shown in Figure 5.4, explain the relationship that Disney seeks to develop with its cast members.
4. Using expectancy theory, explain how Disney seeks to influence the motivation of its cast members.
5. What is important to you in terms of your personal work motivation? How does that which motivates you fit with Disney's approach to motivating cast members?

SOURCE: This case was written by Michael K. McCuddy, The Louis S. and Mary Morgal Professor of Christian Business Ethics, College of Business Administration, Valparaiso University.

1. Adapted from: P. L. Blocklyn, "Making Magic: The Disney Approach to People Management," *Personnel* 65 (1988): 28–35; S. Heise, "Disney Approach to Managing," *Executive Excellence*, 11 (1994): 18–19; R. Henkoff, "Finding, Training, and Keeping the Best Service Workers," *Fortune*, 130 (1994): 110–122; C. M. Solomon, "How Does Disney Do It?" *Personnel Journal*, 68 (1989): 50–57.

References

1. P. M. Fernberg, "Learn to Compete: Training's Vital Role in Business Survival," *Managing Office Technology* 38 (1993): 14–16.
2. R. A. Katzell and D. E. Thompson, "Work Motivation: Theory and Practice," *American Psychologist* 45 (1990): 144–153.
3. J. P. Campbell and R. D. Pritchard, "Motivation Theory in Industrial and Organizational Psychology," in M. D. Dunnette, ed., *Handbook of Industrial and Organizational Psychology* (Chicago: Rand McNally, 1976), 63–130.
4. M. Weber, *The Protestant Ethic and the Spirit of Capitalism* (London: Talcott Parson, tr., 1930).
5. S. Freud, *Civilization and Its Discontents*, trans. and ed. J. Strachey (New York: Norton, 1961).
6. A. D. Mangelsdorff, ed., *Proceedings of the 7th Stress Conference: Training for Psychic Trauma* (San Antonio: U.S. Army Health Services Command, 1989).
7. F. W. Taylor, "Shop Management" (Paper presented at the national meeting of the American Society of Mechanical Engineers, Sarasota, New York, 1903).
8. F. J. Roethlisberger, *Management and Morale* (Cambridge, Mass.: Harvard University Press, 1941).
9. A. Smith, *An Inquiry into the Nature and Causes of the Wealth of Nations*, vol. 10 of *The Harvard Classics*, ed. C. J. Bullock (New York: Collier, 1909).
10. F. W. Taylor, *The Principles of Scientific Management* (New York: Norton, 1911).
11. Hearings before Special Committee of the House of Representatives to Investigage the Taylor and Other Systems of Shop Management under Authority of House Resolution 90, vol. 3, 1377–1508, contains Taylor's testimony before the committee from Thursday, 25 January, through Tuesday, 30 January 1912.
12. A. H. Maslow, "A Theory of Human Motivation," *Psychological Review* 50 (1943): 370–396.
13. W. James, *The Principles of Psychology* (New York: H. Holt & Co., 1890; Cambridge, Mass.: Harvard University Press, 1983).
14. J. Dewey, *Human Nature and Conduct: An Introduction to Social Psychology* (New York: Holt, 1922).
15. S. Freud, *A General Introduction to Psycho-Analysis: A Course of Twenty-Eight Lectures Delivered at the University of Vienna* (New York: Liveright, 1963); A. Adler, *Understanding Human Nature* (Greenwich, Conn.: Fawcett, 1927).
16. L. W. Porter, "A Study of Perceived Need Satisfactions in Bottom and Middle Management Jobs," *Journal of Applied Psychology* 45 (1961): 1–10.
17. E. E. Lawler III and J. L. Suttle, "A Causal Correlational Test of the Need Hierarchy Concept," *Organizational Behavior and Human Performance* 7 (1973): 265–287.
18. D. M. McGregor, *The Human Side of Enterprise* (New York: McGraw-Hill, 1960).
19. D. M. McGregor, "The Human Side of Enterprise," *Management Review*, November 1957, 22–28, 88–92.
20. D. E. Petersen and J. Hillkirk, *A Better Idea: Redefining the Way Americans Work* (Boston: Houghton Mifflin, 1991).
21. G. E. Forward, D. E. Beach, D. A. Gray, and J. C. Quick, "Mentofacturing: A Vision for American Industrial Excellence," *Academy of Management Executive* 5 (1991): 32–44.
22. C. P. Alderfer, *Human Needs in Organizational Settings* (New York: Free Press, 1972).
23. B. Schneider and C. P. Alderfer, "Three Studies of Need Satisfactions in Organizations," *Administrative Science Quarterly* 18 (1973): 489–505.
24. F. Herzberg, B. Mausner, and B. Snyderman, *The Motivation to Work* (New York: Wiley, 1959).
25. F. Herzberg, *Work and the Nature of Man* (Cleveland: World, 1966).
26. R. J. House and L. Wigdor, "Herzberg's Dual-Factor Theory of Job Satisfaction and Motivation: A Review of the Evidence and a Criticism," *Personnel Psychology* 20 (1967): 369–389.
27. H. A. Murray, *Explorations in Personality: A Clinical and Experimental Study of Fifty Men of College Age* (New York: Oxford University Press, 1938).
28. D. C. McClelland, *Motivational Trends in Society* (Morristown, N.J.: General Learning Press, 1971).
29. J. P. Chaplin and T. S. Krawiec, *Systems and Theories of Psychology* (New York: Holt, Rinehart & Winston, 1960).
30. D. C. McClelland, "Achievement Motivation Can Be Learned," *Harvard Business Review* 43 (1965): 6–24.
31. D. C. McClelland and D. Burnham, "Power Is the Great Motivator," *Harvard Business Review* 54 (1976): 100–111.
32. J. Hall and J. Hawker, *Power Management Inventory* (The Woodlands, Tex.: Teleometrics International, 1988).
33. F. Luthans, "Successful versus Effective Real Managers," *Academy of Management Executive* 2 (1988): 127–131.
34. S. Schachter, *The Psychology of Affiliation* (Stanford, Calif.: Stanford University Press, 1959).
35. R. M. Steers, "Murray's Manifest Needs Theory," in R. M. Steers and L. W. Porter, eds., *Motivation and Work Behavior*, 3d ed. (New York: McGraw-Hill, 1983): 42–50.
36. P. M. Blau, *Exchange and Power in Social Life* (New York: Wiley, 1964).
37. A. Etzioni, "A Basis for Comparative Analysis of Complex Organizations," in A. Etzioni, ed., *A Sociological Reader on Complex Organizations*, 2d ed., (New York: Holt, Rinehart & Winston, 1969), 59–76.
38. J. P. Campbell, M. D. Dunnette, E. E. Lawler III, and K. E. Weick, Jr., *Managerial Behavior, Performance and Effectiveness* (New York: McGraw-Hill, 1970).
39. J. S. Adams, "Inequity in Social Exchange," in L. Berkowitz, ed., *Advances in Experimental Social Psychology*, vol. 2 (New York: Academic Press, 1965), 267–299.
40. J. S. Adams, "Toward an Understanding of Inequity," *Journal of Abnormal and Social Psychology* 67 (1963): 422–436.
41. J. Nelson-Horchler, "The Best Man for the Job Is a Man," *Industry Week*, 7 January 1991, 50–52.
42. P. D. Sweeney, D. B. McFarlin, and E. J. Inderrieden, "Using Relative Deprivation Theory to Explain Satisfaction with Income and Pay Level: A Multistudy Examination," *Academy of Management Journal* 33 (1990): 423–436.
43. R. C. Huseman, J. D. Hatfield, and E. A. Miles, "A New Perspective on Equity Theory: The Equity Sensitivity Construct," *Academy of Management Review* 12 (1987): 222–234.

44. K. E. Weick, M. G. Bougon, and G. Maruyama, "The Equity Context," *Organizational Behavior and Human Performance* 15 (1976): 32–65.

45. R. Coles, *Privileged Ones* (Boston: Little, Brown, 1977).

46. J. Greenberg, "Equity and Workplace Status: A Field Experiment," *Journal of Applied Psychology* 73 (1988): 606–613.

47. R. Vecchio, "Predicting Worker Performance in Inequitable Settings," *Academy of Management Review* 7 (1982): 103–110.

48. R. A. Cosier and D. R. Dalton, "Equity Theory and Time: A Reformulation," *Academy of Management Review* 8 (1983): 311–319.

49. J. E. Martin and M. W. Peterson, "Two-Tier Wage Structures: Implications for Equity Theory," *Academy of Management Journal* 30 (1987): 297–315.

50. V. H. Vroom, *Work and Motivation* (New York: Wiley, 1964/1970).

51. U. R. Larson, "Supervisor's Performance Feedback to Subordinates: The Effect of Performance Valence and Outcome Dependence," *Organizational Behavior and Human Decision Processes* 37 (1986): 391–409.

52. M. F. Fadden and B. L. Smith, *High Performance Flying* (Houston: Tenneco Chemicals, 1976).

53. M. C. Kernan and R. G. Lord, "Effects of Valence, Expectancies, and Goal-Performance Discrepancies in Single and Multiple Goal Environments," *Journal of Applied Psychology* 75 (1990): 194–203.

54. T. R. Mitchell, "Expectancy Models of Job Satisfaction, Occupational Preference and Effort: A Theoretical, Methodological, and Empirical Appraisal," *Psychological Bulletin* 81 (1974): 1053–1077.

55. E. D. Pulakos and N. Schmitt, "A Longitudinal Study of a Valence Model Approach for the Prediction of Job Satisfaction of New Employees," *Journal of Applied Psychology* 68 (1983): 307–312.

56. F. J. Landy and W. S. Becker, "Motivation Theory Reconsidered," in L. L. Cummings and B. M. Staw, eds., *Research in Organizational Behavior* 9 (Greenwich, Conn.: JAI Press, 1987), 1–38.

57. L. Kohlberg, "The Cognitive-Developmental Approach to Socialization," in D. A. Goslin, ed., *Handbook of Socialization Theory and Research* (Chicago: Rand McNally, 1969).

58. N. J. Adler, *International Dimensions of Organizational Behavior* (Boston: PWS-KENT, 1991).

59. G. Hofstede, "Motivation, Leadership, and Organization: Do American Theories Apply Abroad?" *Organizational Dynamics* 9 (1980): 42–63.

60. G. H. Hines, "Cross-Cultural Differences in Two-Factor Theory," *Journal of Applied Psychology* 58 (1981): 313–317.

61. Personal communication, Paul McElligatt, Ford Motor Company, 29 January 1996.

CHAPTER

6

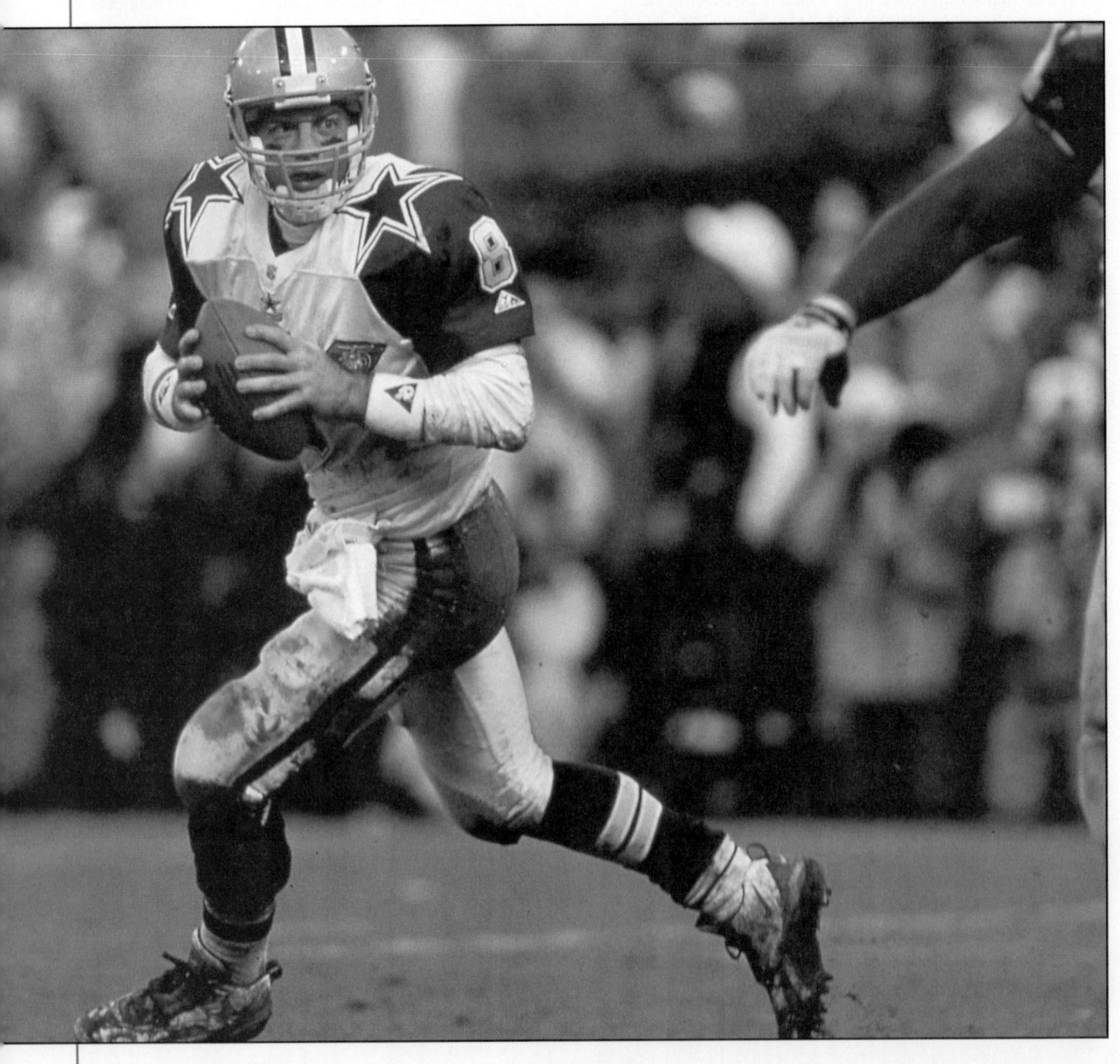

Learning and Performance Management

LEARNING OBJECTIVES

After reading this chapter, you should be able to do the following:

- Define *learning, reinforcement, punishment, extinction,* and *goal setting.*
- Distinguish between classical and operant conditioning.
- Explain the strategies of reinforcement and punishment using positive and negative consequences of behavior.
- Identify the purposes of goal setting and the five characteristics of effective goals.
- Describe effective strategies for giving and receiving performance feedback.
- Compare individual and team-oriented reward systems.
- Describe strategies for correcting poor performance.

OPENING SPOTLIGHT

High Performance at Chaparral Steel

Chaparral Steel Company is arguably the most productive and best-performing steel company in the world. It holds a clear competitive advantage over both foreign and domestic competition. Whereas the average U.S. steel company produces 350 tons of steel per person-year (2,080 hours) and the average Japanese firm produces 600 tons of steel per person-year, Chaparral Steel is able to produce more than 1,100 tons of steel per person-year.

The cooling bed in Chaparral Steel's bar mill allows hot rolled steel bars (red/orange) to cool before further handling.

Some additional indicators of high performance: The average profit margin in the U.S. steel industry is 6 percent; at Chaparral Steel, it is 11 percent. Chaparral steel was the first U.S. steel company to be awarded the Japanese Industrial Standard (JIS) mark on its structural steel products (May 1989). Annual employee turnover in U.S. manufacturing averages 10 percent; at Chaparral Steel it is 8.5 percent.1 With such high levels of performance, where is Chaparral to go from here? ■

Alternate Example
According to Harvard professor John Kotter, "In a rapidly changing and competitive environment, formal K–12 education is very important, but insufficient. Success at work demands huge growth after a terminal degree to learn new approaches, skills, techniques, and more. A turbulent environment offers many opportunities for growth. Those willing to take some risks and to reflect honestly on their experiences." Source: J. Kotter, *The New Rules: How to Succeed in Today's Post-Corporate World*, 1995, New York: The Free Press.

This is the second of two chapters addressing motivation and behavior. Chapter 5 took an endogenous (internal), content-oriented approach to human motivation. This chapter focuses primarily on exogenous (external) causes of behavior. The first section addresses learning theory and the use of reinforcement, punishment, and extinction at work. It also touches on Bandura's social learning theory and Jung's personality approach to learning. The second section presents theory, research, and practice related to goal setting in organizations. The third section addresses the definition and measurement of performance. The fourth section is concerned with rewarding performance. The fifth and concluding section addresses how to correct poor performance.

Learning in Organizations

learning
A change in behavior acquired through experience.

■ **Learning** is a change in behavior acquired through experience. It is not simply the cognitive activity of developing knowledge about a subject. The behaviorist approach to learning assumes that observable behavior is a function of its consequences. Learning has its basis in classical and operant conditioning.

Classical Conditioning

classical conditioning
Modifying behavior so that a conditioned stimulus is paired with an unconditioned stimulus and elicits an unconditioned response.

Classical conditioning is the process of modifying behavior so that a conditioned stimulus is paired with an unconditioned stimulus and elicits an unconditioned response. It is largely the result of the research on animals (primarily dogs) by the Russian physiologist Ivan Pavlov.[2] Pavlov's professional exchanges with Walter B. Cannon and other American researchers during the early 1900s led to the application of his ideas in the United States.[3] Classical conditioning builds on the natural consequence of an unconditioned response to an unconditioned stimulus. In dogs, this might be the natural production of saliva (unconditioned response) in response to the presentation of meat (unconditioned stimulus). By presenting a conditioned stimulus (for example, a bell) simultaneously with the unconditioned stimulus (the meat), the researcher caused the dog to develop a conditioned response (salivation in response to the bell).

Classical conditioning may occur in a similar fashion in humans.[4] For example, a person working at a computer terminal may get lower back tension (unconditioned response) as a result of poor posture (unconditioned stimulus). If the person becomes aware of that tension only when the manager enters the work area (conditioned stimulus), then the person may develop a conditioned response (lower back tension) to the appearance of the manager.

Although this example is logical, classical conditioning has real limitations in its applicability to human behavior in organizations—for at least three reasons. First, humans are more complex than dogs and less amenable to simple cause-and-effect conditioning. Second, the behavioral environments in organizations are complex and not very amenable to single stimulus-response manipulations. Third, complex human decision making makes it possible to override simple conditioning.

Alternate Example
Fortunately for students, we have progressed from the learning approaches of medieval universities. At Oxford and Cambridge universities, you were considered to have learned the material when you were able to recite large passages of verbatim during your classes.

Operant Conditioning

Operant conditioning is the process of modifying behavior through the use of positive or negative consequences following specific behaviors. It is based on the notion that behavior is a function of its consequences,[5] which may be either positive or negative. The consequences of behavior are used to influence, or shape, behavior through three strategies: reinforcement, punishment, and extinction. Organizational behavior modification is a form of operant conditioning used successfully in a variety of organizations to shape behavior.[6]

operant conditioning
Modifying behavior through the use of positive or negative consequences following specific behaviors.

Discussion Consideration
Ask students to identify aspects of their own behavior that were learned through a) classical conditioning and b) operant conditioning.

The Strategies of Reinforcement, Punishment, and Extinction

Reinforcement is used to enhance desirable behavior, and punishment and extinction are used to diminish undesirable behavior. (The three strategies are defined and described in detail later in this section of the chapter.) Organizations, families, and other social systems define and categorize desirable and undesirable behavior. A behavior may be desirable in one context and undesirable in another. For example, a police officer's use of physical force to restrain an unruly adult might be viewed as desirable behavior while his use of the same physical force with a teenager might be viewed as undesirable behavior. Knowing what behavior is desirable and what behavior is undesirable is not always easy. A team of motivational experts was once asked by a military unit to help increase combat soldiers' desire to kill the enemy. The team declined for two reasons. First, its members were not sure they knew how to design such a program. Second, they were uncertain about the social desirability of doing it.[7] The problem posed to the team raises an ethical question about how society should define desirable and undesirable behavior.

Alternate Example
Reinforcement based purely on outcomes can be wrongly used. Some logical, rational decisions may result in a negative outcome. They should not necessarily be punished; instead, the conditions under which they were made should be better understood. Source: J. Hershey and J. Baron, "Judgement by Outcomes: When is it Justified?" Organizational Behavior and Human Decision Processes 53 (1992):89–93.

Reinforcement and punishment are administered through the management of positive and negative consequences of behavior. **Positive consequences** are the results of a person's behavior that the person finds attractive or pleasurable. They might include a pay increase, a bonus, a promotion, a transfer to a more desirable geographical location, or praise from a supervisor. **Negative consequences** are the results of a person's behavior that the person finds unattractive or aversive. They might include disciplinary action, an undesirable transfer, a demotion, or harsh criticism from a supervisor. Positive and negative consequences must be defined for the person receiving them. Therefore, individual, gender, and cultural differences may be important in their classification.

positive consequences
Results of a behavior that a person finds attractive or pleasurable.

negative consequences
Results of a behavior that a person finds unattractive or aversive.

The use of positive and negative consequences following a specific behavior either reinforces or punishes that behavior.[8] Thorndike's law of effect states that

FIGURE 6.1
Reinforcement and Punishment Strategies

	Reinforcement (desirable behavior)	Punishment (undesirable behavior)
Positive consequences	Apply	Withhold
Negative consequences	Withhold	Apply

Points to Emphasize
In learning, there must be a concentrated effort to manage the consequences of behavior. Rollo May, a noted psychologist, said, "praise me or damn me, but don't just ignore me." A similar sentiment was expressed by a professor who said "Cite me good, cite me bad. Just cite me!"

behaviors followed by positive consequences are more likely to recur and behaviors followed by negative consequences are less likely to recur.[9] Figure 6.1 shows how positive and negative consequences may be applied or withheld in the strategies of reinforcement and punishment.

reinforcement
The attempt to develop or strengthen desirable behavior by either bestowing positive consequences or withholding negative consequences.

http://www.marriott.com/

REINFORCEMENT **Reinforcement** is the attempt to develop or strengthen desirable behavior by either bestowing positive consequences or withholding negative consequences. Positive reinforcement results from the application of a positive consequence following a desirable behavior. Bonuses paid at the end of successful business years are an example of positive reinforcement. Marriott Corporation provides positive reinforcement by honoring fifteen to twenty employees each year with its J. Willard Marriott Award of Excellence. Each awardee receives a medallion engraved with the words that express the basic values of the company: dedication, achievement, character, ideals, effort, and perseverance.

Negative reinforcement results from withholding a threatened negative consequence when a desirable behavior occurs. For example, a manager who reduces an employee's pay (negative consequence) if the employee comes to work late (undesirable behavior) and refrains from doing so when the employee is on time (desirable behavior) has negatively reinforced the employee's on-time behavior. The employee avoids the negative consequence (a reduction in pay) by exhibiting the desirable behavior (being on time to work).

Either continuous or intermittent schedules of reinforcement may be used. These are described in Table 6.1.

punishment
The attempt to eliminate or weaken undesirable behavior by either bestowing negative consequences or withholding positive consequences.

Discussion Consideration
Is what individuals do on their own time of any concern in the workplace? What if what they do on their own time becomes evident at work?

PUNISHMENT **Punishment** is the attempt to eliminate or weaken undesirable behavior. It is used in two ways. One way to punish a person is through the application of a negative consequence following an undesirable behavior. For example, a professional athlete who is excessively offensive to an official (undesirable behavior) may be ejected from a game (negative consequence). The other way to punish a person is through the withholding of a positive consequence following an undesirable behavior. For example, a salesperson who makes few visits to companies (undesirable behavior) and whose sales are well below the quota (undesirable behavior) is likely to receive a very small commission check (positive consequence) at the end of the month.

One problem with punishment is that it may have unintended results. Because punishment is discomforting to the individual being punished, the experience of punishment may result in negative psychological, emotional, performance, or behavioral consequences. For example, the person being punished may become angry, hostile, depressed, or despondent. From an organizational standpoint, this result becomes important when the punished person translates negative

TABLE 6.1

Schedules of Reinforcement

SCHEDULE	DESCRIPTION	EFFECTS ON RESPONDING
Continuous		
	Reinforcer follows every response	1. Steady high rate of performance as long as reinforcement follows every response 2. High frequency of reinforcement may lead to early satiation 3. Behavior weakens rapidly (undergoes extinction) when reinforcers are withheld 4. Appropriate for newly emitted, unstable, low-frequency responses
Intermittent		
	Reinforcer does not follow every response	1. Capable of producting high frequencies of responding 2. Low frequency or reinforcement precludes early satiation 3. Appropriate for stable or high-frequency responses
FIXED RATIO	A fixed number of responses must be emitted before reinforcement occurs	1. A fixed ratio of 1:1 (reinforcement occurs after every response) is the same as a continuous schedule 2. Tends to produce a high rate of response that is vigorous and steady
VARIABLE RATIO	A varying or random number of responses must be emitted before reinforcement occurs	Capable of producing a high rate of response that is vigorous, steady, and resistant to extinction
FIXED INTERVAL	The first response after a specific period of time has elapsed is reinforced	Produces an uneven response pattern varying from a very slow, unenergetic response immediately following reinforcement to a very fast, vigorous response immediately preceding reinforcement
VARIABLE INTERVAL	The first response after varying or random periods of time have elapsed is reinforced	Tends to produce a high rate of response that is vigorous, steady, and resistant to extinction

SOURCE: From *Organizational Behavior Modification* by Fred Luthans and Robert Kreitner. Copyright © 1975 by Scott Foresman and Company. Reprinted by permission of Harper Collins Publishers.

emotional and psychological responses into negative actions. A General Motors employee who had been disciplined pulled an emergency cord and shut down an entire assembly line. A hardware store owner was killed by a man he had fired for poor performance. Work slowdowns, sabotage, and subversive behavior are all unintended negative consequences of punishment.

http://www.gm.com

EXTINCTION An alternative to punishing undesirable behavior is **extinction**—the attempt to weaken a behavior by attaching no consequences (either positive or negative) to it. It is equivalent to ignoring the behavior. The rationale for using extinction is that a behavior not followed by any consequence is weakened. However, some patience and time may be needed for it to be effective.

extinction

The attempt to weaken a behavior by attaching no consequences to it.

Extinction may be practiced, for example, by not responding (no consequence) to the sarcasm (behavior) of a colleague. Extinction may be most effective when used in conjunction with the positive reinforcement of desirable behaviors. Therefore, in the example, the best approach might be to compliment the sarcastic colleague for constructive comments (reinforcing desirable behavior) while ignoring the colleague's sarcastic comments (extinguishing undesirable behavior).

ORGANIZATIONAL REALITY

Learning to Play the Business Game

Wednesdays are special days at Springfield Remanufacturing Corp. (SRC) because 40 to 50 of the company's 780 workers play "The Great Game of Business." The focus of the game is financial performance. The SRC Wednesday players, who come from all departments and ranks, share income and expense information for the week with each other. All employees are involved even though the "players" are the ones exchanging information. SRC employees own 32 percent of the company's stock through an ESOP and SRC has been sharing financial information with employees since 1983. Profits and sales growth have climbed approximately 15 percent annually and the stock value has multiplied 18,000 percent. Learning about the financials has paid off.

All employees, from their first days at SRC, are involved in the business game and receive training in understanding the financials, including a four-hour business training course called *Yo-Yo Training*. Because employees learned so well, SRC began an entrepreneurial program in 1989. As of 1995, 12 employee-run companies have been formed in diverse business areas from management consulting to training to one company started by Bev Willis that makes and sells engine rebuilding kits. SRC shares in the profits of these employee-owned enterprises, which were forecasted to be $15 million for 1995. ■

SOURCE: A. Halcrow, "Workers Learn to Play the Business Game," *Personnel Journal* (January 1995): 73

SRC employees do more than work and play business; fishing is a favorite pastime for a number of employees. The sales and marketing group uses an annual bass tournament to partner SRC employees with the top selling engine retailers. This helps build business relations and rewards distributors who sell SRC products.

Extinction is not always the best strategy, however. Punishment might be preferable in cases of dangerous behavior to deliver a swift, clear lesson. It might also be preferable in cases of seriously undesirable behavior, such as employee embezzlement or other unethical behavior.

Bandura's Social Learning Theory

A social learning theory proposed by Albert Bandura is an alternative to the strictly behavioristic approaches of Pavlov and Skinner.[10] Bandura believes learning occurs through the observation of other people and the modeling of their behavior. Executives might teach their subordinates a wide range of behaviors, such as leader-follower interactions and stress management, by exhibiting these behaviors. Since employees look to their supervisors for acceptable norms of behavior, they are likely to pattern their own responses on the supervisor's.

Central to Bandura's social learning theory is the notion of self-efficacy, as defined and discussed in Chapter 3. People with high levels of self-efficacy are more effective at learning than are those with low levels of self-efficacy.[11] According to Bandura, self-efficacy expectations may be enhanced through four means: (1) performance accomplishments (just do it!), (2) vicarious experiences (watch someone else do it), (3) verbal persuasion (be convinced by someone else to do it), or (4) emotional arousal (get excited about doing it). At Springfield Remanufacturing, employees learn through doing as discussed in the accompanying Organizational Reality feature.

Learning and Personality Differences

Our treatment of learning would not be complete without touching on Jung's theory of personality differences (discussed in Chapter 3).[12] Two elements of Jung's theory have important implications for learning.

The first element is the distinction between introverted and extraverted people. Introverts need quiet time to study, concentrate, and reflect on what they are learning. They think best when they are alone. Extraverts need to interact with other people, learning through the process of expressing and exchanging ideas with others. They think best in groups and while they are talking.

The second element is the personality functions of intuition, sensing, thinking, and feeling. These functions are listed in Table 6.2, along with their implications for learning by individuals. The functions of intuition and sensing determine the individual's preference for information gathering. The functions of thinking and feeling determine how the individual evaluates and makes decisions about newly acquired information.[13] Each person has a preferred mode of gathering information and a preferred mode of evaluating and making decisions about that information. For example, an intuitive thinker may want to skim

Discussion Consideration
Should a manager try to draw out the other side of an introvert or extravert in order to create a balance for the individual? Or is it more important to acknowledge and nurture the difference?

Points to Emphasize
Students should recognize that extraverts are not necessarily intellectually "quick". Extroversion and learning are not necessarily related, although they may be linked together as part of an individual's implicit personality theory.

■ **TABLE 6.2**

Personality Functions and Learning

PERSONALITY PREFERENCE	IMPLICATIONS FOR LEARNING BY INDIVIDUALS
Information Gathering	
Intuitors	Prefer theoretical frameworks. Look for the meaning in material. Attempt to understand the grand scheme. Look for possibilities and interrelations.
Sensors	Prefer specific, empirical data. Look for practical applications. Attempt to master details of a subject. Look for what is realistic and doable.
Decision Making	
Thinkers	Prefer analysis of data and information. Work to be fairminded and evenhanded. Seek logical, just conclusions. Do not like to be too personally involved.
Feelers	Prefer interpersonal involvement. Work to be tenderhearted and harmonious. Seek subjective, merciful results. Do not like objective, factual analysis.

SOURCE: O. Kroeger and J. M. Thuesen, *Type Talk: The 16 Personality Types that Determine How We Live, Love, and Work* (New York: Dell Publishing Co., 1988).

CHALLENGE

■ 6.1

Task-Goal Attribute Questionnaire

Listed below is a set of statements that may or may not describe the job or school objectives toward which you are presently working. Please read each statement carefully and rate each on a scale from 1 (agree completely) to 7 (disagree completely) to describe your level of agreement or disagreement with the statement. *Please answer all questions.*

____ **1.** I am allowed a high degree of influence in the determination of my work/school objectives.
____ **2.** I should not have too much difficulty in reaching my work/school objectives; they appear to be fairly easy.
____ **3.** I receive a considerable amount of feedback concerning my quantity of output on the job/in school.
____ **4.** Most of my coworkers and peers try to outperform one another on their assigned work/school goals.
____ **5.** My work/school objectives are very clear and specific; I know exactly what my job/assignment is.
____ **6.** My work/school objectives will require a great deal of effort from me to complete them.
____ **7.** I really have little voice in the formulation of my work/school objectives.
____ **8.** I am provided with a great deal of feedback and guidance on the quality of my work.
____ **9.** I think my work/school objectives are ambiguous and unclear.
____ **10.** It will take a high degree of skill and know-how on my part to attain fully my work/school objectives.
____ **11.** The setting of my work/school goals is pretty much under my own control.
____ **12.** My boss/instructors seldom let(s) me know how well I am doing on my work toward my work/school objectives.
____ **13.** A very competitive atmosphere exists among my peers and me with regard to attaining our respective work/school goals; we all want to do better than anyone else in attaining our goals.
____ **14.** I understand fully which of my work/school objectives are more important than others; I have a clear sense of priorities on these goals.
____ **15.** My work/school objectives are quite difficult to attain.
____ **16.** My supervisor/instructors usually ask(s) for my opinions and thoughts when determining my work/school objectives.

Scoring:

Place your response (1 through 7) in the space provided. For questions 7, 12, 9, and 2, subtract your response from 8 to determine your adjusted score. For each scale (e.g., participation in goal setting), add the responses and divide by the number of questions in the scale.

Discussion Consideration
Is extroversion/introversion a stable trait? Ask students to identify situations when they may be more introverted or extraverted than normal. Ask students if they perceive themselves to be changing on these dimensions of their personality.

research reports about implementing total quality programs and then, based on hunches, decide how to apply the research findings to the organization. A sensing feeler may prefer viewing videotaped interviews with people in companies that implemented total quality programs and then identify people in the organization most likely to be receptive to the approaches presented.

Goal Setting at Work

goal setting
The process of establishing desired results that guide and direct behavior.

■ **Goal setting** is the process of establishing desired results that guide and direct behavior. In organizations, it began with Frederick Taylor's idea that performance standards would lead to higher worker performance.[14] It is based on

CHALLENGE

6.1 continued

Participation in Goal Setting:

Question 1 ___
Question 7 (8– ___) = ___
Question 11 ___
Question 16 ___
Total divided by 4 = ___

Feedback on Goal Effort:

Question 3 ___
Question 8 ___
Question 12 (8– ___) = ___
Total divided by 3 = ___

Peer Competition:

Question 4 ___
Question 13 ___
Total divided by 2 = ___

Goal Specificity:

Question 5 ___
Question 9 (8– ___) ___
Question 14 ___
Total divided by 3 = ___

Goal Difficulty:

Question 2 (8– ___) ___
Question 6 ___
Question 10 ___
Question 15 ___
Total divided by 4 = ___

Interpreting your average scale scores:

6 or 7 is very high on this task-goal attribute.

4 is a moderate level on this task-goal attribute.

1 or 2 is very low on this task-goal attribute.

SOURCE: Adapted from R. M. Steers, "Factors Affecting Job Attitudes in a Goal-Setting Environment," *Academy of Management Journal* 19 (1976): 9.

laboratory studies, field research experiments, and comparative investigations by Edwin Locke, Gary Latham, John M. Ivancevich and others.[15]

Characteristics of Effective Goals

How difficult and specific are your work or school goals? Challenge 6.1 will give you an opportunity to evaluate your goals on five dimensions. Various organizations define the characteristics of effective goals differently. For the former Sanger-Harris, a retail organization, the acronym SMART communicates the approach to effective goals. SMART stands for *S*pecific, *M*easurable, *A*ttainable, *R*ealistic, and *T*ime-bound. Five commonly accepted characteristics of effective goals are specific, challenging, measurable, time-bound, and prioritized.

Alternate Example
Goals should provide "stretch". That is, they should be challenging, yet realistic.

Specific and challenging goals serve to cue or focus the person's attention on exactly what is to be accomplished and to arouse the person to peak performance. People in a wide range of occupations who set specific, challenging goals consistently outperform people who have easy or unspecified goals, as Figure 6.2 shows.

Measureable, quantitative goals are useful as a basis for feedback about goal progress. Qualitative goals are also valuable. The Western Company of North America allowed about 15 percent of a manager's goals to be of a qualitative nature.[16] A qualitative goal might be to improve relationships with customers. Further work might convert the qualitative goal into quantitative measures such as number of complaints or frequency of complimentary letters. However, the qualitative goal may well be sufficient and most meaningful in this case.

Time-bound goals enhance measurability. The time limit may be implicit in the goal or it may need to be made explicit. For example, without the six-month time limit, an insurance salesperson might think the sales goal is for the whole year rather than for six months. Many organizations work on standardized cycles, such as quarters or years, where very explicit time limits are assumed. If there is any uncertainty about the time period of the goal effort, the time limit should be explicitly stated.

Discussion Consideration
Discuss the implications of unrealistic goals in light of the effort-performance expectancy component of the expectancy theory of motivation.

The priority ordering of goals allows for effective decision making about the allocation of resources.[17] As time, energy, or other resources become available, a person can move down the list of goals in descending order. The key concern is with achieving the top-priority goals. Priority helps direct a person's efforts and behavior. Although these characteristics help increase motivation and performance, that is not the only function of goal setting in organizations, however.

Alternate Example
The motivational impact of goal setting can be seen in what has been called the "high performance cycle": The cycle begins with high challenge in the form of specific, difficult goals. If there is commitment to these goals, adequate feedback, high self-efficacy, and suitable task strategies, high performance will result. If high performance leads to desired rewards, high satisfaction will result. Job satisfaction is, in turn, highly associated with an increased propensity to stay on the job. People who are satisfied and stay on the job are then ready and willing to take on new challenges. Thus, the cycle repeats itself. Source: E. Locke and G. Latham, *A Theory of Goal Setting and Task Design,* 1990, Englewood Cliffs: Prentice-Hall.

Goal setting serves one or more of three functions. First, it can increase work motivation and task performance.[18] Second, it can reduce the role stress that is associated with conflicting or confusing expectations.[19] Third, it can improve the accuracy and validity of performance evaluation.[20]

Increasing Work Motivation and Task Performance

Goals are often used to increase employee effort and motivation, which in turn improve task performance. The higher the goal, the better the performance; that is, people work harder to reach difficult goals. The positive relationship between goal difficulty and task performance is depicted in Figure 6.2. Even unreasonable goals may improve motivation, although there is not universal agreement on this point.[21]

Three important behavioral aspects of enhancing performance motivation through goal setting are employee participation, supervisory commitment, and useful performance feedback. Employee participation in goal setting leads to goal acceptance by employees. Goal acceptance is thought to lead to goal commitment and then to goal accomplishment. Special attention has been given to factors that influence commitment to difficult goals, such as participation in the process of setting the difficult goals.[22] Even in the case of assigned goals, goal acceptance and commitment are considered essential prerequisites to goal accomplishment.

Supervisory goal commitment is a reflection of the organization's commitment to goal setting. Organizational commitment is a prerequisite for successful goal-setting programs, such as management by objectives (MBO) programs.[23] The organization must be committed to the program, and the employee and supervisors must be committed to specific work goals as well as to the program. (MBO will be discussed in more detail later in the chapter.)

The supervisor plays a second important role by providing employees with interim performance feedback on progress toward goals. Performance feedback is most useful when the goals are specific, and specific goals improve perfor-

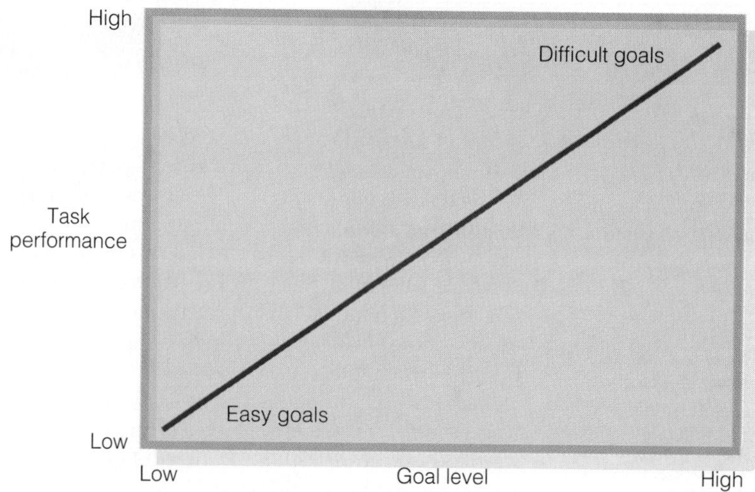

■ **FIGURE 6.2**
Goal Level and Task Performance

mance most when interim feedback is given.[24] For example, assume an insurance salesperson has a goal of selling $500,000 worth of insurance in six months but has achieved sales of only $200,000 after three months. During an interim performance feedback session, the supervisor may help the salesperson identify the fact that he is not focusing his calls on the likeliest prospects. This useful feedback coupled with the specific goal helps the salesperson better focus his efforts to achieve the goal. Feedback is most helpful when it is useful (helping the salesperson identify high probability prospects) and timely (halfway through the performance period).

The accompanying Scientific Foundation feature reports on a study of goal setting, productivity, creativity, expected evaluation, and the presence or absence of coactors. The results are interesting.

Reducing Role Stress of Conflicting and Confusing Expectations

A second function of goal setting is to reduce the role stress associated with conflicting and confusing expectations. This is done by clarifying the task-role expectations communicated to employees. Supervisors, coworkers, and employees are all important sources of task-related information. A fourteen-month evaluation of goal setting in reducing role stress found that conflict, confusion, and absenteeism were all reduced through the use of goal setting.[25]

The improved role clarity resulting from goal setting may be attributable to improved communication between managers and employees. An early study of the MBO goal-setting program at Ford Motor Company found an initial 25 percent lack of agreement between managers and their bosses concerning the definition of the managers' jobs. Through effective goal-setting activities, this lack of agreement was reduced to about 5 percent.[26] At Federal Express, managers are encouraged to include communication-related targets in their annual MBO goal-setting process.[27]

Improving the Accuracy and Validity of Performance Evaluation

The third major function of goal setting is improving the accuracy and validity of performance evaluation. One of the best methods of doing so is to use **management by objectives (MBO)**—a goal-setting program based on interaction

management by objectives (MBO)
A goal-setting program based on interaction and negotiation between employees and managers.

SCIENTIFIC FOUNDATION

Goal Setting for Creativity?

Creativity is often considered an important source of competitive strength for organizations, especially in changing and uncertain times. This research was designed to examine the effects of three factors on creative performance by attempting to answer three basic questions. First, does the presence of others (coactors) have an effect on creative performance? Second, does the anticipation of an evaluation have an effect on creative performance? Third, does setting a creativity goal have an effect on creative performance?

Two studies were designed to answer these questions. In the first study, 84 students worked to develop creative solutions to an in-basket exercise. Some students worked alone and others worked in the presence of other students; some expected to be evaluated and others did not. In the second study, 136 students worked on a similar task. This time a creativity goal was assigned to some of the students and not to others. Two performance measures were used: the degree of solution creativity (innovativeness) and productivity (number of possible solutions).

The results indicated that high levels of creativity occurred when individuals worked alone, and productivity was high when individuals worked alone with no expectation of being evaluated. The highest creativity occurred when individuals had a creativity goal and worked alone. However, productivity was low when individuals worked alone and were assigned a creativity goal. Results were mixed with regard to the effect of expected evaluation. Under the right conditions, goal setting does lead to higher levels of creativity.

SOURCE: C. E. Shalley, "Effects of Coaction, Expected Evaluation, and Goal Setting on Creativity and Productivity," *Academy of Management Journal* 38 (1995): 483–503.

and negotiation between employees and managers. MBO programs have been pervasive in organizations for nearly thirty years.[28]

According to Peter Drucker, who originated the concept, the objectives-setting process begins with the employee writing an "employee's letter" to the manager. The letter would explain the employee's general understanding of the scope of the manager's job, an understanding of the scope of the employee's own job, and the set of specific objectives to be pursued over the next six months or year. After some discussion and negotiation, the manager and the employee would finalize these items into a performance plan.

Discussion Consideration
What if grades were based on a goal negotiated with your professor? What are the potential strengths and weaknesses of an MBO approach to grades?

Drucker considers MBO a participative and interactive process. This does not mean that goal setting begins at the bottom of the organization. It means that goal setting is applicable to all employees, with lower-level organizational members and professional staff having a clear influence over the goal-setting process.[29] (The performance aspect of goal setting is discussed in the next section of the chapter.)

Goal setting programs operate under a variety of names, including goals and controls at Purex, work planning and review at Black & Decker and General Electric, and performance planning and evaluation at Tenneco and IBM. Most of these programs are designed to enhance performance.[30] Their two central ingredients are planning and evaluation.

The planning component consists of organizational and individual goal setting. Organizational goal setting is an essential prerequisite to individual goal setting; the two must be closely linked for the success of both.[31] At Federal Express, all individual objectives must be tied to the overall corporate objectives of people, service, and profit.

In planning, discretionary control is usually given to individuals and departments to develop operational and tactical plans to support the corporate objectives. The emphasis is on formulating a clear, consistent, measurable, and ordered set of goals to articulate *what* to do. It is also assumed that operational support planning helps determine *how* to do it. Intention is a concept used to encompass both the goal (*what*) and the set of pathways that lead to goal attainment (*how*), thus recognizing the importance of both what and how.[32]

The evaluation component consists of interim reviews by managers and employees of goal progress and of formal performance evaluation. The reviews are mid-term assessments designed to help employees take self-corrective action. They are not designed as final or formal performance evaluations. The formal performance evaluation occurs at the close of a reporting period, usually once a year. The Tenneco program is an example of a goal-setting program that systematically incorporates planning and evaluation components.[33]

Because goal-setting programs are somewhat mechanical by nature, they are most easily implemented in stable, predictable industrial settings. Although most programs allow for some flexibility and change, they are less useful in organizations where high levels of unpredictability exist, such as in basic research and development, or where the organization requires substantial adaptation or adjustment. Finally, individual, gender, and cultural differences do not appear to threaten the success of goal-setting programs.[34,35] Thus, goal-setting programs may be widely applied and effective in a diverse work force.

Points to Emphasize
Planning, at any level of the organization, is a two step process. Goal-setting is only one part of this process. Successful planning requires the development of a specific action plan to achieve the goals.

Performance: A Key Construct

■ Goal setting is designed to improve work performance, an important organizational behavior directly related to the production of goods or the delivery of services. Performance is most often thought of as task accomplishment, the term *task* coming from Taylor's early notion of a worker's required activity.[36,37] Taylor considered performance standards and differential piece-rate pay key ingredients in achieving high levels of performance. Robert Yerkes found arousal and stress helpful in improving performance up to an optimum point.[38] Hence, outcomes and effort are both important for good performance. This section focuses on task-oriented performance.

One company that elicits high levels of performance from its people is Federal Express. Chairman, President, and CEO Frederick W. Smith emphasizes People-Service-Profit (P-S-P) and the importance of performance feedback and performance-based rewards in ensuring sustained high levels of performance.

Performance appraisal is the evaluation of a person's performance. Accurate appraisals help supervisors fulfill their dual roles as evaluators and coaches. As a coach, a supervisor is responsible for encouraging employee growth and development. As an evaluator, a supervisor is responsible for making judgments that influence employees' roles in the organization.

performance appraisal
The evaluation of a person's performance.

The major functions of performance appraisals are to give employees feedback on performance, to identify the employees' developmental needs, to make promotion and reward decisions, to make demotion and termination decisions, and to develop information about the organization's selection and placement decisions. Therefore, it is important for performance appraisals to measure performance accurately.

Measuring Performance

Ideally, actual performance and measured performance are the same. Practically, this is seldom the case. Measuring operational performance is easier than measuring managerial performance because of the availability of quantifiable data. Measuring production performance is easier than measuring research and development performance because of the reliability of the measures.

Performance appraisal systems are intended to improve the accuracy of measured performance and increase its agreement with actual performance. The extent of agreement is called the true assessment, as Figure 6.3 shows. The figure also identifies the performance measurement problems that contribute to inaccuracy. They include deficiency, unreliability and invalidity. Deficiency results from overlooking important aspects of a person's actual performance. Unreliability results from poor-quality performance measures. Invalidity results from inaccurate definition of the expected job performance.

■ **FIGURE 6.3**
Actual and Measured Performance

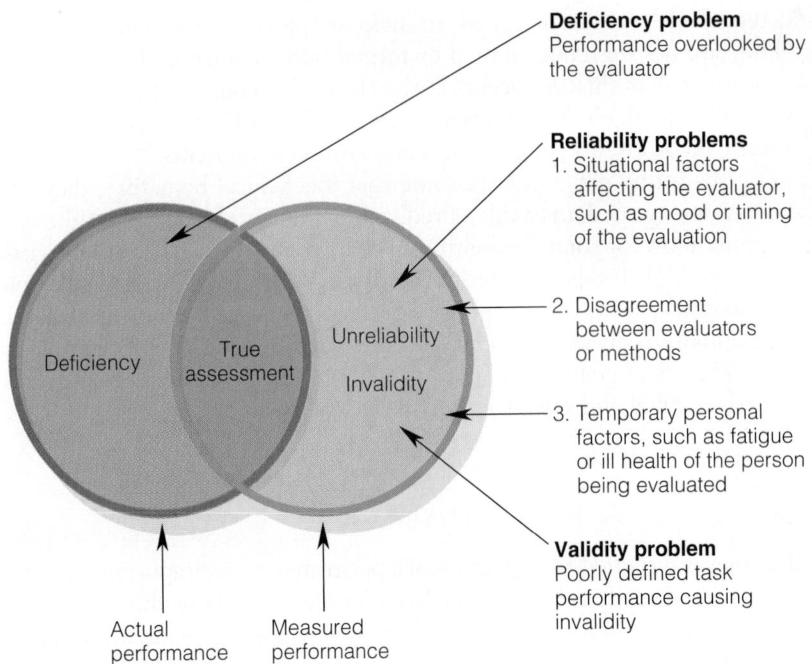

Points to Emphasize
A performance evaluation system can be evaluated by asking two questions: 1) Are we measuring the correct aspects of performance? And 2) Are we measuring accurately? The first question has to do with the validity of the performance appraisal system. The second question has to do with the reliability of the system. Note that the system might be valid, yet not reliable.

Points to Emphasize
Two problems plague traditional, standardized performance appraisal systems. Often they are contaminated, including many aspects of performance that are not important or relevant to the job being evaluated. Performance appraisals may also be deficient, excluding important aspects of performance. By customizing the performance appraisal process, MBO programs can go along way in addressing these problems.

Discussion Consideration
Many organizations are now using a "360" approach to performance appraisal. In this approach, employees are evaluated by superiors, peers, subordinates, themselves, and even customers. If students were allowed to determine grades for one another, would the grades be different from the instructor's? How would the self-evaluations differ from instructor evaluations?

Early performance appraisal systems were often quite biased. See, for example, Table 6.3, which is a sample of officer effectiveness reports from an infantry company in the early 1800s. Even contemporary executive appraisals have a dark side. One study of 82 executives in manufacturing and service companies concluded that senior executives had extraordinary latitude in evaluating the performance of subordinate executives, often using appraisals as political tools to control people and resources.[39]

Performance monitoring systems using modern electronic technology are sometimes used to measure the performance of vehicle operators, computer technicians, and telephone operators. For example, such systems might record the rate of keystrokes or the total number of keystrokes for a computer technician. The people subject to this type of monitoring are in some cases unaware that their performance is being measured. What is appropriate performance monitoring? What constitutes inappropriate electronic spying on the employee? Are people entitled to know when their performance is being measured? The ethics of monitoring performance may differ by culture. The United States and Sweden, for example, respect individual freedom more than Japan and China do. The overriding issue, however, is how far organizations should go in using modern technology to measure human performance.

Goal setting and MBO are results-oriented methods of performance appraisal that do not necessarily rely on modern technology. As with performance monitoring systems, the emphasis is shifted from subjective, judgmental performance dimensions to observable, verifiable results. Goals established in the planning phase of goal setting become the standard against which to measure subsequent performance. However, rigid adherence to a results-oriented approach may risk overlooking performance opportunities.

Another method for improving the accuracy of performance appraisal is to have multiple evaluators contribute to the final appraisal. Superiors, peers, employees, and clients all contribute something unique because each group has a different vantage point. Most traditional evaluations are completed by superiors. Peer and employee evaluations may add a new dimension by covering such areas as cooperation and supervisory style. For example, one mid-level executive behaved very differently in dealing with superiors, peers, and employees. With

■ **TABLE 6.3**

Officer Effectiveness Reports, circa 1813

Alexander Brown—Lt. Col., Comdg.—A good natured man.
Clark Crowell—first Major—A good man, but no officer.
Jess B. Wordsworth—2nd Major—An excellent officer.
Captain Shaw—A man of whom all unite in speaking ill. A knave despised by all.
Captain Thomas Lord—Indifferent, but promises well.
Captain Rockwell—An officer of capacity, but imprudent and a man of violent passions.
1st Lt. Jas. Kearns—Merely good, nothing promising.
1st Lt. Robert Cross—Willing enough—has much to learn—with small capacity.
2nd Lt. Stewart Berry—An ignorant unoffending fellow.
Ensign North—A good young man who does well.

SOURCE: *The Air Officer's Guide, 6th ed.*, copyright 1952, Stackpole Books. Used with permission.

superiors, he was positive, compliant, and deferential. With peers, he was largely indifferent, often ignoring them. With employees, he was tough and demanding, bordering on cruel and abusive. Without each of these perspectives, the executive's performance would not have been accurately assessed.

Federal Express has incorporated a novel and challenging approach to evaluation in its blueprint for service quality. All managers at Federal Express are evaluated by their employees through a survey-feedback-action system. Employees evaluate their managers using a five-point scale on twenty-nine standard statements and ten local option ones. Low ratings suggest problem areas requiring management attention. For example, the following statement received low ratings from employees in 1990: Upper management (directors and above) pays attention to ideas and suggestions from people at my level. CEO Fred Smith became directly involved in addressing this problem area. One of the actions he took to correct the problem was the development of a biweekly employee newsletter.

http://www.fedex.com/

Performance Feedback: A Communication Challenge

Once clearly defined and accurate performance measures are developed, there is still the challenge of performance feedback. Feedback sessions are among the more stressful events for supervisors and employees. Early research at General Electric found employees responded constructively to positive feedback and were defensive over half the time in response to critical or negative feedback. Typical responses to negative feedback included shifting responsibility for the shortcoming or behavior, denying it outright, or providing a wide range of excuses for it.[40]

http://www.ge.com/

Both parties to a performance feedback session should try to make it a constructive learning experience, since positive and negative performance feedback has long-term implications for the employee's performance and for the working relationship. American Airlines follows three guidelines in providing evaluative feedback so the experience is constructive for supervisor and employee alike.[41] First, refer to specific, verbatim statements and specific, observable behaviors displayed by the person receiving the feedback. This enhances the acceptance of the feedback while reducing the chances of denial. Second, focus on changeable behaviors, as opposed to intrinsic or personality-based attributes. People are often more defensive about who they are than what they do. Third, plan and organize for the session ahead of time. Be sure to notify the person who will receive the feedback. Both the leader and the follower should be ready.

http://www.americanair.com/

In addition to these ideas, Tenneco recommends beginning coaching and counseling sessions with something positive.[42] The intent is to reduce defensiveness and enhance useful communication. There is almost always at least one positive element to emphasize. Once the session is under way and rapport is established, then the evaluator can introduce more difficult and negative material. Because people are not perfect, there is always an opportunity for them to learn and to grow through performance feedback sessions. Critical feedback is the basis for improvement and is essential to a performance feedback session.

Self-evaluations are increasingly used for performance feedback, and there is evidence they lead to more satisfying, constructive evaluation interviews and less defensiveness concerning the evaluation process.[43] In addition, self-evaluations may improve job performance through greater commitment to organizational goals. On the other hand, a key criticism of self-evaluations is their low level of agreement with supervisory evaluations.[44] However, high levels of agreement may not necessarily be desirable if what is intended through the overall evaluation process is a full picture of the person's performance.

Developing People and Enhancing Careers

A key function of a good performance appraisal system is to develop people and enhance careers.[45] Developmentally, performance appraisals should emphasize individual growth needs and future performance. If the supervisor is to coach and develop employees effectively, there must be mutual trust. The supervisor must be vulnerable and open to challenge from the subordinate while maintaining a position of responsibility for what is in the subordinate's best interests.[46] The supervisor must also be a skilled, empathetic listener who encourages the employee to talk about hopes and aspirations.[47]

The employee must be able to take active responsibility for future development and growth. This might mean challenging the supervisor's ideas about future development as well as expressing individual preferences and goals. Passive, compliant employees are unable to accept responsibility for themselves or to achieve full emotional development. Individual responsibility is a key characteristic of the Chaparral Steel Company's culture. The company joke is that the company manages by "adultry" (pun intended). Chaparral Steel treats people like adults and expects adult behavior from them.

Key Characteristics of an Effective Appraisal System

An effective performance appraisal system has five key characteristics: validity, reliability, responsiveness, flexibility, and equitableness. Its validity comes from capturing multiple dimensions of a person's job performance. Its reliability comes from capturing evaluations from multiple sources and at different times over the course of the evaluation period. Its responsiveness allows the person being evaluated some input into the final outcome. Its flexibility leaves it open to modification based on new information, such as federal requirements. Its equitability results in fair evaluations against established performance criteria, regardless of individual differences. The accompanying Organizational Reality feature explains the major changes Lyondel Petrochemical made in its performance appraisals.

Rewarding Performance

■ One function of a performance appraisal system is to provide input for reward decisions. If an organization wants good performance, then it must reward good performance. If it does not want bad performance, then it must not reward bad performance. If companies talk "teamwork," "values," and "cus-

ORGANIZATIONAL REALITY

Major Changes in Performance Appraisals

Lyondel Petrochemical made major changes in its performance management system because the company was unhappy with its performance appraisals. One survey found 51 percent of responding companies were similarly dissatisfied, and 64 percent indicated plans to redesign their systems. Many companies redesign their appraisal systems by adopting new scales or adding new performance categories.

Lyondel Petrochemical, a Houston-based energy producer, did not follow this usual process in their redesign. In fact, they eliminated performance ratings and formal appraisals, creating a "dialogue process" instead. Using this dialogue process, supervisors and employees meet frequently and discuss goals, with a focus on the company's four goals: financial success, employee productivity, company responsibility, and customer satisfaction.

In addition, Lyondel Petrochemical separated its performance management system from its pay system. In place of performance-based pay, the company uses market-based pay. There are no caps on salary ranges and no cap on the profit-sharing. Employees receive base salaries tied to market rates for their jobs and, beyond that, profit-sharing and special awards for outstanding contributions add to their annual base.

Lyondel's innovative, major changes in performance appraisal and pay apparently have been well received by employees. The changes also appear consistent with the changing world of business. ■

SOURCE: Reprinted by permission of the publisher, from *HR Focus* (July 1995), Donald J. McNerney, et al. American Management Association, New York.

tomer focus," then they need to reward behaviors related to these ideas. Although this idea is conceptually simple, it can become very complicated in practice. Reward decisions are among the most difficult and complicated decisions made in organizations. They are also among the most important decisions made in organizations.[48]

A Key Organizational Decision Process

Reward and punishment decisions in organizations affect many people throughout the system, not just the persons being rewarded or punished. Reward allocation involves sequential decisions about which people to reward, how to reward them, and when to reward them. Taken together, these decisions shape the behavior of everyone in the organization. This is because of the vicarious learning that occurs as people watch what happens to others, especially when new programs or initiatives are implemented. People carefully watch what happens to peers who make mistakes or have problems with the new system, gauging their own behavior accordingly.

Individual Versus Team Reward Systems

One of the distinguishing characteristics of Americans is the value they place on individualism. Systems that reward individuals are common in organizations in the United States. One of their strengths is that they foster autonomous and independent behavior that may lead to creativity, to novel solutions to old problems, and to distinctive contributions to the organization. Individual reward systems directly affect individual behavior and may encourage competitive striving within a work team. Although motivation and reward techniques in the United States are individually focused, they are often group-focused outside the United States.[49]

Too much competition within a work environment, however, may be dysfunctional. At the Western Company of North America, individual success in the MBO program was tied too tightly to rewards, and individual managers became divisively competitive. For example, some managers took last-minute interdepartmental financial actions in a quarter to meet their objectives, only to cause heartache for other managers whom they caused to miss their objectives. These actions raise ethical questions about how far individual managers should go in serving their own self-interest at the expense of their peers.

Team reward systems solve the problems caused by individual competitive behavior. These systems emphasize cooperation, joint efforts, and the sharing of information, knowledge, and expertise. The Japanese and Chinese cultures, with their collectivist orientations, place greater emphasis than Americans on the individual as an element of the team, not a member apart from the team. Digital Equipment Corporation has a partnership approach to performance appraisals. Self-managed work group members participate in their own appraisal process. This approach emphasizes teamwork and responsibility.

The collectivism of the Japanese and Chinese cultures emphasizes the importance of the individual's contribution to the collective effort of the team. This Japanese work team is learning about new technologies in a television factory.

Some organizations have experimented with individual and group alternative reward systems.[50] At the individual level, these include skill-based and pay-for-knowledge systems. Each emphasizes skills or knowledge possessed by an employee over and above the requirements for the basic job. At the group level, gain-sharing plans emphasize collective cost reduction and allow workers to share in the gains achieved by reducing production or other operating costs. In such plans, everyone shares equally in the collective gain.

The Power of Earning

Points to Emphasize
As we approach the 21st century it is conceivable that employees will place a higher value on leisure time. They may want extended vacation days or increased medical benefits, rather than pay raises.

The purpose behind both individual and team reward systems is to shape productive behavior. Effective performance management can be the lever of change that boosts individual and team achievements in an organization. So, if one wants the rewards available in the organization, then one should work to earn them. Performance management and reward systems assume a demonstrable connection between performance and rewards. Organizations get the performance they reward, not the performance they say they want.[51] Further, when there is no apparent link between performance and rewards, people may begin to believe they are entitled to rewards regardless of how they perform. The concept of entitlement is very different from the concept of earning, which assumes a performance-reward link.

The notion of entitlement at work is counterproductive when taken to the extreme because it counteracts the power of earning.[52] People who believe they are entitled to rewards regardless of their behavior or performance are not motivated to behave constructively. They believe they have a right to be taken care of by someone, whether that is the organization or a specific person. Entitlement engenders passive, irresponsible behavior in people, whereas earning engenders active, responsible, adult behavior. If rewards depend on perfor-

CHALLENGE

■ 6.2

Correcting Poor Performance

At one time or another, each of us has had a poor performance of some kind. It may have been a poor test result in school, a poor presentation at work, or a poor performance in an athletic event. Think of a poor performance event that you have experienced and work through the following three steps.

Step 1. Briefly describe the specific event in some detail. Include why you label it a poor performance (bad score? someone else's evaluation?).

Step 2. Analyze the Poor Performance

a. List all the possible contributing causes to the poor performance. Be specific, such as the room was too hot, you did not get enough sleep, you were not told how to perform the task, etc. You might ask other people for possible ideas, too.

1. ____________ 4. ____________
2. ____________ 5. ____________
3. ____________ 6. ____________
7. ____________

b. Is there a primary cause for the poor performance? What is it?

Step 3. Plan to Correct the Poor Performance

Develop a step-by-step plan of action that specifies what you can change or do differently to improve your performance the next time you have an opportunity. Include seeking help if it is needed. Once your plan is developed, look for an opportunity to execute it.

mance, then people must perform responsibly to receive them. The power of earning rests on a direct link between performance and rewards.

Correcting Poor Performance

■ Often a complicated, difficult challenge for supervisors, correcting poor performance is a three-step process. First, the cause or primary responsibility for the poor performance must be identified. Second, if the primary responsibility is a person's, then the source of the personal problem must be determined. Third, a plan of action to correct the poor performance must be developed. Challenge 6.2 gives you an opportunity to examine a poor performance you have experienced.

Poor performance may result from a variety of causes, the more important being poorly designed work systems, poor selection processes, inadequate training and skills development, lack of personal motivation, and personal problems intruding on the work environment. Not all poor performance is self-motivated; some is induced by the work system. Therefore, a good diagnosis should precede corrective action. For example, it may be that an employee is subject to a work design or selection system that does not allow the person to exhibit good performance. Identifying the cause of the poor performance comes first and should be done in communication with the employee. If the problem is with the system and the supervisor can fix it, then everyone wins as a result.

If the poor performance is not attributable to work design or organizational process problems, then attention should be focused on the employee. At least three possible causes of poor performance can be attributed to the employee. The problem may lie in (1) some aspect of the person's relationship to the organization or supervisor, (2) some area of the employee's personal life, or (3) a training or developmental deficiency. In the latter two cases, poor performance may be treated as a symptom as opposed to a motivated consequence. In such cases, identifying financial problems, family difficulties, or health disorders may enable the supervisor to help the employee solve problems before they become too extensive. Employee Assistance Programs (EAPs) can be helpful to employees managing personal problems and are discussed in Chapter 7 related to managing stress.

Poor performance may also be motivated as a result of an employee's displaced anger or conflict with the organization or supervisor. In such cases, the employee may or may not be aware of the internal reactions causing the problem. In either event, sabotage, work slowdowns, work stoppages, and similar forms of poor performance are the result of such motivated behavior. The supervisor may attribute the cause of the problem to the employee, and the employee may attribute it to the supervisor or organization. To solve motivated performance problems requires treating the poor performance as a symptom with a deeper cause. Resolving the underlying anger or conflict results in the disappearance of the symptom (poor performance).

Attribution and Performance Management

According to attribution theory, as we discussed in Chapter 3, managers make attributions (inferences) concerning employees' behavior and performance.[53,54] The attributions may not always be accurate. For example, an executive with Capital Cities Corporation who had a very positive relationship with his boss was not held responsible for profit problems in his district. The boss attributed the problem to the economy instead.

Alternate Example
The fundamental attribution error refers to our tendency to emphasize dispositional (internal) causes to the behavior of others. This tendency could lead to errors in the performance appraisal process.

Supervisors and employees who share perceptions and attitudes, as in the Capital Cities situation, tend to evaluate each other highly.[55,56] Supervisors and employees who do not share perceptions and attitudes are more likely to blame each other for performance problems.

Figure 6.4 presents an attribution model that specifically addresses how supervisors respond to poor performance. A supervisor who observes poor performance seeks cues about the employee's behavior in three forms: consensus, consistency, and distinctiveness. Consensus is how widespread a behavior is in an organization. Consistency is the frequency of the performance. Distinctiveness is whether a performance problem is unique to a particular task or appears in other aspects of the job. (These cues were first discussed in Chapter 3.)

On the basis of this information, the supervisor makes either an internal (personal) attribution or an external (situational) attribution. Internal attributions might include low effort, lack of commitment, or lack of ability. External attributions are outside the employee's control and might include equipment failure or unrealistic goals. The supervisor then determines the source of responsibility for the performance problem and tries to correct the problem.

Supervisors may choose from a wide range of responses. They can, for example, express personal concern, reprimand the employee, or provide training. Supervisors who attribute the cause of poor performance to a person (an internal cause) will respond more harshly than supervisors who attribute the cause to the work situation (an external cause). Supervisors should try not to make either

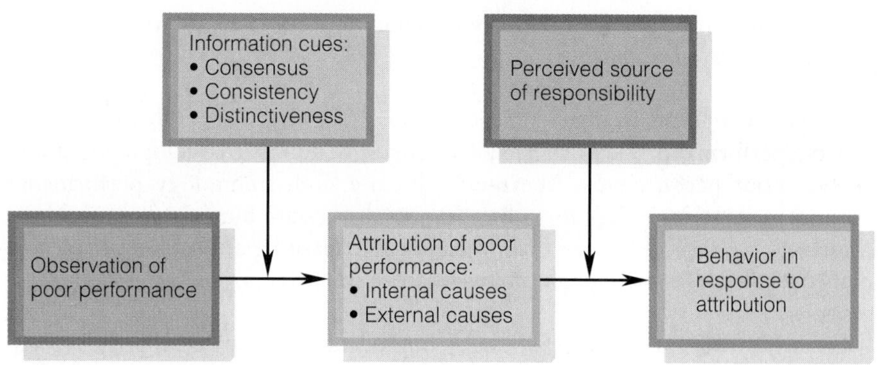

■ **FIGURE 6.4**
Attribution Model

of the two common attribution errors discussed in Chapter 3: the fundamental attribution error and the self-serving bias.

Coaching, Counseling, and Mentoring

Supervisors have important coaching, counseling, and mentoring responsibilities to their subordinates. They should maintain a helping relationship with employees.[57] This relationship may be one where performance-based deficiencies are addressed or one where personal problems that diminish employee performance, such as depression, are addressed.[58] In either case, the supervisors can play a helpful role in employee problem-solving activities without accepting responsibility for the employees' problems. One important form of help is to refer the employee to trained professionals.

Coaching and counseling are among the career and psychosocial functions of a mentoring relationship.[59] **Mentoring** is a work relationship that encourages development and career enhancement for people moving through the career cycle. Mentor relationships typically go through four phases: initiation, cultivation, separation, and redefinition. The relationship can significantly enhance the early development of a newcomer and the mid-career development of an experienced employee. Career development can be enhanced through peer relationships as an alternative to traditional mentoring relationships.[60] Informational, collegial, and special peers aid the individual's development through information sharing, career strategizing, job-related feedback, emotional support, and friendship. Hence, mentors and peers may both play constructive roles in correcting an employee's poor performance and in enhancing overall career development. This mentoring process is discussed in detail in Chapter 17.

mentoring
A work relationship that encourages development and career enhancement for people moving through the career cycle.

Discussion Consideration
Ask students to discuss the role of mentors in their lives. These mentors may be parents, grandparents, teachers, coaches, pastors, or professors. Did their experience with their mentor follow the four phases identified in the text?

Managerial Implications: Performance Management is a Key Task

■ People in organizations learn from the consequences of their actions. Therefore, managers must exercise care in the application of positive and negative consequences, ensuring that they are connected to the behaviors they intend to reward or punish. Managers should also be judicious in the use of punishment and should consider extinction coupled with positive reinforcement as an alternative to punishment for shaping employee behavior. Managers can serve as positive role models for the vicarious learning of employees about ethical behavior and high-quality performance.

Goal-setting activities may be valuable to managers in bringing out the best performance from employees. Managers can use challenging, specific goals for this purpose and must be prepared to provide employees with timely, useful feedback on goal progress so employees will know how they are doing. Goal-setting activities that are misused may create dysfunctional competition in an organization and lead to lower performance.

Good performance evaluation systems are a valuable tool for providing employees with clear feedback on their actions. Managers who rely on valid and reliable performance measures may use them in employee development and to correct poor performance. Managers who use high-technology performance monitoring systems must remember that employees are humans, not machines. Managers are responsible for creating a positive learning atmosphere in performance feedback sessions, and employees are responsible for learning from these sessions.

Finally, managers can use rewards as one of the most powerful positive consequences for shaping employee behavior. If rewards are to improve performance, managers must make a clear connection between specific performance and the rewards. Employees should be expected to earn the rewards they receive; they should expect rewards related to performance quality and skill development.

CLOSING SPOTLIGHT

Restructuring for the Customer

Although Chaparral Steel is a high-performance organization, it has not finished improving, growing, and looking for opportunities to be better than it already is. Many organizations engaged in a wide variety of restructuring, reengineering, and downsizing activities during the early 1990s in response to changes of various kinds. During 1995, Chaparral Steel began an organizational restructuring initiative of its own while maintaining its unique "campus" culture in Midlothian, Texas, that emphasizes learning, education, and trust.[61]

Previously organized along functional lines, Chaparral Steel has set up three separate companies, or business units, within the company.[62] Each of these units is organized around different aspects of the steelmaking operation: structural products, such as bantam beams and wide-flange beams; bar mill products, such as special bar quality rounds; and steelmaking recycled products, such as results from Chaparral's car shredding activities. Three longtime Chaparral executives (Dave Fournie, Peter Wright, and Duff Hunt) have been selected to head each of these three units, respectively.

Chaparral's restructuring activities are aimed at being more focused, responsive, and customer-oriented. When attempting to be the best that you can be, the job is never done and you always need to look for ways to improve, as Chaparral Steel has done. ■

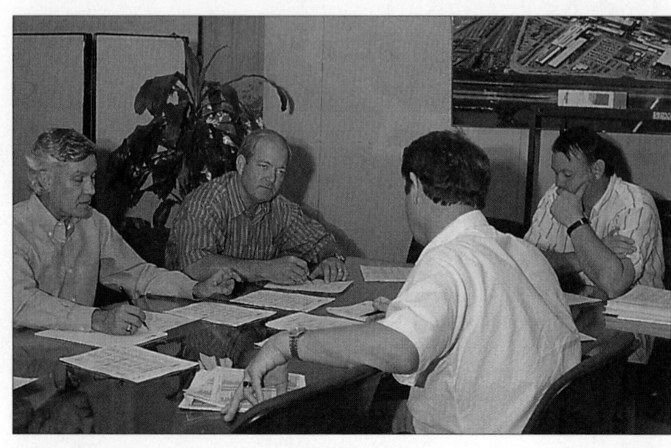

Successful organizational change requires carefully planning, including financial. Chaparral Steel people work and plan together, as in this meeting between (from left) Vice President Dennis Beach, comptroller Larry Clark, supervisor Jack Loteryman, and Dave Fournie.

Chapter Summary

- Learning is a change in behavior acquired through experience.
- The operant conditioning approach to learning states that behavior is a function of its positive and negative consequences.
- Reinforcement is used to develop desirable behavior; punishment and extinction are used to decrease undesirable behavior.
- Bandura's social learning theory suggests that self-efficacy is important to effective learning.
- Goal setting improves work motivation and task performance, reduces role stress, and improves the accuracy and validity of performance appraisal.
- Performance appraisals help organizations develop employees and make decisions about them.
- Problems with performance appraisals include deficiency, poor reliability, and poor validity.
- High-quality performance should be rewarded and poor performance should be corrected.
- Mentoring is a relationship for encouraging development and career enhancement for people moving through the career cycle.

Key Terms

learning (p. 160)
classical conditioning (p. 160)
operant conditioning (p. 161)
positive consequences (p. 161)
negative consequences (p. 161)
reinforcement (p. 162)
punishment (p. 162)
extinction (p. 163)
goal setting (p. 166)
management by objectives (MBO) (p. 169)
performance appraisal (p. 171)
mentoring (p. 179)

Review Questions

1. Define the terms *learning*, *reinforcement*, *punishment*, and *extinction*.
2. What are positive and negative consequences in shaping behavior and how should they be managed? Explain the value of extinction as a strategy.
3. How can self-efficacy be enhanced? How do introverted and extroverted and intuitive and sensing people learn differently?
4. What are the five characteristics of well-developed goals? Why is feedback on goal progress important?
5. What are the purposes for conducting performance appraisals? Who should appraise performance? Why?
6. What possible problems limit accurate performance appraisals? What are five characteristics of a good performance appraisal system?
7. How can supervisors best provide useful performance feedback?
8. How do mentors and peers help people develop and enhance their careers?

Discussion and Communication Questions

1. Which learning approach—the behavioral approach or Bandura's social learning theory—do you find more appropriate for people?
2. Given your personality type, how do you learn best? Do you miss learning some things because of how they are taught?
3. What goals do you set for yourself in your work and personal life? Will you know if you achieve them?
4. If there were a conflict between your self-evaluation and the evaluation given to you by your supervisor or instructor, how would you respond? What, specifically, would you do? What have you learned from your supervisor or instructor during the last reporting period?
5. What rewards are most important to you? How hard are you willing to work to receive them?
6. *(communication question)* Prepare a memo detailing the consequences of behavior in your work or university environment (e.g., grades, awards, suspensions, and scholarships). Include in your memo your classification of these consequences as positive or negative. Should your organization or university change the way it applies these consequences?
7. *(communication question)* Develop an oral presentation about the most current management practices in employee rewards and performance management. Go to the library and read about what at least four (4) different companies are doing in this area. Be prepared to discuss their fit with the text materials.
8. *(communication question)* Interview a manager or supervisor who is responsible for completing performance appraisals on people at work. Ask the manager about the most difficult aspects of performance appraisal and the performance appraisal interview process, and how to manage these difficulties. Include the aspects of his/her job that enable him/her to meet these three different needs.

Ethics Questions

1. Referring to the case of the motivational team asked to teach soldiers to want to kill the enemy: Is this request ethical? Is it socially desirable? Should the team have accepted the assignment? Explain.
2. Suppose the organization you work for simply assigns employees their task goals without consulting them. Is there an ethical problem with this approach? Does the organization have to consult its employees?
3. Assume you are an experienced technical employee with a better understanding of your work than your supervisor has. Further assume that your supervisor sets unachievable performance standards for an inexperienced coworker so the person cannot ever meet them and therefore is fired. What should you do? Is your supervisor's action ethical? Explain.
4. Suppose your company set a performance standard above which it will pay employee bonuses. However, the company did not realize that many employees would be able to reach the standard with hard work and that the bonuses would cost the company much more than expected. Is it fair to lower the bonus rate? Is it fair to increase the performance standard for bonuses after the fact? Explain.

Experiential Exercises

6.1 Positive and Negative Reinforcement

Purpose: To examine the effects of positive and negative reinforcement on behavior change.

1. Two or three volunteers are selected to receive reinforcement from the class while performing a particular task. The volunteers leave the room.
2. The instructor identifies an object for the student volunteers to locate when they return to the room. (The object should be unobtrusive but clearly visible to the class. Some that have worked well are a small triangular piece of paper that was left behind when a notice was torn off a classroom bulletin board, a smudge on the chalkboard, and a chip in the plaster of a classroom wall.)
3. The instructor specifies the reinforcement contingencies that will be in effect when the volunteers return to the room. For negative reinforcement, students should hiss, boo, and throw things (although you should not throw anything harmful) when the first volunteer is moving away from the object; cheer and applaud when the second volunteer is getting closer to the object; and, if a third volunteer is used, use both negative and positive reinforcement.
4. The instructor should assign a student to keep a record of the time it takes each of the volunteers to locate the object.
5. Volunteer number 1 is brought back into the room and is instructed: "Your task is to locate and touch a particular object in the room, and the class has agreed to help you. You may begin."
6. Volunteer number 1 continues to look for the object until it is found while the class assists by giving negative reinforcement.
7. Volunteer number 2 is brought back into the room and is instructed: "Your task is to locate and touch a particular object in the room, and the class has agreed to help you. You may begin."
8. Volunteer number 2 continues to look for the object until it is found while the class assists by giving positive reinforcement.
9. Volunteer number 3 is brought back into the room and is instructed: "Your task is to locate and touch a particular object in the room, and the class has agreed to help you. You may begin."
10. Volunteer number 3 continues to look for the object until it is found while the class assists by giving both positive and negative reinforcement.
11. In a class discussion, answer the following questions:
    a. What were the differences in behavior of the volunteers when different kinds of reinforcement (positive, negative, or both) were used?
    b. What were the emotional reactions of the volunteers to the different kinds of reinforcement?
    c. Which type of reinforcement—positive or negative—is most common in organizations? What effect do you think this has on motivation and productivity?

6.2 Performance Appraisal and Review

This exercise provides an opportunity for you to engage in three performance appraisal and review role-playing sessions. In one session you are the supervisor, in a second session you are an employee, and in a third session you are an observer.

Performance appraisal and review sessions can be challenging for both the supervisor and the employee alike. There are at least three reasons for this. First, the appraisal process is emotional, and employees may become defensive or even hostile during a review session. Second, appraisal systems may be used for one or more reasons, potentially confusing the focus of the review session. Third, errors may creep into the appraisal process, as discussed in the text and summarized in Figure 6.3 on page 000.

There are several steps that supervisors and employees can take to prepare for a constructive performance appraisal and review session. Think about these steps as you read through the role profiles your instructor gives you to prepare for the role plays.

1. Prepare for the session ahead of time.
2. Start with the positive and look for the positive.
3. Practice good, responsive listening.
4. Be ready to engage in problem solving around performance that needs improvement.

The performance appraisal and review role plays give you an opportunity to implement these guidelines. In each case, your instructor will give you a few minutes to prepare and then adequate time to engage in the role play.

VIDEO CASE

Managing and Rewarding Performance at First Bank System[1]

According to Steve League, a marketing executive with First Bank System (FBS), "Banking today is not like banking twenty years ago—a job for life, stick around long enough you get promoted, you get a raise every year—it's totally different. It's very competitive. Very cost conscious. Very performance oriented now."

One of the ways in which these differences are evident is in terms of the linkages between FBS's mission and its performance appraisal and reward systems. First Bank System's mission is basically to broaden market share and to deepen relationships with existing customers by getting them to use more FBS products (e.g., selling the customer a savings plan and credit card in addition to a checking account). Part of the incentive compensation for personal bankers and bank managers is tied to how well this mission is accomplished. Their bonuses reflect the number, types, and dollar value of products sold to customers. Additionally, personal bankers' and bank managers' bonuses are tied to service quality as measured through customer satisfaction surveys.

The people at First Bank System take performance management very seriously. FBS has both informal and formal performance management programs. Under the informal program a manager provides an employee with both positive and critical feedback on a day-by-day, week-by-week, project-by-project basis. With the formal program, performance is reviewed quarterly and annually. Accomplishments, issues, and needs for development are discussed in these formal reviews.

These merit-based performance reviews are tied to employees' compensation, which, according to several FBS executives, is highly motivational. However, one executive says that FBS has experienced "a tendency to pay toward the average so that no one feels badly that he or she is not seen as an above average or superior employee." As partial justification for this, FBS managers say that they do not retain employees who fall below a satisfactory level of performance.

FBS executives believe that, overall, their performance appraisal and reward systems encourage strong employee motivation. Sometimes, however, business conditions have limited First Bank System's flexibility in using its reward system. For example, in earlier years, FBS had to cut some it its workforce and freeze the salaries of the remaining employees. According to Patricia Bauer, an FBS executive, employee motivation remained strong even with the downsizing and salary freeze. This was accomplished by keeping people focused on the task of turning the company around and being a part of the success.

Another approach that FBS uses for encouraging and recognizing superior performance is the Five Star Program. This is a company-wide program in which any employee of the bank can nominate an individual to be recognized for superior job performance. After an extensive interview process, a select few of those nominated are recognized at a special event during the year. FBS also has a similar team recognition program.

DISCUSSION QUESTIONS

1. What advantages and disadvantages do you see in the way that First Bank System assesses the performance of its personal bankers and bank managers?
2. What could FBS managers do to make both the formal and informal feedback sessions as effective as possible?
3. What problems could be created by taking the approach of paying toward the average for merit-based compensation?
4. What value do recognition programs like FBS's Five Star Program have for companies? Explain your answer.
5. How can a business like First Bank System positively influence employee motivation when organizational downsizing is occurring?

SOURCE: This case was written by Michael K. McCuddy, the Louis S. and Mary L. Morgal Professor of Christian Business Ethics, College of Business Administration, Valparaiso University.

1. This case is based on transcripts of interviews that representatives of West Educational Publishing conducted with various First Bank System executives.

References

1. Jeff Roesler, personal communication, 31 January 1996.
2. I. P. Pavlov, *Conditioned Reflexes* (New York: Oxford University Press, 1927).
3. Bradford Cannon, "Walter B. Cannon: Reflections on the Man and His Contributions," *Centennial Session*, American Psychological Association Centennial Convention, Washington, D.C., 1992.
4. B. F. Skinner, *The Behavior of Organisms: An Experimental Analysis* (New York: Appleton-Century-Crofts, 1938).
5. B. F. Skinner, *Science and Human Behavior* (New York: Free Press, 1953).
6. F. Luthans and R. Kreitner, *Organizational Behavior Modification and Beyond* (Glenview, Ill.: Scott, Foresman, 1985).
7. D. C. McClelland, personal communication, 1985.
8. B. F. Skinner, *Contingencies of Reinforcement: A Theoretical Analysis* (New York: Appleton-Century-Crofts, 1969).
9. J. P. Chaplin and T. S. Krawiec, *Systems and Theories of Psychology* (New York: Holt, Rinehart & Winston, 1960).
10. A. Bandura, *Social Learning Theory* (Englewood Cliffs, N.J.: Prentice-Hall, 1977).
11. A. Bandura, "Self-Efficacy: Toward a Unifying Theory of Behavioral Change," *Psychological Review* 84 (1977): 191–215.
12. C. G. Jung, *Psychological Types*, trans. H. G. Baynes (New York: Harcourt Brace, 1923).
13. O. Isachsen and L. V. Berens, *Working Together: A Personality Centered Approach to Management* (Coronado, Calif.: Neworld Management Press, 1988); and O. Krueger and J. M. Thuesen, *Type Talk* (New York: Tilden Press, 1988).
14. E. A. Locke, "The Ideas of Frederick W. Taylor: An Evaluation," *Academy of Management Review* 7 (1982): 14–24.
15. E. A. Locke and G. P. Latham, *A Theory of Goal Setting and Task Performance* (Englewood Cliffs, N.J.: Prentice-Hall, 1990).
16. T. O. Murray, *Management by Objectives: A Systems Approach to Management* (Fort Worth, Tex.: Western Company, n.d.).
17. W. T. Brooks and T. W. Mullins, *High Impact Time Management* (Englewood Cliffs, N.J.: Prentice-Hall, 1989).
18. E. A. Locke, "Toward a Theory of Task Motivation and Incentives," *Organizational Behavior and Human Performance* 3 (1968): 157–189.
19. J. C. Quick, "Dyadic Goal Setting within Organizations: Role Making and Motivational Considerations," *Academy of Management Review* 4 (1979): 369–380.
20. D. McGregor, "An Uneasy Look at Performance Appraisal," *Harvard Business Review* 35 (1957): 89–94.
21. H. Garland, "Influence of Ability, Assigned Goals, and Normative Information on Personal Goals and Performance: A Challenge to the Goal Attainability Assumption," *Journal of Applied Psychology* 68 (1982): 20–30.
22. J. R. Hollenbeck, C. R. Williams, and H. J. Klein, "An Empirical Examination of the Antecedents of Commitment to Difficult Goals," *Journal of Applied Psychology* 74 (1989): 18–23.
23. R. C. Rodgers and J. E. Hunter, "The Impact of Management by Objectives on Organizational Productivity," unpublished paper (Lexington: University of Kentucky, 1989).
24. E. A. Locke, K. N. Shaw, L. M. Saari, and G. P. Latham, "Goal Setting and Task Performance: 1969–1980," *Psychological Bulletin* 90 (1981): 125–152.
25. J. C. Quick, "Dyadic Goal Setting and Role Stress," *Academy of Management Journal* 22 (1979): 241–252.
26. G. S. Odiorne, *Management by Objectives: A System of Managerial Leadership* (New York: Pitman, 1965).
27. American Management Association, *Blueprints for Service Quality: The Federal Express Approach* (New York: American Management Association, 1991).

28. G. P. Latham and G. A. Yukl, "A Review of Research on the Application of Goal Setting in Organizations," *Academy of Management Journal* 18 (1975): 824–845.
29. P. F. Drucker, *The Practice of Management* (New York: Harper & Bros., 1954).
30. R. D. Prichard, P. L. Roth, S. D. Jones, P. J. Galgay, and M. D. Watson, "Designing a Goal-Setting System to Enhance Performance: A Practical Guide," *Organizational Dynamics* 17 (1988): 69–78.
31. C. L. Hughes, *Goal Setting: Key to Individual and Organizational Effectiveness* (New York: American Management Association, 1965).
32. M. E. Tubbs and S. E. Ekeberg, "The Role of Intentions in Work Motivation: Implications for Goal-Setting Theory and Research," *Academy of Management Review* 16 (1991): 180–199.
33. J. M. Ivancevich, J. T. McMahon, J. W. Streidl, and A. D. Szilagyi, "Goal Setting: The Tenneco Approach to Personnel Development and Management Effectiveness," *Organizational Dynamics* 7 (1978): 58–80.
34. J. R. Hollenbeck and A. P. Brief, "The Effects of Individual Differences and Goal Origin on Goal Setting and Performance," *Organizational Behavior and Human Decision Processes* 40 (1987): 392–414.
35. Locke and Latham, *A Theory of Goal Setting and Task Performance.*
36. R. A. Katzell and D. E. Thompson, "Work Motivation: Theory and Practice," *American Psychologist* 45 (1990): 144–153; and M. W. McPherson, "Is Psychology the Science of Behavior? " *American Psychologist* 47 (1992): 329–335.
37. E. A. Locke, "The Ideas of Frederick W. Taylor: An Evaluation," *Academy of Management Review* 7 (1982): 15–16.
38. R. M Yerkes and J. D. Dodson, "The Relation of Strength of Stimulus to Rapidity of Habit-Formation," *Journal of Comparative Neurology and Psychology* 18 (1908): 459–482.
39. D. A. Gioia and C. O. Longenecker, "Delving into the Dark Side: The Politics of Executive Appraisal," *Organizational Dynamics* 22 (1994): 47–58.
40. H. H. Meyer, E. Kay, and J. R. P. French, "Split Roles in Performance Appraisal," *Harvard Business Review* 43 (1965): 123–129.
41. W. A. Fisher, J. C. Quick, L. L. Schkade, and G. W. Ayers, "Developing Administrative Personnel through the Assessment Center Technique," *Personnel Administrator* 25 (1980): 44–46, 62.
42. *Guidelines for Employee Coaching and Counselling* (Houston, Tex.: Tenneco, 1982).
43. M. B. DeGregorio and C. D. Fisher, "Providing Performance Feedback: Reactions to Alternative Methods," *Journal of Management* 14 (1988): 605–616.
44. G. C. Thornton, "The Relationship between Supervisory and Self-Appraisals of Executive Performance," *Personnel Psychology* 21 (1968): 441–455.
45. L. L. Cummings and D. P. Schwab, *Performance in Organizations* (Glenview, Ill.: Scott, Foresman, 1973).
46. L. Hirschhorn, "Leaders and Followers in a Postindustrial Age: A Psychodynamic View," *Journal of Applied Behavioral Science* 26 (1990): 529–542.
47. F. M Jablin, "Superior-Subordinate Communication: The State of the Art," *Psychological Bulletin* 86 (1979): 1201–1222.
48. H. Mintzberg, *The Nature of Managerial Work* (Englewood Cliffs, N.J.: Prentice-Hall, 1973).
49. M. Erez, "Work Motivation from a Cross-Cultural Perspective," in A. M. Bouvy, F. J. R. Van de Vijver, P. Boski, and P. G. Schmitz (eds.), *Journeys into Cross-Cultural Psychology* (Amsterdam, Netherlands: Swets & Zeitlinger, 1994), pp. 386–403.
50. George T. Milkovich and Jerry M. Newman, *Compensation*, 4th ed. (Homewood, Ill.: Irwin, 1993).
51. S. Kerr, "On the Folly of Rewarding A, While Hoping for B," *Academy of Management Journal* 18 (1975): 769–783.
52. J. M. Bardwick, *Danger in the Comfort Zone* (New York: American Management Association, 1991).
53. T. R. Mitchell and R. E. Wood, "An Empirical Test of an Attributional Model of Leaders' Responses to Poor Performance," in *Proceedings of the Academy of Management*, ed. R. C. Huseman (Starkville, Miss.: Academy of Management, 1979), p. 94.
54. M. J. Martinko and W. L. Gardner, "The Leader/Member Attributional Process," *Academy of Management Review* 12 (1987): 235–249.
55. K. N. Wexley, R. A. Alexander, J. P. Greenawalt, and M. A. Couch, "Attitudinal Congruence and Similarity as Related to Interpersonal Evaluations in Manager-Subordinate Dyads," *Academy of Management Journal* 23 (1980): 320–330.
56. H. M. Weiss, "Subordinate Imitation of Supervisor Behavior: The Role of Modeling in Organizational Socialization," *Organizational Behavior and Human Performance* 19 (1977): 89–105.
57. A. G. Athos and J. J. Gabarro, *Interpersonal Behavior: Communication and Understanding in Relationships* (Englewood Cliffs, N.J.: Prentice-Hall, 1978).
58. K. Doherty, "The Good News about Depression," *Business and Health* 3 (1989): 1–4
59. K. E. Kram, "Phases of the Mentor Relationship," *Academy of Management Journal* 26 (1983): 608–625.
60. K. E. Kram and L. A. Isabella, "Mentoring Alternatives: The Role of Peer Relationships in Career Development," *Academy of Management Journal* 28 (1985): 110–132.
61. J. C. Quick and D. A. Gray, "Chaparral Steel Company: Bringing 'World Class Manufacturing' to Steel," *National Productivity Review* 9 (1989–1990): 51–58.
62. Dennis Beach, personal communication, 1 February 1996.

CHAPTER

7

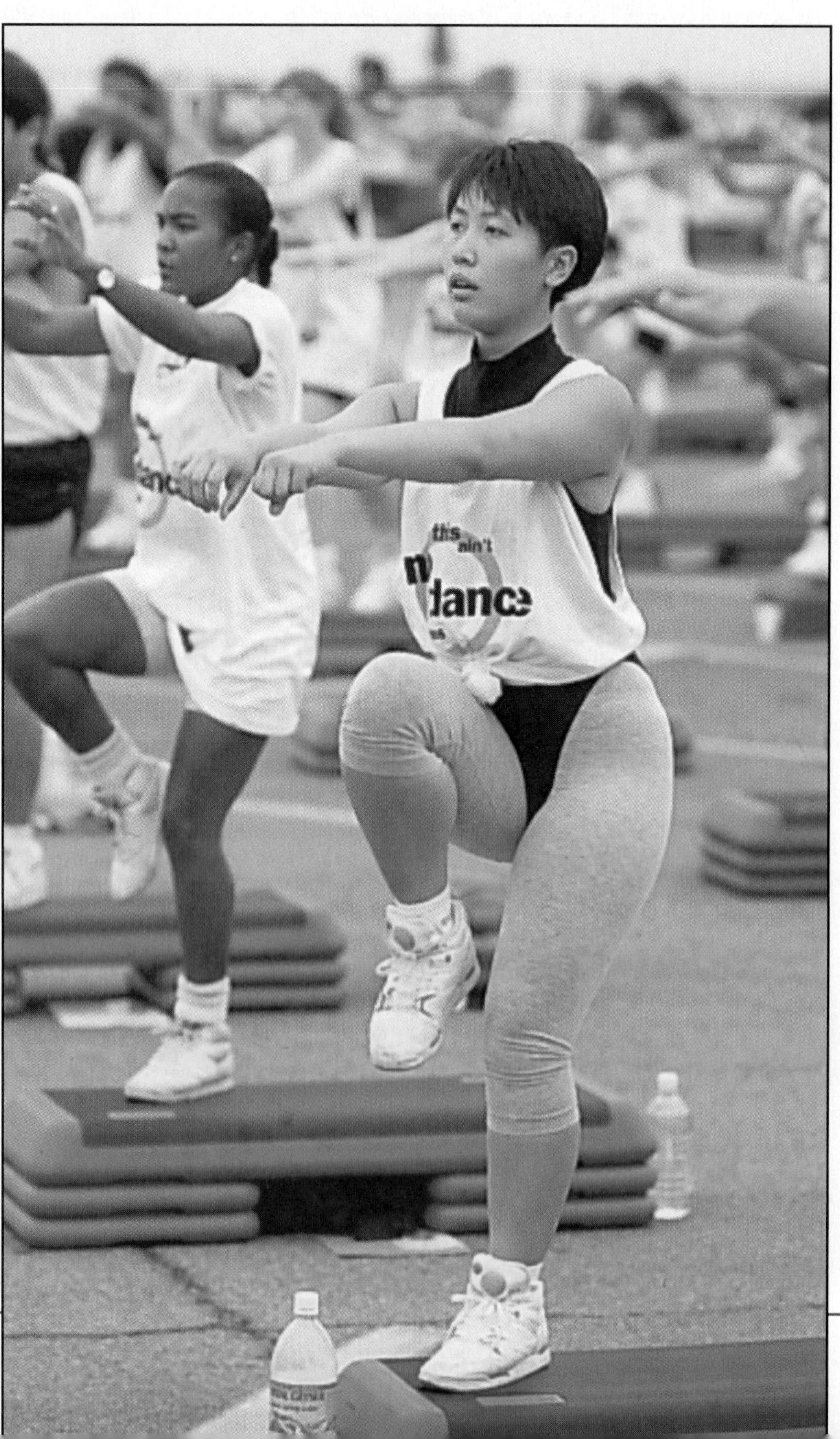

Stress and Well-Being at Work

After reading this chapter, you should be able to do the following:

- Define *stress, distress, strain,* and *eustress.*
- Compare four different approaches to stress.
- Explain the psychophysiology of the stress response.
- Identify work and nonwork causes of stress.
- Describe the benefits of eustress and the costs of distress.
- Discuss four moderators of the stress-strain relationship.
- Distinguish the primary, secondary, and tertiary stages of preventive stress management.
- Discuss organizational and individual methods of preventive stress management.

OPENING SPOTLIGHT

Stress and Challenge in the Financial Markets

http://www.citicorp.com

Citibank recognized that its Third World loans might spell trouble and set aside a $3 billion reserve fund in 1987 to address the potential problem.[1] Although future earnings for Citibank appeared secure, the bank did experience a $1.2 billion loss in 1987. Citibank was not alone in dealing with the challenge of risky Third World loans and, as a global banking and financial leader, its action led the way for other banking and financial institutions to follow suit. The year 1987 was difficult, but it was not a crisis; however, things were to get more stressful for those at Citibank. In fact, the early 1990s may have been Citibank's most challenging years since its founding.

The faltering economy in the early 1990s and unprofitable business loans, particularly in the commercial real estate market, led to a serious financial threat to Citibank and Citicorp's well-being. The immediate response was to engage in cost-cutting for all noncore business operations. These actions were not enough and in 1991, Citibank reported an $885 million loss during its third quarter of operations. At that time, for the first time since 1813, shareholders did not receive their quarterly dividend of 25¢ per share. All businesses go through ups and downs; this was clearly a downer.

The loss capped one of the most stressful and challenging periods in Citibank's long history. Chairman John Reed described the period as "tough, demanding"; it was time for a turnaround. How would Reed and Citibank respond to the challenge? ■

Points to Emphasize
Work-related stress is not just a North American phenomena. Workaholism among Japanese white-collar workers is common. In fact, the Japanese language has a term, karoshi, which means "death from overwork."

Over the past decade, stress has become a significant topic in organizational behavior. This chapter has five major sections, each addressing one aspect of stress. The first section examines the question, What is stress? The discussion includes four approaches to the stress response. The second section reviews the demands and stressors that trigger the stress response at work. The third section examines the performance and health benefits of stress and the individual and organizational forms of distress. The fourth section considers individual difference factors, such as gender and personality hardiness, moderating the stress-distress relationship. The fifth section presents a framework for preventive stress management and reviews a wide range of individual and organizational stress management methods.

What Is Stress?

Discussion Consideration
Are there some jobs or industries that appear to provide more or less distress than others?

stress
The unconscious preparation to fight or flee that a person experiences when faced with any demand.

stressor
The person or event that triggers the stress response.

distress
The adverse psychological, physical, behavioral, and organizational consequences that may arise as a result of stressful events.

strain
Distress.

■ *Stress* is one of the most creatively ambiguous words in the English language, with as many interpretations as there are people who use the word. Even the stress experts do not agree on its definition. Stress carries a negative connotation for some people, as though it were something to be avoided. This is unfortunate, because stress is a great asset in managing legitimate emergencies and achieving peak performance. **Stress,** or the stress response, is the unconscious preparation to fight or flee a person experiences when faced with any demand.[2] A **stressor,** or demand, is the person or event that triggers the stress response. **Distress** or **strain** refers to the adverse psychological, physical, behavioral, and organizational consequences that *may* occur as a result of stressful events. Challenge 7.1 gives you an opportunity to examine how overstressed and angry you may be.

Four Approaches to Stress

The stress response was discovered by Walter B. Cannon early in this century.[3] Later researchers defined stress differently than Cannon. We will review four different approaches to defining stress: the homeostatic/medical, cognitive appraisal, person-environment fit, and psychoanalytic approaches. These four approaches to stress will give you a more complete understanding of what stress really is.

THE HOMEOSTATIC/MEDICAL APPROACH Walter B. Cannon was the medical physiologist who originally discovered stress and called it "the emergency response" or "the militaristic response," arguing that it was rooted in "the fighting emotions." His early writings provide the basis for calling the stress response the *fight-or-flight* response. According to Cannon, stress resulted when

CHALLENGE

■ **7.1**

The Frazzle Factor

Read each of the following statements and rate yourself on a scale of 0 to 3, giving the answer that best describes how you generally feel (3 points for *always*, 2 points for *often*, 1 point for *sometimes*, and 0 points for *never*). Answer as honestly as you can, and do not spend too much time on any one statement.

Am I Overstressed?

____ **1.** I have to make important snap judgements and decisions.
____ **2.** I am not consulted about what happens on my job or in my classes.
____ **3.** I feel I am underpaid.
____ **4.** I feel that no matter how hard I work, the system will mess it up.
____ **5.** I do not get along with some of my coworkers or fellow students.
____ **6.** I do not trust my superiors at work or my professors at school.
____ **7.** The paperwork burden on my job or at school is getting to me.
____ **8.** I feel people outside the job or the university do not respect what I do.

Am I Angry?

____ **1.** I feel that people around me make too many irritating mistakes.
____ **2.** I feel annoyed because I do good work or perform well in school, but no one appreciates it.
____ **3.** When people make me angry, I tell them off.
____ **4.** When I am angry, I say things I know will hurt people.
____ **5.** I lose my temper easily.
____ **6.** I feel like striking out at someone who angers me.
____ **7.** When a coworker or fellow student makes a mistake, I tell him or her about it.
____ **8.** I cannot stand being criticized in public.

SCORING

To find your level of anger and potential for aggressive behavior, add your scores from both quiz parts.

40–48: The red flag is waving, and you had better pay attention. You are in the danger zone. You need guidance from a counselor or mental health professional, and you should be getting it now.

30–39: The yellow flag is up. Your stress and anger levels are too high, and you are feeling increasingly hostile. You are still in control, but it would not take much to trigger a violet flare of temper.

10–29: Relax, you are in the broad normal range. Like most people, you get angry occasionally, but usually with some justification. Sometimes you take overt action, but you are not likely to be unreasonably or excessively aggressive.

0–9: Congratulations! You are in great shape. Your stress and anger are well under control, giving you a laid-back personality not prone to violence.

SOURCE: Questionnaire developed by C. D. Spielberger. Appeared in W. Barnhill, "Early Warning." *The Washington Post*, August 11, 1992, B5.

an external, environmental demand upset the person's natural steady-state balance.[4] He referred to this steady-state balance, or equilibrium, as **homeostasis.** Cannon believed the body was designed with natural defense mechanisms to keep it in homeostasis. He was especially interested in the role of the sympathetic nervous system in activating a person under stressful conditions.[5]

homeostasis

A steady state of bodily functioning and equilibrium.

THE COGNITIVE APPRAISAL APPROACH Richard Lazarus was more concerned with the psychology of stress. He deemphasized the medical and physiological aspects, emphasizing instead the psychological-cognitive aspects of the response.[6] Like Cannon, Lazarus saw stress as a result of a person-environment interaction, and he emphasized the person's cognitive appraisal in classifying persons or events as stressful or not. Individuals differ in their appraisal of events and people. What is stressful for one person may not be stressful for another. Perception and cognitive appraisal are important processes in determining what is stressful, and a person's organizational position can shape such perception. For example, an employee would more likely be stressed by an upset supervisor than another supervisor would be. Lazarus also introduced problem-focused and emotion-focused coping. Problem-focused coping emphasizes managing the stressor, and emotion-focused coping emphasizes managing your response.

THE PERSON-ENVIRONMENT FIT APPROACH Robert Kahn was concerned with the social psychology of stress. His approach emphasized how confusing and conflicting expectations of a person in a social role create stress for the person.[7] He extended the approach to examine a person's fit in the environment. A good person-environment fit occurs when a person's skills and abilities match a clearly defined, consistent set of role expectations. This results in a lack of stress for the person. Stress occurs when the role expectations are confusing and/or conflicting, or when a person's skills and abilities are not able to meet the demands of the social role. After a period of this stress, the person can expect to experience strain, such as strain in the form of depression.

THE PSYCHOANALYTIC APPROACH Harry Levinson defined stress based on Freudian psychoanalytic theory.[8] Levinson believes that two elements of the personality interact to cause stress. The first element is the **ego-ideal,** the embodiment of a person's perfect self. The second element is the **self-image**—how the person really sees himself or herself, both positively and negatively. Although not sharply defined, the ego-ideal encompasses admirable attributes of parental personalities, wished-for and/or imaginable qualities a person would like to possess, and the absence of any negative or distasteful qualities. Stress results from the discrepancy between the idealized self (ego-ideal) and the real self-image; the greater the discrepancy, the more stress a person experiences. More generally, psychoanalytic theory helps us understand the role of unconscious personality factors as causes of stress within a person.

ego-ideal

The embodiment of a person's perfect self.

self-image

How a person sees himself or herself, both positively and negatively.

The Stress Response

Whether activated by an ego-ideal/self-image discrepancy, a poorly defined social role, cognitive appraisal suggesting threat, or a lack of homeostatic balance, the resulting stress response is characterized by a predictable sequence of mind and body events. First, catecholamines, primarily adrenaline and noradrenaline, are released into the bloodstream. Second, these chemical messengers activate the sympathetic nervous system and the endocrine (hormone) system. Third, these two systems work together to create four mind-body changes to prepare one for fight-or-flight:

1. The redirection of the blood to the brain and large-muscle groups and away from the skin, vegetative organs, and extremities.
2. Increased alertness by way of improved vision, hearing, and other sensory processes through the activation of the reticular activating system, a formation in the brainstem (ancient brain) activated under stress.
3. The release of glucose (blood sugar) and fatty acids into the bloodstream to sustain the body during the stressful event.
4. Depression of the immune system, as well as restorative and emergent processes (such as digestion).

This set of four changes shifts the person from a neutral, or naturally defensive, posture to an offensive posture. The stress response can be very functional in

People who cannot get their blood pressure up under the right conditions can be in as much trouble as people who cannot get their blood pressure down. The stress response can be a highly functional, motivational response under the righ conditions, such as when engaged in world class weightlifting.

preparing a person to deal with legitimate emergencies and to achieve peak performance. It is neither inherently bad nor necessarily destructive.

Discussion Consideration
Ask students if they believe there is more stress in the work force today than there was 20 years ago. Why or why not?

Sources of Stress at Work

■ The four approaches to defining stress emphasize demands, or sources of stress, for people at work. We can organize these demands into the general categories of task demands, role demands, interpersonal demands, and physical demands. In addition, the organization needs to be sensitive to nonwork stressors, such as demands from the person's family or nonwork activities. For example, child care considerations are an increasing concern for organizations as more women have gone to work and more men are the primary caregivers. Finally, global factors, such as general economic conditions within a society and the international economy, create widespread stress for individuals. Table 7.1 summarizes the specific demands that we discuss.

Task Demands

Change and lack of control are two of the most stressful demands people face at work.[9] Change leads to uncertainty, a lack of predictability in a person's daily tasks and activities, and may be caused by job insecurity related to difficult economic times. During the 1980s, U.S. Steel had to lay off tens of thousands of workers because of the economic difficulties in the industry resulting from intense international competition. Corporate warfare led to extensive merger, acquisition, and downsizing during the 1980s; this resulted in significant uncertainty for thousands of employees. Technology and technological innovation also create change and uncertainty for many employees, requiring adjustments in training, education, and skill development.

Points to Emphasize
Laid-off employees have referred to the day after being laid off as the day they regained control of their lives. Sometimes the dread of being selected in a layoff is worse than actually being laid off. Some individuals have used their being laid off as the impetus to change careers and do what they always wanted to do.

Lack of control is a second major source of stress, especially in work environments that are difficult and psychologically demanding. The lack of control may be caused by inability to influence the timing of tasks and activities, to select tools or methods for accomplishing the work, to make decisions that influence work outcomes, or to exercise direct action to affect the work outcomes. One study found heart attacks for male workers to be more common in occupations with low job autonomy (lack of control) and high job demands (heavy work loads).[10]

■ **TABLE 7.1**

Work and Nonwork Demands

WORK DEMANDS	
Task Demands	*Role Demands*
Change Lack of control Career progress New technologies Work overload	Role conflict: ■ Interrole ■ Intrarole ■ Person-role Role ambiguity
Interpersonal Demands	*Physical Demands*
Abrasive personalities Sexual harassment Leadership styles	Extreme environments Strenuous activities Hazardous substances
NONWORK DEMANDS	
Family Demands	*Personal Demands*
Marital expectations Child-rearing/day care arrangements Parental care	Religious activities Self-improvement tasks Traumatic events

Concerns over career progress, new technologies, and work overload, (or work underload), are three additional task demands triggering stress for the person at work. Career stress is related to the thinning of mid-managerial ranks in organizations through mergers, acquisitions, and downsizing over the past two decades, causing career gridlock for many.[11] Thinning the organizational ranks often leaves an abundance of work for those who are still employed. Work overload is seen as the leading stressor for people at work. In some cases, the reverse, work underload, can be an equally stressful problem. New technologies also create both career stress and "technostress" for people at work who wonder if they will be replaced by "smart" machines.[12] Although they enhance the organization's productive capacity, new technologies may be viewed as the enemy by workers who must ultimately learn to use them. This creates a real dilemma for management.

Role Demands

Alternate Example
A recent term connected with workplace distress is the survivor syndrome. This is the stress experienced by persons who fear for their jobs in organizations that are downsizing. Survivors may also go through a grieving process for their coworkers who have left the organization.

The social-psychological demands of the work environment may be every bit as stressful as task demands at work. People encounter two major categories of role stress at work: role conflict and role ambiguity.[13] Role conflict results from inconsistent or incompatible expectations communicated to a person. The conflict may be an interrole, intrarole, or person-role conflict.

Interrole conflict is caused by conflicting expectations related to two separate roles, such as employee and parent. For example, the employee with a major sales presentation on Monday and a sick child at home Sunday night is likely to experience interrole conflict.

Intrarole conflict is caused by conflicting expectations related to a single role, such as employee. For example, the manager who presses employees for both very fast work *and* high-quality work may be viewed at some point as creating a conflict for employees.

Ethics violations are likely to cause person-role conflicts. Employees expected to behave in ways that violate personal values, beliefs, or principles experience conflict. The unethical acts of committed employees exemplify this problem. Organizations with high ethical standards, such as Johnson & Johnson, are less

SCIENTIFIC FOUNDATION

Threat to Reputation with One's Supervisor

The premise of this study is that job stressors that threaten an employee's reputation with his or her supervisor are likely to be the source of stress and anxiety for the employee, both at work and at home. Employees characterize threats to reputation as situations that combine the potential for personal loss, negativity, threat to self-esteem, and control by powerful others. Thirty-six raters, primarily working accountants, judged eight job stressors as high or low on threat to reputation. Job stressors rated as high on threat were lack of feedback, training inadequacy, role overload, and role ambiguity. Job stressors rated as low on threat were lack of control, lack of meaningfulness, high interdependency, and role conflict.

Independently, 102 staff accountants rated their exposure to these eight job stressors and how damaging each job stressor might be to their immediate supervisor's view of their competence and dependability (i.e., reputation). In addition, the 102 accountants completed Spielberger's state anxiety measure twice, once for their work environment and once for their home. The findings indicated that work and home anxiety were related, suggesting a work-to-home carryover of anxiety. Work and home anxiety were both significantly correlated with the high-threat job stressors, but not with the low-threat job stressors. Further, work anxiety appeared to mediate the high-threat job stressor to home anxiety relationship, with anxiety at home being highest in the presence of high-threat job stressors and high anxiety at work.

SOURCE: V. J. Doby and R. D. Caplan, "Organizational Stress as Threat to Reputation: Effects on Anxiety at Work and at Home," *Academy of Management Journal* 38 (1995): 1105–1123.

likely to create ethical conflicts for employees. Person-role conflicts and ethics violations create a sense of divided loyalty for an employee.

The second major cause of role stress is role ambiguity. Role ambiguity is the confusion a person experiences related to the expectations of others. Role ambiguity may be caused by not understanding what is expected, not knowing how to do it, or not knowing the result of failure to do it. For example, a new magazine employee asked to copyedit a manuscript for the next issue may experience confusion because of lack of familiarity with copyediting procedures and conventions for the specific magazine.

Alternate Example
The difference of time perspectives varies greatly among cultures. Recognizing and dealing with these differences is crucial to managers seeking productivity through an increasingly diverse work force. Source: D. E. Vinton, "A New Look at Time, Speed, and the Manager," Academy of Management Executive 6, no. 4, (1992):9.

A twenty-one-nation study of middle managers examined their experiences of role conflict, role ambiguity, and role overload. The results indicated that role stress varies more by country than it does by demographic and organizational factors. For example, non-Western managers experience less role ambiguity and more role overload than do their Western counterparts.[14]

Interpersonal Demands

Abrasive personalities, sexual harassment, and the leadership style in the organization are interpersonal demands for people at work.[15] The abrasive person may be an able and talented employee, but one who creates emotional waves that others at work must accommodate. Abrasive personalities stand out at work, and some organizational cultures tolerate them. Organizations are increasingly less tolerant of sexual harassment, a gender-related interpersonal demand. The vast majority of sexual harassment is directed at women in the workplace, creating a stressful working environment for the person being harassed, as well as for others. Leadership styles in organizations, whether authoritarian or participative, create stress for different personality types. Employees who feel secure with firm, directive leadership may be anxious with an open, participative style. Those comfortable with participative leadership may feel restrained by a directive style. Trust is an important characteristic of the leader-follower interpersonal relationship and threat to reputation with one's supervisor may be especially stressful, as seen in the accompanying Scientific Foundation feature.[16]

Alternate Example
Managerial style can be a major source of stress in organizations. IBM's former CEO, John Akers, lost his control in meetings that left middle managers weak with anxiety over upcoming events that he was to undertake for IBM.

Physical Demands

Extreme environments, strenuous activities, and hazardous substances create physical demands for people at work.[17] Work environments that are very hot or very cold place differing physical demands on people and create unique risks. Dehydration is one problem of extremely hot climates, whereas frostbite is one problem of extremely cold climates. The strenuous job of a steelworker and the hazards associated with bomb disposal work are physically demanding in different ways. The unique physical demands of work are often occupation specific, such as the risk of gravitationally induced loss of consciousness for pilots flying the latest generation of high-performance fighters.[18]

Office work has its physical hazards as well. Noisy, crowded offices, such as those of some stock brokerages, can prove stressful to work in. Working with a computer terminal can also be stressful, especially if the ergonomic fit between the person and machine is not correct. Eyestrain, neck stiffness, and arm and wrist problems can occur. Office designs that use partitions (cubicles) rather than full walls can create stress. These systems offer little privacy for the occupant (for example, to conduct employee counseling or performance appraisal sessions) and little protection from interruptions.

Nonwork Demands

Nonwork demands create stress for people, which may carry over into the work environment, or vice versa as we saw in the Scientific Foundation feature.[19] Not all workers are subject to family demands related to marriage, child rearing, and parental care. For those who are, these demands may create role conflicts or overloads that are difficult to manage. For example, the loss of good day care for children may be especially stressful for dual-career families.[20] The accompanying Organizational Reality feature discusses one man's struggle with the tension between his work and his family. As a result of the maturing of the American population, an increasing number of people face the added demand of parental care. Even when one works to achieve an integrative social identity, integrating one's many social roles into a "whole" identity for a more stress-free balance in work and nonwork identities, the process of integration is not an easy one.[21]

In addition to family demands, people have personal demands related to nonwork organizational commitments, such as in churches, synagogues, and public service organizations. These demands become more or less stressful depending on their compatibility with the person's work and family life and their capacity to provide alternative satisfactions for the person. Finally, traumatic events and their aftermath are stressful for people who experience them.[22] Traumatic events need not be catastrophic in nature, although catastrophic events related to war or death of a loved one are traumatic. Job loss, examination failures, and termination of romantic attachments are all traumatic and may lead to distress if not addressed and resolved.[23]

The Consequences of Stress

http://www.bellsouth.com/

■ Contrary to one report, Americans are not failing the stress test, and not all the consequences of stress are bad or destructive.[24] Interestingly, Bell South won the Best of Show television sweepstakes at the 34th International Broadcasting Awards with their commercial entitled "Stress Test." The consequences of healthy, normal stress (called **eustress,** for "euphoria + stress") include a number of performance and health benefits to be added to the more commonly known costs of individual and organizational distress.[25] The benefits of eustress and the costs of distress are listed in Table 7.2. An organization striving for high-

eustress
Healthy, normal stress.

ORGANIZATIONAL REALITY

Tension between Work and Family

Jim Clark was the primary founder of Silicon Graphics in 1982. Rocky Rhodes, a co-founder and chief engineer, found at the age of 41 that he had lots of options. One of these options in 1994 was to help Jim Clark with another start-up: Netscape Communications. Rocky Rhodes passed on that opportunity. Why?

Rhode's life began changing in 1987 when his first of three children, Dustin, was born. While his wife Diane quit her job as a product manager at Apple Computer, Rocky's life became a constant struggle between his work life, which had been nearly all-consuming until then, and his blossoming family life. In the midst of this struggle, in the late 1980s, the Rhodes wrote out the four priorities they agreed were most important in their lives. These were God, family, exercise, and work . . . in that order.

Rocky then examined how he actually spent his time and found that he did not devote time in accordance with his priorities; work seemed to come first. His life was sort of upside down. So he really did turn his life upside down, to live in accord with the priorities he and his wife agreed upon. He is a work-in-progress, attempting to adjust his work life around God, family, and exercise. Working at home during 1992, after the birth of his third child, was not too successful. Going to a part-time work schedule at Silicon Graphics in 1995 helped him achieve a better integration of his work and family life domains. However, there may be no final solution to the tension between work and family.

SOURCE: S. Shellenbarger, "Work & Family," *Wall Street Journal*, January 31, 1996, B1. Reprinted with permission of The Wall Street Journal,

TABLE 7.2

Benefits of Eustress and Costs of Distress

BENEFITS OF EUSTRESS	
Performance	*Health*
Increased arousal Bursts of physical strength	Cardiovascular efficiency Enhanced focus in an emergency
COSTS OF DISTRESS	
Individual	*Organizational*
Psychological disorders Medical illnesses Behavioral problems	Participation problems Performance decrements Compensation awards

quality products and services needs a healthy work force to support the effort. Eustress is one characteristic of healthy people; distress is not.

Performance and Health Benefits of Stress

The Yerkes-Dodson law, shown in Figure 7.1, indicates that stress leads to improved performance up to an optimum point.[26] Beyond the optimum point, further stress and arousal have a detrimental effect on performance. Therefore, healthy amounts of eustress are desirable to improve performance by arousing a person to action. It is in the midrange of the curve that the greatest performance benefits from stress are achieved. Joseph McGrath has suggested that performance declines beyond the midpoint in the Yerkes-Dodson curve because of the increasing difficulty of the task to be performed.[27] The stress response

■ **FIGURE 7.1**
Yerkes-Dodson Law

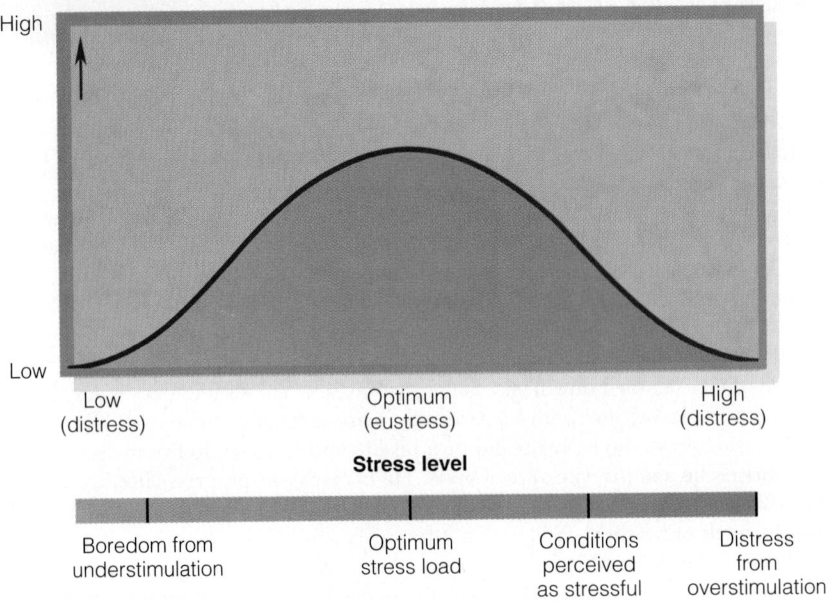

Discussion Consideration
Ask students to identify "eustress" experiences they may have had.

does provide momentary strength and physical force for brief periods of exertion, thus providing a basis for peak performance in athletic competition or other events.

Specific stressful activities, including aerobic exercise, weight training, and flexibility training, improve health and enhance a person's ability to manage stressful demands or situations. Cannon argued that the stress response better prepares soldiers for combat.[28] In survival or combat situations, stress provides one with the necessary energy boost to manage the situation successfully.

The stress response is not inherently bad or destructive. The various individual and organizational forms of distress often associated with the word *stress* are the result of prolonged activation of the stress response, mismanagement of the energy induced by the response, or unique vulnerabilities in a person. We next examine the forms of individual distress first and the forms of organizational distress second.

Individual Distress

Points to Emphasize
The word burnout is probably overused, particularly in regard to individuals who are simply malingering to rationalize failure or boredom.

An extreme preoccupation with work may result in acute individual distress, such as the unique Japanese phenomenon of *karoshi*, or death by overwork.[29] In general, individual distress usually takes one of the three basic forms shown in Table 7.2. Work-related psychological disorders are among the ten leading health disorders and diseases in the United States, according to the National Institute for Occupational Safety and Health.[30] The most common types of psychological distress are depression, burnout, and psychogenic disorders. In the early stages, depression and burnout result in a decline in efficiency; diminished interest in work; fatigue; and an exhausted, run-down feeling. Psychogenic disorders are physical disorders with a genesis, or beginning, in the psyche, or mind. For example, the intense stress of public speaking may result in a psychogenic speech disorder; that is, the person is under so much stress that the mind literally will not allow speech to occur.

A number of medical illnesses have a stress-related component.[31] The most significant medical illnesses of this form are heart disease and strokes, backaches, peptic ulcers, and headaches. Ford Motor Company found that cardiovascular diseases, the leading cause of death in the United States since 1910, constituted only

1.5 percent of the medical incidents among 800 salaried employees at its headquarters but accounted for 29 percent of the reported medical costs.[32] On the positive side, premature death and disability rates have dropped 24 to 36 percent since the mid-1970s. Backaches are a nonfatal medical problem to which stress contributes through the strong muscular contractions related to preparation for fight or flight. Headaches may be related to eyestrain or have a migraine component, but tension headaches are caused by the contraction of the head and neck muscles under stressful conditions. Finally, stress is a contributing factor to peptic ulcers. A popular comedian commented, "I don't get angry; I just grow a tumor!" There is no clear evidence that stress is a direct causal agent in the onset of cancer. However, stress may play an indirect role in the progression of the disease.[33]

Discussion Consideration
Should alcohol and drug abuse problems be handled by courts or through medical and psychological counseling? How much responsibility, or initiative, should an employer take to provide assistance for employees with drug or alcohol related problems?

Behavioral problems are the third form of individual distress. These problems include violence, substance abuse of various kinds, and accidents. Violence need not necessarily be physical to be destructive. Interpersonal conflicts can be a form of nonphysical violence. One study found that conflicts with workmates, neighbors, and other "nonintimates" account for about 80 percent of our bad moods.[34] Ethnic and cultural differences are too often a basis for interpersonal conflicts and may escalate into physical violence in the workplace. For example, some U.S. employees of Arab descent experienced ethnic slurs at work during the Gulf War with Iraq, a largely Arab nation.

It is reported that Her Majesty's Health Service has determined that smoking may cost you more than money. C. Everett Koop came to the same conclusion as U.S. Surgeon General and started a war on smoking. The American Heart Association has determined that "No Smoking" is good for your heart and your health.

Substance abuse ranges from legal behaviors such as alcohol abuse, excessive smoking, and the overuse of prescription drugs to illegal behaviors such as heroin addiction. Former surgeon general C. Everett Koop's war on smoking, begun in the late 1980s, may be warranted from the health-risk standpoint, but it raises an ethical debate about the restriction of individual behavior. How far can the government or society go in restricting individual behavior that has adverse health consequences for many? This is even more problematic in light of recent research results showing the adverse health effects of passive smoking (that is, nonsmokers breathing smoky air).

Accidents, both on and off the job, are another behavioral form of distress that can sometimes be traced to work-related stressors. For example, an unresolved problem at work may continue to preoccupy or distract an employee driving home and result in the employee having an automobile accident.

These three forms of individual distress—psychological disorders, medical illnesses, and behavioral problems—cause a burden of personal suffering. They also cause a collective burden of suffering reflected in organizational distress.

Organizational Distress

The University of Michigan studies on organizational stress identified a variety of indirect costs of mismanaged stress for the organization, such as low morale, dissatisfaction, breakdowns in communication, and disruption of working relationships. Subsequent research at the Survey Research Center at Michigan established behavioral costing guidelines, which specify the direct costs of organizational distress.[35]

Participation problems are the costs associated with absenteeism, tardiness, strikes and work stoppages, and turnover. In the case of absenteeism, the organization may compensate for this participation problem by hiring temporary personnel who take the place of the absentee, thus elevating personnel costs. When considering turnover, a distinction should be made between dysfunctional and

participation problem
A cost associated with absenteeism, tardiness, strikes and work stoppages, and turnover.

functional turnover. Dysfunctional turnover occurs when an organization loses a valuable employee. It is costly for the organization. Replacement costs, including recruiting and retraining, for the valued employee are anywhere from five to seven months of the person's monthly salary. Functional turnover, in contrast, benefits the organization by creating opportunities for new members, new ideas, and fresh approaches. Functional turnover is when an organization loses an employee who has little or no value, or is a problem. Functional turnover is good for the organization. The "up or out" promotion policy for members of some organizations is designed to create functional turnover.

performance decrement
A cost resulting from poor quality or low quantity of production, grievances, and unscheduled machine downtime and repair.

Performance decrements are the costs resulting from poor quality or low quantity of production, grievances, and unscheduled machine downtime and repair. As in the case of medical illnesses, stress is not the only causal agent in these performance decrements. Stress does play a role, however, whether the poor quality or low quantity of production is motivated by distressed employees or by an unconscious response to stress on the job. In California, some employees have the option of taking a "stress leave" rather than filing a grievance against the boss.

compensation award
An organizational cost resulting from court awards for job distress.

Compensation awards are a third organizational cost resulting from court awards for job distress.[36] Given the case law framework for most of the nation's legal system, it takes a history of judgments to determine how far the courts will go in honoring stress-related claims. One former insurance employee in Louisiana filed a federal suit against the company alleging it created a high-strain job for him that resulted in an incapacitating depression.[37] A jury awarded him a $1.5 million judgment that was later overturned by the judge. Stress may have dramatic effects in and on an organization.

Individual Differences in the Stress-Strain Relationship

■ The same stressful events may lead to distress and strain for one person and to excitement and healthy results for another. Individual differences play a central role in the stress-strain relationship. The weak organ hypothesis in medicine, also known as the Achilles' heel phenomenon, suggests that a person breaks down at his or her weakest point. Some individual differences, such as gender and Type A behavior pattern, enhance vulnerability to strain under stressful conditions. Other individual differences, such as personality hardiness and self-reliance, reduce vulnerability to strain under stressful conditions.

Gender Effects

According to Estelle Ramey, women are designed for long, miserable lives, whereas men are designed for short, violent ones.[38] The truth of this is that the life expectancy for American women is approximately seven years greater than for American men. Ramey attributes part of the increased life span to hormonal differences between the sexes.

Alternate Example
As we live longer, we are more likely to extend our working lives. The old concept of "up or out"—meaning a worker must progress up the corporate ladder or leave the company—may need to be altered to accommodate lateral movement and reduced-pressure employment for valuable, experienced employees.

Some literature suggests that there are differences in the stressors to which the two sexes are subject.[39] For example, sexual harassment is a gender-related source of stress for many working women. There is also substantive evidence that the important differences in the sexes are in vulnerabilities.[40] For example, males are more vulnerable at an earlier age to fatal health problems, such as cardiovascular disorders, whereas women report more nonfatal, but long-term and disabling, health problems. Although we can conclude that gender indeed creates a differential vulnerability between the two sexes, it may actually be more important to examine the difference *among* women, or *among* men.[41]

■ **TABLE 7.3**

Type A Behavior Pattern Components

1. Sense of time urgency (a kind of "hurry sickness").
2. The quest for numbers (success is measured by the number of achievements).
3. Status insecurity (feeling unsure of oneself deep down inside).
4. Aggression and hostility expressed in response to frustration and conflict.

Type A Behavior Pattern

Type A behavior pattern is also labeled *coronary-prone behavior*.[42] **Type A behavior pattern** is a complex of personality and behavioral characteristics, including competitiveness, time urgency, social status insecurity, aggression, hostility, and a quest for achievements. Table 7.3 lists four primary components of the Type A behavior pattern.

Type A behavior pattern

A complex of personality and behavioral characteristics, including competitiveness, time urgency, social status insecurity, aggression, hostility, and a quest for achievements.

There are two primary hypotheses concerning the lethal part of the Type A behavior pattern. One hypothesis suggests that the problem is time urgency, whereas the other hypothesis suggests that it is the hostility and aggression. The weight of evidence suggests that hostility and aggression, not time urgency, are the lethal agents.[43] Look back at your result in Challenge 7.1. Are you too angry and overstressed?

The alternative to the Type A behavior pattern is the Type B behavior pattern. People with Type B personalities are relatively free of the Type A behaviors and characteristics identified in Table 7.3. Type B people are less coronary prone, but if they do have a heart attack, they do not appear to recover as well as those with Type A personalities. Organizations can also be characterized as Type A or Type B organizations.[44] Type A individuals in Type B organizations and Type B individuals in Type A organizations experience stress related to a misfit between their personality type and the predominant type of the organization. However, preliminary evidence suggests that Type A individuals in Type A organizations are most at risk of health disorders.

Discussion Consideration

Can a Type A personality change? Should a Type A change?

Type A behavior can be modified. The first step is recognizing that an individual is prone to the Type A pattern. Another possible step in modifying Type A behavior is to spend time with Type B individuals. Type B people often recognize Type A behavior and can help Type A individuals take hassles less seriously and see the humor in situations. Type A individuals can also pace themselves, manage their time well, and try not to do multiple things at once. Focusing only on the task at hand and its completion, rather than worrying about other tasks, can help Type A individuals cope more effectively.

Alternate Example

Greater self-complexity may act as a buffer against stressful events. If an individual has only one or two major identities, any single event is gong to have an impact on most aspects of the self-concept. Source: P. Linville, "Self-Complexity as a Cognitive Buffer Against Stress-related Illness and Depression," *Journal of Personality and Social Psychology* (1987) 52:663–676.

Personality Hardiness

People who have personality hardiness resist strain reactions when subjected to stressful events more effectively than do people who are not hardy.[45] The components of **personality hardiness** are commitment (versus alienation), control (versus powerlessness) and challenge (versus threat). Commitment is a curiosity and engagement with one's environment that leads to the experience of activities as interesting and enjoyable. Control is an ability to influence the process and outcomes of events that leads to the experience of activities as personal choices. Challenge is the viewing of change as a stimulus to personal development, which leads to the experience of activities with openness.

personality hardiness

A personality resistant to distress and characterized by challenge, commitment, and control.

The hardy personality appears to use these three components actively to engage in transformational coping when faced with stressful events.[46] **Transformational coping** is actively changing an event into something less subjectively

transformational coping

A way of managing stressful events by changing them into subjectively less stressful events.

Discussion Consideration
What role, if any, does a person's religious orientation have in managing stress?

stressful by viewing it in a broader life perspective, by altering the course and outcome of the event through action, and/or by achieving greater understanding of the process. The alternative to transformational coping is regressive coping, a much less healthy form of coping with stressful events characterized by a passive avoidance of events by decreasing interaction with the environment. Regressive coping may lead to short-term stress reduction at the cost of long-term healthy life adjustment.

Self-Reliance

self-reliance
A healthy, secure, *interdependent* pattern of behavior related to how people form and maintain supportive attachments with others.

There is increasing evidence that social relationships have an important impact on health and life expectancy.[47] **Self-reliance** is a personality attribute related to how people form and maintain supportive attachments with others. Self-reliance was originally based in attachment theory, a theory about normal human development.[48] The theory identifies three distinct patterns of attachment, and new research suggests that these patterns extend into behavioral strategies during adulthood, in professional as well as personal relationships.[49] Self-reliance results in a secure pattern of attachment and interdependent behavior. Interpersonal attachment is emotional and psychological connectedness to another person. The two insecure patterns of attachment are counterdependence and overdependence.

Self-reliance is a healthy, secure, *interdependent* pattern of behavior. It may appear paradoxical, because a person appears independent while maintaining a host of supportive attachments.[50] Self-reliant people respond to stressful, threatening situations by reaching out to others appropriately. Self-reliance is a flexible, responsive strategy of forming and maintaining multiple, diverse relationships. Self-reliant people are confident, enthusiastic, and persistent in facing challenges.

counterdependence
An unhealthy, insecure pattern of behavior that leads to separation in relationships with other people.

Counterdependence is an unhealthy, insecure pattern of behavior that leads to separation in relationships with other people. Counterdependent people draw into themselves when faced with stressful and threatening situations, attempting to exhibit strength and power. Counterdependence may be characterized as a rigid, dismissing denial of the need for other people in difficult and stressful times. Counterdependent people exhibit a fearless, aggressive, and actively powerful response to challenges.

overdependence
An unhealthy, insecure pattern of behavior that leads to preoccupied attempts to achieve security through relationships.

Discussion Consideration
Ask students to identify their own techniques for handling stressful situations.

Overdependence is also an unhealthy, insecure pattern of behavior. Overdependent people respond to stressful and threatening situations by clinging to other people in any way possible. Overdependence may be characterized as a desperate, preoccupied attempt to achieve a sense of security through relationships. Overdependent people exhibit an active, but disorganized and anxious response to challenges. Overdependence prevents a person from being able to organize and maintain healthy relationships and thus creates much distress. It is interesting to note that both counterdependence and overdependence are exhibited by some military personnel who are experiencing adjustment difficulties during the first thirty days of basic training.[51] In particular, basic military trainees who have the most difficulty have overdependence problems and find it difficult to function on their own during the rigors of training.

Challenge 7.2 gives you an opportunity to examine how self-reliant *(interdependent)*, counterdependent, and/or overdependent you are.

preventive stress management
An organizational philosophy that holds that people and organizations should take joint responsibility for promoting health and preventing distress and strain.

Preventive Stress Management

■ Stress is an inevitable feature of work and personal life. It is neither inherently bad nor destructive. Stress can be managed. The following is the central principle of **preventive stress management:** Individual and organizational distress are

CHALLENGE

■ 7.2

Are You Self-Reliant?

Each of the following questions relates to how you form relationships with people at work, home, and other areas of your life. Please read each statement carefully and rate each on a scale from 0 (Strongly Disagree) to 5 (Strongly Agree) to describe your degree of agreement or disagreement with the statement. *Please answer all 15 questions.*

___ **1.** It is difficult for me to delegate work to others.
___ **2.** Developing close relationships at work will backfire on you.
___ **3.** I avoid depending on other people because I feel crowded by close relationships.
___ **4.** I am frequently suspicious of other people's motives and intentions.
___ **5.** Asking for help makes me feel needy, and I do not like that.
___ **6.** It is difficult for me to leave home or work to go to the other.
___ **7.** People will always be there when I need them.
___ **8.** I regularly and easily spend time with other people during the workday.
___ **9.** I trust at least two other people to have my best interests at heart.
___ **10.** I have a healthy, happy home life.
___ **11.** I need to have colleagues or subordinates close in order to feel secure about my work.
___ **12.** I become very concerned when I have conflict with family members at home.
___ **13.** I get very upset and disturbed if I have conflicts in relationship(s) at work.
___ **14.** I prefer very frequent feedback from my boss to know I am performing well.
___ **15.** I always consult others when I make decisions.

Scoring:
Follow the instructions to determine your score for each subscale of the Self-Reliance Inventory. *Note: Question 6 is used twice in scoring.*

Self-Reliance/Counterdependence
Step 1: Total your responses to Questions 1–6 ____
Step 2: Total your responses to Questions 7–10 ____
Step 3: Subtract your Step 2 total from 20 (20 − ____) = ____
Step 4: Add your results in Steps 1 and 3 ____

Self-Reliance/Overdependence
Step 5: Total your responses to Questions 6 and 11–15 ____
A score lower than 16 in Step 4 or Step 5 indicates self-reliance on that particular subscale.
A score higher than 20 in Step 4 suggests possible counterdependence and a score higher than 20 in Step 5 suggests possible overdependence.

SOURCE: Adapted from J. C. Quick, D. L. Nelson, and J. D. Quick, "The Self-Reliance Inventory," in J. W. Pfeiffer (ed.), *The 1991 Annual: Developing Human Resources* (San Diego: Pfeiffer & Co., 1991), pp. 149–161.

not inevitable. Preventive stress management is an organizational philosophy about people and organizations taking joint responsibility for promoting health and preventing distress and strain. Preventive stress management is rooted in the public health notions of prevention, which were first used in preventive medicine. The three stages of prevention are primary, secondary, and tertiary prevention. A framework for understanding preventive stress management is presented in Figure 7.2, which includes the three stages of prevention in a preventive medicine context, along with these stages in an organizational context.

Points to Emphasize
Locus of control concepts introduced in previous chapters are related to handling stress. Internals are more likely to believe that they can control their outcomes, even when extraordinarily stressful situations have resulted from environmental turbulence.

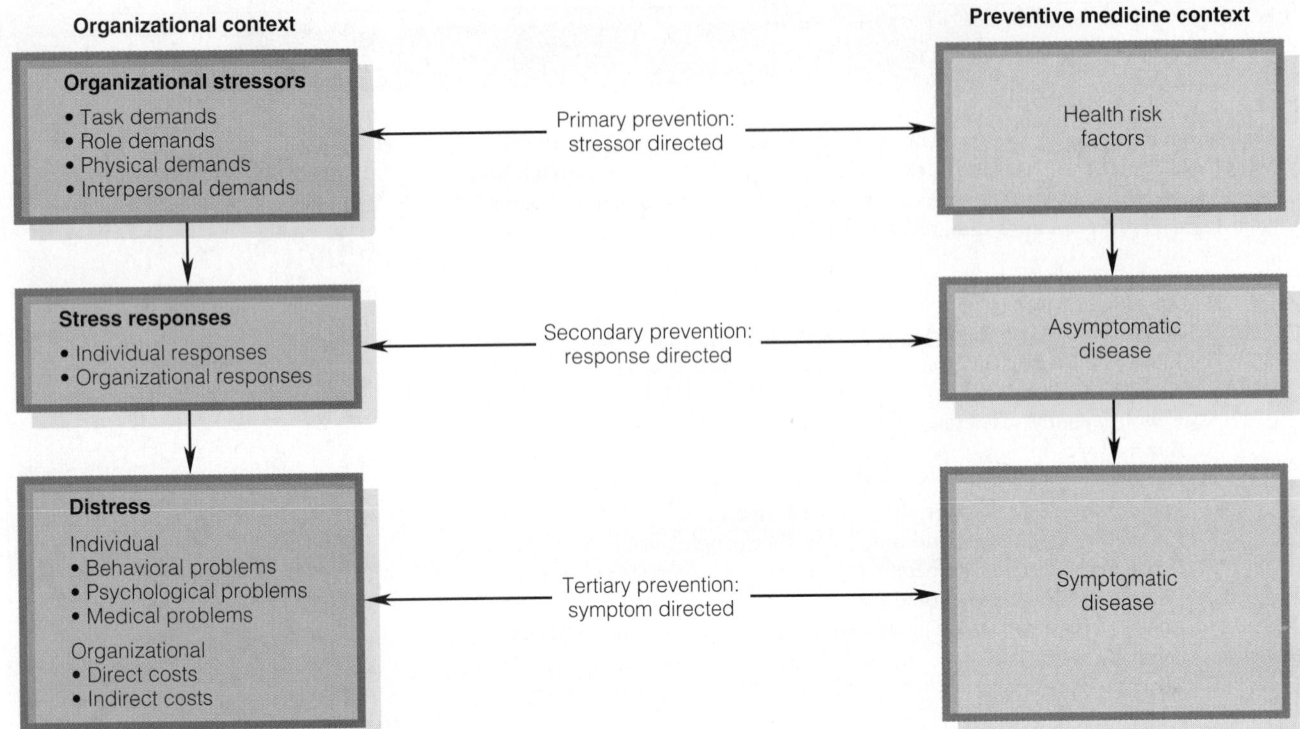

FIGURE 7.2

A Framework for Preventive Stress Management

SOURCE: J. D. Quick, R. S. Horn, and J. C. Quick, "Health Consequences of Stress," *Journal of Organizational Behavior Management* 8, no. 2, figure 1 (Fall 1986): 21. Reprinted with permission of Haworth Press, Inc., 10 Alice Street, Binghamton, NY 13904. Copyright 1986.

primary prevention

The stage in preventive stress management designed to reduce, modify, or eliminate the demand or stressor causing stress.

secondary prevention

The stage in preventive stress management designed to alter or modify the individual's or the organization's response to a demand or stressor.

tertiary prevention

The stage in preventive stress management designed to heal individual or organizational symptoms of distress and strain.

Primary prevention is intended to reduce, modify, or eliminate the demand or stressor causing stress. The idea behind primary prevention is to eliminate or ameliorate the source of a problem. True organizational stress prevention is largely primary in nature, because it changes and shapes the demands the organization places on people at work. **Secondary prevention** is intended to alter or modify the individual's or the organization's response to a demand or stressor. People must learn to manage the inevitable, inalterable work stressors and demands so as to avert distress and strain while promoting health and well-being. **Tertiary prevention** is intended to heal individual or organizational symptoms of distress and strain. The symptoms may range from early warning signs (such as headaches or absenteeism) to more severe forms of distress (such as hypertension, work stoppages, and strikes). Tertiary prevention is therapeutic, aimed at arresting distress and healing the individual, the organization, or both. We will discuss these stages of prevention in the context of organizational prevention, individual prevention, and comprehensive health promotion.

Organizational Stress Prevention

Some organizations are low-stress, healthy ones, whereas other organizations are high-stress ones that may place their employees' health at risk. Organizational stress prevention focuses on people's work demands and ways to reduce distress at work. One comprehensive approach to organizational health and preventive stress management was pioneered in the U.S. Air Force by Major Joyce Adkins, who developed an Organizational Health Center (OHC) at the Sacramento Air Logistics Center.[52] The OHC's goal is to keep people happy, healthy, and on the job, while increasing efficiency and productivity to their highest levels by focusing on workplace stressors, organizational and individual forms of distress, as well as managerial and individual strategies for preventive stress management. The comprehensive, organizational health approach of the OHC addresses primary, secondary, and tertiary prevention. However, most organizational prevention is primary prevention, including job redesign, goal setting, role negotiation, and career management. Two organizational stress prevention methods, team building and social support at work, are secondary prevention. Because team building and career management are discussed extensively in Chapters 9 and 17, respectively, we do not discuss them separately here. Finally, companies such as Kraft, General Foods, and Hardee's Food Systems have developed specific violence prevention programs to combat the rise in workplace violence. The cost of a single episode can amount to $250,000 in lost work time and legal expenses.[53]

JOB REDESIGN The job strain model presented in Figure 7.3 suggests that the combination of high job demands and restricted job decision latitude or worker control leads to a high-strain job. A major concern in job redesign should be to enhance worker control. Increasing worker control reduces distress and strain without necessarily reducing productivity.

Job redesign to increase worker control is one strategy of preventive stress management. It can be accomplished in a number of ways, the most common being to increase job decision latitude. Increased job decision latitude might include greater decision authority over the sequencing of work activities, the timing of work schedules, the selection and sequencing of work tools, or the selection of work teams. A second objective of job redesign should be to reduce uncertainty and increase predictability in the workplace. Uncertainty is a major stressor.

Discussion Consideration
Ask students to evaluate the jobs they have had in terms of the Job Strain Model. Do they agree with the work load/self-determination relationship that is hypothesized in the model?

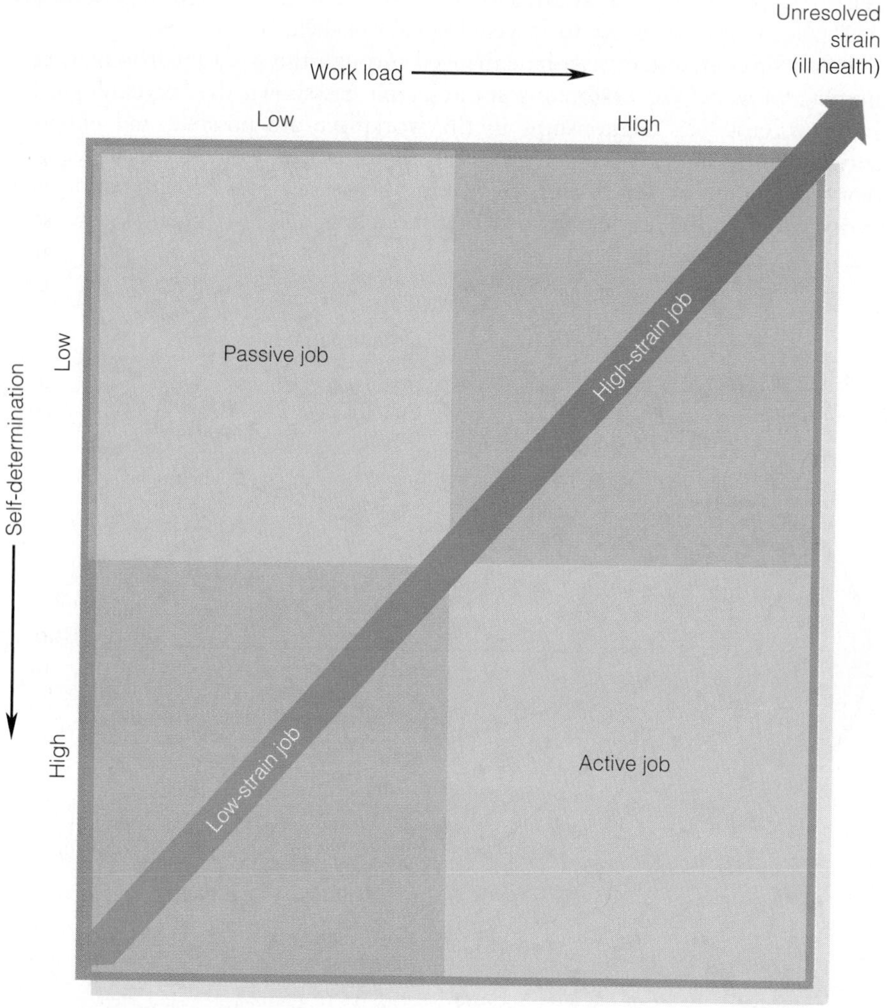

■ **FIGURE 7.3**

Job Strain Model

SOURCE: B. Gardell, "Efficiency and Health Hazards in Mechanized Work," in J. C. Quick, R. S. Bhagat, J. E. Dalton, and J. D.. Quick (eds.), *Work Stress: Health Care Systems in the Workplace* (New York: Praeger, an imprint of Greenwood Publishing Group, Inc., Westport, CT, 1987), p. 60.

GOAL SETTING Organizational preventive stress management can also be achieved through goal-setting activities. These activities are designed to increase task motivation, as discussed in Chapter 6, while reducing the degree of role conflict and ambiguity to which people at work are subject. Goal setting focuses a person's attention while directing energy in a productive channel. Implicit in much of the goal-setting literature is the assumption that people participate in, and accept, their work goals. Chapter 6 addressed goal setting in depth.

Discussion Consideration
Can being under-challenged be distressful?

ROLE NEGOTIATION The organizational development technique of role negotiation has value as a stress management method, because it allows people to modify their work roles.[54] Role negotiation begins with the definition of a specific role, called the focal role, within its organizational context. The person in the focal role then identifies the expectations understood for that role, and key organizational members specify their expectations of the person in the focal role. The actual negotiation follows from the comparison of the role incumbent's expectations and key members' expectations. The points of confusion and conflict are opportunities for clarification and resolution. The final result of the role negotiation process should be a clear, well-defined focal role with which the incumbent and organizational members are both comfortable.

SOCIAL SUPPORT SYSTEMS Team building, discussed in Chapter 9, is one way to develop supportive social relationships in the workplace. However, team building is primarily task oriented, not socioemotional, in nature. Although employees may receive much of their socioemotional support from personal relationships outside the workplace, some socioemotional support within the workplace is also necessary for psychological well-being.

Social support systems can be enhanced through the work environment in a number of ways. For example, some research has shown that psychologically intimate, cross-sex relationships in the workplace are possible and enhance social identity integration.[55] Figure 7.4 identifies key elements in a person's work and nonwork social support system. These relations provide emotional caring, information, evaluative feedback, modeling, and instrumental support.

FIGURE 7.4
Social Support at Work and Home
SOURCE: J. C. Quick and J. D. Quick, *Organizational Stress and Preventive Management* (New York: McGraw-Hill, 1984), p. 205. Reproduced with permission of McGraw-Hill, Inc.

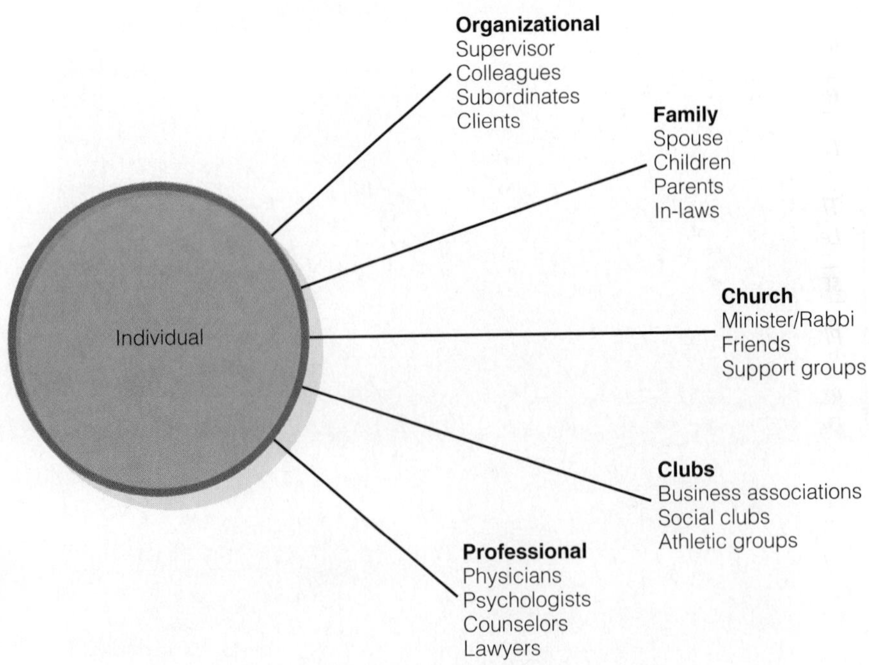

Individual Prevention

Individual prevention focuses on how the person can manage stress before it becomes a problem. Individual prevention can be of a primary, secondary, or tertiary nature. The primary prevention activities we discuss are learned optimism, time management, and leisure time activities. The secondary prevention activities we discuss are physical exercise, relaxation, and diet. The tertiary prevention activities we discuss are opening up and professional help. These eight methods and their benefits are summarized in Table 7.4. In addition, employees may have the option of taking a sabbatical, as described in the accompanying Organizational Reality feature.

LEARNED OPTIMISM Optimism and pessimism are two different thinking styles people use to explain the good and bad events in their lives to themselves.[56] These explanatory styles are habits of thinking learned over time, not inborn attributes. Pessimism is an explanatory style leading to depression, physical health problems, and low levels of achievement. Optimism is an alternative explanatory style that enhances physical health and achievement and averts susceptibility to depression.

Optimistic people avoid distress by understanding the bad events and difficult times in their lives as temporary, limited, and caused by something other than themselves. Optimistic people face difficult times and adversity with hope. Optimistic people take more credit for the good events in their lives; they see these good events as more pervasive and generalized. Learned optimism begins with identifying pessimistic thoughts and then distracting oneself from these thoughts or disputing them with evidence and alternative thoughts. Learned optimism is non-negative thinking.

TIME MANAGEMENT Work overload, the major job stressor, can lead to time pressure and overtime work. Time management skills can help employees make the most effective, efficient use of the time they spend at work. The good time manager is not necessarily the person who gets the most done. Rather, the good

TABLE 7.4

Individual Preventive Stress Management

PRIMARY PREVENTION	
Learned optimism:	Alters the person's internal self-talk and reduces depression.
Time management:	Improves planning and prioritizes activities.
Leisure time activities:	Balance work and nonwork activities.
SECONDARY PREVENTION	
Physical exercise:	Improves cardiovascular function and muscular flexibility.
Relaxation training:	Lowers all indicators of the stress response.
Diet:	Lowers the risk of cardiovascular disease and improves overall physical health.
TERTIARY PREVENTION	
Opening up:	Releases internalized traumas and emotional tensions.
Professional help:	Provides information, emotional support, and therapeutic guidance.

ORGANIZATIONAL REALITY

Sabbaticals: Leave the Stress at Work

Wells Fargo & Co. offers a *Personal Growth Leave (PGL)* sabbatical for employees in good standing for more than 10 years. Xerox Corp. launched an ambitious *Social Service Leave* sabbatical program in 1971.

The Wells Fargo sabbatical program is designed to give employees an opportunity for a combination of rest, relaxation, and personal growth. PGLs are up to three months, with full pay and benefits, in which employees may pursue personal interests. The employee must have a history of commitment to the personal interest for which they take the leave. Leaving their job stress behind for the sabbatical, Wells Fargo employees are able to invest in their own development outside the work environment.

The Xerox leave program has a different focus, designed for their more socially conscious employees. Xerox employees are allowed to take off up to one year, with full salary, while they work for an organization of their choosing. Employees must develop a project for submission to a special committee of cross-functional and cross-divisional employees for approval. Religious and political activities are excluded from consideration at Xerox.

Learning from Xerox's example, Wells Fargo developed their own *Social Service Leave* program and, for example, had a branch manager work for six months with the American Women's Economic Development Corp. The branch manager developed training program components for women and a book about obtaining loans.

SOURCE: C. J. Bachler, "Workers Take Leave of Job Stress," *Personnel Journal* (January 1995): 38–48.

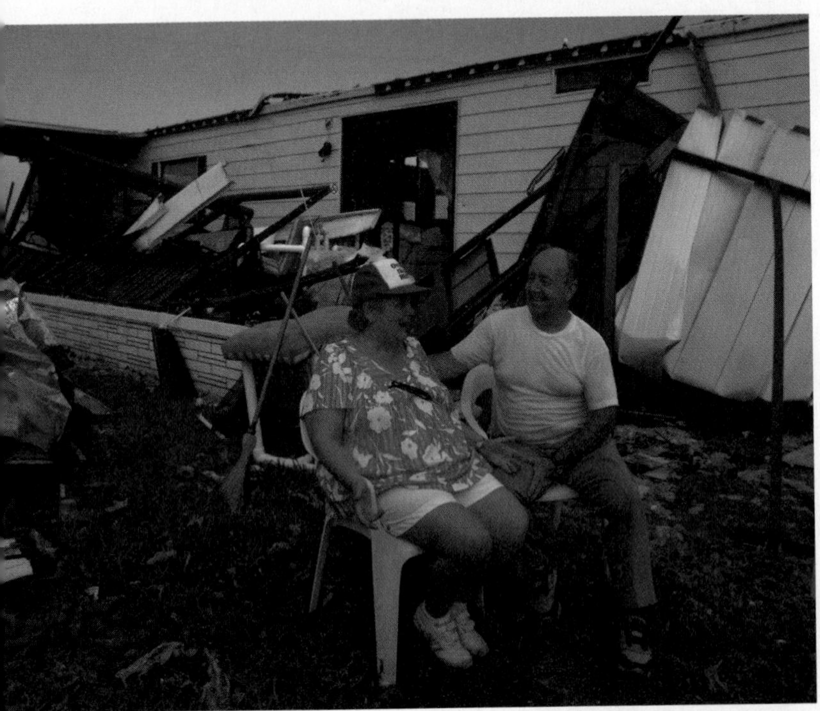

To live with optimism is to live with hope, inspite of adversity. While Hurricane Andrew wrecked their trailer, it did not destroy Helen and Roy Merrick's positive attitude toward life.

time manager is a "macro time manager" who knows the activities that contribute most to his or her long-term life development.[57] Time management enables a person to minimize the stress of work overload and to prioritize work and leisure time activities. Organizing and prioritizing may be the two most important time management skills for successful people managing very busy activity schedules.

LEISURE TIME ACTIVITIES Unremitted striving characterizes many people with a high need for achievement. Leisure time activities provide employees an opportunity for rest and recovery from strenuous activities either at home or at work. Many individuals, when asked what they do with their leisure time, say that they clean the house or mow the lawn. These activities are fine, as long as the individual gets the stress-reducing benefit of pleasure from these activities. Some say our work ethic is a cultural barrier to pleasure.[58] We work longer hours, and two-income families are the norm. Leisure is increasingly a luxury among working people. The key to the effective use of leisure time is enjoyment. Leisure time can be used for spontaneity, joy, and connection with others in our lives.

PHYSICAL EXERCISE Two different types of physical exercise are important secondary stress prevention activities for individuals. First, aerobic exercise

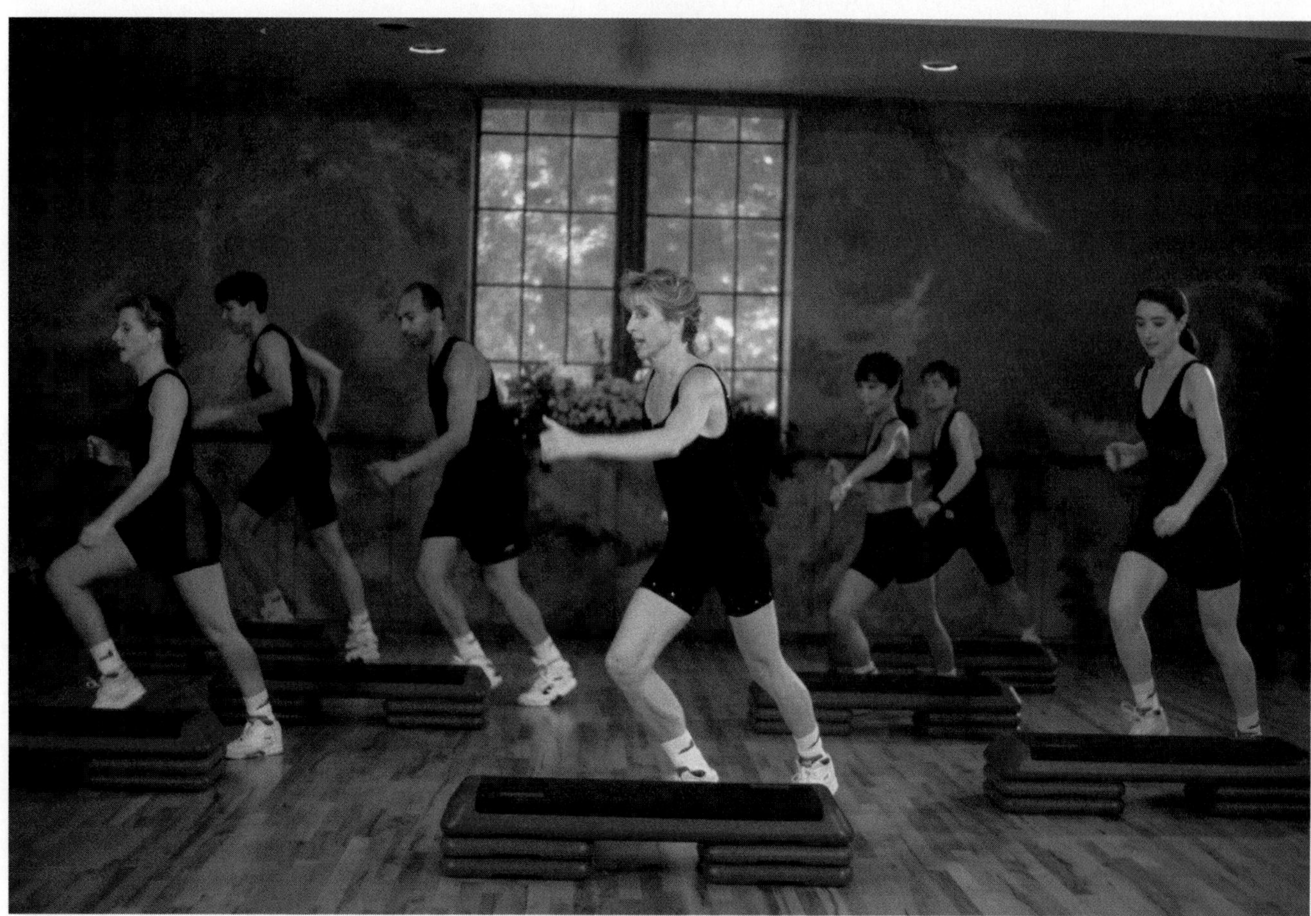

Step aerobics is one form of vigorous exercise that strengthens the cardiovascular system, fitness, and health. According to the American Heart Association, lack of exercise contributes to heart disease, the leading cause of death for American men and women.

improves a person's responsiveness to stressful activities. Kenneth Cooper has long advocated aerobic exercise.[59] Research at the Aerobics Center in Dallas has found that aerobically fit people (1) have lower levels of catecholamines in their blood at rest; (2) have a slower, more efficient cardiovascular system; (3) have a better interaction between their sympathetic and parasympathetic nervous systems; and (4) recover from stressful events more quickly.

Second, flexibility training is important because of the muscular contractions associated with the stress response. One component of the stress response is the contraction of the flexor muscles, which prepares a person to fight or flee. Flexibility training enables a person to stretch and relax these muscles to prevent the accumulation of unnecessary muscular tension.[60] Flexibility exercises help maintain joint mobility, increase strength, and play an important role in the prevention of injury.

RELAXATION TRAINING Herbert Benson was one of the first people to identify the relaxation response as the natural counterresponse to the stress response.[61] In studying Western and Eastern peoples, Benson found that the Judeo-Christian people have elicited this response through their time-honored tradition of prayer, whereas the Eastern people have elicited it through meditation. The relaxation response does not require a theological or religious component. If you have a practice of regular prayer or meditation, you may already elicit the relaxation response regularly. Keep in mind that digestion may interfere with the elicitation of the response, so avoid practicing relaxation shortly after eating.

DIET Diet may play an indirect role in stress and stress management. High sugar content in the diet can stimulate the stress response and foods high in cholesterol can adversely affect blood chemistry. Good dietary practices contribute to a person's overall health, making the person less vulnerable to distress. In his nonsurgical, nonpharmacological approach to reversing heart disease, Dean Ornish proposes a very stringent "reversal diet" for people with identifiable blockage of the arteries.[62] Ornish recommends a somewhat less stringent "prevention diet" as one of four elements for opening up the arteries. Another element in his program is being open in relationships with other people.

OPENING UP Everyone experiences a traumatic, stressful, or painful event in life at one time or another. One of the most therapeutic, curative responses to such an event is to confide in another person.[63] Discussing difficult experiences with another person is not always easy, yet health benefits, immune system improvement, and healing accrue through self-disclosure. In one study comparing those who wrote once a week about traumatic events with those who wrote about nontraumatic events, significant health benefits and reduced absenteeism were found in the first group.[64] Confession need not be through a personal relationship with friends. It may occur through a private diary. For example, a lawyer might write each evening about all of his or her most troubling thoughts, feelings, and emotions during the course of the day. The process of opening up and confessing appears to counter the detrimental effects of stress.

PROFESSIONAL HELP Confession and opening up may occur through professional helping relationships. People who need healing have psychological counseling, career counseling, physical therapy, medical treatment, surgical intervention, and other therapeutic techniques available. Employee assistance programs (EAPs) may be very helpful in referring employees to the appropriate caregivers. Even combat soldiers who experience battle stress reactions severe enough to take them out of action can heal and be ready for subsequent combat duty.[65]The early detection of distress and strain reactions, coupled with prompt professional treatment, can be instrumental in averting permanent physical and psychological damage.

Comprehensive Health Promotion

Whereas organizational stress prevention is aimed at eliminating health risks at work, comprehensive health promotion programs are aimed at establishing a "strong and resistent host" by building on individual prevention and lifestyle change.[66] Physical fitness and exercise programs characterize corporate health promotion programs in the United States and Canada.[67] A health promotion and wellness survey of the 143 accredited medical schools in the United States, Canada, and Puerto Rico found that these programs place the most emphasis on physical well-being and the least emphasis on spiritual well-being.[68] A review of the most intensively researched programs, such as Johnson & Johnson's "Live for Life," AT&T's "TLC," Control Data's "Staywell," and the Coors wellness program, shows a strong emphasis on lifestyle change.[69] Unfortunately, these programs may be among those most at risk in corporate cost-cutting and downsizing programs.

http://www.jnj.com/

Johnson & Johnson's "Live for Life" program is a comprehensive health promotion program with a significant number of educational modules for individuals and groups. Each module addresses a specific topic, such as Type A behavior, exercise, diet (through cooperative activities with the American Heart Association), and risk assessment (through regular risk assessments and health profiles for participants). Johnson & Johnson Health Management, Inc. has found that the health status of employees who are not participating in health promotion programs in the workplace improves if the worksite does have a health promotion program.

Managerial Implications: Stress Without Distress

■ Stress is an inevitable result of work and personal life. Distress is not an inevitable consequence of stressful events, however; in fact, well-managed stress can improve health and performance. Managers must learn how to create healthy stress for employees to facilitate performance and well-being without distress. Managers can help employees by adjusting work loads, avoiding ethical dilemmas, being sensitive to diversity among individuals concerning what is stressful, and being sensitive to employees' personal life demands.

New technologies create demands and stress for employees. Managers can help employees adjust to new technologies by ensuring that their design and implementation are sensitive to employees and that employee involvement is strong.

Managers can be sensitive to early signs of distress at work, such as employee fatigue or changes in work habits, in order to avoid serious forms of distress. The serious forms of distress include violent behavior, psychological depression, and cardiovascular problems. Distress is important to the organization because of the costs associated with turnover and absenteeism, as well as poor-quality production.

Managers should be aware of gender, personality, and behavioral differences when analyzing stress in the workplace. Men and women have different vulnerabilities when it comes to distress. Men, for example, are at greater risk of fatal disorders, and women are more vulnerable to nonfatal disorders, such as depression. Personality hardiness and self-reliance are helpful in managing stressful events.

Managers can use the principles and methods of preventive stress management to create healthier work environments. They can practice several forms of individual stress prevention to create healthier lifestyles for themselves, and they can encourage employees to do the same. Large organizations can create healthier workforces through the implementation of comprehensive health promotion programs. Setting an example is one of the best things a manager can do for employees when it comes to preventive stress management.

CLOSING SPOTLIGHT

John Reed's Five-Point Plan

John Reed and Citibank responded to the stress and challenge of 1990 in a positive and proactive manner.[70] The bank embraced a set of actions to deal with the changing reality in which it found itself. These actions were aimed at stabilizing the bank and then moving it forward. The short-term focus for 1991 and 1992 began by putting 1990 in the two-century history of Citicorp, followed by a dedication to run the bank to overcome its current problems.

John Reed's five-point plan was formulated in January 1991 and was an active approach to dealing with a difficult situation. The five points were:

1. Focus on 1991 and 1992.
2. Reduce the cost base.
3. Build the image as a strongly capitalized company.

4. Maintain strength in core businesses.
5. Maintain strong customer relations.

The five-point plan built on Citibank's historical and organizational strength, calling on the bank's people to focus their collective effort for survival and then success.

Although critics, during that period in Citicorp's history, were engaged in blaming, the follow-on results from the five-point plan silenced these critics with the plan's success over the next two years. Success in this very difficult situation resulted from an acceptance of changing reality, the formulation of a clear plan of action, and then the execution of that plan. ■

Chapter Summary

- Stress is the unconscious preparation to fight or flee when faced with any demand. Distress is the adverse consequence of stress.
- Four approaches to understanding stress are the homeostatic/medical approach, the cognitive appraisal approach, the person-environment fit approach, and the psychoanalytic approach.
- The stress response is a natural mind-body response characterized by four basic mind-body changes.
- Employees face task, role, interpersonal, and physical demands at work, along with nonwork (extraorganizational) demands. Global competition and advanced technologies create new stresses at work.
- Nonwork stressors, such as family problems and work-home conflicts, can affect an individual's work life and home life.
- Stress has health benefits, including enhanced performance.
- Distress is costly to both individuals and organizations.
- Individual diversity requires attention to gender, Type A behavior, personality hardiness, and self-reliance in determining the links between stress and strain.
- Preventive stress management aims to enhance health and reduce distress or strain. Primary prevention focuses on the stressor, secondary prevention focuses on the response to the stressor, and tertiary prevention focuses on symptoms of distress.

Key Terms

stress (p. 188)
stressor (p. 188)
distress (p. 188)
strain (p. 188)
homeostasis (p. 189)
ego-ideal (p. 190)
self-image (p. 190)
eustress (p. 194)
participation problem (p. 197)
performance decrement (p. 198)
compensation award (p. 198)
Type A behavior pattern (p. 199)
personality hardiness (p. 199)
transformational coping (p. 199)
self-reliance (p. 200)
counterdependence (p. 200)
overdependence (p. 200)
preventive stress management (p. 200)
primary prevention (p. 202)
secondary prevention (p. 202)
tertiary prevention (p. 202)

Review Questions

1. Define *stress*, *distress*, *strain*, and *eustress*.
2. Describe four approaches to understanding stress. How does each add something new to our understanding of stress?
3. What are the four changes associated with the stress response?
4. List three demands of each type: task, role, interpersonal, and physical.
5. What is a nonwork demand? How does it affect an individual?
6. Describe the relationship between stress and performance.
7. What are the major medical consequences of distress? The behavioral consequences? The psychological consequences?
8. Why should organizations be concerned about stress at work? What are the costs of distress to organizations?
9. How do gender, the Type A behavior pattern, personality hardiness, and self-reliance moderate the relationship between stress and strain?
10. What is primary prevention? Secondary prevention? Tertiary prevention? Describe major organizational stress prevention methods.
11. Describe eight individual preventive stress management methods.
12. What is involved in comprehensive health promotion programs?

Discussion and Communication Questions

1. Why should organizations help individuals manage stress? Is stress not basically the individual's responsibility?
2. Is there more stress today than in past generations? What evidence is available concerning this question?
3. Discuss the following statement: Employers should be expected to provide stress-free work environments.
4. If an individual claims to have job-related depression, should the company be liable?
5. Do you use any prevention methods to manage stress that are not listed in the chapter?
6. *(communication question)* Write a memo describing the most challenging demands and/or stressors at your workplace (or university). Be specific in fully describing the details of these demands and/or stressors. How might you go about changing these demands and/or stressors?
7. *(communication question)* Interview a medical doctor, a psychologist, or another health care professional about the most common forms of health problems and distress seen in their work. Summarize your interview and compare the results to the categories of distress discussed in the chapter.
8. *(communication question)* Go to the library and read about social support and diaries as ways to manage stressful and/or traumatic events. Develop an oral presentation for class that explains the benefits of each of these approaches for preventive stress management, as well as guidelines for how to practice each.

Ethics Questions

1. Suppose a company knew the health risks associated with very high stress levels in one operation and decided it was willing to pay for employee health problems rather than lower the stress levels. Is this ethical on the company's part? Should employees be informed of the risks?
2. Suppose a company prescribes certain healthy behaviors for all employees, such as regular exercise and the practice of relaxation. Is it ethical for a company to influence these employee behaviors, or does this infringe on their individual rights?
3. Assume that personality hardiness, Type B behavior, and self-reliance are positive personal attributes, and assume further that individuals with these attributes will cope better with stress. Is it appropriate for organizations to use these attributes as hiring criteria? That is, can organizations hire only hardy, self-reliant, Type B people?
4. Assume that a company finds that many employees have lower back problems associated with bending over work benches. In looking into the problem, the company finds that it can either raise the benches so employees bend less or send all the employees to a lower back care class. Should the most cost efficient approach be the one the company chooses? What else should the company consider?

Experiential Exercises

7.1 Sex Role Stressors

The major sources of stress for men and women are not necessarily the same. This exercise will help you identify the similarities and differences in the stressors and perceptions of men and women.

Step 1. Individually, list the major sources of stress for you because of your gender. Be as specific as possible, and within your list, prioritize your stressors.

Step 2. Individually, list what you think are the major sources of stress for those of the opposite sex. Again, be as specific as possible, and prioritize your list.

Step 3. In teams of five or six members of the same sex, share your two lists of stressors. Discuss these stressors, and identify the top five sources of stress for your group because of your gender and the top five sources of stress for those of the opposite sex. Again, be as specific as possible, and prioritize your list.

Step 4. The class will then engage in a cross-team exchange of lists. Look for similarities and differences among the teams in your class as follows. Select one sex to be addressed first. If the females are first, for example, the male groups will post their predictions. This will be followed by the actual stressor lists from the female groups. Then do the same for the other sex.

7.2 Workplace Stress Diagnosis

The following exercise gives you an opportunity to work within a group to compare the work demands and job stressors found in different work settings. Intervention for preventive stress management should always be based on a good diagnosis. This exercise gives you a start in this direction.

Step 1. Rate the degree to which each of the following work demands is a source of stress for you and your coworkers at work. Use a 7-point rating scale for assigning the stressfulness of the work demand, with 7 = very high source of stress, 4 = moderate source of stress, and 1 = very little source of stress.

____ Uncertainty about various aspects of the work environment

____ Lack of control over people, events, or other aspects of work

____ Lack of career opportunities and progress
____ The implementation of new technologies
____ Work overload; that is, too much to do and not enough time
____ Conflicting expectations from one or more people at work
____ Confusing expectations from one or more people at work
____ Dangerous working conditions and/or hazardous substances
____ Sexual harassment by supervisors, coworkers, or others
____ Abrasive personalities and/or political conflicts
____ Rigid, insensitive, unresponsive supervisors or managers

Step 2. Write a brief description of the most stressful event that has occurred in your work environment during the past twelve-month period.

Step 3. The class will form into groups of approximately six members each. Each group elects a spokesperson and then compares the information developed by each person in Steps 1 and 2 above. In the process of this comparison, answer the following questions.

a. What are the similarities between work environments in terms of their most stressful work demands?
b. What are the differences between work environments in terms of their most stressful work demands?
c. Are the most stressful event descriptions similar, or not?

Step 4. Each group will share the results of its answers to the questions in Step 3. Cross-team questions and discussion follow.

Step 5 (Optional). Your instructor may ask you to choose one or another of the work environments in which to develop some preventive stress management strategies. Complete parts a and b below in your group.

a. Identify the best (one to three) preventive stress management strategies to use in the work environment. Why have you chosen them?
b. How should the effectiveness of these strategies be evaluated?

CASE

Downsizing and the Walking Wounded[1]

"AT&T lays off 40,000; IBM, 35,000; and Chase, 12,000." Is this a temporary trend? According to British consultant Charles Handy, America's corporate obsession with cost cutting and downsizing will continue indefinitely. Downsizing won't go away because the forces driving it—changing technology, foreign competition, and Wall Street's obsession with shareholder value—won't go away. In fact, a June 1995 study by the American Management Association revealed that 60 percent of the 1,000 companies it surveyed would eliminate jobs in the subsequent 12 months.

Banking, media/entertainment, retailing, telecommunications, and utilities are among the most vulnerable industries for downsizing. In banking, for instance, tellers, clerks, and their supervisors are most vulnerable to having their positions eliminated through downsizing. And as retailers consolidate, store managers, inventory clerks, and salespeople will see their job eliminated.

Companies undertake downsizing with the expectation of reducing costs, improving productivity, and enhancing profitability. In turn, these businesses should have a much better chance of competing successively and surviving. Indeed, as AT&T's CEO Robert Allen says, "the company had to 'make the necessary, even painful, changes today or forfeit the future.' "

Unfortunately, however, downsizing isn't without its downside—both for those whose jobs are eliminated and those who remain behind. The impact on those who lose their jobs is obvious; the effect on those employees who remain employed is less obvious.

A 1992 survey of 1,141 human resource executives and managers in the United States indicated that employees who survived downsizing displayed distrust, a lack of confidence, doubts about their roles, and a high level of stress. A report by the Families & Work Institute indicates that in the aftermath of downsizing, fear may be partially responsible for frustration, stress, and burnout. Dubbed by some as the *walking wounded,* the survivors of a downsizing "can feel so distrustful, overworked, and insecure that the businesses fail to achieve their projected gains in productivity and profitability." In short, downsizing seemingly saps the life from the very people who are expected to help improve the organization's bottom line.

DISCUSSION QUESTIONS

1. Using Table 7.1, explain how corporate downsizing can become a significant source of stress for those employees who are not terminated.
2. From the organization's perspective, what are the possible consequences of not effectively managing the stress that results from downsizing? What are the possible consequences from the perspective of the employees?
3. What can organizations do to help surviving employees deal with stress that is experienced as a result of downsizing?
4. What can individuals do to cope more effectively with the aftermath of downsizing?
5. Some observers have argued that downsizing constitutes an unethical business practice because many people's jobs and livelihoods are sacrificed for the sake of profits. Where do you stand on this issue? Explain your answer.
6. What do you think you would do if you were downsized out of a job?
7. What do you think you would do if you survived an organizational downsizing?

SOURCE: This case was written by Michael K. McCuddy, the Louis S. and Mary L. Morgal Professor of Christian Business Ethics, Valparaiso University.

1. Adapted from T. Brown, "Creating the 'Sweat Shop' of the '90s," *Industry Week* (March 6, 1995): 31; B. Filipczak, "What the American Worker Thinks," *Training* 31, (1994): 135; R. B. Lieber, "How Safe Is Your Job?" *Fortune*, (April 1, 1996): 72–80; J. S. Lublin, "Walking Wounded: Survivors of Layoffs Battle Angst, Anger, Hurting Productivity," *The Wall Street Journal* (December 6, 1993): A1, A8; J. Norcera, "Living with Layoffs," *Fortune* (April 1, 1996): 69–71; R. J. Pinola, "Building a Winning Team after a Downsizing," *Compensation & Benefits Management* 10 (1994): 54–59; L. Smith and E. M. Davies, "Riskiest Industries," *Fortune* (April 1, 1996): 76; B. Wysocki, Jr., " 'Corporate Anorexia' Takes Toll on Growth," *South Bend Tribune* (July 9, 1995): D1, D2.

References

1. P. Kepos, ed., "Citicorp," in *International Directory of Company Histories: Vol. 9* (London: St. James Press, 1994), pp. 123–126.
2. J. C. Quick and J. D. Quick, *Organizational Stress and Preventive Management* (New York: McGraw-Hill, 1984).
3. S. Benison, A. C. Barger, and E. L. Wolfe, *Walter B. Cannon: The Life and Times of a Young Scientist* (Cambridge, Mass.: Harvard University Press, 1987).
4. W. B. Cannon, "Stresses and Strains of Homeostasis," *American Journal of the Medical Sciences* 189 (1935): 1–14.
5. W. B. Cannon, *The Wisdom of the Body* (New York: Norton, 1932).
6. R. S. Lazarus, *Psychological Stress and the Coping Process* (New York: McGraw-Hill, 1966).
7. D. Katz and R. L. Kahn, *The Social Psychology of Organizations*, 2d ed. (New York: Wiley, 1978), 185–221.
8. H. Levinson, "A Psychoanalytic View of Occupational Stress," *Occupational Mental Health* 3 (1978): 2–13.
9. F. J. Landy, "Work Design and Stress," in G. P. Keita and S. L. Sauter, eds., 1992, *Work and Well-Being: An Agenda for the 1990s* (Washington, D.C.: American Psychological Association), 119–158.
10. T. Theorell and R. A. Karasek, "Current Issues Relating to Psychosocial Job Strain and Cardiovascular Disease," *Journal of Occupational Health Psychology* 1 (1996): 9–26.
11. D. T. Hall and J. Richter, "Career Gridlock: Baby Boomers Hit the Wall," *Academy of Management Executive* 4 (1990): 7–22.
12. S. Zuboff, *In the Age of the Smart Machine: The Future of Work and Power* (New York: Basic Books, 1988).
13. R. L. Kahn, D. M. Wolfe, R. P. Quinn, J. D. Snoek, and R. A. Rosenthal, *Organizational Stress: Studies in Role Conflict and Ambiguity* (New York: Wiley, 1964).
14. M. F. Peterson, et al., "Role Conflict, Ambiguity, and Overload: A 21-Nation Study," *Academy of Management Journal* 38 (1995): 429–452.
15. K. Lewin, R. Lippitt, and R. K. White, "Patterns of Aggressive Behavior in Experimentally Created 'Social Climates,'" *Journal of Social Psychology* 10 (1939): 271–299.
16. L. T. Hosmer, "Trust: The Connecting Link between Organizational Theory and Philosophical Ethics," *Academy of Management Review* 20 (1995): 379–403.
17. R. Gal and A. D. Mangelsdorff, eds., *Handbook of Military Psychology* (Chichester, England, Wiley, 1991); and Dow Chemical, *Who Protects Our Health and Environment?* (Dow Chemical Company, 1980).
18. K. K. Gillingham, "High-G Stress and Orientational Stress: Physiologic Effects of Aerial Maneuvering," *Aviation, Space, and Environmental Medicine* 59 (1988): A10–A20.
19. R. S. Bhagat, S. J. McQuaid, S. Lindholm, and J. Segovis, "Total Life Stress: A Multimethod Validation of the Construct and Its Effect on Organizationally Valued Outcomes and Withdrawal Behaviors," *Journal of Applied Psychology* 70 (1985): 202–214.
20. J. C. Quick, J. R. Joplin, D. A. Gray, and E. C. Cooley, "The Occupational Life Cycle and the Family," in L. L'Abate, ed., *Handbook of Developmental Family Psychology and Psychopathology* (New York: John Wiley, 1993).
21. S. A. Lobel, "Allocation of Investment in Work and Family Roles: Alternative Theories and Implications for Research," *Academy of Management Review* 16 (1991): 507–521.
22. J. W. Pennebaker, C. F. Hughes, and R. C. O'Heeron, "The Psychophysiology of Confession: Linking Inhibitory and Psychosomatic Processes," *Journal of Personality and Social Psychology* 52 (1987): 781–793.
23. R. S. DeFrank and J. E. Pliner, "Job Security, Job Loss, and Outplacement: Implications for Stress and Stress Management," in J. C. Quick, R. S. Bhagat, J. E. Dalton, and J. D. Quick, eds., *Work Stress: Health Care Systems in the Workplace* (New York: Praeger Scientific, 1987), 195–219.
24. "Stress: The Test Americans Are Failing," *Business Week*, April 18, 1988.
25. J. D. Quick, R. S. Horn, and J. C. Quick, "Health Consequences of Stress," *Journal of Organizational Behavior Management* 8 (1986): 19–36.
26. R. M. Yerkes and J. D. Dodson, "The Relation of Strength of Stimulus to Rapidity of Habit-Formation," *Journal of Comparative Neurology and Psychology* 18 (1908): 459–482.
27. J. E. McGrath, "Stress and Behavior in Organizations," in M. D. Dunnette, ed., *Handbook of Industrial and Organizational Psychology* (Chicago: Rand McNally, 1976), 1351–1395.
28. W. B. Cannon, *Bodily Changes in Pain, Hunger, Fear, and Rage* (New York: Appleton, 1915).
29. P. A. Herbig and F. A. Palumbo, "*Karoshi:* Salaryman Sudden Death Syndrome," *Journal of Managerial Psychology* 9 (1994): 11–16.
30. S. Sauter, L. R. Murphy, and J. J. Hurrell, Jr., "Prevention of Work-Related Psychological Distress: A National Strategy Proposed by the National Institute for Occupational Safety and Health," *American Psychologist* 45 (1990): 1146–1158.
31. H. Selye, *Stress in Health and Disease* (Boston: Butterworth, 1976).
32. B. G. Ware and D. L. Block, "Cardiovascular Risk Intervention at a Work Site: The Ford Motor Company Program," *International Journal of Mental Health* 11 (1982): 68–75.
33. B. S. Siegel, *Love, Medicine, and Miracles* (New York: Harper & Row, 1986).
34. N. Bolger, A. DeLongis, R. C. Kessler, and E. A. Schilling, "Effects of Daily Stress on Negative Mood," *Journal of Personality and Social Psychology* 57 (1989): 808–818.
35. B. A. Macy and P. H. Mirvis, "A Methodology for Assessment of Quality of Work Life and Organizational Effectiveness in Behavioral-Economic Terms," *Administrative Science Quarterly* 21 (1976): 212–226.
36. J. M. Ivancevich, M. T. Matteson, and E. Richards, "Who's Liable for Stress on the Job?" *Harvard Business Review* 64 (1985): 60–72.
37. Frank S. Deus v. Allstate Insurance Company, civil action no. 88–2099, U.S. District Court, Western District of Louisiana.

38. E. Ramey, "Gender Differences in Cardiac Disease: The Paradox of Heart Disease in Women." Paper delivered at the Healing the Heart Conference, Boston, 3–5 May 1990.

39. D. L. Nelson and J. C. Quick, "Professional Women: Are Distress and Disease Inevitable?" *Academy of Management Review* 10 (1985): 206–218; and T. D. Jick and L. F. Mitz, "Sex Differences in Work Stress," *Academy of Management Review* 10 (1985): 408–420.

40. L. Verbrugge, "Recent, Present, and Future Health of American Adults," *Annual Review of Public Health* 10 (1989): 333–361.

41. P. A. C. Matuszek, D. L. Nelson, and J. C. Quick, "Gender Differences in Distress: Are We Asking All the Right Questions?" *Journal of Social Behavior and Personality* 10 (1995): 99–120.

42. M. D. Friedman and R. H. Rosenman, *Type A Behavior and Your Heart* (New York: Knopf, 1974).

43. L. Wright, "The Type A Behavior Pattern and Coronary Artery Disease," *American Psychologist* 43 (1988): 2–14.

44. J. M. Ivancevich and M. T. Matteson, "A Type A-B Person–Work Environment Interaction Model for Examining Occupational Stress and Consequences," *Human Relations* 37 (1984): 491–513.

45. S. O. C. Kobasa, "Conceptualization and Measurement of Personality in Job Stress Research," in J. J. Hurrell, Jr., L. R. Murphy, S. L. Sauter, and C. L. Cooper, eds., *Occupational Stress: Issues and Developments in Research* (New York: Taylor & Francis, 1988): 100–109.

46. J. Borysenko, "Personality Hardiness," Lectures in Behavioral Medicine (Boston: Harvard Medical School, 1985).

47. J. S. House, K. R. Landis, and D. Umberson, "Social Relationships and Health," *Science* 241 (1988): 540–545.

48. J. Bowlby, *A Secure Base* (New York: Basic Books, 1988).

49. C. Hazan and P. Shaver, "Love and Work: An Attachment-Theoretical Perspective," *Journal of Personality and Social Psychology* 59 (1990): 270–280.

50. D. L. Nelson and J. C. Quick, "Social Support and Newcomer Adjustment in Organization: Attachment Theory at Work?" *Journal of Organizational Behavior* 12 (1991): 543–554; J. C. Quick, J. R. Joplin, D. L. Nelson, and J. D. Quick, "Behavioral Responses to Anxiety: Self-Reliance, Counterdependence, and Overdependence," *Anxiety, Stress, and Coping* 5 (1992): 41–54; J. C. Quick, D. L. Nelson, and J. D. Quick, *Stress and Challenge at the Top: The Paradox of the Successful Executive* (Chichester, England, Wiley, 1990).

51. J. C. Quick, J. R. Joplin, D. L. Nelson, and J. D. Quick, "Self-reliance for Stress and Combat" (Proceedings of the 8th Combat Stress Conference, U.S. Army Health Services Command, Fort Sam Houston, Texas, 23–27 September 1991): 1–5.

52. K. Hickox, "Content and Competitive," *Airman* (January 1994): 31–33.

53. D. Anfuso, "Deflecting Workplace Violence," *Personnel Journal* 73 (1994): 66–77.

54. W. L. French and C. H. Bell, Jr., *Organizational Development: Behavioral Science Interventions for Organization Improvement*, 4th ed. (Englewood Cliffs, N.J.: Prentice-Hall, 1990).

55. S. A. Lobel and L. St. Clair, "Effects of Family Responsibilities, Gender, and Career Identity Salience on Performance Outcomes of Professionals," *Academy of Management Journal* 35 (1992): 1057–1069.

56. M. E. P. Seligman, *Learned Optimism* (New York: Knopf, 1990).

57. W. T. Brooks and T. W. Mullins, *High-Impact Time Management* (Englewood Cliffs, N.J.: Prentice-Hall, 1989).

58. R. Ornstein and D. Sobel, *Healthy Pleasures* (Reading, Mass.: Addison-Wesley, 1989).

59. K. H. Cooper, *The Aerobic Program for Total Well-Being: Exercise, Diet, Emotional Balance* (New York: M. Evans, 1982).

60. M. Davis, E. R. Eshelman, and M. McKay, *The Relaxation and Stress Reduction Workbook*, 3d ed. (Oakland, Calif.: New Harbinger, 1988).

61. H. Benson, "Your Innate Asset for Combating Stress," *Harvard Business Review* 52 (1974): 49–60.

62. D. Ornish, *Dr. Dean Ornish's Program for Reversing Cardiovascular Disease* (New York: Random House, 1990).

63. J. W. Pennebaker, *Opening Up: The Healing Power of Confiding in Others* (New York: Morrow, 1990).

64. M. E. Francis and J. W. Pennebaker, "Putting Stress into Words: The Impact of Writing on Physiological, Absentee, and Self-Reported Emotional Well-being Measures," *American Journal of Health Promotion* 6 (1992): 280–287.

65. Z. Solomon, B. Oppenheimer, and S. Noy, "Subsequent Military Adjustment of Combat Stress Reaction Casualties: A Nine-Year Follow-Up Study," in N. A. Milgram, ed., *Stress and Coping in Time of War: Generalizations from the Israeli Experience* (New York: Brunner/Mazel, 1986), 84–90.

66. D. Wegman and L. Fine, "Occupational Health in the 1990s," *Annual Review of Public Health* 11 (1990): 89–103.

67. D. Gebhardt and C. Crump, "Employee Fitness and Wellness Programs in the Workplace," *American Psychologist* 45 (1990): 262–272.

68. T. Wolf, H. Randall, and J. Faucett, "A Survey of Health Promotion Programs in U.S. and Canadian Medical Schools," *American Journal of Health Promotion* 3 (1988): 33–36.

69. S. Weiss, J. Fielding, and A. Baum, *Health at Work* (Hillsdale, N.J.: Erlbaum, 1990).

70. J. S. Reed, "Chairman's Letter to Shareholders," *1990 Citicorp Annual Report;* and *CCInvestor* (January/February 1991: 1–4.

INTERNET EXERCISE

In the first assignment, you experimented with a number of different aspects of the Internet. While information sources such as newsgroups, listserv, and gopher are still important, the fastest growing area of the Internet is the World Wide Web (WWW). Many organizations and individuals are establishing home pages. Web pages may be created for commercial, informational, or entertainment reasons. This, and subsequent assignments, will deal mainly with exploring some of the web pages available on the Internet. You will get a chance to find out more about some of the companies (Company Connections) and topics (Topic Trails) discussed in your text. Use your web browser to locate the following companies and topics.

Company Connections

Southwest Airlines
Check out the employee section of this home page. How does the information provided here relate to topics in the text?

Fantastic Foods
How does Fantastic Foods use their home page to promote the vision of their company?

GTE
How does GTE believe they can increase employee productivity?

OSHA
How could managers use the information given at this site to increase employee safety and welfare?

Topic Trails

Sigmund Freud
View his curriculum vitae. What were some of the topics of his research papers?

MBTI
What information on the Myers-Briggs test is available here?

Business Ethics
Check out some of the corporate codes of ethics available on-line. What do they have in common?

Stress
Find Wellspring Media's home page. How could the information here help you manage work-related stress?

E-mail

E-mail your professor and tell him or her what resources are available on the Wellspring Media's home page regarding stress management.

VIDEO COHESION CASE

This section includes four cases dealing with various organizational behavior issues facing PriceCostco, a company resulting from the merger of Price Company and Costco Wholesale. The cases are interrelated, but each can stand alone. Each case is supplemented with videos that present the challenges faced by a corporation formed from two diverse companies seeking to create a single company with a unified philosophy and culture. These cases immediately follow Chapter 18 on page 573.

PART III

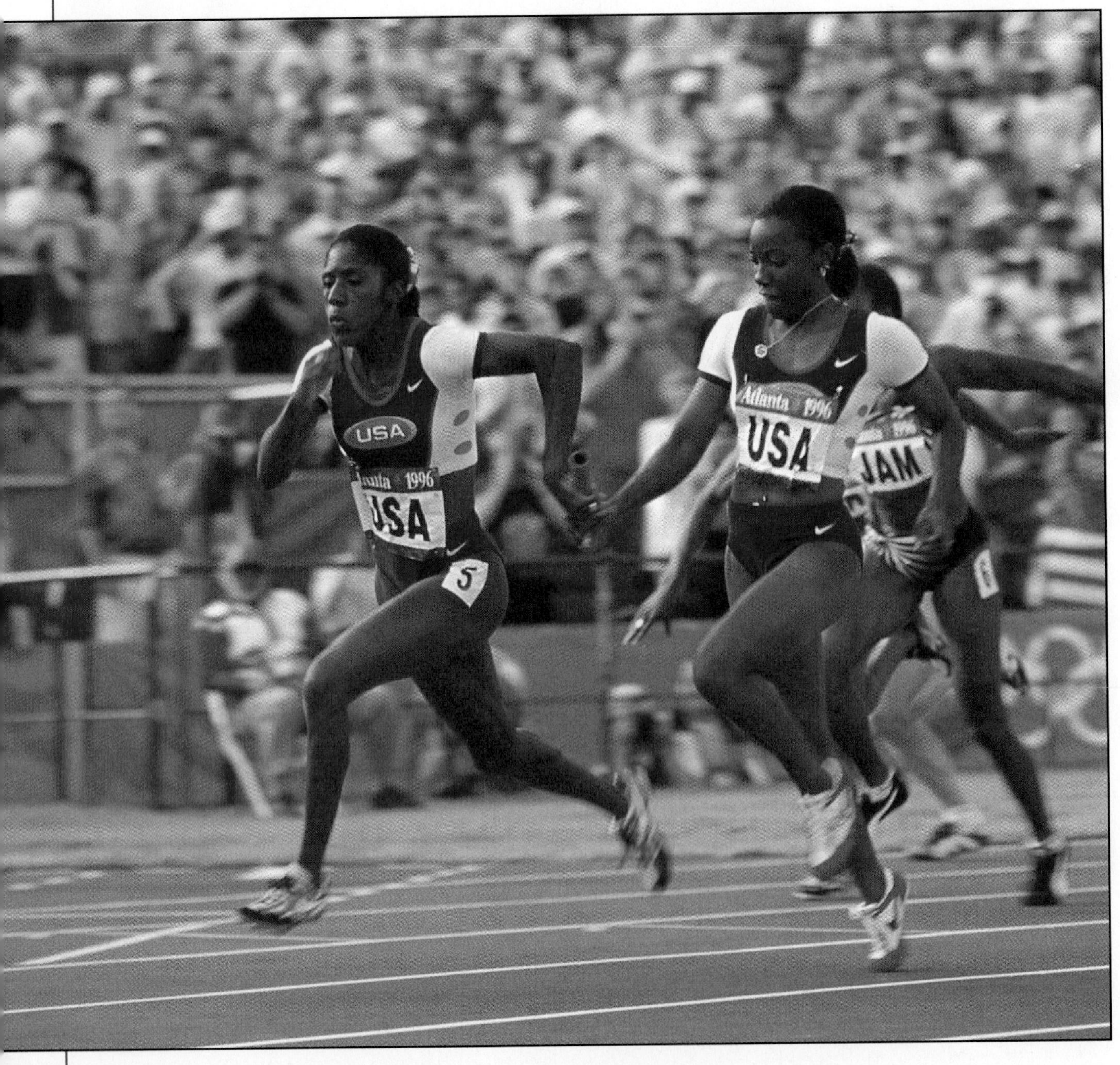

Interpersonal Processes and Behavior

CHAPTER

8

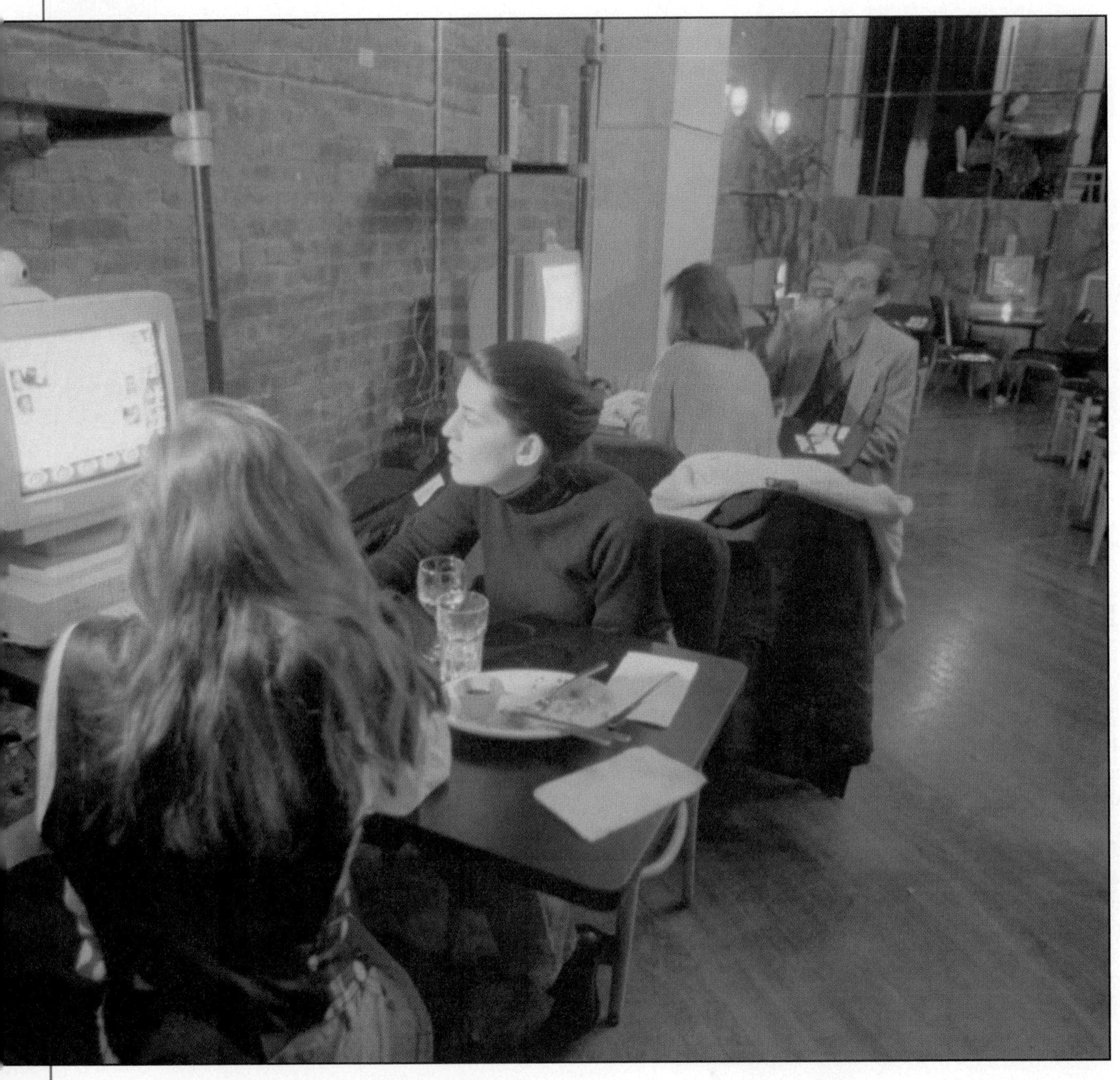

Communication

LEARNING OBJECTIVES

After reading this chapter, you should be able to do the following:

- Understand the roles of the communicator, the receiver, perceptual screens, and the message in interpersonal communication.
- Practice good reflective skills.
- Describe the five communication skills of effective supervisors.
- Explain five barriers to communication and how to overcome them.
- Distinguish between defensive and nondefensive communication.
- Describe contemporary information technologies used by managers.

OPENING SPOTLIGHT

Document Imaging and Information Technology at Chaparral Steel

Between 1973 and 1987, Chaparral Steel grew from a dozen products and about 25 customers to a company offering about 500 basic products to 1,500 customers. The company has well over 2,000 products on its Midlothian, Texas, site at any one time. Along with the growth in steel products went a dramatic growth in paper documents used by the company.

Dave Fournie, a production manager, was given the challenge of converting Chaparral into a paperless office. He developed information technology and management information systems as tools to gain a competitive advantage. He began with a group of fifteen to eighteen people from various departments (accounting, sales, shipping, inventory, the mills, and engineering). This group papered a nine-by-twelve-foot wall with the nearly one hundred pieces of paper needed for interaction with any one customer. The absolute minimum number of completed forms for each customer was eleven pieces of paper, including a mill order, billet order, rolling order, inventory transfer, manifest, and a few others.

Between 1987 and 1990, Chaparral built a relational database on an interactive Digital Equipment Corporation (DEC) system, with which salespeople on the road, some maintenance people at home, and other Chaparral employees could communicate. In addition, thirty customers were allowed on-line access, primarily to check order status. This advance in information technology has given Chaparral access to services such as a rail car monitoring system. The rail car monitoring system allows orders to be computer tracked from the mill to the customer. The information is also immediately available to the customer. In 1992, Larry Clark, vice president and controller, began pushing Chaparral to the next level of high-tech information processing through a document imaging system.[1] Would Chaparral Steel's move to document imaging and a paperless office pay off? The Closing Spotlight provides an answer to this question. ■

The people at Chaparral Steel use the latest information technology to their advantage, but they are also effective in the use of direct, face-to-face interpersonal communication. **Communication** is the evoking of a shared or common meaning in another person. **Interpersonal communication** is communication that occurs between two or more people in an organization. Reading, listening, managing and interpreting information, and serving clients are among the interpersonal communication skills identified by the Department of Labor as being necessary for successful functioning in the workplace.[2]

communication
The evoking of a shared or common meaning in another person.

interpersonal communication
Communication between two or more people in an organization.

Points to Emphasize
Just because you have told someone something, written a memo, sent a fax, or an E-mail does not mean you have communicated. Communication only occurs when you transfer understanding and develop a common meaning between individuals.

This chapter addresses the interpersonal and technological dimensions of communication in organizations. The first section presents an interpersonal communication model and a reflective listening technique intended to improve communication. The next section of the chapter addresses the five communication skills that characterize effective supervisors. The third section examines five barriers to effective communication and gives suggestions for overcoming them. The fourth section compares defensive and nondefensive communication. The fifth section discusses kinds of nonverbal communication. The final section gives an overview of the latest technologies for information managment in organizations.

Interpersonal Communication

■ Interpersonal communication is important in building and sustaining human relationships at work. It cannot be replaced by the advances in information technology and data management that have taken place over the past several decades. The model in this section of the chapter provides a basis for understanding the key elements of interpersonal communication. These elements are the communicator, the receiver, the perceptual screens, and the message. Reflective listening is a valuable tool for improving interpersonal communication.

An Interpersonal Communication Model

Figure 8.1 presents an interpersonal communication model as a basis for the discussion of communication. The model has four basic elements: the communicator, the receiver, perceptual screens, and the message. The **communicator** is the person originating the message. The **receiver** is the person receiving the message. The receiver must interpret and understand the message. **Perceptual screens** are the windows through which we interact with people in the world. The communicator's and the receiver's perceptual screens influence the quality, accuracy, and clarity of the message. The screens influence whether the message sent and the message received are the same or whether distortion occurs in the message. Perceptual screens are composed of the personal factors each person brings to interpersonal communication, such as age, gender, values, beliefs, past

communicator
The person originating a message.

receiver
The person receiving a message.

perceptual screen
A window through which we interact with people that influences the quality, accuracy, and clarity of the communication.

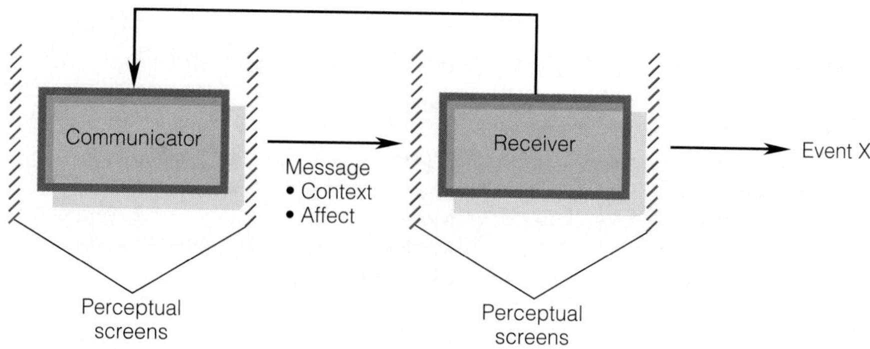

■ **FIGURE 8.1**

A Basic Interpersonal Communication Model

experiences, cultural influences, and individual needs. The extent to which these screens are open or closed significantly influences both the sent and received messages.

The **message** contains the thoughts and feelings that the communicator intends to evoke in the receiver. The message has two primary components. The thought or conceptual component of the message (its content) is contained in the words, ideas, symbols, and concepts chosen to relay the message. The feeling or emotional component of the message (its affect) is contained in the intensity, force, demeanor, and sometimes the gestures of the communicator. This component of the message adds to the conceptual component the emotional overtones, such as joy or anger, fear or pain. This addition often enriches and clarifies the message. The feeling component gives the message its full meaning.

The **feedback loop** may or may not be activated in the model. Feedback occurs when the receiver provides the communicator with a response to the message.

The **language** of the message is increasingly important because of the multinational nature of many organizations. Language is the words, their pronunciation, and the methods of combining them used by a community of people. Language will be addressed as a possible barrier to communication. For example, special language barriers arise for non-Japanese-speaking Americans who work with Japanese workers and for non-Spanish-speaking Canadians who work with Spanish-speaking workers.

Data are the uninterpreted, unanalyzed elements of a message. **Information** is data with meaning to some person who has interpreted or analyzed them. Messages are conveyed through a medium, such as a telephone or face-to-face discussion. Messages differ in **richness**, the ability of the medium to convey the meaning.[3] Table 8.1 compares different media with regard to data capacity and information richness. The accompanying Scientific Foundation feature examines computer-mediated communication and social status.

Reflective Listening

Reflective listening is the skill of carefully listening to another person and repeating back to the speaker the heard message to correct any inaccuracies or misunderstandings. This kind of listening emphasizes the role of the receiver or audience in interpersonal communication. Managers use it to understand other people and help them solve problems at work.[4] Reflective listening enables the listener to understand the communicator's meaning, reduce perceptual distortions, and overcome interpersonal barriers that lead to communication failures. Reflective listening ensures that the meanings of the sent and received messages are the same. Reflecting back the message helps the communicator clarify and sharpen the intended meaning. It is especially useful in problem solving.

Reflective listening can be characterized as personal, feeling oriented, and responsive. First, reflective listening emphasizes the personal elements of the

message

The thoughts and feelings that the communicator is attempting to elicit in the receiver.

feedback loop

The pathway that completes two-way communication.

language

The words, their pronunciation, and the methods of combining them used and understood by a group of people.

data

Uninterpreted and unanalyzed facts.

information

Data that have been interpreted, analyzed, and have meaning to some user.

richness

The ability of a medium or channel to elicit or evoke meaning in the receiver.

reflective listening

A skill intended to help the receiver and communicator clearly and fully understand the message sent.

Discussion Consideration

Is feedback something that should be initiated by the sender or the receiver?

Discussion Consideration

What is the least rich communication channel? What is the richest communication channel? Which communication channel is most frequently used in organizations?

Points to Emphasize

Effective communication requires taking the initiative and the responsibility for the transfer of understanding.

Points to Emphasize
Walter Wriston, former CEO of Citicorp, said it is not difficult to get reports and printouts. The difficulty is getting summarized information that you can use. This illustrates the difference between data and information.

Alternate Example
It has been said that the 500 most commonly used words in the English language have an average of 28 different meanings each. That gives you at least 14,000 chances to miscommunicate in your everyday interactions.

■ **TABLE 8.1**

Communication Media: Information Richness and Data Capacity

MEDIUM	INFORMATION RICHNESS	DATA CAPACITY
Face-to-face discussion	Highest	Lowest
Telephone	High	Low
Electronic mail	Moderate	Moderate
Individualized letter	Moderate	Moderate
Personalized note or memo	Moderate	Moderate
Formal written report	Low	High
Flyer or bulletin	Low	High
Formal numeric report	Lowest	Highest

SOURCE: Adapted by E. A. Gerloff from *Research in Organizational Behavior* 6 (Greenwich, Col., JAI Press, 1984): 191–233, "Information Richness: A New Approach to Managerial Behavior and Organizational Design," Richard L. Daft and R. H. Lengel.

communication process, not the impersonal or abstract elements of the message. The reflective listener demonstrates empathy and concern for the communicator as a person, not an inanimate object. Second, reflective listening emphasizes the feelings communicated in the message. Thoughts and ideas are often the primary focus of a receiver's response, but that is not the case in reflective listening. The receiver should pay special attention to the feeling component of the message. Third, reflective listening emphasizes responding to the communicator, not leading the communicator. Receivers should distinguish their own feelings and thoughts from those of the speaker so as not to confuse the two. The focus must be on the speaker's feelings and thoughts in order to respond to them. A good reflective listener does not lead the speaker according to the listener's own thoughts and feelings.

Four levels of verbal response by the receiver are part of active reflective listening: affirming contact, paraphrasing expressed thoughts and feelings, clarifying implicit thoughts and feelings, and reflecting "core" feelings not fully expressed.[5] Nonverbal behaviors also are useful in reflective listening. Specifically, silence and eye contact are responses that enhance reflective listening.[6]

Each reflective response will be illustrated through the case of a software engineer and her supervisor. The engineer has just discovered a major problem, which is not yet fully defined, in a large information system she is building for a very difficult customer.

AFFIRMING CONTACT The receiver affirms contact with the communicator by using simple statements such as "I see," "Uh-huh," and "Yes, I understand." The purpose of an affirmation response is to communicate attentiveness, not necessarily agreement. In the case of the software engineer, the supervisor might most appropriately use several affirming statements as the engineer begins to talk through the problem. Affirming contact is especially reassuring to a speaker in the early stages of expressing thoughts and feelings about a problem, especially when there may be some associated anxiety or discomfort. As the problem is more fully explored and expressed, it is increasingly useful for the receiver to use additional reflective responses.

PARAPHRASING THE EXPRESSED After an appropriate time, the receiver might paraphrase the expressed thoughts and feelings of the speaker. Paraphrasing is useful because it reflects back to the speaker the thoughts and feelings as the receiver heard them. This verbal response enables the receiver to build greater empathy, openness, and acceptance into the relationship while ensuring the accuracy of the communication process.

In the case of the software engineer, the supervisor may find paraphrasing the engineer's expressed thoughts and feelings particularly useful for both of them

SCIENTIFIC FOUNDATION

Social Status and Computer-Mediated Communication

Social status often has an impact on decisions in face-to-face communication groups, with high-status members exerting more influence than low-status members. These status inequalities appear to be reduced when decisions are made by electronic mail. Computer-mediated (electronic) communication has grown dramatically over the past decade with the development of the Internet and LANs (local area networks) within and between organizations.

Three experiments were conducted to examine whether more equal participation and influence occurred in groups communicating via computer versus communicating face-to-face. In Experiment 1, 59 business students worked in face-to-face groups over two weeks to make two ethical decisions. In Experiment 2, 105 business students worked at computerized workstations networked into three-person groups and completed the same two ethical decisions. In Experiment 3, another 105 business students completed three ethical evaluations of the conduct of a computer professional in a hypothetical situation. The modes of communication were varied over the three tasks by group.

In sharp contrast to previous research, these experiments found that high-status members participated more in group communication than low-status members. This finding held for both face-to-face and computer-mediated communication, regardless of computer technology; for high-status minority as well as high-status majority groups; and for groups in which members were known to each other as well as anonymous to each other. Hence, computer-mediated communication does not appear to eliminate the effects of status difference in groups.

SOURCE: S. P. Weisband, S. K. Schneider, and T. Connolly, "Computer-Mediated Communication and Social Information: Status Salience and Status Differences," *Academy of Management Journal* 38 (1995): 1124–1151.

Students may work on computer terminals to complete research projects for themselves as well as for their professors. Modern information technology makes study at the computer terminal much more common than it was even five years ago.

in developing a clearer understanding of the system problem. For example, the supervisor might say, "I hear you saying that you are very upset about this problem and that you are not yet clear about what is causing it." It is difficult to solve a problem until it is clearly understood.

CLARIFYING THE IMPLICIT People often communicate implicit thoughts and feelings about a problem in addition to their explicitly expressed thoughts and feelings. Implicit thoughts and feelings are not clearly or fully expressed. The receiver may or may not assume that the implicit thoughts and feelings are within the awareness of the speaker. For example, the software engineer may be anxious about how to talk with a difficult customer concerning the system problem. This may be implicit in her discussion with her supervisor because of the

Alternate Example
One of the difficulties of using technology in communication is conveying humor. A set of do's and don'ts connected with E-mail has begun to outline what is acceptable humor. What is implicit in face-to-face communication is difficult to convey through E-mail. This illustrates the richness tradeoff involved with using technology in communication.

previous discussions about this customer. If her anxiety feelings are not expressed, the supervisor may want to clarify them. For example, the supervisor might say, "I hear that you are feeling very upset about the problem and may be worried about the customer's reaction when you inform him." This would help the engineer shift the focus of her attention from the main problem, which is in the software, to the important and related issue of discussing the matter with the customer.

REFLECTING "CORE" FEELINGS Next, the receiver should go beyond the explicit or implicit thoughts and feelings that the speaker is expressing. The receiver, in reflecting the core feelings that the speaker may be experiencing, is reaching beyond the immediate awareness level of the speaker. "Core" feelings are the deepest and most important ones from the speaker's perspective. For example, if the software engineer had not been aware of any anxiety in her relationship with the difficult customer, her supervisor's ability to sense the tension and bring it to the engineer's awareness would exemplify reflecting core feelings.

The receiver runs a risk of overreaching in reflecting core feelings if a secure, empathetic relationship with the speaker does not already exist or if strongly repressed feelings are reflected back. Even if the receiver is correct, the speaker may not want those feelings brought to awareness. Therefore, it is important to exercise caution and care in reflecting core feelings to a speaker.

Points to Emphasize
It has been observed that Americans are not comfortable with silence, that we often feel compelled to fill up the silence with chatter. The notable exception is Native Americans, who could teach us a great deal about silence and patience.

SILENCE Long, extended periods of silence may cause discomfort and be a sign or source of embarrassment, but silence can help both speaker and listener in reflective listening. From the speaker's perspective, silence may be useful in moments of thought or confusion about how to express difficult ideas or feelings. The software engineer may need some patient, silent response as she thinks through what to say next. Listeners can use brief periods of silence to sort out their own thoughts and feelings from those of the speaker. Reflective listening focuses only on the latter. In the case of the software engineer's supervisor, any personal, angry feelings toward the difficult customer should not intrude upon the engineer's immediate problem. Silence provides time to identify and isolate the listener's personal responses and exclude them from the dialogue.

Discussion Consideration
Ask students to research eye contact in various cultures and to compare it with eye contact in the United States. For example, in which cultures is eye contact avoidance between men and women common?

EYE CONTACT Eye contact is a nonverbal behavior that may help open up a relationship and improve communication between two people. The absence of any direct eye contact during an exchange tends to close communication. Cultural and individual differences influence what constitutes appropriate eye contact. For example, some cultures, such as in India, place restrictions on direct eye contact initiated by women or children. Too much direct eye contact, regardless of the individual or culture, has an intimidating effect.

Moderate direct eye contact, therefore, communicates openness and affirmation without causing either speaker or listener to feel intimidated. Periodic aversion of the eyes allows for a sense of privacy and control, even in intense interpersonal communication. Challenge 8.1 gives you an opportunity to evaluate how good a listener you are.

two-way communication
A form of communication in which the communicator and receiver interact.

one-way communication
Communication in which a person sends a message to another person and no questions, feedback, or interaction follow.

One-Way Versus Two-Way Communication

Reflective listening encourages two-way communication. **Two-way communication** is an interactive form of communication in which there is an exchange of thoughts, feelings, or both and through which shared meaning often occurs. Problem-solving and decision-making are often examples of two-way communication. **One-way communication** occurs when a person sends a message to another person and no feedback, questions, or interaction follows. Giving instructions or giving directions are examples of one-way communication. One-

CHALLENGE

■ 8.1

Are You a Good Listener?

Reflective listening is a skill that you can practice and learn. Here are ten tips to help you become a better listener.

1. Stop talking. You cannot listen if your mouth is moving.
2. Put the speaker at ease. Break the ice to help the speaker relax. Smile!
3. Show the speaker you want to listen. Put away your work. Do not look at your watch. Maintain good eye contact.
4. Remove distractions. Close your door. Do not answer the telephone.
5. Empathize with the speaker. Put yourself in the speaker's shoes.
6. Be patient. Not everyone delivers messages at the same pace.
7. Hold your temper. Do not fly off the handle.
8. Go easy on criticism. Criticizing the speaker can stifle communication.
9. Ask questions. Paraphrase and clarify the speaker's message.
10. Stop talking. By this stage, you are probably very tempted to start talking, but do not. Be sure the speaker has finished.

Think of the last time you had a difficult communication with someone at work or school. Evalute yourself in that situation against each of the ten items. Which one(s) do you need to improve on the most?

SOURCE: "Steps to Better Listening," C. Hamilton and B. H. Kleiner, copyright February 1987. Reprinted with permission of *Personnel Journal*.

way communication occurs whenever a person sends a one-directional message to a receiver with no reflective listening or feedback in the communication.

One-way communication is faster, although how much faster depends on the amount and complexity of information communicated and the medium chosen. Even though it is faster, one-way communication is often less accurate than two-way communication. This is especially true for complex tasks where clarifications and iterations may be required for task completion. Where time and accuracy are both important to the successful completion of a task, such as in combat or emergency situations, extensive training prior to execution enhances accuracy and efficiency of execution without two-way communication.[7] Fire fighters and military combat personnel engage extensively in such training to minimize the need for communication during emergencies. These highly trained professionals rely on fast, abbreviated, one-way communication as a shorthand for more complex information. However, this communication only works within the range of situations for which the professionals are specifically trained.

Discussion Consideration
Is most one-way communication that way because of an authority or power difference? What do students believe?

It is difficult to draw general conclusions about people's satisfaction with one-way versus two-way communication. For example, communicators with a stronger need for feedback or who are not uncomfortable with conflicting or confusing questions may find two-way communication more satisfying. In contrast, receivers who believe that a message is very straightforward may be satisfied with one-way communication and dissatisfied with two-way communication because of its lengthy, drawn-out nature.

Five Keys To Effective Supervisory Communication

■ Interpersonal communication between managers and their employees is a critical foundation for effective performance in organizations. One large study of managers in a variety of jobs and industries found that managers with the most effective work units engaged in routine communication within their units, whereas the managers with the highest promotion rates engaged in networking activities with superiors.[8] Another study of male and female banking managers showed that higher performing managers exhibited higher levels of communication skills than lower performing managers. This suggests that higher performing managers are better and less apprehensive communicators than lower performing managers.[9]

A review of the research on manager-employee communication identified five communication skills that distinguish "good" from "bad" supervisors.[10] These skills include being expressive speakers, empathetic listeners, persuasive leaders, sensitive people, and informative managers. Some supervisors are good and effective without possessing each of these skills, and some organizations value one or another skill over the others.

Expressive Speakers

Better supervisors express their thoughts, ideas, and feelings and speak up in meetings. They are comfortable expressing themselves. They tend toward extroversion. Supervisors who are not talkative or who tend toward introversion may at times leave their employees wondering what their supervisors are thinking or how they feel about certain issues. Supervisors who speak out let the people they work with know where they stand, what they believe, and how they feel.

Empathetic Listeners

Points to Emphasize
Ask students to reflect on their MBTI analysis. Is empathetic listening easier for some personality types than for others?

In addition to being expressive speakers, the better supervisors are willing, empathetic listeners. They use reflective listening skills; they are patient with, and responsive to, problems that employees, peers, and others bring to them about their work. They respond to and engage the concerns of other people. For example, the president of a health care operating company estimated that he spends 70 percent of his interpersonal time at work listening to others.[11] He listens empathetically to some personal, as well as work, dilemmas without taking responsibility for others' problems or concerns. Empathetic listeners are able to hear the feelings and emotional dimensions of the messages people send them, as well as the content of the ideas and issues. Better supervisors are approachable and willing to listen to suggestions and complaints.

Persuasive Leaders (and Some Exceptions)

Better supervisors are persuasive leaders rather than directive, autocratic ones. All supervisors and managers must exercise power and influence in organizations if they are to ensure performance and achieve results. These better supervisors are distinguished by their use of persuasive communication when influencing others. Specifically, they encourage others to achieve results instead of telling others what to do. They are not highly directive or manipulative in their influence attempts.

The exceptions to this pattern of communication occur in emergency or high-risk situations, such as life-threatening traumas in medical emergency rooms or in oil rig firefighting. In these cases, the supervisor must be directive and assertive.

Sensitive to Feelings

Better supervisors are also sensitive to the feelings, self-image, and psychological defenses of their employees. Although the supervisor is capable of giving criticism and negative feedback to employees, he or she does it confidentially and constructively. Care is taken to avoid giving critical feedback or reprimanding in public. Those settings are reserved for the praise of employees' accomplishments, honors, and achievements. In this manner, the better supervisors are sensitive to the self-esteem of others. They work to enhance that self-esteem as appropriate to the person's real talents, abilities, and achievements.

Informative Managers

Finally, better supervisors keep those who work for them well informed and are skilled at engaging in the "disseminator" role.[12] This role involves receiving large volumes of information, through a wide range of written and verbal communication media, and then filtering through the information before distributing it appropriately. The failure to filter and disseminate information selectively to employees can lead to either information overload for the employees or a lack of sufficient information for performance and task accomplishment. Better supervisors favor giving advance notice of organizational changes and explaining the rationale for organizational policies. The accompanying Organizational Reality feature shows a no-barrier approach.

Alternate Example
Companies are changing their views about what information is necessary for employees. One approach is that if you want employees to act like owners, you have to give them all the information that any owner would get. Source: J. Case, "The Open-Book Managers," Inc., September 1990, 104–113.

A person may become a good supervisor even in the absence of one of these communication skills. For example, a person with special talents in planning and organizing or in decision making may compensate for a shortcoming in expressiveness or sensitivity. Overall, interpersonal communication is the foundation for human relationships.

Discussion Consideration
Ask students to identify the pros and cons of sharing detailed company information with employees.

Barriers to Communication

■ Barriers to communication are factors that block or significantly distort successful communication. Effective managerial communication skills helps overcome some, but not all, barriers to communication in organizations. These **barriers to communication** in organizations may be temporary and can be overcome. Awareness and recognition are the first steps in formulating ways to overcome the barriers. Five communication barriers are physical separation, status differences, gender differences, cultural diversity, and language. The discussion of each concludes with one or two ways to overcome the barrier.

barriers to communication
Aspects such as physical separation, status differences, gender differences, cultural diversity, and language that can impair effective communication in a workplace.

Physical Separation

The physical separation of people in the work environment poses a barrier to communication. Telephones and technology, such as electronic mail, often help bridge the physical gap. We address a variety of new technologies in the closing section of the chapter. Although telephones and technology can be helpful, they are not as information-rich as face-to-face communication (see Table 8.1).

Periodic face-to-face interactions help overcome physical separation problems, because the communication is much richer, largely because of nonverbal cues. The richer the communication, the less the potential for confusion or misunderstandings. Another way to overcome the barrier of physical separation is through regularly scheduled meetings for people who are organizationally interrelated.

Points to Emphasize
Emphasize to students that we have the technological capability of allowing a large percentage of the work force to fulfill its work responsibilities at home. The problem is resistance to change. For instance, many employees believe they must put in a certain amount of "face time" at the office. That is, they feel they must be seen.

Status Differences

Status differences related to power and the organizational hierarchy pose another barrier to communication among people at work, especially within manager-employee pairs.[13] Because the employee is dependent on the manager as the primary link to the organization, the employee is more likely to distort upward communication than either horizontal or downward communication.[14]

Effective supervisory skills, discussed at the beginning of the chapter, make the supervisor more approachable and help reduce the risk of problems related

Discussion Consideration
Do students feel intimidated when approaching professors for assistance? Is this a function of status differences or some other barrier to effective communication?

ORGANIZATIONAL REALITY

No Barriers at Oticon

Oticon is a highly successful company based in Copenhagen, Denmark, which has revolutionized the hearing-aid industry. Panasonic and Siemens are among its multibillion-dollar competitors. Oticon is a $100 million company whose profits have increased fivefold since 1991 and that set an industry record of 30 percent return on sales. Rather than mass production of conventional hearing aids, Oticon's competitive edge has been its first-to-market obsession and its cutting-edge products, which combine state-of-the-art technology with fashion design. Hence, the sharing and exploiting of knowledge and information is a vital competitive advantage for Oticon, a company that relies on very open, no-barrier communication.

CEO Lars Kolind has neither an office nor a permanent desk, which is true for all Oticon employees. The company does have desks, each equipped with a computer and a telephone, yet none are proprietary. All Oticon's incoming mail is scanned into its computer database and all employees have access to everyone's mail, including Kolind's, as well as their calendars. Project teams are encouraged to tap the database as needed. Each employee, including Kolind, has a personal mobile caddie cart, which is his or her personal filing cabinet on wheels. Armed with his or her personal cart and any desk in Oticon, an employee is ready to go to work. After returning from one two-week trip, Kolind was informed by a clerk that her team had moved his cart to another floor because they needed the desk he had been using. Well, that's life at Oticon . . . no barriers, no doors, and no hierarchical power games. ■

SOURCE: O. Harari, "Open the Doors, Tell the Truth," *Management Review* 84 (1995): 33–35. Reprinted with permission of The Wall Street Journal, © 1996 Dow Jones & Company. All Rights Reserved.

Oticon is a nonbarrier work environment, enabling direct face-to-face and terminal-to-terminal communication a prominent feature of the work environment.

Alternate Example
Even research terminology is sprinkled with status differences. For example, most of the research literature refers to employer/employee communication as superior/subordinate communication.

to status differences. In addition, when employees feel secure, they are more likely to be straightforward in upward communication. The absence of status, power, and hierarchical differences, however, is not a cure-all. New information technologies provide another way to overcome status-difference barriers, because they encourage the formation of nonhierarchical working relationships.[15]

Gender Differences

Communication barriers can be explained in part by differences in conversational styles.[16] Thus, when people of different ethnic or class backgrounds talk to one another, what the receiver understands may not be the same as what the speaker meant. In a similar way, men and women have different conversational styles, which may pose a communication barrier between those of opposite sexes.[17] For example, women prefer to converse face to face, whereas men are comfortable sitting side by side and concentrating on some focal point in front of them. Hence, conversation style differences may result in a failure to communicate between men and women. Again, what is said by one may be understood to have an entirely different meaning by the other. Male-female conversation is really cross-cultural communication.

An important first step to overcoming the gender barrier to communication is developing an awareness of gender-specific differences in conversational style. A second step is to seek clarification of the person's meaning rather than freely interpreting meaning from one's own frame of reference.

Alternate Example
Communication specialist Deborah Tannen suggests that men talking to women is cross-cultural communication. Source: D. Tannen, You Just Don't Understand.

Cultural Diversity

Cultural values and patterns of behavior can be very confusing barriers to communication. Important international differences in work-related values exist between people in the United States, Germany, the United Kingdom, Japan, and other nations.[18] These value differences have implications for motivation, leadership, and teamwork in work organizations.[19] Habitual patterns of interaction within a culture often substitute for communication. Outsiders working in a culture foreign to them often find these habitual patterns confusing and at times bizarre. For example, the German culture places greater value on authority and hierarchical differences. It is therefore more difficult for German workers to engage in direct, open communication with their supervisors than it is for U.S. workers.[20]

A first step to overcoming cultural diversity as a communication barrier is increasing awareness and sensitivity. In addition, companies can provide seminars for expatriate managers as part of their training for overseas assignments. Bernard Isautier, president and CEO of Canadian Occidental Petroleum Ltd., believes that understanding and communication are two keys to success with workplace diversity, which is an essential ingredient for success in international markets.[21]

Alternate Example
Workshops in diversity awareness are among the hottest workshops in the corporate world. One popular exercise is the reverse fishbowl. For example, twelve men from Johnson & Johnson pretended to be women and discussed the difficulties they experienced in their organization. "You feel guilty, frustrated, exhilarated. But you get to communicate at a different level." Source: E. Ehrlich, "Anger, Shouting, and Sometimes Tears," *Business Week*, 6 August 1990, 55.

Language

Language is a central element in communication. It may pose a barrier if its use obscures meaning and distorts intent. Although English is the international language of aviation, it is not the international language of business. Where the native languages of supervisors and employees differ, the risk of barriers to communication exists. Less obvious are subtle distinctions in dialects within the same language, which may cause confusion and miscommunication. For example, the word *lift* means an elevator in Great Britain and a ride in the United States. In a different vein, there are language barriers created across disciplines and professional boundaries by technical terminology. Acronyms may be very useful to those on the inside of a profession or discipline as means of shorthand communication. Technical terms can convey precise meaning between professionals. However, acronyms and technical terms may only serve to confuse, obscure, and derail any attempt at clear understanding for people unfamiliar with their meaning and usage. For example, clinical depression has meaning to a professional psychologist and may have a wide range of meanings to a layperson. Use simple, direct, declarative language. Speak in brief sentences and use terms or words you have heard from your audience. As much as possible, speak in the language of the listener. Do not use jargon or technical language except with those who clearly understand it.

Defensive and Nondefensive Communication

defensive communication

Communication that can be aggressive, attacking and angry, or passive and withdrawing.

nondefensive communication

Communication that is assertive, direct, and powerful.

■ Defensive communication in organizations also can create barriers between people, whereas nondefensive communication helps open up relationships.[22] **Defensive communication** includes both aggressive, attacking, angry communication and passive, withdrawing communication. **Nondefensive communication** is an assertive, direct, powerful form of communication. It is an alternative to defensive communication. Organizations are increasingly engaged in courtroom battles and media exchanges, which are especially fertile settings for defensive communication. Catherine Crier had extensive experience in dealing with defensive people as a trial lawyer and judge. She carried this knowledge over into her position as a news anchor for CNN and then ABC. Her four basic rules are: (1) define the situation; (2) clarify the person's position; (3) acknowledge the person's feelings; and (4) bring the focus back to the facts.

Defensive communication in organizations leads to a wide range of problems, including injured feelings, communication breakdowns, alienation in working relationships, destructive and retaliatory behaviors, nonproductive efforts, and problem-solving failures. When such problems arise in organizations, everyone is prone to blame everyone else for what is not working.[23] The defensive responses of counterattack or sheepish withdrawal derail communication. Such responses tend to lend heat, not light, to the communication. An examination of eight defensive tactics follows the discussion of the two basic patterns of defensiveness in the next section.

Nondefensive communication, in contrast, provides a basis for asserting and defending oneself when attacked, without being defensive. There are appropriate ways to defend oneself against aggression, attack, or abuse. An assertive, nondefensive style restores order, balance, and effectiveness in working relationships. A discussion of nondefensive communication follows the discussion of defensive communication.

Defensive Communication at Work

Defensive communication often elicits defensive communication in response. The two basic patterns of defensiveness are dominant defensiveness and subordinate defensiveness. One must be able to recognize various forms of defensive communication before learning to engage in constructive, nondefensive communication. Challenge 8.2 on page 234–235 helps you examine your defensive communication. Complete it before reading the following text material.

Discussion Consideration
Ask students to think of the most recent defensive communication problem they have dealt with. How did they handle it?

SUBORDINATE DEFENSIVENESS Subordinate defensiveness is characterized by passive, submissive, withdrawing behavior. The psychological attitude of the subordinately defensive person is, "You are right, and I am wrong." People with low self-esteem may be prone to this form of defensive behavior, as well as people at lower organizational levels. When people at lower organizational levels fear sending bad news up the organization, information that is sensitive and critical to organizational performance may be lost.[24] People who are subordinately defensive do not adequately assert their thoughts and feelings in the workplace. Passive-aggressive behavior is a form of defensiveness that begins as subordinate defensiveness and ends up as dominant defensiveness. It is behavior that appears very passive but, in fact, masks underlying aggression and hostility.

DOMINANT DEFENSIVENESS Dominant defensiveness is characterized by active, aggressive, attacking behavior. It is offensive in nature: "The best defense is a good offense." The psychological attitude of the dominantly defensive person is, "I am right, and you are wrong." People who compensate for low self-esteem may exhibit this pattern of behavior, as well as people who are in higher-level positions within the organizational hierarchy.

Junior officers in a regional banking organization described such behavior in the bank chairman, euphemistically called "The Finger." When giving orders or admonishing someone, he would point his index finger in a domineering, intimidating, emphatic manner that caused defensiveness on the part of the recipient.

Defensive Tactics

Unfortunately, defensive tactics are all too common in work organizations. Eight major defensive tactics are summarized in Table 8.2. They might be best understood in the context of a work situation: Joe is in the process of completing a critical report for his boss, and the report's deadline is drawing near. Mary, one of Joe's peers at work, is to provide him with some input for the report, and the department secretary is to prepare a final copy of the report. Each work example in the table is related to this situation.

Points to Emphasize
Individuals who do not want to relinquish their turn in talking to other people never put periods at the end of their sentences. In this way, they are able to control the conversation and responses. These individuals may also interrupt responses that disagree with their position.

Until defensiveness and defensive tactics are recognized for what they are, it is difficult either to change them or to respond to them in nondefensive ways. Defensive tactics are how defensive communication is acted out. In many cases, such tactics raise ethical dilemmas and issues for those involved. For example, is it ethical to raise doubts about another person's values, beliefs, or sexuality? At what point does simple defensiveness become unethical behavior?

Power plays are used by people to control and manipulate others through the use of choice definition (defining the choice another person is allowed to make),

TABLE 8.2

Defensive Tactics

DEFENSIVE TACTIC	SPEAKER	WORK EXAMPLE
Power play	The boss	"Finish this report by month's end or lose your promotion."
Put-down	The boss	"A capable manager would already be done with this report."
Labeling	The boss	"You must be a slow learner. Your report is still not done?"
Raising doubts	The boss	"How can I trust you, Joe, if you can't finish an easy report?"
Misleading information	Joe	"Mary has not gone over with me the information I need from her for the report." (She left him a copy.)
Scapegoating	Joe	"Mary did not give me her input until just today."
Hostile jokes	Joe	"You can't be serious! The report isn't that important."
Deception	Joe	"I gave it to the secretary. Did she lose it?"

CHALLENGE

■ 8.2

What Kind of a Defender Are You?

Not all of our communication is defensive, but each of us has a tendency to engage in either subordinate or dominant defensiveness. The following table presents twelve sets of choices that will help you see whether you tend to be more subordinate or dominant when you communicate defensively.

Complete the questionnaire by allocating 10 points between the two alternatives in each of the twelve rows. For example, if you never ask permission when it is not needed, but you do give or deny permission frequently, you may give yourself 0 and 10 points, respectively, in the third row. However, if you do each of these behaviors about equally, though at different times, you may want to give yourself 5 points for each alternative.

Add your total points for each column. Whichever number is larger identifies your defensive style.

continued on next page

either/or conditions, and overt aggression. The underlying dynamic in power plays is that of domination and control.

A put-down is an effort by the speaker to gain the upper hand in the relationship. Intentionally ignoring another person or pointing out his or her mistakes in a meeting are kinds of put-downs.

Labeling is often used to portray another person as abnormal or deficient. Psychological labels are often used out of context for this purpose, such as calling a person "paranoid," a word that has a specific, clinical meaning.

Raising doubts about a person's abilities, values, preferential orientations, or other aspects of his or her life creates confusion and uncertainty. This tactic tends to lack the specificity and clarity present in labeling.

Giving misleading information is the selective presentation of information designed to leave a false and inaccurate impression in the listener's mind. It is not the same as lying or misinforming. Giving misleading information is one form of deception.

Scapegoating and its companion, buck-passing, are methods of shifting responsibility to the wrong person. Blaming other people is another form of scapegoating or buck-passing.

Hostile jokes should not be confused with good humor, which is both therapeutic and nondefensive. Jokes created at the expense of others are destructive and hostile.

Deception may occur through a variety of means, such as lying or creating an impression or image that is at variance with the truth. Deception can be very useful in military operations, but it can be a destructive force in work organizations.

Nondefensive Communication

Nondefensive communication is a constructive, healthy alternative to defensive communication in working relationships. The person who communicates nondefensively may be characterized as centered, assertive, controlled, informative, realistic, and honest. Nondefensive communication is powerful, because the speaker is exhibiting self-control and self-possession without rejecting the listener. Converting defensive patterns of communication to nondefensive ones is not difficult. It merely takes the awareness and recognition that alternatives to defensiveness exist.

CHALLENGE

■ 8.2 continued

SUBORDINATE DEFENSIVENESS	DOMINANT DEFENSIVENESS
__ Explain, prove, justify your actions, ideas, or feelings more than is required for results wanted.	__ Prove that you're right. *I told you so.* *Now see, that proves my point.*
__ Ask why things are done the way they are, when your really want to change them. *Why don't they . . . ?*	__ Give patient explanations but few answers. *It's always been done this way.* *We tried that before, but . . .*
__ Ask permissions when not needed. *Is it okay with you if . . . ?*	__ Give or deny permission. *Oh, I couldn't let you do that.*
__ Give away decisions, ideas, or power when it would be appropriate to claim them as your own. *Don't you think that . . . ?*	__ Make decisions or take power as your natural right. *The best way to do it is . . .* *Don't argue, just do as I say.*
__ Apologize, feel inadequate, say *I'm sorry* when you're not.	__ Prod people to get the job done. *Don't just stand there . . .*
__ Submit or withdraw when it's not in your best interest. *Whatever you say . . .*	__ Take over a situation or decision even when it's delegated; get arbitrary. *My mind is made up.*
__ Lose your cool, lash out, cry, where it's inappropriate (turning your anger toward yourself).	__ Lose your cool, yell, pound the desk, where it's inappropriate (turning your anger toward others.).
__ Go blank, click off, be at a loss for words just when you want to have a ready response. *I should've said . . .* (afterwards)	__ Shift responsibility for something you should have taken care of yourself. *You've always done it before.* *What're you all of a sudden upset for now?*
__ Use coping humor, hostile jocularity, or put yourself down when "buying time" or honest feedback would get better results. *Why don't you lay off?*	__ Use coping humor, baiting, teasing, hostile jocularity, mimicry—to keep other people off balance so you don't have to deal with them. *What's the matter, can't you take it?*
__ Use self-deprecating adjectives and reactive verbs. *I'm just a . . .* *I'm just doing what I was told.*	__ Impress others with how many important people you know. *The other night at Bigname's party when I was talking to . . .*
__ Use the general *you* and *they* when *I* and personal names would state the situation more clearly. *They really hassle you here.*	__ Don't listen: interpret. Catch the idea of what they're saying, then list rebuttals or redefine their point. *Now what you* really mean *is . . .*
__ Smile to cover up feelings or put yourself down since you don't know what else to do and it's *nice.*	__ Use verbal dominance, if necessary, to make your point. Don't let anyone interrupt what you have to say.
__ TOTAL Subordinate Points	__ TOTAL Dominant Points

The subordinately defensive person needs to learn to be more assertive. This may be done in many ways, of which two examples follow. First, instead of asking for permission to do something, report what you intend to do, and invite confirmation. Second, instead of using self-deprecating words, such as "I'm just following orders," drop the *just,* and convert the message into a self-assertive, declarative statement. Nondefensive communication should be self-affirming without being self-aggrandizing. Some people overcompensate for subordinate defensiveness and inadvertently become domineering.

The person prone to be domineering and dominantly defensive needs to learn to be less aggressive. This may be especially difficult because it requires overcoming the person's sense of "I am right." People who are working to overcome dominant defensiveness should be particularly sensitive to feedback from others about their behavior. There are many ways to change this pattern of behavior. Here are two examples. First, instead of giving and denying permission, give people free rein except in situations where permission is essential as a means of clearing approval or ensuring the security of the task. Second, instead of becoming inappropriately angry, provide information about the adverse consequences of a particular course of action.

Nonverbal Communication

nonverbal communication
All elements of communication that do not involve words.

■ Much defensive and nondefensive communication focuses on the language used. However, most of the meaning in a message (an estimated 65 to 90 percent) is conveyed through nonverbal communication.[25] **Nonverbal communication** includes all elements of communication, such as gestures and the use of space, that do not involve words or do not involve language.[26] The four basic kinds of nonverbal communication are proxemics, kinesics, facial and eye behavior, and paralanguage. They are important topics for managers attempting to understand the types and meanings of nonverbal signals from employees.

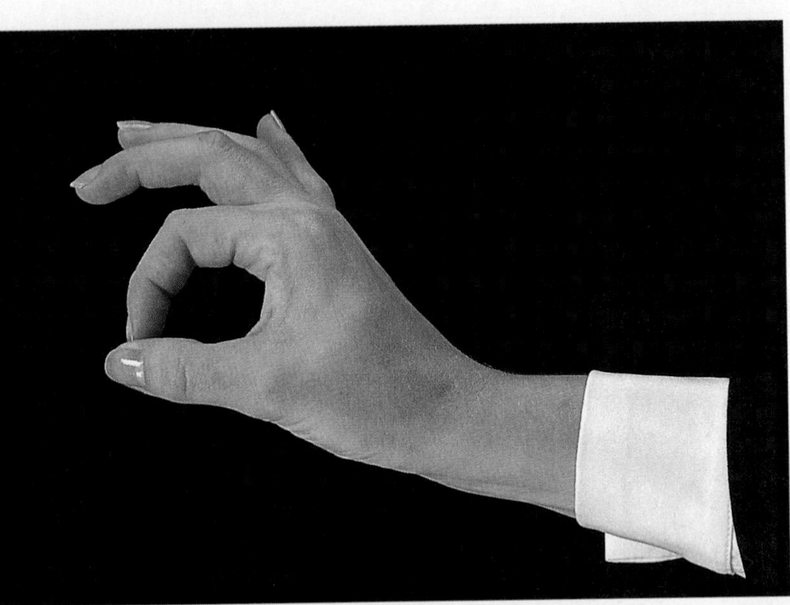

A common affirmation and sign for OK in America, this nonverbal gesture may be an insult to some from other cultures. Gestures, as well as verbal language, must be understood in the context of culture.

Some scholars consider this area of communication to be less scientifically rigorous than other areas of communication. In any case, the interpretation of nonverbal communication is specific to the context of the interaction and the actors. That is, nonverbal cues only give meaning in the context of the situation and the interaction of the actors. It is also important to note that nonverbal behavior is culturally bound. Gestures, facial expressions, and body locations have different meanings in different cultures. The globalization of business means managers should be sensitive to the nonverbal customs of other cultures in which they do business.

Proxemics

Discussion Consideration
Ask students to identify situations in which the verbal message they received was not in congruence with the nonverbal message. Good communicators work hard to send congruent messages.

The study of an individual's perception and use of space, including territorial space, is called *proxemics.*[27] *Territorial space* refers to bands of space extending outward from the body. These bands constitute comfort zones. In each comfort zone, different cultures prefer different types of interaction with others. Figure 8.2 presents four zones of territorial space based on U.S. culture.

The first zone, intimate space, extends outward from the body to about 1½ feet. In this zone, we interact with spouses, significant others, family members,

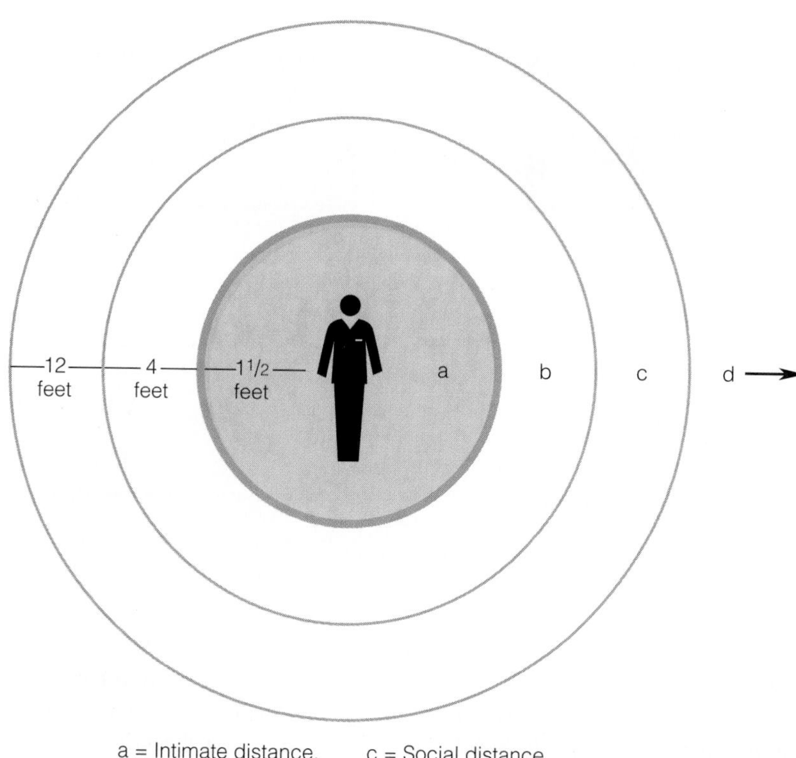

■ **FIGURE 8.2**

Zones of Territorial Space in U.S. Culture

and others with whom we have an intimate relationship. The next zone, the personal distance zone, extends from 1½ feet outward to 4 feet. Friends typically interact within this distance. The third zone, the social distance zone, spans the distance from 4 to 12 feet. We prefer that business associates and acquaintances interact with us in this zone. The final zone is the public distance zone, extending 12 feet from the body outward. Most of us prefer that strangers stay at least 12 feet from us, and we become uncomfortable when they move closer.

Alternate Example
People readily learn the unspoken rules of communication of their society. For example, if there is only one other person on an elevator when you are expected to go to the opposite side of the elevator. If someone violates this norm, you are immediately uncomfortable. Yet, in other cultures, it would be normal to stand at the back of the elevator first, expecting the elevator to fill up.

Territorial space varies greatly across cultures. People often become uncomfortable when operating in territorial spaces different from those in which they are familiar. Edward Hall, a leading proxemics researcher, says Americans working in the Middle East tend to back away to a comfortable conversation distance when interacting with Arabs. Because Arabs's comfortable conversation distance is closer than Americans's, Arabs perceive Americans as cold and aloof. One Arab wondered, "What's the matter? Does he find me somehow offensive?" [28] Personal space tends to be larger in cultures with cool climates, such as the United States, Great Britain, and northern Europe, and smaller in cultures with warm climates, such as southern Europe, the Caribbean, India, or South America.[29]

Our relationships shape our use of territorial space. For example, we hold hands with, or put an arm around, significant others to pull them into intimate space. Conversely, the use of territorial space can shape people's interactions. A 4-foot-wide business desk pushes business interactions into the social distance zone. An exception occurred for one Southwestern Bell manager who met with her seven first-line supervisors around her desk. Being elbow to elbow placed the supervisors in one another's intimate and personal space. They appeared to act more like friends and frequently talked about their children, favorite television shows, and other personal concerns. When the manager moved the staff meeting to a larger room and the spaces around each supervisor were in the social distance zone, the personal exchanges ceased, and they acted more like business associates again.

http://www.swbell.com/

FIGURE 8.3
Seating Dynamics

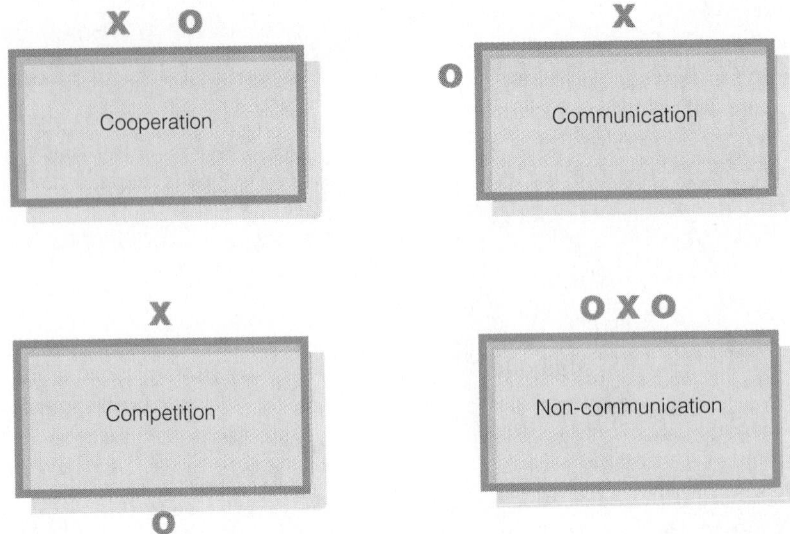

Seating dynamics, another aspect of proxemics, is the art of seating people in certain positions according to the person's purpose in communication. Figure 8.3 depicts some common seating dynamics. To encourage cooperation, you should seat the other party beside you, facing the same direction. To facilitate direct and open communication, seat the other party across a corner of your desk from you or in another place where you will be at right angles. This allows for more honest disclosure. To take a competitive stand with someone, position the person directly across from you. Suppose you hold a meeting around a conference table, and two of the attendees are disrupting your meeting. Where should you seat them? If you place one on each side of yourself, it should stifle the disruptions (unless one is so bold as to lean in front of you to keep chatting).

Kinesics

Kinesics is the study of body movements, including posture.[30] Like proxemics, kinesics is culturally bound; there is no single universal gesture. For example, the U.S. hand signal for "okay" is an insult in other countries. With this in mind, we can interpret some common U.S. gestures. Rubbing one's hands together or exhibiting a sharp intake of breath indicates anticipation. Stress is indicated by a closed hand position (that is, tight fists), hand wringing, or rubbing the temples. Nervousness may be exhibited through drumming fingers, pacing, or jingling coins in the pocket. Perhaps most fun to watch is preening behavior, seen most often in couples on a first date. Preening communicates "I want to look good for you" to the other party and consists of smoothing skirts, straightening the tie, or arranging the hair. No discussion of gestures would be complete without mention of insult gestures—some learned at an early age, much to the anxiety of parents. Sticking out one's tongue and waving fingers with one's thumbs in the ears is a childhood insult gesture.

Facial and Eye Behavior

The face is a rich source of nonverbal communication. Facial expression and eye behavior are used to add cues for the receiver. The face often gives unintended clues to emotions the sender is trying to hide.

Although smiles have universal meaning, frowns, raised eyebrows, and wrinkled foreheads must all be interpreted in conjunction with the actors, the situation, and the culture. One study of Japanese and U.S. students illustrates the point. The students were shown a stress-inducing film, and their facial expressions were videotaped. When alone, the students had almost identical expressions. However, the Japanese students masked their facial expressions of unpleasant feelings much better than did the American students when another person was present.[31]

As mentioned earlier, eye contact can enhance reflective listening, and it varies by culture. A direct gaze indicates honesty and forthrightness in the United States. This may not be true in other cultures. For example, Barbara Walters was uncomfortable interviewing Muammar al-Qaddafi in Libya because he did not look directly at her. However, in Libya, it is a serious offense to look directly at a woman.[32] In Asian cultures it is considered good behavior to bow the head in deference to a superior rather than to look in the supervisor's eyes.

Paralanguage

Paralanguage consists of variations in speech, such as pitch, loudness, tempo, tone, duration, laughing, and crying.[33] People make attributions about the sender by deciphering paralanguage cues. A high-pitched, breathy voice in a female may contribute to the stereotype of the "dumb blonde." Rapid, loud speech may be taken as a sign of nervousness or anger. Interruptions such as "mmm" and "ah-hah" may be used to speed up the speaker so that the receiver can get in a few words. Clucking of the tongue or the "tsk-tsk" sound is used to shame someone. All these cues relate to how something is said.

How Accurately Do We Decode Nonverbal Cues?

Peoples' confidence in their ability to decode nonverbal communication is greater than their accuracy in doing so. Judges with several years' experience in interviewing were asked in one study to watch videotapes of job applicants and to rate the applicants' social skills and motivation levels.[34] The judges were fairly accurate about the social skills, but not about motivation. The judges relied on smiling, gesturing, and speaking as cues to motivation, yet none of these cues are motivation indicators. Thus, incorrectly interpreting nonverbal codes leads to inaccuracy.

Studies of deception emphasize how to use nonverbal cues to interpret whether someone is lying. In one simulation study, customers were asked to detect whether or not automobile salespeople were lying. The customers' ability to detect lies in this study was no better than chance. Does this suggest that salespeople are skilled deceivers who control nonverbal behaviors to prevent detection? [35]

Paul Ekman, a psychologist who has trained judges, Secret Service agents, and polygraphers to detect lies, says that the best way to detect lies is to look for inconsistencies in the nonverbal cues. Rapidly shifting facial expressions and discrepancies between the person's words and body, voice, or facial expressions are some clues.[36]

Nonverbal communication is important for managers because of its impact on the meaning of the message. However, a manager must consider the total message and all media of communication. A message can only be given meaning in context, and cues are easy to misinterpret. Table 8.3 presents common nonverbal behaviors exhibited by managers and how employees may interpret them. Nonverbal cues can give others the wrong signal.

Communicating through New Technologies

■ Nonverbal behaviors can be important in establishing trust in working relationships, but modern technologies may challenge our ability to maintain trust in relationships. New technologies are an essential feature of modern management, as we saw in the Opening Spotlight with the experience of Chaparral

■ **TABLE 8.3**

Common Nonverbal Cues from Manager to Employee

NONVERBAL COMMUNICATION	SIGNAL RECEIVED	REACTION FROM RECEIVER
Manager looks away when talking to the employee	Divided attention	My supervisor is too busy to listen to my problem or simply does not care.
Manager fails to acknowledge greeting from fellow employee.	Unfriendliness.	This person is unapproachable.
Manager glares ominously (i.e., gives the evil eye).	Anger.	Reciprocal anger, fear, or avoidance, depending on who is sending the signal in the organization.
Manager rolls the eyes.	Not taking person seriously.	This person thinks he or she is smarter or better than I am.
Manager sighs deeply.	Disgust or displeasure.	My opinions do not count. I must be stupid or boring to this person.
Manager uses heavy breathing (sometimes accompanied by hand waving).	Anger or heavy stress.	Avoid this person at all costs.
Manager does not maintain eye contact when communicating.	Suspicion or uncertainty.	What does this person have to hide?
Manager crosses arms and leans away.	Apathy or closed-mindedness.	This person already has made up his or her mind; my opinions are not important.
Manager peers over glasses.	Skepticism or distrust.	He or she does not believe what I am saying.
Manager continues to read a report when employee is speaking.	Lack of interest.	My opinions are not important enough to get the supervisor's undivided attention.

SOURCE: "Steps to Better Listening," by C. Hamilton and B. H. Kleiner, © February 1987. Reprinted with permission, *Personnel Journal*, all rights reserved.

Steel. Many organizations around the world are now plugging into the Internet, an electronic and computer-based technology that allows for the easy transfer of information and data across continents. The accompanying Organizational Reality feature is about the Internet in China.

Managers in today's business world have access to more communication tools than ever before. An understanding of the use of these new technologies will influence effective, successful communication during the 1990s and beyond. In addition, it is important to understand how these new technologies affect others' communication and behavior.

ORGANIZATIONAL REALITY

Beijing's Version of the Internet

China Internet Corp. is a small Hong Kong company run by James Chu, a computer scientist educated at UCLA. Mr. Chu is being financially and morally backed by Xinhua New Agency, the official news agency of the People's Republic of China. As the Internet soared globally through cyberspace, slicing across international boundaries, the Chinese became seriously concerned about the insidious threat of barbaric information. Hence, the recruitment of the China Internet Corp. to help screen out undesirable information while keeping what is good on the Internet.

Mr. Chu is pioneering the "intranet," which is an insulated, though not isolated, corner in cyberspace. He is doing this by working to create a for-profit network within the Internet. China Internet Corp.'s ultimate success remains to be seen.

Beijing lives with a real paradox as it seeks to advance in the age of information and communication. On the one hand, it actively seeks out the very latest computer and information hardware, such as in biofeedback equipment for stress management and computers for information processing. On the other hand, it appears almost to avoid the software which is the powerful platform for the Internet. Mr. Chu is attempting to help China live with this paradox by allowing in only what Beijing considers desirable while firewalling that which Beijing considers undesirable. ■

SOURCE: J. Kahn, K. Chen, and M. W. Brauchli, "Chinese Firewall: Beijing Seeks to Build Version of the Internet That Can be Censored," *Wall Street Journal*, January 31, 1996: A1, A6.

The Hong Kong skyline at night is a symbol of advanced technology in the ancient world of the Orient. Beijing would like to control the impact of modern Hong Kong on mainland China, yet is challenged to do so by modern communication technologies.

Written Communication

In the Opening Spotlight, we saw how Chaparral Steel attempted to use new technologies to create a paperless interface with its customers. Some written communication was still required, however. Forms are one category of written communication. Manuals are another. Policy manuals are important in organizations, because they set out guidelines for decision making and rules of actions for organizational members. Operations and procedures manuals explain how to perform various tasks and resolve problems that may occur at work. Reports are a third category of written communication; company annual reports are an example. Reports may summarize the results of a committee's or department's work or provide information on progress toward certain objectives.

Letters and memorandums are briefer, more frequently used categories of written communication in organizations. Letters are a formal means of communication—often with people outside the organization—and may vary substantially in length. Memorandums are another formal means of communication, often to constituencies within the organization. Memos are sometimes used to create a formal, historical record of a specific event or occurrence to which people in the organization may want to refer at some future date. Referring back to Table 8.1, we can conclude that written communication has the advantage of high to moderate data capacity and the possible disadvantage of moderate to low information richness.

Communication Technologies

Computer-mediated communication was once used only by technical specialists but now influences virtually all managers' behavior in the work environment. Informational databases, such as the one in the Opening Spotlight that Chaparral Steel's customers use, are becoming more commonplace. These databases provide a tremendous amount of information with the push of a button. Another example of an informational database is the type of system used in many university libraries, in which books and journals are available through an electronic card catalog.

Electronic mail systems represent another technology; users can leave messages via the computer to be accessed at any time by the receiver. This eliminates the time delay of regular mail and allows for immediate reply. The Internet system is an information network system that links people from many organizations together.

Alternate Example
Roger Ebert, the film reviewer, uses E-mail for his reviews to save time and money. He sends his reviews simultaneously to newspapers across the country. Although faxes are quick and efficient, they do not provide the same level of privacy that E-mail does.

Voice mail systems are another widely used communication mode, especially in sales jobs where people are away from the office. Some voice mail systems even allow the user to retrieve messages from remote locations. Timely retrieval of messages is important. One manager in the office furniture industry had a problem with her voice mail when first learning to use it. She would forget to check it until late in the day. Employees with problems early in the day felt frustrated with her slow response time. When using voice mail, it is important to remember that the receiver may not retrieve the messages in a timely manner. Urgent messages must be delivered directly.

Facsimile (fax) machine systems allow the immediate transmission of documents. This medium allows the sender to communicate facts, graphs, and illustrations very rapidly. Fax machines are used in cars, as well as offices and remote locations.

Car phones are also becoming more commonplace. These permit communication while away from the office and on the commute to and from work. They are used extensively in sales jobs involving travel. Not all reactions to car phones are positive. For example, one oil producer did not want his thinking time while driving disturbed by a car phone.

How Do Communication Technologies Affect Behavior?

new communication technology
The various new technologies—such as electronic mail, voice mail, and fax machines—which are used for interpersonal communication.

The **new communication technologies** provide faster, more immediate access to information than was available in the past. They provide instant exchange of information in minutes or seconds across geographic boundaries and time zones. Schedules and office hours become irrelevant. The normal considerations of time and distance becomes less important in the exchange. Hence, these technologies have important influences on people's behavior.

One aspect of computer-mediated communication is its impersonal nature. The sender interacts with a machine, not a person. Studies show that using these technologies results in an increase in flaming, or making rude or obscene outbursts by computer.[37] Interpersonal skills like tact and graciousness diminish, and managers are more blunt when using electronic media. People who participate in discussions quietly and politely when face to face may become impolite, more intimate, and uninhibited when they communicate using computer conferencing or electronic mail.[38]

Another effect of the new technologies is that the nonverbal cues we rely on to decipher a message are absent. Gesturing, touching, facial expressions, and eye contact are not available, so the emotional element of the message is difficult to access. In addition, clues to power, such as organizational position and departmental membership, may not be available, so the social context of the exchange is altered.

Communication via technologies also changes group interaction. It tends to equalize participation, because group members participate more equally, and charismatic or higher-status members may have less power.[39] Studies of groups that make decisions via computer interaction (computer-mediated groups) have shown that the computer-mediated groups took longer to reach consensus than face-to-face groups. In addition, they were more uninhibited, and there was less influence from any one dominant person. It appears that groups that communicate by computer experience a breakdown of social and organizational barriers.

The potential for overload is particularly great with the new communication technologies. Not only is information available more quickly; the sheer volume of information at the manager's fingertips also is staggering. An individual can easily become overwhelmed by information and must learn to be selective about the information accessed.

The previous Organizational Reality feature about the China Internet Corp. illustrates one paradox of communication technology. Another paradox lies in the danger modern communication technology may pose for managers. The danger is that managers cannot get away from the office as much as in the past, because they are more accessible to coworkers, subordinates, and the boss via telecommunications. Interactions are no longer confined to the 8:00 to 5:00 work hours.

In addition, the use of new technologies encourages polyphasic activity (that is, doing more than one thing at a time).[40] Managers can simultaneously make phone calls, send computer messages, and work on memos. Polyphasic activity has its advantages in terms of getting more done—but only up to a point. Paying attention to more than one task at a time splits a person's attention and may reduce effectiveness. Constantly focusing on multiple tasks can become a habit, making it psychologically difficult for a person to let go of work.

Finally, the new technologies may make people less patient with face-to-face communication. The speed advantage of the electronic media may translate into an expectation of greater speed in all forms of communication. However, individuals may miss the social interaction with others and may find their social needs unmet. Communicating via computer means an absence of small talk; people tend to get to the point right away.

With many of these technologies, the potential for immediate feedback is reduced, and the exchange can become one way. Managers can use the new technologies more effectively by keeping the following hints in mind:

1. Strive for completeness in your message.
2. Build in opportunities for feedback.
3. Do not assume you will get an immediate response.
4. Ask yourself if the communication is really necessary.
5. "Disconnect" yourself from the technology at regular intervals.
6. Provide opportunities for social interaction at work.

Managerial Implications: Communication with Strength and Clarity

■ Interpersonal communication has important implications for the quality of working relationships in organizations. Managers who are sensitive and responsive in communicating with employees encourage the development of trusting, loyal relationships. Managers and employees alike benefit from secure working relations. Managers who are directive, dictatorial, or overbearing with employees, in contrast, are likely to find such behavior counterproductive, especially in periods of change.

Encouraging feedback and practicing reflective listening skills at work can open up communication channels in the work environment. Open communication benefits decision-making processes, because managers are better informed and more likely to base decisions on complete information. Open communication encourages nondefensive relationships, as opposed to defensive relationships, among people at work. Defensive relationships create problems because of the use of tactics that create conflict and division among people.

Managers benefit from sensitivity to employees' nonverbal behavior and territorial space, recognizing that understanding individual and cultural diversity is important in interpreting a person's nonverbal behavior. Seeking verbal clarification on nonverbal cues improves the accuracy of the communication and helps build trusting relationships. In addition, managers benefit from an awareness of their own nonverbal behaviors. Seeking employee feedback about their own nonverbal behavior helps managers provide a message consistent with their intentions.

Managers may complement good interpersonal contact with the appropriate use of new information technology. New information technologies' high data capacity is an advantage in a global workplace. The high information richness of interpersonal contacts is an advantage in a culturally diverse work force. Therefore, managers benefit from both interpersonal and technological media by treating them as complementary modes of communication, not as substitutes for each other.

CLOSING SPOTLIGHT

Downloading Orders, Dumping Paper, Boosting Productivity, and Saving $18,500 a Year

Chaparral has made progress and seen payoffs. By 1993 over sixty customers had information on their orders downloaded each night into their own systems by the Chaparral staff. Chaparral has been able to dump lots of its paper through its document imaging and other high-tech information advances. Hunton's study (cited in the Opening Spotlight) found an annual savings of $18,500. Better yet, Chaparral was able to boost productivity.

Chaparral is now in the information age, yet sometimes the capabilities of the technology are ahead of people's acceptance of it. As future advances in the technology occur, such as larger computer screens, there is a need for advances in people's attitudes, such as greater trust of people and systems in the absence of a hard copy. Even with advancing information technology, however, the need for interpersonal communication and personal exchange continues. The person cannot and should not be taken out of communication.

Chaparral has learned two lessons from its advances in information technology and communication. First, it is best to move in stages, working out the bugs in implementing new information technologies one stage at a time. Second, there are benefits to involving people in planning and implementation, as Dave Fournie found in the work of his group. Once that is done right, the payoffs will be there, both financially and for people's quality of work life. ■

Chapter Summary

- The perceptual screens of communicators and listeners either help clarify or distort a message that is sent and received. Age, gender, and culture influence the sent and received messages.
- Reflective listening involves affirming contact, paraphrasing what is expressed, clarifying the implicit, reflecting "core" feelings, and using appropriate nonverbal behavior to enhance communication.
- The best supervisors talk easily with different kinds of people, listen empathetically, are generally persuasive and not directive, are sensitive to a person's self-esteem, and are communication minded.
- Physical separation, status differences, gender differences, cultural diversity, and language are potential communication barriers that can be overcome.
- Active or passive defensive communication destroys interpersonal relationships, whereas assertive, nondefensive communication leads to clarity.
- Nonverbal communication includes the use of territorial space, seating arrangements, facial gestures, eye contact, and paralanguage. Nonverbal communication varies by nation and culture around the world.
- New communication technologies include electronic mail, voice mail, fax machines, and car phones. High-tech innovations require high-touch responses.

Key Terms

communication (p. 222)
interpersonal communication (p. 222)
communicator (p. 222)
receiver (p. 222)
perceptual screen (p. 222)
message (p. 223)
feedback loop (p. 223)
language (p. 223)
data (p. 223)
information (p. 223)
richness (p. 223)
reflective listening (p. 223)
two-way communication (p. 226)
one-way communication (p. 226)
barriers to communication (p. 229)
defensive communication (p. 232)
nondefensive communication (p. 232)
nonverbal communication (p. 236)
new communication technology (p. 242)

Review Questions

1. What different components of a person's perceptual screens may distort communication?
2. What are the three defining features of reflective listening?
3. What are the four levels of verbal response in reflective listening?
4. Compare one-way communication and two-way communication.
5. What are the five communication skills of effective supervisors?
6. Describe superior and subordinate defensive communication. Describe nondefensive communication.
7. What four kinds of nonverbal communication are important in interpersonal relationships?
8. What are helpful nonverbal behaviors in the communication process? Unhelpful behaviors?
9. Identify at least five new communication technologies.

Discussion and Communication Questions

1. Who is the best communicator you know? Why do you consider that person to be so?
2. Who is the best listener you have ever known? Describe what that person does that makes him or her so good at listening.
3. What methods have you found most helpful in overcoming barriers to communication that are physical? That are status based? That are cultural? That are linguistic?
4. Who makes you the most defensive when you talk with that person? What does the person do that makes you so defensive or uncomfortable?
5. With whom are you the most comfortable and nondefensive in conversation? What does the person do that makes you so comfortable or nondefensive?
6. What nonverbal behaviors do you find most helpful in others when you are attempting to talk with them? When you try to listen to them?

7. *(communication question)* Identify a person at work or at the university who is difficult to talk to and arrange an interview in which you practice good reflective listening skills. Ask the person questions about a topic in which you think he or she is interested. Pay particular attention to being patient, calm, and nonreactive. After the interview, summarize what you learned.
8. *(communication question)* Go to the library and read about communication problems and barriers. Write a memo categorizing the problems and barriers you find in the current literature (last five years). What changes do organizations or people need to make to solve these problems?
9. *(communication question)* Develop a role playing activity for class that demonstrates defensive (dominant or subordinate) and nondefensive communication. Write brief role descriptions that classmates can act out.
10. *(communication question)* Read everything you can find in the library about a new communication technology. Write a two-page memo summarizing what you have learned and the conclusions you draw about the new technology's advantages and disadvantages.

Ethics Questions

1. Suppose that you have heard informally that one of your best friends at work is going to be fired. Should you tell your friend or not?
2. If you believe that someone you are working with is lying about the work and deceiving your boss, but you do not have clear proof of it, what should you do?
3. Assume you are a good, empathetic listener. Someone at work confides in you concerning wrongdoing, yet does not ask your advice about what to do. Should you tell the person what to do? Encourage the person to confess? Report the person?
4. Should you leave confidential messages on a voice mail system in someone's office because you assume that only that person will listen to the voice mail? Can you be confident about the security of an electronic mail system?

Experiential Exercises

8.1 Communicate, Listen, Understand

The following exercise gives you an opportunity to work within a three-person group to do a communication skill-building exercise. You can learn to apply some of the reflective listening and two-way communication materials from the early sections of the chapter, as well as some of the lessons managing difficult communication in a nondefensive manner.

Step 1. The class is formed into three-person groups and each group designates its members "A," "B," and "C." There will be three 5 to 7 minute conversations among the group members: first, between A and B; second, between B and C; third, between C and A. During each conversation, the non-participating group member is to observe and make notes about two communicating group members.

Step 2. Your instructor will give you a list of controversial topics and ask A to pick a topic. A is then asked to discuss her or his position on this topic, with the rationale for the position, with B. B is to practice reflective listening, and engage in listening checks periodically by paraphrasing what he or she understands to be A's position. C should observe whether B is practicing good listening skills or becoming defensive. C should also observe whether A is becoming dominantly defensive in the communication. This should be a two-way communication.

Step 3. Repeat Step 2 with B as communicator, C as listener, and A as observer.

Step 4. Repeat Step 2 with C as communicator, A as listener, and B as observer.

Step 5. After your instructor has had all groups complete Steps 1 through 4, your three-person group should answer the following questions.

a. *Did either the listener or the communicator become visibly (or internally) angry or upset during the discussion?*

b. *What were the biggest challenges for the listeners in the controversial communication? For the communicator?*

c. *What are the most important skill improvements (e.g., better eye contact or more patience) the listener and communicator could have made to improve the quality of understanding achieved through the communication process?*

8.2 Preparing for an Employment-Selection Interview

The purpose of this exercise is to help you develop guidelines for an employment-selection interview. Employment-selection interviews are one of the more important settings in which supervisors and job candidates use applied communication skills. There is always the potential for defensiveness and confusion as well as lack of complete information exchange in this interview. This exercise allows you to think through ways to maximize the value of an employment-selection interview, whether you are the supervisor or the candidate, so that it is a productive experience based on effective applied communication.

Your instructor will form your class into groups of students. Each group should work through steps 1 and 2 of the exercise.

Step 1. *Guidelines for the Supervisor*
Develop a set of guidelines for the supervisor in preparing for and then conducting an employment-selection interview.
Consider the following questions in developing your guidelines.

a. What should the supervisor do before the interview?
b. How should the supervisor act and behave during the interview?
c. What should the supervisor do after the interview?

Step 2. *Guidelines for the Employee*
Develop another set of guidelines for the employee in preparing for and then being involved in an employment-selection interview.
Consider the following questions in developing your guidelines.

a. What should the employee do before the interview?
b. How should the employee act and behave during the interview?
c. What should the employee do after the interview?

Once each group has developed the two sets of guidelines, the instructor will lead the class in a general discussion in which groups share and compare their guidelines. Consider the following questions during this discussion.

1. What similarities are there among the groups for each set of guidelines?
2. What unique or different guidelines have some of the groups developed?
3. What are essential guidelines for conducting an employment-selection interview?

CASE

Promoting Communication with Groupware: Useful or Useless?[1]

Organizational communication and decision making is being revolutionized with the use of various forms of *groupware*—computer technology that can promote collaborative working relationships and participative decision making. Groupware is "software designed for teams of people working together on shared information." It includes electronic mail, electronic bulletin boards, and electronic meeting systems.

Groupware utilizes the potential of a computer network for facilitating communications and promoting cooperation on interdependent tasks. It enables people to share client information, swap leads, do research, keep abreast of news events, and keep tabs on staff assignments. Groupware can also be used to conduct electronic meetings, develop plans, and build group consensus. For example, the IBM System Strategy and Market Analysis Department in Rochester, Minnesota, uses an electronic meeting system "to assist groups in brainstorming, deciding on priorities, and in creating a consensus on a variety of strategic-related topics" within the company and with different customer groups. This IBM unit is enthusiastic about the benefits that can accrue from using an electronic meeting system. They say that the decision-making process is improved because a wider range of alternatives can be generated, participants' positions can be explored in greater depth, participants are kept "on-task," morale is improved as a result of increased participation, issues are resolved more quickly, and complete documentation of the meeting exists.

Groupware also can be used to promote trust, as Bruce Hasenyager, a senior vice president at Chemical Banking Corp., found in the wake of downsizing, reorganization, and an impending merger with Manufacturers Hanover Trust. Though an electronic bulletin board Hasenyager responded to employees' questions and concerns about these organizational actions. Any employee who was on the office computer network could participate in the discussion of issues of concern. Using this open electronic dialog, Hasenyager effectively countered the rumors regarding these decisions. However, after the merger with Manufacturers Hanover Trust, Hasenyager's successor eliminated the bulletin board when he became uncomfortable with the critical comments being made about management. Such openness and participation seemed to be incompatible with the postmerger corporate culture.

Groupware can have tremendous effects on organizational culture. It can help dissolve hierarchical relationships, thereby promoting the sharing of ideas and encouraging broader input into the decision-making process. Groupware also can promote tensions among people if its usage is incompatible with the ways people relate to one another.

Groupware networks can provide every member of the organization with greater access to information and with greater influence on the decision-making process. However, in companies where information is jealously guarded, employees may be reluctant to share their best ideas in network discussions. For instance, some junior employees at Price Waterhouse—a major accounting firm—"wouldn't share information on the network because of the firm's intensely competitive culture." Knowledge was power, and sharing knowledge meant giving up power—power to influence the decision-making process.

How viable is groupware for a particular organization? Michael Schrage, author of *Shared Minds, the New Technologies of Collaboration*, suggests asking the following diagnostic question: "Does that organization value openness or hierarchy, privacy or sharing, cross-functional collaboration or rigid departmental lines of authority?"

DISCUSSION QUESTIONS

1. What are some of the positive and negative behavioral implications of using modern communications technology like groupware?
2. How might an increasing reliance on groupware influence the usage and development of people's interpersonal communication skills?
3. What advantages and disadvantages seem to be associated with the use of groupware?
4. Why should the use of groupware be tailored to the company's organizational culture?
5. Would you be comfortable in working for an organization that is a heavy user of groupware to communicate, to conduct meetings, and to make decisions? Explain your answer.

SOURCE: This case was written by Michael K. McCuddy, the Louis S. and Mary L. Morgal Professor of Christian Business Ethics, College of Business Administration, Valparaiso University.

1. Adapted from S. Gessner, M. McNeilly, and B. Leskee. "Using Electronic Meeting Systems for Collaborative Planning at IBM Rochester," *Planning Review* (January/February 1994): 34–39; J. R. Wilke, "Getting Together: A New Networking Software—Called Groupware—Promises to Change the Way Many of Us Spend Our Workdays," *The Wall Street Journal*, (April 6, 1992): R8; J. R. Wilke, "Shop Talk: Computer Links Erode Hierarchical Nature of Workplace Culture," *The Wall Street Journal*, (December 9, 1993): A1.

References

1. J. E. Hunton, "Setting Up a Paperless Office," *Journal of Accountancy* 178 (1994): 77–85.
2. D. L. Whetzel, "The Department of Labor Identifies Workplace Skills," *The Industrial/Organizational Psychologist* (July 1991): 89–90.
3. *Richness* is a term originally coined by W. D. Bodensteiner, "Information Channel Utilization under Varying Research and Development Project Conditions" (Ph.D. diss., University of Texas at Austin, 1970).
4. A. G. Athos and J. J. Gabarro, *Interpersonal Behavior: Communication and Understanding in Relationships* (Englewood Cliffs, N.J.: Prentice-Hall, 1978); R. Reik, *Listen with the Third Ear* (New York: Pyramid, 1972).
5. Athos and Gabarro, *Interpersonal Behavior*, 432–438.
6. A. Benjamin, *The Helping Interview* (Boston: Houghton Mifflin, 1969).
7. A. D. Mangelsdorff, "Lessons Learned from the Military: Implications for Management" (Distinguished Visiting Lecture, University of Texas at Arlington, 29 January 1993).
8. F. Luthans, "Successful versus Effective Real Managers," *Academy of Management Executive* 2 (1988): 127–132.
9. L. E. Penley, E. R. Alexander, I. E. Jernigan, and C. I. Henwood, "Communication Abilities of Managers: The Relationship of Performance," *Journal of Management* 17 (1991): 57–76.
10. F. M. Jablin, "Superior-Subordinate Communication: The State of the Art," *Psychological Bulletin* 86 (1979): 1201–1222; W. C. Reddin, *Communication within the Organization: An Interpretive Review of Theory and Research* (New York: Industrial Communication Council, 1972).
11. J. C. Quick, D. L. Nelson, and J. D. Quick, *Stress and Challenge at the Top: The Paradox of the Successful Executive* (Chichester, England: Wiley, 1990).
12. H. Mintzberg, *The Nature of Managerial Work* (Englewood Cliffs, N.J.: Prentice-Hall, 1973), 71–75.
13. J. C. Wofford, E. A. Gerloff, and R. C. Cummins, *Organizational Communication: The Keystone to Managerial Effectiveness* (New York: McGraw-Hill, 1977).
14. E. A. Gerloff and J. C. Quick, "Task Role Ambiguity and Conflict in Supervision-Subordinate Relationships," *Journal of Applied Communication Research* 12 (1984): 90–102.
15. E. H. Schein, "Reassessing the 'Divine Rights' of Managers," *Sloan Management Review* 30 (1989): 63–68.

16. D. Tannen, *That's Not What I Mean! How Conversational Style Makes or Breaks Your Relations with Others* (New York: Morrow, 1986).
17. D. Tannen, *You Just Don't Understand* (New York: Ballentine, 1990).
18. G. Hofstede, *Culture's Consequences: International Differences in Work-Related Values* (Beverly Hills, Calif.: Sage Publications, 1980).
19. G. Hofstede, "Motivation, Leadership, and Organization: Do American Theories Apply Abroad?" *Organizational Dynamics* 9 (1980): 42–63.
20. H. Levinson, *Executive* (Cambridge, Mass.: Harvard University Press, 1981).
21. P. Benimadhu, "Adding Value Through Diversity: An Interview with Bernard F. Isautier," *Canadian Business Review* 22 (1995): 6–11.
22. T. Wells, *Keeping Your Cool under Fire: Communicating Nondefensively* (New York: McGraw-Hill, 1980).
23. R. D. Laing, *The Politics of the Family and Other Essays* (New York: Pantheon, 1971).
24. H. S. Schwartz, *Narcissistic Process and Corporate Decay: The Theory of the Organizational Ideal* (New York: New York University Press, 1990).
25. M. L. Knapp, *Nonverbal Communication in Human Interaction* (New York: Holt, Rinehart & Winston, 1978); J. McCroskey and L. Wheeless, *Introduction to Human Communication* (New York: Allyn & Bacon, 1976).
26. A. M. Katz and V. T. Katz, eds., *Foundations of Nonverbal Communication* (Carbondale, Ill.: Southern Illinois University Press, 1983).
27. E. T. Hall, *The Hidden Dimension* (Garden City, N.Y.: Doubleday Anchor, 1966).
28. E. T. Hall, "Proxemics," in A. M. Katz and V. T. Katz, eds., *Foundations of Nonverbal Communication* (Carbondale, Ill.: Southern Illinois University Press, 1983).
29. R. T. Barker and C. G. Pearce, "The Importance of Proxemics at Work," *Supervisory Management* 35 (1990): 10–11.
30. R. L. Birdwhistell, *Kinesics and Context* (Philadelphia: University of Pennsylvania Press, 1970).
31. P. Ekman and W. V. Friesen, "Research on Facial Expressions of Emotion," in A. M. Katz and V. T. Katz, eds., *Foundations of Nonverbal Communication* (Carbondale, Ill.: Southern Illinois University Press, 1983).
32. C. Barnum and N. Wolniansky, "Taking Cues from Body Language," *Management Review* 78 (1989): 59.
33. Katz and Katz, *Foundations of Nonverbal Communication*, 181.
34. R. Gifford, C. F. Ng, and M. Wilkinson, "Nonverbal Cues in the Employment Interview: Links between Applicant Qualities and Interviewer Judgments," *Journal of Applied Psychology* 70 (1985): 729–736.
35. P. J. DePaulo and B. M. DePaulo, "Can Deception by Salespersons and Customers Be Detected through Nonverbal Behavioral Cues?" *Journal of Applied Social Psychology* 19 (1989): 1552–1577.
36. P. Ekman, *Telling Lies* (New York: Norton, 1985); D. Goleman, "Nonverbal Cues Are Easy to Misinterpret," *New York Times*, 17 September 1991, B5.
37. C. Brod, *Technostress: The Human Cost of the Computer Revolution* (Reading, Mass.: Addison-Wesley, 1984).
38. S. Kiesler, "Technology and the Development of Creative Environments," in Y. Ijiri and R. L. Kuhn, eds, *New Directions in Creative and Innovative Management* (Cambridge, Mass.: Ballinger Press, 1988).
39. S. Kiesler, J. Siegel, and T. W. McGuire, "Social Psychological Aspects of Computer-mediated Communication," *American Psychologist* 39 (1984): 1123–1134.
40. B. A. Baldwin, "Managing the Stress of Technology," *CPA Journal*, October 1990, 94.

CHAPTER 9

Work Teams and Groups

LEARNING OBJECTIVES

After reading this chapter, you should be able to do the following:

- Define *group* and *team.*
- Explain four important aspects of group behavior.
- Describe group formation, the four stages of a group's development, and the characteristics of a mature group.
- Discuss quality circles and quality teams.
- Identify the social benefits of group and team membership.
- Explain the task and maintenance functions in teams.
- Discuss empowerment, teamwork, and self-managed teams.
- Explain the importance of upper echelons and top management teams.

OPENING SPOTLIGHT

Ford's Special Vehicle Team (SVT)

Originally designed in the 1960s, the Ford Mustang became a classic success story in American automotive manufacturing. By the 1980s, though, the Mustang had lost some of its edge. During the 1980s, Ford began a major change effort to reinvent itself as a world leader in automotive design and manufacturing. "Quality is Job 1" became Ford Motor Company's slogan for its new drive for world-class quality. Ford's major change and quality revolution led to improved performance, as well as empowerment, involvement, and teamwork among Ford people.

http://www.ford.com/

The sleek, classic beauty of the 1965 red Ford Mustang has as much power today as it did when it rolled off the assembly line. The story of the Ford Mustang is a story of teamwork and success, yesterday and today.

Ford's Special Vehicle Team (SVT) included team members from manufacturing, design, engineering, and marketing. The team's mission was to produce high-performance, limited-edition specialty models from existing Ford platforms. Ford dealerships would be required to apply for and receive SVT status if they wanted to sell the SVT cars. Each specialty model would get expert treatment at each step in the process, from concept to customer. Ford envisioned avid car enthusiasts as the ultimate customers for its line of specialty models. The SVT shattered functional barriers and integrated new vehicle design, manufacture, and sale. What kind of success, if any, would Ford's SVT Concept enjoy?[1] ■

Lee Iacocca received much of the credit for the design of the first Mustang in 1965, but he reported that the venture was a team effort from the beginning.[2] Thus, Ford's use of the SVT 28 years later was no departure from company precedent. Indeed, it is difficult to imagine any work environment in which teams and groups do not play a vital role.

A **group** is two or more people having common interests or objectives.[3] Table 9.1 summarizes the characteristics of a well-functioning, effective group.[4] A **team** is a small number of people with complementary skills who are committed to a common mission, performance goals, and approach for which they hold themselves mutually accountable.[5] Groups emphasize individual leadership,

group

Two or more people with common interests or objectives.

team

A small number of people with complementary skills who are committed to a common mission, performance goals, and approach for which they hold themselves mutually accountable.

■ **TABLE 9.1**

Characteristics of a Well-Functioning, Effective Group

- The atmosphere tends to be relaxed, comfortable, and informal.
- The group's task is well understood and accepted by the members.
- The members listen well to one another; most members participate in a good deal of task-relevant discussion.
- People express both their feelings and their ideas.
- Conflict and disagreement are present and centered around ideas or methods, not personalities or people.
- The group is aware and conscious of its own operation and function.
- Decisions are usually based on consensus, not majority vote.
- When actions are decided, clear assignments are made and accepted by members of the group.

individual accountability, and individual work products. Teams emphasize shared leadership, mutual accountability, and collective work products.

The chapter begins with a traditional discussion in the first two sections of group behavior and group development. The third section discusses teams. The final two sections explore the contemporary team issues of empowerment, self-managed teams, and upper echelon teams.

Group Behavior

■ Group behavior has been a subject of interest in social psychology for a long time, and many different aspects of group behavior have been studied over the years. We now look at four topics relevant to groups functioning in organizations: norms of behavior, group cohesion, social loafing, and loss of individuality. Group behavior topics related to decision making, such as polarization and groupthink, are addressed in Chapter 10.

Discussion Consideration
Have students give examples of organizations in which they were in a group and those in which they experienced a team organization. Can they pinpoint the difference?

Norms of Behavior

The standards that a work group uses to evaluate the behavior of its members are its **norms of behavior.** These norms may be written or unwritten, verbalized or not verbalized, implicit or explicit. So long as individual members of the group understand the norms, the norms can be effective in influencing behavior. Norms may specify what members of a group should do (such as IBM's dress code of a white shirt and dark business suit), or they may specify what members of a group should not do (such as executives not behaving arrogantly with employees).

norms of behavior
The standards that a work group uses to evaluate the behavior of its members.

Norms may exist in any aspect of work group life. They may evolve informally or unconsciously within a group, or they may arise in response to challenges, such as the norm of disciplined behavior by firefighters in responding to a three-alarm fire to protect the group.[6] Performance norms are among the most important group norms from the organization's perspective, as we discuss in a later section of this chapter. Organizational culture and corporate codes of ethics, such as Johnson & Johnson's credo (see Chapter 2), reflect behavioral norms expected within work groups.

Discussion Consideration
To a certain extent this class is a group. What norms have developed in this class thus far?

Group Cohesion

The "interpersonal glue" that makes the members of a group stick together is **group cohesion.** Group cohesion can enhance job satisfaction for members and improve organizational productivity.[7] Highly cohesive groups at work may not have many interpersonal exchanges away from the workplace. However, they are able to control and manage their membership better than work groups low in cohesion. This is due to the strong motivation in highly cohesive groups to maintain good, close relationships with other members. We examine group cohesion in further detail, along with factors leading to high levels of group cohesion, when discussing the common characteristics of well-developed groups.

group cohesion
The "interpersonal glue" that makes members of a group stick together.

Discussion Consideration
Can groups be too cohesive?

Social Loafing

Social loafing occurs when one or more group members rely on the efforts of other group members and fail to contribute their own time, effort, thoughts, or other resources to a group.[8] This may create a real drag on the group's efforts and achievements. Although some scholars argue that social loafing, or free riding, is rational behavior from the individual's standpoint to restore an experience of inequity or when individual efforts are hard to observe, it nevertheless

social loafing
The failure of a group member to contribute personal time, effort, thoughts, or other resources to the group.

Discussion Consideration
What techniques have students used to reduce social loafing in class project groups? Were they successful? Explain.

shortchanges the group, which loses potentially valuable resources possessed by individual members.[9]

A number of methods for countering social loafing exist, such as having identifiable individual contributions to the group product and member self-evaluation systems. For example, if each group member is responsible for a specific input to the group, a member's failure to contribute will be noticed by everyone. If members must formally evaluate their contributions to the group, they are less likely to loaf.

Loss of Individuality

loss of individuality
A social process in which individual group members lose self-awareness and its accompanying sense of accountability, inhibition, and responsibility for individual behavior.

Social loafing may be detrimental to group achievement, but it does not have the potentially explosive effects of **loss of individuality.** Loss of individuality, or deindividuation, is a social process in which individual group members lose self-awareness and its accompanying sense of accountability, inhibition, and responsibility for individual behavior.[10]

When individuality is lost, people may engage in morally reprehensible acts and even violent behavior as committed members of their group or organization. For example, loss of individuality was one of several contributing factors in the violent and aggressive acts that led to the riot that destroyed Los Angeles following the Rodney King verdict in the early 1990s. However, loss of individuality is not always negative or destructive. The loosening of normal ego control mechanisms in the individual may lead to prosocial behavior and heroic acts in dangerous situations.[11] A group that successfully develops into a mature group may not encounter problems with loss of individuality.

Group Formation and Development

■ After its formation, a group goes through predictable stages of development. If successful, it emerges as a mature group. One logical group development model proposes four stages following the group's formation.[12] These stages are mutual acceptance, decision making, motivation and commitment, and control and sanctions. To become a mature group, each of the stages in development must be successfully negotiated.

According to this group development model, a group addresses three issues: interpersonal issues, task issues, and authority issues.[13] The interpersonal issues include matters of trust, personal comfort, and security. The task issues include the mission or purpose of the group, the methods the group employs, and the outcomes expected of the group. The authority issues include decisions about who is in charge, how power and influence are managed, and who has the right to tell whom to do what. This section addresses group formation, each stage of group development, and the characteristics of a mature group.

Alternate Example
There are ways to enhance the learning process of groups so they will function better and make better decisions. The Diversity Council was designed to recognize the different ways people think and how they might respond to problems. The Council gives advice to companies that are moving toward group goals and want to keep diversity as a priority. SOURCE: L. Reynolds, "Companies Will Work Together on Workforce Diversity," HR Focus, December 1992, 7.

Group Formation

Formal and informal groups form in organizations for different reasons. Formal groups are sometimes called official or assigned groups, and informal groups may be called unofficial or emergent groups. Formal groups gather to perform various tasks and include an executive and staff, standing committees of the board of directors, project task forces, and temporary committees. An example of a formal group is the task force assembled by the Hospital Corporation of America during the mid-1980s to examine the mission of the corporation. Headed by a divisional vice president, the task force was composed of 15 members with wide professional and geographic diversity. The task force met approximately once a month for about nine months to complete its task.

Diversity is an important consideration in the formation of groups. For example, Monsanto Agricultural Company (MAC) created a task force titled Valuing Diversity to address subtle discrimination resulting from work force diversity.[14] The original task force was titled Eliminating Subtle Discrimination (ESD) and was composed of 15 women, minorities, and white males. Subtle discrimination might include the use of gender- or culture-specific language. MAC's and the task force's intent was to build on individual differences—whether in terms of gender, race, or culture—in developing a dominant heterogeneous culture. Education and awareness were key ingredients to an understanding that a diverse workforce can be an advantage, not a liability, for a company.

http://www.monsanto.com/

Ethnic diversity has characterized many industrial work groups in the United States since the 1800s. This was especially true during the early years of the 1900s, when waves of immigrant workers came to the country from Germany, Yugoslavia, Italy, Poland, Scotland, the Scandinavian countries, and many other nations.[15] Organizations were challenged to blend these culturally and linguistically diverse peoples into effective work groups.

In addition to ethnic, gender, and cultural diversity, there is interpersonal diversity. Chaparral Steel Company has a strong, stable team of officers who achieved compatibility through interpersonal diversity. Successful interpersonal relationships are the basis of group effort, a key foundation for business success. A group's interpersonal compatibility may be assessed by examining three interpersonal needs: the need for inclusion, the need for control, and the need for affection.[16] For each need, a person has a level of wanting to be included, controlled, or loved, as well as a level of expressing inclusion, control, or love for others. Therefore, each need has two dimensions. A profile of the wanted (W) and expressed (E) dimensions of these three interpersonal needs was developed for the officers at Chaparral Steel. The results are shown in Figure 9.1 and depict the diversity among the officers in these three needs. Rather than treating these differences as negative, the team members developed an appreciation for their differences and became a stronger team. For example, Libor Rostik and Dennis Beach have strong wanted (W) inclusion needs as shown in Figure 9.1. That is, their Inclusion–W scores are high. Gordon Forward and Dick Jaffee have low inclusion needs. That is, their Inclusion–W scores are low. However, Forward has a moderate expressed (E) inclusion need and he is able to satisfy Rostik and Beach's wanted inclusion needs by involving them in work activities. Rostik and Beach will not satisfy their own strong expressed (E) inclusion need with Forward because of his low wanted (W) inclusion need. Hence, they must satisfy their expressed inclusion needs elsewhere.

Gordon Forward (right) and Dennis Beach (left) present an employee award to Dawn Moore in a Chaparral Steel awards ceremony. The officers and employees alike practice teamwork.

Points to Emphasize
Remind students that the MBTI analysis may help them determine the strengths of a team. For example, if a team is structured with all Introverts or Extraverts, it may need an outside facilitator to help begin its discussions.

Informal groups evolve in the work setting to gratify a variety of member needs not met by formal groups. For example, organizational members' inclusion and affection needs might be satisfied through informal athletic or interest groups. Athletic teams representing a department, unit, or company may achieve semiofficial status, such as the American Airlines long-distance running teams who use the corporate logo on their race shirts.

Stages of Group Development

All groups, formal and informal, go through four stages of development: mutual acceptance, decision making, motivation and commitment, and control and sanctions.

■ **FIGURE 9.1**

Interpersonal Needs of the Chaparral Steel Officers

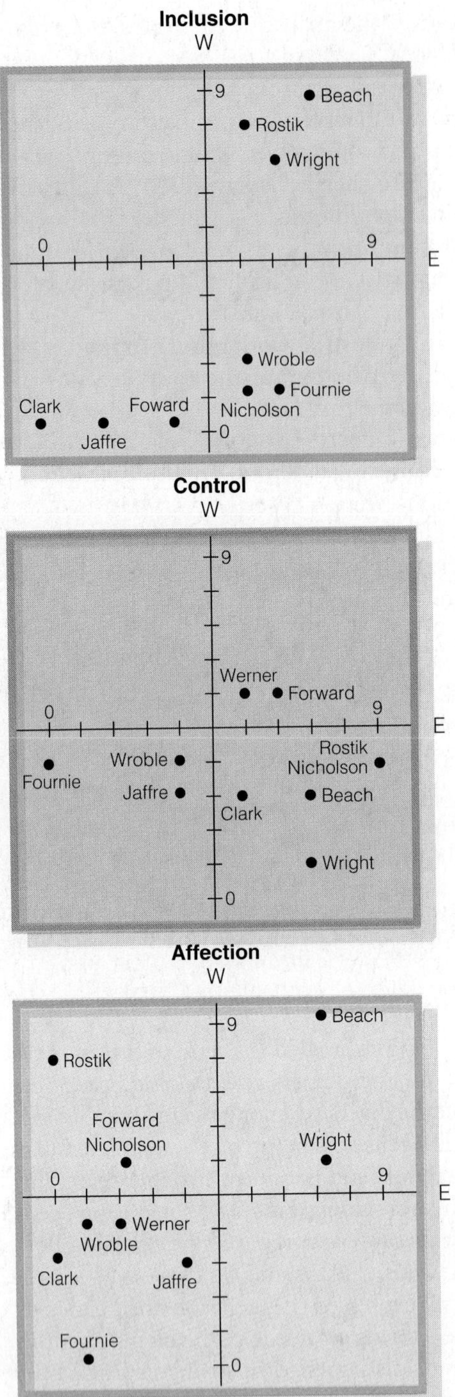

MUTUAL ACCEPTANCE Mutual acceptance is the first stage in a group's development. In this stage, the focus is on the interpersonal relations among the members. Members assess one another with regard to trustworthiness, emotional comfort, and evaluative acceptance. For the Valuing Diversity task force at MAC, trust was one of the early issues to be worked through. The power, influence, and authority issues may also emerge at this point if strong personalities immediately attempt to dominate other group members or dictate the group's agenda. This authority issue is also an interpersonal issue related to trust and acceptance. Once team members establish a comfortable level of mutual trust and acceptance, they can focus their attention on the work of the group.

DECISION MAKING Planning and decision making occur during the second stage of a group's development. The focus turns from interpersonal relations to decision-making activities related to the group's task accomplishment. Specifically, the group must make decisions about what its task is and how to accomplish that task. Wallace Company, an industrial distributor of pipes, valves, and fittings, has found employee teams particularly valuable in this aspect of work life.[17] This second stage may be thought of as the planning stage in a group's development. In addition, the issue of authority often begins to surface during this stage of development, if it did not surface during the first stage. Authority questions the group addresses are ones like these: Who is responsible for what aspects of the group's work? Does the group need one primary leader and spokesperson, or not?

Alternate Example
Many team goals are often focused inward, on the specific work environment. Goal development takes training, and team members need to receive training in problem solving so they can define appropriate goals. SOURCE: H. R. Jessup, "The Road to Results for Teams," *Training and Development*, September, 1992, 67.

http://www.kodak.com

MOTIVATION AND COMMITMENT In the third stage of development, the group has largely resolved the interpersonal and task issues. Member attention is directed to self-motivation and the motivation of other group members for task accomplishment. Some members focus on the task function of initiating activity and ensure that the work of the group really gets moving. Other members contribute to motivation and commitment within the group through maintenance functions such as supporting, encouraging, and recognizing the contributions of their teammates or through establishing the standards that the team may use in evaluating its performance and members.

The latter contribution is illustrated by a 25-member leadership group that monitors "the flow," Eastman Kodak's unique black-and-white film production process named for its layout design. The people who work the flow are called Zebras. With motivation, commitment, and evaluative feedback from the 25-person leadership team, the Zebras substantially enhanced productivity, profitability, and morale.

The emphasis during the motivation and commitment stage of team development is on execution and achievement, whether through a process of questioning and prodding or through facilitation and work load sharing. If key decisions or plans established in the second stage of development need to be revisited, they are. However, this is only done in the context of getting work done.

Runners in the Chemical Bank [now Chase] Corporate Challenge start the race on Park Avenue in New York Saturday, October 9, 1993. Participation in the corporate challenge requires strong motivation and commitment.

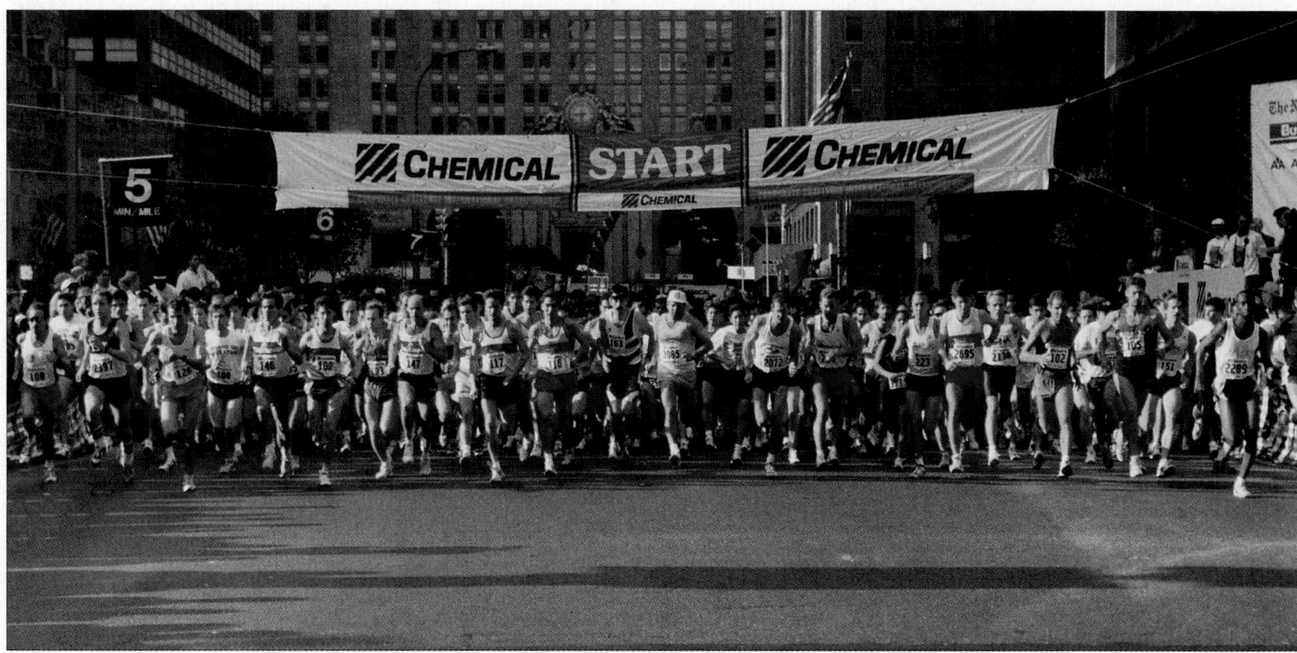

Points to Emphasize
It is important to recognize that groups must develop their own style. This facilitates the development of commitment to goal accomplishment.

Alternate Example
Another model of group development identifies 5 stages: Forming, Storming, Norming, Performing, and Adjourning.

Discussion Consideration
Ask students to reflect on their own experience in a group. Does their experience match the stages of group development portrayed here?

CONTROL AND SANCTIONS In its final stage of development, a group has become a mature, effective, efficient, and productive unit. The group has successfully worked through necessary interpersonal, task, and authority issues. A mature group is characterized by a clear purpose or mission; a well-understood set of norms of behavior; a high level of cohesion; and a clear, but flexible, status structure of leader-follower relationships. A mature group is able to control its members through the judicious application of specific positive and negative sanctions used in response to specific member behaviors. If the group's membership changes, either through a loss of an established member or the inclusion of a newcomer, it may well engage in some activities common in earlier stages of development as it accommodates the newcomer or adjusts to the loss.

Characteristics of a Mature Group

The description of a well-functioning, effective group in Table 9.1 characterizes a mature group. Such a group has four distinguishing characteristics: a clear purpose and mission, well-understood norms and standards of conduct, a high level of group cohesion, and a flexible status structure.

http://www.ibm.com/

PURPOSE AND MISSION The purpose and mission may be assigned to a group (as in the case of Hospital Corporation of America task force's charter to examine the corporate mission) or emerge from within the group (as in the case of the American Airlines long-distance running team). Even in the case of an assigned mission, the group may reexamine, modify, revise, or question the mission. It also may embrace the mission as stated. The importance of mission is exemplified in IBM's Process Quality Management, which requires that a process team of not more than 12 people develop a clear understanding of mission as the first step in the process.[18] The IBM approach demands that all members agree to go in the same direction. The mission statement is converted into a specific agenda, clear goals, and a set of critical success factors. Stating the purpose and mission in the form of specific goals enhances productivity over and above any performance benefits achieved through individual goal setting.[19]

Alternate Example
Connie Gersick has suggested yet another view of group development and performance: punctuated equilibrium. According to this model, groups put forth only a mediocre effort until they reach the halfway point toward a deadline. At this midpoint there is a sharp spike in effort and this increased effort is maintained until the task is completed.

Alternate Example
In most instances, the collective norm has merit over individual ambitions and goals.

BEHAVIORAL NORMS Behavioral norms, which evolve over a period of time, are well-understood standards of behavior within a group.[20] They are benchmarks against which team members are evaluated and judged by other team members. Some behavioral norms become written rules, such as an attendance policy or an ethical code for a team. Other norms remain informal, although they are no less well understood by team members. Dress codes and norms about after-hours socializing may fall in this category. Behavioral norms also evolve around performance and productivity.[21] The group's productivity norm may or may not be consistent with, and supportive of, the organization's productivity standards. A high-performance team sets productivity standards above organizational expectations with the intent to excel. Average teams set productivity standards based upon, and consistent with, organizational expectations. Noncompliant or counterproductive teams may set productivity standards below organizational expectations with the intent of damaging the organization or creating change.

Points to Emphasize
As a group develops and matures, the members often begin to refer to the group as "our group," rather than referring to the group as belonging to the initial leader.

GROUP COHESION Group cohesion was earlier described as the interpersonal attraction binding group members together. It enables a group to exercise effective control over its members in relationship to its behavioral norms and standards. Goal conflict in a group, unpleasant experiences, and domination of a subgroup are among the threats to a group's cohesion. Groups with low levels of cohesion have greater difficulty exercising control over their members and enforcing their standards of behavior. A classic study of cohesiveness in 238

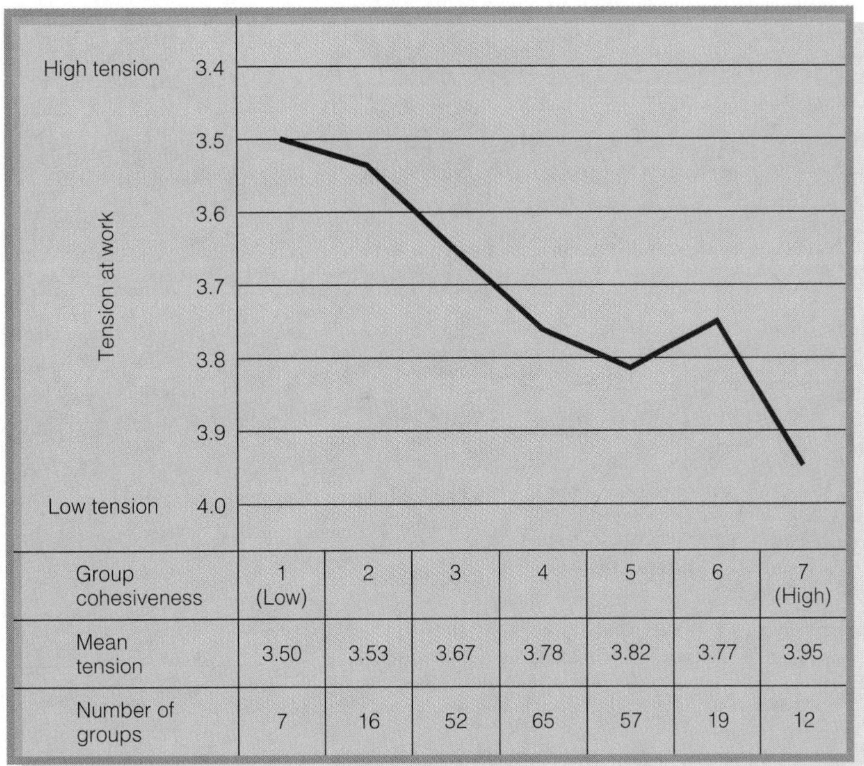

Group cohesiveness	1 (Low)	2	3	4	5	6	7 (High)
Mean tension	3.50	3.53	3.67	3.78	3.82	3.77	3.95
Number of groups	7	16	52	65	57	19	12

Note: Product-moment correlation is .28, and critical ratio is 4.20; p is less than .001.

FIGURE 9.2

Cohesiveness and Work-Related Tension[a]

[a]The measure of tension at work is based on group mean response to the question, "Does your work ever make you feel 'jumpy' or nervous?" A low numerical score represents relatively high tension.

SOURCE: S. E. Seashore, *Group Cohesiveness in the Industrial Work Group* (Ann Arbor, Mich.: University of Michigan, 1954). Research conducted by Stanley E. Seashore at the Institute for Social Research, University of Michigan.

industrial work groups found cohesion to be an important factor influencing anxiety, tension, and productivity within the groups.[22] Specifically, work-related tension and anxiety were lower in teams high in cohesion, and they were higher in teams low in cohesion, as depicted in Figure 9.2. This suggests that cohesion has a calming effect on team members, at least concerning work-related tension and anxiety. In addition, actual productivity was found to vary significantly less in highly cohesive teams, making these teams much more predictable with regard to their productivity. The actual productivity levels were primarily determined by the productivity norms within each work group. That is, highly cohesive groups with high production standards are very productive. Similarly, highly cohesive groups with low productivity standards are unproductive. Member satisfaction, commitment, and communication are better in highly cohesive groups. Groupthink may be a problem in highly cohesive groups and is discussed in Chapter 10. Challenge 9.1 includes the three group cohesion questions from this research project. Complete the Challenge to determine the level of cohesion in a group of which you are a member.

Group cohesion is influenced by a number of factors, most notably time, size, the prestige of the team, external pressure, and internal competition. Group cohesion evolves gradually over time through a group's normal development. Smaller groups—those of 5 or 7 members, for example—are more cohesive than those of over 25, although cohesion does not decline much with size after 40 or more members. Prestige or social status also influences a group's cohesion, with more prestigious groups, such as the U.S. Air Force Thunderbirds or the U.S. Navy Blue Angels, being highly cohesive. However, even groups of very low prestige may be highly cohesive in how they stick together. Finally, external pressure and internal competition influence group cohesion. Although the mechanics' union, pilots, and other internal constituencies at Eastern Airlines had various differences of opinion, they all pulled together in a cohesive fashion in resisting Frank Lorenzo when he came in to reshape the airline before its

Points to Emphasize

Former Citibank CEO Walter Wriston said, "The person who figures out how to harness the collective genius of their organization is going to blow the competition away," SOURCE: J. H. Zenger, "Leadership in a Team Environment," *Training and Development,* October 1991, 48.

CHALLENGE

■ 9.1

How Cohesive Is Your Group?

Think about a group of which you are a member. Answer each of the following questions in relationship to this group by circling the number next to the alternative that most reflects your feelings.

1. Do you feel that you are really a part of your group?

5—Really a part of the group.
4—Included in most ways.
3—Included in some ways, but not in others.
2—Do not feel I really belong.
1—Do not work with any one group of people.

2. If you had a chance to do the same activities in another group, for the same pay if it is a work group, how would you feel about moving?

1—Would want very much to move.
2—Would rather move than stay where I am.
3—Would make no difference to me.
4—Would rather stay where I am than move.
5—Would want very much to stay where I am.

3. How does your group compare with other groups that you are familiar with on each of the following points?

- The way people get along together.
  5—Better than most.
  3—About the same as most.
  1—Not as good as most.
- The way people stick together.
  5—Better than most.
  3—About the same as most.
  1—Not as good as most.
- The way people help one another on the job.
  5—Better than most.
  3—About the same as most.
  1—Not as good as most.

Add up your circled responses. If you have a number of 20 or above, you view your group as highly cohesive. If you have a number between 10 and 19, you view your group's cohesion as average. If you have a number 7 or less, you view your group as very low in cohesion.

SOURCE: Adapted from S. E. Seashore, *Group Cohesiveness in the Industrial Work Group*, University of Michigan, 1954.

demise.[23] Whereas external pressures tend to enhance cohesion, internal competition usually decreases cohesion within a team. This is especially true when there is competition and unresolved conflict over the issue of authority.

status structure

The set of authority and task relations among a group's members.

STATUS STRUCTURE **Status structure** is the set of authority and task relations among a group's members. The status structure may be hierarchical or egalitarian (i.e., democratic), depending on the group. Successful resolution of the authority issue within a team results in a well-understood status structure of leader-follower relationships. Where leadership problems arise, it is important to find solutions and build team leader effectiveness.[24] Whereas groups tend to have one leader, teams tend to share leadership. For example, one person may be the team's task master, who sets the agenda, initiates much of the work activity, and ensures that the team meets its deadlines. Another team member may take a leadership role in maintaining effective interpersonal relationships in the group. Hence, shared leadership is very feasible in teams. An effective status structure results in role interrelatedness among group members.

Points to Emphasize
In mature groups the leadership role is often shared among the group members.

Diversity in a group is healthy, and members may contribute to the collective effort through one of four basic styles.[25] These are the contributor, the collaborator, the communicator, and the challenger. The contributor is data driven, supplies necessary information, and adheres to high performance standards. The collaborator sees the big picture and is able to keep a constant focus on the mission and urge other members to join efforts for mission accomplishment. The communicator listens well, facilitates the group's process, and humanizes the collective effort. The challenger is the devil's advocate who questions everything from the group's mission, purpose, and methods to its ethics. Members may exhibit one or more of these four basic styles over a period of time. In addition, an effective group must have an integrator.[26] This can be especially important in cross-functional teams, where different perspectives carry the seeds of conflict. However, cross-functional teams are not necessarily a problem. Effectively managing cross-functional teams of artists, designers, printers, and financial experts has enabled Hallmark Cards to cut its new-product development time in half.[27]

Emergent leadership in groups was studied among 62 men and 60 women.[28] Groups performed tasks not classified as either masculine or feminine, that is, "sex-neutral" tasks. Men and women both emerged as leaders and neither gender had significantly more emergent leaders. However, group members who described themselves in masculine terms were significantly more likely to emerge as leaders than group members who described themselves in feminine, androgynous (both masculine and feminine), or undifferentiated (neither masculine nor feminine) terms. Hence, gender stereotypes may play a role in emergent leadership.

Teams at Work

■ Teams are task-oriented work groups; they can be formally designated or informally evolved. OshKosh B'Gosh found work teams paid off in its sewing plants, as shown in the accompanying Organizational Reality feature. Both formal and informal teams make important and valuable contributions to the organization and are important to the member need satisfaction. For example, an informal Xerox team from accounting, sales, administration, and distribution saved the company $200 million in inventory costs during 1991 through innovative production and inventory planning.[29]

http://www.xerox.com/

Several kinds of teams exist. One classification scheme uses a sports analogy. Some teams work like baseball teams with set responsibilities, other teams work like football teams through coordinated action, and still other teams work like doubles tennis teams with primary yet flexible responsibilities. Although each type of team may have a useful role in the organization, the individual expert should not be overlooked.[30]

Discussion Consideration
Reflect back on the discussion of high achievers in Chapter 3. Do students think high achievers will have difficulty working in a team environment?

Why Teams?

Teams are very useful in performing work that is complicated, complex, interrelated, and/or more voluminous than one person can handle. Harold Geneen, while chairman of ITT, said, "If I had enough arms and legs and time, I'd do it all myself." Obviously, people working in organizations cannot do everything because of the limitations of arms, legs, time, expertise, knowledge, and other

http://www.ittinfo.com/

ORGANIZATIONAL REALITY

Teams, Technology, and Kids' Clothes

OshKosh B'Gosh is a $365 million–plus company that designs, manufactures, sources, and sells clothes to men, women, children, and families. Founded in 1929, OshKosh B'Gosh has grown steadily over the decades, in its most recent history through several acquisitions in the 1990s. The company's principal products include dresses, blouses, and outerwear for girls and children; shirts and work clothing for boys and men; and outerwear for women. The company also operates family clothing stores.

OshKosh B'Gosh has effectively combined work teams with technology, resulting in 13 of its 14 sewing plants continuing operation in the United States. The company's international subsidiaries include locations in Germany, France, Hong Kong, the Virgin Islands, and the United Kingdom.

The company has experimented with work teams at seven of the domestic sewing plants and has been able to develop measures of effectiveness. The company has tracked unit production systems, mini sew lines, and their progressive bundle system. They found that work teams produced 30 percent more than the sew line, and when work teams were combined with unit production systems, they were even more efficient. However, OshKosh is progressing slowly with implementation of work teams to ensure their success. ■

SOURCE: "Competition is Child's Play for OshKosh," *Daily News Record*, 25 (1995): 17S.

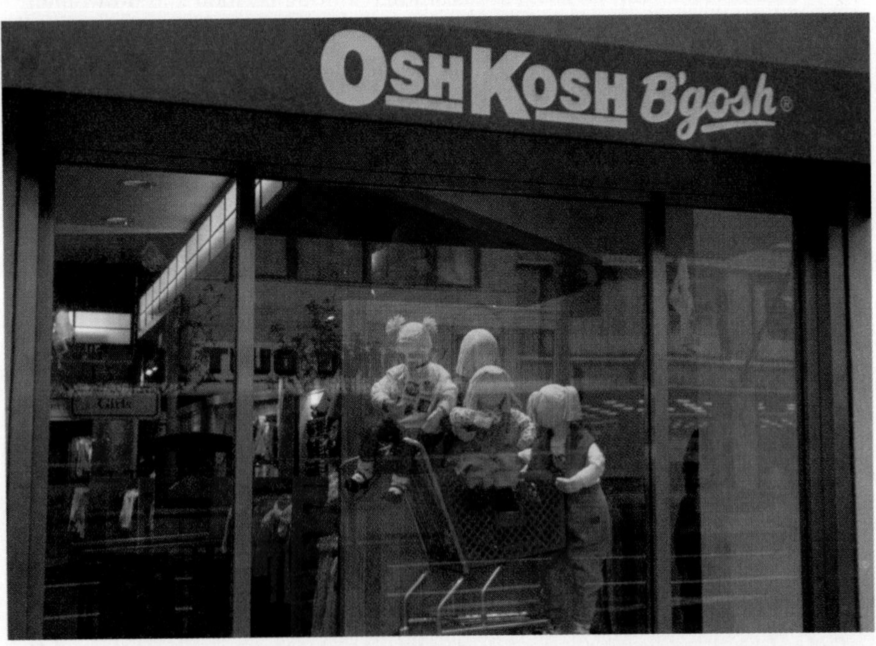

OshKosh B'gosh wants to implement teamwork right, so they do not get in a big hurry. Their success has hinged on combining technology with teamwork, and hard work.

http://www.gm.com/

resources. Individual limitations are overcome through teamwork and collaboration. For example, General Motor's NDH Bearings plant in Sandusky, Ohio, has become a world-class supplier of automotive components in terms of quality, cost, and delivery by emphasizing teamwork, open communication, and advanced technology.[31] In particular, union-management teams, such as the "bid teams," enabled NDH to make impressive gains from 1985 through 1991.

http://www.hp.com/

Teams make important contributions to organizations in work areas that lend themselves to teamwork. Teamwork is a core value at Hewlett-Packard, according to CEO Lew Platt. Complex, interdependent work tasks and activities that require collaboration particularly lend themselves to teamwork. Teams are appropriate where knowledge, talent, skills, and abilities are dispersed across organizational members and require integrated effort for task accomplishment.

■ **TABLE 9.2**

A Comparison of the New Team Environment versus the Old Work Environment

NEW TEAM ENVIRONMENT	OLD WORK ENVIRONMENT
Person comes up with initiatives.	Person follows orders.
Team has considerable authority to chart its own steps.	Team depends on the manager to chart its course.
Members form a team because people learn to collaborate in the face of their emerging right to think for themselves. People both rock the boat and work together.	Members were a team because people conformed to direction set by the manager. No one rocked the boat.
People cooperate by using their thoughts and feelings. They link up through direct talk.	People cooperated by suppressing their thoughts and feelings. They wanted to get along.

SOURCE: Larry Hirschhorn, *Managing in the New Team Environment* (adapted from p. 13), copyright 1991 by Addison Wesley Publishing Company, Inc. Reprinted by permission.

The recent emphasis on team-oriented work environments is based on empowerment with collaboration, not on power and competition. Larry Hirschhorn labels this "the new team environment" founded on a significantly more empowered work force in the industrial sectors of the American economy. This new team environment is compared with the old work environment in Table 9.2.

That teams are necessary is a driving principle of total quality efforts in organizations. Total quality efforts often require the formation of teams—especially cross-functional teams composed of people from different functions, such as manufacturing and design, who are responsible for specific organizational processes. Eastman Kodak Chairman George Fisher believes in the importance of participation and cooperation as foundations for teamwork and a total quality program. Although teams are an essential feature of a total quality work environment, there is a danger of insufficient training and direction if too many teams are formed very quickly. The Dream Team has eight characteristics: consensus, trust, candor, respect, caring, collaboration, meaningful recognition and rewards, and team influence, authority, and business connectedness.[32]

Quality Circles and Teams

Quality circles are one form of team in a total quality program. **Quality circles (QCs)** are small groups of employees who work voluntarily on company time—typically one hour per week—to address quality-related problems such as quality control, cost reduction, production planning and techniques, and even product design. Membership in a QC is typically voluntary and fixed once a circle is formed, although some changes may occur as appropriate. QCs use various problem-solving techniques in which they receive training to address the work-related problems.

quality circle (QC)
A small group of employees who work voluntarily on company time, typically one hour per week, to address work-related problems such as quality control, cost reduction, production planning and techniques, and even product design.

QCs were popularized as a Japanese management method when an American, W. Edward Deming, exported his thinking about QCs to Japan following World War II.[33] QCs became popular in the United States in the 1980s, when companies such as Ford, Hewlett-Packard, and Eastman Kodak implemented them. KL Spring and Stamping Corporation is an automotive industry supplier who has used quality circles and employee involvement for successful productivity improvements.

QCs must deal with substantive issues if they are to be effective; otherwise, employees begin to believe the QC effort is simply a management ploy. QCs do not necessarily require final decision authority to be effective if their recommendations are always considered seriously and implemented when appropriate. One study found QCs to be effective for a period of time, and then their contributions began to diminish.[34] This may suggest that QCs must be reinforced and periodically reenergized to maintain their effectiveness over long periods of time. Decision making in quality circles and **quality teams** is discussed in Chapter 10.

quality team

A team that is part of an organization's structure and is empowered to act on its decisions regarding product and service quality.

Quality teams are different from QCs in that they are more formal, designed and assigned by upper-level management. Quality teams are not voluntary and have more formal power than QCs. Although QCs and quality teams are not intended to provide members with social benefits, all teams in an organization have the potential to afford team members a number of social benefits.

Social Benefits

Two sets of social benefits are available to team or group members. One set of social benefits accrues from achieving psychological intimacy. The other comes from achieving integrated involvement.[35]

psychological intimacy

Emotional and psychological closeness to other team or group members.

Psychological intimacy is emotional and psychological closeness to other team or group members. It results in feelings of affection and warmth, unconditional positive regard, opportunity for emotional expression, openness, security and emotional support, and giving and receiving nuturance. Failure to achieve psychological intimacy results in feelings of emotional isolation and loneliness. This may be especially problematic for chief executives who experience loneliness at the top. Although psychological intimacy is valuable for emotional health and well-being, it need not necessarily be achieved in the work setting.

integrated involvement

Closeness achieved through tasks and activities.

Discussion Consideration

Ask students to reflect on why they join an organization or team. Do their reasons include psychological intimacy and the need for integrated involvement?

Integrated involvement is closeness achieved through tasks and activities. It results in enjoyable and involving activities, social identity and self-definition, being valued for one's skills and abilities, opportunity for power and influence, conditional positive regard, and support for one's beliefs and values. Failure to achieve integrated involvement results in social isolation. Whereas psychological intimacy is more emotion-based, integrated involvement is more behavior- and activity-based. Integrated involvement contributes to social psychological health and well-being.

Psychological intimacy and integrated involvement each contribute to overall health. It is not necessary to achieve both in the same team or group. For example, as a marathon runner while chief executive at Xerox Corporation, David Kearns found integrated involvement with his executive team and psychological intimacy with his athletic companions on long-distance runs.

Teams and groups have two sets of functions that operate to enable members to achieve psychological intimacy and integrated involvement. These are task and maintenance functions.

Points to Emphasize

Early in the life of a group, task functions may be more important as the members try to sort out roles, purposes, and procedures. As the group matures, task functions may not be as important as maintenance functions.

Task and Maintenance Functions

An effective team carries out various task functions to perform its work successfully and various maintenance functions to ensure member satisfaction and a sense of team spirit.[36] Teams that successfully fulfill these functions afford their members the potential for psychological intimacy and integrated involvement. Table 9.3 presents nine task and nine maintenance functions in teams or groups.

task function

An activity directly related to the effective completion of a team's work.

Task functions are those activities directly related to the effective completion of the team's work. For example, the task of initiating activity involves suggesting ideas, defining problems, and proposing approaches and/or solutions to problems. The task of seeking information involves asking for ideas, sugges-

■ **TABLE 9.3**

Task and Maintenance Functions in Teams or Groups

TASK FUNCTIONS	MAINTENANCE FUNCTIONS
Initiating activities	Supporting others
Seeking information	Following others' leads
Giving information	Gatekeeping communication
Elaborating concepts	Setting standards
Coordinating activities	Expressing member feelings
Summarizing ideas	Testing group decisions
Testing ideas	Consensus testing
Evaluating effectiveness	Harmonizing conflict
Diagnosing problems	Reducing tension

tions, information, or facts. Effective teams have members who fulfill various task functions as they are required.

Some task functions are more important at one time in the life of a group, and other functions are more important at other times. For example, during the engineering test periods for new technologies, the engineering team needs members who focus on testing the practical applications of suggestions and those who diagnose problems and suggest solutions.

The effective use of task functions leads to the success of the team, and the failure to use them may lead to disaster. For example, the successful initiation and coordination of an emergency room (ER) team's activities by the senior resident saved the life of a knife wound victim.[37] The victim was stabbed one-quarter inch below the heart, and the ER team acted quickly to stem the bleeding, begin intravenous fluids, and monitor the victim's vital signs. The accompanying Organizational Reality feature profiles the elite Mass General emergency trauma team.

Maintenance functions are those activities essential to the effective, satisfying interpersonal relationships within a team or group. For example, following another group member's lead may be as important as leading others. Communication gatekeepers within a group ensure balanced contributions from all members. Because task activities build tension into teams and groups working together, tension-reduction activities are important to drain off negative or destructive feelings. For example, in a study of 25 work groups over a five-year period, humor and joking behavior were found to enhance the social relationships in the groups.[38] The researchers concluded that performance improvements in the 25 groups indirectly resulted from improved relationships attributable to the humor and joking behaviors. Maintenance functions enhance togetherness, cooperation, and teamwork, enabling members to achieve psychological intimacy while furthering the success of the team. Jody Grant's supportive attitude and comfortable demeanor as chief financial officer of Electronic Data Systems have enabled him to build a strong finance organization in the corporation. Jody is respected for his expertise *and* his ability to build relationships. Both task and maintenance functions are important for successful teams.

maintenance function

An activity essential to effective, satisfying interpersonal relationships within a team or group.

Empowerment and Self-Managed Teams

■ Quality circles and quality teams, as we discussed earlier, are one way to implement teamwork in organizations. Self-managed teams are broad-based work teams that deal with issues beyond quality. Decision making in self-managed teams is also discussed in Chapter 10. General Motor's NDH Bearings plant, for

ORGANIZATIONAL REALITY

Elite Emergency Trauma Team

Mass General is one of the world's finest teaching hospitals. About 200 patients show up at the hospital's emergency room each day, of which about one-third are admitted. A score or so of those admitted, the worst cases, end up in Mass General's trauma center. A triage nurse knows they are in big trouble because of especially traumatic, violent, often life-threatening wounds. A lot of stabbing victims and gunshot victims are rolled into the trauma center on gurneys.

Alasdair Conn, a genial Scotsman, is chief of emergency services at Mass General and presides over the trauma team. He prefers trauma team members with some outside interests, such as sculling or numismatics, that enable the team member to escape the mental rigors of the high performance work demands of the trauma center.

The trauma team consists of doctors, nurses, and technicians who work together in a seamless drama of role-interrelatedness. Highly talented and trained, the team members collaboratively address each new case, with one talking to conscious patients, another setting up an IV, another calling for a consult, and yet another examining the wound(s) and/or fracture(s). As the drama unfolds in the trauma center, one team member often takes charge at some point, plots a strategy for treatment, and guides the team in task activities. Members' adaptive personalities help maintain cohesion in the high-stress trauma center. As violence rises, so does the value of this elite team. ■

SOURCE: K. Labich, "Elite Teams Get the Job Done," *Fortune*, February 19, 1996, 90–99.

Points to Emphasize
"Teams" and "Empowerment" are popular buzzwords, yet many organizations fail to lay the proper foundation or create the supportive atmosphere that is necessary for these programs to function effectively.

example, fostered teamwork by empowering employees to make important decisions at work. The company's approach was to push decision making down throughout the plant.

Empowerment may be thought of as an attribute of a person or of an organization's culture.[39] As an organizational culture attribute, empowerment encourages participation, an essential ingredient for teamwork.[40] Quality Action Teams (QATs) at Federal Express are the primary Quality Improvement Process (QIP) technique used by the company to engage management and hourly employees in four- to ten-member problem-solving teams.[41] The teams are empowered to act and solve problems as specific as charting the best route from the Phoenix airport to the local distribution center or as global as making major software enhancements to the COSMOS IIB on-line package-tracking system.

Empowerment may give employees the power of a lightning strike, but empowered employees must be properly focused through careful planning and preparation before they strike.[42]

Challenge 9.2 includes several items from Federal Express's Survey-Feedback-Action (SFA) survey related to employee empowerment. Complete the Challenge to see if you are empowered.

Foundations for Empowerment

Organizational and individual foundations underlie empowerment that enhances task motivation and performance. The organizational foundations for empowerment include a participative, supportive organizational culture and a team-oriented work design. A participative, supportive work environment is essential because of the uncertainty that empowerment can cause within the organization. Empowerment requires that lower-level organizational members be able to make decisions and take action on those decisions. As operational employees become empowered, it can create real fear, anxiety, or even terror among middle managers in the organization.[43] Senior leadership must create an

CHALLENGE

■ **9.2**

Are You an Empowered Employee?*

Read each of the following statements carefully. Then, to the right, indicate which answer best expresses your level of agreement (5 = strongly agree, 4 = agree, 3 = sometimes agree/sometimes disagree, 2 = disagree, 1 = strongly disagree, and 0 = undecided/do not know). Mark only one answer for each item, and remember to respond to all items. Remember that *work group* means all persons who report to the same manager as you do, regardless of their job titles.

1. I feel free to tell my manager what I think.	5	4	3	2	1	0
2. My manager is willing to listen to my concerns.	5	4	3	2	1	0
3. My manager asks for my ideas about things affecting our work.	5	4	3	2	1	0
4. My manager treats me with respect and dignity.	5	4	3	2	1	0
5. My manager keeps me informed about things I need to know.	5	4	3	2	1	0
6. My manager lets me do my job without interfering.	5	4	3	2	1	0
7. My manager's boss gives us the support we need.	5	4	3	2	1	0
8. Upper management (directors and above) pays attention to ideas and suggestions from people at my level.	5	4	3	2	1	0

Scoring

To determine if you are an empowered employee, add your scores.

32–40: You are empowered! Managers listen when you speak, respect your ideas, and allow you to do your work.

24–31: You have *some* power! Your ideas are considered sometimes and you have some freedom of action.

16–23: You must exercise caution. You cannot speak or act too boldly and your managers appear to exercise close supervision.

8–15: Your wings are clipped! You work in a powerless, restrictive work environment.

*If you are not employed, discuss these questions with a friend who is employed. Is your friend an empowered employee?

SOURCE: *Survey-Feedback-Action (SFA)*, Federal Express Company, Memphis, TN.

organizational culture that is supportive and reassuring for these middle managers as the power dynamics of the system change. If not supported and reassured, the middle managers can become a restraining, disruptive force to empowerment.

A second organizational foundation for empowerment concerns the design of work. The old factory system relied upon work specialization and narrow tasks with the intent of achieving routinized efficiency.[44] This approach to the design of work had some economic advantages, but it also had some distressing disadvantages leading to monotony and fatigue. This approach to the design of work is inconsistent with empowerment and teamwork, because it leads the individual to feel absolved of much responsibility for a whole piece of work. Team-oriented work designs are a key organizational foundation for empowerment, because they lead to broader tasks and a greater sense of responsibility. For example, Volvo builds cars using a team-oriented work design in which each person does many different tasks, and each person has direct responsibility for the finished product.[45] Such work designs create a context for effective empowerment so long as the empowered individuals meet necessary individual prerequisites.

The three individual prerequisites for empowerment include (1) the capability to become psychologically involved in participative activities, (2) the motivation to act autonomously, and (3) the capacity to see the relevance of participation for one's own well-being.[46] First, people must be psychologically equipped to become involved in participative activities if they are to be empowered and become effective team members. Not all people are so predisposed. For example, Germany has an authoritarian tradition that runs counter to participation and empowerment at the individual and group level. General Motors encountered significant difficulties implementing quality circles in its German plants, because workers expected to be directed by supervisors, not to engage in participative problem solving. The German efforts to establish supervisory/worker boards in corporations is an effort to alter this authoritarian tradition.

Alternate Example
Managers may resist efforts to empower employees or create self-directed work teams because these new forms of organizing threaten the power and authority they derive from the traditional organizational hierarchy.

A second individual prerequisite to empowerment and teamwork is the motivation to act autonomously. People with dependent personalities are predisposed to be told what to do and to rely on external motivation rather than internal, intrinsic motivation.[47] These dependent people are not effective team members. The prerequisite of a motivation to act autonomously creates a dynamic tension or paradox for people; they are asked to act autonomously and independently while also subordinating themselves to the team. This is the heart of the conflict between individual autonomy and group membership.[48] Managing the conflict requires balancing the processes of developing individual identity and blending one's identity with other people.

Points to Emphasize
One of the major barriers to implementation of teams is that compensation and performance appraisal systems often continue to emphasize individual performance.

Finally, if empowerment is to work, people must be able to see how it provides a personal benefit to them. The personal payoff for the individual need not be short term. It may be a long-term benefit that they see. Thus, empowerment becomes of instrumental value to the person in achieving work satisfaction; in receiving greater rewards through enhanced organizational profitability; or in reshaping the design of work, and ultimately the organization, to a more humanistic "fit."

Empowerment Skills

Empowerment through employee self-management is an alternative to empowerment through teamwork.[49] Whether through self-management or teamwork, empowerment requires the development of certain skills if it is to be enacted effectively. The first set of skills required for empowerment are competence skills. Mastery and experience in one's chosen discipline and profession provide an essential foundation for empowerment. This means that new employees and trainees should experience only limited empowerment until they demonstrate the capacity to accept more responsibility, a key aspect of empowerment.

Empowerment also requires certain process skills. The most critical process skills for empowerment include negotiating skills, especially with allies, opponents, and adversaries.[50] Allies are the easiest people to negotiate with, because they agree with you about the team's mission, and you can trust their actions and behavior. Opponents require a different negotiating strategy; although you can predict their actions and behavior, they do not agree with your concept of the team's mission. Adversaries are dangerous, difficult people to negotiate with because you cannot predict their actions or behaviors, and they do not agree with your concept of the team's mission.

A third set of empowerment skills is the development of cooperative and helping behaviors.[51] Cooperative people are motivated to maximize the gains for everyone on the team; they engage in encouraging, helpful behavior to bring about that end. The alternatives to cooperation are competitive, individualistic, and egalitarian orientations. Competitive people are motivated to maximize their personal gains regardless of the expense to other people. This can be very counterproductive from the standpoint of the team. Individualistic people are

SCIENTIFIC FOUNDATION

Empowerment and Change at Work

Although the concept of empowerment may be deceptively simple to understand, empowering a workforce may require dramatic change in an organization. This research is based on a study of ten organizations in banking and financial services, the food and grocery business, power and utilities, health care and medical products, television and entertainment, and information services. The keys to empowerment may seem straightforward at first, but they can prove very hard to implement. The key steps to implementation are the formation of an information-sharing culture, the creation of autonomy through structural change, and the establishment of teams to define the new organizational hierarchy. The ten companies in this study experienced real difficulty in the transition from a bureaucratic structure to a flexible, fully empowered one. To bring about the organizational change and empowerment of the workforce required a series of structural changes over several years.

In all ten organizations, empowerment led to improved operational capabilities and renewed competitiveness. Empowerment is all about teaming with other people through sharing information and creating new structures to better use as well as to develop people's talents. Empowerment leads to a feeling of ownership.

The study concluded that for teams to be the hierarchy of the new organizational reality, they must receive direction and training for new skills, encouragement and support for change, and gradual freedom from tight managerial control. They must evolve their own leadership and status structure, and acknowledge the real fear associated with the responsibility of this fundamental change in the organization.

SOURCE: Reprinted by permission of the publisher, from "Navigating the Journey to Empowerment," *Organizational Dynamics*, Spring 1995

motivated to act autonomously, though not necessarily to maximize their personal gains. They are less prone to contribute to the efforts of the team. Egalitarian people are motivated to equalize the outcomes for each team member, which may or may not be beneficial to the team's well-being.

Communication skills are a final set of essential empowerment skills.[52] These skills include self-expression skills and skills in reflective listening. We explored these skills in detail in Chapter 8. Empowerment cannot occur in a team unless members are able to express themselves effectively, as well as listen carefully to one another. Empowering a whole workforce can be a real challenge, as the accompanying Scientific Foundation feature shows.

Self-Managed Teams

self-managed team
A team that makes decisions that were once reserved for managers.

Self-managed teams are ones that make decisions that were once reserved for managers. They are sometimes called *self-directed teams* or *autonomous work groups*. Self-managed teams are one way to implement empowerment in organizations. A one-year study of self-managed teams suggests they have a positive impact on employee attitudes but not on absenteeism or turnover.[53] Evaluative research is helpful in achieving a better understanding of this relatively new way of approaching teamwork and the design of work. Research can help in establishing expectations for self-managed teams. For example, it is probably unreasonable to expect these teams to be fully functional and self-directed in short periods of time. It may take two or three years for new teams to be fully self-directed.[54]

Other evaluations of self-managed teams are more positive. Southwest Industries, a high-technology aerospace manufacturing firm, embarked on a major internal reorganization that included the creation of self-managed teams to fit its high-technology production process. The overall success of Southwest's team approach included a 30 percent increase in shipments, a 30 percent decrease in lead time, a 40 percent decrease in total inventory, a decrease in machinery downtime, and almost a one-third decrease in production costs.[55] Self-managed

Chrysler Motors' oldest plant is in New Castle, Indiana. It was miraculously resurrected through the implementation of self-managed teams as a key foundation in which the union and management cooperated.

http://www.chryslercorp.com/

teams were also the foundation for the miraculous resurrection of Chrysler's oldest plant in New Castle, Indiana, as the United Auto Worker's Union and Chrysler's management forged a partnership for success.[56]

A game (Learning Teams) is available to help people create self-directed teams, learn cooperatively, and master factual information.[57] With no outside help, an engineering team in Texas Instrument's Defense Systems and Electronics Group (DSEG) developed themselves into a highly effective, productive, self-managed team. They then helped DSEG in their successful effort to win a Malcolm Baldrige National Quality Award.

Alternate Example
A major pitfall in implementing teams is the lack of top management involvement and support.

Upper Echelons: Teams at the Top

upper echelon
A top-level executive team in an organization.

■ Self-managed teams at the top of the organization—top-level executive teams—are referred to as **upper echelons.** Organizations are often a reflection of these upper echelons.[58] Upper echelon theory argues that the background characteristics of the top management team can predict organizational characteristics. Furthermore, upper echelons are one key to the strategic success of the organization.[59] Thus, the teams at the top are instrumental in defining the organization over time such that the values, competence, ethics, and unique characteristics of the top management team are eventually reflected throughout the organization. This great power and influence throughout the entire organization makes the top management team a key to the organization's success.

For example, when Lee Iacocca became CEO at Chrysler Corporation, his top management team was assembled to bring about strategic realignment within the corporation by building on Chrysler's historical engineering strength. The dramatic success of Chrysler during the early 1980s was followed by struggle and accommodation during the late 1980s. This raises the question of how long a CEO and the top management team can sustain organizational success.

Hambrick and Fukutomi address this question by examining the dynamic relationship between a CEO's tenure and the success of the organization.[60] They found five seasons in a CEO's tenure: (1) response to a mandate, (2) experimentation, (3) selection of an enduring theme, (4) convergence, and (5) dysfunction. All else being equal, this seasons model has significant implications for organizational performance. Specifically, organizational performance increases with a CEO's tenure to a peak, after which performance declines. This relationship is depicted in Figure 9.3. The peak has been found to come at about seven years—somewhere in the middle of the executive's seasons. As indicated by the

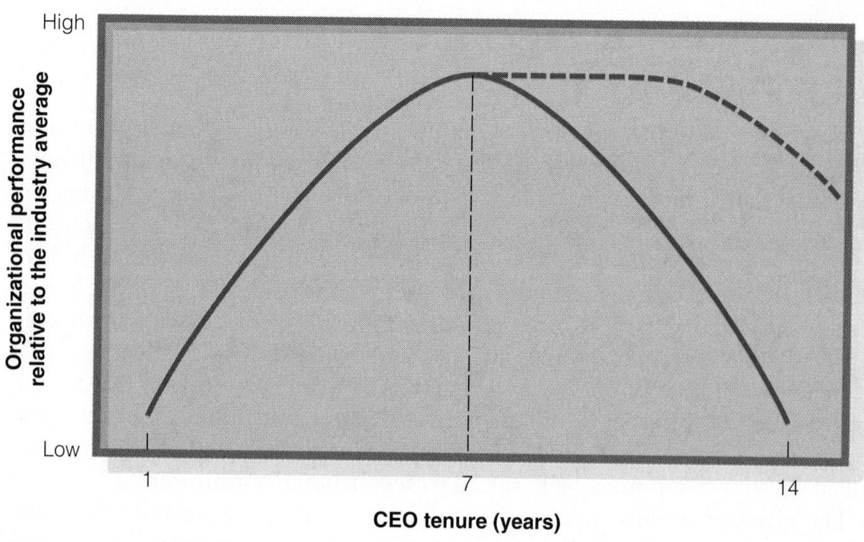

■ **FIGURE 9.3**

Executive Tenure and Organizational Performance

SOURCE: D. Hambrick, The Seasons of an Executive's Tenure, keynote address, the Sixth Annual Texas Conference on Organizations, Lago Vista, Texas, April, 1991.

dotted lines in the figure, the peak may be extended, depending on several factors, such as diversity in the executive's support team.

From an organizational health standpoint, diversity and depth in the top management team enhances the CEO's well-being.[61] From a performance standpoint, the CEO's top management team can influence the timing of the performance peak, the degree of dysfunction during the closing season of the CEO's tenure, and the rate of decline in organizational performance. Diversity and heterogeneity in the top management team help sustain high levels of organizational performance at the peak and help maintain the CEO's vitality. The presence of a "wild turkey" in the top management team can be a particularly positive force. The wild turkey is a devil's advocate who challenges the thinking of the CEO and other top executives and provides a counterpoint during debates. If not shouted down or inhibited, the wild turkey helps the CEO and the team sustain peak performance and retard the CEO's dysfunction and decline. Roger Smith and General Motors lost a possible opportunity to change and improve the corporation's performance by silencing Ross Perot, a wild turkey, after GM's acquisition of EDS. Because Perot's ideas were never implemented at GM, we will never know if they would have been beneficial. Perot was inhibited, and GM's decline continued.

We can conclude that the leadership, composition, and dynamics of the top management team have an important influence on the organization's performance. In some cases, corporations have eliminated the single CEO. For example, in early 1992, Xerox and Microsoft announced plans for a team of executives to function in lieu of a president.[62] Walter Wriston created such a three-member team when he was chairman at Citicorp.

Multicultural Teams

The backgrounds of group members may be quite different in the global workplace. Homogeneous groups in which all members share similar backgrounds are giving way to token groups in which all but one member come from the same background, bicultural groups in which two or more members represent each of two distinct cultures, and multicultural groups in which members represent three or more ethnic backgrounds.[63] Diversity within a group may increase the uncertainty, complexity, and inherent confusion in group processes, making it more difficult for the group to achieve its full, potential productivity.[64] The advantages of culturally diverse groups include the generation of more and better ideas while limiting the risk of groupthink, to be discussed in Chapter 10.

Managerial Implications: Teamwork for Productivity and Quality

■ Work groups and teams are important vehicles through which organizations achieve high-quality performance. The current emphasis on the new team environment, shown in Table 9.2, places unique demands on managers, teams and individuals in leading, working, and managing. Managing these demands requires an understanding of individual diversity and the interrelationships of individuals, teams, and managers, as depicted in the triangle in Figure 9.4. Expectations associated with these three key organizational roles for people at work are different. The first role is as an individual, empowered employee. The second is as an active member of one or more teams. The third is the role of manager or formal supervisor. Earlier in the chapter, we discussed the foundations for teamwork, empowerment, and skills for working in the new team environment. Individual empowerment must be balanced with collaborative teamwork.

The manager in the triangle is responsible for creating a receptive organizational environment for work groups and teams. This requires that the manager achieve a balance between setting limits (so that individuals and teams do not go too far afield) and removing barriers (so that empowered individuals and self-managed teams can accomplish their work). In addition, the manager should establish a flexible charter for each team. Once the charter is established, the manager continues to be available to the team as a coaching resource, as necessary. The manager establishes criteria for evaluating the performance effectiveness of the team, as well as the individuals, being supervised. In an optimum environment, this involves useful and timely performance feedback to teams that carries a sense of equity and fairness with it. The manager's responsibilities are different from the team leader's.

Effective team leaders may guide a work group or share leadership responsibility with their teams, especially self-managed teams. Team leaders are active team members with responsibility for nurturing the development and performance of the team.[65] They require skills different from those of the manager. Whereas the manager establishes the environment in which teams flourish, the team leader teaches, listens, solves problems, manages conflict, and enhances the dynamics of team functioning to ensure the team's success. It is the team leader's task to bring the team to maturity; help the team work through interpersonal, task, and authority issues; and be skilled in nurturing a cohesive, effective team. The skills a team leader requires are the hands-on skills of direct involvement and full membership in the team. Flexibility, delegation, and collaboration are characteristics of healthy teams and team leaders. Increasing globalization

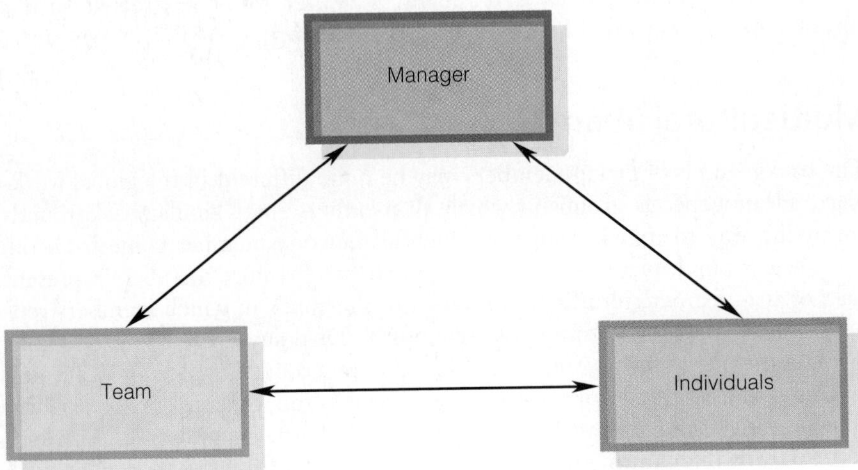

■ **FIGURE 9.4**

The Triangle for Managing in the New Team Environment

SOURCE: Larry Hirchhorn, *Managing in the New Team Environment* (adapted from p. 14), copyright 1991 by Addison Wesley Publishing Company, Inc. Reprinted by permission.

requires team leaders to be skilled at forging teamwork among diverse individuals, whereas managers must be skilled at forging collaboration among diverse groups.

CLOSING SPOTLIGHT

Mustang Cobra—1993 . . . 1996

Janine Bay was the woman Ford selected as chief engineer to take the wheel of the '93 SVT Mustang Cobra.[66] This initial SVT effort had a production run of 5,000 Mustangs. The SVT then followed Bay's success with the Mustang Cobra with the long-rumored "Boss Truck" pickup at about the same time.

The initial successes of the SVT led to three other "co-located team" vehicle programs within Ford, including the new Taurus. The new team approach at Ford was used in "Team Mustang," a new team of automotive planners, designers, and engineers charged with the responsibility of making more revolutionary changes in the 1995 Mustang rather than just working from an existing platform.[67] Ford had seriously considered putting its "Pony Car" out to pasture during mid-1989, but the Mustang still has a lot of miles left.

Ford's SVT announced at the 1996 Chicago Auto Show that a convertible model of the Mustang Cobra would return to the SVT lineup. Ford built only 2,500 Cobra convertibles, 2,450 for sale in the United States and 50 for Canada. While the SVT continues to enjoy team success in conceiving and marketing high-performance road cars for the driving public, they also continue to get wonderful engineering support from SVE (special vehicle engineering). SVE is a highly trained team of 20 or so Ford engineers who spend 75 percent of their time in support of the SVT—another example of teamwork for success at Ford Motor Company. ■

Chapter Summary

- Groups are often composed of diverse people at work. Teams in organizations are a key to enhance quality and achieve success.
- Important aspects of group behavior include norms of behavior, group cohesion, social loafing, and loss of individuality.
- Once a group forms, it goes through four stages of development. If successful, the group emerges as a mature group with a purpose, clear behavioral norms, high cohesion, and a flexible status structure.
- Quality circles, originally popularized in Japan, and quality teams contribute to solving technological and quality problems in the organization.
- Teams provide social benefits for team members, as well as enhance organizational performance.
- Empowerment and teamwork require specific organizational design elements and individual psychological characteristics and skills.
- Upper echelons and top management teams are key players in determining the strategy and performance of an organization. Diversity and a devil's advocate, or "wild turkey," in the top management team enhance organizational performance.
- Managing in the new team environment places new demands on managers, teams, and individuals. Managers must create a supportive and flexible environment for collaborative teams and empowered individuals. Team leaders must nurture the team's development.

Key Terms

group (p. 252)
team (p. 252)
norms of behavior (p. 253)
group cohesion (p. 253)
social loafing (p. 253)
loss of individuality (p. 254)
status structure (p. 260)
quality circle (QC) (p. 263)
quality team (p. 264)
psychological intimacy (p. 264)
integrated involvement (p. 264)
task function (p. 264)
maintenance function (p. 265)
self-managed team (p. 269)
upper echelon (p. 270)

Review Questions

1. What is a group? A team?
2. Explain four aspects of group behavior. How can each aspect help or hinder the group's functioning?
3. Explain what happens in each of the four stages of a group's development. When does the group address interpersonal issues? Task issues? Authority issues?
4. Describe the four characteristics of mature groups.
5. Why are teams important to organizations today? How and why are teams formed?
6. Describe at least five task and five maintenance functions that effective teams must perform.
7. What are the organizational foundations of empowerment and teamwork? The individual foundations?
8. Describe the necessary skills for empowerment and teamwork.
9. What are the benefits and potential drawbacks of self-managed teams?
10. What is the role of the manager in the new team environment? What is the role of the team leader?

Discussion and Communication Questions

1. Which was the most effective group (or team) of which you were a member? What made that group (or team) so effective?
2. Have you ever experienced peer pressure to act more in accordance with the behavioral norms of a group? Have you ever engaged in a little social loafing? Have you ever lost your head and been caught up in a group's destructive actions?
3. Name a company that successfully uses teamwork and empowerment. What has that company done that makes it so successful at teamwork and empowerment? Has its team approach made a difference in its performance? How?
4. Name a person you think is a particularly good team member. What makes this person a good team member? Name a person who is a problem as a team member. What makes this person a problem?
5. Think about your current work environment. Does your work environment use quality circles or self-managed teams? What are the barriers to teamwork and empowerment in that environment? What elements of the environment enhance or encourage teamwork and empowerment? (If you do not work, discuss this question with a friend who does.)
6. *(communication question)* Prepare a memo describing your observations about teams and groups in your workplace or your university. Where have you observed teams or groups to be most effective? Why? What changes might be made at work or in the university to make teams more effective?
7. *(communication question)* Develop an oral presentation about what the most important norms of behavior should be in an academic community and workplace. Be specific. Discuss how these norms should be established and reinforced.
8. *(communication question)* Interview an employee or manager about what he or she believes contributes to cohesiveness in work groups and teams. Ask the person what the conclusions are based on. Be prepared to discuss what you have learned in class.
9. Do you admire the upper echelons in your organization or university? Why or why not? Do they communicate effectively with groups and individuals throughout the organization?

Ethics Questions

1. Assume you know someone who is engaged in social loafing within a group of which you are a member. What should you do? Is this person acting in an unethical manner?
2. Is there a moral dilemma involved in expecting an individual to subordinate his or her individuality and autonomy to the will of the work group or team? Suppose you are a member of a work group or team getting ready to act in a way you believe is unethical or immoral. What should you do? Will you be responsible for the actions of the entire team?
3. Assume that a very mature group decides that it is necessary to resort to threats to one of the members to keep the person in line with the group's norms. Further assume that the behavior of the person in question is not endangering anyone inside or outside the group. Is the proposed group action unethical? What should your position be on the issue?
4. Suppose an empowered employee makes a mistake at your place of work that damages some property but does not hurt anyone. Assuming the employee was empowered to act, should the employee be punished for the unfortunate consequences of the action? Would your answer differ according to whether the employee had or had not been properly trained and supervised before being empowered?

Experiential Exercises

9.1 Tower Building: A Group Dynamics Activity

This exercise gives you an opportunity to study group dynamics in a task-oriented situation. Each group must bring materials to class for building a tower. All materials must fit in a box no greater than eight cubic feet (i.e., 2 ft. × 2 ft. × 2 ft. or 1 ft. × 2 ft. × 4 ft.).

Step 1. Each group is assigned a meeting place and a work place. One or two observers should be assigned in each group. The instructor may assign a manager to each group.

Step 2. Each group plans for the building of the paper tower (no physical construction is allowed during this planning period). Towers will be judged on the basis of height, stability, beauty, and meaning. (Another option is to have the groups do the planning outside of class and come prepared to build the tower.)

Step 3. Each group constructs its tower.

Step 4. Groups inspect other towers, and all individuals rate towers other than their own. See evaluation sheet at right. Each group turns in its point totals (i.e., someone in the group adds up each person's total for all groups rated) to the instructor, and the instructor announces the winner.

Step 5. Group Dynamics Analysis. Observers report observations to their own groups and each group analyzes the group dynamics that occurred during the planning and building of the tower.

Step 6. Groups report on major issues in group dynamics that arose during the tower planning and building. Complete the Tower Building Aftermath questionnaire as homework if requested by your instructor.

	GROUPS							
CRITERIA	1	2	3	4	5	6	7	8
Height								
Stability/ Strength								
Beauty								
Meaning/ Significance								
TOTALS								

Rate each criterion on a scale of 1–10, with 1 being lowest or poorest, and 10 being highest or best.

SOURCE: From *Organizational Behavior and Performance*, 3/e by Andrew D. Szilagyi, Jr. and Marc J. Wallace, Jr.

9.2 Design a Team

The following exercise gives you an opportunity to design a team. Working in a six-person group, address the individual characteristics, team composition, and norms for an effective group whose task is to make recommendations on improving customer relations. The president of a small clothing manufacturer is concerned that his customers are not satisfied enough with the company's responsiveness, product quality, and returned-orders process. He has asked your group to put together a team to address these problems.

Step 1. The class will form into groups of approximately six members each. Each group elects a spokesperson and answers the following questions. The group should spend an equal amount of time on each question.

a. *What characteristics should the individual members of the task team possess?* Members may consider professional competence, skills, department, and/or personality and behavioral characteristics in the group's discussion.

b. *What should the composition of the task team be?* Once your group has addressed individual characteristics, consider the overall composition of the task team. Have special and/or unique competencies, knowledge, skills, and abilities been considered in your deliberations?

c. *What norms of behavior to you think the task team should adopt?* A team's norms of behavior may evolve, or they may be consciously discussed and agreed upon. Take the latter approach.

Step 2. Each group will share the results of its answers to the questions in Step 1. Cross-team questions and discussion follows.

VIDEO CASE

Priority Manufacturing, Inc.[1]

Priority Manufacturing, Inc., located in Wood Dale, Illinois, a Chicago suburb, is in the metal bending business. The company stamps and fabricates precision sheet metal products for customers such as AT&T and General Dynamics.

Founded in 1980, the company was owned by Bruce and Pat Biedar. In September 1986, Bruce died of a sudden heart attack and Pat instantly became sole owner of the business.

Faced with the choice of liquidating the business or operating it herself, Pat Biedar decided to take the plunge—but not without some initial sense of trepidation. Mrs. Biedar had worked on the administrative side of Priority Manufacturing, supervising general office functions. However, she was not experienced with the manufacturing side of the business. Pat readily admitted that she had no "concept of manufacturing processes and costs." Pat Biedar recognized that she could not run the company alone. She needed assistance and guidance.

Teamwork became instrumental for the company's survival. Biedar put together a team of advisors, consisting of CEOs of small manufacturing firms in product lines other than sheet metal stamping and fabricating. This advisory board provided guidance, answered questions and critiqued the company's work. According to Biedar, the advisory board helped to improve the quality and depth of decision making within the company.

Priority Manufacturing also adopted total quality management as an operating philosophy. With its emphasis on customer focus, continuous improvement, and teamwork, total quality management helped the company to address its challenges of a declining customer base, weak revenues, and inexperienced leadership. Teamwork became the vehicle for achieving continuous improvement with the company's processes

This case was written by Michael K. McCuddy, the Louis S. and Mary L. Morgal Professor of Christian Business Ethics, College of Business Administration, Valparaiso University.

[1]This case is based on the *Priority Manufacturing, Inc.* segment of Insights and Inspirations: How Businesses Succeed, The 1995 Blue Chip Enterprise Initiative.

References

1. J. D. Sawyer and T. Rhoades, FAX communication, 12 February 1996.
2. L. Iacocca, *Iacocca: An Autobiography* (New York: Bantam Books, 1984).
3. M. E. Shaw, *Group Dynamics: The Psychology of Small Group Behavior* (New York: McGraw-Hill, 1971).
4. D. M. McGregor, *The Human Side of Enterprise* (New York: McGraw-Hill, 1960).
5. J. R. Katzenbach and D. K. Smith, "The Discipline of Teams," *Harvard Business Review* 71 (1993): 111–120.
6. K. L. Bettenhausen and J. K. Murnighan, "The Development and Stability of Norms in Groups Facing Interpersonal and Structural Challenge," *Administrative Science Quarterly* 36 (1991): 20–35.
7. I. Summers, T. Coffelt, and R. E. Horton, "Work-Group Cohesion," *Psychological Reports* 63 (1988): 627–636.
8. K. H. Price, "Decision Responsibility, Task Responsibility, Identifiability, and Social Loafing," *Organizational Behavior and Human Decision Processes* 40 (1987): 330–345.
9. R. Albanese and D. D. Van Fleet, "Rational Behavior in Groups: The Free-Riding Tendency," *Academy of Management Review* 10 (1985): 244–255.
10. E. Diener, "Deindividuation, Self-Awareness, and Disinhibition," *Journal of Personality and Social Psychology* 37 (1979): 1160–1171.
11. S. Prentice-Dunn and R. W. Rogers, "Deindividuation and the Self-Regulation of Behavior," in P. Paulus, ed., *Psychology of Group Influence* (Hillsdale, N.J.: Erlbaum, 1989), 87–109.
12. B. M. Bass and E. C. Ryterband, *Organizational Psychology* 2d ed. (Boston: Allyn & Bacon, 1979); B. W. Tuckman, "Developmental Sequences in Small Groups," *Psychological Bulletin* 63 (1963): 384–399.
13. W. G. Bennis and H. A. Shepard, "A Theory of Group Development," *Human Relations* 9 (1956): 415–438.
14. S. Caudron, "Monsanto Responds to Diversity," *Personnel Journal* (November 1990): 72–80.
15. W. P. Anthony, "Managing Diversity, Then and Now," *Wall Street Journal*, 3 July 1992, A8.

and products, and for promoting and sustaining its customer focus. In fact, Pat Biedar says that "The most important thing we did was putting a team together. It's a team-oriented company."

With the assistance of a state of Illinois development grant, Pat brought in experts to train the employees in total quality management techniques. Pat and her daughter, Patte, who joined the business after her father's death and became Vice President of Operations, also took classes to improve their management and supervisory skills. Much of their training was aimed at improving their abilities to lead in a team environment.

In reflecting on how she has overcome the obstacles she has faced, Pat Biedar provides some insight into her relationships with employees. She says, "I need people. They're my biggest asset. And I depend on them totally. I try not to step in their way." Perhaps these are Pat Biedar's guidelines for fostering effective teamwork.

Teamwork has paid off for Priority Manufacturing. The company is recognized for its quality products—it is highly regarded as a world-class manufacturer. Indeed, the company has received a top quality rating from 36 client companies. Priority Manufacturing now has 42 major customers as compared to three when Pat Biedar took over the business. Sales volume has doubled. Employment has more than doubled. The company now has 48 employees as compared to 22 employees when Pat Biedar took over the company upon her husband's death. In reflecting on these results and how they were achieved, Pat Biedar says, "My husband would have been proud."

DISCUSSION QUESTIONS

1. How has Pat Biedar fostered teamwork at Priority Manufacturing?
2. Using Table 9.1, discuss the extent to which the characteristics of well-functioning, effective groups might apply to Priority Manufacturing's advisory board. Also discuss the extent to which these characteristics might apply to the company's employee teams.
3. To what extent is Pat Biedar empowering her employees? Explain your answer.
4. What individual and organizational foundations of empowerment appear to exist at Priority Manufacturing?
5. Using Figure 9.4 as a point of departure, explain how Priority Manufacturing achieved the success that it did after Pat Biedar became sole owner of the company.

16. W. C. Schutz, "Interpersonal Underworld," *Harvard Business Review* 36 (1958): 123–135.
17. D. Nichols, "Quality Program Sparked Company Turnaround," *Personnel* (October 1991): 24. For a commentary on Wallace's hard times and subsequent emergence from Chapter 11 bankruptcy, see R. C. Hill, "When the Going Gets Tough: A Baldrige Award Winner on the Line," *Academy of Management Executive* 7 (1993): 75–79.
18. M. Hardaker and B. K. Ward, "How to Make a Team Work," *Harvard Business Review* 65 (1987): 112–120.
19. C. R. Gowen, "Managing Work Group Performance by Individual Goals and Group Goals for an Interdependent Group Task," *Journal of Organizational Behavior Management* 7 (1986): 5–27.
20. K. L. Bettenhausen and J. K. Murnighan, "The Emergence of Norms in Competitive Decision-Making Groups," *Administrative Science Quarterly* 30 (1985): 350–372; K. L. Bettenhausen, "Five Years of Groups Research: What We Have Learned and What Needs to Be Addressed," *Journal of Management* 17 (1991): 345–381.
21. J. E. McGrath, *Groups: Interaction and Performance* (Englewood Cliffs, N.J.: Prentice-Hall, 1984).
22. S. E. Seashore, *Group Cohesiveness in the Industrial Work Group* (Ann Arbor, Mich.: University of Michigan, 1954).
23. J. C. Quick, "Crafting an Organizational Culture: Herb's Hand at Southwest Airlines," *Organizational Dynamics* 21 (1992): 45–56.
24. N. Steckler and N. Fondas, "Building Team Leader Effectiveness: A Diagnostic Tool," *Organizational Dynamics* 23 (1995): 20–35.
25. G. Parker, *Team Players and Teamwork* (San Francisco: Jossey-Bass, 1990).
26. N. R. F. Maier, "Assets and Liabilities in Group Problem Solving: The Need for an Integrative Function," *Psychological Review* 74 (1967): 239–249.
27. T. A. Stewart, "The Search for the Organization of Tomorrow," *Fortune*, 18 May 1992, 92–98.
28. J. R. Goktepe and C. E. Schneier, "Role of Sex, Gender Roles, and Attraction in Predicting Emergent Leaders," *Journal of Applied Psychology* 74 (1989): 165–167.
29. B. Dumaine, "The Bureaucracy Busters," *Fortune*, 17 June 1991, 36.
30. P. F. Drucker, "There's More Than One Kind of Team," *Wall Street Journal*, February 11, 1992, A16.

31. J. H. Sheridan, "A Star in the GM Heavens," *Industry Week*, 18 March 1991, 50–54.
32. O. Harari, "The Dream Team," *Management Review*, (October 1995): 29–31.
33. W. L. Mohr and H. Mohr, *Quality Circles: Changing Images of People at Work* (Reading, Mass.: Addison-Wesley, 1983).
34. R. W. Griffin, "A Longitudinal Assessment of the Consequences of Quality Circles in an Industrial Setting," *Academy of Management Journal* 31 (1988): 338–358.
35. P. Shaver and D. Buhrmester, "Loneliness, Sex-Role Orientation, and Group Life: A Social Needs Perspective," in P. Paulus, ed., *Basic Group Processes* (New York: Springer-Verlag, 1985), 259–288.
36. W. R. Lassey, "Dimensions of Leadership," in W. R. Lassey and R. R. Fernandez, eds., *Leadership and Social Change* (La Jolla, Calif.: University Associates, 1976), 10–15.
37. J. D. Quick, G. Moorhead, J. C. Quick, E. A. Gerloff, K. L. Mattox, and C. Mullins, "Decision Making among Emergency Room Residents: Preliminary Observations and a Decision Model," *Journal of Medical Education* 58 (1983): 117–125.
38. W. J. Duncan and J. P. Feisal, "No Laughing Matter: Patterns of Humor in the Workplace," *Organizational Dynamics* 17 (1989): 18–30.
39. K. W. Thomas and B. A. Velthouse, "Cognitive Elements of Empowerment: An 'Interpretive' Model of Intrinsic Task Motivation," *Academy of Management Review* 15 (1990): 666–681.
40. R. R. Blake, J. S. Mouton, and R. L. Allen, *Spectacular Teamwork: How to Develop the Leadership Skills for Team Success* (New York: Wiley, 1987).
41. American Management Association, *Blueprints for Service Quality: The Federal Express Approach*, AMA Management Briefing (New York: AMA, 1991).
42. W. C. Byham, *ZAPP! The Human Lightning of Empowerment* (Pittsburgh: Developmental Dimensions, 1989).
43. T. L. Brown, "Fearful of 'Empowerment': Should Managers Be Terrified?" *Industry Week*, 18 June 1990, 12.
44. L. Hirschhorn, "Stresses and Patterns of Adjustment in the Postindustrial Factory," in G. M. Green and F. Baker, eds., *Work, Health, and Productivity* (New York: Oxford University Press, 1991), 115–126.
45. P. G. Gyllenhammar, *People at Work* (Reading, Mass.: Addison-Wesley, 1977).
46. R. Tannenbaum and F. Massarik, "Participation by Subordinates in the Managerial Decision-Making Process," *Canadian Journal of Economics and Political Science* 16 (1950): 408–418.
47. H. Levinson, *Executive* (Cambridge, Mass.: Harvard University Press, 1981).
48. S. Freud, *Civilization and Its Discontents*, ed. and trans. James Strachey (New York: Norton, 1961).
49. F. Shipper and C. C. Manz, "Employee Self-Management without Formally Designated Teams: An Alternative Road to Empowerment," *Organizational Dynamics* (Winter 1992): 48–62.
50. P. Block, *The Empowered Manager: Positive Political Skills at Work* (San Francisco: Jossey-Bass, 1987).
51. V. J. Derlega and J. Grzelak, eds., *Cooperation and Helping Behavior: Theories and Research* (New York: Academic Press, 1982).
52. A. G. Athos and J. J. Gabarro, *Interpersonal Behavior: Communication and Understanding in Relationships* (Englewood Cliffs, N.J.: Prentice-Hall, 1978).
53. J. L. Cordery, W. S. Mueller, and L. M. Smith, "Attitudinal and Behavioral Effects of Autonomous Group Working: A Longitudinal Field Study," *Academy of Management Journal* 34 (1991): 464–476.
54. B. Hughes, "25 Stepping Stones for Self-Directed Work Teams," *Training* 28 (1991): 44–46.
55. R. M. Robinson, S. L. Oswald, K. S. Swinehart, and J. Thomas, "Southwest Industries: Creating High-Performance Teams for High-Technology Production," *Planning Review*, published by the Planning Forum, Nov.–Dec. 1991, 19, 10–47.
56. A. Lienert, "Forging a New Partnership," *Management Review* 83 (1994): 39–43.
57. S. Thiagaraian, "A Game for Cooperative Learning," *Training and Development*, (May 1992), 35–41.
58. D. C. Hambrick and P. Mason, "Upper Echelons: The Organization as a Reflection of Its Top Managers," *Academy of Management Review* 9 (1984): 193–206.
59. D. C. Hambrick, "The Top Management Team: Key to Strategic Success," *California Management Review* 30 (1987): 88–108.
60. D. C. Hambrick and G. D. S. Fukutomi, "The Seasons of a CEO's Tenure," *Academy of Management Review* 16 (1991): 719–742.
61. J. C. Quick, D. L. Nelson, and J. D. Quick, "Successful Executives: How Independent?" *Academy of Management Executive* 1 (1987): 139–145.
62. A. Bennett, "Firms Run by Executive Teams Can Reap Rewards, Incur Risks," *Wall Street Journal*, 5 February 1991, B1, B2.
63. N. J. Adler, *International Dimensions of Organizational Behavior* (Boston: PWS-KENT, 1991).
64. I. D. Steiner, *Group Process and Productivity* (New York: Academic Press, 1972).
65. J. W. Pfeiffer and C. Nolde, eds., *The Encyclopedia of Team-Development Activities* (San Diego: University Associates, 1991).
66. J. Keebler, "Mustang Cobra Bows, Woman at the Wheel," *Automotive News* (January 25, 1993): 44.
67. P. Ingrassia and N. Templin, "Running Strong," *Wall Street Journal*, 16 July 1992, A1, A6.

CHAPTER 10

Decision Making by Individuals and Groups

LEARNING OBJECTIVES

After reading this chapter, you should be able to do the following:

- Explain the assumptions of bounded rationality.
- Describe Jung's cognitive styles and how they affect managerial decision making.
- Understand the role of creativity in decision making, and practice ways to increase your own creativity.
- Identify the advantages and disadvantages of group decision making.
- Discuss the symptoms of groupthink and ways to prevent it.
- Evaluate the strengths and weaknesses of several group decision-making techniques.
- Describe the effects that expert systems and group decision support systems have on decision making organizations.
- Utilize an "ethics check" for examining managerial decisions.

OPENING SPOTLIGHT

Going Global at Federal Express: A Bad Decision?

In 1989, Fred Smith, founder of Federal Express Corporation, considered buying Tiger International's Flying Tiger cargo line. Flying Tiger held landing rights in Australia, Malaysia, and the Philippines, which are hard to obtain, and these routes were essential for global expansion.

http://www.fedex.com/

Smith and his management team, in their decision process, identified four risks. First, there would be problems integrating the two companies' pilot seniority lists. Second, there would be tremendous costs in maintaining Tiger's old planes and revamping its computer system. Third, some freight forwarders in Tiger's airport-to-airport business would probably defect, threatened by Federal's door-to-door service. Finally, the traditional airfreight market would have to remain stable while the transition was completed.

The team made a risky decision and bought Flying Tiger. Critics said FedEx paid $880 million for a fleet of old planes and a sagging company. Furthermore, Tiger's work force was unionized, whereas Federal Express's was not. This would cause problems in integrating the two companies' employees. Maintaining Tiger's antiquated aircraft would cost a fortune. Fred Smith and his team found that putting the two companies together was more difficult that expected, taking more time, money, and effort. FedEx's overseas operations lost $629 million in the first three years. Was the decision a disaster? We will follow up in the Closing Spotlight.[1] ■

The Decision-Making Process

programmed decision

A simple, routine matter for which a manager has an established decision rule.

nonprogrammed decision

A new, complex decision that requires a creative solution.

■ Decision making is a critical activity in the lives of managers. The decisions a manager faces can range from very simple, routine matters for which the manager has an established decision rule (**programmed decisions**) to new and complex decisions that require creative solutions (**nonprogrammed decisions**).[2] Scheduling lunch hours for one's work group is a programmed decision. The manager performs the decision activity on a daily basis, using an established procedure with the same clear goal in mind. The Federal Express management team's decision to buy Flying Tiger in the Opening Spotlight was certainly a nonprogrammed decision. The decision to acquire the company was unique, was unstructured, and required considerable judgment. Regardless of the type of decision made, it is helpful to understand as much as possible about how individuals and groups make decisions.

Decision making is a process involving a series of steps, as shown in Figure 10.1. The first step is recognition of the problem; that is, the manager realizes that a decision must be made. Identification of the real problem is important; otherwise, the manager may be reacting to symptoms and firefighting rather than dealing with the root cause of the problem. It is also important at this stage to identify the objective of the decision. In other words, the manager must determine what is to be accomplished by the decision.

The second step in the decision-making process is gathering information relevant to the problem. The manager must pull together sufficient information about why the problem occurred. This involves conducting a thorough diagnosis of the situation and going on a fact-finding mission.

The third step is listing and evaluating alternative courses of action. During this step, a thorough "what if" analysis should also be conducted to determine the various factors that could influence the outcome. It is important to generate a wide range of options and creative solutions in order to be able to move on to the fourth step.

Alternate Example
One indicator of stress in decision making is constant requests for help. Some individuals never have enough assistance or information to override their fear of decision making.

Next, the manager selects the alternative that best meets the decision objective. If the problem has been diagnosed correctly and sufficient alternatives have been identified, this step is much easier.

Finally, the solution is implemented. The situation must then be monitored to see whether the decision met its objective. Consistent monitoring and periodic feedback is an essential part of the follow-up process.

Decision making can be stressful. Managers must make decisions with significant risk and uncertainty, and often without full information. They must trust and rely on others in arriving at their decisions, but they are ultimately respon-

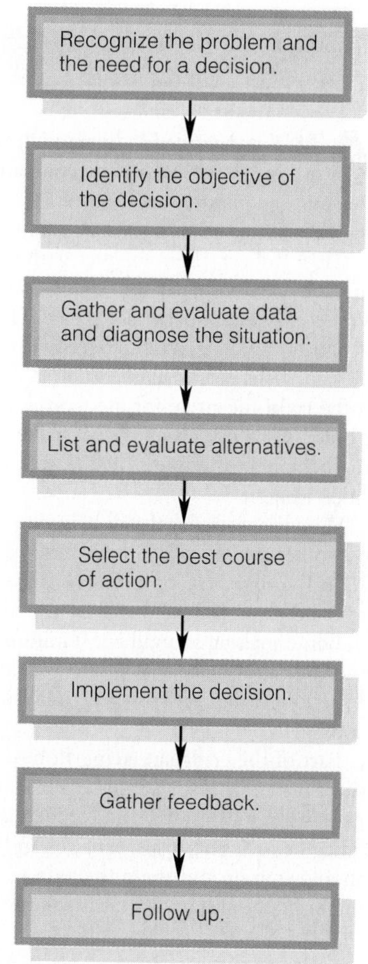

■ **FIGURE 10.1**
The Decision-Making Process

sible. And often, they meet with considerable criticism. The Organizational Reality feature presents the case of Robert Allen, CEO of AT&T, who like other CEOs endures the stress of making decisions that affect thousands of people.

http://www.att.com/

Models of Decision Making

■ The success of any organization depends on managers' abilities to make **effective decisions**. An effective decision is timely, is acceptable to the individuals affected by it, and meets the desired objective.[3] This section describes three models of decision making: the rational model, the bounded rationality model, and the garbage can model.

effective decision
A timely decision that meets a desired objective and is acceptable to those individuals affected by it.

Rational Model

Rationality refers to a logical, step-by-step approach to decision making, with a thorough analysis of alternatives and their consequences. The rational model of decision making comes from classic economic theory and contends that the decision maker is completely rational in his or her approach. The rational model has the following important assumptions:

1. The outcome will be completely rational.
2. The decision maker has a consistent system of preferences, which is used to choose the best alternative.
3. The decision maker is aware of all the possible alternatives.

rationality
A logical, step-by-step approach to decision making, with a thorough analysis of alternatives and their consequences.

Discussion Consideration
Ask students to reflect on a recent decision they had to make. How closely did their decision making process follow the rational model?

ORGANIZATIONAL REALITY

Taking the Heat for Decisions at AT&T

AT&T announced a shocking decision: It would fire 30,000 people and cut its payroll by 40,000 jobs. The company would split into separate long-distance, equipment, and computer companies, and the job cuts followed that decision. The stock market reacted to the news by adding $6 billion to AT&T's stock market value.

CEO Robert Allen was met with considerable criticism for his decision. The stock market reaction increased Allen's own stockholdings and options by about $5 million. When asked about the fact that the layoffs would make him richer, he reflected on the decision. "Did I make the decision [in order] to increase my personal wealth? Hell, no," he said. "Increasing shareowner value is the right incentive for me to have at AT&T. Is it the right incentive for me to affect 40,000 people? . . . I don't know. . . . Is it fair? . . . I don't know if it's fair. I don't make the rules . . . it's the worst part of my job. I have the personal experience of saying to people, 'There's no place for you here.' It's not fun. I don't like it."

Why the need for the downsizing? AT&T's $7.5 billion purchase of NCR mainframe computer company five years ago may have been a bad decision. Allen concedes that AT&T took a bath on NCR because "we didn't make it work." First, AT&T had tried to build a computer business internally, and failed. Then it bought NCR, which was at the time making around $350 million. After the purchase, nothing went right. Last year the computer business lost an estimated $600 million before taxes—not counting the $1.6 billion that it cost to restructure and get out of the business of making personal computers.

Part of the criticism facing Bob Allen and other CEOs who make downsizing decisions has to do with fairness. Is it fair that companies are eviscerating their payrolls, people are losing jobs, and top managers retain high salaries? Some don't think so. They believe that top executives and boards of directors, who make such decisions, should step up and share the pain with employees who are affected. Shared sacrifice might go a long way toward making these decisions a little more palatable. ■

SOURCES: A. Sloan, "For Whom the Bell Tolls," *Newsweek*, January 15, 1996: 44–45; C. J. Loomis, "AT&T Has No Clothes," *Fortune*, February, 5, 1996: 78–80.

4. The decision maker can calculate the probability of success for each alternative.[4]

In the rational model, the decision maker strives to optimize, that is, to select the best possible alternative.

Given the assumptions of the rational model, it is unrealistic. There are time constraints and limits to human knowledge and information-processing capabilities. In addition, a manager's preferences and needs change often. The rational model is thus an ideal that managers strive for in making decisions. It captures the way a decision should be made but does not reflect the reality of managerial decision making.[5]

Bounded Rationality Model

Discussion Consideration
Ask students to identify common heuristics, or rules of thumb, that they use in their decision making.

Recognizing the deficiencies of the rational model, Herbert Simon suggested that there are limits upon how rational a decision maker can actually be. His decision theory, the bounded rationality model, earned a Nobel Prize in 1978.

Simon's model, also referred to as the "administrative man" theory, rests on the idea that there are constraints that force a decision maker to be less than completely rational. The bounded rationality model has four assumptions:

1. Managers select the first alternative that is satisfactory.

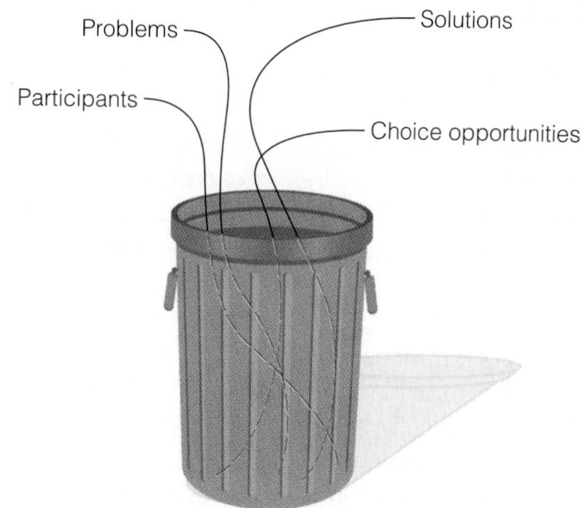

■ **FIGURE 10.2**

The Garbage Can Model

SOURCE: Reprinted from "A Garbage Can Model of Organizational Choice," M. D. Cohen, J. G. March, and J. P. Olsen. Published in *Administrative Science Quarterly* 17 (March 1972) 1–25 by permission of *Administrative Science Quarterly*.

2. Managers recognize that their conception of the world is simple.
3. Managers are comfortable making decisions without determining all the alternatives.
4. Managers make decisions by rules of thumb or heuristics.

Bounded rationality assumes that managers **satisfice**; that is, they select the first alternative that is "good enough," because the costs of optimizing in terms of time and effort are too great.[6] Further, the theory assumes that managers develop shortcuts, called **heuristics**, to make decisions in order to save mental activity. Heuristics are rules of thumb that allow managers to make decisions based on what has worked in past experiences.

Does the bounded rationality model more realistically portray the managerial decision process? Research indicates that it does.[7] One of the reasons that managers face limits to their rationality is because they must make decisions under risk and time pressure. The situation they find themselves in is highly uncertain, and the probability of success is not known.

bounded rationality

A theory that suggests that there are limits upon how rational a decision maker can actually be.

satisfice

To select the first alternative that is "good enough," because the costs in time and effort are too great to optimize.

heuristics

Shortcuts in decision making that save mental activity.

Garbage Can Model

Sometimes the decision-making process in organizations appears to be haphazard and unpredictable. In the **garbage can model,** decisions are random and unsystematic.[8] Figure 10.2 depicts the garbage can model. In this model, the organization is a garbage can in which problems, solutions, participants, and choice opportunities are floating around randomly. If the four factors happen to connect, a decision is made.[9] The quality of the decision depends on timing. The right participants must find the right solution to the right problem at the right time.

The garbage can model illustrates the idea that not all organizational decisions are made in a step-by-step, systematic fashion. Especially under conditions of high uncertainty, the decision process may be chaotic. Some decisions appear to happen out of sheer luck.

garbage can model

A theory that contends that decisions in organizations are random and unsystematic.

Points to Emphasize

The research process used by social scientists parallels the decision making process in many ways. The actual process involves elements of each of the decision making models presented here.

Decision Making and Risk

■ Fred Smith's team faced many risks in their decision to buy Flying Tiger. Would the two groups of employees mesh well? What would be their competitors' reactions? Could Federal Express generate enough international business to make a profit, given the costliness of the acquisition? The uncertainty of these issues made it a risky decision.

Risk and the Manager

risk aversion

The tendency to choose options that entail fewer risks and less uncertainty.

Individuals differ in terms of their willingness to take risks. Some people experience **risk aversion**. They choose options that entail fewer risks, preferring familiarity and certainty. Other individuals are risk takers; that is, they accept greater potential for loss in decisions, tolerate greater uncertainty, and in general are more likely to make risky decisions.

Research indicates that women are more averse to risk taking than men and that older, more experienced managers are more risk averse than younger managers. There is also some evidence that successful managers take more risks than unsuccessful managers.[10] However, the tendency to take risks or avoid them is only part of behavior toward risk. Risk taking is influenced not only by an individual's tendency but also by the specific situation the decision maker faces.[11]

The way managers behave in response to uncertainty and risk has important implications for organizations. Many individuals find uncertainty stressful, and one of the negative consequences of distress in organizations is faulty decision making by managers. One way to manage the decision-making behavior of employees is to model effective decision making under uncertainty by displaying the desired behavior. This communicates to employees the acceptable level of risk-taking behavior in the organization.

Upper-level managers face a tough task in managing risk-taking behavior. By discouraging lower-level managers from taking risks, they may stifle creativty and innovation. However, if upper-level managers are going to encourage risk taking, they must allow employees to fail without fear of punishment. One way to accomplish this is to consider failure "enlightened trial and error."[12] The key is establishing a consistent attitude toward risk within the organization.

When individuals take risks, losses may occur. Suppose an oil producer thinks there is an opportunity to uncover oil by reentering an old drilling site. She gathers a group of investors, she shows them the logs, and they chip in to finance the venture. The reentry is drilled to a certain depth, and nothing is found. Convinced they did not drill deep enough, the producer goes back to the investors and requests additional financial backing to continue drilling. The investors consent, and she drills deeper, only to find nothing. She approaches the investors, and after lengthy discussion, they agree to provide more money to drill deeper. Why do decision makers sometimes throw good money after bad? Why do they continue to provide resources to what looks like a losing venture?

Escalation of Commitment

escalation of commitment

The tendency to continue to commit resources to a losing course of action.

Continuing to commit resources to a losing course of action is known as **escalation of commitment**.[13] A situation often cited as an example is former President Lyndon Johnson's continued commitment of troops and money to the Vietnam War, even though many advisors had warned that U.S. involvement was a losing effort.

Alternate Example

Escalation may be related to personality. Political scientist James David Barber suggests that active-negative personalities, such as LBJ and Nixon, are prone to intense rigidification when faced with a crisis. This rigidification leads to escalation of commitment. SOURCE: J. D. Barber, The Presidential Character,

In situations characterized by escalation of commitment, individuals who make decisions that turn out to be poor choices tend to hold fast to those choices, even when substantial costs are incurred.[14] Why does escalation of commitment occur? One explanation is offered by cognitive dissonance theory, as we discussed in Chapter 4. This theory assumes that humans dislike inconsistency, and that when there is inconsistency among their attitudes or inconsistency between their attitudes and behavior, they strive to reduce the dissonance.[15]

Hanging on to a poor decision can be costly to organizations. Organizations can deal with escalation of commitment in several ways. One is to split the responsibility for decisions about projects. One individual can make the initial decision, and another individual can make subsequent decisions on the project. Another suggestion is to provide individuals with a graceful exit from poor decisions so that their images are not threatened. One way of accomplishing this is to reward people who admit to poor decisions before escalating their commitment to them. A recent study also suggested that having groups, rather than individuals, make an initial investment decision would reduce escalation. Support was found for this idea. Participants in group decision making may experience a diffusion of responsibility for the failed decision rather than feeling personally responsible; thus, they can pull out of a bad decision without threatening their image.[16]

Discussion Consideration
Ask students for examples of escalation of commitment. How is this escalation different from stubbornness?

We have seen that there are limits to how rational a manager can be in making decisions. Most managerial decisions involve considerable risk, and individuals react differently to risk situations.

Jung's Cognitive Styles

■ In Chapter 3 we introduced Jungian theory as a way of understanding and appreciating differences among individuals. This theory is especially useful in pointing out that individuals have different styles of making decisions. Carl Jung's original theory identified two styles of information gathering (sensing and intuiting) and two styles of making judgments (thinking and feeling). You already know what each individual preference means. Jung contended that individuals prefer one style of perceiving and one style of judging.[17] The combination of a perceiving style and a judging style is called a **cognitive style**. There are four cognitive styles: sensing/thinking (ST), sensing/feeling (SF), intuiting/thinking (NT), and intuiting/feeling (NF). Let us look at how each of the cognitive styles affects managerial decision making.[18]

Discussion Consideration
Ask students to compare cognitive styles with the three models of decision making presented earlier. Are certain types more prone to the rational or garbage can models?

cognitive style
An individual's preference for gathering information and evaluating alternatives.

STs rely on facts. They conduct an impersonal analysis of the situation and then make an analytical, objective decision. The ST cognitive style is valuable in organizations because it produces a clear, simple solution. STs remember details and seldom make factual errors. Their weakness is that they may alienate others because of their tendency to ignore interpersonal aspects of decisions. In addition, they tend to avoid risks.

SFs also gather factual information, but they make judgments in terms of how they affect people. They place great importance on interpersonal relationships but also take a practical approach to gathering information for problem solving. The SFs' strength in decision making lies in their ability to handle interpersonal problems well and their ability to take calculated risks. SFs may have trouble accepting new ideas that break the rules in the organization.

NTs focus on the alternative possibilities in a situation and then evaluate the possibilities objectively and impersonally. NTs love to initiate ideas, and they like to focus on the long term. They are innovative and will take risks. Weaknesses of NTs include their tendencies to ignore arguments based on facts and to ignore the feelings of others.

NFs also search out alternative possibilities, but they evaluate the possibilities in terms of how they will affect the people involved. They enjoy participative decision making and are committed to developing their employees. However, NFs may be prone to making decisions based on personal preferences rather than on more objective data. They may also become too responsive to the needs of others.

Research tends to support the existence of these four cognitive styles. One study asked managers to describe their ideal organization, and researchers found strong similarities in the description of managers with the same cognitive style.[19] STs wanted an organization that relied on facts and details and that exercised impersonal methods of control. SFs focused on facts, too, but they did so in terms of the relationships within the organization. NTs emphasized broad issues and described impersonal, idealistic organizations. NFs described an organization that would serve humankind well and focused on general, humanistic values.

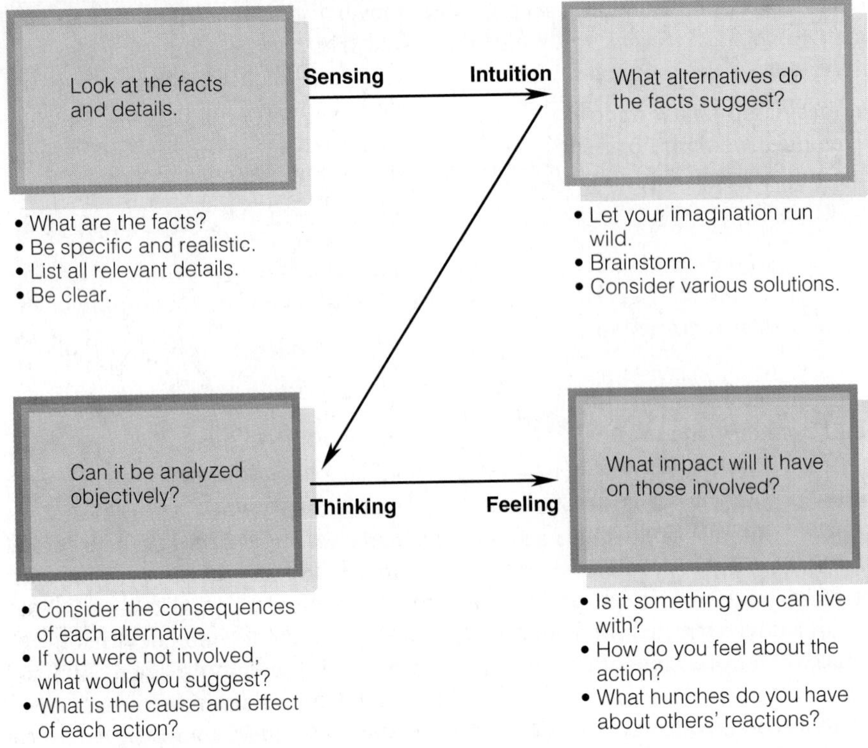

FIGURE 10.3

The Z Problem-Solving Model

SOURCE: From *Type Talk at Work* by Otto Kroeger and Janet M. Thuesen. Copyright © 1992 by Otto Kroeger and Janet M. Thuesen. Used by permission of Dell Books, a division of Bantam Doubleday Dell Publishing Group, Inc.

Other studies have found that MBA students with different cognitive styles exhibited these different styles in making strategic planning decisions and in making production decisions in a computer-simulated manufacturing environment.[20]

All four cognitive styles have much to contribute to organizational decision making.[21] Isabel Briggs Myers, creator of the MBTI, also developed the Z problem-solving model, which capitalizes on the strengths of the four separate preferences (sensing, intuiting, thinking, and feeling). By using the Z problem-solving model, managers can use both their preferences and nonpreferences to make decisions more effectively. The Z model is presented in Figure 10.3.

According to this model, good problem solving has four steps:

1. *Examine the facts and details.* Use sensing to gather information about the problem.
2. *Generate alternatives.* Use intuiting to develop possibilities.
3. *Analyze the alternatives objectively.* Use thinking to logically determine the effects of each alternative.
4. *Weigh the impact.* Use feeling to determine how the people involved will be affected.

Points to Emphasize
Selective exposure may impact the decision making process by limiting the number of options that are actually considered.

Using the Z model can help an individual develop his or her nonpreferences. Another way to use the Z model is to rely on others to perform the nonpreferred activities. For example, an individual who is an NF might want to turn to a trusted NT for help in analyzing alternatives objectively.

Other Individual Influences on Decision Making

In addition to the cognitive styles just examined, many other individual differences affect a manager's decision making. Other personality characteristics, attitudes, and values, along with all of the individual differences variables that were discussed in Chapters 3 and 4, have implications for managerial decision making. Two particular individual influences that can enhance decision-making effectiveness will be highlighted in this section: intuition and creativity.

The Role of Intuition

There is some evidence that managers use their **intuition** to make decisions. Henry Mintzberg, in his work on managerial roles, found that in many cases managers do not appear to use a systematic, step-by-step approach to decision making. Rather, Mintzberg argued, managers make judgments based on "hunches."[22] Daniel Isenberg studied the way senior managers make decisions and found that intuition was used extensively, especially as a mechanism to evaluate decisions made more rationally.[23] Robert Beck studied the way BankAmerica managers made decisions about the future direction of the company following the deregulation of the banking industry. Beck described their use of intuition as an antidote to "analysis paralysis," or the tendency to analyze decisions rather than developing innovative solutions.[24]

intuition

A fast, positive force in decision making utilized at a level below consciousness that involves learned patterns of information.

Discussion Consideration

What is the role of intuition in decision making?

Just what is intuition? In Jungian theory, intuiting (N) is one preference used to gather data. This is only one way that the concept of intuition has been applied to managerial decision making, and it is perhaps the most widely researched form of the concept of intuition. There are, however, many definitions of *intuition* in the managerial literature. Chester Barnard, one of the early influential management researchers, argued that intuition's main attributes were speed and the inability of the decision maker to determine how the decision was made.[25] Other researchers have contended that intuition occurs at an unconscious level, and this is why the decision maker cannot verbalize how the decision was made.[26]

Intuition has been variously described as follows:

- The ability to know or recognize quickly and readily the possibilities of a situation.[27]
- Smooth automatic performance of learned behavior sequences.[28]
- Simply analyses frozen into habit and into the capacity for rapid response through recognition.[29]

These definitions share some common assumptions. First, there seems to be a notion that intuition is fast. Second, intuition is utilized at a level below consciousness. Third, there seems to be agreement that intuition involves learned patterns of information. Fourth, intuition appears to be a positive force in decision making.

The use of intuition may lead to more ethical decisions. Intuition allows an individual to take on another's role with ease, and role taking is a fundamental part of developing moral reasoning. You may recall from Chapter 4 the role of cognitive moral development in ethical decision making. One study found a strong link between cognitive moral development and intuition. The development of new perspectives through intuition leads to higher moral growth, and thus to more ethical decisions.[30]

One question that arises is whether managers can be taught to use their intuition. Weston Agor, who has conducted workshops on developing intuitive skills in managers, has attained positive results in organizations such as Tenneco and the city of Phoenix. Agor suggests relaxation techniques, using images to guide the mind, and taking creative pauses before making a decision.[31] A recent review of the research on intuition suggests that although intuition itself cannot be taught, managers can be trained to rely more fully on the promptings of their intuition.[32]

Intuition is an elusive concept, and one with many definitions. There is an interesting paradox regarding intuition. Some researchers view "rational" methods as preferable to intuition, yet satisfaction with a rational decision is usually determined by how the decision feels intuitively.[33] Intuition appears to have a positive effect on managerial decision making, yet researchers need to agree on a common definition and conduct further research to increase our knowledge of the role of intuition at work and the influence of experience on our intuitive capabilities.

Creativity at Work

creativity
A process influenced by individual and organizational factors that results in the production of novel and useful ideas, products, or both.

Points to Emphasize
To create means to bring into existence.

Creativity is a process influenced by individual and organizational factors that results in the production of novel and useful ideas, products, or both.[34] The social and technological changes that organizations face require creative decisions.[35] Managers of the future need to develop special competencies to deal with the turbulence of change, and one of these important competencies is the ability to promote creativity in organizations.[36]

Creativity is a process that is at least in part unconscious. The four stages of the creative process are preparation, incubation, illumination, and verification.[37] Preparation means seeking out new experiences and opportunities to learn, because creativity grows from a base of knowledge. Travel and educational opportunities of all kinds open the individual's mind. Incubation is a process of reflective thought and is often conducted unconsciously. During incubation, the individual engages in other pursuits while the mind considers the problem and works on it. Illumination occurs when the individual senses an insight for solving the problem. Finally, verification is conducted to determine if the solution or idea is valid. This is accomplished by thinking through the implications of the decision, presenting the idea to another person, or trying out the decision. There are both individual and organizational influences on the creative process.

At Hallmark Cards, creativity is an essential rather than a luxury. Hallmark recognizes employee individuality, encourages work/home life balance, and promotes open communication. To design new card lines, the company brings together cross-functional teams of people who were previously separated by departments, floors, and buildings. These teams form support networks in which creativity flourishes.

INDIVIDUAL INFLUENCES Several individual variables are related to creativity. One group of factors involves the cognitive processes that creative individuals tend to use. One cognitive process is divergent thinking, meaning the individual's ability to generate several potential solutions to a problem.[38] In addition, associational abilities and the use of imagery are associated with creativity.[39] Unconscious processes such as dreams are also essential cognitive processes related to creative thinking.[40]

Personality factors have also been related to creativity in studies of individuals from several different occupations. These characteristics include intellectual and artistic values, breadth of interests, high energy, concern with achievement, independence of judgment, intuition, self-confidence, and a creative self-image.[41] Tolerance of ambiguity, intrinsic motivation, risk taking, and a desire for recognition are also associated with creativity.[42]

There is also evidence that people who are in a good mood are more creative. One study found that individuals who were in a good mood were more successful at creative problem solving than people whose mood was neutral.[43]

ORGANIZATIONAL INFLUENCES The organizational environment in which people work can either support creativity or impede creative efforts. Creativity killers include focusing on how work is going to be evaluated, being watched while you are working, competing with other people in win-lose situations, and being given limits on how you can do your work. In contrast, creativity facilitators include feelings of autonomy, being part of a team with diverse skills, and having supervisors who are creative role models.[44] Supportive supervision and support from peers are related to creativity.[45] Flexible organizational structures and participative decision making have also been associated with creativity.[46]

Studies of the role of organizational rewards in encouraging creativity have mixed results. Some studies have shown that monetary incentives improve creative performance, whereas others have found that material rewards do not influence innovative activity.[47] Still other studies have indicated that explicitly contracting to obtain a reward led to lower levels of creativity when compared with contracting for no reward, being presented with just the task, or being presented with both the task and receiving the reward later.[48] Organizations can therefore enhance individuals' creative decision making by providing a supportive environment, participative decision making, and a flexible structure.

Alternate Example
Creative people allow time for the incubation of ideas. Seymour Cray, founder of Cray Computers, divided his time between creating the biggest, fastest, most powerful computer in the world and digging a tunnel underneath his house. It took him an hour or so to dig four inches, but he believed that effort helped him solve his computer problems. SOURCE: P. Russell and R. Evans, *The Creative Manager* (San Francisco, Jossey-Bass, 1992), 52.

INDIVIDUAL/ORGANIZATION FIT Research has indicated that creative performance is highest when there is a match, or fit, between the individual and organizational influences on creativity. For example, when individuals who desire to be creative are matched with an organization that values creative ideas, the result is more creative performance.[49]

Points to Emphasize
At one time, the research and development department was considered the only creative department in organizations. Today, all members of the organization must contribute to and support the creative efforts required to maintain a competitive advantage.

One mistaken assumption that many people have regarding creativity is that either you have it or you do not. Research refutes this myth and has shown that individuals can be trained to be more creative.[50] One company that has found success in this way is Frito-Lay. Frito-Lay offers three courses in creative problem solving and trains its own trainers to hold creativity workshops within each plant. The company saved $500 million dollars during the first six years of its creativity training effort and believes this is directly related to the employees' creative problem-solving skills.[51] Challenge 10.1 allows you to practice your own creative problem-solving skills.

http://www.fritolay.com/

Part of creativity training involves learning to open up mental locks that keep us from generating creative alternatives to a decision or problem. The following are some mental locks that diminish creativity:

- Searching for the "right" answer.
- Trying to be logical.
- Following the rules.
- Avoiding ambiguity.
- Striving for practicality.
- Being afraid to look foolish.
- Avoiding problems outside our own expertise.
- Fearing failure.
- Believing we are not really creative.
- Not making play a part of work.[52]

Note that many of these mental locks stem from values within organizations. Organizations can facilitate creative decision making in many ways. Rewarding creativity, allowing employees to fail, making work more fun, and providing creativity training are a few suggestions.

3M is a company that consistently ranks among the top ten in *Fortune's* annual list of most admired corporations. It earned this reputation through innovation: more than one-quarter of 3M's sales are from products less than four years old. Post-It Notes, for example, were created by a worker who wanted little adhesive papers to mark hymns for church service. He thought of another worker who had perfected a light adhesive, and the two spent their "free time" developing Post-It Notes. Last year 3M sold more than $100 million of them. The Organizational Reality feature shows how 3M manages creative people.

http://www.3M.com/

CHALLENGE

10.1 Creative Problem Solving

Each of the following problems is an equation that can be solved by substituting the appropriate words for the letters. Have fun with them!

Examples: 3F = 1Y (3 feet = 1 yard.)
4LC = GL (4 leaf clover = Good luck.)

1. M + M + NH + V + C + RI = NE.
2. "1B in the H = 2 in the B."
3. 8D − 24H = 1W.
4. 3P = 6.
5. HH & MH at 12 = N or M.
6. 4J + 4Q + 4K = All the FC.
7. S & M & T & W & T & F & S are D of W.
8. A + N + AF + MC + CG = AF.
9. T = LS State.
10. 23Y − 3Y = 2D.
11. E − 8 = Z.
12. Y + 2D = T.
13. C + 6D = NYE.
14. Y − S − S − A = W.
15. A & E were the G of E.
16. My FL and South P are both MC.
17. "NN = GN."
18. N + P + SM = S of C.
19. 1 + 6Z = 1M.
20. "R = R = R."
21. AL & JG & WM & JK were all A.
22. N + V + P + A + A + C + P + I = P of S.
23. S + H of R = USC.

(Your instructor can provide the solution to this Challenge.)

SOURCE: Roger Von Oech, *A Whack on the Side of the Head* (New York: Warner, 1983). Used with permission.

Creativity is a global concern. Poland, for example, is undergoing a major shift from a centrally planned economy and monoparty rule to a market economy and Western-style democracy. One of the major concerns for Polish mangers is creativity. Finding ingenious solutions and having the ability to think creatively can be a question of life or death for Polish organizations, which are now making the transition to a faster pace of learning and change.[53]

Japanese companies manage creativity in a much different way than do North American firms. Min Basadur visited several major Japanese companies, including Matsushita, Hitachi, Toyota, and others, to conduct comparative research on organizational creativity in Japan and North America. He found several differences between the two cultures. First, Japanese companies place a strong emphasis on problem finding. Companies in North America, in contrast, are more reluctant to identify problems, because rewards often go to individuals who appear not to have many problems. Furthermore, Japanese companies have a structured mechanism for encouraging problem finding. Workers are given cards on which to write down problems or areas of discontent, and these are posted on a wall. When others notice a problem that interests them, they join forces to solve it.

Another difference that Basadur found involves rewards. In North America, the motivating factor for suggestions is money. A few employees submit ideas

ORGANIZATIONAL REALITY

3M's Ten Commandments for Managing Creative People

3M is one of the most visionary and adaptive companies in the world, and it owes its success to its creative employees. The company makes 66,000 products as diverse as fire hose linings, surgical gowns, bingo supplies, and Scotch tape. So what is 3M's secret?

3M keeps the magic going using ten commandments for managing creative people. In a nutshell, they are:

1. **Give folks time to follow their muse.** Technicians are free to devote 15 percent of their time to any project they wish.
2. **Create a culture of cooperation.** Everyone is encouraged to call up any other employee and tap into their expertise. Part of every person's job is to share knowledge—on the phone, in person, by e-mail, or any other way.
3. **Measure your results.** Each of 45 business units measures not only sales, earnings, and market share, but also what each business unit has done that is new.
4. **Stay ahead of the customer.** The most interesting products are ones that people need but can't articulate that they need.
5. **Stage a lot of celebrations.** The top awards are given on 3M's Oscar night, where some innovators are inducted into the Carlton Society, a hall of fame for company immortals.
6. **Be honest and know when to say no.** Managers decide early if an idea just won't make it commercially, and tell the person who came up with it. The creator can then shop the idea to another part of the company, which might pick it up.
7. **Make the company a lifetime career.** 3M rarely lays off people, and depends on long-term employees who know the 3M philosophy. They reason that it's tough to fire a lot of people and then ask the survivors to be innovative.
8. **Give your best managers assignments overseas.** Half of the company's annual sales come from outside the U.S. The company believes that you have to live abroad to learn that customers have different tastes and values, and that there are different ways of accomplishing goals.
9. **Keep increasing R&D spending.** 3M has for 20 straight years, even in the tough times.
10. **Don't follow everything Wall Street tells you.** Play it prudently so you have a cushion of money to let your technicians chase their dreams.

3M operates very closely to these ten ideas. Their approach can be summed up easily: Hire good people, and leave them alone. If you put fences around people, you get sheep. ■

SOURCE: "Ten Commandments of Managing Creative People," *Fortune*, January 16, 1995: 135–16.

3M rewards creative behavior in many ways. In 1972, the company established the Golden Step Award to acknowledge, emphasize and accelerate development of new markets and products.

that save a company large sums of money and reap large cash rewards. In Japan, all employees participate, and monetary rewards are small. Every suggestion gets a reward. For the Japanese, the most motivating rewards are intrinsic: accomplishment, recognition, and personal growth.[54]

Both intuition and creativity are important influences on managerial decision making. Both concepts require additional research so that managers can better understand how to use intuition and creativity, as well as how to encourage their employees to use them to make more effective decisions.

Participation in Decision Making

■ We have examined several features of individual decision making. In organizations, however, not all decisions are made by individuals acting alone. For one thing, managers work with employees who may participate in decision making. This section discusses the effects of employee participation and the appropriate level of participation for given circumstances.

The Effects of Participation

participative decision making
Decision making in which individuals who are affected by decisions influence the making of those decisions.

Participative decision making occurs when individuals who are affected by decisions influence the making of those decisions.[55] Participation is associated with greater feelings of autonomy and meaningfulness of work.[56] In addition, participative management has been found to increase employee creativity and job satisfaction.[57] Some studies have reported a positive link between participation and productivity.[58]

It is also important to acknowledge that some individuals do not respond well to participative decision making. They prefer instead to have managers make the decisions.[59] Ralph Stayer at Johnsonville Foods learned this when he attempted to move his company toward participative management. He announced to his management team that they would be responsible for making their own decisions; yet two years after the announcement, his plan was not working. He had nurtured the managers' inability to make decisions. Stayer said, "I didn't really want them to make independent decisions. I wanted them to make the decisions I would have made." He ended up replacing three top managers with people who could not read his mind and who were strong enough to call his bluff.[60]

The Vroom-Yetton-Jago Normative Decision Model

Points to Emphasize
The Vroom-Yetton-Jago model is a decision tree designed to tell a manager what method to use when making a decision.

How does a manager know when to have employees participate in the decision making process? Victor Vroom, Phillip Yetton, and Arthur Jago developed and refined the normative decision model, which helps managers determine the appropriate decision-making strategy to use.[61] In their model, they describe five forms of decision making. Two forms are autocratic (AI and AII), two are consultative (CI and CII), and one is a group method (G). The five forms of decision making follow:

- *The AI form.* The manager makes the decision alone, using whatever information is available at the time. This is the most authoritarian method.
- *The AII form.* The manager seeks information from employees or peers and then makes the decision. Employees may or may not know what the problem is before providing the information to the manager.
- *The CI form.* The manager explains the problem to appropriate peers or employees in a one-on-one format. The manager makes the decision, which may or may not reflect the others' inputs.

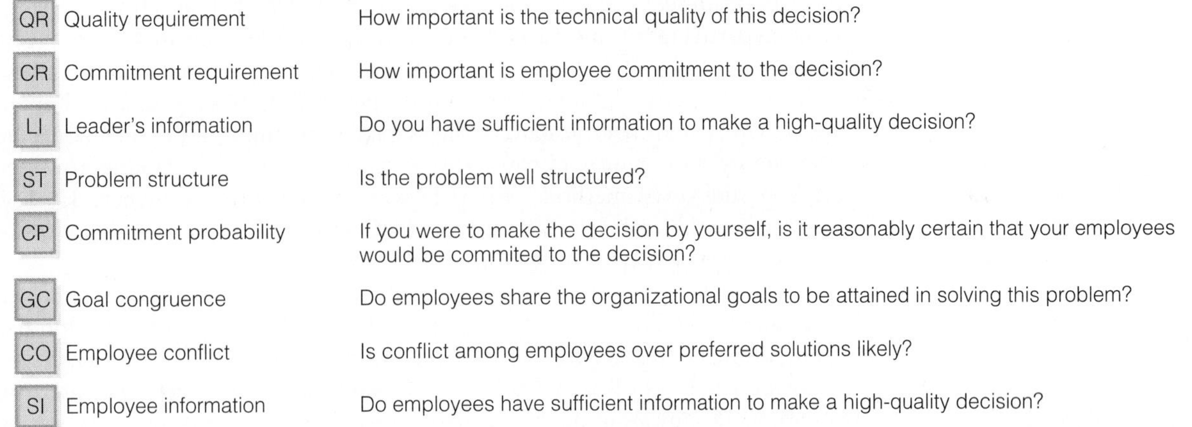

QR Quality requirement
How important is the technical quality of this decision?
CR Commitment requirement
How important is employee commitment to the decision?
LI Leader's information
Do you have sufficient information to make a high-quality decision?
ST Problem structure
Is the problem well structured?
CP Commitment probability
If you were to make the decision by yourself, is it reasonably certain that your employees would be commited to the decision?
GC Goal congruence
Do employees share the organizational goals to be attained in solving this problem?
CO Employee conflict
Is conflict among employees over preferred solutions likely?
SI Employee information
Do employees have sufficient information to make a high-quality decision?

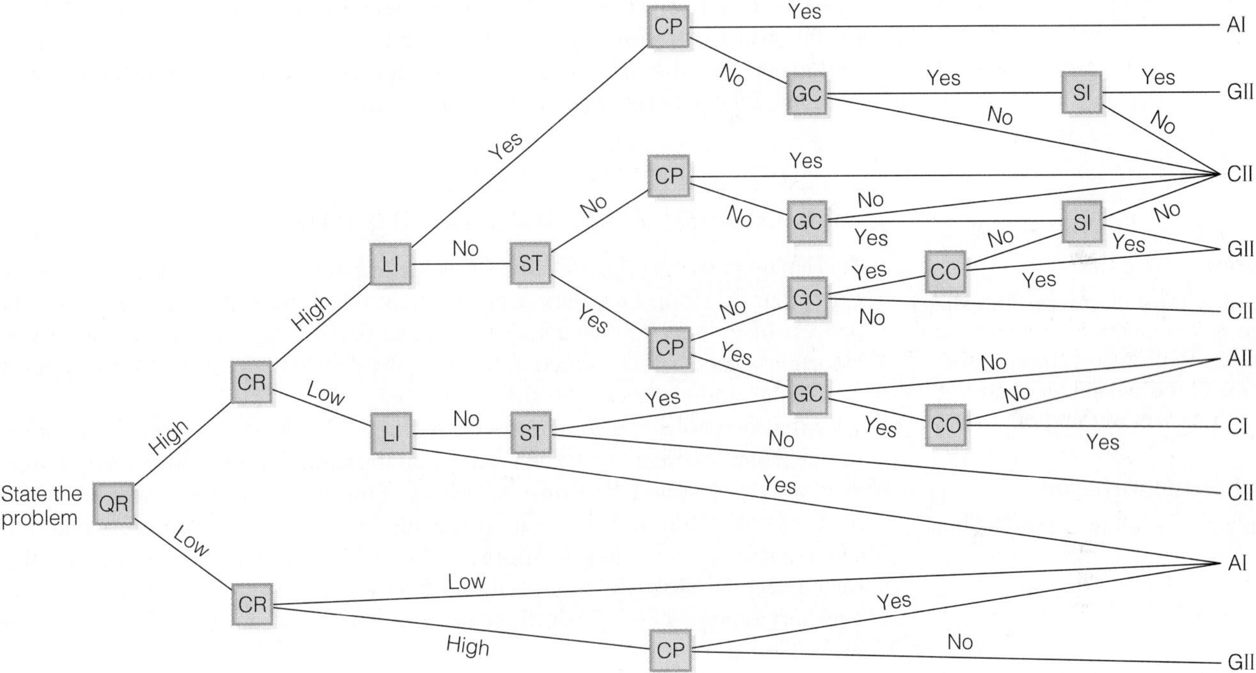

■ **FIGURE 10.4**

The Vroom-Yetton-Jago Normative Decision Model

SOURCE: Reprinted from *The New Leadership: Managing Participation in Organizations* by Victor H. Vroom and Arthur G. Jago, 1988, Englewood Cliffs, NJ: Prentice-Hall. Copyright 1987 by V. H. Vroom and A. G. Jago. Used with permission of the authors.

- *The CII form.* The manager explains the problem to employees or peers as a group. The manager makes the decision, which may or may not reflect the others' inputs.
- *The G form.* The manager explains the problem to employees and peers as a group, and the group makes the final decision.

The key to the normative decision model is that a manager should use the decision method most appropriate for a given decision situation. The manager arrives at the proper method by working through the decision tree shown in Figure 10.4. Each node in the decision tree asks the manager to answer a question about the decision situation. The questions reflect key attributes of the decision situation: time, quality, commitment, and information. Working through the decision tree leads to a prescribed decision style at the end of the path.

This version of the normative decision model is relatively new, so it is too early to ascertain how well it is supported by research. However, studies have supported an earlier version of the model proposed in 1973. Managers who were trained to diagnose the key attributes of the decision situation were better able to select the appropriate level of participation than managers who had not

Discussion Consideration

Do managers use a formal process, such as the normative model, to decide how to make decisions? Or do they have a dominant or preferred style they use in all situations?

received training.[62] In addition, research has shown that selecting the correct level of participation increases the effectiveness of decision making.[63] A study conducted in a large department store found that managers who used a decision style prescribed by the model had higher-performing work groups.[64] Research has also indicated that the skills of the manager are important in normative decision theory. For managers with strong conflict management skills, the use of more participative methods led to higher employee performance. However, managers with weak conflict management skills who used participative styles had more poorly performing employees.[65]

The best way to learn about the normative decision model is to practice using it. Challenge 10.2 gives you an opportunity to work through the decision tree.

In summary, the normative decision model emphasizes the importance of choosing the level of participation in decision making most appropriate to the situation. It shows managers that they must evaluate the decision thoroughly before choosing a process for reaching a decision. Research on earlier versions of the model is positive, and the new version appears to have promise. Given that group decision making is sometimes appropriate, we now turn to an examination of the process of group decision making.

The Group Decision-Making Process

synergy
A positive force in groups that occurs when group members stimulate new solutions to problems through the process of mutual influence and encouragement in the group.

social decision schemes
Simple rules used to determine final group decisions.

■ Managers use groups to make decisions for several reasons. One is for **synergy**; that is, group members stimulate new solutions to problems through the process of mutual influence and encouragement in the group. Another reason for using a group is to gain commitment to a decision. Groups also bring more knowledge and experience to the problem-solving situation.

Group decisions can sometimes be predicted by comparing the views of the initial group members with the final group decision. These simple relationships are known as **social decision schemes**. One social decision scheme is the majority-wins rule, in which the group supports whatever position is taken by the majority of its members. Another scheme, the truth-wins rule, predicts that the correct decision will emerge as an increasing number of members realize its appropriateness. The two-thirds-majority rule means that the decision favored by two-thirds or more of the members is supported. Finally, the first-shift rule states that members support a decision represented by the first shift in opinion shown by a member.

Research indicates that these social decision schemes can predict a group decision as much as 80 percent of the time.[66] Current research is aimed at discovering which rules are used in particular types of tasks. For example, studies indicate that the majority-wins rule is used most often in judgment tasks (that is, when the decision is a matter of preference or opinion), whereas the truth-wins rule predicts decisions best when the task is an intellective one (that is, when the decision has a correct answer).[67]

Advantages and Disadvantages of Group Decision Making

Discussion Consideration
Ask students if they prefer individual or group decision making. Under what conditions would they prefer one over the other?

Both advantages and disadvantages are associated with group decision making. The advantages include (1) more knowledge and information through the pooling of group member resources; (2) increased acceptance of, and commitment to, the decision, because the members had a voice in it; and (3) greater understanding of the decision, because members were involved in the various stages of the decision process. The disadvantages of group decision making include (1) pressure within the group to conform and fit in; (2) domination of the group by one forceful member or a dominant clique, who may ramrod the decision;

CHALLENGE

■ **10.2**

Apply the Normative Decision Model

Read the following case. Then, using Figure 10.4, work through the normative decision model to determine which decision making style to use.

You are the public relations manager for a software company that has just developed a new and revolutionary product. In fact, all indications are that this product will completely change the way people use computers.

The problem is how to market the product, because it is so vastly different. It is not clear whether previous marketing methods would work or not. There is considerable disagreement among your employees on what approach to use.

Each of your five employees has been talking to different advertising agencies, and each one has what he or she thinks is the absolute best advertising/marketing program.

Which decision style would you use in determining how to market your product? (Your instructor can provide the solution to this Challenge.)

SOURCE: D. Marcic, *Organizational Behavior: Experiences and Cases* (St. Paul: West, 1989), 166–170.

and (3) the amount of time required, because a group is slower than an individual to make a decision.[68]

Given these advantages and disadvantages, should an individual or a group make a decision? The Vroom-Yetton-Jago model is one tool for making this judgment. There is also substantial empirical research indicating that whether a group or an individual should be used depends on the type of task involved. For judgment tasks requiring an estimate or a prediction, groups are usually superior to individuals because of the breadth of experience that multiple individuals bring to the problem.[69] However, other studies have indicated that on tasks that have a correct solution, the most competent individual outperforms the group.[70] A recent study calls this finding into question. Much of the previous research on groups had been conducted in the laboratory, where group members interacted only for short periods of time. The researchers wanted to know how a longer experience in the group would affect decisions. Their study showed that groups who worked together for longer periods of time outperformed the most competent member 70 percent of the time. As groups gained experience, the best members became less important to the group's success.[71] This study demonstrated that experience in the group is an important variable to consider when evaluating the individual versus group decision-making question.

Given the emphasis on teams in the workplace, many managers believe that groups produce better decisions than do individuals, yet the evidence is mixed. It is evident that more research needs to be conducted in organizational settings to help answer this question.

Two potential liabilities are found in group decision making: groupthink and group polarization. These problems are discussed in the following sections.

Groupthink

One liability of a cohesive group is its tendency to develop **groupthink**, a dysfunctional process. Irving Janis, the originator of the groupthink concept, describes groupthink as "a deterioration of mental efficiencey, reality testing, and moral judgment" resulting from in-group pressures.[72]

groupthink

A deterioration of mental efficiency, reality testing, and moral judgment resulting from in-group pressures.

Certain conditions favor the development of groupthink. One of the antecedents is high cohesiveness. Cohesive groups tend to avoid conflicts and to

Points to Emphasize
The Abilene paradox is an updated version of groupthink. This paradox states that it is our inability to handle agreement (not disagreement) that keeps us from taking action.

demand conformity. Other antecedents include directive leadership, high stress, insulation of the group, and lack of methodical procedures for developing and evaluating alternatives. Two other conditions that encourage groupthink are having to make a highly consequential decision and time constraints.[73] A highly consequential decision is one that will have a great impact on the group members and on outside parties. When group members feel that they have a limited time in which to make a decision, they may rush through the process. These antecedents cause members to prefer concurrence in decisions and to fail to evaluate one another's suggestions critically. A group suffering from groupthink shows recognizable symptoms. Table 10.1 presents these symptoms and makes suggestions on how to avoid groupthink.[74]

A recent incident that has been examined for these symptoms of groupthink is the space shuttle *Challenger* disaster. On January 28, 1986, seventy-three seconds into its flight, the *Challenger* exploded, killing all seven members of its crew. The evidence pointed toward an O-ring seal that was still cold from nighttime temperatures and failed to do its job. A presidential commission was convened, and its investigation cited flawed decision making as a primary cause of the accident.

An analysis of the *Challenger* incident indicated that the negative symptoms of groupthink increased during the twenty-four hours prior to the decision to launch the spacecraft.[75] National Aeronautics and Space Administration (NASA) management officials were warned by engineers that the launch should be canceled because the O-rings would not withstand the temperatures. The

TABLE 10.1

Symptoms of Groupthink and How to Prevent It

SYMPTOMS OF GROUPTHINK

- *Illusions of invulnerability.* Group members feel they are above criticism. This symptom leads to excessive optimism and risk taking.
- *Illusions of group morality.* Group members feel they are moral in their actions and therefore above reproach. This symptom leads the group to ignore the ethical implications of their decisions.
- *Illusions of unanimity.* Group members believe there is unanimous agreement on the decisions. Silence is misconstrued as consent.
- *Rationalization.* Group members concoct explanations for their decisions to make them appear rational and correct. The results are that other alternatives are not considered, and there is an unwillingness to reconsider the group's assumptions.
- *Stereotyping the enemy.* Competitors are stereotyped as evil or stupid. This leads the group to underestimate its opposition.
- *Self-censorship.* Members do not express their doubts or concerns about the course of action. This prevents critical analysis of the decisions.
- *Peer pressure.* Any members who express doubts or concerns are pressured by other group members, who question their loyalty.
- *Mindguards.* Some members take it upon themselves to protect the group from negative feedback. Group members are thus shielded from information that might lead them to question their actions.

GUIDELINES FOR PREVENTING GROUPTHINK

- Ask each group member to assume the role of the critical evaluator who actively voices objections or doubts.
- Have the leader avoid stating his or her position on the issue prior to the group decision.
- Create several groups that work on the decision simultaneously.
- Bring in outside experts to evaluate the group process.
- Appoint a devil's advocate to question the group's course of action consistently.
- Evaluate the competition carefully, posing as many different motivations and intentions as possible.
- Once consensus is reached, encourage the group to rethink its position by reexamining the alternatives.

SOURCE: Irving L. Janis, *Groupthink: Psychological Studies of Policy Decisions and Fiascoes,* 2d ed. Copyright © 1982 by Houghton Mifflin Company. Used with permission.

engineers were pressured by their bosses to stifle their dissent, and their opinions were devalued. Further, the decision to launch was made by polling managers—engineers were not polled. There was overconfidence among the decision makers because of the record of success at NASA. Some managers knew that the rocket casings had been ordered to be redesigned, but this information was withheld from other decision makers.

Consequences of groupthink include an incomplete survey of alternatives, failure to evaluate the risks of the preferred course of action, biased information processing, and a failure to work out contingency plans. The overall result of groupthink is defective decision making. This was evident in the *Challenger* situation. The group considered only two alternatives: launch or no launch. They failed to consider the risks of their decision to launch the shuttle, and they did not develop any contingency plans.

Table 10.1 presents Janis's guidelines for avoiding groupthink. Many of these suggestions center around the notion of ensuring that decisions are evaluated completely, with opportunities for discussion from all group members. This strategy helps encourage members to evaluate one another's ideas critically.

Janis has used the groupthink framework to conduct historical analyses of several political and military fiascoes, including the Bay of Pigs invasion, the Vietnam War, and Watergate. One review of the decision situation in the *Challenger* incident proposed that two variables, time and leadership style, are important to include.[76] When a decision must be made quickly, there is more potential for groupthink. Leadership style can either promote groupthink (if the leader makes his or her opinion known up front) or avoid groupthink (if the leader encourages open and frank discussion).

There are few empirical studies of groupthink, and most of these involved students in a laboratory setting. More applied research may be seen in the future, however, as a questionnaire has been developed to measure the constructs associated with groupthink.[77] Janis's work on groupthink has led to several interdisciplinary efforts at understanding policy decisions.[78] The work underscores the need to examine multiple explanations for failed decisions.

Discussion Consideration
What steps can be taken to avoid faulty decision making?

Group Polarization

Another group phenomenon was discovered by a graduate student. His study showed that groups made riskier decisions; in fact, the group and each individual accepted greater levels of risk following a group discussion of the issue. Subsequent studies uncovered another shift—toward caution. Thus, group discussion produced shifts both toward more risky positions and toward more cautious positions.[79] Further research revealed that individual group member attitudes simply became more extreme following group discussion. Individuals who were initially against an issue became more radically opposed, and individuals who were in favor of the issue became more strongly supportive following discussion. These shifts came to be known as **group polarization**.[80]

group polarization
The tendency for group discussion to produce shifts toward more extreme attitudes among members.

The tendency toward polarization has important implications for group decision making. Groups whose initial views lean a certain way can be expected to adopt more extreme views following interaction.

Several ideas have been proposed to explain why group polarization occurs. One explanation is the social comparison approach. Prior to group discussion, individuals believe they hold better views than the other members. During group discussion, they see that their views are not so far from average, so they shift to more extreme positions.[81] A second explanation is the persuasive arguments view. It contends that group discussion reinforces the initial views of the members, so they take a more extreme position.[82] Both explanations are supported by research. It may be that both processes, along with others, cause the group to develop more polarized attitudes.

Alternate Example
George Bush would assign members of his staff to analyze various aspects of an issue without telling them his preference. This was an attempt to make sure the issues were analyzed thoroughly, with all options considered, rather than merely supporting the President's position.

Group polarization leads groups to adopt extreme attitudes. In some cases, this can be disastrous. For instance, if individuals are leaning toward a dangerous decision, they are likely to support it more strongly following discussion.

Both groupthink and group polarization are potential liabilities of group decision making. However, several techniques can be used to help prevent or control these two liabilities.

Techniques for Group Decision Making

■ Once a manager has determined that a group decision approach should be used, he or she can determine the technique that is best suited to the decision situation. Seven techniques will be briefly summarized: brainstorming, nominal group technique, Delphi technique, devil's advocacy, dialectical inquiry, quality circles and quality teams, and self-managed teams.

Brainstorming

brainstorming

A technique for generating as many ideas as possible on a given subject, while suspending evaluation until all the ideas have been suggested.

Brainstorming is a good technique for generating alternatives. The idea behind **brainstorming** is to generate as many ideas as possible, suspending evaluation until all of the ideas have been suggested. Participants are encouraged to build upon the suggestions of others, and imagination is emphasized. Groups that use brainstorming have been shown to produce significantly more ideas than groups that do not.[83]

One recent trend is the use of electronic brainstorming instead of verbal brainstorming in groups. Electronic brainstorming overcomes two common problems that can produce group brainstorming failure: production blocking and evaluation apprehension. In verbal brainstorming, individuals are exposed to the inputs of others. While listening to others, individuals are distracted from their own ideas. This is referred to as production blocking. When ideas are recorded electronically, participants are free from hearing the interruptions of others; thus production blocking is reduced. Some individuals suffer from evaluation apprehension in brainstorming groups. They fear that others might respond negatively to their ideas. In electronic brainstorming, input is anonymous, so evaluation apprehension is reduced. Studies indicate that electronic brainstorming groups outperform face-to-face brainstorming groups in the number of ideas generated.[84] Later in this chapter we will examine the effects of group decision support systems in more detail.

Nominal Group Technique

nominal group technique (NGT)

A structured approach to group decision making that focuses on generating alternatives and choosing one.

A structured approach to decision making that focuses on generating alternatives and choosing one is called **nominal group technique (NGT).** NGT has the following discrete steps:

1. Individuals silently list their ideas.
2. Ideas are written on a chart one at a time until all ideas are listed.
3. Discussion is permitted, but only to clarify the ideas. No criticism is allowed.
4. A written vote is taken.

NGT is a good technique to use in a situation where group members fear criticism from others.[85]

Delphi Technique

Delphi technique

Gathering the judgments of experts for use in decision making.

The **Delphi technique** originated at the Rand Corporation to gather the judgments of experts for use in decision making. Experts at remote locations respond to a questionnaire. A coordinator summarizes the responses to the questionnaire, and the summary is sent back to the experts. The experts then rate the various alternatives generated, and the coordinator tabulates the results. The Delphi technique is valuable in its ability to generate a number of independent judgments without the requirement of a face-to-face meeting.[86]

Discussion Consideration
Ask students when they would use the Delphi technique over the nominal group technique.

Devil's Advocacy

In the **devil's advocacy** decision method, a group or individual is given the role of critic. This devil's advocate has the task of coming up with the potential problems of a proposed decision. This helps organizations avoid costly mistakes in decision making by identifying potential pitfalls in advance.[87] As we discussed in Chapter 9, a devil's advocate who challenges the CEO and top management team can help sustain the vitality and performance of the upper echelon.

devil's advocacy

A technique for preventing groupthink in which a group or individual is given the role of critic during decision making.

Dialectical Inquiry

Dialectical inquiry is essentially a debate between two opposing sets of recommendations. Although it sets up a conflict, it is a constructive approach, because it brings out the benefits and limitations of both sets of ideas.[88] When using this technique, it is important to guard against a win-lose attitude and to concentrate on reaching the most effective solution for all concerned. Recent research has shown that the way a decision is framed (that is, win-win versus win-lose) is very important. A decision's outcome could be viewed as a gain or a loss, depending on the way the decision is framed.[89]

dialectical inquiry

A debate between two opposing sets of recommendations.

Quality Circles and Quality Teams

As you recall from Chapter 9, quality circles are small groups that voluntarily meet to provide input for solving quality or production problems. Quality circles are also a way of extending participative decision making into teams. Managers often listen to recommendations from quality circles and implement the suggestions. The rewards for the suggestions are intrinsic—involvement in the decision-making process is the primary reward.

Quality circles are often generated from the bottom up; that is, they provide advice to managers, who still retain decision-making authority. As such, quality circles are not empowered to implement their own recommendations. They operate in parallel fashion to the organization's structure, and they rely on voluntary participation.[90] In Japan, quality circles have been integrated into the organization instead of added on. This may be one reason for Japan's success with this technique.

Points to Emphasize
Time constraints may prevent managers from using group decision making techniques.

Quality teams, in contrast, are included in total quality management and other quality improvement efforts as part of a change in the organization's structure. Quality teams are generated from the top down and are empowered to act on their own recommendations. Whereas quality circles emphasize the generation of ideas, quality teams make data-based decisions about improving product and service quality. Various decision-making techniques are employed in quality teams. Brainstorming, flowcharts, and cause-and-effect diagrams help pinpoint problems that affect quality.

Quality circles and quality teams are methods for using groups in the decision-making process. Self-managed teams take the concept of participation one step further.

Self-Managed Teams

Another group decision-making method is the use of self-managed teams, which we also discussed in Chapter 9. The decision-making activities of self-managed teams are more broadly focused than those of quality circles and quality teams, which usually emphasize quality and production problems. Self-managed teams make many of the decisions that were once reserved for managers, such as work scheduling, job assignments, and staffing. Unlike quality circles, whose role is an advisory one, self-managed teams are delegated authority in the organization's decision-making process.

Many organizations have claimed success with self-managed teams. At Northern Telecom, revenues rose 63 percent and sales increased 26 percent following the implementation of self-managed teams.[91] Preliminary research evidence is also encouraging. An analysis of seventy studies concluded that self-managed teams positively affected productivity and attitudes toward self-management. However, the analysis indicated no significant effects of self-managed teams on job satisfaction, absenteeism, or turnover.[92]

Self-managed teams, like any cohesive group, can fall victim to groupthink. An antidote for groupthink in self-managed teams has been proposed, called teamthink. The idea is that through managing the team's internal dialogue, mental imagery, and belief system, more effective decisions can be made. Teamthink involves constructive, critical, synergistic thinking. It requires a balanced focus on both the teams and individuals. Essentially, it is careful management of group thought. The symptoms of teamthink are the opposite of those of groupthink. They include encouragement of divergent views, discussion of collective doubts, utilization of nonstereotypical views, and recognition of the ethical consequences of decisions. Research is underway to determine whether self-managed teams that are trained in the teamthink concept make more effective decisions.[93]

Before choosing a group decision-making technique, the manager should carefully evaluate the group members and the decision situation. Then the best method for accomplishing the objectives of the group decision-making process can be selected. If the goal is generating a large number of alternatives, for example, brainstorming would be a good choice. If group members are reluctant to contribute ideas, the nominal group technique would be appropriate. The need for expert input would be best facilitated by the Delphi technique. To guard against groupthink, devil's advocacy or dialectical inquiry would be effective. Decisions that concern quality or production would benefit from the advice of quality circles or the empowered decisions of quality teams. Finally, a manager who wants to provide total empowerment to a group should consider self-managed teams.

Cultural Issues in Decision Making

■ Styles of decision making vary greatly among cultures. Many of the dimensions proposed by Hofstede that were presented in Chapter 2 affect decision making. Uncertainty avoidance, for example, can affect the way people view decisions. In the U.S., a culture with low uncertainty avoidance, decisions are seen as opportunities for change. In contrast, cultures such as those of Indonesia and Malaysia attempt to accept situations as they are rather than to change them.[94] Power distance also affects decision making. In more hierarchical cultures, such as India, top-level managers make decisions. In countries with low power distance, lower level employees make many decisions. The Swedish culture exemplifies this type.

The individualist/collectivist dimension has implications for decision making. Japan, with its collectivist emphasis, favors group decisions. The U.S. has a more difficult time with group decisions because it is an individualistic culture. Time orientation affects the frame of reference of the decision. In China, with its long-term view, decisions are made with the future in mind. In the U.S., many decisions are made considering only the short term.

The masculine/feminine dimension can be compared to the Jungian thinking/feeling preferences for decision making. Masculine cultures, as in many Latin American countries, value quick, assertive decisions. Feminine cultures, as in many Scandinavian countries, value decisions that reflect concern for others.

Managers should learn as much as possible about the decision processes in other cultures. NAFTA, for example, has opened many trade barriers with Mexico. In Mexican organizations, decision-making authority is centralized, autocratic, and retained in small groups of top managers. As a consequence, Mexican employees are reluctant to participate in decision making, and often wait to be told what to do rather than take a risk. In addition, joint ventures with family-owned *grupos* (large groups of businesses) can be challenging. It may be difficult to identify the critical decision maker in the family and to determine how much decision-making authority is held by the *grupo's* family board.[95]

http://www.dupont.com/
http://www.digital.com/
http://www.campbell soup.com//
http://www.ti.com/

Technological Aids to Decision Making

■ Many computerized decision tools are available to managers. These systems can be used to support the decision-making process in organizations.

Expert Systems

Artificial intelligence is used to develop an expert system, which is a programmed decision tool. The system is set up using decision rules, and the effectiveness of the expert system is highly dependent on its design. Because expert systems are sources of knowledge and experience and not just passive software, the organization must decide who is responsible for the decisions made by expert systems. Organizations must therefore be concerned about the liability for using the recommendations of expert systems.

An expert system for use in an organization can be developed in many ways. DuPont, for example, uses a dispersed design whereby the users of the system are primarily responsible for its design. Digital Equipment Corporation, in contrast, created a separate department of specialists to develop expert systems for the company.[96]

Campbell Soup Company, like other organizations in the food industry, faces intense competition. Production downtime must be minimized. One particular problem Campbell Soup faced was that its hydrostatic canned food product sterilizers, 70 feet tall and packed with equipment, incurred a lot of downtime because of malfunctions, which affected the bottom line. The pending retirement of the company's 44-year veteran expert diagnostician forced Campbell to do something before his expertise walked out the door with him. The company enlisted the help of Texas Instruments to design an expert system that would "clone" the diagnostician's expertise.

Campbell Soup's "COOKER" is an expert system that controls its hydrostatic canned food product sterilizers. The company cloned their diagnostician's expertise before he retired and built the "COOKER" to retain that expertise.

The design team watched the diagnostician perform his job and conducted extensive interviews with him over a period of several weeks. From his expertise a series of rules was devised and built into the expert system. TI's project team used knowledge of engineering and careful selection of expert system hardware and software to develop "COOKER." The expert system reduced equipment downtime from days to hours.[97]

Expert systems hold great potential for affecting managerial decisions. Thus, managers must carefully scrutinize the expert system rather than simply accepting its decisions.

Group Decision Support Systems

Another tool for decision making focuses on helping groups make decisions. A group decision support system (GDSS) uses computer support and communication facilities to support group decision-making processes in either face-to-face meetings or dispersed meetings. The GDSS has been shown to affect conflict management within a group by depersonalizing the issue and by forcing the group to discuss its conflict management process.[98] It has been suggested that team decisions should improve by using a GDSS, because the use of software pushes team members to structure a decision that otherwise would have been made ad hoc.[99]

Boeing is one company that has seen the benefits of GDSS. By using new network software called groupware, Boeing has reduced the time needed to complete team projects by 91 percent. The company was interested in groupware because of its experience in team meetings: 20 percent of the members did 80 percent of the talking, and potentially valuable team members kept quiet. Groupware eliminated the problem. Meetings are now held in a conference room with a computer at every place. Everyone can speak at once via the computer. Ideas accumulate on each screen and comments are anonymous, which encourages even shy team members to contribute.[100]

Do introverts react differently to a GDSS than extraverts? The study described in the Scientific Foundation feature addressed this question. It points out that individuals respond differently to technological aids to decision making.

The success of GDSS as an aid to decision making depends on a number of factors. Organizations in which people are open to change and in which managers attach importance to flexible and creative decision processes are more likely to benefit. Evidence also shows that a GDSS that encourages full participation and promotes raising questions and expressing concerns is more likely to be successful. Further, managers should carefully consider the group's size and the type of task in planning for a GDSS. In the initial stages of decision making, such as generating alternatives, larger groups may work well with a GDSS. For more complex problem solving and choice making, however, small groups (fifteen members or fewer) are more effective.[101]

In a networked meeting like this one at Boeing, participants do their talking on screen. Using the groupware, employees can challenge the boss since nobody knows who said what.

SCIENTIFIC FOUNDATION

Introverts, Extraverts, and GDSS

How do personality characteristics influence individuals' feelings about group decision support systems? The authors of this study focused on extraverts and introverts to see whether they reacted differently to the use of electronically supported meetings. Students in a large public university participated in a laboratory experiment. In small groups, they generated solutions to difficult ethical decisions for which there is no single correct answer. The task, therefore, encouraged a great deal of discussion. The students completed the Myers-Briggs Type Indicator to determine whether they were introverts or extraverts. They were randomly mixed in small groups. First, they tackled an ethical dilemma in a group using a GDSS. The group used the GDSS to generate suggested solutions, and then the group members removed suggestions that had a low likelihood of solving the ethical problem. The members then voted on the suggestions that survived. Upon completion of the GDSS session, the subjects moved to a conference room and tackled a similar ethical dilemma in a face-to-face group using the same procedure. To ensure that the scenarios used did not influence the results, the order of their use was varied.

The results were interesting. Introverts felt best able to contribute with the GDSS. While introverts may be more uncomfortable in group discussions than extraverts, the GDSS environment gave them opportunity for equal participation. All of the participants produced more original solutions with the GDSS, but generated more discussion in the non-GDSS environment. If the quality of proposed solutions is important, the GDSS appears to provide the best forum to accomplish this. It supports idea generation with fewer comments. On the other hand, if the organization prefers more discussion and embellishment, face-to-face meetings might be better.

SOURCE: R. E. Yellen, M. Winniford, and C. C. Sanford, "Extraversion and Introversion in Electronically Supported Meetings," *Information & Management* 28 (1995): 63–74.

Ethical Issues in Decision Making

One criterion that should be applied to decision making is the ethical implications of the decision. Ethical decision making in organizations is influenced by many factors, including individual differences and organizational rewards and punishments.

Kenneth Blanchard and Norman Vincent Peale proposed an "ethics check" for decision makers in their book *The Power of Ethical Management*.[102] They contend that the decision maker should ponder three questions:

1. Is it legal? (Will I be violating the law or company policy?)
2. Is it balanced? (Is it fair to all concerned in the short term and long term? Does it promote win-win relationships?)
3. How will it make me feel about myself? (Will it make me proud of my actions? How will I feel when others become aware of the decision?)

Groups can also make decisions that are unethical. Beech-Nut, for example, admitted selling millions of jars of "phony" apple juice that contained cheap, adulterated concentrate. Groupthink may have been responsible for this unethical decision. Beech-Nut was losing money, and its managers believed that other companies were selling fake juice. They were convinced that their fake juice was safe for consumers and that no laboratory test could conclusively discriminate real juice from artificial ingredients. Normally a reputable company, Beech-Nut ignored caution and conscience in favor of bottom-line mentality, ignored dissent, and thus suffered damage to its reputation because of unethical practices.[103]

http://www.beechnut.com/

Unethical group decisions like the one at Beech-Nut can be prevented by using the techniques for overcoming groupthink. Appointing a devil's advocate who constantly questions the group's course of action can help bring ethical issues to the surface. Setting up a dialectical inquiry between two subgroups can head off unethical decisions by leading the group to question its course of action.

In summary, all decisions, whether made by individuals or by groups, must be evaluated for their ethics. Organizations should reinforce ethical decision making among employees by encouraging and rewarding it. Socialization processes should convey to newcomers the ethical standards of behavior in the organization. Groups should use devil's advocates and dialectical methods to reduce the potential for groupthink and the unethical decisions that may result. Effective and ethical decisions are not mutually exclusive.

Managerial Implications: Decision Making Is a Critical Activity

■ Decision making is important at all levels of every organization. At times managers may have the luxury of optimizing (selecting the best alternative), but more often they are forced to satisfice (select the alternative that is good enough). And, at times, the decision process can even seem unpredictable and random.

Individuals differ in their preferences for risk, as well as in their styles of information gathering and making judgments. Understanding individual differences can help managers maximize strengths in employee decision styles and build teams that capitalize on strengths. Creativity is one such strength. It can be encouraged by providing employees with a supportive environment that nourishes innovative ideas. Creativity training has been used in some organizations with positive results.

Some decisions are best made by individuals and some by teams or groups. The task of the manager is to diagnose the situation and implement the appropriate level of participation. To do this effectively, managers should know the advantages and disadvantages of various group decision-making techniques and should minimize the potential for groupthink. Finally, decisions made by individuals or groups should be analyzed to see whether or not they are ethical.

CLOSING SPOTLIGHT

The Risky Decision Pays Off at FedEx

Despite the risks faced in acquiring Flying Tiger, Federal Express has become a global overnight delivery system. Customers use a computerized just-in-time inventory system to track goods delivered overnight or second day. FedEx's risky decision looks smart now, since rival United Parcel Service has found obtaining foreign landing rights difficult. Federal Express now operates in over 185 countries. It has overhauled its management structure so that decisions are made by senior executives and their staffs in three regions: the Americas, Europe/Africa, and Asia/Pacific. In the past, these decisions were made by the international marketing staff at the Memphis headquarters.

Rapid growth in the Asia/Pacific market has included the opening of two Asian express-freight hubs, one at Taipei and one at Subic Bay in the Philippines. The Subic Bay and Taipei facilities will operate as an Asian network, feeding packages to FedEx's Anchorage station for customs clearance before entering the domestic network. China is pivotal to the company's long-term strategy in Asia, and FedEx's takeover of Evergreen International's routes to Beijing and Shanghai mark the only direct flights into China for a U.S. cargo carrier.

The risky decision to go global by purchasing Flying Tiger has paid off well. FedEx has become a global carrier by taking calculated risks and pursuing an aggressive strategy of global expansion.[104] ■

Chapter Summary

- Bounded rationality assumes that there are limits to how rational managers can be.
- The garbage can model shows that under high uncertainty, decision making in organizations can be an unsystematic process.
- Jung's cognitive styles can be used to help explain individual differences in gathering information and evaluating alternatives.
- Intuition and creativity are positive influences on decision making and should be encouraged in organizations.
- Managers should carefully determine the appropriate level of participation in the decision-making process. They can use the normative decision model to accomplish this.
- Techniques such as brainstorming, nominal group technique, Delphi technique, devil's advocacy, dialectical inquiry, quality circles and teams, and self-managed teams can help managers reap the benefits of group methods while limiting the possibilities of groupthink and group polarization.
- Technology is providing assistance to managerial decision making, especially through expert systems and group decision support systems. More research is needed to determine the effects of these technologies.
- Managers should carefully weigh the ethical issues surrounding decisions and encourage ethical decision making throughout the organization.

Key Terms

programmed decision (p. 282)
nonprogrammed decision (p. 282)
effective decision (p. 283)
rationality (p. 283)
bounded rationality (p. 285)
satisfice (p. 285)
heuristics (p. 285)
garbage can model (p. 285)
risk aversion (p. 286)
escalation of commitment (p. 286)
cognitive style (p. 287)
intuition (p. 289)
creativity (p. 290)
participative decision making (p. 294)
synergy (p. 296)
social decision schemes (p. 296)
groupthink (p. 297)
group polarization (p. 299)
brainstorming (p. 300)
nominal group technique (NGT) (p. 300)
Delphi technique (p. 300)
devil's advocacy (p. 301)
dialectical inquiry (p. 301)

Review Questions

1. Compare the garbage can model with the bounded rationality model. Compare the usefulness of these models in today's organizations.
2. List and describe Jung's four cognitive styles. How does the Z problem-solving model capitalize on the strengths of the four preferences?
3. What are the individual and organizational influences on creativity?
4. According to the normative decision model, what situational variables affect the level of participation in decision making?
5. Describe the advantages and disadvantages of group decision making.
6. Describe the symptoms of groupthink and actions that can be taken to prevent it.
7. What techniques can be used to improve group decisions?

Discussion and Communication Questions

1. Which model of decision making do you think is used most often in organizations? Why?
2. How will you most likely make decisions based on your cognitive style? What might you overlook using your preferred approach?
3. How can organizations encourage creative decision making?
4. Review the Scientific Foundation feature. How does it contribute to our knowledge of group decision support systems? Do you think the same thing happens in organizational settings? Why or why not?
5. What are some organizations that use expert systems? Group decision support systems? How will these two technologies affect managerial decision making?
6. Review the Opening and Closing Spotlights on Federal Express. Using the Vroom-Yetton-Jago model in Figure 10.4, analyze the decision to buy Flying Tiger. What additional information could you have used for the model?
7. *(communication question)* Form a team of four persons. Go to your library and find two examples of recent decisions made in organizations: one that you consider a good decision, and one that you consider a bad decision. Two members should work on the good decision, and two on the bad decision. Each pair should write a brief description of the decision. Then write a summary of what went right, what went wrong, and what could be done to improve the decision process. Compare and contrast your two examples in a presentation to the class.
8. *(comunication question)* Reflect on your own experience in groups and groupthink. Describe the situation in which you encountered groupthink, what symptoms were present, and the outcome of the situation. What remedies for groupthink would you prescribe? Summarize your answers in a memo to your instructor.

Ethics Questions

1. Think of a decision made by a group that you feel was an unethical one. What factors led to the unethical decision? Evaluate whether groupthink may have been a factor by examining the antecedents, symptoms, and consequences of groupthink.
2. How can organizations encourage ethical decision making?
3. How do cultural differences affect ethical decision making?
4. Describe groupthink as an ethical problem.
5. Whose responsibility is it to ensure that employees make ethical decisions?
6. Using the "ethics check," evaluate the decision to launch the *Challenger*. How could a knowledge of ethical decision making have aided the individuals who made this decision?

Experiential Exercises

10.1 Making a Layoff Decision

Purpose

In this exercise, you will examine how to weigh a set of facts and make a difficult personnel decision about laying off valued employees during a time of financial hardship. You will also examine your own values and criteria used in the decision-making process.

The Problem

Walker Space (WSI) is a medium-sized firm located in Connecticut. The firm essentially has been a subcontractor on many large space contracts that have been acquired by firms like North American Rockwell and others.

With the cutback in many of the National Aeronautics and Space Administration programs, Walker has an excess of employees. Stuart Tartaro, the head of one of the sections, has been told by his superior that he must reduce his section of engineers from nine to six. He is looking at the following summaries of their vitae and pondering how he will make this decision:

1. *Roger Allison*, age twenty-six, married, two children. Allison has been with WSI for a year and a half. He is a very good engineer, with a degree from Rensselaer Polytech. He has held two prior jobs and lost both of them because of cutbacks in the space program. He moved to Connecticut from California to take this job. Allison is well liked by his coworkers.

2. *Dave Jones*, age twenty-four, single. Jones is an African-American, and the company looked hard to get him because of affirmative action pressure. He is not very popular with his coworkers. Because he has been employed less than a year, not too much is known about his work. On his one evaluation (which was average), Jones accused his supervisor of bias against African-Americans. He is a graduate of the Detroit Institute of Technology.

3. *William Foster*, age fifty-three, married, three children. Foster is a graduate of "the school of hard knocks." After getting out of World War II, he started to go to school. However, his family expenses were too high, so he dropped out. Foster has worked at the company for twenty years. His ratings were excellent for fifteen years. The last five years they have been average. Foster feels his supervisor grades him down because he does not "have sheepskins covering his office walls."

4. *Donald Boyer*, age thirty-two, married, no children. Boyer is well liked by his coworkers. He has been at WSI five years, and he has a B.S. and M.S. in engineering from Purdue University. Boyer's ratings have been mixed. Some supervisors rated him high and some average. Boyer's wife is an M.D.

5. *Ann Shuster*, age twenty-nine, single. Shuster is a real worker, but a loner. She has a B.S. in engineering from the University of California. She is working on her M.S. at night, always trying to improve her technical skills. Her performance ratings were above average for the three years she has been employed at WSI.

6. *Sherman Soltis*, age thirty-seven, divorced, two children. He has a B.S. in engineering from Ohio State University. Soltis is very active in community affairs: Scouts, Little League, and United Way. He is a friend of the vice president through church work. His ratings have been average, although some recent ones indicate that he is out of date. He is well liked and has been employed at WSI for fourteen years.

7. *Warren Fortuna*, age forty-four, married, five children. He has a B.S. in engineering from Georgia Tech. Fortuna headed this section at one time. He worked so hard that he had a heart attack. Under doctor's orders, he resigned from the supervisory position. Since then he has done good work, though because of his health, he is a bit slower than the others. Now and then he must spend extra time on a project, because he did get out of date during the eight years he headed the section. His performance evaluations for the last two years have been above average. He has been employed at WSI for fourteen years.

8. *Robert Treharne*, age forty-seven, single. He began an engineering degree at MIT but had to drop out for financial reasons. He tries hard to stay current by regular reading of engineering journals and taking all the short courses the company and nearby colleges offer. His performance evaluations have varied, but they tend to be average to slightly above average. He is a loner, and Tartaro thinks this has negatively affected his performance evaluations. He has been employed at WSI sixteen years.

9. *Sandra Rosen*, age twenty-two, single. She has a B.S. in engineering technology from the Rochester Institute of Technology. Rosen has been employed less than a year. She is enthusiastic, a very good worker, and well liked by her coworkers. She is well regarded by Tartaro.

Tartaro does not quite know what to do. He sees the good points of each of his section members. Most have been good employees. They all can pretty much do one another's work. No one has special training.

He is fearful that the section will hear about this and morale will drop. Work would fall off. He does not even want to talk to his wife about it, in case she would let something slip. Tartaro has come to you, Edmund Graves, personnel manager at WSI, for some guidelines on this decision—legal, moral, and best personnel practice.

Assignment

You are Edmund Graves. Write a report with your recommendations for termination and a careful analysis of the criteria for the decision. You should also carefully explain to Tartaro how you would go about the terminations and what you would consider reasonable termination pay. You should also advise him about the pension implications of this decision. Generally, fifteen years' service entitles you to at least partial pension.

SOURCE: W. F. Glueck, *Cases and Exercises in Personnel* (Dallas: Business Publications, 1978), 24–26.

10.2 The Wilderness Experience

Try to imagine yourself in the situation depicted. Assume that you are alone and have a minimum of equipment, except where specified. The season is fall. The days are warm and dry, but the nights are cold. Circle the letter beside the best answer.

1. You have strayed from your party in a trackless timber. You have no special signaling equipment. The best way to attempt to contact your friends is to:
- **a.** call "help" loudly but in a low register.
- **b.** yell or scream as loud as you can.
- **c.** whistle loudly and shrilly.

2. You are in "snake country." Your best action to avoid snakes is to:
- **a.** make a lot of noise with your feet.
- **b.** walk softly and quietly.
- **c.** travel at night.

3. You are hungry and lost in wild country. The best rule for determining which plants are safe to eat (those you don't recognize) is to:
- **a.** try anything you see the birds eat.
- **b.** eat anything except plants with bright red berries.
- **c.** put a bit of the plant on your lower lip for five minutes; if it seems all right, try a little.

4. The day becomes dry and hot. You have a full canteen of water (about 1 liter) with you. You should:
- **a.** ration it—about a cupful a day.
- **b.** not drink until you stop for the night, then drink what you think you need.
- **c.** drink as much as you think you need when you need it.

5. Your water is gone; you become very thirsty. You finally come to a dried-up watercourse. Your best chance of finding water is to:
- **a.** dig anywhere in the stream bed.
- **b.** dig up plant and tree roots near the bank.
- **c.** dig in the stream bed at the outside of a bend.

6. You decide to walk out of the wild country by following a series of ravines where a water supply is available. Night is coming on. The best place to make camp is:
- **a.** next to the water supply in the ravine.
- **b.** high on a ridge.
- **c.** midway up the slope.

7. Your flashlight glows dimly as you are about to make your way back to your campsite after a brief foraging trip. Darkness comes quickly in the woods and the surroundings seem unfamiliar. You should:
- **a.** head back at once, keeping the light on, hoping the light will glow enough for you to make landmarks.
- **b.** put the batteries under your armpits to warm them, and then replace them in the flashlight.
- **c.** shine your light for a few seconds, try to get the scene in mind, move in the darkness, and repeat the process.

8. An early snow confines you to your small tent. You doze with your small stove going. There is danger if the flame is:
- **a.** yellow.
- **b.** blue.
- **c.** red.

9. You must ford a river that has a strong current, large rocks, and some white water. After carefully selecting your crossing spot, you should:
- **a.** leave your boots and pack on.
- **b.** take your boots and pack off.
- **c.** take off your pack, but leave your boots on.

10. In waist-deep water with a strong current, when crossing the stream, you should face:
- **a.** upstream.
- **b.** across the stream.
- **c.** downstream.

11. You find yourself rimrocked; your only route is up. The way is mossy, slippery rock. You should try it:
- **a.** barefoot.
- **b.** with boots on.
- **c.** in stocking feet.

12. Unarmed and unsuspecting, you surprise a large bear prowling around your campsite. As the bear rears up about ten meters from you, you should:
- **a.** run.
- **b.** climb the nearest tree.
- **c.** freeze, but be ready to back away slowly.

After you have completed the worksheet, your instructor will help you form groups of five or six members. Then each group should go through the worksheet and agree on a correct answer for each question.

SOURCE: Reprinted from J. W. Pfeiffer and J. E. Jones (eds.) *The 1976 Annual Handbook for Group Facilitators*, San Diego, CA: Pfeiffer & Company, 1976. Used with permission.

CASE

The Newton MessagePad: A Good Decision or Not?[1]

In late 1993, Michael H. Spindler, the new chief executive officer at Apple Computer, "might have been expected to concentrate on the PC business and let products from nontraditional technologies—such as the much-maligned Newton MessagePad, a handheld personal digital assistant (notetaker)—evolve slowly into a new line of business." Instead, Spindler made the *gutsy* decision to put more resources—including Apple's most creative people—into the development of the MessagePad. Even with more corporate resources behind the product, first-year sales were expected to be only about 1 percent of Apple's annual revenues. Moreover, Apple lost $188 million in the third quarter of 1993 and made a $2.7 million profit the fourth quarter.

A gutsy decision, yes! But was it the right decision for Apple's survival and success?

According to Forrester Research, the early handheld personal digital assistants (PDAs) had to overcome several problems including "incomplete communications capabilities, cumbersome desktop synchronization, the unfulfilled promise of handwriting recognition, a lack of useful application and high cost." Users, for instance, had to write their own applications software. With regard to handwriting recognition, Waverly Deutsche, an analyst at Forrester Research, says, "As an input device, the pen is miserable. It isn't good for anything more than checking boxes and signatures."

Peter Ferrara, chief operating officer of Granum Communications, started using the first Newton because he thought it was a great technological idea. However, Ferrara had to practice daily for nearly a month before the device could recognize his handwriting at an acceptable level. Stewart Alsop, a columnist who writes about the computer industry, stopped using his Newton MessagePad because it didn't work. Alsop said the Newton could not synchronize names in his networked database or appointments in his networked scheduler. He also complained about problems with Newton's handwriting recognition as well as paging and e-mail forwarding services.

Apple Computer fixed the problems, marketing version 2.0 of the Newton. Albert Lellimo, another computer industry columnist, regards the second version of the Newton MessagePad as "one of the most versatile PDAs available"—primarily because of its third-party support in terms of both software and hardware attachments. However, Kevin Burden, also a computer industry columnist, maintains that unless the MessagePad is equipped with custom-designed software, it does not have any significant business applications. According to Stewart Alsop, "The challenge for Apple involves persuading enough people to take a look at this version; its predecessor is considered a failed product by virtually everybody."

DISCUSSION QUESTIONS

1. Using the notions of risk and escalation of commitment, how would you evaluate Michael Spindler's original decision to put additional corporate resources into the development of the Newton MessagePad? Using the same two concepts, how would you evaluate the decision to develop a second version of the MessagePad?
2. How would you describe the decisions regarding the Newton MessagePad in terms of the rational, bounded rationality, and garbage can models of decisions making?
3. How could Apple Computer have used the Z problem-solving model shown in Figure 10.3 as an aid to evaluating the failure of the first version of the Newton?
4. Do you think Spindler's original decision on developing the Newton MessagePad was a good decision? Why or why not? Do you think the decision to develop a second version of the MessagePad was a good decision? Why or why not?

SOURCE: This case was written by Michael McCuddy, the Louis S. and Mary L. Morgal Professor of Christian Business Ethics, College of Business Administration, Valparaiso University.

1. Adapted from S. Alsop, "Realizing the Gravity of Its PDA Problems, Apple Has Drawn Me Back to Newton," *Infoworld* (November 6, 1995): 138; K. Burden, "Custom Programs Broaden MessagePad's Appeal," *Computerworld* (July 3, 1995): 76; A. Lellimo, Jr., "PDAs: The Next Generation," *Network World* (March 15, 1995): 63–66; A. Radding, "Getting a Grip on Handhelds," *Computerworld* (July 3, 1995): 72–75; A. L. Sprout, "Getting the Most Out of Newton," *Fortune* (July 25, 1994): 237; M. A. Verespej, "Gutsy Decisions of 1993," *Industry Week* (February 7, 1994): 26–40.

References

1. A. Biesada, "Fed Ex: Pride Goeth . . . ," *Financial World*, 4 September 1990, 38–41.
2. H. A. Simon, *The New Science of Management Decision* (New York: Harper & Row, 1960).
3. G. Huber, *Managerial Decision Making* (Glenview, Ill.: Scott, Foresman, 1980).
4. H. A. Simon, *Administrative Behavior* (New York: Macmillan, 1957).
5. E. F. Harrison, *The Managerial Decision-Making Process* (Boston: Houghton Mifflin, 1981).
6. R. L. Ackoff, "The Art and Science of Mess Management," *Interfaces* (February 1981): 20–26.
7. R. M. Cyert and J. G. March, eds., *A Behavioral Theory of the Firm* (Englewood Cliffs, N.J.: Prentice-Hall, 1963).
8. M. D. Cohen, J. G. March, and J. P. Olsen, "A Garbage Can Model of Organizational Choice," *Administrative Science Quarterly* 17 (1972): 1–25.
9. J. G. March and J. P. Olsen, "Garbage Can Models of Decision Making in Organizations," in J. G. March and R. Weissinger-Baylon, eds., *Ambiguity and Command* (Marshfield, Mass.: Pitman, 1986), 11–53.
10. K. R. MacCrimmon and D. Wehrung, *Taking Risks* (New York: Free Press, 1986).
11. P. Slovic, "Information Processing, Situation Specificity and the Generality of Risk-Taking Behavior," *Journal of Personality and Social Psychology* 22 (1972): 128–134.
12. T. S. Perry, "How Small Firms Innovate: Designing a Culture for Creativity," *Research Technology Management* 28 (1995): 14–17.
13. B. M. Staw, "Knee-Deep in the Big Muddy: A Study of Escalating Commitment to a Chosen Course of Action," *Organizational Behavior and Human Performance* 16 (1976): 27–44; B. M. Staw, "The Escalation of Commitment to a Course of Action," *Academy of Management Review* 6 (1981): 577–587.
14. B. M. Staw and J. Ross, "Understanding Behavior in Escalation Situations," *Science* 246 (1989): 216–220.
15. L. Festinger, *A Theory of Cognitive Dissonance* (Evanston, Ill.: Row, Peterson, 1957).
16. G. Whyte, "Diffusion of Responsibility: Effects on the Escalation Tendency," *Journal of Applied Psychology* 76 (1991): 408–415.
17. C. G. Jung, *Psychological Types* (London: Routledge and Kegan Paul, 1923).
18. W. Taggart and D. Robey, "Minds and Managers: On the Dual Nature of Human Information Processing and Management," *Academy of Management Review* 6 (1981): 187–195; D. Hellreigel and J. W. Slocum, Jr., "Managerial Problem-Solving Styles," *Business Horizons* 18 (1975): 29–37.
19. I. I. Mitroff and R. H. Kilmann, "On Organization Stories: An Approach to the Design and Analysis of Organization through Myths and Stories," in R. H. Killman, L. R. Pondy, and D. P. Slevin, eds., *The Management of Organization Design* (New York: Elsevier–North Holland, 1976).
20. B. K. Blaylock and L. P. Rees, "Cognitive Style and the Usefulness of Information," *Decision Sciences* 15 (1984): 74–91; D. L. Davis, S. J. Grove, and P. A. Knowles, "An Experimental Application of Personality Type as an Analogue for Decision-Making Style," *Psychological Reports* 66 (1990): 167–175.
21. I. B. Myers, *Gifts Differing* (Palo Alto, Calif.: Consulting Psychologists Press, 1980).
22. H. Mintzberg, "Planning on the Left Side and Managing on the Right," *Harvard Business Review* 54 (1976): 51–63.
23. D. J. Isenberg, "How Senior Managers Think," *Harvard Business Review* 62 (1984): 81–90.
24. R. N. Beck, "Visions, Values, and Strategies: Changing Attitudes and Culture," *Academy of Managment Executive* 1 (1987): 33–41.
25. C. I. Barnard, *The Functions of the Executive* (Cambridge, Mass.: Harvard University Press, 1938).
26. R. Rowan, *The Intuitive Manager* (New York: Little, Brown, 1986).
27. W. H. Agor, *Intuition in Organizations* (Newbury Park, Calif.: Sage, 1989).
28. Isenberg, "How Senior Managers Think," 81–90.
29. H. A. Simon, Making Management Decisions: The Role of Intuition and Emotion," *Academy of Management Executive* 1 (1987): 57–64.
30. J. L. Redford, R. H. McPhierson, R. G. Frankiewicz, and J. Gaa, "Intuition and Moral Development," *Journal of Psychology* 129 (1994): 91–101.
31. W. H. Agor, "How Top Executives Use Their Intuition to Make Important Decisions," *Business Horizons* 29 (1986): 49–53.
32. O. Behling and N. L. Eckel, "Making Sense Out of Intuition," *Academy of Management Executive* 5 (1991): 46–54.
33. L. R. Beach, *Image Theory: Decision Making in Personal and Organizational Contexts* (Chichester, England: Wiley, 1990).
34. L. Livingstone, "Person-Environment Fit on the Dimension of Creativity: Relationships with Strain, Job Satisfaction, and Performance" (Ph.D. diss., Oklahoma State University, 1992).
35. M. A. West and J. L. Farr, "Innovation at Work," in M. A. West and J. L. Farr, eds., *Innovation and Creativity at Work: Psychological and Organizational Strategies* (New York: Wiley, 1990), 3–13.
36. G. Morgan, *Riding the Waves of Change* (San Francisco: Jossey-Bass, 1988).
37. G. Wallas, *The Art of Thought* (New York: Harcourt Brace, 1926).
38. M. D. Mumford and S. B. Gustafson, "Creativity Syndrome: Integration, Application, and Innovation," *Psychological Bulletin* 103 (1988): 27–43.
39. T. Poze, "Analogical Connections—The Essence of Creativity," *Journal of Creative Behavior* 17 (1983): 240–241.
40. I. Sladeczek and G. Domino, "Creativity, Sleep, and Primary Process Thinking in Dreams," *Journal of Creative Behavior* 19 (1985): 38–46.
41. F. Barron and D. M. Harrington, "Creativity, Intelligence, and Personality," *Annual Review of Psychology* 32 (1981): 439–476.

42. R. J. Sternberg, "A Three-Faced Model of Creativity," in R. J. Sternberg, ed., *The Nature of Creativity* (London: Cambridge University Press, 1988), 125–147.
43. A. M. Isen, K. A. Daubman, and G. P. Nowicki, "Positive Affect Facilitates Creative Problem Solving," *Journal of Personality and Social Psychology* 52 (1987): 1122–1131.
44. T. Stevens, "Creativity Killers," *Industry Week*, January 23, 1995: 63.
45. T. M. Amabile, "Creativity Motivation in Research and Development" (Paper presented at the annual meeting of the American Psychological Association, Toronto, 1984).
46. R. M. Kanter, *The Change Masters* (New York: Simon and Schuster, 1983); R. F. Lovelace, "Stimulating Creativity through Managerial Intervention," *R & D Management* 16 (1986): 161–174.
47. D. M. Harrington, "Creativity, Analogical Thinking, and Muscular Metaphors," *Journal of Mental Imagery* 6 (1981): 121–126; Kanter, *Change Masters.*
48. T. M. Amabile, B. A. Hennessey, and B. S. Grossman, "Social Influences on Creativity: The Effects of Contracted-for Reward," *Journal of Personality and Social Psychology* 50 (1986): 14–23.
49. Livingstone, "Person-Environment Fit."
50. R. L. Firestein, "Effects of Creative Problem-Solving Training on Communication Behaviors in Small Groups," *Small Group Research* (November 1989): 507–521.
51. C. M. Solomon, "What an Idea: Creativity Training," *Personal Journal* 69 (1990): 64–71.
52. R. von Oech, *A Whack on the Side of the Head* (New York: Warner, 1983).
53. M. Kostera, M. Proppe, and M. Szatkowski, "Staging the New Romantic Hero in the Old Cynical Theatre: On Managers, Roles, and Change in Poland," *Journal of Organizational Behavior* 16 (1995): 631–646.
54. M. Basadur, "Managing Creativity: A Japanese Model," *Academy of Management Executive* 6 (1992): 29–42.
55. P. E. Conner, "Decision-Making Participation Patterns: The Role of Organizational Context," *Academy of Management Journal* 35 (1992): 218–231.
56. M. Sashkin, "Participative Management Is an Ethical Imperative," *Organizational Dynamics*, Spring 1984, 4–22.
57. D. Plunkett, "The Creative Organization: An Empirical Investigation of the Importance of Participation in Decision Making," *Journal of Creative Behavior* 24 (1990): 140–148; J. A. Wagner III and R. Z. Gooding, "Shared Influence and Organizational Behavior: A Meta-Analysis of Situational Variables Expected to Moderate Participation-Outcome Relationships," *Academy of Management Journal* 29 (1987): 524–541.
58. C. R. Leana, E. A. Locke, and D. M. Schweiger, "Fact and Fiction in Analyzing Research on Participative Decision Making: A Critique of Cotton, Vollrath, Froggatt, Lengnick-Hall, and Jennings," *Academy of Management Review* 15 (1990): 137–146; J. L. Cotton, D. A. Vollrath, M. L. Lengnick-Hall, and K. L. Froggatt, "Fact: The Form of Participation Does Matter—A Rebuttal to Leana, Locke, and Schweiger," *Academy of Management Review* 15 (1990): 147–153.
59. D. Collins, R. A. Ross, and T. L. Ross, "Who Wants Participative Management?" *Group and Organization Studies* 14 (1989): 422–445.
60. R. Stayer, "How I Learned to Let My Workers Lead," *Harvard Business Review* (Novermber-December 1990): 66–83.
61. V. H. Vroom and P. W. Yetton, *Leadership and Decision Making* (Pittsburg: University of Pittsburg Press, 1973); V. H. Vroom and A. G. Jago, *The New Leadership: Managing Participation in Organizations* (Englewood Cliffs, N.J.: Prentice-Hall, 1988).
62. V. H. Vroom, "A New Look in Managerial Decision Making," *Organizational Dynamics* (Spring 1973): 66–80.
63. R. H. Field, "A Test of the Vroom-Yetton Normative Model of Leadership," *Journal of Applied Psychology* 67 (1982): 523–532.
64. R. J. Paul and Y. M. Ebadi, "Leadership Decision Making in a Service Organization: A Field Test of the Vroom-Yetton Model," *Journal of Occupational Psychology* 62 (1989): 201–211.
65. A. Crouch and P. Yetton, "Manager Behavior, Leadership Style, and Subordinate Performance: An Empirical Extension of the Vroom-Yetton Conflict Rule," *Organizational Behavior and Human Decision Processes* 39 (1987): 384–396.
66. G. Stasser, L. A. Taylor and C. Hanna, "Information Sampling in Structured and Unstructured Discussion of Three- and Six-Person Groups," *Journal of Personality and Social Psychology* 57 (1989): 67–78.
67. E. Kirchler and J. H. Davis, "The Influence of Member Status Differences and Task Type on Group Consensus and Member Position Change," *Journal of Personality and Social Psychology* 51 (1986): 83–91.
68. R. F. Maier, "Assets and Liabilities in Group Problem Solving," *Psychological Review* 74 (1967): 239–249.
69. M. E. Shaw, *Group Dynamics: The Psychology of Small Group Behavior*, 3d ed. (New York: McGraw-Hill, 1981).
70. P. W. Yetton and P. C. Bottger, "Individual versus Group Problem Solving: An Empirical Test of a Best Member Strategy," *Organizational Behavior and Human Performance* 29 (1982): 307–321.
71. W. Watson, L. Michaelson, and W. Sharp, "Member Compentence, Group Interaction, and Group Decision Making: A Longitudinal Study," *Journal of Applied Psychology* 76 (1991): 803–809.
72. I. Janis, *Victims of Groupthink* (Boston: Houghton Mifflin, 1972).
73. C. P. Neck and G. Moorhead, "Groupthink Remodeled: The Importance of Leadership, Time Pressure, and Methodical Decision Making Procedures," *Human Relations* 48 (1995): 537–557.
74. I. Janis, *Groupthink*, 2d ed. (Boston: Houghton Mifflin, 1982).
75. J. K. Esser and J. S. Lindoerfer, "Groupthink and the Space Shuttle *Challenger* Accident: Toward a Quantitative Case Analysis," *Journal of Behavioral Decision Making* 2 (1989): 167–177.
76. G. Moorhead, R. Ference, and C. P. Neck, "Group Decision Fiascoes Continue: Space Shuttle *Challenger* and a Revised Groupthink Framework," *Human Relations* 44 (1991): 539–550.

77. J. R. Montanari and G. Moorhead, "Development of the Groupthink Assessment Inventory," *Educational and Psychological Measurement* 49 (1989): 209–219.
78. P. t'Hart, "Irving L. Janis' Victims of Groupthink," *Political Psychology* 12 (1991): 247–278.
79. J. A. F. Stoner, "Risky and Cautious Shifts in Group Decisions: The Influence of Widely Held Values," *Journal of Experimental Social Psychology* 4 (1968): 442–459.
80. S. Moscovici and M. Zavalloni, "The Group as a Polarizer of Attitudes," *Journal of Personality and Social Psychology* 12 (1969): 125–135.
81. G. R. Goethals and M. P. Zanna, "The Role of Social Comparison in Choice of Shifts," *Journal of Personality and Social Psychology* 37 (1979): 1469–1476.
82. A. Vinokur and E. Burnstein, "Effects of Partially Shared Persuasive Arguments on Group-Induced Shifts: A Problem-Solving Approach," *Journal of Personality and Social Psychology* 29 (1974): 305–315.
83. T. Bouchard, "Whatever Happened to Brainstorming?" *Journal of Creative Behavior* 5 (1971): 182–189.
84. K. L. Siau, "Group Creativity and Technology," *Journal of Creative Behavior* 29 (1995): 201-216.
85. A. Van de Ven and A. Delbecq, "The Effectiveness of Nominal, Delphi and Interacting Group Decision-Making Processes," *Academy of Management Journal* 17 (1974): 605–621.
86. A. L. Delbecq, A. H. Van de Ven, and D. H. Gustafson, *Group Techniques for Program Planning: A Guide to Nominal, Group, and Delphi Processes* (Glenview, Ill.: Scott, Foresman, 1975).
87. R. A. Cosier and C. R. Schwenk, "Agreement and Thinking Alike: Ingredients for Poor Decisions," *Academy of Management Executive* 4 (1990): 69–74.
88. D. M. Schweiger, W. R. Sandburg, and J. W. Ragan, "Group Approaches for Improving Strategic Decision Making: A Comparative Analysis of Dialectical Inquiry, Devil's Advocacy, and Consensus," *Academy of Management Journal* 29 (1986): 149–159.
89. G. Whyte, "Decision Failures: Why They Occur and How to Prevent Them," *Academy of Management Executive* 5 (1991): 23–31.
90. E. E. Lawler III and S. A. Mohrman, "Quality Circles: After the Honeymoon," *Organizational Dynamics* (Spring 1987): 42–54.
91. J. Schilder, "Work Teams Boost Productivity," *Personnel Journal* 71 (1992): 67–72.
92. P. S. Goodman, R. Devadas, and T. L. Griffith-Hughson, "Groups and Productivity: Analyzing the Effectiveness of Self-Managed Teams," in J. P. Campbell, R. J. Campbell, and Associates, eds., *Productivity in Organizations* (San Francisco: Jossey-Bass, 1988), 295–327.
93. C. C. Manz and C. P. Neck, "Teamthink: Beyond the Groupthink Syndrome in Self-Managed Teams," *Journal of Managerial Psychology* 10 (1995): 7–15.
94. N. Adler, *International Dimensions of Organizational Behavior*, 2d ed. (Boston: PWS-Kent, 1991).
95. G. K. Stephens and C. R. Greer, "Doing Business in Mexico: Understanding Cultural Differences," *Organization Dynamics* 24 (1995): 39–55.
96. C. L. Meador and E. G. Mahler, "Choosing an Expert System's Game Plan," *Datamation* 36 (1990): 64–69.
97. "How Organizations Are Becoming More Efficient Using Expert Systems," *I/S Analyzer Case Studies* 36 (1995): 2–6.
98. M. S. Poole, M. Holmes, and G. DeSanctis, "Conflict Management in a Computer-supported Meeting Environment," *Management Science* 37 (1991): 926–953.
99. R. Johansen, *Leading Business Teams: Process, Technology, and Team Effectiveness* (Menlo Park, Calif.: Institute for the Future, 1990).
100. D. Kirkpatrick, "Here Comes the Payoff from PCs," *Fortune*, March 23, 1992: 93–102.
101. A. T. McCartt and J. Rohrbaugh, "Managerial Openness to Change and the Introduction of GDSS: Explaining Initial Success and Failure in Decision Conferencing," *Organization Science* 6 (1995): 569–584.
102. K. Blanchard and N. V. Peale, *The Power of Ethical Management* (New York: Fawcett Crest, 1988).
103. R. R. Sims, "Linking Groupthink to Unethical Behavior in Organizations," *Journal of Business Ethics* 11 (1992): 651–662.
104. M. Mecham, "FedEx Selects Taipei as Second Asian Hub," *Aviation Week & Space Technology*, June 19, 1995: 36.

CHAPTER

11

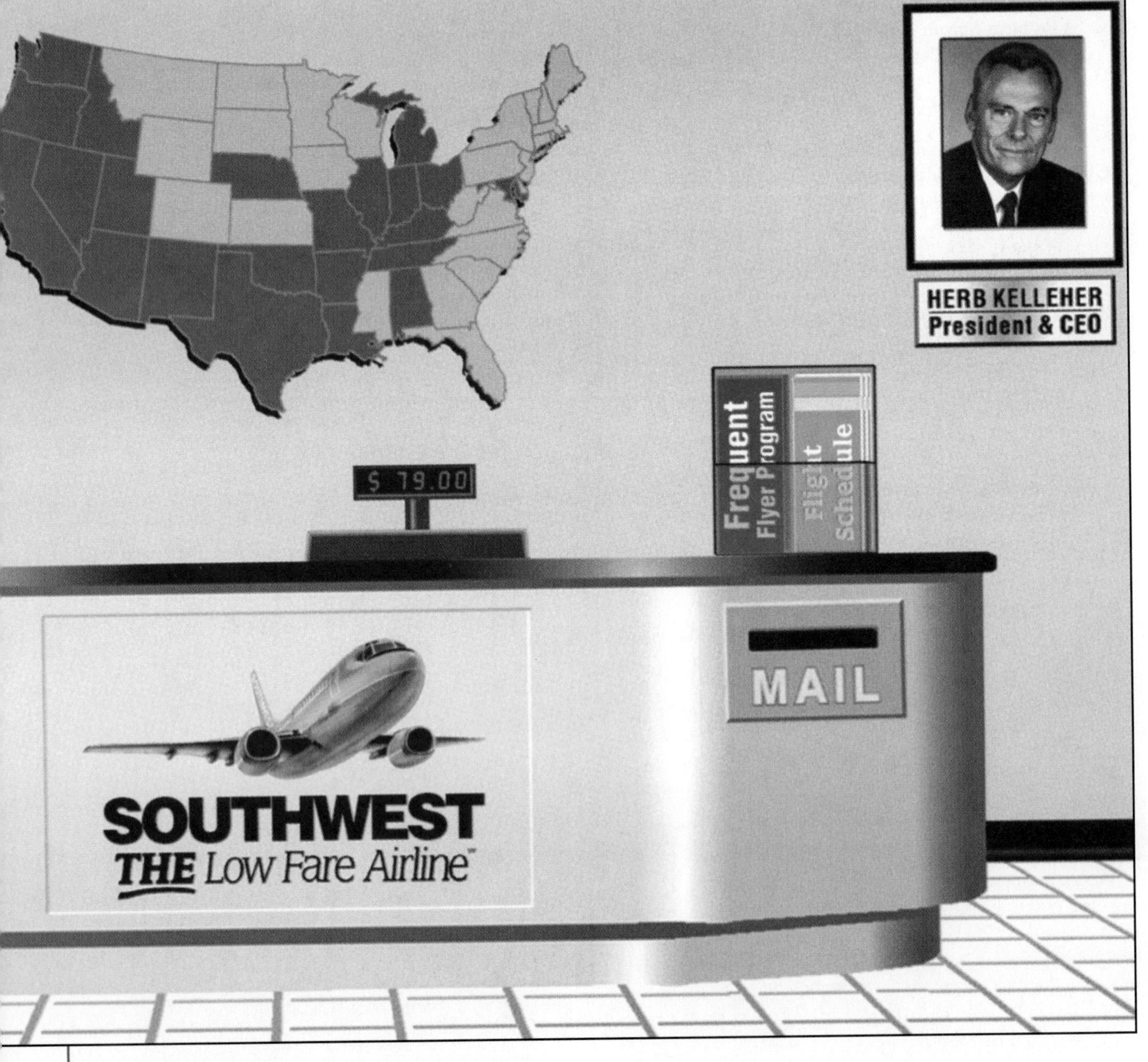
HERB KELLEHER
President & CEO
$ 79.00
Frequent
Flyer Program
Flight
Schedule
MAIL
SOUTHWEST
THE Low Fare Airline™

Power and Political Behavior

LEARNING OBJECTIVES

After reading this chapter, you should be able to do the following:

- Distinguish between power, influence, and authority.
- Describe the interpersonal and intergroup sources of power.
- Understand the ethical use of power.
- Explain Etzioni's organizational-level theory of power.
- Identify symbols of power and powerlessness in organizations.
- Define organizational politics and understand the major influence tactics.
- Develop a plan for managing employee-boss relationships.
- Discuss the ways managers can empower others.

OPENING SPOTLIGHT

People Power at Southwest Airlines

http://www.iflyswa.com/

Southwest Airlines has a unique organizational culture. Herb Kelleher, the president, chief executive officer, and chairman of the board, has created an airline where all people are considered important. For example, the company has a "people department," not a personnel department. Many people at Southwest have influence over selection decisions.

When the company hires new pilots, they bring existing Southwest pilots into the decision. They participate voluntarily and often on their own time because of their dedication to the airline. The reservations agent who books the prospective pilot's flight to Dallas for the interview has input into the hiring decision. The coordinator who arranges the pilot's interview schedule contributes as well. The receptionist who greets the pilot as he arrives may have a say in the final decision.

Alternate Example
The acceptance of hierarchy and power is almost automatic in most situations. A professor who had been a lieutenant colonel in the military had a difficult time adjusting to a nonmilitary way of life. For example, he automatically stood up when the dean of the college entered a faculty meeting.

The culture at Southwest Airlines is such that all people are accorded respect. Each person, regardless of job description or role, is a vital link in the success of the entire airline. Herb Kelleher believes that employees are most effective when they have significant power. "Take the organizational pyramid and turn it upside down . . . . at the bottom, you've got the people at headquarters. Up there, at the top, you've got the people who are out there in the field on the front lines. They're the ones who make things happen. We're the supply corps. We supply the heroes, period. The heroes are out there."[1]

In the Closing Spotlight, we'll examine employee empowerment Southwest-style. ■

The Concept of Power

power
The ability to influence another person.

influence
The process of affecting the thoughts, behavior, and feelings of another person.

authority
The right to influence another person.

■ **Power** is the ability to influence someone else. As an exchange relationship, it occurs in transactions between an agent and a target. The agent is the person using the power, and the target is the recipient of the attempt to use power.[2]

Because power is an ability, individuals can learn to use it effectively. **Influence** is the process of affecting the thoughts, behavior, and feelings of another person. **Authority** is the right to influence another person.[3] It is important to understand the subtle differences among these terms. For instance, a manager may have authority but no power. She may have the right, by virtue of her position as boss, to tell someone what to do. But she may not have the skill or ability to influence other people.

zone of indifference
The range in which attempts to influence a person will be perceived as legitimate and will be acted on without a great deal of thought.

Discussion Consideration
Ask students to differentiate between power and authority, and between power and influence.

Points to Emphasize
Often there are people in organizations that have tremendous power, yet they have no authority.

In a relationship between the agent and the target, there are many influence attempts that the target considers legitimate. Working forty hours per week, greeting customers, solving problems, and collecting bills are actions that, when requested by the manager, are considered legitimate by a customer service representative. Requests such as these fall within the employee's **zone of indifference**—the range in which attempts to influence the employee are perceived as legitimate and are acted on without a great deal of thought.[4] The employee accepts that the manager has the authority to request such behaviors and complies with the requests. Some requests, however, fall outside the zone of indifference, so the manager must work to enlarge the employee's zone of indifference. Enlarging the zone is accomplished with power (an ability) rather than with authority (a right).

Suppose the manager asks the employee to purchase a birthday gift for the manager's wife or to overcharge a customer for a service call. The employee may think that the manager has no right to ask these things. These requests fall outside the zone of indifference; they're viewed as extraordinary, and the manager has to operate from outside the authority base to induce the employee to fulfill them. In some cases, no power base is enough to induce the employee to comply, especially if the behaviors requested by the manager are considered unethical by the employee.

Failures to understand power and politics can be costly, as seen in the Organizational Reality feature. Managers must learn as much as possible about power and politics to be able to use them effectively, and to manage the inevitable political behavior in organizations.

Points to Emphasize
French and Raven point out that in any situation where power is being exerted, it is likely that more than one type of power is usually at work.

Forms and Sources of Power in Organizations

■ Individuals have many forms of power to use in their work settings. Some of them are interpersonal—used in interactions with others. One of the earliest and most influential theories of power comes from French and Raven, who tried to determine the sources of a power a manager uses to influence other people.

ORGANIZATIONAL REALITY

A Great Moment in Career Suicide

Chairman Jack Welch of GE often spoke passionately about a company without boundaries, but one engineer became a little too inspired by this vision. The engineer decided that GE really needed a Department of Creativity and Innovation that would function to solicit suggestions from employees.

The engineer's supervisors rejected his proposal, so he went to GE's annual board of directors' meeting and nominated himself to the board. Referring to Jack Welch as "the naked emperor," the engineer claimed to be "a dumb lieutenant who will be able to tell (Welch) when he is naked." He failed in his attempt to be elected to the board.

Undaunted, the engineer went back to his office and circulated a survey, via e-mail, asking 5400 employees to evaluate GE's employee innovation initiatives. "I thought the guys at the top would see that this guy was pushing and pushing, and they would let me make a real presentation to them," the engineer said. But GE had heard enough . . . and pushed the engineer out the door for a huge unauthorized use of e-mail. ■

SOURCE: T. Carvell, "Great Moments in Career Suicide," *Fortune* (January 15, 1996): 40.

Interpersonal Forms of Power

French and Raven identified five forms of interpersonal power that managers use. They are reward, coercive, legitimate, referent, and expert power.[5]

Reward power is power based on the agent's ability to control rewards that a target wants. For example, managers control the rewards of salary increases, bonuses, and promotions. Reward power can lead to better performance, but only as long as the employee sees a clear and strong link between performance and rewards. To use reward power effectively, then, the manager should be explicit about the behavior being rewarded and should make the connection between the behavior and the reward clear.

reward power
Power based on an agent's ability to control rewards that a target wants.

Coercive power is power that is based on the agent's ability to cause the target to have an unpleasant experience. To coerce someone into doing something means to force the person to do it, often with threats of punishment. Managers using coercive power may verbally abuse employees or withhold support from them.

coercive power
Power that is based on an agent's ability to cause an unpleasant experience for a target.

Legitimate power, which is similar to authority, is power that is based on position and mutual agreement. The agent and target agree that the agent has the right to influence the target. It doesn't matter that a manager thinks he has the right to influence his employees; for legitimate power to be effective, the employees must also believe the manager has the right to tell them what to do. In Native American societies, the chieftain has legitimate power; tribe members believe in his right to influence the decisions in their lives.

legitimate power
Power that is based on position and mutual agreement; agent and target agree that the agent has the right to influence the target.

Referent power is an elusive power that is based on interpersonal attraction. The agent has referent power over the target because the target identifies with or wants to be like the agent. Charismatic individuals are often thought to have referent power. Interestingly, the agent need not be superior to the target in any way. People who use referent power well are most often individualistic and respected by the target.

referent power
An elusive power that is based on interpersonal attraction.

Expert power is the power that exists when the agent has information or knowledge that the target needs. For expert power to work, three conditions must be in place. First, the target must trust that the information given is accurate. Second, the information involved must be relevant and useful to the target. Third, the target's perception of the agent as an expert is crucial. As a manager, you may believe you are an expert, but if your employees do not share this view, then your expert power will not be effective.

expert power
The power that exists when an agent has information or knowledge that the target needs.

Magic Johnson uses his referent power for a very worthy cause. His charisma has helped him educate thousands of young people about AIDS prevention.

Discussion Consideration
Does power reside in the agent or the perceiver?

Which type of interpersonal power is most effective? This is the question that research has focused on since French and Raven introduced their five forms of power. Some of the results are surprising. Reward power and coercive power have similar effects.[6] Both lead to compliance. That is, employees will do what the manager asks them to, at least temporarily, if the manager offers a reward or threatens them with punishment. However, reliance on these sources of power is dangerous because it may require the manager to be physically present and watchful in order to apply rewards or punishment when the behavior occurs. Constant surveillance creates an uncomfortable situation for managers and employees and eventually results in a dependency relationship. Employees will not work unless the manager is present.

Legitimate power also leads to compliance. When told "Do this because I'm your boss," most employees will comply. However, the use of legitimate power has not been linked to organizational effectiveness or to employee satisfaction.[7] In organizations where managers rely heavily on legitimate power, organizational goals are not necessarily met.

Points to Emphasize
Power is a potential that does not have to be actualized in order to have an effect.

Referent power is linked with organizational effectiveness. However, it is the most dangerous power because it can be too extensive and intensive in altering the behavior of others. Charismatic leaders need an accompanying sense of responsibility for others. Magic Johnson's referent power has made him a powerful spokesman for AIDS prevention, especially among young people.

Alternate Example
Power can also be understood as function of dependency. The more dependent an individual, A, is on another person, B, the more power B will have over A.

Expert power has been called the power of the future.[8] Of the five forms of power, it has the strongest relationship with performance and satisfaction. It is through expert power that vital skills, abilities, and knowledge are passed on within the organization. Employees internalize what they observe and learn from managers they perceive to be experts.

Discussion Consideration
Is it possible for a subordinate to have power over his or her manager? How?

The results on the effectiveness of these five forms of power pose a challenge in organizations. The least effective power bases—legitimate, reward, and coercive—are the ones most likely to be used by managers.[9] Managers inherit these power bases when they take a supervisory job, and they are part of the position. In contrast, the most effective power bases—referent and expert—are ones that must be developed and strengthened through interpersonal relationships with employees.

Using Power Ethically

Managers can work at developing all five of these forms of power for future use. The key to using them well is using them ethically, as Table 11.1 shows. Coercive power, for example, requires careful administration if it is to be used in an ethical manner. Employees should be informed of the rules in advance, and any punishment should be used consistently, uniformly, and privately. The key to using all five types of interpersonal power ethically is to be sensitive to employees' concerns and to communicate well.

Determining whether a power-related behavior is ethical is complex. Another way to look at the ethics surrounding the use of power is to ask three questions that show the criteria for examining power-related behaviors:[10]

1. *Does the behavior produce a good outcome for people both inside and outside the organization?* This question represents the criterion of *utilitarian outcomes.* The behavior should result in the greatest good for the greatest number of people. If the power-related behavior serves only the individual's self-interest and fails to help the organization reach its goals, it is considered unethical. A

Discussion Consideration
Ask students to identify the types of power associated with famous individuals such as Michael Jordan.

TABLE 11.1

Guidelines for the Ethical Use of Power

FORM OF POWER	GUIDELINES FOR USE
Reward power	Verify compliance. Make feasible, reasonable requests. Make only ethical requests. Offer rewards desired by subordinates. Offer only credible rewards.
Coercive power	Inform subordinates of rules and penalties. Warn before punishing. Administer punishment consistently and uniformly. Understand the situation before acting. Maintain credibility. Fit punishment to the infraction. Punish in private.
Legitimate power	Be cordial and polite. Be confident. Be clear and follow up to verify understanding. Make sure request is appropriate. Explain reasons for request. Follow proper channels. Exercise power consistently. Enforce compliance. Be sensitive to subordinates' concerns.
Referent power	Treat subordinates fairly. Defend subordinates' interests. Be sensitive to subordinates' needs and feelings. Select subordinates similar to oneself. Engage in role modeling.
Expert power	Maintain credibility. Act confident and decisive. Keep informed. Recognize employee concerns. Avoid threatening subordinates' self-esteem.

SOURCE: Gary A. Yukl, *Leadership in Organizations,* Copyright 1981, pp. 44–58, adapted by permission of Prentice Hall, Englewood Cliffs, NJ.

salesperson might be tempted to discount a product deeply in order to make a sale that would win a contest. Doing so would be in her self-interest but would not benefit the organization.

2. *Does the behavior respect the rights of all parties?* This question emphasizes the criterion of *individual rights.* Free speech, privacy, and due process are individual rights that are to be respected, and power-related behaviors that violate these rights are considered unethical.
3. *Does the behavior treat all parties equitably and fairly?* This question represents the criterion of *distributive justice.* Power-related behavior that treats one party arbitrarily or benefits one party at the expense of another is unethical. Granting a day of vacation to one employee in a busy week in which co-workers must struggle to cover for him might be considered unethical.

Discussion Consideration
Ask students to identify examples of the unethical use of power.

To be considered ethical, power-related behavior must meet all three criteria. If the behavior fails to meet the criteria, then alternate actions should be considered. Unfortunately, most power-related behaviors are not easy to analyze. Conflicts may exist among the criteria; for example, a behavior may maximize the greatest good for the greatest number of people but may not treat all parties equitably. Individual rights may need to be sacrificed for the good of the organization. A CEO may need to be removed from power for the organization to be saved. Still, these criteria can be used on a case-by-case basis to sort through the complex ethical issues surrounding the use of power.

Points to Emphasize
The concept of power is value free and neutral. It is how power is used that determines whether it will have a constructive or destructive impact on the organization.

McClelland's Two Faces of Power

We turn now to a theory of power that takes a strong stand on the "right" versus "wrong" kind of power to use in organizations. David McClelland has spent a great deal of his career studying the need for power and the ways managers use power. As was discussed in Chapter 5, he believes that there are two distinct faces of power, one negative and one positive.[11] The negative face of power is **personal power**—power used for personal gain. Managers who use personal power are commonly described as "power hungry." Personal power is a win-lose form of power in which the manager tends to treat others as objects to be utilized to get ahead. It is based on the traditional notion of power as domination over others.

personal power
Power used for personal gain.

The positive face of power is **social power**—power used to create motivation or to accomplish group goals. McClelland clearly favors the use of social power by managers. He has found that the best managers are those who have a high need for social power coupled with a relatively low need for affiliation. In addition, he has found that managers who use power successfully have four power-oriented characteristics:

social power
Power used to create motivation or to accomplish group goals.

1. *Belief in the authority system.* They believe that the institution is important and that its authority system is valid. They are comfortable influencing and being influenced. The source of their power is the authority system of which they are a part.
2. *Preference for work and discipline.* They like their work and are very orderly. They have a basic value preference for the Protestant work ethic, believing that work is good for a person over and beyond its income-producing value.
3. *Altruism.* They publicly put the company and its needs before their own needs. They are able to do this because they see their own well-being as integrally tied to the corporate well-being.
4. *Belief in justice.* They believe justice is to be sought above all else. People should receive that to which they are entitled and that which they earn.

Alternate Example
Employees will have to adjust to working with a social power manager after working for a personal power manager. Personal power managers require submissive rule observers. Social power managers want employees to help determine the rules. SOURCE: A. Toffler, "Powershift," *Newsweek,* 15 October 1990, 90.

McClelland takes a definite stand on the proper use of power by managers. When power is used for the good of the group, rather than for individual gain, it is positive. McClelland's approach to power is basically psychological in nature, focusing on the needs and drives of the individual.

Intergroup Sources of Power

Groups or teams within an organization can also use power from several sources. One source of intergroup power is control of *critical resources*.[12] When one group controls an important resource that another group desires, the first group holds power. Controlling resources needed by another group allows the power-holding group to influence the actions of the less powerful group.

Salancik and Pfeffer, who proposed this resource dependency model, conducted a study of university budgeting decisions. Various departments within a university have power by virtue of their national ranking, their ability to win outside grant monies, and their success in attracting promising graduate students. Departments that obtain these critical outside resources are awarded more internal resources from within the university.[13] Thus, one source of group power is control over valued resources.

Groups also have power to the extent that they control **strategic contingencies**—activities that other groups depend on in order to complete their tasks.[14] The dean's office, for example, may control the number of faculty positions to be filled in each department of a college. The departmental hiring plans are thus contingent on approval from the dean's office. In this case, the dean's office controls the strategic contingency of faculty hiring, and thus has power.

strategic contingencies
Activities that other groups depend on in order to complete their tasks.

Three factors can give a group control over a strategic contingency.[15] One is the *ability to cope with uncertainty*. If a group can help another group deal with uncertainty, it has power. One organizational group that has gained power in recent years is the legal department. Faced with increasing government regulations and fears of litigation, many other departments seek guidance from the legal department.

Another factor that can give a group control power is a *high degree of centrality* within the organization. If a group's functioning is important to the organization's success, it has high centrality. The sales force in a computer firm, for example, has power because of its immediate effect on the firm's operations and because other groups (accounting and servicing groups, for example) depend on its activities.

The third factor that can give a group power is *nonsubstitutability*—the extent to which a group performs a function that is indispensable to an organization. A team of computer specialists may be powerful because of its expertise with a system. It may have specialized experience that another team cannot provide.

The strategic contingencies model thus shows that groups hold power over other groups when they can reduce uncertainty, when their functioning is central to the organization's success, and when the group's activities are difficult to replace.[16]

Etzioni's Power Analysis

■ Amitai Etzioni takes a more sociological orientation to power. Etzioni has developed a theory of power analysis.[17] He says that there are three types of organizational power and three types of organizational involvement, or membership, that will lead to either congruent or incongruent uses of power. The three types of organizational power are the following:

1. *Coercive power*—influencing members by forcing them to do something under threat of punishment, or through fear intimidation.
2. *Utilitarian power*—influencing members by providing them with rewards and benefits.
3. *Normative power*—influencing members by using knowledge that they want very much to belong to the organization and by letting them know that what they are expected to do is the "right" thing to do.

FIGURE 11.1

Etzioni's Power Analysis

SOURCE: Amitai Etzioni, *Modern Organizations,* copyright 1964, pp. 59–61. Adapted by permission of Prentice Hall, Englewood Cliffs, NJ.

Type of power	Type of membership: Alienative	Calculative	Moral
Coercive	●		
Utilitarian		●	
Normative			●

Along with these three types of organizational power, Etzioni proposes that we can classify organizations by the type of membership they have:

1. *Alienative membership.* The members have hostile, negative feelings about being in the organization. They don't want to be there. Prisons are a good example of alienative memberships.
2. *Calculative membership.* Members weigh the benefits and limitations of belonging to the organization. Businesses are good examples of organizations with calculative memberships.
3. *Moral membership.* Members have such positive feelings about organizational membership that they are willing to deny their own needs. Organizations with many volunteer workers, such as the American Heart Association, are examples of moral memberships. Religious groups are another example.

Etzioni argues that you should match the type of organizational power to the type of membership in the organization in order to achieve congruence. Figure 11.1 shows the matches in his power analysis theory.

In an alienative membership, members have hostile feelings. In prisons, for example, Etzioni would contend that coercive power is the appropriate type to use.

A calculative membership is characterized by an analysis of the good and bad aspects of being in the organization. In the business partnership example, each partner weighs the benefits from the partnership against the costs entailed in the contractual arrangement. Utilitarian, or reward-based, power is the most appropriate type to use.

In a moral membership, the members have strong positive feelings about the particular cause or goal of the organization. Normative power is the most appropriate to use because it capitalizes on the members' desires to belong.

Etzioni's power analysis is an organizational-level theory. It emphasizes that the characteristics of an organization play a role in determining the type of power appropriate for use in the organization. Etzioni's theory is controversial in its contention that a single type of power is appropriate in any organization.

Alternate Example

One of the reasons security guards dress in uniforms is to symbolize power. If they look like police, maybe they will be obeyed as police are.
SOURCE: J. Pfeffer, Managing with Power (Boston: Harvard Business School Press, 1992), 132.

Symbols of Power

■ Organization charts show who has authority, but they do not reveal much about who has power. We'll now look at two very different ideas about the symbols of power. The first one comes from Rosabeth Moss Kanter. It is a scholarly approach to determining who has power and who feels powerless. The second is a semiserious look at the tangible symbols of power by Michael Korda.

Kanter's Symbols of Power

Kanter provides several characteristics of powerful people in organizations: [18]

1. *Ability to intercede for someone in trouble.* An individual who can pull someone out of a jam has power.
2. *Ability to get placements for favored employees.* Getting a key promotion for an employee is a sign of power.
3. *Exceeding budget limitations.* A manager who can go above budget limits without being reprimanded has power.
4. *Procuring above-average raises for employees.* One faculty member reported that her department head distributed 10 percent raises to the most productive faculty members although the budget allowed for only 4 percent increases. "I don't know how he did it; he must have pull," she said.
5. *Getting items on the agenda at meetings.* If a manager can raise issues for action at meetings, it's a sign of power.
6. *Access to early information.* Having information before anyone else does is a signal that a manager is plugged in to key sources.
7. *Having top managers seek out their opinion.* When top managers have a problem, they may ask for advice from lower-level managers. The managers they turn to have power.

Points to Emphasize
Kanter also has caveats to accompany the uses of power. Hiring others like ourselves results in unity in perspective, which can increase the power of a department. On the other hand, it can thwart creativity and innovation.

A theme that runs through Kanter's list is doing things for others: for people in trouble, for employees, for bosses. There is an active, other-directed element in her symbols of power.

You can use Kanter's symbols of power to identify powerful people in organizations. They can be particularly useful in finding a mentor who can effectively use power.

Kanter's Symbols of Powerlessness

Kanter also wrote about symptoms of **powerlessness**—a lack of power—in managers at different levels of the organization. First-line supervisors, for example, often display three symptoms of powerlessness: overly close supervision, inflexible adherence to the rules, and a tendency to do the job themselves rather than training their employees to do it. Staff professionals such as accountants and lawyers display different symptoms of powerlessness. When they feel powerless, they tend to resist change and try to protect their turf. Top executives can also feel powerless. They show symptoms such as focusing on budget cutting, punishing others, and using dictatorial, top-down communication.

powerlessness
A lack of power.

Employees at any level can feel powerless. When caught in powerless jobs, they may react passively and display overdependence on their boss.[19] In contrast, they may become frustrated and disrupt the work group.[20] The key to overcoming powerlessness is to share power and delegate tasks to employees.

Identifying powerful executives is not always easy. Lunching with employees is Hai Min Lee, President of Samsung USA.

Korda's Symbols of Power

Michael Korda takes a different look at symbols of power in organizations.[21] He discusses three unusual symbols: office furnishings, time power, and standing by.

Furniture is not just physically useful; it also conveys a message about power. Locked file cabinets are signs that the manager has important and confidential information in the office. A rectangular (rather than round) conference table enables the most important person to sit at the head of the table. The size of one's desk may convey the amount of power. Most executives prefer large, expensive desks.

Discussion Consideration
Ask students to identify the symbols of power that they observe in the offices of their professors or in the dean's office.

Time power means using clocks and watches as power symbols. Korda says that the biggest compliment a busy executive can pay a visitor is to remove his watch and place it face down on the desk, thereby communicating "my time is yours." He also notes that the less powerful the executive, the more intricate the watch; moreover, managers who are really secure in their power wear no watch at all, since they believe nothing important can happen without them. A full calendar is also proof of power. Personal planners are left open on the desk to display busy schedules.

Discussion Consideration
Ask students to describe two situations, one in which they felt powerless and one in which they felt powerful.

Standing by is a game in which people are obliged to stay close to their phones so that an executive can have access to them. The idea is that the more you can impose your schedule on other people, the more power you have. In fact, Korda defines *power* as follows: There are more people who inconvenience themselves on your behalf than there are people on whose behalf you would inconvenience yourself. Closely tied to this is the ability to make others perform simple tasks for you, such as getting your coffee or fetching the mail.

Both Kanter's and Korda's perspectives can be used to identify people who hold power in organizations. By identifying powerful people and learning from their modeled behavior, newcomers can learn the norms of power use in the organization.

Political Behavior in Organizations

organizational politics
The use of power and influence in organizations.

political behavior
Actions not officially sanctioned by an organization that are taken to influence others in order to meet one's personal goals.

■ Like power, the term *politics* in organizations may conjure up a few negative images. However, **organizational politics** is not necessarily negative; it is the use of power and influence in organizations. As people try to acquire power and expand their power base, they use various tactics and strategies. Some are sanctioned (acceptable to the organization); others are not. **Political behavior** is actions not officially sanctioned by an organization that are taken to influence others in order to meet one's personal goals.[22]

Points to Emphasize
Politics, like power, is not necessarily bad. In fact, some politics are potentially useful, or constructive, to the organization.

Politics is a controversial topic among managers. Some managers take a favorable view of political behavior; others see it as detrimental to the organization. In a study of managers, 53 percent reported that politics had a positive impact on the achievement of the organization's goals.[23] In contrast, 44 percent reported that politics distracted organization members from focusing on goal achievement. In a different study, managers displayed conflicting attitudes toward politics in organizations. Over 89 percent agreed that workplace politics were common in most organizations and that successful executives must be good politicians. However, 59 percent indicated that workplaces that were free of politics were more satisfying to work in.[24] These studies point out the controversial nature of political behavior in organizations.

Many organizational conditions encourage political activity. Among them are unclear goals, autocratic decision making, ambiguous lines of authority, scarce resources, and uncertainty.[25] Even supposedly objective activities may involve politics. One such activity is the performance appraisal process. A study of sixty executives who had extensive experience in employee evaluation indicated that political considerations were nearly always part of the performance appraisal process.[26]

Discussion Consideration
Ask students whether they believe that political savvy is desirable in the workplace.

Individuals who use power in organizations are organizational politicians. Challenge 11.1 shows the personal characteristics of effective organizational politicians and can help you assess your own political potential.

CHALLENGE

■ 11.1

Evaluate Your Political Potential

Examine the following table and answer the questions that follow it.

PERSONAL CHARACTERISTICS OF EFFECTIVE POLITICAL ACTORS

Personal Characteristic	*Behavioral Example*
Articulate	■ Must be able to clearly communicate ideas.
Sensitive	■ Must be sensitive to other individuals, situations, and opportunities.
Socially adept	■ Must understand the social norms of the organization and behave so as to be perceived by influential others as "fitting in well."
Competent	■ Must have the necessary skills and qualifications.
Popular	■ Must be liked or admired by others in the organization.
Extraverted	■ Must be interested in what happens outside of him or her.
Self-confident	■ Must have confidence in his or her abilities.
Aggressive	■ Must be self-assertive and forceful.
Ambitious	■ Must be eager to attain success.
Devious	■ Must be willing to use any tactic to get his or her way.
"Organization man or woman"	■ Must emphasize the well-being of the organization.
Highly intelligent	■ Must be able to use his or her knowledge to solve problems.
Logical	■ Must be capable of reasoning.

1. Which characteristics do you possess? Which do you need to work on? Ask a friend what characteristics you possess.
2. On the basis of the table, are you an effective political actor? Explain.
3. Can we assume that all of these characteristics are worth having?

SOURCE: R. N. Allen, D. L. Madison, L. W. Porter, P. A. Renwick, and B. T. Mayes, "Organizational Politics: Tactics and Characteristics of its Actors," *California Management Review*, Fall 1979, 77–83. Copyright 1979 by The Regents of the University of California. Adapted from *California Management Review*, Vol. 22, No. 1. By permission of the regents.

Maccoby's Four Political Types

Michael Maccoby offers another view of organizational politicians. In his book *The Gamesman*, Maccoby describes four distinct types of organizational politicians.[27] A manager who recognizes them is better able to understand the behavior of others in the organization. The four types are the craftsman, the jungle fighter, the company man, and the gamesman.

The *craftsman* is often a technical specialist who likes detail and precision. The person is usually quiet, sincere, modest, and practical. The goal of the craftsman is to be a good provider, and often the individual goes along with goals she or he doesn't quite believe in. The craftsman is the least politically active of the four types.

The *jungle fighter* desires success at any cost. Unafraid to step on others to get ahead, this fighter believes employees should be used to get ahead in the company. There are two types of jungle fighters: foxes and lions. Foxes make their nests in the organization and maneuver from this safe base. Lions conquer others' territories and build empires.

As a politician, the *company man or woman* is conservative. The person's goal is the protection of self and company. In fact, this individual's identity rests with the powerful, protective company. The concern of such people is for humans; however, they are more involved with security than success and may miss opportunities that arise.

The *gamesman* likes contests and views business as a game. This individual takes calculated risks and thrives on challenge and competition. Gamesmen tend to be charismatic and to motivate their employees with enthusiasm. They love to talk about business tactics and strategies.

The major contribution of Maccoby's work is that it shows that individuals differ in their behavior as political actors. Craftsmen, driven by achievement, are the least political. Company men or women, possessing a strong desire for affiliation, also may not exhibit a lot of political behavior. In contrast, jungle fighters and gamesmen, although very different in behavior, are apt to be active politicians.

Influence Tactics

Influence is the process of affecting the thoughts, behavior, or feelings of another person. That other person could be the boss (upward influence), an employee (downward influence), or a coworker (lateral influence). There are eight basic types of influence tactics. They are listed and described in Table 11.2.[28]

Discussion Consideration
How does influence differ from power?

Research has shown that the four tactics used most frequently are consultation, rational persuasion, inspirational appeals, and ingratiation, regardless of the target of the influence attempt. Thus, individuals do not differentiate among bosses, subordinates, and peers in terms of the tactic they choose. Upward appeals and coalition tactics are used moderately. Exchange tactics are used least often.

Some of the influence tactics are used for impression management, which was described in Chapter 3. In impression management, individuals use influence tactics to control others' impressions of them. Ingratiation is an example of one tactic often used for impression management. Ingratiation can take many forms, including flattery, opinion conformity, and subservient behavior.[29] Exchange is another influence tactic that may be used for impression management. Offering to do favors for someone in an effort to create a favorable impression is an exchange tactic.

Discussion Consideration
Ask students to identify the influence tactics they use most often. Which tactics seem to work best? Which tactics are used on them most often?

Which influence tactics are more effective? It depends on the target of the influence attempt and the objective. Individuals use different tactics for different purposes, and they use different tactics for different people. Influence attempts with subordinates, for example, usually involve assigning tasks or changing behavior. With peers, the objective is often to request assistance. With superiors, influence attempts are often made to request approval, resources, political support, or personal benefits. Rational persuasion and coalition tactics are used most often to get support from peers and superiors to change company policy. Consultation and inspirational appeals are particularly effective for gaining support and resources for a new project.[30] Overall, the most effective tactic in terms of achieving objectives is rational persuasion, while pressure seems to be the least effective.

One way in which subordinates often use influence attempts is in trying to convince their supervisors of their promotability. Evidence indicates that rational persuasion has a positive effect on supervisors' assessments of promotability.

■ **TABLE 11.2**

Influence Tactics Used in Organizations

TACTICS	DESCRIPTION	EXAMPLES
Pressure	The person uses demands, threats, or intimidation to convince you to comply with a request or to support a proposal.	If you don't do this, you're fired. You have until 5:00 to change your mind, or I'm going without you.
Upward appeals	The person seeks to persuade you that the request is approved by higher management, or appeals to higher management for assistance in gaining your compliance with the request.	I'm reporting you to my boss. My boss supports this idea.
Exchange	The person makes an explicit or implicit promise that you will receive rewards or tangible benefits if you comply with a request or support a proposal, or reminds you of a prior favor to be reciprocated.	You owe me a favor. I'll take you to lunch if you'll support me on this.
Coalition	The person seeks the aid of others to persuade you to do something or uses the support of others as an argument for you to agree also.	All the other supervisors agree with me. I'll ask you in front of the whole committee.
Ingratiation	The person seeks to get you in a good mood or to think favorably of him or her before asking you to do something.	Only you can do this job right. I can always count on you, so I have another request.
Rational persuasion	The person uses logical arguments and factual evidence to persuade you that a proposal or request is viable and likely to result in the attainment of task objectives.	This new procedure will save us $150,000 in overhead. It makes sense to hire John; he has the most experience.
Inspirational appeals	The person makes an emotional request or proposal that arouses enthusiasm by appealing to your values and ideals, or by increasing your confidence that you can do it.	Being environmentally conscious is the right thing. Getting that account will be tough, but I know you can do it.
Consultation	The person seeks your participation in making a decision or planning how to implement a proposed policy, strategy, or change.	This new attendance plan is controversial. How can we make it more acceptable? What do you think we can do to make our workers less fearful of the new robots on the production line?

SOURCE: First two columns from G. Yukl and C. M. Falbe, "Influence Tactics and Objectives in Upward, Downward, and Lateral Influence Attempts," *Journal of Applied Psychology* 5 (1990): 132–140. Copyright 1990 by the American Psychological Association. Reprinted by permission.

Ingratiation, a softer tactic, has a negative effect on promotability—supervisors may see their subordinate's ingratiation attempts as self-serving attempts to get ahead.[31]

There is evidence that men and women view politics and influence attempts differently. Men tend to view political behavior more favorably than do women. When both men and women witness political behavior, they view it more positively if the agent is of their gender and the target is of the opposite gender.[32]

There is also some preliminary evidence that different cultures prefer different influence tactics at work. One study found that American managers dealing with a tardy employee tended to rely on pressure tactics such as "If you don't start reporting on time for work, I will have no choice but to start docking your pay." In contrast, Japanese managers relied on influence tactics that either

SCIENTIFIC FOUNDATION

Cultural Differences in Innovation Championing Strategies

Innovation has the capacity to alter the distribution of power in organizations, and there is often resistance to new ideas because of the uncertainty of the innovation process. This creates the need for someone to overcome resistance to change by using personal influence. Innovation champions, who do this, use various behaviors to promote innovation.

The increasing globalization of innovation efforts in multinational corporations has focused attention on the need to know more about the championing process in other cultures. The authors of this study examined three of Hofstede's cultural attributes, individualism/collectivism, power distance, and uncertainty avoidance, in terms of the championing process. Specifically, they hypothesized the following:

H1. The greater the collectivism of a society, the more people will prefer champions to make cross-functional appeals for the support of the innovation effort.

H2. The higher the power distance of a society, the more people prefer champions to gather support for the innovation among those in authority before beginning work on an innovation.

H3. The higher the uncertainty avoidance of a society, the more people prefer that champions work within the organization's rules and standard operating procedures to develop the innovation.

A survey was used in the study, and 1,228 individuals from 30 countries participated. The survey was translated into nine different languages to capture the variations in cultures. Results supported the hypotheses. In collectivist cultures, people prefer champions to gather support for innovation by appealing to a variety of groups for support. The more uncertainty accepting a society is, the more people in it prefer champions to overcome resistance by violating organizational norms and rules. The more power distant a society is, the more people prefer champions to garner support from those in authority.

Senior managers in multinational firms need to learn how to harness diversity. The success rates of innovations depend on the ability of champions to gain the support of others. Learning culturally appropriate innovation championing strategies is important for managers as business globalizes.

SOURCE: S. Shane, S. Venkataraman, and I. MacMillan, "Cultural Differences in Innovation Championing Strategies," *Journal of Management* 21 (1995): 931–952.

appealed to the employee's sense of duty ("It is your duty as a responsible employee of this company to begin work on time") or emphasized a consultative approach ("Is there anything I can do to help you overcome the problems that are preventing you from coming to work on time?").[33]

One situation in which influence strategies are essential is in championing innovations. A champion is someone who takes personal risks to overcome resistance to innovations in organizations. There are cultural differences in championing strategies, as shown in the Scientific Foundation feature.

How can a manager use influence tactics well? First, a manager can develop and maintain open lines of communication in all directions: upward, downward, and lateral. Then, the manager can treat the targets of influence attempts—whether managers, employees, or peers—with basic respect. Finally, the manager can understand that influence relationships are reciprocal—they are two-way relationships. As long as the influence attempts are directed toward organizational goals, the process of influence can be advantageous to all involved.

Managing Political Behavior in Organizations

Politics cannot and should not be eliminated from organizations. Managers can, however, take a proactive stance and manage the political behavior that inevitably occurs.[34]

Open communication is one key to managing political behavior. Uncertainty is a condition that tends to increase political behavior, and communication that reduces the uncertainty is important. One form of communication that will help is to clarify the sanctioned and nonsanctioned political behaviors in the organization. For example, you may want to encourage social power as opposed to personal power.[35]

Another key is to clarify expectations regarding performance. This can be accomplished through the use of clear, quantifiable goals and through the establishment of a clear connection between goal accomplishment and rewards.[36]

Participative management is yet another key. Often, people engage in political behavior when they feel excluded from decision-making processes in the organization. By including them, you will encourage positive input and eliminate behind-the-scenes maneuvering.

Encouraging cooperation among work groups is another strategy for managing political behavior. Managers can instill a unity of purpose among work teams by rewarding cooperative behavior and by implementing activities that emphasize the integration of team efforts toward common goals.[37]

Managing scarce resources well is also important. An obvious solution to the problem of scarce resources is to increase the resource pool, but few managers have this luxury. Clarifying the resource allocation process and making the connection between performance and resources explicit can help discourage dysfunctional political behavior.

Managing political behavior at work is important. The perception of dysfunctional political behavior can lead to dissatisfaction.[38] When employees perceive that there are dominant interest groups or cliques at work, they are less satisfied with pay and promotions. When they believe that the organization's reward practices are influenced by political behavior, they are less satisfied with their supervisors. In addition, when employees believe that their coworkers are exhibiting increased political behavior, they are less satisfied with their coworkers. Open communication, clear expectations about performance and rewards, participative decision-making practices, work group cooperation, and effective management of scarce resources can help managers prevent the negative consequences of political behavior.

Managing Up: Managing The Boss

■ One of the least discussed aspects of power and politics is the relationship between you and your boss. This is a crucial relationship, because your boss is your most important link with the rest of the organization.[39] The employee-boss relationship is one of mutual dependence; you depend on your boss to give you performance feedback, provide resources, and supply critical information. She depends on you for performance, information, and support. Because it's a mutual relationship, you should take an active role in managing it. Too often, the management of this relationship is left to the boss; but if the relationship doesn't meet your needs, chances are you haven't taken the responsibility to manage it proactively.

Points to Emphasize
Point out the difference between manipulation and coercion of superiors or employees.

Table 11.3 shows the basic steps to take in managing your relationship with your boss. The first step is to try to understand as much as you can about your boss. What are the person's goals and objectives? What kind of pressures does the person face in the job? Many individuals naively expect the boss to be perfect and are disappointed when they find that this is not the case. What are the boss's strengths, weaknesses, and blind spots? Because this is an emotionally charged relationship, it is difficult to be objective; but this is a critical step in forging an effective working relationship. What is the boss's preferred work style? Does the person prefer everything in writing or hate detail? Does the boss prefer that you make appointments, or is dropping in at the boss's office acceptable? The point is to gather as much information about your boss as you can and to try to put yourself in that person's shoes.

■ **TABLE 11.3**

Managing Your Relationship with Your Boss

MAKE SURE YOU UNDERSTAND YOUR BOSS AND HER CONTEXT, INCLUDING:
Her goals and objectives. The pressures on her. Her strengths, weaknesses, blind spots. Her preferred work style.
ASSESS YOURSELF AND YOUR NEEDS, INCLUDING:
Your own strengths and weaknesses. Your personal style. Your predisposition toward dependence on authority figures.
DEVELOP AND MAINTAIN A RELATIONSHIP THAT:
Fits both your needs and styles. Is characterized by mutual expectations. Keeps your boss informed. Is based on dependability and honesty. Selectively uses your boss's time and resources.

SOURCE: J. J. Gabarro and J. P. Kotter, "Managing Your Boss," *Harvard Business Review,* (January–February 1980): 92–100.

The second step in managing this important relationship is to assess yourself and your own needs much in the same way you analyzed your boss's. What are your strengths, weaknesses, and blind spots? What is your work style? How do you normally relate to authority figures? Some of us have tendencies toward counterdependence; that is, we rebel against the boss as an authority and view the boss as a hindrance to our performance. Or, in contrast, we might take an overdependent stance, passively accepting the boss-employee relationships and treating the boss as an all-wise, protective parent. What is your tendency? Knowing how you react to authority figures can help you understand your interactions with your boss.

Once you have done a careful self-analysis and tried to understand your boss, the next step is to work to develop an effective relationship. Both parties' needs and styles must be accommodated. A fundraiser for a large volunteer organization related a story about a new boss, describing him as cold, aloof, unorganized, and inept. She made repeated attempts to meet with him and clarify expectations, and his usual reply was that he didn't have the time. Frustrated, she almost looked for a new job. "I just can't reach him!" was her refrain. Then she stepped back to consider her boss's and her own styles. Being an intuitive-feeling type of person, she prefers constant feedback and reinforcement from others. Her boss, an intuitive-thinker, works comfortably without feedback from others and has a tendency to fail to praise or reward others. She sat down with him and cautiously discussed the differences in their needs. This discussion became the basis for working out a comfortable relationship. "I still don't like him, but I understand him better," she said.

Another aspect of managing the relationship involves working out mutual expectations. One key activity is to develop a plan for work objectives and have the boss agree to it.[40] It is important to do things right, but it is also important to do the right things. Neither party to the relationship is a mind reader, and clarifying the goals is a crucial step.

Keeping the boss informed is also a priority. No one likes to be caught off guard, and there are several ways to keep the boss informed. Give the boss a weekly to-do list as a reminder of the progress towards goals. When you read something pertaining to your work, clip it out for the boss. Most busy executives appreciate being given materials they don't have time to find for themselves. Give the boss interim reports, and let the boss know if the work schedule is slipping. Don't wait until it's too late to take action.

The employee-boss relationship must be based on dependability and honesty. This means giving and receiving positive and negative feedback. Most of us are reluctant to give any feedback to the boss, but positive feedback is welcomed at the top. Negative feedback, while tougher to initiate, can clear the air. If given in a problem-solving format, it can even bring about a closer relationship.[41]

One university professor was constantly bombarded by the department head's requests that she serve on committees. When she complained about this to a colleague, she was told, "It's your fault; you need to learn how to say no." She went to the department head, explained that the committee work was keeping her from being an effective researcher and teacher, and asked that he reassign other faculty members to the committees. The department head was astonished that he had relied on her so heavily. "I just didn't realize that you were on so many committees already. Thanks for pointing it out. We need to spread these responsibilities around better."

Another point about negative feedback is that it is better to give it directly, rather than behind the boss's back. If the boss never gets the information, how can the problem be corrected?

Being considerate of the boss's time is important. Before running into the person's office, ask yourself if the meeting is necessary at that particular time. Does the boss need the information right now? Could you supply the information in a note? Is it a matter you could handle yourself? Another good time management technique is to submit an agenda before your meeting with the boss; that way, the boss can select an appropriate time slot and will have time to think about the items.

Finally, remember that the boss is on the same team you are. The golden rule is to make the boss look good, because you expect the boss to do the same for you.

Sharing Power: Empowerment

■ Another positive strategy for managing political behavior is **empowerment**— sharing power within an organization. As modern organizations grow flatter, eliminating layers of management, empowerment becomes more and more important. Jay Conger defines *empowerment* as "creating conditions for heightened motivation through the development of a strong sense of personal self-efficacy." [42] This means sharing power in such a way that individuals learn to believe in their ability to do the job. The driving idea of empowerment is that the individuals closest to the work and to the customers should make the decisions and that this makes the best use of employees' skills and talents.[43] You can empower yourself by developing your sense of self-efficacy. Challenge 11.2 helps you assess your progress in terms of self-empowerment.

empowerment
Sharing power within an organization.

Empowerment is easy to advocate but difficult to put into practice. Conger offers some guidelines on how leaders can empower others.

First, managers should express confidence in employees and set high performance expectations. Positive expectations can go a long way toward enabling good performance, as the Pygmalion effect shows (Chapter 3).

Second, managers should create opportunities for employees to participate in decision making. This means participation in the forms of both voice and choice. Employees should not only be asked to contribute their opinions about any issue; they should also have a vote in the decision that is made. One method for increasing participation is using self-managed teams, as we discussed in Chapter 9.

Alternate Example
Remind students that not everyone in an organization wants to be empowered. Some individuals may want parameters spelled out, and others may be more comfortable with traditional hierarchy.

CHALLENGE

■ 11.2

Are You Self-Empowered?

Check either A or B to indicate how you usually are in these situations:

1. If someone disagrees with me in a class or a meeting, I
   a. immediately back down
   b. explain my position further
2. When I have an idea for a project I
   a. typically take a great deal of time to start it
   b. get going on it fairly quickly
3. If my boss or teacher tells me to do something which I think is wrong I
   a. do it anyway, telling myself he or she is "the boss"
   b. ask for clarification and explain my position
4. When a complicated problem arises, I usually tell myself
   a. I can take care of it
   b. I will not be able to solve it
5. When I am around people of higher authority, I often
   a. feel intimidated and defer to them
   b. enjoy meeting important people
6. As I awake in the morning, I usually feel
   a. alert and ready to conquer almost anything
   b. tired and have a hard time getting myself motivated
7. During an argument I
   a. put a great deal of energy into "winning"
   b. try to listen to the other side and see if we have any points of agreement
8. When I meet new people I
   a. always wonder what they are "really" up to
   b. try to learn what they are about and give them the benefit of a doubt until they prove otherwise
9. During the day I often
   a. criticize myself on what I am doing or thinking
   b. think positive thoughts about myself
10. When someone else does a great job I
    a. find myself picking apart that person and looking for faults
    b. often give a sincere compliment
11. When I am working in a group, I try to
    a. do a better job than the others
    b. help the group function more effectively
12. If someone pays me a compliment I typically
    a. try not to appear boastful and I downplay the compliment
    b. respond with a positive "thank you" or similar response
13. I like to be around people who
    a. challenge me and make me question what I do
    b. give me respect
14. In love relationships I prefer the other person
    a. have his/her own selected interests
    b. do pretty much what I do
15. During a crisis I try to
    a. resolve the problem
    b. find someone to blame
16. After seeing a movie with friends I
    a. wait to see what they say before I decide whether I liked it
    b. am ready to talk about my reactions right away
17. When work deadlines are approaching I typically
    a. get flustered and worry about completion
    b. buckle down and work until the job is done

CHALLENGE

18. If a job comes up I am interested in I
   a. go for it and apply
   b. tell myself I am not qualified enough

19. When someone treats me unkindly or unfairly I
   a. try to rectify the situation
   b. tell other people about the injustice

20. If a difficult conflict situation or problem arises, I
   a. try not to think about it, hoping it will resolve itself
   b. look at various options and may ask others for advice before I figure out what to do

Scoring:

Score one point for each of the following circled:
1b, 2b, 3b, 4a, 5b, 6a, 7b, 8b, 9b, 10b, 11b, 12b, 13a, 14a, 15a, 16b, 17b, 18a, 19a, 20b.

Analysis of Scoring

16–20 You are a take-charge person and generally make the most of opportunities. When others tell you something cannot be done, you may take this as a challenge and do it anyway. You see the world as an oyster with many pearls to harvest.

11–15 You try hard, but sometimes your negative attitude prevents you from getting involved in productive projects. Many times you take responsibility, but there are situations where you look to others to take care of problems.

0–10 You complain too much and are usually focused on the "worst case scenario." To you the world is controlled by fate and no matter what you do it seems to get you nowhere, so you let other people develop opportunities. You need to start seeing the positive qualities in yourself and in others and see yourself as the "master of your fate."

Third, managers should remove bureaucratic constraints that stifle autonomy. Often, companies have antiquated rules and policies that prevent employees from managing themselves. An example is a collection agency where a manager's signature was once required to approve long-term payment arrangements for delinquent customers. Collectors, who spoke directly with customers, were the best judges of whether the payment arrangements were workable, and having to consult a manager made them feel closely supervised and powerless. The rule was dropped, and collections increased.

Fourth, managers should set inspirational or meaningful goals. When individuals feel they "own" a goal, they are more willing to take personal responsibility for it.

Empowerment is a matter of degree. Jobs can be thought of in two dimensions: job content and job context. Job content consists of the tasks and procedures necessary for doing a particular job. Job context is broader. It is the reason the organization needs the job and includes the way the job fits into the organization's mission, goals, and objectives. These two dimensions are depicted in Figure 11.2, the Employee Empowerment Grid.

Both axes of the grid contain the major steps in the decision-making process. As shown on the horizontal axis, decision-making authority over job content increases in terms of greater involvement in the decision-making process. Similarly, the vertical axis shows that authority over job context increases with

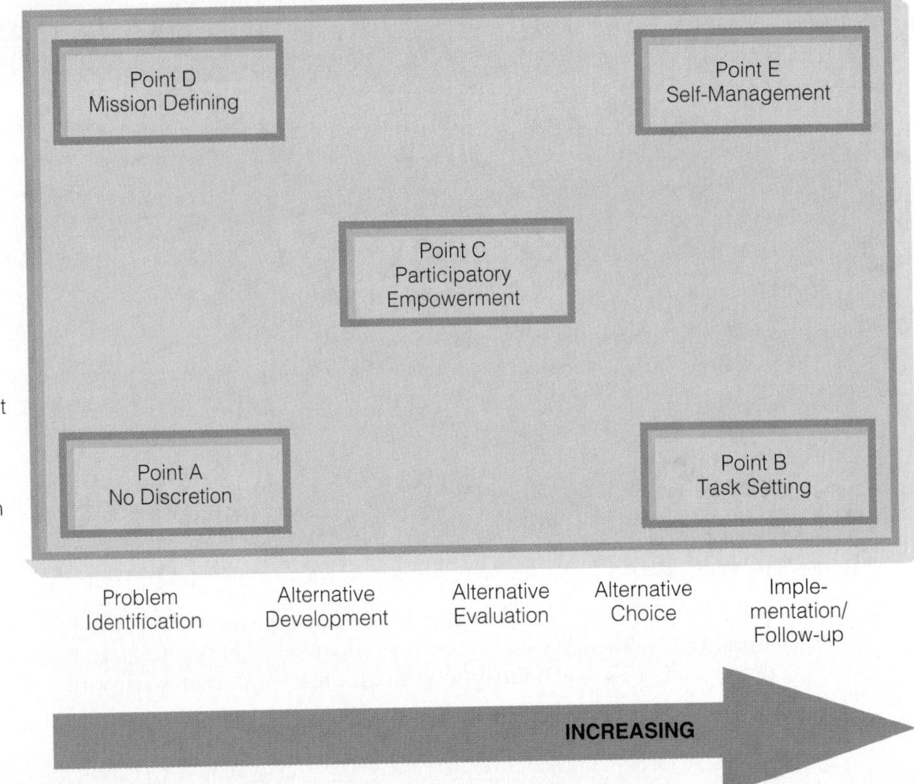

FIGURE 11.2
Employee Empowerment Grid

greater involvement in that decision-making process. Combining job content and job context authority in this way produces five points that vary in terms of the degree of empowerment.[44]

No Discretion (point A) represents the traditional, assembly-line job: highly routine and repetitive, with no decision-making power. Recall from Chapter 7 that if these jobs have a demanding pace and if workers have no discretion, distress will result.

Task setting (point B) is the essence of most empowerment programs in organizations today. In this case, the worker is empowered to make decisions about the best way to get the job done, but has no decision responsibility for the job context.

Participatory Empowerment (point C) represents a situation that is typical of autonomous work groups that have some decision-making power over both job content and job context. Their involvement is in problem identification, developing alternatives, and evaluating alternatives, but actual choice of alternatives is often beyond their power. Participatory empowerment can lead to job satisfaction and productivity. The Saturn plan in Spring Hill, Tennessee, is one success story in this category, as presented in the Organizational Reality feature.

Mission Defining (point D) is an unusual case of empowerment and is seldom seen. Here, employees have power over job context but not job content. An example would be a unionized team that is asked to decide whether their jobs could be better done by an outside vendor. Deciding to outsource would dramatically affect the mission of the company, but would not affect job content, which is specified in the union contract. Assuring these employees of continued employment regardless of their decision would be necessary for this case of empowerment.

Self-Management (point E) represents total decision-making control over both job content and job context. It is the ultimate expression of trust. One

ORGANIZATIONAL REALITY

Empowerment the Saturn Way

The Saturn Corporation of Spring Hill, Tennessee, is a subsidiary of General Motors that is as renowned for the way it produces cars as it is for the cars it produces. At Saturn, all work is accomplished by work units, consisting of about 15 team members and a work unit counselor. The counselors have some management functions like managing daily production, managing conflicts, and monitoring budget, quality, and safety issues. However, the work unit makes decisions by consensus, and the counselor is more of an executor working for the unit than a manager working for upper management.

Work units are empowered to perform about 30 functions for which all team members are responsible. Each Saturn team will:

- Design its own jobs.
- Plan and assign work.
- Control its own material and inventory.
- Perform maintenance on its equipment.
- Make hiring decisions.

All Saturn members have the power to "stop the line" if they see a quality problem. Although this is not uncommon in other plants, at Saturn, if you stop the line, you are responsible for fixing the problem. You can't pass it off to a manager or to another department. This means that all team members must keep in constant contact with suppliers, engineers, customers, and end users.

Empowerment without ability doesn't work, so Saturn gives all new team members 320 hours of training their first year, and at least 92 hours of training per year thereafter. Workers are trained in conflict management, problem solving, and interviewing—subjects that in other companies are often reserved only for managers. The aim of Saturn's approach is to broaden the employees' skills and help each one maximize his or her potential.

Although making decisions by team consensus is not the fastest method, it has paid off for Saturn. Once a decision is made, Saturn members are strongly committed to it because they were directly involved in the process. Most important, all Saturn employees feel that they are, to some degree, in control of the operation of the company. ■

SOURCE: "Enriching and Empowering Employees—The Saturn Way," *Personnel Journal* (September 1995): 32; "Saturn's Rings," *Supervisory Management* (August 1994): 8–9. Reprinted by permission of the publisher from *Supervisory Management*.

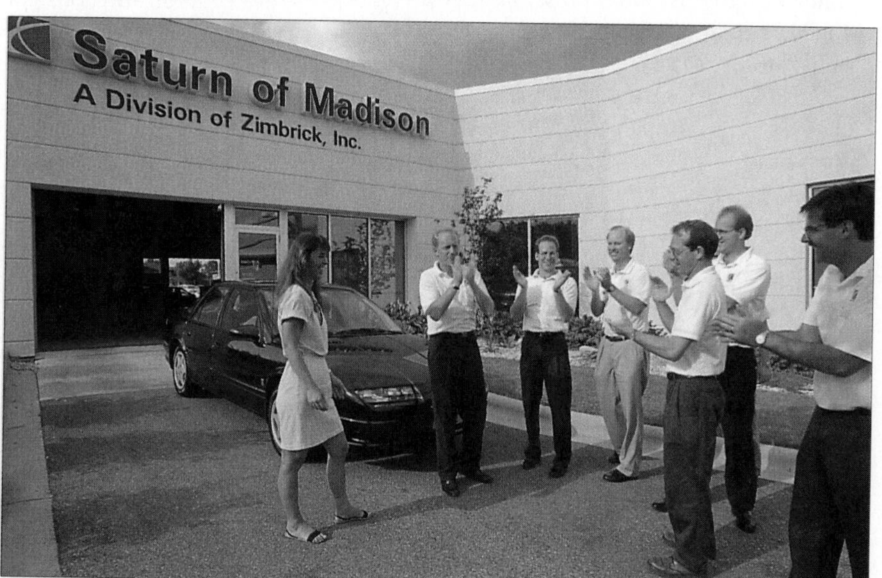

The Saturn Corporation is as famous for its empowered teams as it is for its cars. Teams take great pride in the quality of the cars they produce, and share that pride with new car owners.

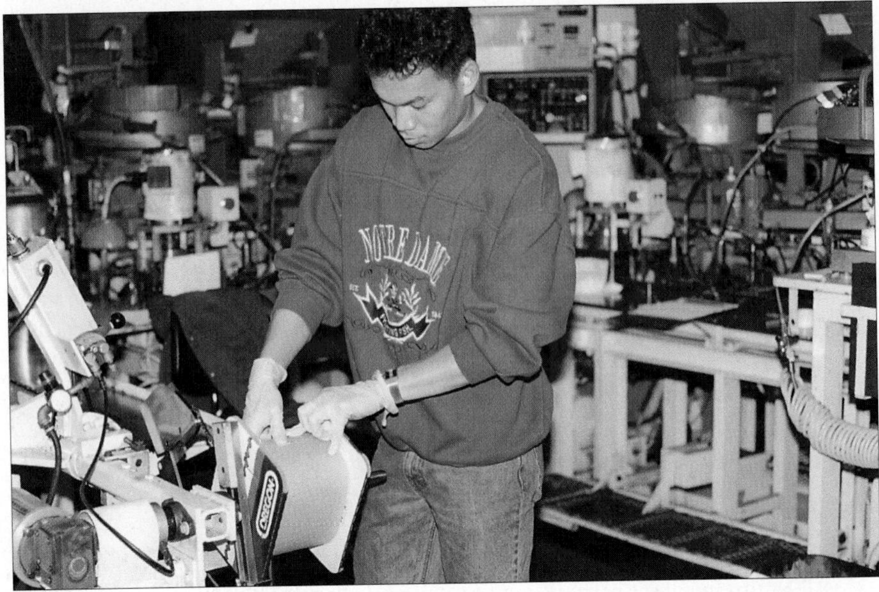

Companies that are concerned about product quality empower employees to diagnose and solve quality problems. At Oregon Cutting Systems, managers encourage employees to take risks; they would rather employees ask forgiveness than permission.

example is Chaparral Steel, where employees redesign their own jobs to add value to the organization.

Empowerment should begin with job content and proceed to job context. Because the work force is so diverse, managers should recognize that some employees are more ready for empowerment than others. Managers must diagnose situations and determine the degree of empowerment to extend to employees.

One organization that practices empowerment successfully is Square D Company, an electronics technology company of 20,000 employees.[45] Square D created Vision College in 1987 to focus on personal accountability for the company's vision: "Dedicated to growth, committed to quality." Vision College provides an opportunity for Square D employees to compare their current state with their vision, or desired state. All Square D employees participate in two-day Vision College sessions, in which the employees provide information about what works, what doesn't work, and what needs improvement in the company. They also discuss and define their own role in that improvement process. The establishment of Vision College to promote empowerment has moved accountability to the lowest levels of the organization.

At Oregon Cutting Systems, empowerment is a key element of the quality process. The company designs and manufactures cutting tools and holds half of the world's market in chains for saws. In this company, machine operators use statistical process control to improve product quality. Operators are empowered to gather their own data, find the causes of problems, make decisions, and act to fix the problems. Managers at Oregon Cutting Systems prefer that employees ask for forgiveness rather than permission. Empowerment is essential to an organizational culture that supports quality.

The empowerment process also carries with it a risk of failure. When you delegate responsibility and authority, you must be prepared to allow employees to fail; and failure is not something most managers tolerate well. At Levi Strauss, an employee failed to order enough fabric to meet a production run on jeans. The manager sat down with the employee and found out what had gone wrong and how to prevent that problem in the future. She did this in a nonthreatening way, without blaming or fingerpointing.[46] Coaching and counseling following a failure can turn it into a learning experience.

Managerial Implications: Using Power Effectively

■ Managers must depend on others to get things done. John Kotter argues that managers therefore need to develop power strategies to operate effectively.[47] Kotter offers some guidelines for managing dependence on others and for using power successfully:

- *Use power in ethical ways.* People have certain assumptions about the use of power. One way of using the various forms of power ethically is by applying the criteria of utilitarian outcomes, individual rights, and distributive justice.
- *Understand and use all of the various types of power and influence.* Successful managers diagnose the situation, understand the people involved, and choose a compatible influence method.
- *Seek out jobs that allow you to develop your power skills.* Recognize that managerial positions are dependent ones, and look for positions that allow you to focus on a critical issue or problem.
- *Use power tempered by maturity and self-control.* Power for its own sake should not be a goal, nor should power be used for self-aggrandizement.
- *Accept that influencing people is an important part of the management job.* Power means getting things accomplished; it is not a dirty word. Acquiring and using power well is a key to managerial success.

Mastering the power and politics within an organization takes respect and patience. When all people are treated as important, the total amount of power within the organization will increase.

In the Opening Spotlight, the pilot who applied for a job with Southwest Airlines assumed his expertise and good relationships with peers would win him the job. He was mistaken, as the Closing Spotlight shows.

CLOSING SPOTLIGHT

Empowerment and Employee Ownership at Southwest Airlines

At Southwest Airlines, their internal philosophy is Positively Outrageous Service (P.O.S.): For employees to make customers happy, Southwest must ensure employees' happiness first. This is accomplished in a number of ways. Two of them are empowerment and employee ownership.

Southwest employees are empowered to make decisions to provide P.O.S. A few years ago, severe weather led to numerous flight delays. Employees invented the LUV cart—a small cart filled with coffee, soft drinks, peanuts, and other goodies. After passing out complimentary drinks and snacks to customers waiting for their flights, employees entertained the customers with games and prizes. This was so well received by customers that it became a Southwest tradition. Empowering employees gives them the freedom to take matters into their own hands and innovate.

There is one surefire way to give employees the power to think and act like owners: Make them owners. Studies show that companies with significant employee ownership, like Southwest, outperform both their industry peers and the broad-based stock indices. Employee owners focus on customer needs and the good of the entire organization.

Southwest extends empowerment to its customers through its "Southwest Airlines Home Gate," a new site on the Internet's World Wide Web. The site dispenses information like route maps, job listings, discount packages, and tidbits about the company. Customers can even book their own flights using Southwest's ticketless booking system.[48] ■

Chapter Summary

- Power is the ability to influence others. Influence is the process of affecting the thoughts, behavior, and feelings of others. Authority is the right to influence others.
- French and Raven's five forms of interpersonal power are reward, coercive, legitimate, referent, and expert power.
- The key to using all of these types of power well is to use them ethically.
- McClelland believes personal power is negative and social power is positive.
- Intergroup power sources include control of critical resources and strategic contingencies.
- According to Etzioni, an important factor in deciding the type of power to use is the characteristics of the organization.
- Recognizing symbols of both power and powerlessness is a key diagnostic skill for managers.
- Organizational politics is an inevitable feature of work life. Political behavior consists of actions not officially sanctioned that are taken to influence others in order to meet personal goals. Managers should take a proactive role in managing politics.
- The employee-boss relationship is an important political relationship. Employees can use their skills to develop more effective working relationships with their bosses.
- Empowerment is a positive strategy for sharing power throughout the organization.

Key Terms

power (p. 316)
influence (p. 316)
authority (p. 316)
zone of indifference (p. 317)
reward power (p. 317)
coercive power (p. 317)
legitimate power (p. 317)
referent power (p. 317)
expert power (p. 317)
personal power (p. 320)
social power (p. 320)
strategic contingencies (p. 321)
powerlessness (p. 323)
organizational politics (p. 324)
political behavior (p. 324)
empowerment (p. 331)

Review Questions

1. What are the five types of power according to French and Raven? What are the effects of these types of power?
2. What are the intergroup sources of power?
3. Distinguish between personal and social power. What are the four power-oriented characteristics of the best managers?
4. Identify Etzioni's types of power and types of membership used to achieve congruence.
5. According to Rosabeth Moss Kanter, what are the symbols of power? The symptoms of powerlessness?
6. Describe the four political types of people Michael Maccoby discusses.
7. What are some ways to empower people at work?

Discussion and Communication Questions

1. Who is the most powerful person you know personally? What is it that makes the person so powerful?
2. What kinds of membership (alienative, calculative, moral) do you currently have? Is the power used in these relationships congruent?
3. What do McClelland's theory and Etzioni's theory have in common?
4. Do you experience yourself as powerful, powerless, or both? On what symbols or symptoms are you basing your perception?
5. Are people in your work environment empowered? How could they become more empowered?
6. Chapter 2 discussed power distance as a dimension of cultural differences. How would empowerment efforts be different in a country with high power distance?
7. *(communication question)* Review the Organizational Reality feature, "A Great Moment in Career Suicide." Pair up with a partner from your class. Using the concepts in this chapter, develop a role-play with one person taking on the role of engineer in the Organizational Reality, and one person tak-

ing on the role of an expert in organizational politics. The engineer should describe what happened in greater detail, and the expert should enlighten the engineer by explaining what the engineer needs to know about power and political behavior. Be prepared to present your role-play to the class.

8. *(communication question)* Think of a person you admire. Write a newspaper feature analyzing their use of power in terms of the ideas presented in the chapter.

Ethics Questions

1. Which of French and Raven's five types of power has the most potential for abuse? How can the abuse be prevented?
2. Under what circumstances is it ethical to manipulate people for the good of the organization?
3. Are moral memberships the only ethical organizational memberships? That is, can alienative and calculative memberships be ethical? Explain.
4. What are the most common forms of political behavior that you see in your work or school environment? Are they ethical or unethical? Explain.
5. Is it possible to have an organization where all power is equally shared, or is the unequal distribution of power a necessary evil in organizations? Explain.

Experiential Exercises

11.1 Social Power Role Plays

1. Divide the class into five groups of equal size, each of which is assigned one of the French and Raven types of power.

2. Read the following paragraph and prepare an influence plan using the type of power that has been assigned to your group. When you have finished your planning, select one member to play the role of instructor. Then choose from your own or another group a "student" who is to be the recipient of the "instructor's" efforts.

You are an instructor in a college class and have become aware that a potentially good student has been repeatedly absent from class and sometimes is unprepared when he is there. He seems to be satisfied with the grade he is getting, but you would like to see him attend regularly, be better prepared, and thus do better in the class. You even feel that the student might get really turned on to pursuing a career in this field, which is an exciting one for you. You are respected and liked by your students, and it irritates you that this person treats your dedicated teaching with such a cavalier attitude. You want to influence the student to start attending regularly.

3. Role-playing.
   a. Each group role-plays its influence plan.
   b. During the role-playing, members in other groups should think of themselves as the student being influenced. Fill out the following "Reaction to Influence Questionnaire" for each role-playing episode, including your own.

4. Tabulate the results of the questionnaire within your group. For each role-playing effort, determine how many people thought the power used was reward, coercive, and so on, then add up each member's score for item 2, then for items 3, 4, and 5.

5. Group discussion.
   a. As a class, discuss which influence strategy is the most effective in compliance, long-lasting effect, acceptable attitude, and enhanced relationships.
   b. What are the likely side-effects of each type of influence strategy?

Reaction to Influence Questionnaire

Role-Play #1

1. Type of power used (mark one): Role-Plays

	1	2	3	4	5
Reward—Ability to influence because of potential reward.					
Coercive—Ability to influence because of capacity to coerce or punish.					
Legitimate—Stems from formal position in organization.					
Referent—Comes from admiration and liking.					
Expert—Comes from superior knowledge or ability to get things done.					

Think of yourself on the receiving end of the influence attempt just described and record your own reaction with an "X" in the appropriate box.

2. As a result of this influence attempt I will . . .
   definitely not comply — definitely comply
   1 2 3 4 5
3. Any change that does come about will be . . .
   temporary — long-lasting
   1 2 3 4 5
4. My own personal reaction is . . .
   resistant — accepting
   1 2 3 4 5
5. As a result of this influence attempt, my relationship with the instructor will probably be . . .
   worse — better
   1 2 3 4 5

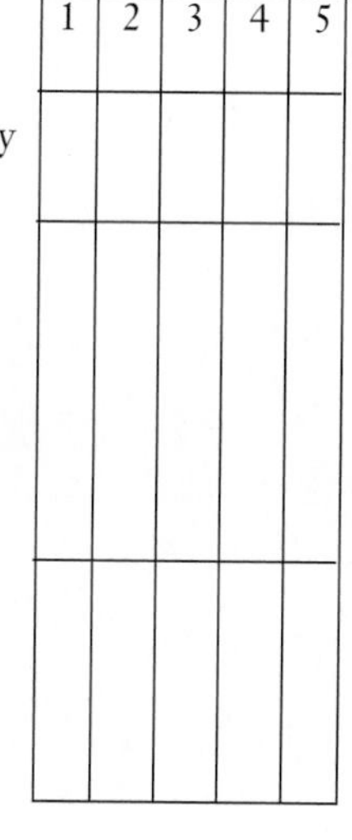

SOURCE: Adapted with permission from Gib Akin, *Exchange* 3, No. 4 (1978): 38–39.

11.2 Empowerment in the Classroom

1. Divide the class into groups of six people.

2. Each group is to brainstorm ways in which students might be more empowered in the classroom. The ideas do not have to be either feasible or reasonable. They can be as imaginative as possible.

3. Each group should now analyze each of the empowerment ideas for feasibility, paying attention to administrative or other constraints that may hamper implementation. This feasibility discussion might include ideas about how the college or university could be altered.

4. Each group should present its empowerment ideas along with its feasibility analysis. Questions of clarification for each group should follow each presentation.

5. Discuss the following questions as a class:

   a. Who is threatened by the power changes caused by empowerment?

   b. Are there unintended or adverse consequences of empowerment? Explain.

VIDEO CASE

Employee Empowerment at Oregon Cutting Systems[1]

Located in Portland, Oregon, Oregon Cutting Systems focuses its business on "cutting technology, the science of designing and manufacturing cutting tools for various applications." A major producer of blades and chains for chain saws, OCS developed its products under patent protection.

By the early 1980s, however, OCS had developed a history of ignoring customer complaints. As Jim Osterman, president of OCS, observed, "When someone came in with a problem or complaint, we were certain it had to be their problem, not our product problem. As a consequence, we earned a reputation in the field of not covering our products."

Until the early to mid-1980s OCS ignored the customers' problems and needs. Charlie Nicholson, division vice president for quality, says that OCS "made a lot of assumptions regarding end users' needs and expectations." This contributed to OCS's business problems because there actually are a "lot of different segments that demand different types of products."

Recognizing that they had to become more customer focused, OCS has changed its view. Now the customers' problems are the company's problems and OCS works very hard at trying to solve them. In an effort to improve efficiency and product quality, Oregon Cutting Systems implemented just-in-time (JIT) manufacturing and statistical process control (SPC) procedures. JIT was implemented first, then SPC.

At Oregon Cutting Systems, SPC is used as an operating tool rather than as an engineering or management tool—it is one means that OCS uses to empower employees. SPC is an aid to serving internal customers in the manufacturing chain. Operators are encouraged to identify problems and solve them without management input. They spend 5 to 10 percent of their time collecting data, using control charts, analyzing data, identifying problems, and acting on those problems.

OCS's approach to employee empowerment is also reflected in its decision-making process. Decisions are pushed down to the lowest possible level and teams are involved in the decision process. Jim Osterman advocates that employees should make decisions and then ask for forgiveness if they are wrong, rather than not making any decisions at all or asking for permission to make decisions. This has changed how supervisors, like Judy Rankin, do their jobs. She points out that now, "I'm a coach and trainer. . . . We make decisions as a team, and make better decisions."

Osterman, the company president, maintains that people are empowered to feel good about what they're doing. "Our people really do put in the extra effort," he says. Moreover, employees feel they have made a difference. According to Charlie Clough, OCS's manager of industrial engineering, "The best experts you can hire are on the floor already." One operator observes that, "If you let the person building the product have input on the product, they are going to feel closer to it and strive to produce a better product." And the chronic customer problems of the past are nonexistent now.

DISCUSSION QUESTIONS

1. What sources of power do Oregon Cutting Systems' executives, managers, and supervisors seem to use? What sources of power are available to the production employees?
2. How does OCS empower its employees? Explain your answer in the context of the employee empowerment grid shown in Figure 11.2.
3. Why might empowering employees contribute to an organization's success? To the employees' success?
4. How, if at all, can employee empowerment create problems for an organization? For the employees?
5. How do production employees at OCS exercise influence over their coworkers? Over their supervisors and higher-level managers?

SOURCE: This case was written by Michael K. McCuddy, the Louis S. and Mary L. Morgal Professor of Christian Business Ethics, College of Business Administration, Valparaiso University.

1. This case is based on the *Oregon Cutting Systems* segment of the Association for Manufacturing Excellence video entitled *We're Getting Closer.*

References

1. "Southwest Airlines' Herb Kelleher: Unorthodoxy at Work," *Management Review* (January 1995): 9–12.
2. G. C. Homans, "Social Behavior as Exchange," *American Journal of Sociology* 63 (1958): 597–606.
3. R. D. Middlemist and M. A. Hitt, *Organizational Behavior: Managerial Strategies for Performance* (St. Paul, Minn., West Publishing, 1988).
4. C. Barnard, *The Functions of the Executive* (Cambridge, Mass., Harvard University Press, 1938).
5. J. R. P. French and B. Raven, "The Bases of Social Power," in D. Cartwright, ed., *Group Dynamics: Research and Theory* (Evanston, Ill.: Row, Peterson, 1962); T. R. Hinkin and C. A. Schriesheim, "Development and Application of New Scales to Measure the French and Raven (1959) Bases of Social Power," *Journal of Applied Psychology* 74 (1989): 561–567.
6. P. M. Podsakoff and C. A. Schriesheim, "Field Studies of French and Raven's Bases of Power: Critique, Reanalysis, and Suggestions for Future Research," *Psychological Bulletin* 97 (1985): 387–411.
7. M. A. Rahim, "Relationships of Leader Power to Compliance and Satisfaction with Supervision: Evidence from a National Sample of Managers," *Journal of Management* 15 (1989): 545–556.
8. C. Argyris, "Management Information Systems: The Challenge to Rationality and Emotionality," *Management Science* 17 (1971): 275–292; J. Naisbitt and P. Aburdene, *Megatrends 2000* (New York: Morrow, 1990).
9. P. P. Carson, K. D. Carson, E. L. Knight, and C. W. Roe, "Power in Organizations: A Look Through the TQM Lens," *Quality Progress* (November 1995): 73–78.
10. M. Velasquez, D. J. Moberg, and G. F. Cavanaugh, "Organizational Statesmanship and Dirty Politics: Ethical Guidelines for the Organizational Politician," *Organizational Dynamics* 11 (1982): 65–79.
11. D. E. McClelland, *Power: The Inner Experience* (New York: Irvington, 1975).
12. J. Pfeffer and G. Salancik, *The External Control of Organizations* (New York: Harper & Row, 1978).
13. G. Salancik and J. Pfeffer, "The Bases and Uses of Power in Organizational Decision Making," *Administrative Science Quarterly* 15 (1971): 216–229.
14. R. H. Miles, *Macro Organizational Behavior* (Glenview, Ill.: Scott, Foresman, 1980).
15. D. Hickson, C. Hinings, C. Lee, R. E. Schneck, and J. M. Pennings, "A Strategic Contingencies Theory of Intraorganizational Power," *Administrative Science Quarterly* 14 (1971): 219–220.
16. C. R. Hinings, D. J. Hickson, J. M. Pennings, and R. E. Schneck, "Structural Conditions of Intraorganizational Power," *Administrative Science Quarterly* 19 (1974): 22–44.
17. A. Etzioni, *Modern Organizations* (Englewood Cliffs, N.J.: Prentice-Hall, 1964).
18. R. Kanter, "Power Failure in Management Circuits," *Harvard Business Review*, July–August 1979, 31–54.
19. L. Mainiero, "Coping with Powerlessness: The Relationship of Gender and Job Dependency to Empowerment Strategy Usage," *Administrative Science Quarterly* 31 (1986): 633–653.
20. B. E. Ashforth, "The Experience of Powerlessness in Organizations," *Organizational Behavior and Human Decision Processes* 43 (1989): 207–242.
21. M. Korda, *Power: How to Get It, How to Use It* (New York: Random House, 1975).
22. B. T. Mayes and R. T. Allen, "Toward a Definition of Organizational Politics," *Academy of Management Review* 2 (1977): 672–678.
23. D. L. Madison, R. W. Allen, L. W. Porter, and B. T. Mayes, "Organizational Politics: An Exploration of Managers' Perceptions," *Human Relations* 33 (1980): 92–107.
24. J. Gandz and V. Murray, "The Experience of Workplace Politics," *Academy of Management Journal* 23 (1980): 237–251.
25. D. A. Ralston, "Employee Ingratiation: The Role of Management," *Academy of Management Review* 10 (1985): 477–487; D. R. Beeman and T. W. Sharkey, "The Use and Abuse of Corporate Politics," *Business Horizons*, (March–April 1987): 25–35.
26. C. O. Longnecker, H. P. Sims, and D. A. Gioia, "Behind the Mask: The Politics of Employee Appraisal," *Academy of Management Executive* 1 (1987): 183–193.
27. M. Maccoby, *The Gamesman* (New York: Simon & Schuster, 1976).
28. D. Kipnis, S. M. Schmidt, and I. Wilkinson, "Intraorganizational Influence Tactics: Explorations in Getting One's Way," *Journal of Applied Psychology* 65 (1980): 440–452; D. Kipnis, S. Schmidt, C. Swaffin-Smith, and I. Wilkinson, "Patterns of Managerial Influence: Shotgun Managers, Tacticians, and Bystanders," *Organizational Dynamics* (Winter 1984): 60–67; G. Yukl and C. M. Falbe, "Influence Tactics and Objectives in Upward, Downward, and Lateral Influence Attempts," *Journal of Applied Psychology* 2 (1990): 132–140.
29. G. R. Ferris and T. A. Judge, "Personnel/Human Resources Management: A Political Influence Perspective," *Journal of Management* 17 (1991): 447–488.
30. G. Yukl, P. J. Guinan, and D. Sottolano, "Influence Tactics Used for Different Objectives with Subordinates, Peers, and Superiors," *Groups & Organization Management* 20 (1995): 272–296.
31. R. A. Thacker and S. J. Wayne, "An Examination of the Relationship Between Upward Influence Tactics and Assessments of Promotability," *Journal of Management* 21 (1995): 739–756.
32. A. Drory and D. Beaty, "Gender Differences in the Perception of Organizational Influence Tactics," *Journal of Organizational Behavior* 12 (1991): 249–258.
33. R. Y. Hirokawa and A. Miyahara, "A Comparison of Influence Strategies Utilized by Managers in American and Japanese Organizations," *Communication Quarterly* 34 (1986): 250–265.
34. K. Kumar and M. S. Thibodeaux, "Organizational Politics and Planned Organizational Change," *Group and Organization Studies* 15 (1990): 354–365.

35. McClelland, *Power.*
36. Beeman and Sharkey, "Use and Abuse of Corporate Politics," 37.
37. C. P. Parker, R. L. Dipboye, and S. L. Jackson, "Perceptions of Organizational Politics: An Investigation of Antecedents and Consequences," *Journal of Management* 21 (1995): 891–912.
38. J. Zhou and G. R. Ferris, "The Dimensions and Consequences of Organizational Politics Perceptions: A Confirmatory Analysis," *Journal of Applied Social Psychology* 25 (1995): 1747–1764.
39. J. J. Gabarro and J. P. Kotter, "Managing Your Boss," *Harvard Business Review* (January–February 1980): 92–100.
40. P. Newman, "How to Manage Your Boss," Peat, Marwick, Mitchell & Company's *Management Focus* (May–June 1980): 36–37.
41. F. Bertolome, "When You Think the Boss Is Wrong," *Personnel Journal* 69 (1990): 66–73.
42. J. Conger and R. Kanungo, *Charismatic Leadership: The Elusive Factor in Organizational Effectiveness* (New York: Jossey-Bass, 1988).
43. T. Brown, "Fearful of Empowerment," *Industry Week* 239 (1990): 12.
44. R. C. Ford and M. D. Fottler, "Empowerment: A Matter of Degree," *Academy of Management Executive* 9 (1995): 21–31.
45. J. T. McKenna, "Smart Scarecrows: The Wizardry of Empowerment," *Industry Week,* 16 July 1990, 8–19.
46. B. Dumaine, "The Bureaucracy Busters," *Fortune,* 17 June 1991, 36–50.
47. J. P. Kotter, "Power, Dependence, and Effective Management," *Harvard Business Review* 55 (1977): 125–136; J. P. Kotter, *Power and Influence* (New York: Free Press, 1985).
48. J. L. Lederer and C. R. Weinberg, "Equity-Based Pay: The Compensation-Based Paradigm for the Re-Engineered Corporation," *Chief Executive* (April 1995): 36–39; S. Krajewski, "Southwest Gets Wired," *Adweek,* March 27 (1995): 2.

CHAPTER

12

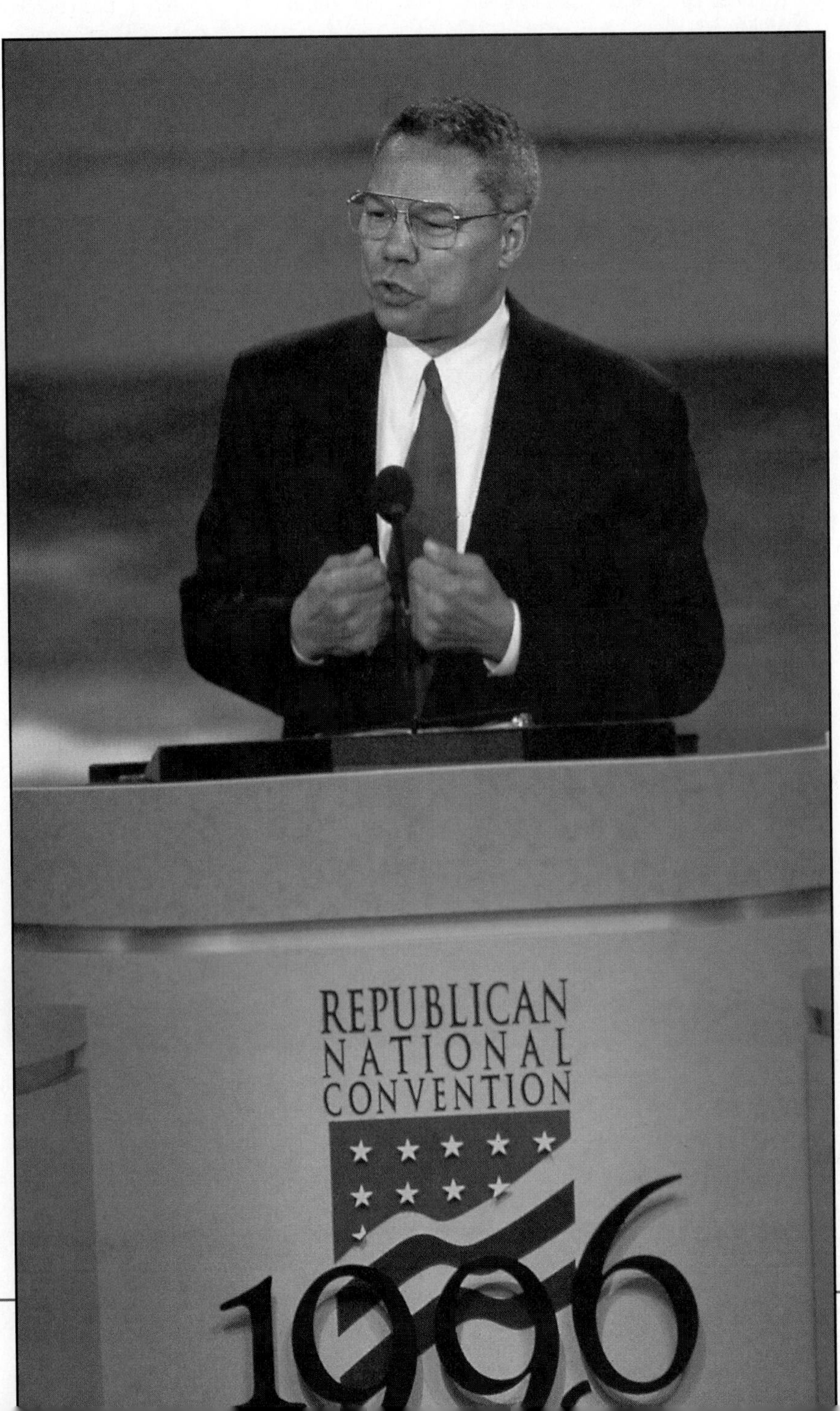

Leadership and Followership

LEARNING OBJECTIVES

After reading this chapter, you should be able to do the following:

- Define *leadership* and *followership.*
- Discuss the differences between leadership and management.
- Distinguish among transformational, transactional, and charismatic leaders.
- Compare autocratic, democratic, and laissez-faire leadership.
- Explain initiating structure and consideration, as well as P-oriented and M-oriented leader behaviors.
- Compare the five leadership styles in the managerial grid.
- Explain Fiedler's contingency theory of leadership.
- Distinguish among three Type IV leadership theories: the path-goal theory, the Vroom-Yetton-Jago theory, and the situational leadership model.
- Discuss the characteristics of effective and dynamic followers.

OPENING SPOTLIGHT

Leadership and Vision in Changing Times

http://www.motorola.com

In the early 1980s, Motorola was in a change process aimed at transforming itself into a healthier, more effective organization. Envisioning change is both exciting and confusing at the same time.[1] At the officers meeting in 1983, former Motorola chairman and CEO Bob Galvin gave a leadership speech to his top executives. His remarks captured several core ideas about leadership and followership. Galvin argued that a leader inherits freedom and, with that freedom, a commensurate amount of responsibility. He suggested that only time can prove the merit of leader's stewardship. If one is to lead, it implies that others are to follow. Leaders and followers are coactors in a larger organizational drama.

However, is the leader a breed apart or, rather, a better follower? For Galvin, the leader is an observer, a listener, a student, a mimic, and a product of experience. Galvin sees two paradoxes in leadership. First, to lead well presumes the ability to follow smartly. Second, the leader is a finite person with apparently infinite influence. Did Galvin have a clear vision for Motorola? ■

leadership
The process of guiding and directing the behavior of people in the work environment.

formal leadership
Officially sanctioned leadership based on the power and authority of a formal position.

informal leadership
Unofficial leadership accorded to a person by other members of the organization.

followership
The process of being guided and directed by a leader in the work environment.

Leadership in organizations is the process of guiding and directing the behavior of people in the work environment. The first section of the chapter distinguishes leadership from management. **Formal leadership** occurs when an organization officially bestows upon a leader the power and authority to guide and direct others in the organization. **Informal leadership** occurs when others in an organization unofficially accord a person the power and influence to guide and direct their behavior. Leadership is among the most researched topics in organizational behavior and one of the least understood social processes in organizations.

Sections two through five examine four types of leadership theories: Type I theories (universal trait theories), Type II theories (universal behavior theories), Type III theories (situational trait theories), and Type IV theories (situational behavior theories). The sixth section summarizes guidelines for leadership in organizations. The final section of the chapter focuses on the process of followership. **Followership** in organizations is the process of being guided and directed by a leader in the work environment. Leaders and followers are companions in these processes.

Leadership and Management

Points to Emphasize
Leadership is not necessarily tied to an organizational position. A leader can be a person who emerges from a team meeting with creative ideas. A leader may be one only for a moment.

■ John Kotter suggests that leadership and management are two distinct, yet complementary systems of action in organizations.[2] Specifically, he believes that effective leadership produces useful change in organizations (as exemplified by Lee Iacocca at Chrysler Corporation in the early 1980s) and that good management controls complexity in the organization and its environment (as exemplified by Jack Welch at General Electric). Healthy organizations need both effective leadership and good management.

For Kotter, the management process involves (1) planning and budgeting, (2) organizing and staffing, and (3) controlling and problem solving. The management process reduces uncertainty and stabilizes an organization. Alfred P.

Jack Welch (right), Chairman of General Electric, is a master manager who effectively deals with the complexity of GE's many businesses and the diversity of GE's many environments.

ORGANIZATIONAL REALITY

Privatization and Leadership in Siberia

Governmental organizations around the world are being challenged to change the way they are doing business and providing services. This has been especially true throughout Eastern Europe and Latin America as well as in the United States and Canada. Privatization is one way in which governments are changing how they do business, taking governmental services and moving them into the private sector of the nation's economy.

A new leadership team at Primorski Sugar Corporation in Siberia, Russia is one excellent example of successful privatization. The new leadership team at Primorski has transformed the sugar refinery into a diversified world-class company. Primorski, like many governmentally owned enterprises under the old Soviet Union's economic system, had a dismal and discouraging history of chronic problems. These problems included antiquated equipment, low levels of employee productivity, and little leadership.

The new director of Primorski was selected from outside the company, once it was privatized. He challenged the entrenched managers and employees to change and to create a true private enterprise, or to leave. Most left; not the new director. The new leadership team is continuing to transform the old Soviet plant and Primorski is becoming a diversified, world-class organization. ■

SOURCE: T. Broersma, "Creating the Future: How Organizations Are Meeting the Challenge," *Training & Development* 49 (1995): 40.

Sloan's integration and stabilization of General Motors after its early growth years is an example of good management.

In contrast, the leadership process involves (1) setting a direction for the organization; (2) aligning people with that direction through communication; and (3) motivating people to action, partly through empowerment and partly through basic need gratification. The leadership process creates uncertainty and change in an organization. Donald Peterson's championing of a quality revolution at Ford Motor Company is an example of effective leadership. Leadership may not necessarily be limited to one person; for example, General Electric Medical Systems Group (GEMS) uses the Global Leadership Program to train leaders for global operations, focusing on cross-cultural and language skills.[3] GEMS is just one of many companies focusing on leadership training for global operations. This training requires different skills from traditional leadership training and the privatization of government services requires still different skills. The accompanying Organizational Reality feature shows the importance of leadership in the changing environment of privatization.

This chapter emphasizes leadership, rather than management. It uses an organization scheme to classify leadership theories because there are so many of them.[4] Figure 12.1 presents this organizing scheme, which relies on two underlying dimensions. The first dimension divides the theories into those concerned with the leader's traits or personality versus those concerned with the leader's behavior. The second dimension divides the theories into those that may be universal for all leadership situations and those that are situationally specific. The situationally specific theories, often called contingency theories, began emerging after 1948.[5]

When both dimensions are considered, four types of leadership theories emerge, as illustrated in Figure 12.1. Type I theories are universal trait theories; Type II are universal behavioral theories; Type III are contingent trait theories; and Type IV are contingent behavioral theories. Each type of theory is discussed in a separate section of the chapter.

■ **FIGURE 12.1**

A Typology for Leadership Theories

SOURCE: A. G. Jago, "Leadership Perspectives in Theory and Research," *Management Science* 22 (1982): 316. Used with permission.

		Degree of generalizability	
		Universal	Contingent
Leader attribute	Traits	Type I	Type III
	Behaviors	Type II	Type IV

Discussion Consideration
What is the relationship between leadership and power? Is it possible to be a leader without power?

Discussion Consideration
Ask students to differentiate between managers and leaders by giving examples of well-known individuals in politics, science or other fields. For example, Steven Jobs, founder of Apple Computer, was considered an innovative leader, yet a meager manager.

George C. Marshall, World War II general and later secretary of state, comes to mind as a great leader whose traits enabled him to be successful in the military and as a statesman. In contrast, John DeLorean was a very successful automotive executive who rose to the top ranks of General Motors Corporation only to become a failure as an entrepreneur designing and building his own cars. These examples suggest that some individuals may be good leaders in different situations and some individuals may not. Hence, the situation and the leader may be important considerations in leadership.

All leadership theories in one way or another address the issue of how followers receive necessary guidance and good feelings from their leaders. They assume the leader is the primary source of guidance and good feelings. It is possible, however, that followers receive the necessary guidance and good feelings from alternative sources in the work environment.[6] Task substitutes for leadership include unambiguous, routine work. Organizational substitutes for task-oriented behavior include formal rules, regulations, and procedures. Organizational substitutes for relationship-oriented behavior include a closely knit, cohesive work group.

Type I Theories

Alternate Example
Most organizations are over managed and under led.

Alternate Example
Historians have proposed a "great man" theory of leadership that is based on the idea that those who lead successfully do so because they have sufficient charisma, intelligence, or some other trait or ability.

■ Type I theories of leadership were the first attempts at understanding leadership. These theories of leadership attempt to identify the traits and/or inherent attributes of leaders, regardless of the leaders' situation or circumstances, as well as the impact of these traits and/or styles on the followers. Early Type I theories focused on a leader's physical attributes, personality, and abilities. Recently, a renewed interest in Type I theories has focused attention on the distinctions between leaders and managers, as well as on charismatic leadership. The implications of Type I theories for organizations involve selection issues rather than training and development issues.

Physical Attributes, Personality, and Abilities

The first studies of leadership attempted to identify what physical attributes, personality characteristics, and abilities distinguished leaders from other members of a group.[7] The physical attributes considered have been height, weight, physique, energy, health, appearance, and even age. This line of research yielded some interesting findings. However, very few valid generalizations emerged from this line of inquiry. Therefore, there is insufficient evidence to conclude that leaders can be distinguished from followers on the basis of physical attributes.

Leader personality characteristics that have been examined include originality, adaptability, introversion-extroversion, dominance, self-confidence, integrity, conviction, mood optimism, and emotional control. There is some evidence that leaders may be more adaptable and self-confident than the average group member.

With regard to leader abilities, attention has been devoted to such constructs as social skills, intelligence, scholarship, speech fluency, cooperativeness, and insight. In this area, there is some evidence that leaders are more intelligent, verbal, and cooperative and have a higher level of scholarship than the average group member.

These conclusions suggest traits leaders possess, but the findings are neither strong nor uniform. For each attribute or trait claimed to distinguish leaders from followers, there were always at least one or two studies with contradictory findings. This suggests a limitation in being able to identify universal, distinguishing attributes of leaders.

Alternate Example
Another approach to leadership is called "Zeitgeist" or spirit of the times. This approach de-emphasizes the role of individual leaders in history, and focuses instead on the culmination of economic, cultural, and social forces.

Leaders and Managers

A more recent examination of personality attributes distinguishes leaders from managers. Specifically, Abraham Zaleznik argues that leaders and managers are fundamentally different types of personalities.[8] Both make a valuable contribution to an organization, and each one's contribution is different. Whereas **leaders** agitate for change and new approaches, **managers** advocate stability and the status quo. There is a dynamic tension between leaders and managers that makes it difficult for each to understand the other. Leaders and managers differ along four separate dimensions of personality: attitudes toward goals, conceptions of work, relationships with other people, and sense of self. The differences between these two personality types are summarized in Table 12.1.

Zaleznik's distinction between leaders and managers is similar to the distinction made between transactional and transformational leaders, or between leadership and supervision.[9] Transactional leaders use formal rewards and punishments to

leader
An advocate for change and new approaches to problems.

manager
An advocate for stability and the status quo.

Points to Emphasize
Although there is little empirical support for trait approaches to leadership, most have little difficulty identifying the characteristics of effective leaders we have known. Thus, certain traits may be part of our implicit theories of leadership.

■ **TABLE 12.1**

Leaders and Managers

PERSONALITY DIMENSION	MANAGER	LEADER
Attitudes toward goals	Has an impersonal, passive, functional attitude; believes goals arise out of necessity and reality	Has a personal and active attitude; believes goals arise from desire and imagination
Conceptions of work	Views work as an enabling process that combines people, ideas, and things; seeks moderate risk through coordination and balance	Looks for fresh approaches to old problems; seeks high-risk positions, especially with high payoffs
Relationships with others	Avoids solitary work activity, preferring to work with others; avoids close, intense relationships; avoids conflict	Is comfortable in solitary work activity; encourages close, intense working relationships; is not conflict averse
Sense of self	Is once born; makes a straightforward life adjustment; accepts life as it is	Is twice born; engages in a struggle for a sense of order in life; questions life

SOURCE: A. Zaleznik, "Managers and Leaders: Are They Different?" *Harvard Business Review* 55 (1977): 67–77.

Discussion Consideration
Can an individual be both a manager and a leader?

http://www.wal-mart.com/

Discussion Consideration
Ask students which is more important to an effective organization: Management or Leadership?

manage followers; they formally or informally engage in deal making and contractual obligations. Transformational leaders inspire and excite followers to high levels of performance. These leaders rely on their personal attributes instead of their official position to manage followers. For example, the late Sam Walton may be considered the transformational leader and the visionary heart of Wal-Mart. Certainly he changed the way the United States did business in retailing. However, as in the case of Wal-Mart, it becomes an organizational challenge to figure out a way to institutionalize a transformational leader's style and vision.[10] The accompanying Scientific Foundation feature discusses an award-winning theoretical article aimed at a cognitive interpretation of transactional and transformational leadership theories.

There is some evidence that leaders may learn transformational leadership and benefit from its power to inspire followers to perform beyond expectations.[11] As a young student at Texas A&M University, for example, Henry Cisneros began developing the leadership skills that would later enable him to inspire his diverse followers as mayor of San Antonio; cochair of the National Hispanic Leadership Agenda; and most recently, President Bill Clinton's secretary of housing and urban development.[12] Cisneros believes that studying the history and biographies of great leaders can enable a person to develop transformational leadership skills. As U.S. corporations increasingly operate in a global economy, there is a greater demand for leaders who can practice transformational leadership by converting their visions into reality.[13]

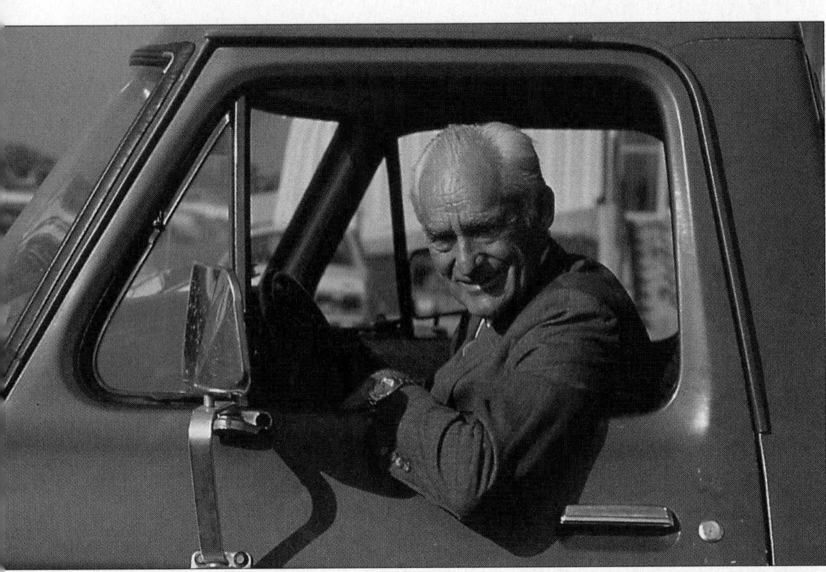

The late Sam Walton was a transformational leader who revolutionized retail sales through Wal-Mart. Wal-Mart's challenge has been to institutionalize the style of leadership which Sam Walton provided.

If the distinction between leaders and managers is accepted, an organizational dilemma results. Specifically, bureaucratic organizations foster the development of managers to the exclusion of leaders, leaving a leadership gap in organizations and society.[14] Because leaders challenge established ways of working, they are a source of uncertainty, anxiety, and discomfort to the organization, and they challenge its stability. Leaders want to change the established order to improve the system. While at General Motors, John DeLorean never fully accepted the GM way of doing things; he was a leader who agitated for improvements in the system. DeLorean was less concerned with appearances, which were important at GM, than he was with substance in automotive manufacturing. However, too much agitation led to his early departure from General Motors. The dilemma for an organization is how to draw on the strengths and contributions of each type of personality without alienating either type.

http://www.gm.com/

Women Leaders

Alternate Example:
The creation of settings that promote discussion, encourage opinions, and distribute power is associated with a "feminine" style of leadership. SOURCE: "In Praise of Followership," Psychology Today, September 1992, 10.

If leaders and managers are different, do women and men lead differently? Historical stereotypes persist and people characterize successful managers with more male-oriented attributes than female-oriented attributes.[15] Although legitimate gender differences may exist, the same leadership traits may be interpreted differently in a man and a woman because of stereotypes. The real issue should be leader behaviors that are not bound by gender stereotypes.[16]

Women who describe their leadership style in transformational terms may be very successful in traditional or nontraditional organizations.[17] Women leaders are more likely than men to include and energize people, helping them feel important. Women leaders have learned out of necessity to lead without formal

SCIENTIFIC FOUNDATION

A Cognitive Interpretation of Leadership

Good science is founded on good theory and original data. Recognized with an award from the Center for Creative Leadership, this article adds an important new framework for theorizing about transformational and transactional leadership behaviors. The authors have 18 testable propositions about six mediators in the relationships between feedback, environmental inputs, and leadership behaviors. The crux of the article is the theory that because transformational and transactional leaders think differently, they act and behave differently.

Transformational and transactional leaders think differently about themselves and their followers. Transformational leaders' thoughts emphasize charismatic behavior, individualized consideration, intellectual stimulation, and empowerment; transactional leaders' thoughts emphasize directiveness, social exchange, work assignment, and contingent rewards. Transformational leaders' thoughts about followers emphasize loyalty, self-respect, self-confidence, trust, overall purpose, uniqueness, intellectual capability, and creativity; transactional leaders' thoughts about followers emphasize goal difficulty and commitment, specific task skills and knowledge, work assignment, and effort-performance-reward relationships.

Finally, there are three other cognitive differences between these two types of leaders. Transformational leaders are more abstract, manage diverse and complex inputs better, and emphasize vision over goals. Transactional leaders are less abstract, less able to manage diverse and complex inputs, and emphasize goals over vision.

SOURCE: J. C. Wofford and V. L. Goodwin, "A Cognitive Interpretation of Transactional and Transformational Leadership Theories," *Leadership Quarterly* 5 (1994): 161–186.

McBride, Zapata, and Zinkowski (left to right) are three women leaders of FTI (Flight Time International), a Boston-based service that tracks and hires available charter transits. FTI specializes in filling large planes (eg, DC-10s), yet handles corporate jets and small propeller aircraft too.

authority, so they do not covet formal authority. Because women have traditionally been excluded from very top level leadership in corporations, they often go out and build their own organizations. Anita Roddick did exactly that when she built The Body Shop, a large international organization.

Charismatic Leadership

Anita Roddick is a charismatic leader who created a vision and sold it to customers and followers alike, motivating her followers to fulfill the vision. **Charismatic**

charismatic leadership
The use, by a leader, of personal abilities and talents in order to have profound and extraordinary effects on followers.

leadership results when a leader uses the force of personal abilities and talents to have profound and extraordinary effects on followers.[18] Some scholars see transformational leadership and charismatic leadership as very similar, but others believe they are different. *Charisma* is a Greek word meaning "gift"; the charismatic leader's unique and powerful gifts are the source of their great influence with followers.[19] In fact, followers often view the charismatic leader as one who possesses superhuman, or even mystical, qualities.[20] Charismatic leaders rely heavily on referent power, discussed in Chapter 11. Followers often accept unconditionally the mission and directions of the leader, suspending their own discriminatory judgment. Hence, charismatic leadership carries with it not only great potential for high levels of achievement and performance on the part of followers but also shadowy risks of destructive courses of action that might harm followers or other people.

Franklin Delano Roosevelt (1882-1945) was the 32nd President of the United States and a towering world leader during the dark days of World War II. His leadership transformed the United States and the free world.

Charismatic leadership falls to those who are chosen (are born with the "gift" of charisma) or who cultivate that gift. Some say charismatic leaders are born, and others say they are taught.

Recent efforts have attempted to demystify charismatic leadership and distinguish its two faces.[21] The ugly face of charisma is revealed in the personalized power motivations of Adolf Hitler in Nazi Germany and David Koresh of the Branch Davidian cult in Waco, Texas. Both men led their followers into struggle, conflict, and death. The brighter face of charisma is revealed in the socialized power motivations of U.S. President Franklin D. Roosevelt and of Cable News Network (CNN) entrepreneur Ted Turner, who has built a large business empire. Peter Drucker has thoughtfully described President Roosevelt and other leaders' styles from firsthand experience. Whereas charismatic leaders with socialized power motivation are concerned about the collective well-being of their followers, charismatic leaders with a personalized power motivation are driven by the need for personal gain and glorification. The former are constructive forces for organizational improvement, whereas the latter may be narcissistic leaders who abuse their power by manipulating and taking advantage of their followers.[22]

Discussion Consideration
Ask students to use the two faces of power introduced in chapter 11 to evaluate the following charismatic leaders: Martin Luther King, Jr., David Koresh, Franklin D. Roosevelt, Adolph Hitler.

Charismatic leadership, like other Type I theories, does not address attributes of the situation that may create contingencies for the exercise of leadership. Whereas the early Type I theories focused on a leader's physical attributes, personality, and abilities, subsequent Type I theories examined leaders from psychodynamic and power motivation perspectives. All Type I theories are concerned with inherent attributes of leaders. Type II theories of leadership shift the focus from traits and attributes to actions and behaviors.

Type II Theories

■ Type II theories of leadership are concerned with describing leaders' actions and behaviors, often from the perspective of the followers. Like Type I theories, Type II theories exclusively emphasize the leader, as opposed to situational characteristics. Although Type II theories depend in some cases on the descriptions by followers of their leaders, these theories do not consider characteristics of the followers themselves or of the leadership situation in understanding the leadership process. The first Type II theory classified leaders according to one of three basic leadership styles, whereas subsequent Type II theories examined common behavioral dimensions of all leaders. Type II theories help organizations train and develop leaders rather than select them.

Leadership Style and Emotional Climate at Work

The earliest research on leadership style, conducted by Kurt Lewin and his students, identified three basic styles: autocratic, democratic, and laissez-faire.[23] Each leader uses one of these three basic styles when approaching a group of followers in a leadership situation. The specific situation is not an important consideration, because the leader's style does not vary with the situation. Rather, the leader's style is a universal trait taken into all situations. The **autocratic style** is directive, strong, and controlling in relationships. Leaders with an autocratic style use rules and regulations to run the work environment. Followers have little discretionary influence over the nature of the work, its accomplishment, or other aspects of the work environment. The leader with a **democratic style** is collaborative, responsive, and interactive in relationships and emphasizes rules and regulations less than the autocratic leader. Followers have a high degree of discretionary influence, although the leader has ultimate authority and responsibility. The leader with a **laissez-faire style** leads through nonleadership. A laissez-faire leader abdicates the authority and responsibility of the position.

autocratic style

A style of leadership in which the leader uses strong, directive, controlling actions to enforce the rules, regulations, activities, and relationships in the work environment.

democratic style

A style of leadership in which the leader takes collaborative, reciprocal, interactive actions with followers concerning the work and work environment.

laissez-faire style

A style of leadership in which the leader fails to accept the responsibilities of the position.

Subsequent leadership research has used somewhat different terminology for the same leadership styles: an autocratic style has been labeled boss-centered, job-centered, authoritarian, and even dictatorial.[24] All these labels refer to the same basic traits of autocratic leadership. Likewise, a democratic style has been labeled subordinate-centered, employee-centered, and participative. All these labels refer to the same basic traits of democratic leadership. The laissez-faire style of leadership has not had a comparable alternative set of labels. It is uniformly referred to as laissez-faire leadership.

This approach to the study of leadership, developed at the University of Michigan, suggests that the leader's style has very important implications for the emotional atmosphere of the work environment and, therefore, for the followers who work under each style of leader. Comparing the work environments under autocratic and democratic leadership is easier than attempting to compare either with the work environment under laissez-faire leadership. The most pronounced consequence of laissez-faire leadership tends to be chaos in the work environment, although there are exceptions.

An autocratic leadership style leads to a work environment characterized by constant influence attempts on the part of the leader, either through direct, close supervision or through the use of many written and unwritten rules and regulations for behavior. The resulting restrictive work environment can create high levels of tension for followers. High tension may affect followers in one of two ways in the work environment. Either the followers strongly inhibit their tension and suppress any conflict at work (which leads to a superficially calm atmosphere), or they express their tension (which results in periodic outbursts of intense conflict and aggression). The pathway the followers choose is in part determined by the strength of the leader. In either case, the autocratic style leads to a restriction of the physical and psychological discretion that followers feel. Finally, leader-follower relationships are often rigid in authoritarian environments. When not taken to an extreme, autocratic leadership can provide structure in the work environment and direction for followers who need clear, explicit guidelines for action.

In comparison with an autocratic leadership style, a democratic leadership style leads to a work environment characterized by fewer influence attempts by

Discussion Consideration
Because laissez faire leadership is the most ambiguous of the three types, have students elaborate on its values.

Discussion Consideration
Are there situations when autocratic or laissez faire leadership would be appropriate?

the leader. The leader exhibits less direct or less close supervision and establishes fewer written or unwritten rules and regulations for behavior. This pattern of influence leads to lower levels of tension among followers. Nonetheless, tension may still exist and be manifested in expressed conflict, usually over ideas and issues. The conflict tends not to be personalized. Followers in a democratic work environment are less inhibited and experience a much greater sense of physical and psychological freedom than are followers in an autocratic work environment. Finally, there is flexibility and spontaneity in the relationships between the leader and followers in the democratic work environment. For those who need more structure, however, a democratic work environment may elicit uncertainty and anxiety.

Leadership Behaviors

Points to Emphasize
Although similar, the Ohio State and Michigan studies differ in the range in which they predict behavior. The Ohio studies see the dimensions of leadership as coexisting; the Michigan studies seem them as mutually exclusive.

initiating structure
Leader behavior aimed at defining and organizing work relationships and roles, as well as establishing clear patterns of organization, communication, and ways of getting things done.

consideration
Leader behavior aimed at nurturing friendly, warm working relationships, as well as encouraging mutual trust and interpersonal respect within the work unit.

The leadership research program at Ohio State University measured several specific leader behaviors as an alternative to a generalized leader style, such as autocratic, as was done at Michigan. The initial Ohio State research studied aircrews and pilots.[25] The aircrew members, as followers, were asked a wide range of questions about their lead pilots using the Leader Behavior Description Questionnaire (LBDQ). The results using the LBDQ suggested that there were two important underlying dimensions of leader behaviors.[26] These were labeled initiating structure and consideration.

Initiating structure is leader behavior aimed at defining and organizing work relationships and roles, as well as establishing clear patterns of organization, communication, and ways of getting things done. **Consideration** is leader behavior aimed at nurturing friendly, warm working relationships, as well as encouraging mutual trust and interpersonal respect within the work unit. These two leader behaviors are independent of each other. That is, a leader may be high on both, low on both, or high on one while low on the other. The Ohio State studies were intended to describe leader behavior, not to evaluate or judge behavior.

The Ohio State approach to the study of leadership suggested that leader behavior was open to change and modification, because it was not an enduring trait or attribute. In a study at International Harvester Company, Edwin Fleishman found that consideration behaviors could be improved through a training program for the company's supervisors.[27] Although the training resulted in changes in both initiating structure and consideration, the changes in either attitude or behavior were not permanent. When back in the work environment, the supervisors tended toward increased initiating structure behavior and less consideration. The conclusion was that the leadership climate at the company was a more important determinant of leader behaviors than was the training. Therefore, upper management's influence on the behaviors of middle managers and supervisors is important. This logic has recently led some corporations (for example, General Electric) to establish desired leader behaviors directly at the top of the organization.[28]

Leadership Styles in Japan

P-oriented behavior
Leader behavior that encourages a fast work pace, emphasizes good quality and high accuracy, works toward high-quantity production, and demonstrates concern for rules and regulations.

M-oriented behavior
Leader behavior that is sensitive to employees' feelings, emphasizes comfort in the work environment, works to reduce stress levels, and demonstrates appreciation for follower contributions.

Shortly after World War II, a program of research was begun in Japan to examine whether U.S. leadership approaches could be generalized in Japanese organizations. This led to a 30-year program of research that was labeled the Performance-Maintenance (PM) theory of leadership; **P-oriented behavior** and **M-oriented behavior** are characterized in Table 12.2. Although not exactly the same, initiating structure and P-oriented leader behavior are similar; consideration and M-oriented leader behavior are also similar. According to the

■ **TABLE 12.2**

Characteristics of P-Oriented and M-Oriented Leadership

P-ORIENTED LEADERSHIP
Encourages fast work pace Emphasizes good quality and high accuracy Works toward high-quantity production Demonstrates concern for rules and regulations
M-ORIENTED LEADERSHIP
Is sensitive to employees' feelings Emphasizes comfort in the work environment Works to reduce stress levels Demonstrates appreciation for follower contributions

SOURCE: Reprinted from "The Performance-Maintenance (PM) Theory of Leadership: Review of a Japanese Research Program by J. Misumi and M. F. Peterson published in *Administrative Science Quarterly* 30 (1985): 207 by permission of Administrative Science Quarterly © 1985.

Japanese researchers, autocratic leaders are those who emphasize P-oriented behavior to the exclusion of M-oriented behavior, whereas democratic leaders are those who emphasize M-oriented behavior, though not necessarily to the exclusion of P-oriented behavior. Laissez-faire leaders are those who do not exhibit either P-oriented or M-oriented behaviors.

The Japanese researchers studied leadership styles in private enterprises, local government, the postal service, secondary school classrooms, family systems, and sports groups. Their findings suggest that the leadership styles of lower- and middle-level managers affect employee performance in Japan more than in the United States. In addition, the researchers concluded that autocratic leadership may be less successful in Japanese companies than in some U.S. companies.

What distinguishes the Japanese application of Kurt Lewin's original theory is the use of two independent aspects of a leader's behavior as the basis for classifying the leader into an autocratic, democratic, or laissez-faire style. The measurement of two or more dimensions of a leader's behavior is very similar to the Ohio State leader behavior studies begun during the 1950s. Before we turn to a discussion of these studies, take a few minutes to complete Challenge 12.1. This exercise gives you an opportunity to examine your supervisor's or professor's P-oriented and M-oriented behaviors.

The Managerial Grid

The Ohio State leadership studies and the subsequent Japanese leadership approaches were behavioral formulations. An attitudinal formulation called the **Managerial Grid** was developed by Robert Blake and Jane Mouton.[29] The two underlying dimensions of the grid are labeled Concern for Production and Concern for People. These two attitudinal dimensions are coupled through an interaction process. The five distinct managerial styles shown in Figure 12.2 parallel five orientations to interpersonal relationships of fight (9,1), flight (1,1), depending (1,9), pairing (5,5), and work (9,9) observed in previous clinical practice by Bion.

The **organization man manager (5,5)** works for adequate organizational performance by balancing getting work done and maintaining morale. This manager goes along to get along, conforming to and maintaining the status quo. The **authority-obedience manager (9,1)** emphasizes production and works to achieve high levels of efficiency in operations by minimizing any interference from the human element. Production maximization is the hallmark of this manager. The **country club manager (1,9)** gives thoughtful attention to the needs

Managerial Grid
An approach to understanding a manager's concern for production and concern for people.

organization man manager (5,5)
A manager who maintains the status quo.

authority-obedience manager (9,1)
A manager who emphasizes efficient production.

country club manager (1,9)
A manager who creates a happy, comfortable work environment.

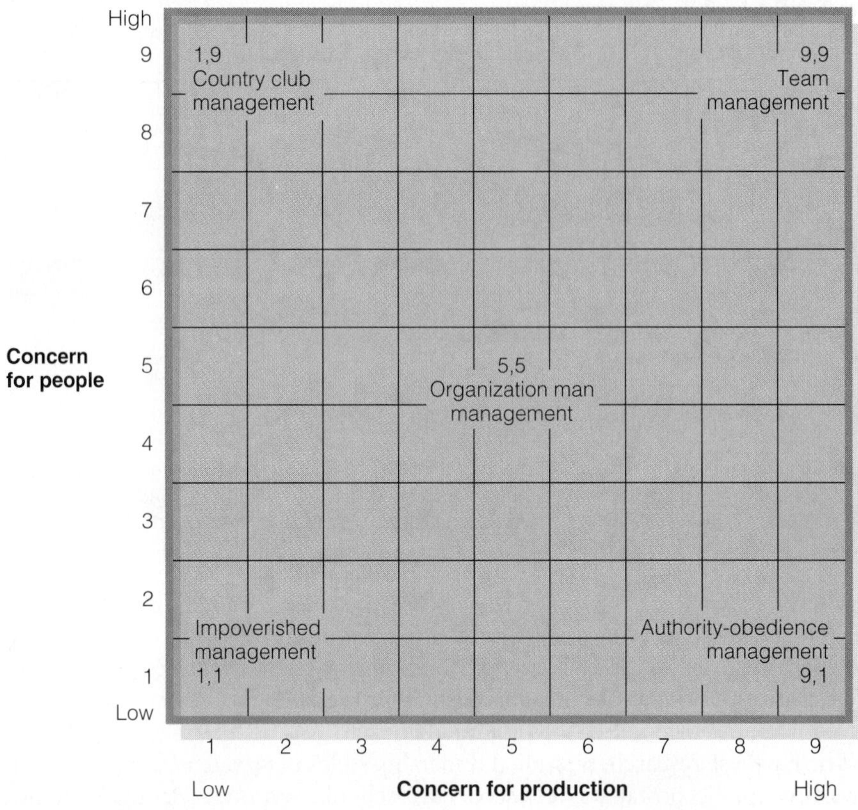

■ **FIGURE 12.2**

The Managerial Grid

SOURCE: The Leadership Grid® figure from *Leadership Dilemmas—Grid Solutions,* by Robert R. Blake and Anne Adams McCanse. Houston: Gulf Publishing Company, p. 29. Copyright © 1991, by Scientific Methods, Inc. Reproduced by permission of the owners.

of people and their relationships so as to create a comfortable working environment. Good feelings are the hallmark of this manager. The **team manager (9,9)** emphasizes high levels of work accomplishment through committed, trustworthy people; there is no trade-off between people and production. Finally, the **impoverished manager (1,1)** exerts the minimum effort to get essential work done while maintaining organizational membership. This style of management is similar to the laissez-faire style and is a form of abdication of responsibility.

team manager (9,9)

A manager who builds a highly productive team of committed people.

impoverished manager (1,1)

A manager who exerts just enough effort to avoid being fired.

Points to Emphasize

Blake and Mouton would have the 9,9 orientation, where individual have a high concern for both production and people, as the optimal one.

The Managerial Grid is distinguished from the original Ohio State research in two important ways. First, it has attitudinal overtones that are not present in the original research. Whereas the LBDQ aims to describe behavior, the grid addresses both the behavior and the attitude of the leader. Second, the Ohio State approach is fundamentally descriptive and nonevaluative, whereas the grid is normative and prescriptive. Specifically, the grid evaluates the team manager (9,9) as the very best style of managerial behavior. This is the basis on which the grid has been used for team building and leadership training in organizational development, which are discussed in Chapter 18. As an organizational development method, the grid aims to transform the leadership structure of the organization and the manner in which teams throughout the organization are led and managed.

Type III Theories

■ Type III theories of leadership are concerned with identifying the situationally specific conditions in which leaders with particular traits are effective. Type III theories classify leaders according to particular traits or attributes, as do Type I theories. However, Type III theories are contingency theories, as opposed to universal theories. They have a dual focus: the leader and the situation in which

CHALLENGE

■ **12.1**

How Does Your Supervisor Lead?

Answer the following sixteen questions concerning your supervisor's (or professor's) leadership behaviors on the 7-point Likert scale. Then complete the summary to examine your supervisor's behaviors.

	Not At All						Very Much
1. Is your superior strict about observing regulations?	1	2	3	4	5	6	7
2. To what extent does your superior give you instructions and orders?	1	2	3	4	5	6	7
3. Is your superior strict about the amount of work you do?	1	2	3	4	5	6	7
4. Does your superior urge you to complete your work by the time he or she has specified?	1	2	3	4	5	6	7
5. Does your superior try to make you work to your maximum capacity?	1	2	3	4	5	6	7
6. When you do an inadequate job, does your superior focus on the inadequate way the job was done instead of on your personality?	1	2	3	4	5	6	7
7. Does your superior ask you for reports about the progress of your work?	1	2	3	4	5	6	7
8. Does your superior work out precise plans for goal achievement each month?	1	2	3	4	5	6	7
9. Can you talk freely with your superior about your work?	1	2	3	4	5	6	7
10. Generally, does your superior support you?	1	2	3	4	5	6	7
11. Is your superior concerned about your personal problems?	1	2	3	4	5	6	7
12. Do you think your superior trusts you?	1	2	3	4	5	6	7
13. Does your superior give you recognition when you do your job well?	1	2	3	4	5	6	7
14. When a problem arises in your workplace, does your superior ask your opinion about how to solve it?	1	2	3	4	5	6	7
15. Is your superior concerned about your future benefits like promotions and pay raises?	1	2	3	4	5	6	7
16. Does your superior treat you fairly?	1	2	3	4	5	6	7

Add up your answers to Questions 1 through 8. This total indicates your supervisor's performance orientation:

P-orientation = ________

Add up your answers to Questions 9 through 16. This total indicates your supervisor's maintenance orientation:

M-orientation = ________

A score above 40 is high, and a score below 20 is low.

SOURCE: J. Misumi and M. F. Peterson, "The Performance-Maintenance (PM) Theory of Leadership," *Administrative Science Quarterly* 30 (1985): 207.

the leader works. The central concern of Type III theories is how the leader's traits interact with situational factors in determining team effectiveness in task performance. Fiedler's contingency theory is the one Type III leadership theory developed to date. Its implications for organizations concern how to select the right leader for the situation.

Fiedler's Contingency Theory

Points to Emphasize
Students often misunderstand the LPC score. It does not mean that the employee is not productive. It simply means that if the rater had his or her choice, they would not want to work with the least preferred coworker.

Fiedler's contingency theory of leadership proposes that the fit between the leader's need structure and the favorableness of the leader's situation determine the team's effectiveness in work accomplishment. This theory assumes that leaders are task-oriented or relationship-oriented, depending upon how the leaders obtain their primary need gratification.[30] Task-oriented leaders are primarily gratified by accomplishing tasks and getting work done. Relationship-oriented leaders are primarily gratified by developing good, comfortable interpersonal relationships. Accordingly, the effectiveness of both types of leaders depends on the favorableness of their situation. The theory classifies the favorableness of the leader's situation according to the leader's position power, the structure of the team's task, and the quality of the leader-follower relationships.

least preferred coworker (LPC)
The person a leader has least preferred to work with over his or her career.

THE LEAST PREFERRED COWORKER Fiedler classifies leaders using the Least Preferred Coworker (LPC) Scale.[31] The LPC Scale is a projective technique through which a leader is asked to think about the person with whom he or she can work least well (the **least preferred coworker,** or **LPC**). This is not necessarily the person the leader likes least; rather, it is the person with whom the leader had the most difficulty getting the job done.

The leader is asked to describe this least preferred coworker using sixteen eight-point bipolar adjective sets. Three of these bipolar adjective sets follow (the leader marks the blank most descriptive of the least preferred coworker):

Pleasant : : : : : : : : : Unpleasant
Efficient : : : : : : : : : Inefficient
Gloomy : : : : : : : : : Cheerful

Points to Emphasize
The LPC score has been widely criticized. Many question if it is really measuring a leadership style. Some students who have completed the LPC scale have suggested that it measures their mood more than anything else.

Leaders who describe their least preferred coworker in positive terms (that is, pleasant, efficient, cheerful, and so on) are classified as high LPC, or relationship-oriented, leaders. Those who describe their least preferred coworkers in negative terms (that is, unpleasant, inefficient, gloomy, and so on) are classified as low LPC, or task-oriented, leaders.

The LPC score is a controversial element in contingency theory. It has been critiqued conceptually and methodologically, because it is a projective technique with lower measurement reliability, along with situational favorableness.[32]

task structure
The degree of clarity, or ambiguity, in the work activitie assigned to the group.

position power
The authority associated with the leader's formal position in the organization.

leader-member relations
The quality of interpersonal relationships among a leader and the group members.

SITUATIONAL FAVORABLENESS The leader's situation has three dimensions: task structure, position power, and leader-member relations. Based on these three dimensions, the situation is either favorable or unfavorable for the leader. **Task structure** refers to the number and clarity of rules, regulations, and procedures for getting the work done. **Position power** refers to the leader's legitimate authority to evaluate and reward performance, punish errors, and demote group members.

The quality of **leader-member relations** is measured by the Group-Atmosphere Scale, composed of nine eight-point bipolar adjective sets. Three of these bipolar adjective sets follow:

Friendly : : : : : : : : : Unfriendly
Accepting : : : : : : : : : Rejecting
Warm : : : : : : : : : Cold

A favorable leadership situation is one with a structured task for the work group, strong position power for the leader, and good leader-member relations. In contrast, an unfavorable leadership situation is one with an unstructured task, weak position power for the leader, and moderately poor leader-member relations. Between these two extremes, the leadership situation has varying degrees of moderate favorableness for the leader.

Leadership Effectiveness

The contingency theory suggests that low and high LPC leaders are each effective if placed in the right situation.[33] Specifically, low LPC (task-oriented) leaders are most effective in either very favorable or very unfavorable leadership situations. In contrast, high LPC (relationship-oriented) leaders are most effective in situations of intermediate favorableness. Figure 12.3 shows the nature of these relationships and suggests that leadership effectiveness is determined by the degree of fit between the leader and the situation.

What, then, is to be done if there is a misfit? That is, what happens when a low LPC leader is in a moderately favorable situation or when a high LPC leader is in a highly favorable or highly unfavorable situation? It is unlikely that the leader can be changed, according to the theory, because the leader's need structure is an enduring trait requiring intense psychological intervention to alter. This leaves the situation as the preferred point of intervention. Specifically, Fiedler recommends that the leader's situation be reengineered to fit the leader's basic predisposition.[34] Hence, a moderately favorable situation would be reengineered to be more favorable and therefore more suitable for the low LPC leader. The highly favorable or highly unfavorable situation would be changed to one that is moderately favorable, and therefore more suitable for the high LPC leader.

Discussion Consideration
For Fiedler, a leader's style is fixed or stable. Do you agree?

Fiedler's contingency theory is a Type III theory because he considers the leaders' inherent traits, not their behaviors, in considering a fit with the leadership situation. His theory makes an important contribution in drawing our attention to the leader's situation.

■ **FIGURE 12.3**

Leadership Effectiveness in the Contingency Theory

SOURCE: F. E. Fiedler, *A Theory of Leader Effectiveness* (New York: McGraw-Hill, 1964). Reprinted with permission of the author.

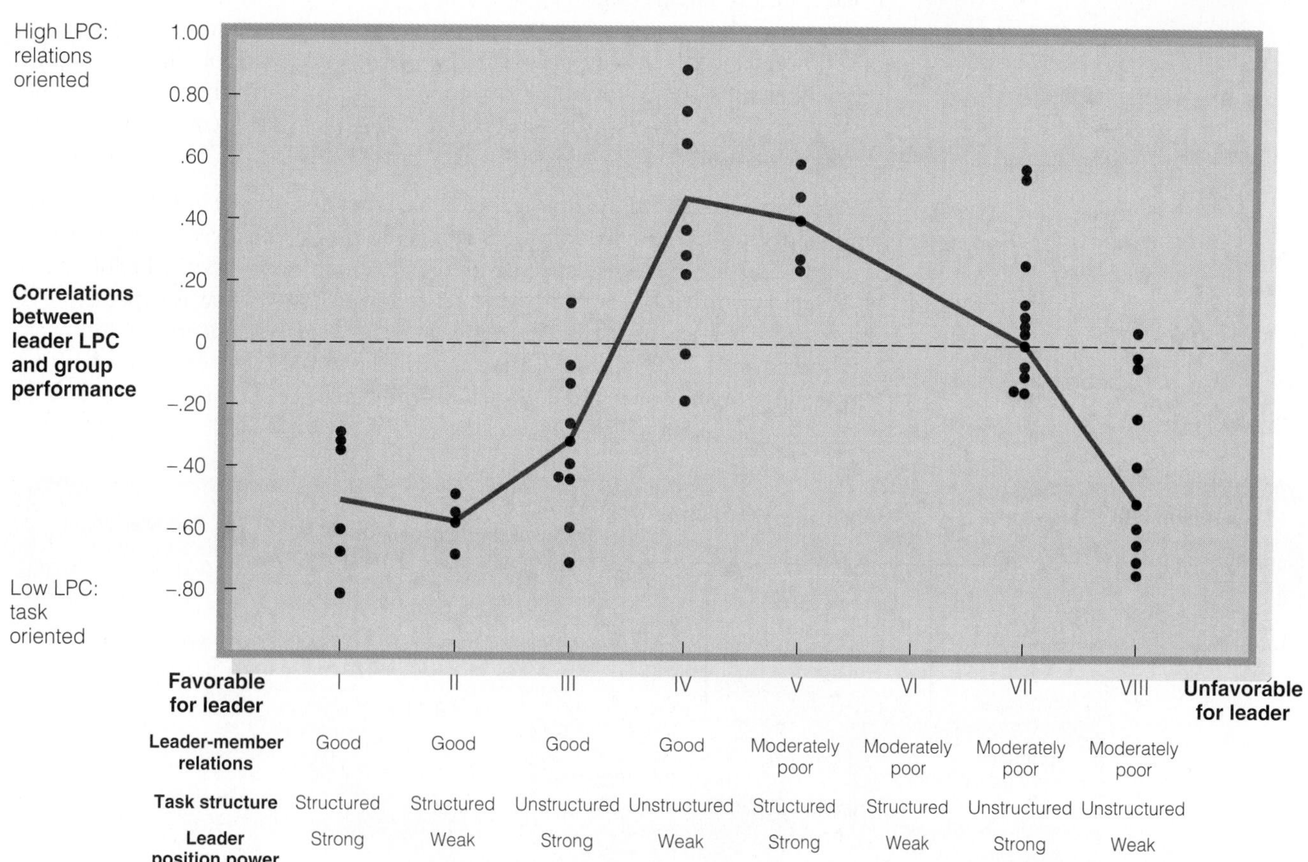

Type IV Theories

■ Type IV theories of leadership are concerned with identifying the specific leader behaviors that are most effective in specific leadership situations. A number of leader behaviors are considered important by different Type IV theories. Like Type III theories, Type IV theories are considered contingency theories, as opposed to universal theories. The central concern in the Type IV theories is the behavioral contingencies of the leader that yield the most effective performance by the followers. This section considers three specific Type IV theories. They are Robert House's path-goal theory, the Vroom-Yetton-Jago normative decision theory, and the situational leadership model developed by Paul Hersey and Kenneth Blanchard. As with Type II theories, the implications for organizations of Type IV theories concern how to train and develop leaders rather than how to select them.

The Path-Goal Theory

Robert House advocates a path-goal theory of leader effectiveness based on an expectancy theory of motivation.[35] From the perspective of path-goal theory, the basic role of the leader is to enhance follower motivation so that the followers are able to experience need gratification. The leader uses the most appropriate of four leader behavior styles to help followers clarify the paths that lead them to work and personal goals. The key concepts in the theory are shown in Figure 12.4.

The path-goal theory is based on the following two propositions:

- *Proposition 1.* Leader behavior is acceptable and satisfying to followers to the extent that they see it as an immediate source of satisfaction or as instrumental to future satisfaction.
- *Proposition 2.* Leader behavior is motivational to the extent that (1) it makes followers' need satisfaction contingent on effective performance and (2) it complements the followers' environment by providing the coaching, guidance, support, and rewards necessary for effective performance—rewards not otherwise available.

A leader selects from the four leader behavior styles, shown in Figure 12.4, the one that is most helpful to followers at a given time. The directive style is used when the leader must give specific guidance about work tasks, schedule work, maintain performance standards, and let followers know what is expected. The supportive style is used when the leader needs to express concern for followers' well-being and social status. The participative style is used when the leader must engage in problem solving and mutual decision-making activities with followers.

■ **FIGURE 12.4**

The Path-Goal Theory of Leadership

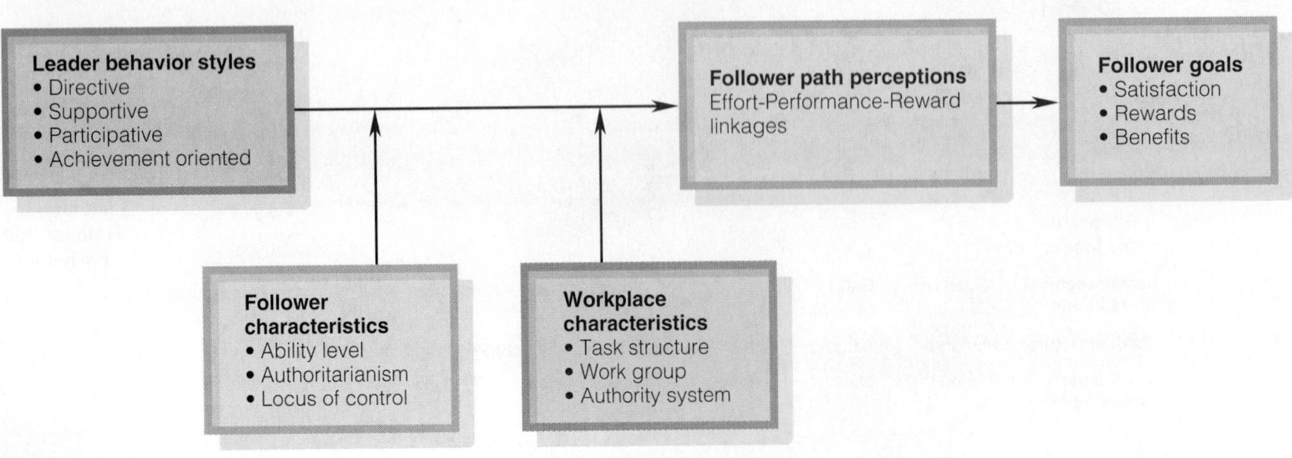

The achievement-oriented style is used when the leader must set challenging goals for followers, expect very high levels of performance, and show strong confidence in the followers.

In selecting the appropriate leader behavior style, the leader must consider characteristics of the followers and the work environment. A few characteristics are included in Figure 12.4. Let us look at four examples. In Example 1, the followers are inexperienced and working on an ambiguous, unstructured task. The leader in this situation might best use a directive style. In Example 2, the task is structured, and the followers are experienced and able. Here the leader might better use a supportive style. In Example 3, the followers are experienced and able, yet the task is confusing and unstructured. The leader in this situation may be most helpful in using a participative style. In Example 4, the followers are highly trained professionals, and the task is a difficult, yet achievable one. The leader in this situation might best use an achievement-oriented style. The leader always chooses the leader behavior style that helps followers achieve their goals.

The path-goal theory assumes that leaders adapt their behavior and style to fit the characteristics of the followers and the environment in which they work. Actual tests of the path-goal theory and its propositions provide conflicting evidence.[36] Hence, it is premature either to fully accept or fully reject the theory at this point. The path-goal theory does have intuitive appeal and offers a number of constructive ideas for leaders who lead a variety of followers in a variety of work environments.

Vroom-Yetton-Jago Normative Decision Theory

The Vroom-Yetton-Jago normative decision theory was discussed in Chapter 10, "Decision Making by Individuals and Groups," because a core element of the theory proposes five alternative decision-making processes. These five processes and the decision process flowchart, or decision tree, are contained in Chapter 10. From a leadership perspective, the Vroom-Yetton-Jago theory recognizes the potential benefits of authoritarian, as well as democratic, styles of leader behavior.[37] The key situational determinants of the appropriate leader behavior within the theory are the quality of the decision to be made, the acceptance of that decision by employees, the time available for the decision, and the information available to the manager.

Discussion Consideration
Is the normative theory a practical theory? That is, can leaders afford to analyze each situation to determine the appropriate decision style?

Although the theory offers very explicit predictions, as well as prescriptions, for leaders, its utility is limited to the leader decision situation. The theory offers no guidance for leaders in nondecision situations where interaction with followers is required for task accomplishment.

One test of the normative decision theory supported it based on leader perceptions of a recent decision process but failed to support the theory based on follower perceptions of the same process.[38] Vroom and Jago created a new model that substantially improves the original by adding a number of objectives that leaders may choose to seek, such as cost reduction.[39]

The Situational Leadership Model

The situational leadership model, developed by Paul Hersey and Kenneth Blanchard, suggests that the leader's behavior should be adjusted to the maturity level of the followers.[40] The model employs two dimensions of leader behavior as used in the Ohio State studies; one dimension is task- or production-oriented, and the other is relationship- or people-oriented. Follower maturity is categorized into four levels, as shown in Figure 12.5. Follower maturity is determined by the ability and willingness of the followers to accept responsibility for completing their work. Followers who are unable and unwilling are the least mature, and those who are both able and willing are the most mature. The four styles of

Alternate Example
The situational model has also been called the life cycle theory of leadership. This suggests that as a follower matures, a leader's style should also change.

■ **FIGURE 12.5**

The Situational Leadership Model: The Hersey-Blanchard Model

SOURCE: P. Hersey and K. H. Blanchard, *Management of Organizational Behavior: Utilizing Human Resources,* 3d ed., Copyright 1977, p. 170. Adapted by permission of Prentice Hall, Englewood Cliffs, NJ.

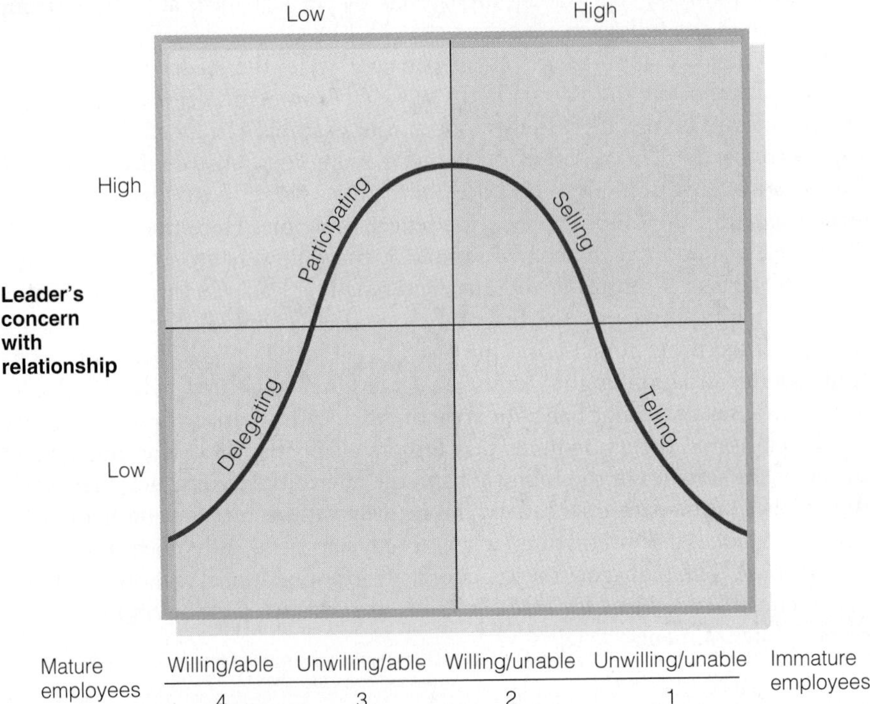

leader behavior associated with each level of follower maturity are depicted in the figure as well.

According to the situational leadership model, a leader should use a telling style of leadership with immature followers who are unable and unwilling to take responsibility for completing their work. This style is characterized by high concern with the task and strong initiating structure behavior, coupled with low concern with relationships and little consideration behavior. As followers mature to the second level, the leader should use a selling style, in which there is high concern with both the task and relationships. The able but unwilling followers are the next most mature and require a participating style from the leader. This style is characterized by high concern with relationships and low concern with the task. Finally, the most mature followers are ones who are both able and willing, thus requiring a delegating style of leadership. The leader employing this style of leadership shows low concern with the task and relationships, because the followers accept responsibility.

Points to Emphasize
The situational model of leadership is based on the task relevant maturity of followers. Can one assume that upper level managers are more mature than operational level managers?

One key limitation of the situational leadership model is the absence of central hypotheses that could be tested, which would make it a more valid, reliable theory of leadership.[41] However, the theory has intuitive appeal and is widely used for training and development in corporations. In addition, the theory focuses attention on followers as important participants, if not determinants, of the leadership process.

Points to Emphasize
Fiedler's theory assumes that a leader's style is fixed. The situational theory assumes that style is flexible. In fact, a leader must be flexible in order to be effective according to the situational model.

Guidelines for Leadership

Discussion Consideration
Can a leader's style change to meet the follower level of maturity as suggested by the situational theory proposes?

■ Leadership is an important topic in organizational behavior and an important contributor to organizational effectiveness. When artifacts are eliminated, studies of leadership succession show a moderately strong leader influence on organizational performance.[42] Corporate leaders also set the ethical tone of their organizations, as shown in the accompanying Organizational Reality. With this said, it is important to recognize that other factors also influence organizational

ORGANIZATIONAL REALITY

Ethics and Corporate Leadership

Corporate leaders play a central role in setting the ethical tone and moral values for their organizations. The Johnson & Johnson Credo was presented in Chapter 2 as one basis for ethical behavior at work. As chairman and CEO of Johnson & Johnson, James Burke played a pivotal role in the 1970s and 1980s in modeling ethical leadership at the company. His undergraduate education was at Holy Cross, a Jesuit college where he received important ethical and moral education. His business education came through his graduate work at Harvard Business School.

Burke called Johnson & Johnson executives to a series of Credo challenge meetings in which the significance and meaning of the Credo, at that time 30 years old, was revisited. The importance of reaffirming the ethical and moral basis for the Credo was clear a decade later when Burke and Johnson & Johnson had to face the two Tylenol crises.

Burke concluded from the successes he and Johnson & Johnson had in managing these crises that every relationship that works is based on trust. Further, he believes that trust grows on a groundwork of moral behavior. Finally, as CEO of a company with a long history of institutional trust, he believes that it is the corporate executive's responsibility to maintain the history of trust compiled over the years. Johnson & Johnson ranked No. 1 in the *Fortune* list of most admired corporations in corporate leadership, in no small part due to the ethical and moral values modeled by James Burke as J&J's corporate leader. ■

SOURCE: P. B. Murphy and G. Enderle, "Managerial Ethical Leadership: Examples Do Matter," *Business Ethics Quarterly* 5 (1995): 117–128. Reprinted by permission of Kluwer Academic Publishers.

performance. These include environmental factors (such as general economic conditions) and technological factors (such as efficiency).

Leaders face a paradox of privilege and accountability with their positions.[43] Horton addresses the paradox through various dilemmas involved in decision making, planning, delegation, team building, and ambition. Although no hard or fast leadership rule emerges from either his treatment of these dilemmas or from the extensive research of the past century, five useful guidelines do appear warranted.

First, leaders and organizations should appreciate the unique attributes, predispositions, and talents of each leader. No two leaders are the same, and there is value in this diversity.

Second, although there appears to be no single best style of leadership, there are organizational preferences in terms of style. Leaders should be chosen who challenge the organizational culture, when necessary, without destroying it.

Third, participative, considerate leader behaviors that demonstrate a concern for people appear to enhance the health and well-being of followers in the work environment. This does not imply, however, that a leader must ignore the team's work tasks.

Fourth, different leadership situations call for different leadership talents and behaviors. This may result in different individuals taking the leader role, depending on the specific situation in which the team finds itself.

Fifth, good leaders are likely to be good followers. Although there are distinctions between their social roles, the attributes and behaviors of leaders and followers may not be as distinct as is sometimes thought.

Followership

■ In contrast to leadership, the topic of followership has not been extensively researched. Much of the leadership literature suggests that leader and follower roles are highly differentiated. The traditional view casts followers as passive, whereas a more contemporary view casts the follower role as an active one with potential for leadership.[44] The follower role has alternatively been cast as one of self-leadership in which the follower assumes responsibility for influencing his or her own performance.[45] Mike Walsh, CEO of Tenneco, sounds as if he is encouraging self-leadership when exhorting employees to think boldly and set higher goals in a slow-growth economy. Walsh recognizes that this makes leaders more visible and vulnerable, but also more effective. Organizational programs such as empowerment and self-managed work teams may be used to further activate the follower role.[46]

http://www.tenneco.com

Alternate Example
An alternative definition of leadership has been developed by Robert Lord of Akron University: Leadership is the process of being perceived as a leader.

It is increasingly difficult to think of followers as passive agents of willful leaders. One study of leader-follower dynamics over a three-month period actually found leaders responding to follower performance rather than causing or initiating it.[47] Followers are an active component of the leadership process, and we need to expand our core knowledge about followership even further.

This section examines different types of followers and the characteristics of a dynamic subordinate. As we examine the follower role, keep in mind that blind, unquestioning followership may lead to destructive, and even antisocial, behavior.[48]

Types of Followers

Contemporary work environments are ones in which followers recognize their interdependence with leaders and learn to challenge them while at the same time respecting the leaders' authority.[49] Effective followers are active, responsible, and autonomous in their behavior and critical in their thinking without being insubordinate or disrespectful. Effective followers and four other types of followers are identified based on two dimensions: (1) activity versus passivity and (2) independent, critical thinking versus dependent, uncritical thinking.[50] Figure 12.6 shows these follower types.

Alienated followers are ones who think independently and critically, yet are very passive in their behavior. As a result, they become psychologically and emotionally distanced from their leaders. Alienated followers are potentially disrup-

■ **FIGURE 12.6**

Five Types of Followers

SOURCE: R. E. Kelley, "In Praise of Followers," *Harvard Business Review* 66 (1988): 145.

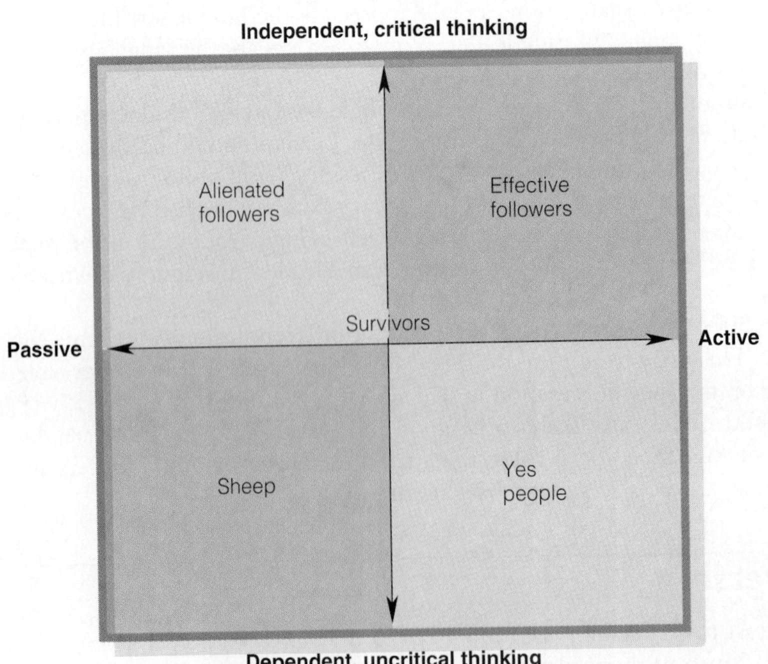

tive and a threat to the health of the organization. Sheep are followers who do not think independently or critically and are passive in their behavior. They simply do as they are told by their leaders. In a sense, they are slaves to the system. Yes people are followers who also do not think independently or critically, yet are very active in their behavior. They uncritically reinforce the thinking and ideas of their leaders with enthusiasm, never questioning or challenging the wisdom of the leaders' ideas and proposals. Yes people are the most dangerous to a leader because they are the most likely to give a false positive reaction and give no warning of potential pitfalls. Survivors are followers who are the least disruptive and the lowest-risk followers in an organization. They perpetually sample the wind, and their motto is "Better safe than sorry."

Effective followers are the most valuable to a leader and an organization because of their active contributions. Effective followers share four essential qualities. First, they practice self-management and self-responsibility. A leader can delegate to an effective follower without anxiety about the outcome. Second, they are committed to both the organization and a purpose, principle, or person outside themselves. Effective followers are not self-centered or self-aggrandizing. There is a risk, however, when the follower is committed to a purpose or principle at odds with the organization. Third, effective followers invest in their own competence and professionalism and focus their energy for maximum impact. Effective followers look for challenges and ways in which to add to their talents or abilities. Fourth, they are courageous, honest, and credible. Challenge 12.2 gives you an opportunity to consider your effectiveness as a follower.

Effective followers might be thought of as self-leaders who do not require close supervision.[51] The notion of self-leadership, or superleadership, blurs the distinction between leaders and followers. There is a complementary concept of caring leadership.[32] Caring leadership focuses attention on the followers, demonstrating concern for their development and well-being. Caring leadership is follower-centered, not self-centered. The caring leader is able to develop dynamic followers.

Alternate Example

Jesus said that he came not to be served, but to serve others and give himself for his followers. This is the essence of servant leadership.

The Dynamic Follower

The traditional stereotype of the follower or employee is of someone in a powerless and dependent role rather than in a potent, active, significant role. The latter is a more contemporary, healthy role in which the follower is dynamic.[53] The **dynamic follower** is a responsible steward of his or her job, is effective in managing the relationship with the boss, and practices responsible self-management.

dynamic follower

A follower who is a responsible steward of his or her job, is effective in managing the relationship with the boss, and practices self-management.

A responsible job steward is one who masters the content of his or her work and possesses or develops the skills required to do a good job. Once prepared, a dynamic follower then does a good job without being led. The dynamic follower is a self-starter.

The dynamic follower becomes a trusted advisor to the boss by keeping the supervisor well informed and building trust and dependability into the relationship. He or she is open to constructive criticism and solicits performance feedback. The dynamic follower shares needs and is responsible.

Self-management requires acquiring self-awareness and control of one's own feelings and behavior. It means being nondefensive and taking risks by challenging the supervisor and the organization.

Dynamic followers are effective in managing the relationship with their bosses along the lines discussed in Chapter 11, aiming to achieve the best possible results for the follower, the boss, and the organization. It takes time and patience to nurture a good relationship between a follower and a supervisor. Once this relationship has been developed, it is a valuable resource for both. Therefore, the follower should be selective in the use of the supervisor's time and resources while always keeping the supervisor informed about work.

CHALLENGE

■ 12.2

Are You an Effective Follower?

To determine whether or not you are an effective follower, read the text section on "Types of Followers," look back at your self-reliance results on Challenge 7.2, and work through the following four steps. Answer each question in the four steps yes or no.

Step 1. Self-Management and Self-Responsibility

_____ Do you take the initiative at work?
_____ Do you challenge the system at work when appropriate?
_____ Do you ask questions when you need more information?
_____ Do you successfully bring your projects to completion?

Step 2. Commitment beyond Yourself

_____ Are you committed to your boss' and company's success?
_____ Is there a higher purpose in life that you value deeply?
_____ Is there a principle(s) that you will not compromise?
_____ Is there a person at work or elsewhere you admire greatly?

Step 3. Self-Development

_____ Do you attend a professional development class annually?
_____ Do you have a program of self-study or structured learning?
_____ Do you take at least one class each semester in the year?
_____ Have you identified new skills to learn for your job?

Step 4. Courage and Honesty

_____ Have you disagreed with your boss twice this year?
_____ Have you taken two unpopular positions at work this year?
_____ Have you given critical feedback to someone, kindly?
_____ Have you taken one risk at work to do a better job?

Scoring:
Count the number of "yes" answers in Steps 1 through 4: ____
If you have 10 to 16 "yes" answers, this would suggest that you are an effective follower. If you have 7 or fewer "yes" answers, this may suggest that you fall into one of the other four categories of followers.

People who are self-reliant may also be effective followers and effective followers may also be self-reliant. If you were an effective follower, were you also self-reliant in Challenge 7.2? If you were not self-reliant in Challenge 7.2, did you fall into other than the effective follower category?

SOURCE: Adapted from R. E. Kelley, "In Praise of Followers," *Harvard Business Review* 66 (1988): 142–148.

Cultural Differences in Leadership

■ In Chapter 5 we noted a number of cultural differences in several motivation theories. Parallel differences do not appear to exist in the area of leadership. Earlier in this chapter we noted similar findings when applying American leadership studies in Japan, along with some differences. The People's Republic of China is another country in which American leadership theories have been said to apply.[54] However, some of the groundbreaking research on leadership and culture concluded that ethnic differences were more important than national or industrial ones.[55] For example, David Kearns became convinced that the Japanese copier industry had targeted Xerox Corporation for elimination from that industry.[56] Convinced he was in the battle for Xerox's life, Kearns introduced Leadership-through-Quality to Xerox in the early 1980s after learning from Fuji Xerox that quality improvements would not increase real costs.[57] Kearns's leadership came at the right time to revolutionize Xerox's culture. The situational approaches to leadership would lead to the conclusion that a leader must factor in culture as an important situational variable when exercising influence

http://www.xerox.com

and authority. Thus, global leaders should expect to be flexible enough to alter their approaches when crossing national boundaries and working with people from foreign cultures.[58]

Managerial Implications: Leaders and Followers as Partners

■ The chapter includes guidelines for leaders and followers, because both affect the quality of work performed and the success, and even survival, of the organization. The actions of national and international competitors and government regulations also affect the success of the organization.

There is no one best leadership theory. Many theories have been proposed, because not one of them works in every situation. One theory may be useful in one manufacturing firm, whereas another is most useful in another manufacturing firm. The many theories of leadership can be thought of as tools of the trade to be applied selectively by the leader in the most appropriate way. Properly applied, each theory is of some value to the user.

The 1990s is a period of significant transition for American industries. They must increasingly learn from other countries and cultures about leadership and followership. Some concepts appear to be cross-culturally applicable, whereas others may not be. Leadership within American corporations is changing, too, as more women assume positions of leadership. Women may lead differently than men, and both men and women can benefit from building on their unique strengths and talents.

Followers are equally important partners in the leadership process, for without followers, who would leaders lead? The role of the follower is one deserving greater respect, dignity, and understanding than presently exists. Effective followers keep leaders out of trouble and advance the cause of leaders with vision and imagination.

CLOSING SPOTLIGHT

Visionary Leader as Change Strategist

Change strategists are leaders who sense the environment in which their organizations operate and create a vision for their organization's future.[59] As we saw in the Scientific Foundation feature, thinking in a visionary way characterizes transformational leaders. Visionary leaders create a broad, and not necessarily precise, framework within which organizational change may then occur. Motorola's Galvin is one of these visionary leaders who is a change strategist and an enabler for the tactical followers who provide detail and precision to the vision, then implement it.

Motorola is an organization that exemplifies excellence in quality, but in the 1980s it was an organization suffering from a bureaucratic structure, intermittent customer feedback, negative supplier relations, unfocused training and a lack of quality commitment. Motorola needed to change yet Galvin did not have a clear, precise vision for Motorola's future. However, Motorola's top management responded to a challenge Galvin issued at the 1983 meeting and formulated a vision that focused on reduction of cycle time and defects within specific periods and participative management. Quality improved ten times by 1989 and 100 times by 1991. The results of the initiatives included new performance measurement tools, a reduced and more positive supplier base, better teamwork, quality beyond Baldridge standards and a quality function elevated to top management status.[60] A visionary leader, Galvin was also a change strategist for Motorola. ■

Chapter Summary

- Leadership is the process of guiding and directing the behavior of followers in organizations. Followership is the process of being guided and directed by a leader. Leadership and followership involve people, not technology.
- A leader creates meaningful change in organizations, whereas a manager controls complexity. Charismatic leaders have a profound impact on their followers.
- Autocratic leaders create high pressure for followers, whereas democratic leaders create healthier environments for followers.
- Two distinct dimensions of leader behavior are labeled initiating structure and consideration. Roughly the same behaviors are labeled P-oriented behavior and M-oriented behavior, respectively, in Japan.
- The five styles in the Managerial Grid are organization man manager, authority-obedience manager, country club manager, team manager, and impoverished manager.
- According to the contingency theory, task-oriented leaders are most effective in highly favorable or highly unfavorable leadership situations, and relationship-oriented leaders are most effective in moderately favorable leadership situations.
- The path-goal theory, Vroom-Yetton-Jago theory, and situational leadership model say that a leader should adjust his or her behavior to the situation and should appreciate diversity among followers.
- Effective, dynamic followers are competent and active in their work, assertive, independent thinkers, sensitive to their bosses' needs and demands, and responsible self-managers.

Key Terms

leadership (p. 346)
formal leadership (p. 346)
informal leadership (p. 346)
followership (p. 346)
leader (p. 349)
manager (p. 349)
charismatic leadership (p. 352)
autocratic style (p. 353)
democratic style (p. 353)
laissez-faire style (p. 353)
initiating structure (p. 354)
consideration (p. 354)
P-oriented behavior (p. 354)
M-oriented behavior (p. 354)
Managerial Grid (p. 355)
organization man manager (p. 355)
authority-obedience manager (p. 355)
country club manager (p. 355)
team manager (p. 356)
impoverished manager (p. 356)
least preferred coworker (LPC) (p. 358)
task structure (p. 358)
position power (p. 358)
leader-member relations (p. 358)
dynamic follower (p. 365)

Review Questions

1. Define *leadership* and *followership*. Distinguish between formal leadership and informal leadership.
2. What are the differences between, and the contributions of, leaders and managers in organizations? How do leaders and managers differ? How do charismatic leaders affect their followers?
3. Describe the differences between autocratic and democratic work environments. How do they differ from a laissez-faire workplace?
4. Define *initiating structure* and *consideration* as leader behaviors. How do they compare with P-oriented behavior and M-oriented behavior?
5. Describe the organization man manager, authority-obedience manager, country club manager, team manager, and impoverished manager.
6. How does the LPC scale measure leadership style? What are the three dimensions of the leader's situation?
7. Describe the alternative decision strategies used by a leader in the Vroom-Yetton-Jago normative decision theory.
8. Compare House's path-goal theory of leadership with the situational leadership model.
9. Describe alienated followers, sheep, yes people, survivors, and effective followers.

Discussion and Communication Questions

1. Do you (or would you want to) work in an autocratic, democratic, or laissez-faire work environment? What might be the advantages of each work environment? The disadvantages?
2. Is your supervisor or professor someone who is high in concern for production? High in concern for people? What is his or her Managerial Grid style?
3. What decision strategies does your supervisor use to make decisions? Are they consistent or inconsistent with the Vroom-Yetton-Jago model?
4. Discuss the similarities and differences between effective leadership and dynamic followership. Are you dynamic?
5. Describe the relationship you have with your supervisor or professor. What is the best part of the relationship? The worst part? What could you do to make the relationship better?
6. *(communication question)* Who is the leader you admire the most? Write a description of this person including his or

her characteristics and attributes that you admire. Note any aspects of this leader or his/her behavior that you find less than wholly admirable.

7. *(communication question)* Refresh yourself on the distinction between leaders (also called transformational leaders) and managers (also called transactional leaders) in the text. Then go to the library and read about four contemporary business leaders. Prepare a brief summary of each and classify them as leaders or managers.

8. *(communication question)* Interview a supervisor or manager about the best follower the supervisor or manager has worked with. Ask questions about the characteristics and behaviors that made this person such a good follower. Note in particular how this follower responds to change. Be prepared to present your interview results in class.

Ethics Questions

1. Is it ethical for leaders to tell followers unilaterally what to do without asking their opinions or getting any input from them?
2. Is it acceptable for a leader to take credit for the work of subordinates who are being supervised?
3. If a leader is using a delegating leadership style and big problems develop in the team's work, is the leader still responsible for what happens?
4. If a follower disagrees with the supervisor's directions, is the follower obligated to follow those directions anyway? Or is the follower obligated to be disobedient while adhering to a moral principle?
5. What should you do if your supervisor acts in an unethical or illegal matter? Talk with the supervisor? Immediately report the action to the company's ethics committee?

Experiential Exercises

12.1 National Culture and Leadership

Effective leadership often varies by national culture, as Hofstede's research has shown. This exercise gives you the opportunity to examine your own and your group's leadership orientation compared to norms from ten countries, including the United States.

Exercise Schedule

1. Preparation (before class)
   Complete the 29-item questionnaire.
2. Individual and Group Scoring
   Your instructor will lead you through the scoring of the questionnaire, both individually and as a group.
3. Comparison of Effective Leadership Patterns by Nation
   Your instructor leads a discussion on Hofstede's value system and presents the culture dimension scores for the ten countries.

In the questionnaire below, please indicate the extent to which you agree or disagree with each statement. For example, if you strongly agree with a particular statement, circle the 5 next to the statement.

1 = strongly disagree
2 = disagree
3 = neither agree nor disagree
4 = agree
5 = strongly agree

QUESTIONNAIRE 2	STRONGLY AGREE				STRONGLY DISAGREE
1. It is important to have job instructions spelled out in detail so that employees always know what they are expected to do.	1	2	3	4	5
2. Managers expect employees to closely follow instructions and procedures	1	2	3	4	5
3. Rules and regulations are important because they inform employees what the organization expects of them.	1	2	3	4	5
4. Standard operating procedures are helpful to employees on the job.	1	2	3	4	5
5. Instructions for operations are important for employees on the job.	1	2	3	4	5
6. Group welfare is more important than individual rewards.	1	2	3	4	5
7. Group success is more important than individual success.	1	2	3	4	5
8. Being accepted by the members of your work group is very important.	1	2	3	4	5

9. Employees should pursue their own goals only after considering the welfare of the group.	1	2	3	4	5
10. Managers should encourage group loyalty even if individual goals suffer.	1	2	3	4	5
11. Individuals may be expected to give up their goals in order to benefit group success.	1	2	3	4	5
12. Managers should make most decisions without consulting subordinates.	1	2	3	4	5
13. Managers should frequently use authority and power when dealing with subordinates.	1	2	3	4	5
14. Managers should seldom ask for the opinions of employees.	1	2	3	4	5
15. Managers should avoid off-the-job social contacts with employees.	1	2	3	4	5
16. Employees should not disagree with management decisions.	1	2	3	4	5
17. Managers should not delegate important tasks to employees.	1	2	3	4	5
18. Managers should help employees with their family problems.	1	2	3	4	5
19. Managers should see to it that employees are adequately clothed and fed.	1	2	3	4	5
20. A manager should help employees solve their personal problems.	1	2	3	4	5
21. Management should see that all employees receive health care.	1	2	3	4	5
22. Management should see that children of employees have an adequate education.					
23. Management should provide legal assistance for employees who get into trouble with the law.	1	2	3	4	5
24. Managers should take care of their employees as they would their children.	1	2	3	4	5
25. Meetings are usually run more effectively when they are chaired by a man.	1	2	3	4	5
26. It is more important for men to have a professional career than it is for women to have a professional career.	1	2	3	4	5
27. Men usually solve problems with logical analysis; women usually solve problems with intuition.	1	2	3	4	5
28. Solving organizational problems usually requires an active, forcible approach, which is typical of men.	1	2	3	4	5
29. It is preferable to have a man, rather than a woman, in a high-level position.	1	2	3	4	5

SOURCE: By Peter Dorfman, *Advances in International Comparative Management*, vol. 3, pages 127–150. Copyright 1988 by JAI Press Inc. Used with permission. D. Marcic and S. M. Puffer, "Dimensions of National Culture and Effective Leadership Patterns: Hofstede Revisited," *Management International* (Minneapolis/St. Paul: West Publishing, 1994): 10–15. All rights reserved. May not be reproduced without written permission of the publisher. For more information, contact West Publishing, Publications Dept., 610 Opperman Drive, St. Paul, MN 55164.

12.2 Leadership and Influence

In order to get a better idea of what your leadership style is and how productive it would be, fill out the questionnaire below. If you are currently a manager or have been a manager, answer the questions considering "members" to be your employees. If you have never been a manager, think of situations when you were a leader in an organization and consider "members" to be people working for you.

Response choices for each item:

A = always B = often C = occasionally D = seldom E = never

	A	B	C	D	E
1. I would act as the spokesperson of the group.					
2. I would allow the members complete freedom in their work.					
3. I would encourage overtime work.					
4. I would permit the members to use their own judgment in solving problems.					
5. I would encourage the use of uniform procedures.					
6. I would needle members for greater effort.					
7. I would stress being ahead of competing groups.					
8. I would let the members do their work the way they think best.					
9. I would speak as the representative of the group.					
10. I would be able to tolerate postponement and uncertainty.					
11. I would try out my ideas in the group.					
12. I would turn the members loose on a job, and let them go on it.					
13. I would work hard for a promotion.					
14. I would get swamped by details.					
15. I would speak for the group when visitors are present.					
16. I would be reluctant to allow the members any freedom of action.					
17. I would keep the work moving at a rapid pace.					
18. I would let some members have authority that I should keep.					
19. I would settle conflicts when they occur in the group.					
20. I would allow the group a high degree of initiative.					
21. I would represent the group at outside meetings.					
22. I would be willing to make changes.					
23. I would decide what will be done and how it will be done.					
24. I would trust the members to exercise good judgment.					
25. I would push for increased production.					
26. I would refuse to explain my actions.					
27. Things usually turn out as I predict.					
28. I would permit the group to set its own pace.					
29. I would assign group members to particular tasks.					
30. I would act without consulting the group.					
31. I would ask the members to work harder.					
32. I would schedule the work to be done.					
33. I would persuade others that my ideas are to their advantage.					
34. I would urge the group to beat its previous record.					
35. I would ask that group members follow standard rules and regulations.					

Scoring

People oriented: Place a check mark behind the number if you answered either A or B to any of these questions.

Question # 2 ____ 10 ____ 22 ____
4 ____ 12 ____ 24 ____
6 ____ 18 ____ 28 ____
8 ____ 20 ____

Place a check behind the number if you answered either D or E to any of these questions.

14 ____ 16 ____ 26 ____ 30 ____

Count your checks to get your total people-oriented score. ____

Task oriented: Place a check mark behind the number if you answered either A or B to any of these questions.

3 ____ 7 ____ 11 ____ 13 ____
17 ____ 25 ____ 29 ____ 31 ____
34 ____

Place a check behind the number if you answered C or D to any of these questions.

1 ____ 5 ____ 9 ____ 15 ____
19 ____ 21 ____ 23 ____ 27 ____
32 ____ 33 ____ 35 ____

Count your check marks to get your total task-oriented score. ____

Range	*Range*		
People 0–7;	Task 0–10	You are not involved enough in either the task or the people.	Uninvolved
People 0–7;	Task 10–20	You tend to be autocratic, a whip-snapper. You get the job done, but at a high emotional cost.	Task-oriented
People 8–15;	Task 0–10	People are happy in their work, but sometimes at the expense of productivity.	People-oriented
People 8–15;	Task 10–20	People enjoy working for you and are productive. They naturally expend energy because they get positive reinforcement for doing a good job.	Balanced

As a leader, most people tend to be more task-oriented or more people-oriented. Task-orientation is concerned with getting the job done, while people-orientation focuses on group interactions and the needs of individual workers.

Effective leaders, however, are able to use both styles, depending on the situation. There may be time when a rush job demands great attention placed on task completion. During a time of low morale, though, sensitivity to workers' problems would be more appropriate. The best managers are able to balance both task and people concerns. Therefore a high score on both would show this balance. Ultimately, you will gain respect, admiration and productivity from your workers.

Exercise Schedule

1. Preparation (before class)
   Complete and score inventory.
2. Group discussion
   The class should form four groups based on the scores on the Leadership Style Inventory. Each group will be given a separate task.

Uninvolved: Devise strategies for developing task-oriented and people-oriented styles.

Task-oriented: How can you develop a more people-oriented style? What problems might occur if you do not do so?

People-oriented: How can you develop a more task-oriented style? What problems might occur if you do not do so?

Balanced: Do you see any potential problems with your style? Are you a fully developed leader?

SOURCE: Copyright 1988 by Dorothy Marcic. Adapted with permission from Thomas Sergiovanni, Richard Metzcus and Larry Burden. "Toward a Particularistic Approach to Leadership Style: Some Findings," *American Educational Research Journal*, Vol. 6(1), January 1969, American Educational Research Association, Washington D.C.

VIDEO CASE

Jeff Goodman: President and CEO of IBAX Health Care Systems[1]

IBAX Health Care Systems, a company formed by a merger of IBM and Baxter Health Care, markets Health Care Information System software to hospitals and physicians. The company's software products are designed to manage financial, patient accounting, and clinical information.

After the merger, IBAX operated in a very traditional mode. The company was organized around functions with well-defined boundaries. Senior managers made decisions to be implemented by others. Lower-level organizational members tended to ask permission before making a decision. In short, IBAX was managed in a top-down fashion.

IBAX's top-down orientation is amply illustrated with the budgetary process. Senior management would decide on the budget and then mandate achievement of those budgetary goals. Dialog or consensus building were absent from the budgetary process. The managerial perspective was essentially, "These are your numbers for the year," now you "go figure out how to make them."

Unfortunately, IBAX's top-down leadership approach helped foster an atmosphere of mistrust and contributed to poor employee morale. In addition, IBAX was operating at a significant financial loss while experiencing problems with customer satisfaction and product quality.

In 1991, Jeff Goodman was hired as president and CEO of IBAX with the charge of fixing the customer satisfaction problem and eliminating the financial losses. He soon discovered that the problems were more severe than he had originally thought.

IBAX employees expressed concern because morale was low. Goodman's reaction was: "Good! Because anybody with high morale—when we're losing $23 million—probably shouldn't be working." Goodman believed that high morale should come from performing well and making the company better.

Although Goodman believes that the company's financial performance should affect employee morale, he also believes that other factors are influential as well. He describes his approach to building morale as one of "building trust and sharing and being totally open."

Turning IBAX around was Goodman's challenge. His strategy consisted of eliminating the artificial boundaries in the organization and creating autonomous business units. People in the business units were empowered through the use of high-performance work teams that relied on self-directed efforts. Leadership practices were changed to emphasize coaching, guiding, and counseling rather than delegation and direction.

By the end of 1992, IBAX had six independent business units that were run by employee teams rather than by general managers. Using the bottom-up approach to budgeting implemented by Goodman, these teams developed their own business plans for 1993, projecting their expected revenues and costs. Senior managers made sure that the individual unit plans fit with IBAX's total profile. But senior managers also empowered, coached, and mentored people in the business units as they worked toward achieving their budgetary goals.

Empowering people is a critical element of Jeff Goodman's approach to leadership. He says that "Top-down leadership—in my opinion—doesn't work well anymore. We had to transfer the leadership to the people running the business." Goodman's approach was to invert the organizational pyramid—employee business teams were at the top and senior management was at the bottom supporting the business teams.

In summarizing his view of leadership, Goodman says, "There's just two things that I try to do religiously. The first is to be impeccably honest. . . . The second is to always protect the integrity of the people" with whom one deals. "I think that if you bring honesty and respect to your job, and then maybe throw in a little spice called 'developing them' and 'trying to make them as good as they can be,' that's leadership."

DISCUSSION QUESTIONS

1. In what ways is Jeff Goodman a leader? In what ways is he a manager?
2. Using Figure 12.6, analyze the nature of followership in the pre-Goodman era at IBAX. Repeat the followership analysis for the Goodman era.
3. What do you think Jeff Goodman means by "being impeccably honest" and "protecting the integrity of people"?
4. What skills would you personally need to develop to become a leader like Jeff Goodman? What could you do to develop those skills?
5. What do you think is the most important leadership lesson in this case? Explain your answer.

SOURCE: This case was written by Michael K. McCuddy, the Louis S. and Mary L. Morgal Professor of Christian Business Ethics, College of Business Administration, Valparaiso, University.

1. This case is based on transcripts of interviews that representatives of West Educational Publishing conducted with various IBAX Health Care System executives.

References

1. R. M. Kanter, B. A. Stein, and T. D. Jick, *The Challenge of Organizational Change* (New York: The Free Press, 1992).
2. J. P. Kotter, "What Leaders Really Do," *Harvard Business Review* 68 (1990): 103–111.
3. Jennifer J. Laabs, "GE Medical Systems," winner of the 1992 Optimas Award from *Personnel Journal* (January 1992): 55.
4. A. G. Jago, "Leadership: Perspectives in Theory and Research," *Management Science* 28 (1982): 315–336.
5. R. M. Stogdill, *Stogdill's Handbook of Leadership: A Survey of Theory and Research*, rev. B. M. Bass (New York: Free Press, 1981).
6. S. Kerr and J. Jermier, "Substitutes for Leadership: Their Meaning and Measurement," *Organizational Behavior and Human Performance* 22 (1978): 376–403.
7. R. M. Stogdill, "Personal Factors Associated with Leadership: A Survey of the Literature," *Journal of Psychology* 25 (1948): 35–71.
8. A. Zaleznik, "HBR Classic—Managers and Leaders: Are They Different?" *Harvard Business Review* 70 (1992): 126–135.
9. J. M. Burns, *Leadership* (New York: Harper & Row, 1978); T. O. Jacobs, *Leadership and Exchange in Formal Organizations* (Alexandria, Va.: Human Resources Research Organization, 1971).
10. N. Tichy and M. A. DeVanna, *The Transformational Leader* (New York: Wiley, 1986).
11. B. M. Bass, "From Transactional to Transformational Leadership: Learning to Share the Vision," *Organizational Dynamics* 19 (1990): 19–31; B. M. Bass, *Leadership and Performance beyond Expectations* (New York: Free Press, 1985).
12. J. R. Joplin, "Developing Effective Leadership: An Interview with Henry Cisneros," *Academy of Management Executive* 7 (1993): 84–92.
13. W. Bennis, "Managing the Dream: Leadership in the 21st Century," *Training* 27 (1990): 43–48.
14. A. Zaleznik, "The Leadership Gap," *Academy of Management Executive* 4 (1990): 7–22.
15. M. E. Heilman, C. J. Block, R. F. Martell, and M. C. Simon, "Has Anything Changed? Current Characteristics of Men, Women, and Managers," *Journal of Applied Psychology* 74 (1989): 935–942.
16. L. Putnam and J. S. Heiner, "Women in Management: The Fallacy of the Train Approach," *MSU Business Topics*, (Summer 1976): 47–53.
17. J. B. Rosener, "Ways Women Lead," *Harvard Business Review* 68 (1990): 119–125.
18. R. J. House and M. L. Baetz, "Leadership: Some Empirical Generalizations and New Research Directions," in B. M. Staw, ed., *Research in Organizational Behavior*, vol. 1 (Greenwood, Conn.: JAI Press, 1979), 399–401.
19. J. A. Conger and R. N. Kanungo, "Toward a Behavioral Theory of Charismatic Leadership in Organizational Settings," *Academy of Management Review* 12 (1987): 637–647.
20. A. R. Willner, *The Spellbinders: Charismatic Political Leadership* (New Haven, Conn.: Yale University Press, 1984).
21. J. M. Howell, "Two Faces of Charisma: Socialized and Personalized Leadership in Organizations," in J. A. Conger, ed., *Charismatic Leadership: Behind the Mystique of Exceptional Leadership* (San Francisco: Jossey-Bass, 1988).
22. D. Sankowsky, "The Charismatic Leader as Narcissist: Understanding the Abuse of Power," *Organizational Dynamics* 23 (1995): 57–71.
23. K. Lewin, R. Lippitt, and R. K. White, "Patterns of Aggressive Behavior in Experimentally Created "Social Climates," *Journal of Social Psychology* 10 (1939): 271–299.
24. R. Likert, *New Patterns of Management* (New York: McGraw-Hill, 1961); R. Tannenbaum and W. H. Schmidt, "How to Choose a Leadership Pattern," *Harvard Business Review* 51 (1973): 162–180.
25. R. M. Stodgill and A. E. Coons, eds., *Leader Behavior: Its Description and Measurement*, research monograph no. 88 (Columbus, Ohio: Bureau of Business Research, The Ohio State University, 1957).
26. A. W. Halpin and J. Winer, "A Factorial Study of the Leader Behavior Description Questionnaire," in R. M. Stogdill and A. E. Coons, eds., *Leader Behavior: Its Description and Measurement*, research monograph no. 88 (Columbus, Ohio: Bureau of Business Research, The Ohio State University, 1957), 39–51.
27. E. A. Fleishman, "Leadership Climate, Human Relations Training, and Supervisory Behavior," *Personnel Psychology* 6 (1953): 205–222.
28. N. Tichy and R. Charan, "Speed, Simplicity, Self-Confidence: An Interview with Jack Welch," *Harvard Business Review* 67 (1989): 112–121.
29. R. R. Blake and J. S. Mouton, *The Managerial Grid III: The Key to Leadership Excellence* (Houston: Gulf, 1985).
30. F. E. Fiedler, *A Theory of Leader Effectiveness* (New York: McGraw-Hill, 1964).
31. F. E. Fiedler, *Personality, Motivational Systems, and Behavior of High and Low LPC Persons*, tech. rep. no. 70-12 (Seattle: University of Washington, 1970).
32. J. T. McMahon, "The Contingency Theory: Logic and Method Revisited," *Personnel Psychology* 25 (1972): 697–710; L. H. Peters, D. D. Hartke, and J. T. Pohlman, "Fiedler's Contingency Theory of Leadership: An Application of the Meta-analysis Procedures of Schmidt and Hunter," *Psychological Bulletin* 97 (1985): 224–285.
33. F. E. Fiedler, "The Contingency Model and the Dynamics of the Leadership Process," in L. Berkowitz, ed., *Advances in Experimental and Social Psychology*, vol. 11 (New York: Academic Press, 1978).
34. F. E. Fiedler, "Engineering the Job to Fit the Manager," *Harvard Business Review* 43 (1965): 115–122.
35. R. J. House, "A Path-Goal Theory of Leader Effectiveness," *Administrative Science Quarterly* 16 (1971): 321–338; R. J. House and T. R. Mitchell, "Path-Goal Theory of Leadership," *Journal of Contemporary Business* 3 (1974): 81–97.
36. C. A. Schriescheim and V. M. Von Glinow, "The Path-Goal Theory of Leadership: A Theoretical and Empirical Analysis," *Academy of Management Journal* 20 (1977): 398–405; E. Valenzi and G. Dessler, "Relationships of

Leader Behavior, Subordinate Role Ambiguity, and Subordinate Job Satisfaction," *Academy of Management Journal* 21 (1978): 671–678; N. R. F. Maier, *Leadership Methods and Skills* (New York: McGraw-Hill, 1963).

37. V. H. Vroom and P. W. Yetton, *Leadership and Decision Making* (Pittsburgh: University of Pittsburgh, 1973).
38. R. H. G. Field and R. J. House, "A Test of the Vroom-Yetton Model Using Manager and Subordinate Reports," *Journal of Applied Psychology* 75 (1990): 362–366.
39. V. H. Vroom and A. G. Jago, *The New Leadership: Managing Participation in Organizations* (Englewood Cliffs, N.J.: Prentice-Hall, 1988).
40. P. Hersey and K. H. Blanchard, "Life Cycle Theory of Leadership," *Training and Development Journal* 23 (1969): 26–34; P. Hersey and K. H. Blanchard, *Management of Organizational Behavior: Utilizing Human Resources*, 3d ed. (Englewood Cliffs, N.J.: Prentice-Hall, 1977).
41. B. M. Bass, *Bass and Stogdill's Handbook of Leadership: Theory, Research, and Managerial Applications*, 3d ed. (New York: Free Press, 1990).
42. G. A. Yukl, *Leadership in Organizations*, 2d ed. (Englewood Cliffs, N.J.: Prentice-Hall, 1989).
43. T. R. Horton, *The CEO Paradox: The Privilege and Accountability of Leadership* (New York: American Management Association, 1992).
44. E. P. Hollander and L. R. Offerman, "Power and Leadership in Organizations: Relationships in Transition," *American Psychologist* 45 (1990): 179–189.
45. C. Manz, "Self-Leadership: Toward an Expanded Theory of Self-Influence Processes in Organizations," *Academy of Management Review* 11 (1986): 585–600.
46. C. C. Manz and H. P. Sims, "Leading Workers to Lead Themselves: The External Leadership of Self-Managing Work Teams," *Administrative Science Quarterly* 32 (1987): 106–128.
47. C. N. Greene, "The Reciprocal Nature of Influence between Leader and Subordinate," *Journal of Applied Psychology* 60 (1975): 187–193.
48. H. S. Schwartz, "Antisocial Actions of Committed Organizational Participants," in *Narcissistic Process and Corporate Decay* (New York: NYU Press, 1990): 31–45.
49. L. Hirschhorn, "Leaders and Followers in a Postindustrial Age: A Psychodynamic View," *Journal of Applied Behavioral Science* 26 (1990): 529–542.
50. R. E. Kelley, "In Praise of Followers," *Harvard Business Review* 66 (1988): 142–148.
51. C. C. Manz and H. P. Sims, "SuperLeadership: Beyond the Myth of Heroic Leadership," *Organizational Dynamics* 20 (1991): 18–35.
52. J. Chain, General (Retired), former Commander-in-Chief of the Strategic Air Command, in the commissioning address for A.F.R.O.T.C. cadets, Texas Christian University, 10 May 1996.
53. W. J. Crockett, "Dynamic Subordinancy," *Training and Development Journal* (May 1981): 155–164.
54. T. K. Oh, "Theory Y in the People's Republic of China," *California Management Review* 19 (1976): 77–84.
55. M. Haire, E. E. Ghiselli, and L. W. Porter, "Cultural Patterns in the Role of the Manager," *Industrial Relations* 2 (1963): 95–117.
56. D. T. Kearns and D. A. Nadler, *Prophets in the Dark: How Xerox Reinvented Itself and Beat Back the Japanese* (New York: Harper Business, 1992).
57. D. T. Kearns, "Leadership through Quality," *Academy of Management Executive* 4 (1990): 86–89.
58. N. J. Adler, *International Dimensions in Organizational Behavior* (Boston: PWS-KENT, 1991).
59. R. M. Kanter, B. A. Stein, and T. A. Jick, "Chapter 11: Sensing the Environment, Creating Visions: Change Strategists," in *The Challenge of Organizational Change* (New York: The Free Press, 1992): pp. 395–428.
60. "Communicators of Quality," *Management Decision* 32 (1994): 20–21.

CHAPTER

13

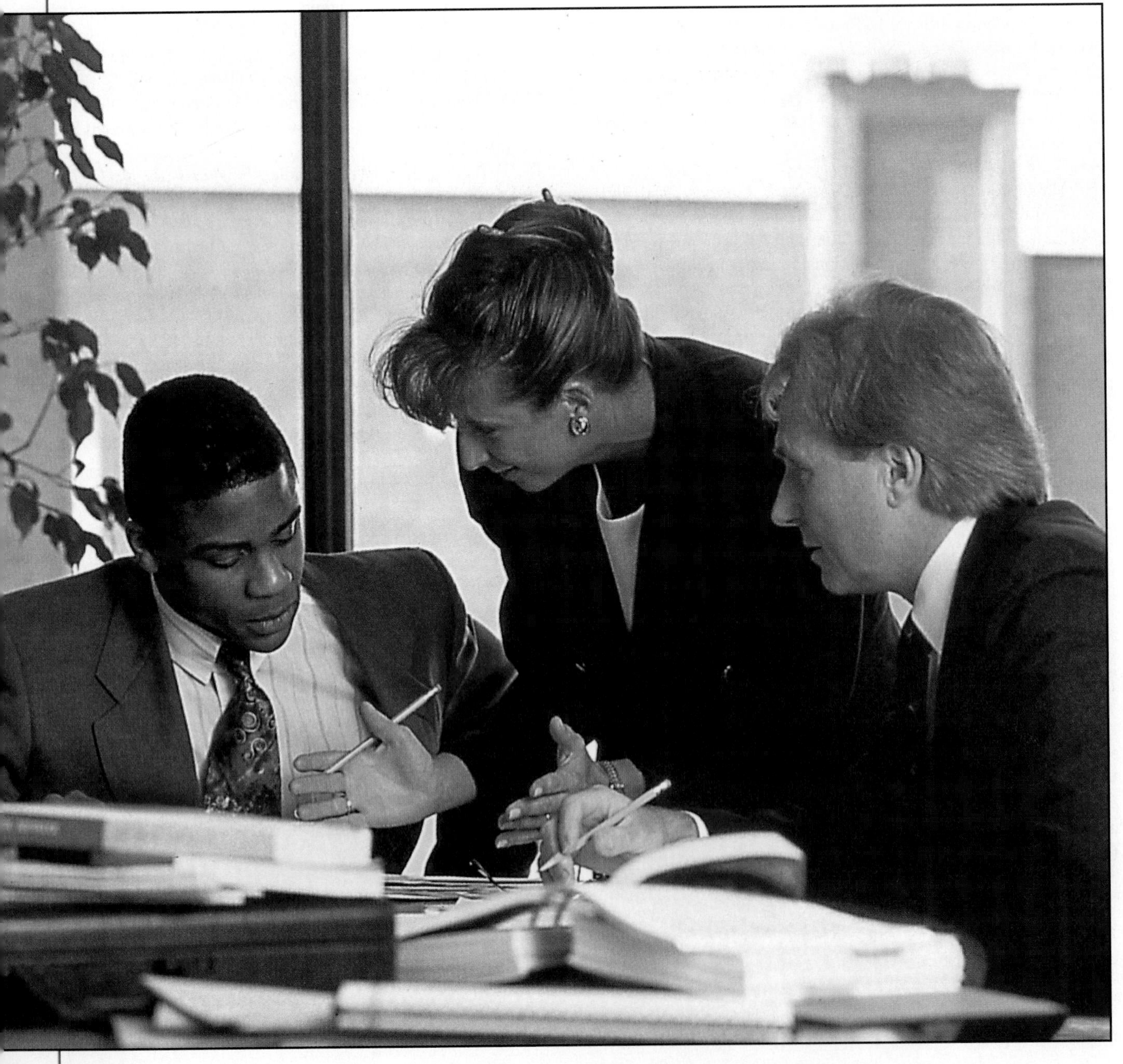

Conflict at Work

LEARNING OBJECTIVES

After reading this chapter, you should be able to do the following:

- Diagnose functional versus dysfunctional conflict, and identify the different forms of conflict.
- Identify the causes of conflict in organizations.
- Understand the defense mechanisms that individuals exhibit when they engage in interpersonal conflict.
- Construct an action plan for dealing with difficult people.
- Conduct an effective role analysis.
- Describe effective and ineffective techniques for managing conflict.
- Understand five styles of conflict management, and diagnose your own preferred style.

OPENING SPOTLIGHT

Managing Conflict from Day One at Southwest Airlines

http://www.iflyswa.com

Although incorporated in 1967 as Air Southwest Company, Southwest Airlines did not fly its inaugural routes until 1971. The four years from 1967 through 1971 can be characterized as the "Period of Lift-off" for Southwest. An intense legal battle was being fought on the ground in what was at the time a highly regulated industry. (It was not until the 1978 Airline Deregulation Act that the industry became deregulated.)

Southwest's competitors were Braniff, Trans Texas, and Continental Airlines. These three carriers waged their ground conflict, mostly during 1968 and 1969, to keep Southwest out of the air. The Texas Airline Commission (TAC) granted Southwest its application to fly on February 20, 1968. The very next day, the three opponents obtained a temporary restraining order prohibiting TAC from delivering Southwest's certificate. The three opponents were also successful in the Texas State District Court and the state court of civil appeals.

Finally, in 1970, the Texas Supreme Court unanimously overturned the lower court rulings, and the U.S. Supreme Court denied Braniff's and Texas International's appeals of the Texas Supreme Court ruling. Southwest Airlines had clearly won the ground war. ■

The Nature of Conflicts in Organizations

conflict

Any situation in which incompatible goals, attitudes, emotions, or behaviors lead to disagreement or opposition between two or more parties.

Points to Emphasize

As with the concepts of stress, power, and politics, conflict often has negative connotations. Yet, conflict can be constructive, as well as destructive.

■ All of us have experienced conflict of various types, yet we probably fail to recognize the variety of conflicts that occur in organizations. **Conflict** is defined as any situation in which incompatible goals, attitudes, emotions, or behaviors lead to disagreement or opposition between two or more parties.[1]

Today's organizations may face greater potential for conflict than ever before in history. The marketplace, with its increasing competition and globalization, magnifies differences among people in terms of personality, values, attitudes, perceptions, languages, cultures, and national backgrounds.[2] With the increasing diversity of the workforce, furthermore, comes potential incompatibility and conflict.

Importance of Conflict Management Skills for the Manager

Estimates show that managers spend about 21 percent of their time dealing with conflict.[3] That is the equivalent of one day every week. And conflict management skills are a major predictor of managerial success.[4] The accompanying Organizational Reality feature describes how "emotional intelligence" relates to the ability to manage conflict.

Alternate Example

"Resolving conflict is rarely about who is right. It is about acknowledgment and appreciation of differences." SOURCE: T. Crum, The Magic of Conflict, cited in D. Knick and C. Altizer, "Classroom Confrontations," *Training and Development,* February 1993, 17–20.

Functional versus Dysfunctional Conflict

Not all conflict is bad. In fact, some types of conflict encourage new solutions to problems and enhance the creativity in the organization. In these cases, managers will want to encourage the conflicts.[5] Therefore, managers should stimulate functional conflict and prevent or resolve dysfunctional conflict. This is the key to conflict management. However, the difficulty lies in trying to tell the difference between dysfunctional and functional conflicts. The consequences of conflict can be positive or negative, as shown in Table 13.1.

functional conflict

A healthy, constructive disagreement between two or more people.

Functional conflict is a healthy, constructive disagreement between two or more people. A recent study of twenty corporations revealed that few managers

■ **TABLE 13.1**

Consequences of Conflict

POSITIVE CONSEQUENCES	NEGATIVE CONSEQUENCES
■ Leads to new ideas	■ Diverts energy from work
■ Stimulates creativity	■ Threatens psychological well-being
■ Motivates change	■ Wastes resources
■ Promotes organizational vitality	■ Creates a negative climate
■ Helps individuals and groups establish identities	■ Breaks down group cohesion
■ Serves as a safety value to indicate problems	■ Can increase hostility and aggressive behaviors

ORGANIZATIONAL REALITY

Did a Lack of EQ Really Cost Him His Job?

Dick Snyder was the head of Simon & Schuster, the giant publishing house. He pushed the company to higher and higher earnings, and in that regard he was extremely successful. However, for years he was unable to keep himself from degrading and humiliating employees. Viacom eventually bought Simon & Schuster, and Frank Biondi, Viacom's CEO, fired Snyder. In explaining to an interviewer why he had done so, he said that Snyder was not a team player. What if Snyder had been able to double S&S's business? Biondi replied that he still would have axed him.

Snyder lacked what author Daniel Goleman terms "emotional intelligence" (EQ)—the power not only to control emotions but also to perceive them. EQ has five dimensions: knowing one's emotions and controlling them, recognizing emotions in others (empathy) and controlling them, and self-motivation. Goleman contends that incompetence as a manager is most likely a lack of EQ rather than IQ. EQ skills are essential in managing conflict. People who lack emotional intelligence, especially empathy or the ability to see life from another person's perspective, are more likely to be causes of conflict rather than managers of conflict.

SOURCES: A. Farnham, "Are You Smart Enough to Keep Your Job?" *Fortune*, January 15, 1996, 34–48; and D. Goleman, *Emotional Intelligence* (New York: Bantam Books, 1995).

understand the ways in which conflict can benefit an organization.[6] Functional conflict can produce new ideas, learning, and growth among individuals. When individuals engage in constructive conflict, they develop a better awareness of themselves and others. In addition, functional conflict can improve working relationships, because when two parties work through their disagreements, they feel they have accomplished something together. By releasing tensions and solving problems in working together, morale is improved.[7] Functional conflict can lead to innovation and positive change for the organization.[8] Because it tends to encourage creativity among individuals, this positive form of conflict can translate into increased productivity.[9] A key for recognizing functional conflict is that it is often cognitive in origin; that is, it arises from someone challenging old policies or thinking of new ways to approach problems.

Dysfunctional conflict is an unhealthy, destructive disagreement between two or more people. Its danger is that it takes the focus away from the work to be done and places the focus on the conflict itself and the parties involved. Excessive conflict drains energy that could be used more productively. A key for recognizing a dysfunctional conflict is that its origin is often emotional or behavioral. Disagreements that involve personalized anger and resentment directed at specific individuals rather than specific ideas are dysfunctional.[10] Individuals involved in dysfunctional conflict tend to act before thinking, and they often rely on threats, deception, and verbal abuse to communicate. In dysfunctional conflict, the losses to both parties may exceed any potential gain from the conflict.

dysfunctional conflict
An unhealthy, destructive disagreement between two or more people.

Discussion Consideration
Ask students to identify examples of functional and dysfunctional conflict from their own experience.

Diagnosing conflict as good or bad is not easy. The manager must look at the issue, the context of the conflict, and the parties involved. The following questions can be used to diagnose the nature of the conflict a manager faces:

- Are the parties approaching the conflict from a hostile standpoint?
- Is the outcome likely to be a negative one for the organization?
- Do the potential losses of the parties exceed any potential gains?
- Is energy being diverted from goal accomplishment?

Discussion Consideration
Ask students for examples of when group conflict that is not well managed might lead to "mob behavior."

If the majority of the answers to these questions are yes, then the conflict is probably dysfunctional. Once the manager has diagnosed the type of conflict, he or she can either work to resolve it (if it is dysfunctional) or to stimulate it (if it is functional).

One occasion in which managers should work to stimulate conflict is when they suspect their group is suffering from groupthink, discussed in Chapter 10.[12] When a group fails to consider alternative solutions and becomes stagnant in its thinking, it might benefit from healthy disagreements. Teams exhibiting symptoms of groupthink should be encouraged to consider creative problem solving and should appoint a devil's advocate to point out opposing perspectives. These actions can help stimulate constructive conflict in a group. Evidence indicates that structured decision-making techniques like *dialectical* inquiry can be used to stimulate cognitive conflict, as shown in the Scientific Foundation feature.

Causes of Conflict in Organizations

■ Conflict is pervasive in organizations. To manage it effectively, managers should understand the many sources of conflict. They can be classified into two broad categories: structural factors, which stem from the nature of the organization and the way in which work is organized, and personal factors, which arise from differences among individuals. Figure 13.1 summarizes the causes of conflict within each category.

Structural Factors

The causes of conflict related to the organization's structure include specialization, interdependence, common resources, goal differences, authority relationships, status inconsistencies, and jurisdictional ambiguities.

SPECIALIZATION When jobs are highly specialized, employees become experts at certain tasks. For example, at one software company, there is one specialist for databases, one for statistical packages, and another for expert systems. Highly specialized jobs can lead to conflict, because people have little awareness of the tasks that others perform.

A classic conflict of specialization is one between salespeople and engineers. Engineers are technical specialists responsible for product design and quality. Salespeople are marketing experts and liaisons with customers. Salespeople are often accused of making delivery promises to customers that engineers cannot keep because the sales force lacks the technical knowledge necessary to develop realistic delivery deadlines.

INTERDEPENDENCE Work that is interdependent requires groups or individuals to depend on one another to accomplish goals.[12] Depending on other people to get work done is fine when the process works smoothly. However, when there is a problem, it becomes very easy to blame the other party, and conflict

■ **FIGURE 13.1**

Causes of Conflict in Organizations

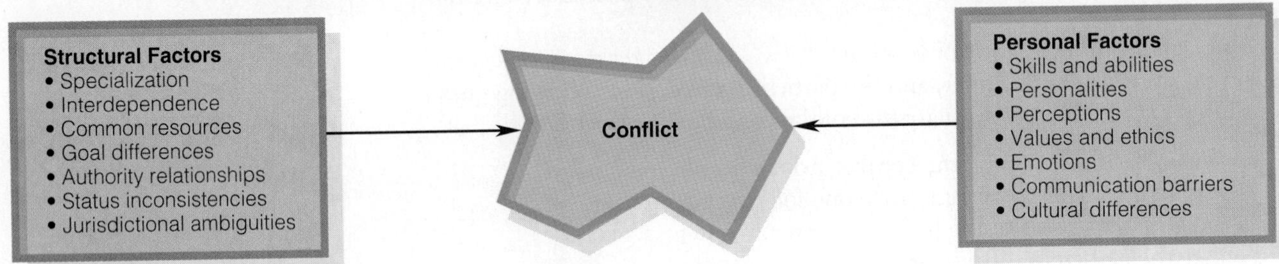

SCIENTIFIC FOUNDATION

Structured Conflict in Groups Can Have Positive Effects

Many groups experience cognitive conflict as members try to reach solutions to complex problems. Some group decision-making techniques provide a forum for this conflict, while others are more unstructured. In dialectical inquiry, the group is divided into two subgroups that debate each other until both groups agree on a solution. In the consensus method, participants are told to treat conflict as a positive part of decision making and to try to reach consensus rather than to make a hasty decision by voting, flipping coins, or by using other simple techniques. Thus dialectical inquiry is a more structured way of introducing conflict into the decision-making process. In this study it was predicted that dialectical inquiry would strengthen group consensus, increase individuals' commitment to the group's decision, and increase members' satisfaction with the group.

Thirty-eight four-person groups of undergraduate business students participated in the study during their senior-level capstone course. The student groups were asked to work on a case exercise that involved a realistic managerial scenario. Their tasks were to develop solutions to the case. Nineteen of the groups used the consensus method and nineteen used the dialectical inquiry method. Assignments to groups and to decision-making methods were made randomly.

The results supported the hypotheses. Group consensus on the decision, individual acceptance of the decision, and member satisfaction with the group were higher in the dialectical inquiry groups than in the consensus groups. It seems that providing a structured way of introducing conflict in a group can have positive results. Acceptance of solutions, commitment to them, and member satisfaction can contribute to the long-term effectiveness of the group. The downside is that the dialectical inquiry method, because it is more structured, is more complicated and may be met with less enthusiasm by group members.

SOURCE: R. L. Priem, D. A. Harrison, and N. K. Muir, "Structured Conflict and Consensus Outcomes in Group Decision Making," *Journal of Management* 21 (1995): 691–710.

escalates. In a garment manufacturing plant, for example, when the fabric cutters get behind in their work, the workers who sew the garments are delayed as well. Considerable frustration may result when the workers at the sewing machines feel their efforts are being blocked by the cutters' slow pace.

COMMON RESOURCES Any time multiple parties must share resources, there is potential for conflict.[13] This potential is enhanced when the shared resources become scarce. One resource often shared by managers is secretarial support. It is not uncommon for a secretary to support ten or more managers, each of whom believes his or her work is most important. This puts pressure on the secretaries and leads to potential conflicts in prioritizing and scheduling work.

GOAL DIFFERENCES When work groups have different goals, these goals may be incompatible. For example, in one cable television company, the salesperson's goal was to sell as many new installations as possible. This created problems for the service department, because its goal was timely installations. With increasing sales, the service department's work load became backed up, and orders were delayed. Often these types of conflicts occur because individuals do not have knowledge of another department's objectives.

AUTHORITY RELATIONSHIPS The nature of a traditional boss-employee relationship brings to mind a vision of a hierarchy or of a boss who is superior to the employee. For many employees, this relationship is not a comfortable one, because another individual has the right to tell them what to do. Some people resent authority more than others, and obviously this creates conflicts. In addition, some bosses are more autocratic than others; this compounds the potential for conflict in the relationship. As organizations move toward the team approach and empowerment, there should be less potential for conflict from authority relationships.

STATUS INCONSISTENCIES Some organizations have a strong status difference between management and nonmanagement workers. Managers may enjoy privileges—such as flexible schedules, personal telephone calls at work, and longer lunch hours—that are not available to nonmanagement employees. This may result in resentment and conflict.

jurisdictional ambiguity
The presence of unclear lines of responsibility within an organization.

JURISDICTIONAL AMBIGUITIES Have you ever telephoned a company with a problem and had your call transferred through several different people and departments? This situation illustrates **jurisdictional ambiguity**—that is, unclear lines of responsibility within an organization.[14] When a problem occurs for which there is no definite source of responsibility, workers tend to "pass the buck," or avoid dealing with the problem. Conflicts emerge over responsibility for the problem.

The factors just discussed are structural in that they arise from the ways in which work is organized. Other conflicts come from differences among individuals.

Personal Factors

The causes of conflict that arise from individual differences include skills and abilities, personalities, perceptions, values and ethics, emotions and communication barriers.

SKILLS AND ABILITIES The work force is composed of individuals with varying levels of skills and ability. Diversity in skills and abilities may be positive for the organization, but it also holds potential for conflict, especially when jobs are interdependent. Experienced, competent workers may find it difficult to work alongside new and unskilled recruits. Workers can become resentful when their new boss, fresh from college, knows a lot about managing people but is unfamiliar with the technology with which they are working.

PERSONALITIES Individuals do not leave their personalities at the doorstep when they enter the workplace. Personality conflicts are realities in organizations. To expect that you will like all of your coworkers may be a naive expectation, as would be the expectation that they will all like you.

One personality trait that many people find difficult to deal with is abrasiveness.[15] An abrasive person is one who ignores the interpersonal aspects of work and the feelings of colleagues. Abrasive individuals are often achievement oriented and hardworking, but their perfectionist, critical style often leaves others feeling unimportant. This style creates stress and strain for those around the abrasive person.[16]

Discussion Consideration
Ask students to identify specific perception and personality issues that have led to conflict in their lives.

PERCEPTIONS Differences in perception can also lead to conflict. One area in which perceptions can differ is the perception of what motivates employees. If managers and workers do not have a shared perception of what motivates people, the reward system can create conflicts. Managers usually provide what they think employees want rather than what employees really want.

VALUES AND ETHICS Differences in values and ethics can be sources of disagreement. Older workers, for example, value company loyalty and probably would not take a sick day when they were not really ill. Younger workers, valuing mobility, like the concept of "mental health days," or calling in sick to get away from work. This may not be true for all workers, but it illustrates that differences in values can lead to conflict.

Most people have their own sets of values and ethics. The extent to which they apply these ethics in the workplace varies. Some people have strong desires for approval from others and will work to meet others' ethical standards. Some people are relatively unconcerned with approval from others and strongly apply their own ethical standards. Still others operate seemingly without regard to ethics or values.[17] When conflicts over values or ethics do arise, heated disagreement is common because of the personal nature of the differences.

EMOTIONS The moods of others can be a source of conflict in the workplace. Problems at home often spill over into the work arena, and the related moods can be hard for others to deal with.

COMMUNICATION BARRIERS Communication barriers such as physical separation and language can create distortions in messages, and these can lead to conflict. Another communication barrier is value judgment, in which a listener assigns a worth to a message before it is received. For example, suppose a team member is a chronic complainer. When this individual enters the manager's office, the manager is likely to devalue the message before it is even delivered. Conflict can then emerge. Many other communication barriers can lead to conflict. These were discussed in Chapter 8.

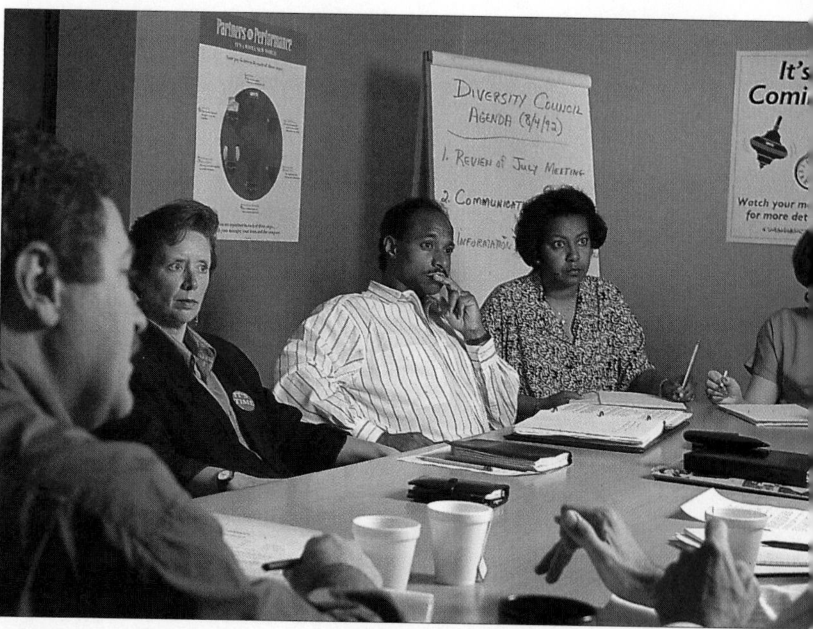

Diversity in the workplace can lead to conflict from differences in values and perceptions. Levi-Strauss & Co., uses diversity councils like this one to help employees improve communication issues.

Globalization and Conflict

■ Large transnational corporations employ many different ethnic and cultural groups. In these multiethnic corporations, the widely differing cultures represent vast differences among individuals, so the potential for conflict increases.[18] As indicated in Chapter 2, Hofstede has identified five dimensions along which cultural differences may emerge: individualism/collectivism, power distance, uncertainty avoidance, masculinity/femininity, and long-term/short-term orientation.[19] These cultural differences have many implications for conflict management in organizations.

Individualism means that people believe that their individual interests take priority over society's interests. Collectivism, in contrast, means that people put the good of the group first. For example, the United States is a highly individualistic culture, whereas Japan is a very collectivist culture. The individualism/collectivism dimension of cultural differences strongly influences conflict management behavior. People from collectivist cultures tend to display a more cooperative approach to managing conflict.[20]

Alternate Example
One of the inherent disadvantages of ethnocentricism is the belief that we are always right in conflicts. Most countries at war claim God is on their side.

Hofstede's second dimension of cultural differences is power distance. In cultures with high power distance, individuals accept that people in organizations have varying levels of power. In contrast, in cultures with low power distance, individuals do not automatically respect those in positions of authority. For example, the United States is a country of low power distance, whereas Brazil is a country with a high power distance. Differences in power distance can lead to conflict. Imagine a U.S. employee managed by a Brazilian supervisor who expects deferential behavior. The supervisor would expect automatic respect based on legitimate power. When this respect was not given, conflict would arise.

Uncertainty avoidance also varies by culture. In the United States, employees can tolerate high levels of uncertainty. However, employees in Israel tend to prefer certainty in their work settings. A U.S.–based multinational firm might run into conflicts operating in Israel. Suppose such a firm were installing a new technology. Its expatriate workers from the United States would tolerate the uncertainty of the technological transition better than would their Israeli coworkers, and this might lead to conflicts among the employees.

Masculinity versus femininity illustrates the contrast between preferences for assertiveness and material goods versus preferences for human capital and quality of life. The United States is a masculine society, whereas Sweden is considered a feminine society. Adjustment to the assertive interpersonal style of U.S. workers may be difficult for Swedish coworkers.

Discussion Consideration
When conflicts arise between two cultures, how do you decide which culture's values are appropriate?

Conflicts can also arise between cultures that vary in their time orientation of values. China, for example, has a long-term orientation; the Chinese prefer values that focus on the future, such as saving and persistence. The United States and Russia, in contrast, have short-term orientations. These cultures emphasize values in the past and present, such as respect for tradition and fulfillment of social obligations. Conflicts can arise when managers fail to understand the nature of differences in values.

An organization whose work force consists of multiple ethnicities and cultures holds potential for many types of conflict because of the sheer volume of individual differences among workers. The key to managing conflict in a multicultural work force is understanding cultural differences and appreciating their value.

Forms of Conflict in Organizations

■ Conflict can take on any of several different forms in an organization, including interorganizational, intergroup, interpersonal, and intrapersonal conflicts. It is important to note that the prefix *inter* means "between," whereas the prefix *intra* means "within."

Interorganizational Conflict

interorganizational conflict
Conflict that occurs between two or more organizations.

Conflict that occurs between two or more organizations is called **interorganizational conflict.** The Southwest Airlines example in the Opening Spotlight is one illustration of this form of conflict. Other examples of interorganizational conflict are corporate takeover attempts, such as AT&T's struggle to gain control of NCR. Although the takeover was finally accomplished, it proved to be a tough one for AT&T, because in one meeting AT&T could not gather enough shareholder votes to oust the majority of NCR's board.[21] Competition among organizations also can spur interorganizational conflict, as seen in the ongoing rivalries between the U.S. and Japanese automakers.

http://www.att.com

Conflicts between a company and a union may constitute interorganizational conflict. In Germany during February 1992, the powerful IG Metall union of steelworkers endorsed a strike over higher wages. The strike especially threatened Volkswagen and Daimler-Benz, which alerted workers that production standstills might be forthcoming because of lack of steel reserves.[22]

Intergroup Conflict

intergroup conflict
Conflict that occurs between groups or teams in an organization.

When conflict occurs between groups or teams, it is known as **intergroup conflict**. Conflict between groups can have predictable effects within each group, such as increased group cohesiveness, increased focus on tasks, and increased loyalty to the group.[23] In addition, groups in conflict tend to develop an "us against them" mentality whereby each sees the other team as the enemy, becomes more hostile, and decreases its communication with the other group.

Competition between groups must be managed carefully so that it does not escalate into dysfunctional conflict. Research has shown that when groups compete for a goal that only one group can achieve, negative consequences like territoriality, aggression, and prejudice toward the other group can result.[24]

Interpersonal Conflict

Conflict between two or more people is **interpersonal conflict**. Many individual differences lead to conflict between people, including personalities, attitudes, values, perceptions, and the other differences we discussed in Chapters 3 and 4. Later in this chapter, we look at defense mechanisms that individuals exhibit in interpersonal conflict and at ways to cope with difficult people.

Intrapersonal Conflict

When conflict occurs within an individual, it is called **intrapersonal conflict**. There are several types of intrapersonal conflict, including interrole, intrarole, and person-role conflicts. A role is a set of expectations placed on an individual by others.[25] The person occupying the focal role is the role incumbent, and the individuals who place expectations on the person are role senders. Figure 13.2 depicts a set of role relationships.

Interrole conflict occurs when a person experiences conflict among the multiple roles in his or her life. One interrole conflict that many employees experience is work/home conflict, in which their role as worker clashes with their role as spouse or parent.[26] For example, when a child gets sick at school, the parent often must leave work to care for the child.

Intrarole conflict is conflict within a single role. It often arises when a person receives conflicting messages from role senders about how to perform a certain role. Suppose a manager receives counsel from her department head that she needs to socialize less with the nonmanagement employees. She also is told by her project manager that she needs to be a better team member, and that she can accomplish this by socializing more with the other nonmanagement team members. This situation is one of intrarole conflict.

Person-role conflict occurs when an individual in a particular role is expected to perform behaviors that clash with his or her values.[27] Salespeople, for example, may be required to offer the most expensive item in the sales line

interpersonal conflict
Conflict that occurs between two or more individuals.

intrapersonal conflict
Conflict that occurs within an individual.

interrole conflict
A person's experience of conflict among the multiple roles in his or her life.

intrarole conflict
Conflict that occurs within a single role, such as when a person receives conflicting messages from role senders about how to perform a certain role.

person-role conflict
Conflict that occurs when an individual is expected to perform behaviors in a certain role that conflict with his or her personal values.

FIGURE 13.2

An Organization Member's Role Set

SOURCE: J. C. Quick and J. D. Quick, *Organizational Stress and Preventive Management* (New York: McGraw-Hill, 1948): 205. Reproduced with permission of McGraw Hill, Inc.

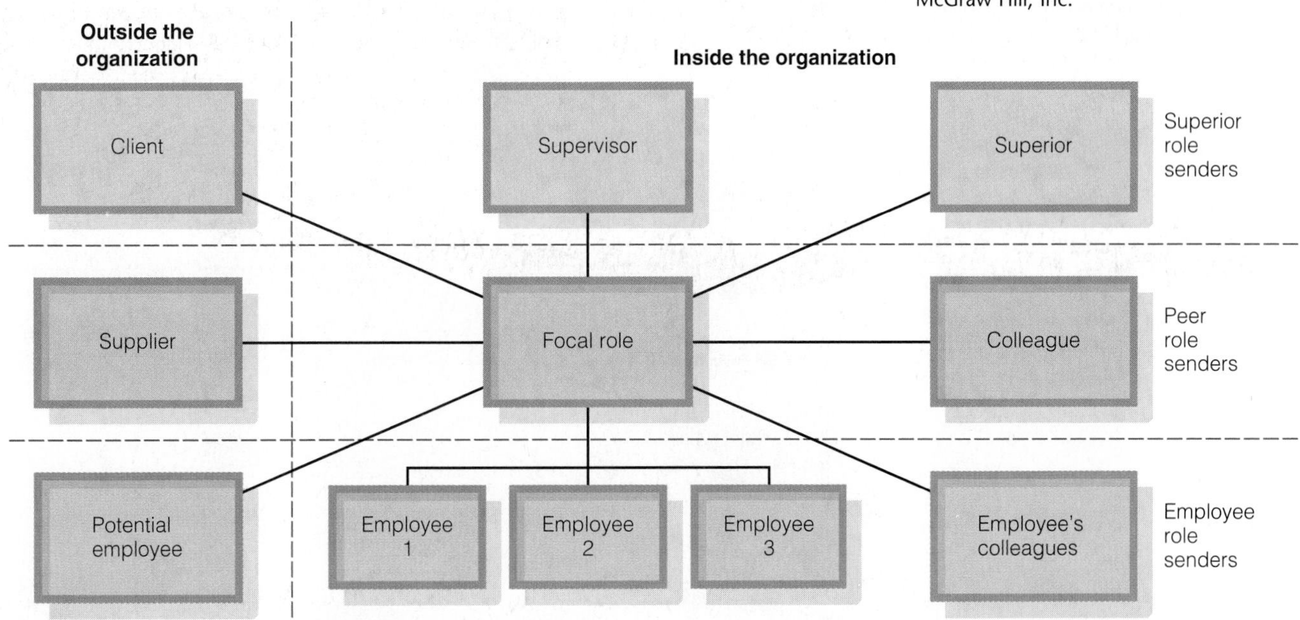

first to the customer, even when it is apparent that the customer does not want or cannot afford the item. A computer salesman may be required to offer a large, elaborate system to a student he knows is on a tight budget. This may conflict with the salesman's values, and he may experience person-role conflict.

Discussion Consideration
Of the forms of conflict listed, which creates the most distress for students?

All these forms of conflict can be managed. An understanding of the many forms is a first step. The next section focuses more extensively on interpersonal conflict because of its pervasiveness in organizations.

Interpersonal Conflict

Points to Emphasize
Some students from other countries experience intrarole conflict in classes with high levels of student participation. They may come from cultures where the professor is not to be questioned and is expected to have all the answers.

■ When a conflict occurs between two or more people, it is known as interpersonal conflict. To manage interpersonal conflict, it is helpful to understand power networks in organizations, defense mechanisms exhibited by individuals, and ways to cope with difficult people.

Power Networks

According to Mastenbroek, individuals in organizations are organized in three basic types of power networks.[28] Based on these power relationships, certain kinds of conflict tend to emerge. Figure 13.3 illustrates three basic kinds of power relationships in organizations.

The first relationship is equal versus equal, in which there is a horizontal balance of power among the parties. An example of this type of relationship would be a conflict between individuals from two different project teams. The behavioral tendency is toward suboptimization; that is, the focus is on a win-lose approach to problems, and each party tries to maximize its power at the expense of the other party. Interventions like improving coordination between the parties and working toward common interests can help manage these conflicts.

■ **FIGURE 13.3**

Power Relationships in Organizations

SOURCE: W. F. G. Mastenbroek, *Conflict Management and Organizational Development.* Copyright © 1987. John Wiley and Sons, Ltd. Reprinted by permission of John Wiley and Sons, Ltd.

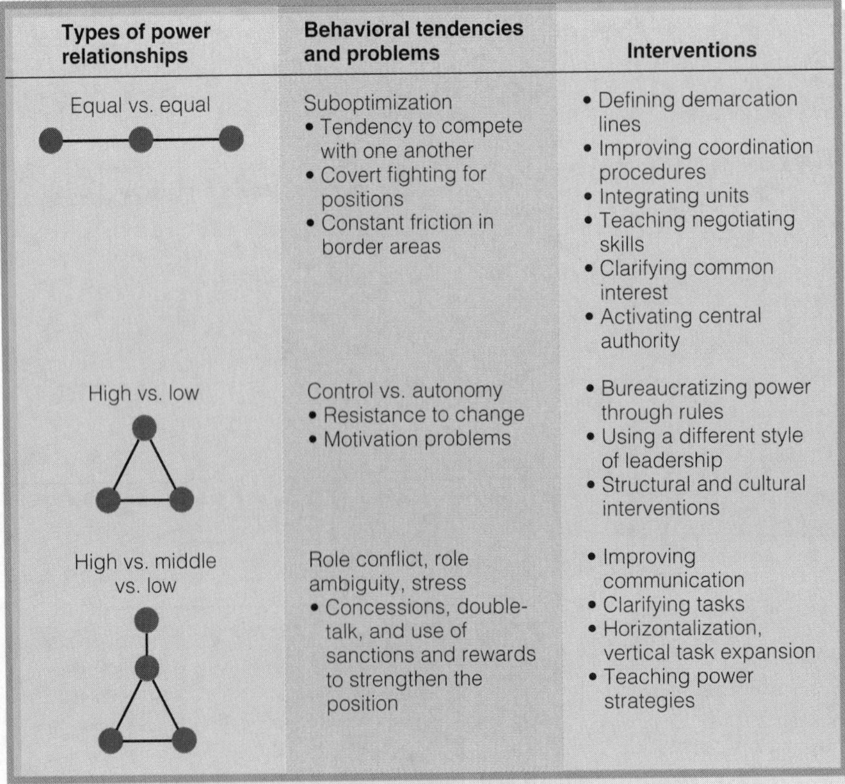

Types of power relationships	Behavioral tendencies and problems	Interventions
Equal vs. equal	Suboptimization • Tendency to compete with one another • Covert fighting for positions • Constant friction in border areas	• Defining demarcation lines • Improving coordination procedures • Integrating units • Teaching negotiating skills • Clarifying common interest • Activating central authority
High vs. low	Control vs. autonomy • Resistance to change • Motivation problems	• Bureaucratizing power through rules • Using a different style of leadership • Structural and cultural interventions
High vs. middle vs. low	Role conflict, role ambiguity, stress • Concessions, double-talk, and use of sanctions and rewards to strengthen the position	• Improving communication • Clarifying tasks • Horizontalization, vertical task expansion • Teaching power strategies

The second power network is high versus low, or a powerful versus a less powerful relationship. Conflicts that merge here take the basic form of the powerful individuals trying to control others, with the less powerful people trying to become more autonomous. Organizations typically respond to these conflicts by tightening the rules. However, the more successful ways of managing these conflicts are to try a different style of leadership, such as a coaching and counseling style, or to change the structure to a more decentralized one.

Discussion Consideration
Are women and minority groups at a disadvantage in power networks?

The third power network is high versus middle versus low. This power network illustrates the classic conflicts felt by middle managers. Two particular conflicts are evident for middle managers: role conflict, in which conflicting expectations are placed on the manager from bosses and employees, and role ambiguity, in which the expectations of the boss are unclear. Improved communication among all parties can reduce role conflict and ambiguity. In addition, middle managers can benefit from education in positive ways to influence others.

Knowing the typical kinds of conflicts that arise in various kinds of relationships can help a manager diagnose conflicts and devise appropriate ways to manage them. The Organizational Reality feature describes a conflict at Kiwi International Airlines that threatened the company's survival. As you can see, Kiwi's employee owners saw the power structure differently than did the members of the voting trust that controlled the company.

Points to Emphasize
One of the major reasons conflicts are not resolved in negotiations is that we typically wait too long to express them. This results in emotional approaches or defense mechanisms.

Defense Mechanisms

When individuals are involved in conflict with another human being, frustration often results.[29] Conflicts can often arise within the context of a performance appraisal session. Most people do not react well to negative feedback, as was illustrated in a classic study.[30] In this study, when employees were given criticism about their work, over 50 percent of their responses were defensive.

When individuals are frustrated, as they often are in interpersonal conflict, they respond by exhibiting defense mechanisms.[31] Defense mechanisms are common reactions to the frustration that accompanies conflict. Table 13.2 illustrates several defense mechanisms seen in organizations.

Aggressive mechanisms are aimed at attacking the source of the conflict. Some of these are fixation, displacement, and negativism. In **fixation**, an individual fixates on the conflict, or keeps up a dysfunctional behavior that obviously will not solve the conflict. An example of fixation occurred in a university, where a faculty member became embroiled in a battle with the dean because the faculty member felt he had not received a large enough salary increase. He persisted in writing angry letters to the dean, whose hands were tied because of a low budget allocation to the college. **Displacement** means directing anger toward someone who is not the source of the conflict. For example, a manager may respond harshly to an employee after a telephone confrontation with an angry customer. Another aggressive defense mechanism is **negativism,** which is active or passive resistance. Negativism is illustrated by a manager who, when appointed to a committee on which she did not want to serve, made negative comments throughout the meeting.

Compromise mechanisms are used by individuals to make the best of a conflict situation. Three compromise mechanisms include compensation, identification, and rationalization. **Compensation** occurs when an individual tries to make up for an inadequacy by putting increased energy into another activity. Compensation can be seen when a person makes up for a bad relationship at home by spending more time at the office. **Identification** occurs when one individual patterns his or her behavior after another's. One supervisor at a construction firm, not wanting to acknowledge consciously that she was not likely to be promoted, mimicked the behavior of her boss, even going so far as to buy a car just like the boss's. **Rationalization** is trying to justify one's behavior by constructing bogus

fixation
An aggressive mechanism in which an individual keeps up a dysfunctional behavior that obviously will not solve the conflict.

displacement
An aggressive mechanism in which an individual directs his or her anger toward someone who is not the source of the conflict.

negativism
An aggressive mechanism in which a person responds with pessimism to any attempt at solving a problem.

compensation
A compromise mechanism in which an individual attempts to make up for a negative situation by devoting himself or herself to another pursuit with increased vigor.

identification
A compromise mechanism whereby an individual patterns his or her behavior after another's.

rationalization
A compromise mechanism characterized by trying to justify one's behavior by constructing bogus reasons for it.

ORGANIZATIONAL REALITY

Employee-Owners with No Voice Stir Things Up at Kiwi

Kiwi International Airlines was started in 1992 when Robert Iverson and some of his fellow pilots pooled their money following the collapse of Eastern Airlines. Employee ownership was the theme of the venture. Pilots and other highly paid employees had to invest $50,000 and other employees had to invest $5,000. Customer service was great—pilots helped clean the planes, and employees volunteered to work at half pay to help the airline survive the fare wars. The company won top honors in quality surveys.

Kiwi is no longer one big happy family. Robert Iverson, along with several of his top executives, was dismissed and escorted out the door in the "Groundhog Day Massacre." A $24 million loss in 1994 almost led to bankruptcy. Since then, Kiwi has gone through four top executives in a single year. What caused the problems?

Many feel that conflict over employee ownership is the root of the problems. Although the company is 100 percent employee-owned, workers have no voice. Kiwi's founders gave all the decision-making power to seven pilot-directors in a "voting trust." These seven people control virtually everything the airline does. Employees who were forced to invest in the company felt that their investments entitled them to equal say in running the company. Many employees ignored the directives of management. Pilots refused to fly charter trips, and flight attendants refused to make promotional announcements. Meetings at Kiwi dragged on for hours because every "owner" wanted to have a say. Employees gave free tickets to charities without permission. Former CEO Iverson has said, "One of the stupidest things I ever did was call everybody owners . . . an owner is somebody who thinks he can exercise gratuitous control."

Kiwi is starved for capital and is struggling to gain momentum. A new CEO, the fourth in a year, was hired from outside the company. Jerry Murphy intends to instill a new degree of discipline at Kiwi. "I think one needs to recognize that this company is employee-run, but you need to run it as a business . . . I don't care who owns it. A line needs to be drawn." It remains to be seen whether drawing the line will save the airline.

SOURCES: A. Bryant, "One Big Happy Family No Longer," *New York Times*, March 22, 1995, D1-2; C. Quintanilla, "Kiwi's Pilots are Bailing Out of the Company Cockpit," *Wall Street Journal*, September 19, 1995, B4-3.

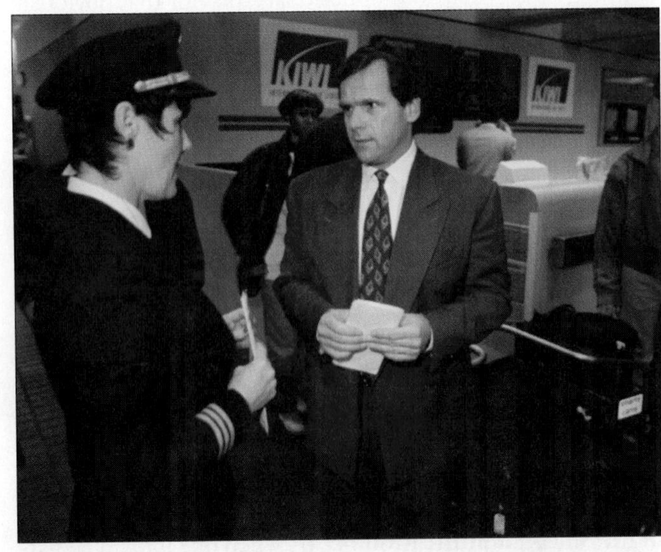

Kiwi International Airlines has seen both good and bad days, in terms of conflict. Multiple employee-owners all wanted to have their say in running the airline, and the ensuing conflicts threatened the airline's survival.

■ **TABLE 13.2**

Common Defense Mechanisms

DEFENSE MECHANISM	PSYCHOLOGICAL PROCESS
	Aggressive Mechanisms
• Fixation	Person maintains a persistent, nonadjustive reaction even though all the cues indicate the behavior will not cope with the problem.
• Displacement	Individual redirects pent-up emotions toward persons, ideas, or objects other than the primary source of the emotion.
• Negativism	Person uses active or passive resistance, operating unconsciously.
	Compromise Mechanisms
• Compensation	Individual devotes himself or herself to a pursuit with increased vigor to make up for some feeling of real or imagined inadequacy.
• Identification	Individual enhances own self-esteem by patterning behavior after another's, frequently also internalizing the values and beliefs of the other person; also vicariously shares the glories or suffering in the disappointments of other individuals or groups.
• Rationalization	Person justifies inconsistent or undesirable behavior, beliefs, statements, and motivations by providing acceptable explanations for them.
	Withdrawal Mechanisms
• Flight or withdrawal	Person leaves the field in which frustration, anxiety, or conflict is experienced, either physically or psychologically.
• Conversion	Emotional conflicts are expressed in muscular, sensory, or bodily symptoms of disability, malfunctioning, or pain.
• Fantasy	Person daydreams or uses other forms of imaginative activity to obtain an escape from reality and obtain imagined satisfactions.

SOURCE: Adapted from Timothy W. Costello and Sheldon S. Zalkind, "Psychology in Administration: A Research Orientation." (First appeared in *Journal of Conflict Resolution,* III, 1959, pp. 148–149).

reasons for it. Employees may rationalize unethical behavior like padding their expense accounts because "everyone else does it."

Withdrawal mechanisms are exhibited when frustrated individuals try to flee from a conflict using either physical or psychological means. Flight, conversion, and fantasy are examples of withdrawal mechanisms. Physically escaping a conflict is **flight**. An employee who takes a day off after a blowup with the boss is an example. **Conversion** is a process whereby emotional conflicts become expressed in physical symptoms. Most of us have experienced the conversion reaction of a headache following an emotional exchange with another person. **Fantasy** is an escape by daydreaming. An excellent example of fantasy was shown in the movie *9 to 5*, in which Dolly Parton, Lily Tomlin, and Jane Fonda played characters who fantasized about torturing their boss because he was such a tyrant.

Knowledge of these defense mechanisms can be extremely beneficial to a manager. By understanding the ways in which people typically react to interpersonal conflict, managers can be prepared for employees' reactions and help them uncover their feelings about a conflict.

Discussion Consideration

Ask students to reflect on their own behavior. Which of the defense mechanisms do they commonly use?

flight

A withdrawal mechanism that entails physically escaping a conflict.

conversion

A withdrawal mechanism in which emotional conflicts that are expressed in physical symptoms.

fantasy

A withdrawal mechanism that provides an escape from a conflict through daydreaming.

Coping with Difficult People

Many interpersonal conflicts arise when one person finds another person's behavior uncomfortable, irritating, or bothersome in one way or another. Robert Bramson has identified seven basic types of difficult people that may be encountered at work.[32] Table 13.3 presents seven types of difficult people, along with suggestions for coping with them.

Alternate Example
Some employees agree to do things they don't want to do. This results in internalized conflict and grudges. A superagreeable person may leave the impression that the other individual has won in a situation; yet, the conflict is merely delayed.
SOURCE: K. Rottenberger, "How do you Handle Conflicts with Superiors and Subordinates?" *Sales and Marketing Management*, July 1992, 32–33.

Hostile-aggressives bully other people by bombarding them with cutting remarks, or throwing a tantrum when things do not go their way. Their focus is on attacking the other party in a conflict. Openly emotional, they use these displays to create discomfort or surprise in their adversaries. Underlying their behavior is a strong sense of "shoulds," internal rules about the way things ought to be. A key to dealing with hostile-aggressives is to recognize the behavior and not to be drawn into it yourself.

Complainers gripe constantly but never take action about what they complain about, usually because they feel powerless or they do not want to take responsibility. You may want to hear complainers out and let them know you understand their feelings, but do not get drawn into pitying them. Use a problem solving stance. For instance, a manager might say, "Joan, what do you want the outcome of our meeting to be? What action needs to be taken?" This focuses the complainer on solutions, not complaints.

Clams are silent and unresponsive when asked for opinions. They react to conflict by closing up (like their namesakes) and refusing to discuss problems. The challenge in coping with clams is getting them to open up and talk. Open-ended questions are invaluable, as is patience in allowing them their silence for a reasonable time. If a coworker is avoiding you and has refused to talk, "Are you angry with me?" may not be a good question. "Why are you avoiding me?" may be better. If no response is forthcoming, you might try direct action. "Since you won't discuss this, I'm going to assume that there's nothing wrong and sign us both up for the company volleyball team."

Superagreeables are often charming individuals who are sincere and helpful to your face, but they fail to do what they promise when you leave. A service manager at an auto dealership may listen attentively to the problems you report with your new car, dutifully write them down, and assure you that they will be taken care of. When you pick up the car, however, none of the problems are resolved. Does this sound familiar? These people are often conflict avoiders and make unrealistic promises to avoid a confrontation. Be prepared to compromise on a solution, and make sure it is workable. Finally, if you get a humorous response from a superagreeable, look for the hidden meaning in it.

Negativists respond to any attempts to solve a problem with pessimism. They are dangerous, because their negativism is contagious, and you may lose your optimism about solving the problem in interacting with them. A problem-solving mode is appropriate in this case; let the negativist bring up alternative solutions. Play devil's advocate, bringing up the negative aspects yourself. You may also want to ask, "What is the worst that might happen?" When the negativists are convinced that they can handle even the worst-case scenario, they may feel more in control.

Know-it-alls display superior attitudes, wanting you to know that they know everything there is to know about everything. If they really know what they are talking about, they are bulldozers. Bulldozers overrun individuals with their blustery style, and they are most aggravating because they are always right. To cope with bulldozers, you need to be prepared. They will respect you if you have done your homework. Phony experts are known as balloons. Balloons only think they know everything. To deal with them, state your position as your own perception of the situation. It is also important to allow the balloon to save face when deflated, so confront the balloon in private. A new professor, when asked to explain a particular statistical technique to his new colleagues, provided a

TABLE 13.3

Coping Tactics for Dealing with Difficult People

HOSTILE-AGGRESSIVE:
■ Stand up for yourself. ■ Give them time to run down. ■ Use self-assertive language. ■ Avoid a direct confrontation.
COMPLAINERS:
■ Listen attentively. ■ Acknowledge their feelings. ■ Avoid complaining with them. ■ State the facts without apology. ■ Use a problem-solving mode.
CLAMS:
■ Ask open-ended questions. ■ Be patient in waiting for a response. ■ Ask more open-ended questions. ■ If no response occurs, tell clams what you plan to do, because no discussion has taken place.
SUPERAGREEABLES:
■ In a nonthreatening manner, work hard to find out why they will not take action. ■ Let them know you value them as people. ■ Be ready to compromise and negotiate, and do not allow them to make unrealistic commitments. ■ Try to discern the hidden meaning in their humor.
NEGATIVISTS:
■ Do not be dragged into their despair. ■ Do not try to cajole them out of their negativism. ■ Discuss the problem thoroughly, without offering solutions. ■ When alternatives are discussed, bring up the negative side yourself. ■ Be ready to take action alone, without their agreement.
KNOW-IT-ALLS:
Bulldozers: ■ Prepare yourself. ■ Listen and paraphrase their main points. ■ Use the questioning form to raise problems. *Balloons:* ■ State facts or opinions as your own perceptions of reality. ■ Find a way for balloons to save face. ■ Confront balloons, alone, not in public.
INDECISIVE STALLERS:
■ Raise the issue of why they are hesitant. ■ If you are the problem, ask for help. ■ Keep the action steps in your own hands. ■ Possibly remove the staller from the situation.

SOURCE: From *Coping with Difficult People,* Robert M. Bramson. Copyright © 1981 by Robert M. Bramson. Used by permission of Doubleday, a division of Bantum Doubleday Dell Publishing Group, Inc.

faulty explanation. This new professor was a balloon, eager to display his expertise. A wise, seasoned professor took the newcomer aside after the presentation and said, "I think my old pal Professor Windbag at State U. misinformed you on that statistic. Let me show you a book I have that explains it." The new professor's face was saved and his factual knowledge enhanced.

Points to Emphasize
Technology and information may provide convenient excuses for stalling when we are not getting our way. That is, we state that we do not have enough information to make an informed decision.

Indecisive stallers put off decisions until they have no choice, or they fail to come to a decision at all. Stallers often are genuinely concerned about others and are afraid that no matter what they decide, they will alienate or fail to please someone. The key in coping with stallers is to uncover the reasons for their hesitation. You must take responsibility to ensure that the staller follows through. If stallers are too disruptive, you may want to remove them from the decision situation.

In coping with difficult people, it is important to identify the reasons you perceive them as difficult. Bramson's framework helps accompish this. In addition, you should analyze your response to the difficult person. Challenge 13.1 can help you proactively manage a relationship with a difficult person in your life.

Intrapersonal Conflict

■ Intrapersonal conflict, or conflict within an individual related to social roles, can be managed with careful self analysis and diagnosis of the situation. Two actions in particular can help prevent or resolve intrapersonal conflicts.

First, when seeking a new job, applicants should find out as much as possible about the values of the organization.[33] Many person-role conflicts center around differences between the organization's values and the individual's values. Research has shown that when there is a good fit between the values of the individual and the organization, the individual is more satisfied and committed and is less likely to leave the organization.[34]

Second, to manage intrarole or interrole conflicts, role analysis is a good tool.[35] In role analysis, the individual asks the various role senders what they expect of him or her. The outcomes are clearer work roles and the reduction of conflict and ambiguity.[36]

Conflict Management Strategies and Techniques

■ Several strategies can be used to manage conflict in organizations. We examine both effective and ineffective ways of managing conflict.

One way to evaluate conflict management strategies is to examine the win or loss potential for the parties involved, as well as for the organization. To do so, we can use the framework of competitive versus cooperative strategies. Table 13.4 depicts the two strategies and four different conflict scenarios. The competitive strategy is founded on assumptions of win-lose and entails less-than-honest communication, distrust, and a rigid position from both parties.[37] The

■ **TABLE 13.4**

Win-Lose versus Win-Win Strategies

STRATEGY	DEPARTMENT A	DEPARTMENT B	ORGANIZATION
Competitive	Lose	Lose	Lose
	Lose	Win	Lose
	Win	Lose	Lose
Cooperative	Win–	Win–	Win

CHALLENGE

1. Describe, in as much detail as you can, the behavior of a difficult person in your life.
2. What kind of difficult person is he or she? What are some possible reasons for his or her behavior?
3. Think of your own behavior in past interactions with that person. What kind of defense mechanisms do you exhibit? In what situations is the interaction more positive? In what situations does the interaction seem worse?
4. What coping behavior will be most useful in coping with the difficult person you have described?
5. Review your answer to Question 3. What do you need to change in your own behavior to make the interactions more positive?
6. What specifically will you do to cope with this difficult person? By what date?

13.1

Action Plan for Coping with Difficult People

cooperative strategy is founded on different assumptions: the potential for win-win outcomes, honest communication, trust, openness to risk and vulnerability, and the notion that the whole may be greater than the sum of the parts.

Suppose there is a conflict in a telephone company between service representatives (who deal with customers calling in with problems) and installers (who go to customers' homes to put in telephones). The service representatives (Department A) feel that the installers are not doing quality work and that this lack of quality increases the customer complaints that the service reps must handle. The installers (Department B) feel that the service representatives make unreasonable promises to customers about scheduling their telephone installations.

If no action is taken, both departments and the company as a whole are in a losing mode. Customer complaints will continue to increase, and hostilities between the departments will continue. This is a lose-lose approach.

If the installers demand that the service reps adhere strictly to a reasonable schedule for taking customer orders, it will eliminate part of the conflict. Or, if the service reps insist that the installers begin a service quality program, part of the conflict will be handled. Both of these scenarios, however, are win-lose approaches that do not completely solve the conflict. One group gets its demands satisfied, whereas the other group does not; therefore, the company ends up in a losing posture regarding the conflict.

To construct a win-win solution, the groups must cooperate. The service representatives could adhere to a reasonable schedule, consulting the installers when exceptional cases arise. The installers could institute a service quality program, which would help reduce the complaint calls fielded by the service representatives. This represents a win-win solution whereby the company is in a winning position following the conflict. Both parties have conceded something (note the "win−" in Table 13.4), but the conflict has been resolved with a positive outcome.

Alternate Example
Women are typically advancers of and succeeders at the win-win approach to conflict, in part because they are good at picking up subtle cues that indicate how well negotiations are going. SOURCE: "Women at the Table," *Psychology Today,* September-October 1992, 11.

Consistently adopting a win-lose, competitive approach to interpersonal conflict can be dangerous. Seeking mutual benefits and cooperation can be a much more effective strategy.

Ineffective Techniques

There are many techniques for dealing with conflict. Before turning to techniques that work, it should be recognized that some actions commonly taken in organizations to deal with conflict are not effective.[38]

nonaction
Doing nothing in hopes that a conflict with disappear.

Nonaction is doing nothing in hopes that the conflict will disappear. This is not generally a good technique, because most conflicts do not go away, and the individuals involved in the conflict react with frustration.

secrecy
Attempting to hide a conflict or an issue that has the potential to create conflict.

Secrecy, or trying to keep a conflict out of view of most people, only creates suspicion. An example is an organizational policy of pay secrecy. In some organizations, discussion of salary is grounds for dismissal. When this is the case, employees suspect that the company has something to hide.

administrative orbiting
Delaying action on a conflict by buying time.

Administrative orbiting is delaying action on a conflict by buying time, usually by telling the individuals involved that the problem is being worked on or that the boss is still thinking about the issue. Like nonaction, this technique leads to frustration and resentment.

due process nonaction
A procedure set up to address conflicts that is so costly, time-consuming, or personally risky that no one will use it.

Due process nonaction is a procedure set up to address conflicts that is so costly, time-consuming, or personally risky that no one will use it. Some companies' sexual harassment policies are examples of this technique. To file a sexual harassment complaint, detailed paperwork is required, the accuser must go through appropriate channels, and the accuser risks being branded a troublemaker. Thus, the company has a procedure for handling complaints (due process), but no one uses it (nonaction).

character assassination
An attempt to label or discredit an opponent.

Character assassination is an attempt to label or discredit an opponent. In the confirmation hearings of Supreme Court Justice Clarence Thomas, for example, attempts at character assassination were made upon Anita Hill by referring to her as a spurned woman and by saying she lived in fantasy. Justice Thomas was also a victim of character assassination; he was portrayed as a womanizer and a perpetrator of sexual harassment. Character assassination can backfire and make the individual who uses it appear dishonest and cruel.

Effective Techniques

Fortunately, there are effective conflict management techniques. These include appealing to superordinate goals, expanding resources, changing personnel, changing structure, and confronting and negotiating.

superordinate goal
An organizational goal that is more important to both parties in a conflict than their individual or group goals.

SUPERORDINATE GOALS An organizational goal that is more important to both parties in a conflict than their individual or group goals is a **superordinate goal.**[39] Superordinate goals cannot be achieved by an individual or by one group alone. The achievement of these goals requires cooperation by both parties.

One effective technique for resolving conflict is to appeal to a superordinate goal—in effect, to focus the parties on a larger issue on which they both agree. This helps them realize their similarities rather than their differences.

In the conflict between service representatives and telephone installers that was discussed earlier, appealing to a superordinate goal would be an effective technique for resolving the conflict. Both departments can agree that superior customer service is a goal worthy of pursuit and that this goal cannot be achieved unless telephones are installed properly and in a timely manner, and customer complaints are handled effectively. Quality service requires that both departments cooperate to achieve the goal.

EXPANDING RESOURCES One conflict resolution technique is so simple that it may be overlooked. If the conflict's source is common or scarce resources, providing more resources may be a solution. Of course, managers working with tight budgets may not have the luxury of obtaining additional resources. Nevertheless, it is a technique to be considered. In the example earlier in this chapter, one solution to the conflict among managers over secretarial support would be to hire more secretaries.

CHANGING PERSONNEL Sometimes a conflict is prolonged and severe, and efforts at resolution fail. In such cases, it may be appropriate to change personnel. Transferring or firing an individual may be the best solution, but only after due process.

CHANGING STRUCTURE Another way to resolve a conflict is to change the structure of the organization. One way of accomplishing this is to create an integrator role. An integrator is a liaison between groups with very different interests. In severe conflicts, it may be best that the integrator be a neutral third party.[40] Creating the integrator role is a way of opening dialogue between groups that have difficulty communicating.

Using cross-functional teams is another way of changing the organization's structure to manage conflict. In the old methods of designing new products in organizations, many departments had to contribute, and delays resulted from difficulties in coordinating the activities of the various departments. Using a cross-functional team made up of members from different departments improves coordination and reduces delays by allowing many activities to be performed at the same time rather than sequentially.[41] The team approach allows members from different departments to work together and reduces the potential for conflict.

CONFRONTING AND NEGOTIATING Some conflicts require confrontation and negotiation between the parties. Both these strategies require skill on the part of the negotiator and careful planning before engaging in negotiations. The process of negotiating involves an open discussion of problem solutions, and the outcome often is an exchange in which both parties work toward a mutually beneficial solution.

Discussion Consideration
Which of the effective techniques of conflict resolution are the easiest to use ?

Negotiation is a joint process of finding a mutually acceptable solution to a complex conflict. Negotiating is a useful strategy under the following conditions:

- There are two or more parties. Negotiation is primarily an interpersonal or intergroup process.
- There is a conflict of interest between the parties such that what one party wants is not what the other party wants.
- The parties are willing to negotiate because they believe they can use their influence to obtain a better outcome than by simply taking the side of the other party.
- They prefer to work together than to fight openly, give in, break off contact, or take the dispute to a higher authority.

There are two major negotiating approaches: distributive bargaining and integrative negotiation.[42] **Distributive bargaining** is an approach in which the goals of one party are in direct conflict with the goals of the other party. Resources are limited, and each party wants to maximize its share of the resources (get its part of the pie). It is a competitive or win-lose approach to negotiations. Sometimes distributive bargaining causes negotiators to focus so much on their differences that they ignore their common ground. In these cases, distributive bargaining can become counterproductive. The reality is, however, that some situations are distributive in nature, particularly when the parties are interdependent. If a negotiator wants to maximize the value of a single deal and is not worried about maintaining a good relationship with the other party, distributive bargaining may be an option.

distributive bargaining
A negotiation approach in which the goals of the parties are in conflict, and each party seeks to maximize its resources.

In contrast, **integrative negotiation** is an approach in which the parties' goals are not seen as mutually exclusive and in which the focus is on making it possible for both sides to achieve their objectives. Integrative negotiation focuses on the merits of the issues and is a win-win approach (how can we make the pie bigger?). There are preconditions for integrative negotiation to be successful. These include having a common goal, faith in one's own problem-solving

integrative negotiation
A negotiation approach that focuses on the merits of the issues and seeks a win-win solution.

abilities, a belief in the validity of the other party's position, motivation to work together, mutual trust, and clear communication.

Conflict Management Styles

■ Managers have at their disposal a variety of conflict management styles: avoiding, accommodating, competing, compromising, and collaborating. One way of classifying styles of conflict management is to examine the styles' assertiveness (the extent to which you want your goals met) and cooperativeness (the extent to which you want to see the other party's concerns met).[43] Figure 13.4 graphs the five conflict management styles using these two dimensions. Table 13.5 lists appropriate situations for using each conflict management style.

Avoiding

Avoiding is a style low on both assertiveness and cooperativeness. Avoiding is a deliberate decision to take no action on a conflict or to stay out of a conflict situation. One example of an organization that avoided conflict occurred in 1973 and 1974, when Exxon officials quietly withdrew their executives from Argentina because of the increased rate of kidnapping of U.S. executives.[44] In certain situations, it may be appropriate to avoid a conflict. For example, when the parties are angry and need time to cool down, it may be best to use avoidance. There is a potential danger in using an avoiding style too often, however. Research shows that overuse of this style results in negative evaluations from others in the workplace.[45]

Accommodating

A style in which you are concerned that the other party's goals be met but relatively unconcerned with getting your own way is called accommodating. It is cooperative but unassertive. Appropriate situations for accommodating include

■ **FIGURE 13.4**

Conflict Management Styles

SOURCE: K. W. Thomas, "Conflict and Conflict Management," in M. D. Dunnette, *Handbook of Industrial and Organizational Psychology,* 900 (Chicago, IL: Rand McNally, 1976). Used with permission of M. D. Dunnette.

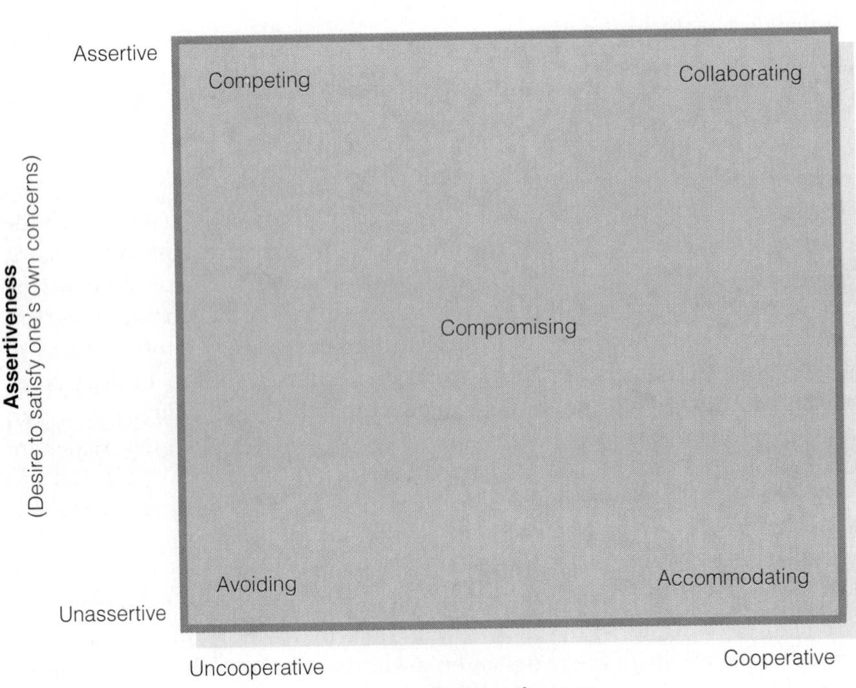

■ TABLE 13.5

Uses of Five Styles of Conflict Management

CONFLICT-HANDLING STYLE	APPROPRIATE SITUATION
Competing	1. When quick, decisive action is vital (e.g., emergencies). 2. On important issues where unpopular actions need implementing (e.g., cost cutting, enforcing unpopular rules, discipline). 3. On issues vital to company welfare when you know you are right. 4. Against people who take advantage of non-competitive behavior.
Collaborating	1. To find an integrative solution when both sets of concerns are too important to be compromised. 2. When your objective is to learn. 3. To merge insights from people with different perspectives. 4. To gain commitment by incorporating concerns into a consensus. 5. To work through feelings that have interfered with a relationship.
Compromising	1. When goals are important, but not worth the effort or potential disruption of more assertive modes. 2. When opponents with equal power are committed to mutually exclusive goals. 3. To achieve temporary settlements to complex issues. 4. To arrive at expedient solutions under time pressure. 5. As a backup when collaboration or competition is unsuccessful.
Avoiding	1. When an issue is trivial, or more important issues are pressing. 2. When you perceive no chance of satisfying your concerns. 3. When potential disruption outweighs the benefits of resolution. 4. To let people cool down and regain perspective. 5. When gathering information supersedes immediate decision. 6. When others can resolve the conflict more effectively. 7. When issues seem tangential or symptomatic of other issues.
Accommodating	1. When you find you are wrong—to allow a better position to be heard, to learn, and to show your reasonableness. 2. When issues are more important to others than to yourself—to satisfy others and maintain cooperation. 3. To build social credits for later issues. 4. To minimize loss when you are outmatched and losing. 5. When harmony and stability are especially important. 6. To allow employees to develop by learning from mistakes.

SOURCE: D. Tjosvold "The Conflict Positive Organization," © 1991 Addison-Wesley Publishing Company Inc. Reprinted by permission Addison-Wesley Publishing Company Inc.

Alternate Example
Many view accommodating as aligning with the superagreeables. Yet, in many instances, it is an appropriate strategy. For example, if the relationship is more important than the issue, accommodating may be valuable. It is also good for training individuals to learn from their mistakes and to collect social credits for the future.

http://www.shell.com

times when you find you are wrong, when you want to let the other party have his or her way in order to remind the individual that he or she owes you similar treatment later, or when the relationship is important. Overreliance on accommodating has its dangers. If managers constantly defer to others, others may lose respect for them. In addition, accommodating managers may become frustrated because their own needs are never met, and they may lose self-esteem.[46]

Competing

Competing is a style that is very assertive and uncooperative. You want to satisfy your own interests and are willing to do so at the other party's expense. In an emergency or in situations where you know you are right, it may be appropriate to put your foot down. For example, environmentalists forced Shell Oil Company to scrap its plans to build a refinery in Delaware after a bitter "To Hell With Shell" campaign.[47] Relying solely on competing strategies is dangerous. Managers who do so may become reluctant to admit when they are wrong and may find themselves surrounded by people who are afraid to disagree with them.

Compromising

The compromising style is intermediate in both assertiveness and cooperativeness, because each party must give up something to reach a solution to the conflict. Compromises are often made in the final hours of union-management negotiations, when time is of the essence. Compromise is also an effective backup style when efforts toward collaboration are not successful.[48]

Collaborating

Points to Emphasize
As with leadership styles, we may have a dominant or preferred style for conflict management. However, our preferred style may not always be appropriate. Thus, we may have to get outside our personal comfort zone to handle a conflict situation effectively.

A win-win style that is high on both assertiveness and cooperativeness is known as collaborating. Working toward collaborating involves an open and thorough discussion of the conflict and arriving at a solution that is satisfactory to both parties. Situations where collaboration may be effective include times when both parties need to be committed to a final solution or when a combination of different perspectives can be formed into a solution.

Research on the five styles of conflict management indicates that although most managers favor a certain style, they have the capacity to change styles as the situation demands.[49] A study of project managers found that managers who used a combination of competing and avoiding styles were seen as ineffective by the engineers who worked on their project teams.[50] In another study of conflicts between R&D project managers and technical staff, competing and avoiding styles resulted in more frequent conflict and lower performance, whereas the collaborating style resulted in less frequent conflict and better performance.[51] Use Challenge 13.2 to assess your dominant conflict management style.

Cultural differences also influence the use of different styles of conflict management. For example, one study compared Turkish and Jordanian managers with U.S. managers. All three groups preferred the collaborating style. Turkish managers also reported frequent use of the competing style, whereas Jordanian and U.S. managers reported that it was one of their least used styles.[52]

The human resources manager of one U.S. telecommunications company's office in Singapore engaged a consultant to investigate the conflict in the office.[53] Twenty-two expatriates from the U.S. and Canada and 38 Singaporeans worked in the office. The consultant used the Thomas model (Figure 13.4) and distributed questionnaires to all managers to determine their conflict management styles. The results were not surprising: The expatriate managers preferred the competing, collaborating, and compromising styles, while the Asians preferred the avoiding and accommodating styles.

CHALLENGE

■ **13.2**

What Is Your Conflict-Handling Style?

Instructions:
For each of the 15 items, indicate how often you rely on that tactic by circling the appropriate number.

	Rarely Always
1. I argue my case with my coworkers to show the merits of my position.	1—2—3—4—5
2. I negotiate with my coworkers so that a compromise can be reached.	1—2—3—4—5
3. I try to satisfy the expectations of my coworkers.	1—2—3—4—5
4. I try to investigate an issue with my coworkers to find a solution acceptable to us.	1—2—3—4—5
5. I am firm in pursuing my side of the issue.	1—2—3—4—5
6. I attempt to avoid being "put on the spot" and try to keep my conflict with my coworkers to myself.	1—2—3—4—5
7. I hold on to my solution to a problem.	1—2—3—4—5
8. I use "give and take" so that a compromise can be made.	1—2—3—4—5
9. I exchange accurate information with my coworkers to solve a problem together.	1—2—3—4—5
10. I avoid open discussion of my differences with my coworkers.	1—2—3—4—5
11. I accommodate the wishes of my coworkers.	1—2—3—4—5
12. I try to bring all our concerns out in the open so that the issues can be resolved in the best possible way.	1—2—3—4—5
13. I propose a middle ground for breaking deadlocks.	1—2—3—4—5
14. I go along with the suggestions of my coworkers.	1—2—3—4—5
15. I try to keep my disagreements with my coworkers to myself in order to avoid hard feelings.	1—2—3—4—5

Scoring Key:

Collaborating		Accommodating		Competing	
Item	**Score**	**Item**	**Score**	**Item**	**Score**
4.	___	3.	___	1.	___
9.	___	11.	___	5.	___
12.	___	14.	___	7.	___
Total =	___	Total =	___	Total =	___

Avoiding		Compromising	
Item	**Score**	**Item**	**Score**
6.	___	2.	___
10.	___	8.	___
15.	___	13.	___
Total =	___	Total =	___

Your primary conflict-handling style is: _______________
(The category with the highest total.)
Your backup conflict-handling style is: _______________
(The category with the second highest total.)

SOURCE: Adapted from M. A. Rahim, "A Measure of Styles of Handling Interpersonal Conflict," *Academy of Management Journal* (June 1983): 368–76.

Workshops were conducted within the firm to develop an understanding of the differences and how the differences negatively affected the firm. The Asians interpreted the results as the passion of Americans to "shout first and ask questions later." They felt that the Americans had an arrogant attitude and could not handle having their ideas rejected. The Asians attributed their own styles to their cultural background. Americans attributed the results as representing the stereotypical view of Asians as unassertive and timid, and they viewed their own results as their desire to "get things out in the open."

The process opened a dialogue between the two groups, who began to work on the idea of harmony through conflict. They began to discard the traditional stereotypes in favor of shared meanings and mutual understanding.

It is important to remember that preventing and resolving dysfunctional conflict is only half the task of effective conflict management. Stimulating functional conflict is the other half.

Managerial Implications: Creating a Conflict-Positive Organization

■ Dean Tjosvold argues that well-managed conflict adds to an organization's innovation and productivity.[54] He discusses procedures for making conflict positive. Too many organizations take a win-lose, competitive approach to conflict or avoid conflict altogether. These two approaches view conflict as negative. A positive view of conflict, in contrast, leads to win-win solutions. Figure 13.5 illustrates these three approaches to conflict management.

Four interrelated steps are involved in creating a conflict-positive organization:

1. *Value diversity and confront differences.* Differences should be seen as opportunities for innovation, and diversity should be celebrated. Open and honest confrontations bring out differences, and they are essential for positive conflict.
2. *Seek mutual benefits, and unite behind cooperative goals.* Conflicts have to be managed together. Through conflict, individuals learn how much they depend on one another. Even when employees share goals, they may differ on how to accomplish the goals. The important point is that they are moving toward the same objectives. Joint rewards should be given to the whole team for cooperative behavior.
3. *Empower employees to feel confident and skillful.* People must be made to feel that they control their conflicts and that they can deal with their differences productively. When they do so, they should be recognized.
4. *Take stock to reward success and learn from mistakes.* Employees should be encouraged to appreciate one another's strengths and weaknesses and to talk directly about them. They should celebrate their conflict managment successes and work out plans for ways they can improve in the future.

Alternate Example
A conflict positive organization is one where ideas win and lose, but the people remain intact.

Tjosvold believes that a conflict-positive organization has competitive advantages for the future.

■ **FIGURE 13.5**

Three Organization Views of Conflict

SOURCE: D. Tjosvold, *The Conflict-Positive Organization,* Copyright © by Addison-Wesley Publishing Company, Inc.

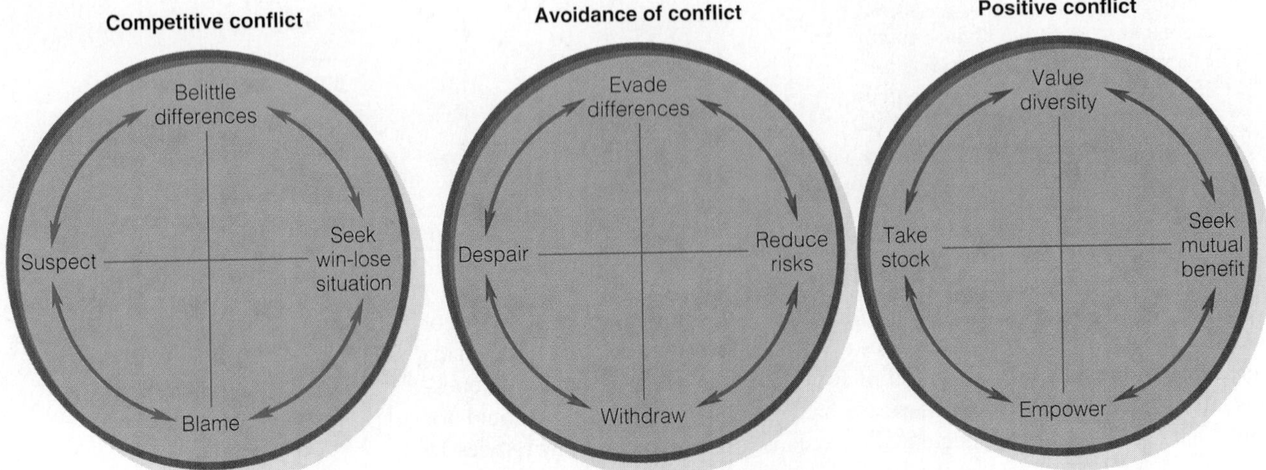

CLOSING SPOTLIGHT

Negotiating an Unprecedented Agreement at Southwest

Since Southwest Airlines' early struggle to fly, the airline has been extremely successful. It has consistently won Triple Crown Awards (best on-time record, best baggage handling, and fewest customer complaints in a single month). In the lean years for the airline industry, it has been the only major airline to turn a profit. Part of Southwest's success can be attributed to good labor-management relations and to CEO Herb Kelleher's hands-on approach to negotiations.

Employee ownership is the central feature of Southwest's labor relations strategy. Last year Kelleher negotiated a new agreement with the Southwest Airlines Pilots Association that was unprecedented. In the 10-year agreement, pilots will receive no pay raises over the first five years of the contract. They will receive guaranteed increases of 3 percent per year in 1999, 2001, and 2003. Over the life of the agreement, pilots will be eligible for additional compensation based on Southwest's profitability. The real benefit to the pilots is in stock options to acquire up to 1.4 million shares of Southwest stock in each year of the agreement, with the option price fixed upon the signing of the contract. As Southwest's stock price rises, so will the value of the options.

Clearly, the agreement is a win for both the pilots and Southwest. The pilots stand to gain with the stock options, and Southwest will save significantly in labor costs in an era where cutting costs is the key to survival.[55]

Every day is casual dress day at Southwest Airlines' Dallas headquarters. Herb Kelleher's open and informal style of interacting with employees creates a culture that encourages win-win solutions to conflicts.

Chapter Summary

- Conflict management skills are keys to management success. The manager's task is to stimulate functional conflict and prevent or resolve dysfunctional conflict.
- Structural causes of conflict include specialization, interdependence, common resources, goal differences, authority relationships, status inconsistencies, and jurisdictional ambiguities.
- Personal factors that lead to conflict include differences in skills and abilities, personalities, perceptions, or values and ethics; emotions; communication barriers; and cultural differences. The increasing diversity of the work force and globalization of business have potential to increase conflict arising from these differences.
- The levels of conflict include interorganizational, intergroup, interpersonal, and intrapersonal.
- Individuals engaged in interpersonal conflict often display aggressive, compromise, or withdrawal defense mechanisms.
- In coping with a difficult person, it is important to identify the reasons the person is perceived as difficult and to analyze the response to the difficult person.
- Ineffective techniques for managing conflict include nonaction, secrecy, administrative orbiting, due process nonaction, and character assassination.
- Effective techniques for managing conflict include appealing to superordinate goals, expanding resources, changing personnel, changing structure, and confronting and negotiating.
- In negotiating, managers can use a variety of conflict management styles, including avoiding, accommodating, competing, compromising, and collaborating.
- Managers should strive to create a conflict-positive organization—one that values diversity, empowers employees, and seeks win-win solutions to conflicts.

Key Terms

conflict (p. 378)
functional conflict (p. 378)
dysfunctional conflict (p. 379)
jurisdictional ambiguity (p. 382)
interorganizational conflict (p. 384)
intergroup conflict (p. 384)
interpersonal conflict (p. 385)
intrapersonal conflict (p. 385)
interrole conflict (p. 385)
intrarole conflict (p. 385)
person-role conflict (p. 385)
fixation (p. 387)
displacement (p. 387)
negativism (p. 387)
compensation (p. 387)
identification (p. 387)
rationalization (p. 387)
flight (p. 389)
conversion (p. 389)
fantasy (p. 389)
nonaction (p. 394)
secrecy (p. 394)
administrative orbiting (p. 394)
due process nonaction (p. 394)
character assassination (p. 394)
superordinate goal (p. 394)
distributive bargaining (p. 395)
integrative negotiation (p. 395)

Review Questions

1. Discuss the differences between functional and dysfunctional conflict. Why should a manager understand conflict?
2. Identify the structural and personal factors that contribute to conflict.
3. Discuss the four major forms of conflict in organizations.
4. What defense mechanisms do people use in interpersonal conflict?
5. Characterize the different types of difficult people who may cause conflict at work.
6. What are the most effective techniques for managing conflict at work? What are some ineffective techniques?
7. Identify and discuss five styles of conflict management.

Discussion and Communication Questions

1. What causes you the most conflict at work or school?
2. Identify the different interrole, intrarole, and person-role conflicts that you experience.
3. Who is the most difficult person for you to deal with in your life? Why? How could you more effectively deal with that person?
4. What methods have you found most personally helpful in dealing with difficult people at school or work? At home? In social situations?
5. Are you comfortable with your preferred conflict management style? Would you consider modifying it?
6. *(communication question)* Think of a person with whom you have had a recent conflict. Write a letter to this person, attempting to resolve the conflict. Use the concepts from the chapter to accomplish your objective. Be sure to address whether the conflict is functional or dysfunctional, what styles each party has used, effective strategies for resolving the conflict, and ineffective strategies that should be avoided.
7. *(communication question)* Develop an action plan for dealing with a difficult person in your life. Using Table 13.3, determine the type of difficult person you are dealing with. Prepare a one-page action plan indicating the specific steps you will take to improve your interaction with this person.

Ethics Questions

1. What kind of ethical conflicts have you experienced at school or work? At home?
2. Is it ethical to avoid a conflict?
3. How can you stimulate conflict in an ethical manner?
4. Evaluate the following techniques in terms of their implications for ethical behavior: nonaction, secrecy, administrative orbiting, and changing personnel.
5. Suppose an employee comes to you with a sexual harassment complaint. You know that your company has a policy in place, but the policy is so complicated and risky that it is hardly worth using. What should you do?
6. In what situations is the competing style of conflict management appropriate? What unethical behaviors might be associated with this style? How can these behaviors be avoided?

Experiential Exercises

13.1 Conflicts over Unethical Behavior

Many conflicts in work organizations arise over differences in beliefs concerning what constitutes ethical versus unethical behavior. The following questionnaire provides a list of behaviors that you or your coworkers might engage in when working for a company. Go over each item, and circle the number that best indicates the frequency with which you personally would (or do, if you work now) engage in that behavior. Then put an *X* over the number you think represents how often your coworkers would (or do) engage in that behavior. Finally, put a check mark beside the item (in the "Needs Control" column) if you believe that management should control that behavior.

	AT EVERY OPPORTUNITY	OFTEN	ABOUT HALF THE TIME	SELDOM	NEVER	NEEDS CONTROL
1. Passing blame for errors to an innocent coworker.	5	4	3	2	1	______
2. Divulging confidential information.	5	4	3	2	1	______
3. Falsifying time/quality/quantity reports.	5	4	3	2	1	______
4. Claiming credit for someone else's work.	5	4	3	2	1	______
5. Padding an expense account by over 10 percent.	5	4	3	2	1	______
6. Pilfering company materials and supplies.	5	4	3	2	1	______
7. Accepting gifts/favors in exchange for preferential treatment.	5	4	3	2	1	______
8. Giving gifts/favors in exchange for preferential treatment.	5	4	3	2	1	______
9. Padding an expense account by up to 10 percent.	5	4	3	2	1	______
10. Authorizing a subordinate to violate company rules.	5	4	3	2	1	______
11. Calling in sick to take a day off.	5	4	3	2	1	______
12. Concealing one's errors.	5	4	3	2	1	______
13. Taking longer than necessary to do a job.	5	4	3	2	1	______
14. Using company services for personal use.	5	4	3	2	1	______
15. Doing personal business on company time.	5	4	3	2	1	______
16. Taking extra personal time (lunch hour, breaks, early departure, and so forth).	5	4	3	2	1	______
17. Not reporting others' violations of company policies and rules.	5	4	3	2	1	______
18. Overlooking a superior's violation of policy to prove loyalty to the boss.	5	4	3	2	1	______

Discussion Questions

1. Would (do) your coworkers seem to engage in these behaviors more often than you would (do)? Why do you have this perception?
2. Which behaviors tend to be most frequent?
3. How are the most frequent behaviors different from the behaviors engaged in less frequently?
4. What are the most important items for managers to control? How should managers control these behaviors?
5. Select a particular behavior from the list. Have two people debate whether the behavior is ethical or not.
6. Given the behaviors in the list, what types of conflicts could emerge if the behaviors occurred frequently?

SOURCE: L. R. Jauch, S. A. Coltrin, A. G. Bedeian, and W. F. Glueck, "Controlling Ethical Behavior," *The Managerial Experience*, 3d ed. (Hinsdale, Ill.: Dryden Press, 1983).

13.2 The World Bank Game: An Intergroup Negotiation

The purposes of this exercise are to learn about conflict and trust between groups and to practice negotiation skills. In the course of the exercise, money will be won or lost. Your team's objective is to win as much money as it can. Your team will be paired with another team, and both teams will receive identical instructions. After reading these instructions, each team will have 10 minutes to plan its strategy.

Each team is assumed to have contributed $50 million to the World Bank. Teams may have to pay more or may receive money from the World Bank, depending on the outcome.

Each team will receive 20 cards. These cards are the weapons. Each card has a marked side (*X*) and an unmarked side. The marked side signifies that the weapon is armed; the unmarked side signifies that the weapon is unarmed.

At the beginning, each team will place 10 of its 20 weapons in their unarmed position (marked side up) and the remaining 10 in their unarmed position (marked side down). The weapons will remain in the team's possession and out of sight of the other team at all times.

The game will consist of *rounds* and *moves*. Each round will be composed of seven moves by each team. There will be two or more rounds in the game, depending on the time available. Payoffs will be determined and recorded after each round. The rules are as follows:

1. A move consists of turning 2, 1, or 0 of the team's weapons from armed to unarmed status, or vice versa.
2. Each team has 1.5 minutes for each move. There is a 30-second period between each move. At the end of the 1.5 minutes, the team must have turned 2, 1, or 0 of its weapons from armed to unarmed status or from unarmed to armed status. If the team fails to move in the allotted time, no change can be made in weapon status until the next move.
3. The 2-minute length of the period between the beginning of one move and the beginning of the next is unalterable.

FINANCES

The funds each team has contributed to the World Bank are to be allocated in the following manner: $30 million will be returned to each team to be used as the team's treasury during the course of the game, and $20 million will be retained for the operation of the World Bank.

PAYOFFS

1. If there is an attack:
   - **a.** Each team may announce an attack on the other team by notifying the banker during the 30 seconds following any 1.5-minute period used to decide upon the move (including the seventh, or final, decision period in any round). The choice of each team during the decision period just ended counts as a move. An attack may not be made during negotiations.
   - **b.** If there is an attack by one or both teams, two things happen: (1) the round ends, and (2) the World Bank assesses a penalty of $2.5 million on each team.
   - **c.** The team with the greater number of armed weapons wins $1.5 million for each armed weapon it has over and above the number of armed weapons of the other team. These funds are paid directly from the treasury of the losing team to the treasury of the winning team. The banker will manage the transfer of funds.
2. If there is no attack:
   At the end of each round (seven moves), each team's treasury will receive from the World Bank $1 million for each of its weapons that is at that point unarmed; and each team's treasury will pay to the World Bank $1 million for each of its weapons remaining armed.

NEGOTIATIONS

Between moves, each team will have the opportunity to communicate with the other team through its negotiations. Either team may call for negotiations by notifying the banker during any of the 30-second periods between decisions. A team is free to accept or reject any invitation to negotiate.

Negotiators from both teams are required to meet after the third and sixth moves (after the 30-second period following the move, if there is no attack).

Negotiations can last no longer than 3 minutes. When the two negotiators return to their teams, the 1.5-minute decision period for the next move will begin once again.

Negotiators are bound only by (a) the 3-minute time limit for negotiations and (b) their required appearance after the third and sixth moves. They are always free to say whatever is necessary to benefit themselves or their teams. The teams are not bound by agreements made by their negotiators, even when those agreements are made in good faith.

SPECIAL ROLES

Each team as 10 minutes to organize itself and plan team strategy. During this period, before the first round begins, each team must choose persons to fill the following roles:

- A *negotiator*—activities stated above.
- A *representative*—to communicate the team's decisions to the banker.
- A *recorder*—to record the moves of the team and to keep a running balance of the team's treasury.
- A *treasurer* to execute all financial transactions with the banker.

The instructor will serve as the banker for the World Bank and will signal the beginning of each of the rounds.

At the end of the game, each participant should complete the following questionnaire, which assesses reactions to the World Bank Game.

WORLD BANK QUESTIONNAIRE

1. To what extent are you satisfied with your team's strategy?

Highly dissatisfied	1	2	3	4	5	6	7	Highly satisfied

2. To what extent do you believe the other team is trustworthy?

Highly untrustworthy	1	2	3	4	5	6	7	Highly trustworthy

3. To what extent are you satisfied with the performance of your negotiator?

Highly dissatisfied 1 2 3 4 5 6 7 Highly satisfied

4. To what extent was there a consensus on your team regarding its moves?

Very little 1 2 3 4 5 6 7 A great deal

5. To what extent do you trust the other members of your team?

Very little 1 2 3 4 5 6 7 A great deal

6. Select one word that describes how you feel about your team: ____________.

7. Select one word that describes how you feel about the other team: ____________.

Negotiators only:

How did you see the other team's negotiator?

Phony and insincere 1 2 3 4 5 6 7 Authentic and sincere

At the end of the game, the class will reconvene and discuss team members,' responses to the World Bank Questionnaire. In addition, the following questions are to be addressed:

1. What was each team's strategy for winning? What strategy was most effective?
2. Contrast the outcomes in terms of win/win solutions to conflict versus win/lose solutions.

SOURCE: Adapted by permission from N. H. Berkowitz and H. A. Hornstein, "World Bank: An Intergroup Negotiation," in J. W. Pfeiffer and J. E. Jones (eds.), *The 1975 Handbook for Group Facilitators* (San Diego: Pfeiffer), 58–62.

WORLD BANK RECORD SHEET

		Round One		Round Two		Round Three		Round Four	
		Armed	Unarmed	Armed	Unarmed	Armed	Unarmed	Armed	Unarmed
	Move	10	10	10	10	10	10	10	10
	1								
	2								
Required Negotiation	3								
	4								
	5								
Required Negotiation	6								
	7								

		Round One	Round Two	Round Three	Round Four
Funds in Team Treasury	$30 million				
Funds of Other Team	$30 million				
Funds in World Bank	$40 million				

CASE

Caterpiller, Inc., and the UAW[1]

On June 21, 1994, approximately 14,500 members of the United Auto Workers union went on strike against Caterpillar, Inc., a manufacturer of excavators, bulldozers, and other heavy-duty construction equipment. This was but one more event in a recent history of contentious labor-management relations at Caterpillar.

An earlier five-month-long strike ended in April, 1992, when the company threatened to permanently replace the striking workers. Donald Fites, Caterpillar's CEO, "refused to grant the same job-security pledges the UAW had won from Deere & Co.," citing the need for cost containment in order to compete in the global market. The defeated strikers returned to work without a contract. Then, taking a hard line, Fites imposed a contract settlement and introduced efficiency measures, threatening some 1,500 strikers' jobs.

Although the UAW had been defeated, Caterpillar was not gracious in victory. "[I]nstead of soothing the feelings of defeated workers, Cat . . . disciplined and fired union members for mostly petty actions" like wearing T-shirts and buttons with slogans that disparaged the company or said "Permanently Replace Fites." Caterpillar's disciplinary actions resulted in 89 complaints to the National Labor Relations Board.

Meanwhile, union leaders tried to get the workers to follow work rules to the letter, thereby slowing down production. Union members, however, ignored the UAW leaders, and "neither productivity or quality suffered."

Underlying the contentious labor-management relations was the substantive conflict regarding job security. Fites still refused to grant the job security that the UAW members wanted. Moreover, Caterpillar played on the workers' fears of job loss even while hiring more than 1,000 new workers.

Labor-management relations continued to deteriorate and UAW members went out on strike on June 21, 1994. Caterpillar's management maintained production by using office workers who had gained production experience during the 1992 strike, temporary replacement workers, new hires, and defecting union members. Caterpillar's production was 14 percent higher in the second half of 1994 as compared to the first half of the year.

As the strike lengthened, the UAW dipped into its $1 billion strike fund, tripling strike pay to $1,200 a month—a sum that covered the monthly bills of many striking workers who lived in rural or semirural areas. And as time went on the number of strikers dwindled—to about 10,500 in early October of 1994 and then to 9,000 in January of 1995.

Caterpillar had "the upper hand, having proved it could build product without the union." In the second quarter of 1995, net profits were at a historical high for any three-month period in Cat's corporate history. In late November of 1995, the dispute "was close to being settled largely because of leadership shifts at the UAW." Stephen Yokich, the new UAW president, wanted to end the disastrous 18-month-old strike. Caterpillar's management planned "to give strikers a new proposal that insiders say is almost exactly the same as the one rejected by the UAW in 1992." Would union members swallow their pride, and accept Cat's plan?

DISCUSSION QUESTIONS

1. What were the causes of the conflict from Caterpillar's viewpoint? From the UAW's viewpoint?
2. What conflict management strategy (or strategies) did the UAW use? What was effective? Why? What was ineffective? Why?
3. What conflict management strategy (or strategies) did the UAW use? What was effective? Why? What was ineffective? Why?
4. What conflict management style (or styles) did Caterpillar CEO Donald Fites use? Using Table 13.5, discuss whether or not this style was appropriate for the situation that Fites faced.
5. What conflict management styles did other Caterpillar executives use? What conflict management styles did UAW members and leaders use? Were these conflict resolution styles appropriate for this situation?
6. What would Caterpillar need to do to create a conflict-positive organization?

SOURCE: This case was written by Michael K. McCuddy, the Louis S. and Mary L. Morgal Professor of Christian Business Ethics, College of Business Administration, Valparaiso University.

1. Adapted from H. S. Byrne, "A Still-Fat Cat," *Barron's*, (August 7, 1995): 13; R. Grover, "Much Ado about Pettiness," *Business Week*, (July 4, 1994): 34, 36; K. Kelly, "Cat is Purring, but They're Hissing on the Floor," *Business Week*, (May 16, 1994): 33; K. Kelly, "For Now, the UAW Can't Keep Cat from Purring," *Business Week*, (October 3, 1994): 57; K. Kelly, "A New Life for Cat?" *Business Week*, (February 6, 1995): 38–39; K. Kelly, "Caught in Cat's Claws," *Business Week*, (December 4, 1995): 38.

References

1. Definition adapted from D. Hellriegel, J. W. Slocum, Jr., and R. W. Woodman, *Organizational Behavior* (St. Paul: West, 1992), and from R. D. Middlemist and M. A. Hitt, *Organizational Behavior* (St. Paul: West, 1988).
2. D. Tjosvold, *The Conflict-Positive Organization* (Reading, Mass.: Addison-Wesley, 1991).
3. K. Thomas and W. Schmidt, "A Survey of Managerial Interests with Respect to Conflict," *Academy of Management Journal* 19 (1976): 315–318; G. L. Lippitt, "Managing Conflict in Today's Organizations," *Training and Development Journal* 36 (1982): 66–74.
4. M. Rajim, "A Measure of Styles of Handling Interpersonal Conflict," *Academy of Management Journal* 26 (1983): 368–376.
5. S. P. Robbins, *Managing Organizational Conflict* (Englewood Cliffs, N.J.: Prentice-Hall, 1974).
6. C. Morrill, "Learning from Managerial Conflict," *New Management* 3 (1988): 45–49.
7. Tjosvold, *The Conflict-Positive Organization*, 4.
8. R. A. Cosier and D. R. Dalton, "Positive Effects of Conflict: A Field Experiment," *International Journal of Conflict Management* 1 (1990): 81–92.
9. D. Tjosvold, "Making Conflict Productive," *Personnel Administrator* 29 (1984): 121–130.
10. A. C. Amason, W. A. Hochwarter, K. R. Thompson, and A. W. Harrison, "Conflict: An Important Dimension in Successful Management Teams," *Organizational Dynamics* 24 (1995): 25–35.
11. I. Janis, *Groupthink*, 2d ed. (Boston: Houghton Mifflin, 1982).
12. J. D. Thompson, *Organizations in Action* (New York: McGraw-Hill, 1967).
13. G. Walker and L. Poppo, "Profit Centers, Single-Source Suppliers, and Transaction Costs," *Administrative Science Quarterly* 36 (1991): 66–87.
14. R. Miles, *Macro Organizational Behavior* (Glenview, Ill.: Scott, Foresman, 1980).
15. H. Levinson, "The Abrasive Personality," *Harvard Business Review* 56 (1978): 86–94.
16. J. C. Quick and J. D. Quick, *Organizational Stress and Preventive Management* (New York: McGraw-Hill, 1984).
17. F. N. Brady, "Aesthetic Components of Management Ethics," *Academy of Management Review* 11 (1986): 337–344.
18. V. K. Raizada, "Multi-ethnic Corporations and Inter-ethnic Conflict," *Human Resource Management* 20 (1981): 24–27; T. Cox, Jr., "The Multicultural Organization," *Academy of Management Executive* 5 (1991): 34–47.
19. G. Hofstede, *Culture's Consequences: International Differences in Work-related Values* (Beverly Hills, Calif.: Sage, 1980); G. Hofstede and M. H. Bond, "The Confucius Connection: From Cultural Roots to Economic Growth," *Organizational Dynamics*, Spring 1988, 4–21; G. Hofstede, "Cultural Constraints in Management Theories," *Academy of Management Executive* 7 (1993): 81–94.
20. T. H. Cox, S. A. Lobel, and P. L. McLead, "Effects of Ethnic Group Cultural Differences on Cooperative and Competitive Behavior in a Group Task," *Academy of Management Journal* 34 (1991): 827–847.
21. "AT&T's Bid for NCR: Round Thirteen," *Economist*, 20 April 1991, 68–69.
22. A. Choi, "Steelworkers of Germany Endorse Strike," *Wall Street Journal*, 3 February 1992, A6.
23. M. Sherif, *Intergroup Conflict and Cooperation* (Norman, Okla.: University Book Exchange, 1977).
24. M. Sherif and C. W. Sherif, *Social Psychology* (New York: Harper & Row, 1969).
25. D. Katz and R. Kahn, *The Social Psychology of Organizations*, 2d ed. (New York: Wiley, 1978).
26. D. L. Nelson and J. C. Quick, "Professional Women: Are Distress and Disease Inevitable?" *Academy of Management Review* 10 (1985): 206–218; D. L. Nelson and M. A. Hitt, "Employed Women and Stress: Implications for Enhancing Women's Mental Health in the Workplace," in J. C. Quick, J. Hurrell, and L. A. Murphy, eds., *Stress and Well-being at Work: Assessments and Interventions for Occupational Mental Health* (Washington, D.C.: American Psychological Association, 1992).
27. R. L. Kahn et al., *Organizational Stress: Studies in Role Conflict and Ambiguity* (New York: Wiley, 1964).
28. W. F. G. Mastenbroek, *Conflict Management and Organization Development* (Chichester, England: Wiley, 1987).
29. K. Thomas, "Conflict and Conflict Management," in M. D. Dunnette, ed., *Handbook of Industrial and Organizational Psychology* (New York: Wiley, 1976).
30. H. H. Meyer, E. Kay, and J. R. P. French, "Split Roles in Performance Appraisal," *Harvard Business Review* 43 (1965): 123–129.
31. T. W. Costello and S. S. Zalkind, *Psychology in Administration: A Research Orientation* (Englewood Cliffs, N.J.: Prentice-Hall, 1963).
32. R. Bramson, *Coping with Difficult People* (New York: Dell, 1981).
33. B. Schneider, "The People Make the Place," *Personnel Psychology* 40 (1987): 437–453.
34. C. A. O'Reilly, J. Chatman, and D. F. Caldwell, "People and Organizational Culture: A Profile Comparison Approach to Assessing Person-Organization Fit," *Academy of Management Journal* 34 (1991): 487–516.
35. I. Dayal and J. M. Thomas, "Operation KPE: Developing a New Organization," *Journal of Applied Behavioral Science* 4 (1968): 473–506.
36. R. H. Miles, "Role Requirements as Sources of Organizational Stress," *Journal of Applied Psychology* 61 (1976): 172–179.
37. H. S. Baum, "Organizational Politics against Organizational Culture: A Psychoanalytic Perspective," *Human Resource Management* 28 (1989): 191–200.
38. R. Miles, *Macro Organizational Behavior*; R. Steers, *Introduction to Organizational Behavior*, 4th ed. (Glenview, Ill.: HarperCollins, 1991).
39. A. Tyerman and C. Spencer, "A Critical Text of the Sherrif's Robber's Cave Experiments: Intergroup Competition and Cooperation between Groups of Well-acquainted Individuals," *Small Group Behavior* 14 (1983): 515–531; R. M. Kramer, "Intergroup Relations and Organizational Dilemmas: The Role of Categorization Processes," in B. Staw and L. Cummings, eds., *Research in*

Organizational Behavior 13 (Greenwich, Conn.: JAI Press, 1991), 191–228.

40. R. Blake and J. Mouton, "Overcoming Group Warefare," *Harvard Business Review* 64 (1984): 98–108.
41. D. G. Ancona and D. Caldwell, "Improving the Performance of New Product Teams," *Research Technology Management* 33 (1990): 25–29.
42. R. J. Lewicki, J. A. Litterer, J. W. Minton, and D. M. Saunders, *Negotiation,* 2 ed. (Burr Ridge, Ill.: Irwin, 1994).
43. K. W. Thomas, "Conflict and Conflict Management," in M. D. Dunnette, ed., *Handbook of Industrial and Organizational Psychology* (Chicago: Rand McNally, 1976), 900.
44. T. N. Gladwin and I. Walter, "How Multinationals Can Manage Social and Political Forces," *Journal of Business Strategy* 1 (1980): 54–68.
45. R. A. Baron, S. P. Fortin, R. L. Frei, L. A. Hauver, and M. L. Shack, "Reducing Organizational Conflict: The Role of Socially Induced Positive Affect," *International Journal of Conflict Management* 1 (1990): 133–152.
46. S. L. Phillips and R. L. Elledge, *The Team Building Source Book* (San Diego: University Associates, 1989).
47. Gladwin and Walter, "How Multinationals Can Manage," 228.
48. K. W. Thomas, "Toward Multidimensional Values in Teaching: The Example of Conflict Behaviors," *Academy of Management Review* 2 (1977): 484–490.
49. W. King and E. Miles, "What We Know and Don't Know about Measuring Conflict," *Management Communication Quarterly* 4 (1990): 222–243.
50. J. Barker, D. Tjosvold, and I. R. Andrews, "Conflict Approaches of Effective and Ineffective Project Managers: A Field Study in a Matrix Organization," *Journal of Management Studies* 25 (1988): 167–178.
51. M. Chan, "Intergroup Conflict and Conflict Management in the R&D Divisions of Four Aerospace Companies," *IEEE Transactions on Engineering Management* 36 (1989): 95–104.
52. M. K. Kozan, "Cultural Influences on Styles of Handling Interpersonal Conflicts: Comparisons among Jordanian, Turkish, and U.S. Managers," *Human Relations* 42 (1989): 787–799.
53. S. McKenna, "The Business Impact of Management Attitudes Towards Dealing with Conflict: A Cross-Cultural Assessment," *Journal of Managerial Psychology* 10 (1995): 22–27.
54. Tjosvold, *The Conflict-Positive Organization.*
55. "Southwest Moves the Goalposts," *Air Transport World* (January 1995): 7.

INTERNET EXERCISE

This assignment deals with many of the interpersonal aspects of organizational behavior examined in section III of the text. These are only a few of the websites that are available. Using your Web browser, find the following sites and take some time to follow the links displayed.

Company Connections

China Internet Corporation
What services are provided here that would help managers better communicate with their Chinese counterparts?

Ford Motor Company
How has Ford made use of the ideas of W. Edward Deming?

Outward Bound
What programs are offered for team development?

AT&T
What information is available here that gives you a sense of what factors affect AT&T's business decisions?

Saturn Corporation
How does their website express their corporate culture?

Motorola
What information can you find on their leadership style from this web page?

Microsoft
How is their leadership style expressed in their home page?

Topic Trails

Netiquette
What are the rules of the web?

TQM
Find the University of Michigan Quality Gopher. What information on teams is available?

Organizational politics
Many universities now have courses dealing with organizational politics. Find the organizational politics courses at the University of Pennsylvania and at Duke University. What do these courses have in common?

Leadership
Find the Center for Creative Leadership. What is their mission and how do they assist organizations with leadership issues?

Conflict resolution/negotiation
Find information on negotiation at Harvard University. What resources are available here that pertain to negotiation and conflict resolution?

VIDEO COHESION CASE

This section includes four cases dealing with various organizational behavior issues facing PriceCostco, a company resulting from the merger of Price Company and Costco Wholesale. The cases are interrelated, but each can stand alone. Each case is supplemented with videos that present the challenges faced by a corporation formed from two diverse companies seeking to create a single company with a unified philosophy and culture. These cases immediately follow Chapter 18 on page 573.

PART IV

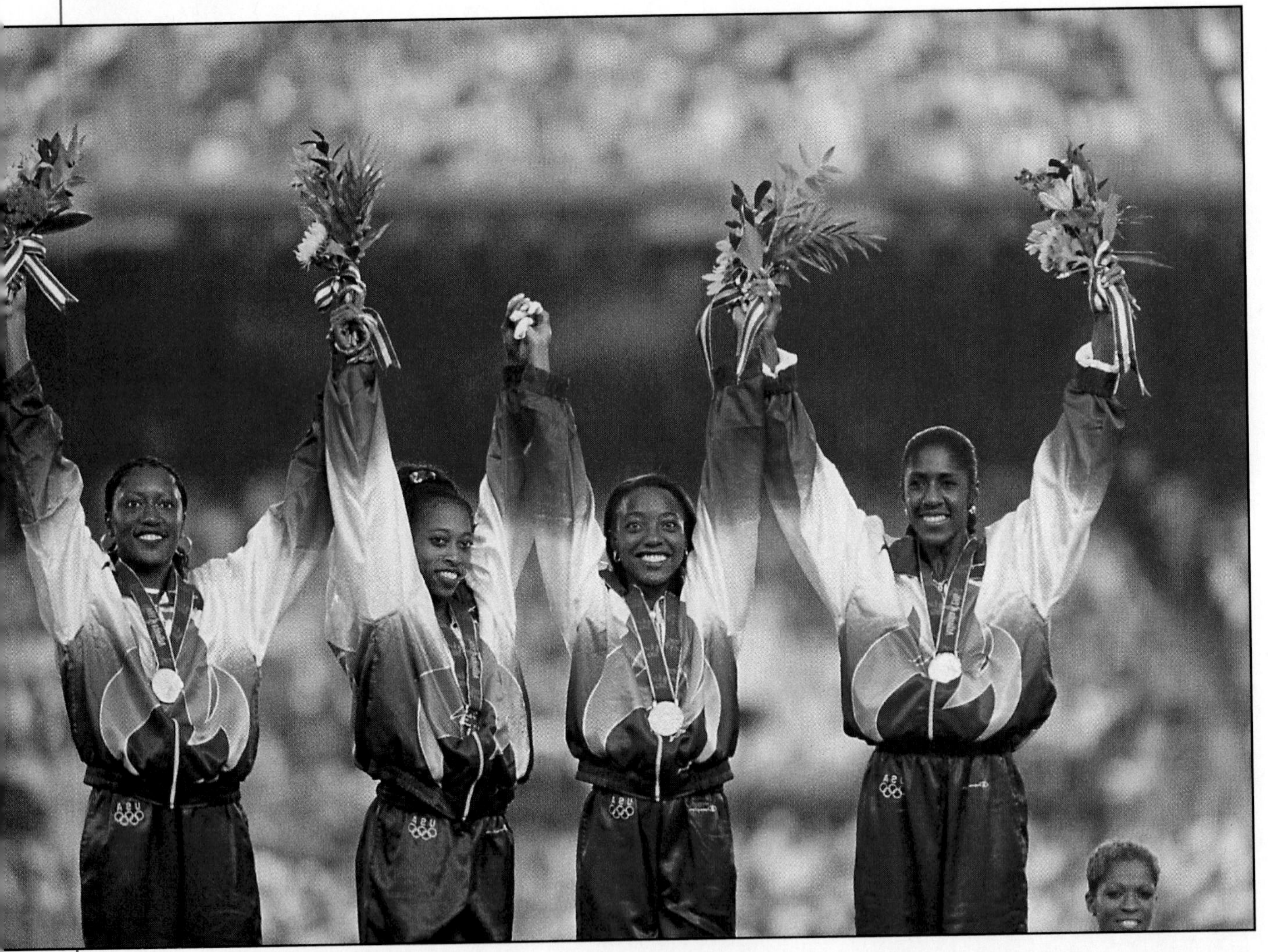

Organizational Processes and Structure

CHAPTER

14

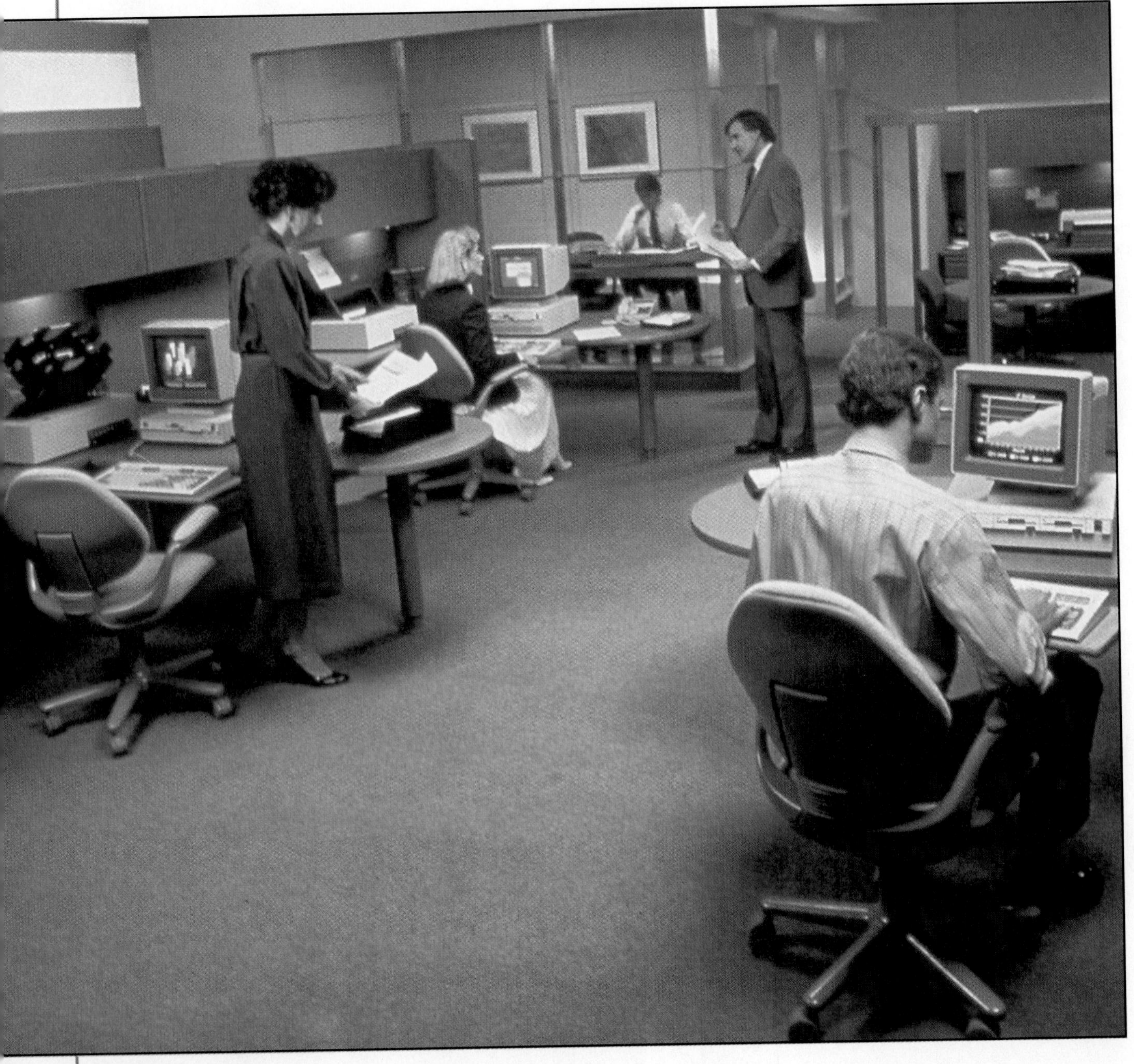

Jobs and the Design of Work

LEARNING OBJECTIVES

After reading this chapter, you should be able to do the following:

- Define the term *job,* and identify six patterns of defining *work.*
- Discuss the four traditional approaches to job design.
- Describe the job characteristics model.
- Compare the social information-processing (SIP) model with traditional job design approaches.
- Explain the interdisciplinary approach to job design.
- Compare Japanese, German, and Scandinavian approaches to work.
- Explain how job control, uncertainty, and conflict can be managed for employee well-being.
- Discuss five emerging issues in the design of work.

OPENING SPOTLIGHT

"Quality Is Job 1"

http://www.ford.com

During the early 1980s, Ford Motor Company teetered on the brink of collapse, along with Chrysler Corporation. At the same time, Ford was on the eve of a miraculous resurgence in the motor vehicle industry. The change had begun in 1978, when Philip Caldwell, Ford's president at the time, placed "quality—number 1" at the top of his private checklist for discussion with senior management. *Job 1* is car-making jargon for the first car of a new model as it begins its run down the assembly line. When Caldwell captured the notion "Quality Is Job 1," he was saying that quality was the very first component Ford Motor Company put in each and every one of its products.

Caldwell carried the concept even further: "The quality I am talking about is not limited to products or to our manufacturing assembly plants. Quality is an ethic, a course of action to govern everything we do."[1] What were the implications of "Quality Is Job 1" for the tens of thousands of jobs at Ford? How would Ford employees respond to the challenge? ■

job
A set of specified work and task activities that engage an individual in an organization.

Job 1 has a specific meaning in the context of the automotive industry. What does *job* mean in general? A **job** is defined as an employee's specific work and task activities in an organization. A job is not the same as an organizational position or a career. *Organizational position* identifies a job in relation to other parts of the organization; *career* refers to a sequence of job experiences over time.

This chapter focuses on jobs and the design of work as elements of the organization's structure. Jobs help people define their work and become integrated into the organization. The first section in the chapter examines the meaning of work in organizations. The second major section addresses four traditional approaches to job design developed between the late 1800s and the 1970s. The third major section examines four alternative approaches to job design developed over the past couple of decades. The final section addresses emerging issues in job design.

Work in Organizations

work
Mental or physical activity that has productive results.

■ **Work** is effortful, productive activity resulting in a product or a service. Work is one important reason why organizations exist. A job is composed of a set of specific tasks, each of which is an assigned piece of work to be done in a specific time period. Work is an especially important human endeavor, according to Sigmund Freud, because it has a more powerful effect than any other aspect of human life in binding a person to reality: "In his work he is at least securely attached to a part of reality, the human community."[2]

Work has different meanings for different people. For all people, work is organized into jobs, and jobs fit into the larger structure of an organization. The structure of jobs is the concern of this chapter, and the structure of the organization is the concern of the next chapter. Both chapters emphasize organizations as sets of task and authority relationships through which people get work done.

The Meaning of Work

the meaning of work
The way a person interprets and understands the value of work as part of life.

Alternate Example
North Americans often define their self-worth by their work, linking their definition of success to their career. A striking alternative to this view has been provided by Chuck Swindoll, a popular pastor-author and now president of Dallas Theological Seminary. According to Swindoll, success meant being a good husband, a good daddy, and teaching God's word. Notice that his work (teaching God's word) was third on his list.

The meaning of work differs from person to person. One recent study found six patterns people follow in defining *work*, and these help explain the cultural differences in people's motivation to work.[3] Pattern A people define *work* as an activity in which value comes from performance and for which a person is accountable. It is generally self-directed and devoid of negative affect. Pattern B people define *work* as an activity that provides a person with positive personal affect and identity. Work contributes to society and is not unpleasant. Pattern C people define *work* as an activity from which profit accrues to others by its performance and that may be done in various settings other than a working place. Work is usually physically strenuous and somewhat compulsive. Pattern D people define work as primarily a physical activity a person must do that is directed by others and generally performed in a working place. Work is usually devoid of positive affect and is unpleasantly connected to performance. Pattern E people define *work* as a physically and mentally strenuous activity. It is generally unpleasant and devoid of positive affect. Pattern F people define *work* as an activity constrained to specific time periods that does not bring positive affect through its performance.

These six patterns were studied in six different countries: Belgium, the Federal Republic of Germany, Israel, Japan, the Netherlands, and the United States. Table 14.1 summarizes the percentage of workers in each country who defined *work* according to each of the six patterns. An examination of the table shows that a small percentage of workers in all six countries used either Pattern E or Pattern F to define *work*. Furthermore, there are significant differences among countries in how *work* is defined. In the Netherlands, *work* is defined most positively and with the most balanced personal and collective reasons for doing it. *Work* is defined least positively and with the most collective reason for doing it in Germany and Japan. Belgium, Israel, and the United States represent a middle position between these two. Future international studies should include Middle Eastern countries, India, Central and South American countries, and other Asian countries to better represent the world's cultures.

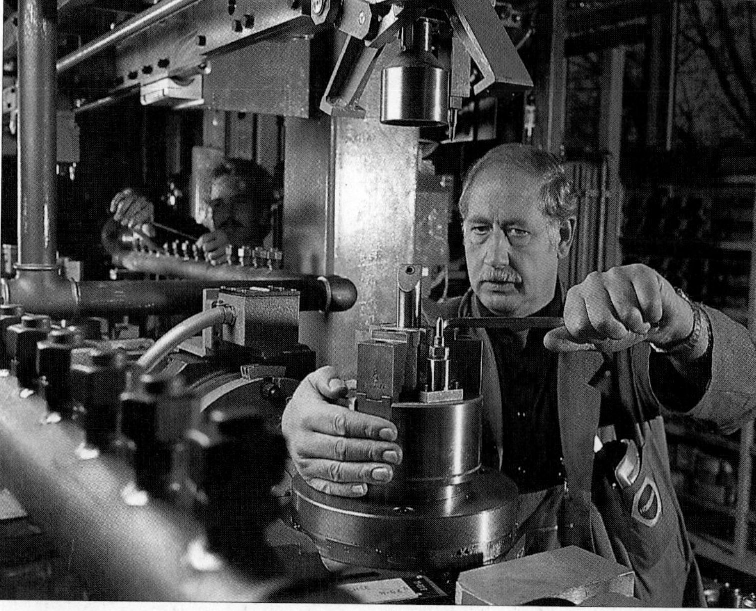

How work is defined and the unique ways in which people work vary by country. Germans are known for their precision engineering and fine craftsmanship, as exemplified by this German worker in a tooling plant.

Another international study of 5,550 people across ten occupational groups in 20 different countries completed the Work Value Scales (WVS).[4] The WVS is composed of thirteen items measuring various aspects of the work environment, such as responsibility and job security. The study found two common basic work dimensions across cultures. Work content is one dimension, measured by items such as "the amount of responsibility on the job." Job context is the other dimension, measured by items such as "the policies of my company." This finding suggests that people in many cultures distinguish between the nature of the work itself and elements of

■ TABLE 14.1

Work Definition Patterns by Nation

SAMPLE	PATTERN[a]					
	A	B	C	D	E	F
TOTAL SAMPLE (N = 4,950)	**11%**	**28%**	**18%**	**22%**	**11%**	**12%**
Nation						
Belgium	8%	40%	13%	19%	11%	9%
Federal Republic of Germany	8	26	13	28	11	14
Israel	4	22	33	23	9	9
Japan	21	11	13	29	10	17
The Netherlands	15	43	12	11	9	9
United States	8	30	19	19	12	11

NOTE: X^2 = 680.98 (25 degrees of freedom). P<.0001 Significance level

[a]In Pattern A, work is valued for its performance. The person is accountable and generally self-directed. In Pattern B, work provides a person with positive affect and identity. It contributes to society. In Pattern C, work provides profit to others by its performance. It is physical and not confined to a working place. In Pattern D, work is a required physical activity directed by others and generally unpleasant. In Pattern E, work is physically and mentally strenuous. It is generally unpleasant. In Pattern F, work is constrained to specific time periods. It does not bring positive affect through performance.

SOURCE: G. W. England and I. Harpaz, "How Working is Defined: National Contexts and Demographic and Organizational Role Influences," *Journal of Organizational Behavior,* 11 (1990), p. 262. Copyright © 1990, John Wiley & Sons, Ltd. Reprinted by permission of John Wiley & Sons, Ltd.

the context in which work is done. This supports Herzberg's two-factor theory of motivation (see Chapter 5) and his job enrichment method discussed later in this chapter. Thus, although differences in the meaning of *work* exist among countries, similarities exist across countries in understanding the structure in which work is done.

Jobs in Organizations

Discussion Consideration
Ask students to distinguish between jobs and careers.

Task and authority relationships define an organization's structure. Jobs are the basic building blocks of this task-authority structure and are considered the micro-structural element to which employees most directly relate. Jobs are usually designed to complement and support other jobs in the organization. Isolated jobs are rare. However, one such isolated job was identified at Coastal Corporation during the early 1970s. Shortly after Oscar Wyatt moved the company from Corpus Christi, Texas, to Houston, Coastal developed organizational charts and job descriptions because the company had grown so large. In the process of charting the organization's structure, it was discovered that the beloved corporate economist reported to no one. Everyone assumed he worked for someone else. Such peculiarities are rare.

Jobs in organizations are interdependent and designed to make a contribution to the organization's overall mission and goals. For salespeople to be successful, the production people must be effective. For production people to be effective, the material department must be effective. These interdependencies require careful planning and design so that all of the "pieces of work" fit together into a whole. For example, if an envelope salesperson takes an order for 1 million envelopes from John Hancock Life Insurance Company and promises a two-week delivery date without knowing that the production department cannot meet that deadline, the salesperson dooms the company to failure in meeting John Hancock's expectations. The central concerns of this chapter are designing work and structuring jobs to prevent such problems and to ensure employee well-being.

Chapter 15 addresses the larger issues in the design of organizations. In particular, it examines the competing processes of differentiation and integration in organizations. Differentiation is the process of subdividing and departmentalizing the work of an organization. Jobs result from differentiation, which is necessary because no one can do it all (contrary to the famous statement made by Harold Geneen, former chairman of ITT: "If I had enough arms and legs and time, I'd do it all myself"). Even small organizations must divide work so that each person is able to accomplish a manageable piece of the whole. At the same time the organization divides up the work, it must also integrate those pieces back into a whole. Integration is the process of connecting jobs and departments into a coordinated, cohesive whole. For example, if the envelope salesperson had coordinated with the production manager before finalizing the order with John Hancock, the company could have met the customer's expectations, and integration would have occurred.

Traditional Approaches to Job Design

■ Failure to differentiate, integrate, or do both, may result in badly designed jobs, which in turn cause a variety of performance problems in organizations. Good job design helps avoid these problems, improve productivity, and enhance employee well-being. Four approaches to job design developed during this century are scientific management, job enlargement/job rotation, job enrichment, and the job characteristics theory. Each approach offers unique benefits to the organization, the employee, or both. Each approach also has limitations and drawbacks. The later job design approaches were developed to overcome the limitations of earlier approaches. For example, job enlargement is intended to overcome the problem of boredom associated with scientific management's narrowly defined approach to jobs.

Scientific Management

Scientific management, an approach to work design advocated by Frederick Taylor from the late 1800s through 1915, emphasized work simplification. **Work simplification** is the standardization and the narrow, explicit specification of task activities for workers.[5] Jobs designed through scientific management have a limited number of tasks, and each task is scientifically specified so the worker is not required to think or deliberate. According to Taylor, the role of management and the industrial engineer is to calibrate and define each task carefully. The role of the worker is to execute the task. The elements of scientific management, such as time and motion studies, differential piece rate systems of pay, and the scientific selection of workers, all focus on the efficient use of labor to the economic benefit of the corporation. Some employees like scientifically designed jobs and one study found employees satisfied with various aspects of repetitive work.[6]

work simplification
Standardization and the narrow, explicit specification of task activities for workers.

Points to Emphasize
Work simplification may be rooted in the assumptions managers have about their employees. For instance, theory X and theory Y assumptions have substantially different implications for the design of work.

Two arguments supported the efficient and standardized job design approach of scientific management in the early days of the American industrial revolution. The first argument was that work simplification allowed workers of diverse ethnic and skill backgrounds to work together in a systematic way. Large industrial organizations had to design ways to blend the large waves of European immigrants of the late 1800s into a productive workforce. Work simplification avoided having workers engage in problem-solving or decision-making activities, which would have been difficult, because no one language united all immigrants. Germans, Scots, Hungarians, and Poles might have a difficult time in a quality circle without a common language.[7] Taylor's unique approach to work standardization allowed immigrants of various linguistic and ethnic descents to be blended into a functional workforce.

The second argument for scientific management was that work simplification led to production efficiency in the organization and, therefore, to higher profits. This economic argument for work simplification tended to treat labor as a means of production and dehumanized it.

A fundamental limitation of scientific management is that it undervalues the human capacity for thought and ingenuity. Jobs designed through scientific management use only a portion of a person's capabilities. This underutilization makes work boring, monotonous, and understimulating. The failure to fully utilize the workers' capacity in a constructive fashion may cause a variety of work problems. A contemporary example of a work problem resulting from underutilization and boredom is the intentional installation of Coke bottles in the car doors on an automobile assembly line.

Job Enlargement/Job Rotation

Job enlargement proposes to overcome the limitations of overspecialized work, such as boredom.[8] **Job enlargement** is a method of job design that increases the number of tasks in a job. **Job rotation**, a variation of job enlargement, exposes a worker to a variety of specialized job tasks over time. The reasoning for these approaches to the problems of overspecialization is as follows. First, the core problem with overspecialized work was believed to be lack of variety. That is, jobs designed by scientific management were too narrow and limited in the number of tasks and activities assigned to each worker. Second, a lack of variety led to

job enlargement
A method of job design that increases the number of activities in a job to overcome the boredom of overspecialized work.

job rotation
A variation of job enlargement in which workers are exposed to a variety of specialized jobs over time.

Alternate Example
Thomson Consumer Electronics experienced a jump in accidents and workers' compensation costs. Job rotation helped the company reduce the number of accidents by eliminating repetitive motion and increasing job variety. SOURCE: L. Hazzard, J. Mautz, and D. Wrightsman, "Job Rotation cuts Cumulative Trauma Cases," *Personnel Journal,* February 1992, 29.

understimulation and underutilization of the worker. Third, the worker would be more stimulated and better utilized by increasing the variety in the job. Variety could be increased by increasing the number of activities or by rotating the worker through different jobs. For example, job enlargement for a lathe operator in a steel plant might include selecting the steel pieces to be turned and performing all of the maintenance work on the lathe. An example of job rotation might occur in a small bank where an employee might take new accounts one day, serve as a cashier another day, and process loan applications on a third day.

One of the first studies of the problem of repetitive work was done at IBM after World War II. The company implemented a job enlargement program during the war and evaluated the effort after six years.[9] The two most important results were a significant increase in product quality and a reduction in idle time, both for people and for machines. Less obvious and measurable are the benefits of job enlargement to IBM through enhanced worker status and improved manager-worker communication. Therefore, job enlargement does counter the problems of work specialization.

A later study examined the effects of mass production jobs on assembly line workers in the automotive industry.[10] Mass production jobs have six characteristics: mechanically controlled work pace, repetitiveness, minimum skill requirements, predetermined tools and techniques, minute division of the production process, and a requirement for surface mental attention, rather than thoughtful concentration. The researchers conducted 180 private interviews with assembly line workers and found generally positive attitudes toward pay, security, and supervision. They concluded that job enlargement and job rotation would improve other job aspects, such as repetition and a mechanical work pace.

cross-training
A variation of job enlargement in which workers are trained in different specialized tasks or activities.

Job rotation and **cross-training** programs are variations of job enlargement. Job rotation may be a proactive means for enhancing work experiences for career development, as discussed in the accompanying Scientific Foundation feature. In cross-training, workers are trained in different specialized tasks or activities. All three kinds of programs horizontally enlarge jobs; that is, the number and variety of an employee's tasks and activities are increased. Graphics Controls Corporation developed a flexible work force through cross-training which enabled the company to maintain high levels of production.[11]

Job Enrichment

job enrichment
Designing or redesigning jobs by incorporating motivational factors into them.

Discussion Consideration
Can every job be enriched? Ask students to discuss how the following jobs might be enriched: toll booth operator, data entry clerk, ticket taker.

Whereas job enlargement increases the number of job activities through horizontal loading, job enrichment increases the amount of job responsibility through vertical loading. **Job enrichment** is a job design or redesign method aimed at increasing the motivational factors in a job. Job enrichment builds on Herzberg's two-factor theory of motivation, which distinguished between motivational and hygienic factors for people at work. Whereas job enlargement recommends increasing and varying the number of activities a person does, job enrichment recommends increasing the recognition, responsibility, and opportunity for achievement. For example, enlarging the lathe operator's job means adding maintenance activities, and enriching the job means having the operator meet with customers who buy the products.

Herzberg believes that only certain jobs should be enriched, and the first step is to select the jobs appropriate for job enrichment.[12] He recognizes that some people prefer simple jobs. Once jobs are selected for enrichment, management should brainstorm about possible changes, revise the list to include only specific changes related to motivational factors, and screen out generalities and suggestions related to simply increasing activities or numbers of tasks. Those whose jobs are to be enriched should not participate in this process because of a conflict of interest. Two key problems can arise in the implementation of job enrichment. First, an initial drop in performance can be expected as workers accom-

SCIENTIFIC FOUNDATION

Job Rotation and Career Success

Work assignments are a primary source of career learning for many employees, contributing to their career development and success. Job rotations, one form of work assignment policy, are lateral transfers of employees between jobs in an organization. This field research study examined (1) the factors that predicted the number of job rotations for a group of employees and (2) the effects of job rotations on subsequent career success.

The researchers studied 255 executives, managers, and professionals in the financial function of a large pharmaceutical company. The company did have a promotion-from-within policy, with an emphasis on developing generalists. The average age of the study group was 39 years; the average tenure was 13 years; 97 percent had a bachelor's degree, and 55 percent had a graduate degree.

The researchers expected that younger employees, early in their careers, with high education and high job performance, would have more job rotations than would older employees, later in their careers, with less education and lower job performance. The data largely supported this expectation. In addition, the researchers expected that frequent job rotations would be positively related to faster promotions and salary growth. The data provided support for this expectation.

Job rotations are a form of career development that may be more common for employees in the early part of their career and more common for high-performing employees. Job rotations have tangible benefits for employees in the form of salary increases and promotions.

SOURCE: M. A. Campion, L. Cheraskin, and M. J. Stevens, "Career-Related Antecedents and Outcomes of Job Rotation," *Academy of Management Journal* 37 (1994): 1518–1542.

Eli Lilly and Company is a large pharmaceutical company with a promotion-from-within staffing strategy and an emphasis on developing generalists. However, there are many highly technical jobs within the organization that must be done, and done well, to insure the company's success.

modate to the change. Second, first-line supervisors may experience some anxiety or hostility as a result of employees' increased responsibility.

A seven-year implementation study of job enrichment at AT&T found the approach beneficial.[13] Job enrichment required a big change in management style, and AT&T found that it could not ignore hygienic factors in the work environment just because it was enriching existing jobs. Whereas the AT&T experience with job enrichment was positive, a critical review of job enrichment did not find that to be the case generally.[14] One problem with job enrichment as a strategy for work design is that it is based on an oversimplified motivational theory. Another problem is the lack of consideration for individual differences among employees. Job enrichment, like scientific management's work specialization and job enlargement/job rotation, is a universal approach to the design of work and thus does not differentiate among individuals.

http://www.att.com

Points to Emphasize

One of the major problems with enrichment is getting the commitment and resources to make a long-term change. "Some top executives believe that job enrichment involves too many changes to a job classification plan and costs too much money." SOURCE: J. Cunningham and T. Eberle, "A Guide to Job Enrichment and Redesign," *Personnel,* February 1990, 262.

Job Characteristics Theory

The job characteristics theory is a traditional approach to the design of work initiated during the mid-1960s that makes a significant departure from the three earlier approaches. It emphasizes the interaction between the individual and specific attributes of the job; therefore, it is a person-job fit model rather than a universal job design model. Its earliest origins were in a research study of 470 workers in 47 different jobs across 11 industries.[15] The study measured and classified relevant task characteristics for these 47 jobs and found four core job characteristics: job variety, autonomy, responsibility, and interpersonal interaction. The study also found that core job characteristics did not affect all workers in the same way. A worker's values, religious beliefs, and ethnic background influenced how the worker responded to the job. Specifically, workers with rural values and strong religious beliefs preferred jobs high in core characteristics, and workers with urban values and weaker religious beliefs preferred jobs low in core characteristics.

Points to Emphasize
The Hackman and Oldham model assumes that employees are satisfied with the general environment in which they work. Thus, a satisfactory environment may be a prerequisite for a job redesign program to be effective. From Herzberg's perspective, the hygiene factors may have to be in place before the motivators will work.

Richard Hackman and his colleagues modified the original model by including three critical psychological states of the individual and refining the measurement of core job characteristics. The result is the **Job Characteristics Model** shown in Figure 14.1.[16] The **Job Diagnostic Survey (JDS)** was developed to diagnose jobs by measuring the five core job characteristics and three critical psychological states shown in the model. The core job characteristics stimulate the critical psychological states in the manner shown in Figure 14.1. This results in varying personal and work outcomes, as identified in the figure.

Job Characteristics Model
A framework for understanding person-job fit through the interaction of core job dimensions with critical psychological states within a person.

Job Diagnostic Survey (JDS)
The survey instrument designed to measure the elements in the Job Characteristics Model.

The five core job characteristics are defined as follows:

1. *Skill variety*. The degree to which a job includes different activities and involves the use of multiple skills and talents of the employee.
2. *Task identity*. The degree to which the job requires completion of a whole and identifiable piece of work—that is, doing a job from beginning to end with a tangible outcome.
3. *Task significance*. The degree to which the job has a substantial impact on the lives or work of other people, whether in the immediate organization or in the external environment.
4. *Autonomy*. The degree to which the job provides substantial freedom, independence, and discretion of the employee in scheduling the work and in determining the procedures to be used in carrying it out.
5. *Feedback from the job itself*. The degree to which carrying out the work activities results in the employee's obtaining direct and clear information about the effectiveness of his or her performance.

Points to Emphasize
Unless all five factors of the job characteristics model are considered, the model may have only short-term success.

Discussion Consideration
Ask student which element of the Job Characteristics Model is most important to them.

Hackman and his colleagues say that the five core job characteristics interact to determine an overall Motivating Potential Score (MPS) for a specific job. The MPS indicates a job's potential for motivating incumbents. An individual's MPS is determined by the following equation:

$$\text{MPS} = \frac{\begin{bmatrix}\text{Skill}\\ \text{variety}\end{bmatrix} + \begin{bmatrix}\text{Task}\\ \text{identity}\end{bmatrix} + \begin{bmatrix}\text{Task}\\ \text{significance}\end{bmatrix}}{3} \times [\text{Autonomy}] \times [\text{Feedback}].$$

Challenge 14.1 enables you to answer five questions from the JDS short form to get an idea about the motivating potential of your present job or any job you have held.

The Job Characteristics Model includes *growth need strength* (the desire to grow and fully develop one's abilities) as a moderator. People with a high growth need strength respond favorably to jobs with high MPSs, and individuals with low growth need strength respond less favorably to such jobs. The job charac-

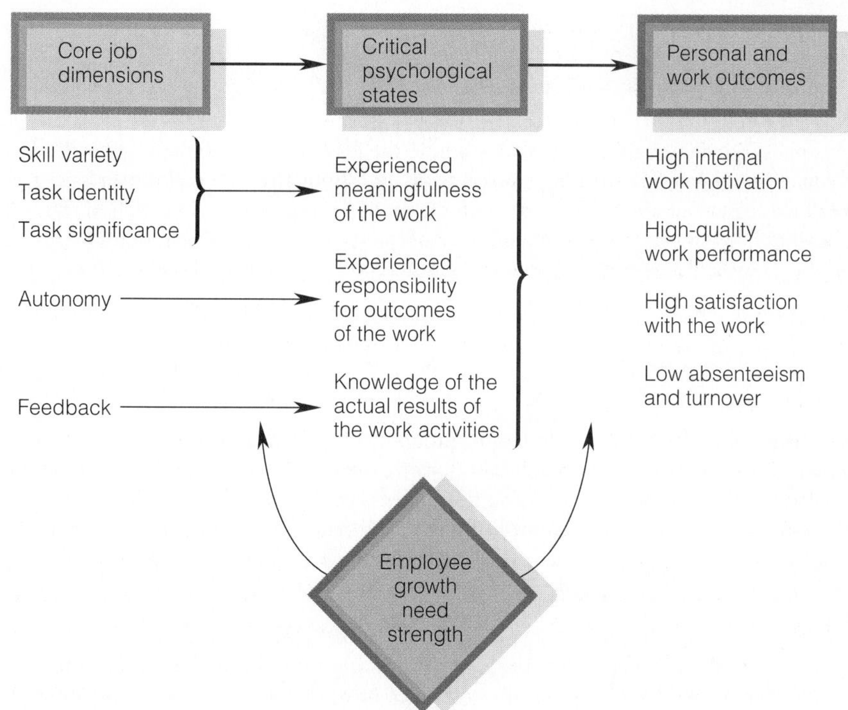

■ **FIGURE 14.1**

The Job Characteristics Model

SOURCE: J. R. Hackman and G. R. Oldham, "The Relationship Among Core Job Dimensions, the Critical Psychological States, and On-the-Job Outcomes," *The Job Diagnostic Survey: An Instrument for the Diagnosis of Jobs and the Evaluation of Job Redesign Projects,* Yale University, (1974), 3. Used with permission.

teristics theory further suggests that core job dimensions stimulate three critical psychological states according to the relationships specified in the model. These critical psychological states are defined as follows:

1. *Experienced meaningfulness of the work*, or the degree to which the employee experiences the job as one that is generally meaningful, valuable, and worthwhile.
2. *Experienced responsibility for work outcomes*, or the degree to which the employee feels personally accountable and responsible for the results of the work he or she does.
3. *Knowledge of results*, or the degree to which the employee knows and understands, on a continuous basis, how effectively he or she is performing the job.

In one early study, Hackman and Oldham administered the JDS to 658 employees working on 62 different jobs in seven business organizations.[17] The JDS was useful for job redesign efforts through one or more of five implementing concepts: (1) the combining of tasks into larger jobs, (2) forming natural work teams to increase task identity and task significance, (3) establishing relationships with customers, (4) loading jobs vertically with more responsibility, and/or (5) opening feedback channels for the job incumbent. For example, if an automotive mechanic received little feedback on the quality of repair work performed, one redesign strategy would be to solicit customer feedback one month after each repair.

Points to Emphasize

People whose jobs are high on the five core dimensions are generally more motivated, more satisfied, and more productive than others.

In an international study, the Job Characteristics Model was tested in a sample of 57 jobs from 37 organizations in Hong Kong.[18] Job incumbents each completed the JDS, and their supervisors completed the Job Rating Form (JRF).[19] The JRF, a supervisory version of the JDS, asks the supervisor to rate the employee's job. The study supported the model in general. However, task significance was not a reliable core job dimension in this study, which suggests either national differences in the measurement of important job dimensions or cultural biases about work. This result may also suggest value differences between American and Asian people with regard to jobs.

CHALLENGE

14.1

Diagnosing Your Job

This questionnaire challenges you to examine the motivating potential in your job. If you are not currently working, complete the questionnaire for any job you have ever held for which you want to examine the motivating potential. For each of the following five questions, circle the number of the most accurate description of the job. Be as objective as you can in describing the job by answering these questions.

1. How much *autonomy* is there in the job? That is, to what extent does the job permit a person to decide *on his or her own* how to go about doing the work?

1	2	3	4	5	6	7
Very little; the job gives a person almost no personal say about how and when the work is done.			Moderate autonomy; many things are standardized and not under the control of the person, but he or she can make some decisions about the work.			Very much; the job gives the person almost complete responsibility for deciding how and when the work is done.

2. To what extent does the job involve doing a *"whole"* and *identifiable piece of work?* That is, is the job a complete piece of work that has an obvious beginning and end? Or is it a small *part* of the overall piece of work, which is finished by other people or by automatic machines?

1	2	3	4	5	6	7
The job is only a tiny part in the overall piece of work; the results of the person's activities cannot be seen in the final product or service.			The job is a moderate-sized "chunk" of the overall piece of work; the person's own contribution can be seen in the final outcome.			The job involves doing the whole piece of work, from start to finish; the results of the person's activities are easily seen in the final product or service.

3. How much *variety* is there in the job? That is, to what extent does the job require a person to do many different things at work, using a variety of his or her skills and talents?

1	2	3	4	5	6	7
Very little; the job requires the person to do the same routine things over and over again.			Moderate variety.			Very much; the job requires the person to do many different things, using a number of different skills and talents.

Discussion Consideration
One of the assumptions many of the models make is that all people want enriched work. Ask students for examples of situations in which individuals do not want enriched work.

An alternative to the Job Characteristics Model is the Job Characteristics Inventory (JCI) developed by Henry Sims and Andrew Szilagyi.[20] The JCI primarily measures core job characteristics. It is not as comprehensive as the JDS, because it does not incorporate critical psychological states, personal and work outcomes, or employee needs. The JCI does give some consideration to structural and individual variables that affect the relationship between core job characteristics and the individual.[21] One comparative analysis of the two models found similarities in the measures and in the models' predictions.[22] The comparative analysis also found two differences. First, the variety scales in the two models appear to have different effects on performance. Second, the autonomy scales in the two models appear to have different effects on employee satisfaction. Overall, the two models together support the usefulness of a person-job fit approach to the design of work over the earlier, universal theories.

CHALLENGE

■ **14.1 continued**

4. In general, how *significant or important* is the job? That is, are the results of the person's work likely to affect significantly the lives or well-being of other people?

1	2	3	4	5	6	7
Not at all significant; the outcome of the work is *not* likely to affect anyone in any important way.			Moderately significant.			Highly significant; the outcome of the work can affect other people in very important ways.

5. To what extent does *doing the job itself* provide the person with information about his or her work performance? That is, does the actual *work itself* provide clues about how well the person is doing—aside from any feedback co-workers or supervisors may provide?

1	2	3	4	5	6	7
Very little; the job itself is set up so a person could work forever without finding out how well he or she was doing.			Moderately; sometimes doing the job provides feedback to the person; sometimes it does not.			Very much; the job is set up so that a person gets almost constant feedback as he or she works about how well he or she is doing.

To score your questionnaire, place your responses to Questions 3, 2, 4, 1, and 5, respectively, in the blank spaces in the following equation:

$$\text{Motivating Potential Score (MPS)} = \frac{\overset{Q\#3}{[\ \ ]} + \overset{Q\#2}{[\ \ ]} + \overset{Q\#4}{[\ \ ]}}{3} \times \overset{Q\#1}{[\ \ ]} \times \overset{Q\#5}{[\ \ ]} = \underline{\qquad}.$$

If the MPS for the job you rated is between

- 200 and 343, it is high in motivating potential.
- 120 and 199, it is moderate in motivating potential.
- 0 And 119, it is low in motivating potential.

SOURCE: J. R. Hackman and G. R. Oldham, "The Job Diagnostic Survey: An Instrument for the Diagnosis of Jobs and the Evaluation of Job Redesign Projects," *Technical Report No. 4* (New Haven, Conn.: Department of Administrative Sciences, Yale University, 1974), 2–3 of the Short Form.

Alternative Approaches to Job Design

■ Because each of the traditional job design approaches has limitations, several alternative approaches to job design have emerged over the past couple of decades. This section examines four of these alternatives. First, it examines the social information-processing model. Second, it reviews the interdisciplinary approach of Michael Campion and Paul Thayer. Their approach builds on the traditional job design approaches. Third, this section examines the international perspectives of the Japanese, the Germans, and the Scandinavians. Finally, it focuses on the health and well-being aspects of work design. An emerging fifth approach to the design of work through teams and autonomous work groups was addressed in Chapter 9. George Fisher, chairman of Eastman Kodak,

http://www.kodak.com

believes that jobs in today's workplace must be designed for a world that has moved beyond the industrial age of mass production.

Social Information Processing

social information-processing (SIP) model

A model that suggests that the important job factors depend in part on what others tell a person about the job.

The traditional approaches to the design of work emphasize objective core job characteristics. In contrast, the **social information-processing (SIP) model** emphasizes the interpersonal aspects of work design. Specifically, the SIP model says that what others tell us about our jobs is important.[23] The SIP model has four basic premises about the work environment.[24] First, other people provide cues we use to understand the work environment. Second, other people help us judge what is important in our jobs. Third, other people tell us how they see our jobs. Fourth, other people's positive and negative feedback helps us understand our feelings about our jobs.

People's perceptions and reactions to their jobs are shaped by information from other people in the work environment.[25] In other words, what others believe about a person's job may be important to understanding the person's perceptions of, and reactions to, the job. This does not mean that objective job characteristics are unimportant; rather, it means that others can modify the way these characteristics affect us. For example, one study of task complexity found that the objective complexity of a task must be distinguished from the subjective task complexity experienced by the employee.[26] While objective task complexity may be a motivator, the presence of others in the work environment, social interaction, or even daydreaming may be important additional sources of motivation. The SIP model makes an important contribution to the design of work by emphasizing the importance of other people and the social context of work. In some cases, these aspects of the work environment may be more important than objective core job characteristics. For example, the subjective feedback of other people about how difficult a particular task is may be more important to a person's motivation to perform than an objective probability estimate of the task's difficulty.

Interdisciplinary Approach

The interdisciplinary approach to job design of Michael Campion and Paul Thayer builds on the traditional job design approaches and does not emphasize the social aspects of the work environment. Four approaches—the mechanistic, motivational, biological, and perceptual/motor approaches—are necessary, they say, because no one approach can solve all performance problems caused by poorly designed jobs. Each approach has its benefits, as well as its limitations.

The interdisciplinary approach allows the job designer or manager to consider trade-offs and alternatives among the approaches based on desired outcomes. If a manager finds poor performance a problem, for example, the manager should analyze the job to ensure a design aimed at improving performance. The interdisciplinary approach is important because badly designed jobs cause far more performance problems than managers realize.[27]

Table 14.2 summarizes the positive and negative outcomes of each job design approach. The mechanistic and motivational approaches to job design are very similar to scientific management's work simplification and to the Job Characteristics Model, respectively. Because these were discussed earlier in the chapter, they are not further elaborated here.

Alternate Example

Another element of the biological approach is ergonomics—the study of the physical environment of work.

The biological approach to job design emphasizes the person's interaction with physical aspects of the work environment and is concerned with the amount of physical exertion, such as lifting and muscular effort, required by the position. For example, an analysis of medical claims at Chaparral Steel Company identified lower back problems as the most common physical problem

TABLE 14.2

Summary of Outcomes from Various Job Design Approaches

JOB DESIGN APPROACH (DISCIPLINE)	POSITIVE OUTCOMES	NEGATIVE OUTCOMES
Mechanistic Approach (mechanical engineering)	Decreased training time Higher personnel utilization levels Lower likelihood of error Less chance of mental overload Lower stress levels	Lower job satisfaction Lower motivation Higher absenteeism
Motivational Approach (industrial psychology)	Higher job satisfaction Higher motivation Greater job involvement Higher job performance Lower absenteeism	Increased training time Lower personnel utilization levels Greater chance of errors Greater chance of mental overload and stress
Biological Approach (biology)	Less physical effort Less physical fatigue Fewer health complaints Fewer medical incidents Lower absenteeism Higher job satisfaction	Higher financial costs because of changes in equipment or job environment
Perceptual Motor Approach (experimental psychology)	Lower likelihood of error Lower likelihood of accidents Less chance of mental stress Lower training time Higher personnel utilization levels	Lower job satisfaction Lower motivation

SOURCE: Reprinted with permission of publisher, from *Organizational Dynamics*, Winter/1987 © 1987. American Management Association, New York. All rights reserved.

experienced by steel makers and managers alike. As a result, the company instituted an education and exercise program under expert guidance to improve care of the lower back. Program graduates received back cushions for their chairs with "Chaparral Steel Company" embossed on them.[28] The accompanying Organizational Reality feature discusses Herman Miller's revolutionary chair design, which supports not only the lower back but other parts of the seated human body. Lower back problems associated with improper lifting may be costly, but they are not fatal. Campion describes a more catastrophic problem in the case of Three Mile Island, when nuclear materials contaminated the surrounding area and threatened disaster. Campion concluded that poor design of the control room operator's job caused the disaster.

The perceptual/motor approach to job design also emphasizes the person's interaction with physical aspects of the work environment and is based on engineering that considers human factors such as strength or coordination, ergonomics, and experimental psychology. This approach addresses how people mentally process information acquired from the physical work environment through perceptual and motor skills. The approach emphasizes perception and fine motor skills, as opposed to the gross motor skills and muscle strength emphasized in the mechanistic approach. The perceptual/motor approach is more likely to be relevant to operational and technical work, which may tax a person's concentration and attention, than to managerial, administrative, and custodial jobs, which are less likely to strain concentration and attention. For example, keyboard operations and data entry jobs are where this approach may be very applicable.

One study using the interdisciplinary approach to improve jobs evaluated 377 clerical, 80 managerial, and 90 analytical positions.[29] The jobs were improved

ORGANIZATIONAL REALITY

Herman Miller's Aeron Chair

Industrial engineers can play an important role in the ergonomics and design of essential office equipment. Whereas Chaparral Steel uses education, exercise, and lower back cushions on conventional chairs, Herman Miller has attempted to revolutionize a central feature of the office work environment—the office chair.

The inspiration for Herman Miller's chair came from the observation that traditional work chairs do not fit 40–50 percent of the population. As a result Don Chadwick and Bill Stumpf designed a chair called Aeron, which comes in three different sizes: small, medium, and large. The Aeron has a Kinemat tilt mechanism that spontaneously supports any preferred posture, anywhere from the work-intensive forward position to the fully reclined position for thinking.

Unlike ordinary chairs that use the traditional fabric-covered foam cushioning, Aeron has a see-through, meshlike Pellicle material that conforms to the individual's shape, equally distributing body pressure on the chair's seat and back. Parts of Aeron are recyclable and parts are made of recycled materials. The Aeron has easy controls to adjust seat height, tilt-tension, tilt limit, each armrest independently, and the lumbar pad. So the Aeron attends to the lower back in addition to all other parts of the seated human body.

SOURCE: J. Teresko, "Emerging Technologies," *Industry Week*, February 27, 1995, 1–2.

Herman Miller has attempted to revolutionize the office chair through an innovative, inspirational design and construction called the Aeron Chair.

by combining tasks and adding ancillary duties. The improved jobs provided greater motivation for the incumbents and were better from a perceptual/motor standpoint. However, the jobs were poorly designed from a mechanical engineering standpoint, and they were unaffected from a biological standpoint. Again, the interdisciplinary approach considers trade-offs and alternatives when evaluating job redesign efforts.

Japanese, German, and Scandinavian Perspectives

Each nation or ethnic group has a unique way of understanding and designing work.[30] As organizations become more global and international, an appreciation of the perspectives of other nations is increasingly important. The Japanese,

Germans, and Scandinavians in particular have distinctive perspectives on the designing and organizing of work. Each country's perspective is forged within its unique cultural and economic system, and each is distinct from the approaches used in North America during the twentieth century.

The Japanese began harnessing their productive energies during the 1950s by drawing on the product quality ideas of W. Edwards Deming.[31] In addition, the central government became actively involved in the economic resurgence of Japan, and it encouraged companies to conquer industries rather than to maximize profits.[32] Such an industrial policy built on the Japanese cultural ethic of collectivism has implications for how work is done. Whereas Frederick Taylor and his successors in the United States emphasized the job of an individual worker, the Japanese work system emphasizes the strategic level and encourages collective and cooperative working arrangements.[33] As may be seen in Table 14.1, the Japanese emphasize performance, accountability, and other- or self-directedness in defining work, whereas Americans emphasize the positive affect, personal identity, and social benefits of work.

The German approach to work has been shaped by Germany's unique educational system, cultural values, and economic system. The Germans are a highly educated and well-organized people. For example, their educational system has a multitrack design with technical and university alternatives. The German economic system has a strong emphasis on free enterprise, private property rights, and management-labor cooperation. A comparison of voluntary and mandated management-labor cooperation in Germany found productivity superior in the former type of cooperation.[34] The Germans value hierarchy and authority relationships and, as a result, are generally disciplined.[35] Germany's workers are highly unionized, and their discipline and efficiency have enabled Germany to be highly productive while its workers labor substantially fewer hours than do Americans.

Discussion Consideration
Of the Japanese, German, and Scandinavian perspectives, which one would students be most comfortable in? Least comfortable in?

The traditional German approach to work design was **technocentric**, an approach that placed technology and engineering at the center of job design decisions. Recently, German industrial engineers have moved to a more **anthropocentric** approach, which places human considerations at the center of job design decisions. The former approach uses a natural scientific process in the design of work, whereas the latter relies on a more humanistic process, as shown in Figure 14.2.[36] In the anthropocentric approach, work is evaluated using the criteria of practicability and worker satisfaction at the individual level and the criteria of endurability and acceptability at the group level. Figure 14.2 also identifies problem areas and disciplines concerned with each aspect of the work design.

technocentric
Placing technology and engineering at the center of job design decisions.

anthropocentric
Placing human considerations at the center of job design decisions.

The Scandinavian cultural values and economic system stand in contrast to the German system. The social democratic tradition in Scandinavia during this century has emphasized social concern rather than industrial efficiency. The Scandinavians place great emphasis on a work design model that encourages high degrees of worker control and good social support systems for workers.[37] Lennart Levi believes that circumstantial and inferential scientific evidence is sufficiently strong as a basis for legislative and policy action for redesign intended to enhance worker well-being. An example of such action for promoting good working environments and occupational health, Swedish Government Bill 1976/77:149, states "Work should be safe both physically and mentally, *but also* provide opportunities for involvement, job satisfaction, and personal development." More recently, the Swedish Working Life Fund was set up by a 1991 decree from the Swedish Parliament to fund research, intervention programs, and demonstration projects in work design. For example, a study of Stockholm police on shift schedules going from a daily, counterclockwise to a clockwise rotation, which was more compatible with human biology, resulted in improved sleep, less fatigue, lower systolic blood pressure, and lower blood levels of

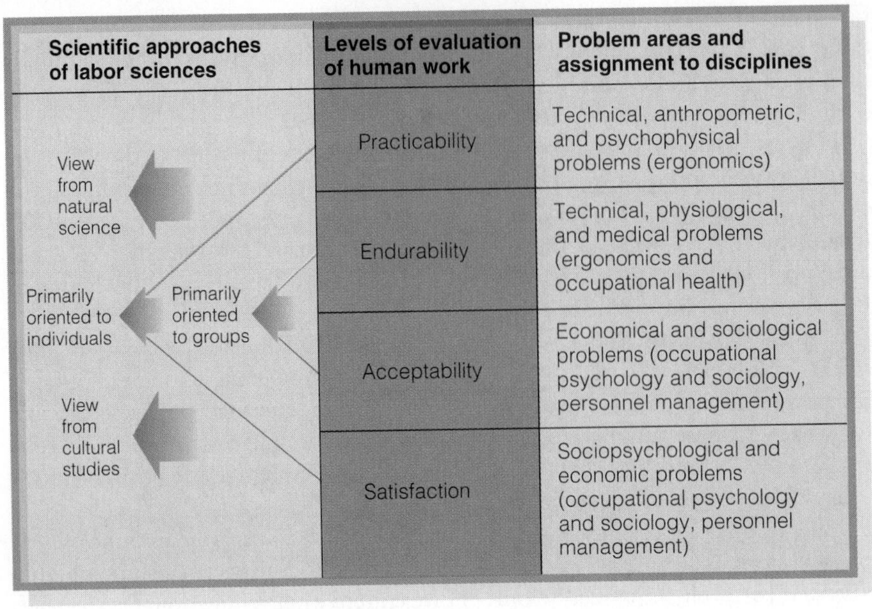

■ **FIGURE 14.2**

Hierarchical Model of Criteria for the Evaluation of Human Work

SOURCE: H. Luczak, "'Good Work' Design: An Ergonomic, Industrial Engineering Perspective," in J. C. Quick, L. R. Murphy, and J. J. Hurrell, eds., *Stress and Well-Being at Work* (Washington, D.C.): American Psychological Association. Reprinted by permission.

Scientific approaches of labor sciences	Levels of evaluation of human work	Problem areas and assignment to disciplines
View from natural science	Practicability	Technical, anthropometric, and psychophysical problems (ergonomics)
Primarily oriented to individuals	Endurability	Technical, physiological, and medical problems (ergonomics and occupational health)
Primarily oriented to groups	Acceptability	Economical and sociological problems (occupational psychology and sociology, personnel management)
View from cultural studies	Satisfaction	Sociopsychological and economic problems (occupational psychology and sociology, personnel management)

triglycerides and glucose.[38] Hence, the work redesign improved the police officers' health.

Work Design and Well-Being

American social scientists have had concerns like those of the Scandinavians with regard to the effects of work and job design on health and well-being. This issue was discussed briefly in Chapter 7. Economic and industry-specific upheavals in the United States during the past two decades led to job loss and unemployment, and the adverse health impact of these factors has received attention.[39] Attention also has been devoted to the effects of specific work design parameters on psychological health.[40] Frank Landy believes that organizations should work to redesign jobs to increase worker control and reduce worker uncertainty, while at the same time managing conflict and task/job demands. These objectives can be achieved in several ways.

Alternate Example
Most managers would agree philosophically with the concept of sharing information with employees. However, one of the major criticisms by victims of downsizing and restructuring is the reluctance of managers to let employees know about the impending decisions.

Control in work organizations can be increased by: (1) giving workers the opportunity to control several aspects of the work and the workplace; (2) designing machines and tasks with optimal response times and/or ranges; and (3) implementing performance-monitoring systems as a source of relevant feedback to workers. Uncertainty can be reduced by: (1) providing employees with timely and complete information needed for their work; (2) making clear and unambiguous work assignments; (3) improving communication at shift change time, and (4) increasing employee access to information sources. Conflict at work can be managed through: (1) participative decision making to reduce conflict; (2) the use of supportive supervisory styles to resolve conflict; and (3) sufficient resource availability to meet work demands, thus preventing conflict. Task/job design can be improved by enhancing core job characteristics and not patterning service work after assembly line work.

Task uncertainty was shown to have an adverse effect on morale in a study of 629 employment security work units in California and Wisconsin.[41] More important, the study showed that morale was better predicted by considering both the overall design of the work unit and the task uncertainty. This study suggests that if one work design parameter, such as task uncertainty, is a problem in a job, its adverse effects on people may be mitigated by other work design parameters. For example, higher pay may offset an employee's frustration with a difficult coworker, or a friendly, supportive working environment may offset frus-

CHALLENGE

■ **14.2**

Is Your Work Environment A Healthy One?

To determine whether or not yours is a healthy work environment, read the text section on "Work Design and Well-Being," then complete the following four steps. Answer each question in the five steps "Yes" or "No."

Step 1. Control and Influence
____ Do you have influence over the pace of your work?
____ Are system response times neither too fast nor too slow?
____ Do you have a say in your work assignments and goals?
____ Is there an opportunity for you to comment on your performance appraisal?

Step 2. Information and Uncertainty
____ Do you receive timely information to complete your work?
____ Do you receive complete information for your work assignments?
____ Is there adequate planning for changes that affect you at work?
____ Do you have access to all the information you need at work?

Step 3. Conflict at Work
____ Does the company apply policies clearly and consistently?
____ Are job descriptions and task assignments clear and unambiguous?
____ Are there adequate policies and procedures for the resolution of conflicts?
____ Is your work environment an open, participative one?

Step 4. Job Scope and Task Design
____ Is there adequate variety in your work activities and/or assignments?
____ Do you receive timely, constructive feedback on your work?
____ Is your work important to the overall mission of the company?
____ Do you work on more than one small piece of a big project?

Scoring:
Count the number of "yes" answers in Steps 1 through 4: ______
If you have 10 to 16 "yes" answers this would suggest that your work environment is a psychologically healthy one.
If you have 7 or fewer "yes" answers this may suggest that your work environment is not as psychologically healthy as it could be.

tration with low pay. Challenge 14.2 provides you with an opportunity to evaluate how psychologically healthy your work environment is.

Emerging Issues in the Design of Work

■ A number of issues related to specific aspects of the design of work have emerged over the past several years. Rather than being comprehensive ways to address job design or worker well-being, these issues address one or another aspect of a job. They are not interrelated. The emerging issues addressed are task revision, telecommuting, alternative work patterns, technostress, and skill development.

Task Revision

task revision
The modification of incorrectly specified roles or jobs.

A new concept in the design of work is **task revision.**[42] Task revision is an innovative way to modify an incorrectly specified role or job. Task revision assumes that organizational roles and job expectations may be correctly or incorrectly defined. Furthermore, a person's behavior in a work role has very different performance consequences depending on whether the role is correctly or incorrectly defined. Table 14.3 sets out the performance consequences of three categories of

■ **TABLE 14.3**

Performance Consequences of Role Behaviors

ROLE CHARACTERISTICS	STANDARD ROLE BEHAVIOR (Meets Expectations)	EXTRAROLE BEHAVIOR (Goes beyond Expectations)	COUNTER-ROLE BEHAVIOR (Differs from Expected)
Correctly Specified Role	Ordinary good performance	Excellent performance (organizational citizenship and prosocial behavior)	Poor performance (deviance, dissent, and grievance)
Incorrectly specified role	Poor performance (bureaucratic behavior)	Very poor performance (bureaucratic zeal)	Excellent performance (task revision and redirection, role innovation)

SOURCE: R. M. Staw and R. D. Boettger, "Task Revision: A Neglected Form of Work Performance," *Academy of Management Journal* 33 (1990): 536.

role behaviors based on the definition of the role or job. As indicated in the table, standard role behavior leads to good performance if the role is correctly defined, and it leads to poor performance if the role is incorrectly defined. These performances go to the extreme when incumbents exhibit extreme behavior in their jobs.[43] Going to extremes leads one to exceed expectations and display extraordinary behavior (extrarole behavior); this results in either excellent performance or very poor performance, depending on the accuracy of the defined role.

counter-role behavior

Deviant behavior in either a correctly or incorrectly defined job or role.

Counter-role behavior is when the incumbent acts contrary to the expectations of the role or exhibits deviant behavior. This is a problem if the role is correctly defined. For example, poor performance occurred on a hospital ward when the nursing supervisor failed to check the administration of all medications for the nurses she was supervising, resulting in one near fatality because a patient was not given required medication by a charge nurse. The nursing supervisor exhibited counter-role behavior in believing she could simply trust the nurses and did not have to double-check their actions. The omission was caught on the next shift. When a role or task is correctly defined (for example, double-checking medication administration), counter-role behavior leads to poor performance.

Discussion Consideration

Is task revision related to employees' fear that they will "work themselves out of a job"?

Task revision is counter-role behavior in an incorrectly specified role and is a useful way to correct for the problem in the role specification (see Table 14.3). Task revision is a form of role innovation that modifies the job to achieve a better performance. Task revision is the basis for long-term adaptation when the current specifications of a job are no longer applicable.[44] For example, the traditional role for a surgeon is to complete surgical procedures in an accurate and efficient manner. Based on this definition, socio-emotional caregiving is counter-role behavior on the part of the surgeon. However, if the traditional role were to be labeled incorrect, the surgeon's task revision through socio-emotional caregiving would be viewed as leading to much better medical care for patients.

Telecommuting

Telecommuting, as noted in Chapter 2, is when employees work at home or in other locations geographically separate from their company's main location. Telecommuting may entail working in a combination of home, satellite office, and main office locations. This flexible arrangement is designed to achieve a better fit between the needs of the individual employee and the organization's task demands.

Executives have practiced forms of telecommuting for years. For example, Jonathan Fielding, while serving as a professor at UCLA and working for Johnson & Johnson, telecommuted between offices in Berkley, California;

Brunswick, New Jersey; and other locations throughout the country and the world. A number of companies, such as AT&T in Phoenix and Bell Atlantic, started pilot programs in telecommuting for a wide range of employees.These flexible arrangements help some companies respond to changing demographics and a shrinking labor pool. The Travelers Companies was one of the first companies to try telecommuting and is considered an industry leader in telecommuting. Because of their confidence in employees, The Travelers has reaped rewards from telecommuting, including higher productivity, reduced absenteeism, expanded opportunities for disabled workers, and an increased ability to attract and retain talent.[45]

http://www.travelers.com

Pacific Bell has tried telecommuting on a large scale.[46] In 1990, Pacific Bell had 1,500 managers who telecommuted. For example, an employee might work at home four days a week as an information systems designer and spend one day a week at the main office location in meetings, work exchanges, and coordination with others. Of 3,000 Pacific Bell managers responding to a mail survey, 87 percent said telecommuting would reduce employee stress, 70 percent said it would increase job satisfaction while reducing absenteeism, and 64 percent said it would increase productivity.

Telecommuting is neither a cure-all nor a universally feasible alternative. Many telecommuters feel a sense of social isolation. Furthermore, not all forms of work are amenable to telecommuting. For example, firefighters and police officers must be at their duty stations to be successful in their work. Employees for whom telecommuting is not a viable option within a company may feel jealous of those able to telecommute. In addition, it may have the potential to create the sweatshops of the twenty-first century. Telecommuting is a novel, emerging issue.

Alternate Example
One advantage of telecommuting is that disabled individuals can be employed in jobs they might otherwise not have been able to do.

Alternative Work Patterns

Job sharing is an alternative work pattern in which there is more than one person occupying a single job. Job sharing may be an alternative to telecommuting for addressing demographic and labor pool concerns. Job sharing is found throughout a wide range of managerial and professional jobs, as well as in production and service jobs. It is not common among senior executives.

job sharing
An alternative work pattern in which there is more than one person occupying a single job.

The four-day workweek is a second type of alternative work schedule. Information systems personnel at the United Services Automobile Association (USAA) in San Antonio, Texas, work four 10-hour days and enjoy a three-day weekend. This arrangement provides the benefit of more time for those who want to balance work and family life through weekend travel. However, the longer workdays may be a drawback for employees with many family or social activities on weekday evenings. Hence, the four-day workweek has both benefits and limitations.

Flextime is a third alternative work pattern. Flextime, in which employees can set their own daily work schedules, has been applied in numerous ways in work organizations. For example, many companies in highly concentrated urban areas, like Houston, Los Angeles, and New York City, allow employees to set their own daily work schedules as long as they start their eight hours at any 30-minute interval from 6:00 A.M. to 9:00 A.M. This arrangement is designed to ease traffic and commuting pressures. It also is somewhat responsive to individual biorhythms, allowing early risers to go to work early and nighthawks to work late. Typically, 9:00 A.M. to 3:00 P.M. is the required core working time for everyone in the company. Flextime options take many forms in organizations, depending on the nature of the work and the coordination requirements in various jobs. Even in companies without formal flextime programs, flextime may be an individual option arranged between supervisor and subordinate. For example, a first-line supervisor who wants to complete a college degree may negotiate a

flextime
An alternative work pattern through which employees can set their own daily work schedules.

Alternate Example
Results from a study of nurses found that in terms of job stress and job satisfaction, those working fixed shifts appeared to be better off than those working rotating shifts.
SOURCE: M. Jamal and V. Baba, "Shiftwork and Department-type Related Job Stress, Work Attitudes, and Behavioral Intentions: A Study of Nurses," *Journal of Organizational Behavior* 13 (1992): 449–464.

work schedule accommodating both job requirements and course schedules at the university. Flextime options may be more likely for high performers who assure their bosses that work quality and productivity will not suffer.[47]

Technology at Work

virtual office

A mobile platform of computer, telecommunication, and information technology and services.

technostress

The stress caused by new and advancing technologies in the workplace.

New technologies are changing the face of work environments, dramatically in some cases. As forces for change, new technologies are a double-edged sword that can be used to improve job performance, or to create stress. On the positive side, modern technologies are helping to revolutionize the way jobs are designed and the way work gets done. The **virtual office** is a mobile platform of computer, telecommunication, and information technology and services at the disposal of mobile workforce members to conduct business virtually anywhere, anytime, globally. The accompanying Organizational Reality feature describes AT&T's Virtual Workplace Program.

Technostress is stress caused by new and advancing technologies in the workplace, most often information technologies.[48] For example, the widespread use of electronic bulletin boards as a forum for rumors of layoffs may cause feelings of uncertainty and anxiety (technostress). However, the same electronic bulletin boards can be an important source of information and uncertainty reduction for workers.

New information technologies enable organizations to monitor employee work performance, even if the employee is not aware of the monitoring.[49] These new technologies also allow organizations to tie pay to performance as it is electronically monitored.[50] The Office of Technology Assessment suggests three guidelines for making electronic workplace monitoring, especially of performance, less distressful.[51] First, workers should participate in the introduction of the monitoring system. Second, performance standards should be seen as fair. Third, performance records should be used to improve performance, not to punish the performer.

Skill Development

Problems in work system design are often seen as the source of frustration for those dealing with technostress.[52] However, system and technical problems are not the only sources of technostress in new information technologies. Some experts see a growing gap between the skills demanded by new technologies and the skills possessed by employees in jobs using these technologies.[53] Although technical skills are important and are emphasized in many training programs, the largest sector of the economy is actually service-oriented, and service jobs require interpersonal skills. Managers also use a wide range of nontechnical skills to be effective in their work.[54] Therefore, any discussion of jobs and the design of work must recognize the importance of incumbent skills and abilities to meet the demands of the work. Organizations must consider the talents and skills of their employees when they engage in job design efforts. The two issues of employee skill development and job design are interrelated. The knowledge and information requirements for jobs of the future are especially high.

Discussion Consideration

Can creativity and innovation be learned?

Managerial Implications: The Changing Nature of Work

■ Work is an important aspect of a healthy life. The two central needs in human nature are to engage in productive work and to form healthy relationships with others. Work means different things to different ethnic and national groups. Therefore, job design efforts must be sensitive to cultural values and beliefs.

ORGANIZATIONAL REALITY

AT&T's Virtual Office

Mobile workforces are an increasingly common characteristic of the global industrial landscape. Their range, maneuverability, and flexibility is a real advantage for many companies. However, their effectiveness hinges on access to essential information through computer and telecommunications technologies. Once automated and activated, mobile workforces can range over the global industrial landscape in virtual offices. The virtual office promises to revolutionize the design of jobs and the workplace.

AT&T Global Information Solutions plans to deliver a broad initiative that mixes the essential technologies and services through computers and telecommunications to enable companies to create virtual office platforms for their mobile workforces. AT&T has a five-tier Virtual Workplace Program that promises to combine (1) network services, (2) notebook computers, (3) communications products, (4) support services, and (5) application software into a one-stop solution for companies looking to manage their mobile computer environments. The first three tiers of the program deal with integrating PCs, peripherals, and communications products. The fourth layer partners AT&T with three client/server applications: (1) Adaptive Strategies Inc.'s MobileSync, (2) XcelleNet Inc.'s RemoteWare and (3) Brock Control Systems Inc.'s TakeControl. AT&T will offer its customers seven-day, around-the-clock support to help integrate the varying products.

SOURCE: L. DiCarlo, "AT&T Maps Virtual Office Environment," *PC Week*, February 27, 1995, 1–2.

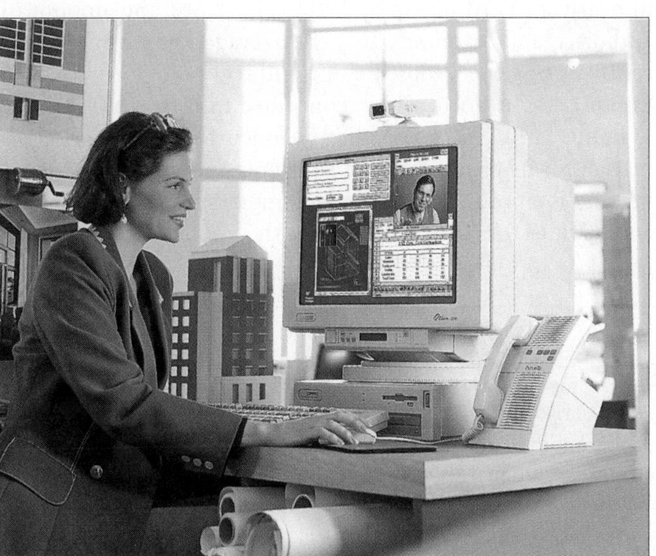

Virtual offices are here today for women and men who are on the move. Designed and used primarily by mobile employees, the core of the virtual office is essential information and telecommunication technologies.

In crafting work tasks and assignments, managers should make an effort to fit the jobs to the people who are doing them. There are no universally accepted ways to design work, and early efforts to find them have been replaced by a number of alternatives. Early approaches to job design were valuable for manufacturing and administrative jobs of mid-1900s. However, the changing nature of work in the United States challenges managers to find new ways to define work and design jobs.

The distinguishing feature of job design in the foreseeable future is flexibility. Dramatic global, economic, and organizational change dictates that managers be flexible in the design of work in their organizations. Jobs must be designed to fit the larger organizational structures discussed in Chapter 15. Organizations must ask, does the job support the organization's mission? Employees must ask, does the job meet my short- and long-term needs?

Technology is one of the distinguishing features of the modern workplace. Advances in information, mechanical, and computer technology are transforming work into a highly scientific endeavor demanding employees who are highly educated, knowledgeable workers. American workers can expect these technological advances to continue during their lifetimes and should expect to meet the challenge through continuous skill development and enhancement.

CLOSING SPOTLIGHT

Concurrent Engineering: The Next Transformation at Ford

The people at Ford Motor Company responded very positively to the transformation of how work would be done at Ford. Fully 80 percent of the improvements in Ford's quality and productivity from 1981 through 1989 were attributable to the contributions of the people—not the technology. Estimates were that quality was up 65 percent in 1988 over 1980. One of the contributing factors was the implementation of employee involvement programs, which empowered employees to have significant input in their work and work processes. The unions at Ford embraced these programs, which were in place in nearly all Ford plants by 1989. Therefore, the amount of responsibility, authority, and autonomy that the average Ford worker had increased significantly during the 1980s. People and technology combined in the transformation process at Ford, which continued into the next decade.

In the early 1990s, Ford began concurrent engineering to reduce time-to-market for its products while continuing to improve quality.[55] Concurrent engineering is a product development approach in which engineers work on design and manufacturability simultaneously. People and technology transform Ford. ■

Chapter Summary

- Different countries have different preferences for one or more of six distinct patterns of defining *work*.
- Scientific management, job enlargement/job rotation, job enrichment, and the job characteristics theory are traditional American approaches to the design of work and the management of workforce diversity.
- The social information processing (SIP) model suggests that information from others and the social context are important in a job.
- The interdisciplinary approach draws on mechanical engineering, industrial psychology, experimental psychology, and biology in considering the advantages and disadvantages of job design efforts.
- The cultural values and social organizations in Japan, Germany, and Scandinavia lead to unique approaches to the design of work.
- Control, uncertainty, conflict, and job/task demands are important job design parameters to consider when designing work for the well-being of the workers.
- Task revision, telecommuting, alternative work patterns, technostress, and skill development are emerging issues in the design of work and the use of information technology.

Key Terms

job (p. 416)
work (p. 416)
the meaning of work (p. 416)
work simplification (p. 419)
job enlargement (p. 419)
job rotation (p. 419)
cross-training (p. 420)
job enrichment (p. 420)
Job Characteristics Model (p. 422)
Job Diagnostic Survey (JDS) (p. 422)
social information-processing (SIP) model (p. 426)
technocentric (p. 429)
anthropocentric (p. 429)
task revision (p. 431)
counter-role behavior (p. 432)
job sharing (p. 433)
flextime (p. 433)
virtual office (p. 434)
technostress (p. 434)

Review Questions

1. Define a job in its organizational context.
2. Describe six patterns of working that have been studied in different countries.
3. Describe four traditional approaches to the design of work in America.
4. Identify and define the five core job dimensions and the three critical psychological states in the Job Characteristics Model.
5. What are the salient features of the social information-processing (SIP) model of job design?
6. List the positive and negative outcomes of the four job design approaches considered by the interdisciplinary model.
7. How do the Japanese, German, and Scandinavian approaches to work differ from one another and from the American approach?
8. Describe the key job design parameters considered when examining the effects of work design on health and well-being.
9. What are five emerging issues in jobs and the design of work?

Discussion and Communication Questions

1. Is there ever one best way to design a particular job?
2. What should managers learn from the traditional approaches to the design of work used in the United States?
3. It is possible for American companies to apply approaches to the design of work that were developed in other countries?
4. What is the most important emerging issue in the design of work?
5. *(communication question)* Go to the library and read about new approaches to jobs, such as job sharing. Prepare a memo comparing what you have learned from your library reading to one or more approaches to job design discussed in the chapter. What changes in approaches to jobs and job design do you notice from this comparison?
6. *(communication question)* Interview an employee in your organization or another organization and develop an oral presentation about how the job the employee is doing could be enriched. Make sure you ask questions about all aspects of the employee's work (e.g., what specific tasks are done and with whom the employee interacts on the job).
7. *(communication question)* Based on the materials in the chapter, prepare a memo detailing the advantages and disadvantages of flextime job arrangements. In a second part of the memo, identify the specific conditions and characteristics required for a successful flextime program. Would you like to work under a flextime arrangement?

Ethics Questions

1. Assume that a company is planning to redesign all of the jobs in one department based on the advice of a major consulting firm. Should the company discuss the job redesign plans with employees before implementing them? Should the employees have been consulted prior to hiring the consulting firm?
2. Assume that a company is aware of certain psychological or physical risks associated with a job, such as respiratory problems and cancer risk associated with the installation of asbestos. Assume also that the medical costs for workers will not be too great. Is it ethical not to warn employees about the possible health risks? Would it make a difference if the risks were less permanent, such as lower back tension or temporarily altered vision?
3. Suppose that the design of a particular job exposed the employee to a health or safety risk and that the redesign of the job would cost the company more than paying the medical claims if the employee were injured or hurt. Should the company tell employees doing the job about its decision not to redesign the job to make it safer? Is it ethical for the company not to redesign the job?
4. Assume that a company has many older, mature workers. Rather than retrain them in new technologies, the company wants to replace the older workers with younger ones. Should this be allowed?

Experiential Exercises

14.1 Chaos and the Manager's Job

Managers' jobs in the 1990s are increasingly chaotic as a result of high rates of change, uncertainty, and turbulence. Some managers thrive on change and chaos while others have a difficult time responding to high rates of change and uncertainty in a positive manner. The 24-item questionnaire gives you an opportunity to evaluate how you would react to a manager's job that is rather chaotic.

EXERCISE SCHEDULE

1. Preparation (preclass)
   Complete the 24-item questionnaire.
2. Individual Scoring
   Give yourself 4 points for each A, 3 points for each B, 2 points for each C, 1 point for each D, and 0 points for each E. Compute the total, divide by 24, and round to one decimal place.
3. Group Discussion
   Your instructor may have you discuss your scores in groups of six students. The higher your score, the more you respond positively to change and chaos; the lower your score, the more difficulty you would have responding to this manager's job in a positive manner. In addition, answer the following questions.
   a. If you could redesign this manager's job, what are the two or three aspects of the job that you would change first?
   b. What are the two or three aspects of the job that you would feel no need to change?

SOURCE: D. Marcic, "Option B. Quality and the New Management Paradigm," *Organizational Behavior: Experiences and Cases, 4th ed.* (Minneapolis/St. Paul: West Publishing, 1995): 296–297.

A MANAGER'S JOB[a]

Listed below are some statements a 37-year-old manager made about his job at a large and successful corporation. If your job had these characteristics, how would you react to them? After each statement are five letters, A–E. Circle the letter that best describes how you would react according to the following scale:

A. I would enjoy this very much; it's completely acceptable.
B. This would be enjoyable and acceptable most of the time.
C. I'd have no reaction one way or another, or it would be about equally enjoyable and unpleasant.
D. This feature would be somewhat unpleasant for me.
E. This feature would be very unpleasant for me.

1. I regularly spend 30–40 percent of my time in meetings. A B C D E
2. A year and a half ago, my job did not exist, and I have been essentially inventing it as I go along. A B C D E
3. The responsibilities I either assume or am assigned consistently exceed the authority I have for discharging them. A B C D E
4. At any given moment in my job, I average about a dozen phone calls to be returned. A B C D E
5. There seems to be very little relation in my job between the quality of my performance and my actual pay and fringe benefits. A B C D E
6. I need about two weeks of management training a year to stay current in my job. A B C D E
7. Because we have very effective equal employment opportunity in my company and because it is thoroughly multinational, my job consistently brings me into close contact at a professional level with people of many races, ethnic groups, and nationalities and of both sexes. A B C D E
8. There is no objective way to measure my effectiveness. A B C D E
9. I report to three different bosses for different aspects of my job, and each has an equal say in my performance appraisal. A B C D E
10. On average, about a third of my time is spent dealing with unexpected emergencies that force all scheduled work to be postponed. A B C D E
11. When I need to meet with the people who report to me, it takes my secretary most of a day to find a time when we are all available, and even then I have yet to have a meeting where everyone is present for the entire meeting. A B C D E
12. The college degree I earned in preparation for this type of work is now obsolete, and I probably should return for another degree. A B C D E

[a]By Peter B. Vaill in *Managing as a Performing Art: New Ideas for a World of Chaotic Change*, published by Jossey-Bass, 1989. Used with permission of the publisher.

13. My job requires that I absorb about 100–200 pages a week of technical material. A B C D E
14. I am out of town overnight at least one night a week. A B C D E
15. My department is so interdependent with several other departments in the company that all distinctions about which department is responsible for which tasks are quite arbitrary. A B C D E
16. I will probably get a promotion in about a year to a job in another division that has most of these same characteristics. A B C D E
17. During the period of my employment here, either the entire company or the division I worked in has been reorganized every year or so. A B C D E
18. While I face several possible promotions, I have no real career path. A B C D E
19. While there are several possible promotions I can see ahead of me, I think I have no realistic chance of getting to the top levels of the company. A B C D E
20. While I have many ideas about how to make things work better, I have no direct influence on either the business policies or the personnel policies that govern my division. A B C D E
21. My company has recently put in an "assessment center" where I and other managers must go through an extensive battery of psychological tests to assess our potential. A B C D E
22. My company is a defendant in an antitrust suit, and if the case comes to trial, I will probably have to testify about some decisions that were made a few years ago. A B C D E
23. Advanced computer and other electronic office technology is continually being introduced into my division, necessitating constant learning on my part. A B C D E
24. The computer terminal and screen I have in my office can be monitored in my boss' office without my knowledge. A B C D E

14.2 A Job Redesign Effort

This activity will help you consider ways in which work can be redesigned to improve its impact on people and its benefit to the organization. Consider the following case:

> Eddie is a quality control inspector for an automotive assembly line. His job is to inspect the body, interior, and engine of cars as they roll off the assembly line. Sometimes late in the day, especially on Thursdays and Fridays, Eddie lets assembly problems slip past him. In addition, Eddie's back feels sore at the end of the day, and sometimes he is very stiff in the morning. There are times when he is not sure whether he is seeing a serious problem or just a glitch.

As a five-person team, your job is to evaluate two alternative approaches to redesigning Eddie's job using theories presented in the chapter. Answer the following questions as a team. Your team should be prepared to present its recommendations to the class as a whole.

Discussion Questions

Your instructor will lead a class discussion of each of the following questions:

1. For this particular job, which are the two best models to use in a redesign effort? Why?
2. Does your team need any additional information before it begins to redesign Eddie's job? If so, what information do you need?
3. Using the two models you chose in Question 1, what would your team specifically recommend to redesign Eddie's job?

VIDEO CASE

Steelcase's Team-Oriented Manufacturing Cells[1]

Steelcase, a leading designer and manufacturer of office furniture, implemented significant changes in its manufacturing process in order to better satisfy customer needs. As Rob Pew, head of Steelcase operations, observed, "Now customers are demanding more specialized kinds of requirements. . . . We have to change manufacturing processes to roll with that."

In the past, Steelcase had designed jobs around simplicity, with employees doing routine, repetitive tasks all day. "What happened because of that," according to Bill Baxter, director of manufacturing planning, was "we ended up with very complex processes." Because of the complex processes, lots of inventory and lots of support people were needed.

With the new manufacturing process, Steelcase has flexible and well-trained people who can be trusted and who can do a multitude of tasks. How did Steelcase alter its manufacturing process in order to achieve these outcomes?

The new manufacturing process arranges operations by product rather than function so that there are focus factories or manufacturing cells within factories. Within each focus factory all the necessary production processes are linked together for manufacturing a particular product. The manufacturing cells are run by self-directed teams of employees. These work teams are responsible for making decisions and solving problems on their own. Problems tend to be resolved quickly and effectively within the work teams.

The manufacturing cell design also takes a broad view of who the customers are. In addition to purchasers or end users, customers include the next operation in the production process. With this perspective, Steelcase employees work toward achieving world-class performance in every step of the production process. Commenting on their quality focus, Jerry Myers, president and CEO of Steelcase, says: "World-class performance means providing customers"—both external and internal—"with the products and services that fully satisfy their needs."

Steelcase's pursuit of world-class performance can be seen in the work of a three-person team that produces chair rings, an important structural component of office chairs. This three-person team handles eight operations that were formerly performed by 12 workers. This team runs the chair ring production process from beginning to end, and has maintained output quantity while achieving zero defect quality and absolutely eliminating scrap.

The new work system has had other beneficial effects as well. For instance, Tracey Wood, an upholstery trimmer, now does three tasks instead of one. He likes the new job arrangement because it is easier on his body not having to perform the same repetitive motions all the time. Many employees now take considerable initiative in solving problems and improving the manufacturing process. Rob Pew, head of Steelcase operations, points out that even long-time employees are coming up with new ideas. For example, a 30-year veteran interviewed customers in the next department to get ideas for satisfying their needs.

Using self-directed work teams to run the manufacturing cells also means that fewer layers of supervision are needed. In fact, now supervisors serve as coaches and trainers, and help to implement cross-functional ideas.

However, Steelcase's supervisors have had more difficulty with the changes than the production employees. Because they were asked to adopt a new philosophy of management, some of the supervisors perceived a loss of control, power, and decision-making authority. Tom Lahuis, a Steelcase performance facilitator, observes that the biggest challenge was getting some of the supervisors to make the transition from their old way of doing business to the new way of doing business—which is involving people in making decisions. Still, many supervisors have learned to thrive in the team system.

In reflecting on the manufacturing approach adopted by Steelcase, Jerry Myers, the president and CEO, stresses that the new system relies heavily on communication and the "power of the individual to bring change to the business." Anyone in the organization can implement changes to move Steelcase toward world-class performance. Yet, as another Steelcase manager says, "We're not, in the textbook sense, a world-class manufacturing plant. But we're as busy as anybody is at getting there."

DISCUSSION QUESTIONS

1. Using the job characteristics model, analyze and discuss the job design implications of Steelcase's use of manufacturing cells.
2. What useful lessons about job design can be derived from this case?
3. The case indicates that some of the supervisors presented the biggest challenge to Steelcase's implementation of the employee-managed manufacturing cells. Explain why this would be such a challenge and how it could be overcome.
4. Why do you think the production workers so enthusiastically embraced the new manufacturing system?
5. Although it apparently was not a problem at Steelcase, why might some production workers be inclined to resist job design changes like those implemented at this company?

SOURCE: This case was written by Michael K. McCuddy, the Louis S. and Mary L. Morgal Professor of Christian Business Ethics, College of Business Administration, Valparaiso University.

1. This case is based on the *Steelcase* segment of the Association for Manufacturing Excellence video entitled *We're Getting Closer.*

References

1. A. F. Doody and R. Bingaman, *Reinventing the Wheels: Ford's Spectacular Comeback* (Cambridge, Mass., Ballinger Press, 1988), 31.
2. S. Freud, *Civilization and Its Discontents* (London: Hogarth Press, 1930), 34.
3. G. W. England and I. Harpaz, "How Working Is Defined: National Contexts and Demographic and Organizational Role Influences," *Journal of Organizational Behavior* 11 (1990): 253–266.
4. L. R. Gomez-Mejia, "The Cross-Cultural Structure of Task-Related and Contextual Constructs," *Journal of Psychology* 120 (1986): 5–19.
5. F. W. Taylor, *The Principles of Scientific Management* (New York: Norton, 1911).
6. A. N. Turner and A. L. Miclette, "Sources of Satisfaction in Repetitive Work," *Occupational Psychology* 36 (1962): 215–231.
7. T. Bell, *Out of This Furnace* (Pittsburgh: University of Pittsburgh Press, 1941).
8. N. D. Warren, "Job Simplification versus Job Enlargement," *Journal of Industrial Engineering* 9 (1958): 435–439.
9. C. R. Walker, "The Problem of the Repetitive Job," *Harvard Business Review* 28 (1950): 54–58.
10. C. R. Walker and R. H. Guest, *The Man on the Assembly Line* (Cambridge, Mass., Harvard University Press, 1952).
11. E. Santora, "Keep Up Production Through Cross-Training," *Personnel Journal* (June 1992): 162–166.
12. F. Herzberg, "One More Time: How Do You Motivate Employees?" *Harvard Business Review* 46 (1968): 53–62.
13. R. N. Ford, "Job Enrichment Lessons from AT&T," *Harvard Business Review* 51 (1973): 96–106.
14. R. J. House and L. A. Wigdor, "Herzberg's Dual-Factor Theory of Job Satisfaction and Motivation: A Review of the Evidence and a Criticism," *Personnel Psychology* 20 (1967): 369–389.
15. A. N. Turner and P. R. Lawrence, *Industrial Jobs and the Worker* (Cambridge, Mass., Harvard University Press, 1965).
16. J. R. Hackman and G. R. Oldham, "The Job Diagnostic Survey: An Instrument for the Diagnosis of Jobs and the Evaluation of Job Redesign Projects," *Technical Report No. 4* (New Haven, Conn.: Department of Administrative Sciences, Yale University, 1974).
17. J. R. Hackman and G. R. Oldham, "Development of the Job Diagnostic Survey," *Journal of Applied Psychology* 60 (1975): 159–170.
18. P. H. Birnbaum, J.-L. Farh, and G. Y. Y. Wong, "The Job Characteristics Model in Hong Kong," *Journal of Applied Psychology* 71 (1986): 598–605.
19. J. R. Hackman and G. R. Oldham, *Work Design* (Reading, Mass.: Addison-Wesley, 1980).
20. H. P. Sims, A. D. Szilagyi, and R. T. Keller, "The Measurement of Job Characteristics," *Academy of Management Journal* 19 (1976): 195–212.
21. H. P. Sims and A. D. Szilagyi, "Job Characteristic Relationships: Individual and Structural Moderators," *Organizational Behavior and Human Performance* 17 (1976): 211–230.
22. Y. Fried, "Meta-Analytic Comparison of the Job Diagnostic Survey and Job Characteristic Inventory as Correlates of Work Satisfaction and Performance," *Journal of Applied Psychology* 76 (1991): 690–698.
23. G. R. Salancik and J. Pfeffer, "A Social Information Processing Approach to Job Attitudes and Task Design," *Administrative Science Quarterly* 23 (1978): 224–253.
24. J. Pfeffer, "Management as Symbolic Action: The Creation and Maintenance of Organizational Paradigms," in L. L. Cummings and B. M. Staw, eds., *Research in Organizational Behavior*, Vol. 3 (Greenwich, Conn.: JAI Press, 1981), 1–52.
25. J. Thomas and R. Griffin, "The Social Information Processing Model of Task Design: A Review of the Literature," *Academy of Management Review* 8 (1983): 672–682.
26. D. J. Campbell, "Task Complexity: A Review and Analysis," *Academy of Management Review* 13 (1988): 40–52.
27. M. A. Campion and P. W. Thayer, "Job Design: Approaches, Outcomes, and Trade-offs," *Organizational Dynamics* 16 (1987): 66–79.
28. D. E. Beach, personal communication, 3 September 1992.
29. M. A. Campion and C. L. McClelland, "Interdisciplinary Examination of the Costs and Benefits of Enlarged Jobs: A Job Design Quasi-Experiment," *Journal of Applied Psychology* 76 (1991): 186–199.
30. B. Kohut, *Country Competitiveness: Organizing of Work* (New York: Oxford University Press, 1993).
31. W. E. Deming, *Out of the Crisis* (Cambridge, Mass.: MIT Press, 1986).
32. L. Thurow, *Head to Head: The Coming Economic Battle among Japan, Europe, and America* (New York: Morrow, 1992).
33. M. A. Fruin, *The Japanese Enterprise System—Competitive Strategies and Cooperative Structures* (New York: Oxford University Press, 1992).
34. E. Furubotn, "Codetermination and the Modern Theory of the Firm: A Property-Rights Analysis," *Journal of Business* 61 (1988): 165–181.
35. H. Levinson, *Executive: The Guide to Responsive Management* (Cambridge, Mass.: Harvard University Press, 1981).
36. H. Luczak, "'Good Work' Design: An Ergonomic, Industrial Engineering Perspective," in J. C. Quick, L. R. Murphy and J. J. Hurrell, eds., *Stress and Well-Being at Work* (Washington, D.C.: American Psychological Association, 1992), 96–112.
37. B. Gardell, "Scandinavian Research on Stress in Working Life" (Paper presented at the IRRA Symposium on Stress in Working Life, Denver, September 1980).
38. L. Levi, "Psychosocial, Occupational, Environmental, and Health Concepts; Research Results; and Applications," in G. P. Keita and S. L. Sauter, eds. *Work and Well-Being: An Agenda for the 1990s* (Washington, D.C.: American Psychological Association, 1992), 199–211.
39. R. L. Kahn, *Work and Health* (New York: Wiley, 1981).
40. F. J. Landy, "Work Design and Stress," in G. P. Keita and S. L. Sauter, eds., *Work and Well-Being: An Agenda for the 1990s* (Washington, D.C.: American Psychological Association, 1992), 119–158.

41. C. Gresov, R. Drazin, and A. H. Van de Ven, "Work-Unit Task Uncertainty, Design, and Morale," *Organizational Studies* 10 (1989): 45–62.
42. B. M. Staw and R. D. Boettger, "Task Revision: A Neglected Form of Work Performance," *Academy of Management Journal* 33 (1990): 534–559.
43. H. S. Schwartz, "Job Involvement as Obsession Compulsion," *Academy of Management Review* 7 (1982): 429–432.
44. C. J. Nemeth and B. M. Staw, "The Tradeoffs of Social Control and Innovation in Groups and Organizations," in L. Berkowitz, ed., *Advances in Experimental Social Psychology*, Vol. 22 (New York: Academic Press, 1989), 175–210.
45. S. Caudron, "Working at Home Pays Off," *Personnel Journal* (November 1992): 40–47.
46. D. S. Bailey and J. Foley, "Pacific Bell Works Long Distance," *HRMagazine*, August 1990, 50–52.
47. S. M. Pollan and M. Levine, "Asking for Flextime," *Working Women*, February 1994, 48.
48. S. Zuboff, *In the Age of the Smart Machine: The Future of Work and Power* (New York: Basic Books, 1988).
49. B. A. Gutek and S. J. Winter, "Computer Use, Control over Computers, and Job Satisfaction," in S. Oskamp and S. Spacapan, eds., *People's Reactions to Technology in Factories, Offices, and Aerospace: The Claremont Symposium on Applied Social Psychology* (Newbury Park, Calif., Sage, 1990), 121–144.
50. L. M. Schleifer and B. C. Amick III, "System Response Time and Method of Pay: Stress Effects in Computer-based Tasks," *International Journal of Human-Computer Interaction* 1 (1989): 23–39.
51. M. J. Smith and P. C. Carayon, "Electronic Monitoring of Worker Performance: A Review of the Potential Effects on Job Design and Stress" (Working paper developed for U.S. Congress, Office of Technology Assessment, Washington, D. C., 1990).
52. M. J. Smith and G. Salvendy, *Work with Computers: Organizational, Management, Stress, and Health Aspects* (New York: Elsevier Press, 1989).
53. D. M. Herold, "Using Technology to Improve our Management of Labor Market Trends," in M. Greller, ed., "Managing Careers with a Changing Workforce," *Journal of Organizational Change Management* 3 (1990), 44–57.
54. D. A. Whetten and K. S. Camerson, *Developing Management Skills* (New York: HarperCollins, 1993).
55. R. E. Anderson, "HRD's Role in Concurrent Engineering," *Training & Development* 47 (1993): 49–54.

CHAPTER

15

Organizational Design and Structure

LEARNING OBJECTIVES

After reading this chapter, you should be able to do the following:

- Define the organizational design processes of differentiation and interpretation.
- Discuss six basic design dimensions of an organization.
- Briefly describe five structural configurations for organizations.
- Describe four contextual variables for an organization.
- Explain the four forces reshaping organizations.
- Discuss emerging organizational structures.
- Identify the two cautions about the effect of organizational structures on people.

OPENING SPOTLIGHT

Citibank and China: Then . . . and Now?

Citibank has a 200-plus-year history in the United States, beginning with a state banking charter. The bank grew and prospered during the early decades of the nineteenth century, but it did not receive a national charter until 1865, at the close of the Civil War, taking the name National City Bank of New York (NCB). As a national bank, NCB continued to grow in size, financial assets, and branches through the latter part of the nineteenth century. However, it was not until the Federal Reserve Act of 1913 that NCB and other

http://www.citicorp.com

federally chartered banks were allowed to grow internationally . . . to go global. NCB established a branch in Buenos Aires, Argentina, in 1914. The bank went fully international when it acquired a controlling interest in International Banking Corporation, which had a banking network from London to Singapore. Therefore, Citibank could now trace a Shanghai, China, branch back to 1902 and a Beijing, China, branch back to 1909. All of Citibank's China branches were closed as a result of World War II. After the war and Mao Tse-Tung's political victory, the People's Republic of China remained closed to Citibank. With the thawing of relations between the United States and China, would Citibank return to the Chinese mainland? ■

organizational design

The process of constructing and adjusting an organization's structure to achieve its goals.

organizational structure

The linking of departments and jobs within an organization.

Points to Emphasize

A useful way to clarify this distinction is to think of design as the process and structure as the result of the process.

contextual variables

A set of characteristics that influences the organization's design processes.

Organizational design is the process of constructing and adjusting an organization's structure to achieve its goals. The design process begins with the organization's goals, which are broken into tasks as the basis for jobs, as discussed in Chapter 14. Jobs are grouped into departments, and departments are linked to form the **organizational structure.**

The first section of the chapter examines the design processes of differentiation and integration. The second section addresses the six basic design dimensions of an organization's structure. The organization's structure gives it the form to fulfill its function in the environment. As Louis Sullivan, the father of the skyscraper, said, "Form ever follows function." The third section of the chapter presents five structural configurations for organizations. Based on its mission and purpose, an organization determines the best structural configuration for its unique situation. The fourth section examines size, technology, environment, and strategy and goals as **contextual variables** influencing organizational design. When the organization's contextual variables change, the organization must redesign itself to meet new demands and functions. The fifth section examines five forces shaping organizations today. The final section notes several areas about which managers should be cautious with regard to structural weaknesses and dysfunctional structural constellations.

Key Organizational Design Processes

■ Differentiation is the design process of breaking the organizational goals into tasks. Integration is the design process of linking the tasks together to form a structure that supports goal accomplishment. These two processes are the keys to successful organizational design. The organizational structure is designed to prevent chaos through an orderly set of reporting relationships and communication channels. Understanding the key design processes and organizational structure helps a person understand the larger working environment and may prevent confusion in the organization.

The organization chart is the most visible representation of the organization's structure and underlying components. Most organizations have a series of organization charts showing reporting relationships throughout the system. The underlying components are (1) formal lines of authority and responsibility (the organizational structure designates reporting relationships by the way jobs and departments are grouped) and (2) formal systems of communication, coordination, and integration (the organizational structure designates the expected patterns of formal interaction among employees).[1]

Differentiation

differentiation

The process of deciding how to divide the work in an organization.

Differentiation is the process of deciding how to divide the work in an organization.[2] Differentiation ensures that all essential organizational tasks are assigned to one or more jobs and that the tasks receive the attention they need.

■ **TABLE 15.1**

Differentiation between Marketing and Engineering

BASIS FOR DIFFERENCE	MARKETING	ENGINEERING
Goal orientation	Sales volume	Design
Time orientation	Long run	Medium run
Interpersonal orientation	People-oriented	Task-oriented
Structure	Less formal	More formal

Many dimensions of differentiation have been considered in organizations. Lawrence and Lorsch found four dimensions of differentiation in one study: (1) manager's goal orientation, (2) time orientation, (3) interpersonal orientation, and (4) formality of structure.[3] Table 15.1 shows some typical differences in orientation for various functional areas of an organization. Three different forms of differentiation are horizontal, vertical, and spatial.

Horizontal differentiation is the degree of differentiation between organizational subunits and is based on employees' specialized knowledge, education, or training. For example, two university professors who teach specialized subjects in different academic departments are subject to horizontal differentiation. Horizontal differentiation increases with specialization and departmentation.

Specialization refers to the particular grouping of activities performed by an individual.[4] The degree of specialization or the division of labor in the organization gives an indication of how much training is needed, what the scope of a job is, and what individual characteristics are needed for job holders. Specialization can also lead to the development of a specialized vocabulary, as well as other behavioral norms. As the two college professors specialize in their subjects, abbreviations or acronyms take on unique meanings. For example, *OB* means "organizational behavior" to a professor of management, and it means "obstetrics" to a professor of medicine.

Points to Emphasize
There is a difference between job specialization and person specialization. Person specialization occurs when an individual becomes skilled in a specific task-related field.

Usually, the more specialized the jobs within an organization, the more departments are differentiated within that organization (the greater the departmentation). Departmentation can be by function, product, service, client, geography, process, or some combination of these. A large organization may departmentalize its structure using all or most of these methods at different levels of the organization.

Vertical differentiation is the difference in authority and responsibility in the organizational hierarchy. Vertical differentiation occurs, for example, between a chief executive and a maintenance supervisor. Tall, narrow organizations have greater vertical differentiation, and flat, wide organizations have less vertical differentiation. The height of the organization is also influenced by level of horizontal differentiation and span of control. The span of control defines the number of subordinates a manager can and should supervise.[5]

Alternate Example
Graicunas, a Lithuanian management consultant, determined mathematically that in the span of control the number of potential interactions between the manager and the subordinate increases geometrically as the number of subordinates increases. Thus, 3 subordinates means 18 possible relationships, 4 subordinates means 44, and 18 subordinates means 2,359,602 possible relationships.

Tall structures—those with narrow spans of control—tend to be characterized by closer supervision and tighter controls. In addition, the communication becomes more burdensome, since directives and information must be passed through more layers. The banking industry has often had tall structures. Flat structures—those with wider spans of control—have simpler communication chains and reduced promotion opportunities due to fewer levels of management. Sears is an organization that has gone to a flat structure. With the loss of over a million middle management positions in organizations during the 1980s, many organizations are now flatter. The degree of vertical differentiation affects organizational effectiveness, but there is no consistent finding that flatter or taller organizations are better.[6] Organizational size, type of jobs, skills and personal characteristics of employees and degree of freedom must all be considered in determining organizational effectiveness.[7]

http://www.bc.com

Spatial differentiation is the geographic dispersion of an organization's offices, plants, and personnel. A Boise-Cascade salesperson in New York and one in Portland experience spatial differentiation. An increase in the number of locations increases the difficulty in organizational design but may be necessary for organizational goal achievement or organizational protection. For example, if an organization wants to expand into a different country, it may be in its best interest to form a separate subsidiary that is partially owned and managed by citizens of that country. Few U.S. citizens think of Shell Oil Company as being a subsidiary of Royal Dutch Shell, a company whose international headquarters is in the Netherlands.

Spatial differentiation may give an organization political and legal advantages in a country because of the identification of a company as a local company. Distance is as important as political and legal issues in making spatial differentiation decisions. For example, a salesperson in Lubbock, Texas, would have a hard time servicing accounts in Beaumont, Texas (over 500 miles away), whereas a salesperson in Delaware might be able to cover all of that state, as well as parts of one or two others.

http://www.cocacola.com

Horizontal, vertical, and spatial differentiation indicate the amount of width, height, and breadth an organizational structure needs. Just because an organization is highly differentiated along one of these dimensions does not mean it must be highly differentiated along all three. The university environment, for example, is generally characterized by great horizontal differentiation but relatively little vertical and spatial differentiation. A company such as Coca-Cola is characterized by a great deal of all three types of differentiation. The more structurally differentiated an organization is, the more complex it is.[8]

Points to Emphasize
The larger and more complex the organization, the more likely it will have many rules and procedures and a distinct chain of command.

Complexity refers to the number of activities, subunits, or subsystems within the organization. Lawrence and Lorsch suggest that an organization's complexity should mirror the complexity of its environment. As the complexity of an organization increases, its need for mechanisms to link and coordinate the differentiated parts also increases. If these links do not exist, the departments or differentiated parts of the organization can lose sight of the organization's larger mission, and the organization runs the risk of chaos. Designing and building linkage and coordination mechanisms is known as *integration*.

Integration

integration
The process of coordinating the different parts of an organization.

Integration is the process of coordinating the different parts of an organization. Integration mechanisms are designed to achieve unity among individuals and groups in various jobs, departments, and divisions in the accomplishment of organizational goals and tasks.[9] Integration helps keep the organization in a state of dynamic equilibrium, a condition in which all the parts of the organization are interrelated and balanced.[10]

Vertical linkages are used to integrate activities up and down the organizational chain of command. A variety of structural devices can be used to achieve vertical linkage. These include hierarchical referral, rules and procedures, plans and schedules, positions added to the structure of the organization, and management information systems.[11]

The vertical lines on an organization chart indicate the lines of hierarchical referral up and down the organization. When there is a problem that employees do not know how to solve, it can be referred up the organization for consideration and resolution. Work that needs to be assigned is usually delegated down the chain of command as indicated by the vertical lines.

Rules and procedures, as well as plans and schedules, provide standing information for employees without direct communication. These vertical integrators, for example an employee handbook, communicate to employees standard information or information that they can understand on their own. These integrators allow managers to have wider spans of control, because the managers do not have to inform each employee of what is expected and when it is expected. These vertical integrators encourage managers to use management by exception—to make decisions when employees bring problems up the hierarchy. Military organizations depend heavily on vertical linkages. The army, for example, has a well-defined chain of command. Certain duties are expected to be carried out, and proper paperwork is to be in place. However, in times of crisis, much more information is processed, and the proper paperwork becomes secondary to "getting the job done." Vertical linkages help individuals understand their roles in the organization, especially in times of crisis.

Adding positions to the hierarchy is used as a vertical integrator when a manager becomes overloaded by hierarchical referral or problems arise in the chain of command. Positions may be added, such as "assistant to," or another level may be added. Adding levels to the hierarchy often reflects growth and increasing complexity. This action tends to reduce the span of control, thus allowing more communication and closer supervision.

Management information systems that are designed to process information up and down the organization also serve as a vertical linkage mechanism. With the advent of computers and network technology, it has become easier for managers and employees to communicate through written reports that are entered into a network and then electronically compiled for managers in the hierarchy. Electronic mail systems allow managers and employees greater access to one another without having to be in the same place at the same time or even attached by telephone. These types of systems make information processing up and down the organization more efficient.

Alternate Example
According to Lawrence and Lorsch, as differentiation increases, the need to integrate also increases. Yet, differentiation and integration seem to work against each other.

Generally, the taller the organization, the more vertical integration mechanisms are needed. This is because the chains of command and communication are longer. Additional length requires more linkages to minimize the potential for misunderstandings and miscommunications.

Horizontal integration mechanisms provide the communication and coordination that is necessary for links across jobs and departments in the organization.[12] The need for horizontal integration mechanisms increases as the complexity of the organization increases. Within the design of the organization, the horizontal linkages are built with the inclusion of liaison roles, task forces, integrator positions, and teams.

A liaison role is created when a person in one department or area of the organization has the responsibility for coordinating with another department (for example, a liaison between the engineering and production departments). Task forces are temporary committees composed of representatives from multiple departments who assemble to address a specific problem affecting these departments.[13]

A stronger device for integration is to develop a person or department designed to be an integrator. In most organizations, the integrator has a good deal of responsibility, but not much authority. Such an individual must have the ability to get people together to resolve differences within the perspective of organizational goals.[14]

Discussion Consideration
Has the networking of personal computers served to decentralize or centralize organizations? How does it affect vertical integration?

The strongest method of horizontal integration is through teams. Horizontal teams cut across existing lines of organizational structure to create new entities that make organizational decisions. An example of this is in product development. A team may be formed that includes marketing, research, design, and production personnel. Ford used such a cross-functional team, discussed in detail in Chapter 9, to develop the Taurus automobile, which was designed to regain market share in the United States. The information exchanged by such a product development team should lead to a product that is acceptable to a wider range of organizational groups, as well as to customers.[15]

Discussion Consideration
How do the integration requirements of manufacturing organizations differ from those of service organizations?

These six young Ford designers can be electronically linked to other Ford design studios from Turin, Italy to Melbourne, Australia. In this "GLOBAL STUDIO" environment, these young Ford team members design vehicles for people living in a changing world.

FORD DESIGNERS FROM LEFT TO RIGHT: SUSAN K. WESTFALL, DAVID HILTON, GARY BRADDOCK, SOO KANG, PAUL ARNONE, AARON WALKER

Alternate Example
Team members need explicit information about reporting and performance feedback responsibilities that might vary between their team and their traditional supervisor.

The use of these linkage mechanisms varies from organization to organization, as well as within areas of the same organization. In general, the flatter the organization, the more necessary horizontal integration mechanisms are.

Basic Design Dimensions

■ Differentiation, then, is the process of dividing work in the organization, and integration is the process of coordinating work in the organization. From a structural perspective, every manager and organization looks for the best combination of differentiation and integration for accomplishing the goals of the organization. There are many ways to approach this process. One way is to establish a desired level of each structural dimension on a high to low continuum and then develop a structure that meets the desired configuration. These structural dimensions include the following:[16]

formalization
The degree to which the organization has official rules, regulations, and procedures.

centralization
The degree to which decisions are made at the top of the organization.

specialization
The degree to which jobs are narrowly defined and depend on unique expertise.

standardization
The degree to which work activities are accomplished in a routine fashion.

complexity
The degree to which many different types of activities occur in the organization.

1. **Formalization**: the degree to which an employee's role is defined by formal documentation (procedures, job descriptions, manuals, and regulations).
2. **Centralization**: the extent to which decision-making authority has been delegated to lower levels of an organization. An organization is centralized if the decisions are made at the top of the organization and decentralized if decision making is pushed down to lower levels in the organization.
3. **Specialization**: the degree to which organizational tasks are subdivided into separate jobs. The division of labor and the degree to which formal job descriptions spell out job requirements indicate the level of specialization in the organization.
4. **Standardization**: the extent to which work activities are described and performed routinely in the same way. Highly standardized organizations have little variation in the defining of jobs.
5. **Complexity**: the number of activities within the organization and how much differentiation is needed within the organization.

SCIENTIFIC FOUNDATION

Trust and Implicit Moral Duty

Trust is essential to interpersonal and group behavior. It is an equally essential ingredient in organizational theory and institutional transactions. Trust is based on the underlying assumption of an implicit moral duty, which makes a precise definition difficult. A clear understanding of trust requires a familiarity with philosophical ethics and moral philosophy, which this article provides.

Although trust never appears in the organizational design literature as a key structural variable, this article argues that trust is a linchpin for organization, economic, and social structures. The organizational theory literature does suggest that trust is generally expressed as an optimistic expectation about the outcome of an event or the behavior of another person or organization. Trust is generally associated with willing cooperation and with the benefits resulting from that cooperation. Trust is generally difficult to enforce.

Trust is an important foundation for ethical behavior in organizations. Virtuous actions that contribute to collective well-being in an organization are founded on an individual moral duty to act in a trustworthy fashion. Whereas it is clear that moral behavior is doing what is *right* and immoral behavior is doing what is *wrong*, it is much less clear in organizational practice to determine which specific acts and behaviors are *moral* and which ones are *immoral*. Thus, trust is an implicitly important connective variable in the organization.

SOURCE: L. T. Hosmer, "Trust: The Connecting Link between Organizational Theory and Philosophical Ethics," *Academy of Management Review* 5 (1995): 379–403.

6. **Hierarchy of authority**: the degree of vertical differentiation through reporting relationships and the span of control within the structure of the organization.

hierarchy of authority
The degree of vertical differentiation across levels of management.

An organization that is high on formalization, centralization, specialization, standardization, and complexity and has a tall hierarchy of authority is said to be highly bureaucratic. Bureaucracies are not in and of themselves bad; however, they are often tainted by abuse and red tape. The Internal Revenue Service is often described as bureaucratic. An organization that is on the opposite end of each of these continua is very flexible and loose. Control is very hard to implement and maintain in such an organization, but at certain times such an organization is appropriate. The research and development departments in many organizations are often more flexible than other departments in order to stimulate creativity. An important organizational variable, which is not included in the structural dimensions, is trust. The accompanying Scientific Foundation feature discusses the importance of trust in organizational theory.

Discussion Consideration
Using a scale ranging from 1(low) to 5(high), ask students to their university on the six dimensions of organizational structure.

Discussion Consideration
Is a bureaucratic organization more difficult to change than a nonbureaucratic organization?

Another approach to the process of accomplishing organizational goals is to describe what is and is not important to the success of the organization rather than worry about specific characteristics. Henry Mintzberg feels that the following questions can guide managers in designing formal structures that fit each organization's unique set of circumstances:[17]

1. How many tasks should a given position in the organization contain, and how specialized should each task be?
2. How standardized should the work content of each position be?
3. What skills, abilities, knowledge, and training should be required for each position?
4. What should be the basis for the grouping of positions within the organization into units, departments, divisions, and so on?
5. How large should each unit be, and what should the span of control be (that is, how many individuals should report to each manager)?
6. How much standardization should be required in the output of each position?
7. What mechanisms should be established to help individuals in different positions and units to adjust to the needs of other individuals?

CHALLENGE

■ 15.1

How Decentralized Is Your Company?

Decentralization is one of the key design dimensions in an organization. It is closely related to several behavioral dimensions of an organization, such as leadership style, degree of participative decision making, and the nature of power and politics within the organization.

The following questionnaire allows you to get an idea about how decentralized your organization is. (If you do not have a job, have a friend who does work complete the questionnaire to see how decentralized his or her organization is.) Which level in your organization has the authority to make each of the following eleven decisions? Answer the questionnaire by circling one of the following:

0 = The board of directors makes the decision.
1 = The CEO makes the decision.
2 = The division/functional manager makes the decision.
3 = A subdepartment head makes the decision.
4 = The first-level supervisor makes the decision.
5 = Operators on the shop floor make the decision.

Decision Concerning:	Circle Appropriate Level					
a. The number of workers required.	0	1	2	3	4	5
b. Whether to employ a worker.	0	1	2	3	4	5
c. Internal labor disputes.	0	1	2	3	4	5
d. Overtime worked at shop level.	0	1	2	3	4	5
e. Delivery dates and order priority.	0	1	2	3	4	5
f. Production planning.	0	1	2	3	4	5
g. Dismissal of a worker.	0	1	2	3	4	5
h. Methods of personnel selection.	0	1	2	3	4	5
i. Method of work to be used.	0	1	2	3	4	5
j. Machinery or equipment to be used.	0	1	2	3	4	5
k. Allocation of work among workers.	0	1	2	3	4	5

Add up all your circled numbers. Total = ______. The higher your number (for example, 45 or more), the more decentralized your organization. The lower your number (for example, 25 or less), the more centralized your organization.

SOURCE: D. Miller and C. Droge, "Psychological and Traditional Determinants of Structure," *Administrative Science Quarterly* 31 (1986): 558.

8. How centralized or decentralized should decision-making power be in the chain of authority? Should most of the decisions be made at the top of the organization (centralized) or be made down in the chain of authority (decentralized)?

The manager who can answer these questions has a good understanding of how the organization should implement the basic structural dimensions. These basic design dimensions act in combination with one another and are not entirely independent characteristics of an organization. Challenge 15.1 gives you (or a friend) an opportunity to consider how decentralized your company is.

Five Structural Configurations

■ Differentiation, integration, and the basic design dimensions combine to yield various structural configurations. Mintzberg proposes five structural configurations: the simple structure, the machine bureaucracy, the professional bureaucracy, the divisionalized form, and the adhocracy.[18] Table 15.2 summa-

■ **TABLE 15.2**

Five Structural Configurations of Organization

STRUCTURAL CONFIGURATION	PRIME COORDINATING MECHANISM	KEY PART OF ORGANIZATION	TYPE OF DECENTRALIZATION
Simple structure	Direct supervision	Upper echelon	Centralization
Machine bureaucracy	Standardization of work processes	Technical staff	Limited horizontal decentralization
Professional bureaucracy	Standardization of skills	Operating Level	Vertical and horizontal decentralization
Divisionalized form	Standardization of outputs	Middle Level	Limited vertical decentralization
Adhocracy	Mutual adjustment	Support staff	Selective decentralization

SOURCE: H. Mintzberg, *The Structuring of Organizations* (Englewood Cliffs, N.J.): Prentice Hall, 1979), 301.

rizes the prime coordinating mechanism, the key part of the organization, and the type of decentralization for each of these structural configurations. The five fundamental elements of the organization, for Mintzberg, are the upper echelon; the middle level; the operating core, where work is accomplished; the technical staff; and the support staff. Each configuration affects people in the organization somewhat differently.

Simple Structure

The **simple structure** is an organization with little technical and support staff, strong centralization of decision making in the upper echelon, and a minimal middle level. This structure has minimum of vertical differentiation of authority and minimum formalization. It achieves coordination through direct supervision, often by the chief executive in the upper echelon. An example of a simple structure is a small, independent landscape practice in which one or two landscape architects supervise the vast majority of work with no middle-level managers. Even an organization with as few as 30 people can become dysfunctional as a simple structure after an extended period.

simple structure

A centralized form of organization that emphasizes the upper echelon and direct supervision.

Points to Emphasize

Most organizations pass through the simple structure in their formative years. It is the riskiest structure because it is often based on whims.

Machine Bureaucracy

The **machine bureaucracy** is an organization with a well-defined technical and support staff differentiated from the line operations of the organization, limited horizontal decentralization of decision making, and a well-defined hierarchy of authority. The technical staff is powerful in a machine bureaucracy. There is strong formalization through policies, procedures, rules, and regulations. Coordination is achieved through the standardization of work processes. An example of a machine bureaucracy is an automobile assembly plant, with routinized operating tasks. The strength of the machine bureaucracy is efficiency of operation in stable, unchanging environments. The weakness of the machine bureaucracy is its slow responsiveness to external changes and to individual employee preferences and ideas.

machine bureaucracy

A moderately decentralized form of organization that emphasizes the technical staff and standardization of work processes.

Professional Bureaucracy

The **professional bureaucracy** emphasizes the expertise of the professionals in the operating core of the organization. The technical and support staffs serve the professionals. There is both vertical and horizontal differentiation in the

professional bureaucracy

A decentralized form of organization that emphasizes the operating level and standardization of skills.

Alternate Example
One of the difficulties hospitals face is the professional bureaucracy. Physicians typically are loyal to their profession rather than to the hospitals in which they practice.

professional bureaucracy. Coordination is achieved through the standardization of the professionals' skills. Examples of professional bureaucracies are hospitals and universities. The doctors, nurses, and professors are given wide latitude to pursue their work based on professional training and indoctrination through professional training programs. Large accounting firms may fall into the category of professional bureaucracies.

Divisionalized Form

divisionalized form
A moderately decentralized form of organization that emphasizes the middle level and standardization of outputs.

The **divisionalized form** is a loosely coupled, composite structural configuration.[19] It is a configuration composed of divisions, each of which may have its own structural configuration. Each division is designed to respond to the market in which it operates. There is vertical decentralization from the upper echelon to the middle of the organization, and the middle level of management is the key part of the organization. This form of organization may have one division that is a machine bureaucracy, one that is an adhocracy, and one that is a simple structure. An example of this form of organization is Valero Energy Corporation, which produces natural gas and owns an oil refinery in south Texas. The divisionalized organization uses standardization of outputs as its coordinating mechanism.

Discussion Consideration
Which of the five basic configurations best represents the structure of your university?

Adhocracy

adhocracy
A selectively decentralized form of organization that emphasizes the support staff and mutual adjustment among people.

The **adhocracy** is a highly organic, rather than mechanistic, configuration with minimal formalization and order. It is designed to fuse interdisciplinary experts into smoothly functioning ad hoc project teams. Liaison devices are the primary mechanism for integrating the project teams in an adhocracy through a process of mutual adjustment. There is a high degree of horizontal specialization based on formal training and expertise. Selective decentralization of the project teams occurs within the adhocracy. An example of this form of organization is the National Aeronautics and Space Administration (NASA), composed of many talented experts who work in small teams on a wide range of projects related to America's space agenda.

Contextual Variables

■ The basic design dimensions and the resulting structural configurations play out in the context of the organization's internal and external environments. Four contextual variables influence the success of an organization's design: size, technology, environment, and strategy and goals. These variables provide a manager with challenges in considering an organizational design, although they are not necessarily determinants of structure. As the content of the organization changes, so should the structural design. Also, the amount of change in the contextual variables throughout the life of the organization influences the amount of change needed in the basic dimensions of the organization's structure.[20]

Size

The total number of employees is the appropriate definition of size when discussing the design of organizational structure. This is logical, because people and their interactions are the building blocks of structure. Other measures, such as net assets, production rates, and total sales, are usually highly correlated with the total number of employees but may not reflect the actual number of interpersonal relationships that are necessary to effectively structure an organization.

http://www.eds.com

Electronic Data Systems (EDS) began as an entrepreneurial venture of H. Ross Perot and had grown into an internationally prominent provider of

This is a view of the Mission Control Center at NASA's Johnson Space Center, Houston, Texas. Flight director John P. Shannon (left center) passes on information to astronaut Marc Gameau, STS-70 spacecraft communicator (CAPCOM).

information technology services when it was bought by General Motors Corporation (GM) in the early 1980s. Nearly half of EDS's revenues came from GM at the time of the buyout. The early culture of EDS placed a premium on technical competence, high achievement drive, an entrepreneurial attitude, and a maverick spirit. EDS is continuing to grow and is once again changing, asserting its independence of GM, and becoming an autonomous company once again.

http://www.gm.com

Discussion Consideration

Would students prefer to work in a large organization or a small organization? Why?

Although there is some argument over the degree of influence that size has on organizational structure, there is no argument that it does influence design options. In one study, Meyer found size of the organization to be the most important of all variables considered in influencing the organization's structure and design.[21] Other researchers argue that the decision to expand the organization's business causes an increase in size as the structure is adjusted to accommodate the planned growth.[22] Downsizing is a planned strategy to reduce the size of an organization. Closing operations, as discussed in the accompanying Organizational Reality feature, is another way the size of an organization may shrink.

How much influence size exerts on the organization's structure is not as important as the relationship between size and the design dimensions of structure. In other words, when exploring structural alternatives, what should the manager know about designing structures for large and small organizations?

Table 15.3 illustrates the relationships among each of the design dimensions and organizational size. Formalization, specialization, and standardization all tend to be greater in larger organizations, because they are necessary to control

■ **TABLE 15.3**

Relationship between Organizational Size and Basic Design Dimensions

BASIC DESIGN DIMENSIONS	SMALL ORGANIZATIONS	LARGE ORGANIZATIONS
Formalization	Less	More
Centralization	High	Low
Specialization	Low	High
Standardization	Low	High
Complexity	Low	High
Hierarchy of authority	Flat	Tall

ORGANIZATIONAL REALITY

Nissan Shuts Mexican Factories

Organizations do not inevitably grow in size. There are times when the best organizational strategy is to resize, downsize, and/or curtail operations in some markets. The devaluation of the Mexican peso precipitated an economic crisis that had ripple effects throughout the Mexican economy and affected Mexico's relationships with its trading partners.

In early January, 1995, Fort Motor Company announced the closure of its small-car assembly plant in Mexico. This announcement followed one by Volkswagen de Mexico that suspended production of all model cars in Mexico by the German company.

Nissan, the Japanese company, had two automotive assembly plants in Mexico. The economic crisis led to a price dispute between Nissan and its Mexican suppliers. This dispute in turn led to a shortage of parts in the assembly plants.

Conducting business in different national markets carries uncertainties and complications, which may lead to closing operations for various periods of time. As the Mexican economy becomes stronger and more stable, Nissan is likely to continue to expand the size of its business operations there. ■

SOURCE: Associated Press, "Nissan is Third Automaker to Shut Factories Temporarily in Mexico," *Dallas Morning News*, January 24, 1995, 7D.

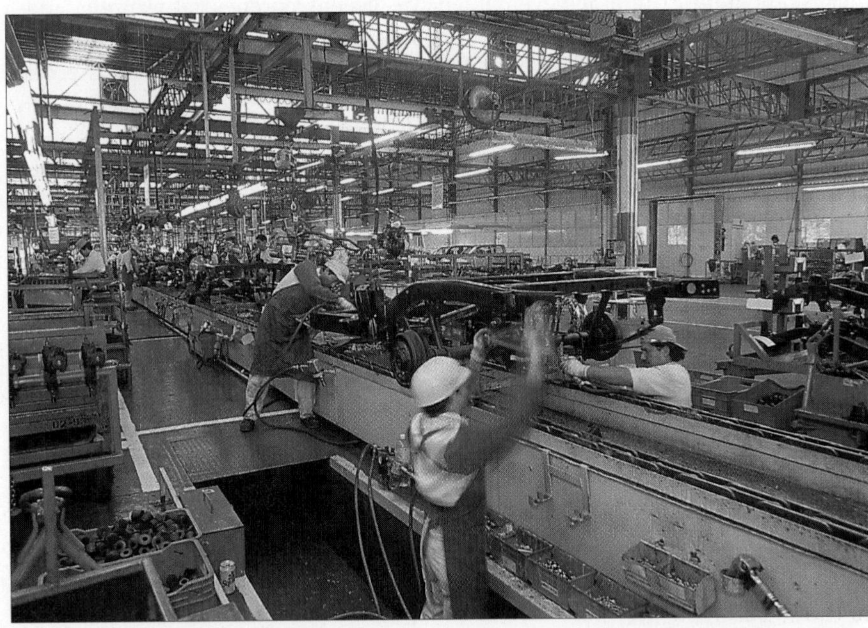

This 1994 photo shows Mexican workers at the Nissan Plant in Cuernavaca's CIVAC Industrial Park actively involved in automobile assembly. As the Mexican economy grows and strengthens, foreign businesses will expand as well.

http://www.mcdonalds.com

activities within the organization. For example, documentation, rules, written policies and procedures, and detailed job descriptions are more likely to be used in larger organizations than is relying on personal observation by the manager. The more relationships that have to be managed by the structure, the more formalized and standardized the processes need to be. McDonald's has several volumes that describe how to make all its products, how to greet customers, how to maintain the facilities, and so on. This level of standardization, formalization, and specialization helps McDonald's maintain the same quality of product no matter where a restaurant is located. In contrast, at a small, locally owned café, your hamburger and french fries may taste a little different every time you visit. This is evidence of a lack of standardization.

Formalization and specialization also help a large organization decentralize decision making. Because of the complexity and number of decisions in a large organization, formalization and specialization are used to set parameters for decision making at lower levels. Can you imagine the chaos if Robert Crandall, CEO of American Airlines, had to make every decision about flights, food, or ticketing procedures for the airline? By decentralizing decision making, the larger organization adds horizontal and vertical complexity, but not necessarily spatial complexity. However, it is more common for a large organization to have more geographic dispersion.

http://www.americanair.com

Another dimension of design, hierarchy of authority, is related to complexity. As size increases, complexity increases; thus, more levels are added to the hierarchy of authority. This keeps the span of control from getting too large. However, there is a balancing force, because formalization and specialization are added. The more formalized, standardized, and specialized the roles within the organization, the wider the span of control can be.

Balancing the design dimensions relative to size is a perplexing problem with few simple answers. This balancing becomes even more difficult when other contextual variables are taken into account.

Technology

An organization's technology is an important contextual variable in determining the organization's structure, as noted in Chapter 2.[23] Technology is defined as the tools, techniques, and actions used by an organization to transform inputs into outputs.[24] The inputs of the organization include human resources, machines, materials, information, and money. The outputs are the products and services that the organization offers to the external environment. Determining the relationship between technology and structure is complicated, because different departments may employ very different technologies. As organizations become larger, there is greater variation in technologies across units in the organization. Joan Woodward, Charles Perrow, and James Thompson have developed ways to understand traditional organizational technologies. More work is needed to understand better the contemporary engineering, research and development, and knowledge-based technologies of the information age.

Woodward introduced one of the best-known classification schemes for technology, identifying three types: unit, mass, or process production. Unit technology is small-batch manufacturing technology and, sometimes, made-to-order production. Examples include Smith and Wesson's arms manufacture or the manufacture of fine furniture. Mass technology is large-batch manufacturing technology. Examples include American automotive assembly lines or latex glove production. Process production is continuous-production processes. Examples include oil refining and beer making. Woodward classified unit technology as the least complex, mass technology as more complex, and process technology as the most complex. The more complex the organization's technology, the more complex the administrative component or structure of the organization needs to be.[25]

The computer aided design (CAD) of products is one technological advance which has reduced product design costs. Technology is one important contextual variable in the design of organizations.

Perrow proposed an alternative to Woodward's scheme based on two variables: task variability and problem analyzability. Task variability considers the number of exceptions encountered in doing the tasks within a job. Problem analyzability examines the types of search procedures followed to find ways to respond to task exceptions. For example, for some exceptions encountered while doing a task, the appropriate response is easy to find. If you are driving down a

Points to Emphasize
Technology has changed organizations in drastic ways. Many organizations are centralizing because of the capacity and efficiency of large relational databases. On the other hand, the networking of personal computers is enabling organizations to decentralize.

street and see a sign that says, "Detour—Bridge Out," it is very easy to respond to the task variability. However, when Thomas Edison was designing the first electric light bulb, the problem analyzability was very high for his task.

Perrow went on further to identify the key aspects of structure that could be modified to the technology. These four structural elements are (1) the amount of discretion that an individual can exercise to complete a task, (2) the power of groups to control the unit's goals and strategies, (3) the level of interdependence among groups, and (4) the extent to which organizational units coordinate work using either feedback or planning. Figure 15.1 summarizes Perrow's findings about types of technology and basic design dimensions.[26]

technological interdependence
The degree of interrelatedness of the organization's various technological elements.

Thompson offered yet another view of technology and its relationship to organizational design. This view is based on the concept of **technological interdependence** (i.e., the degree of interrelatedness of the organization's various technological elements) and the pattern of an organization's work flows. Thompson's research suggests that greater technological interdependence leads to greater organizational complexity and that the problems of this greater complexity may be offset by decentralized decision making.[27]

The research of these three early scholars on the influence of technology on organizational design can be combined into one integrating concept—routineness in the process of changing inputs into outputs in an organization. This routineness has a very strong relationship with organizational structure. The more routine and repetitive the tasks of the organization, the higher the degree of formalization that is possible; the more centralized, specialized, and standardized the organization can be; and the more hierarchical levels with wider spans of control that are possible.

However, an important caveat to the discussion of technology has emerged since the work of Woodward, Perrow, and Thompson: The advancement of information technology has influenced how organizations transform inputs into outputs. The introduction of computer-integrated networks, CAD/CAM systems, and computer-integrated manufacturing has broadened the span of con-

■ **FIGURE 15.1**

Summary of Perrow's Findings about the Relationship between Technology and Basic Design Dimensions

SOURCE: Built from C. Perrow, "A Framework for the Comparative Analysis of Organizations," *American Sociological Review,* April 1967, 194–208.

Problem Analyzability	Task Variability: Few Exceptions	Task Variability: Many Exceptions
Ill-defined and Unanalyzable	Craft 1. Moderate 2. Moderate 3. Moderate 4. Low-moderate 5. High 6. Low	Nonroutine 1. Low 2. Low 3. Low 4. Low 5. High 6. Low
Well-defined and Analyzable	Routine 1. High 2. High 3. Moderate 4. High 5. Low 6. High	Engineering 1. Moderate 2. Moderate 3. High 4. Moderate 5. Moderate 6. Moderate

Key:
1. Formalization
2. Centralization
3. Specialization
4. Standardization
5. Complexity
6. Hierarchy of authority

trol, flattened the organizational hierarchy, decentralized decision making, and lowered the amount of specialization and standardization.[28]

Environment

The third contextual variable for organizational design is **environment**. The environment of an organization is most easily defined as anything outside the boundaries of that organization. Different aspects of the environment have varying degrees of influence on the organization's structure. The general environment includes all conditions that may have an impact on the organization. These conditions could include economic factors, political considerations, ecological changes, sociocultural demands, and governmental regulation.

environment

Anything outside the boundaries of an organization.

Discussion Consideration
Have students identify the general and the task environment for the university.

When aspects of the general environment become more focused in areas of direct interest to the organization, those aspects become part of the **task environment**, or specific environment. The task environment is that part of the environment that is directly relevant to the organization. Typically, this level of environment includes stakeholders such as unions, customers, suppliers, competitors, government regulatory agencies, and trade associations.

task environment

The elements of an organization's environment that are related to its goal attainment.

The domain of the organization refers to the area the organization claims for itself with respect to how it fits into its relevant environments. The domain is particularly important because it is defined by the organization, and it influences how the organization perceives and acts within its environments.[29] For example, Wal-Mart and Neiman-Marcus both sell clothing apparel, but their domains are very different.

The organization's perceptions of its environment and the actual environment may not be the same. The environment that the manager perceives is the environment that the organization responds to and organizes for.[30] Therefore, two organizations may be in relatively the same environment from an objective standpoint, but if the managers perceive differences, the organizations may enact very different structures to deal with this same environment.

The perception of **environmental uncertainty** or the perception of the lack of environmental uncertainty is how the contextual variable of environment most influences organizational design. Some organizations have relatively static environments with little uncertainty, whereas others are so dynamic that no one is sure what tomorrow may bring. Binney and Smith, for example, has made relatively the same product for over 50 years with very few changes in the product design or packaging. The environment for its Crayola products is relatively static. In fact, customers rebelled when the company tried to get rid of some old colors and add new ones. In contrast, in the last ten years, those who compete in the airline industry have encountered deregulation, mergers, bankruptcies, safety changes, changes in cost and price structures, changes in customer and employee demographics, and changes in global competition. The uncertainty of the environment of the major airlines has been relatively high during this last decade.

environmental uncertainty

The amount and rate of change in the organization's environment.

http://www.crayola.com

The amount of uncertainty in the environment influences the structural dimensions. Burns and Stalker labeled two structural extremes that are appropriate for the extremes of environmental uncertainty—mechanistic structure and organic structure.[31] Table 15.4 compares the structural dimensions of these two extremes. The mechanistic and organic structures are opposite ends of a continuum of organizational design possibilities. Although the general premise of environmental uncertainty and structural dimensions has been upheld by research, the organization must make adjustments for the realities of its perceived environment when designing its structure.[32]

Points to Emphasize
According to the environmental imperative, structure is a function of environment. Thus, an organizations structure should reflect the complexity of the environment in which the organization operates.

The question for those trying to design organizational structures is how to determine environmental uncertainty. Dess and Beard defined three dimensions of environment that should be measured in assessing the degree of uncertainty:

■ **TABLE 15.4**

Mechanistic and Organic Organizational Forms

BASIC DESIGN DIMENSIONS	MECHANISTIC	ORGANIC
Formalization	High	Low
Centralization	High	Low
Specialization	High	Low
Standardization	High	Low
Complexity	Low	High
Hierarchy of authority	Strong, tall	Weak, flat

capacity, volatility, and complexity.[33] The capacity of the environment reflects the abundance or scarcity of resources. If resources abound, the environment supports expansion, mistakes, or both. In contrast, in times of scarcity, the environment demands survival of the fittest. Volatility is the degree of instability. The airline industry, as described above, is in a volatile environment. This makes it difficult for managers to know what needs to be done. The complexity of the environment refers to the differences and variability among environmental elements.

If the organization's environment is uncertain, dynamic, and complex, and resources are scarce, the manager needs an organic structure that it is better able to adapt to its environment. Such a structure allows the manager to monitor the environment from a number of internal perspectives, thus helping the organization maintain flexibility in responding to environmental changes.[34]

Strategy and Goals

The fourth contextual variable that influences how the design dimensions of structure should be enacted is the strategies and goals of the organization. Strategies and goals provide legitimacy to the organization, as well as employee direction, decision guidelines, and criteria for performance.[35] In addition, strategies and goals help the organization fit into its environment.

In recent years, more understanding about the contextual influence of strategies and goals has been developed. This has led to the definition of several strategic dimensions that influence structure. One of the most recent of these definitions was put forth by Danny Miller.[36] The dimensions and the implications of strategy on organizational structure are shown in Table 15.5.

http://www.apple.com

For example, when Apple Computer introduced personal computers to the market, it was very innovative in its strategies. The structure of the organization was relatively flat and very informal. Apple had Friday afternoon beer and popcorn discussion sessions, and eccentric behavior was easily accepted. However, as the personal computer market became more competitive, the structure of Apple changed to help it differentiate its products and to help control costs. Steve Jobs, one of Apple's founders, had a set of innovative strategies and structures that were no longer appropriate. The board of directors recruited John Scully, a marketing expert from PepsiCo, to help Apple better compete in the market it had created. Once again in 1996, Apple is under new leadership and in the throws of attempting to reinvent itself.

http://www.pepsico.com

Limitations exist, however, on how much strategies and goals influence structure. Because the structure of the organization includes the formal information-processing channels in the organization, it stands to reason that the need to change strategies may not be communicated throughout the organization. In such a case, the organization's structure influences its strategic choice.

The inefficiency of the structure to perceive environmental changes may even lead to organizational failure. In the airline industry, several carriers failed to

■ **TABLE 15.5**

Miller's Integrative Framework of Structural and Strategic Dimensions

STRATEGIC DIMENSION	PREDICTED STRUCTURAL CHARACTERISTICS
Innovation—to understand and manage new processes and technologies	Low formalization Decentralization Flat hierarchy
Market differentiation—to specialize in customer preferences	Moderate to high complexity Moderate to high formalization Moderate centralization
Cost control—to produce standardized products efficiently	High formalization High centralization High standardization Low complexity

SOURCE: D. Miller, "The Structural and Environmental Correlates of Business Strategy," *Strategic Management Journal* 8 (1987): 55–76.

■ **TABLE 15.6**

Examples of How Structure Affects the Strategic Decision Process

FORMALIZATION

As the level of formalization increases, so does the probability of the following:

1. The strategic decision process will become reactive to crisis rather than proactive through opportunities.
2. Strategic moves will be incremental and precise.
3. Differentiation in the organization will not be balanced with integrative mechanisms.
4. Only environmental crises that are in areas monitored by the formal organizational systems will be acted upon.

CENTRALIZATION

As the level of centralization increases, so does the probability of the following:

1. The strategic decision process will be initiated by only a few dominant individuals.
2. The decision process will be goal-oriented and rational.
3. The strategic process will be constrained by the limitations of top managers.

COMPLEXITY

As the level of complexity increases, so does the probability of the following:

1. The strategic decision process will become more politicized.
2. The organization will find it more difficult to recognize environmental opportunities and threats.
3. The constraints on good decision processes will be multiplied by the limitations of each individual within the organization.

SOURCE: Adapted from J. Fredrickson, "The Strategic Decision Process and Organizational Structure," *Academy of Management Review* (1986): 284.

adjust quickly enough to deregulation and the highly competitive marketplace. Only those airlines that were generally viewed as lean structures with good information-processing systems have flourished in the last ten turbulent years. Examples of how different design dimensions can affect the strategic decision process are listed in Table 15.6.

■ **FIGURE 15.2**

The Relationship among Key Organizational Design Elements

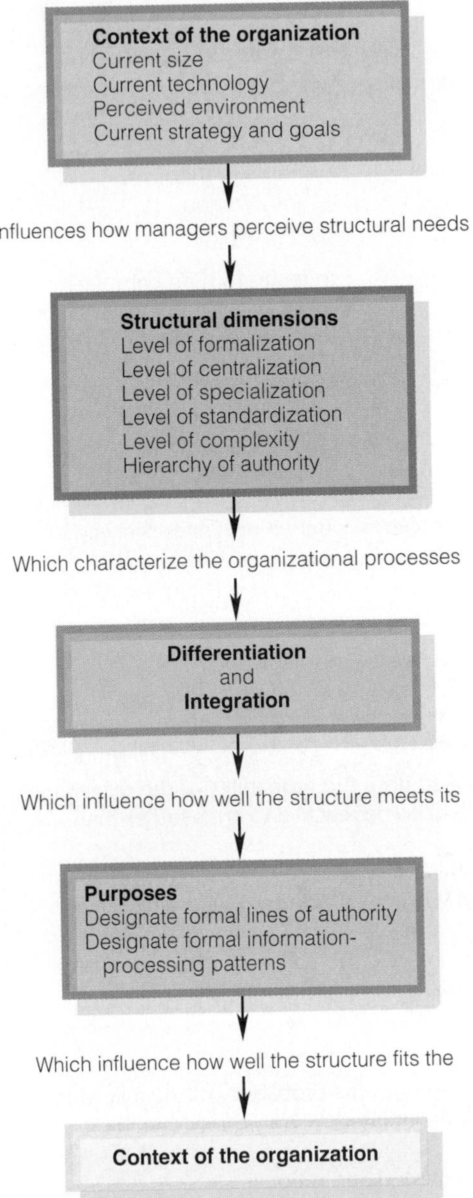

Discussion Consideration

What are the structural implications for organizations operating in an environment of increased global competition?

The four contextual variables—size, technology, environment, and strategy and goals—combine to influence the design process. However, the existing structure of the organization influences how the organization interprets and reacts to information about each of the variables. Each of the contextual variables is represented by management researchers who claim that it is the most important variable in determining the best structural design. Because of the difficulty in studying the interactions of the four contextual dimensions and the complexity of organizational structures, the argument about which variable is most important continues.

What is apparent is that there must be some level of fit between the structure and the contextual dimensions of the organization. The better the fit, the more likely that the organization will achieve its short-run goals. In addition, the better the fit, the more likely that the organization will process information and design appropriate organizational roles for long-term prosperity, as indicated in Figure 15.2.

Forces Reshaping Organizations

■ Managers and researchers traditionally examine organizational design and structure within the framework of basic design dimensions and contextual variables. Several forces reshaping organizations are causing managers to go beyond the traditional frameworks and to examine ways to make organizations more responsive to customer needs. Some of these forces include shorter life cycles within the organization, globalization, and rapid changes in information technology. These forces together increase the demands on process capabilities within the organization and emerging organizational structures.[37]

Life Cycles in Organizations

Organizations are dynamic entities. As such, they ebb and flow through different stages. Usually, researchers think of these stages as **organizational life cycles**. The total organization has a life cycle that begins at birth, moves through growth and maturity to decline, and possibly experiences revival.[38]

organizational life cycle
The differing stages of an organization's life from birth to death.

Organizational subunits may have very similar life cycles. Because of changes in technology and product design, many organizational subunits are experiencing shorter life cycles, especially those that are product-based. Hence, the subunits that compose the organization will change more rapidly than in the past. These shorter life cycles enable the organization to respond quickly to external demands and changes.

Alternate Example
An additional stage, maturity, may be added to the development of organizations. At present, we are only beginning to understand this stage. The future may extend the stages beyond maturity.

As a new organization or subunit is born, the structure is organic and informal. If the organization or subunit is successful, it grows and matures. This usually leads to formalization, specialization, standardization, complexity, and a more mechanistic structure. However, if the environment changes, the organization must be able to respond. A mechanistic structure is not able to respond to a dynamic environment as well as an organic one. If the organization or subunit does respond, it becomes more organic and revives; if not, it declines and possibly dies.

Discussion Consideration
Ask students to discuss where on the organizational life cycle the university is.

Shorter life cycles put more pressure on the organization to be both flexible and efficient at the same time. At each stage the organization differs in its strategies and goals, as well as in its structural emphasis. The effective manager is able to use the redesign process to keep abreast of the needs for structural change.

Discussion Consideration
What does it take to revive an organization?

Globalization

Another force that is reshaping organizations is the globalization of organizations and markets. In other words, organizations operate worldwide rather than in just one country or region. Such globalization makes spatial differentiation even more of a reality for organizations. Besides the obvious geographic differences, there may be deep cultural and value system differences. This adds another type of complexity to the structural design process and necessitates the creation of integrating mechanisms for people to be able to understand and interpret one another, as well as coordinate with one another.

The choice of structure for managing an international business is generally based on choices concerning the following three factors:

1. *The level of vertical differentiation.* A hierarchy of authority must be created that clarifies the responsibilities of both domestic and foreign managers.
2. *The level of horizontal differentiation.* Foreign and domestic operations should be grouped in such a way that the company effectively serves the needs of all customers.
3. *The degree of formalization, specialization, standardization, and centralization.* The global structure must allow decisions to be made in the most appropriate area

of the organization. However, controls must be in place that reflect the strategies and goals of the parent firm.[39]

Changes in Information Processing Technologies

Many of the changes in information-processing technologies have allowed organizations to move into new product and market areas more quickly. However, just as shorter life cycles and globalization have caused new concerns for designing organizational structures, so has the increased availability of advanced information-processing technologies.

Historically, as new capabilities in information processing have emerged, new forms of organizational structures also have emerged.[40] The impact of advanced information-processing technologies on the structure of organizations is already being felt. More integration and coordination is evident, because managers worldwide can be connected through computerized networks. The basic design dimensions also have been affected as follows:

1. The hierarchy of authority has been flattened.
2. The basis of centralization has been changed. Now managers can use technology to acquire more information and make more decisions, or they can use technology to push information and decision making lower in the hierarchy and thus decrease centralization.
3. Less specialization and standardization are needed, because people using advanced information-processing technologies have more sophisticated jobs that require a broader understanding of how the organization gets work done.[41]

Alternate Example
The aging workforce will have an increasing impact on the structure of organizations, forcing companies to reconsider hierarchical structures. SOURCE: "The Rising Tide of Older Workers," *Nation's Business*, September 1992, 22.

Demands on Organizational Processes

Because of the forces reshaping organizations, managers find themselves trying to meet what seem to be conflicting goals: an efficiency orientation that results in on-time delivery *and* a quality orientation that results in customized, high-quality goods or services.[42] Efficiency and customization traditionally have been seen by managers as being conflicting demands.

To meet these conflicting demands, organizations need to become "dynamically stable."[43] To do so, an organization must have managers who see their roles as architects who clearly understand the "how" of the organizing process. Managers must combine long-term thinking with flexible and quick responses that help improve process and know-how. The organizational structure must help define, at least to some degree, roles for managers who hope to successfully address the conflicting demands of dynamic stability. The differences between the structural roles of managers today and managers of the future is illustrated in Table 15.7. Challenge 15.2 allows you to examine the ways managers in your organization currently operate on the job.

Alternate Example
One of the difficulties foreign managers have with domestic hierarchies is the "glass ceiling." Many foreign managers believe that they might not be able to advance beyond a certain level if they work in a company that is based in a different country.

Emerging Organizational Structures

The demands on managers and on process capabilities place demands on structures. The emphasis in tomorrow's organizations will be on organizing around processes, a key tenet of total quality management (TQM). This process orientation emerges from the combination of three streams of applied organizational design: high-performance, self-managed teams; managing processes rather than functions; and the evolution of information technology.

Discussion Consideration
What are the implications of the Americans with Disabilities Act for organizational design processes? What accommodations will be required as more disabled workers enter the workforce?

Horizontal companies are an emerging organizational structure. Frank Ostroff and Doug Smith of McKinsey and Company developed a ten-step blueprint for a horizontal company.[44] The steps are as follows: (1) organize primarily around process, not task; (2) flatten the hierarchy by minimizing subdivision

CHALLENGE

15.2

Managers of Today and the Future

Are the roles for managers in your organization more oriented toward today or toward the future? (If you do not work, think of an organization where you have worked or talk with a friend about managerial roles in his or her organization.)

Step 1. Reread Table 15.7, and check which orientation (today or future) predominates in your organization for each of the following seven characteristics:

	Today	Future
1. Boss-employee relationships.	______	______
2. Getting work accomplished.	______	______
3. Messenger versus problem solver.	______	______
4. Basis for task accomplishment.	______	______
5. Narrow versus broad functional focus.	______	______
6. Adherence to channels of authority.	______	______
7. Controlling versus coaching subordinates.	______	______

Step 2. Examine the degree of consistency across all seven characteristics. Could the organization make one or two structural changes to achieve a better alignment of the manager's role with today or with the future?

Step 3. Identify one manager in your organization who fits very well into the organization's ideal manager's role. What does this manager do that creates a good person-role fit?

Step 4. Identify one manager in your organization who does not fit very well into the organization's ideal manager's role. What does this manager do that creates a poor person-role fit?

TABLE 15.7

Structural Roles of Managers Today versus Managers of the Future

ROLES OF MANAGERS TODAY
1. Strictly adhering to boss-employee relationships. **2.** Getting things done by giving orders. **3.** Carrying messages up and down the hierarchy. **4.** Performing a prescribed set of tasks according to a job description. **5.** Having a narrow functional focus. **6.** Going through channels, one by one by one. **7.** Controlling subordinates.
ROLES OF FUTURE MANAGERS
1. Having hierarchical relationships subordinated to functional and peer relationships. **2.** Getting things done by negotiating. **3.** Solving problems and making decisions. **4.** Creating the job by developing entrepreneurial projects. **5.** Having broad cross-functional collaboration. **6.** Emphasizing speed and flexibility. **7.** Coaching one's workers.

SOURCE: Reprinted by permission of the publisher, from *Management Review,* January 1991 © 1991. Thomas R. Horton. American Management Association, New York. All rights reserved.

ORGANIZATIONAL REALITY

Horizontal Organization in Sweden

The prestigious Karolinska Hospital in Stockholm, Sweden, faced financial difficulties in 1992 with a 20 percent reduction in funding. This change in funding challenged Jan Lindsten, Karolinska's chief executive, to reexamine the way in which the hospital was organized. He was deeply concerned about the quality of patient care in the face of the reductions in funding.

Over several years, the hospital and its staff reorganized their work around patient flow rather than around the doctors and the medical departments. At one point, due to a major decentralization, Karolinska housed 47 departments. Lindsten brought that number down to 11. With the new horizontal organization, a patient sees a surgeon and doctor of internal medicine at the same time, rather than being shuttled from one department or office to the other. More radically, nurse coordinators proactively minimize the number of visits a patient must make by looking for inefficiencies in the system. Some doctors at Karolinska are still not quite comfortable reporting to a nurse on administrative matters, which the nurse coordinator concept requires. However, doctors and surgeons now concentrate on clinical matters, not administrative matters.

While the hospital closed 3 of its 15 operating theaters through the reorganization, the number of operations increased by 3,000 annually, up 25 percent. Change in hospitals, and other organizations, may not come easily, yet can be very successful. ■

SOURCE: R. Rao, "The Struggle to Create an Organization for the 21st Century," *Fortune*, April 3, 1995, 90–99.

of processes and arranging teams in parallel; (3) make senior managers responsible for processes and process performance; (4) use customer satisfaction as the basic link to performance objectives and evaluation; (5) make teams the focus of organizational performance and design; (6) break down vertical barriers in the organization; (7) encourage employees to develop multiple competencies; (8) inform and train people on a just-in-time, need-to-perform basis; (9) maximize contacts for everyone in the organization with suppliers and customers; and (10) reward both individual skills and team performance. Horizontal organization can be applied to all sectors of the economy, as the accompanying Organizational Reality feature shows.

The modular corporation is an alternative to the vertically integrated company. Companies that focus on their distinctive competence and on the distinctive value they add to a product or service can outsource (i.e., allow external suppliers to provide) a wide range of activities that are not part of their core business. These companies become modular corporations and exploit their distinctive expertise.[45] For example, Nike considers its competitive strengths to be the design and marketing of fine athletic shoes. Nike outsources the production of shoes they design to non-Nike-owned factories worldwide.

Cautionary Notes about Structure

■ This chapter has identified the purposes of structure, the processes of organizational design, and the dimensions and contexts that must be considered in structure. In addition, it has looked at forces and trends in organizational design. Two cautionary notes are important for the student of organizational behavior. First, an organizational structure may be weak or deficient. In general, if the structure is out of alignment with its contextual variables, one or more of the following four symptoms appears. First, decision making is delayed because the hierarchy is overloaded and too much information is being funneled through one or two channels. Second, decision making lacks quality, because information linkages are not providing the correct information to the right person in the right format. Third, the organization does not respond innovatively to a changing environment, especially when coordinated effort is lacking across departments. Fourth, a great deal of conflict is evident when departments are working against one another rather than working for the strategies and goals of the organization as a whole; the structure is often at fault.

The second caution is that the personality of the chief executive may adversely affect the structure of the organization. Five dysfunctional combinations of personality and organization have been identified: the paranoid, the depressive, the dramatic, the compulsive, and the schizoid.[46] Each of these personality-organization constellations can create problems for the people who work in the organization. For example, in a paranoid constellation, people are suspicious of each other, and distrust in working relationships may interfere with effective communication and task accomplishment. For another example, in a depressive constellation, people feel depressed and inhibited in their work activities, which can lead to low levels of productivity and task accomplishment.

Managerial Implications: Fitting People and Structures Together

■ Organizations are complex social systems composed of numerous interrelated components. They can be complicated to understand. Managers who design, develop, and improve organizations must have a mastery of the basic concepts related to the anatomy and processes of organizational functioning. It is essential for executives at the top to have a clear concept of how the organization can be differentiated and then integrated into a cohesive whole.

People can work better in organizations if they understand how their jobs and departments relate to other jobs and teams in the organization. An understanding of the whole organization enables people to better relate their contribution to the overall mission of the organization and to compensate for structural deficiencies that may exist in the organization.

Different structural configurations place unique demands on the people who work within them. The diversity of people in work organizations suggests that some people are better suited for a simple structure, others are better suited to a professional bureaucracy, and still others are most productive in an adhocracy. Organizational structures are not independent of the people who work within them. This is especially true as organizations become more global in their orientation.

Managers must pay attention to the technology of the organization's work, the amount of change occurring in the organization's environment, and the regulatory pressures created by governmental agencies as the managers design effective organizations and subunits to meet emerging international demands and a diverse, multicultural workforce.

CLOSING SPOTLIGHT

Beijing, China . . . 1995

By the 1940s, Citibank was one of the biggest foreign banks in China with 14 branches in nine cities. When Citibank inaugurated its full-service commercial branch in Beijing during October, 1995, it was resurrecting an operation that began nearly 100 years ago in the Chinese capital.[47] Citibank was the only U.S. bank with a Beijing branch at the time of the resurrection. Beijing was not Citibank's only Chinese presence on the eve of the twenty-first century. The bank already had established branches in Shanghai and Shenzhen, as well as representative offices in Guangzhou and Xiamen. However, the rules for Chinese operations are somewhat different than in the United States. Under Chinese regulations, Citibank is limited to project and international trade financing, and cannot accept deposits nor do business in local Chinese currency. International and global operations in banking, as in other businesses, require structural and operational adjustments across international borders, as Citibank has done to grow its business in China.

Chapter Summary

- Three basic types of differentiation occur in organizations: horizontal, vertical, and spatial.
- The greater the complexity of an organization because of its degree of differentiation, the greater the need for integration.
- Formalization, centralization, specialization, standardization, complexity, and hierarchy of authority are the six basic design dimensions in an organization.
- Simple structure, machine bureaucracy, professional bureaucracy, divisionalized form, and adhocracy are five structural configurations of an organization.
- The contextual variables important to organizational design are size, technology, environment, and strategy and goals.
- Life cycles, globalization, changes in information-processing technologies, and demands on process capabilities are forces reshaping organizations today.
- New, emerging organizational structures differ from the traditional ones.
- Organizational structures may be inherently weak or chief executives may create personality-organization constellations that adversely affect employees.

Key Terms

organizational design (p. 446)
organizational structure (p. 446)
contextual variables (p. 446)
differentiation (p. 446)
integration (p. 448)
formalization (p. 450)
centralization (p. 450)
specialization (p. 450)
standardization (p. 450)
complexity (p. 450)
hierarchy of authority (p. 451)
simple structure (p. 453)
machine bureaucracy (p. 453)
professional bureaucracy (p. 453)
divisionalized form (p. 454)
adhocracy (p. 454)
technological interdependence (p. 458)
environment (p. 459)
task environment (p. 459)
environmental uncertainty (p. 459)
organizational life cycle (p. 463)

Review Questions

1. Define the processes of differentiation and integration.
2. Describe the six basic dimensions of organizational design.
3. Discuss five structural configurations from the chapter.
4. Discuss the effects of the four contextual variables on the basic design dimensions.
5. Identify four forces that are reshaping organizations today.
6. Discuss the nature of emerging organizational structures.
7. List four symptoms of structural weakness and five unhealthy personality-organization combinations.

Discussion and Communication Questions

1. How would you characterize the organization you work for (or your college) on each of the basic design dimensions? For example, is it a very formal organization or an informal organization?
2. How do the size, technology, and strategy and goals of your organization affect you? Or do they not affect you?
3. What are domestic or international competitive factors or changes in information-processing technologies that affect you or your organization?
4. Does your company display any one or more of the four symptoms of structural deficiency discussed at the end of the chapter?
5. *(communication question)* Write a memo classifying and describing the structural configuration of your university based on the five choices in Table 15.2. Do you need more information than you have to be comfortable with your classification and description? Where could you get the information?
6. *(communication question)* Interview an administrator in your college or university about possible changes in size (Will the college or university get bigger? smaller?) and technology (Is the college or university making a significant investment in information technology?). What effects do they anticipate from these changes? Be prepared to present your results orally to the class.

Ethics Questions

1. For what types of individual behavior is it ethical for an organization to have formal rules and regulations? For what types of individual behavior is it unethical for an organization to have formal rules and regulations?
2. Should legal limits be set to prevent large companies from engaging in very competitive behavior to drive small companies out of business?
3. As an organization changes its structure over time, how much commitment should it show to employees who need to be retrained to fit into the new system? Or is it acceptable for the organization to hire new people to fit the new structure?
4. Suppose an employee complains about organizational design problems and suggests a solution. The organization is redesigned accordingly, but that employee's department is eliminated. Is it ethical for the company to terminate the employee? Should the company always make room for a person who has a beneficial idea for the organization?

Experiential Exercises

15.1 Words-in-Sentences Company

Purpose:
To design an organization for a particular task and carry through to production; to compare design elements with effectiveness.

Group Size:
Any number of groups of six to 14 persons

Time Required:
50–90 minutes

Related Topics:
Dynamics within Groups, Work Motivation

Background

You are a small company that manufactures words and then packages them in meaningful English-language sentences. Market research has established that sentences of at least three words but not more than six words are in demand. Therefore, packaging, distribution, and sales should be set up for three- to six-word sentences.

The "words-in-sentences" industry is highly competitive; several new firms have recently entered what appears to be an expanding market. Since raw materials, technology, and pricing are all standard for the industry, your ability to compete depends on two factors: (1) volume and (2) quality.

YOUR TASK

Your group must design and particiapte in running a WIS company. You should design your organization to be as efficient as possible during each ten-minute production run. After the first production run, you will have an opportunity to reorganize your company if you want.

Raw materials

For each production you will be given a "raw material word or phrase." The letters found in the word or phrase serve as raw materials available to produce new words in sentences. For example, if the raw material word is "organization," you could produce the words and sentence: "Nat ran to a zoo."

Production Standards

There are several rules that have to be followed in producing "words-in-sentences." If these rules are not followed, your output will not meet production specifications and will not pass quality-control inspection.

1. The same letter may appear only as often in a manufactured word as it appears in the raw material word or phrase, for example, "organization" has two o's. Thus "zoo" is legitimate, but not "zoonosis." It has too many o's and s's.
2. Raw material letters can be used again in different manufactured words.
3. A manufactured word may be used only once in a sentence and in only one sentence during a production run; if a word—for example, "a"— is used once in a sentence, it is out of stock.
4. A new word may not be made by adding "s" to form the plural of an already manufactured word.
5. A word is defined by its spelling, not its meaning.
6. Nonsense words or nonsense sentences are unacceptable.
7. All words must be in the English language.
8. Names and places are acceptable.
9. Slang is not acceptable.

Measuring Performance
The output of your WIS company is measured by the total number of acceptable words that are packaged in sentences. The sentences must be legible, listed on no more than two sheets of paper, and handed to the Quality Control Review board at the completion of each production run.

Delivery
Delivery must be made to the Quality Control Review Board thirty seconds after the end of each production run, or else all points are lost.

Quality Control
If any word in a sentence does not meet the standards set forth above, all the words in the sentence will be rejected. The Quality Control Review Board (composed of one member from each company) is the final arbiter of acceptability. In the event of a tie on the Review Board, a coin toss will determine the outcome.

EXERCISE SCHEDULE

	Unit Time	*Total Time*
1. Form groups, organizations, and assign workplaces Groups should have between six and fourteen members (if there are more than 11–12 persons in a group, assign one or two observers). Each group is a company.	**2–5 min**	**2–5 min**
2. Read "Background" Ask the instructor about any points that need clarification.	**5 min**	**10 min**
3. Design organizations Design your organizations using as many members as you see fit to produce your "words-in-sentences." You may want to consider the following. a. What is your objective? b. What technology would work here? c. What technology would work here? d. What type of division of labor is effective? Assign one member of your group to serve on the Quality Review Board. This person may also take part in production runs.	**7–15 min**	**14–25 min**
4. Production Run #1 The instructor will hand each WIS company a sheet with a raw material word or pharase. When the instructor announces "Begin production," you are to manufacture as many words as possible and package them in sentences for delivery to the Quality Control Review Board. You will have ten minutes. When the instructor announces "Stop production," you will have 30 seconds to deliver your output to the Quality Control Review Board. Output received after 30 seconds does not meet the delivery schedule and will not be counted.	**7–10 min**	**21–35 min**
5. Quality Review Board meets, evaulates output While that is going on, groups discuss what happened during the previous production run.	**5–10 min**	**26–45 min**
6. Companies evaluate performance and type of organization Groups may choose to restructure and reorganize for the next production run.	**5–10 min**	**31–55 min**
7. Production run #2 (same as Production Run #1)	**7–10 min**	**38–65 min**
8. Quality Review Board meets Quality Review Board evaluates output while groups draw their organization charts (for Runs #1 and #2) on the board.	**5–10 min**	**43–75 min**
9. Class discussion Instructor leads discussion of exercise as a whole. Discuss the following questions: a. What were the companies' scores for Runs #1 and #2? b. What type of structure did the "winning" company have? Did it reorganize for Run #2? c. What type of task was there? Technology? Environment? d. What would Joan Woodward, Henry Mintzberg, Frederick Taylor, Lawrence and Lorsch, or Burns and Stalker say about WIS Company organization?	**7–15 min**	**43–75 min**

SOURCE: Dorothy Marcic, *Organizational Behavior Experiences and Cases*, Fourth Edition (St. Paul: West, 1995), 303–305.

15.2 Design and Build a Castle

This exercise is intended to give your group an opportunity to design an organization and produce a product.

Your group is one of three product-development teams working within the research and development division of the GTM (General Turret and Moat) Corporation. GTM has decided to enter new markets by expanding the product line to include fully designed and produced castles, rather than selling components to other companies, as it has in the past.

Each of the three teams has been asked to design a castle for the company to produce and sell. Given limited resources, the company cannot put more than one design on the market. Therefore, the company will have to decide which of the three designs it will use, discarding the other two designs.

Your task is to develop and design a castle. You will have forty-five minutes to produce a finished product. At the end of this period, several typical consumers, picked by scientific sampling techniques, will judge which is the best design. Before the consumers make their choice, each group will have one to two minutes to make a sales presentation.

Step 1. Each group is designated either 1, 2, or 3. The instructor will provide group members a memorandum appropriate for their group. One (or two for larger groups) observer is selected for each group. Observers read their materials.

Step 2. Groups design their organization in order to complete their goal.

Step 3. Each group designs its own castle and draws it on newsprint.

Step 4. "Typical consumers" (may be observers) tour building locations and hear sales pitches. Judges caucus to determine winner.

Step 5. Groups meet again and write up their central goal statement. They also write the organization chart on newsprint with the goal written beneath. These are posted around the room.

Step 6. Instructor leads a class discussion on how the different memos affected organization design. Which design seemed most effective for this task?

NOTE: Your instructor may allow more time and actually have you *build* the castles.

SOURCE: Dorothy Marcic and Richard C. Housley, *Organizational Behavior Experiences and Cases* (St. Paul: West, 1989), 221–225.

CASE

Eastman Chemical's Pizza Chart[1]

Eastman Chemical Co., the tenth largest chemical company in the United States in terms of sales, manufactures and markets over 400 fibers, chemicals, and plastics worldwide. As a $4 billion company in the early 1990s, Eastman estimated that it could grow into a $7 billion a year company by the year 2000 without redesigning its functional organization. However, with some significant redesign Eastman executives believed they could become a $15–$20 billion a year business by 2000. Consequently, Eastman executives decided to make "*big* changes, *radical* changes" in the way the company worked.

In the process of reinventing their organization, Eastman executives decided to change the company's focus from product lines to markets and customers. They also decided to retain the company's core competencies in the areas of manufacturing, customer interaction, and technology. Eastman also wanted to retain its functional expertise, its strong emphasis on teamwork, and its distinctive culture, known as the Eastman Way.

How could Eastman become customer- and market-focused while retaining its core competencies, functional expertise, sense of teamwork, and culture? For the Eastman executives, the answer was to be found in one of the basic food groups—pizza!

The creators of Eastman Chemical's new organization structure affectionately call it the "pizza chart." According to Eastman's president, the organization chart "looks like a pizza with lots of pepperoni sitting on it" and is "circular to show that everyone is equal." Each piece of pepperoni typically represents a cross-functional team responsible for managing a business, a geographical area, a function, or a core competence.

In creating its pizza chart, Eastman placed the president at the center of the pizza with six sets of interconnected groups reporting directly to the president. Two of the groups—the specialty business group and the industrial business group—represent two major business segments. A third group—the worldwide business support group—was created to foster globalization. A functional management group capitalizes on Eastman's functional expertise. Another group of teams—administration and staff—provides coordinating and support services for the other Eastman teams. Cross-functional core competency teams were established to ensure that core competencies were being utilized and refined throughout the company. All the teams are equally important in Eastman's organizational design, which was really an interconnected network of self-directed teams.

Eastman Chemical's pepperoni pizza organization has enabled the company to become market-focused, pursue global expansion, seek faster growth, maintain functional excellence, and leverage its core competencies more than ever before. Eastman executives believe they have developed into a company that "knows how to deal with the turbulence of changing markets and changing technologies."

DISCUSSION QUESTIONS

1. How does Eastman Chemical Co. utilize differentiation and integration in its pepperoni pizza organization?
2. How would you describe Eastman's pizza chart in terms of formalization, centralization, specialization, standardization, complexity, and hierarchy of authority?
3. How do the contextual variables of size, technology, environment, strategy, and goals seem to influence Eastman Chemical's organization design?
4. What advantages and disadvantages do you think are associated with Eastman's pizza organization?
5. A pepperoni pizza is a useful metaphor for describing Eastman Chemical's organization structure. Other organizations have different structural designs. What other metaphors might be useful for understanding other kinds of structural designs? Explain your answer.

SOURCE: This case was written by Michael K. McCuddy, the Louis S. and Mary L. Morgal Professor of Christian Business Ethics, College of Business Administration, Valparaiso University.

1. Adapted from J. D. Beckham, "Redefining Work in the Integrated Delivery System," *Healthcare Forum* 38 (1995): 76–82; J. D. Holmes, and G. E. McGraw, "Whitewater Ahead: Eastman Prepares for Turbulent Times," *Research-Technology Management* 37 (1994): 20–24; Eastman Chemical Co., *Quality* (January 1994): 24–26.

References

1. J. Child, *Organization* (New York: Harper & Row, 1984).
2. P. Lawrence and J. Lorsch, "Differentiation and Integration in Complex Organizations," *Administrative Science Quarterly* (June 1967): 1–47.
3. P. Lawrence and J. Lorsch, *Organization and Environment: Managing Differentiation and Integration* (Boston, Mass.: Harvard University Press, 1967).
4. J. Hage, "An Axiomatic Theory of Organizations," *Administrative Science Quarterly* (December 1965): 289–320.
5. W. Ouchi and J. Dowling, "Defining the Span of Control," *Administrative Science Quarterly* (September 1974): 357–365.
6. L. Porter and E. Lawler III, "Properties of Organization Structure in Relation to Job Attitudes and Job Behavior," *Psychological Bulletin* (July 1965): 23–51.
7. J. Ivancevich and J. Donnelly, Jr., "Relation of Organization and Structure to Job Satisfaction, Anxiety-Stress, and Performance," *Administrative Science Quarterly* 20 (1975): 272–280.
8. R. Dewar and J. Hage, "Size, Technology, Complexity, and Structural Differentiation: Toward a Theoretical Synthesis," *Administrative Science Quarterly* 23 (1978): 111–136.
9. Lawrence and Lorsch, "Differentiation and Integration," 1–47.
10. Lawrence and Lorsch, "Differentiation and Integration," 1–47.
11. J. Galbraith, *Designing Complex Organizations* (Reading, Mass.: Addison-Wesley, 1973).
12. Galbraith, *Designing Complex Organizations.*
13. W. Altier, "Task Forces: An Effective Management Tool," *Management Review* (February 1987): 26–32.
14. P. Lawrence and J. Lorsch, "New Managerial Job: The Integrator," *Harvard Business Review* 45 (1967): 142–151.
15. J. Lorsch and P. Lawrence, "Organizing for Product Innovation," *Harvard Business Review* 43 (1965): 110–111.
16. D. Pugh, D. Hickson, C. Hinnings, and C. Turner, "Dimensions of Organization Structure," *Administrative Science Quarterly* (1968): 65–91; R. Daft, *Organization Theory and Design*, 4th ed. (St. Paul, MN: West Publishing Company, 1992); B. Reimann, "Dimensions of Structure in Effective Organizations: Some Empirical Evidence," *Academy of Management Journal* (1974): 693–708; S. Robbins, *Organization Theory: The Structure and Design of Organizations*, 3rd ed. (Englewood Cliffs, NJ: Prentice-Hall, 1990).
17. H. Mintzberg, *The Structuring of Organizations* (Englewood Cliffs, NJ: Prentice-Hall, 1979).
18. H. Mintzberg, *The Structuring of Organizations.*
19. K. Weick, "Educational Institutions as Loosely Coupled Systems," *Administrative Science Quarterly* (1976): 1–19.
20. D. Miller and C. Droge, "Psychological and Traditional Determinants of Structure," *Administrative Science Quarterly* (1986): 540; H. Tosi, Jr. and J. Slocum, Jr., "Contingency Theory: Some Suggested Directions," *Journal of Management* (Spring 1984): 9–26.
21. M. Meyer, "Size and the Structure of Organizations: A Causal Analysis," *American Sociological Review*, (August 1972): 434–441.
22. J. Beyer and H. Trice, "A Reexamination of the Relations between Size and Various Components of Organizational Complexity," *Administrative Science Quarterly* 24 (1979): 48–64; B. Mayhew, R. Levinger, J. McPherson, and T. James, "Systems Size and Structural Differentiation in Formal Organizations: A Baseline Generator for Two Major Theoretical Propositions," *American Sociological Review* (October 1972): 26–43.
23. J. Woodward, *Industrial Organization: Theory and Practices* (London: Oxford University Press, 1965).
24. C. Perrow, "A Framework for the Comparative Analysis of Organizations," *American Sociological Review* (April 1967): 194–208; D. Rosseau, "Assessment of Technology in Organizations: Closed versus Open Systems Approaches," *Academy of Management Review* 4 (1979): 531–542.
25. Woodward, *Industrial Organization.*
26. Perrow, "A Framework for the Comparative Analysis of Organizations," 194–208.
27. J. D. Thompson, *Organizations in Action* (New York: McGraw-Hill, 1967).
28. P. Nemetz and L. Fry, "Flexible Manufacturing Organizations: Implication for Strategy Formulation and Organization Design," *Academy of Management Review* 13 (1988): 627–638; G. Huber, "The Nature and Design of Post-Industrial Organizations," *Management Science* 30 (1984): 934.
29. Thompson, *Organizations in Action.*
30. H. Downey, D. Hellriegel, and J. Slocum, Jr., "Environmental Uncertainty: The Construct and Its Application," *Administrative Science Quarterly* 20 (1975): 613–629.
31. T. Burns and G. Stalker, *The Management of Innovation* (London: Tavistock, 1961); Mintzberg, *Structuring of Organizations.*
32. M. Chandler and L. Sayles, *Managing Large Systems* (New York: Harper & Row, 1971).
33. G. Dess and D. Beard, "Dimensions of Organizational Task Environments," *Administrative Science Quarterly* 29 (1984): 52–73.
34. J. Courtright, G. Fairhurst, and L. Rogers, "Interaction Patterns in Organic and Mechanistic Systems," *Academy of Management Journal* 32 (1989): 773–802.
35. R. Daft, *Organization Theory and Design*, 4th ed. (St. Paul: West 1992).
36. D. Miller, "The Structural and Environmental Correlates of Business Strategy," *Strategic Management Journal* 8 (1987): 55–76.
37. A. Boynton and B. Victor, "Beyond Flexibility: Building and Managing a Dynamically Stable Organization," *California Management Review* 8 (Fall 1991): 53–66.
38. D. Miller and P. Friesen, "A Longitudinal Study of the Corporate Life Cycle," *Management Science* 30 (1984): 1161–1183.
39. C. Hill and G. Jones, *Strategic Management Theory*, 2d ed. (Boston: Houghton Mifflin, 1992).
40. A. Chandler, *The Visible Hand: The Managerial Revolution in American Business* (Cambridge, Mass.: Harvard University Press, 1977).
41. Daft, *Organization Theory and Design.*
42. S. Davis, *Future Perfect* (Reading, Mass.: Addison-Wesley, 1987).
43. Boynton and Victor, "Beyond Flexibility," 53–66.
44. T. Stewart, "The Search for the Organization of Tomorrow," *Fortune*, 18 May 1992, 92–98.
45. S. Tully, "The Modular Corporation," *Fortune*, 8 February 1993, 106–115; and R. L. Bunning and R. S. Althisar, "Modules: A Team Module for Manufacturing," *Personnel Journal* (1990): 90–96.
46. M. F. R. Kets de Vries and D. Miller, "Personality, Culture, and Organization," *Academy of Management Review* 11 (1986): 266–279.
47. J. M. Morris, Personal Communication, 1 March 1996.

CHAPTER 16

Organizational Culture

LEARNING OBJECTIVES

After reading this chapter, you should be able to do the following:

- Define *organizational culture* and explain its three levels.
- Identify the four functions of culture within an organization.
- Explain the relationship between organizational culture and performance.
- Contrast the characteristics of adaptive and nonadaptive cultures.
- Describe five ways leaders reinforce organizational culture.
- Describe the three stages of organizational socialization and the ways culture is communicated in each step.
- Identify ways of assessing organizational culture.
- Explain actions managers can take to change organizational culture.

OPENING SPOTLIGHT

Chaparral Steel's Mentofacturing Culture

Chaparral Steel believes that the human mind is the most crucial resource in the organization. The company's emphasis is on mentofacturing, which means "made by mind," as opposed to manufacturing, or made by the hand. Chaparral is a learning organization, and it has a unique organizational culture that supports its vision. Five core values permeate the entire company. The first is *trust in people to be responsible.* This value is exemplified in the fact that all employees are on salary and are treated as adults. The second value is *take risks for achievement and success.* Individual differences are celebrated at the company, and the unconventional is valued. Mistakes are seen as opportunities to learn. The third value is *challenge individuals to grow in knowledge and expertise.* In the goal-setting program at the company, production and maintenance employees set goals with supervisory and management personnel, and they are empowered to achieve them. Individuals and work teams determine ways to reach the goals. The fourth value is *be open to learning and to teaching.* Chaparral makes a heavy investment in employee training, and every individual has an education matrix that includes specific learning goals. The final value is *make work fun and pleasurable.* The work environment includes informal dress and an emphasis on teamwork rather than hierarchy. These key values guide the progress at Chaparral.[1] The Closing Spotlight reveals how key employees perpetuate Chaparral's culture. ■

The Key Role of Organizational Culture

Alternate Example
The concept of organizational culture has been advanced through the field of organizational behavior. In fact, part of the study of culture has been attached to the concept of how to change or strengthen the existing culture through leadership.

■ The concept of organizational culture has its roots in cultural anthropology. Just as there are cultures in larger human society, there seem to be cultures within organizations. These cultures are similar to societal cultures. They are shared, communicated through symbols, and passed down from generation to generation of employees.

The concept of cultures in organizations was alluded to as early as the Hawthorne Studies, which described work group culture. However, the topic came into its own during the early 1970s, when managers and researchers alike began to search for keys to survival for organizations in a competitive and turbulent environment. Then, in the early 1980s, several books on corporate culture were published, including Deal and Kennedy's *Corporate Cultures*,[2] Ouchi's *Theory Z*,[3] and Peters and Waterman's *In Search of Excellence*.[4] These books found wide audiences, and research began in earnest on the elusive topic of organizational cultures. Executives indicated that these cultures were real and could be managed.[5]

Culture and Its Levels

Many definitions of *organizational culture* have been proposed. Most of them agree that there are several levels of culture and that these levels differ in terms of their visibility and their ability to be changed. The definition adopted in this chapter is that **organizational (corporate) culture** is a pattern of basic assumptions that are considered valid and that are taught to new members as the way to perceive, think, and feel in the organization.[6]

organizational (corporate) culture
A pattern of basic assumptions that are considered valid and that are taught to new members as the way to perceive, think, and feel in the organization.

Edgar Schein, in his comprehensive book on organizational culture and leadership, suggests that organizational culture has three levels. His view of culture is presented in Figure 16.1. The levels range from visible artifacts and creations to testable values to invisible and even preconscious basic assumptions. To achieve a complete understanding of an organization's culture, all three levels must be studied.

Discussion Consideration
Ask students if their university has an identifiable culture. What are the artifacts of the school's culture?

Artifacts

Symbols of culture in the physical and social work environment are called **artifacts**. They are the most visible and accessible level of culture. The key to understanding culture through artifacts lies in figuring out what they mean. Artifacts are also the most frequently studied manifestation of organizational culture, perhaps because of their accessibility. Among the artifacts of culture are personal enactment, ceremonies and rites, stories, rituals, and symbols.[7]

artifacts
Symbols of culture in the physical and social work environment.

PERSONAL ENACTMENT Culture may be understood, in part, through an examination of the behavior of organization members. Personal enactment is

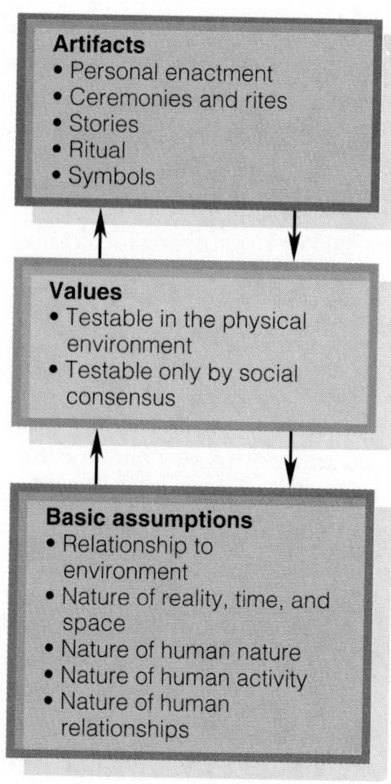

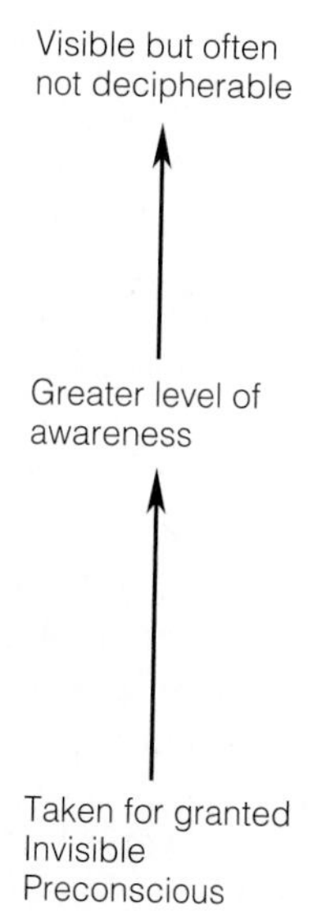

■ **FIGURE 16.1**

Levels of Organizational Culture

SOURCE: Edgar H. Schein, *Organizational Culture and Leadership: A Dynamic View,* Fig. 1, p. 14. Copyright 1985 by Jossey-Bass, Inc., Publishers. ISBN 0-87589-639-1.

behavior that reflects the organization's values. In particular, personal enactment by the top managers lends insight into these values. If, for example, customer service is highly valued, then the CEO may be seen going the extra mile for the customer, as did the late Sam Walton of Wal-Mart. He reinforced quality service by visiting stores often and recognizing individual employees. The CEO transmits values to others in the organization through modeling appropriate behavior.

http://www.walmart.com

Boone Pickens, CEO of Mesa Petroleum, values physical fitness for its psychological and spiritual benefits and believes a physically fit work force leads to economic benefits for the company. He established a fitness center for employees and is a regular participant at the center. His presence has resulted in fitness participation by three-quarters of Mesa's employees—and cost savings for the company.[8]

Modeled behavior is a powerful learning tool for employees, as Bandura's social learning theory demonstrated.[9] As we saw in Chapter 5, individuals learn vicariously by observing others' behavior and patterning their own behavior similarly. The values reflected in that behavior can permeate the entire employee population.

CEREMONIES AND RITES Relatively elaborate sets of activities that are enacted time and again on important occasions are known as organizational ceremonies and rites.[10] These occasions provide opportunities to reward and recognize employees whose behavior is congruent with the values of the company. Ceremonies and rites send a message that individuals who both espouse and exhibit corporate values are heroes to be admired.

The ceremonies also bond organization members together. Southwestern Bell emphasizes the importance of management training to the company. Training classes are kicked off by a high-ranking executive (a rite of renewal), and completion of the classes is signaled by a graduation ceremony (a rite of passage). Six kinds of rites in organizations have been identified:[11]

1. *Rites of passage* show that an individual's status has changed. Retirement dinners are an example.

2. *Rites of enhancement* reinforce the achievement of individuals. An example is the awarding of certificates to sales contest winners.
3. *Rites of renewal* emphasize change in the organization and commitment to learning and growth. An example is the opening of a new corporate training center.
4. *Rites of integration* unite diverse groups or teams within the organization and renew commitment to the larger organization. Company functions such as annual picnics fall into this category.
5. *Rites of conflict reduction* focus on dealing with conflicts or disagreements that arise naturally in organizations. Examples are grievance hearings and the negotiation of union contracts.
6. *Rites of degradation* are used by some organizations to visibly punish persons who fail to adhere to values and norms of behavior. Some CEOs, for example, are replaced quite publicly for unethical conduct or for failure to achieve organizational goals. Japanese employees who perform poorly in some organizations are given ribbons of shame as punishment.

http://www.marykay.com

Mary Kay Cosmetics holds extravagant annual seminars that exemplify several of these rites. Mary Kay Ash, founder of the company, has described these ceremonies as "a combination of the Academy Awards, the Miss America pageant, and a Broadway opening."[12] Each seminar has an elaborate script and a theme expressing a particular corporate value. Several nights of awards ceremonies are held, culminating in the crowning of the director and consultant queens, who receive mink coats and diamonds. The message sent out by these ceremonies is a clear one. Mary Kay Cosmetics' goals are sales performance, personal attention to both organization members and customers, and creating opportunities that give every employee the ability to excel.

Points to Emphasize
University cultures are rich with stories that solidify employees' and students' opinion of their institutions. Have students relate stories about professors, administrators, student associations, buildings, or any other aspect of campus life.

STORIES Some researchers have argued that the most effective way to reinforce organizational values is through stories.[13] Stories give meaning and identity to organizations as they are told and retold, especially in orienting new employees. Part of the strength of organizational stories is that the listeners are left to draw their own conclusions—a powerful communication tool.[14]

Often, the stories told are about the CEO's behavior. One story passed down at Monsanto is about Jack Hanley, who, upon taking over the reins of the company, wanted to make it more professional. He went so far as to remove a toothpick dispenser from the company cafeteria because he thought it was not in keeping with a professional image.

Other stories reinforce such values as customer service. IBM once had a client company whose machine went down one afternoon in the midst of payroll processing. Paychecks were to be distributed the following day. As the story goes, IBM flew in another machine and personnel, who worked all night to ensure that the client's payroll was distributed on time.[15]

Research by Joanne Martin and her colleagues has indicated that certain themes appear in stories across different types of organizations:[16]

1. *Stories about the boss.* These stories may reflect whether or not the boss is "human" or how the boss reacts to mistakes.
2. *Stories about getting fired.* Events leading to employee firings are recounted.
3. *Stories about how the company deals with employees who have to relocate.* These stories relate to the company's actions toward employees who have to move—whether or not the company is helpful and takes family and other personal concerns into account.
4. *Stories about whether lower-level employees can rise to the top.* Often, these stories describe a person who started out at the bottom and eventually became the CEO.

5. *Stories about how the company deals with crisis situations.* The example at IBM of the client crisis shows how the company overcomes obstacles.
6. *Stories about how status considerations work when rules are broken.* Tom Watson, Sr., chief executive officer of IBM, was once confronted by a security guard because he was not wearing an ID badge.

These are the themes that can emerge when stories are passed down. The information from these stories serves to guide the behavior of organization members.

Discussion Consideration
Do students believe informal organizations are more people-oriented than formal organizations? Have them provide examples to support their views.

RITUALS Everyday organizational practices that are repeated over and over are rituals. They are usually unwritten, but they send a clear message about "the way we do things around here." While some companies insist that people address each other by their titles (Mr., Mrs., Ms., Miss) and surnames to reinforce a professional image, others prefer that employees operate on a first-name basis—from the top manager on down. Hewlett-Packard values open communication, so its employees address one another by first names only.

The Charles Machine Works, producer of Ditch Witch underground excavation equipment, values informality, teamwork, and a flat organizational structure. One ritual practiced in the company is that a manager's employees are not referred to as subordinates. The idea that one person is lower than others is in opposition to the value placed on teamwork, so the workers are referred to as employees or team members.

As everyday practices, rituals reinforce the organizational culture. Insiders who commonly practice the rituals may be unaware of their subtle influence, but outsiders recognize it easily.

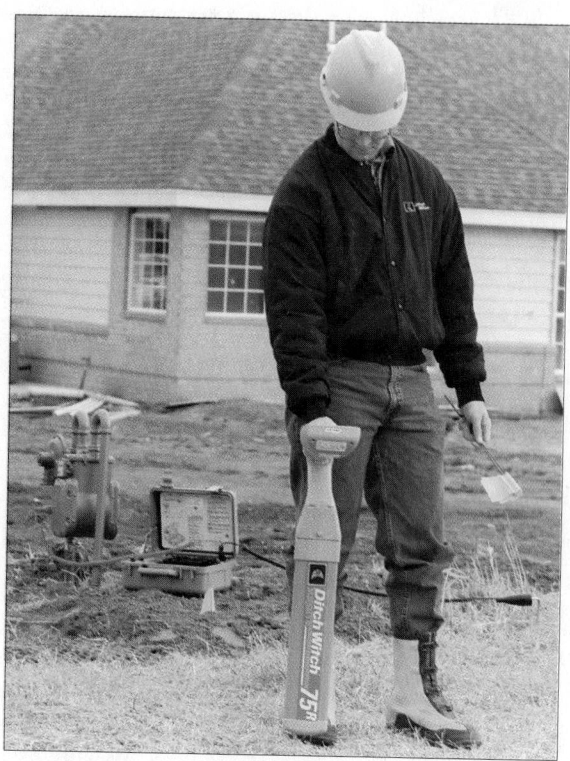

At Charles Machine Works, makers of Ditch Witch equipment, they ditched the term "subordinate" in favor of "team member." Their organizational culture is one of empowerment and teamwork.

SYMBOLS Symbols communicate organizational culture by unspoken messages. Southwest Airlines has used symbols in several ways. During its early years, the airline emphasized its customer service value by using the heart symbol (the "Love" airline) and love bites (peanuts). More recently, the airline has taken on the theme of fun. Flight attendants wear casual sports clothes in corporate colors. Low fares are "fun fares," and weekend getaways are "fun packs." Some aircraft are painted to resemble Shamu the whale, underscoring the fun image.

At Mary Kay Cosmetics, a meaningful symbol is the diamond bumblebee pin awarded to top performers. Engineers have argued that a bumblebee's wings are too small and its body is too heavy for the bee to fly, but the bumblebee flies somehow. The symbol represents success achieved despite great obstacles.

Symbols may be only mental images. At Southwestern Bell, company loyalty is valued. Longtime company employees are referred to as "bleeding blue and gold" (company colors).

Discussion Consideration
Ask students to analyze the university mascot as a symbol. How about their high school team names and mascots?

Personal enactment, rites and ceremonies, stories, rituals, and symbols serve to reinforce the values that are the next level of culture.

Alternate Example
Texas A&M is a university with a strong culture. Among their rituals are midnight yell practice, bonfires before the annual game with Texas, and the 12th man tradition.

Values

Values are the second, and deeper, level of culture. They reflect a person's underlying beliefs of what should be or should not be. Values are often consciously articulated, both in conversation and in a company's mission statement or annual report. However, there may be a difference between a company's **espoused values** (what the members say they value) and its **enacted values** (values reflected in the way the members actually behave).[17] Values also may be reflected in the behavior of individuals, which is an artifact of culture.

espoused values
What members of an organization say they value.

enacted values
Values reflected in the way individuals actually behave.

SCIENTIFIC FOUNDATION

A Culture That Values Teamwork Performs Better

One area of interest to many managers and scholars alike is whether there is a link between organizational culture and performance. In this study, the researchers focused on a large electric utility to see whether certain values that were part of the organization's culture were related to performance. The values included in the study were teamwork, trust and credibility, and common goals.

Twelve organizations within the electrical utility participated in the study. A survey was administered to 884 employees in these twelve organizations at two different times, one year apart. This permitted the researchers to assess the stability of the values. The performance data were collected for the two fiscal years for each of the twelve service organizations. The performance measure was a summary of five objective performance indicators: operations, customer accounting, support services, marketing, and employee safety and health.

The researchers correlated the values with the performance indicators. The results showed that teamwork was the major aspect of organizational culture that was related to performance. In this electric utility, an organizational culture that emphasizes teamwork was more conducive to organizational effectiveness than one that does not foster cooperative behaviors. Helping others, sharing information and resources, and working as a team enhanced performance in the utility. Future studies will need to address whether this holds true for other types of organizations.

SOURCE: M. M. Petty, N. A. Beadles II, D. F. Chapman, C. M. Lowery, and D. W. Connell, "Relationships Between Organizational Culture and Organizational Performance," *Psychological Reports* 76 (1995): 483–492.

http://www.levi.com

Alternate Example
Congruence between espoused values and enacted values is critical. For example, LBJ often said publicly that he would not send American boys to Viet Nam to do a job that should be done by Asian boys. Despite these public statements, privately LBJ was escalating the war commitment. This lack of congruence undermined his credibility with the public.

One company that emphasizes values is Levi Strauss. Its values are espoused in a formal aspirations statement and are enacted by its employees from the CEO down. At Levi Strauss, the values include diversity, ethical behavior, recognition for individuals and teams, and empowerment, among others. The result of practicing these values has been positive. Employees' work is more creative and entrepreneurial. Business has never been better. One-third of the reward package for managers depends on their ability to manage "aspirationally"—based on the company's aspirations.

Values underlie the adaptable and innovative culture at Levi Strauss. As guides for behavior, they are reinforced in the aspirations statement and in the reward system of the organization. Work force diversity is valued at Levi Strauss. A former strong supporter of the Boy Scouts of America, the company discontinued its funding after the Scouts were shown to discriminate on the basis of sexual orientation. Mary Gross, a Levi Strauss spokesperson, expressed the company's position on valuing diversity: "One of the family values of this company is treating people who are different from you the same as you'd like to be treated. Tolerance is a pretty important family value."[18]

Do values make a difference in performance? The Scientific Foundation feature reports a study that addressed this issue. For the large utility company in the study, teamwork was the value that paid off.

Assumptions

assumptions
Deeply held beliefs that guide behavior and tell members of an organization how to perceive and think about things.

Assumptions are the deeply held beliefs that guide behavior and tell members of an organization how to perceive and think about things. As the deepest and most fundamental level of an organization's culture, according to Schein, they are the essence of culture. They are so strongly held that a member behaving in any fashion that would violate them would be unthinkable. Another characteristic of assumptions is that they are often unconscious. Organization members may not be aware of their assumptions and may be reluctant or unable to discuss them or change them.

CHALLENGE

■ **16.1**

Analyzing the Three Levels of Culture

Select an organization you respect. Analyze its culture using the following dimensions.

The artifacts of ______________ 's culture are as follows:

Personal enactment:

Rites and ceremonies:

Stories:

Rituals:

Symbols:

The values embedded in ______________ 's culture are as follows:

The assumptions of ______________ 's culture are as follows:

1. On what information did you base your analysis?
2. How complete is your view of this organization's culture?

Chaparral Steel's values reflect three basic assumptions. The first is that people are basically good; this assumption is reflected in the company's emphasis on trust. The second assumption is that people want opportunities to learn and grow, as is seen in the value placed on education and training. The third assumption is that people are motivated by opportunities to learn and by work that is challenging and enjoyable, as reflected in Chaparral's goal-setting program.

To fully decipher an organization's culture, one must examine all three levels: artifacts, values, and assumptions. Challenge 16.1 offers insight into analyzing an organization's culture using Schein's framework.

Functions and Effects of Organizational Culture

■ In an organization, culture serves four basic functions. First, culture provides a sense of identity to members and increases their commitment to the organization.[19] When employees internalize the values of the company, they find their work intrinsically rewarding and identify with their fellow workers. Motivation is enhanced, and employees are more committed.[20]

Second, culture is a sense-making device for organization members. It provides a way for employees to interpret the meaning of organizational events.[21]

Third, culture reinforces the values in the organization. At Westinghouse's Commercial Nuclear Fuel Division, for example, a cultural change was undertaken to achieve total quality as the number one value. All employees were involved in creating the quality plan, which in 1988 won the coveted Baldrige National Quality Award.[22]

http://www.westinghouse.com

Finally, culture serves as a control mechanism for shaping behavior. Norms that guide behavior are part of culture. At Westinghouse, employee suggestions increased fivefold following the emphasis on total quality. It became a norm to think of ways to improve processes at the division.

The effects of organizational culture are hotly debated by organizational behaviorists and researchers. It seems that managers attest strongly to the positive effects of culture in organizations, but it is difficult to quantify these effects. Recently, John Kotter and James Heskett reviewed three theories about the relationship between organizational culture and performance and the evidence that either supports or refutes these theories.[23] The three are the strong culture perspective, the fit perspective, and the adaptation perspective.

The Strong Culture Perspective

strong culture

An organizational culture with a consensus on the values that drive the company and with an intensity that is recognizable even to outsiders.

The strong culture perspective states that organizations with "strong" cultures perform better than other organizations.[24] A **strong culture** is an organizational culture with a consensus on the values that drive the company and with an intensity that is recognizable even to outsiders. Thus, a strong culture is deeply held and widely shared. It also is highly resistant to change. One example of a strong culture is IBM's. Its culture is one we are all familiar with: conservative, with a loyal workforce and an emphasis on customer service.

Strong cultures are thought to facilitate performance for three reasons. First, these cultures are characterized by goal alignment; that is, all employees share common goals. Second, strong cultures create a high level of motivation because of the values shared by the members. Third, strong cultures provide control without the oppressive effects of a bureaucracy.

To test the strong culture hypothesis, Kotter and Heskett selected 207 firms from a wide variety of industries. They used a questionnaire to calculate a culture strength index for each firm, and they correlated that index with the firm's economic performance over a twelve-year period. They concluded that strong cultures were associated with positive long-term economic performance, but only modestly.

There are also two perplexing questions about the strong culture perspectives. First, what can be said about evidence showing that strong economic performance can create strong cultures, rather than the reverse? Second, what if the strong culture leads the firm down the wrong path? Sears, for example, is an organization with a strong culture. In recent years, however, it has focused inward, ignoring competition and consumer preferences and damaging its performance.[25]

The Fit Perspective

The "fit" perspective argues that a culture is good only if it fits the industry's or the firm's strategy. For example, a culture that values a traditional hierarchical structure and stability would not work well in the computer manufacturing industry, which demands fast response and a lean, flat organization. Three particular characteristics of an industry may affect culture: the competitive environment, customer requirements, and societal expectations.[26] In the computer industry, firms face a highly competitive environment, customers who require highly reliable products, and a society that expects state-of-the-art technology and high-quality service. These characteristics affect the culture in computer manufacturing companies.

A study of twelve large U.S. firms indicated that cultures consistent with industry conditions help managers make better decisions. It also indicated that cultures need not change as long as the industry doesn't change. However, if the industry does change, many cultures change too slowly to avoid negative effects on firms' performance.[27]

The fit perspective is useful in explaining short-term performance but not long-term performance. It also indicates that it is difficult to change culture quickly, especially if the culture is widely shared and deeply held. But it doesn't explain how firms can adapt to environmental change.

The Adaptation Perspective

The third theory about culture and performance is the adaptation perspective. Its theme is that only cultures that help organizations adapt to environmental change are associated with excellent performance. An **adaptive culture** is a culture that encourages confidence and risk taking among employees,[28] has leadership that produces change,[29] and focuses on the changing needs of customers.[30] 3M is a company with an adaptive culture, in that it encourages new product ideas from all levels within the company.

To test the adaptation perspective, Kotter and Heskett interviewed industry analysts about the cultures of twenty-two firms. The contrast between adaptive cultures and nonadaptive cultures was striking. The results of the study are summarized in Table 16.1.

Adaptive cultures facilitate change to meet the needs of three groups of constituents: stockholders, customers, and employees. Nonadaptive cultures are characterized by cautious management that tries to protect its own interests. Adaptive firms showed significantly better long-term economic performance in Kotter and Heskett's study. One contrast that can be made is between Hewlett-Packard, a high performer, and Xerox, a lower performer. Hewlett-Packard was viewed by the industry analysts as valuing excellent leadership more than Xerox did and as valuing all three key constituencies more than Xerox did. Economic performance from 1977 through 1988 suported this difference: HP's index of annual net income growth was 40.2, as compared to Xerox's 13.1. Kotter and Heskett concluded that the cultures that promote long-term performance are those that are most adaptive.

adaptive culture

An organizational culture that encourages confidence and risk taking among employees, has leadership that produces change, and focuses on the changing needs of customers.

Alternate Example

Many organizations offer cash rewards for cost cutting suggestions.

http://www.hp.com

Alternate Example

Joanne Martin offers an interesting alternative to the mainstream view of organizational culture. She suggests that there are three perspectives through which an organizational culture can be analyzed. The integration perspective emphasizes consistency and common meanings that are shared among the organization's members. The differentiation perspective describes cultural manifestations as sometimes inconsistent. The fragmentation perspective focuses on ambiguity as the essence of organizational culture. SOURCE: J. Martin, *Cultures in Organizations: Three Perspectives* (1992), New York: Oxford University Press.

■ **TABLE 16.1**

Adaptive versus Nonadaptive Organizational Cultures

	ADAPTIVE ORGANIZATIONAL CULTURES	NONADAPTIVE ORGANIZATIONAL CULTURES
Core Values	Most managers care deeply about customers, stockholders, and employees, They also strongly value people and processes that can create useful change (e.g., leadership up and down the management hierarchy).	Most managers care mainly about themselves, their immediate work group, or some product (or technology) associated with that work group. They value the orderly and risk-reducing management process much more highly than leadership initiatives.
Common Behavior	Managers pay close attention to all their constituencies, especially customers, and initiate change when needed to serve their legitimate interests, even if that entails taking some risks.	Managers tend to behave somewhat insularly, politically, and bureaucratically. As a result, they do not change their strategies quickly to adjust to or take advantage of changes in their business environments.

SOURCE: Reprinted with the permission of The Free Press, a Division of Macmillan, Inc. From *Corporate Culture and Performance* by John P. Kotter and James L. Heskett. Copyright © 1992 by Kotter Associates, Inc. and James L. Heskett.

Given that high-performing cultures are adaptive ones, it is important to know how managers can develop adaptive cultures. In the next section, we will examine the leader's role in managing organizational culture.

The Leader's Role in Shaping and Reinforcing Culture

■ According to Edgar Schein, leaders play crucial roles in shaping and reinforcing culture.[31] The five most important elements in managing culture are these: (1) what leaders pay attention to; (2) how leaders react to crises; (3) how leaders behave; (4) how leaders allocate rewards; and (5) how leaders hire and fire individuals.

What Leaders Pay Attention To

Leaders in an organization communicate their priorities, values, and beliefs through the themes that consistently emerge from what they focus on. These themes are reflected in what they notice, comment on, measure, and control. The late Ray Kroc, founder of McDonald's, paid attention to detail. He built the company on the basis of a vision of providing identical, high-quality hamburgers at low cost.[32] Through careful training, quality control, and even special measuring cups, he honed his company's expertise so that the Big Mac in Miami would be the same as the Big Mac in Moscow.

Points to Emphasize
Impression management is related to developing culture. Leaders who are conscious of the impression they leave help their employees to figure out what is valued.

If leaders are consistent in what they pay attention to, measure, and control, employees receive clear signals about what is important in the organization. If, however, leaders are inconsistent, employees spend a lot of time trying to decipher and find meaning in the inconsistent signals.

How Leaders React to Crises

The way leaders deal with crises communicates a powerful message about culture. Emotions are heightened during a crisis, and learning is intense. In Lee Iacocca's effort to turn Chrysler around, the company perceived itself to be in crisis. Iacocca appealed for a government bailout, framing his argument in such a way that the government's refusal would be seen as a lack of commitment to businesses and to America's competitive position.[33] Iacocca had articulated Chrysler's mission as protecting America's jobs, and his reaction to the crisis underscored Chrysler's value that the free enterprise system should be protected.

Discussion Consideration
Ask students to identify ways in which their university president or college dean has attempted to shape the culture of their organization.

Difficult economic times present crises for many companies and illustrate their different values. Some organizations do everything possible to prevent laying off workers. Others may claim that employees are important but quickly institute major layoffs at the first signal of an economic downturn. Employees may perceive that the company shows its true colors in a crisis and thus may pay careful attention to the reactions of their leaders.

How Leaders Behave

Through role modeling, teaching, and coaching, leaders reinforce the values that support the organizational culture. Employees often emulate leaders' behavior and look to the leaders for cues to appropriate behavior. Ebby Halliday, founder and president of Ebby Halliday Realtors, based in Dallas, believes strongly in giving back to the community. This belief, along with behavior that backs it up, has been a key contributor to her success. Halliday is heavily

ORGANIZATIONAL REALITY

Empowerment Pays Off at Chrysler

Chrysler is the most profitable automaker in the world on a per vehicle basis. A few years ago, it was near death. Things are looking up now, however. While Toyota leads the world in quality, Chrysler is catching up fast. Last year's earnings were up 246 percent and sales were far above previous records. Employees have turned out a fleet of hot-selling new models: the Neon subcompact, Ram pickup, and hand-built Viper convertible. When asked how the company accomplished its turnaround, CEO Robert Eaton replies, "If I had to use one word, it's empowerment. That's the biggest reason."

When Chrysler creates a new model, it forms a team of about 700 people from engineering, design, manufacturing, marketing, and finance, including specialists of all kinds. These self-contained, multidisciplinary groups have a vice president who acts as a "godfather" or advisor, but the group organizes as it sees fit. The group works out a contract with managers that sets out objectives, and the team is turned loose to work. As a result, every single vehicle has come in below its investment target and its cost-per-car target. When teams have the power to create the car and the responsibility to meet the budget, they meet it.

Empowerment was in full swing when Robert Eaton arrived at Chrysler, but it has become even more important during his leadership. One payoff is speed to market. It used to take Chrysler five years to get a car into production. Now it takes 2½ years or less. That even beats the Japanese, according to CEO Eaton.

Global expansion is the vision at Chrysler, which is growing at a rate of 20 percent abroad. Chrysler is exploring many foreign ventures in Southeast Asia and in South America. As Eaton surveys the global auto market, he concludes that Chrysler's success will ultimately come down to people. "What will make all the difference in business will be how well you train your workforce, how well you motivate—and how well you empower." ■

SOURCE: M. Loeb, "Empowerment That Pays Off," *Fortune*, March 20, 1995: 145–146.

Chrysler CEO Robert Eaton shines up a new Ram pickup, one of the company's best selling vehicles. Eaton claims that empowerment is the number one reason for Chrysler's success.

invested in community activities, including beautification, education, and other efforts to help improve the lives of people in Dallas. She also encourages and supports community involvement on the part of all of her employees.[34]

Leaders who "walk the walk" earn the respect of their employees. The Organizational Reality feature shows how Chrysler CEO Robert Eaton reinforces empowerment by turning his employees loose to be creative.

How Leaders Allocate Rewards

To ensure that values are accepted, leaders should reward behavior that is consistent with the values. Some companies, for example, may claim that they use a pay-for-performance system that distributes rewards on the basis of performance. When the time comes for raises, however, the increases are awarded according to length of service with the company. Imagine the feelings of a high-performing newcomer who has heard leaders espouse the value of rewarding individual performance and then receives only a tiny raise.

Some companies may value teamwork. They form cross-functional teams and empower these teams to make important decisions. However, when performance is appraised, the criteria for rating employees focus on individual performance. This sends a confusing signal to employees about the company's culture: Is individual performance valued, or is teamwork the key?

How Leaders Hire and Fire Individuals

A powerful way that leaders reinforce culture lies in the selection of newcomers to the organization. Leaders often unconsciously look for individuals who are similar to current organizational members in terms of values and assumptions. Some companies hire individuals on the recommendation of a current employee; this tends to perpetuate the culture because the new employees typically hold similar values. Promotion-from-within policies also serve to reinforce organizational culture.

Alternate Example: Sudden termination is used in situations where individuals might have access to important company information. Often, employees are escorted off the premises immediately.

The way a company fires an employee and the rationale behind the firing also communicates the culture. Some companies deal with poor performers by trying to find them a place within the organization where they can perform better and make a contribution. Other companies seem to operate under the philosophy that those who cannot perform are out quickly.

The reasons for terminations may not be directly communicated to other employees, but curiosity leads to speculation. An employee who displays unethical behavior and is caught may simply be reprimanded even though such behavior is clearly against the organization's values. This may be viewed by other employees as a failure to reinforce the values within the organization.

http://www.iflyswa.com

All of these elements are ways leaders act to shape the culture within the organization. One leader who has shaped a distinctive organizational culture is Herb Kelleher of Southwest Airlines. Kelleher has appeared at company parties as Elvis Presley and Roy Orbison, singing "Jailhouse Rock" and "Pretty Woman." When Robert Crandall, CEO of American Airlines (and a Rhode Island native), asked him what he was going to do with the whale droppings from Southwest's freshly painted Shamu airplane, Kelleher's response was, "I am going to turn it into chocolate mousse and feed it to Yankees from Rhode Island." To follow up, he sent a tub of chocolate mousse to Crandall's office, along with a king-size Shamu spoon. His leadership has made humor and altruism two key values at Southwest Airlines.[35]

Kelleher's leadership has established a unique culture at Southwest Airlines. Southwest's costs are the lowest of any major airline, its people are the best paid, and the annual turnover is the industry's lowest. In a turbulent industry, Southwest is a major player.[36]

Organizational Socialization

■ We have seen that leaders play key roles in shaping an organization's culture. Another process that perpetuates culture is the way it is handed down from generation to generation of employees. Newcomers learn the culture through **orga-**

nizational socialization—the process by which newcomers are transformed from outsiders to participating, effective members of the organization.[37] The process is also a vehicle for bringing newcomers into the organizational culture. As we saw earlier, cultural socialization begins with the careful selection of newcomers who are likely to reinforce the organizational culture.[38] Once selected, newcomers pass through the socialization process.

organizational socialization

The process by which newcomers are transformed from outsiders to participating, effective members of the organization.

The Stages of the Socialization Process

The organizational socialization process is generally described as having three stages: anticipatory socialization, encounter, and change and acquisition. Figure 16.2 presents a model of the process and the key concerns at each stage of it.[39] It also describes the outcomes of the process, which will be discussed in the next section of the chapter.

ANTICIPATORY SOCIALIZATION **Anticipatory socialization**, the first stage, encompasses all of the learning that takes place prior to the newcomer's first day on the job. It includes the newcomer's expectations. The two key concerns at this stage are realism and congruence.

anticipatory socialization

The first socialization stage, which encompasses all of the learning that takes place prior to the newcomer's first day on the job.

Realism is the degree to which a newcomer holds realistic expectations about the job and about the organization. One thing newcomers should receive information about during entry into the organization is the culture. Information about values at this stage can help newcomers begin to construct a scheme for interpreting their organizational experiences. A deeper understanding of the organization's culture will be possible through time and experience in the organization.

There are two types of *congruence* between an individual and an organization. The first is congruence between the individual's abilities and the demands of the job. The second is the fit between the organization's values and the individual's values. Value congruence is particularly important for organizational culture. It is also important in terms of newcomer adjustment. Newcomers whose values match the company's values are more satisfied with their new jobs, adjust more quickly, and say they intend to remain with the firm longer.[40]

Alternate Example

A Harvard MBA went to work for Pepsi. On his first day of work, he asked where the Coke machine was. He was informed that they did not have Coke machines at the Pepsi company.

It has even been suggested that employees should be hired to fit the culture of the organization, not just the requirements of the job. This is practiced extensively in Korean chaebols, which are conglomerate groups. Each chaebol has a

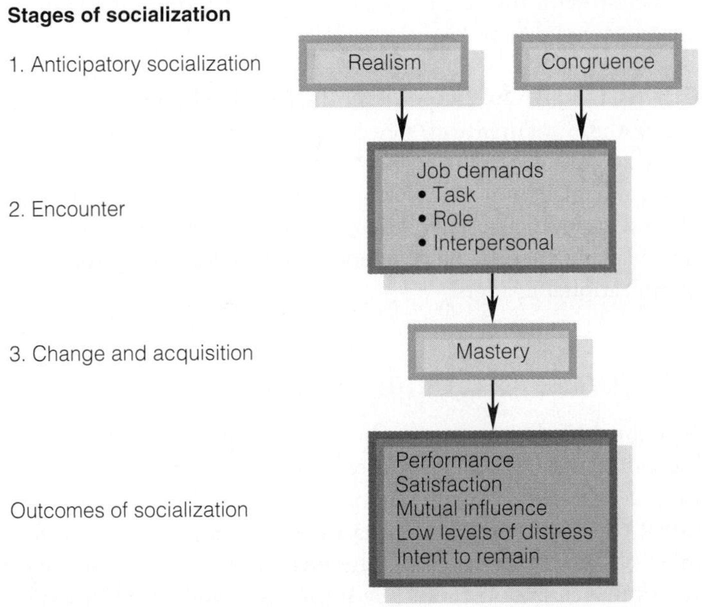

■ **FIGURE 16.2**

The Organizational Socialization Process: Stages and Outcomes

SOURCE: Reprinted by permission of the publisher, from "Organizational Dynamics," Autumn 1989, © 1989. John B. Cullen. American Management Association, New York. All rights reserved.

unique culture and selects newcomers in part on the basis of personality criteria. The Hanjin group, for example, looks for newcomers who exhibit patriotism and serviceship. Korean Airlines (KAL) is a member of the Hanjin group, which also has other transportation subsidiaries. At KAL, employees are expected to act as civilian diplomats; they are required to master a foreign language and to go abroad at least once. Polished manners and refined language are required, and female employees are forbidden to wear jeans even off duty.[41]

encounter

The second socialization stage, in which the newcomer learns the tasks associated with the job, clarifies roles, and establishes new relationships at work.

Points to Emphasize
There are some difficulties in the "fit" approach to hiring. If individuals can contribute only on the basis of the existing culture, it will be difficult to encourage diversity in the workforce. For example, does a disabled individual fit into a culture with a strong emphasis on a bowling or softball league?

Points to Emphasize
Fit actually has three levels. Level 1 involves the fit between an employee's skill level and the requirements of the job. Level 2 involves the fit between the rewards offered by the job, both tangible and intangible, and the needs of the employee. Level 3 involves the fit between the organization's values and the individual's personal value system.

Points to Emphasize
Self-monitoring may be particularly useful when starting a new job.

ENCOUNTER The second stage of socialization, **encounter**, is when newcomers learn the tasks associated with the job, clarify their roles, and establish new relationships at work. This stage commences on the first day at work and is thought to encompass the first six to nine months on the new job. Newcomers face task demands, role demands, and interpersonal demands during this period.

Task demands involve the actual work performed. Learning to perform tasks is related to the organization's culture. In some organizations, considerable latitude is given to newcomers to experiment with new ways to do the job, and value is placed on creativity. In others, newcomers are expected to learn their tasks using established procedures. Newcomers may also need guidance from the culture about work hours. Is there a value placed on putting in long hours, or is leaving work at 5:00 to spend time with family more the norm?

Role demands involve the expectations placed on newcomers. Newcomers may not know exactly what is expected of them (role ambiguity) or may receive conflicting expectations from other individuals (role conflict). The way newcomers approach these demands depends in part on the culture of the organization. Are newcomers expected to operate with considerable uncertainty, or is the manager expected to clarify the newcomers' roles? Some cultures even put newcomers through considerable stress in the socialization process, including humility-inducing experiences, so newcomers will be more open to accepting the firm's values and norms. Long hours, tiring travel schedules, and an overload of work are part of some socialization practices.

Interpersonal demands arise from relationships at work. Politics, leadership style, and group pressure are interpersonal demands. All of them reflect the values and assumptions that operate within the organization. Most organizations have basic assumptions about the nature of human relationships. The Korean chaebol Lucky-Goldstar strongly values harmony in relationships and in society, and its decision-making policy emphasizes unanimity.

In the encounter stage, the expectations formed in anticipatory socialization may clash with the realities of the job. It is a time of facing the task, role, and interpersonal demands of the new job.

change and acquisition

The third socialization stage, in which the newcomer begins to master the demands of the job.

CHANGE AND ACQUISITION In the third and final stage of socialization, **change and acquisition**, newcomers begin to master the demands of the job. They become proficient at managing their tasks, clarifying and negotiating their roles, and engaging in relationships at work. The completion of the socialization process varies widely, depending on the individual, the job, and the organization. Its end is signaled by newcomers being considered by themselves and others as organizational insiders.

Outcomes of Socialization

Newcomers who are successfully socialized should exhibit good performance, high job satisfaction, and the intention to stay with the organization. In addition, they should exhibit low levels of distress symptoms.[42] High levels of organizational commitment are also marks of successful socialization.[43] This commitment is facilitated throughout the socialization process by the communication of values that newcomers can buy into. Successful socialization is also signaled by mutual influence; that is, the newcomers have made adjustments in the job and organization to accommodate their knowledge and personalities. Newcomers are expected to leave their mark on the organization and not be completely conforming.

This is something of a paradox for organizations socializing individuals into their cultures. Organizations desire strong cultures but also want to allow the unique qualities of newcomers to affect the work situation. This can be accomplished by creating a culture that values empowerment and that encourages newcomers to apply their creative potential to the new job.[44]

Socialization as Cultural Communication

Socialization is a powerful cultural communication tool. While the transmission of information about cultural artifacts is relatively easy, the transmission of values is more difficult. The communication of organizational assumptions is almost impossible, since organization members themselves may not be consciously aware of them.

The primary purpose of socialization is the transmission of core values to new organization members.[45] Newcomers are exposed to these values through the role models they interact with, the training they receive, and the behavior they observe being rewarded and punished. Newcomers are vigilant observers, seeking clues to the organization's culture and consistency in the cultural messages they receive. If they are expected to adopt these values, it is essential that the message reflect the underlying values of the organization.

One company known for its culture is the Walt Disney Company. Disney transmits its culture to employees though careful selection, socialization, and training. The Disney culture is built around customer service, and its image serves as a filtering process for applicants. Peer interviews are used to learn how applicants interact with each other. Disney tries to secure a good fit between employee values and the organization's culture. To remind employees of the image they are trying to project, employees are referred to as "cast members" and they occupy a "role." They work either "on stage" or "backstage" and wear "costumes," rather than uniforms. Disney operates its own "universities," which are attended by all new employees. Once trained at a Disney university, cast members are paired with role models to continue their learning on-site.

The Disney culture is built around customer service and "Disney Courtesy." Outstanding cast members become instructors at Disney "universities" and teach their peers while in full costume.

http://www.disney.com

Companies such as Disney use the socialization process to communicate messages about organizational culture. Both individuals and organizations can take certain actions to ensure the success of the socialization process. Socialization is explored further in the following chapter, on career management.

Assessing Organizational Culture

■ While some organizational scientists would argue for assessing organizational culture with quantitative methods, others would say that organizational culture must be assessed with qualitative methods.[46] Quantitative methods, such as questionnaires, are valuable because of their precision, comparability, and objectivity. Qualitative methods, such as interviews and observations, are valuable because of their detail, descriptiveness, and uniqueness.

Two widely used quantitative assessment instruments are the Organizational Culture Inventory (OCI) and the Kilmann-Saxton Culture-Gap Survey. Both

Discussion Consideration
Is a strong culture always an asset? Under what situations would a strong culture be a liability?

assess the behavioral norms of organizational cultures, as opposed to the artifacts, values, or assumptions of the organization.

Organizational Culture Inventory

The OCI focuses on behaviors that help employees fit into the organization and meet the expectations of coworkers. Using Maslow's motivational need hierarchy as its basis, it measures twelve cultural styles. The two underlying dimensions of the OCI are task/people and security/satisfaction. There are four satisfaction cultural styles and eight security cultural styles.

A self-report instrument, the OCI contains 120 questions. It provides an individual assessment of culture and may be aggregated to the work group and to the organizational level.[47] It has been used in firms throughout North America, Western Europe, New Zealand, and Thailand, as well as in U.S. military units, the Federal Aviation Administration, and nonprofit organizations.

Kilmann-Saxton Culture-Gap Survey

The Kilmann-Saxton Culture-Gap Survey focuses on what actually happens and on the expectations of others in the organization.[48] Its two underlying dimensions are technical/human, and time (the short term versus the long term). With these two dimensions, the actual operating norms and the ideal norms in four areas are assessed. The areas are task support (short-term technical norms), task innovation (long-term technical norms), social relationships (short-term human orientation norms), and personal freedom (long-term human orientation norms). Significant gaps in any of the four areas are used as a point of departure for cultural change to improve performance, job satisfaction, and morale.

A self-report instrument, the Gap Survey provides an individual assessment of culture and may be aggregated to the work group. It has been used in firms throughout the United States and in nonprofit organizations.

Triangulation

triangulation
The use of multiple methods to measure organizational culture.

A study of a rehabilitation center in a 400-bed hospital incorporated **triangulation** (the use of multiple methods to measure organizational culture) to improve inclusiveness and accuracy in measuring the organizational culture.[49] Triangulation has been used by anthropologists, sociologists, and other behavioral scientists to study organizational culture. Its name comes from the navigational technique of using multiple reference points to locate an object. In the rehabilitation center study, the three methods used to triangulate on the culture were (1) obtrusive observations by eight trained observers, which provided an outsider perspective; (2) self-administered questionnaires, which provided quantitative insider information; and (3) personal interviews with the center's staff, which provided qualitative contextual information.

The study showed that each of the three methods made unique contributions toward the discovery of the rehabilitation center's culture. The complete picture could not have been drawn with just a single technique. Triangulation can lead to a better understanding of the phenomenon of culture and is the best approach to assessing organizational culture.

Changing Organizational Culture

■ Changing situations may require changes in the existing culture of an organization. With rapid environmental changes such as globalization, workforce diversity, and technological innovation, the fundamental assumptions and basic values that drive the organization may need to be altered. One particular situation that may require cultural change is a merger or acquisition. The blending of two distinct organizational cultures may prove difficult.

When Mellon Bank Corporation and Dreyfus Corporation joined forces, it was heralded as a natural fit between a bank and a mutual funds company, representing the wave of the future. The combined companies were envisioned to be a financial services powerhouse. Early stages, however, indicated a clash of organizational cultures. Mellon had little understanding of the mutual funds industry. Its culture, characterized as bean-counting and technocratic, collided with Dreyfus' more loose and informal culture. Mellon's emphasis was on expense reduction, while Dreyfus' focus was on business promotion. If the two companies can bring about a unified culture, the acquisition could work. Mellon brings to the table greater business discipline, while Dreyfus brings entrepreneurial direct marketing skills. The challenge of working through the clash of cultures will ultimately decide the success of the venture.[50]

Discussion Consideration
Ask students how easy they think it would be to change an organizational culture.

Another situation that may require alterations in culture is an organization's employment of people from different countries. Research indicates that some organizational cultures actually enhance differences in national cultures.[51] One study compared foreign employees working in a multinational organization to employees working in different organizations within their own countries. The assumption was that employees from the various countries working for the same multinational organization would be more similar than employees working in diverse organizations in their native countries. The results were surprising, in that there were significantly greater differences between the employees of the multinational than there were between managers working for different companies within their native countries. In the multinational, Swedes became more Swedish, Americans became more American, and so forth. It appears that employees enhance their national culture traditions even when working within a single organizational culture.[52]

Changing an organization's culture is feasible but difficult.[53] One reason for the difficulty is that assumptions—the deepest level of culture—are often unconscious. As such, they are often nonconfrontable and nondebatable. Another reason for the difficulty is that culture is deeply ingrained and behavioral norms and rewards are well learned.[54] In a sense, employees must unlearn the old norms before they can learn new ones. Managers who want to change the culture should look first to the ways culture is maintained.

A model for cultural change that summarizes the interventions managers can use is presented in Figure 16.3. In this model, the numbers represent the actions managers can take. There are two basic approaches to changing the existing culture: (1) helping current members buy into a new set of values (actions 1, 2, and 3); or (2) adding newcomers and socializing them into the organization, and removing current members as appropriate (actions 4 and 5).[55]

The first action is to change behavior in the organization. However, even if behavior does change, this change is not sufficient for cultural change to occur. Behavior is an artifact (level 1) of culture. Individuals may change their behavior but not the values that drive it. They may rationalize, "I'm only doing this because my manager wants me to."

Therefore, managers must use action 2, which is to examine the justifications for the changed behavior. Are employees buying into the new set of values, or are they just complying?

The third action, cultural communication, is extremely important. All of the artifacts (personal enactment, stories, rites and ceremonies, rituals, and symbols) must send a consistent message about the new values and beliefs. It is crucial that the communication be credible; that is, managers must live the new values rather than just talking about them. The communication must also be persuasive. Individuals may resist cultural change and may have to be persuaded to try the new behavior by someone they respect and can identify with.

■ **FIGURE 16.3**

Interventions for Changing Organizational Culture

SOURCE: Vijay Sathe, "How to Decipher and Change Corporate Culture," in R. H. Kilmann, M. J. Saxton, R. Serpa, and Associates, *Gaining Control of the Corporate Culture,* Fig. 1, p. 245. Copyright 1985 by Jossey-Bass, Inc., Publishers. ISBN 0-87589-666-9.

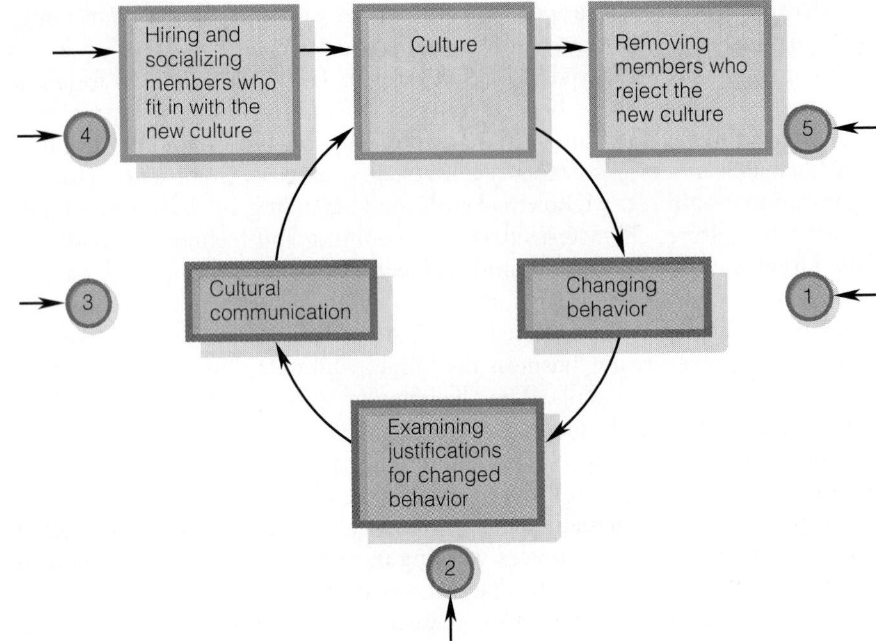

The two remaining actions (4 and 5) involve shaping the workforce to fit the intended culture. First, organizations can revise their selection strategies to more accurately reflect the new culture. Second, the organization can identify individuals who resist the cultural change or who are no longer comfortable with the values in the organization. This is not intended to be a ruthless pursuit; it should be a gradual and subtle change that takes considerable time. Changing personnel in the organization is a lengthy process; it cannot be done effectively in a short period of time without considerable problems.

Evaluating the success of cultural change may be best done by looking at behavior. Culture change can be assumed to be successful if the behavior is intrinisically motivated—on "automatic pilot." If the new behavior would persist even if rewards were not present, and if the employees have internalized the new value system, then the behavior is probably intrinisically motivated. If employees automatically respond to a crisis in ways consistent with the corporate culture, then the cultural change effort can be deemed successful.

http://www.att.com

One organization that has changed its culture is AT&T. In 1984, the courts ordered the breakup of AT&T. Prior to the breakup, the company operated in a stable environment with low levels of uncertainty. The organization was a highly structured bureaucracy. The culture emphasized lifetime employment, promotion from within, and loyalty. AT&T faced minimal competition, and it offered individual security. When the courts ordered AT&T to divest its Bell operating companies, the old culture was no longer effective. The company had to move toward a culture that holds individuals accountable for their performance. Change at AT&T was painful and slow, but it was necessary for the company to be able to operate in the new competitive environment.[56] Changing environments may bring about changes in organizational culture. Microsoft, with its rapid growth, is a company whose culture may change, as seen in the Organizational Reality feature.

Given the current business environment, managers may want to focus on three particular cultural modifications. They are (1) support for a global view of business, (2) reinforcement of ethical behavior, and (3) empowerment of employees to excel in product and service quality.

ORGANIZATIONAL REALITY

Culture Change at Microsoft?

Perhaps one of the most recognizable organizational cultures of modern times is that of Microsoft Corporation. The Microsoft Campus in Redmond, Washington, is a hive of creative energy surrounded by tall pines. The dominant members of this culture are the software developers, called "wild ducks," who design software as a team. The fact that people are the most important asset is so well ingrained that no one bothers to talk about it. And collaboration within Microsoft is also ingrained. Terminology like "autonomous work teams" is unnecessary—it's simply the way the company works.

The "wild ducks" are charged with making software that is "seamless" or user friendly, and managers operate with a "seamless" philosophy. They interfere with the wild ducks as little as possible. Empowerment underlies Microsoft's ability to recruit and retain wild ducks, who are automatically assigned a mentor to help them learn to function as a member of the team. All the latest equipment, the opportunity to do state of the art development, flexible work hours, attractive surroundings, little bureaucracy, and a highly creative environment also attract the wild ducks. Microsoft works hard at making its campus environment as employee-friendly as possible.

As Microsoft grows, can it sustain this culture? Many companies that start out small and creative end up large, bureaucratic, and rigid. Only time will tell if Microsoft will go this route. The culture faces one of its biggest challenges as Microsoft shifts its emphasis to CD-ROM products. Bill Gates has predicted that by the year 2000, home-based CD-ROM products will make up over 50 percent of Microsoft's revenues. The company has already had success with several products like Encarta and Microsoft Complete Baseball. Microsoft Home, the brand name for the Microsoft Consumer Division, expects a boom. Typical home PC users own more than 20 CD-ROM titles.

Microsoft's leap into CD-ROM may cause a rapid change in the company's internal culture. Developers are accustomed to collaborating with each other and jealously protecting their technology from the outside world until it is ready to be sold. CD-ROM titles, however, are rich in content and require the skills of many companies, scholars, and artists. Microsoft Home has to go outside and team up with many experts to accomplish its tasks. Working collaboratively with outsiders may be a challenge for Microsoft. And developers, in particular, who are used to interacting with their own kind, may have problems relating to a variety of scholars and artists. Making CD-ROMs is more like being a movie production company, which may require Microsoft's strong culture to adapt. ■

SOURCE: Reprinted with permission from the September 1992 issue of *Training* magazine. Copyright 1992. Lakewood Publications, Minneapolis, MN. All rights reserved. Not for resale.

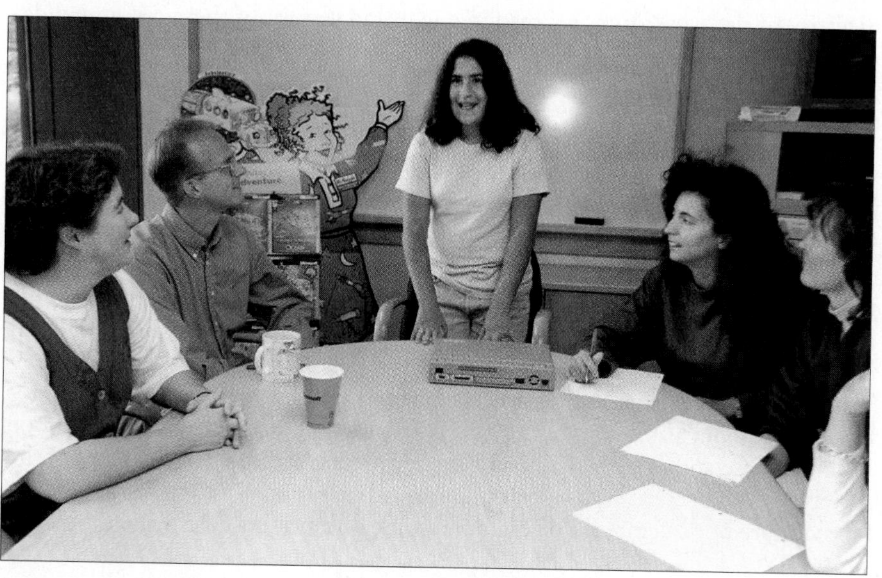

In a conference room at Microsoft's headquarters, 12-year-old Leah Mosner consults with staff members about products and market trends. Microsoft's informal culture extends to its child consultants, who often work from home and E-mail their evaluations of Microsoft's products for young people.

Developing a Global Organizational Culture

The values that drive the organizational culture should support a global view of the company and its efforts. To do so, the values should be clear to everyone involved, so everyone understands them. The values should also be strongly supported at the top. Management should embody the shared values and reward employees who support the global view. Finally, the values should be consistent over time. Consistent values give an organization a unifying theme that competitors may be unable to emulate.[57]

Global corporations suffer from the conflicting pressures of centralization and decentralization. An overarching corporate culture that integrates the decentralized subsidiaries in locations around the world can be an asset in the increasingly competitive global marketplace.

Following are six specific guidelines for managers who want to create a global culture:[58]

1. Create a clear and simple mission statement. A shared mission can unite individuals from diverse cultural backgrounds.
2. Create systems that ensure an effective flow of information. Coordination councils and global task forces can be used to ensure that information flows throughout the geographically dispersed organization are consistent.
3. Create "matrix minds" among managers; that is, broaden managers' minds to allow them to think globally. IBM does this through temporary overseas assignments. Managers with international experience share that experience when they return to the home organization.
4. Develop global career paths. This means ensuring not only that home country executives go overseas but also that executives from other countries rotate into service in the home office.
5. Use cultural differences as a major asset. Digital Equipment Corporation, for example, has transferred its research and development functions to Italy to take advantage of the free-flowing Italian management style that encourages creativity. Its manufacturing operations go to Germany, which offers a more systematic management style.
6. Implement worldwide management education and team development programs. Unified training efforts that emphasize corporate values can help establish a shared identity among employees.

These guidelines are specifically aimed toward multinational organizations that want to create a global corporate culture. Other organizations can also benefit from them. Companies that want to broaden employees' views or to use the diversity of the workforce as a resource will find several of these recommendations advantageous.

Developing an Ethical Organizational Culture

The organizational culture can have profound effects on the ethical behavior of organization members.[59] When a company's culture promotes ethical norms, individuals behave accordingly. The integration of ethics into the culture is usually achieved by codes of conduct, as we discussed in Chapter 2, and by ethics training. Most ethics training courses include three elements: messages from the CEO touting ethical business practices, discussion of the company's code of ethics, and procedures for reporting unethical behavior.[60]

Managers can encourage ethical behavior by being good role models for employees. They can institute the philosophy that ethical behavior makes good business sense and puts the company in congruence with the larger values of the society.[61] Managers can also communicate that rationalizations for unethical behavior are not tolerated. For example, some salespersons justify padding their expense accounts because everyone else does it. Declaring these justifications illegitimate sends a clear message about the lack of tolerance for such behavior. Communication is a key ingredient in an ethical organizational culture. Disseminating the code of ethics, keeping employees informed of ethical issues, and involving all levels of employees in solving ethical dilemmas can keep ethics at the forefront of culture.

Trust is another key to effectively managing ethical behavior, especially in cultures that encourage whistle-blowing (as we saw in Chapter 2). Employees must trust that whistle-blowers will be protected, that procedures used to investigate ethical problems will be fair, and that management will take action to solve problems that are uncovered.

Managers can reward ethical behavior on the part of the employees and punish individuals who behave unethically. Ethical decision making can also be integrated into the performance appraisal system.

The reasons most often cited for unethical corporate conduct are interesting.[62] They include the belief that a behavior is not really unethical, that it is in the organization's best interest, that it will not be discovered, and that the organization will support it because it offers a good outcome for the organization. An ethical corporate culture can eliminate the viability of these excuses through clear communication of the boundaries of ethical conduct, the selection of employees who support the ethical culture, the rewarding of ethical behavior on the part of the organization members, and the conspicuous punishment of members who engage in unethical behavior.

Organizations that seek to encourage ethical behavior can do so by using their organizational culture. By completing Challenge 16.2, you can assess the ethical culture of an organization you're familiar with.

Developing a Culture of Empowerment and Quality

Throughout this book, we have seen that successful organizations promote a culture that empowers employees and excels in product and service quality. Motorola and Federal Express are prime examples. Empowerment serves to unleash employees' creativity and productivity. It requires eliminating traditional hierarchical notions of power.

General Motors' Cadillac division experienced a massive cultural change over a short period of time. In 1985, the company installed state-of-the-art robotics technology at its Hamtramck Assembly Center.[63] The idea was to use tomorrow's technology to build the Cadillac of the future. The plant, intended to be a technology showcase, turned into a technology disaster. Robots went haywire, spray-painting one another, smashing windshields, and destroying cars. Computer systems had bugs that led to body parts being installed on the wrong cars.

http://www.gm.com

The new technology was considered a total failure, and the reason cited for the failure was that "people issues" were not addressed. The technology was yanked. The plant was redesigned to develop a balance between technology and people. Extensive employee involvement and a teamwork approach to design were used to empower employees throughout the Cadillac division.

Managers decided to incorporate input from assemblers in the product design process.[64] Designers, product development engineers, and assembly workers came together in teams to design the new car models. Once the cars were designed, the rest of the assembly workers were consulted a year and a half prior to the scheduled date of production. The designs were then revised to improve the cars' quality. On the Seville and El Dorado models alone, over 300 modifications were made.

Teams were also used to improve quality once a model went into production. A team made up of engineers, assemblers, and supervisors worked on a continuous

CHALLENGE

■ 16.2

Organizational Culture and Ethics

Think about the organization you currently work for or one you know something about and complete the following Ethical Climate Questionnaire.

Please use the scale below and write the number that best represents your answer in the space next to each item.

To what extent are the following statements true about your company?

Completely false	Mostly false	Somewhat false	Somewhat true	Mostly true	Completely true
0	1	2	3	4	5

____ **1.** In this company, people are expected to follow their own personal and moral beliefs.
____ **2.** People are expected to do anything to further the company's interests.
____ **3.** In this company, people look out for each other's good.
____ **4.** It is very important here to follow strictly the company's rules and procedures.
____ **5.** In this company, people protect their own interests above other considerations.
____ **6.** The first consideration is whether a decision violates any law.
____ **7.** Everyone is expected to stick by company rules and procedures.
____ **8.** The most efficient way is always the right way in this company.
____ **9.** Our major consideration is what is best for everyone in the company.
____ **10.** In this company, the law or ethical code of the profession is the major consideration.
____ **11.** It is expected at this company that employees will always do what is right for the customer and the public.

To score the questionnaire, first add up your responses to questions 1, 3, 6, 9, 10, and 11. This is subtotal number 1. Next, reverse the scores on questions 2, 4, 5, 7, and 8 (5 = 0, 4 = 1, 3 = 2, 2 = 3, 1 = 4, 0 = 5). Add the reverse scores to form subtotal number 2. Add subtotal number 1 to subtotal number 2 for an overall score.

Subtotal 1 ______ + Subtotal 2 ______ = Overall Score ______ .

Overall scores can range from 0 to 55. The higher the score, the more the organization's culture encourages ethical behavior.

SOURCE: J. B. Cullen, B. Victor, and C. Stephens, "An Ethical Weather Report: Assessing the Organization's Ethical Climate." Reprinted with permission of publisher, from *Organizational Dynamics*, Autumn/1989 © 1989. American Management Association, New York.

quality improvement process that targeted electrical system problems. The team effort reduced defects by 90 percent. Employee involvement was the key to the turnaround of Cadillac's culture. The original culture, emphasizing technology as the means for success, was replaced with a culture that emphasizes empowerment and product quality. One of the results was the 1990 Malcolm Baldrige National Quality Award.

Managers can learn from the experience of Cadillac that employee empowerment is a key to achieving quality. Involving employees in decision making, removing obstacles to their performance, and communicating the value of product and service quality reinforces the values of empowerment and quality in the organizational culture.

Managerial Implications: The Organizational Culture Challenge

■ Managing organizational culture is a key challenge for leaders in today's organizations. With the trend toward downsizing and restructuring, maintaining an organizational culture in the face of change is difficult. In addition, such challenges as globalization, workforce diversity, technology, and managing ethical behavior often require that an organization change its culture. Adaptive cultures that can respond to changes in the environment can lead the way in terms of organizational performance.

Managers have at their disposal many techniques for managing organizational culture. These techniques range from manipulating the artifacts of culture, such as ceremonies and symbols, to communicating the values that guide the organization. The socialization process is a powerful cultural communication process. Managers are models who communicate the organizational culture to employees through personal enactment. Their modeled behavior sets the norms for the other employees to follow. Their leadership is essential for developing a culture that values diversity, supports empowerment, fosters innovations in product and service quality, and promotes ethical behavior.

CLOSING SPOTLIGHT

Chaparral's Emphasis on Learning Supports Its Culture

Chaparral is one of the world's most productive steel companies. It is a learning organization, one that emphasizes continual growth and development. Employees are trained to understand the whole process of steel making. The company runs a training program that teaches team members what happens to a piece of steel as it moves through the operation, in addition to accounting, finance, and sales. This helps employees see how their jobs affect the welfare of the whole company. This shared understanding of how the entire organization works promotes unity and trust.

Chaparral runs a program called "K through 90" that includes 85 percent of the employees. The people who do the training are front-line supervisors who take sabbaticals to teach everything from vector mathematics to credit management to Spanish. Rewards are based on pay for skills, rather than automatic raises, to encourage learning. Chaparral employees are encouraged to use the knowledge in the workplace, acquire additional skills, take on additional responsibility, and keep learning. A company that prides itself on mentofacturing depends on minds that continually learn.[65] ■

Chapter Summary

- Organizational (corporate) culture is a pattern of basic assumptions that are considered valid and that are taught to new members as the way to perceive, think, and feel in the organization.
- The most visible and accessible level of culture is artifacts, which include personal enactment, ceremonies and rites, stories, rituals, and symbols.
- Organizational culture has four functions: giving members a sense of identity and increasing their commitment, serving as a sense-making device for members, reinforcing organizational values, and serving as a control mechanism for shaping behavior.
- Three theories about the relationship between culture and performance are the strong culture perspective, the fit perspective, and the adaptation perspective.
- Leaders shape and reinforce culture by what they pay attention to, how they react to crises, how they behave, how they allocate rewards, and how they hire and fire individuals.

- Organizational socialization is the process by which newcomers become participating, effective members of the organization. Its three stages are anticipatory socialization, encounter, and change and acquisition. Each stage plays a unique role in communicating organizational culture.
- The Organizational Culture Inventory and Kilmann-Saxton Culture-Gap Survey are two quantitative instruments for assessing organizational culture. Triangulation, using multiple methods for assessing culture, is an effective measurement strategy.
- It is difficult but not impossible to change organizational culture. Managers can do so by helping current members buy into a new set of values, by adding newcomers and socializing them into the organization, and by removing current members as appropriate.

Key Terms

organizational (corporate) culture (p. 476)
artifacts (p. 476)
espoused values (p. 479)
enacted values (p. 479)
assumptions (p. 480)
strong culture (p. 482)
adaptive culture (p. 483)
organizational socialization (p. 487)
anticipatory socialization (p. 487)
encounter (p. 488)
change and acquisition (p. 488)
triangulation (p. 490)

Review Questions

1. What is mentofacturing? How does it relate to the organizational culture of Chaparral Steel?
2. Explain the three levels of organizational culture. How can each level of culture be measured?
3. Describe five artifacts of culture and give an example of each.
4. Explain three theories about the relationship between organizational culture and performance. What does the research evidence say about each one?
5. Contrast adaptive and nonadaptive cultures.
6. How can leaders shape organizational culture?
7. Describe the three stages of organizational socialization. How is culture communicated in each stage?
8. How can managers assess the organizational culture? What actions can they take to change the organizational culture?
9. How does a manager know that cultural change has been successful?
10. What can managers do to develop a global organizational culture?

Discussion and Communication Questions

1. Name a company with a visible organizational culture. What do you think are the company's values? Has the culture contributed to the organization's performance? Explain.
2. Name a leader you think manages organizational culture well. How does the leader do this? Use Schein's description of ways leaders reinforce culture to analyze the leader's behavior.
3. Suppose you want to change your organization's culture. What sort of resistance would you expect from employees? How would you deal with this resistance?
4. Given Schein's three levels, can we ever truly understand an organization's culture? Explain.
5. To what extent is culture manageable? Changeable?
6. *(communication question)* Use Challenge 16.1 to analyze the culture of an organization you respect. Now, assume you have been hired by that organization to develop a socialization program for newcomers that will orient them into that organization's culture. Develop an outline for your socialization program, including the content of the program, ways to deliver the content, and the stages of socialization in which the cultural information will be presented.
7. *(communication question)* Select an organization that you might like to work for. Learn as much as you can about that company's culture, using library resources, contacts within the company, and as many creative means as you can. Prepare a brief presentation to the class summarizing the culture.

Ethics Questions

1. Are rites of degradation ethical?
2. Is it ethical to influence individual's values through the organizational culture? If culture shapes behavior, is managing culture a manipulative tactic? Explain.
3. How can leaders use organizational culture as a vehicle for encouraging ethical behavior?
4. Korean chaebols hire individuals to fit their cultures. To what extent might this practice be considered unethical in the United States?
5. One way of changing culture is to remove members who do not change with the culture. How can this be done ethically?

Experiential Exercises

16.1 Identifying Behavioral Norms

This exercise asks you to identify campus norms at your university. Every organization or group has a set of norms that help determine individuals' behavior. A norm is an unwritten rule for behavior in a group. When a norm is not followed, negative feedback is given. It may include negative comments, stares, harassment, and exclusion.

1. As a group, brainstorm all the norms you can think of in the following areas:

Dress
Studying
Classroom behavior
Weekend activities
Living arrangements
Dating (who asks whom)
Eating on campus versus off campus
Campus activities
Relationships with faculty
Transportation

2. How did you initially get this information?
3. What happens to students who don't follow these norms?
4. What values can be inferred from these norms?

SOURCE: Adapted from D. Marcic, *Organizational Behavior: Experiences and Cases* (St. Paul, Minn.: West Publishing, 1989).

16.2 Contrasting Organizational Cultures

To complete this exercise, groups of four or five students should be formed. Each group should select one of the following pairs of organizations:

American Airlines and Northwest Airlines
Anheuser-Busch and Coors
Hewlett-Packard and Xerox
Albertsons and Winn-Dixie
Dayton-Hudson (Target) and J. C. Penney

Use your university library's resources to gather information about the companies' cultures.

Contrast the cultures of the two organizations using the following dimensions:

- Strength of the culture.
- Fit of the culture with the industry's environment.
- Adaptiveness of the culture.

Which of the two is the better performer? On what did you base your conclusion? How does the performance of each relate to its organizational culture?

SOURCE: Reprinted with the permission of The Free Press, a Division of Macmillan, Inc. From *Corporate Culture and Performance* by John P. Kotter and James L. Heskett.

VIDEO CASE

Cultural Transformation at Cadillac[1]

On December 13, 1990, John Grettenberger, Cadillac's general manger, announced to Cadillac's employees that the company had won the Malcolm Baldridge National Quality Award. Winning the award capped a dramatic turnaround of the Cadillac Motor Division of General Motors. Fighting quality problems and a platform production mentality that was unresponsive to customers' needs and desires, Cadillac launched sweeping organizational changes. As part of its efforts to produce a better quality, more distinctive product and to better serve its customers, Cadillac transformed and revitalized its organizational culture.

A key element of the new culture is its definition of the customer. Cadillac does not confine its definition of the customer to the end-user. Instead, Cadillac focuses on both internal and external customers. It is concerned with both external consumers of the product and internal departments and individuals that utilize a subassembly from a previous process.

In discussing Cadillac's customer focus, Rosetta Riley, director of customer satisfaction, observes that "You must have quality to achieve customer satisfaction. But also you must have service. You must support your product. You must care for the customer." As part of its customer focus Cadillac makes a competitive tool out of its efforts to correct absolutely anything that is wrong. For example, Joe Stetler is one of many production operators who make follow-up calls to external customers. And Cadillac operates a 24-hour road service hotline.

Cadillac also tries to create a win/win situation for the manufacturer and dealer. According to Rosetta Riley, this is done by "meeting customer requirements" and by "being there when the customer needs you."

Of course, the customer focus applies to employees as well as to end-users of the product. According to Bob Dorn, chief engineer, "The first definition of our customers was the operators in the plant." He continues, "Our job is to make them (the production workers) more effective." The internal customer focus also stresses employee involvement. For example, assembly operators participate in group discussions about quality improvement during their lunch break. And employees, like Joe Stetler, call Cadillac's customers.

Cadillac's new culture is built around cooperation and mutual interest, unlike the adversarial ways of the old culture. Bill Bailey, an electrical coordinator and a United Auto Workers (UAW) member, provides an interesting contrast of the old and new cultures. He describes the old Cadillac culture as a "Mom and Dad philosophy." "Mom and Dad tell you to do as you are told—if you don't, some disciplinary action will be taken. Now we communicate back and forth."

In developing the new culture, Cadillac's management realized "the union was not the enemy" and the union realized "management was not the enemy." Both realized that they had mutual and overlapping interests.

This is reflected in a cornerstone of Cadillac's new culture—a concept known as "growing the green." This concept, which is both an artistic and an agricultural metaphor, uses colors to depict management's objectives, the union's objectives, and their common objectives. Management's objectives are depicted in blue, the union's objectives in yellow, and their overlapping objectives in green (which is derived by mixing blue and yellow). From this "green common ground" a sturdy tree (organization) grows.

Another key element of the new culture is simultaneous engineering, symbolized with a three-legged stool. The legs represent the three components of simultaneous engineering: engineering, suppliers, and the plant process. Every leg must be in place for the stool to stand; without any one leg, the stool is dysfunctional. So it is with the Cadillac organization. Engineering, suppliers, and the plant process have to be in place and work together for the organization to function effectively.

Simultaneous engineering fosters communication among engineering, suppliers, and the operating personnel in the plant process. On *jeans day*, for example, plant executives and engineers work side by side with the operators on the production line. This facilitates communication and enables the executives and engineers to better understand the challenges faced by the operating technicians. As one Cadillac employee says, jeans days provide the "opportunity to resolve issues by communicating directly in a hands-on setting."

Another example of the positive effects of simultaneous coordination and communication involves the improvements in the overhead system (i.e. headliner, assist handles, map lights, visors, fasteners, etc.) used in Cadillacs. Through simultaneous engineering, this overhead system supplied added value by combining 65 separate parts into one outsourced subassembly.

In describing Cadillac's turnaround success, Bill Bailey, a UAW member, says, "The quality award was given to the process as well as the product. The process is people." And another UAW member indicates, "What turned Cadillac around is the people." Now, as Cadillac seeks to engineer, produce, and market the world's finest automobiles, it ". . . hopes the focus on employees and customers will give it a window of opportunity to compete and prosper."

DISCUSSION QUESTIONS

1. Which cultural perspective—strong, fit, or adaptation—does Cadillac seem to be using? Explain your answer.
2. What roles do you think Cadillac's leaders have assumed in transforming the company's culture?
3. What challenges do you think Cadillac encountered in trying to transform its culture?
4. What advantages and disadvantages might exist with Cadillac's present culture?
5. What should Cadillac do if it wishes to maintain its present culture?

SOURCE: This case was written by Micheal K. McCuddy, the Louis S. and Mary L. Morgal Professor of Christian Business Ethics, College of Business Administration, Valparaiso University.

1. This case is based on the *Cadillac* segment of the Association for Manufacturing Excellence video entitled *We're Getting Closer.*

References

1. G. E. Forward, D. E. Beach, D. A. Gray, and J. C. Quick, "Mentofacturing: A Vision for American Industrial Excellence," *Academy of Management Executive* 5 (1991): 32–44.
2. T. E. Deal and A. A. Kennedy, *Corporate Cultures* (Reading, Mass.: Addison-Wesley, 1982).
3. W. Ouchi, *Theory Z* (Reading, Mass.: Addison-Wesley, 1981).
4. T. J. Peters and R. H. Waterman, *In Search of Excellence* (New York: Harper & Row, 1982).
5. M. Gardner, "Creating a Corporate Culture for the Eighties," *Business Horizons* (January–February 1985): 59–63.
6. Definition adapted from E. H. Schein, *Organizational Culture and Leadership* (San Francisco: Jossey-Bass, 1985), p. 9.
7. C. D. Sutton and D. L. Nelson, "Elements of the Cultural Network: The Communicators of Corporate Values," *Leadership and Organization Development* 11 (1990): 3–10.
8. B. Pickens, *Boone* (Boston: Houghton Mifflin, 1987).
9. A. Bandura, *Social Learning Theory* (Englewood Cliffs, N.J.: Prentice-Hall, 1977).
10. J. M. Beyer and H. M. Trice, "How an Organization's Rites Reveal Its Culture," *Organizational Dynamics* 16 (1987): 5–24.
11. H. M. Trice and J. M. Beyer, "Studying Organizational Cultures through Rites and Ceremonials," *Academy of Management Review* 9 (1984): 653–669.
12. M. K. Ash, *Mary Kay* (New York: Harper & Row, 1981).
13. H. Levinson and S. Rosenthal, *CEO: Corporate Leadership in Action* (New York: Basic Books, 1984).
14. V. Sathe, "Implications of Corporate Culture: A Manager's Guide to Action," *Organizational Dynamics* 12 (1987): 5–23.
15. Sutton and Nelson, "Elements of the Cultural Network."
16. J. Martin, M. S. Feldman, M. J. Hatch, and S. B. Sitkin, "The Uniqueness Paradox in Organizational Stories," *Administrative Science Quarterly* 28 (1983): 438–453.
17. C. Argyris and D. A. Schon, *Organizational Learning* (Reading, Mass.: Addison-Wesley, 1978).
18. "Sounds Like a New Woman," *New Woman*, February 1993, 144.
19. L. Smircich, "Concepts of Culture and Organizational Analysis," *Administrative Science Quarterly* (1983): 339–358.
20. Y. Weiner and Y. Vardi, "Relationships between Organizational Culture and Individual Motivation: A Conceptual Integration," *Psychological Reports* 67 (1990): 295–306.
21. M. R. Louis, "Surprise and Sense Making: What Newcomers Experience in Entering Unfamiliar Organizational Settings," *Administrative Science Quarterly* 25 (1980): 209–264.
22. E. Segalla, "All for Quality and Quality for All," *Training and Development Journal* (September 1989): 36–45.
23. J. P. Kotter and J. L. Heskett, *Corporate Culture and Performance* (New York: Free Press, 1992).
24. Deal and Kennedy, *Corporate Cultures.*
25. D. R. Katz, *The Big Store* (New York: Viking, 1987).
26. G. G. Gordon, "Industry Determinants of Organizational Culture," *Academy of Management Review* 16 (1991): 396–415.
27. G. Donaldson and J. Lorsch, *Decision Making at the Top* (New York: Basic Books, 1983).
28. R. H. Kilman, M. J. Saxton, and R. Serpa, eds., *Gaining Control of the Corporate Culture* (San Francisco: Jossey-Bass, 1986).
29. J. P. Kotter, *A Force for Change: How Leadership Differs from Management* (New York: Free Press, 1990); R. M. Kanter, *The Change Masters* (New York: Simon & Schuster, 1983).
30. T. Peters and N. Austin, *A Passion for Excellence: The Leadership Difference* (New York: Random House, 1985).
31. Schein, *Organizational Culture and Leadership.*
32. W. A. Cohen, *The Art of the Leader* (Englewood Cliffs, N.J.: Prentice-Hall, 1990).
33. J. Conger, "Inspiring Others: The Language of Leadership," *Academy of Management Executive* 5 (1991): 31–45.
34. J. C. Quick, D. L. Nelson, and J. D. Quick, *Stress and Challenge at the Top: The Paradox of the Successful Executive* (Chichester, England: Wiley, 1990).
35. J. C. Quick, "Crafting an Organizational Culture: Herb's Hand at Southwest Airlines," *Organizational Dynamics* (Autumn 1992): 45–56.
36. E. O. Welles, "Captain Marvel," *Inc.*, January 1992, 44–47.
37. D. C. Feldman, "The Multiple Socialization of Organization Members," *Academy of Management Review* 6 (1981): 309–318.
38. R. Pascale, "The Paradox of Corporate Culture: Reconciling Ourselves to Socialization," *California Management Review* 27 (1985): 26–41.
39. D. L. Nelson, "Organizational Socialization: A Stress Perspective," *Journal of Occupational Behavior* 8 (1987): 311–324.
40. J. Chatman, "Matching People and Organizations: Selection and Socialization in Public Accounting Firms," *Administrative Science Quarterly* 36 (1991): 459–484.
41. S. M. Lee, S. Yoo, and T. M. Lee, "Korean Chaebols: Corporate Values and Strategies," *Organizational Dynamics* 19 (1991): 36–50.
42. D. L. Nelson, J. C. Quick, and M. E. Eakin, "A Longitudinal Study of Newcomer Role Adjustment in U.S. Organizations," *Work and Stress* 2 (1988): 239–253.
43. N. J. Allen and J. P. Meyer, "Organizational Socialization Tactics: A Longitudinal Analysis of Links to Newcomers' Commitment and Role Orientation," *Academy of Management Journal* 33 (1990): 847–858.
44. D. E. Bowen, G. E. Ledford, Jr., and B. R. Nathan, "Hiring for the Organization, Not the Job," *Academy of Management Executive* 5 (1991): 35–51.
45. Y. Weiner, "Forms of Value Systems: A Focus on Organizational Effectiveness and Cultural Change and Maintenance," *Academy of Management Review* 13 (1988): 534–545; J. E. Hebden, "Adopting an Organization's Culture: The Socialization of Graduate Trainees," *Organizational Dynamics* (Summer 1986): 46–72.
46. D. M. Rousseau, "Assessing Organizational Culture: The Case for Multiple Methods," in B. Schneider, ed., *Organizational Climate and Culture* (San Francisco: Jossey-Bass, 1990).

47. R. A. Cooke and D. M. Rousseau, "Behavioral Norms and Expectations: A Quantitative Approach to the Assessment of Organizational Culture," *Group and Organizational Studies* 12 (1988): 245–273.
48. R. H. Kilmann and M. J. Saxton, *Kilmann-Saxton Culture-Gap Survey* (Pittsburgh: Organizational Design Consultants, 1983).
49. W.J. Duncan, "Organizational Culture: 'Getting a Fix' on an Elusive Concept," *Academy of Management Executive* 3 (1989): 229–236.
50. P. L. Zweig, "Tense Scenes from a Marriage," *Business Week*, January 16, 1995: 66–67.
51. N. J. Adler, *International Dimensions of Organizational Behavior*, 2d ed. (Boston: PWS Kent, 1991).
52. A. Laurent, "The Cultural Diversity of Western Conceptions of Management," *International Studies of Management and Organization* 13 (1983): 75–96.
53. P. Bate, "Using the Culture Concept in an Organization Development Setting," *Journal of Applied Behavior Science* 26 (1990): 83–106.
54. K. R. Thompson and F. Luthans, "Organizational Culture: A Behavioral Perspective," in B. Schneider, ed., *Organizational Climate and Culture* (San Francisco: Jossey-Bass, 1990).
55. V. Sathe, "How to Decipher and Change Organizational Culture," in R. H. Kilman et al., *Managing Corporate Cultures* (San Francisco: Jossey-Bass, 1985).
56. J. B. Shaw, C. D. Fisher, and W. A. Randolph, "From Maternalism to Accountability: The Changing Cultures of Ma Bell and Mother Russia," *Academy of Management Executive* 5 (1991): 7–20.
57. D. Lei, J. W. Slocum, Jr., and R. W. Slater, "Global Strategy and Reward Systems: The Key Roles of Management Development and Corporate Culture," *Organizational Dynamics* 19 (1990): 27–41.
58. S. H. Rhinesmith, "Going Global from the Inside Out," *Training and Development Journal* 45 (1991): 42–47.
59. L. K. Trevino and K. A. Nelson, *Managing Business Ethics: Straight Talk about How to Do It Right* (New York: John Wiley & Sons, 1995).
60. S. J. Harrington, "What Corporate America Is Teaching about Ethics," *Academy of Management Executive* 5 (1991): 21–30.
61. A. Bhide and H. H. Stevenson, "Why Be Honest if Honesty Doesn't Pay?" *Harvard Business Review*, (September–October 1990): 121–129.
62. S. W. Gellerman, "Why Good Managers Make Bad Ethical Choices," *Harvard Business Review* 64 (1986): 85–90.
63. J. Teresko, "Best Plants: Cadillac," *Industry Week*, 21 October 1991, 29–32.
64. M. Krebs, "Cadillac Starts Down a New Road," *Industry Week*, 5 August 1991, 18–23.
65. "The Learning Organization," *Chief Executive* (March 1995): 54–64; D. K. Denton, "Creating a System for Continuous Improvement," *Business Horizons* (January–February 1995): 16–21.

CHAPTER

17

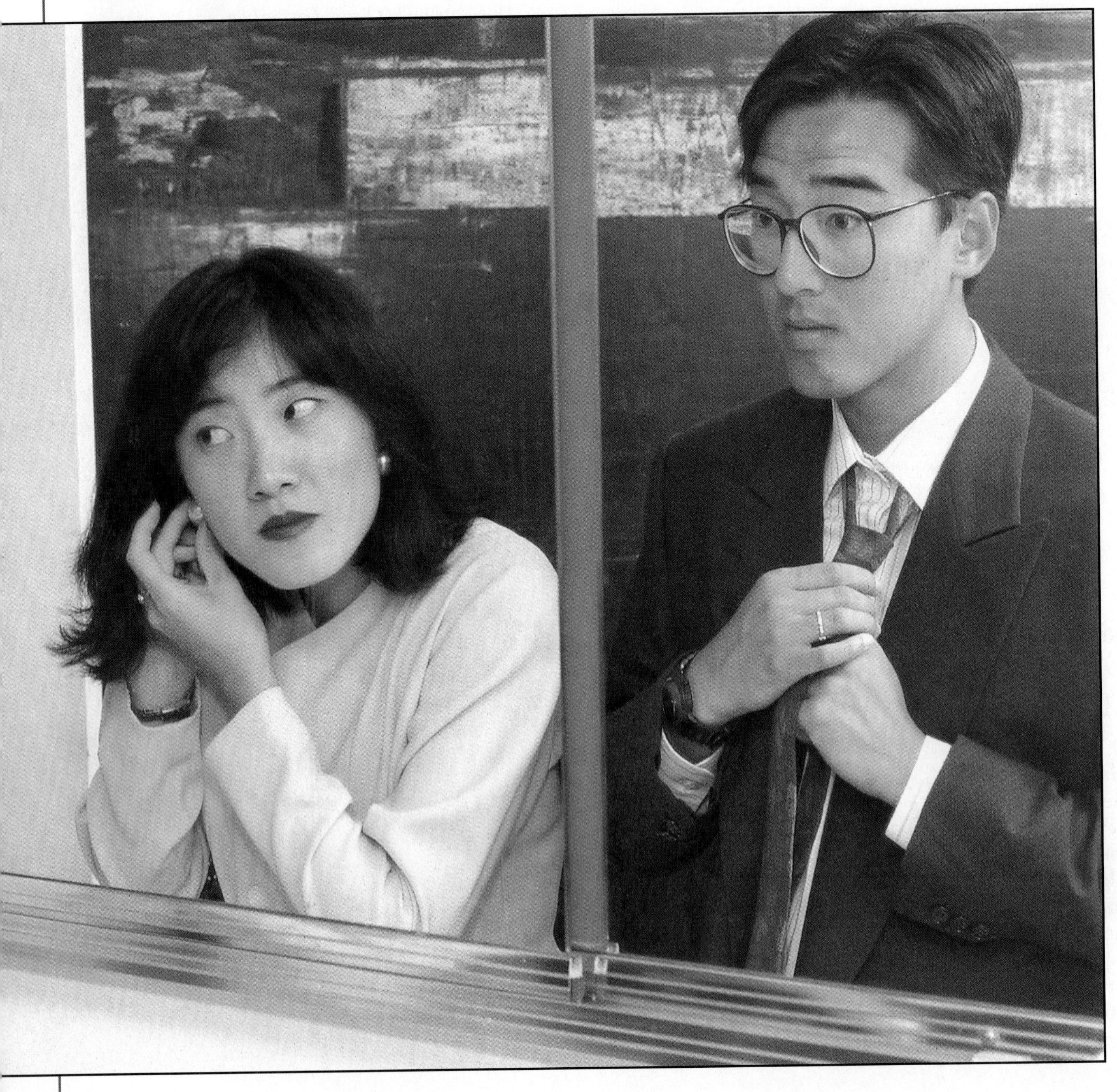

Career Management

After reading this chapter, you should be able to do the following:

- Define *career* and *career management.*
- Explain occupational and organizational choice decisions.
- Describe the four stages of the career model.
- Explain the psychological contract.
- Describe how mentors help organizational newcomers.
- Describe ways to manage conflicts between work and home.
- Explain how career anchors help form a career identity.

OPENING SPOTLIGHT

Motorola's Commitment to Training

Motorola University is a global network of 300 professionals who train Motorola's employees in a wide variety of skills. It is admired as one of the premier training organizations in the world. An examination of the manufacturing skills training area alone is mind-boggling. Worldwide, the company employs 60,000 manufacturing associates who work with an array of products including pagers, cellular phones, two-way radios, semiconductors, and base-station equipment. Three-day training courses teach employees how to run the company's robotic assembly lines. Motorola invested significant funds in duplicating its leading-edge automated machinery in classrooms and laboratory facilities in Schaumburg, IL, Singapore, and Boynton Beach, FL. Students travel to the facilities to learn to set up, start, and shut down the lines. This hands-on training experience proved extremely valuable.

Motorola continues to introduce leading-edge products like the personal digital assistant shown here. A major contributor to Motorola's success is its substantial investment in training and career development activities.

Motorola's steady growth has spurred an increased need for the training. It is expensive, however, to send the employees to the sites for the three-day seminars. The company attempted to keep up with the demand for training by recreating the classrooms and labs at other sites, but problems with the cost and difficulty in obtaining equipment made the process too slow. Motorola's central problem was this: How could they distribute the training to people quickly enough and still have a hands-on training environment? The Closing Spotlight will present Motorola's innovative solution to the dilemma. ■

Careers as Joint Responsibilities

Alternate Example
Students should be aware that the rules for job seeking have changed. Many in the work force need to practice self-marketing. Advertisements, the traditional approach to job seeking, pay off only 5 percent of the time. SOURCE: M. Messmer, "Proper Self-marketing Key to Job Move," *Computerworld,* January 11, 1993, 47.

■ Career management is an integral activity in our lives. There are three reasons why it is important to understand careers. First, if we know what to look forward to over the course of our careers, we can take a proactive approach to planning and managing them. Second, as managers, we need to understand the experiences of our employees and colleagues as they pass through the various stages of careers over their life spans. Third, career management is good business. It makes good financial sense to have highly trained employees keep up with their fields so that organizations can protect valuable investments in human resources. Motorola's massive investment in training, as shown in the Opening Spotlight, reflects the company's commitment to helping employees remain productive and competitive in their careers.

career
The pattern of work-related experiences that span the course of a person's life.

A **career** is a pattern of work-related experiences that span the course of a person's life.[1] There are two elements in a career: the objective element and the subjective element.[2] The objective element of the career is the observable, concrete environment. For example, you can manage a career by getting training to improve your skills. In contrast, the subjective element involves your perception of the situation. Rather than getting training (an objective element), you might change your aspirations (a subjective element). Thus, both objective events and the individual's perception of those events are important in defining a career.

career management
A lifelong process of learning about self, jobs, and organizations; setting personal career goals; developing strategies for achieving the goals, and revising the goals based on work and life experiences.

Career management is a lifelong process of learning about self, jobs, and organizations; setting personal career goals; developing strategies for achieving the goals; and revising the goals based on work and life experiences.[3] Whose responsibility is career management? It is tempting to place the responsibility on individuals, and it is appropriate. However, it is also the organization's duty to form partnerships with individuals in managing their careers. Careers are made up of exchanges between individuals and organizations. Inherent in these exchanges is the idea of reciprocity, or give and take.

The balance between individuals and organizations in terms of managing careers has shifted in recent times. With restructuring and reengineering has come a new perspective of careers and career management.

The New Career

■ The time of the fast track to the top of the hierarchical organization is past. Also gone is the idea of lifetime employment in a single organization. Today's environment demands leaner organizations. The paternalistic attitude that organizations take care of employees no longer exists. Individuals now take on more responsibility for managing their own careers. The concept of the career is undergoing a paradigm shift, as shown in Table 17.1. The old career is giving way to a new career characterized by discrete exchange, occupational excellence, organizational empowerment, and project allegiance.[4]

Discrete exchange occurs when an organization gains productivity while a person gains work experience. It is a short-term arrangement that recognizes that job skills change in value, and that renegotiation of the relationship must occur as conditions change. This contrasts sharply with the mutual loyalty contract of the old career paradigm in which employee loyalty was exchanged for job security.

Occupational excellence means continually honing skills that can be marketed across organizations. The individual identifies more with the occupation (I am an engineer) than the organization (I am an IBMer). In contrast, the old one-employer focus meant that training was company-specific rather than preparing the person for future job opportunities.

Organizational empowerment means that power flows down to business units and in turn to employees. Employees are expected to add value and help the organization remain competitive by being innovative and creative. The old top-down approach meant that control and strategizing were only done by the top managers, and individual initiative might be viewed as disloyalty or disrespect.

Project allegiance means that both individuals and organizations are committed to the successful completion of a project. The firm's gain is the project outcome; the individual's gain is experience and shared success. On project completion, the project team breaks up as individuals move on to new projects. Under the old paradigm, corporate allegiance was paramount. The needs of projects were overshadowed by corporate policies and procedures. Work groups were long-term, and keeping the group together was often a more important goal than project completion.

It may be premature to say that the old career paradigm is dead. There are still many organizations in which vertical career progression is the norm; however, we are in a time of transition in which the new paradigm is replacing the old one. This means that individuals must prepare for the new career and manage their careers with change in mind.

Becoming Your Own Career Coach

The best way to stay employed is to see yourself as being in business for yourself, even if you work for someone else. Know what skills you can package for other employers, and what you can do to ensure that your skills are state-of-the-art. Organizations need employees who have acquired multiple skills and are adept at more than one job. Employers want employees who demonstrated competence in dealing with change.[5] To be successful, think of organizational change not as a disruption to your work, but instead as the central focus of your work. You will also need to develop self-reliance, as we discussed in Chapter 7, to deal effectively with the stress of change. Self-reliant individuals take an interdependent approach to relationships and are comfortable both giving and receiving support from others.

Alternate Example
Many companies are organizing career workshops. These workshops can build confidence and self-esteem. SOURCE: J. Hansel, "Getting Employees to Take Charge of Their Careers," *Training and Development*, February 1993, 51–54.

The people who will be most successful in the new career paradigm are individuals who are flexible, team-oriented (rather than hierarchical), energized by change, and tolerant of ambiguity. Those who will become frustrated in the new career are individuals who are rigid in their thinking and learning styles, and

■ **TABLE 17.1**

The New versus Old Career Paradigms

NEW CAREER PARADIGM	OLD CAREER PARADIGM
Discrete exchange means:	*The mutual loyalty contract meant:*
■ explicit exchange of specified rewards in return for task performance ■ basing job rewards on the current market value of the work being performed ■ engaging in disclosure and renegotiation on both sides as the employment relationship unfolds ■ exercising flexibility as each party's interests and market circumstances change	■ implicit trading of employee compliance in return for job security ■ allowing job rewards to be routinely deferred into the future ■ leaving the mutual loyalty assumptions as a political barrier to renegotiation ■ assuming employment and career opportunities are standardized and prescribed by the firm
Occupational excellence means:	*The one-employer focus meant:*
■ performance of current jobs in return for developing new occupational expertise ■ employees identifying with and focusing on what is happening in their adopted occupation ■ emphasizing occupational skill development over the local demands of any particular firm ■ getting training in anticipation of future job opportunities; having training lead jobs	■ relying on the firm to specify jobs and their associated occupational skill base ■ employees identifying with and focusing on what is happening in their particular firm ■ forgoing technical or functional development in favor of firm-specific learning ■ doing the job first to be entitled to new training: making training follow jobs
Organizational empowerment means:	*The top-down firm meant*
■ strategic positioning is dispersed to separate business units ■ everyone is responsible for adding value and improving competitiveness ■ business units are free to cultivate their own markets ■ new enterprise, spinoffs, and alliance building are broadly encouraged	■ strategic direction is subordinated to "corporate headquarters" ■ competitiveness and added value are the responsibility of corporate experts ■ business unit marketing depends on the corporate agenda ■ independent enterprise is discouraged, and likely to be viewed as disloyalty
Project allegiance means:	*Corporate allegiance meant:*
■ shared employer and employee commitment to the overarching goal of the project ■ a successful outcome of the project is more important than holding the project team together ■ financial and reputational rewards stem directly from project outcomes ■ upon project completion, organization and reporting arrangements are broken up	■ project goals are subordinated to corporate policy and organizational constraints ■ being loyal to the work group can be more important that the project itself ■ financial and reputational rewards stem from being a "good soldier" regardless of results ■ social relationships within corporate boundaries are actively encouraged

who have high needs for control.[6] A commitment to continuous, lifelong learning will prevent you from becoming a professional dinosaur. An intentional and purposeful commitment to taking charge of your professional life will be necessary in managing the new career.

Before turning to the stages of an individual's career, we will examine the process of preparation for the world of work. Prior to beginning a career, individuals must make several important decisions.

Preparing for the World of Work

■ When viewed from one perspective, you might say that we spend our youth preparing for the world of work. Educational experiences and personal life experiences help an individual develop the skills and maturity needed to enter a career. Preparation for work is a developmental process that gradually unfolds over time.[7] As the time approaches for beginning a career, individuals face two difficult decisions: the choice of occupation and the choice of organization.

Points to Emphasize
The principles of goal-setting and planning developed in chapter 6 can also be applied to the career planning process.

Occupational Choice

In choosing an occupation, individuals assess their needs, values, abilities, and preferences and attempt to match them with an occupation that provides a fit. Personality plays a role in the selection of occupation. John Holland's theory of occupational choice contends that there are six types of personalities and that each personality is characterized by a set of interests and values.[8] Holland's six types are as follows:

Points to Emphasize
Students need to realize that they probably will not work for one company all their lives. In fact, they may experience some rather radical career changes. Seminaries are booming with men and women who have left the corporate world to pursue second careers in ministry-related work.

1. *Realistic:* stable, persistent, and materialistic.
2. *Artistic:* imaginative, emotional, and impulsive.
3. *Investigative:* curious, analytical, and independent.
4. *Enterprising:* ambitious, energetic, and adventurous.
5. *Social:* generous, cooperative, and sociable.
6. *Conventional:* efficient, practical, and obedient.

Holland also states that occupations can be classified using this typology. For example, realistic occupations include mechanic, restaurant server, and mechanical engineer. Artistic occupations include architect, voice coach, and interior designer. Investigative occupations include physicist, surgeon, and economist. Real estate agent, human resource manager, and lawyer are enterprising occupations. The social occupations include counselor, social worker, and member of the clergy. Conventional occupations include word processor, accountant, and data entry operator.

Discussion Consideration
Ask students which of Holland's six types best describes them. What type of jobs would seem to be good fits for each of these types?

An assumption that drives Holland's theory is that people choose occupations that match their own personalities. A mismatch occurs when, for example, an artistic personality ends up working in real estate sales, an enterprising occupation. The artistic individual would become dissatisfied and move toward an occupation more likely to satisfy his or her needs, such as interior designer.

Although personality is a major influence on occupational choice, it is not the only influence. There are a host of other influences, including social class, parents' occupations, economic conditions, and geography.[9] Once a choice of occupation has been made, another major decision individuals face is the choice of organizations.

Organizational Choice and Entry

Several theories of how individuals choose organizations exist, ranging from theories that postulate very logical and rational choice processes to those that offer seemingly irrational processes. Expectancy theory, which we discussed in Chapter 5, can be applied to organizational choice.[10] According to the expectancy theory view, individuals choose organizations that maximize positive outcomes and avoid negative outcomes. Job candidates calculate the probability that an organization will provide a certain outcome and then compare the probabilities across organizations.

Discussion Consideration
Ask students if they are willing to select the organization they want to work for in the same way they selected the university they are attending.

Other theories propose that people select organizations in a much less rational fashion. Job candidates may satisfice, that is, select the first organization that meets one or two important criteria and then justify their choice by distorting their perceptions.[11]

The method of selecting an organization varies greatly among individuals and may reflect a combination of the expectancy theory and theories that postulate less rational approaches. Entry into an organization is further complicated by the conflicts that occur between individuals and organizations during the process. Figure 17.1 illustrates these potential conflicts. The arrows in the figure illustrate four types of conflicts that can occur as individuals choose organizations and organizations choose individuals. The first two conflicts (1 and 2) occur between individuals and organizations. The first is a conflict between the organization's effort to attract candidates and the individual's choice of an organization. The individual needs complete and accurate information to make a good choice, but the organization may not provide it. The organization is trying to attract a large number of qualified candidates, so it presents itself in an overly attractive way.

Discussion Consideration
Ask students to identify the criteria that will be important for them when selecting an organization to work for.

The second conflict is between the individual's attempt to attract several organizations and the organization's need to select the best candidate. Individuals want good offers, so they do not disclose their faults. They describe their preferred job in terms of the organization's opening instead of describing a job they would really prefer.

Conflicts 3 and 4 are conflicts internal to the two parties. The third is a conflict between the organization's desire to recruit a large pool of qualified applicants and the organization's need to select and retain the best candidate. In recruiting, organizations tend to give only positive information, and this results in mismatches between the individual and the organization. The fourth conflict is internal to the individual; it is between the individual's desire for several job offers and the need to make a good choice. When individuals present themselves as overly attractive, they risk being offered positions that are poor fits in terms of their skills and career goals.[12]

The organizational choice and entry process is very complex due to the nature of these conflicts. Partial responsibility for preventing these conflicts rests with the individual. Individuals should conduct thorough research of the organiza-

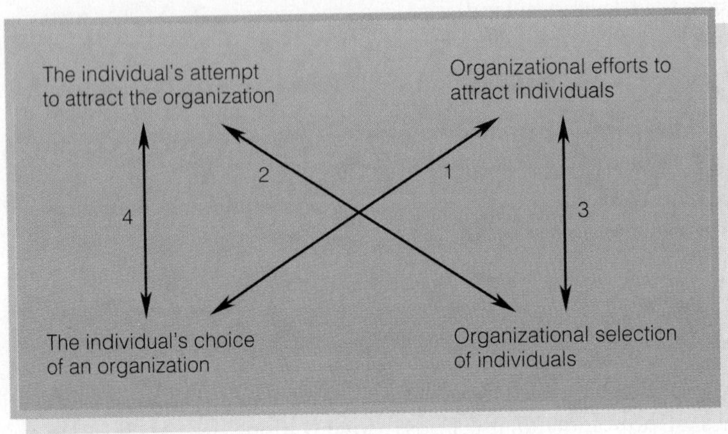

FIGURE 17.1

Conflicts during Organizational Entry

SOURCE: L. W. Porter, E. E. Lawler III, and J. R. Hackman, *Behavior in Organizations* (New York: McGraw-Hill, Inc., 1975): 134. Reproduced with permission of The McGraw-Hill Companies.

CHALLENGE

■ 17.1

Checklist for Building or Evaluating Your Résumé

The following checklist can be used to create or evaluate your résumé. Go over your résumé carefully, using the criteria listed. Then, for any area you rated "average" or "poor," revise your résumé to make it "excellent." Alternatively, you may want to have a friend evaluate your résumé using the checklist.

	RATING			
	Excellent	*Average*	*Poor*	SUGGESTIONS FOR IMPROVEMENT
Does it stress accomplishments over skills and duties?				
Is the résumé clear? Is it easy to get a picture of the writer's qualifications?				
Is irrelevant personal information left out?				
Does it avoid self-evaluation?				
Is the language clear and understandable?				
Does it emphasize benefits for a potential employer?				
Is it well printed on good, professional-looking stock?				
Does the layout invite attention? Do strong points stand out?				
Is the industry/product line of past employers clear?				
Do the sentences begin with action words?				
Does it sell the writer's problem-solving skills?				

SOURCE: T. Jackson, *Not Just Another Job: How to Invent a Career That Works for You* (New York: Times Books, 1992), 194.

tion through published reports and industry analyses. Individuals also should conduct a careful self-analysis and be as honest as possible with organizations to ensure a good match. Challenge 17.1 presents a checklist you can use to prepare or evaluate your résumé. It can help you paint a clear and accurate picture of your skills and experience.

Partial responsibility for good matches also rests with the organization. One way of avoiding the conflicts and mismatches is to utilize a realistic job preview.

Realistic Job Previews

The conflicts just discussed may result in unrealistic expectations on the part of the candidate. People entering the world of work may expect, for example, that they will receive explicit directions from their boss, only to find that they are left with ambiguity about how to do the job. They may expect that promotions will be based on performance and find that promotions are based mainly on political considerations. A recent study illustrated that newly recruited graduates to a British oil company had unrealistic expectations about their jobs in terms of management content. The recruits expected to be given managerial responsibilities right away; however, this was not the case. They were gradually given managerial responsibility over time.[13]

realistic job preview (RJP)

Both positive and negative information given to potential employees about the job they are applying for, thereby giving them a realistic picture of the job.

Giving potential employees a realistic picture of the job they are applying for is known as a **realistic job preview (RJP).** When candidates are given both positive and negative information, they can make more effective job choices. Traditional recruiting practices produce unrealistically high expectations, which produce low job satisfaction when these unrealistic expectations hit the reality of the job situation. RJPs tend to create expectations that are much closer to reality, and they increase the numbers of candidates who withdraw from further consideration.[14] This occurs because candidates with unrealistic expectations tend to look for employment elsewhere.

RJPs can also be thought of as inoculation against disappointment. If new recruits know what to expect in the new job, they can prepare for the experience. Ultimately, this can result in more effective matches, lower turnover, and higher commitment and satisfaction.[15]

Job candidates who receive RJPs view the organization as honest and also have a greater ability to cope with the demands of the job.[16] RJPs perform another important function: uncertainty reduction.[17] Knowing what to expect, both good and bad, gives a newcomer a sense of control that is important to job satisfaction and performance.

In summary, the needs and goals of individuals and organizations can clash during entry into the organization. To avoid potential mismatches, individuals should conduct a careful self-analysis and provide accurate information about themselves to potential employers. Organizations should present realistic job previews to show candidates both the positive and negative aspects of the job, along with the potential career paths available to the employee.

After entry into the organization, individuals embark on their careers. A person's work life can be traced through successive stages, as we see in the career stage model.

establishment

The first stage of a person's career, in which the person learns the job and begins to fit into the organization and occupation.

advancement

The second, highly achievement-oriented career stage in which people focus on increasing their competence.

maintenance

The third stage in an individual's career in which the individual tries to maintain productivity while evaluating progress toward career goals.

The Career Stage Model

■ A common way of understanding careers is viewing them as a series of stages that individuals pass through in their working lives.[18] Figure 17.2 presents the career stage model, which will form the basis for our discussion in the remainder of this chapter.[19] The career stage model shows that individuals pass through four stages in their careers: establishment, advancement, maintenance, and withdrawal. It is important to note that the age ranges shown are approximations; that is, the timing of the career transitions varies greatly between individuals.

Establishment is the first stage of a person's career. The activities that occur in this stage center around learning the job and fitting into the organization and occupation. **Advancement** is a highly achievement-oriented stage in which people focus on increasing their competence. **The maintenance** stage finds the individual trying to maintain productivity while evaluating progress toward

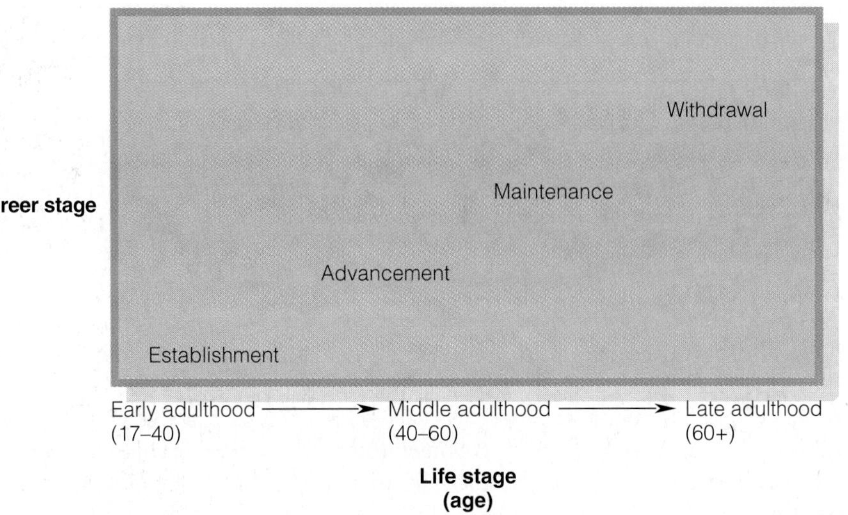

■ **FIGURE 17.2**

The Career Stage Model

career goals. The **withdrawal** stage involves contemplation of retirement or possible career change.

withdrawal
The final stage in an individual's career, in which the individual contemplates retirement or possible career changes.

Along the horizontal axis in Figure 17.2 are the corresponding life stages for each career stage. These life stages are based on the pioneering research on adult development conducted by Levinson and his colleagues. Levinson conducted extensive biographical interviews to trace the life stages of men and women. He interpreted his research in two books, *The Seasons of a Man's Life* and *The Seasons of a Woman's Life.*[20] Levinson's life stages are characterized by an alternating pattern of stability and transition.[21] Throughout the discussion of career stages that follows, we weave in the transitions of Levinson's life stages. Work and personal life are inseparable, and to understand a person's career experiences, we must also examine the unfolding of the person's personal experiences.

You can see that adult development provides unique challenges for the individual and that there may be considerable overlap between the stages. Now let us examine each career stage in detail.

Discussion Consideration
Ask students if they would have difficulty supervising employees who were considerably older than they are.

The Establishment Stage

■ During the establishment stage, the individual begins a career as a newcomer to the organization. This is a period of great dependence on others, as the individual is learning about the job and the organization. The establishment stage usually occurs during the beginning of the early adulthood years (ages eighteen to twenty-five). During this time, Levinson notes, an important personal life transition into adulthood occurs: the individual begins to separate from his or her parents and becomes less emotionally and financially dependent. Following this period is a fairly stable time of exploring the adult role and settling down.

The transition from school to work is a part of the establishment stage. Many graduates find the transition to be a memorable experience. The following description was provided by a newly graduated individual who went to work at a large public utility:

> We all tried to one-up each other about jobs we had just accepted . . . bragging that we had the highest salary, the best management training program, the most desirable coworkers, the most upward mobility . . . and believed we were destined to become future corporate leaders. . . . Every Friday after work we met for happy hour to visit and relate the events of the week. It is interesting to look at how the mood of those happy hours changed over the first few months . . . at first, we jockeyed for position in terms of telling stories about how great these new jobs were, or how weird our

> bosses were. . . . Gradually, things quieted down at happy hour. The mood went from "Wow, isn't this great" to "What in the world have we gotten ourselves into?" There began to be general agreement that business wasn't all it was cracked up to be.[22]

Establishment is thus a time of big transitions in both personal and work life. At work, three major tasks face the newcomer: negotiating effective psychological contracts, managing the stress of socialization, and making a transition from organizational outsider to organizational insider.

Psychological Contracts

psychological contract

An implicit agreement between an individual and an organization that specifies what each is expected to give and receive in the relationship.

A **psychological contract** is an implicit agreement between the individual and the organization that specifies what each is expected to give and receive in the relationship.[23] Individuals expect to receive salary, status, advancement opportunities, and challenging work to meet their needs. Organizations expect to receive time, energy, talents, and loyalty in order to meet their goals. Working out the psychological contract with the organization begins with entry, but the contract is modified as the individual proceeds through the career.

Discussion Consideration
Do students feel they have have a psychological contract in the courses they take?

The psychological contract is evolving in accordance with the paradigm shift to the new career. Employability has replaced the idea of employment security. Employees' skills should be continually enhanced and updated so that when companies restructure, people can find new jobs, whether with the same company or with another firm. This places a premium on training. If an employee takes charge of her own employability by keeping her skills updated and varied, she also builds more security with her current employer. And if a company provides training and learning opportunities, it is more likely to retain good employees.

Psychological contracts also form and exist between individuals.[24] During the establishment stage, newcomers form attachment relationships with many people in the organization. Working out effective psychological contracts within each relationship is important. Newcomers need social support in many forms and from many sources. Table 17.2 shows the type of psychological contracts, in the form of social support, that newcomers may work out with key insiders in the organization.

Discussion Consideration
Contracts involve responsibilities for both parties. What responsibilities do students feel employees should bring to the contract?

Points to Emphasize
It is important for newcomers to look for cues about an organization's value system.

One common newcomer concern, for example, is whose behavior to watch for cues to appropriate behavior. Senior colleagues can provide modeling support by displaying behavior that the newcomer can emulate. This is only one of many types of support that newcomers need. Newcomers should contract with others to receive each of the needed types of support so that they can adjust to the new job. Organizations should help newcomers form relationships early and should encourage the psychological contracting process between newcomers and insiders.

The Stress of Socialization

In Chapter 16 on organizational culture and socialization, we discussed three phases that newcomers go through in adjusting to a new organization: anticipatory socialization, encounter, and change and acquisition. (You may want to refer to Figure 16.2 for review.) Another way to look at these three phases is to examine the kinds of stress newcomers experience during each stage.[25]

In anticipatory socialization, the newcomer is gathering information from various sources about the job and organization. The likely stressor in this stage is ambiguity, so the provision of accurate information is important. During this stage, the psychological contract is formed. It is essential that both parties go into it with good intentions of keeping up their end of the agreement.

In the encounter phase, the demands of the job in terms of the role, task, interpersonal relationships, and physical setting become apparent to the new-

■ **TABLE 17.2**

Newcomer-Insider Psychological Contracts for Social Support

TYPE OF SUPPORT	FUNCTION OF SUPPORTIVE ATTACHMENTS	NEWCOMER CONCERN	EXAMPLES OF INSIDER RESPONSE/ACTION
Protection from stressors	Direct assistance in terms of resources, time, labor, or environmental modification	What are the major risks/ threats in this environment?	*Supervisor* cues newcomer in to risks/threats
Informational	Provision of information necessary for managing demands	What do I need to know to get things done?	*Mentor* provides advice on informal political climate in organization
Evaluative	Feedback on both personal and professional role performances	How am I doing?	*Supervisor* provides day-to-day performance feedback during first week on new job
Modeling	Evidence of behavioral standards provided through modeled behavior	Who do I follow?	Newcomer is apprenticed to *senior colleague*
Emotional	Empathy, esteem, caring, or love	Do I matter? Who cares if I'm here or not?	*Other newcomers* empathize with and encourage individual when reality shock sets in

SOURCE: D. L. Nelson, J. C. Quick, and J. R. Joplin, "Psychological Contracting and Newcomer Socialization: An Attachment Theory Foundation," *Journal of Social Behavior and Personality* 6 (1991): 65.

comer. The expectations formed in anticipatory socialization may clash with the realities of organizational life, and reality shock can occur.[26] This very predictble "surprise" reaction may find the new employee thinking, "What have I gotten myself into?"[27] The degree of reality shock depends on the expectations formed in the anticipatory socialization stage. If these expectations are unrealistic or unmet, reality shock may be a problem.

In the change and acquisition phase, the newcomer begins to master the demands of the job. Newcomers need to feel that they have some means of control over job demands.

Easing the Transition from Outsider to Insider

Being a newcomer in an organization is stressful. The process of becoming a functioning member of the organization takes time, and the newcomer needs support in making the transition. A successful transition from outsider to insider can be ensured if both the newcomer and the organization work together to smooth the way.

INDIVIDUAL ACTIONS Newcomers should ask about the negative side of the job if they were not given a realistic job preview. In particular, newcomers should ask about the stressful aspects of the job. Other employees are good sources of this information. Research has shown that newcomers who underestimate the stressfulness of job demands do not adjust well.[28] In addition, newcomers should present honest and accurate information about their own weaknesses. Both actions can promote good matches.

During the encounter phase, newcomers must prepare for reality shock. Realizing that slight depression is natural when adjusting to a new job can help alleviate the distress. Newcomers can also plan ways to cope with job stress ahead of time. If, for example, long assignments away from home are typical, newcomers can plan for these trips in advance. Part of the plan for dealing with reality shock should include ways to seek support from others. Networking with other newcomers who empathize can help individuals cope with the stress of the new job.

In the change and acquisition stage of adjusting to a new organization, newcomers should set realistic goals and take credit for the successes that occur as they master the job. Newcomers must seek feedback on job performance from their supervisors and coworkers. Organizations also can assist newcomers in their transition from outsiders to insiders.

ORGANIZATIONAL ACTIONS Realistic job previews start the relationship between the newcomer and the organization with integrity and honesty. Careful recruitment and selection of new employees can help ensure good matches.

During the encounter phase, organizations should provide early job assignments that present opportunities for the new recruit to succeed. Newcomers who experience success in training gain increased self-efficacy and adjust to the new job more effectively.[29] Newcomers who face early job challenges successfully tend to be higher performers later in their careers.[30] Phil Barry, president of Compro Insurance Services of San Jose, California, has been training new managers for thirty years. He recommends that new managers sit in on meetings one level higher to gain a larger perspective on the business. This technique sends a message to the new manager that the company communicates openly and is not secretive.[31] Providing encouragement and feedback to the newcomer during this stage is crucial. The immediate supervisor, peers, other newcomers, and support staff are important sources of support during encounter.[32]

During the change and acquisition phase, rewards are important. Organizations should tie the newcomers' rewards as explicitly as possible to performance.[33] Feedback is also crucial. Newcomers should receive daily, consistent feedback. This communicates that the organization is concerned about their progress and wants to help them learn the ropes along the way.

The establishment stage marks the beginning of an individual's career. Its noteworthy transitions include the transition from school to work, from dependence on parents to dependence on self, from organizational outsider to organizational insider. Negotiating sound psychological contracts and planning for the stress of adjusting to a new organization can help newcomers start off successfully. Once they have met their need to fit in, individuals move on to the advancement stage of their career.

The Advancement Stage

■ The advancement stage is a period when many individuals strive for achievement. They seek greater responsibility and authority and strive for upward mobility. Usually around age thirty, an important life transition occurs.[34] Individuals reassess their goals and feel the need to make changes in their career dreams. The transition at age thirty is followed by a period of stability during which the individual tries to find a role in adult society and wants to succeed in the career. During this stage, several issues are important: exploring career paths, finding a mentor, working out dual-career partnerships, and managing conflicts between work and personal life.

Career Paths and Career Ladders

career path

A sequence of job experiences that an employee moves along during his or her career.

Career paths are sequences of job experiences along which employees move during their careers.[35] At the advancement stage, individuals examine their career dreams and the paths they must follow to achieve those dreams. For example, suppose a person's dream is to become a top executive in the pharmaceutical industry. She majors in chemistry in undergraduate school and takes a job with a nationally recognized firm. After she has adjusted to her job as a quality control chemist, she reevaluates her plan and decides that further education is necessary. She plans to pursue an MBA degree part-time, hoping to gain expertise in management. From there, she hopes to be promoted to a supervisory position within her current firm. If this does not occur within five years, she will consider moving to a different pharmaceutical company. An alternate route would be to try to transfer to a sales positon, from which she might advance into management.

Alternate Example
The traditional career ladder is no longer available in many organizations, thus individuals no longer feel the same level of loyalty to their organization.

A **career ladder** is a structured series of job positions through which an individual progresses in an organization. For example, at Southwestern Bell, it is customary to move through a series of alternating line and staff supervisory assignments to advance toward upper management. Supervisors in customer service might be assigned next to the training staff and then rotate back as line supervisors in network services to gain experience in different departments.

career ladder
A structured series of job positions through which an individual progresses in an organization.

Some companies use the traditional concept of career ladders to help employees advance in their careers. Other organizations take a more contemporary approach to career advancement. Sony encourages creativity from its engineers by using nontraditional career paths. At Sony, individuals have the freedom to move on to interesting and challenging job assignments without notifying their supervisors. If they join a new project team, their current boss is expected to let them move on. This self-promotion philosophy at Sony is seen as a key to high levels of innovation and creative new product designs.

Another approach used by some companies to develop skills is the idea of a "career lattice"—an approach to building compentencies by moving laterally through different departments in the organization or by moving through different projects. Top management support for the career lattice is essential, because in traditional terms an employee who has made several lateral moves might not be viewed with favor. However, the career lattice approach is an effective way to develop an array of skills to ensure one's employability.[36]

Discussion Consideration
Do students have a career path and ladder in mind? Have them do a quick timeline to see where they think they will be in two, five, and ten years.

Whether through career ladders or career lattices, the advancement stage involves developing a portfolio of valued skills to increase one's employability. The acompanying Organizational Reality feature details the skills that are prized at Xerox.

Points to Emphasize
Recent research refutes some of the rigid categories said to exist in the stages of career development and the ladders to success. Advancement seems to have more to do with individual experience than age. SOURCE: A. Rosenfeld and E. Stark, "The Prime of Our Lives," in R. Sims, D. White, and D. Bednar, (Eds.), *Readings in Organizational Behavior* (Boston: Allyn & Bacon, 1992).

Exploring career paths is one important activity in advancement. Another crucial activity during advancement is finding a mentor.

Finding a Mentor

A **mentor** is an individual who provides guidance, coaching, counseling, and friendship to a protégé. Mentors are important to career success because they perform both career and psychosocial functions.[37]

mentor
An individual who provides guidance, coaching, counseling, and friendship to a protégé.

The career functions provided by a mentor include sponsorship, facilitating exposure and visibility, coaching, and protection. Sponsorship means actively helping the individual get job experiences and promotions. Facilitating exposure and visibility means providing opportunities for the protégé to develop relationships with key figures in the organization in order to advance. Coaching involves providing advice in both career and job performance. Protection is provided by shielding the protégé from potentially damaging experiences. Career functions are particularly important to the protégé's future success. One study found that the amount of career coaching received by protégés was related to more promotions and higher salaries four years later.[38]

The mentor also performs psychosocial functions. Role modeling occurs when the mentor displays behavior for the protégé to emulate. This facilitates social learning. Acceptance and confirmation is important to both the mentor and protégé. When the protégé feels accepted by the mentor, it fosters a sense

ORGANIZATIONAL REALITY

How to Get Ahead at Xerox

The new Xerox organization rewards people on a suite of skills, not solely on either technical or managerial skills. Each employee is rated from 0 to 5 on the following inventory of skills:

BUSINESS SKILLS

- **Business Knowledge:** Understands business principles (including financial management), industry, and economic influences.
- **Customer Requirements:** Demonstrates understanding of customer plans, problems, processes, and requirements.
- **Vision, Goals, and Objectives:** Understands vision, goals, and objectives of the corporation.

TECHNICAL SKILLS

- **Technology:** Employs new, as well as tested and proven, technologies. Pursues appropriate technical solutions to meet customer requirements. Understands and supports the information management technical architecture.
- **Technical Currency:** Acquires general knowledge in all current and emerging technologies, with particular emphasis on integration and end-to-end customer solutions.

LEADERSHIP SKILLS

- **Proactive Leadership and Positive Influence:** Makes things happen. Looks for ways to increase the value of self and others.
- **Quality Processes/Tools/Measurements:** Understands that doing things right the first time is central to the team's ability to deliver a competitive advantage to the business. Applies quality principles and tools. Manages by fact, conducts root cause analyses.
- **Teamwork:** Recognizes the importance of teams. Able to build teams that recognize diverse stakeholder needs and include cross-functional members with shared goals. Establishes and uses networks, alliances, coalitions, and teams to increase productivity, quality, and customer satisfaction.
- **Strategic Thinking:** Deals with ideas at an abstract level. Conceptualizes "what could be." Translates that into plans and direction.
- **Deliver Business Results:** Prepares detailed plans. Dedicated to completing deliverables on time, within cost, and with quality.
- **Decision-Making:** Makes sound decisions with available information, knowledge. Open to influence, change. Assumes responsibility for decisions.
- **Creativity:** Looks for and supports new and better ways of doing things.
- **Risk-Taking:** Willing to take calculated risks and act quickly to seize business opportunities as they arise. Learns from mistakes.
- **Communication:** Interprets correctly what people are thinking and feeling even when it is not obvious from what they say. Expresses ideas and concepts clearly and persuasively.
- **Staff Development:** Is able to identify, attract, retain, and develop talented people. Values diversity. ■

SOURCE: "How to Get Ahead at Xerox," *Datamation*, January 15, 1995: 47.

of pride. Likewise, positive regard and appreciation from the junior colleague provide a sense of satisfaction for the mentor. Counseling by a mentor helps the protégé explore personal issues that arise and require assistance. Friendship is another psychosocial function that benefits both mentor and protégé alike.

Some companies have formal mentoring programs in which a junior employee is assigned to a senior employee who serves as mentor. Dow Jones uses a "quad" system that matches a high-level mentor with a group of three employees: a white man, a white or minority woman, and a minority man or woman. If an employee does not have rapport with the mentor in the quad, that employee still may relate to the two members of the quad. Capitalizing on diversity makes the quad mentoring system successful.[39] Douglas Aircraft also uses a formal mentoring system, as shown in the Organizational Reality feature.

Discussion Consideration
Ask students to reflect on mentors they have had. How did they find these mentors? Or, did the mentors seek them out?

Mentoring programs are also effective ways of addressing the challenge of workforce diversity. The mentoring process, however, presents unique problems, including the availability of mentors, issues of language and acculturation, and cultural sensitivity, for minority groups such as Hispanic-Americans. Adding to this challenge is the substantial diversity within the Hispanic-American population in terms of country of origin and country of birth.[40] Companies can make the mentoring process easier for minority workers by creating formal programs that address special needs in the mentoring process and by creating a culture that values diversity, as was discussed in Chapter 16.

Although some companies have formal mentoring programs, junior employees more often are left to negotiate their own mentoring relationships. The barriers to finding a mentor include lack of access to mentors, fear of initiating a mentoring relationship, and fear that supervisors or coworkers might not approve of the mentoring relationship. Individuals may also be afraid to initiate a mentoring relationship because it might be misconstrued as a sexual advance by the potential mentor or others. This is a fear of potential mentors as well. Some are unwilling to develop a relationship because of their own or because of the protégé's gender. Women report more of these barriers than men, and individuals who lack previous experience report more barriers to finding a mentor.[41]

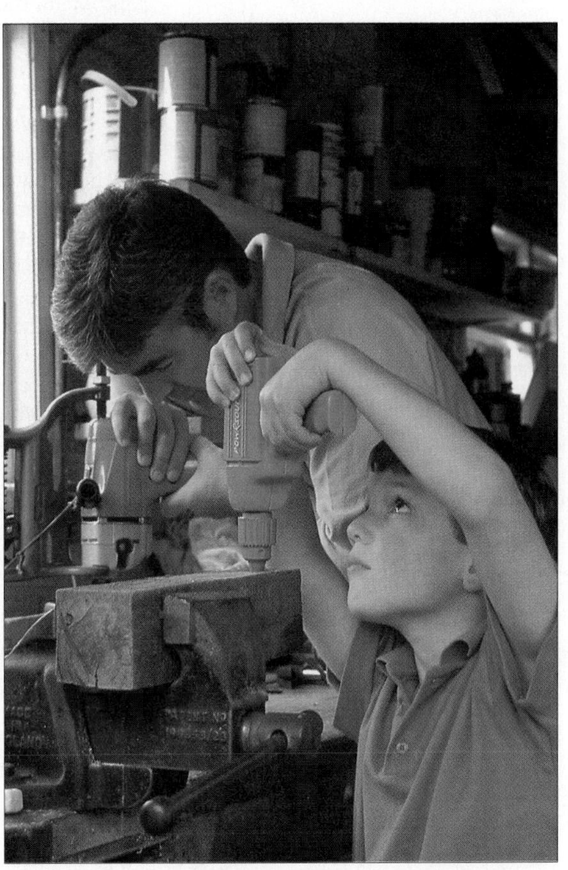

Mentor/protégé relationships form early in life as children look to their parents as a natural way to learn. Similarly, the role modeling, coaching, and counseling provided by mentors can equip protégés with the skills they need for career success in organizations.

Organizations can encourage junior workers to approach mentors by providing opportunities for them to interact with senior colleagues. The immediate supervisor is not always the best mentor for an individual, so exposure to other senior workers is important. Seminars, multilevel teams, and social events can serve as vehicles for bringing together potential mentors and protégés.

Mentoring relationships go through a series of phases: initiation, cultivation, separation, and redefinition. There is no fixed time length for each phase, because each relationship is unique. In the initiation phase, the mentoring relationship begins to take on significance for both the mentor and the protégé. In the cultivation phase, the relationship becomes more meaningful, and the protégé shows rapid progress because of the career and psychosocial support provided by the mentor. Protégés influence mentors as well. The Scientific Foundation feature presents a study that examined the tactics used by protégés to influence their mentors.

In the separation phase, the protégé feels the need to assert independence and work more autonomously. Separation can be voluntary, or it can result from an involuntary change (the protégé or mentor may be promoted or transferred). The separation phase can be difficult if it is resisted, either by the mentor (who is reluctant to let go of the relationship), or by the protégé (who resents the mentor's withdrawal of support). Separation can proceed smoothly and naturally or can result from a conflict that disrupts the mentoring relationship.

The redefinition phase occurs if separation has been successful. In this phase, the relationship takes on a new identity as both parties consider themselves colleagues or friends. The mentor feels pride in the protégé, and the protégé develops a deeper appreciation for the support from the mentor.

Points to Emphasize
We will probably never be able to repay the mentors in our lives. However, we can pass it on by becoming mentors ourselves.

Why are mentors so important? Aside from the support they provide, the research shows that mentors are important to the protégé's future success. For example, studies have demonstrated that individuals with mentors have higher

ORGANIZATIONAL REALITY

Mentoring Is Part of the Culture at Douglas Aircraft

At Douglas Aircraft Company in Long Beach, California, mentoring is a tradition. Two important elements have ingrained mentoring in the organization's culture. First, senior management's support of mentoring is frequent, visible, and unwavering. Second, mentoring is part of the long-term strategic plan published by the CEO of Douglas's parent company, McDonnell Douglas.

At Douglas Aircraft, mentoring is the vehicle for moving knowledge through the organization from the people who have the most learning and experience. Management identifies high-performing employees, using criteria like readiness for promotion. Potential mentors are senior managers who volunteer their time. Before they join the program, they must outline the knowledge and guidance they believe they can contribute to the program. Mentorees select three potential mentors from the list of volunteers. A steering team matches the mentorees with mentors. The team can assign no more than two mentorees to a single mentor, and the mentor must be outside a mentoree's direct chain of command. This is because managers are already coaching and mentoring employees in their own work groups, and it avoids the awkward situation of being mentored by one's boss's boss.

Another benefit of Douglas's mentoring program is that supervisors are involved. Supervisors and mentorees jointly set developmental objectives, and these objectives are used by the mentoree and mentor as well. For example, suppose a mentoree in the manufacturing group determines, along with her supervisor, that she needs exposure to the financial aspects of the business. The mentoree is matched with an executive from the finance group.

In a recent evaluation, feedback from the mentorees showed an 80 percent overall satisfaction rating with the mentoring program. The most frequently mentioned concern from the mentorees was that time constraints limited their ability to schedule meetings with their mentors.

Douglas Aircraft's mentoring program is not a static one. It is revised and improved every year. In one-year cycles, mentors, mentorees, and supervisors receive ongoing instruction, counseling, support, and follow-through. ■

SOURCE: A. H. Geiger-DuMond and S. K. Boyle, "Mentoring: A Practitioner's Guide," *Training & Development* (March 1995): 51–54. Copyright March 1995, *Training and Development*, American Society for Training and Development. Reprinted with permission. All rights reserved.

promotion rates and higher incomes than individuals who do not have mentors.[42] Individuals with mentors also are better decision makers.[43]

During the advancement stage, many individuals face another transition: they settle into a relationship with a life partner. This lifestyle transition requires adjustment in many respects: learning to live with another person, being concerned with someone besides yourself, dealing with an extended family, and many other demands. The partnership can be particularly stressful if both members are career-oriented.

Dual-Career Partnerships

dual-career partnership
A relationship in which both people have important career roles.

The two-career lifestyle has increased in recent years due in part to the need for two incomes to maintain a preferred standard of living. **Dual-career partnerships** are relationships in which both people have important career roles. This type of partnership can be mutually beneficial, but it can also be stressful. Often these stresses center around stereotypes that providing income is a man's responsibility and taking care of the home is the woman's domain.

One stressor in a dual-career partnership is time pressure. When both partners work outside the home, there may be a time crunch in fitting in work, family, and

SCIENTIFIC FOUNDATION

What Tactics Do Protégés Use to Influence Their Mentors?

Although we know that mentors contribute both career and psychological functions to mentoring relationships, we know less about protégés' contributions to the relationships. This study investigated upward influence tactics used by protégés to preserve mentoring relationships with senior colleagues. Four types of mentoring relationships were examined: (1) protégés in formal mentoring relationships with their supervisors (formal supervisory protégés), (2) protégés receiving informal mentoring from their supervisors (informal supervisory protégés), (3) protégés receiving mentoring from other senior employees (nonsupervisory protégés), and (4) subordinates receiving no mentoring (nonprotégés).

Five groups of upward maintenance tactics were investigated. *Personal tactics* included informal communication such as joking, sharing personal experiences, and interaction at social events. *Direct tactics* involved unedited communication of personal views, such as expressing opinions, expectations, and perceptions of injustices. *Regulative tactics* involved efforts to limit or manage contact, communication, and emotional displays with superiors (censoring or distorting messages, avoiding the delivery of bad news, overlooking negative comments and mood swings). *Contractual tactics* involved formal communication such as clarifying responsibilities, sticking to agreements, sharing credit for success, accepting criticism, and showing respect. *Extracontractual tactics* involved a willingness to exceed supervisor expectations (finishing work before deadlines, maintaining a flexible schedule, relieving the boss of burdens).

A survey was used to measure protégé status and influence tactics, along with demographic characteristics. The survey respondents were 259 managerial and professional employees from a variety of organizations in the banking, insurance, health, manufacturing, and education industries. The median age of the respondents was between 30 and 34 years, and 60 percent of the respondents were men.

The results showed that informal supervisory protégés used a distinctive pattern of tactics to maintain stability in their mentoring relationships. They were more likely to report using direct and extracontractual tactics and less likely to report using regulative and contractual techniques than were formal supervisory protégés, nonsupervisory protégés, and nonprotégés. These results imply that informal mentoring relationships between supervisors and protégés provide a nonthreatening context in which protégés can directly challenge and question their mentors (use direct tactics) and not have to perform "emotional work" to manage the relationship (use regulative tactics). In addition, protégés in formal mentoring relationships with supervisors used the same tactics as nonprotégés, suggesting that they felt no more comfortable in the relationships with their supervisors than those who received no mentoring at all.

The study has implications for mentoring programs in organizations. First, mentoring relationships with supervisors that develop naturally provide a nonthreatening way for protégés to challenge their mentors and to exceed performance expectations. Second, protégés in formal mentoring relationships may experience relational conflicts that make them less willing to express their emotions. Organizations with formal mentoring programs can use communication training programs to help protégés and mentors alike to develop open communications in the relationship.

SOURCE: B. J. Tepper, "Upward Maintenance Tactics in Supervisory Mentoring and Nonmentoring Relationships," *Academy of Management Journal* 38 (1995): 1191–1205.

leisure time. Another potential problem is jealousy. When one partner's career blooms before the other's, the partner may feel threatened.[44] Another issue to work out is whose career takes precedence. For example, what happens if one partner is transferred to another city? Must the other partner make a move that might threaten his or her own career in order to be with the individual who was transferred? Who, if anyone, will stay home and take care of a new baby?

Alternate Example
An often overlooked aspect of international jobs is the adjustment processes that spouses and children have to make when an employee accepts an international assignment.

Working out a dual-career partnership takes careful planning and consistent communication between the partners. Each partner must serve as a source of social support for the other. Couples can also turn to other family members, friends, and professionals for support if the need arises.

Work-Home Conflicts

An issue related to dual-career partnerships that is faced throughout the career cycle, but often first encountered in the advancement phase, is the conflicts that

Intergenerational daycare centers like this one at Minnequa Medicenter are places where young and old alike share daily experiences like games, cooking, and arts and crafts. These progressive programs offer great potential in meeting the needs of senior citizens and children.

occur between work and personal life. Experiencing a great deal of work-home conflict negatively affects an individual's overall quality of life.[45] Responsibilities at home can clash with responsibilities at work, and these conflicts must be planned for. For example, suppose a child gets sick at school. Who will pick up the child and stay home with him or her? Couples must work together to resolve these conflicts.

Work-home conflicts are particular problems for working women.[46] Women have been quicker to share the provider role than men have been to share responsibilities at home.[47] When working women experience work-home conflict, their performance declines, and they suffer more strain. Work-home conflicts are different in Japan than in the United States. In Japan, women are expected to leave the work force at an early age to marry and raise a family. Women who work after having children are looked down upon.[48] This attitude is slowly changing, and Japanese women are turning to temporary employment to balance their work and home responsibilities.

flexible work schedule

A work schedule that allows employees discretion in order to accommodate personal concerns.

To help individuals deal with work-home conflict, companies can offer **flexible work schedules.**[49] These programs, such as flextime, which we discussed in Chapter 14, give employees freedom to take care of personal concerns while still getting their work done. Company-sponsored child care is another way to help. Companies with on-site day care centers include Johnson & Johnson and Campbell Soup. Whereas large companies may offer corporate day care, small companies can also assist their workers by providing referral services for locating the type of child care the workers need. For smaller organizations, this is a cost-effective alternative.[50] At the very least, companies can be sensitive to work-home conflicts and handle them on a case-by-case basis with flexibility and concern.

eldercare

Assistance in caring for elderly parents and/or other elderly relatives.

Discussion Consideration

Ask students to reflect on the various interrole conflicts they may experience between home and work.

A program of increasing interest that organizations can provide is **eldercare.** Often workers find themselves part of the sandwich generation: They are expected to care for both their children and their elderly parents. This extremely stressful role is reported more often by women than men.[51] The need for eldercare is a significant nationwide problem in the United States.[52] Companies have taken a variety of approaches to assisting employees with eldercare. PepsiCo has in-house seminars to provide information, a resource guide, and a hotline to a university center on aging.

DuPont is an example of a company concerned about the balance between work and home. DuPont conducted a survey of its employees and found that the need for company change was great. The majority of employees said that they had difficulty finding child care that conformed to their work hours, that they had difficulty attending school activities, and that many of their ten- to thirteen-year-olds were left alone routinely after school. Concerns over day care can create extreme stress for workers and can also decrease their productivity.[53] DuPont formed a company-wide committee that made twenty-three recommendations for action, including flexible work arrangements, more benefit options for child care and eldercare, and the incorporation of work and family topics in training sessions. DuPont is currently implementing these recomendations.[54]

The advancement stage is filled with the challenges of finding a mentor, balancing dual-career partnerships, and dealing with work-home conflicts. Developmental changes that occur in either the late advancement stage or the early maintenance stage can prove stressful, too. The midlife transition, which takes place approximately between ages forty and forty-five, is often a time of crisis. Levinson points out three major changes that contribute to the midlife transition. First, people realize that their lives are half over and that they are mortal. Second, age forty is considered by people in their twenties and thirties to be "over the hill" and not part of the youthful culture. Finally, people reassess their dreams and evaluate how close they have come to achieving those dreams. All these factors make up the midlife transition.

Alternate Example
Companies are beginning to view assistance programs as long-term benefits. Helping employees balance their personal lives with work seems like common sense. "A worker who isn't distracted by worries over baby-sitting or caring for a parent is better able to focus on the job." SOURCE: M. Galen, A. Palmer, A. Cuneo, and M. Maremont, "Work and Family," *Business Week,* 28 June 1993, 80–88.

The Maintenance Stage

■ *Maintenance* may be a misnomer for this career stage, because some people continue to grow in their careers, although the growth is usually not at the rate it was earlier. A career crisis at midlife may accompany the midlife transition. A senior product manager at Borden found himself in such a crisis and described it this way: "When I was in college, I had thought in terms of being president of a company. . . . But at Borden I felt used and cornered. Most of the guys in the next two rungs above me had either an MBA or 15 to 20 years of experience in the food business. My long-term plans stalled."[55]

Some individuals who reach a career crisis are burned out, and a month's vacation will help, according to Carolyn Smith Paschal, who owns an executive search firm. She recommends that companies give employees in this stage sabbaticals instead of bonuses. This would help rejuvenate them.

Some individuals reach the maintenance stage with a sense of achievement and contentment, feeling no need to strive for further upward mobility. Whether the maintenance stage is a time of crisis or contentment, however, there are two issues to grapple with: sustaining performance and becoming a mentor.

Sustaining Performance

Remaining productive is a key concern for individuals in the maintenance stage. This becomes challenging when one reaches a **career plateau,** a point where the probability of moving further up the hierarchy is low. Some people handle career plateauing fairly well, but others may become frustrated, bored, and dissatisfied with their jobs.

career plateau
A point in an individual's career in which the probability of moving further up the hierarchy is low.

To keep employees productive, organizations can provide challenges and opportunities for learning. Lateral moves are one option. Another option is to involve the employee in project teams that provide new tasks and skill development. The key is keeping the work stimulating and involving. Individuals at this stage also need continued affirmation of their value to the organization. They need to know that their contributions are significant and appreciated.[56]

Becoming a Mentor

During maintenance, individuals can make a contribution by sharing their wealth of knowledge and experience with others. Opportunities to be mentors to new employees can keep senior workers motivated and involved in the organization. It is important for organizations to reward mentors for the time and energy they expend. Some employees adapt naturally to the mentor role, but others may need training on how to coach and counsel junior workers.

Kathy Kram notes that there are four keys to the success of a formal mentoring program. First, participation should be voluntary. No one should be forced to enter a mentoring relationship, and careful matching of mentors and protégés is important. Second, support from top executives is needed to convey the intent of the program and its role in career development. Third, training should be provided to mentors so they understand the functions of the relationship. Finally, a graceful exit should be provided for mismatches or for people in mentoring relationships that have fulfilled their purpose.[57]

Maintenance is a time of transition, like all career stages. It can be managed by individuals who know what to expect and plan to remain productive, as well as by organizations that focus on maximizing employee involvement in work. According to Levinson, during the latter part of the maintenance stage, another life transition occurs. The age fifty transition is another time of reevaluating the dream and working further on the issues raised in the midlife transition. Following the age fifty transition is a fairly stable period. During this time, individuals begin to plan seriously for withdrawing from their careers.

The Withdrawal Stage

Discussion Consideration
Ask students to compare their parents' or grandparents' career withdrawal stage with what they think the stage will be like for them.

■ The withdrawal stage usually occurs later in life and signals that a long period of continuous employment will soon come to a close. Older workers may face discrimination and stereotyping. They may be viewed by others as less productive, more resistant to change, and less motivated. However, older workers are one of the most undervalued groups in the workforce. They can provide continuity in the midst of change and can serve as mentors and role models to younger generations of employees.

Discrimination against older workers is prohibited under the Age Discrimination in Employment Act.[58] Organizations must create a culture that values older workers' contributions. With their level of experience, strong work ethic, and loyalty, these workers have much to contribute. In fact, older workers have lower rates of tardiness and absenteeism, are more safety conscious, and are more satisfied with their jobs than are younger workers.[59]

Retirement is a very individual decision, with some individuals retiring as early as age forty and some never leaving the workforce. Some individuals withdraw from work gradually by scaling back their work hours or by working part-time. Some retire and change careers. The key to making transitions at this career stage is careful planning.

Planning for Change

http://www.bc.com

The decision to retire is an individual one, but the need for planning is universal. A retired sales executive from Boise-Cascade said that the best advice is to "plan no unplanned retirement."[60] This means carefully planning not only the transition but also the activities you will be involved in once the transition is made. All options should be open for consideration. One recent trend is the need for temporary top-level executives. Some companies are hiring senior managers from the outside on a temporary basis. The qualities of a good temporary executive include substantial high-level management experience, financial security that allows the executive to choose only assignments that really interest him or her, and a willingness to relocate.[61] Some individuals at the withdrawal stage find this an attractive option.

Planning for retirement should include not only financial planning but also a plan for psychologically withdrawing from work. The pursuit of hobbies and travel, volunteer work, or more time with extended family can all be part of the plan. The key is to plan early and carefully, as well as to anticipate the transition with a positive attitude and a full slate of desirable activities.

Retirement

The decision to retire can focus on early retirement, traditional retirement at age sixty-five, or postponed retirement. With many organizations downsizing, forced early retirements are increasing. Factors that influence the decision of when to retire include company policy, financial considerations, family support or pressure, health, and opportunities for other productive activities.[62]

During the withdrawal stage, the individual faces a major life transition that Levinson refers to as the late adulthood transition (ages sixty to sixty-five). One's own mortality becomes a major concern and the loss of one's family members and friends becomes more frequent. There is a major psychological development task to be accomplished during this transition. The person works to achieve a sense of integrity in life—that is, the person works to find the encompassing meaning and value in life.

Retirement can be stressful. Besides the fact that it is a major life transition, there are stressors involved, such as dual-career considerations, income uncertainty, declining physical capacity, and spouse's concerns and anxieties. Knowing what to expect can help a retiree cope with these stressors. Careful planning and knowing what to expect can produce a transition into a meaningful and rewarding retirement.

Retirement need not be a complete cessation of work. Many alternative work arrangements can be considered, and many companies offer flexibility in these options. Phased retirement, such as part-time work, consulting, and mentoring, will probably become more common as large numbers of baby boomers near retirement. Not all baby boomers will want to retire, and many organizations

Many retirees spend time giving something back to their communities. These ladies are volunteer kitchen workers for Meals on Wheels, an organization that provides and delivers meals for the elderly.

will not be able to afford the loss of large numbers of experienced employees at once.

Now that you understand the career stage model, you can begin to conduct your own career planning. It is never too early to start.

Career Anchors

career anchors

A network of self-perceived talents, motives, and values that guide an individual's career decisions.

■ Much of an individual's self-concept rests upon a career. Over the course of the career, career anchors are developed. **Career anchors** are self-perceived talents, motives, and values that guide an individual's career decisions.[63] Edgar Schein developed the concept of career anchors based on a twelve-year study of MBA graduates from the Massachusetts Institute of Technology (MIT). Schein found great diversity in the graduates' career histories but great similarities in the way they explained the career decisions they had made.[64] From extensive interviews with the graduates, Schein developed five career anchors:

1. *Technical/functional competence.* Individuals who hold this career anchor want to specialize in a given functional area (for example, finance or marketing) and become competent. The idea of general management does not interest them.
2. *Managerial competence.* Adapting this career anchor means individuals want general management responsibility. They want to see their efforts have an impact on organizational effectiveness.
3. *Autonomy and independence.* Freedom is the key to this career anchor, and often these individuals are uncomfortable working in large organizations. Autonomous careers like writer, professor, or consultant attract these individuals.
4. *Creativity.* Individuals holding this career anchor feel a strong need to create something. They are often entrepreneurs.
5. *Security/stability.* Long-term career stability, whether in a single organization or in a single geographic area, fits people with this career anchor. Some government jobs provide this type of security.

Discussion Consideration
Ask students which of the five career anchors best describes them.

Career anchors emerge over time and may be modified by work or life experiences.[65] The importance of knowing your career anchor is that it can help you find a match between yourself and an organization. For example, individuals with creativity as an anchor may find themselves stifled in bureaucratic organizations. Textbook sales may not be the place for an individual with a security anchor because of the frequent travel and seasonal nature of the business.

Managerial Implications: Managing Your Career

■ The challenges of globalization, diversity, technology, and ethics have provided unique opportunities and threats for career management. The ongoing restructuring of American organizations with its accompanying downsizing has resulted in a reduction of 25 percent of the jobs held in the Fortune 500 companies, which translates into 3.7 million fewer workers in 1992 than in 1981.[66] The flattening of the organizational hierarchy has resulted in fewer opportunities for promotion. Forty-year careers with one organization, a phenomenon baby boomers saw their parents experience, are becoming less and less the norm. Negotiating the turbulent waters of the U.S. employment market will be a challenge in the foreseeable future.

Many industries are experiencing sinking employment, but there are some bright spots. According to Labor Department projections, the U.S. economy

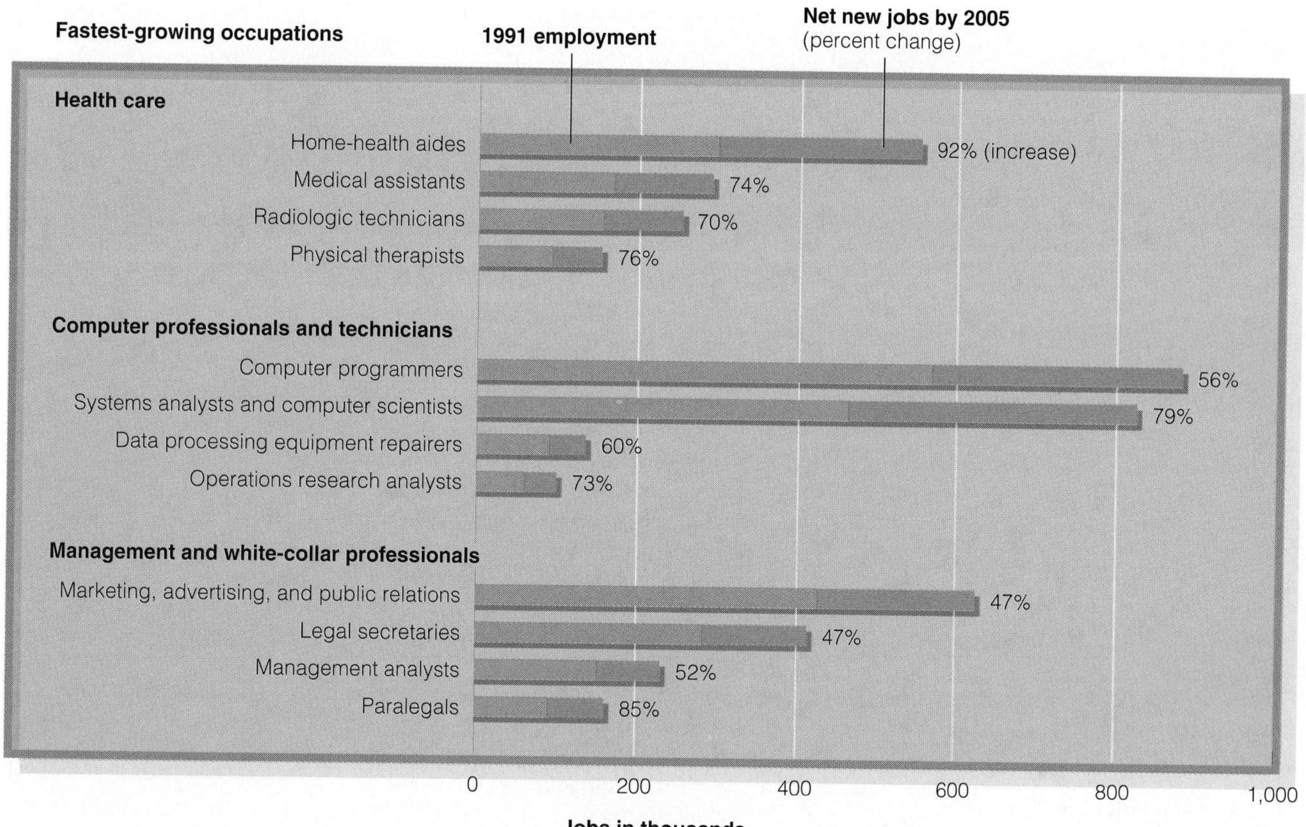

■ **FIGURE 17.3**

The Hottest Job Prospects

SOURCE: Bureau of Labor Statistics and Louis S. Richman, "The Hottest Job Prospects," *Fortune,* 12 July 1993, 53.

will add approximately 25 million jobs by the year 2005, with most of them in service industries. Figure 17.3 shows where the new jobs will be found.

Allen S. Grove, CEO of Intel Corporation, suggests that as a general rule, you must accept that no matter where you work, you are not an employee. Instead, you are in a business with one employee: yourself. You face tremendous competition with millions of other businesses. You own your career as a sole proprietor. Grove poses three key questions that are central to managing your career:

1. Continually ask, *Am I adding real value?* You add real value by continually looking for ways to make things truly better in your organization. In principle, every hour of your work day should be spent increasing the value of the output of the people for whom you're responsible.
2. Continually ask, *Am I plugged into what's happening around me?* Inside the company? The industry? Are you a node in a network of plugged-in people, or are you floating around by yourself?
3. *Are you trying new ideas, new techniques and new technologies?* Try them personally—don't just read about them.[67]

The key to survival is to add more value everyday, and to be flexible. You can use Challenge 17.2 to assess the current state of your flexibility skills.

CHALLENGE

■ 17.2

Assess Your Flexibility Skills

Use the following scale to rate the frequency with which you perform the behaviors described in each question. Place the corresponding number (1–7) in the blank preceding the statement.

Rarely	Irregularly	Occasionally	Usually	Frequently	Almost Always	Consistently
1	2	3	4	5	6	7

____ **1.** I manage a variety of assignments with varying demands and complexities.
____ **2.** I adjust work plans to account for new circumstances.
____ **3.** I modify rules and procedures in order to meet operational needs and goals.
____ **4.** I work with ambiguous assignments when necessary and use these when possible to further my goals and objectives.
____ **5.** I rearrange work or personal schedules to meet deadlines.
____ **6.** In emergencies, I respond to the most pressing needs first.
____ **7.** I change my priorities to accommodate unexpected events.
____ **8.** I manage my personal work overload by seeking assistance or by delegating responsibility to others.
____ **9.** I vary the way I deal with others according to their needs and personalities.
____ **10.** I help others improve their job performance or I assign tasks that will further their development.
____ **11.** I accept the authority of my manager but continue to demonstrate my initiative and assertiveness.
____ **12.** I work well with all types of personalities.
____ **13.** I measure my performance on the job against the feedback I receive.
____ **14.** I correct performance deficits that have been brought to my attention.
____ **15.** When I disagree with my manager's appraisal of my work, I discuss our differences.
____ **16.** I seek training and assignments that can help me improve my job-related skills.
____ **17.** In disagreements concerning work-related issues, I look at matters impersonally and concentrate on the facts.
____ **18.** I make compromises to get problems moving toward resolution.
____ **19.** I look for new and better ways to accomplish my duties and responsibilities.
____ **20.** I offer to negotiate all areas of disagreement.

■ **FIGURE A**

Flexible Behaviors Questionnaire (FBQ) Scoring

Skill Area	Items	Score
Working with new, changing, and ambiguous situations	1, 2, 3, 4	
Working under pressure	5, 6, 7, 8	
Dealing with different personal styles	9, 10, 11, 12	
Handling feedback	13, 14, 15, 16	
Resolving conflicts	17, 18, 19, 20	
	TOTAL SCORE	

CHALLENGE

■ 17.2 continued

Total Score				
Lowest score				Highest score
20	50	80	110	140

Category Scores

Working with new, changing, and ambiguous situations				
4	10	16	22	28

Working under pressure				
4	10	16	22	28

Dealing with different personality styles				
4	10	16	22	28

Handling feedback				
4	10	16	22	28

Resolving conflicts				
4	10	16	22	28

■ **FIGURE B**

Flexible Behaviors Questionnaire (FBQ) Evaluation

FBQ Scoring

The scoring sheet in Figure A summarizes your responses for the FBQ. It will help you identify your existing strengths and pinpoint areas that need improvement.

FBQ Evaluation

Figure B shows score lines for your total score and for each category measured on the FBQ. Each line shows a continuum from the lowest score to the highest.

The score lines in Figure B show graphically where you stand with regard to the five flexible behaviors. If you have been honest with yourself, you now have a better idea of your relative strengths and weaknesses in the categories that make up the skills of flexibility.

SOURCE: P. M. Fandt, *Management Skills: Practice and Experience*, p. 431–433. St. Paul, MN: West Publishing, 1994.

CLOSING SPOTLIGHT

Motorola Finds Its Training Solution in Virtual Reality

Motorola began exploring technologies that could extend the reach of its hands-on training program. Virtual reality, because of its ability to give learners a three-dimensional learning experience, was appealing. Designers created a virtual model that replicated the actions of the laboratory machinery. When the student turns on a power switch, the corresponding lights or equipment are powered. On the virtual assembly line, students hear the same whirs, clicks, and hums they would hear if they were using real equipment.

A test of the virtual model was conducted using three groups of students. A control group used the "real" lab equipment. A second group looked at the model on the computer screen in two dimensions and used a mouse to navigate though the model. A third group was outfitted with head-mount displays to view the virtual world. They used a "tracker," a device that tracks head movements so the user can turn his or her head to scan the virtual space without having to use a mouse. After training, all students were taken to the real lab to start up, run, and shut down the robotic assembly line. They were graded on the number or errors they made and the steps they missed. The results were impressive. The third group of students—those who used the head-mounted devices—outperformed the other groups.

Motorola continues to innovate its training techniques. New peripherals will be tried, including an input glove to give students a more natural way to activate the machinery. Developing a virtual world and the accompanying equipment costs between $30,000 and $100,000. Still, it's far less expensive than building new training laboratories with actual equipment. Computer models are also easier to modify as manufacturing technologies evolve.

The virtual reality approach will allow Motorola to extend training to every manufacturing facility from Europe to Asia. Because virtual reality is individually driven, it allows trainees the chance to practice at their own pace, and to experience working the line as though they were in the real manufacturing environment.[68] ■

Chapter Summary

- Career management is a joint responsibility of individuals and organizations.
- Good matches between individuals and organizations can be promoted with a realistic job preview (RJP).
- There are four stages in an individual's career: establishment, advancement, maintenance, and withdrawal. Each stage has unique challenges.
- Psychological contracts are implicit agreements between individuals and organizations.
- Mentoring is crucial to both the career success of young workers and the needs of older workers.
- Childcare, eldercare, and flexible work schedules can help employees manage work-home conflicts.
- Career anchors help an individual form a career identity and formulate an effective career plan.

Key Terms

career (p. 506)
career management (p. 506)
realistic job preview (RJP) (p. 512)
establishment (p. 512)
advancement (p. 512)
maintenance (p. 512)
withdrawal (p. 513)
psychological contract (p. 514)
career path (p. 516)
career ladder (p. 517)
mentor (p. 517)
dual-career partnership (p. 520)
flexible work schedule (p. 522)
eldercare (p. 522)
career plateau (p. 523)
career anchors (p. 526)

Discussion and Communication Questions

1. What do you think will be the most stressful career stage? What type of stressors led you to make this choice?
2. Does the career stage model have exceptions? In other words, can it be applied to all careers? If not, what are the exceptions?
3. Do men and women have different expectations of a dual-career partnership? How do these expectations differ?
4. Given the downsizing and restructuring in many organizations, how can organizations help employees with career management if there are fewer opportunities for promotion?
5. How has each of the four challenges (globalization, diversity, technology, and ethics) affected career management in recent years?
6. *(communication question)* Contact the human resources manager of a local business. Ask if he or she would take a few minutes to discuss some issues about résumés with you. Structure your discussion around the following questions:

   a. How often do your encounter "padded" résumés? What is the most common "padding" and how do you react to it?
   b. Do you verify the information on résumés? How do you do this? How long does it take for you to be sure that an applicant has been honest about his/her qualifications?
   c. What would you do if you found that a productive, loyal employee had lied on a résumé when he or she applied for a job? Is "résumé fraud" an offense that warrants firing?

   Summarize the findings from your interview in a memo to your instructor.
7. *(communication question)* Select an individual in the field you want to work in, or in a company you might want to work for. Contact the individual and ask if you might take a minute of their time for some career advice. Ask them the following two questions, along with others you design yourself. First, how has the idea of a "career" changed over the past few years? Second, what advice would they give to college students just beginning a new career? Be prepared to present your interview results in class.

Ethics Questions

1. You are leaving your current job to look for employment elsewhere. Should you tell your current employer? Is it ethical not to reveal your job search to your employer?
2. You are a manager, and one of your employees is an older worker about sixty years old. You have noticed that his performance is slipping, and other workers have been complaining about his errors. Is it ethical to discuss retirement with him? Under what circumstances is it ethical to pressure an employee to retire?
3. You are interviewing a job candidate who inquires about the career paths within your organization. A natural next step from the job she is seeking would be middle management, but you know that your company is flattening its hierarchy and that most middle-management jobs will be eliminated. You are afraid that this information will discourage this very talented candidate from taking the job. What should you do?
4. One of your employees has been a disruptive influence on the work group, yet he has decent performance. He wants to be promoted to a supervisory position, and two positions are available: one in your department and one in another location. Your inclination is to nominate him for the position in the other department and reveal nothing of his disruptive nature in order to transfer him away from your department. Discuss the ethical implications of this course of action.

Experiential Exercises

17.1 The Individual-Organizational Dialogue

The purpose of this exercise is to help you gain experience in working out a psychological contract from both perspectives—the individual's and the organization's.

Students should form groups of six to eight members. Within each group, half of the students will be job candidates, and half will represent organization members (insiders).

Step 1. Each half should make two lists as follows:

List 1, candidate version. What information should you, as a job candidate, provide the organization to start an effective psychological contract?

List 2, candidate version. What information should you, as a job candidate, seek from the organization?

List 1, insider version. What information should you, as an organization insider, seek from potential employees?

List 2, insider version. What information should you, as an organization insider, provide to potential employees to start an effective psychological contract?

Step 2. Within each group, compare lists by matching the two versions of List 1. What were the similarities and differences in your lists? Then compare List 2 from each half of the group. What were the similarities and differences in these lists?

Step 3. Review the lists, and select the most difficult information to obtain from the candidate and the organization. Select one person to play the candidate and one to play the insider. First, have the candidate role-play an interaction with the insider in which the candidate tries to get the difficult information from the organization. Then have the insider try to obtain the difficult information from the candidate.

Step 4. Reconvene as a class, and discuss the following questions:

1. What did you find to be the most difficult questions asked by candidates?
2. What did you find to be the most difficult questions asked by insiders?
3. What information is necessary for an effective psychological contract?
4. What keeps each party from fully disclosing the information needed for a good psychological contract?
5. What can organizations do to facilitate the process of forming good psychological contracts?
6. What can individuals do to facilitate the process?

17.2 The Ethics of Résumés and Recommendations

The purpose of this exercise is to explore ethical issues concerning résumés and recommendations. First, read the following brief introductory scenario.

Jason Eckerle returned to his desk from lunch with a single mission in mind: to select the half-dozen best candidates for a regional customer service manager's position. As he hung up his suit jacket, Eckerle sized up the stack of résumés and recommendations he'd been dealing with all morning—more than a hundred of them.

The work had been slow but steady, gradually forming into three distinct piles: one contained absolute rejects (not enough work experience, wrong academic credentials, or poor recommendations from former employers), the second contained a few definite candidates for personal interviews, while the third held the applications of those about whom he still had questions or reservations.

His task for the afternoon—selecting three more applicants to bring to the company headquarters for interviews—was complicated by the résumés and recommendation letters themselves. Some questions were obvious: "This guy lists five years' full-time sales and marketing experience, yet he's only 22 years old. How can he go to school full-time and have that kind of experience?" Here's another: "This young lady says she went to school at the Sorbonne in Paris for two years; yet on the application form, under the heading 'Foreign Languages' she's checked 'none.'" Here's one more: "This fella says he has a degree from the University of Texas, yet nowhere on his résumé does he say he lived or spent time there. Did he get that diploma by correspondence?"

Other issues are even more mysterious: "This young lady's résumé lists education and work experience, but there's a three-year gap from 1989 to 1992. What's that all about? Is she trying to conceal something, or just absent minded?" As Eckerle thumbed through another résumé, he noticed the application form declaring "fluency in Japanese, French, and Spanish." "How do you get to be *fluent* in a language unless you've lived where it's spoken?" he wondered. The résumé didn't list any of those languages as native, nor did the application mention living abroad.

"Some of this stuff is outright fraud," he observed. As he sifted through the "reject" pile, Eckerle pulled out one application with an education block that lists a degree the applicant didn't have. "When we checked," he said, "they told us he was close to finishing a master's degree, but he hadn't yet finished his thesis. The applicant said he had the degree in hand." Another listed work experience no one could verify. "This guy's résumé says he was a client service representative for Litiplex, Inc. of Boston, but the phone book doesn't list any firm by that name, no one in our business has ever heard of them, and we can't check out his claims. I asked the applicant about the company, and he says, 'Maybe they went out of business.'"

Résumés weren't Eckerle's only problem. Recommendations were almost as bad. "Letters of recommendation aren't particularly useful," he said. "In the first place, almost no one is dumb enough to ask for a recommendation from someone who'll give them a bad one. Second, most recommenders write in broad, general, vague terms that don't tell me much about an applicant's work history, aptitude, or potential. They use glowing, nonspecific words that tell me the applicant's a marvelous human being but don't say whether the guy's had any comparable work experience that I could use to help make a decision."

Eckerle mentioned one other recommendation problem. "Most of the people who write letters in support of a job applicant are fairly close friends of the applicant. They'll often say things that are laudatory, but just aren't true. By the time you're done reading the letter, you'd think the young man in question could walk on water. When he comes for an interview, he can't get his own name straight." Excessive praise in letters of recommendation, Eckerle noted, can be expensive for a firm when the recommendation just doesn't reflect the applicant's true potential. "It costs us nearly $1,000 to bring in an entry-level management candidate for interviews," he said, "and it's my job to make sure we don't bring in someone who's just not competitive." Inflated recommendations, he thought, can make that job much more difficult.

Next, the class should be divided into ten groups. Each group will be assigned one ethical issue. The group should formulate an answer to the dilemma and be ready to present the group's solution to the class.

1. Is a job applicant obligated to list *all employment* or *every work experience* on a résumé? What about jobs in which an applicant has had a bad relationship with a supervisor? Is it fair to "load up" a résumé only with positive work experience?
2. What if an applicant has been fired? Is a résumé *required* to reveal the exact circumstances under which he or she left the job?
3. Is it ethical to list educational institutions or degree programs that an applicant has attended but not completed? How much detail is necessary? Should an applicant explain *why* he or she left a degree program or school without finishing?
4. Is a job applicant *obliged* to list offenses against the law on a résumé? What about convictions or incarceration—say 90 days' jail time for DWI?
5. Under such résumé categories as "Foreign Languages," how does an applicant determine whether he or she is

"fluent," "conversant," or merely "familiar with" a language? Do the same general rules apply to listing technical skills, such as computer languages and software applications?

6. In a letter of recommendation, is it ethical to lavish praise on a young man or woman, just because you know the person is in need of a job? Conversely, does faint praise mean that a job applicant will likely be refused?
7. Is it better to turn away a student for asking for a letter of recommendation, or should you do what's *honest* and tell a graduate school (or potential employer) exactly what you think of the person?
8. Is a résumé something like a *certificate of authenticity*, listing specifics and details with absolute adherence to honesty and accuracy, or is it more like a *sales brochure*, offering the best possible picture of a person in search of employment?
9. How well do you have to know someone before you can write an authentic, honest letter or recommendation? Is there a minimum time requirement before you can do so in good conscience?
10. Is the author of a letter of recommendation required to reveal *everything relevant* that he or she knows about an applicant? What about character or integrity flaws that may stand in the way of a job applicant's success? To whom is the author of such letters obligated? To the potential employer or to the applicant?

SOURCE: J. S. O'Rourke, "The Ethics of Résumés and Recommendations: When Do Filler and Fluff Become Deceptions and Lies?" *Business Communication Quarterly* 58 (1995): 54–56.

VIDEO CASE

The Minnesota Twins: Pursuing A Career in Sports Management[1]

Sports management is a "very tough industry to break into," says Bill Matere, vice president of marketing for the Minnesota Twins professional baseball franchise. In any professional sport, the number of management positions is limited by the number of teams in the league. In professional baseball, for example, there are 28 major league teams, and thus only 28 VPs of marketing, 28 VPs of operations, 28 promotions managers, and so forth. Although these people have other staffers working for them, the number of positions is limited. The Twins, for instance, employ 55 full-time people on the management side of their operation.

In baseball, each major league team also has several minor league affiliates that provide additional opportunities for sports management careers. However, minor league teams have even fewer management positions available.

Sports management also is a difficult career field to break into because of low turnover rates among existing employees. Laura Day, the Twins promotions manager, observes that in her four years with the franchise only three full-time positions have opened up. Commenting on the difficulty in breaking into the sports management industry, Day says, "I certainly don't mean to be a dragon slayer here . . . , but it is the reality that we face in today's working situation."

With these constraints on professional sports management opportunities, what can aspiring individuals do to enhance their chances of successful career entry and development? Day, the promotions manager, suggests that students who desire a career in sports management should get as much business experience as they can through paid or unpaid internships. Matere, the Twins marketing VP, urges people to acquire some meaningful, broad-based experience in other corporate settings before getting into professional sports management. He points out that professional sports franchises do not invest a lot of time in training and developing front office people so that they can be strong managers and leaders in the organization. Instead, people need to have "good, quality training and experience in . . . a good, solid corporation" before getting into the sports management industry, says Matere. Sherry Rood, the Twins MIS manager, echoes this sentiment. She indicates that, in new hires, she looks for someone whose career is information systems, not baseball.

Kevin Mather, vice president of finance, indicates that one way to "chase your dream" of professional sports management is to work your way up through the minor league system. If a person is "willing to go to a smaller town and put up with minor league baseball," a lot can be learned on the sports management side because there is an opportunity to wear every hat—doing the books, selling tickets, taking care of the balls and bats, and so on.

Baseball is part of the entertainment industry. Unlike companies in other industries, working in baseball provides a more relaxed atmosphere. Says Rood, the Twins MIS manager, "On days when we are having an afternoon game, if you want to go out and watch a couple of innings of a game, you can do that; whereas, if you work somewhere else, you can't leave your job and go to the ballpark and pick up an inning or two."

But people should not get into sports management just because they love sports. Jobs in this field are very demanding. Says Jerry Bell, president of the Minnesota Twins franchise, "Just because someone is a good fan does not mean they are going to be a good employee in the major league sports setting. . . . If you don't like this work, you will not be successful at it because you're going to spend an awful lot of time. When other people are off at the lake and having their weekends off, we work nights and weekends during the season. In the off-season, the challenge is to prepare for the next season."

Matere, the marketing VP, suggests that people should have a long-term perspective on their careers, whether or not it's in the field of sports management. He recommends that people ask themselves, "Where do I want to be ten years from now, and does this company provide me the biggest opportunity to advance and take on additional responsibility? . . . Where do I want to be, not only personally, but also in a business setting; how do I get there?" And more importantly than anything, "How do I do it with . . . a lot of integrity?"

DISCUSSION QUESTIONS

1. What challenges and obstacles seem to exist for someone who wishes to pursue a sports management career?
2. Assume that you are interested in a career in sports management. Using the facts of the case along with the career stage model shown in Figure 17.2, explain how you might expect your career to develop. (You may wish to give special emphasis to the establishment and advancement stages.)
3. In reference to your analysis in question 2, what could you do to facilitate effective movement through the career stages? What might an employer do to facilitate effective movement through the career stages?
4. What advice do you think the Minnesota Twins executives would give people regarding self-management of their careers, particularly in the sports management industry?

SOURCE: This case was written by Michael K. McCuddy, the Louis S. and Mary L. Morgal Professor of Christian Business Ethics, College of Business Administration, Valparaiso University.

1. This case is based on transcripts of interviews that representatives of West Educational Publishing conducted with various Minnesota Twins executives.

References

1. J. H. Greenhaus, *Career Management* (Hinsdale, Ill.: CBS College Press, 1987).
2. D. T. Hall, *Careers in Organizations* (Pacific Palisades, Calif.: Goodyear, 1976).
3. Greenhaus, *Career Management;* T. G. Gutteridge and F. L. Otte, "Organizational Career Development: What's Going On Out There?" *Training and Development Journal* 37 (1983): 22–26.
4. M. B. Arthur, P. H. Claman, and R. J. DeFillippi, "Intelligent Enterprise, Intelligent Careers," *Academy of Management Executive* (November 1995): 7–22.
5. P. Buhler, "Managing in the '90s, " *Supervision* (July 1995): 24–26.
6. R. Koonce, "Becoming Your Own Career Coach," *Training & Development* 49 (1995): 18–25.
7. D. E. Super, *The Psychology of Careers* (New York: Harper & Row, 1957); D. E. Super and M. J. Bohn, Jr., *Occupational Psychology* (Belmont, Calif.: Wadsworth, 1970).
8. J. L. Holland, *The Psychology of Vocational Choice* (Waltham, Mass.: Blaisdell, 1966); J. L. Holland, *Making Vocational Choices: A Theory of Careers* (Englewood Cliffs, N.J.: Prentice-Hall, 1973).
9. S. H. Osipow, *Theories of Career Development* (Englewood Cliffs, N.J. Prentice-Hall, 1973).
10. J. P. Wanous, T. L. Keon, and J. C. Latack, "Expectancy Theory and Occupational/Organizational Choices: A Review and Test," *Organizational Behavior and Human Performance* 32 (1983): 66–86.
11. P. O. Soelberg, "Unprogrammed Decision Making," *Industrial Management Review* 8 (1967): 19–29.
12. J. P. Wanous, *Organizational Entry: Recruitment, Selection, and Socialization of Newcomers* (Reading, Mass.: Addison-Wesley, 1980).
13. N. Nicholson and J. Arnold, "From Expectation to Experience: Graduates Entering a Large Corporation," *Journal of Organizational Behavior* 12 (1991): 413–429.
14. S. L. Premack and J. P. Wanous, "A Meta-Analysis of Realistic Job Preview Experiments," *Journal of Applied Psychology* 70 (1985): 706–719.
15. J. P. Wanous and A. Colella, "Organizational Entry Research: Current Status and Future Directions," in K. R. Rowland and G. R. Ferris, eds., *Research in Personnel and Human Resources Management* (New York: JAI Press, 1989), 59–120; R. J. Vandenberg and V. Scarpello, "The Matching Model: An Examination of the Processes Underlying Realistic Job Previews," *Journal of Applied Psychology* 75 (1990): 60–67.
16. J. A. Breaugh, "Realistic Job Previews: A Critical Appraisal and Future Research Directions," *Academy of Management Review* 8 (1983): 612–619.
17. G. R. Jones, "Socialization Tactics, Self-Efficacy, and Newcomers' Adjustment to Organizations," *Academy of Management Journal* 29 (1986): 262–279.
18. J. O. Crites, "A Comprehensive Model of Career Adjustment in Early Adulthood," *Journal of Vocational Behavior* 9 (1976): 105–118; S. Cytrynbaum and J. O. Crites, "The Utility of Adult Development in Understanding Career Adjustment Process," in M. B. Arthur, D. T. Hall, and B. S. Lawrence, eds., *Handbook of Career Theory* (Cambridge: Cambridge University Press, 1989), 66–88.
19. D. E. Super, "A Life-Span, Life-Space Approach to Career Development," *Journal of Vocational Behavior* 16 (1980): 282–298; L. Baird and K. Kram, "Career Dynamics: Managing the Superior/Subordinate Relationship," *Organizational Dynamics* 11 (1983): 46–64.
20. D. J. Levinson, *The Seasons of a Man's Life* (New York: Knopf, 1978); D. J. Levinson, *The Seasons of a Woman's Life*, in press.
21. D. J. Levinson, "A Conception of Adult Development," *American Psychologist* 41 (1986): 3–13.
22. D. L. Nelson, "Adjusting to a New Organization: Easing the Transition from Outsider to Insider," in J. C. Quick, R. E. Hess, J. Hermalin, and J. D. Quick, eds., *Career Stress in Changing Times* (New York: Haworth Press, 1990), 61–86.
23. J. P. Kotter, "The Psychological Contract: Managing the Joining Up Process," *California Management Review* 15 (1973): 91–99.
24. D. M. Rousseau, "New Hire Perceptions of Their Own and Their Employers' Obligations: A Study of Psychological Contracts," *Journal of Organizational Behavior* 11 (1990): 389–400; D. L. Nelson, J. C. Quick, and J. R. Joplin, "Psychological Contracting and Newcomer Socialization: An Attachment Theory Foundation," *Journal of Social Behavior and Personality* 6 (1991): 55–72.
25. D. L. Nelson, "Organizational Socialization: A Stress Perspective," *Journal of Occupational Behavior* 8 (1987): 311–324.
26. R. A. Dean, K. R. Ferris, and C. Konstans, "Reality Shock: Reducing the Organizational Commitment of Professionals," *Personnel Administrator* 30 (1985): 139–148.
27. Nelson, "Adjusting to a New Organization," 61–86.
28. D. L. Nelson and C. D. Sutton, "The Relationship between Newcomer Expectations of Job Stressors and Adjustment to the New Job," *Work and Stress* 5 (1991): 241–254.
29. A. M. Saks, "Longitudinal Field Investigation of the Moderating and Mediating Effects of Self-Efficacy on the Relationship Between Training and Newcomer Adjustment," *Journal of Applied Psychology* 80 (1995): 211–225.
30. G. F. Dreher and R. D. Bretz, Jr., "Cognitive Ability and Career Attainment: Moderating Effects of Early Career Success," *Journal of Applied Psychology* 76 (1991): 392–397.
31. R. Maynard, "Help Newcomers Learn the Ropes," *Nation's Business*, August 1991, 32–33.
32. D. L. Nelson and J. C. Quick, "Social Support and Newcomer Adjustment in Organizations: Attachment Theory at Work?" *Journal of Organizational Behavior* 12 (1991): 543–554.
33. R. Pascale, "The Paradox of Corporate Culture: Reconciling Ourselves to Socialization," *California Management Review* 27 (1985): 27–41.
34. Levinson, "A Conception of Adult Development," 3–13.
35. J. W. Walker, "Let's Get Realistic about Career Paths," *Human Resource Management* 15 (1976): 2–7.

36. B. Filipczak, "You're on Your Own," *Training* (January 1995): 29–36.
37. K. E. Kram, *Mentoring at Work: Developmental Relationships in Organizational Life* (Glenview, Ill.: Scott, Foresman, 1985).
38. C. Orpen, "The Effects of Monitoring on Employees' Career Success," *Journal of Social Psychology* 135 (1995): 667–668.
39. M. Granfield, "90s Mentoring: Circles and Quads," *Working Woman* (November 1992): 15.
40. S. B. Knouse, "The Mentoring Process for Hispanics," in S. B. Knouse, P. Rosenfield, and A. L. Culbertson, eds., *Hispanics in the Workplace* (Newbury Park, Calif.: Sage Publications, 1992), 137–150.
41. B. R. Ragins and J. L. Cotton, "Easier Said Than Done: Gender Differences in Perceived Barriers to Gaining a Mentor," *Academy of Management Journal* 34 (1991): 939–951.
42. W. Whiteley, T. W. Dougherty, and G. F. Dreher, "Relationship of Career Mentoring and Socioeconomic Origin to Managers' and Professionals' Early Career Progress," *Academy of Management Journal* 34 (1991): 331–351; G. F. Dreher and R. A. Ash, "A Comparative Study of Mentoring among Men and Women in Managerial, Professional, and Technical Positions," *Journal of Applied Psychology* 75 (1990): 539–546; T. A. Scandura, "Mentorship and Career Mobility: An Empirical Investigation," *Journal of Organizational Behavior* 13 (1992): 169–174.
43. D. D. Horgan and R. J. Simeon, "Mentoring and Participation: An Application of the Vroom-Yetton Model," *Journal of Business and Psychology* 5 (1990): 63–84.
44. F. S. Hall and D. T. Hall, *The Two-Career Couple* (Reading, Mass.: Addison-Wesley, 1979).
45. R. W. Rice, M. R. Frone, and D. B. McFarlin, "Work-Nonwork Conflict and the Perceived Quality of Life," *Journal of Organizational Behavior* 13 (1992): 155–168.
46. D. L. Nelson, J. C. Quick, M. A. Hitt, and D. Moesel, "Politics, Lack of Career Progress, and Work/Home Conflict: Stress and Strain for Working Women," *Sex Roles* 23 (1990): 169–185.
47. L. E. Duxbury and C. A. Higgins, "Gender Differences in Work-Family Conflict," *Journal of Applied Psychology* 76 (1991): 60–74.
48. J. E. Rehfeld, "What Working for a Japanese Company Taught Me," *Harvard Business Review* (November–December 1990): 167–172.
49. D. L. Nelson and M. A. Hitt, "Employed Women and Stress: Implications for Enhancing Women's Mental Health in the Workplace," in J. C. Quick, L. R. Murphy, and J. J. Hurrell, eds., *Stress and Well-Being at Work: Assessments and Interventions for Occupational Mental Health* (Washington, D.C.: American Psychological Association, 1992), 164–177.
50. D. Machan, "The Mommy and Daddy Track," *Forbes*, 6 April 1990, 162.
51. E. M. Brody, M. H. Kleban, P. T. Johnsen, C. Hoffman, and C. B. Schoonover, "Work Status and Parental Care: A Comparison of Four Groups of Women," *Gerontological Society of America* 27 (1987): 201–208; J. W. Anastas, J. L. Gibson, and P. J. Larson, "Working Families and Eldercare: A National Perspective in an Aging America," *Social Work* 35 (1990): 405–411.
52. P. Schroeder, "Toward a National Family Policy," *American Psychologist* 44 (1989): 1410–1413.
53. Korsek, E. E., "Diversity in child care assistance needs: Employee problems, preferences, and work-related outcomes," *Personnel Psychology* 43 (1990): 769–791.
54. D. T. Hall, "Promoting Work/Family Balance: An Organization-Change Approach," *Organizational Dynamics*, (Winter 1990): 5–18.
55. J. Kaplan, "Hitting the Wall at Forty," *Business Month* 136 (1990): 52–58.
56. M. B. Arthur and K. E. Kram, "Reciprocity at Work: The Separate Yet Inseparable Possibilities for Individual and Organizational Development," in M. B. Arthur, D. T. Hall, and B. S. Lawrence, eds. *Handbook of Career Theory* (Cambridge: Cambridge University Press, 1989).
57. K. E. Kram, "Phases of the Mentoring Relationship," *Academy of Management Review* 26 (1983): 608–625.
58. B. Rosen and T. Jerdee, *Older Employees: New Roles for Valued Resources* (Homewood, Ill.: Irwin, 1985).
59. J. W. Gilsdorf, "The New Generation: Older Workers," *Training and Development Journal* (March 1992): 77–79.
60. J. F. Quick, "Time to Move On?" in J. C. Quick, R. E. Hess, J. Hermalin, and J. D. Quick, eds., *Career Stress in Changing Times* (New York: Haworth Press, 1990), 239–250.
61. D. Machan, "Rent-an-Exec," *Forbes*, 22 January 1990, 132–133.
62. E. McGoldrick and C. L. Cooper, "Why Retire Early?" in J. C. Quick, R. E. Hess, J. Hermalin, and J. D. Quick, eds., *Career Stress in Changing Times* (New York: Haworth Press, 1990), 219–238.
63. E. Schein, *Career Anchors* (San Diego: University Associates, 1985).
64. G. W. Dalton, "Developmental Views of Careers in Organizations," in M. B. Arthur, D. T. Hall, and B. S. Lawrence, eds., *Handbook of Career Theory* (Cambridge: Cambridge University Press, 1989), 89–109.
65. D. C. Feldman, "Careers in Organizations: Recent Trends and Future Directions," *Journal of Management* 15 (1989): 135–156.
66. B. O'Reilly, "The Job Drought," *Fortune*, 24 August 1992, 62–74.
67. A. S. Grove, "A High-Tech CEO Updates His Views on Managing and Careers," *Fortune*, September 18, 1995: 229–230.
68. N. Adams, "Lessons from the Virtual World," *Training* (June 1995): 45–48.

CHAPTER 18

DILBERT®
BY
SCOTT ADAMS

WALLY, I'M PROMOTING YOU TO DIRECTOR OF THE ENGINEERING QUALITY GROUP!

YES!

WAIT A MINUTE. I THOUGHT YOU WERE GOING TO ELIMINATE THAT GROUP.

YOUR ASSIGNMENT IS TO FIRE THEM ALL.

AAAGH! THAT WILL BE HIDEOUS!

AND WHEN I'M DONE YOU WON'T NEED A DIRECTOR. THEN YOU'LL FIRE ME!

YOU HAVE MY WORD THAT I WILL NOT FIRE YOU.
5/29

HI, GUYS.
THAT WOULD BE A JOB FOR EXECUTIVE DIRECTOR DILBERT.

Managing Change

LEARNING OBJECTIVES

After reading this chapter, you should be able to do the following:

- Identify the major external and internal forces for change in organizations.
- Define the terms *incremental change, strategic change, transformational change,* and *change agent.*
- Describe the major reasons individuals resist change, and discuss methods organizations can use to manage resistance.
- Apply force field analysis to a problem.
- Explain Lewin's organizational change model.
- Describe the use of organizational diagnosis and needs analysis as a first step in organizational development.
- Discuss the major organization development interventions.
- Identify the ethical issues that must be considered in organization development efforts.

OPENING SPOTLIGHT

Changes, Both Large and Small, Lead to Success at Federal Express

Managing change is a key competency that characterizes Federal Express. One goal that FedEx had was to wean itself from paper. This constituted a massive change. Managers knew that they needed an automated system to accomplish this goal, but computers often generate an ever greater glut of paper, especially when they automate already inefficient processes.

The company developed what many experts deem the most sophisticated automated human resources system in the world. PRISM is the 93,000-employee system. It offers more than 550 online screens that guide employees through a myriad of transactions. Using PRISM, managers can track job applicants and enter information on new hires. There are also online services for affirmative action reporting, job bidding, training, merit reviews, job descriptions, and employee action surveys, to name only a few. Employees can update their own personnel records, sign up for benefits, and bid for new jobs from anywhere within FedEx. Electronic imaging technology has facilitated the transition to the paperless system. Clerks feed about 10,000 pages a day into PRISM, and an optical disk jukebox provides sophisticated data storage, holding 114 disks, each with a 66,000-image capacity. As a result, human resources managers worldwide can examine résumés and personnel records.

PRISM fundamentally changed the way FedEx works, especially within the human resources department. Even as FedEx has grown, that department hasn't grown, and it hasn't replaced people with technology. The jobs in the HR department, however, have grown more technical.[1]

Not all changes at FedEx are as massive as the transition to PRISM. The Closing Spotlight relates how a simple change had a big impact for the company. ■

Forces for Change in Organizations

■ Change has become the norm in most organizations. Plant closings, business failures, mergers and acquisitions, and downsizing have become experiences common to American companies. *Adaptiveness*, *flexibility*, and *responsiveness* are terms used to describe the organizations that will succeed in meeting the competitive challenges that businesses face.[2] In the past, organizations could succeed by claiming excellence in one area—quality, reliability, or cost, for example—but this is not the case today. The current environment demands excellence in all areas, and organizations like Federal Express are taking steps to achieve this goal.

As we saw in Chapter 1, change is what's on managers' minds. The pursuit of organizational effectiveness through downsizing, restructuring, reengineering, productivity management, cycle-time reduction, and other efforts, is paramount. Organizations are in tremendous states of turmoil and transition, and all members are affected. The downsizing spree of recent years may have left firms leaner but not necessarily richer. While downsizing can increase shareholder value by better aligning costs with revenues, the effective organizations are the ones that excel at new product innovation—the systematic innovators.[3]

Organizations also must deal with ethical, environmental, and other social issues. Competition is becoming fierce, and companies can no longer afford to rest on their laurels. At American Airlines, a series of programs has been developed to ensure that the company constantly reevaluates and changes its operating methods to prevent the company from stagnating. GE holds off-site Work-Out sessions with groups of managers and employees whose goal is to make GE a faster, less complex organization that can respond effectively to change. In the WorkOut sessions, employees recommend specific changes, explain why they are needed, and propose ways the changes can be implemented. Top management must make an immediate response: an approval, a disapproval (with an explanation), or a request for more information. The GE WorkOut sessions eliminate the barriers that keep employees from contributing to change.

http://www.americanair.com

http://www.ge.com

There are two basic forms of change in organizations. **Planned change** is change resulting from a deliberate decision to alter the organization. Companies that wish to move from a traditional hierarchical structure to one that facilitates self-managed teams must use a proactive, carefully orchestrated approach. Not all change is planned, however. **Unplanned change** is imposed on the organization and is often unforeseen. Changes in government regulations and changes in the economy, for example, are often unplanned. Responsiveness to unplanned change requires tremendous flexibility and adaptability on the part of organiza-

planned change

Change resulting from a deliberate decision to alter the organization.

unplanned change

Change that is imposed on the organization and is often unforeseen.

tions. Managers must be prepared to handle both planned and unplanned forms of change in organizations.

Forces for change can come from many sources. Some of these are external, arising from outside the company, whereas others are internal, arising from sources within the organization.

Discussion Consideration
Do students feel that planned change is less stressful than unplanned change?

External Forces

The four major managerial challenges we have described throughout the book are major external forces for change. Globalization, workforce diversity, technological change, and managing ethical behavior are challenges that precipitate change in organizations.

GLOBALIZATION The power players in the global market are the multinational and transnational organizations. Conoco recently formed a joint venture with Arkhangelskgeologia, a Russian firm, to develop a new oil field in Russia. This partnership, named Polar Lights, is the first of its kind. It will explore a geographic area where there is no existing production, and its investment could total $3 billion.[4] Expanding into ventures such as this one requires extreme adaptability and flexibility on the part of both parties to the agreement.

Conoco's joint venture with a Russian firm resulted in a partnership called "Polar Lights" that will explore new oil fields in Russia. Many firms have responded to the challenge of globalization by combining forces in world markets.

New opportunities are not limited to the former Soviet Union, however, and the United States is but one nation in the drive to open new markets. Japan and Germany are responding to global competition in powerful ways, and the emergence of the European Community as a powerful trading group will have a profound impact on world markets. By joining with their European neighbors, companies in smaller countries will begin to make major progress in world markets, thus increasing the fierce competition that already exists.

Another example of a company taking giant strides in terms of the global marketplace is IBS. As managing director of IBS (a software and services business based in Sweden), Steffan Edberg has expanded his company by acquiring small, well-positioned firms in several European countries. He uses cross-border contracts and a wealth of experience in the industry to stay on top. The acquired firms retain their own management but draw on the capital and experience of other offices. Edberg maintains a low overhead and considers himself headquartered "wherever I happen to be." [5] IBS is just one of many companies that are beginning to look at the world as their marketplace.

All of these changes, along with others, have led companies to rethink the borders of their markets and to encourage their employees to think globally. Jack Welch of GE has called for a boundaryless company, in which there are no mental distinctions between domestic and foreign operations or between managers and employees.[6] The thought that drives the boundaryless company is that barriers that get in the way of people's working together should be removed. Globalizing an organization means rethinking the most efficient ways to use resources, disseminate and gather information, and develop people. It requires not only structural changes but also changes in the minds of employees.

Points to Emphasize
Often the workplace expectations of and pressures on black women are enormous. People with double diversity characteristics are often imposed on to fulfill many service roles, such as on committees, as mentors, and as company figureheads. SOURCE: J. Martin and G. Hall, "Thinking Black, Thinking Internal, Thinking Feminist," *Journal of Counseling Psychology* 39 (1992): 509–514.

WORKFORCE DIVERSITY Related to globalization is the challenge of workforce diversity. As we have seen throughout this book, workforce diversity is a powerful force for change in organizations. Let us recap the demographic trends contributing to workforce diversity that we discussed at length in Chapter 2. First, the workforce will see increased participation from females, as the majority of new workers will be female.[7] Second, the workforce will be more culturally diverse than ever. Part of this is attributable to globalization, but in addition, U.S. demographics are changing. The participation of African-Americans and Hispanic-Americans is increasing in record numbers. Third, the workforce is aging. There will be fewer young workers, and more middle-aged Americans working.[8]

Alternate Example
Government regulation can be a force for change. The passage of the Americans with Disabilities Act (ADA) required organizations to provide accommodations for individuals with disabilities.

These trends point toward an increasingly diverse workforce in terms of age, gender, and culture. Managing diversity effectively requires that organizations help employees view differences as valuable assets. Monsanto is a leader in managing diversity and it uses a formal diversity program to accomplish its goals. Managers at Monsanto are evaluted and rewarded based on how effectively they train and promote women.

The *Seattle Times* won a prestigious award for its diversity management efforts. The Organizational Reality feature presents the company's story.

Successfully managing workforce diversity means enabling all workers, including physically and mentally disabled employees, to reach their potential. Marriott Corporation considers disabled individuals as untapped gold mine and is proud that its turnover rate among disabled employees is only 8 percent.[9] Part of Marriott's success is due to its practice of pairing new disabled workers with managers who serve as coaches for the newcomers.

TECHNOLOGICAL CHANGE Rapid technological innovation is another force for change in organizations, and those who fail to keep pace can quickly fall behind. The technological competition between the United States and Japan is heated. There is a widely held perception that the United States is closing the quality gap with Japan. However, Japanese manufacturers are said to have moved beyond quality to flexibility as a new strategy. Manufacturing innovations seem to pass through stages from quality (doing it right) to reliability (always doing it right) to flexibility (adding variety and speed). At Toshiba, in Japan, flexibility means making a greater variety of products with the same equipment and employees. In Toshiba's Ōme plant, workers assemble nine different word processors on one line and twenty different laptop computers on another.[10] Flexibility gives organizations a competitive edge through the ability to read the market quickly and respond faster than competitors.

http://www.toshiba.com

Technological innovations bring about profound change because they are not just changes in the way work is performed. Instead, the innovation process promotes associated changes in work relationships and organizational structures.[11] The team approach adopted by many organizations, including Levi Strauss, leads to flatter structures, decentralized decision making, and more open communication between leaders and team members.

Alternate Example
Technological change has implications for everyone, including technically competent individuals. For example, many systems analysts have hand drawn their flow diagrams for years, and are resisting the use of on-line tools.

Alternate Example
A subtle criticism of computer conferencing is that it keeps people from traveling and visiting with colleagues. This replacement of the interpersonal with the technological is rarely recognized when the costs of travel versus computer conferencing are compared.

MANAGING ETHICAL BEHAVIOR Recent ethical scandals have brought ethical behavior in organizations to the forefront of public consciousness. Ethical issues, however, are not always public and monumental. Employees face ethical dilemmas in their daily work lives. The need to manage ethical behavior has brought about several changes in organizations. Most center around the idea that an organization must create a culture that encourages ethical behavior.

One organization with an innovative approach to ethics communication is Texas Instruments. TI introduced "Instant Experience," an internal communication tool to help employees learn about ethical behavior from each other. Instant Experience uses the corporate electronic mail system to transmit weekly information about ethical issues via T-News, the company's worldwide electronic newspaper. It feature anonymous ethical questions and the ethics offices' responses. Instant Experience also allows employees to interact with one

ORGANIZATIONAL REALITY

The *Seattle Times* Changes with the Times

The Seattle Times Company is one newspaper firm that has recognized the need for change and done something about it. In the newspaper industry, papers must reflect the diversity of the communities to which they provide information. They must reflect that diversity with their news coverage or risk losing their readers' interest and their advertisers' support. Operating within Seattle, which has 20 percent racial minorities, the paper has put into place policies and procedures for hiring and maintaining a diverse workforce. The rationale for the change is that for information to be fair, appropriate, and objective, it should be reported by the same kind of population that reads it.

A diversity committee composed of reporters, editors, and photographers meets regularly to evaluate the *Seattle Times*' content and to educate the rest of the newsroom staff about diversity issues. In addition, the paper instituted a content audit that evaluates the frequency and manner of representation of women and people of color in photographs. Early audits showed that minorities were pictured far too infrequently and were pictured with a disproportionate number of negative articles. The audit results in improvement in the frequency of minority representation and their portrayal in neutral or positive situations. And, as a result, the *Seattle Times* has improved as a newspaper. The diversity training and content audits helped the Seattle Times Company to win the coveted Personnel Journal Optimas Award for excellence in managing change. ■

SOURCE: D. Anfuso, "Awareness Effort Puts Diversity in the News," *Personnel Journal* (January 1995): 76.

another. In addition, weekly articles are archived so that new employees, or anyone with an ethics question, can refer to them. Instant Experience allows everyone at TI to learn about ethics from the open exchange.[12]

Society expects organizations to maintain ethical behavior both internally and in relationships with other organizations. Ethical behavior is expected in relationships with customers, the environment, and society. These expectations may be informal, or they may come in the form of increased legal requirements.

Discussion Consideration
Which force for change do students perceive as the strongest? What other forces for change do students believe will be at work during their careers?

These four challenges are forces that place pressures to change on organizations. There are other forces as well. Legal developments, changing stakeholder expectations, and shifting consumer demands are forces that can also lead to change.[13] Other powerful forces for change originate from within the organization.

Internal Forces

Pressures for change that originate inside the organization are generally recognizable in the form of signals indicating that something needs to be altered.

Declining effectiveness is a pressure to change. A company that experiences its third quarterly loss within a fiscal year is undoubtedly motivated to do something about it. Some companies react by instituting layoffs and massive cost-cutting programs, whereas others look at the bigger picture, view the loss as symptomatic of an underlying problem, and seek out the cause of the problem.

A crisis also may stimulate change in an organization. Strikes or walkouts may lead management to change the wage structure. The resignation of a key decision maker is one crisis that causes the company to rethink the composition of its management team and its role in the organization. A much-publicized crisis that led to change with Exxon was the oil spill accident with Exxon's *Valdez*. The accident brought about many changes in Exxon's environmental policies.

Changes in employee expectations also can trigger change in organizations. A company that hires a group of young newcomers may be met with a set of expectations very different from those expressed by older workers. The workforce is more educated than ever before. Although this has its advantages, workers with more education demand more of employers. Today's workforce is also concerned with career and family balance issues, such as dependent care. The many sources of workforce diversity hold potential for a host of differing expectations among employees.

Changes in the work climate at an organization can also stimulate change. A workforce that seems lethargic, unmotivated, and dissatisfied is a symptom that must be addressed. This symptom is common in organizations that have experienced layoffs. Workers who have escaped a layoff may grieve for those who have lost their jobs and may find it hard to continue to be productive. They may fear that they will be laid off as well, and many feel insecure in their jobs.

Change Is Inevitable

■ We have seen that organizations face substantial pressures to change from both external and internal sources. Change in organizations is inevitable, but change is a process that can be managed. The scope of change can vary from small to quantum.

The Scope of Change

incremental change

Change of a relatively small scope, such as making small improvements.

strategic change

Change of a larger scale, such as organizational restructuring.

transformational change

Change in which the organization moves to a radically different, and sometimes unknown, future state.

Change can be of a relatively small scope, such as a modification in a work procedure (an **incremental change).** Such changes, in essence, are a fine-tuning of the organization, or the making of small improvements. Change also can be of a larger scale, such as the restructuring of an organization (a **strategic change).**[14] In strategic change, the organization moves from an old state to a known new state during a controlled period of time. Strategic change usually involves a series of transition steps.

The most massive scope of change is **transformational change,** in which the organization moves to a radically different, and sometimes unknown, future state.[15] In transformational change, the organization's mission, culture, goals, structure, and leadership may all change dramatically.[16]

Many organizations undertake transformational change in order to meet the competitive challenge of globalization. In 1982, British Airways faced two extreme external pressures. One pressure was the deregulation of international air traffic, with resulting fare wars among airlines. Another pressure was the British government's decision to take British Airways from government to private ownership. British Airways made radical changes in its structure, systems, culture, and mission in order to survive the competitive challenge.[17] The Organizational Reality feature describes transformational change at St. Francis Regional Medical Center.

The Change Agent's Role

change agent

The individual or group who undertakes the task of introducing and managing a change in an organization.

The individual or group who undertakes the task of introducing and managing a change in an organization is known as a **change agent.** Change agents can be internal, such as managers or employees who are appointed to oversee the change process. In her book *The Change Masters*, Rosabeth Moss Kanter notes that at companies like Hewlett-Packard and Polaroid, managers and employees alike are developing the needed skills to produce change and innovation in the organization.[18] Change agents can also be external, such as outside consultants.

Internal change agents have certain advantages in managing the change process. They know the organization's past history, its political system, and its culture. Because they must live with the results of their change efforts, internal change agents are likely to be very careful about managing change. There are

ORGANIZATIONAL REALITY

Reorganization as Rebirth

Like many organizations in the 1980s, St. Francis Regional Medical Center of Wichita, Kansas, tried downsizing. A layoff of 400 people was a horrible experience, both for those who left and for those who stayed. The 1990s brought a change in the health care environment, and the hospital's administration needed to change the structure and culture in order to remain competitive.

The management team remapped the ideal management structure to run things without regard to the structure that was actually in place. To make such radical change work, they defined specific job titles, but not specific people. They dissolved the old organizational chart and created a new one, unveiling a chart that had all the new titles on it with no names. Those who wanted to be part of the new organization had to apply for whatever position they felt they were most qualified to fill. Imaging having to apply to a company you'd been with for fifteen years! The restructuring also meant a rethinking of corporate culture. An examination of culture revealed that making decisions at the hospital became bogged down by management and dictated by policy. Eliminating old policies allowed the team to look at things as possibilities rather than restrictions. Two task forces were formed to look at service lines and functional realignment. A consulting firm was called in to help the hospital make the transition. The consulting firm helped strategize and create a time line for the changes.

At the reorganizational meeting, each employee was given an 80-page bound booklet complete with vision statement, the new organizational chart, timetable, reorganization fact sheet, copies of all position descriptions, and a question and answer section. The result was terror, confusion, upheaval, and little by little, understanding, cooperation, and success. Instead of approaching the reorganization as a shameful secret, the task forces highlighted the changes in the new culture and tied the internal changes to the changes in the health care industry. Each week "The Grapevine: Reorganization Update" was distributed. On the first official day of the new organization, employees were given flowers and a message stating "Today starts a new beginning focused on you."

The new corporate culture involves management by contact. The new VPs walk the hallways and touch base constantly with what's going on. The result of the reorganization is decision making at lower levels, which results in faster actions. No more ideas die because of red tape. The reorganization is fluid and ongoing, with employees and managers still incorporating the new management philosophy and corporate culture into their daily work lives. ■

SOURCE: M. S. Egan, "Reorganization as Rebirth," *HR Magazine* (January 1995): 84–88.

disadvantages, however, to using internal change agents. They may be associated with certain factions within the organization and may easily be accused of favoritism. Furthermore, internal change agents may be too close to the situation to have an objective view of what needs to be done.

In a recent study, interviews were conducted with 150 internal change agents at 30 organizations. The researchers focused on middle managers as change agents because to make large-scale changes, organizations need a critical mass of change leaders in the middle of the company. Change leaders, as the researchers call them, tend to be young, in the 25 to 40 age range. They are more flexible than ordinary general managers, and much more people-oriented. A high number of change leaders are women. The change leaders have a balance of technical and interpersonal skills. They are tough decision makers who focus on performance results. They also know how to energize people and get them aligned in the same direction. They get more out of people than ordinary managers can. In addition, they have the ability to operate in more than one leadership style and can shift from a team mode to command and control, depending on the situation. They are also comfortable with uncertainty.[19]

External change agents bring an outsider's objective view to the organization. They may be preferred by employees because of their impartiality. External change agents face certain problems, including their limited knowledge of the organization's history. In addition, they may be viewed with suspicion by organization members. External change agents have more power in directing changes if employees perceive the change agents as being trustworthy, possessing important expertise, having a track record that establishes credibility, and being similar to them.[20]

The Process of Change in Organizations

■ Once an organization has made the decision to change, careful planning and analysis must take place. Part of the planning involves the recognition that individuals, when faced with change, often resist. Some individuals are more open to change, in general, than others.

The challenge of managing the change process involves harnessing the energy of diverse individuals who hold a variety of views of change. It is important to recognize that most changes will be met with varying degrees of resistance and to understand the basis of resistance to change.

Resistance to Change

People often resist change in a rational response based on self-interest. However, there are countless other reasons people resist change. Many of these center around the notion of reactance—that is, a negative reaction that occurs when individuals feel that their personal freedom is threatened.[21] Some of the major reasons for resisting change follow.

FEAR OF THE UNKOWN Change often brings with it substantial uncertainty. Employees facing a technological change, such as the introduction of a new computer system, may resist the change simply because it introduces ambiguity into what was once a comfortable situation for them. This is especially a problem when there has been a lack of communication about the change.

FEAR OF LOSS When a change is impending, some employees may fear losing their jobs, particularly when an advanced technology like robotics is introduced. Employees also may fear losing their status because of a change.[22] Computer systems experts, for example, may feel threatened when they feel their expertise is eroded by the installation of a more user friendly networked information system. Another common fear is that changes may diminish the positive qualities the individual enjoys in the job. Computerizing the customer service positions at Southwestern Bell, for example, threatened the autonomy that representatives previously enjoyed.

FEAR OF FAILURE Some employees fear changes because they fear their own failure. Introducing computers into the workplace often arouses individuals' self-doubts about their ability to interact with the computer.[23] Resistance can also stem from a fear that the change itself will not really take place. In one large library that was undergoing a major automation effort, employees had their doubts as to whether the vendor could really deliver the state-of-the-art system that was promised. In this case, the implementation never became a reality—the employees' fears were well founded.[24]

DISRUPTION OF INTERPERSONAL RELATIONSHIPS Employees may resist change that threatens to limit meaningful interpersonal relationships on the job. Librarians facing the automation effort described previously feared that once the computerized system was implemented, they would not be able to interact as they did when they had to go to another floor of the library to get help finding a resource. In the new system, with the touch of a few buttons on the computer, they would get their information without consulting another librarian.

PERSONALITY CONFLICTS When the change agent's personality engenders negative reactions, employees may resist the change.[26] A change agent who appears insensitive to employee concerns and feelings may meet considerable resistance, because employees perceive that their needs are not being taken into account.

POLITICS Organizational change may also shift the existing balance of power in the organization. Individuals or groups who hold power under the current arrangement may be threatened with losing these political advantages in the advent of change.

CULTURAL ASSUMPTIONS AND VALUES Sometimes cultural assumptions and values can be impediments to change, particularly if the assumptions underlying the change are alien to employees. This form of resistance can be very difficult to overcome, because some cultural assumptions are unconscious. As we discussed in Chapter 2, some cultures tend to avoid uncertainty. In Mexican and Greek cultures, for example, change that creates a great deal of uncertainty may be met with great resistance.

Points to Emphasize
When organizations are changing, it is likely that employees will experience several of the fears and other factors that often lead to resistance.

Some individuals are more tolerant of ambiguity. You can assess your own attitude toward ambiguity by using Challenge 18.1.

We have described several sources of resistance to change. The reasons for resistance are as diverse as the workforce itself and vary with individuals and organizations. The challenge for managers is introducing change in a positive manner and managing employee resistance.

Managing Resistance to Change

The traditional view of resistance to change treated it as something to be overcome, and many organizational attempts to reduce the resistance have only served to intensify it. The contemporary view holds that resistance is simply a form of feedback and that this feedback can be used very productively to manage the change process.[26] One key to managing resistance is to plan for it and to be ready with a variety of strategies for using the resistance as feedback and helping employees negotiate the transition. Three key strategies for managing resistance to change are communication, participation, and empathy and support.[27]

Communication about impending change is essential if employees are to adjust effectively. The details of the change should be provided, but equally important is the rationale behind the change. Employees want to know why change is needed. If there is no good reason for it, why should they favor the change? Providing accurate and timely information about the change can help prevent unfounded fears and potentially damaging rumors from developing. It is also beneficial to inform people about the potential consequences of the change. Educating employees on new work procedures is often helpful. Studies on the introduction of computers in the workplace indicate that providing employees with opportunities for hands-on practice helps alleviate fears about the new technology. Employees who have experience with computers display more positive attitudes and greater efficacy—a sense that they can master their new tasks.[28]

Points to Emphasize
Resistance may be a form of feedback or a request for additional information. Recognizing this, managers should attempt to proactively provide as much information about changing situations as possible.

There is substantial research support underscoring the importance of participation in the change process. In a classic study, workers in a garment factory

CHALLENGE

■ 18.1

Tolerance for Ambiguity

Tolerance for Ambiguity Survey Form

Please read each of the following statements carefully. Then rate each of them in terms of the extent to which you either agree or disagree with the statement using the following scale:

Completely Disagree			Neither Agree nor Disagree			Completely Agree
1	2	3	4	5	6	7

Place the number that best describes your degree of agreement or disagreement in the blank to the left of each statement.

____ **1.** An expert who doesn't come up with a definite answer probably doesn't know much.
____ **2.** I would like to live in a foreign country for a while.
____ **3.** The sooner we all acquire similar values and ideals the better.
____ **4.** A good teacher is one who makes you wonder about your way of looking at things.
____ **5.** I like parties where I know most of the people more than ones where all or most of the people are complete strangers.
____ **6.** Teachers or supervisors who hand out vague assignments give a chance for one to show initiative and originality.
____ **7.** A person who leads an even, regular life in which few surprises or unexpected happenings arise really has a lot to be grateful for.
____ **8.** Many of our most important decisions are based upon insufficient information.
____ **9.** There is really no such thing as a problem that can't be solved.
____ **10.** People who fit their lives to a schedule probably miss most of the joy of living.
____ **11.** A good job is one where what is to be done and how it is to be done are always clear.
____ **12.** It is more fun to tackle a complicated problem than to solve a simple one.
____ **13.** In the long run, it is possible to get more done by tackling small, simple problems rather than large and complicated ones.
____ **14.** Often the most interesting and stimulating people are those who don't mind being different and original.
____ **15.** What we are used to is always preferable to what is unfamiliar.

Scoring: For even-numbered questions, add the total points.
For odd-numbered questions, use reverse scoring and add the total points.
Your score is the total of the even- and odd-numbered questions.

Alternate Example
A major criticism in the area of restructuring and layoffs is that managers usually wait too long to tell employees what lies ahead. Managers may mistakenly think that employees do not need to know, or already know, that a major change is in the air.

were introduced to change in three different ways. One group was simply told about the new procedure, one group was introduced to the change by a trained worker, and one group was allowed to help plan the implementation of the new production. The results were dramatic. The third group, those who participated in the change, adopted the new method more quickly, was more productive, and experienced no turnover.[29] Participation helps employees become involved in the change and establish a feeling of ownership in the process. When employees are allowed to participate, they are more committed to the change.

Another strategy for managing resistance is providing empathy and support to employees who have trouble dealing with the change. Active listening, as was discussed in Chapter 8, is an excellent tool for identifying the reasons behind resistance and for uncovering fears. An expression of concerns about the change can provide important feedback that managers can use to improve the change

CHALLENGE ■ **18.1 continued**

Norms Using the Tolerance for Ambiguity Scale

Source: The Tolerance for Ambiguity Scale

Basis: The survey asks 15 questions about personal and work-oriented situations with ambiguity. You were asked to rate each situation on a scale from one (tolerant) to seven (intolerant). (Alternating questions have the response scale reversed.) The index scores the items. A perfectly tolerant person would score 15 and a perfectly intolerant person 105. Scores between 20 and 80 are reported with means of 45. The responses to the even-numbered questions with 7 minus the score are added to the response for the odd-numbered questions.

The Scale:

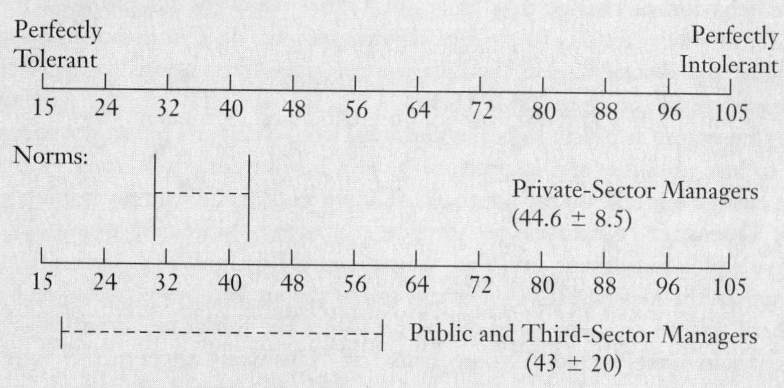

SOURCE: D. Marcic, *Organizational Behavior: Experiences and Cases*, p. 339–340. St. Paul, MN: West Publishing, 1992. Adapted from Paul Nutt. Used with permission.

process. Emotional support and encouragement can help an employee deal with the anxiety that is a natural response to change. Employees who experience severe reactions to change can benefit from talking with a counselor. Some companies provide counseling through their employee assistance plans.

Open communication, participation, and emotional support can go a long way toward managing resistance to change. Managers must realize that some resistance is inevitable, however, and should plan ways to deal with resistance early in the change process.

Managing resistance to change is a long and often arduous process. GTE Mobilnet faced substantial resistance to change when it implemented its customer connection initiative, with the goal of building a cellular-phone network that ranks first in customer service. The change agent, Ben Powell, and his teammates tried to persuade staffers at Mobilnet's 350 service centers to send new cellular phones out the door with fully charged batteries in them. The salespeople liked the idea—they could tell customers that their phones were ready to use when they sold them. Service workers, however, balked at the idea because they were the ones who had to install the batteries.

Powell and his team essentially repeated the following dialogue 350 times: "You can't see why you need to bother with installing the batteries? Here are sales figures showing how much revenue we lose by making customers wait to use their phones. The average customer calls everybody he knows when he first gets the thing, like a kid with a new toy—but only if it has a charged battery in it. Don't have room to stock all those batteries? We'll help you redesign your workspace to accommodate them. Can't predict how many of which battery you'll need on hand at any given time? We'll provide data to help you with those projections. Can't afford any of this to come out of your operating budget? We'll fund it for you."

Powell says, "When you meet this kind of resistance, the only thing you can do is keep plugging away. . . . Finally, in the last six months or so we have been getting to the point where we're really changing how we do business. But it's taken years. Not weeks. Not months. On a day-to-day basis, it feels like bowling in sand."[30]

Behavioral Reactions to Change

In spite of attempts to minimize the resistance to change in an organization, some reactions to change are inevitable. Negative reactions may be manifested in overt behavior, or change may be resisted more passively. People show four basic, identifiable reactions to change: disengagement, disidentification, disenchantment, and disorientation.[31] Managers can use interventions to deal with these reactions, as shown in Table 18.1.

disengagement

Psychological withdrawal from change.

Points to Emphasize

Many seniors in college suffer from a form of disengagement from the university. They know they need to become active in job seeking; yet, they delay, avoiding the inevitable.

Disengagement is psychological withdrawal from change. The employee may appear to lose initiative and interest in the job. Employees who disengage may fear the change but take on the approach of doing nothing and simply hoping for the best. Disengaged employees are physically present but mentally absent. They lack drive and commitment, and they simply comply without real psychological investment in their work. Disengagement can be recognized by behaviors such as being hard to find or doing only the basics to get the job done. Typical disengagement statements include "No problem" or "This won't affect me."

The basic managerial strategy for dealing with disengaged individuals is to confront them with their reaction and draw them out so that they can identify the concerns that need to be addressed. Disengaged employees may not be aware of the change in their behavior, and they need to be assured of your intentions. Drawing them out and helping them air their feelings can lead to productive discussions. Disengaged people seldom become cheerleaders for the change, but they can be brought closer to accepting and working with a change by open communication with an empathetic manager who is willing to listen.

disidentification

Feeling that one's identify is being threatened by a change.

Alternate Example

Disidentification is a key to outplacement counseling. Many individuals cannot move on to the next step during the first few days of outplacement. They will continually refer to the past as if they were still part of the decision making process.

Another reaction to change is **disidentification.** Individuals reacting in this way feel that their identity has been threatened by the change, and they feel very vulnerable. Many times they cling to a past procedure because they had a sense of mastery over it, and it gave them a sense of security. "My job is completely changed" and "I used to . . ." are verbal indications of disidentification. Disidentified employees often display sadness and worry. They may appear to be sulking and dwelling in the past by reminiscing about the old ways of doing things.

Because disidentified employees are so vulnerable, they often feel like victims in the change process. Managers can help them through the transition by encouraging them to explore their feelings and helping them transfer their positive feelings into the new situation. One way to do this is to help them identify what it is they liked in the old situation, as well as to show them how it is possible to have the same positive experience in the new situation. Disidentified employees need to see that work itself and emotion are separable—that is, that they can let go of old ways and experience positive reactions to new ways of performing their jobs.

disenchantment

Feeling negativity or anger toward a change.

Disenchantment is also a common reaction to change. It is usually expressed as negativity or anger. Disenchanted employees realize that the past is gone, and they are mad about it. They may try to enlist the support of other employees by forming coalitions. Destructive behaviors like sabotage and backstabbing may

■ **TABLE 18.1**

Reactions to Change and Managerial Interventions

REACTION	EXPRESSION	MANAGERIAL INTERVENTION
Disengagement	Withdrawal	Confront, identify
Disidentification	Sadness, worry	Explore, transfer
Disenchantment	Anger	Neutralize, acknowledge
Disorientation	Confusion	Explain, plan

SOURCE: Adapted from H. Woodward and S. Buchholz, *Aftershock: Helping People through Corporate Change,* p. 15. Copyright © 1987 John Wiley & Sons, Inc. Reprinted with permission of John Wiley & Sons, Inc.

result. Typical verbal signs of disenchantment are "This will never work" and "I'm getting out of this company as soon as I can." The anger of a disenchanted person may be directly expressed in organizational cultures where it is permissible to do so. This behavior tends to get the issues out in the open. More often, however, cultures view the expression of emotion at work as improper and unbusinesslike. In these cultures, the anger is suppressed and emerges in more passive-aggressive ways, such as badmouthing and starting rumors. One of the particular dangers of disenchantment is that it is quite contagious in the workplace.

It is often difficult to reason with disenchanted employees. Thus, the first step in managing this reaction is to bring these employees from their highly negative, emotionally charged state to a more neutral state. To neutralize the reaction does not mean to dismiss it; rather, it means to allow the individuals to let off the necessary steam so that they can come to terms with their anger. The second part of the strategy for dealing with disenchanted employees is to acknowledge that their anger is normal and that you do not hold it against them. Sometimes disenchantment is a mask for one of the other three reactions, and it must be worked through to get to the core of the employee's reaction.

A final reaction to change is **disorientation.** Disorientated employees are lost and confused, and often they are unsure of their feelings. They waste energy trying to figure out what to do instead of how to do things. Disoriented individuals ask a lot of questions and become very detail-oriented. They may appear to need a good deal of guidance and may leave their work undone until all of their questions have been answered. "Analysis paralysis" is characteristic of disoriented employees. They feel that they have lost touch with the priorities of the company, and they may want to analyze the change to death before acting on it. Disoriented employees may ask questions like "Now what do I do?" or "What do I do first?"

disorientation

Feelings of loss and confusion due to a change.

Disorientation is a common reaction among people who are used to clear goals and unambiguous directions. When change is introduced, it creates uncertainty and a lack of clarity. The managerial strategy for dealing with this reaction is to explain the change in a way that minimizes the ambiguity that is present. The information about the change needs to be put into a framework or an overall vision so that the disoriented individual can see where he or she fits into the grand scheme of things. Once the disoriented employee sees the broader context of the change, you can plan a series of steps to help this employee adjust. The employee needs a sense of priorities to work on.

Managers need to be able to diagnose these four reactions to change. Because each reaction brings with it significant and different concerns, no single universal strategy can help all employees adjust. By recognizing each reaction and applying the appropriate strategy, it is possible to help even strong resisters work through a transition successfully.

Lewin's Change Model

Kurt Lewin developed a model of the change process that has stood the test of time and continues to influence the way organizations manage planned change. Lewin's model is based on the idea of force field analysis.[32] Figure 18.1 shows a force field analysis of a decision to engage in exercise behavior.

Discussion Consideration
Often, when change efforts encounter difficulties, it is because managers have not spent enough time on the unfreezing portion of the model. Ask students for examples from their personal experience of times when unfreezing was not attempted in a change event.

This model contends that a person's behavior is the product of two opposing forces; one force pushes toward preserving the status quo, and another force pushes for change. When the two opposing forces are approximately equal, current behavior is maintained. For behavioral change to occur, the forces maintaining status quo must be overcome. This can be accomplished by increasing the forces for change, by weakening the forces for status quo, or by a combination of these actions. Challenge 18.2 asks you to apply force field analysis to a problem in your life.

Lewin's change model is a three-step process, as shown in Figure 18.2. The process begins with **unfreezing,** which is a crucial first hurdle in the change process. Unfreezing involves encouraging individuals to discard old behaviors by shaking up the equilibrium state that maintains the status quo. Organizations often accomplish unfreezing by eliminating the rewards for current behavior and showing that current behavior is not valued. Unfreezing on the part of individuals is an acceptance that change needs to occur. In essence, individuals surrender by allowing the boundaries of their status quo to be opened in preparation for change.[33]

unfreezing
The first step in Lewin's change model, which involves encouraging individuals to discard old behaviors by shaking up the equilibrium state that maintains the status quo.

The second step in the change process is **moving.** In the moving stage, new attitudes, values, and behaviors are substituted for old ones. Organizations accomplish moving by initiating new options and explaining the rationale for the change, as well as by providing training to help employees develop the new skills they need. Employees should be given the overarching vision for the change so that they can establish their roles within the new organizational structure and processes.[34]

moving
The second step in Lewin's change model, in which new attitudes, values, and behaviors are substituted for old ones.

Refreezing is the final step in the change process. In this step, new attitudes, values, and behaviors are established as the new status quo. The new ways of operating are cemented in and reinforced. Managers should ensure that the organizational culture and formal reward systems encourage the new behaviors and avoid rewarding the old ways of operating. Changes in the reward structure may be needed to ensure that the organization is not rewarding the old behaviors and merely hoping for the new behaviors. A study by Exxon Research and Engineering showed that framing and displaying a mission statement in managers' offices may eventually change the behavior of 2 percent of the managers.

refreezing
The final step in Lewin's change model, which involves the establishment of new attitudes, values, and behaviors as the new status quo.

FIGURE 18.1
Force Field Analysis of a Decision to Engage in Exercise

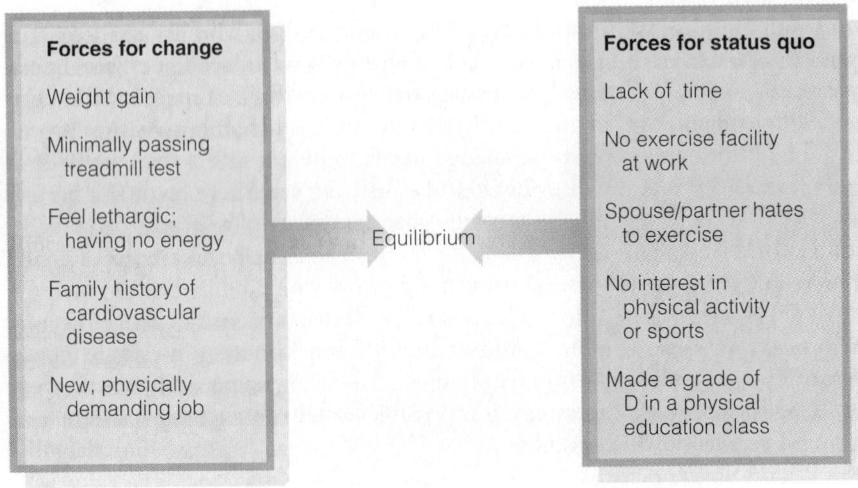

CHALLENGE

■ **18.2**

Applying Force Field Analysis

Think of a problem you are currently facing. An example would be trying to increase the amount of study time you devote to a particular class.

1. Describe the problem, as specifically as possible.
2. List the forces driving change on the arrows at the left side of the diagram.
3. List the forces restraining change on the arrows at the right side of the diagram.
4. What can you do, specifically, to remove the obstacles to change?
5. What can you do to increase the forces driving change?
6. What benefits can be derived from breaking a problem down into forces driving change and forces restraining change?

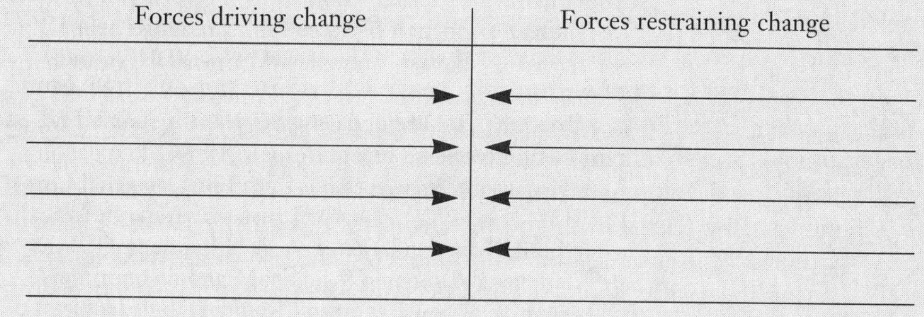

■ **FIGURE 18.2**

Lewin's Change Model

Unfreezing	Moving	Refreezing
Reducing forces for status quo	Developing new attitudes, values, and behaviors	Reinforcing new attitudes, values, and behaviors

In contrast, changing managers' evaluation and reward systems will change the behavior of 55 percent of the managers almost overnight.[35]

Monsanto's approach to increasing opportunities for women within the company is an illustration of how to use the Lewin model effectively. First, Monsanto emphasized unfreezing by helping employees debunk negative stereotypes about women in business. This also helped overcome resistance to change. Second, Monsanto moved employees' attitudes and behaviors by diversity training in which differences were emphasized as positive, and supervisors learned ways of training and developing female employees. Third, Monsanto changed its reward system so that managers were evaluated and paid according to how they coached and promoted women, which helped refreeze the new attitudes and behaviors.

http://www.monsanto.com

Lewin's model proposes that for change efforts to be successful, the three-stage process must be completed. Failures in efforts to change can be traced back to one of the three stages. Successful change thus requires that old behaviors be discarded, new behaviors be introduced, and these new behaviors be institutionalized and rewarded. This is a learning process, and the learning theories discussed in Chapter 6 certainly apply. Skinner's work helps us understand how to encourage new behaviors and extinguish old ones by using reinforcers. Bandura's social learning theory points out the importance of modeling. Managers should model appropriate behavior, because employees look to them and pattern their own behavior after the managers' behavior.

Organizations that wish to change can select from a variety of methods to make a change become reality. Organization development is a method that consists of various programs for making organizations more effective.

Organization Development Interventions

organizational development (OD)

A systematic approach to organizational improvement that applies behavioral science theory and research in order to increase individual and organizational well-being and effectiveness.

Alternate Example

The force field analysis technique is an excellent tool for unfreezing a system. When the need for change and the forces against the change are made explicit, employees are more receptive to the change. Thus, force field analysis can be a useful communication tool.

■ **Organization development (OD)** is a systematic approach to organizational improvement that applies behavioral science theory and research in order to increase individual and organizational well-being and effectiveness.[36] This definition implies certain characteristics. First, OD is a systematic approach to planned change. It is a structured cycle of diagnosing organizational problems and opportunities and then applying expertise to them. Second, OD is grounded in solid research and theory. It involves the application of our knowledge of behavioral science to the challenges that organizations face. Third, OD recognizes the reciprocal relationship between individuals and organizations. It acknowledges that for organizations to change, individuals must change. Finally, OD is goal-oriented. It is a process that seeks to improve both individual and organizational well-being and effectiveness.

Organization development has a rich history. Some of the early work in OD was conducted by Kurt Lewin and his associates during the 1940s. This work was continued by Rensis Likert, who pioneered the use of attitude surveys in OD. During the 1950s, Eric Trist and his colleagues at the Tavistock Institute in London focused on the technical and social aspects of organizations and how they affect the quality of work life. These programs on the quality of work life migrated to the United States during the 1960s. During this time, a 200-member OD network was established, and it has grown to over 2,000 members today. As the number of practitioners has increased, so has the number of different OD methods. One compendium of organizational change methods estimates that over 300 different methods have been used.[37]

Organization development is also being used internationally. OD has been applied in Canada, Sweden, Norway, Germany, Japan, Australia, Israel, and Mexico, among others. Some OD methods are difficult to implement in other cultures. As OD becomes more internationally widespread, we will increase our knowledge of how culture affects the success of different OD approaches.

Prior to deciding on a method of intervention, managers must carefully diagnose the problem they are attempting to address. Diagnosis and needs analysis is a critical first step in any OD intervention. Following this, an intervention method is chosen and applied. Finally, a thorough follow-up of the OD process is conducted. Figure 18.3 presents the OD cycle, a continuous process of moving the organization and its employees toward effective functioning.

Diagnosis and Needs Analysis

Before any intervention is planned, a thorough organizational diagnosis should be conducted. Diagnosis is an essential first step for any organization development intervention.[38] The term *diagnosis* comes from *dia* (through) and *gnosis* (knowledge of). Thus, the diagnosis should pinpoint specific problems and areas in need of improvement. Problems can arise in any part of the organization. Six areas to examine carefully are the organization's purpose, structure, reward system, support systems, relationships, and leadership.[39]

Harry Levinson's diagnostic approach asserts that the process should begin by identifying where the pain (the problem) in the organization is, what it is like, how long it has been happening, and what has already been done about it.[40] Then a four-part, comprehensive diagnosis can begin. The first part of the diagnosis is an understanding of the organization's history. The second part is an

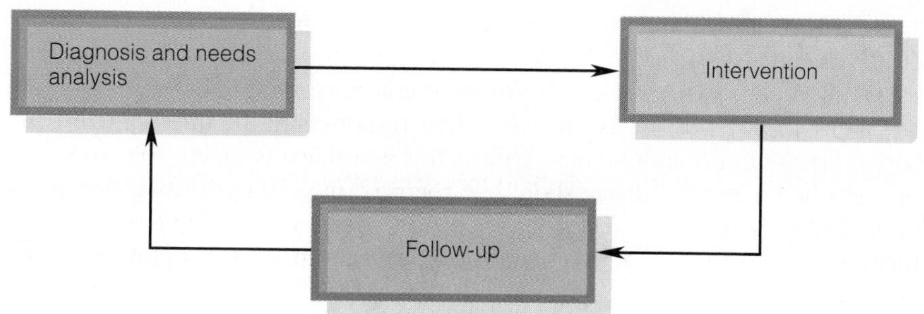

■ **FIGURE 18.3**

The Organization Development Cycle

analysis of the organization as a whole to obtain data about the structure and processes of the organization. The third part is the gathering of interpretive data about attitudes, relationships, and current organizational functioning. The fourth part of the diagnosis is an analysis of the data and conclusions. The data in each stage of the diagnosis can be gathered using a variety of methods, including observation, interviews, questionnaires, and archival records.

The diagnostic process may yield the conclusion that change is necessary. As part of the diagnosis, it is important to address the following issues:

- What are the forces for change?
- What are the forces preserving the status quo?
- What are the most likely sources of resistance to change?
- What are the goals to be accomplished by the change?

This information constitutes a force field analysis, as discussed earlier in the chapter.

A needs analysis is another crucial step in managing change. This is an analysis of the skills and competencies that employees must have to achieve the goals of the change. A needs analysis is essential because interventions such as training programs must target these skills and competencies.

Hundreds of alternative OD intervention methods exist. One way of classifying these methods is by the target of change. The target of change may be the organization, groups within the organization, or individuals.

Organization- and Group-Focused Techinques

Some OD intervention methods emphasize changing the organization itself or changing the work groups within the organization. Intervention methods in this category are survey feedback, management by objectives, product and service quality programs, team building, and process consultation.

SURVEY FEEDBACK A widely used intervention method whereby employee attitudes are solicited using a questionnaire is known as **survey feedback.** Once the data are collected, they are analyzed and fed back to the employees to diagnose problems and plan other interventions. Survey feedback is often used as an exploratory tool and then is combined with some other intervention. The effectiveness of survey feedback in actually improving outcomes (absenteeism or productivity, for example) increases substantially when this method is combined with other interventions.[41]

survey feedback
A widely used method of intervention whereby employee attitudes are solicited using a questionnaire.

Discussion Consideration
Ask students what it would take to get them to respond to a survey that takes ten minutes to complete.

Some surveys are developed by managers within the organization and tailored to a specific problem or issue. Well-established and widely used surveys also are available for use. Two such surveys are the Survey of Organizations and the Michigan Organizational Assessment Questionnaire, both of which were developed at the University of Michigan's Institute for Social Research.[42] A large body of research indicates that these surveys have good reliability and validity, and they are useful tools for gathering employees' perceptions of their work environments.

For survey feedback to be an effective method, certain guidelines should be used. Employees must be assured that their responses to the questionnaire will be confidential and anonymous. Unless this assurance is given, the responses may not be honest. Feedback should be reported in a group format; that is, no individual responses should be identified. Employees must be able to trust that there will be no negative repercussions from their responses. Employees should be informed of the purpose of the survey. Failing to do this can set up unrealistic expectations about the changes that might come from the surveys.

In addition, management must be prepared to follow up on the survey results. If some things cannot be changed, the rationale (for example, prohibitive cost) must be explained to the employees. Without appropriate follow-through, employees will not take the survey process seriously the next time.

management by objectives (MBO)
An organization-wide intervention technique that involves joint goal setting between employees and managers.

MANAGEMENT BY OBJECTIVES As an organization-wide technique, **management by objectives (MBO)** involves joint goal setting between employees and managers. The MBO process includes the setting of initial objectives, periodic progress reviews, and problem solving to remove any obstacles to goal achievement.[43] All these steps are joint efforts between managers and employees.

MBO is a valuable intervention because it meets three needs. First, it clarifies what is expected of employees. This reduces role conflict and ambiguity. Second, MBO provides knowledge of results, an essential ingredient in effective job performance. Finally, MBO provides an opportunity for coaching and counseling by the manager. The problem-solving approach encourages open communication and discussion of obstacles to goal achievement.[44]

Companies that have used MBO successfully include Tenneco, Mobil Oil, and General Electric. The success of MBO in effecting organizational results hinges on the linking of individual goals to the goals of the organization. MBO is usually tailored to the organization; as such, MBO programs may appear to differ widely across organizations.[45] However, the programs all focus on joint goal setting and evaluation. There is a caution to be exercised in using MBO programs. An excessive emphasis on goal achievement can result in cut-throat competition among employees, falsification of results, and striving for results at any cost. In addition, top management support is essential if the program aspires to be more than just an exercise in red tape.

quality program
A program that embeds product and service quality excellence into the organizational culture.

PRODUCT AND SERVICE QUALITY PROGRAMS **Quality programs**—programs that embed product and service quality excellence into the organized culture—are assuming key roles in the organization development efforts of many companies. For example, the success or failure of a service company may depend on the quality of customer service it provides.[46] The quality revolution consists of programs that entail two steps. The first step is to raise aspirations about the product and service quality, both within the company and among its customers. If the organization is to improve, employees must be committed to product and service quality excellence, and customers must expect it. The second step is to embed product and service quality excellence in the organizational culture, using continual improvement tools such as benchmarking to change habits, attitudes, skills, and knowledge. Benchmarking is comparing products and processes with those of other companies in order to imitate and improve on them. Xerox uses benchmarking to improve the product quality of its copiers. Service quality improvement programs can lead to competitive advantage, increased productivity, enhanced employee morale, and word-of-mouth advertising from satisfied customers. One company known for service quality is Gateway 2000, a mail-order computer business based in North Sioux City, South Dakota. The company provides toll-free technical support for the life of the cus-

http://www.gwdk.com/

tomer's Gateway computer system, and it is reputed to have the best-qualified technical support staff in the industry.

The Ritz-Carlton® Hotel Company integrates its comprehensive service quality program into marketing and business objectives. The Atlanta-based company manages twenty-eight luxury hotels and won the 1992 Malcolm Baldrige Award for service quality. Key elements of Ritz-Carlton's quality program include participatory executive leadership, thorough information gathering, coordinated execution, and employees who are empowered to "move heaven and earth" to satisfy customers.[47]

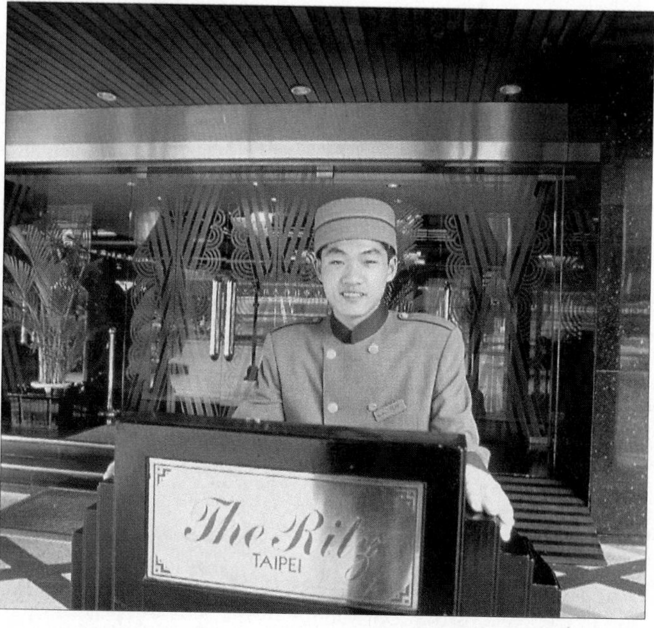

Employees at Ritz-Carlton Hotels are empowered to "move heaven and earth" to satisfy customers. Quality teams are in place at all levels of the company.

At Ritz-Carlton, the company president and thirteen senior executives make up the senior quality management team, which meets weekly to focus on service quality. Quality goals are established at all levels of the company. The crucial product and service requirements of travel consumers are translated into Ritz-Carlton Gold Standards, which include a credo, a motto, three steps of service, and twenty Ritz-Carlton Basics. These standards guide service quality throughout the organization.

Employees are required to act on a customer complaint at once and are empowered to provide "instant pacification," no matter what it takes. Quality teams set action plans at all levels of the company. Each hotel has a quality leader, who serves as a resource to the quality teams. Daily quality production reports provide an early warning system for identifying areas that need quality improvement.

The Ritz-Carlton program has all of the hallmarks of an excellent service quality program: committed leadership, empowered teams and employees, carefully researched standards and goals, and constant monitoring. The company has reaped rewards from its excellent service; it received 121 quality-related awards in 1991, along with best-in-industry rankings from all three major hotel-ranking organizations.

After celebrating an award as the best hotel in the world, Ritz-Carlton did not stop its quality improvement process. At one hotel, the chief complaint was that room service was always late. A quality team was put together, including a cook, a waiter, and a room service order taker. They studied how the process flowed. Then it was discovered that the service elevator was slow. So they brought an engineer and a representative from the elevator company into the team. They found the elevators worked well. Next they posted a team member in the elevator 24 hours a day for a week. Every time the door opened, the team member had to find out why. Finally, a team member noticed that housemen who helped the maids got on the elevator a lot. It turned out that the housemen were stealing towels from other floors because their maids needed more. The problem with room service was that the hotel didn't own enough towels. Ritz-Carlton bought more towels, and room service complaints fell 50 percent.[48]

TEAM BUILDING As an organization development intervention, **team building** can improve the effectiveness of work groups. Team building usually begins with a diagnostic process through which team members identify problems, and it continues with the team's planning actions to take in order to resolve those problems. The OD practitioner in team building serves as a facilitator, and the work itself is completed by team members.[49]

team building
An intervention designed to improve the effectiveness of a work group.

Discussion Consideration
Ask students to discuss their experiences with group projects in college and then compare them with the team-building concepts. Which components were missing? In retrospect, could they have built "teams" out of their groups?

Team building is a very popular OD method. A recent survey of Fortune 500 companies indicated that human resource managers considered team building the most successful OD technique.[50] Four areas in team building are critical to the success of the intervention:

1. Team building should develop communication that facilitates respect for other members' input and the desire to work for the good of the team.
2. Team building should encourage member interaction and mutual interdependence.
3. Team building should emphasize team goals. Team members should learn one another's responsibilities so that the team can deal adaptively with crisis situations.
4. Team building must provide examples of effective and ineffective teamwork, and it should stress flexibility.[51]

One popular technique for team building is the use of outdoor challenges. Participants go through a series of outdoor activities, such as climbing a 14-foot wall. Similar physical challenges require the participants to work as a team and focus on trust, communication, decision making, and leadership. GE and Weyerhaeuser use outdoor challenges at the beginning of their team-building courses, and later in the training, team members apply what they have learned to actual business situations.[52]

Because team building is a relatively new intervention, it is difficult to assess its effectiveness. Preliminary studies, however, indicate that team building can improve group processes.[53]

process consultation

An OD method that helps managers and employers improve the processes that are used in organizations.

Points to Emphasize

One of the reasons that outside consultants are used is for trust and confidentiality. These consultants are careful to ensure that individuals' comments and concerns are not reported inappropriately to superiors. Additionally, outside consultants can also bring fresh ideas to the organization because they are not bound to the organizations norms and hierarchy.

PROCESS CONSULTATION Pioneered by Edgar Schein, **process consultation** is an OD method that helps managers and employees improve the processes that are used in organizations.[54] The processes most often targeted are communication, conflict resolution, decision making, group interaction, and leadership.

One of the distinguishing features of the process consultation approach is that an outside consultant is used. The role of the consultant is to help employees help themselves. The consultant guides the organization members in examining the processes in the organization and in refining them. The steps in process consultation are entering the organization, defining the relationship, choosing an approach, gathering data and diagnosing problems, intervening, and gradually leaving the organization.

Process consultation is an interactive technique between employees and an outside consultant, so it is seldom used as a sole OD method. Most often, it is used in combination with other OD interventions.

All the preceding OD methods focus on changing the organization or the work group. Other OD methods are aimed at facilitating change within individuals.

Individual-Focused Techniques

Organization development efforts that are targeted toward individuals include skills training, sensitivity training, management development training, role negotiation, job redesign, stress management programs, and career planning.

skills training

Increasing the job knowledge, skills, and abilities that are necessary to do a job effectively.

SKILLS TRAINING The key question addressed by **skills training** is, "What knowledge, skills, and abilities are necessary to do this job effectively?" Skills training is accomplished either in formal classroom settings or on the job. The challenge of integrating skills training into organization development is the rapid change that most organizations face. The job knowledge in most positions requires continual updates to keep pace with rapid change.

Federal Express depends on 45,000 employees in 700 different locations across 135 countries to deliver 100 percent customer satisfaction. The company is constantly changing its products and services, sometimes at the rate of 1,700 changes per year. FedEx decided to accomplish its mission using interactive video training and job skills testing. The video training consists of twenty-five laser disks updated with a CD-ROM every six weeks. Employees find the interactive video training easy to use, convenient, and individualized. FedEx has found it to be economical, by eliminating travel expenses and the need for instructors. In job skills testing, every customer service employee takes a test every six months via computer. The test generates a unique prescription that informs employees what they do well and how they need to improve. It also directs employees to the interactive video lesson they need to practice to improve their skills.[55]

SENSITIVITY TRAINING Also called T-group training, **sensitivity training** is designed to help individuals understand how their behavior affects others. In a typical session, groups of ten to twelve strangers (T-groups) are formed. Participants from the same organization are placed in different T-groups. The trainer serves as a resource person but does not engage in structuring behaviors. The members are left on their own to work out the interaction in the group, and they are encouraged to concentrate on the "here and now" of the experience and on openness with other group members. It is important that the trainer be well qualified to monitor the group's progress. The trainer intervenes only to help move the group forward.[56]

sensitivity training

An intervention designed to help individuals understand how their behavior affects others.

The outcome of sensitivity training should be an increased sensitivity to others, and in some cases this has been demonstrated. In other cases, however, the new and better ways of dealing with others did not persist on the job. When people returned to their jobs, which rewarded the old behaviors, the new behavior patterns were quickly extinguished. There are also side effects from T-groups. Because they result in emotional exposure, some participants feel vulnerable and react negatively to the extreme personal nature of the interactions.

Sensitivity training is less popular today than it was in the early 1980s.[57] It can still be used, however, to help managers deal with current challenges like cultural, gender, age, and ability diversity. T-groups can help employees understand others better, become aware of their own feelings and perceptions, and improve communication.

MANAGEMENT DEVELOPMENT TRAINING **Management development** encompasses a host of techniques designed to enhance a manager's skills on the job. Management development training generally focuses on four types of learning: verbal information, intellectual skills, attitudes, and development. Verbal information that is disseminated in training, such as information on leadership theory, can be assessed with objective measures like tests. Intellectual skills, such as how to conduct a performance appraisal in a specific format, can be evaluated by performance demonstrations. Attitudes, such as attitudes toward workforce diversity, can be assessed via questionnaires. Development—a change in self-knowledge and behavior—is more difficult to evaluate. It can be assessed, however, by descriptive reports from the manager, performance appraisals from the manager's supervisor, and organizational outcomes.[58]

management development

A host of techniques for enhancing managers' skills in an organization.

Development as a manager requires an integration of classroom learning with on-the-job experiences. One way of accomplishing development is through the use of action learning, a technique that was pioneered in Europe.[59] In action learning, managers take on unfamiliar problems or familiar problems in unfamiliar settings. The managers work on the problems and meet weekly in small groups made up of individuals from different organizations. The outcome of action learning is that managers learn about themselves through the challenges of their comrades. Other techniques that provide active learning for participants are simulation, business games, role-playing, and case studies.[60]

Management development can be conducted in a formal classroom setting or consist of on-the-job training. If a classroom setting is used, it is essential that follow-up be done to ensure that the skills transfer to the job. Some ways to accomplish this are presented in the Scientific Foundation feature.

SCIENTIFIC FOUNDATION

Making Sure Management Training Works

One of the key criteria for evaluating any management development effort is transfer of training; that is, the degree to which trainees apply the new skills they've learned when they return to the job. This study examined whether the climate and culture of the organization could influence transfers of management training.

Climate is the employee's perception of the immediate work environment. A positive transfer climate is one in which social cues such as interactions among trainees, peers, and supervisors prompt trainees to apply their training to the jobs. The more positive the interactions, the more likely the employee will demonstrate the trained behaviors and skills. A continuous-learning culture is an organizational culture in which learning is an essential responsibility in every employee's job, and all members share the perception that learning is an important part of everyday work life. The researchers in this study hypothesized the following: (1) A positive transfer-of-training climate will be related to greater transfer of training (posttraining behaviors); and (2) a continuous learning culture will be related to greater transfer of training (posttraining behaviors).

Participants in the study were supermarket managers. A total of 104 management trainees were included, along with 104 supervisors and 297 of the trainees' coworkers. Thus a total of 505 managers from 52 stores were involved in the study. Three weeks before attending training, trainees and their supervisors completed a measure of supervisory behaviors. Next, the trainees attended a management training program. At the end of the training, trainees completed a climate and culture questionnaire and were asked to distribute the questionnaire to four or five managerial coworkers and their supervisor. Then six to eight weeks after the training, each trainee and his or her supervisor completed a post-training behavior questionnaire.

The results showed that both positive transfer-of-training and continuous learning culture were related to post-training behaviors. Trainees who worked in a climate that encouraged them to display their learned behaviors and in a culture that valued continuous learning demonstrated more of their newly-acquired skills on their jobs. Thus, the work environment can be structured to encourage transfer of training. Specifically, organizations should examine their work environments to make sure that trainees receive social support for practicing their new skills on the job.

SOURCE: J. B. Tracey, S. I. Tannenbaum, and M. J. Kavanaugh, "Applying Training Skills on the Job: The Importance of the Work Environment," *Journal of Applied Psychology* 80 (1995): 239–252.

Management development should be based on a careful needs assessment. The content of the program should focus on the skills that managers must possess to be successful in the future.

role negotiation

A technique whereby individuals meet and clarify their psychological contract.

ROLE NEGOTIATION Individuals who work together sometimes have differing expectations of one another within the working relationship. **Role negotiation** is a simple technique whereby individuals meet and clarify their psychological contract. In doing this, the expectations of each party are clarified and negotiated. The outcome of role negotiation is a better understanding between the two parties of what each can be expected to give and receive in the reciprocal relationship. When both parties have a mutual agreement on expectations, there is less ambiguity in the process of working together.

job redesign

An OD intervention method that alters jobs to improve the fit between individual skills and the demands of the job.

JOB REDESIGN As an OD intervention method, **job redesign** emphasizes the fit between individual skills and the demands of the job. Chapter 14 outlined several approaches to job design. Many of these methods are used as OD techniques for realigning task demands and individual capabilities, or for redesigning jobs to fit new techniques or organization structures better.

One company that has undergone tremendous change is Harley-Davidson. The motorcycle manufacturer was close to financial disaster when it engaged in a radical restructuring effort. The company essentially threw out the old hierarchies and traditional jobs, opted for a leaner organization, and redesigned jobs to allow employees more participation and control. The company credits its renewed success, in part, to its redesign efforts.[61]

Steelcase, the world's leading designer and manufacturer of office furniture, used job redesign as a key component of its comprehensive change from a traditional manufacturing system to a "factory within a factory" design. In the old system, jobs were designed around the principle of task simplicity and specialization. In the new design, operations are arranged by products, with each factory run by a self-managed team. Employees' jobs are now flexible, team oriented, and characterized by high levels of empowerment.

HEALTH PROMOTION PROGRAMS As organizations have become increasingly concerned with the costs of distress in the workplace, health promotion programs have become a part of larger organization development efforts. In Chapter 7, we examined stress and strain at work. Companies that have successfully integrated health promotion programs into their organizations include AT&T, Caterpillar Tractor, Kimberly-Clark, and Johnson & Johnson.

The components of health promotion and stress management programs vary widely. They can include education about stress and coping, diagnosis of the causes of stress, relaxation training, company-provided exercise programs, and employee assistance programs. These efforts all focus on helping employees manage stress before it becomes a problem.

CAREER PLANNING Matching an individual's career aspirations with the opportunities in the organization is career planning. This proactive approach to career management is often part of an organization's development efforts. Career planning is a joint responsibility of organizations and individuals. Companies like IBM, Travelers Insurance, and 3M have implemented career planning programs.

Career planning activities benefit the organization, as well as its individuals. Through counseling sessions, employees identify their skills and skill deficiencies. The organization then can plan its training and development efforts based on this information. In addition, the process can be used to identify and nurture talented employees for potential promotion.

Managers can choose from a host of organization development techniques to facilitate organizational change. Some of these techniques are aimed toward organizations or groups, and others focus on individuals. Large-scale changes in organizations require the use of multiple techniques. For example, implementing a new technology like robotics may require simultaneous changes in the structure of the organization, the configuration of work groups, and individual attitudes.

We should recognize at this point that the organization development methods just described are means to an end. Programs do not drive change; business needs do. The OD methods are merely vehicles for moving the organization and its employees in a more effective direction.

Ethical Considerations in Organization Development

■ Organization development is a process of helping organizations improve. It may involve resistance to change, shifts in power, losses of control, and redefinition of tasks.[62] These are all sensitive issues. Further, the change agent, whether a manager from within the organization or a consultant from outside, is in a position of directing the change. Such a position carries the potential for misuse of power. The ethical concerns surrounding the use of organization development center around four issues.[63]

The first issue is the selection of the OD method to be used. Every change agent has inherent biases about particular methods, but these biases must not enter into the decision process. The OD method used must be carefully chosen in accordance with the problem as diagnosed, the organization's culture, and the employees concerned. All alternatives should be given fair consideration in the choice of a method. In addition, the OD practitioner should never use a method he or she is not skilled in delivering. Using a method you are not an expert in is unethical, because the client assumes you are.

The second ethical issue is voluntary participation. No employee should be forced to participate in any OD intervention.[64] To make an informed decision about participation, employees should be given information about the nature of the intervention and what will be expected of them. They should also be afforded the option to discontinue their participation at any time they so choose.

The third issue of ethical concern is confidentiality. Change agents gather a wealth of information during organizational diagnoses and interventions. Successful change agents develop a trusting relationship with employees. They may receive privileged information, sometimes unknowingly. It is unethical for a change agent to reveal information in order to give some group or individual political advantage or to enhance the change agent's own standing. Consultants should not reveal information about an organization to its competitors. The use of information gathered from OD efforts is a sensitive issue and presents ethical dilemmas.

A final ethical concern in OD is the potential for manipulation by the change agent. Because any change process involves influence, some individuals may feel manipulated. The key to alleviating the potential for manipulation is open communication. Participants should be given complete knowledge of the rationale for change, what they can expect of the change process, and what the intervention will entail. No actions should be taken that limit the participants' freedom of choice.[65]

Are Organization Development Efforts Effective?

■ Because organization development is designed to help organizations manage change, it is important to evaluate the effectiveness of these efforts. The success of any OD intervention depends on a host of factors, including the technique used, the competence of the change agent, the organization's readiness for change, and top management commitment. No single method of OD is effective in every instance. Instead, multiple-method OD approaches are recommended, because they allow organizations to capitalize on the benefits of several approaches.[66]

Recent efforts to evaluate OD efforts have focused on outcomes such as productivity. One review of over 200 interventions indicated that worker productivity improved in 87 percent of the cases.[67] A separate analysis of ninety-eight of these interventions revealed impressive productivity increases.[68] We can conclude that when properly applied and managed, organization development programs have positive effects on performance.[69]

Managerial Implications: Managing Change

■ Several guidelines can be used to facilitate the success of management change efforts.[70] First, managers should recognize the forces for change. These forces can come from a combination of sources both internal and external to the organization.

A shared vision of the change should be developed that includes participation by all employees in the planning process. Top management must be committed to the change and should visibly demonstrate support, because employees look to these leaders to model appropriate behavior. A comprehensive diagnosis and needs analysis should be conducted. The company then must ensure that there are adequate resources for carrying out the change.

Resistance to change should be planned for and managed. Communication, participation, and empathetic support are ways of helping employees adjust. The reward system within the organization must be carefully evaluated to ensure that new behaviors, rather than old ones, are being reinforced. Participation in the change process should also be recognized and rewarded.

The organization development technique used should be carefully selected to meet the goals of the change. Finally, organization development efforts should be managed in an ethical manner and should preserve employees' privacy and freedom of choice. By using these guidelines, managers can meet the challenges of managing change while enhancing productivity in their organizations.

CLOSING SPOTLIGHT

A Little Change Makes a Big Difference

Throughout the book, we have highlighted many changes at Federal Express, from their global push to their state-of-the-art package tracking and human resource management systems. Clearly, the company's ability to manage change has contributed to its success.

Federal Express made one seemingly small change with big results. In 1994 it changed its marketing name and made "FedEx" perhaps the world's most visible new logo. FedEx kept its distinctive colors but got rid of the slanted, cumbersome graphics that were designed in the 1960s. The new visual system is cleaner, more modern, and more confident. And it is simpler—note how much easier it is to specify "FedEx" (only two syllables) than United States Postal Service (eight syllables). The power of the FedEx identity communicates worldwide leadership in the overnight delivery business.[71]

Federal Express manages both large-scale and small-scale changes well. The development of its sophisticated human resources system, PRISM, constituted a massive change. On a smaller scale, the company changed its logo to "FedEx" with excellent results.

Chapter Summary

- Organizations face many pressures to change. Some forces are external, including globalization, workforce diversity, technological innovation, and ethics. Other forces are internal, such as declining effectiveness, crises, changing employee expectations, and changing work climate.
- Organizations face both planned and unplanned change. Change can be of an incremental, strategic, or transformational nature. The individual who directs the change, known as a change agent, can be internal or external to the organization.
- Individuals resist change for many reasons, and many of these reasons are rooted in fear. Organizations can help manage resistance by educating workers and openly communicating the change, encouraging worker participation in the change efforts, and providing empathy and support to those who have difficulty dealing with change.
- Reactions to change may be manifested in behaviors reflecting disengagement, disidentification, disenchantment, and disorientation. Managers can use separate interventions targeted toward each reaction.
- Force field analysis states that when the forces for change are balanced by the forces restraining change, an equilibrium state exists. For change to occur, the forces for change must increase, or the restraining forces must decrease.
- Lewin's change model proposes three stages of change: unfreezing, moving, and refreezing.
- A thorough diagnosis and needs analysis is a critical first step in any organization development (OD) intervention.
- OD interventions targeted toward organizations and groups include survey feedback, management by objectives, product and service quality programs, team building, and process consultation.
- OD interventions that focus on individuals include skills training, sensitivity training, management development training, role negotiation, job redesign, stress management programs, and career planning.
- OD efforts should be managed ethically and should preserve individual freedom of choice and privacy.
- When properly conducted, organization development can have positive effects on performance.

Key Terms

planned change (p. 540)
unplanned change (p. 540)
incremental change (p. 544)
strategic change (p. 544)
transformational change (p. 544)
change agent (p. 544)
disengagement (p. 550)
disidentification (p. 550)
disenchantment (p. 550)
disorientation (p. 551)
unfreezing (p. 552)
moving (p. 552)
refreezing (p. 552)
organization development (OD) (p. 554)
survey feedback (p. 555)
management by objectives (MBO) (p. 556)
quality program (p. 556)
team building (p. 557)
process consultation (p. 558)
skills training (p. 558)
sensitivity training (p. 559)
management development (p. 559)
role negotiation (p. 560)
job redesign (p. 560)

Review Questions

1. What are the major external and internal forces for change in organizations?
2. Contrast incremental, strategic, and transformational change.
3. What is a change agent? Who plays this role?
4. What are the major reasons individuals resist change? How can organizations deal with resistance?
5. Name the four behavioral reactions to change. Describe the behavioral signs of each reaction and an organizational strategy for dealing with each reaction.
6. Describe force field analysis and its relationship to Lewin's change model.
7. What is organization development? Why is it undertaken by organizations?
8. Name six areas to be critically examined in any comprehensive organizational diagnosis.
9. What are the major organization-focused and group-focused OD intervention methods? The major individual-focused methods?
10. Which OD intervention is most effective?

Discussion and Communication Questions

1. What are the major external forces for change in today's organizations?
2. What are the advantages of using an external change agent? An internal change agent?
3. Review Challenge 18.1. What can you learn from this Challenge about how individuals' tolerance for ambiguity can lead to resistance?
4. Can organizations prevent resistance to change? If so, how?
5. What organization development techniques are the easiest to implement? What techniques are the most difficult to implement? Why?
6. Suppose your organization experiences a dramatic increase in absenteeism rates. How would you diagnose the underlying problem?
7. The quality movement has played a major role in changing U.S. organizations. Analyze the internal and external forces for change regarding product and service quality.
8. If you were in charge of designing the ideal management development program, what topics would you include? Why?
9. *(communication question)* Go to your university library and find an article that describes an organization that has gone through change and managed it well. Develop an "Organizational Reality" feature of your own about the example you find using the format in the book. Prepare a brief oral presentation of your Organizational Reality for your class.
10. *(communication question)* Think of a change you would like to make in your life. Using Figure 18.1 as a guide, prepare your own force field analysis for that change. How will you overcome the forces for the status quo? How will you make sure to "refreeze" following the change? Summarize your analysis in an action plan.

Ethics Questions

1. What constitutes abuse of a change agent's power? How can organizations prevent this?
2. Is it ethical to coerce individuals to change in organizations?
3. You are leading a management development seminar, and the supervisor of one of the participants asks how his employee is performing in the seminar. Should you reveal this information?
4. Suppose you are a consultant, and an organization asks you to deliver a team-building intervention. You know a little about team building, but not a lot. You do know that a competitor will probably get the job if you do not do it. What should you do?
5. Suppose you are a consultant, and a company asks you to assist in rewriting its policies and procedures manual to help eliminate the company's excessive absenteeism. From your limited knowledge about the company, you suspect that the problem lies elsewhere, and that changing the manual will not solve the problem. What should you do?

Experiential Exercises

18.1 Organizational Diagnosis of the University

The purpose of this exercise is to give you experience in organizational diagnosis. Assume that your team has been hired to conduct a diagnosis of problem areas in your university and to make preliminary recommendations for organization development interventions.

Each team member should complete the following University Profile. Then, as a team, evaluate the strengths and weaknesses within each area (academics, teaching, social, cultural, and administrative) using the accompanying University Diagnosis form. Finally, make recommendations concerning organization development interventions for each area. Be as specific as possible in both your diagnosis and your recommendations. Each team should then present its diagnosis to the class.

UNIVERSITY PROFILE

Not True 1 2 3 4 5 Very True

I. Academics

1 2 3 4 5 1. There is a wide range of courses to choose from.

1 2 3 4 5 2. Classroom standards are too easy.

1 2 3 4 5 3. The library is adequate.

1 2 3 4 5 4. Textbooks are helpful.

II. Teachers

1 2 3 4 5 1. Teachers here are committed to quality instruction.

1 2 3 4 5 2. We have a high-quality faculty.

III. Social

1 2 3 4 5 1. Students are friendly to one another.

1 2 3 4 5 2. It is difficult to make friends.

1 2 3 4 5 3. Faculty get involved in student activities.

1 2 3 4 5 4. Too much energy goes into drinking and goofing off.

IV. Cultural Events

1 2 3 4 5 1. There are ample activities on campus.

1 2 3 4 5 2. Student activities are boring.

1 2 3 4 5 3. The administration places a high value on student activities.

1 2 3 4 5 4. Too much emphasis is placed on sports.

1 2 3 4 5 5. We need more "cultural" activities.

V. Organizational/Management

1 2 3 4 5 1. Decision making is shared at all levels of the organization.

1 2 3 4 5 2. There is unity and cohesiveness among departments and units.

1 2 3 4 5 3. Too many departmental clashes hamper the organization's effectiveness.

1 2 3 4 5 4. Students have a say in many decisions.

1 2 3 4 5 5. The budgeting process seems fair.

1 2 3 4 5 6. Recruiting and staffing are handled thoughtfully, with student needs in mind.

University Diagnosis

	STRENGTH	WEAKNESS	INTERVENTION
1. Academic			
2. Teaching			
3. Social			
4. Cultural			
5. Administrative			

SOURCE: D. Marcic, *Organizational Behavior: Experiences and Cases*, 326–329 (St. Paul: West Publishing Company, 1989).

18.2 Team Building for Team Effectiveness

This exercise will allow you and your team to engage in an organization development activity for team building. The two parts of the exercise are diagnosis and intervention.

Part 1. Diagnosis

Working as a team, complete the following four steps:

1. Describe how you have worked together this semester as a team.

2. What has your team done especially well? What has enabled this?

3. What problems or conflicts have you had as a team? (Be specific.) What was the cause of the problems your team experienced? Have the conflicts been over ideas, methods, or people?

4. Would you assess the overall effectiveness of your team as excellent, good, fair, poor, or a disaster? Explain your effectiveness rating.

Part 2. Intervention

A diagnosis provides the basis for intervention and action in organization development. Team building is a way to improve the relationships and effectiveness of teams at work. It is concerned with the results of work activities and the relationships among the members of the team. Complete the following three steps as a team.

Step 1. Answer the following questions with regard to the relationships within the team:

a. How could conflicts have been handled better?

b. How could specific relationships have been improved?

c. How could the interpersonal atmosphere of the team have been improved?

Step 2. Answer the following questions with regard to the results of the team's work:

a. How could the team have been more effective?

b. Are there any team process changes that would have improved the team's effectiveness?

c. Are there any team structure changes that would have improved the team's effectiveness?

Step 3. Answer the following questions with regard to the work environment in your place of employment:

a. What have you learned about team building that you can apply there?

b. What have you learned about team building that would not be applicable there?

CASE

Managing Cultural Change at IBM[1]

For decades, the culture of International Business Machines (IBM) was embedded in three basic beliefs: "Pursue excellence; provide the best customer service; and, above all, show employees 'respect for the individual.'" So ingrained were these basic beliefs that Thomas J. Waston, Jr., the son of IBM's founder, once observed that in order to succeed, IBM was willing to change everything but its basic beliefs.

As late as the early 1990s, IBM labored "mightily to preserve the Watson culture." For instance, as part of its strong employee orientation, IBM tried to maintain its tradition of no layoffs—sometimes with a transfer to an unglamorous job but nonetheless a job at IBM. Edward Kaszuba, a 16-year IBM veteran, suggests, "If you ever have a layoff at IBM, it would not only destroy the company, it would traumatize the people who are left behind."

Also in the early 1990s, IBM's revenues and profit margins were falling while its cost of goods sold was rising. IBM was struggling with its poorest performance ever, suffering from lost market share. In response, the company cut thousands and thousands of jobs through natural attrition and buyouts for early retirements. In the midst of this corporate struggle, Louis V. Gerstner, Jr., was recruited away from RJR Nabisco Holdings Corp. to become IBM's chief executive officer.

Just months after he became IBM's CEO, Gerstner replaced the three basic beliefs with eight corporate principles:

- The marketplace is the driving force behind everything we do.
- At our core, we are a technology company with an overriding commitment to quality.
- Our primary measures of success are customer satisfaction and shareholder value.
- We operate as an entrepreneurial organization with a minimum of bureaucracy and a never-ending focus on productivity.
- We never lose sight of our strategic vision.
- We think and act with a sense of urgency.
- Outstanding, dedicated people make it all happen, particularly when they work together as a team.
- We are sensitive to the needs of all employees and to the communities in which we operate.

Gerstner also recruited Gerald Czarnecki, at the time CEO of Bank of America Hawaii, to lead the cultural revolution embodied in these eight principles. However, after struggling for about a year with cultural change and not achieving much progress, Czarnecki resigned under pressure. The resistance to cultural change that Czarnecki encountered is perhaps epitomized by one veteran IBM executive. He says, "I'm so tired of people taking the ax to the old IBM."

In commenting on IBM's struggle with changing its corporate culture, David Noer, vice president of training for the Center for Creative Leadership, indicates, "Culture has to change from within. Unless IBM is prepared to accept a fundamental shift, one person can't change it." Some observers argue that real change must come from the bottom of the organization—"real change must bubble up from the bottom and spread through . . ." the company. Indeed, thousands of IBM employees were apparently eager to rebuild the struggling company. Still, "People have been conditioned into dependence at IBM. They need to learn not to be that way."

DISCUSSION QUESTIONS

1. What forces was Louis Gerstner responding to in his efforts to change IBM's culture?
2. What behavioral reactions to change do you think would occur at IBM? Why would they occur? How could Gerstner's management team deal with these behavioral reactions?
3. Why might IBM employees—particularly the long-time veterans—resist Gerstner's cultural change efforts?
4. What do you think of the idea that change needs to start at the bottom rather than the top of the organization? What advantages and disadvantages do you see in change being initiated in a bottom-up manner? What advantages and disadvantages do you see in change being initiated in a top-down fashion?
5. How would you evaluate Louis Gerstner as a change agent?
6. How could Gerstner have used force field analysis as an aid to understanding and managing cultural change at IBM?

SOURCE: This case was written by Michael K. McCuddy, the Louis S. and Mary L. Morgal Professor of Christian Business Ethics, College of Business Administration, Valparaiso University.

1. Adapted from L. Hays, "Blue Blood: IBM's Finance Chief, Ax in Hand, Scours Empire for Costs to Cut," *The Wall Street Journal* (January 26, 1994): A1, A4; L. Hays, "Blue Period: Gerstner is Struggling as He Tries to Change Ingrained IBM Culture," *The Wall Street Journal* (May 13, 1994): A1, A5; D. Kirkpatrick, "Gerstner's New Vision for IBM," *Fortune* (November 15, 1993): 119–126; M. A. Miller, "True Blues; Hard Times Threaten IBM's Long Tradition of Eschewing Layoffs," *The Wall Street Journal* (July 31, 1992): A1.

References

1. S. Greengard, "Federal Express Makes Its Workflow Automation Package Work," *Personnel Journal* (July 1994): 32N.
2. M. A. Verespej, "When Change Becomes the Norm," *Industry Week*, 16 March 1992, 35–38.
3. E. Davis, "What's on American Managers' Minds," *Management Review* (April 1995): 14–20.
4. "Conoco Plans to Develop Oil Fields in Russia: Cost of Up to $3 Billion," *Journal Record*, 19 June 1992, 16.
5. J. A. Belasco, *Teaching the Elephant to Dance* (New York: Crown, 1990).
6. L. Hirschhorn and T. Gilmore, "The New Boundaries of the 'Boundaryless' Company," *Harvard Business Review* (May–June 1992): 104–115.
7. L. R. Offerman and M. Gowing, "Organizations of the Future: Changes and Challenges," *American Psychologist* (February 1990): 95–108.
8. W. B. Johnston, "Global Work Force 2000: The New World Labor Market," *Harvard Business Review*, (March–April 1991): 115–127.
9. N. J. Perry, "The Workers of the Future," *Fortune* (Spring/Summer 1991): 68–72.
10. T. A. Stewart, "Brace for Japan's Hot New Strategy," *Fortune*, 21 September 1992, 63–74.
11. R. M. Kanter, "Improving the Development, Acceptance, and Use of New Technology: Organizational and Interorganizational Challenges," in *People and Technology in the Workplace* (Washington, D. C.: National Academy Press, 1991), 15–56.
12. L. K. Trevino and K. A. Nelson, *Managing Business Ethics: Straight Talk about How to Do It Right* (New York: John Wiley & Sons, 1995).
13. S. A. Mohrman and A. M. Mohrman, Jr., "The Environment as an Agent of Change," in A. M. Morhman, Jr., et al., eds., *Large-Scale Organizational Change* (San Francisco: Jossey-Bass, 1989), 35–47.
14. D. Nadler, "Organizational Frame-Bending: Types of Change in the Complex Organization," in R. Kilmann and T. Covin, eds., *Corporate Transformation* (San Francisco: Jossey-Bass, 1988), 66–83.
15. L. Ackerman, "Development, Transition, or Transformation: The Question of Change in Organizations," *OD Practitioner* (December 1986): 1–8.
16. T. D. Jick, *Managing Change* (Homewood, Ill., Irwin, 1993), 3.
17. L. D. Goodstein and W. W. Burke, "Creating Successful Organizational Change," *Organizational Dynamics* (Spring 1991): 4–17.
18. R. M. Kanter, *The Change Masters* (New York: Simon and Schuster, 1983).
19. J. R. Katzenbach, *Real Change Leaders* (New York: Times Business, 1995).
20. M. Beer, *Organization Change and Development: A Systems View* (Santa Monica, Calif.: Goodyear, 1980), 78.
21. J. W. Brehm, *A Theory of Psychological Reactance* (New York: Academic Press, 1966).
22. J. A. Klein, "Why Supervisors Resist Employee Involvement," *Harvard Business Review* 62 (1984): 87–95.
23. S. Zuboff, "New Worlds of Computer-Mediated Work," *Harvard Business Review* 60 (1982): 142–152.
24. D. L. Nelson and M. A. White, "Management of Technological Innovation: Individual Attitudes, Stress, and Work Group Attributes," *Journal of High Technology Management Research* 1 (1990): 137–148.
25. J. Stanislao and B. C. Stanislao, "Dealing with Resistance to Change," *Business Horizons* (July–August 1983): 74–78.
26. D. Klein, "Some Notes on the Dynamics of Resistance to Change: The Defender Role," in W. G. Bennis, K. D. Benne, R. Chin, and K. E. Corey, eds., *The Planning of Change*, 3d ed. (New York: Holt, Rinehart & Winston, 1969), 117–124.
27. T. G. Cummings and E. F. Huse, *Organizational Development and Change* (St. Paul: West, 1989).
28. L. Livingstone, M. A. White, and D. L. Nelson, "The Effects of Delayed Implementation on Employee Attitudes toward Computer Innovations" (Working paper, Oklahoma State University, 1992); A. Rafaeli, "Employee Attitudes toward Working with Computers," *Journal of Occupational Behavior* (April 1986): 89–106.
29. L. Coch and J. P. French, "Overcoming Resistance to Change," *Human Relations* 1 (1948): 512–532.
30. A. B. Fisher, "Making Change Stick," *Fortune*, April 17, 1995: 121–131.
31. J. P. Kotter and L. A. Schlesinger, "Choosing Strategies for Change," *Harvard Business Review* 57 (1979): 109–112; W. Bridges, *Transitions: Making Sense of Life's Changes* (Reading, Mass.: Addison-Wesley, 1980); H. Woodward and S. Buchholz, *Aftershock: Helping People through Corporate Change* (New York: Wiley, 1987).
32. K. Lewin, "Frontiers in Group Dynamics," *Human Relations* 1 (1947): 5–41.
33. W. McWhinney, "Meta-Praxis: A Framework for Making Complex Changes," in A. M. Mohrman, Jr., et al., eds., *Large-Scale Organizational Change* (San Francisco: Jossey-Bass, 1989), 154–199.
34. M. Beer and E. Walton, "Developing the Competitive Organization: Interventions and Strategies," *American Psychologist* 45 (1990): 154–161.
35. B. Bertsch and R. Williams, "How Multinational CEOs Make Change Programs Stick," *Long Range Planning* 27 (1994): 12–24.
36. W. L. French and C. H. Bell, *Organization Development: Behavioral Science Interventions for Organization Improvement*, 4th ed. (Englewood Cliffs, N.J.: Prentice-Hall, 1990); W. W. Burke, *Organization Development: A Normative View* (Reading, Mass., Addison-Wesley, 1987).
37. A. Huczynski, *Encyclopedia of Organizational Change Methods* (Brookfield, Vt.: Gower, 1987).
38. A. O. Manzini, *Organizational Diagnosis* (New York: AMACOM, 1988).
39. M. R. Weisbord, "Organizational Diagnosis: Six Places to Look for Trouble with or without a Theory," *Group and Organization Studies* (December 1976): 430–444.
40. H. Levinson, *Organizational Diagnosis* (Cambridge, Mass.: Harvard University Press, 1972).

41. J. Nicholas, "The Comparative Impact of Organization Development Interventions," *Academy of Management Review* 7 (1982): 531–542.
42. C. Cammann, M. Fichman, G. D. Jenkins, and J. Klesh, "Assessing the Attitudes and Perceptions of Organization Members," in S. Seashore, E. Lawler III, P. Mirvis, and C. Cammann, eds., *Assessing Organizational Change: A Guide to Methods, Measures, and Practices* (New York: Wiley, 1983), 71–138.
43. G. Odiorne, *Management by Objectives* (Marshfield, Mass.: Pitman, 1965).
44. E. Huse, "Putting in a Management Development Program That Works," *California Management Review* 9 (1966): 73–80.
45. J. P. Muczyk and B. C. Reimann, "MBO as a Complement to Effective Leadership," *Academy of Management Executive* (May 1989): 131–138.
46. L. L. Berry and A. Parasuraman, "Prescriptions for a Service Quality Revolution in America," *Organizational Dynamics* 20 (1992): 5–15.
47. "Five Companies Win 1992 Baldridge Quality Awards," *Business America,* 2 November 1992, 7–16.
48. D. M. Anderson, "Hidden Forces," *Success* (April 1995): 12.
49. W. G. Dyer, *Team Building: Issues and Alternatives,* 2d ed. (Reading, Mass., Addison-Wesley, 1987).
50. E. Stephan, G. Mills, R. W. Pace, and L. Ralphs, "HRD in the Fortune 500: A Survey," *Training and Development Journal* (January 1988): 26–32.
51. R. Swezey and E. Salas, eds., *Teams: Their Training and Performance* (Norwood, N.J.: Ablex, 1991).
52. M. Whitmire and P. R. Nienstedt, "Lead Leaders into the '90s," *Personnel Journal* (May 1991): 80–85.
53. E. Salas, T. L. Dickinson, S. I. Tannenbaum, and S. A. Converse, *A Meta-Analysis of Team Performance and Training,* Naval Training System Center Technical Reports (Orlando, Fla., U.S. Government, 1991).
54. E. Schein, *Its Role in Organization Development,* vol. 1 of *Process Consultation* (Reading, Mass:, Addison-Wesley, 1988).
55. D. Filipowski "How Federal Express Makes Your Package Its Most Important," *Personnel Journal* (February 1992): 40–46; P. Galagan, "Training Delivers Results to Federal Express," *Training and Development* (December 1991): 27–33.
56. J. Campbell and M. Dunnette, "Effectiveness of T-Group Experiences in Managerial Training and Development," *Psychological Bulletin* 70 (1968): 73–103.
57. R. T. Golembiewski, *Organization Development* (New Brunswick, N.J.: Transaction Publishers, 1989).
58. N. M. Dixon, "Evaluation and Management Development," in J. Pfeiffer, ed., *The 1991 Annual: Developing Human Resources* (San Diego: University Associates, 1991), 287–296.
59. R. W. Revans, *Action Learning* (London: Blonde and Briggs, 1980).
60. I. L. Goldstein, *Training in Organizations,* 3d ed. (Pacific Grove, Calif., Brooks/Cole, 1993).
61. C. Steinburg, "Taking Charge of Change," *Training and Development* (March 1992): 26–32.
62. D. A. Nadler, "Concepts for the Management of Organizational Change," in J. R. Hackman, E. E. Lawler III, and L. W. Porter, eds., *Perspectives on Organizational Behavior* (New York: McGraw-Hill, 1983).
63. Cummings and Huse, *Organizational Development;* P. E. Connor and L. K. Lake, *Managing Organizational Change* (New York: Praeger, 1988).
64. R. L. Lowman, "Ethical Human Resource Practice in Organizational Settings," in D. W. Bray, ed., *Working with Organizations* (New York: Guilford Press, 1991).
65. H. Kelman, "Manipulation of Human Behavior: An Ethical Dilemma for the Social Scientist," in W. Bennis, K. Benne, and R. Chin, eds., *The Planning of Change* (New York: Holt, Rinehart, & Winston, 1969).
66. J. B. Nicholas, "The Comparative Impact of Organization Development Interventions on Hard Criteria Measures," *Academy of Management Review* (October 1982): 531–542.
67. R. A. Katzell and R. A. Guzzo, "Psychological Approaches to Worker Productivity," *American Psychologist* 38 (1983): 468–472.
68. R. A. Guzzo, R. D. Jette, and R. A. Katzell, "The Effects of Psychologically Based Intervention Programs on Worker Productivity," *Personnel Psychology* 38 (1985): 275–291.
69. Goldstein, *Training in Organizations.*
70. T. Covin and R. H. Kilmann, "Participant Perceptions of Positive and Negative Influences on Large-Scale Change," *Group and Organization Studies* 15 (1990): 233–248.
71. T. Spaeth, "What Does It All Mean?" *Across the Board* (February 1995): 53–55.

INTERNET EXERCISE

The assignments for this section will provide you with information on more macro organizational issues. There are many websites available to help manager with job and structural design problems. Other sites help employees deal with changes and manage their careers more effectively.

Company Connections

Chrysler Corporation
What information is available about technology and job design at Chrysler Corporation?

Coca-Cola
What information is available on their mission and structure?

NASA
What does their organizational structure look like?

Levi Strauss
How does this website reflect the information discussed in the text?

Du Pont
What information on careers and jobs at Du Pont is available here?

Marriott Corporation
Explore this site. How has Marriott changed to better adapt to its environment?

Topic Trails

W. Edward Deming
What can you learn here about Deming's approach to quality and job design?

Telecommuting
What are the keys listed at the Ohio State website for successful telecommuting?

Downsizing
What guidelines are offered at the Princeton website on downsizing?

Cultural Diversity
How could an organization benefit from the information offered by the National Center for Research on Cultural Diversity?

Career Management
Find the On-line Career Center. What career resources are available at this website?

Organizational Development
How could an organization use the links listed at the Bowling Green State University website?

VIDEO COHESION CASE

This section includes four cases dealing with various organizational behavior issues facing PriceCostco, a company resulting from the merger of Price Company and Costco Wholesale. The cases are interrelated, but each can stand alone. Each case is supplemented with videos that present the challenges faced by a corporation formed from two diverse companies seeking to create a single company with a unified philosophy and culture. These cases immediately follow Chapter 18 on page 573.

VIDEO COHESION CASE—PART I

PriceCostco (A)

PriceCostco, a chain of warehouse clubs serving both businesses and individuals in selected occupations, was formed in October, 1993 by the merger of Price Company and Costco Wholesale. Similar in size, each company owned and operated approximately 100 warehouses. Each company also had about $7 billion in annual sales. Both companies had similar standards for conducting business, namely, being very efficient in product handling, keeping margins low, and treating employees well.

Price Company also had interests in real estate development, primarily shopping centers. However, the main focus of their operations was on warehouse clubs.

In describing the nature of the warehouse club business, Jim Sinegal, chief executive officer, says, "We essentially set up our business . . . to be a cash and carry business to bring a lot of products under one roof for the small business person." PriceCostco provides products to be used in the operation of their businesses, to be sold in their businesses, or for personal consumption. These customers are known as business or wholesale members.

In addition to the business members of the warehouse club, there are other individuals who are qualified for membership on the basis of their occupation. These customers are called Gold Star members.

On a worldwide basis, PriceCostco has over 10 million members or accounts—but there may be more than one person on an account. Since members pay $30 or $35 a year to shop at PriceCostco they tend to be loyal, repeat customers. The membership fees represent about 2 percent of sales, which, in turn, permits the company to lower prices by 2 percent, thus helping to keep prices low. Over 85 percent of the business members and over 75 percent of the Gold Star members renew their memberships each year. The goal is to increase these percentages to 90 percent and 80 percent, respectively.

According to Jim Sinegal, "In every market in the world, not just the United States, the people that own businesses are at the top end of the demographic scale." A third of PriceCostco's customers are businesses, but they generate two-thirds of the company's sales volume. The other third of sales volume is generated by Gold Star members, who make up two-thirds of the customers.

Richard Galanti, PriceCostco's chief financial officer, indicates that " . . . the whole premise of the warehouse club is to continue to drive down the costs and therefore to be able to drive down the selling prices to our . . . members." PriceCostco doesn't price merchandise below cost. Says Galanti, "If we can't make a little money and sell it to you at the most competitive price, we just won't sell that item."

Dick Disertio, vice president of merchandising (marketing), adds, "Price is very key to our overall strategy. Quality and value, however, are even more important than price." He continues, "If someone carries an item at a very low price, we try to get a better item. We always try to make the item better. Better quality to separate ourselves from our wholesale club competitors."

PriceCostco competes with all types of low-cost providers of goods. They compete head-to-head with Sam's Club, a subsidiary of WalMart, and BJ's. They also compete with grocery stores, computer stores, hardware stores; super centers like WalMart, Target, and Kmart; and specialty stores like Office Depot, Toys R Us, and PetSmart. Rather than carrying a lot of items in each product category, PriceCostco selects the best item in the category and makes it available at the best price. People shop at PriceCostco for value.

At PriceCostco, the expenses average 9 percent of the sales dollar. At competitors like WalMart, Target, and Kmart, expenses range from 15 percent to 21 percent of sales. Supermarkets tend to be in the 18 percent range and expenses at traditional department stores might be as high as 40 percent. PriceCostco tries to eliminate or at least minimize the types of expenses incurred by these other retailers. The company does not advertise like traditional retail outlets but does do some direct mail advertising to its members. This costs about one-tenth of 1 percent of sales as compared to 2–5 percent of sales in traditional retail formats. Occupancy costs are lower because they locate warehouses off the beaten path rather than in prime retail locations. Labor cost savings are generated through high labor productivity—for example, forklift operators simply put pallets of merchandise on the floor for members' self-service. Inventory shrinkage is less than three-tenths of 1 percent of sales as compared to other retail formats that range from 1 to 3 percent of sales.

PriceCostco also has a limit—currently at 15 percent—on how much it will mark up goods. The markups range from 2 percent to 15 percent above costs, with an average of 9.5 percent to 10 percent. Local warehouses price shop competitors on a weekly basis, and buyers use this information to determine whether or not to match those prices. Markup decisions are based on the competitive environment.

PriceCostco aims to compete on the basis of low cost, low prices, and high value. Don Burdick, vice president/corporate counsel, summarizes the PriceCostco approach to doing business: "PriceCostco is dedicated to being the lowest cost provider out there. . . . Buy better and lower the price. Handle it less and lower the price."

PriceCostco is currently about a $17 billion company in terms of sales. It has over 50,000 employees.

Prior to the merger, Price Company had some unionized employees in California and several east coast states. They were represented under a collective bargaining agreement with the Teamsters Union. Costco, however, developed in a nonunion environment. With the merger of the two companies, about 70 percent of the employees are nonunion and about 30 percent are unionized. The Teamsters still represent the union members.

In addition to its United States locations, PriceCostco currently has 19 locations in western Canada, 25 locations in eastern Canada, 13 locations in Mexico, three locations in the United Kingdom (two in England and one in Scotland), and one location in Seoul, South Korea. They also are developing a location in Taichung, Taiwan. Costco Wholesale started the Canadian businesses about a decade ago. Price Company developed the Mexican operations.

One of the challenges in having both domestic and international operations is the industry's regulatory environment. Don Burdick, vice president/corporate counsel, says that the warehouse club industry is more heavily regulated in the United States than in any other country. He adds, however, that PriceCostco sees the law as a minimum standard. For example, with regard to employees, Burdick observes, "The policy with respect to doing the right thing for the employees and accommodating the employees goes far beyond what the law says."

PriceCostco tries to be fair and consistent in its treatment of employees. For instance, the company tries to follow the same sexual harassment policy throughout the world—that is, providing an environment that is safe for workers.

Taking care of employees is just one aspect of PriceCostco's way of doing business. Perhaps their overall philosophy can be best captured through their mission statement. According to Jim Sinegal, the CEO, if PriceCostco does four things—obey the law, take care of customers, take care of employees, and respect the vendors—it will be taking care of its shareholders. Adds John Matthews, senior vice president of human resources, "We're going to conduct our business in a way that's fair to our shareholders, to our employees, to our members, and to our communities."

DISCUSSION QUESTIONS

1. What is PriceCostco's business philosophy and approach? How does their business philosophy and approach help them to compete in the marketplace? What are the strengths and weaknesses of PriceCostco's business philosophy and approach?
2. What lessons about leading and managing organizations does PriceCostco provide?
3. What challenges do you think PriceCostco will encounter as it continues to move into global markets? How should PriceCostco respond to these challenges?
4. How does workforce diversity appear to influence PriceCostco's operations? How is the issue of workforce diversity related to PriceCostco's move toward increased globalization of their operations?
5. How could PriceCostco use technology to further drive down their operating costs?
6. What types of ethical dilemmas are likely to be encountered in a warehouse club operation? How do you think PriceCostco's managers would deal with these ethical dilemmas? How would you, personally, deal with these ethical dilemmas?
7. Which of the organizational challenges—globalization, workforce diversity, emerging technologies, and ethical dilemmas—are likely to have the greatest impact on PriceCostco's future operations? Explain your answer.

SOURCE: This case was written by Michael K. McCuddy, the Louis S. and Mary L. Morgal Professor of Christian Business Ethics, College of Business Administration, Valparaiso University. This case is based on transcripts of interviews that representatives of West Educational Publishing conducted with various PriceCostco executives.

VIDEO COHESION CASE—PART II

PriceCostco (B)

When they entered into the merger agreement, Price Company and Costco Wholesale adopted an extraordinary policy of not laying off any employees as a result of the merger. It meant moving a lot of people around and consolidating functions, but no one lost their job because of the merger. This is but one aspect of PriceCostco's commitment to people. PriceCostco's approach to hiring and developing employees as well as motivating and compensating them also vividly illustrates the company's commitment to people. The company's values and attitudes are embodied in their business practices and policies.

Hiring and Developing Employees

In describing PriceCostco's approach to hiring and developing employees, John Matthews, senior vice president of human resources, says they "bring people in at entry level positions and . . . bring them through the organization and . . . grow them ourselves." About 80 percent of PriceCostco's promotions are made from within the company. Most promotions are based purely on performance.

PriceCostco spends a lot of time and energy on the orientation process so that new employees are effectively acclimated to the company's culture and the way it does business. New hires are aligned with experienced peers—called big brothers or big sisters—to help them through the process. Once people complete the orientation, they receive on-the-job training in several different functional areas in the warehouse environment.

PriceCostco has formal training sessions for supervisors to help them understand leadership functions, motivational tools, how to deal with interpersonal relationships, and various legal issues that pertain to hiring and managing employees. As supervisors move up through the organization these skills are reinforced with further training programs.

Motivating and Compensating Employees

A lot of PriceCostco's positions are entry-level so the company does several things to maintain motivation for these employees. The company stresses that employees are part of a team and they encourage the team to do well. Job assignments are rotated among employees. Experienced employees are empowered by having them become big brothers and big sisters in the orientation program. Employees are encouraged to share their ideas for improving the organization.

The wage scale for hourly employees—about 95 percent of the workforce—"is very competitive and significantly above market rates." Says John Matthews, "We choose to start an individual at a higher level because we feel that's what's fair and an equitable beginning wage." PriceCostco also moves people to the top of the wage scale more rapidly than many other organizations because they believe that it is the fairest approach.

The base pay of salaried workers—who represent about 5 percent of PriceCostco's workforce—is established according to their functional area of expertise, making sure that the rates are equitable with the marketplace. Don Burdick, vice president/corporate counsel, notes that "all of management is compensated at very small base salaries." Senior executives are compensated at a multiple of about 20 times the lowest level annual employee. Managers, however, receive "bonus compensation if the company exceeds its performance standards, and that judgment is made by outside directors."

PriceCostco also emphasizes performance in the compensation of its directors. The company pays fairly small directors' fees in comparison to other companies. In addition to these fees, however, all of the directors receive stock options. This helps align the directors' interest with that of the shareholders.

Values and Attitudes

PriceCostco is a major advocate for United Way—a key vehicle for distributing money to a variety of charitable causes. In 1994 the company also raised "$2 million for 54 children's hospitals throughout the United States and Canada." The company also participates in Fresh Start, an adopt-a-school program in the United States. In this program, a PriceCostco warehouse adopts a school in its market area and provides each child in the school with a backpack full of supplies at the beginning of the school year. PriceCostco also "encourages its employees to be active on their own in their favorite charities."

PriceCostco's humane values and attitudes extend to the vendors and contractors with whom it does business. For instance, in developing the warehouse club network and other real estate interests, PriceCostco has built hundreds of buildings. The company's policy is that their general contractor and all their subcontractors will pay at least 90 percent of the Davis-Bacon standard. As Don Burdick points out, "there is an understanding that it costs PriceCostco more to do that but senior management feels very strongly that it's the right thing to do."

PriceCostco's sensitivity to others' attitudes and values carries over into its international operations. Differences in the cultures and customs of countries are viewed as important. In the host country, says Franz Lazarus, executive vice president of northwest region and international, "our members would be very offended if we didn't abide by their cultural differences and acknowledge their special holidays and . . . special religious beliefs." Reflecting the perspective of PriceCostco, Lazarus observes that the company must understand the culture of the country in which it is doing business.

Within the organization itself, PriceCostco strives for a nondiscriminatory working environment. Burdick, the company's corporate counsel, indicates that "we have made a conscientious effort to adopt fair workplace standards" in order to make a comfortable working environment for people of different backgrounds. John Matthews, the human resources senior vice president, adds that while PriceCostco does not have an affirmative action program, it strives to provide a working environment that is free of any form of discrimination.

Perhaps the values and attitudes of PriceCostco can be best summarized in the musings of Don Burdick. He says that PriceCostco tries to be fair with its own employees as well as with the outside people who work with and for the company.

Overall, PriceCostco's commitment to people—whether they are employees, customers, vendors, or contractors—is an essential ingredient of its business philosophy and practices. According to Jim Sinegal, the company's chief executive officer, PriceCostco's most important asset is very good people who are committed to and involved with the business. While this observation is about PriceCostco's employees, the sentiment it expresses might also extend to the company's customers, vendors, and contractors.

DISCUSSION QUESTIONS

1. PriceCostco is very committed to people. What are the strengths and weaknesses of an organization having such a high level of commitment to people?
2. Do you think PriceCostco could retain its strong commitment to people if it relied more heavily on technology? Explain your answer.
3. What challenges would an increasingly diverse workforce pose for PriceCostco's hiring and employee development practices? For its motivation and compensation practices?
4. To what extent are PriceCostco's hiring and employee development practices as well as its motivation and compensation practices transferable throughout the world? What problems, if any, might PriceCostco encounter in attempting to transfer these practices to warehouse clubs established in new global markets?
5. What underlying ethical principles seem to govern PriceCostco's relationships with the various stakeholders of the business? Do you think these ethical principles are appropriate for guiding a business? Explain your answer.
6. Would you like to work for an organization like PriceCostco? Why or why not?

SOURCE: This case was written by Michael K. McCuddy, the Louis S. and Mary L. Morgal Professor of Christian Business Ethics, College of Business Administration, Valparaiso University. This case is based on transcripts of interviews that representatives of West Educational Publishing conducted with various PriceCostco executives.

VIDEO COHESION CASE—PART III

PriceCostco (C)

The merger of Price Company and Costco Wholesale challenged the executives, managers, and hourly employees of the organization in a number of ways, including possible system redundancies, communication problems, establishing and maintaining an ethical culture, and managing global growth.

System Redundancies

There were more similarities than differences in the operations of Costco Wholesale and Price Company before the merger. Although both companies were well managed, each had areas of superiority. Jim Sinegal, CEO of PriceCostco, says, "Our challenge was to try to find those areas where we were doing things well in one company and incorporate it into the total picture."

"We did not categorically or summarily throw out anything in terms of systems," observes Sinegal. Instead the company thoroughly studied the whole process before taking any action. One decision was to consolidate the management information systems (MIS) departments of the two merged companies, but it proved to be more difficult than they had anticipated.

In the process of overcoming these difficulties, new initiatives were developed. PriceCostco used a decision support system in the past, but it is now considering implementing an executive information system (EIS) to enable users to easily access the information they want. Initially, the EIS will be developed for top executives, then more information and capabilities will be added to the system to enable more people—at least down to the buying level—to become users of the system.

Communications

The merger had a tremendous impact on communications. Sinegal says that with the merger the need for communication became more apparent than ever. Loyalties had to be transferred from Price Company and Costco Wholesale to PriceCostco. Achieving this required the members of the two merged companies to communicate effectively with each other.

Bob Craves, senior vice president of membership and marketing, observes that clear and understandable communication is essential "when you're managing a business, and when you are being managed." And Franz Lazarus, executive vice president of northwest region and international, suggests that managers must be able to communicate with the people they supervise as well as with their own supervisors. Managers, he says, "have to be able to take in a lot of information and digest it and feed it back" in an understandable fashion to those who work for them.

John Matthews, senior vice president of human resources, cites the open door policy as a key element of PriceCostco's communication process. He says, "One of the essential ingredients to our success and to employee morale within the organization is that . . . we strive to maintain an open door policy for as many issues as we possibly can."

Establishing and Maintaining an Ethical Culture

PriceCostco's executives set the tone for ethical behavior throughout the organization. "Top management at PriceCostco is very involved in setting the standards for conduct in the company." They take the leadership role in clearly defining acceptable and expected conduct.

The company has a zero tolerance policy regarding the acceptance of gratuities. This policy applies across the board—whether it's lunch, tickets to an NCAA tournament, a condo in Hawaii, or $100,000 under the table. "If people take gratuities, it's grounds for discipline or termination and . . . management follows the same policy in . . . the conduct of their own affairs," says Don Burdick, vice president/corporate counsel.

PriceCostco communicates their ethical policy to employees with a simple motto: "What we do in business first has to be fair and reasonable, and second it has to be within the law."

Managing Global Growth

For PriceCostco, some aspects of managing global growth remain the same across countries. Both the strategy of providing merchandise at the best possible price and technology of the business remain the same from country to country.

However, PriceCostco has encountered its share of challenges in the global marketplace. Sometimes the company did not have a good forecast of market potential. For instance, when PriceCostco entered the United Kingdom market, it did not know what to expect in terms of sales volume. It hired more employees than were needed, and consequently had to lay off some employees. However, all laid-off employees who had satisfactory performance are being offered jobs in other PriceCostco units as they open.

PriceCostco has also encountered different regulations and standards than it has been accustomed to in the United States. Product labeling standards differ outside the United States, even in Canada and Mexico. For example, in Canada, all labels have to be bilingual—French and English. Bilingual labeling requirements exist in most other countries as well.

"The American standards often differ from the international standards for both product labeling and even in some cases ingredients." The challenge is not so much "how to make the foreign product meet the U.S. standards but rather . . . how that product is going to be attractive in the foreign market." PriceCostco works very closely with its vendors to ensure that products both appeal to the market and comply with regulations and standards.

Product liability is another issue that affects PriceCostco's global growth. "As PriceCostco moves into the international arena, the responsibility and product liability issues will undoubtedly change." U.S. product liability standards are higher than in many other nations of the world. PriceCostco tries to make sure their vendors assume responsibility for the products they supply. And for safety's sake, PriceCostco will not carry a product that's not approved by Underwriters Laboratories (UL). Nonetheless, PriceCostco will "find a way to do the right thing for the member" even if a vendor doesn't take responsibility for the product it supplied.

Another global challenge is the development of supplier relationships. Richard Galanti, chief financial officer, recalls what happened when PriceCostco entered the Canadian market. Galanti says that "in many instances manufacturers up there were fearful of selling to us knowing that their other retail customers would be upset." Over time, however, those barriers have disintegrated, in part because of PriceCostco's global purchasing power. Interestingly, the company encountered the same procurement obstacles when it went into the United Kingdom.

Whether dealing with global growth, the establishment and maintenance of an ethical culture, the need for effective communications, or system redundancies, PriceCostco executives have tackled these challenges with enthusiasm.

DISCUSSION QUESTIONS

1. Assume that you are a PriceCostco executive. Could you have anticipated the system redundancy, communication, ethical culture, and global growth issues that the company encountered? Explain your answer.
2. How can the use of decision-making technology like an executive information system (EIS) help executives in managing domestic operations? In managing international operations?
3. How could PriceCostco executives, managers, and hourly employees use knowledge about power and political behavior, conflict resolution, and teamwork to deal with the various challenges of global growth?
4. Why is effective communication and effective leadership so crucial to effectively merging two organizations?
5. What are the advantages and disadvantages of having a zero tolerance ethics policy that applies to all employees?
6. What role should leaders play in establishing and maintaining an ethical culture within a company? What role should followers play in establishing and maintaining an ethical culture?

SOURCE: This case was written by Michael K. McCuddy, the Louis S. and Mary L. Morgal Professor of Christian Business Ethics, College of Business Administration, Valparaiso University. This case is based on transcripts of interviews that representatives of West Educational Publishing conducted with various PriceCostco executives.

VIDEO COHESION CASE—PART IV

PriceCostco (D)

In reflecting on the merger of Price Company and Costco Wholesale, Jim Sinegal, chief executive officer of PriceCostco, points out that it was done with a lot of thought and deliberation. Since the two companies were very similar in terms of business philosophy and their approaches to many important issues, they decided to enter into a merger agreement. Nonetheless, the two companies had their differences, and that created some managerial challenges as the merger took place. Commenting on this, Sinegal says, "but even when you're very close and you have the same general approach to the business, it proves that the differences become bigger than the similarities and you have to attack that."

In the first few months after the merger, considerable progress was made in integrating the two organizations. According to Don Burdick, vice president/corporate counsel, the merger went very well from an operational standpoint—or the warehouse level. He believes that the operational aspect of the merger went well primarily because the two companies had similar cultures.

PriceCostco's culture is very simple, says Jim Sinegal. "It is a company that's on a first-name basis. We not only encourage it, we insist upon it." Everyone wears a name badge, however, because the company has a large number of employees and it's difficult for people to remember everybody's name. PriceCostco also has an open door policy "and every employee is entitled to appeal to any member of management on any issue." Any employee having over two years' service cannot be terminated unless it is approved by a senior member of management. "There's a lot of value placed on the people within the organization," emphasizes the CEO.

Sinegal says that maintaining this type of culture during the merger was difficult. Even though the cultures of Costco Wholesale and Price Company were similar, people's loyalties were to different individuals.

According to Richard Galanti, chief financial officer, the two biggest things that PriceCostco accomplished after the merger were to adopt an automated warehouse receiving system that was developed by Costco and a front-end scanning system that was developed by Price Club. In both instances, PriceCostco spent about $25 million to install hardware and software to make the transition to a more automated system.

Prior to the merger, Price Company was headquartered in San Diego and Costco Wholesale was headquartered in Seattle. Rather than eliminating one home office, both remained open with certain functions being performed in one office and other functions being performed in the other office. This aspect of the merger proved to be quite difficult, and was perhaps a harbinger of things to come.

Several months after the merger, progress on resolving issues slowed considerably and there were too many remaining differences concerning how the business should be run. "We were fighting about too many issues," says PriceCostco's CEO. "In the best interest of the company, that couldn't go on. We determined that it was necessary to develop a different structure and that structure involved the spin-off."

The Price Company had some real estate—primarily shopping centers—that was outside the warehouse club business. Shortly after the merger, people began to clearly understand that differences existed regarding the strategic issue of whether or not to continue developing shopping centers. In December, 1994, the company's development of shopping centers was spun off as Price Enterprises. This enabled PriceCostco to get the remaining operations "back on track to reduce expenses and to operate more efficiently." Just as Price Company and Costco Wholesale had done when they merged, no one was laid off when Price Enterprises was spun off from PriceCostco.

With the real estate development interests spun off, PriceCostco could devote its attention to developing and managing the warehouse club business, particularly in the global marketplace. The company expects a 10 percent annual growth rate for the next few years in the United States and Canada. It expects to double the 13 units in Mexico, and to pursue numerous opportunities in Asia and Europe.

PriceCostco is approaching the global marketplace as both a source of potential customers and a source of potential suppliers. In order to be successful entrants into overseas markets, PriceCostco is taking a long-term approach to developing relationships with foreign suppliers. "As the business grows and as more locations are added, you become more important to the vendor," says Franz Lazarus, executive vice president of the northwest region and international.

PriceCostco tries to have a joint venture partner in each country in which it operates. The company seeks a partner who has experience in the country's politics, real estate, and customs. Nonetheless, PriceCostco retains a controlling majority interest in the operation and infuses its business philosophy and practices into the new operation.

As Franz Lazarus says, "Initially, when we start to do business in a foreign country, we will send some . . . current management employees . . . on an expatriate basis . . . until local people can be trained to take over those jobs."

PriceCostco would like to adopt the same ethical standards for its operations throughout the world. This "would include issues like child labor even though it may not be prohibited in a foreign country." In dealing with these types of ethical issues, PriceCostco has been aggressive about understanding their suppliers' operational practices. Company executives admit, however, that their monitoring is probably not perfect.

Clearly, PriceCostco has many challenges and opportunities in the global arena as well as in the United States. Addressing these challenges and taking advantage of these opportunities means that PriceCostco must continue to adapt and change while retaining the essential features of its business philosophy and business approach. Will PriceCostco rise to the occasion?

DISCUSSION QUESTIONS

1. What useful managerial and organizational lessons are provided by the Price Company and Costco Wholesale merger? Why are these lessons useful?
2. How could the adoption of technology—like the automated warehouse receiving system and the front-end scanning system—help PriceCostco carry out its business approach of minimizing product handling, keeping margins low, and treating employees well?
3. How should PriceCostco's organization structure be designed to accommodate the company's anticipated growth as well as promote effective and efficient operations?
4. Will PriceCostco's organizational culture need to change in any way to accommodate the company's anticipated growth in domestic and global operations? If so, how will the culture need to change?
5. What is your opinion regarding PriceCostco's desire to have uniform ethical standards across its domestic and international operations? What could or should be done if these desired standards are in conflict with the ethical standards and practices of a foreign location?
6. In your opinion, what implications will PriceCostco's growth plans have for the major organizational challenges of globalization, workforce diversity, emerging technologies, and ethical dilemmas? How should PriceCostco respond to these implications?
7. Suppose that you are a PriceCostco executive who has responsibility for managing the company's planned change process. What change issues would you focus on? Why would you focus on these issues? What change techniques might be useful to you? Explain your answer.

SOURCE: This case was written by Michael K. McCuddy, the Louis S. and Mary L. Morgal Professor of Christian Business Ethics, College of Business Administration, Valparaiso University. This case is based on transcripts of interviews that representatives of West Educational Publishing conducted with various PriceCostco executives.

A Brief Historical Perspective

Organizational behavior may be traced back thousands of years, as noted in Sterba's analysis of the ancient Mesopotamian temple corporations. However, we will focus on the modern history of organizational behavior, which dates to the late 1800s. One of the more important series of studies conducted during this period was the Hawthorne Studies. As these and other studies have unfolded, the six disciplines discussed in Chapter 1 of the text have contributed to the advancement of organizational behavior. An overview of the progress during the past century is presented in Table A.1 and the accompanying text. This is followed by a discussion of the Hawthorne Studies.

One Hundred Years of Progress

■ Progress in any discipline, practice, or field of study is measured by significant events, discoveries, and contributions over time. The history of organizational behavior begins, as noted in Table A.1, with the work of Frederick Taylor

Ancient Mesopotamians were perhaps the first people to evolve a methodical, disciplined approach to the management of large-scale, complex organizations. The success and longevity of their temple corporations, such as the one pictured here, provide dramatic testimony to the versatility and effectiveness of concepts and techniques which they developed to manage organizational behavior.

■ **TABLE A.1**

One Hundred Years of Progress in Organizational Behavior

1890s	■ Frederick Taylor's development of scientific management
1900s	■ Max Weber's concept of bureaucracy and the Protestant ethic
1910s	■ Walter Cannon's discovery of the "emergency (stress) response"
1920s	■ Elton Mayo's illumination studies in the textile industry
	■ The Hawthorne Studies at Western Electric Company
1930s	■ Kurt Lewin's, Ronald Lippitt's, and Ralph White's early leadership studies
1940s	■ Abraham Maslow's need hierarchy motivation theory
	■ B. F. Skinner's formulation of the behavioral approach
	■ Charles Walker's and Robert Guest's studies of routine work
1950s	■ Ralph Stogdill's Ohio State leadership studies
	■ Douglas McGregor's examination of the human side of enterprise
	■ Frederick Herzberg's two-factor theory of motivation and job enrichment
1960s	■ Arthur Turner's and Paul Lawrence's studies of diverse industrial jobs
	■ Robert Blake's and Jane Mouton's managerial grid
	■ Patricia Cain Smith's studies of satisfaction in work and retirement
	■ Fred Fiedler's contingency theory of leadership
1970s	■ J. Richard Hackman's and Greg Oldham's job characteristics theory
	■ Edward Lawler's approach to pay and organizational effectiveness
	■ Robert House's path-goal and charismatic theories of leadership
1980s	■ Peter Block's political skills for empowered managers
	■ Charles Manz's approach to self-managed work teams
	■ Edgar Schein's approach to leadership and organizational culture

in scientific management at Midvale Steel Company, Bethlehem Steel Company, and elsewhere.[1] Taylor applied engineering principles to the study of people and their behavior at work. He pioneered the use of performance standards for workers, set up differential piece-rate systems of pay, and argued for the scientific selection of employees. His ultimate hope was for an improvement in labor-management relationships in American industry. Taylor's lasting contributions include organizational goal-setting programs, incentive pay systems, and modern employee selection techniques.

The late 1800s also saw the United States make the transition from an agricultural to an industrial society and Taylor was part of this transformation process. About the same time Taylor was developing a uniquely American approach to the design of work, Max Weber was undertaking a classic work on religion and capitalism in Germany.[2] Weber's lasting legacies to management and organizational behavior are found in his notions of bureaucracies and the Protestant ethic, the latter an important feature of Chapter 5 in the text. Another major event of this era, as noted in Table A.1, was Walter Cannon's discovery of the stress response in about 1915. This discovery laid a foundation for psychosomatic medicine, industrial hygiene, and an understanding of the emotional components of health at work and play.[3] Finally, the first quarter of the twentieth century saw the initiation of the Hawthorne Studies, a major research advancement in understanding people at work.[4] The Hawthorne Studies are discussed in some depth in the second half of this brief history.

Beginning at the end of the 1930s and extending through the 1950s, as noted in Table A.1, came a series of major contributions to the understanding of leadership, motivation, and behavior in organizations.[5] Lewin, Lippitt, and White's early examination of autocratic, democratic, and laissez-faire leadership styles was followed over a decade later by Ralph Stogdill's extensive studies at Ohio State University focusing on leader behaviors. This marked a point of departure from earlier leadership studies, which had focused on the traits of the leader. Abraham Maslow proposed a need hierarchy of human motivation during the early 1940s, which was one foundation for Douglas McGregor's theorizing in the 1950s about assumptions concerning the human side of a business enterprise. The 1950s was the decade in which Frederick Herzberg developed a new theory of motivation, which he later translated into an approach to job design, called job enrichment. This is quite different from the approach to designing work that Charles Walker and Robert Guest formulated a decade earlier in response to the problems they found with routine work. Attention was also given to group dynamics during this era in an effort to explain small group behavior.[6]

The 1960s and 1970s saw continued attention to theories of motivation, leadership, the design of work, and job satisfaction.[7] For example, Arthur Turner and Paul Lawrence's studies of diverse industrial jobs in various industries was a forerunner for the research program of Richard Hackman and Greg Oldham, which led to their job characteristics theory a decade later. Robert Blake and Jane Mouton's managerial grid was a variation on the Ohio State leadership studies of a decade earlier, while Fred Fiedler's contingency theory of leadership was an entirely new approach to leadership that emerged during the 1960s. Robert House proposed path-goal and charismatic theories of leadership during this era, and Edward Lawler drew attention to the importance of pay in performance and organizational effectiveness.

The 1980s saw attention shift to organizational culture, teamwork, and political skills in organizations. Peter Block drew our attention to the political skills required to empower managers in increasingly challenging working environments while Charles Manz directed attention to teamwork and self-managed teams. Leadership continued to be an important topic and Edgar Schein formulated a framework for understanding how leaders created, embedded, and maintained an organizational culture. Throughout the changing and unfolding story of the study of organizational behavior during the twentieth century there has been a common theme: How do we understand people, their psychology, and their behavior in the workplace?[8]

The intention of this brief historical review and timeline in Table A.1 is to give you a sense of perspective on the drama of unfolding research programs, topics, and investigators who have brought us to the present state of knowledge and practice in organizational behavior. Although the text addresses the field in a topical manner by chapter, we think it important that students of organizational behavior have a sense of historical perspective over the whole field. We now turn to the Hawthorne Studies, one of the seminal research programs from the early part of the century.

The Hawthorne Studies

■ Initiated in 1925 with a grant from Western Electric, the Hawthorne Studies were among the most significant advances in the understanding of organizational behavior during the past century. They were preceded by a series of studies of illumination conducted by Elton Mayo in the textile industry of Philadelphia. The research at the Hawthorne Works (an industrial manufacturing facility in Cicero, Illinois) was directed by Fritz Roethlisberger and consisted

This view of a cord-finishing department is typical of those departments at the Hawthorne Works which were almost entirely staffed by women. Approximately 100 women sit four abreast at long tables, each with a bundle of cord and a small machine in front of them to finish the cord. This photo was taken in December 1925, just as the groundbreaking Hawthorne Studies were getting under way.

of four separate studies over a seven-year period.[9] These studies included (1) experiments in illumination, (2) the relay assembly test room study, (3) experiments in interviewing workers, and (4) the bank wiring room study. We will briefly examine this research program.

Experiments in Illumination

The experiments in illumination were a direct follow-up of Mayo's earlier work in the textile industry. At Hawthorne, the experiments in illumination consisted of a series of studies of test groups, in which the researchers varied illumination levels, and control groups, in which conditions were held constant. The purpose was to examine the relation of the quality and quantity of illumination to the efficiency of industrial workers. The experiments began in 1925 and extended over several years.

The researchers were surprised to discover that productivity increased to roughly the same rate in both test and control groups. It was only in the final experiment, where they decreased illumination levels to 0.06 footcandle (roughly moonlight intensity), that an appreciable decline in output occurred. The anticipated finding of a positive, linear relationship between illumination and industrial efficiency was simply not found. The researchers concluded that the results were "screwy" in the absence of this simple, direct cause-and-effect relationship.

It is from these first experiments that the term *Hawthorne Effect* was coined, referring originally to the fact that people's knowledge that they are being studied leads them to modify their behavior. A closer consideration of the Hawthorne Effect reveals that it is poorly understood and has taken on different meanings with the passage of time.[10] Hence, it has become somewhat an imprecise concept.

Relay Assembly Test Room Study

The researchers next set out to study workers segregated according to a range of working condition variables, such as work room temperature and humidity, work schedule, rest breaks, and food consumption. The researchers chose five women in the relay assembly test room and kept careful records of the predictor variables, as well as output (measuring the time it took each woman to assemble a telephone relay of approximately forty parts).

Again, there was little the researchers were able to conclude from the actual data in this study in terms of a relationship between the predictor variables and industrial efficiency. However, they began to suspect that employee attitudes and sentiments were critically important variables not previously accounted for. Therefore, the researchers underwent a radical change of thought.

Experiments in Interviewing Workers

In 1928, a number of the researchers began a program of going into the workforce, without their normal tools and equipment, for the purpose of getting the workers to talk about what was important to them. Nearly 20,000 workers were interviewed over a period of two years, and in this interviewing process a major breakthrough occurred. The interview study was a form of research in which the investigators did not have a set of preconceptions concerning what they would find, as was the case in the two earlier phases of research. Rather, they set out to sympathetically and skillfully listen to what each worker was saying. As the interviewing progressed, the researchers discovered that the workers would open up and talk freely about what were the most important, and at times problematic, issues on their minds. The researchers discovered a rich and intriguing world previously unexamined within the Hawthorne Works.

Ultimately, Roethlisberger and his colleagues formulated guidelines for the conduct of interviews, and these guidelines became the basis for contemporary interviewing and active listening skills.[11] The discovery of the informal organization and its relationship to the formal organization began during the interview study. This led to a richer understanding of the social, interpersonal dynamics of people at work.

The Bank Wiring Room Study

The concluding study at Hawthorne was significant because it confirmed the importance of one aspect of the informal organization on worker productivity. Specifically, the researchers studied workers in the bank wiring room and found that the behavioral norms set by the work group had a powerful influence over the productivity of the group. The higher the norms, the greater the productivity. The lower the norms, the lower the productivity. The power of the peer group and the importance of group influence on individual behavior and productivity were confirmed in the bank wiring room.

The Hawthorne Studies laid a foundation for understanding people's social and psychological behavior in the workplace. Some of the methods used at Hawthorne, such as the experimental design methods and the interviewing technique, are used today for research in organizations. However, the discipline of organizational behavior is more than the psychology of people at work and more than the sociology of their behavior in organizations. Organizational behavior emerges from a wide range of interdisciplinary influences.

References

1. F. W. Taylor, *The Principles of Scientific Management* (New York: Norton, 1911).

2. M. Weber, *The Protestant Ethic and the Spirit of Capitalism* (London: Talcott Parson, tr., 1930).

3. W. B. Cannon, *Bodily Changes in Pain, Hunger, Fear, and Rage* (New York: Appleton, 1915).
4. F. J. Roethlisberger and W. J. Dickson, *Management and the Worker* (Cambridge, Mass.: Harvard University Press, 1939).
5. K. Lewin, R. Lippitt, and R. K. White, "Patterns of Aggressive Behavior in Experimentally Created 'Social Climates,' " *Journal of Social Psychology* 10 (1939): 271–299; A. H. Maslow, *Motivation and Personality* (New York: Harper & Row, 1954); F. Herzberg, B. Mausner, and B. Snyderman, *The Motivation to Work*, 2d ed. (New York: Wiley, 1959); E. A. Locke, "Toward a Theory of Task Motivation and Incentives," *Organizational Behavior and Human Performance* 3 (1968): 157–189; R. M. Stogdill, *Handbook of Leadership: A Survey of Theory and Research* (New York: Free Press, 1974); G. A. Yukl, *Leadership in Organizations*, 3d ed. (Englewood Cliffs, N.J.: Prentice-Hall, 1995).
6. G. C. Homans, *The Human Group* (New York: Harcourt Brace Jovanovich, 1950).
7. J. R. Hackman and G. Oldham, *Work Redesign* (Reading, Mass.: Addison-Wesley, 1980); P. C. Smith, L. M. Kendall, and C. L. Hulin, *The Measurement of Satisfaction in Work and Retirement* (Chicago: Rand McNally, 1969).
8. N. R. F. Maier, *Psychology in Industry: A Psychological Approach to Industrial Problems*, 2nd ed. (Boston: Houghton Mifflin, 1955).
9. F. J. Roethlisberger, *Management and Morale* (Cambridge, Mass: Harvard University Press, 1941).
10. J. G. Adair, "The Hawthorne Effect: A Reconsideration of Methodological Artifact," *Journal of Applied Psychology* 69 (1984): 334–345.
11. F. J. Roethlisberger, W. J. Dickson, and H. A. Wright, *Management and the Worker: An Account of a Research Program Conducted by the Western Electric Company, Hawthorne Works, Chicago* (Cambridge, Mass.: Harvard University Press, 1950); A. G. Athos and J. J. Gabarro, *Interpersonal Behavior: Communication and Understanding in Relationships* (Englewood Cliffs, N.J.: Prentice-Hall, 1978).

How Do We Know What We Know about Organizational Behavior?

By Uma Sekaran

This book has examined the skills and knowledge that managers need to be successful in their jobs. But how do you know how much faith you should have in all the information you acquire from textbooks and management journals? Are some theories and statements more applicable than others? Even when applicable, will they apply at all times and under all circumstances? You can find answers to these important questions once you know the foundation on which theories and assertions rest. This appendix provides that foundation. It first examines why managers need to know about research, and then discusses the basis for knowledge in this field. It then looks at the research process and research design and ends with a discussion of how research knowledge affects you.

Why Managers Should Know About Research

■ Why is it necessary for you to know about research? First, this knowledge helps you determine how much of what is offered in textbooks is of practical use to you as a manager. Second, a basic understanding of how good empirical research is done can make you an effective manager by helping you to make intelligent decisions about research proposals and reports that reach your desk. Third, it enables you to become an informed and discriminating consumer of research articles published in the management journals that you need to read to keep up with new ideas and technology. For your convenience, a list of the current academic and practitioner-oriented journals that frequently publish articles in organizational behavior is provided in Table B–1.

Understanding scientific research methods enables you to differentiate between good and appropriate research, which you can apply in your setting, and flawed or inappropriate research, which you cannot use. Moreover, knowledge of techniques such as sampling design enables you to decide whether the results of a study using a particular type of sample in certain types of organizations is applicable to your setting.

Managers need to understand, predict, and control the research-oriented problems in their environment. Some of these problems may be relatively simple and can be solved through simple data gathering and analysis. Others may be relatively complex, needing the assistance of researchers or consultants. In either

TABLE B–1

Journals with Organizational Behavior Articles

ACADEMIC JOURNALS	PRACTITIONER-ORIENTED JOURNALS
Academy of Management Journal	Academy of Management Executive
Academy of Management Review	Business Horizons
Administrative Science Quarterly	California Management Review
Advances in International Comparative Management	Columbia Journal of World Business
American Journal of Small Business Behavioral Science	Harvard Business Review
Group and Organization Studies	Human Resource Development Quarterly
Human Relations	Industrial Relations
Human Resource Management	Industry Week
Human Resource Management Review	Organizational Dynamics
Human Resource Planning	Personnel Journal
Industrial and Labor Relations Review	SAM Advanced Management Journal
International Journal of Management	Sloan Management Review
Journal of Applied Behavioral Science	Supervision
Journal of Applied Business Research	Training
Journal of Applied Psychology	Training and Development Journal
Journal of Business	
Journal of Business Ethics	
Journal of Business Research	
Journal of Human Resource Management	
Journal of International Business Studies	
Journal of Management	
Journal of Management Studies	
Journal of Occupational Psychology	
Journal of Organizational Behavior	
Journal of Organizational Behavior Management	
Journal of Vocational Behavior	
Organizational Behavior and Human Decision Processes	
Personnel Administrator	
Sex Roles	
Women in Business	

case, without some basic knowledge of scientific research, managers will be unable to solve the problems themselves or to work effectively with consultants.

Managers need to discuss their problems with consultants in a useful way. This includes informing the problem solvers right at the start of the consulting process of any constraints (such as company records that are off-limits to outsiders) or of types of recommendations that will not be considered (such as laying off or hiring more people). Such discussions not only save time but also help the managers and researchers start off on the right foot. Managers who don't understand the important aspects of research will not be equipped to anticipate and forestall the inevitable hurdles in manager-researcher interactions. Also, paying a consultant handsomely for a research report will not help the company unless the manager is capable of determining how much scientific value can be placed on the findings. For these and other reasons, a working knowledge of the scientific research process and research design is necessary.

Our Basis for Knowledge

■ Observation and scientific data gathering have led to some of our knowledge about management. For instance, very early on, Frederick Winslow Taylor observed, studied, experimented, and demonstrated that coal-mining operations could be more efficiently managed by changing the way men shoveled coal—changing how the shovel was handled, how the body movements were made, and so on. The era of scientific management that Taylor's work ushered in provided much knowledge about how management could improve efficiency. This type of knowledge is not easy to come by, however, when we are examining employees' feelings, attitudes, and behaviors. Our knowledge of organizational behavior stems instead from armchair theories, case studies, and scientific research.

Armchair Theories

In trying to understand organizational behavior, management experts and scholars initially resorted to *armchair theorizing*—theorizing based on the observation of various phenomena and behaviors in the workplace. For instance, Douglas McGregor, through observation and experience, theorized that managers have two different world views of employees. Some managers (Theory X) assume that employees are by nature lazy and not very bright, that they dislike responsibility and prefer to be led rather than to lead, and that they resist change. Other managers (Theory Y) assume that employees have the opposite characteristics. McGregor's concept of Theory X and Theory Y managers has become a classic armchair theory.

Few people either totally accept or totally dispute this theory because of the lack of hard data to either substantiate or negate this interesting notion. Armchair theories are based on natural observation with no systematic experimentation and hence are not very useful for application in organizations.

Case Studies

Case studies—studies that examine the environment and background in which events occur in specific organizations in a particular period of time—help us to understand behavior in those organizations at that time. For example, we could study a particular organization in depth to determine the contributing factors that led to its fast recovery after a prolonged recession. We might find several factors, including price reductions, the offering of good incentives to a highly motivated work force, and the taking of big risks. However, the findings from this one-time study of an organization offer only limited knowledge about fast recovery from recessions because the findings may not hold true for other organizations or for even the same organization at another time. The replication of case studies is almost impossible, since environmental and background factors are rarely the same from organization to organization. Most of the companies whose problems you have been asked to solve are from real cases written by management scholars who studied the companies. The solutions they found may not work for other organizations experiencing similar problems because of differences in size, technology, environment, labor force, clientele, and other internal and external factors. However, through case studies, we do gather information and gain insights and knowledge that might help us to develop theories and test them later.

Scientific Research

Empirical or data-based *scientific research* identifies a problem and solves it after a systematic gathering and analysis of the relevant data. This type of research offers in-depth understanding, confidence in the findings, and the capability of applying the knowledge gained to similar organizations. Scientific research is the main focus of this appendix.

Scientific Inquiry

■ Scientific inquiry involves a well-planned and well-organized systematic effort to identify and solve a problem. It encompasses a series of well-thought-out and carefully executed activities that help to solve the problem—as opposed to the symptoms—that is identified.

Purposes of Scientific Research: Applied and Basic Research

Scientific inquiry can be undertaken for two different purposes: to solve an existing problem that a particular organization faces, or to examine problems that organizations generally encounter and to generate solutions, thereby expanding the knowledge base. Research undertaken to solve an existing problem in a specific setting is *applied research*. In this type of research, the findings are immediately applied to solve the problem. Many professors acting as consultants to organizations do applied research.

Research undertaken to add information to our existing base of knowledge is *basic research*. A large number of issues are of common interest to many organizations—for example, how to increase the productivity of a diverse work force or how to eradicate sexual harassment in the workplace. The knowledge gained from research on such general issues can become useful later for application in organizational settings, but that is not the primary goal of basic research. The goal is to generate knowledge with which to build better theories that can be tested later. Basic research is often published in academic journals.

The Two Faces of Science: Theory and Empirical Research

Theory and empirical research are the two faces of science. Organizations benefit when good theories are developed and then substantiated through scientific research, because the results can then be confidently used for problem solving.

THEORY A *theory* is a postulated network of associations among various factors that a researcher is interested in investigating. For example, given what has been published thus far, you might theorize that self-confident employees perceive their work environment positively, which fosters their productivity, which in turn generates more profits for the company. In constructing this theory, you have postulated a positive relationship between (a) the self-confidence of employees and their positive attitude toward their work environment, (b) their attitude toward the work environment and their productivity, and (c) their productivity and the company's profits.

No doubt, this theory appeals to common sense; but in order to establish whether or not it holds true, we need to actually test it in organizations. Thus, theories offer the basis for doing scientific, data-based research; and the theories and research together add to our knowledge. Conducting empirical research without the basis of sound theories does not steer us in the right direction, and building theories without empirically testing them limits their value.

The usefulness of good theories cannot be overstated. A good theory is formulated only after a careful examination of all the previous research and writings on the topic of interest, so that no factor already established as important is inadvertently omitted. Theory building offers unique opportunities to look at phenomena from different perspectives or to add new dimensions to existing ways of examining a phenomenon. New insights and creative ideas for theory building can come through personal observation, through intuition, or even through informal discussions with employees.

Testable theories are theories whose hypothesized relationships among measurable variables can be empirically tested and verified. When tested and substantiated repeatedly, such theories become the foundation on which subsequent theory building progresses. The next issue of interest is how theories are affirmed through empirical research.

EMPIRICAL RESEARCH As we have just seen, theories are of no practical use unless we have confidence that they work and can be applied to problem solving in organizational settings. Empirical research allows us to test the value of theories.

Empirical research is research that involves identifying the factors to be studied, gathering the relevant data, analyzing them, and drawing conclusions from the results of data analysis. It could involve simple qualitative analysis of the data, or it could be more complex, using a hypothetico-deductive approach. In *qualitative analysis*, responses to open-ended questions are obtained and meaningfully classified, and certain conclusions are drawn. In the *hypothetico-deductive approach*, a problem is identified, defined, and studied in depth; then, a theory is formulated; from that theory, testable hypotheses are generated; next, a research design is developed, relevant data are gathered and analyzed, results are interpreted, and conclusions (or deductions) are drawn from the results. Figure B–1 illustrates this approach.

To be called "scientific," research should conform to certain basic principles. It should be conducted objectively (without subjective biases). It should have a good and rigorous design (which we will examine shortly). It should be testable; that is, the conjectured relationships among factors in a setting should be capable of being tested. It should be replicable; that is, the results must be similar each time similar research is conducted. Finally, the findings should be generalizable (applicable to similar settings). It goes without saying, then, that scientific research offers precision (a good degree of exactitude) and a high degree of confidence in the results of the research (i.e. the researcher can say that 95 percent of the times, the results generated by the research will hold true, with only a 5 percent chance of its not being so).

The Research Process

■ The research process starts with a definition of the problem. To help define the problem, the researcher may interview people and study published materials in the area of interest in order to better understand what is happening in the environment. After defining the problem in clear and precise terms, the researcher develops a theoretical framework, generates hypotheses, creates the research design, collects data, analyzes data, interprets results, and draws conclusions.

Problem Definition

The first job for the researcher is to define the problem. Often, however, it is difficult to precisely state the specific research question to be investigated. The researcher might simply know the broad area of interest—for instance, discrimination—without being clear about which aspect of discrimination to study. In order to focus on the issue to be investigated, the researcher might need to collect some preliminary information that will help to narrow down the issue.

FIGURE B–1

Steps in the Hypothetico-Deductive Approach to Research

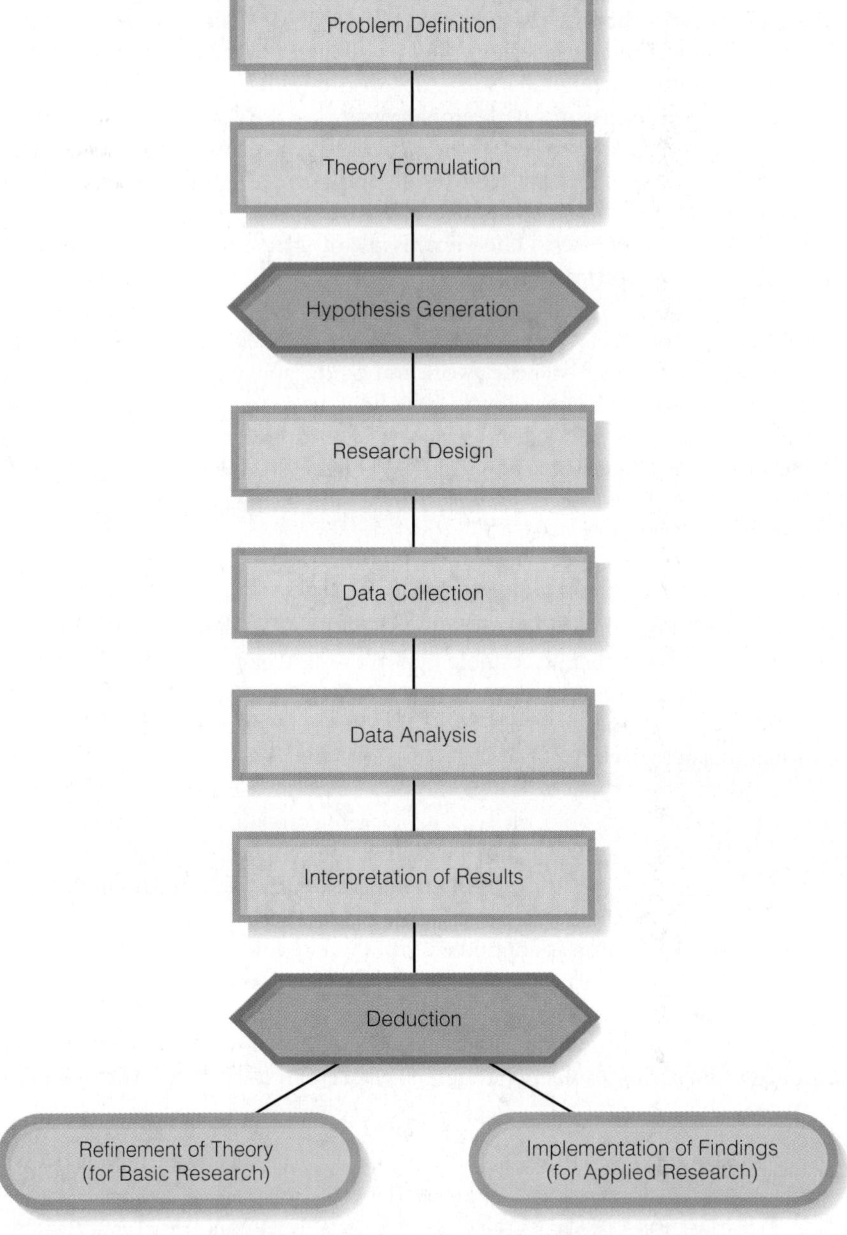

Such information can be obtained by interviewing people in organizations and by doing a literature survey. For example, employees of different gender, race, age, physical ability, and the like may be interviewed to determine the specific aspect of discrimination on which to focus. These interviews also provide insight into what the employees (rather than the researchers) consider important. The literature survey ensures that no pertinent variable is inadvertently omitted and that there is a credible and defensible basis for the research to be done. The researcher conducts an exhaustive search for all the published work in the area of interest to determine what research has been done thus far in the particular area and with what results. The search consumes a lot of time, as one must wade through several psychological, sociological, anthropological, and other relevant journals.

With all this information in hand, the researcher is now ready to define the problem. A well-defined, precise problem statement is a must for any study. The problem definition for the broad topic of discrimination could be this: *What are the important factors that contribute to employees' beliefs that they are being discriminated against by their immediate supervisor in cross-gender or cross-racial supervisor-employee relationships?*

Theoretical Framework

The next step is to develop a theoretical framework for the study. It involves focusing on the pertinent variables for the study and discussing the anticipated or theorized network of connections among the variables. For the discrimination problem, the framework might identify three factors related to employees' beliefs that they were discriminated against by the supervisor: (a) the level of mutual trust that is perceived by the employee to exist between the supervisor and employee (high to low), (b) the manner in which the supervisor offers performance feedback to the employee (in a forthright and helpful manner rather than in a derogatory and hurtful way), and (c) the extent to which the supervisor plays the role of mentor to the employee (training the subordinate and promoting the person's interests in career advancement to being indifferent toward the employee's career progress).

A network of logical connections among these four variables of interest to the study—discrimination (the dependent variable) and trust, performance feedback, and mentoring (the three independent variables)—can then be formulated. These connections with the anticipated nature and direction of the relationships among the variables are postulated in the theoretical framework.

Hypotheses

On the basis of the theoretical framework, the researcher next generates hypotheses. A *hypothesis* is a testable statement of the conjectured relationship between two or more variables. It is derived from the connections postulated in the theoretical framework. An example of a hypothesis is this: The more the employee perceives the supervisor as performing the mentoring role, the less the employee will feel discriminated against by the supervisor. The statement can be tested through data gathering and correlational analysis to see if it is supported.

Research Design

The next step in the research process is research design. Because this step is complex, it is covered in a separate section of the chapter, after the research process.

Data Collection

After creating the research design, the researcher must gather the relevant data. In our example of the discrimination problem, we would collect data on the four variables of interest from employees in one or more organizations, we would obtain information about their race and gender and that of their supervisors, and we would seek such demographic data as age, educational level, and position in the organization. This information helps us describe the sample and enable us to see later if demographic characteristics make a difference in the results. For example, we might discover during data analysis that older employees sense less discrimination than their younger counterparts. Such information could even provide a basis for further theory development.

Data Analysis

Having collected the data, the researcher must next analyze them, using statistical procedures, to test whether the hypotheses have been substantiated. In the case of the discrimination hypothesis, if a correlational analysis between the variables of mentoring and discrimination indicates a significant negative correlation, the hypothesis will have been supported; that is, we have been correct in conjecturing that the more the supervisor is perceived as a mentor, the less the employee feels discriminated against. Each of the hypotheses formulated from the theoretical framework is tested, and the results are examined.

Interpreting Results and Drawing Conclusions

The final step is to interpret the results of the data analysis and draw conclusions about them. In our example, if a significant negative relationship is indeed found between mentoring and discrimination, then one of our conclusions might be that mentoring helps fight feelings of discrimination. We might therefore recommend that if the organization wants to create a climate where employees do not feel discriminated against, supervisors should actively engage in mentoring. If the organization accepts this recommendation, it might conduct training programs to make supervisors better mentors. By testing and substantiating each of the hypotheses, we might find a multitude of solutions to overcome the perception of discrimination by employees.

Summary

We can see that every step in the research process is important. Unless the problem is well defined, the research endeavor will be fruitless. If a thorough literature survey is not done, a defensible theoretical framework cannot be developed and useful hypotheses cannot be generated—which compromises effective problem solving. Using the correct methods in data gathering and analysis and drawing relevant conclusions are all indispensable methodological steps for conducting empirical research. We next examine some of the research design issues which are integral to conducting good research.

Research Design

■ Issues regarding research design relate particularly to how the variables are measured, how the data are collected, what sampling design is used, and how the data are analyzed. Before decisions in these areas are made, some details about the nature and purpose of the study have to be determined so there is a good match between the purpose of the study and the design choices. If the research design does not mesh with the research goals, the right solutions will not be found.

Important Concepts in Research Design

Five important concepts in research design must be understood before an adequate design can be created: nature of study, study setting, types of study, researcher interference, and time horizon. The *nature of study* is the purpose of the study—whether it is to establish correlations among variables or causation. The *study setting* could be either the environment in which the phenomena studied normally and naturally occur—*the field*—or it could be in a contrived, artificial setting—the laboratory. The *type of study* is either experimental (to establish causal connections) or correlational (to establish correlations). Experiments can be conducted in an artificial setting—a *lab experiment*, or it could be conducted in the organization itself where events naturally occur—*field experiment. Researcher interference* is the extent to which the researcher manipulates the independent variable and controls other contaminating factors in the study setting that are likely to affect the cause-effect relationship. The *time horizon* is the number of data collection points in the study; the study could be either one-shot (various types of data are collected only once during the investigation) or longitudinal (same or similar data are collected more than once from the same system during the course of the study).

Purpose of Study and Design Choices

One of the primary issues to consider before making any research design decision is the purpose of the study. Is the research to establish a causal relationship (that variable X causes variable Y), or is it to detect any correlations that might exist between two or more variables? A study to establish a cause-effect relationship differs in many areas (for example, the setting, type of study, extent of researcher interference with the ongoing processes, and time frame of the study) from a study to examine correlations among factors. Figure B–2 depicts the fit between the goal of the study and the characteristics of the study.

Causal Studies

Studies conducted to detect causal relationships call for an experimental design, considerable researcher interference, and a longitudinal time span. The design could consist of laboratory experiments, field experiments, or simulations.

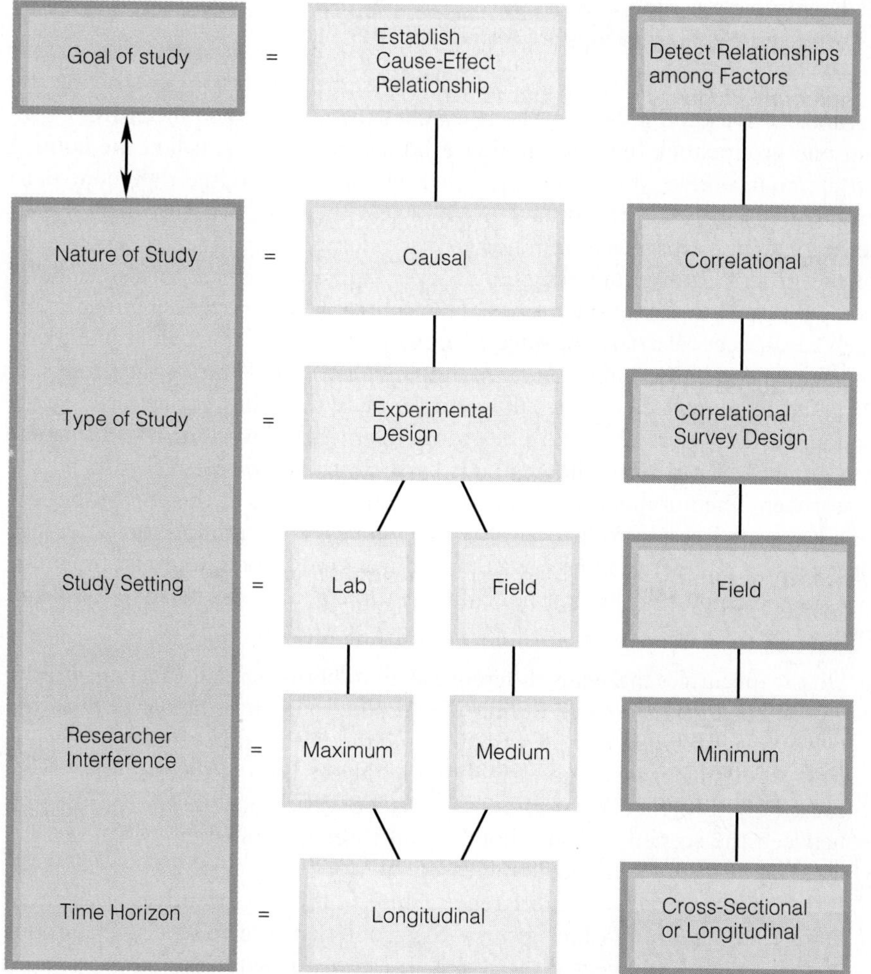

FIGURE B–2
Fit between Goal of Study and Study Characteristics

LABORATORY EXPERIMENTS A rigorous causal study may call for a *laboratory experiment*, where participants are exposed to an artificial environment and an artificial stimulus in order to establish a cause-effect relationship. The experiment is set up with maximum researcher interference; both manipulation and controls (described later) are used, and data are collected from the subjects more than once during the experiment (longitudinally). Following is an example of how a lab experiment is conducted.

Suppose a manager wants to know which of two incentives—offering stock options or giving a bonus—would better improve employee productivity. To determine this, the manager has to experiment with each of the two types of incentives to see which offers better results. Not knowing how to proceed, the manager might hire a researcher, who is likely to recommend conducting a lab experiment first, and then a field experiment. The lab experiment firmly establishes the causal relationship, and the field experiment confirms whether or not the causal relationship established during the lab experiment holds good in the organizational setting.

To set up a lab experiment in which thirty subjects participate, the following is done:

1. An artificial setting is created. It will consist of three conference rooms in which the experiment is conducted after regular work hours.
2. A simple job—assembling cardboard houses—is given to the subjects who take part in the experiment for two hours.
3. The subjects receive an imaginary bonus in the form of cardboard chips and stock options in the form of fake certificates.
4. Each subject is randomly assigned to one of the three conference rooms, so three ten-member groups are formed.

For the first hour, all three groups will be assigned the task of assembling the cardboard houses. Thereafter, the researcher manipulates the incentives—giving one group stock options; another a bonus; and a third, called the control group, no incentives at all. The researcher has already exercised tight control to ensure that all three groups have more or less the same types of members in terms of ability, experience, and the like by randomly assigning members to each of the groups. In random assignment, every member has an equal chance of being assigned to any of the groups. This control helps avoid contamination of the cause-effect relationship, since all factors that might affect the causal relationship (age, ability, and so on) are randomly distributed among the groups.

The data are collected at two different times, in the following manner. At the end of the first hour, when all three groups have worked without any incentives, the number of cardboard houses built by each group will be recorded by the researcher. The numbers are again counted and recorded at the end of the second hour, after the introduction of the incentives. Determining the difference between the number of houses assembled during the second hour and the number assembled during the first hour for the three groups clarifies the following two issues:

- Do the incentives make any difference at all to performance? Obviously, if the performance has increased during the second hour for either or both of the two groups provided with incentives, while there is no difference for the control group, then it is safe to surmise that either or both of the incentives have caused performance to rise. If there is no difference in the production between the second and first hour for all three groups, then, of course, the incentives have not caused an increase in performance.
- If the incentives do make a difference, which of the two incentives has worked better? By examining which group—the group that received the stock options or the group that received the bonus—performed better during the second

hour, we know which of the two incentives worked better. The incentive that increases performance more will obviously be preferred by the company.

Since all possible contaminating factors have been controlled by the random assignment of members to the three groups, the cause-effect relationships found can be accepted with a high degree of confidence.

FIELD EXPERIMENTS What occurred in the tightly controlled artificial lab setting may or may not happen in an organizational setting, where many of the factors (such as employees' ages and experience) cannot be controlled and the jobs to be done might be quite complex. But having established a strong causal relationship in the lab setting, the researcher is eager to see if the causal relationship found in the lab setting is generalizable to the organization, or field setting.

For the field experiment, three experimental cells (three branches or departments of the company, or whatever other units are appropriate for the organization) can be chosen. Real bonus and stock options can be offered to two groups, while the third group is treated as a control group and given no incentives. Work performance data can be collected for the three cells before the incentives are introduced and again six months after the incentives are introduced.

While it is possible to manipulate the incentive in a field experiment, it is not possible to control the contaminating factors (ability, experience, and so on). Since employees are already placed, members cannot be randomly assigned to the three units. Under the circumstances, researcher interference can be only partial, since the independent variable can be manipulated but other factors cannot be controlled. Even manipulating the independent variable is not easy, because people in organizations get suspicious and anxious as the word spreads that some strange changes are being made at some sites. Not only does this cause apprehension among employees, but it may also produce invalid results. Because of these difficulties, very few field experiments are conducted in organizational behavior research. However, if the manipulation is successful and the results of the field experiment are similar to those of the lab experiment, the manager can confidently introduce the changes needed to obtain the desired results.

If you read journal articles describing experimental designs, you will want to see how well the manipulations were done (were the independent variables successfully manipulated, or did the subjects see through the manipulations?) and how tightly the contaminating variables were controlled. If the subjects in the various groups differed in some characteristics that are relevant to the cause-effect relationship, then it cannot be said with confidence that only the manipulated independent variable caused the dependent variable. Other factors in the setting might also have influenced the dependent variable, and they might be impossible to trace.[1]

SIMULATIONS Somewhere between lab and field experiments are *simulations*—experiments that are conducted in settings that closely resemble field settings. The specially created settings look much like actual environments in which events normally occur—for example, offices with desks, computers, and phones. Members of the experimental group are randomly selected and exposed to real-world experiences over a period of time, during which their behavior is studied. A free simulation for studying leadership styles, called "Looking Glass," has been used in management classes. This simulation enables students to study different kinds of behavior as the researcher manipulates some of the stimuli while allowing the flow of events to be governed by the reactions of the participants.[2]

Correlational Studies

Researchers and managers may not be interested in establishing causal connections. Instead, they may want to understand, describe, or predict occurrences in the workplace. In general, they want to know which factors are related to desirable outcomes (such as employee loyalty to the organization) and which to undesirable outcomes (such as high turnover rates). *Correlational studies* are studies that are not specifically geared toward establishing cause-effect relationships. Such studies may be *exploratory*—trying to understand certain relationships; *descriptive*—trying to describe certain phenomena at the workplace; or *analytical*—focusing on testing hypotheses. Correlational studies are always conducted in the field setting with minimum researcher interference, and they can be either one-shot or longitudinal. The vast majority of the research articles published in organizational behavior journals are field studies examining correlations among factors.

To conduct a scientific study, whether causal or correlational, certain research design decisions must be made. As Figure B–3 shows, these decisions involve measurement, issues, data collection methods, sampling design, and data analysis procedures.

Measurement Issues

We saw earlier that it is difficult to measure attitudes, feelings, and other abstract concepts. Since the measurement of variables in the organizational sciences is not as exact as in the physical sciences, management research cannot be completely scientific. It is possible, however, to minimize biases in measurement by carefully developing valid and reliable measures for even abstract concepts. The primary aspects in measurement are: operational definition, the "goodness" of measures, and the measurement techniques to be used.

OPERATIONAL DEFINITION Attitudes such as job satisfaction and organizational commitment do not easily lend themselves to measurement. To measure them, we first need to translate them into observable behaviors. *Operational definition* is the reduction of the level of abstraction of concepts so as to identify the observable behaviors and measure them.

For example, how can we measure the motivational level of individuals? We know that highly motivated people engage in the following types of behaviors, among others: They are driven by work, and they keep persevering even if they initially fail to accomplish what they want. We can measure the abstract concept of motivation by developing an instrument that asks subjects to respond to several suitably worded questions tapping these behaviors.[3] Most of the abstract concepts that are important to the study of organizational behavior have been operationally defined by scholars, who have developed "good" instruments for measuring them.[4]

■ **FIGURE B–3**

Research Design Decisions

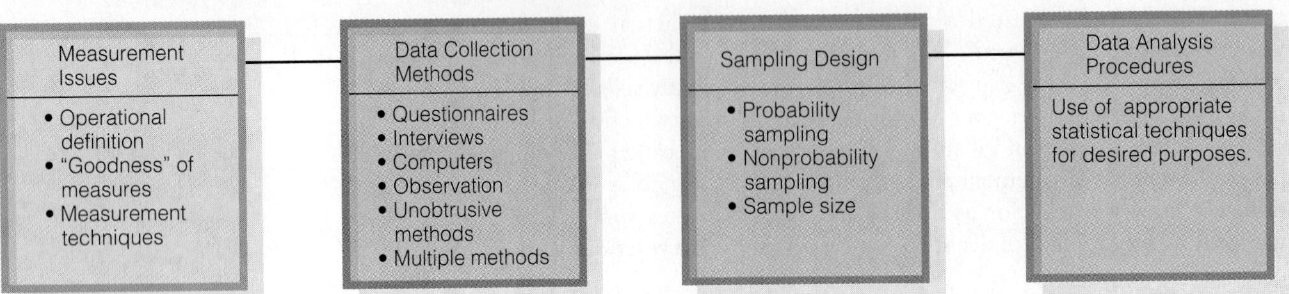

"GOODNESS" OF MEASURES "Good" measurement instruments offer researchers the confidence that they do indeed measure what is desired to be measured and in a thorough and accurate manner. The goodness of instruments is established through their validity and reliability.

Validity is our confidence that the instrument used does indeed measure the concept it is supposed to measure. For instance, if a twenty-item instrument is developed to measure job satisfaction, we need to know that it does indeed measure job satisfaction, not employees' general happiness.

Researchers usually establish various types of validity for the measures they use. Among them are content validity, criterion-related validity, predictive validity, construct validity, and convergent and discriminant validity. Journal articles often explain the types of validity established for the instrument used, especially if it is newly developed. In general, only such measures as are both valid and reliable are frequently used by researchers.[5]

Reliability is the ability of an instrument to accurately and stably measure a concept over time and across situations. For example, it is not enough for an instrument to measure job satisfaction; it must do so consistently and accurately time and again in all settings. Most researchers discuss the reliability of their instruments in terms of stability and consistency. Test-retest reliability is one indicator of the stability of a measure over time, and Cronbach's alpha, and split-half reliability, indicates the internal consistency of instruments. These are the terms you are likely to come across in published empirical research.

Authors of studies usually provide details of the measures they use, and at a minimum cite their source. Journal editors and reviewers try to ensure that studies to be published have used valid and reliable measures. Discriminating readers of journals reporting empirical studies pay attention to the "goodness" of the measures. If variables are not validly and reliably measured, how can we place any confidence in the results of the study?

MEASUREMENT TECHNIQUES Concepts are not measured solely through questionnaires or interviews. Sometimes, in order to tap certain ideas, feelings, and thoughts that are not easily verbalized, researchers use *projective tests*—Word association, sentence completion, thematic apperception tests, and ink-blot tests are some familiar projective tests. In word association (e.g. **Work** could be associated with excitement or drudgery,) and sentence completion (**"I Like** ——") tests, the respondent is believed to give answers based on deeply embedded feelings, attitudes, and orientations. Marketing researchers use these techniques to assess consumer preferences. Thematic apperception tests and ink-blot tests ask the subject to offer a story or interpret an ink blot. They can be interpreted only by trained psychologists.

Data Collection Methods

Data can be collected through questionnaires, interviews, computers, observation, unobtrusive methods, or a combination of these. The most frequently used method in organizational behavior research is questionnaires.

QUESTIONNAIRES A *questionnaire* is a written set of questions to which respondents record their answers, usually within a close range of alternatives given to them. Questionnaires can be mailed to respondents or administered personally.

Mail questionnaires are commonly used because of the large number of people who can be reached economically even when they are geographically dispersed. As a rule, however, they do not elicit a good response rate, even when stamped, self-addressed envelopes are enclosed for their return. (Researchers sometimes even include, as a small token of their appreciation, a $1 bill.) A 30 percent response rate for mail questionnaires is considered good. Mail responses generally fall far short of even this low percentage. Because of the low response rate, certain types of nonresponse biases can creep into research. For example, we cannot know if those who responded to the survey differ from those who did not. Thus, we cannot be sure that the data are representative of the population we are trying to study.

Personally administered questionnaires are questionnaires given to groups of subjects by the researcher, who collects the responses immediately after completion. This method assures practically a 100 percent response rate. However, many organizations are reluctant to spare company time for the research effort unless the study is of vital importance to them.

INTERVIEWS *Interviews* have the potential to elicit a good deal of information. In *structured interviews*, specific questions are asked of all respondents, and the responses are noted down by the interviewer. In *unstructured interviews*, there is no predetermined format; questions are framed according to responses given to the previous question. Structured interviews are conducted when the interviewer knows precisely what sort of information is needed. They are efficient in terms of the amount of time involved in both obtaining the required information and categorizing the data obtained. Unstructured interviews are conducted when the researcher wants to explore a problem or become more knowledgeable about particular situations.

Face-to-face interviews offer the researcher the advantage of being able to observe the interviewees as they respond to questions. Nonverbal messages transmitted by the interviewees can be observed and explored further. *Telephone interviews*, on the other hand, help the researcher reach a vast number of geographically dispersed individuals. In both face-to-face and telephone interviews, certain types of biases can enter. The way a question is worded and asked, the inflection of a voice, the frame of mind of the interviewee at the time the interview is conducted, and other factors can all contribute to biases in the data.

COMPUTERS *Computer-assisted interviewing* and *computer-aided surveys* will become more popular in the future as more and more people become comfortable using their computers at home and responding to questions contained on diskettes. Interview and questionnaire methods of data collection are greatly facilitated through computers. However, computer literacy of respondents is prerequisite for using computer-assisted data collection techniques effectively.

OBSERVATIONAL SURVEYS *Observational surveys* are another data collection method whereby information is obtained without asking questions of subjects. In this method, the researcher observes firsthand what is going on and how people are behaving in the work setting. The data are collected by either nonparticipant observers (researchers who observe behavior as outsiders) or participant observers (integral members of the work team). An example of a nonparticipant study is one done by Henry Mintzberg, who observed the nature of managerial work over a period of time.

Like interviews, observational surveys can be either structured or unstructured. In a structured observational survey, the observer identifies the factors that are to be observed. For example, the observer might want to note the number of times a manager gives instructions to staff members and how much time this takes. In an unstructured observational survey, the observer might simply want to know how the manager spends the day at the workplace and might jot down all the activities the manager engages in and the time periods and frequencies involved.

Observational studies help prevent respondent bias, since information is not given by the subjects directly. Any bias that might creep in through the self-consciousness of subjects usually lasts only a few days. Then, subjects begin to function and behave normally, oblivious to the presence of the observer.

However, observer fatigue and observer bias cannot be totally avoided in observational studies. Moreover, when several observers are involved in a large research project, inter-observer reliability could become an issue for concern; different observers might interpret and categorize the same behavior differently. This problem can be minimized by training the observers before the start of the project.

UNOBTRUSIVE METHODS Data collection by *unobtrusive methods* offers valid and reliable information; bias is minimized because the source of the data is tangible elements rather than people. For example, the usage of library books can be determined by the wear and tear on them, a source of information more reliable than surveys of users of the library. The number of cans or bottles of beer in the recycling bins outside houses on garbage collection days would offer a good idea of the beer consumption patterns in households. The personnel records of a company would indicate the absenteeism patterns of employees. Unobtrusive methods thus have the potential to offer the most reliable and unbiased data. They are, however, time-consuming and labor-intensive; also, the researcher must obtain the company's permission to gain access to such data.

MULTIPLE METHODS Each data collection method has advantages and disadvantages. The best approach is using multiple methods of collecting data, since it offers researchers a chance to cross-check the information obtained through the various methods. This approach, however, is expensive and hence is used infrequently in organizational behavior research.

When you read journal articles, you should assess the data collection methods used by the researchers to determine if they are adequate. Authors of published studies often discuss the limitations of their research and the biases they have attempted to minimize. The biases could relate to the types of measures used, the data collection methods adopted, the sampling design, and other research process and design issues. Sophisticated managers pay attention to all research design details in order to evaluate the quality of the research.

Sampling Design

Sampling is the process of drawing a limited number of subjects from a larger population, or universe. Since researchers cannot possibly survey the entire universe of people they are interested in studying, they usually draw a sample of subjects from the population for investigation. The sampling design used makes a difference in the generalizability of the findings and determines the usefulness and scientific nature of the study. Sample size is another important issue. There are two broad categories of sampling—probability sampling and nonprobability sampling.

PROBABILITY SAMPLING *Probability sampling* is sampling that ensures that the elements in the population have some known chance, or probability, of being selected for the sample. Because of this, probability sampling designs offer more generalizability than nonprobability designs. There are many probability designs. The *simple random sampling* design, wherein every element in the population has a known and equal chance of being chosen, lends itself to the greatest generalizability. However, other probability designs can be more efficient and offer good generalizability as well. Among them are systematic sampling, stratified random sampling, cluster sampling, and area sampling.

In *systematic sampling*, every *n*th element in the population is chosen as a subject. In *stratified random sampling*, the population is first divided into meaningful strata (for example, blue-collar and white-collar employees); a sample is then drawn from each stratum using either simple random sampling or systematic sampling. *Cluster sampling* is the random selection of chunks (clusters or groups) of elements from the population; every chunk has an equal chance of being selected, and all the members in each chosen chunk participate in the research. For example, in an attitude survey, three departments in an organization can be randomly chosen; all the members of the three departments are the subjects. *Area sampling* is cluster sampling confined to particular geographical areas, such as counties or city blocks. Marketing researchers use cluster and area sampling extensively for surveys.

NONPROBABILITY SAMPLING For some research projects, probability sampling may be impossible or inappropriate. In such cases, *nonprobability* sampling may be used, even if generalizability is impaired or lost. Nonprobability sampling is one where the subjects do not have a known probability of being chosen for the study. For instance, the sample of subjects in a study of sexual harassment must come from those who have experienced such harassment; there is nothing to be gained by researching all the employees of the organization. When the choice of subjects for a study involves a limited number of people who are in a position to provide the required information, a probability sampling design is infeasible. The results of such a study are not generalizable; nevertheless, this type of sampling is the best way to learn about certain problems, such as sexual harassment.

Nonprobability sampling includes convenience sampling, judgment sampling, and quota sampling. In *convenience sampling*, information is collected from whoever is conveniently available. In *judgment sampling*, subjects who are in the best position to provide the required information are chosen. In *quota sampling*, people from different groups—some of which are underrepresented—are sampled for comparison purposes. One example might be a study of middle-class African-Americans and whites.

As noted earlier, nonprobability sampling does not lend itself to generalizability. In reading research articles, you should determine the type of sampling design being used and how much generalizability the author claims for the research.

SAMPLE SIZE Another critical issue in sampling is *sample size*. Too small or too large a sample could distort the results of the research. Tables providing ideal sample sizes for desired levels of precision and confidence are available to researchers. In examining any business report or journal article, you should note the sampling design and the sample size used by the researcher to assess the generalizability of the findings.

Data Analysis Procedures

Beyond good measures, appropriate data collection methods, and an acceptable sampling design, a good research project should also have suitable *data analysis procedures*. Some data cannot be subjected to sophisticated statistical tests. Two examples are data collected on a *nominal scale*, that divides subjects into mutually exclusive groups, such as men and women or the poor and the rich; and data collected on an *ordinal scale*, that rank-orders the subjects and indicates a preference (X is better than Y). Various simple ways are available to analyze such data that are qualitative or nonparametric in nature. For instance, if we have categorized under distinct heading the verbal responses of organizational members to an open-ended question on how they perceive their work environment, a frequency count of the responses in each category would be adequate to describe how the work environment is perceived. Likewise, to detect if the gender of the worker (male versus female) is independent of members' commitment to the organization (less committed versus more committed) a simple X^2 (chi-square) test would suffice.

Sophisticated statistical tests are possible when data have been gathered on interval or ratio scales. Data collected on interval scales—through individuals' responses to questions on equal-appearing multipoint scales—allow for the computation of the arithmetic mean and standard deviation. Data collected on ratio scales also allow us to compute proportions and ratios. For example, an individual who weighs 250 pounds is twice as heavy as one who weighs 125 pounds. Pearson correlations can be calculated, and multiple regression and many multivariate analyses can be made with data obtained on interval and ratio scales. These sorts of analyses cannot be made with data obtained on nominal and ratio scales. Illustrations of the four scales appear in Figure B–4.

One decision that needs to be made before collecting the data is: What kinds of analyses are needed to find answers to the research question? This decision will determine which scales should be used in data collection. Sometimes researchers are tempted to apply more sophisticated statistical analyses to data that do not lend themselves to such analyses (this includes sample sizes below 30). Using inappropriate methods can negatively affect the interpretation of the results and can compromise the problem solution.

Biases in Interpretation of Results

Thus far, we have examined the biases that would result from poor research process and design decisions. Another source of bias is in the interpretation of results. Objectivity plays a large part in the validity of interpretations from the results of data analysis. Objectivity may be difficult, however, if the results of the study do not substantiate the theories painstakingly developed by the researcher.

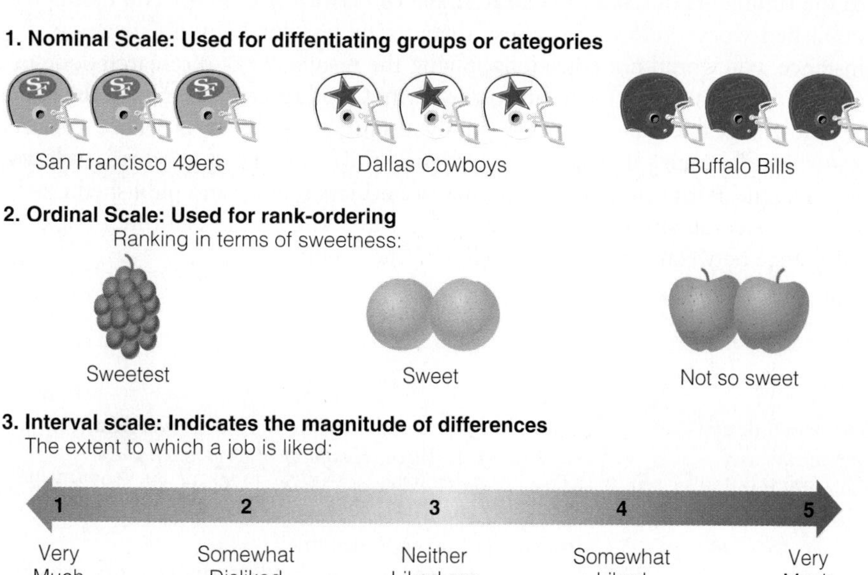

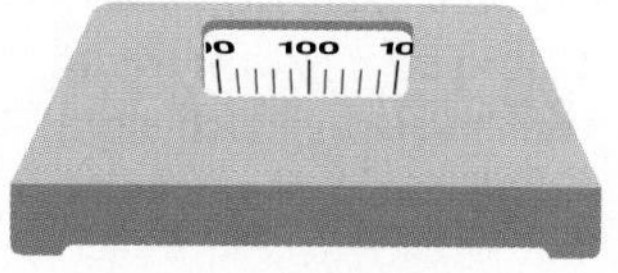

FIGURE B–4
Illustrations of Four Data Analysis Scales

When data analysis does not substantiate one or more of the hypotheses generated, the researcher may be tempted to downplay the results or try to explain them away. For example, a researcher may say that the results were actually in the expected direction even though they were not statistically significant. If a hypothesis has not passed the appropriate statistical test, the hypothesis is just not substantiated, regardless of whether the results were in the theorized direction. When authors try to explain their results, you have to decide for yourself whether the explanations offered are valid.

Organizational Behavior Research and You

■ It is seldom possible to do completely scientific research in the field of organizational behavior. First, adherence to good research design principles may not always be possible, since certain choices (such as obtaining the most representative sample for better generalizability or utilizing the best data collection methods) may be beyond the researcher's control. Second, attitudes and feelings cannot be measured accurately. Hence there are likely to be several types of biases in research in this field. However, by paying careful attention to the research process and rigorously making good research design choices, we are able to minimize the biases and enhance the objectivity, testability, replicability, precision and confidence, and generalizability of our research.

Bias can enter at every stage of the process, from problem definition to problem solution. Errors can creep into experimental designs by way of poor or inadequate manipulations and controls. They can enter into measurement, data collection, sampling, data analysis, interpretation of results, and the drawing of conclusions therefrom.

Unless managers are knowledgeable about some of the methodological flaws that can adversely affect research results, they may inappropriately apply the conclusions drawn in published research to their own settings. Having been exposed to the rudiments of scientific research, *you* can critically examine and evaluate all published works before you assess their usefulness for your organization. For instance, you would not consider applying the results of good research done in a service organization to a manufacturing firm. Good research results in the hands of knowledgeable managers are highly useful tools. That is where research knowledge becomes invaluable. By grasping the essentials of good research, you will become a discriminating consumer of business reports and published articles and can become an effective manager. Research knowledge can often make the difference between managerial excellence and mediocrity.

References

1. Two sources for further reference on experimental design are D. T. Campbell and J. C. Stanley, *Experimental and Quasi-Experimental Designs for Research* (Chicago: Rand McNally, 1966); and T. D. Cook and D. T. Campbell, *Quasi-Experimentation: Design and Analysis Issues for Field Settings* (Boston: Houghton Mifflin, 1979).
2. M. L. Lombardo, M. McCall, and D. L. DeVries, *Looking Glass* (Glenview, Ill.: Scott, Foresman, 1983).
3. Elaboration of how such measures are developed is beyond the scope of this appendix but can be found in U. Sekaran, *Research Methods for Business: A Skill Building Approach*, 2d ed. (New York: Wiley, 1992).
4. Several measures are available in *Psychological Measurement Yearbooks;* J. L. Price, *Handbook of Organizational Measurement* (Lexington, Mass.: D. C. Heath, 1972; and *Michigan Organizational Assessment Packages* (Ann Arbor: Institute of Survey Research).
5. One such instrument is the Job Descriptive Index, which is used to measure job satisfaction. It was developed by P. C. Smith, L. Kendall, and C. Hulin. See their book *The Measurement of Satisfaction in Work and Retirement* (Chicago: Rand McNally, 1969), pp. 79–84.

Glossary

adaptive culture An organizational culture that encourages confidence and risk taking among employees, has leadership that produces change, and focuses on the changing needs of customers.
adhocracy A selectively decentralized form of organization that emphasizes the support staff and mutual adjustment among people.
administrative orbiting Delaying action on a conflict by buying time.
advancement The second, highly achievement-oriented career stage in which people focus on increasing their competence.
affect The emotional component of an attitude.
affective commitment The type of organizational commitment that is based on an individual's desire to remain in an organization.
anthropocentric Placing human considerations at the center of job design decisions.
anthropology The science of the learned behavior of human beings.
anticipatory socialization The first socialization stage, which encompasses all of the learning that takes place prior to the newcomer's first day on the job.
artifacts Symbols of culture in the physical and social work environment.
assumptions Deeply held beliefs that guide behavior and tell members of an organization how to perceive and think about things.
attitudes Individuals' general affective, cognitive, and intentional responses toward objects, other people, themselves, or social issues.
attribution theory A theory that explains how individuals pinpoint the causes of the behavior of themselves and others.
authority The right to influence another person.
authority-obedience manager (9,1) A manager who emphasizes efficient production.
autocratic style A style of leadership in which the leader uses strong, directive, controlling actions to enforce the rules, regulations, activities, and relationships in the work environment.

barriers to communication Aspects such as physical separation, status differences, gender differences, cultural diversity, and language that can impair effective communication in a workplace.
behavioral measures Personality assessments that involve observing an individual's behavior in a controlled situation.
benevolent An individual who is comfortable with an equity ratio less than that of his or her comparison other.
bounded rationality A theory that suggests that there are limits upon how rational a decision maker can actually be.
brainstorming A technique for generating as many ideas as possible on a given subject, while suspending evaluation until all the ideas have been suggested.
by higher-order needs.

career The pattern of work-related experiences that span the course of a person's life.
career anchors A network of self-perceived talents, motives, and values that guide an individual's career decisions.
career ladder A structured series of job positions through which an individual progresses in an organization.
career management A lifelong process of learning about self, jobs, and organizations; setting personal career goals; developing strategies for achieving the goals, and revising the goals based on work and life experiences.
career path A sequence of job experiences that an employee moves along during his or her career.
career plateau A point in an individual's career in which the probability of moving further up the hierarchy is low.
centralization The degree to which decisions are made at the top of the organization.
challenge The call to competition, context, or battle.
change The transportation or modification of an organization and/or its stakeholders.
change agent The individual or group who undertakes the task of introducing and managing a change in an organization.
change and acquisition The third socialization stage, in which the newcomer begins to master the demands of the job.
character assassination An attempt to label or discredit an opponent.
charismatic leadership The use, by a leader, of personal abilities and talents in order to have profound and extraordinary effects on followers.
classical conditioning Modifying behavior so that a conditioned stimulus is paired with an unconditioned stimulus and elicits an unconditioned response.
coercive power Power that is based on an agent's ability to cause an unpleasant experience for a target.

cognitive dissonance A state of tension that is produced when an individual experiences conflict between attitudes and behavior.
cognitive moral development The process of moving through stages of maturity in terms of making ethical decisions.
cognitive style An individual's preference for gathering information and evaluating alternatives.
collectivism A cultural orientation in which individuals belong to tightly knit social frameworks, and they depend strongly on large extended families or clans.
communication The evoking of a shared or common meaning in another person.
communicator The person originating a message.
compensation A compromise mechanism in which an individual attempts to make up for a negative situation by devoting himself or herself to another pursuit with increased vigor.
compensation award An organizational cost resulting from court awards for job distress.
complexity The degree to which many different types of activities occur in the organization.
conflict Any situation in which incompatible goals, attitudes, emotions, or behaviors lead to disagreement or opposition between two or more parties.
consensus An informational cue indicating the extent to which peers in the same situation behave in a similar fashion.
consequential theory An ethical theory that emphasizes the consequences or results of behavior.
consideration Leader behavior aimed at nurturing friendly, warm working relationships, as well as encouraging mutual trust and interpersonal respect within the work unit.
consistency An informational cue indicating the frequency of behavior over time.
contextual variables A set of characteristics that influences the organization's design processes.
continuance commitment The type of organizational commitment that is based on the fact that an individual cannot afford to leave.
conversion A withdrawal mechanism in which emotional conflicts that are expressed in physical symptoms.
counter-role behavior Deviant behavior in either a correctly or incorrectly defined job or role.
counterdependence An unhealthy, insecure pattern of behavior that leads to separation in relationships with other people.
country club manager (1,9) A manager who creates a happy, comfortable work environment.
creativity A process influenced by individual and organizational factors that results in the production of novel and useful ideas, products, or both.
cross-training A variation of job enlargement in which workers are trained in different specialized tasks or activities.
cultural theory An ethical theory that emphasizes respect for different cultural values.

data Uninterpreted and unanalyzed facts.
defensive communication Communication that canbe aggressive, attacking and angry, or passive and withdrawing.
Delphi technique Gathering the judgments of experts for use in decision making.
democratic style A style of leadership in which the leader takes collaborative, reciprocal, interactive actions with followers concerning the work and work environment.
devil's advocacy A technique for preventing groupthink in which a group or individual is given the role of critic during decision making.
dialectical inquiry A debate between two opposing sets of recommendations.
differentiation The process of deciding how to divide the work in an organization.
discounting principle The assumption that an individual's behavior is accounted for by the situation.
disenchantment Feeling negativity or anger toward a change.
disengagement Psychological withdrawal from change.
disidentification Feeling that one's identify is being threatened by a change.
disorientation Feelings of loss and confusion due to a change.
displacement An aggressive mechanism in which an individual directs his or her anger toward someone who is not the source of the conflict.
distinctiveness An informational cue indicating the degree to which an individual behaves the same way in other situations.
distress The adverse psychological, physical, behavioral, and organizational consequences that may arise as a result of stressful events.
distributive bargaining A negotiation approach in which the goals of the parties are in conflict, and each party seeks to maximize its resources.
distributive justice The fairness of the outcomes that individuals receive in an organization.
diversity All forms of individual differences, including culture, gender, age, ability, personality, religious affiliation, economic class, social status, military attachment, and sexual orientation.
divisionalized form A moderately decentralized form of organization that emphasizes the middle level and standardization of outputs.
dual-career partnership A relationship in which both people have important career roles.
due process nonaction A procedure set up to address conflicts that is so costly, time-consuming, or personally risky that no one will use it.
dynamic follower A follower who is a responsible steward of his or her job, is effective in managing the relationship with the boss, and practices self-management.
dysfunctional conflict An unhealthy, destructive disagreement between two or more people.

effective decision A timely decision that meets a desired objective and is acceptable to those individuals affected by it.
ego-ideal The embodiment of a person's perfect self.
eldercare Assistance in caring for elderly parents and/or other elderly relatives.
empowerment Sharing power within an organization.
enacted values Values reflected in the way individuals actually behave.
encounter The second socialization stage, in which the newcomer learns the tasks associated with the job, clarifies roles, and establishes new relationships at work.

endogenous process One of an individual's many internal attributes and characteristics that may help predict his or her behavior.
engineering The applied science of energy and matter.
entitled An individual who is comfortable with an equity ratio greater than that of his or her comparison other.
environment Anything outside the boundaries of an organization.
environmental uncertainty The amount and rate of change in the organization's environment.
equity sensitive An individual who prefers an equity ratio equal to that of his or her comparison other.
escalation of commitment The tendency to continue to commit resources to a losing course of action.
espoused values What members of an organization say they value.
establishment The first stage of a person's career, in which the person learns the job and begins to fit into the organization and occupation.
ethical behavior Acting in ways consistent with one's personal values and the commonly held values of the organization and society.
eustress Healthy, normal stress.
exogenous cause A factor external to an individual that may help predict his or her behavior.
expatriate manager A manager who works in a country other than his or her home country.
expectancy The belief that effort leads to performance.
expert power The power that exists when an agent has information or knowledge that the target needs.
expert system A computer-based application that uses a representation of human expertise in a specialized field of knowledge to solve problems.
extinction The attempt to weaken a behavior by attaching no consequences to it.
extraversion A preference indicating that an individual is energized by interaction with other people.

fantasy A withdrawal mechanism that provides an escape from a conflict through daydreaming.
feedback loop The pathway that completes two-way communication.
feeling Making decisions in a personal, value-oriented way.
femininity The cultural orientation in which relationships and concern for others are valued.
first-impression error The tendency to form lasting opinions about an individual based on initial perceptions.
fixation An aggressive mechanism in which an individual keeps up a dysfunctional behavior that obviously will not solve the conflict.
flexible work schedule A work schedule that allows employees discretion in order to accommodate personal concerns.
flextime An alternative work pattern through which employees can set their own daily work schedules.
flight A withdrawal mechanism that entails physically escaping a conflict.
followership The process of being guided and directed by a leader in the work environment.
formal leadership Officially sanctioned leadership based on the power and authority of a formal position.
formal organization The part of the organization that has legitimacy and official recognition.
formalization The degree to which the organization has official rules, regulations, and procedures.
functional conflict A healthy, constructive disagreement between two or more people.
fundamental attribution error The tendency to make attributions to internal causes when focusing on someone else's behavior.

garbage can model A theory that contends that decisions in organizations are random and unsystematic.
glass ceiling A transparent barrier that keeps women from rising above a certain level in organizations.
goal setting The process of establishing desired results that guide and direct behavior.
group Two or more people with common interests or objectives.
group cohesion The "interpersonal glue" that makes members of a group stick together.
group polarization The tendency for group discussion to produce shifts toward more extreme attitudes among members.
groupthink A deterioration of mental efficiency, reality testing, and moral judgment resulting from in-group pressures.
guanxi The Chinese practice of building networks for social exchange.

Hawthorne Studies Studies conducted during the 1920s and 1930s that discovered the existence of the informal organization.
heuristics Shortcuts in decision making that save mental activity.
hierarchy of authority The degree of vertical differentiation across levels of management.
homeostasis A steady state of bodily functioning and equilibrium.
humanistic theory The personality theory that emphasizes individual growth and improvement.
hygiene factor A work condition related to dissatisfaction caused by discomfort or pain.

identification A compromise mechanism whereby an individual patterns his or her behavior after another's.
implicit personality theory Opinions formed about other people that are based on our own mini-theories about how people behave.
impoverished manager (1,1) A manager who exerts just enough effort to avoid being fired.
impression management The process by which individuals try to control the impression others have of them.
incremental change Change of a relatively small scope, such as making small improvements.
individual differences The way in which factors such as skills, abilities, personalities, perceptions, attitudes, values, and ethics differ from one individual to another.
individualism A cultural orientation in which people belong to loose social frameworks, and their primary concern is for themselves and their families.

inequity The situation in which a person perceives he or she is receiving less than he or she is giving, or is giving less than he or she is receiving.
influence The process of affecting the thoughts, behavior, and feelings of another person.
informal leadership Unofficial leadership accorded to a person by other members of the organization.
informal organization The unofficial part of the organization.
information Data that have been interpreted, analyzed, and have meaning to some user.
initiating structure Leader behavior aimed at defining and organizing work relationships and roles, as well as establishing clear patterns of organization, communication, and ways of getting things done.
instrumental values Values that represent the acceptable behaviors to be used in achieving some end state.
instrumentality The belief that performance is related to rewards.
integrated involvement Closeness achieved through tasks and activities.
integration The process of coordinating the different parts of an organization.
integrative approach The broad theory that describes personality as a composite of an individual's psychological processes.
integrative negotiation A negotiation approach that focuses on the merits of the issues and seeks a win-win solution.
interactional psychology The psychological approach that emphasizes that in order to understand human behavior, we must know something about the person and about the situation.
intergroup conflict Conflict that occurs between groups or teams in an organization.
interorganizational conflict Conflict that occurs between two or more organizations.
interpersonal communication Communication between two or more people in an organization.
interpersonal conflict Conflict that occurs between two or more individuals.
interrole conflict A person's experience of conflict among the multiple roles in his or her life.
intrapersonal conflict Conflict that occurs within an individual.
intrarole conflict Conflict that occurs within a single role, such as when a person receives conflicting messages from role senders about how to perform a certain role.
introversion A preference indicating that an individual is energized by time alone.
intuiting Gathering information through "sixth sense" and focusing on what could be rather than what actually exists.
intuition A fast, positive force in decision making utilized at a level below consciousness that involves learned patterns of information.

job A set of specified work and task activities that engage an individual in an organization.
Job Characteristics Model A framework for understanding person-job fit through the interaction of core job dimensions with critical psychological states within a person.
Job Diagnostic Survey (JDS) The survey instrument designed to measure the elements in the Job Characteristics Model.
job enlargement A method of job design that increases the number of activities in a job to overcome the boredom of overspecialized work.
job enrichment Designing or redesigning jobs by incorporating motivational factors into them.
job redesign An OD intervention method that alters jobs to improve the fit between individual skills and the demands of the job.
job rotation A variation of job enlargement in which workers are exposed to a variety of specialized jobs over time.
job satisfaction A pleasurable or positive emotional state resulting from the appraisal of one's job or job experiences.
job sharing An alternative work pattern in which there is more than one person occupying a single job.
judging Preferring closure and completion in making decisions.
jurisdictional ambiguity The presence of unclear lines of responsibility within an organization.

laissez-faire style A style of leadership in which the leader fails to accept the responsibilities of the position.
language The words, their pronunciation, and the methods of combining them used and understood by a group of people.
leader An advocate for change and new approaches to problems.
leader-member relations The quality of interpersonal relationships among a leader and the group members.
leadership The process of guiding and directing the behavior of people in the work environment.
learning A change in behavior acquired through experience.
least preferred coworker (LPC) The person a leader has least preferred to work with over his or her career.
legitimate power Power that is based on position and mutual agreement; agent and target agree that the agent has the right to influence the target.
locus of control An individual's generalized belief about internal control (self-control) versus external control (control by the situation or by others).
loss of individuality A social process in which individual group members lose self-awareness and its accompanying sense of accountability, inhibition, and responsibility for individual behavior.

M-oriented behavior Leader behavior that is sensitive to employees' feelings, emphasizes comfort in the work environment, works to reduce stress levels, and demonstrates appreciation for follower contributions.
Machiavellianism A personality characteristic indicating one's willingness to do whatever it takes to get one's own way.
machine bureaucracy A moderately decentralized form of organization that emphasizes the technical staff and standardization of work processes.
maintenance The third stage in an individual's career in which the individual tries to maintain productivity while evaluating progress toward career goals.
maintenance function An activity essential to effective, satisfying interpersonal relationships within a team or group.
management The study of overseeing activities and supervising people in organizations.

management by objectives (MBO) A goal-setting program based on interaction and negotiation between employees and managers.
management development A host of techniques for enhancing managers' skills in an organization.
manager An advocate for stability and the status quo.
Managerial Grid An approach to understanding a manager's concern for production and concern for people.
masculinity The cultural orientation in which assertiveness and materialism are valued.
meaning of work The way a person interprets and understands the value of work as part of life.
medicine The applied science of healing or treatment of diseases to enhance an individual's health and well-being.
mentor An individual who provides guidance, coaching, counseling, and friendship to a protégé.
mentoring A work relationship that encourages development and career enhancement for people moving through the career cycle.
message The thoughts and feelings that the communicator is attempting to elicit in the receiver.
moral maturity The measure of a person's cognitive moral development.
motivation The process of arousing and sustaining goal-directed behavior.
motivation factor A work condition related to satisfaction of the need for psychological growth.
moving The second step in Lewin's change model, in which new attitudes, values, and behaviors are substituted for old ones.
Myers-Briggs Type Indicator (MBTI) An instrument developed to measure Carl Jung's theory of individual differences.

need for achievement A manifest (easily perceived) need that concerns individuals' issues of excellence, competition, challenging goals, persistence, and overcoming difficulties.
need for affiliation A manifest (easily perceived) need that concerns an individual's need to establish and maintain warm, close, intimate relationships with other people.
need for power A manifest (easily perceived) need that concerns an individual's need to make an impact on others, influence others, change people or events, and
need hierarchy The theory that behavior is determined by a progression of physical, social, and psychological needs.
negative affect An individual's tendency to accentuate the negative aspects of himself or herself, other people, and the world in general.
negative consequences Results of a behavior that a person finds unattractive or aversive.
negativism An aggressive mechanism in which a person responds with pessimism to any attempt at solving a problem.
nominal group technique (NGT) A structured approach to group decision making that focuses on generating alternatives and choosing one.
nonaction Doing nothing in hopes that a conflict with disappear.
nondefensive communication Communication that is assertive, direct, and powerful.
nonprogrammed decision A new, complex decision that requires a creative solution.
nonverbal communication All elements of communication that do not involve words.
norms of behavior The standards that a work group uses to evaluate the behavior of its members.

objective knowledge Knowledge that results from research and scholarly activities.
one-way communication Communication in which a person sends a message to another person and no questions, feedback, or interaction follow.
operant conditioning Modifying behavior through the use of positive or negative consequences following specific behaviors.
organization manager (5,5) A manager who maintains the status quo.
organizational behavior The study of individual behavior and group dynamics in organizational settings.
organizational citizenship behavior Behavior that is above and beyond the call of duty.
organizational commitment The strength of an individual's identification with an organization.
organizational (corporate) culture A pattern of basic assumptions that are considered valid and that are taught to new members as the way to perceive, think, and feel in the organization.
organizational design The process of constructing and adjusting an organization's structure to achieve its goals.
organizational development (OD) A systematic approach to organizational improvement that applies behavioral science theory and research in order to increase individual and organizational well-being and effectiveness.
organizational life cycle The differing stages of an organization's life from birth to death.
organizational politics The use of power and influence in organizations.
organizational socialization The process by which newcomers are transformed from outsiders to participating, effective members of the organization.
organizational structure The linking of departments and jobs within an organization.
overdependence An unhealthy, insecure pattern of behavior that leads to preoccupied attempts to achieve security through relationships.

P-oriented behavior Leader behavior that encourages a fast work pace, emphasizes good quality and high accuracy, works toward high-quantity production, and demonstrates concern for rules and regulations.
participation problem A cost associated with absenteeism, tardiness, strikes and work stoppages, and turnover.
participative decision making Decision making in which individuals who are affected by decisions influence the making of those decisions.
perceiving Preferring to explore many alternatives and flexibility.
perceptual screen A window through which we interact with people that influences the quality, accuracy, and clarity of the communication.
performance appraisal The evaluation of a person's performance.

performance decrement A cost resulting from poor quality or low quantity of production, grievances, and unscheduled machine downtime and repair.
person-role conflict Conflict that occurs when an individual is expected to perform behaviors in a certain role that conflict with his or her personal values.
personal power Power used for personal gain.
personality A relatively stable set of characteristics that influences an individual's behavior.
personality hardiness A personality resistant to distress and characterized by challenge, commitment, and control.
planned change Change resulting from a deliberate decision to alter the organization.
political behavior Actions not officially sanctioned by an organization that are taken to influence others in order to meet one's personal goals.
position power The authority associated with the leader's formal position in the organization.
positive affect An individual's tendency to accentuate the positive aspects of himself or herself, other people, and the world in general.
positive consequences Results of a behavior that a person finds attractive or pleasurable.
power The ability to influence another person.
power distance The degree to which a culture accepts unequal distribution of power.
powerlessness A lack of power.
preventive stress management An organizational philosophy that holds that people and organizations should take joint responsibility for promoting health and preventing distress and strain.
primary prevention The stage in preventive stress management designed to reduce, modify, or eliminate the demand or stressor causing stress.
procedural justice The fairness of the process by which outcomes are allocated in an organization.
process consultation An OD method that helps managers and employers improve the processes that are used in organizations.
professional bureaucracy A decentralized form of organization that emphasizes the operating level and standardization of skills.
programmed decision A simple, routine matter for which a manager has an established decision rule.
projective test A personality test that elicits an individual's response to abstract stimuli.
psychoanalysis Sigmund Freud's method for delving into the unconscious mind to understand better a person's motives and needs.
psychodynamic theory The personality theory that emphasizes the unconscious determinants of behavior.
psychological contract An implicit agreement between an individual and an organization that specifies what each is expected to give and receive in the relationship.
psychological intimacy Emotional and psychological closeness to other team or group members.
psychology The science of human behavior.
punishment The attempt to eliminate or weaken undesirable behavior by either bestowing negative consequences or withholding positive consequences.

quality circle (QC) A small group of employees who work voluntarily on company time, typically one hour per week, to address work-related problems such as quality control, cost reduction, production planning and techniques, and even product design.
quality program A program that embeds product and service quality excellence into the organizational culture.
quality team A team that is part of an organization's structure and is empowered to act on its decisions regarding product and service quality.

rationality A logical, step-by-step approach to decision making, with a thorough analysis of alternatives and their consequences.
rationalization A compromise mechanism characterized by trying to justify one's behavior by constructing bogus reasons for it.
realistic job preview (RJP) Both positive and negative information given to potential employees about the job they are applying for, thereby giving them a realistic picture of the job.
receiver The person receiving a message.
referent power An elusive power that is based on interpersonal attraction.
reflective listening A skill intended to help the receiver and communicator clearly and fully understand the message sent.
refreezing The final step in Lewin's change model, which involves the establishment of new attitudes, values, and behaviors as the new status quo.
reinforcement The attempt to develop or strengthen desirable behavior by either bestowing positive consequences or withholding negative consequences.
reinvention The creative application of new technology.
reward power Power based on an agent's ability to control rewards that a target wants.
richness The ability of a medium or channel to elicit or evoke meaning in the receiver.
risk aversion The tendency to choose options that entail fewer risks and less uncertainty.
robotics The use of robots in organizations.
role negotiation A technique whereby individuals meet and clarify their psychological contract.
rule-based theory An ethical theory that emphasizes the character of the act itself rather than its effects.

satisfice To select the first alternative that is "good enough," because the costs in time and effort are too great to optimize.
secondary prevention The stage in preventive stress management designed to alter or modify the individual's or the organization's response to a demand or stressor.
secrecy Attempting to hide a conflict or an issue that has the potential to create conflict.
selective perception The process of selecting information that supports our individual viewpoints while discounting information that threatens our viewpoints.
self-efficacy An individual's beliefs and expectancies about his or her ability to accomplish a specific task effectively.
self-esteem An individual's general feeling of self-worth.
self-fulfilling prophecy The situation in which our expectations about people affect our interaction with them in such a way that our expectations are fulfilled.

self-image How a person sees himself or herself, both positively and negatively.
self-interest What is in the best interest and benefit to an individual.
self-managed team A team that makes decisions that were once reserved for managers.
self-monitoring The extent to which people base their behavior on cues from other people and situations.
self-reliance A healthy, secure, *interdependent* pattern of behavior related to how people form and maintain supportive attachments with others.
self-report questionnaire A common personality assessment that involves an individual's responses to a series of questions.
self-serving bias The tendency to attribute one's own successes to internal causes and one's failures to external causes.
sensing Gathering information through the five senses.
sensitivity training An intervention designed to help individuals understand how their behavior affects others.
simple structure A centralized form of organization that emphasizes the upper echelon and direct supervision.
skill development The mastery of abilities essential to successful functioning in organizations.
skills training Increasing the job knowledge, skills, and abilities that are necessary to do a job effectively.
social decision schemes Simple rules used to determine final group decisions.
social information-processing (SIP) model A model that suggests that the important job factors depend in part on what others tell a person about the job.
social learning The process of deriving attitudes from family, peer groups, religious organizations, and culture.
social loafing The failure of a group member to contribute personal time, effort, thoughts, or other resources to the group.
social perception The process of interpreting information about another person.
social power Power used to create motivation or to accomplish group goals.
social responsibility The obligation of an organization to behave in ethical ways.
sociology The science of society.
specialization The degree to which jobs are narrowly defined and depend on unique expertise.
standardization The degree to which work activities are accomplished in a routine fashion.
status structure The set of authority and task relations among a group's members.
stereotype A generalization about a group of people.
strain Distress.
strategic change Change of a larger scale, such as organizational restructuring
strategic contingencies Activities that other groups depend on in order to complete their tasks.
stress The unconscious preparation to fight or flee that a person experiences when faced with any demand.
stressor The person or event that triggers the stress response.
strong culture An organizational culture with a consensus on the values that drive the company and with an intensity that is recognizable even to outsiders.
strong situation A situation that overwhelms the effects of individual personalities by providing strong cues for appropriate behavior.
structure The manner in which an organization's work is designed at the micro level, as well as how departments, divisions, and the overall organization are designed at the macro level.
superordinate goal An organizational goal that is more important to both parties in a conflict than their individual or group goals.
survey feedback A widely used method of intervention whereby employee attitudes are solicited using a questionnaire.
synergy A positive force in groups that occurs when group members stimulate new solutions to problems through the process of mutual influence and encouragement in the group.

task An organization's mission, purpose, or goal for existing.
task environment The elements of an organization's environment that are related to its goal attainment.
task function An activity directly related to the effective completion of a team's work.
task revision The modification of incorrectly specified roles or jobs.
task structure The degree of clarity, or ambiguity, in the work activitie assigned to the group.
team A small number of people with complementary skills who are committed to a common mission, performance goals, and approach for which they hold themselves mutually accountable.
team building An intervention designed to improve the effectiveness of a work group.
team manager (9,9) A manager who builds a highly productive team of committed people.
technocentric Placing technology and engineering at the center of job design decisions.
technological interdependence The degree of interrelatedness of the organization's various technological elements.
technology The intellectual and mechanical processes used by an organization to transform inputs into products or services that meet organizational goals.
technostress The stress caused by new and advancing technologies in the workplace.
telecommuting Transmitting work from a home computer to the office using a modem.
terminal values Values that represent the goals to be achieved, or the end states of existence.
tertiary prevention The stage in preventive stress management designed to heal individual or organizational symptoms of distress and strain.
Theory X A set of assumptions of how to manage individuals who are motivated by lower-order needs.
Theory Y A set of assumptions of how to manage individuals who are motivated by higher-order needs.
thinking Making decisions in a logical, objective fashion.
time orientation Whether a culture's values are oriented toward the future (long-term orientation) or toward the past and present (short-term orientation)
total quality management The total dedication to continuous improvement and to customers so that the customers' needs are met and their expectations exceeded.

trait theory The personality theory that states that in order to understand individuals, we must break down behavior patterns into a series of observable traits.
transformational change Change in which the organization moves to a radically different, and sometimes unknown, future state.
transformational coping A way of managing stressful events by changing them into subjectively less stressful events.
transnational organization An organization in which the global viewpoint supersedes national issues.
triangulation The use of multiple methods to measure organizational culture.
two-way communication A form of communication in which the communicator and receiver interact.
Type A behavior pattern A complex of personality and behavioral characteristics, including competitiveness, time urgency, social status insecurity, aggression, hostility, and a quest for achievements.

uncertainty avoidance The degree to which a culture tolerates ambiguity and uncertainty.
unfreezing The first step in Lewin's change model, which involves encouraging individuals to discard old behaviors by shaking up the equilibrium state that maintains the status quo.
unplanned change Change that is imposed on the organization and is often unforeseen.
upper echelon A top-level executive team in an organization.

valence The value or importance one places on a particular reward.
values Enduring beliefs that a specific mode of conduct or end state of existence is personally or socially preferable to an opposite or converse mode of conduct or end state of existence.
virtual office A mobile platform of computer, telecommunication, and information technology and services.

whistle-blower An employee who informs authorities of the wrongdoings of his or her company or coworkers.
withdrawal The final stage in an individual's career, in which the individual contemplates retirement or possible career changes.
work Mental or physical activity that has productive results.
work simplification Standardization and the narrow, explicit specification of task activities for workers.

zone of indifference The range in which attempts to influence a person will be perceived as legitimate and will be acted on without a great deal of thought.

Name Index

L

M

N

O

P

T

U

V

W

Y

Z

Company Index

Subject Index

Q

R

S

T

U

V

W

Y

Z

Photo Credits

cover Tony Stone/©Robert E. Daemmrich; **2** Duomo/David Madison; **4** Courtesy of IBM; **7** UniPhoto Picture Agency/©Llewellyn; **14** Courtesy of Chaparral Steel; **16** Courtesy of IBM; **19** Photo Researchers/©Will & Deni McIntyre; **30** Richard Nowitz/Corbis; **36** Gamma Liaison Network/© Carol Halebian; **41** Mark Jenkinson; **42** PhotoEdit/©Michael Newman; **54** Sygma; **68** Duomo/Brad Mangin; **70** B&N Enterprises; **73** Courtesy of Southwest Airlines; **76** Fantastic Foods; **77** Photo Researchers/©Gregory Dimijian; **89** PhotoEdit/©Michael Newman; **101** © Giboux/Liason; **104** AP Photo/The Oprah Winfrey Show, George Burns; **110** The Gamma Liaison Network/©William Snyder; **115** Courtesy of Albany Ladder; **116** AP Photo/Peter Zuzga; **118** The Granger Collection, New York; **130** Photo Researchers/©Rafael Macia 1995; **132** Reuters/Paul Barker/Archive Photos; **150** Ron Sonntag Public Relations; **152** Ford Motors; **158** Gamma Liaison/©G. Rose; **160** Courtesy of Chaparral Steel; **164** Courtesy of Springfield Manufacturing; **176** ©Tony Stone Images/Charles Grupton; **180** Courtesy of Chaparral Steel; **186** Photo Edit/©David Young-Wolff; **191** Gamma/© J.O. Atlanta 96; **197** The Picture Cube/©Eunice Harris; **206** Tony Arruza/Corbis; **207** Karl Weatherly/Corbis; **218** Mike Powell/Allsport; **220** Kevin Fleming/©Corbis; **225** Visuals Unlimited; **230** Oticon; **236** Photo Researchers/©Dick Luria Photography; **241** Visuals Unlimited/© Kjell Sandved; **250** George Hall/Corbis; **252** Stock Boston/©Bill Horsman; **255** Courtesy of Chaparral Steel; **257** AP Photo/Ed Bailey; **262** Gail Mooney/©Corbis; **270** Courtesy of Chrysler; **280** Courtesy of FedEx; **290** Courtesy of Hallmark Cards, Inc; **293** Courtesy of 3M; **303** Courtesy of Campbell Soup; **304** ©Phil Schofield; **314** Courtesy of Southwest Airlines; **318** ©Giboux/Gamma Liaison; **323** ©Ken Kerbs Photography; **335** Gamma Liaison/Schnepf; **336** Courtesy of Oregon Cutting Systems; **344** Gamma Liaison/©Joe Traver; **346** Reuters/Mike Theiler/Archive Photos; **350** Gamma Liaison/©Marc Francoeur; **351** David Zadig; **352** The Granger Collection; **376** Liaison International/© PBJ Pictures; **383** Photo Edit/© Mark Richards; **388** AP Photo/Jayson Mellom; **393** Biely E. Barnes/Photo Edit; **401** AP Photo/Tim Sharp; **412** Duomo/Steven E. Sutton; **414** Courtesy of IBM; **417** Stock Boston/© Nubar Alexanian; **421** Roger Ressmeyer/©Corbis ; **428** Hedrich-Blessing/Nick Merrick. Courtesy of Herman Miller, Inc.; **435** Courtesy of Picture Tel; **444** Courtesy of Citibank; **450** Courtesy of Ford Motors; **455** Courtesy of NASA; **456** Courtesy of Nissan; **457** Courtesy of IBM; **474** Courtesy of Mary Kay; **479** Courtesy of Ditch Witch; **485** The Gamma Liaison Network/© Joe Caputo; **489** Ben Van Hook/Black Star; **493** Therese Frare NYT Pictures; **504** PhotoEdit/©Robert Brenner; **506** Courtesy of Motorola; **519** ©Tony Stone Images/Ian Shaw; **522** Gamma Liaison; **525** ©Daemmrich/Uniphotos; **538** Scott Adams/United Features Syndicate; **541** Courtesy of Conoco; **557** Sygma; **563** Cindy Charles/PhotoEdit; **563** Tom McCarthy/PhotoEdit; **A-1** The Granger Collection; **A-4** Property of AT&T Archives. Reprinted with permission of AT&T.

GREENLAND
(DEN.)
ALASKA
(U.S.)
CANADA
UNITED
STATES
ATLANTIC
OCEAN
BAHAMAS
MEXICO
CUBA
DOMINICAN REP.
PUERTO RICO
HAWAII
(U.S.)
HAITI
ST. KITTS
BELIZE
VIRGIN ISLANDS
ANTIGUA
GUATEMALA
HONDURAS
ST. LUCIA
DOMINICA
BARBADOS
EL SALVADOR
NICARAGUA
ST. VINCENT
GRENADA
PACIFIC
COSTA RICA
TRINIDAD & TOBAGO
GUYANA
PANAMA
VENEZUELA
SURINAME
FR. GUYANA
COLOMBIA
ECUADOR
OCEAN
PERU
BRAZIL
NAURU
KIRIBATI
SOLOMON
ISLANDS
TUVALU
TOKELAU
WEST.
SAMOA
AM.
SAMOA
VANUATU
FIJI
COOK
IS.
(N.Z.)
TONGA
NIUE
(N.Z.)
FRENCH
POLYNESIA
NEW
CALEDONIA
BOLIVIA
PARAGUAY
PITCAIRN
(U.K.)
URUGUAY
CHILE
ARGENTINA
NEW
ZEALAND
FALKLAND IS.
(U.K.)